SOCIAL GERONTOLOGY

A MULTIDISCIPLINARY PERSPECTIVE

Nancy R. Hooyman
University of Washington

H. Asuman Kiyak
University of Washington

Allyn and Bacon
Boston   London   Toronto   Sydney   Tokyo   Singapore

Senior Editor: Jeff Lasser
Editor in Chief, Social Sciences: Karen Hanson
Editorial Assistant: Andrea Christie
Marketing Manager: Judeth Hall
Editorial Production Service: Bernadine Richey Publishing Services
Manufacturing Buyer: Suzanne Lareau
Cover Administrator: Linda Knowles
Electronic Composition: Omegatype Typography, Inc.

Library of Congress Cataloging-in-Publication Data

Hooyman, Nancy R.
    Social gerontology : a multidisciplinary perspective / Nancy R. Hooyman, H. Asuman Kiyak.—[6th ed.].
       p. cm.
    Includes bibliographical references and index.
    ISBN 0-205-33625-6 (alk. paper)
    1. Gerontology. 2. Aging. 3. Aged—United States. I. Kiyak, H. Asuman, 1951- II. Title.

HQ1061 .H583 2001
305.26—dc21

                                                           2001037304

Printed in the United States of America

10 9 8 7 6 5 4 3 2 1   RRD-VA 06 05 04 03 02 01

Photo Credits
Photo credits may be found on page xviii, which should be considered an extension of the copyright page.

In memory of my son, Chris, and in celebration
of my children, Kevin and Mani

—NRH

In memory of my parents, Yahya and Leman Kiyak,
and with gratitude to Lara and Joe

—HAK

ABOUT THE AUTHORS

Nancy R. Hooyman   Nancy R. Hooyman is professor and dean at the School of Social Work at the University of Washington in Seattle. Her Ph.D. is in sociology and social work from the University of Michigan. She is nationally recognized for her scholarship in aging, issues related to family caregiving, gender inequities in caregiving, feminist social work practice, and administration. In addition to this textbook, Dr. Hooyman is the coauthor of *Taking Care of Aging Family Members* and *Feminist Perspectives on Family Care: Policies for Gender Justice* and has edited *Feminist Social Work Practice in Clinical Settings*. She has published over 80 articles and chapters related to gerontology and women's issues. Her research interests are in family caregiving of persons with chronic disabilities, feminist practice models, and older women's issues. She is a Fellow in the Gerontological Society, and, in 1998, she received the Career Achievement Award from the Association for Gerontology in Social Work Education.

H. Asuman Kiyak   H. Asuman Kiyak is Director of the Institute on Aging, professor in the School of Dentistry, and adjunct professor in the Departments of Architecture and Psychology at the University of Washington. She obtained her Ph.D. in psychology at Wayne State University. Professor Kiyak has been the recipient of major research grants from NIH, AOA, and private foundations in the areas of health promotion and health service utilization by older adults, and in person–environment adaptation to Alzheimer's disease by patients and their caregivers. She has published over 100 articles and 30 chapters in these areas and is known nationally and internationally for her research on geriatric dental care and the application of psychological theory to health promotion. In 2000 she received the Distinguished Scientist Award from the International Association for Dental Research, and has served as president of the Geriatric Oral Research and Behavioral Sciences and Health Services Research Groups of IADR.

Contents

CHAPTER 4

MANAGING CHRONIC DISEASES AND PROMOTING WELL-BEING IN OLD AGE   101

PART THREE   THE PSYCHOLOGICAL CONTEXT OF SOCIAL AGING   147

CHAPTER 5

COGNITIVE CHANGES WITH AGING   150

CHAPTER **6**

PERSONALITY AND MENTAL HEALTH IN OLD AGE   176

CHAPTER **7**

LOVE, INTIMACY, AND SEXUALITY IN OLD AGE   227

PART FOUR   THE SOCIAL CONTEXT OF AGING   251

CHAPTER **8** SOCIAL THEORIES OF AGING   255

CHAPTER **9** THE IMPORTANCE OF SOCIAL SUPPORTS: FAMILY, FRIENDS, AND NEIGHBORS   276

CHAPTER 10

OPPORTUNITIES AND STRESSES OF INFORMAL CAREGIVING   308

CHAPTER 11

LIVING ARRANGEMENTS AND SOCIAL INTERACTIONS   329

CHAPTER **12**

PRODUCTIVE AGING: PAID AND NONPAID ROLES AND ACTIVITIES   364

CHAPTER **13**

DEATH, DYING, BEREAVEMENT, AND WIDOWHOOD   415

PART FIVE   THE SOCIETAL CONTEXT OF AGING   503

CHAPTER 16 SOCIAL POLICIES TO ADDRESS SOCIAL PROBLEMS   506

CHAPTER 17 HEALTH AND LONG-TERM CARE POLICY AND PROGRAMS   538

PREFACE

Aging is a complex and fascinating process, one that we will all experience. It is complex because of its many facets—physiological, emotional, cognitive, economic, and interpersonal—that influence our social functioning and well-being. It is a fascinating process because these changes will occur differently in each one of us. There is considerable truth to the statement that, as we grow older, we become more unlike each other.

Aging is also a process that attracts the attention of the media, politicians, business and industry, and the general public, largely because we live in a rapidly aging society. Changes in the numbers and proportion of older people in our population have numerous implications for societal structures, including the family, health and social services, long-term care, pension and retirement practices, political processes, recreational services, and housing. In addition, these changes are of growing concern because of the problems of poverty, inadequate housing, and chronic disease faced by some older people—particularly women, ethnic minorities, the oldest-old, and those living alone. Public officials as well as individuals in the private sector are faced with the challenge of planning for a future when there will be more people over age 65 than ever before.

These changes have also meant that most colleges and universities now offer courses in *gerontology*, the study of aging. The goal of many of these courses is to prepare students to understand the process of aging and the diversity among older people and to work effectively with older adults. These programs also attempt to enhance students' personal understanding of their own and others' aging. Frequently, students take such a course sim-

ply to meet a requirement, not realizing how relevant the aging process is to their own lives. Thus, instructors are often faced with the need to help students see the connection between learning about aging and understanding their own behavior, the behavior of their relatives, and often the behavior of their clients.

This book grew out of our experiences in teaching gerontology courses to undergraduate students. In doing so, we were unable to locate a textbook that conveyed the excitement and relevance of understanding the aging process or one that adequately addressed the biological, physiological, psychological, and social aspects of aging. For years, we were frustrated by the lack of a text that was comprehensive, thorough, and current in its review of the rapidly growing research on older adults. As a sociologist/social worker and a psychologist, we have been committed to developing a text that could be useful to a wide range of disciplines, including nursing, social work, sociology, psychology, health education, and the allied health professions.

AIMS AND FOCUS

The primary focus of this book is *social* gerontology. As the title implies, however, our goal is to present the diversities of the aging experience and the older population in a multidisciplinary manner. It is our premise that an examination of the social lives of older people requires a basic understanding of the historical, cultural, biological, physiological, psychological, and social contexts of aging. It is important to understand the changes that occur within the aging individual, how these changes influence interactions with social and physical environments, and how the older person is, in turn, affected by such interactions. Throughout this book, the impact of these dynamic interactions between older people and their environments on their quality of life is a unifying theme.

Social gerontology encompasses a wide range of topics with exciting research in so many domains. This book does not cover all these areas, but rather highlights major research findings that illuminate the processes of aging. Through such factual information, we intend to dispel some of the myths and negative attitudes about aging. We also hope to encourage the reader to pursue this field, both academically and for the personal rewards that come from gaining insight into older people's lives. Because the field is so complex and rapidly changing, more recent research findings may appear to contradict earlier studies. We have attempted to be thorough in presenting a multiplicity of theoretical perspectives and empirical data to ensure that the reader has as full and accurate a picture of the field as possible.

FEATURES

This book begins by reviewing major demographic, historical, and cross-cultural changes, and their implications for the development of the field of social gerontology, as well as methods used to study aging and older people. We then turn to the major biological and physiological changes that affect older people's daily functioning, as well as their risk of chronic diseases and consequent utilization of health and long-term care services. The third section considers psychological changes, particularly in learning and memory, personality, mental health, and sexuality. Given our emphasis on how such physical and psychological changes affect the social aspects of aging, the fourth section examines social theories of aging, the social context of the family, friends, and other intergenerational supports, new living arrangements, productivity in the later years, and the conditions under which people die. Throughout the book, the differential effects that these changes have on women and ethnic mi-

norities are identified, with two chapters focusing specifically on such differences. We conclude by turning to the larger context of social, health, and long-term care policies and future implications for the field. To highlight the application of research findings to everyday situations, each chapter integrates discussions of both the policy and practice implications of the aging process. Vignettes of older people in different situations bring to life many of the concepts introduced in these chapters.

NEW TO THIS EDITION

The positive response of students and faculty to the first five editions suggests that we have been successful in achieving our goals for this book. Based on the responses of faculty who have used *Social Gerontology* in different colleges across the United States, the sixth edition represents a major change. The book is designed to be completed in a 16-week semester, but readers can proceed at a faster pace through the chapters. The chapter on social theories has been expanded and updated to include recent theoretical developments, including feminist and social constructionist perspectives. New research findings are presented on extending both years and quality of life, achieving successful aging, and encouraging productivity through both paid and unpaid activities. Exciting developments on early diagnosis and treatment of dementias are also discussed. A new chapter on caregiving for and by older adults has been added. This chapter addresses issues of the costs and benefits of caregiving, its stresses, and help for caregivers. Housing options for older people, especially those needing help with managing their chronic diseases and home maintenance, have expanded in the past ten years. Today, older people needing long-term care can choose among several alternatives to nursing homes. These are presented in the new edition. Both the strengths and challenges facing older women and ethnic minorities are presented. Given the dramatically changing political arena, the chapters on social, health, and long-term care policies have been rewritten to reflect contemporary policy debates, to address the need for home and community-based care alternatives to institutionalization, and to take account of the increasing diversity of the older population. The increased attention given to differences in the aging process by gender, ethnicity, and socioeconomic status, and to social, health, and long-term policy debates in this edition, is a reflection of the dramatic demographic and economic changes facing us in the twenty-first century.

In addition, we have attempted to make this book more "reader friendly." Pages are broken up by more vignettes; by bulleted summaries of major points; and by "Points to Ponder," issues for readers to consider related to the topic addressed. Each chapter begins with clearly "bulleted" points to be covered in the chapter. The glossary has been reduced in length, while more resources, especially internet resources, have been added at the end of each chapter, and described more fully in the companion website for this text: www.ablongman.com/hooyman.

ANNENBERG/CPB TELECOURSE

Social Gerontology is being offered as part of the Annenberg/CPB college-level telecourse *Growing Old in a New Age,* broadcast on PBS.

Growing Old in a New Age is a thirteen-part public television series and college-level course that provides an understanding of the processes of aging, of old age as a stage of life, and of the impact of aging on society. The course responds to the demographic wave that is sweeping our nation and our world, exploring questions about what roles people will play in their eighth, ninth, and tenth decades, and how institutions may evolve to address their needs. *Growing Old in a New Age* also offers opportunities for the student and viewer to examine personal attitudes toward aging and older people. Material contributed by outstanding social scientists, medical professionals, and clinicians provides a multidisciplinary, multicultural approach. Extensive interviews with older people themselves support this cross-cultural and comprehensive introduction to gerontology.

In addition to *Social Gerontology,* a student *Telecourse Study Guide* is available through most college bookstores. *A Telecourse Faculty Guide* is available without charge to those who license the telecourse. The programs may be purchased on videocassettes by calling the Annenberg/CPB Collection at 1-800-LEARNER. Off-air taping licenses may be acquired from either the Annenberg CPB Collection or the PBS Adult Learning Service. Colleges and universities may license the use of *Growing Old in a New Age* as a telecourse for college credit through the PBS Adult Learning Service (1-800-257-2578; in Virginia, 1-703-739-5363).

ACKNOWLEDGMENTS

We are grateful to the many people who have contributed significantly to the successful completion of the sixth edition of *Social Gerontology.* In particular, we thank Valerie Higgins, Pat Kline, Diane Broderick, Asantawa Antobam, Madeline Galbraith, Erin Wallace, Alison Beck, Mildred Berto, and Jane Braziunas for assisting us with library research and the technical aspects of the revisions. Their willingness to "pitch in" and do whatever tasks were necessary was a tremendous support. Our families have been a mainstay of support throughout the preparation of all the editions of this book. And Gnanamani (Mani) Hooyman, who joined the Hooyman family during the last edition, has never known her mother not to be working on THE BIG BOOK!

We appreciate the assistance from the staff associated with the Center on Aging, University of Hawaii at Manoa, who have chosen our text for the first national telecourse on aging, *Growing Old in a New Age.* In particular, we thank Dr. Kathryn Braun, author of the student and faculty guides for the telecourse, for her efforts in changing the Student Guide to reflect the changes made in earlier editions, and Dr. Michael Cheang for his work on the new edition.

We want to thank the following reviewers of the sixth edition for their helpful comments in reviewing the book: Joyce Hickson, Columbus State University; and William C. Hays, Wichita State University; and our colleagues Charley Enlet, Leonard Poon, Boaz Kahana, and Eric Kingson for giving us feedback that they have received from students who have used the textbook.

THE FIELD OF SOCIAL GERONTOLOGY

TOWARD UNDERSTANDING AGING

From the perspective of youth and middle age, old age seems a remote and, to some, an undesirable period of life. Throughout history, humans have tried to prolong youth and to delay aging. The attempts to discover a substance to rejuvenate the body and mind have driven explorers to far corners of the globe and have inspired alchemists and scientists to search for ways to restore youth and extend life. Indeed, the discovery of Florida by Ponce de Leon in 1513 was an accident, as he searched for a fountain in Bimini whose waters were rumored to bring back one's youth. Medieval Latin alchemists believed that eating gold could add years to life and spent many years trying to produce a digestible form of gold. In the seventeenth century, a popular belief was that smelling fresh earth each morning could prolong one's youth. The theme of prolonging or restoring youth is evident today in advertisements for skin creams, soaps, vitamins, and certain foods; in the popularity of cosmetic surgery; in books and movies that feature attractive, youthful-looking older characters; and even in medical research that is testing technological methods to replace depleted hormones in older people in an attempt to rejuvenate aging skin and physical and sexual functioning. One organization, by its name, reveals its bias that aging is a disease or process that can be fought or prevented. The International Academy of Anti-Aging Medicine actually promotes preventive and naturopathic medicine, but its name suggests a more negative view of aging than does its goal.

Most people are unprepared for the physical and cognitive signs of aging. As Leo Tolstoy noted, "Old age is the most unexpected of all things that happen to a man."

All these concerns point to underlying fears of aging. Many of our concerns and fears arise from misconceptions about what happens to our bodies, our minds, our status in society, and our social lives as we reach our seventies, eighties, and beyond. They arise, in part, from negative attitudes toward older people within our own culture. These attitudes are sometimes identified as manifestations of **ageism,** a term that was coined by Robert Butler, the first Director of the National Institute on Aging, to describe stereotypes about old age. As is true for sexism and racism, ageism attributes certain characteristics to all members of a group solely because of a characteristic they share—in this case, their age. In fact, ageism is one prejudice that we are all likely to encounter sooner or later, regardless of our gender, ethnic minority status, social class, or sexual orientation. A frequent result of ageism is discriminatory behavior against the target group (i.e., older persons). For example, some aging advocates have argued that older, experienced workers are encouraged to retire early because of stereotypes about older people's abilities and productivity. Instead, advocates suggest that employers should consider each worker's skills and experience when organizational restructuring requires layoffs.

To distinguish the realities of aging from the social stereotypes surrounding this process requires an understanding of the "normal" changes that can be expected in the aging body, in mental and emotional functioning, and in social interactions and status. Aging can then be understood as a phase of growth and development—a universal biological phenomenon. Accordingly, the normal processes due to age alone need to be differentiated from pathological changes or disease. As life expectancy increases, as the older proportion of our population grows, and as more of us can look forward to becoming older ourselves, concerns and questions about the aging process continue to attract widespread public and professional attention.

1

THE GROWTH OF SOCIAL GERONTOLOGY

This chapter includes

- Definitions of aging
- Definitions of gerontology, social gerontology, and geriatrics
- The person–environment perspective used throughout this book
- Reasons for studying social gerontology
- Demographic patterns within the United States and worldwide
- Life expectancy, life span, and longevity in health or disease
- Development of the field of gerontology
- Research methods and designs for studying older adults
- The importance of representative samples for social gerontological research

THE FIELD OF GERONTOLOGY

The growing interest in understanding the process of aging has given rise to the multidisciplinary field of **gerontology,** the study of the biological, psychological, and social aspects of aging. Gerontologists include researchers and practitioners in such diverse fields as biology, medicine, nursing, dentistry, physical and occupational therapy, psychology, psychiatry, sociology, economics, political science, and social work. These individuals are concerned with many aspects of aging, from studying and describing the cellular processes involved to seeking ways to improve the quality of life for older people. **Geriatrics** focuses on how to prevent or manage the diseases of aging. The field has become a specialty in medicine, nursing, and dentistry and is receiving more attention with the increase in the number of older people who have long-term health problems.

Gerontologists view aging in terms of four distinct processes that are examined throughout this book:

• *Chronological aging* is the definition of aging on the basis of a person's years from birth. Thus, a 75-year-old is chronologically older than a 45-year-old. Chronological age is not necessarily related to a person's biological or physical age, nor to his or her psychological or social age, as we will emphasize throughout this book. For example, we may remark that someone "looks younger (or older)" or "acts younger (or older)" than her or his age. This implies that the individual's *biological* or *psychological* or *social age* is incongruent with the *chronological age*.

• *Biological aging* refers to the physical changes that reduce the efficiency of organ systems, such as the lungs, heart, and circulatory system. A major cause of biological aging is the decline in the number of cell replications as an organism becomes chronologically older. Another factor is the loss of certain types of cells that do not replicate. This type of aging can be determined by measuring the efficiency and functional abilities of an individual's organ systems, as well as physical activity levels. Indeed, some have referred to this as *functional aging* (Hayflick, 1996).

• *Psychological aging* includes the changes that occur in sensory and perceptual processes, mental functioning (e.g., memory, learning, and intelligence), adaptive capacity, and personality. Thus, an individual who is intellectually active and adapts well to new situations can be considered psychologically young.

• *Social aging* refers to an individual's changing roles and relationships with family and friends, in both paid and unpaid productive roles, and within organizations such as religious and political groups. As people age chronologically, biologically, and psychologically, their social roles and relationships also alter. The social context, which can vary considerably for different people, determines the meaning of aging for an individual and whether the aging experience will be primarily negative or positive.

Social gerontologists study the impact of changes on both older people and social structures. They also study social attitudes toward aging and the effects of these attitudes on older adults. For example, as a society, we have tended to undervalue older people and to assume that most of them are less intelligent than younger people; that they are unemployable, nonproductive, uninterested in interacting with younger people, forgetful, and asexual. As a result, they have been limited in their access to activities such as jobs in high-tech fields. The research reviewed throughout this book demonstrates that these stereotypes are not true for the great majority of older adults and that many continue to participate actively in society.

With the rapid growth in the number and diversity of older persons, societal myths and stereotypes have been challenged. The public has become increasingly aware of older citizens' strengths and contributions. Accordingly, the status of older people and the way they are viewed by other segments of the U.S. population are changing. Contemporary advertising, for example, reflects the changing status of older people from a group that is viewed as weak, ill, and poor to one perceived as politically and economically powerful and, therefore, a growing market.

As older people have become more politically active and as age-based advocacy groups have emerged, they have influenced not only public perceptions, but also policies and programs such as Social Security and Medicare. In the past 50 years, organized groups of older people have helped make changes in retirement and pension policies, housing options, health and long-term care policy, education, and other services. As described in Chapter 12, age-based advocacy is being replaced by cross-generational collaboration today. Such political and attitudinal changes, which can profoundly transform the condition of older people, are also important issues in the study of social gerontology.

Equally significant in this area of study are the social and health problems that continue to affect a large percentage of older people. Even though older adults today are financially better off than they were 50 years ago, almost 11 percent still fall below the U.S. government's official poverty line. Poverty is an even greater problem for women, older people of color, those living alone, and the oldest of the old. Although less than 5 percent of the older population resides in nursing homes at any given time, the number who will require long-term care at some point in their lives is increasing. Growing percentages of older people in the community face chronic diseases that may limit their daily activities. At the same time, however, health and long-term care costs have escalated. In general, older people pay a higher proportion of their income for health and long-term care than they have at any time in the past, and often lack access to publicly supported home- and community-based services. Therefore, many gerontologists are also concerned with developing public policy and practice interventions to address these problems.

SOCIAL GERONTOLOGY

The purpose of this book is to introduce you to *social gerontology*. This term was first used by Clark Tibbitts in 1954 to describe the area of gerontology that is concerned with the impact of social and sociocultural conditions on the process of aging and with the social consequences of this process. This field has grown as we have recognized the extent to which aging differs across cultures and societies.

Social gerontologists are interested in how the older population and the diversity of aging experiences both affect and are affected by the social structure. As discussed later in this chapter, older people are now the fastest-growing population segment in the United States. This fact has far-reaching social implications for health and long-term care, the workplace, pension and retirement practices, community facilities, and patterns of government spending. Already, it has led to new specialties in health care and long-term care; the growth of specialized services such as assisted living and adult day health programs; and a leisure industry aimed at the older population. Changes in

the sociopolitical structure, in turn, affect characteristics of the older population. For example, the greater availability of secondary and higher education, health promotion programs, and employment-based pensions offers hope that future generations of older people will be better educated, healthier, and economically more secure than the current generation.

WHAT IS AGING?

Contrary to the messages on birthday cards, aging does not start at age 40 or 65. Even though we are less conscious of age-related changes in earlier stages of our lives, we are all aging from the moment of birth. In fact, **aging** in general refers to changes that take place in the organism throughout the lifespan—good, bad and neutral. Younger stages are referred to as *development* or *maturation*, because the individual develops and matures, both socially and physically, from birth through adolescence. After age 30, additional changes occur that reflect normal declines in all organ systems. This is called **senescence.** Senescence happens gradually throughout the body, ultimately reducing the viability of different bodily systems and increasing their vulnerability to disease. This is the final stage in the development of an organism (International Longevity Center, 1999).

Our place in the social structure also changes throughout our life span. Every society is *age-graded*; that is, it assigns different roles, expectations, opportunities, status, and constraints to people of different ages. For example, there are common societal expectations about the appropriate age to attend school, begin work, have children, and retire—even though many people deviate from these expectations, and some of these expectations change over time. To call someone a *toddler, child, young adult,* or an *old person* is to imply a full range of social characteristics. As we age, we pass through a sequence of defined stages, each with its own social norms and characteristics. In sum, age is a social construct with social meanings and social implications.

POINTS TO PONDER

For each age group below, think of one activity or event that you think is typical for that age. These might include marriage, attending school, learning to ride a bike. Then think of an activity or event that is not so typical:

	TYPICAL	ATYPICAL
Toddler (ages 2–4)		
Child (ages 4–12)		
Young adult (ages 18–24)		
Old person (age 65+)		

The specific effects of age grading, or age stratification, vary across different cultures and historical time periods. A primitive society, for instance, has very different expectations associated with stages of childhood, adolescence, and old age from our contemporary American cultures. Even within our own culture, those who are old today have different experiences of aging than previous or future groups of older people. The term **cohort** is used to describe groups of people who were born at approximately the same time and therefore share many common experiences. For example, current cohorts of older persons have experienced the Great Depression, World War II, and the Korean War. These experiences have shaped their lives. Its members include large numbers of immigrants who came to the United States in the first third of the twentieth century, and many who have grown up in rural areas. Their average levels of education are lower than those of later generations. Such factors set today's older population apart from other cohorts and must be taken into account in any studies of the aging process.

The Older Population Is Diverse

Throughout this book, we will refer to the phenomenon of aging and the population of older people. These terms are based, to some extent, on chronological criteria, but, more importantly, on individual differences in social, psychological, and biological functioning. In fact, each of us differs somewhat in the way we define old age. You may know an 80-year-old who seems youthful and a 50-year-old whom you consider old. Older people also define themselves differently. Some individuals, even in their eighties, do not want to associate with "those old people," whereas others readily join age-based organizations and are proud of the years they have lived. There are significant differences among the "young-old" (ages 65 to 74), the "old-old" (ages 75 to 84), and the "oldest-old" (ages 85 and over) (Riley & Riley, 1986). In addition, diversity exists even within these divisions.

Older people vary greatly in their health status, their productive activities, and their family situations. Some are still employed full- or part-time; most are retired. Most are healthy; some are frail, confused, or homebound. Most still live in a house or apartment; a small percentage are in nursing homes. Some receive large incomes from pensions and investments; most depend primarily on Social Security and have little discretionary income. Most men over age 65 are married, whereas women are more likely to become widowed and live alone as they age. For all these reasons, we cannot consider the social aspects of aging without also assessing the impact of individual variables such as physiological changes, health status, psychological well-being, socioeconomic class, gender, and ethnic

---

POINTS TO PONDER

Discuss with friends and family some common terms used to describe older adults, such as "elderly," "old folks," and "elders." What images of aging and older people do these terms convey?

---

minority status. Recognizing this, many chapters in this book focus on biological, physiological, health, psychological, gender, and ethnic minority characteristics of older persons that influence their social functioning.

It is likewise impossible to define aging only in chronological terms, since chronological age only partially reflects the biological, psychological, and sociological processes that define life stages. Although the terms *elders, elderly,* and *older persons* are often used to mean those over 65 years in chronological age, this book is based on the principle that aging is a complex process that involves many different factors and is unique to each individual. Rather than chronological age, the more important distinction may be between the ability to function independently or not—that is, the ability to perform activities of daily living that require cognitive and physical well-being.

A PERSON–ENVIRONMENT PERSPECTIVE ON SOCIAL GERONTOLOGY

Consistent with the perspective of the interaction of physiological, psychological, and social changes with aging, this textbook will approach topics in social gerontology from a person–environment perspective. A **person–environment perspective** suggests that the environment is not a static backdrop but changes continually as the older person takes from it what he or she needs, controls what can be manipulated, and adjusts to conditions that cannot be changed. Adaptation thus implies a dual process in which the individual adjusts to some characteristics of the social and physical environment (e.g., completing the numerous forms re-

quired by Medicare), and brings about changes in others (e.g., lobbying to expand Medicare benefits to cover prescription drugs).

Environmental Press

The **competence model** is one useful way to view the dynamic interactions between the person's physical and psychological characteristics and the social and physical environment. This model was first proposed by Lawton and Nahemow (1973), and examined further by Lawton (1989) and by Parmelee and Lawton (1990). *Environment* in this model, which is shown in Figure 1.1, may refer to the larger society, the community, the neighborhood, or the home. **Environmental press** refers to the demands that social and physical environments make on the individual to adapt, respond, or change. The environmental press model can be approached from a variety of disciplinary perspectives. A concept fundamental to social work, for example, is that of human behavior and the environment, and the need to develop practice and policy interventions that achieve a better fit between the person and his or her social environment. Health care providers are increasingly aware of the necessity to take account of social and physical environmental factors (e.g., family and living situation) in their assessments of health problems.

Architects and advocates for persons with disabilities are developing ways to make physical environments more accessible for older people. Psychologists are interested in how physical and social environments may be modified to maximize the older person's ability to learn new tasks and perform familiar ones such as driving, taking tests, and self-care. Sociologists study ways that the

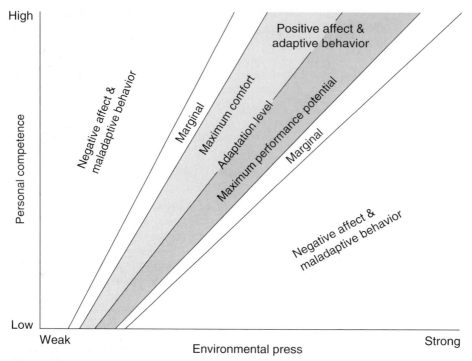

FIGURE 1.1   **Diagrammatic Representation of the Behavioral and Affective Outcomes of Person–Environment Transactions**

SOURCE: M. P. Lawton and L. Nahemow, Ecology and the aging process. In C. Eisdorfer and M. P. Lawton (Eds.), *Psychology of adult development and aging* (Washington, D.C.: American Psychological Association, 1973), p. 661. Copyright 1973 by the American Psychological Association. Reprinted by permission of the author and publisher.

macro-environment (larger political and economic structures) affects and is affected by an individual's interactions with it. Because the concepts of this model are so basic to understanding the position of older people and to developing ways to improve the quality of their lives, such environmental interactions are referred to throughout this text.

The environmental press in such settings can range from minimal to quite high. For example, very little environmental press is present in an institutional setting where an individual is not responsible for self-care, such as personal grooming and housekeeping, and has few resources to stimulate the senses or challenge the mind. Other environments can create a great deal of press—for example, a multigenerational household in which the older person plays a pivotal role. Living in a fa-

miliar setting with few visitors generates low levels of environmental press. An increase in the number of people sharing the living arrangement or a move to a new home increases the environmental demands. As the demands change, the individual must adapt to the changes in order to maintain one's sense of competence.

Individuals perform at their maximum level when the environmental press slightly exceeds the level at which they adapt. In other words, the environment challenges them to test their limits but does not overwhelm them. If the level of environmental demand becomes too high, the individual experiences excessive stress or overload. When the environmental press is far below the individual's adaptation level, sensory deprivation, boredom, learned helplessness, and dependence on others may result. However, a situation of mild to moderate stress, just below the person's adaptation level, results in maximum comfort. It is important to challenge the individual in this situation as well, to prevent a decline to boredom and inadequate stimulation. In either situation—too much or too little environmental press—the person or the environment must change, if the individual's adaptive capacity is to be restored and quality of life enhanced.

Individual competence is another concept central to this model. This is defined by Lawton and Nahemow (1973) as the theoretical upper limit of an individual's abilities to function in the areas of health, social behavior, and cognition. Some of the abilities needed to adapt to environmental press include good health, effective problem-solving and learning skills, job performance, and the ability to manage the basic activities of daily living such as dressing, grooming, and cooking (Parmelee and Lawton, 1990). As suggested by the model in Figure 1.1, the higher a person's competence, the higher the levels of environmental press that can be tolerated. Thus, an older person with multiple physical disabilities and chronic illnesses has reduced physical competence, thereby limiting the level of social and physical demands with which he or she can cope.

Environmental Interventions

The competence model has numerous implications for identifying interventions to enhance older adults' lives. Most services for older people are oriented toward minimizing environmental demands and increasing supports. These services may focus on changing the physical or the social environment, or both. Physical environmental modifications,

such as ramps and handrails, and community services, such as Meals-on-Wheels and escort vans, are relatively simple ways to reestablish the older person's level of adaptation and to ease the burdens of daily coping. Such arrangements are undoubtedly essential to the well-being of some older people who require supports in the form of environmental adaptations or occasional assistance from family and paid caregivers to enhance their independence. For example, many older people with chronic conditions are able to remain in their own homes because of environmental modifications such as emergency systems that allow them to call for help, vans equipped for wheelchairs, computers that aid them with communication, and medication reminders. Other examples of both environmental and individual interventions to enhance older people's choices are considered throughout this text.

A fine line exists, however, between minimizing excessive environmental press and creating an environment that is not stimulating or is "too easy" to navigate. Well-intentioned families, for example, may do too much for the older person, assuming responsibility for daily activities, so that their older relative no longer has to exert any effort and may no longer feel he or she is a contributing family member. Likewise, professionals and family members may try to shield the older person from experiencing too many changes. For example, they may presume that an older person is too set in her or his ways to adjust to sharing a residence, thereby denying the person the opportunity to learn about and make an independent decision on home-sharing options. Well-intentioned nursing home staff may not challenge residents to perform such daily tasks as getting out of bed or going to the dining hall. Protective efforts such as these can remove

---

POINTS TO PONDER

Think about your own home. In what ways would it create high environmental press for an older person with multiple health problems? How could you change it to make it more congruent with the older user's level of personal competence, in order to help him or her achieve positive affect and adaptive behavior?

necessary levels of environmental press, with the result that the person's social, psychological, and physical levels of functioning may decline. Under-stimulating conditions, then, can be as negative in their effects on older people as those in which there is excessive environmental press.

ORGANIZATION OF THE TEXT

This book is divided into five parts:

• Part One is a general introduction to the field of social gerontology and the demographics of an aging society, and includes a brief history of the field, the growth of the older population, a dis-cussion of research methods and designs, and de-scriptions of aging in other historical periods and cultures.

• Part Two addresses the physiological changes that influence social aging. It begins with a review of normal age-related changes in the body's major organ systems, including changes in the sensory sys-tem and their social/environmental effects. It also discusses the chronic diseases that occur most fre-quently among older people, how these diseases can be managed, factors that influence health care be-havior (e.g., when and why older people are likely to seek professional care), and health promotion programs aimed at improving physical, psycholog-ical, and social functioning among older people.

• In Part Three, we move to the psychological context of aging, including normal and disease-re-lated changes in cognitive functioning (learning, intelligence, and memory), theories of personality development and coping styles, mental health is-sues of importance to the older population, and the use of mental health services, as well as love, intimacy, and sexuality in the later years.

• Part Four explores the social issues of aging, beginning with a discussion of current social the-ories of aging, the importance of family, friends, and neighbors for elders, informal caregiving of older adults, and how the array of housing arrange-ments for older adults affects their social interac-tions and sense of competence. Issues related to

productivity, employment, retirement, and income are next explored, followed by a review of unpaid productive roles in the community, in education, in religious institutions, and in politics. This part concludes with topics related to death, dying, and widowhood. The last two chapters of Part Four present the challenges and strengths of older eth-nic minorities and women.

• Part Five goes beyond the individual's social context to address societal perspectives, particu-larly social, health, and long-term care policy is-sues of importance to the older population, and contemporary policy debates. The Epilogue fo-cuses on emerging trends in aging and society's re-sponses to future generations or cohorts of older people, especially the aging of the baby boomers.

Each part begins with an introduction to the key issues of aging that are discussed in that sec-tion. In order to emphasize the variations in phys-iological, psychological, social, and societal aspects of aging, vignettes of older people representing these differences are presented. Throughout each chapter, the diversity of the older population and of the aging process itself is highlighted in terms of chronological age, gender, culture, ethnic minority status, and sexual orientation. Where appropriate, the dynamic interaction between older people and their environment is emphasized. How age-related changes are measured and methods for improving measurement in this field are also discussed. Each chapter concludes with a glossary of key terms that have been introduced as well as web-based and print resources. Look for boxes on some pages that illustrate some of the concepts introduced in the chapters, as well as "Points to Ponder." These ex-ercises can help you apply what you are learning to your own experiences.

WHY STUDY AGING?

As you begin this text, you may find it useful to think about your own motivations for learning about older adults and the aging process. You may be in a required course, questioning its relevance, and approaching this text as something you must read to satisfy requirements. Or you may have personal reasons for wishing to learn about aging. You may be concerned about your own age-related changes, wondering whether reduced energy or alterations in physical features are inevitable with age. After all, since middle and old age together encompass a longer time span than any other stage of our lives, it is important that we understand and prepare for these years. Perhaps you are looking forward to the freedom made possible by retirement and the "empty nest." Through increased knowledge about the aging process, you may be hoping to make decisions that can enhance your own positive adaptation to aging and old age. Or perhaps you are interested in assisting aging relatives, friends, and neighbors, wanting to know what can be done to help them maintain their independence, what housing options exist for them, and how you can improve your caregiving abilities.

Learning about aging not only gives us insight into our own interpersonal relationships, self-esteem, competence, and meaningful activities as we grow older; it also helps us comprehend the aging process of our parents, grandparents, clients, patients, and friends. It is important to recognize that change and growth take place throughout the life course, and that the concerns of older people are not distinct from those of the young, but represent a continuation of earlier life periods. Such understanding can improve our effectiveness in communicating with relatives, friends, or professionals. In addition, such knowledge can help change any assumptions or stereotypes we may hold about behavior appropriate to various ages.

Perhaps you wish to work professionally with older people, but are unsure how your interests can fit in with the needs of the older population. The final chapter of this book, the Epilogue, discusses careers in gerontology. If you are already working with older people, you may genuinely enjoy your work, but you may be concerned about the social and economic problems facing some older adults and thus feel a responsibility to change these negative social conditions. As a pro-fessional or future professional working with older people, you are probably eager to learn more about policy and practice issues that can enhance their quality of life and life satisfaction.

Regardless of your motivations for reading this text, chances are that, like most Americans, you have some misconceptions about older people and the aging process. As products of our youth-oriented society, we have all sensed the pervasiveness of negative attitudes about aging, although our own personal experiences with older people may counter many stereotypes and myths. By studying aging and older people, you will not only become more aware of the older population's competence in many areas, but also be able to differentiate the normal changes that are associated with the aging process from pathological or disease-related changes. Such an understanding may serve to reduce some of your own fears about aging, as well as positively affect your professional and personal interactions with older people.

Our challenge as educators and authors is to present you with the facts and the concepts that will give you a more accurate picture of the experience of aging in U.S. society. We also want to convey to you the excitement and importance of learning about the field of aging. We hope that by the time you have completed this text, you will have acquired information that strengthens positive attitudes toward living and working with older people and toward your own experience of aging. First, we will turn to the demographic changes that are resulting in the largest population of people aged 65 and older in history, not just in the United States, but also throughout the world.

GROWTH OF THE OLDER POPULATION

The growing size of the older population is the single most important factor affecting current interest in the field of gerontology. In 1900, people over 65 accounted for approximately 4 percent of the United States population—less than one in twenty-five. One hundred years later, this segment of our population has grown to almost 35 million, or just under 13 percent of the United States (U.S. Administration on Aging, 2000). This represents a twelve-fold increase in the older population during this period, compared with a threefold increase in the population under age 65. During the next 10 years, however, the population over 65 is expected to grow more slowly than it did between 1950 and 2000. After 2010, as the baby boom generation begins to reach old age, the population over 65 will again increase significantly. Thus, demographers predict that by 2030 the population aged 65 and older will grow to 70 million, representing a 100 percent increase over 30 years, compared with a 30 percent growth in the total population.*

Changes in Life Expectancy

Why have these changes in the older population occurred? Chiefly because people are living longer. In 1900, the average **life expectancy** at birth in the United States (i.e., the average length of time one could expect to live if one were born that year) was 47 years. At that time, there were approximately 772,000 people between the ages of 75 and 84 in the United States, and only 123,000 aged 85 and older. In 1998 there were over 4.1 million in the oldest group. The average life expectancy is now much longer. Females born in 1998 can expect to reach age 79.5, and men, age 73.8. Life expectancy at age 65 is an additional 19.2 years for women and 15.8 years for men (U.S. Bureau of the Census, 1998b, 2000). About four out of five individuals can now expect to reach age 65, at which point there is a better than 50 percent chance of living past age 80.

According to the Census Bureau, life expectancy at birth is expected to increase from the current 76.7 years to 77.6 in 2005 and to 82.6 in 2050. Sex differences in life expectancy have declined since 1980, when females born that year could expect to live 7.4 years more than men; in

1998 the difference was less than 7 years. Projections by the Census Bureau assume a fairly constant 6- to 7-year difference in life expectancy well into the future. Therefore, females born in 2005 are expected to reach age 81; males in that birth cohort will reach age 74. Even in the year 2050, however, male life expectancy will be less than 80 years, whereas women will achieve 84.3 years (U.S. Bureau of the Census, 1996b). Of course, these projections do not take into account potentially new diseases that could differentially increase mortality risks for men and women. For example, if AIDS continues to be a fatal disease that infects younger men more than women, there could be a much greater sex differential in life expectancy. On the other hand, death rates due to hypertension and stroke have already started to decline because of lifestyle changes. Since both conditions are somewhat more likely to affect men, these factors may narrow the sex differential and increase life expectancy even more, for both men and women. Nevertheless, the trend illustrated in Figure 1.2, where women outnumber men at every age after 55, will continue well into this century.

Most of the gains in life expectancy have occurred in the younger ages. For example, during the period from 1900 to 1998, the average life expectancy at birth increased from 47 years to 76 years. In contrast, gains in life expectancy beyond age 65 during this same period have been relatively modest, from about 12.3 to 17.6 years between 1900 and 1998. Gender differences are particularly striking; older men added 3.4 years and women 6.8 years to their life expectancy from 1900 to 1993. The gains that occurred in the early years of life are largely attributable to the eradication in the prior century of many diseases that caused high infant and childhood mortality. On the other hand, increases in survival beyond age 65 may increase significantly in future cohorts, when heart disease and cancer become more chronic and less fatal diseases in adulthood. Already there has been an acceleration of years gained. Between 1900 and 1960 only 2.4 years were gained beyond age 65, while the gain since 1960 has been 3.2 years.

*Estimates by the Urban Institute and the Census Bureau range from a low of 64.3 million to 69.3 million (National Academy, 1999).

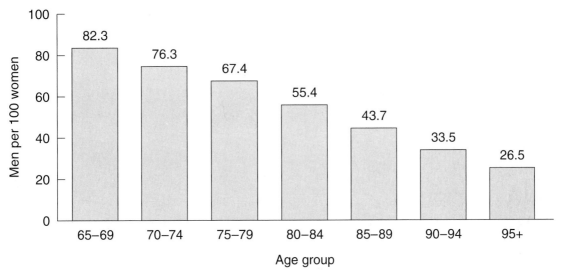

FIGURE 1.2   **Number of Men per 100 Women by Age: 1994**
SOURCE: U.S. Bureau of the Census, 1994.

This shift results mostly from advances in medicine. A hundred years ago, adults generally died from acute diseases, with influenza and pneumonia the principal killers. Few people survived these diseases long enough to need care for chronic or long-term conditions. Today, death from acute diseases is rare. Maternal, infant, and early childhood death rates have also declined considerably. The result is a growing number of people who survive to old age, often with one or more health problems requiring long-term care. The evidence from epidemiological studies suggests that older Americans are receiving better health care than their counterparts in other developed countries. As a result, white Americans at age 80 have a greater life expectancy (women = 9.1 years, men = 7 years) than 80-year-olds in Sweden, Japan, France, and England, even though life expectancy at birth is higher in Sweden and Japan (Manton and Vaupel, 1995).

Maximum Life Span

It is important to distinguish life expectancy from **maximum life span.** While life expectancy is a probability estimate based on environmental conditions such as disease and health care, as described previously, maximum life span is the maximum number of years a given species could expect to live if environmental hazards were eliminated. There appears to be a maximum biologically determined life span for cells that comprise the organism, so that even with the elimination of all diseases, we could not expect to live much beyond 120 years. For these reasons, more and more persons will expect to live longer, but the maximum number of years they can expect to live will not be increased in the foreseeable future unless, of course, some extraordinary and unanticipated biological discoveries occur. Research on some biological factors that may increase longevity for future cohorts is discussed in Chapter 3.

Perhaps the most important goal of health planners and practitioners should be to approach a rectangular survival curve, that is, the "ideal curve." That is, as seen in the survival curve in Figure 1.3, developments in medicine, public hygiene, and health have already increased the percentage of people surviving into the later years. The ideal situation is one where all people would survive to

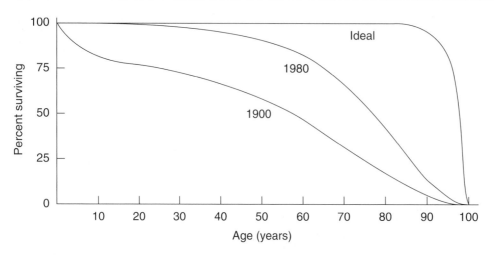

FIGURE 1.3 Increasing Rectangularization of the Survival Curve
SOURCE: Adapted from L. Hayflick, The cell biology of human aging. *Scientific American*, 1980, 242, p. 60, by permission of the publisher.

MORE FORMER U.S. PRESIDENTS AND FIRST LADIES ARE ALIVE TODAY

One example of the increasing likelihood of survival beyond age 65 is the current number of past U.S. presidents who are still alive. In early 2001, five were still alive, from Ronald Reagan at age 90 to Gerald Ford at 87, George Bush and Jimmy Carter at age 76, and Bill Clinton at 55. This was not the case at any other point in U.S. history. As an illustration of greater longevity among women beyond age 65, in early 2001 there are six surviving former first ladies.

Picture taken during a dinner in honor of the 200th Anniversary of the White House. Associated Press AP

the maximum life span, creating a "rectangular curve." The survival curves of developed countries serve as a model for developing countries; that is, about 50 percent of all babies born today in developed countries will reach age 80, or two-thirds of the maximum life span of 120 years (Hayflick, 1996). We are approaching this ideal curve, but it will not be achieved until the diseases of youth and middle age—including cancer, heart disease, diabetes, and kidney diseases—can be totally prevented or at least managed as chronic conditions.

THE OLDEST-OLD

Ages 85 and Older

The population aged 85 and older, also referred to as the "oldest-old," has grown more rapidly than any other age group in our country. In 1998, of the 34.4 million persons aged 65 and over in the United States:

- Twelve million or 35 percent were age 75 to 84.
- Twelve percent were age 85 and over (U.S. Bureau of the Census, 1999a).

Since World War II, mortality rates in adulthood have declined significantly, resulting in an unprecedented number of people who are reaching advanced old age and who are most likely to require long-term care.

- The oldest-old population of Americans has increased by a factor of 23.
- The old-old (ages 75–84) have increased twelvefold.
- The young-old (ages 65–74) increased eightfold.

Those over 85 have increased by more than 300 percent from 1960 to 2000, to 4.3 million. They are expected to reach 8.5 million in 2030. Projections vary depending on predictions about changes in chronic disease morbidity and mortality rates (U.S. Bureau of the Census, 1999a).

This tremendous growth in the oldest-old will take place *before* the influx of baby boomers reaches old age, because this latter group will not begin to turn age 85 until after 2030. The baby boom generation is generally accepted as those born between 1946 and 1964, and currently numbers 69 million. By the year 2050, when the survivors of this generation are age 85 and older, they

---

WHO ARE THE OLDEST-OLD?

- Not surprisingly, the great majority are women (70 percent).
- Their educational level is lower than for those aged 65 to 74 (8.6 years vs. 12.1 in 1990),
- Most are widowed, divorced, or never married (77.2 percent vs. 62 percent).
- Their mean personal income is lower than for other, older cohorts,
- A high proportion live below or near poverty (19 percent of married persons 85 and older were classified as poor or near poor in 1998, compared with 11 percent of their counterparts aged 65–69) (SSA.gov/policy/pubs, 2000).

- The current cohort of oldest-old includes 15 percent who are foreign born. Many immigrated from Italy, Poland, Russia, and other European countries in the early 1900s, while others are later immigrants from China, Japan, the Philippines, Vietnam, and Mexico. The usual problems of aging may be exacerbated for these non-native speakers of English as they try to communicate with health care providers. Misdiagnosis of physical, psychological, and cognitive disorders may occur in such cases.

are expected to number 19 million, or 5 percent of the total U.S. population (U.S. Bureau of the Census, 1999c). This represents a 500 percent increase within 60 years. The impact of such a surge in the oldest-old on the demand for health services, especially hospitals and long-term care settings, will be dramatic.

It is also important to consider the distribution of selected age groups now and in the future. The young-old (ages 65–74) currently represent 53 percent of the older population; those over 85 make up 12 percent. In contrast, the corresponding proportions in 2050 are projected to be 44 percent young-old and 23 percent oldest-old (see Figure 1.4).

Because they are more likely to have multiple health problems that often result in physical frailty, and because up to 50 percent of the oldest-old may have some form of cognitive impairment, this group is disproportionately represented in institutional settings such as nursing homes, assisted living, and hospitals (Carr, Goate, Phil, and Morris, 1997). Almost 25 percent live in a long-term care setting, and they make up more than 50 percent of the population of nursing homes. How-

ever, the incidence of institutionalization among African Americans aged 85 and older is only about half this rate (12 percent). The oldest-old blacks are far more likely to be living with relatives other than a spouse (40 percent). Very few of the oldest-old (regardless of ethnic minority status) live with a spouse, compared with nearly 60 percent of all people over age 65 (U.S. Administration on Aging, 2000). Even among those living in the community, functional health is more impaired in the oldest-old. However, as shown in later chapters, future cohorts of the oldest-old are likely to be healthier and more active than today's population.

Centenarians

Projections by the Census Bureau (1999a) also suggest a substantial increase in the population of "centenarians," people aged 100 or older. In 2000, it was estimated that about 70,000 people have reached this age, and about 324,000 will do so by 2030. Even with this fivefold increase, however, the population over 100 will still represent less than 1 percent of the U.S. population in 2030. Baby boomers are expected to survive to age 100

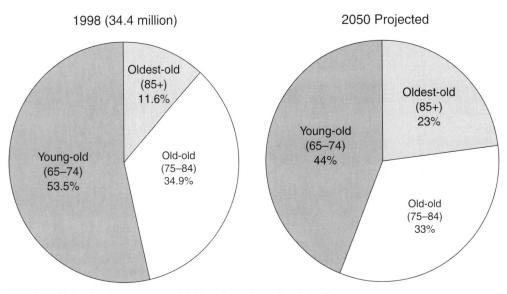

1998 (34.4 million)

2050 Projected

FIGURE 1.4   **Percentage of Older Americans by Age Group**
SOURCE: U.S. Administration on Aging, 2000.

A growing number of multigenerational families are headed by centenarians.

at rates never before achieved; one in 26 can expect to live to be 100, by 2025, compared with one in 500 at the turn of the century.

As more and more Americans become centenarians, there is growing interest in their genetics and the lifestyle that may have influenced their longevity. Data from the Georgia Centenarian Study support other findings of greater survival among women, as well as race crossover effects in advanced old age. In this follow-up of 137 people aged 100 at entry into the study, African American women survived longest beyond age 100. On average, they survived twice as many months as white men, who lived the shortest time beyond 100. White women had the next best survival rates, and lived slightly longer than African American men (Poon et al., 2000).

The New England Centenarian Study points to genetic factors that determine how well the older person copes with disease (Perls, 1995; Perls and Silver, 1999; Perls and Wood, 1996). As shown in Figure 1.5, the model proposed by this study suggests that the oldest-old are hardy because they have a higher threshold for disease and show slower rates of disease progression than their peers who develop chronic diseases at a younger age and die earlier. Perls and colleagues illustrate this hypothesis with the case of a 103-year-old man who displayed few symptoms of Alzheimer's

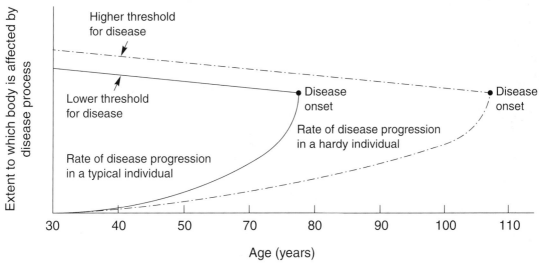

FIGURE 1.5   Response to Chronic Disease among Elders Who Survive to Age 100 vs Nonsurvivors
SOURCE: Adapted from Perls, 1995.

disease; however, at autopsy this man's brain had a high level of neurofibrillary tangles, which are a hallmark of this disease.

Older men who survive to age 90, in particular, represent the hardiest segment of their birth cohort. Between ages 65 and 89, women score higher on tests of cognitive function. However, after age 90, men perform far better on these tests. Even at age 80, 44 percent of men were found to be robust and independent, compared with 28 percent of women. Contrary to the prior belief prevalent in gerontology that dementia is a concomitant of advanced age, it appears that as many as 30 percent of centenarians have no memory problems, 20 percent have some, and 50 percent have serious problems. In one study of 69 centenarians who were tested for dementia, six subsequently died. None of these robust elders showed significant signs of dementia, either in their neuropsychological testing or in the neuropathological studies of their brains (Samuelsson et al., 1997; Silver, Newell, Hyman, Growdon, Hedley, and Perls, 1998; Suzman, Willis, and Manton, 1992). Indeed, other researchers who have studied dementia in older adults have suggested that the genetic mutations most closely associated with Alzheimer's disease are not present in the oldest-old. Environmental factors that emerge much later in life appear to cause dementia in these survivors (Kaye, 1997).

Further evidence for the robustness of centenarians comes from the New England Centenarian Study and a similar assessment of centenarians in Sweden (Samuelsson et al., 1997). Of the 79 people who were age 100 or older in the former study, all lived independently into their early 90s and, on average, took only one medication. In the Swedish Centenarian Study:

- Fifty-two percent were able to perform their activities of daily living with little or no assistance.
- Thirty-nine percent had a disorder of the circulatory system.
- Eighty percent had problems with vision and hearing.

Centenarians appear to be healthy for a longer period of time, although almost 50 percent live in nursing homes, compared with 25 percent of all persons aged 85 and older (U.S. Bureau of the Census, 1999a). Death generally occurs quickly rather than lingering. Indeed, a major study of medical expenditures for the last two years of life found the average cost to be nearly three times greater for people who died at age 70 than for those who live past 100 (Lubitz and Riley, 1993).

Population Pyramids

The increase in longevity is partly responsible for an unusually rapid rise in the *median age* of the U.S. population—from 28 in 1970 to 35.3 in 2000—meaning that half the population was older than 35 and half younger in 1997. From an historical perspective, a 7-year increase in the median age over a 30-year period is a noteworthy demographic event. The other key factors contributing to this rise include a dramatic decline in the birth rate after the mid-1960s, high birth rates in the periods from 1890 to 1915 and just after World War II (these baby boomers are now all older than the median), and the large number of immigrants before the 1920s.

As stated earlier in this chapter, the baby boom generation (currently aged 34 to 52) will

---

MANY CENTENARIANS ARE ACTIVE IN THEIR COMMUNITIES

In one assisted-living facility, two centenarians are active participants in that community. They join in most of the social activities, enjoy local outings, and have numerous friends who visit them. They regularly go to the exercise room after dinner, pedaling on stationary bikes while reading or watching the news.

dominate the age distribution in the United States in the next three decades. In fact, between 2010 and 2030, they will form the "senior boom" and swell the ranks of the 65-plus generation to the point that one in five Americans will be old. The projected growth in the older population will increase the median age of the U.S. population from 36 in 2000 to age 37 by 2010. If current fertility and immigration levels remain stable, the only age groups to experience significant growth in the next century will be those older than 55 (U.S. Bureau of the Census, 1999a).

One of the most dramatic examples of the changing age distribution of the American population is the shift in the proportion of older adults in relation to the proportion of young persons, as illustrated in Figure 1.6. In 1900, when approximately 4 percent of the population was age 65 and over, young persons aged 0 to 17 years made up 40 percent of the population. By 1994, reduced birth rates in the 1970s and 1980s had resulted in a decrease of young persons to 25 percent of the population. The U.S. Census Bureau predicts that, by 2030, the proportion of young and old persons will be almost equal, with those aged 0 to 17 forming 22 percent of the population and older adults forming 21 percent. Indeed, in 1990 the proportion of people under age 14 was the same as those aged 60 or older (U.S. Bureau of the Census, 1996b). After 2030, if current trends continue, the death rate will be greater than the birth rate.

One way of illustrating the changing proportions of young and old persons in the population is the *population pyramid*. Figure 1.7 contrasts the population pyramid for 1975 and those for the years 2010, 2030, and 2050. Each horizontal bar in these pyramids represents a 10-year *birth cohort* (i.e., people born within the same 10-year period). By comparing these bars, we can determine the relative proportion of each birth cohort. As you can see in the first graph, the distribution of the population in 1975 had already moved from a true pyramid to one with a bulge in the 10- to 30-year-old group; this represents the large group of baby boomers. This pyramid grows more column-like over the years, as shown in the other three

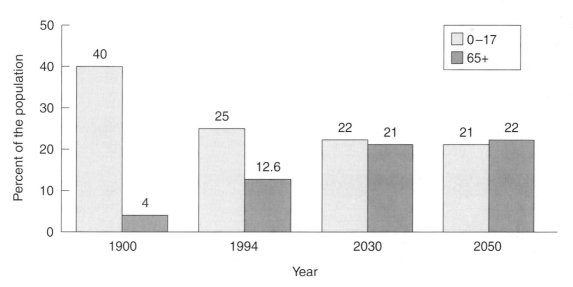

FIGURE 1.6 **Actual and Projected Distribution of Children and Elderly in the Population: 1900–2050**

SOURCE: G. Spencer, U.S. Bureau of the Census, Projections of the population of the United States, by age, sex, and race: 1983–2080. *Current Population Reports,* Series P-25-1104, 1993.

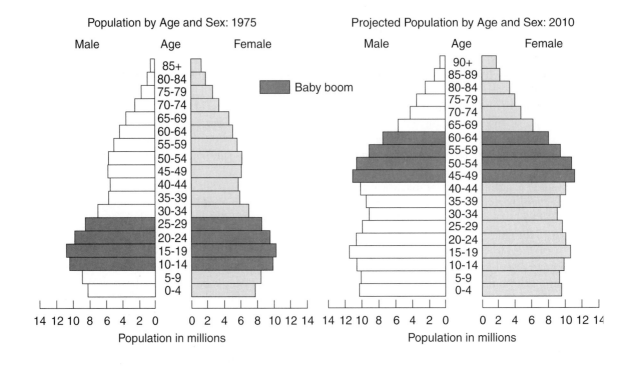

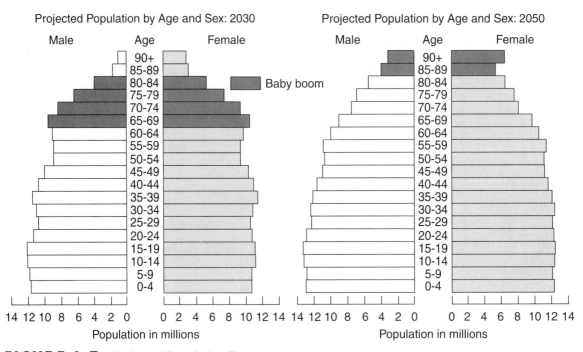

FIGURE 1.7 **Projected Population Figures**

SOURCES: U.S. Bureau of the Census, Preliminary Estimates of the Population of the United States by Age, Sex, and Race: 1970–1981. *Current Population Reports,* Series P-25, No. 917. U.S. Government Printing Office, Washington, DC, 1982. Jennifer C. Day, U.S. Bureau of the Census, Population Projections of the United States by Age, Sex, Race, and Hispanic Origin: 1993–2050. *Current Population Reports,* P-25-1104. U.S. Government Printing Office, Washington, DC, 1993 (middle series projections).

graphs. These changes reflect the aging of the baby boomers (note the "pig in a python" phenomenon as this group moves up the age ladder), combined with declining birth rates and reduced death rates for older cohorts.

DEPENDENCY RATIOS

One aspect of the changing age distribution in our population that has raised public concern is the so-called *dependency ratio*, or "elderly support ratio." The way this ratio has generally been used is to indicate the relationship between the proportion of the population that is employed (defined as "productive" members of society) and the proportion that is not in the workforce (and is thus viewed as "dependent"). This rough estimate is obtained by comparing the percent of the population aged 18 to 64 (the working years) to the proportion under age 18 (yielding the childhood dependency ratio) and over 65 (yielding the old-age dependency ratio). This ratio has increased steadily, such that proportionately fewer employed persons appear to support older persons today. In 1910, the ratio was less than .10 (i.e., ten working people per older person), compared with .21 in 1995 (i.e., five working people per older person). Assuming that the lower birth rate continues, this trend will be apparent in the early part of this century, as the baby boom cohort reaches old age. By the year 2020, a ratio of .28 (or fewer than four working people per retired person) is expected (U.S. Administration on Aging, 2000). These changes since 1960, along with projections through 2050, are illustrated in Figure 1.8.

Such a crude measure of dependency rates is problematic, however. Many younger and older persons are actually in the labor force and not dependent, while many people of labor-force age may not be employed. Another flaw is that dependency ratios do not take account of the labor-force participation rates of different groups; for example, the rates of women aged 16 and older are expected to increase in this century, while those of men are projected to remain steady. When these variations are taken into account, the total dependency ratio in the year 2050 will remain lower than recent historical levels, even though it increases as the population ages. Moreover, despite population aging, those under the age of 16 will continue to constitute the largest "dependent" group into this century. Therefore, we need to be

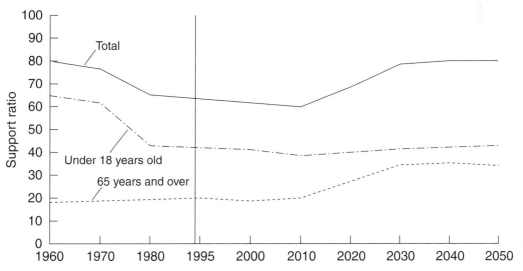

FIGURE 1.8 **Number of Dependents per 100 Persons Aged 18–64 Years:**
Estimates, 1960–1980; Projections, 1995 to 2050
SOURCE: U.S. Bureau of the Census, Current Population Reports, Series P-25, No. 1130, 1996.

cautious when policy makers predict "burdens" on the younger population and blame rising costs of public pension programs primarily on the changing dependency ratio (National Academy, 1999; Quinn, 1996).

POPULATION TRENDS

In addition to the proportional growth of the older population in general, other demographic trends are of interest to gerontologists. These include statistics related to the social, ethnic, racial, gender, and geographic distribution of older populations. In this section, we will review some of these trends, beginning with the demographics of ethnic minorities in the United States.

Ethnic Minorities

Because of lifelong differences in access to health care and preventive health services, elders of color have a lower life expectancy than whites. For example, in 1998, life expectancy at birth was 80 years for white females and 74.8 for African American females. White males could expect to live 74.5 years, compared with 67.6 years for their black counterparts. Nevertheless, the greatest improvement in life expectancy between 1997 and 1998 occurred for the latter group, an increase of 0.4 years. White males showed no change in life expectancy during that same period (U.S. Bureau of the Census, 2000).

Today, ethnic minorities comprise 16 percent of the population over age 65; they include a smaller proportion of older people and a larger proportion of younger adults than the white population. In 1998, 14.8 percent of whites, but only 8.4 percent of African Americans and 5.8 percent of Hispanics were age 65 and over. The difference results primarily from the higher fertility and mortality rates among the nonwhite population under age 65 than among the white population under 65. However, the recently released 2000 census figures suggest that the proportion of older persons will increase at a *higher* rate for the nonwhite population than for the white population. This is partly because of the large percent of children in these groups, who, unlike their parents and especially their grandparents, are expected to reach old age (U.S. Bureau of the Census, 2000). Figures 1.9 and 1.10 illustrate these differential patterns of growth. A more detailed description of ethnic minority populations is provided in Chapter 14.

Geographic Distribution

Demographic information on the location of older populations is important for a variety of reasons. For example, the differing needs of rural and urban older people may affect research designs as well as local government policy decisions. Statistical information on older populations state-to-state is necessary in planning for the distribution of federal funds. Comparison of demographic patterns in different nations and cultures may provide insights into various aspects of the aging process. The following are some of the most salient statistics on the geographic distribution of older adults today. The implications of these changes will be considered in later chapters, including their impact on living arrangements, social, health and long-term care policies, and cross-cultural issues.

Although older adults live in every state and region of the United States and represent 13 percent of the total U.S. population, they are not evenly distributed:

- The Northeast continues to be the region with the oldest population; those over 65 represent 14 percent of its population.
- The western states have approximately 11 percent elders (U.S. Administration on Aging, 2000).

About 52 percent of all persons 65 and older lived in nine states in 1998:

- California (3.5 million older residents)
- Florida (2.7 million)
- New York (2.4 million)

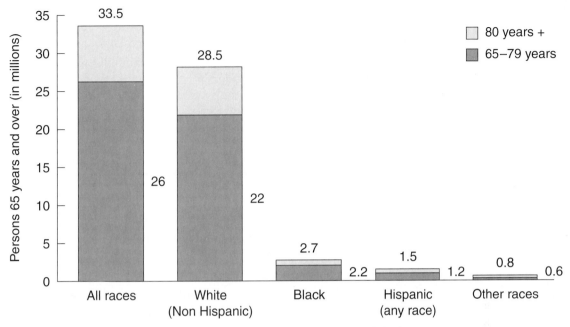

FIGURE 1.9 **Persons 65 Years and Over: 1995 (numbers in million)**
SOURCE: U.S. Bureau of the Census, modified and actual age, sex, race, and Hispanic origin data, 1996.

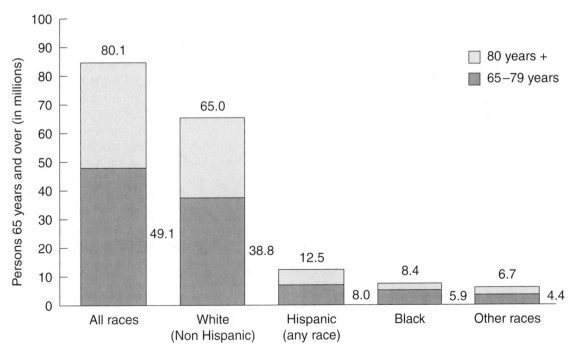

FIGURE 1.10 **Persons 65 Years and Over: 2050 (numbers in millions).**
Hispanics are also included in racial group totals.
SOURCE: U.S. Bureau of the Census, Middle series projections (1993).

- Pennsylvania and Texas (about 2 million in each)
- Ohio, Illinois, Michigan, and New Jersey (over 1 million each)

This does not necessarily mean that all these states have a higher *proportion* of older Americans than the national average, but their absolute numbers are large. Some states have a much higher proportion of residents over 65 than the national average. For example, in 1998 they represented:

- 18.3 percent of the population in Florida
- almost 16 percent in Pennsylvania and Rhode Island
- approximately 15 percent in West Virginia, Iowa, Arkansas, North and South Dakota, and Connecticut

In contrast, elders represented just 5.5 percent of the population of Alaska and 8.8 percent of the population of Utah (U.S. Administration on Aging, 2000).

Because of these disparate proportions of older adults in their states' population, it is not surprising that Florida has the highest median age in the United States (37.6 years), and Utah the lowest (26.8 years). In some cases, such as that of Florida, migration of retired persons to the state explains the increase, whereas in others, such as West Virginia and South Dakota, migration of younger persons out of the state leaves a greater proportion of older people. More than 20 percent of some rural counties in these states are over age 65. Other states may simply reflect the generalized

"graying of America." These regional differences are expected to continue in this century.

Residential relocation is relatively rare for older people in the United States. In a typical year, less than 5 percent of people aged 65 and older move, compared with 18 percent of people under age 65 (U.S. Administration on Aging, 2000). The movement that occurs tends to be within the same region of the country and the same types of environment; that is, people over age 65 generally move from one metropolitan area to another or from one rural community to another. These trends and their implications for well-being in the later years are described further in Chapter 11 and the Epilogue.

Educational and Economic Status

In 1960, less than 20 percent of the population over age 65 had finished high school. By 1998, 67 percent of the new cohort aged 65 and older had completed high school and 15 percent held a bachelor's degree, with only slight gender differences. However, racial and generational differences are striking. Among whites who were age 65 and older in 1998, 69 percent had completed high school, compared with 43 percent of African Americans and 30 percent of Hispanics in this age group (U.S. Administration on Aging, 2000). Because of historical patterns of discrimination in educational opportunities, a disproportionate ratio of older persons of color today have less than a high school education. Thus, 63 percent of African Americans and 70 percent of Hispanics in this age group did not complete high school, compared with only 33 percent of white elders (AARP,

---

POINTS TO PONDER

The majority of older people, 77 percent in 1998, lived in metropolitan areas. About 28 percent lived in cities, 49 percent in suburbs, and 23 percent in rural areas. Despite their low distribution in rural communities, older adults make up a greater percentage of rural populations than in the general population: 15 percent of all rural residents vs. 13 percent of the total U.S. population (AARP, 2000). What do you think accounts for this higher proportion of elders in rural communities?

1999). Because educational level is so closely associated with economic well-being, these ethnic differences have a major impact on poverty levels of older persons of color. Other implications of these gaps in educational attainment are discussed further in Chapter 14.

Not surprisingly, people aged 65 to 69 are more educated today than the old-old and oldest-old. Two-thirds of the former (67 percent) have at least a high school education, compared with 52 percent of their older peers. For this reason, the median educational level today is 12.1 years for the young-old, 10.5 years for the old-old, and 8.6 years for the oldest-old (age 85+). Women in all older cohorts of whites and African Americans (but not Hispanics) are more likely than men to have completed high school. The situation shifts for college education. Because of cultural values in previous generations, fewer white women age 65 and older have college degrees than do white men. Among African Americans the pattern is mixed; for those 70 and older, more black women than men have completed college while for the 65- to 69-year-olds, fewer have completed college (U.S. Bureau of the Census, 1998a). It is noteworthy that an even greater proportion of people over 25 today (75 percent) have at least a high school education. This suggests that future generations of older people will be better educated—many with college degrees—than their grandparents are today. The implications of this shift for political activism, employment, and the nature of productive roles are explored in the Epilogue.

In 1998 only 16 percent of men and 8 percent of women aged 65 and older were in the labor force. This represents a steady decline in labor-force participation, even with the removal of mandatory retirement from most jobs in 1986. However, part-time work is an increasingly attractive option for 54 percent of older people (48 percent of men and 62 percent of women) employed in a part-time or temporary capacity (U.S. Administration on Aging, 2000).

Social Security remains the major source of income for many older Americans; in 1998 only 21 percent said that their primary source was earnings from employment and 43 percent from private pensions. In fact, increases in Social Security benefits along with annual cost-of-living adjustments are major factors underlying the improved economic status of the older population. Currently, almost 11 percent of older people subsist on incomes below the poverty level, compared to 35 percent in the late 1950s, and equal to the poverty rate of Americans aged 18–64. Another 6.3 percent of older Americans are classified as "near-poor" with income levels between poverty and 125 percent of the poverty level (U.S. Administration on Aging, 2000). The improved economic status of the older population as a whole masks the growing rates of poverty among older women, elders of color, the oldest-old, and those living alone. Older women in 1998 were almost twice as likely to be poor as men (12.8 percent vs. 7.2 percent). Older African Americans and Hispanics are far more likely to be poor than whites (26.4 percent, 22 percent, and 8.2 percent, respectively). Poverty is higher among elders in central cities (13.8 percent) and in rural communities (12.5 percent). The combination of ethnicity and marital status displays even more disparities; for example, in 1998 the median income for a white married couple aged 65 and older was $32,398, compared with $22,102 for older African American households. The current and projected economic status of the older population is discussed in detail in Chapters 12, 13, and 14.

WORLDWIDE TRENDS

All world regions are experiencing an increase in the absolute and relative size of their older populations. The number of persons age 65 or older in the world is expected to increase from 357 million in 1990 to 761 million in 2025. This will result in a world population in which one out of every seven people will be 65 years of age or older by the year 2025 (U.S. Bureau of the Census, 1999b).

The current numbers and expected growth of the older population differ substantially between the industrialized and developing countries. Currently 60 percent of older adults live in developing countries, projected to increase to 75 percent by 2020. For example, in 2000 the population aged 65 and older for most Western European countries was estimated to be greater than 15 percent:

- Italy currently has the highest proportion of elders in the world (18.2 percent).
- Greece has 17.2 percent.
- Belgium is home to 17.1 percent.
- Japan has 17 percent (U.S. Bureau of the Census, 1999b).

In contrast, Sub-Saharan Africa and South Asia each counted only 3 percent of their population aged 65 or over. The median age of these regions also varies:

- The median age is 23.5 worldwide.
- It is 37 in Western Europe.
- It is 32 in the United States.
- It is 20 in Latin America.

In Africa, with continued high fertility and high mortality rates, the median age will remain around 20 in the year 2020, while that of other countries will rise (U.S. Bureau of the Census, 1999b).

At the same time, the less developed regions of the world expect to show a nearly fivefold increase in their oldest population, from 3.8 percent in 1975 to 17 percent in 2075. An even greater rise in the proportion of the old-old (ages 75–84) and oldest-old (85+) is expected in these countries,

from the current 0.5 percent to 3.5 percent in 2075. Reasons for this increase in developing countries include:

- improved sanitation
- medical care
- immunizations
- better nutrition

By the year 2020, only 25 percent of the world's older adults are expected to reside in industrialized nations, while 75 percent will live in developing countries. It is important to note, however, that the less developed regions of the world are currently coping with the tremendous impact of high fertility rates. Even with the continued high infant mortality rates in these countries, children under 15 represent 37 percent of the population in less developed regions, compared with 22 percent in more developed regions.

As noted above, the improved life expectancy in industrial nations, which has increased by 6 years for men and 8.5 years for women since 1953, has resulted in a dramatic increase in the older population. The rate has grown more rapidly over the past 20 years, with a significant impact on the availability of workers to support retired persons. If current retirement patterns continue, the dependency ratio for older retired persons will drop from 3.5 workers to support one retiree in 1990 to about 2 in 2030 in the industrialized countries of Europe. In Japan, the pyramid will become even more rectangular, with a decline from 4 to 2 workers in the next 30 years. In con-

---

JAPAN'S EXPERIENCES WITH AN AGING POPULATION

Japan is experiencing the most rapid rate of population aging in the world. In 1970, 7 percent of its population was 65 or older, but this increased to 17 percent in 2000. This group will comprise 26 percent of Japan's population by 2020. Even more striking is the prediction that 7.2 percent will be age 80 and older in 2020, compared with 4.1 percent in the U.S. (U.S. Bureau of the Census, 1996a). Japan's median age is currently 41, compared with 35 for the United States. Japan also has the highest life expectancy at birth: 80.2 years (U.S. Bureau of the Census, 1999b).

trast, the ratio in the United States will drop from the current 5 workers to 3 during this same period. These changes will place tremendous demands on the social security systems, government-subsidized health care, and pension programs of these nations. They may need to develop incentives for later retirement, which may be difficult, considering the trend toward early retirement in most industrial nations. It may also be necessary for developed countries to permit more immigration of young workers from the developing world and to provide training in the technology required by these countries. However, this is a controversial proposal for countries where immigrants often are not easily assimilated because of languages, religions, and cultures divergent from those of the host country.

Therefore, it is not surprising that in countries with the lowest birthrates and the highest proportions of people aged 65 and older, where one would expect large numbers of foreign-born workers, they represent less than 10 percent of the total population. In 1995, 1.7 percent of Italy's, 1.1 percent of Japan's, and 8.8 percent of Germany's residents were foreign-born (OECD, 1995). In 2000 the Interior Ministry of Germany established a Migrant Commission comprised of academic experts, labor union and business leaders, as well as foreign nationals in Germany. The task of this commission is to make recommendations regarding future immigration policy for much-needed younger workers.

Other countries are implementing new programs for elder care. With a growing population of people over 65, combined with fewer children to care for them, China has increased its publicly funded housing for childless elders. A private residential care facility industry is also emerging in response to the anticipated 16 percent older population by 2030. In Singapore a more radical approach to caring for a growing older population has emerged. In 1997 the government opened a special court where older persons can bring legal claims against their children for not providing assistance in their old age.

IMPACT OF DEMOGRAPHIC TRENDS IN THE UNITED STATES

As discussed later in this book, the growth of older populations has wide-ranging implications. The impact of demographic changes in the United States is most striking in terms of federal spending. The growth in numbers and proportions of older people has already placed pressures on our health, long-term care, and social service systems, as discussed in Chapters 16 and 17. Although some expenditures are directly related to the high cost of health care, the increase in life expectancy also has changed people's expectations about the quality of life in late adulthood. Increasingly in our society, those facing retirement anticipate living 20 to 30 years in relatively good health, with adequate retirement incomes. When these expectations are not met, because of catastrophic medical costs, widowhood, or a retirement income eroded by inflation, older adults may not be prepared to manage a change in their lifestyles. For other segments of the older population, particularly women and elders of color, old age may represent a continuation of a lifetime of poverty or near-poverty. Fortunately, for most older people, the problems associated with old age, particularly chronic illness and the attendant costs, are forestalled until their 70s and 80s. Nevertheless, rapid growth in numbers of frail elders, the majority of whom are women, may severely strain the health and income systems designed to provide resources in old age.

LONGEVITY IN HEALTH OR DISEASE?

Future cohorts of older people may be healthier and more independent well into their eighties and nineties. A strong argument was put forth to this effect by Fries (1980, 1990), who suggests that more people will achieve the maximum life span in future years because of healthier lifestyles and better health care during their youth and middle years. Furthermore, Fries argues that future

---

INTERNATIONAL COMPARISONS

The United States has a lower healthy life expectancy than countries such as Japan, Australia, Sweden, France, and Italy. Japan's advantage in healthy life ex- pectancy has been attributed to lower rates of smoking and heart disease among older cohorts (AARP, 2000).

---

cohorts will have fewer debilitating illnesses and will, in fact, experience a phenomenon he labelled **compression of morbidity** (i.e., experiencing only a few years of major illness in very old age). These older adults of the future may therefore expect to die a "natural death," or death due to the natural wearing out of all organ systems by approximately age 100. If this process does occur, it will have a significant impact on both the type of health and long-term care services needed by future genera- tions of older people and their ability to experience productive aging. Long-term care needs may be re- duced, with more subacute care facilities and short-term home health services required.

Indeed, some evidence from a review of large national health surveys indicates that the older population today is generally healthier than pre- vious cohorts. An analysis of two large longitudi- nal health surveys—the Longitudinal Study on Aging and the National Health Interview Survey (NHIS)—from 1982 through 1993 for respon- dents who were age 70 and older in each year, re- veals that rates of disability are declining or stabilizing. At the same time, recovery from acute disabilities (e.g., due to falls) is improving. This may be due to more aggressive rehabilitation ef- forts for older adults in recent years (Crimmins, Saito, and Reynolds, 1997), and is consistent with the findings of another analysis of national health surveys. In a comparison of responses to the Na- tional Long-term Care Survey from 1982 through 1999, there was a notable decline in disability rates, from 26 percent in 1982 to 20 percent in 1996 (Manton and Gu, 2001). This means that future generations of the oldest-old may have lower health care expenditures and less reliance on long-term care services.

The concept of **active versus dependent life ex- pectancy** (Katz et al., 1983) is useful in this con- text. Katz and others distinguish between merely living a long life and living a healthy old age. This can also be conceptualized as adding life to years, not just years to life. Instead of death, they define the endpoint of "active" life expectancy as the loss of independence or the need to rely on others for most activities of daily living. Life expectancy has increased beyond age 65, but about a third of the years lived will be in a dependent state (WHO, 1995). For example:

- A 65-year-old woman today has approxi- mately 19.2 years remaining, 13.2 in active life expectancy, 6 in dependency.
- A 65-year-old man can look forward to living 15.8 more years, about one-third of these in a dependent state.

Not surprisingly, differences in life conditions of older persons with inadequate income and those above the median income have led to the conclusion that active life expectancy differs by 1 to 2.5 years between the poor and nonpoor. This may result in a growing bimodal distribution of older people remaining healthier and free of dis- ease (as predicted by Fries), and another, probably larger distribution of older adults surviving dis- eases that would have been fatal years ago, but liv- ing with "battle scars." This latter group may be the segment of the population that is distorting projections for compressed morbidity; as we have seen in the reviews of NHIS findings, this latter group also appears to be increasing in size. This is probably the segment of the older population that will require long-term care in the future.

HOW AGING AND OLDER ADULTS ARE STUDIED

You are undoubtedly aware that more researchers are studying older people and the process of aging now than in the past. Some of the concerns that have motivated this increasing professional interest in the field have probably influenced your own decision to study gerontology. In this section we turn to the question of how the older population is studied: What are the particular challenges of social gerontological research, and how are they addressed? Methods of conducting research in this field are described. The net effect of this information is to give you a basic orientation to the field of aging, how it has developed, and methods of studying the older population.

Development of the Field

Although the scientific study of social gerontology is relatively recent, it has its roots in biological studies of the aging processes and in the psychology of human development. Biologists have long explored the reasons for aging in living organisms. Several key publications and research studies are milestones in the history of the field.

One of the first textbooks on aging, *The History of Life and Death,* was written in the thirteenth century by Roger Bacon. With great foresight, Bacon suggested that life expectancy could be extended if health practices, such as personal and public hygiene, were improved. The first scientist to explain aging as a developmental process, rather than as stagnation or deterioration, was a nineteenth-century Belgian mathematician–statistician named Adolph Quetelet. His interest in age and creative achievement preceded the study of these issues by social scientists by 100 years. His training in the field of statistics also led him to consider the problems of **cross-sectional research**—that is, the collection of data on people of different ages at one time, instead of **longitudinal research,** the study of the same person over a period of months or years.

These problems are examined in greater detail in the next section of this chapter.

One of the first laboratory studies of aging was undertaken in the 1920s by the Russian physiologist Ivan Pavlov. Pavlov is best known for his research with animals, which has provided the foundation for stimulus-response theories of behavior. Recognizing that the ability of older animals to learn and distinguish a response differed from that of younger animals, Pavlov explored the reasons for these differences in animal brains. The work of Raymond Pearl and colleagues in the 1920s established the insect *Drosophila* (or fruit fly) as an ideal animal model for studying biological aging and longevity. During this era, in 1922, American psychologist G. Stanley Hall published one of the first books on the social–psychological aspects of aging in the United States. Titled *Senescence, the Last Half of Life*, it remains a landmark text in social gerontology because it provided the experimental framework for examining changes in cognitive processes and social and personality functions.

Historical Forces of the Late Nineteenth and Early Twentieth Centuries

Two important forces led to the expansion of research in social gerontology in the late nineteenth and early twentieth centuries:

- the growth of the population over age 65 (as described earlier)
- the emergence of retirement policies

Changes in policies toward older adults were first evident in many European countries (e.g., Germany) where age-based social services and health insurance programs were developed. In contrast, these changes did not occur in the United States until the 1930s. In 1900, the focus on economic growth and the immediate problems of establishing workers' rights and child welfare laws took precedence over improving the welfare of older people. The prevailing belief in this country had been that families should be responsible for their aging members.

However, the Great Depression of the 1930s brought to policy makers the stark realization that families struck by unemployment and homelessness could not be responsible for their elders. The older segments of society suffered a disproportionate share of the economic blight of the Depression. New concern for the needs of the aging population was exemplified by the Social Security system, established in 1935 to help people maintain a minimal level of economic security after retirement. Early work in social gerontology dealt largely with social and economic problems of aging. For example, E. V. Cowdry's *Problems of Ageing,* published in 1939, focused on society's treatment of older people and their particular needs. It amazes us today that the second edition of Cowdry's book, published in 1942, contained all the research knowledge available on aging at that time!

FORMAL DEVELOPMENT OF THE FIELD

As society grew more aware of issues facing the older population, the formal study of aging emerged in the 1940s. In 1945, the Gerontological Society of America (GSA) was founded, bringing together the small group of researchers and practitioners who were interested in gerontology and geriatrics at that time. Gerontology became a division of the American Psychological Association in 1945 and, later, of the American Sociological Association.

The *Journal of Gerontology,* which the GSA began publishing in 1946, served as the first vehicle for transmitting new knowledge in this growing field. In 1988 it became two journals,

reflecting the growth of gerontology. Today numerous others are devoted to the study of aging and to the concerns of those who work with older people. An indicator of the knowledge explosion in the field is that the literature on aging published between 1950 and 1960 equalled that of the previous 115 years (Birren and Clayton, 1975). An effort to compile a bibliography of biomedical and social research from 1954 to 1974 produced 50,000 titles (Woodruff, 1975). Today, the burgeoning periodicals in diverse disciplines focused on gerontology have resulted in an exponential growth of research publications in this field. Gerontology has become increasingly more interdisciplinary; that is, specialists in diverse areas of the basic, clinical, behavioral, and social sciences are working together on research projects focused on specific aspects of aging (Birren, 1996).

Major Research Centers Founded

Research in gerontology assumed greater significance after these developments, and an interest in the social factors associated with aging grew in the late 1950s and early 1960s. In 1946, a national gerontology research center, headed by the late Nathan Shock, a leader in geriatric medicine, was established at Baltimore City Hospital by the National Institutes of Health. This federally funded research center undertook several studies of physiological aspects of aging, using a cross-sectional approach.

In 1958, Dr. Shock and his colleagues began a longitudinal study of physiological changes in healthy, middle-aged and older men living in the community, by testing them every two years on numerous physiological parameters. They later started to examine the cognitive, personality, and

---

THE GERONTOLOGICAL SOCIETY OF AMERICA

Today, the GSA has about 6000 members. It is the major professional association for people in diverse disciplines focused on research in aging. The GSA's mission is "to add life to years, not just years to life." This emphasizes the goal of most gerontologists—to enhance quality of life in the later years, not just to extend life.

social–psychological characteristics of these men. Much later, in 1978, older women were included in their samples. Known as the **Baltimore Longitudinal Studies of Aging,** these assessments of changes associated with healthy aging are still continuing, now under the direction of the National Institute on Aging. More than 2200 volunteers, men and women, aged 20 to 90, have participated or are currently participating in this ongoing study of the basic processes of aging. On average, these volunteers remain in the study for 13 years. More recently, ethnic minorities have been recruited as subjects; 13 percent are African Americans, mostly in the younger cohorts. The results of this ongoing research effort continue to provide valuable information about normal age-related changes in physiological and psychological functions. As more persons of color in this longitudinal study grow older, they will provide valuable insights into the process of normal, age-related changes versus disease in these populations.

Concurrently with the Baltimore Longitudinal Studies, several university-based centers were developed to study the aging process and the needs of older adults. One of the first, the Duke University Center on Aging, was founded in 1955 by one of the pioneers in gerontology, Ewald Busse. This center focused initially on physiological aging and on mental health, but has also examined many social aspects of aging.

The University of Chicago, under Robert Havighurst's direction, developed the first research center devoted exclusively to the social aspects of aging. The Kansas City studies of adult development, discussed in Chapters 6 and 8, represent the first major social-psychological studies of adult development, and were conducted by researchers from the Chicago center. Research and training centers on aging have since evolved at many other universities, generally stimulated by government sponsorship of gerontological research through the National Institute on Aging (established in 1974), the National Institute of Mental Health (which established its center for studies of the mental health of the aging in 1976), and the Administration on Aging (established in 1965).

RESEARCH METHODS

Before examining the issues and areas of special concern to social gerontologists, we first consider the ways in which such information about the aging process is gathered. The topic of research methodologies in gerontology may seem an advanced one to introduce in a basic text, but in fact, it is essential to understanding the meaning and validity of information presented throughout this book.

The study of aging presents particular conceptual and methodological difficulties. A major one is how research is designed and data interpreted regarding age changes. A point that complicates research in aging and also produces some misleading interpretations of data is how to distinguish *age changes* from *age differences*. This differentiation is necessary if we are to understand the process of aging and the conditions under which age differences occur. If we wish to determine what changes or effects are experienced as an individual moves from middle age to old age and to advanced old age, we must examine the same individual over a period of years, or at least months. In order to understand age changes, longitudinal research is necessary—that is, the repeated measurement of the same person over a specified period of time.

Many older adults participate in research that could benefit others.

Unfortunately, the time and cost of such studies prevent many researchers from undertaking longitudinal research. Instead, much of the research in this field focuses on age differences, by comparing people of different chronological ages at the same measurement period. These studies, cross-sectional in nature, are the most common ones in gerontology.

The unique problems inherent in how gerontological research is designed and how data are interpreted are evident in the following question: Given that aging in humans is a complex process that proceeds quite differently among individuals in varied geographic, cultural, and historic settings, and that it occurs over a time span as long as 100 to 120 years, how does one study it? Obviously, scientists cannot follow successive generations—or even a single generation of subjects—throughout their life span. Nor can they be expected to address the entire range of variables that affect aging—including lifestyle, social class, cultural beliefs, public policies, and so on—in a single study.

The Age/Period/Cohort Problem

The problem in each case is that of distinguishing *age differences* (ways that one generation differs from another) from *age changes* (ways that people normally change over time). This has been referred to as the "age/period/cohort" problem. (The word *cohort*, you will recall, refers to those people born at roughly the same time. *Period* refers to the effects of the specific historical period involved.) The concept of cohort is an important one in gerontology because historical events differentiate one cohort from another in attitudes and behaviors. Those people in the same cohort are likely to be more similar to each other because of comparable social forces acting on them during a given era.

Cross-Sectional Studies

As noted earlier, the most common approach to studying aging is cross-sectional; that is, researchers compare a number of subjects of different ages on the same characteristics in order to determine age-related differences. One reason that cross-sectional studies are frequently used is that, compared to other designs, data can be readily gathered. Some examples might include a comparison of the lung capacity of men aged 30 with those who are aged 40, 50, 60, 70, and 80, or a study comparing church attendance by American adults under age 65 with those over age 65. The average differences among different age groups in each study might suggest conclusions about the changes that come with age.

The danger with such cross-sectional studies is that these differences might not be due to the process of aging, but rather to particular cultural and historical conditions that shaped each group of subjects being studied. For example, a higher rate of church attendance among today's older adults than among younger adults probably reflects a change in social attitudes toward attending church, as opposed to an increased need for spiritual and religious life as one grows older.

Even in studies of biological factors, such as lung capacity, many intervening variables may threaten the validity of comparative results. In this case, they include the effects of exercise, smoking, and other lifestyle factors, genetic inheritance, and exposure to pollution (this, in turn, might be a product of work environments and social class) on relevant outcome variables.

The major limitation of cross-sectional studies occurs when differences among younger and older respondents are erroneously attributed to growing old; for example, some researchers have found that the older the respondent, the lower his or her score on intelligence tests. As a result, cognitive abilities have been misinterpreted as declining with age. In fact, such differences may be due to the lower educational levels and higher test anxiety of this cohort of older adults compared to younger adults, not to age. This is an example of *confounding*, or a joint effect of two variables on an outcome of interest. In this case, age effects are confounded by the impact of cohort differences. Because many issues in social gerontology center on distinguishing age from cohort effects, a number of research designs have emerged that attempt to do this. They include "longitudinal" and "sequential" designs.

Longitudinal Studies: Design and Limitations

Longitudinal designs permit inferences about *age changes*. They eliminate cohort effects by studying the same people over time. Each row in Table 1.1 represents a separate longitudinal study in which a given cohort (e.g., A, B, or C) is measured once every 10 years. Despite the advantages of longitudinal designs over the cross-sectional approach, they still have limitations. First, the longitudinal method does not allow a distinction between age and time of testing. Second, it cannot separate the effects of events extraneous to the study that influence people's responses in a particular measurement period.

Another problem with longitudinal studies is the potential for practice effects. This problem occurs in studies that administer aptitude or knowledge tests, where repeated measurement with the same test improves the test-taker's performance because of familiarity or practice. For example, a psychologist who is interested in age-related changes in intelligence could expect to obtain improvements in people's scores if the same test is administered several times, with a brief interval (e.g., less than one year) between tests. In such cases, it is difficult to relate the changes to maturation unless the tests can be varied or parallel forms of the same tests can be used.

TABLE 1.1 **Alternative Research Designs in Aging**

Cohort Born in	TIME OF MEASUREMENT			
	1970	1980	1990	2000
1920	A_1	A_2		
1930		B_1	B_2	
1940		C_1	C_2	C_3
1950				D_4

Cross-sectional: Cohorts A, B, and C are measured in 1980. *Longitudinal:* Cohort A is measured in 1970 and 1980; or Cohort B is measured in 1980 and 1990; or Cohort C is measured in 1980, 1990, and 2000. *Cohort-sequential:* Cohort A is measured in 1970 and 1980; Cohort B is measured in 1980 and 1990. *Time-sequential:* Cohorts B and C are measured in 1980; Cohorts C and D are measured in 2000. *Cross-sequential:* Cohorts B and C are both measured in 1980 and 1990.

SOURCE: Adapted from K. W. Schaie (Ed.), *Longitudinal studies of adult psychological development* (New York: Guilford Press, 1983).

Longitudinal studies also present the problem of *attrition*, or dropout. Individuals in experimental studies and respondents in surveys that are administered repeatedly may drop out for many reasons—death, illness, loss of interest, or frustration with poor performance. To the extent that people who drop out are not different from the original sample in terms of demographic characteristics, health status, and intelligence, the researcher can still generalize from the results obtained with the remaining sample. However,

AN EXAMPLE OF MISINTERPRETING LONGITUDINAL DATA

Imagine a study that attempted to determine attitudes about retirement. If a sample of 55-year-old workers had been interviewed in 1980, before mandatory retirement was changed to age 70, and again in 1990, after mandatory retirement was eliminated, it would be difficult to determine whether the changes in the workers' attitudes toward retirement occurred because of their increased age and proximity to retirement, or because of the modifications in retirement laws during this period.

more often it is the case that dropouts differ significantly from those who stay until the end. As we shall see in Chapter 5, those who drop out of longitudinal studies are more likely:

- to be in poorer health,
- to score lower on intelligence tests, and
- to be more socially isolated.

In contrast, older participants who remain in a longitudinal study are generally:

- more educated,
- healthier, and
- motivated.

This is known as the problem of **selective dropout.** While many researchers have pointed to the potential bias introduced by selective dropout, others have suggested that the results of such longitudinal data provide a positive developmental image about aging (Cooney, Schaie, and Willis, 1988; Schaie, 1996).

Sequential Designs

Some alternative research designs have emerged in response to the problems of cross-sectional and longitudinal methods. One is the category of **sequential research designs** (Schaie, 1967, 1973,

1977, 1983). These include the cohort-sequential, time-sequential, and cross-sequential methods, which are illustrated in Tables 1.1 and 1.2.

A *cohort-sequential* design is an extension of the longitudinal design, whereby two or more cohorts are followed for a period of time, so that measurements are taken of different cohorts at the same ages, but at different points in time.

The *time-sequential* design is useful for distinguishing between age and time of measurement or historical factors. It can be used to determine if changes obtained are due to aging or to historical factors. The researcher using this design would compare two or more cross-sectional samples at two or more measurement periods. Time-sequential designs do not prevent the confounding of age and cohort effects, but it is acceptable to use this method where one would not expect age differences to be confused with cohort differences.

The third technique proposed by Schaie (1983) is the *cross-sequential* design, which combines cross-sectional and longitudinal designs. This approach is an improvement over both the traditional cross-sectional and longitudinal designs, but it still confounds age and time of measurement effects. These three sequential designs are becoming more widely used by gerontological researchers, especially in studies of intelligence. Table 1.2 summarizes potential confounding effects in each of these methods.

TABLE 1.2   Potential Confounding Effects in Developmental Studies

Design	CONFOUNDING EFFECT		
	Age × Cohort Confounded	Age × Time of Measurement Confounded	Cohort × Time of Measurement Confounded
Cross-sectional	Yes	No	No
Longitudinal	No	Yes	No
Cohort-sequential	No	No	Yes
Time-sequential	Yes	No	No
Cross-sequential	No	Yes	No

SOURCE: Adapted from M. F. Elias, P. K. Elias, and J. W. Elias, *Basic processes in adult developmental psychology* (St. Louis: C. V. Mosby, 1977).

EXAMPLE OF A COHORT-SEQUENTIAL DESIGN

An investigator may wish to compare changing attitudes toward federal aging policies among the cohort born in 1930 and the cohort born in 1940 and follow each one for 10 years, from 1980 to 1990 for the first cohort, and from 1990 to 2000 for the second. This approach is useful for many social gerontological studies in which age and cohort must be distinguished.

However, it still does not separate the effects of cohort from historical effects or time of measurement. As a result, historical events that occurred just before one cohort entered a study (in this case, the Great Depression), but later than another cohort entered, may influence each cohort's attitude scores differently.

EXAMPLE OF A TIME-SEQUENTIAL DESIGN

A group of 70-year-olds and a group of 60-year-olds might be compared on their attitudes toward religious activities in 1990. The latter group then could be compared with a new group of 60-year-olds in

2000. This would give some information on how people approaching old age at two different historical periods view the role of religion in their lives.

EXAMPLE OF A CROSS-SEQUENTIAL DESIGN

A researcher interested in examining the effects of cohort and historical factors on attitudes toward federal aging policy might compare two groups: people who were age 40 and 50 in 1990, and the same people in 2000 when they are age 50 and 60, respec-

tively. This would permit the assessment of cohort and historical factors concurrently, with one providing information on changes from age 40 to 50, and the other representing changes from age 50 to 60.

Despite the growth of new research methods, much of social gerontology is based on cross-sectional studies. For this reason, it is important to read carefully the description of a study and its results in order to make accurate inferences about age changes as opposed to age differences, and to determine whether the differences found between groups of different ages are due to cohort effects or to the true effects of aging.

Problems with Representative Samples of Older Persons in Research

Accurate sampling can be difficult with older populations. If the sample is not representative, the results are of questionable validity. However, comprehensive lists of older people are not readily available. Membership lists from organizations such as AARP tend to overrepresent those who are healthy, white, and financially secure. Studies in institutions, such as nursing homes and adult day centers, tend to overrepresent those with chronic impairments. Because whites represent 84 percent of the population over age 65 today, it is not surprising that they are more readily available for research.

Reaching older persons of color through organizational lists can be especially difficult. More effective means of recruiting these groups include the active participation of community leaders such as ministers and respected elders in churches attended by the population of interest. The problem of ensuring diverse samples of research participants is compounded by the mistrust toward research among many elders of color. Many African Americans, in particular, remember the unethical practices of the Tuskegee Syphilis Study in the early twentieth century and are reluctant to participate in research today, despite significant improvements in the ethics of human research. Researchers must be sensitive to these issues when attempting to recruit elders of color into research projects. For example, older African Americans:

- Prefer to participate in social science studies more than in clinical research.
- May need transportation to the research site.
- Feel more comfortable when African Americans are represented on the research staff (Burnette, 1998).

Such disproportionate focus on whites and lack of data on ethnic minorities has slowed the development of gerontological theories that consider the impact of race, ethnicity, and culture on the aging process. Yet, even as researchers and funding agencies emphasize the need to include more people of color in all types of research, multiple confounding factors must be considered. For example, Hispanic elders represent U.S.-born as well as immigrant populations who have come here from countries as diverse as Mexico, Cuba, and Argentina. Therefore, any research that includes ethnic minorities must distinguish among subgroups by language, place of birth, and religion, not just the broader categories of Hispanic, African American, and Asian. It is not necessary to include all possible subgroups of a particular ethnic minority population in a given study. However, it behooves the researcher to state clearly who is represented, in order to assure appropriate generalizability of the findings.

The problem of *measurement equivalence* in gerontological research is compounded when the sample includes elders of color. As will be discussed in Chapters 5 and 6, many tests of intelligence, memory, and personality traits were originally developed for testing younger populations. As a result, they may not be appropriate for older cohorts whose educational level is generally lower and whose educational and cultural experiences as children differed widely from newer cohorts. In order to achieve equivalence of tests and measures for diverse age groups, gerontologists have spent many years testing the *validity* of existing measures for this population—modifying them and developing new tests as needed. Similar work with elders of color has not been undertaken as extensively. Although there has been some work to assure linguistic equivalence, researchers have not spent as much time on testing the *conceptual equivalence* of these measures (i.e., that people of different ethnic backgrounds see the same meaning or concepts underlying a particular test). If we are to understand ethnic differences in aging, it is important to use valid measures that mean the same thing to all groups participating in research.

The problem of *selective survival* affects most studies of older people. Over time, the birth cohort loses members, so that those who remain are not necessarily representative of all members of the original group. Those who survive, for example, probably were healthiest at birth, and maintained their good health throughout their lives—all variables that tend to be associated with higher socioeconomic status.

Even when an adequate sample is located, older respondents may vary in their memories or

---

POINTS TO PONDER

Think about some studies that are reported in newspapers, such as surveys of voter preferences. In the 2000 presidential election, several national polls reported the likelihood of "older voters" choosing one candidate or another. Did these surveys reflect the diversity among older voters, or put them into a monolithic block that distinguished them from another diverse group, "middle-class voters"?

attention spans; such variations can interfere with conducting interviews or tests. Ethical issues and unique difficulties arise in interviewing frail elders, yet there are no ethical guidelines specifically aimed at research with older adults. The issue of informed consent becomes meaningless when dealing with a confused or a severely medically compromised older person. In such cases, family members or guardians must take an active role in judging the risks and benefits of research for frail older persons. An additional problem is that studies of the old-old may be influenced by *terminal drop,* a decline in some tests of intelligence shortly before death (Botwinick, 1984; White and Cunningham, 1988). Since death becomes increasingly likely with age, terminal drop will manifest as a gradual decline in performance test scores with age in cross-sectional designs. In longitudinal studies, this problem may result in an overestimation of performance abilities in the later years because those who survive are likely to represent the physically and cognitively most capable older individual (Schaie, 1996). This problem is explored further in Chapter 5.

Further refinement of research methodologies is a challenging task for social gerontologists. As progress is made in this area, the quality of data with which to study aging will continually improve.

SUMMARY AND IMPLICATIONS

A primary reason for the growing interest in gerontology is the increase in the population over age 65. This growth results from a reduction in infant and child mortality and improved treatment of acute diseases of childhood and adulthood, which in turn increases the proportion of people living to age 65 and beyond. In the United States, average life expectancy from birth has increased from 47 years in 1900 to 78 in 1998, with women continuing to outlive men. The growth in the population over age 85 has been most dramatic, reflecting major achievements in disease prevention and health care since the turn of the twentieth century. More recently, there has been increased at-

tention on centenarians. Those who live to be 100 and older may have a biological advantage over their peers who die at a younger age. Studies have found greater tolerance to stress and fewer chronic illnesses in centenarians. Elders of color in the United States and older persons in developing nations are less likely to live beyond age 65 than whites and those in industrialized nations, but population projections anticipate a much higher rate of growth for these groups in the next 20 years.

The growth in the numbers and proportions of older people, especially the oldest-old, will require that both public and private policies affecting employment and retirement, health and long-term care, and social services be modified to meet the needs and improve the quality of life of those who are living longer. Fundamental issues will have to be resolved about who will receive what societal resources and what will be the roles of the private and public sectors for sharing responsibilities of elder care. In many industrialized countries, controversial questions of immigration policy will need to be addressed as birth rates decline dramatically among native-born citizens.

Gerontology has grown as a field of study since early philosophers and scientists first explored the reasons for changes experienced with advancing age. Roger Bacon in the thirteenth century, Adolph Quetelet in the early nineteenth century, Botkin in the late nineteenth century, and Ivan Pavlov and G. Stanley Hall in the early twentieth century made pioneering contributions to this field. During the early 1900s, in Europe and the United States, the impact of an increasing aging population on social and health resources began to be felt. Social gerontological research has expanded since the 1940s, paralleling the rapid growth of the older population and its needs.

The growing older population and associated social concerns have stimulated great interest in gerontological research. However, existing research methodologies are limited in their ability to distinguish the process of aging per se from cohort, time, and measurement effects. Cross-sectional research designs are most often used in this field, but these can provide information only on age differences, not on age changes. Longitudinal designs are necessary for understanding age changes, but they suffer from the possibility of subject attrition and the effects of measuring the same individual numerous times. Newer methods in social gerontology, known as cohort-sequential, time-sequential, and cross-sequential designs, test multiple cohorts or age groups over time. They also are limited by possible confounding effects, but represent considerable improvement over traditional research designs.

Because research methods in gerontology have improved, today there is a better understanding of many aspects of aging. Research findings to date provide the empirical background for the theories and topics to be covered in the remaining chapters. Despite the recent explosion of knowledge in gerontology, there are many gaps in what is known about older people and the aging process. The problem is particularly acute in our understanding of aging among ethnic minority populations. Throughout the text, we will call attention to areas in which additional research is needed.

GLOSSARY

active versus dependent life expectancy   a way of describing expected length of life, the term *active* denoting a manner of living that is relatively healthy and independent in contrast to being *dependent* on help from others

ageism   attitudes, beliefs, and conceptions of the nature and characteristics of older persons that are prejudicial, distorting their actual characteristics, abilities, etc.

aging   changes that occur to an organism during its life span, from development to maturation to senescence

Baltimore Longitudinal Studies of Aging   a federally funded longitudinal study that has examined physiological, cognitive, and personality changes in healthy, middle-aged and older men since 1958, and in women since 1978

cohort   a group of people of the same generation sharing a statistical trait such as age, ethnicity, or socioeconomic status (for example, all African American women between the ages of 60 and 65 in 1999)

competence model   a conception or description of the way persons perform, focusing on their abilities vis-á-vis the demands of the environment

compression of morbidity   given a certain length of life, a term referring to relatively long periods of healthy, active, high-quality existence and relatively short periods of illness and dependency in the last few years of life

cross-sectional research   research that examines or compares characteristics of people at a given point in time and attempts to identify factors associated with contrasting characteristics of different groupings of people

environmental press   features of the social, technological, natural environment that place demands on people

geriatrics   clinical study and treatment of older people and the diseases that affect them

gerontology   the field of study that focuses on understanding the biological, psychological, social, and political factors that influence older people's lives

life expectancy   the average length of time persons, defined by age, sex, ethnic group, and socioeconomic status in a given society, are expected to live

longitudinal research   research that follows the same individual, over time, to measure change in specific variables

maximum life span   biologically programmed maximum number of years that each species can expect to live

person–environment (P–E) perspective   a model for understanding the behavior of people based on the idea that persons are affected by personal characteristics, such as health, attitudes, and beliefs, as they interact with and are affected by the characteristics of the cultural, social, political, and economic environment

sequential research designs   research designs that combine features of cross-sectional and longitudinal research designs to overcome some of the problems encountered in using those designs

RESOURCES

See the companion Website for this text at <www.ablongman.com/hooyman> for information about the following:

- ACTION—Older Americans Volunteer Programs
- Alliance for Aging Research
- American Federation for Aging Research

- Gerontological Society of America
- Grey Panthers
- MedWeb: Geriatrics
- National Institute on Aging (NIA)

REFERENCES

AARP. *Global Aging Report.* 2000, *5*, 4–5.

AARP. *A profile of older Americans: 1999.* Washington, DC, 2000.

Birren, J. E. History of gerontology. In J. E. Birren (Ed.), *Encyclopedia of gerontology,* Vol. 1. San Diego: Academic Press, 1996.

Birren, J. E., and Clayton, V. History of gerontology. In D. S. Woodruff and J. E. Birren (Eds.), *Aging: Scientific perspectives and social issues.* New York: Van Nostrand, 1975.

Botwinick, J. *Cognitive processes in maturity and old age* (3rd ed.). New York: Springer, 1984.

Burnette, D. Conceptual and methodological considerations in research with non-white ethnic elders. *Journal of Social Service Research,* 1998, *23,* 71–91.

Carr, D. B., Goate, A., Phil, D., and Morris, J. C. Current concepts in the pathogenesis of Alzheimer's disease. *American Journal of Medicine,* 1997, *103,* 3S–10S.

Cooney, T. M., Schaie, K. W., and Willis, S. L. The relationship between prior functioning on cognitive and personality dimensions and subject attrition in longitudinal research. *Journals of Gerontology,* 1988, *43,* P12–17.

Crimmins, E. M., Saito, Y., and Reynolds, S. L. Further evidence on the prevalence and incidence of disability among older Americans from two sources: The LSOA and the NHIS. *Journals of Gerontology,* 1997, *52B,* S59–S71.

Fries, J. F. Aging, natural death, and the compression of morbidity. *New England Journal of Medicine,* 1980, *303,* 130–135.

Fries, J. F. The compression of morbidity: Near or far? *Milbank Quarterly,* 1990, *67,* 208–232.

Fries, J. F., and Crapo, L. M. *Vitality and aging.* San Francisco: W. H. Freeman, 1981.

Hayflick, L. *How and why we age* (2nd ed.). New York: Ballantine Books, 1996.

International Longevity Center–USA. *The aging factor in health and disease.* (Report of an interdisciplinary workshop). New York: The Center, 1999.

Katz, S., Branch, L. G., Branson, M. H., Papsidero, J. A., Beck, J. C., and Greer, D. S. Active life expectancy. *New England Journal of Medicine,* 1983, *309,* 1218–1224.

Kaye, J. A. Oldest-old healthy brain function. *Archives of Neurology,* 1997, *54,* 1217–1221.

Lawton, M. P. Behavior-relevant ecological factors. In K. W. Schaie and C. Scholar (Eds.). *Social structure and aging: Psychological processes.* Hillsdale, NJ: Erlbaum, 1989.

Lawton, M. P., and Nahemow, L. Ecology and the aging process. In C. Eisdorfer and M. P. Lawton (Eds.), *Pychology of adult development and aging.* Washington, DC: American Psychological Association, 1973, 619–674.

Lubitz, J. D., and Riley, G. F. Trends in Medicare payments in the last year of life. *New England Journal of Medicine,* 1993, *328,* 1092–1096.

Manton, K. G. and Gu, X. L. Changes in the prevalence of chronic disability in U.S. black and non-black population above age 65 from 1982 to 1999. *Proceedings of the National Academy of Sciences,* Online article #1522, May 8, 2001.

Manton, K. G., and Vaupel, J. W. Survival after the age of 80 in the United States, Sweden, France, England, and Japan. *New England Journal of Medicine,* 1995, *333,* 1232–1235.

National Academy on an Aging Society. *Demography is not destiny.* Washington, DC: Gerontological Society of America, 1999.

National Center for Health Statistics (NCHS). Deaths: Final data for 1998. *National Vital and Health Statistics Reports,* July 2000a.

National Center for Health Statistics (NCHS). Life expectancy at birth: 1940–1998. *National Vital and Health Statistics Reports,* July 2000b.

Organization for Economic Cooperation and Development (OECD). *The OECD Observer,* 1995, No. 192.

Parmelee, P. A., and Lawton, M. P. The design of special environments for the aged. In J. E. Birren and K. W. Schaie (Eds.), *Handbook of the psychology of aging* (3rd ed.). San Diego: Academic Press, 1990.

Perls, T. T. The oldest old. *Scientific American,* 1995, 70–75.

Perls, T. T. and Silver, M. H. *Living to 100: Lessons in living to your maximum potential at any age.* New York: Basic Books, 1999.

Perls, T. T., and Wood, E. R. Acute care costs of the oldest old: They cost less, their care intensity is less, and they go to nonteaching hospitals. *Archives of Internal Medicine,* 1996, *156,* 754–760.

Poon, L. W., Johnson, M. A., Davey, A., Dawson, D. V., Siegler, I. C., and Martin, P. Psychosocial predictors of survival among centenarians. In P. Martin, A. Rott, B. Hagberg, and K. Mongan (Eds), *Centenarians*. New York: Springer Publishing, 2000.

Quinn, J. *Entitlements and the federal budget: Securing our future*. Washington, DC: National Academy on Aging, 1996.

Riley, M. W., and Riley, J. Longevity and social structure: The potential of the added years. In A. Pifer and L. Bronte (Eds.), *Our aging society: Paradox and promise*. New York: W.W. Norton, 1986.

Samuelsson, S. M., Baur, B., Hagberg, B., Samuelsson, G., Norbeck, B., Brun, A., Gustafson, L., and Risberg, J. The Swedish Centenarian Study: A multidisciplinary study of five consecutive cohorts at the age of 100. *International Journal of Aging and Human Development*, 1997, *45*, 223–253.

Schaie, K. W. Age changes and age differences. *The Gerontologist*, 1967, *7*, 128–132.

Schaie, K. W. *Intellectual development in adulthood*. Cambridge: Cambridge University Press, 1996.

Schaie, K. W. (Ed.), *Longitudinal studies of adult psychological development*. New York: Guilford Press, 1983.

Schaie, K. W. Methodological problems in descriptive developmental research on adulthood and aging. In J. R. Nesselroade and H. W. Reese (Eds.), *Lifespan developmental psychology: Methodological issues*. New York: Academic Press, 1973.

Schaie, K. W. Quasi-experimental research designs in the psychology of aging. In J. E. Birren and K. W. Schaie (Eds.), *Handbook of the psychology of aging*. New York: Van Nostrand Reinhold, 1977.

Silver, M. H., Newell, K., Hyman, B., Growdon, J., Hedley, E. T., and Perls, T. Unraveling the mystery of cognitive changes in old age. *International Psychogeriatrics*, 1998, *10*, 25–41.

Social Security Administration, Office of Research and Statistics. *Income of the Population 5 and Older, 1994*. SSA Publications, No. 13–11871, January 1996.

Social Security Administration Web Site: www.ssa.gov/policy. Office of Policy publications. April 2001.

Suzman, R. M., Willis, D. P., and Manton, K. G. (Eds.), *The oldest old*. New York: Oxford University Press, 1992.

U.S. Adminstration on Aging. National Aging Information Center, *Aging in the twenty-first century*. Washington, DC: 1996.

U.S. Administration on Aging Web Page, http://www.aoa.gov/aoa/stats/profile. July 2000.

U.S. Bureau of the Census. American housing survey for the United States in 1991. *Current Housing Reports*, Series H150/91, 1993a.

U.S. Bureau of the Census. Centenarians in the United States. *Current Population Reports*, P23, No. 199RV, 1999a.

U.S. Bureau of the Census. Comparative international statistics. *Statistical Abstract of the United States*, 1999b.

U.S. Bureau of the Census. Educational attainment in the U.S.: March 1998. *Current Population Reports*, P20, No. 513, 1998a.

U.S. Bureau of the Census. *Global Aging into the 21st Century*. Washington, DC: U.S. Department of Commerce, 1996a.

U.S. Bureau of the Census. *International Brief: Gender and Aging*. IB/98–2. Washington, DC: U.S. Department of Commerce, 1998b.

U.S. Bureau of the Census. Life expectancy at birth: United States 1940, 1950, 1960, 1970, and 1998. *National Vital Statistics Reports*, 48, No. 11, 2000.

U.S. Bureau of the Census. Population projections of the U.S. 1998. *Current Population Reports*, P60, No. 198, 1999c.

U.S. Bureau of the Census. Population projections of the U.S., by age, sex, race, and Hispanic origin data: 1993 to 2050. *Current Population Reports*, P25, No.1104, 1993b.

U.S. Bureau of the Census. Population projections of the U.S., by age, sex, race, and Hispanic origin data: 1995 to 2050. *Current Population Reports*, P25, No. 1130, 1996b.

U.S. Bureau of the Census Web Page, http://www.census.gov/ October 1997.

U.S. Bureau of Labor Statistics. *Employment and earnings*, January 1994.

White, N., and Cunningham, W. R. Is terminal drop pervasive or specific? *Journals of Gerontology*, 1988, *44*, S141–144.

Woodruff, D. Introduction: Multidisciplinary perspectives of aging. In D. Woodruff and J. Birren (Eds.), *Aging: Scientific perspectives and social issues*. New York: Van Nostrand, 1975.

World Health Organization (WHO). *World Health Report: 1995*. 1996.

2 HISTORICAL AND CROSS-CULTURAL ISSUES IN AGING

This chapter includes

- The role of older people in stable, preliterate, or primitive societies
- Elders in some non-western cultures
- Changes in the social roles of older persons
- Societal norms regarding aging
- Older adults' expectations of society
- Contrasting perspectives regarding the impact of modernization on the relationship between older persons and the larger society
- Both historical and cross-cultural views

The experience of aging is dramatically different from earlier historical periods. The social and economic roles of older persons, their interactions with families and the larger social system where they live are in many ways profoundly different today from previous generations. Until relatively recently, only a minority of people lived long enough to be considered old. As the number of older people has grown and as social values have changed, the authority and power of older adults in society have also shifted.

The experiences of older adults differ cross-culturally as well as historically. That is, in addition to historical changes, significant cultural variations affect the social position of older persons. Perhaps the greatest differences in the status of older adults are between traditional societies and those of the modern Western world, with its rapidly changing values and norms. Examining the different ways that other societies, both historical and contemporary, have dealt with issues affecting their elders can shed light on the process of aging in our society. The emergence of "comparative sociocultural gerontology" or an "anthropology of aging" has served to refute some of the myths of the "good old days" presumed to exist in historical times and in contemporary nonindustrial societies. It begins to differentiate what aspects of aging are universal or biological as opposed to which factors are largely shaped by the sociocultural system (Sokolovsky, 1997).

Understanding how aging in contemporary American society differs from that experienced elsewhere, and which factors are socioculturally determined, can also suggest strategies for improving environments in which to grow old. Within the constraints of this one chapter, we can only glance at a few other cultures. For a more complete view, we urge you to turn to the expanding literature on the anthropology of aging (Fry, 1996; Sokolovsky, 1997). While this chapter explores aging cross-culturally and historically, Chapter 14 focuses on the cultural diversity represented by older ethnic minorities within contemporary American society.

OLD AGE HISTORICALLY

Old Age in Ancient Cultures

Although our knowledge of aging in prehistoric and primitive societies is limited, we know that people of advanced age were rare, with most dying before the age of 35. Nevertheless, there were always a few people perceived to be old, although they were probably chronologically relatively young, since maturity and death came quickly in the lives of people struggling to survive in harsh environments. Those few elders were treated with respect, in a manner that reflected a sense of sacred obligation. During ceremonial occasions, elders were seated in positions of high honor and served as the clan's memory. The belief that an older person was a mediator between this world and the next gave added prestige to elders by conferring on them the role of witch doctors or priests.

Even though positive attitudes toward the young-old were widespread, nonsupportive or death-hastening behavior was shown toward those who survived beyond an "intact" stage of life. This stage of old-old age was often referred to as the "sleeping period." No longer able to contribute to the common welfare and look after themselves, older people were then viewed as useless, "overaged," or "already dead," and were sometimes treated brutally. Those who outlived their usefulness were a heavy burden in societies that existed close to the edge of subsistence, particularly those in harsh climates with little agriculture, or with no system of **social stratification** (Barker, 1997; Glascock, 1997).

The practice of **geronticide** or **senecide**—the deliberate destruction of older community members—was viewed as functional and, for many traditional societies, was often performed with great reverence or ceremony. In a minority of primitive tribes, the frail were killed outright; in most, they were abandoned, neglected, or encouraged to commit suicide, and the burial place was often converted into an ancestral shrine. Consistent with the coexistence of positive attitudes toward the old along with their nonsupportive treatment, geronticide in many societies often occurred under the older person's direction and by a close relative, usually a son. Examples of geronticide, abandon-

---

EXAMPLES OF DEATH-HASTENING BEHAVIOR IN HISTORIC PERIODS

In some rural areas of ancient Japan, older people were carried into the mountains and left there to die.

It was not unusual for aged Eskimos to walk off into the snow when famine and disease placed great burdens on the tribe.

GERONTICIDE WITH REVERENCE

Ritual sacrifice was used to kill the oldest members perceived to be a burden among the Ojibwa Indians of Lake Winnipeg and the Siriono of the Bolivian rain forest.

---

ment, and forsaking support to the oldest-old were reported in remote cultures as recently as the twentieth century (Glascock, 1997).

Old Age in Greek and Roman Cultures

In Greek and Roman classical cultures, 80 percent of the population perished before reaching the stage of life that we now consider to be middle age. Nevertheless, our chronological conception of age, with *old* defined as age 65 and over, began during this period. Age implied power in the ancient cities, which were ruled by councils of elders who derived their authority from their years. Within the family, the eldest male's authority was nearly absolute, and the young were dependent on the old by custom and by law. However, only the elite members of society, not the peasants, benefited from the respect accorded age by the community.

Some idea of the changing status of older people in ancient Greek society can be obtained by analyzing how old and young were depicted in Greek tragedy. In her book, *Time in Greek Tragedy*, de Romilly (1968) points to an evolution of views about age from Aeschylus in the late sixth and early fifth centuries B.C., to Euripides in the mid- to late fifth century B.C. For Aeschylus, age brought with it wisdom, especially about justice and prudence.

Although he refers to the destructive influences of age, particularly loss of physical strength, Aeschylus insists that such physical decline has no impact on the older person's mind or spirit. In contrast, Sophocles' tragedies, which were written during the middle of the fifth century, depict old age as distasteful, a time of decline in physical and mental functioning. For Sophocles, youth is the only period of life characterized by true happiness. Later, in Euripides' plays, older people are both wise and weak. Older characters of Euripides long for eternal youth; old age is described as miserable, bitter, and painful. The shift from Aeschylus' admiration of old age to the exaltation of youth and denigration of old age by Sophocles and Euripides may be a reflection of the growth of democracy in fifth-century Greece (and, consequently, a growing belief in social equality) as well as of the heroism of young men in the wars of that era.

This coincided with the Classical period, when beauty, youth, and strength were idealized in the visual arts. Greek mythology also depicts the old as tyrannical and wicked, the ultimate enemy in many myths. The gift of immortality was cherished only if it meant rejuvenation or eternal youth. Greek and later Roman mythology contrasted the eternal youthfulness of the gods with the gradual deterioration of mortals.

AGING IN GREEK MYTHOLOGY

In the myth of Eos and Tithonus, Eos (or Aurora), the goddess of dawn, fell in love with Tithonus, a mortal. She prevailed on Zeus to grant him immortality but forgot to ask that he remain eternally young like her. She left him when he became very old and frail, and eventually turned him into a grasshopper. Presumably this was a better fate for the ancient Greeks and Romans than remaining a feeble old man.

Old Age in Medieval Europe

Little is known about the role of older people during the medieval period, except that life expectancy was even shorter than in the Greek and Roman eras. To a large extent, increasing urbanization and related problems of sanitation and disease were responsible for the high death rates before people reached old age. Nevertheless, older people were more likely than the young to survive the Black Plague and other epidemics, creating a disproportionate population of elders and arousing bitterness among the young. This shift also resulted in more extended family living arrangements (Minois, 1989).

The nobility lived longer than the common people during the Middle Ages, largely because of better standards of living. Furthermore, the general populace was more likely to die of war or the numerous diseases that plagued this era. The nobility had the freedom to flee such conditions. For the small proportion of poor people who did manage to survive, old age was a cruel period of life.

To the extent that the prevailing attitudes toward older persons in that historical period can be inferred from art, one would have to conclude that old age was depicted as ugly, weak, and deceptive. During the Renaissance, artists and poets reestablished links with Classical Greece, contrasting the beauty of youth with the unattractiveness and weakness they, like the ancient Greeks, saw in old age. Many of Shakespeare's plays, including *Hamlet*, *Othello*, and *As You Like It*, portray a contrast between the vitality and energy of youth versus the weakness and immobility of old age.

Old Age in Colonial America

In seventeenth- and eighteenth-century America, old age was treated with deference and respect, in part because it was so rare. This attitude has been described as one of veneration, an emotion closer to awe than affection and a form of worship deeply embedded in the Judeo-Christian ethic of early America. The Puritans, for example, viewed old age as a sign of God's favor and assumed that youth would inevitably defer to age. Old men occupied the highest public offices, as well as positions of authority within the family, until they died; fathers waited until their sixties before giving their land to the eldest son. Church seats were given to the old. The primary basis of the power enjoyed by older people in colonial times was their control of property, especially productive farmland. In this agricultural society, such control amounted to the ability to dominate all key institutions—the family, the church, the economy, and the polity.

Even though the oldest members of society were exalted by law and custom in colonial times, they received little affection or love from younger people; in fact, most were kept at an emotional distance. In reserving power and prestige for older persons, society in many ways created this separation between young and old. Elders frequently

---

SHAKESPEARE'S VIEW OF AGING

In Shakespeare's play, *As You Like It*, youth evolves from an impulsive boy to soldier, to the fifth age "full of wise saws and modern instances." The sixth age is depicted as weak, with "his big manly voice, turning again toward childish treble." The seventh and final stage "is second childishness and mere oblivion, sans teeth, sans eyes, sans taste, sans everything." Thus, Shakespeare's view of old age is that of decline and uselessness; this may reflect the attitude of sixteenth-century Europe that the old were a burden to a community struggling with food shortages and high death rates among its infants and young soldiers. Perhaps most striking is Shakespeare's attribution of wisdom and perspective to middle age, in contrast to the beliefs of pre-Classical and Hellenistic Greek playwrights and philosophers that old age is the time of greatest wisdom.

Older people in traditional societies symbolize power and wisdom.

complained that they had lived to become strangers in their communities. Old age was not a time of serenity, but rather anxiety about adequately fulfilling social obligations and keeping faith with God (Achenbaum, 1996).

This pattern persisted until about 1770, when attitudes toward the older population began to change and the relative status of youth was elevated. Indications of this change included:

- Church-seating arrangements that had favored the old were abolished.
- The first mandatory retirement laws for legislators were passed.
- The eldest son no longer automatically inherited the family property.
- New fashions were introduced that flattered youth—a change from the white wigs and broadwaisted coats that favored older men.
- New words appeared that negatively portrayed elders, such as *codger* and *fuddy-duddy*.
- Family portraits of all members were placed on the same horizontal plane rather than po-

sitioning the oldest male members to stand over women and children (Fischer, 1978).

A major demographic change occurred in approximately 1810, when the median age began to rise, creating a greater percentage of the population older than the typical "old" age of 40 or 50. This was due primarily to a declining birth rate, not a falling death rate. After 1810, the median age advanced at a constant annual rate, approximately 0.4 percent per year, until about 1950 (Fischer, 1978); this has been attributed to reductions in the impact of diseases. A dramatic change was that parents began to live beyond the period of their children's dependency, for the first time in history experiencing relatively good health at the time their children left the family home.

THE EFFECTS OF MODERNIZATION

As the foregoing historical examples suggest, definitions of old age—as well as the authority exercised by older people—largely rested on the material and political resources controlled by older members of society. These resources include:

- traditional skills and knowledge
- security bestowed by property rights
- civil and political power
- food for communal sharing
- information control
- general welfare from routine services performed by older people such as child care

Within the constraints set by the social environment and its ideology, older people's social rank was generally determined by the balance between the cost of maintaining them and the societal contributions they were perceived to make. As age became a less important criterion for determining access to and control of valued resources, older members of society lost some of their status and authority.

A number of explanations have been advanced for the declining status of the old in our society.

Modernization theory is a major explanation. One of the first comparative analyses that raised this issue was reported by Leo Simmons in *The Role of the Aged in Primitive Society* (1945). He noted that the status of older persons, as reflected in their resources and the honor bestowed upon them, varied inversely with the degree of technology, social and economic diversity, and occupational specialization (or modernization) in a given society. As society becomes more modernized, according to this theory, older people lose political and social power, influence, and leadership. These social changes also may lead to disengagement of aging persons from community life. In addition, younger and older generations become increasingly separated socially, morally, and intellectually. Youth is glorified as the embodiment of progress and achievement, as well as the means to attain such progress. Modernization theory has been advanced primarily by Cowgill (1974a, 1974b, 1986), and is defined by Cowgill (1974a) as:

> The transformation of a total society from a relatively rural way of life based on animate power, limited technology, relatively undifferentiated institutions, parochial and traditional outlook and values, toward a predominantly urban way of life, based on inanimate sources of power, highly differentiated institutions, matched by segmented individual roles, and a cosmopolitan outlook which emphasizes efficiency and progress (p. 127).

The characteristics of modernization that contribute to lower status for older people were identified by Cowgill as:

* health technology
* scientific technology as applied in economic production and distribution
* urbanization
* literacy and mass education

According to Cowgill, the application of *health technology* reduced infant mortality and maternal deaths, and prolonged adult life, thereby increasing the number of older persons. With more older people in the labor market, competition for jobs between generations intensified, and retirement developed as a means of forcing older people out of the labor market.

Scientific technology creates new jobs primarily for the young, with older workers more likely to remain in traditional occupations that become obsolete. The rapid development of industries that rely on high technology today and the gap between generations in the use of computers illustrate this phenomenon. Unable to perform the socially valued role of contributors to the workforce, many older workers feel marginalized and alienated.

In the early stages of modernization, when the society is relatively rural, young people are attracted to urban areas, whereas older parents and grandparents remain on the family farm or in rural communities. The resulting residential segregation of the generations has a dramatic impact on family interactions. The geographical and occupational mobility of the young, in turn, leads to increased social distance between generations and to a reduced status of the old.

Finally, modernization is characterized by efforts to promote *literacy and education,* which tend to be targeted toward the young. As younger generations acquire more education than their parents, they begin to occupy higher-status positions. Intellectual and moral differences between the generations increase, with older members of society experiencing reduced leadership roles and influence (Cowgill, 1974a, 1974b).

Some social historians have criticized modernization theory, arguing that it idealizes the past and ignores the fact that older people in many preindustrial societies were treated harshly and at the whim of younger family members (Albert and Cattell, 1994; Kertzer and Laslett, 1994). However, there is considerable empirical support for this theory. For example, rapid urbanization in many developing countries has dislodged the tradition of family support for many older people. Modern migration programs in India, while providing resources for young and old, have resulted in younger

ROLE CHANGES AND OLDER WOMEN

Evidence of intergenerational conflict is reflected in suicide rates among older women. Although the rate among women in the United States *drops* from 11.6 per 100,000 among those aged 40–50 to 6.6 per 100,000 among women over 65, the suicide rate *in-* *creases* dramatically in Japan, tripling from 11.6 to 39.3 per 100,000. In Taiwan there is also a striking increase, from 10.4 to 34.6 per 100,000 in this same age range (Hu, 1995).

people obtaining more education and creating a sense of superiority over their illiterate elders. Rapid urbanization has left almost 30 percent of old people in rural areas in India without family nearby to care for them (Dandekar, 1996; Vincentnathan and Vincentnathan, 1994). Meanwhile, families who eke out a meager living in urban areas have little with which to assist their elders who live with them. For example, 33 percent of older women in Mexico's urban areas were found to have no personal income, and 12 percent earned $5.00 or less per month in 1992 (Bialik, 1992). Even in the economically more successful countries of East Asia, such as Japan and Taiwan, older people may live in three-generational households but not necessarily feel welcome in these settings.

Occupation and education appear to have a reversed J-shaped relationship to modernization. In the early phases of rapid social change (illustrated by nations such as Turkey and the Philippines), the occupational and educational status of older adults shows a decline, but then later improves (exemplified by New Zealand, Canada, and the United States). This suggests that, as societies move beyond an initial state of rapid modernization, status differences between generations decrease and the relative status of older people may rise, particularly when reinforced by social policies such as Social Security. Similarly, the financial status of older Americans has steadily improved since World War II. It may be that societies in advanced stages of modernization become more aware of the older population's devalued status. Thus, through public education, social policies, and the media, they attempt to create more op-

portunities for and positive images of older people. This has already begun in the United States, with advertising and television programs increasingly portraying older persons as vital, active, and involved. The combination of low unemployment rates in the late twentieth and early twenty-first century and more positive attitudes about aging have resulted in more employers seeking older people for part-time service work.

Alternatives to Modernization Theory

More recent analyses of older people's status in nonindustrial societies have found that conditions for high status did not always apply. For example, differences often existed between the prestige of the old and the way they were actually treated; over 60 percent of the 41 nonindustrial societies examined by Glascock (1997) had some form of nonsupportive treatment (ranging from insults to killing) for the old, even though older members were also respected in many of these cultures. Death-hastening activities are often justified by claims that they are directed toward elders who are no longer active and productive and are a liability to society and their families. Most societies have some norms of favorable treatment toward their elders, but considerable variability exists in practice. For example, filial piety in China and Taiwan was not always manifest, but was affected by family resources and the number of living children (Ikels, 1997). The coexistence of high status and bad treatment in many traditional societies can be partially explained in terms of differential behavior toward the young-old versus old-old, noted in our earlier discussion of traditional societies that abandoned or murdered their frail elders.

Class and gender differences also come into play. For instance, the norms of filial piety were more often practiced by wealthy families in traditional rural China. Despite the Confucian reverence for age, older people in lower-class families had fewer resources to give them status. The importance of women's household responsibilities throughout life may explain their relatively higher status in old age than men's (Cool and McCabe, 1987).

Turning to contemporary China, there has been a major transformation of life for older people in that country. The "political economy" has had an impact on elders' status as government policies have been altered. For example, women have benefited from changes such as not having to submit to arranged marriages or having their feet bound. Their work opportunities have expanded by opening up more jobs to women. National social insurance also benefits older Chinese citizens. But not all changes have had positive effects. Rules limiting family size and the breaking up of communes have had negative consequences for the childless older population in particular. As noted in Chapter 1, both the Chinese government and entrepreneurs have begun to build group housing for childless elders. These effects are expected to continue as future cohorts of older people contend with fewer children to care for them in times of need. These changes will also impact multigenerational living arrangements in China (Ikels, 1997).

Another alternative to modernization theory is that the development of state or nation represented a shift in older people's roles (Dickerson-Putnam, 1994; Fry, 1996). With the movement from kin-based societies to modern states and capitalist economies in the nineteenth century, labor became a commodity that was sold in exchange for economic security rather than for the security of an extended family. Such marketplace exchanges also created competition between old and young for jobs; this led to the emergence of retirement laws in nineteenth-century Europe that served to

formally remove older people from competition for jobs. The emergence of social security programs in capitalist economies was intended to provide a safety net for retired people that could reduce their dependence on kin and prevent the older person from reentering the job market. At the same time, social security and pension plans that emerged later have provided a stabilizing effect for older people and their families (Achenbaum, 1996).

Ideal of Equality versus Status of Age in America

In his now classic historical analysis, Fischer (1978) formulated reasons other than modernization for explaining changes between generations in American society. He argues that these changes cannot be attributed to modernization, because the decline in older people's status occurred before industrialization and urbanization. He also contends that the increase in numbers of older people does not fully explain the shifts in attitudes toward the old. Instead, he suggests that the emphasis on youthfulness that characterizes our society can be partially attributed to our cultural values of liberty and equality. Both of these values run counter to a hierarchy of authority based on age.

According to Fischer, the elevated status of older persons in earlier historical periods gradually became supplanted in the late eighteenth and early nineteenth centuries by an emerging ideal of age equality. The fundamental change was caused by the social and intellectual forces unleashed by revolutions in America and France. The spirit of equality was dramatically expressed in public fetes borrowed from the French Revolution, where a symbolic harmony of youth and age was celebrated in elaborate rituals of young and old exchanging food (Fischer, 1978).

However, although our society's ideology was egalitarian, economic inequalities actually grew in the nineteenth century. For example, economic status became the basis of seating arrangements in public meetings. Individualistic pursuits of wealth created countervailing forces to a sense of community that had previously been founded on the power of elders. Thus, the age equality that had initially replaced veneration of elders was later supplanted by a celebration of youthfulness and a derogation of age. Inequalities based on age reemerged, but this time to the advantage of youth. Growing contempt toward older people in the mid-1800s is vividly illustrated by Thoreau's (1856) conclusion, "Age is no better, hardly so well qualified for an instructor of youth, for it has not profited as much as it has lost." Heroes and legends centered on younger men, such as Daniel Boone. Social trends in the early twentieth century, such as the development of retirement policies, mass education, and residential segregation of generations, furthered perceptions of older people as useless, with the cult of youth reaching its peak in the 1960s. One irony was that as the economic and social conditions of many older adults declined, their ties of family affection, especially between grandparents and grandchildren, often grew stronger (Fischer, 1978).

Other Perspectives on Historical Change

Historians and gerontologists have questioned whether a critical turning point in age relations occurred between 1770 and 1830 (Achenbaum, 1996). Achenbaum, for example, has taken a position somewhere between Fischer's view and modernization theory regarding the change in status of older adults in the United States. He has identified social trends similar to those documented by Fischer, stating that prior to the middle of the nineteenth century, elders were venerated because of their experiences and were actively involved in socially useful roles. A decline in their status, Achenbaum asserts, occurred during the post–Civil War era. The growing emphasis on efficiency and impersonality in bureaucracies, along with increased misperceptions about senility, furthered a perception of old age as obsolescence. Both Fischer and Achenbaum suggest that it is not possible to establish a firm relationship between modernization and older people's status; rather, they maintain that

Many older women in China continue in self-employed positions.

Americans have always been ambivalent about old age. Shifting beliefs and values are viewed as more salient in accounting for loss in status than are changes in the economic and political structures that occurred with modernization.

These contrasting perspectives of social gerontologists and anthropologists suggest that there is not a simple "before and after" relationship in the meaning and significance of old age between preindustrial and modern societies (Achenbaum, 1996). People in preindustrial societies who, by reason of social class, lacked property and power undoubtedly suffered from loss of status, regardless of their age. For such persons, modernization brought less improvement in status than for older people who were better educated and of higher socioeconomic background. Such inequities continue to be problematic, particularly among persons of color within our society. Cultural gerontologists have emphasized that modernization is not a linear process, but proceeds at different rates and through varied stages, each of which may have a different impact on older people's status (Fry, 1996).

In addition, cross-cultural evidence shows that cultural values can mitigate many of the negative effects of modernization on older people. This is illustrated in modern, industrialized, and urban

Japanese society. Confucian values of filial piety and ancestor worship have helped to maintain older persons' relatively high status and integration in family life, as well as their leadership in national politics. Traditional values of reciprocity and lifelong indebtedness to one's parents are a major reason for continued three-generational households in Japan (Akiyama, Antonucci, and Campbell 1997).

Political ideology may also be an intervening variable. This is illustrated by the effect of Communist party policies in Maoist China, which at first villified older people but eventually sought them to work with the young to promote the Cultural Revolution. Despite their emphasis on collectivization, the Communist leaders did not provide a comprehensive welfare program for older people, especially those in rural China. Families were expected to provide care for their elders, except for those who were childless in their old age. However, as modernization and especially urbanization continued in China after the 1950s, societal views of and governmental benefits to older persons improved (Ikels, 1997).

In sum, the effects of modernization historically do not appear to be uniform or unidirectional. As shown in the next section, many contemporary cultures are still struggling to define satisfying roles for their rapidly increasing populations of older people. Changing values and declining resources result in conflicting attitudes toward their older members in many transitional societies.

A CROSS-CULTURAL VIEW OF OLD AGE IN CONTEMPORARY SOCIETIES

As we have discussed, every society defines people as old on some basis, whether chronological, functional, or generational, and assigns that group a particular set of rights, privileges, and duties that differ from those of its younger members. For example, older persons in our society today qualify for Social Security and Medicare on the basis of their age. In some religious groups, only the oldest members are permitted to perform the most sacred rituals. Societies generally distinguish two, sometimes three, classes of elders:

- those who are no longer fully productive economically, but are physically and mentally able to attend to their daily needs
- those who are totally dependent, who require custodial care, and who are regarded as social burdens and thus may be negatively treated
- those who continue to participate actively in the economy of the social system, through farming or self-employment, care of grandchildren, or household maintenance, while younger adults work outside the home

Older people who can no longer work but who control resources essential to fulfill the needs of younger group members generally offset the societal costs incurred in maintaining them. In some social systems, political, judicial, or ritual power and privileges are vested in older people as a group, and this serves to mediate social costs. For instance, in societies such as those of East Africa, politically powerful positions are automatically assigned to men who reach a certain age (Keith, 1990). In other societies, the old do not inherently have privileges, but gain power as individuals, often through diplomatic skills and contacts with powerful others. The following examples from other cultures illustrate the balance between the costs and contributions made by older adults:

- In the subsistence society of the Chipewyan Indians of Canada, older men are accorded low status, and old age is despised and feared. This is primarily because older men, who are no longer able to hunt, are perceived as unproductive, costing society more than they contribute. Dependent on the contributions of each tribal member, the Chipewyans have sometimes been forced to abandon their old when faced with a choice between the death of older men and that of the entire tribe.

• Unlike older men, Chipewyan older women are still able to perform customary domestic and gathering tasks that do not require physical vigor. As a result, aging does not produce as substantial a decline in the status of older women as in that of older men.

• Unlike Chipewyan men, older men among the Asmats of coastal New Guinea are able to assert political leadership in kinship and local groups even after their hunting skills have deteriorated. The primary reason for this difference is that the Asmat economy is less precarious, so that older men can still acquire resources to protect their position in old age (Amoss and Harrell, 1981).

• In Australia, the traditional respect accorded to older people in the Aborigine culture has resulted in a valuable role for older women. In one Aborigine community in central Australia, a group of women, all over age 70, have formed a night patrol that intervenes to stop rowdy parties and disco activity that result in excessive drinking and violence. These peacekeepers receive more cooperation from the young perpetrators than do police, and community leaders report a decline in assaults and arrests for drunken behavior over the past ten years since this group began its work (AARP, 2000).

• A recent study of Zulu grandmothers and their grandchildren in South Africa reveals that older women play a valuable role in Zulu culture. Their pensions are a steady source of family income, and grandmothers provide an important caregiving function. Despite their contributions, these older women reported feeling that younger Zulus did not respect them. Grandchildren reported a schism between their new values of individualism and traditional tribal values of kinship held by their grandmothers (AARP, 1999).

In other cultures, respect toward intact elders may be promoted, but a subtle acceptance of benign neglect may result in the demise of older persons who are physically and/or cognitively impaired. An ethnographic analysis of Niue, an independent Polynesian island, revealed significant discrepancies between the status of older people who were in good health and had important social and political functions, and those who were too frail to care for themselves. Although medical services are free on Niue, families and neighbors did not summon visiting doctors and public health nurses, even for infected sores, painful joints, and other treatable conditions in these frail elders. The basic needs of cognitively impaired elders were even more frequently ignored. This may stem from values of reciprocity. Like other societies where reciprocity is crucial for intergenerational exchanges, the frail elders of Niue can no longer contribute to the group's well-being (Barker, 1997). Therefore, such neglect may be seen as a way of merely hastening the inevitable death of these weaker members of that society (Glascock, 1997).

Importance of Social Position and the Control of Property

The control of property is a means to achieve power in most societies. In both past and present times, older people have used their rights over property to guarantee their security by compelling others to support them or to provide them with goods and services. For example, among the Etal

---

TRADITIONAL EXTENDED HOUSEHOLDS IN CHINA

The position of the aging father in the Chinese family depends almost entirely on the political and economic power he wields. Elders in wealthy Chinese households and those with substantial pensions to contribute to family expenses enjoy higher status within the family and are better able to control the lives of their adult children than those in poor households (Olson, 1990).

Islanders in Micronesia, the old try to keep enough property to ensure continued care by younger members who hope to inherit it (Nason, 1981). In the Gwembe Tonga tribe in Zambia, males were formerly able to secure their positions by accumulating land and livestock. As their lineage land became covered by water, however, forced relocation cost many older people their exclusive control of property, and the old became dependent on sons and nephews, who acquired better land at the time of flooding (Colson and Scudder, 1981). In other societies, the leadership of males derives from their positions within the family.

Substantial class differences exist in elders' power in many countries. In addition, the extended family structure confers status on older members, even in the face of modernization. As economic resources decline and class differences disappear in such traditional cultures as China, with increasing modernization, filial piety may become undermined. For example, the growing pressures of limited housing and low income in China appear to be having a negative effect on younger generations' attitudes toward old people. In such instances, increased provision of public housing, health care, old-age pension plans, and policies that support family care of elders may serve to reduce tensions between generations.

Older persons from traditional cultures who immigrate to Western countries face even more problems adjusting to the loss of power. In the past 28 years, waves of Indochinese refugees have come to the United States from countries experiencing political strife and unrest. Older people who arrived with younger family members have had more difficulties in becoming part of the culture. Property and other resources in their native lands that afforded them importance and power have been stripped from them. Being in the United States has brought them a different life than the one they might have expected for their later years. These older refugees do not have the ability to provide material goods, land, or other financial support, which has traditionally given them status (Yee, 1997). Accordingly, traditional power has

been eroded as families have started new lives in this culture. Indeed, financial self-sufficiency is a major determinant of adjustment to life in the United States among older Indochinese refugees, regardless of education, gender, and English proficiency (Tran, 1992). Refugees from Russia and other countries of the former Soviet Union are also struggling with the adjustment to their loss of status in their host country.

Knowledge as a Source of Power

Control over knowledge, especially ritual and religious knowledge, is another source of power. The aged Shaman is an example, revered in many societies for knowledge or wisdom. The importance of older members of society in maintaining cultural values is illustrated in India, where traditional Hindu law prescribes a four-stage life cycle for high-caste men: student, householder, ascetic, and mendicant. In the last two stages, older religious men are expected to renounce worldly attachments to seek enlightenment in isolated retreats. This practice ensures that the pursuit of the highest form of knowledge is limited to older men of higher castes (Sokolovsky, 1997). As another example, the !Kung Bushmen value the storytelling ability of those age 45 and over, because the stories are considered to contain the accumulated knowledge of the people. Information and stories are the older person's resource that can be exchanged for food and security (Biesele and Howell, 1981).

Knowledge as the basis of older people's power has been challenged in many traditional societies by Western technological and scientific expertise (Cowgill, 1974a). For example, the older farmer who passes on to his children traditional methods of growing crops may be dismayed to find that they ignore this advice and rely on new agricultural methods and products. Examples in which the relevance of traditional knowledge declines with modernization abound in many fields: farming, fishing, construction, housekeeping, even childrearing. They include the Tong elders of Zambia who

GAINS AND LOSSES WITH INCREASED WORK ROLES

Women in Ganga in Papua New Guinea have assumed a larger role in local coffee production. However, these changes in their work lives have affected their traditional control over the rituals of education and initiation for younger girls. This was once an important part of their knowledge base and power. What was previously provided by a group of older women is now acted out by a young girl's closest relatives. Consequently the power base of older women in shaping the lives of young women has eroded (Dickerson-Putnam, 1994).

lost status due to the flooding of their old habitat and the outmoding of their specialized knowledge (Colson and Scudder, 1981), older people in Taiwan who are less knowledgeable in new commercial and industrial contexts (Harrell, 1981), and many native North American groups faced with changing patterns of production and consumption. Among western Irish peasants, the once dignified movement of the older couple to the sacred "west room" of the house, which signified high esteem, has been replaced by "warehousing" of elders in institutions (Scheper-Hughes, 1987).

Among some cultural groups, however, such as the Coast Salish Indians of Washington, a revival of interest and pride in native identity and religion has occurred, thus raising the esteem of elders who possess ritual knowledge. For example, they are the only ones who know the words and steps for many traditional songs and dances (Amoss and Harrell, 1981; Keith, 1990). Knowledge of the group's culture, particularly its arts and handicrafts, native songs and epics, has enhanced the social status of older persons in these societies; furthermore, the traditions of reverence for old age and wisdom remain strong, overriding the impact of modernization on older people's roles. The timing of such a revival is critical, however. A similar revival among Plains Indians did not have comparable positive consequences for the tribe's older members who were no longer expert in traditional ways (Keith, 1990).

The growing desire for ethnic or tribal identity among many Native Americans, which has led to a conscious restoration of old forms, illustrates that modernization does not automatically erode the status of the elders. Similarly, the search for one's heritage or roots has led to increased contacts between younger generations seeking this information from older persons who often are a great repository of family histories.

Cultural and historical factors can also mitigate the presumed negative consequences of modernization for older people. For example, in Samoa, despite the influx of U.S. aid, industries, and educational programs designed to promote modernization, the cultural system has been flexible enough to maintain older persons as a viable part of society. This has largely been due to the

Older grandparents in rural China serve a vital role as full-time caregivers for their grandchildren.

POINTS TO PONDER

Think about immigrant groups in the United States. In what ways are elders in such families involved or not involved in the lives of their children and grandchildren? What impact do a common language and shared cultural values have on their interactions?

persistence of the traditional *matai* family system, which involves the elders in leadership roles within large bilateral kinship groups, and a village council that accords older Samoans respect and power (Holmes and Rhoads, 1987). The traditional family system has combined with Samoan values of reciprocity in social relationships and an acceptance of dependency in old age to retain high status among Samoan elders.

Indeed, modernization has not resulted in the disintegration of extended families in most non-Western societies, including the rapidly developing Asian and Third World countries. Extended families in rural Thailand and Zimbabwe have adapted to the need for adult children to migrate to the cities for jobs by creating "skip-generation households," where grandparents remain in their rural homes, caring for grandchildren, while their adult children work in urban settings. This reciprocal dependency has also proved useful for many Asians and Eastern European refugee families in the United States where grandparents have immigrated with their adult children to provide regular child care to grandchildren in the extended family (Hashimoto, 1991, 1993).

The way that older people react to change can serve to maintain or improve their position. Among the Sherpa in Tibet, for example, as younger sons move away from the community, and are not available to share households and care for the old, the old resist the traditional division of property and tend to keep the younger sons' shares for themselves. Sherpa elders are also becoming proponents of birth control; since they cannot count on sons to take care of them as they wish, they prefer to share their property among fewer children, keeping more for themselves (Keith, 1990).

EFFECTS OF CULTURE AND MODERNIZATION: THE CASE OF JAPAN

In other situations, the buffering effects of culture on modernization are less distinct. For example, the issue of modernization and aging in contemporary Japan is particularly complex. Older adults have high status and prestige. Values adopted from Confucianism are viewed as linking the old to a family system that emphasizes filial devotion, in which the dependence of elders in this "second privileged period" is accepted (Ogawa and Retherford, 1993). This perspective has been criticized, however, as being based on cultural values and census figures that reflect intergenerational harmony rather than systematic anthropological or social research (Sokolovsky, 1997).

Indeed, the rapid demographic shifts in Japan that have made it one of the world's oldest populations (as described in Chapter 1) and the growth in the numbers of working women (41 percent currently) have altered traditional conceptions of old age and reduced the positive influences of cultural values on intergenerational relations. For instance, the modernization of Japanese society has resulted in increased economic demands on the nuclear family. This is compounded by the fact that the unprecedented numbers of older people in Japan today have increased the societal costs of maintaining older members, and have created dilemmas for younger family members who are responsible for their support.

The majority of middle-aged persons in Japan still believe that care of older parents is the children's responsibility. Indeed, negligence toward one's parents is a source of great public shame in Japan. Society also assumes responsibility for the care of Japan's elders; all those over 70 receive free basic medical services. The Japanese government provides incentives for home care by families; they can receive subsidies to remodel their homes in order to accommodate joint households as well as a tax credit for providing elder parent care (Maeda and Shimizu, 1992). For these reasons, the proportion of older parents living in multigenerational households is higher than in any other industrialized nation. In 1994, 60 percent of people over age 65 lived with their children and grandchildren, but this is a decline from 1985, when 69 percent of older households were multigenerational. Meanwhile, the number of households consisting only of the older couple has grown. In 1994 they made up 24 percent of older households, compared with 19 percent in 1985 (Jenike, 1997).

The number of nursing homes and long-stay hospitals in Japan has also grown rapidly. These trends suggest that traditional customs of caring for aging parents in adult children's homes are slowly changing. The percentage of parents living with children has declined, due to urbanization, industrialization, the growing number of employed women, and the declining number of children since 1950. Urban–rural differences in family expectations are demonstrated by the fact that 25 percent of people age 75 and older in Tokyo live alone, compared with 15 percent in rural regions. Institutionalization in any form is viewed as abandonment by many older people. As a result, most elder care still takes place in private homes.

Middle-aged women are the primary caregivers to Japanese elders, as in most other countries. As more older adults live longer, they may increasingly require goods and services at the perceived expense of younger members and may place even greater demands on middle-aged women in Japanese society. With the increased proportion of educated, professional women and newer cohorts influenced more by Western values than by Confucianism, many women do not want to leave their jobs to become caregivers to their parents or par-

ents-in-law. Because of public concerns about long-term care needs for its growing population of oldest-old, the Japanese Diet passed the Public Long Term Care Insurance Act in 1997 (Maeda, 1998). This national policy guarantees comprehensive long-term care for all Japanese persons aged 65 or older, and for those aged 40–64 who may require long-term care. Funding is provided by a combination of mandatory insurance premiums paid by older persons (estimated to be approximately equivalent to $19 per month in 2000 and $27 in 2010) and taxes that will be paid to federal, prefecture, and municipal governments. Users of this service also must co-pay 10 percent of all incurred expenses.

This bold new legislation in Japan was implemented in April 2000, so its impact cannot yet be determined. The current shortage of nursing homes, home health agencies, and care managers need to be addressed to fully implement this program. Nevertheless, if it succeeds, this universal long-term care program is expected to relieve the burden on Japanese families and hospitals, where most long-term care occurs. The program is being watched closely by policy makers in the United States and in other developed countries to see if it can serve as a model for caring for their increasing populations of oldest-old.

SUMMARY AND IMPLICATIONS

These brief examples from diverse cultures around the world illustrate how each society responds to its aging members within the constraints set by both the natural environment and the larger human environment of social and technological change. A basic principle governing the status of older adults appears to be the effort to achieve a balance between older people's contributions to the society and the costs of supporting them. As will be discussed in detail in Chapter 10, however, the family plays an important role in supporting the old in most societies. Historical and cross-cultural evidence also suggests that maximum social participation of older adults in society results in greater acceptance and respect of elders by the young in most cultures.

The extent to which older citizens are engaged in society appears to vary with the nature of their power resources, such as their material possessions, knowledge, and social authority. In most of their exchanges, older people seek to maintain reciprocity and to be active independent agents in the management of their own lives. That is, they prefer to give money, time, or other resources in exchange for services or materials. This theoretical perspective, described as social exchange theory in Chapter 8, suggests that modern society should seek ways to increase older people's exchange resources so that they are valued by society. For example, maximizing the social value and productivity of the old in our society might include retraining older adults, developing innovative educational programs for older learners (see Chapter 5), and creating opportunities for part-time employment (see Chapter 12).

Control of resources as a basis for social interactions between members of a society is important throughout the life cycle. However, it becomes even more crucial in old age, because retirement generally results in a decline in one's level of control over material and social resources. As their physical strength diminishes and their social world correspondingly shrinks, many older people face the challenge of altering their environments and using their capacities in ways that will help them to maintain reciprocal exchanges and to protect their competence and independence. This may be an even greater problem for older refugees who may still have full physical and cognitive functions, but have lost material resources in their homeland that would have given them power and prestige. These attempts to maintain control over one's environment in the face of changing personal capacities and resources are consistent with the person–environment model presented in Chapter 1. This issue will be discussed in detail in subsequent chapters on biological, psychological, and social changes with aging.

The growth of Japan's older population, combined with the effects of modernization and economic demands on the nuclear family, has resulted in major legislation to support long-term care for frail Japanese elders. Efforts to provide options in long-term care for U.S. elders are described in Chapters 11 and 17.

GLOSSARY

geronticide (or senecide)   inducing the death of old persons, as practiced in some ancient cultures

modernization theory   advances in technology, applied sciences, urbanization, and literacy which, in this context, are related to a decline in the status of older people

social stratification   divisions among people (e.g., by age, ethnic group) for purposes of maintaining distinctions between different strata by significant characteristics of those strata

REFERENCES

AARP. Adapting to a new social order. *Global aging report*, 1999, 4, 6

AARP. *Global aging report*, 2000, 5, 5.

Achenbaum, W. A. Historical perspectives on aging. In R. H. Binstock and L. K., George (Eds.), *Handbook of aging and the social sciences* (4th ed.). San Diego: Academic Press, 1996.

Akiyama, H., Antonucci, T. C., and Campbell, R. Exchange and reciprocity among two generations of Japanese and American women. In J. Sokolovsky (Ed.), *The cultural context of aging* (3rd ed.). Westport, CT: Bergin and Garvey, 1997.

Albert, S. M., and Cattell, M. G. *Old age in global perspective.* New York: G. K. Hall and Co., 1994.

Amoss, P., and Harrell, S. (Eds.). *Other ways of growing old.* Stanford, CA: Stanford University Press, 1981.

Barker, J. C. Between humans and ghosts: The decrepit elderly in a Polynesian society. In J. Sokolovsky (Ed.), *The cultural context of aging.* Westport, CT: Bergin and Garvey, 1997.

Bialik, R. Family care of the elderly in Mexico. In J. Kosberg (Ed.), *Family care of the elderly.* Newbury Park, CA: Sage, 1992.

Biesele, M., and Howell, N. The old people give you life: Aging among !Kung hunters-gatherers. In P. Amoss and S. Harrell (Eds.), *Other ways of growing old*. Stanford, CA: Stanford University Press, 1981.

Colson, E., and Scudder, T. Old age in Gwemba District, Zambia. In P. Amoss and S. Harrell (Eds.), *Other ways of growing old*. Stanford, CA: Stanford University Press, 1981.

Cool, L., and McCabe, J. The "scheming hag" and the "dear old thing." The anthropology of aging women. In J. Sokolovsky (Ed.), *Growing old in different cultures*. Acton, MA: Copley, 1987.

Cowgill, D. Aging and modernization: A revision of the theory. In J. F. Gubrium (Ed.), *Late life communities and environmental policy*. Springfield, IL: Charles C. Thomas, 1974a.

Cowgill, D. *Aging around the world*. Belmont, CA: Wadsworth, 1986.

Cowgill, D. The aging of populations and societies. In F. Eisele (Ed.), *Political consequences of aging. The annals of the American Academy of Political and Social Science*, 1974b, *415*, 1–18.

Dandekar, K. *The elderly in India*. Thousand Oaks, CA: Sage, 1996.

de Romilly, J. *Time in Greek tragedy*. Ithaca, NY: Cornell University Press, 1968.

Dickerson-Putnam, J. Old women at the top: An exploration of age stratification among Bena Bena women. *Journal of Cross-Cultural Gerontology*, 1994, *9*, 193–205.

Fischer, D. H. *Growing old in America*. Oxford: Oxford University Press, 1978.

Fry, C. L. Age, aging, and culture. In R. H. Binstock and L. K. George (Eds.), *Handbook of aging and the social sciences* (4th ed.). San Diego: Academic Press, 1996.

Glascock, A. P. When is killing acceptable: The moral dilemma surrounding assisted suicide in America and other societies. In J. Sokolovsky (Ed.), *The cultural context of aging* (3rd ed.). Westport, CT: Bergin and Garvey, 1997.

Harrell, S. Growing old in rural Taiwan. In P. Amoss and S. Harrell (Eds.), *Other ways of growing old*. Stanford, CA: Stanford University Press, 1981.

Hashimoto, A. Family relations in later life: A cross-cultural perspective. *Generations*, 1993, *17*, 24–26.

Hashimoto, A. Living arrangements of the aged in seven developing countries. *Journal of Cross-Cultural Gerontology*, 1991, *6*, 359–381.

Holmes, L., and Rhoads, E. Aging and change in Samoa. In J. Sokolovsky (Ed.), *Growing old in different societies*. Acton, MA: Copley, 1987.

Hu, Y. H. Elderly suicide risk in family context: A critique of the Asian family care model. *Journal of Cross-Cultural Gerontology*, 1995, *10*, 199–217.

Ikels, C. Long-term care and the disabled elderly in urban China. In J. Sokolovsky (Ed.), *The cultural context of aging* (3rd ed.). Westport, CT: Bergin and Garvey, 1997.

Jenike, B. R. Gender and duty in Japan's aged society: The experience of family caregivers. In J. Sokolovsky (Ed.), *The cultural context of aging* (3rd ed.). Westport, CT: Bergin and Garvey, 1997.

Keith, J. Age in social and cultural context: Anthropological perspectives. In R. Binstock and L. George (Eds.), *Handbook of aging and the social sciences* (3rd ed.). New York: Academic Press, 1990.

Kertzer, D., and Laslett, P. (Eds.). *Demography, society and old age*. Berkeley: University of California Press, 1994.

Maeda, D. Recent policy of long term care in Japan. Paper presented at meetings of the American Public Health Association. Washington DC: November, 1998.

Maeda, D., and Shimizu, Y. Family support for elderly people in Japan. In H. Kendig, A. Hashimoto, and L. Coppard (Eds.), *Family support for the elderly; The international experience*. Oxford: Oxford University Press, 1992.

Minois, G. *History of old age*. Cambridge, England: Polity Press, 1989.

Nason, J. D. Respected elder or old person: Aging in a Micronesian community. In P. Amoss and S. Harrell (Eds.), *Other ways of growing old*. Stanford, CA: Stanford University Press, 1981.

Ogawa, N., and Retherford, R. Care of the elderly in Japan: Changing norms and expectations. *Journal of Marriage and the Family*, 1993, *55*, 585–597.

Olson, P. The elderly in the People's Republic of China. In J. Sokolovsky (Ed.), *The cultural context of aging* (2nd ed.). New York: Bergin and Garvey, 1990.

Scheper-Hughes, N. Deposed kings: The demise of the rural Irish gerontocracy. In J. Sokolovsky (Ed.), *Growing old in different societies*. Acton, MA: Copley, 1987.

Simmons, L. W. *The role of the aged in primitive society*. New Haven, CT: Yale University Press, 1945.

Sokolovsky, J. (Ed.) *The cultural context of aging* (3rd ed.). Westport, CT: Bergin and Garvey, 1997.

Thoreau, H. D. *Walden*. New York: New American Library, 1856, Chapter 1, p. 8.

Tran, T. V. Adjustment among different age and ethnic groups of Indochinese in the United States. *The Gerontologist*, 1992, 32, 508–518.

Vincentnathan, S. G., and Vincentnathan, L. Equality and hierarchy in untouchable intergenerational relations and conflict resolutions. *Journal of Cross-Cultural Gerontology*, 1994, 9, 1–19.

Yee, B. W. K., The social and cultural context of adaptive aging by Southeast Asian elders. In J. Sokolovsky (Ed.), *The cultural context of aging* (3rd ed.). Westport, CT: Bergin and Garvey, 1997.

THE BIOLOGICAL AND PHYSIOLOGICAL CONTEXT OF SOCIAL AGING

If we are to understand how older people differ from younger age groups, and why the field of gerontology has evolved as a separate discipline, we must first review the normal changes in biological and physiological structures as well as diseases that impair these systems and affect the day-to-day functioning of older persons. Part Two provides this necessary background.

• Chapter 3 describes normal changes in major organ systems and how they influence older persons' ability to perform activities of daily living and to interact with their social and physical environments. This area of research has received considerable attention as scientists have explored the basic processes of aging. Numerous theories have emerged to explain observable changes such as wrinkles, gray hair, stooped shoulders, and slower response time, as well as changes in other biological functions that can only be inferred from tests of physiologic function. These include changes in the heart, lungs, kidneys, and bones. There are many normal changes in these organ systems within the same person that do not imply disease,

but in fact may slow down the older adult. Furthermore, significant differences have been observed among people and among organ systems within the same person in the degree of change experienced. The effects of vigorous exercise and an active lifestyle on the extent of physical aging are discussed.

• Chapter 3 also highlights some of the exciting new discoveries in biological research that show the potential of modifying cellular processes and using human growth hormones to slow down aging and even increase the maximum life span of humans.

• Age-related changes in the five major senses are also discussed in Chapter 3. Because sensory functions are so critical for our daily interactions with our social and physical environments, and because many of the normal declines observed in sensory systems are a model of changes throughout the body, it is useful to focus on each sensory system and its role in linking individuals with their environments. Recommendations are made for modifying the environment and for communicating with older people who are experiencing significant declines in vision, hearing, taste, smell, touch, and kinesthetic functioning.

• Chapter 4 focuses on secondary aging—diseases of the organ systems described in Chapter 3, and how these diseases can affect older people's social functioning. Acute and chronic diseases are differentiated, and the impact of these diseases on the demand for health and social services among different segments of the older population is presented. The growing problem of AIDS among older persons and implications for long-term care are discussed in this chapter. Because automobile accidents among older people often result from psychomotor changes associated with aging, methods to reduce auto fatalities through new programs in driver training and through better environmental design are considered.

• Chapter 4 also provides some striking statistics on older people's use of health services, barriers to their use, and recommendations for enhancing appropriate utilization of services. Most existing medical, dental, and mental health services do not adequately address the special needs of the older population, especially those with low income and less education. As a result, older people who could benefit most from the services fail to use them.

• Health promotion has proved successful in maintaining and even improving older people's health in many areas, including exercise, prevention of falls and osteoporosis, and nutrition. Chapter 4 describes some of these programs and the research evidence for the benefits of health promotion.

Throughout Part Two, the tremendous variations in how people age physically are emphasized. Because of lifestyle, environmental, and genetic factors, some people will show dramatic declines in all their organ systems at a relatively early age. Most older people, however, will experience slower rates of decline and at different levels across the organ systems. For example, some people may suffer from chronic heart disease, yet at the same time maintain strong bones and muscle strength.

In contrast, others may require medications for painful osteoarthritis, even as their heart and lungs remain in excellent condition. The following vignettes illustrate these variations.

A HEALTHY OLDER PERSON

Mrs. Hill is an 80-year-old widow and retired librarian. She has been slightly deaf all her life, has some recent loss of vision, and has high blood pressure that is managed by regular use of antihypertensive medications. Despite her minor physical limitations, Mrs. Hill is able to volunteer at the local library, where she spends two afternoons each week reading new books to children aged 4–6. She can still drive, but prefers walking to most places, so she can get her exercise. Active in the local senior center, she was one of the first participants in a health promotion project for older adults. Now she helps teach an exercise class at the center three times a week. She rarely visits the doctor except for a semiannual checkup and medication review. She does admit that she has less energy than in her middle years, but for the most part, she accepts these changes and adjusts her physical activities accordingly. Her son-in-law has made some minor modifications in her home, especially in the height and location of kitchen shelves, so that her daily routines do not place her at risk for a fall or tire her out too much. Friends and relatives are frequently telling her how she does not look her age; she, in turn, becomes impatient with older people who stay home all the time, watch TV, and complain. She is usually optimistic about her situation, and believes that each person can control how well or poorly he or she faces old age.

AN OLDER PERSON WITH CHRONIC ILLNESS

Mr. Jones, age 70, had a stroke at age 65 and is paralyzed on his left side, so he is unable to walk. The stroke has also left him with slightly slurred speech and some personality changes. His wife states that he is not the kind, gentle man she used to know. He has to be lifted from bed to chair and recently became incontinent. His wife first tried to care for him at home, but after he became incontinent, she felt she could no longer handle the responsibility and made the difficult decision to move him to a nearby nursing home. Both Mr. and Mrs. Jones are having difficulty adjusting to the nursing home placement. Since Mr. Jones remains mentally alert and aware of all the changes, he continually expresses his frustration with his physical limitations and with his forced retirement and reduced income. Their children live in another state and have been unable to help their mother with the daily care or the financial burden of the nursing home. As their financial resources dwindle, Mr. and Mrs. Jones are facing the need to apply for Medicaid to cover nursing home costs. Mr. Jones starts to cry easily, sobbing that he is losing control of his life and that his life was never meant to be like this. Mrs. Jones feels angry that her caregiving efforts have not been appreciated and that her husband is so difficult.

These two vignettes point to the complexity of physiological aging. Chronological age is often a poor predictor of health and functional status, as illustrated by Mrs. Hill's excellent functional and emotional health and Mr. Jones's situation of physical dependency, even though he is 10 years younger than Mrs. Hill. As noted above, Part Two describes these variations in physiological aging. It contrasts these with changes due to disease, and presents factors that influence health care status in the later years.

3

THE SOCIAL CONSEQUENCES OF PHYSICAL AGING

This chapter includes

- Major theories of biological aging
- Research on reversing the effects of biological aging
- Effects of aging on body composition
- Aging in different organ systems and the impact of these changes on normal functions
- The implications of these changes for older people's functions and ability to interact with their social and physical environments
- Ways in which the environment can be modified to help accommodate the biological changes experienced by most older people

For most people, aging is defined only by its visible signs—graying hair, balding among some men, sagging and wrinkled skin, stooped shoulders, and a slower walk or shuffling gait. Although these are the most visible signs of old age among humans, there are numerous other changes that occur in our internal organs—the heart, lungs, kidneys, stomach, bladder, and central nervous system. These changes are not as easy to detect because they are not visible. In fact, x-rays and computer-assisted images of organ systems are not very useful for showing most changes that take place. It is primarily by measuring the functional capacity of these systems (i.e., the performance capacity of the heart, lungs, kidneys, and other organs) that their relative efficiency across the life span can be determined. This chapter describes normal changes that all of us experience in our biological systems as we age. In the next chapter, the diseases of aging that may impair organ functions more than would be expected from normal aging are discussed.

As noted in Chapter 1, biological aging, or **senescence,** is defined as the normal process of changes over time in the body and its components. It is a gradual process common to all living organisms that eventually affects an individual's functioning vis-à-vis the environment but does not necessarily result in disease or death. It is not, in itself, a disease. But aging and disease are often linked in most people's minds, since declines in organ capacity and internal protective mechanisms do make us more vulnerable to sickness. Because certain diseases such as Alzheimer's, arthritis, and heart conditions have a higher incidence with age, we may erroneously equate age with disease. However, a more accurate conception of the aging process is a gradual accumulation of irreversible functional losses to which the average person tries to accommodate in some socially acceptable manner. Conversely, people may attempt to alter their physical and social environments by reducing the demands placed on their remaining functional capacity (e.g., relocating to a one-story home or apartment to avoid stairs, driving only during the day, avoiding crowds). This is consistent with the person–environment model of aging; as their physical competence declines, older people may simplify their physical environment to reestablish homeostasis or their comfort zone.

Individual differences are evident in the rate and severity of physical changes, as illustrated by the vignettes of Mrs. Hill and Mr. Jones. Not all people show the same degree of change in any given organ system, nor do all the systems decline at the same rate and at the same time. Individual aging depends largely on genetic inheritance, nutrition and diet, physical activity, and environment. Thus, while one 78-year-old feels "old" because of aches and pains due to arthritis but uses her excellent cognitive skills at work every day, another 78-year-old may retain her physical ability but be institutionalized due to advanced dementia. One way of understanding these variations in bi-

ological aging is to examine the major theories that have been advanced to explain the changes in all living organisms over time.

BIOLOGICAL THEORIES OF AGING

Popular culture, as reflected in books and magazines, is full of stories about "anti-aging hormones," "fighting aging," and "preventing death." The problem with these optimistic projections is that no single scientific theory has yet been able to explain what causes aging and death. Without a clear understanding of this process, it is impossible to prevent, fight, or certainly to stop this normal mechanisim of all living organisms.

The process of aging is complex and multidimensional, involving significant loss and decline in some physiological functions, and minimal change in others. Scientists have long attempted to find the causes for this process. A theme of some theories is that aging is a process that is programmed into the genetic structure of each species. Other theories state that aging represents an accumulation of stimuli from the environment that produce stress on the organism. Any theory of aging must be based on the scientific method, using systematic tests of hypotheses and empirical observations. In addition, Bernard Strehler (1986) has proposed four requirements that biological theories must meet, in order to be considered viable:

1. The process must be universal; that is, all members of a species must experience the phenomenon.
2. The process must be deleterious, or result in physiological decline.
3. The process must be progressive, that is, losses must be gradual over time.
4. Finally, the losses must be intrinsic, that is, they cannot be corrected by the organism.

These guidelines are helpful for excluding biological phenomena that are different from aging per se. For example, they help to distinguish disease from normal aging. While diseases are often deleterious, progressive, and intrinsic, they are not universal (e.g., not all older adults will develop arthritis or Alzheimer's disease). Each of the following theories meets these criteria, although the evidence to support them is not always clear. Even though these theories help our understanding of aging, none of them is totally adequate for explaining what *causes* aging. The theories that will be discussed in this section are based on extensive research with animals or humans:

- Wear and tear
- Autoimmune
- Cross-linkage
- Free radical
- Cellular aging

The **wear and tear theory** suggests that, like a machine, the organism simply wears out over time (Wilson, 1974). In this model, aging is a preprogrammed process; that is, each species has a biological clock that determines its maximum life span and the rate at which each organ system will deteriorate. For example, fruit flies (drosophilae) have a natural life span of a few hours, butterflies a few weeks, dogs up to 20 years, and humans about 120 years. This process is compounded by the effects of environmental stress on the organism (e.g., nutritional deficiencies). Cells continually wear out, and existing cells cannot repair damaged components within themselves. This is particularly true in tissues that are located in the striated skeletal and heart muscle and throughout the nervous system; these tissues are composed of cells that cannot undergo cell division. As we will see later, these systems are most likely to experience significant decline in their ability to function effectively with age.

One of the earliest theories of biological aging, the **autoimmune theory,** proposes that aging is a function of the body's immune system becoming defective over time and attacking not just foreign proteins, bacteria, and viruses, but also producing antibodies against itself. Older people become more susceptible to infections. This explanation of

the immune system is consistent with the process of many diseases that increase with age, such as cancer, diabetes, and rheumatoid arthritis (Finch, 1990). Nevertheless, this theory does not explain why the immune system becomes defective with age; only the effects of this change are described. For example, the thymus gland, which controls production of disease-fighting white blood cells, shrinks with aging, but the *reasons* for both this reduction in size and why more older people do not suffer from autoimmune diseases are unclear.

The **cross-linkage theory** (Bjorksten, 1974) focuses on the changes in the protein called *collagen* with age. Collagen is an important connective tissue found in most organ systems; indeed, about one-third of all the protein in our body is collagen. As a person ages, there are clearly observable changes in collagen, for instance, wrinkling of the skin. These changes lead to a loss of elasticity in blood vessels, muscle tissue, skin, the lens of the eye, and other organs, and to slower wound healing. Another visible effect of changes in collagen is that the nose and ears tend to increase in size. Proponents of this theory argue that these changes are due to the binding of essential molecules in the cells through the accumulation of cross-linking compounds, which in turn slows the process of normal cell functions and shows signs of aging. These cross-links are necessary to join together the parallel molecules of collagen. However, in older animals and humans these links increase, making the tissue less pliable and rigid, as seen in wrinkled skin.

An extension of cross-linkage theory is the **free radical theory** of aging (Finch 1990; Harman, 1981). Free radicals are highly reactive molecules that break off in cells and possess an unpaired electron. Produced normally by the use of oxygen within the cell, they interact with other cell molecules and may cause DNA mutations, cross-linking of connective tissue, changes in protein behavior, and other damage. Such reactions continue until one free radical pairs with another or meets an *antioxidant*. These are chemical inhibitors that can safely absorb the extra electron and prevent oxygen from combining with susceptible molecules to form free radicals. It has been proposed that the ingestion of antioxidants such as vitamin E, beta carotene, and selenium can inhibit free radical damage; this can then slow the aging process by delaying the loss of immune function and reducing the incidence of many diseases associated with aging (Cutler and Cutler, 1983; Harman, 1981).

Nevertheless, it appears that free radicals are not totally destroyed. Those that survive in the organism damage the proteins needed to make cells in the body by interacting with the oxygen used to produce protein. As a result, free radicals may destroy the fragile process of building cells and the DNA strands that transmit messages of genes. Some have argued that this continuous pounding by dangerous oxidants wears away the organism over time, not just by interfering with cell-building but also by requiring antioxidants to be ever-vigilant. This damage to cell tissue by free radicals has been implicated in normal aging, as well as in the development of some cancers, heart disease, Alzheimer's disease, and Parkinson's disease.

Molecular biologists have explored this theory further by splicing genes to measure the cumulative effects of free radicals in cells, with the goal of developing ways to counter these effects. It may be that synthetic antioxidants can be developed and administered to older people as the body's natural supply is depleted. Animal studies have shown dramatic enhancements of memory and physical activity with high doses of antioxidants. For example, two drugs containing the enzymes superoxide dismutase and catabase (known to have antioxidant properties) have been found to extend the lifespan of worms by more than 50 percent. These drugs may also be effective in reducing the damage caused by strokes or Parkinson's disease (Melov et al., 2000). Until research with mice supports the promising results emerging from worm studies, it is difficult to predict whether humans will experience similar benefits. It may be that the free radical theory holds the greatest promise for slowing the aging process in the future. However, while increasing the intake of an-

tioxidants may eventually result in more people achieving their *life expectancy*, there is no evidence that the *maximum life span* of 120 years would increase (Hayflick, 1996).

The **cellular aging theory** suggests that aging occurs as cells slow their number of replications. Hayflick and Moorehead (1961) first reported that cells grown in culture (i.e., in controlled laboratory environments) undergo a finite number of replications, approaching 50 doublings. Cells from older subjects replicate even fewer times, as do cells derived from individuals with progeria and Werner Syndrome—both rare genetic anomalies in which aging is accelerated and death may occur by age 15 to 20 in the former and by 40 to 50 in the latter condition. It appears that cells are programmed to follow a biological clock and stop replicating after a given number of times. In addition, proponents of this theory point out that each cell has a given level of DNA that is eventually depleted. This in turn reduces the production of RNA, which is essential for producing enzymes necessary for cellular functioning. Hence, the loss of DNA and subsequent reduction of RNA eventually result in cell death (Goldstein and Reis, 1984).

Of all the theories of physiological aging, cellular aging appears to explain best what is going on. The role of cell replication, RNA production, and telomeres loss in aging is widely accepted in the scientific community. It should not be assumed, however, that the step from understanding to reversing the process of aging will be achieved soon. It is often erroneously assumed that scientific discoveries of the *cause* of a particular physiological process or disease can immediately lead to *changing* or reversing that condition. Unfortunately, that step is a difficult one to make, as evidenced by progress in cancer research. Scientists have long observed the structural changes in cancer cells, but the reasons for these changes are far from being understood. Without a clear understanding of *why* a particular biological process takes place, it is impossible to move toward reversing that process. However, some hope is offered by recent scientific research that successfully forced cells to produce

telomerase, the enzyme responsible for rebuilding telomeres and in this manner continued cell replication. The reverse process may be effective in preventing the rapid proliferation of cancer cells. Researchers have recently found methods of inhibiting or blocking the production of this enzyme (Bodnar et al., 1998).

CAN AGING BE REVERSED OR DELAYED?

Growth Hormones

Genetic researchers have made great strides in the past 30 years in their understanding of the aging process. Indeed, contrary to our long-held assumptions about aging, many scientists have become convinced that aging is *reversible.* New research on telomeres is one example of this development. Another approach is the possibility of introducing new hormones into the body to replace the depleted hormones in genes that serve as chemical messengers. Researchers at the National Institute on Aging, Veterans Administration centers, and universities around the country are testing the effects of injecting growth hormones into aging animals and humans. So far, many startling discoveries have been made, such as increased lean muscle mass and vertebral bone density, and reduced fat levels. These changes in turn led to increased activity and vigor. While these effects are short-lived, it may not be long before a human growth hormone is marketed that can safely be administered on a regular basis, like daily doses of vitamins.

One promising compound that is being tested by U.S. and French researchers is the hormone dehydroepiandrosterone, or DHEA. This hormone is secreted by the adrenal glands, and the body converts it into testosterone and estrogen. Production of DHEA increases from age 7 to 30, when it stabilizes, then begins to decline. By the age of 80, the body has less than 5 percent of the level of DHEA it produced in its peak. Animal studies have shown that administering DHEA to adult mice results in increased activity levels and learning speed. Human studies are just beginning. Preliminary studies in which DHEA was given orally have shown improved sleep, greater energy, increased sexual activity, and greater tolerance of stress. It may also increase production of an insulin-like growth factor that stimulates cell growth and cell division. The effects were sustained up to three months in these studies (Morales et al., 1995). Research evidence is currently not sufficient to recommend the regular, long-term use of DHEA. Side effects in these short-term studies included liver problems, growth of facial hair in women, and enlarged prostate and breasts among some men, especially at higher doses. Those effects may be due to DHEA's stimulation of testosterone and estrogen. While these and other experiments with growth hormones and other compounds are still in their infancy, they offer promise of extending active life expectancy for future cohorts of older adults. That is, they may not add years to the human life span, but will more likely add life to the years available to each individual.

Caloric Restriction

Several studies using animal models (mice, fruit flies, fish) have demonstrated that reducing caloric intake by 65 percent increased the life span of

---

POINTS TO PONDER

How would you feel if the aging process could be reversed? What might happen to society if more people could achieve the maximum life span of 120 years? What are some of the ethical and resource allocation issues raised by scientific efforts to reverse or slow the aging process?

LEARNING FROM MASTER ATHLETES

Nearly 12,000 athletes age 50 and older competed in the 1999 Senior Olympics in Orlando. Among those who broke records are 88-year-old Leon Joslin, a shotput thrower who claims his recent return to competitive track and field sports has eliminated his migraines and asthma. Some of these competitors in the Senior Olympics have been lifelong athletes, in-cluding 86-year-old Ross Carter, who played guard for an NFL team in the 1930s. Whether they have main-tained their physical activity levels since their youth or began in middle age, older **master athletes** can teach gerontologists much about the effects of healthy lifestyles on biological aging.

---

experimental animals by as much as 35 percent. Dietary restriction did not, however, include limiting nutrients in these studies. Caloric restriction that was accomplished mostly through reducing fat intake has been found to be most successful in extending the life of experimental animals without causing malnutrition. Yet, it is evident from these studies that restriction of fat, protein, or carbohydrate intake alone is not sufficient; total caloric intake must also be reduced. Nor have the same benefits been found from merely increasing the intake of antioxidants or specific vitamins. The benefits of caloric restriction are greatest when it is initiated at birth; however, even when mice were placed on such diets in middle age, their maximum life span increased by 10 to 20 percent (Weindruch, 1996). In fact, caloric restriction has even been found to extend the reproductive capacity of female mice (McShane, Wilson, and Wise, 1999).

Until the results of longitudinal studies with primates are available, these conclusions are not generalizable to humans. The first such major study with primates is an ongoing one by researchers at the Baltimore Longitudinal Studies Gerontology Research Center (Lane et al., 1997; Lane et al., 1996, 1995; Weed et al., 1997). This study has examined the effects of feeding Rhesus monkeys 30 percent less than their normal caloric intake. After 6 years on this diet, these monkeys showed higher activity levels, lower body temperature, improved glucose metabolism, and a slower decline in DHEA levels produced by the adrenal glands than an age-matched control group of monkeys that were fed freely, with no caloric restrictions.

These results provide the first evidence in primates that caloric restriction may have anti-aging effects by slowing down metabolism, thereby reducing the number of free radicals created in the organism. Lower caloric intake may also maintain the production of adrenal steroids such as DHEA without artificially replacing them. Caloric restriction also reduces the growth of tumors, delays kidney dysfunction, decreases loss of muscle mass, and slows other age-related changes ordinarily found in these animals. It delays the onset of autoimmune disease, hypertension, cataracts, glaucoma, and cancers in these animals. These studies offer further support that caloric restriction may be useful for humans in improving their active life expectancy (Ausman and Russell, 1990; Li and Wolf, 1997).

RESEARCH ON PHYSIOLOGICAL CHANGES WITH AGE

It is difficult to distinguish normal, age-related changes in many human functions from changes that are secondary to disease or other factors. Until the late 1950s, much of our knowledge about aging came from cross-sectional comparisons of healthy young persons with institutionalized or community-dwelling older populations who had multiple chronic diseases. These comparisons led to the not-surprising conclusion that the organ systems of older persons function less efficiently than those of younger persons.

Since the 1950s, a series of longitudinal studies have been undertaken with healthy younger and middle-aged persons to determine changes in various physiological parameters. The first of these studies began in 1958 at the Gerontology Research Center in Baltimore, as described in Chapter 1 (Shock, 1962). The initial sample of 600 healthy males between the ages of 20 and 96 was expanded in 1978 to include females. Today, many of the people in the original sample are still participating in the study. Another longitudinal study began in 1955 at Duke University's Center for the Study of Aging, with a sample composed entirely of older adults. Some of these individuals were followed every two years for more than 20 years (Palmore, 1974, 1985). Many other researchers around the country are now examining physiological functions longitudinally. The information in this chapter is derived from their work.

Aging in Body Composition

In this section, we will review *normal* changes in the human body, both visible and invisible. These include changes in:

- muscle mass, fat tissue, and water (body composition)
- skin
- hair

CHANGES IN BODY COMPOSITION   Although individuals vary greatly in body weight and composition, the proportion of body weight contributed by water generally declines for both men and women: on the average, from 60 percent to 54 percent in men, and from 52 percent to 46 percent in women (Blumberg, 1996). Lean body mass in muscle tissue is lost, whereas the proportion of fat increases (see Figure 3.1). This decline in muscle mass and increase in fat is known as "sarcopenia."

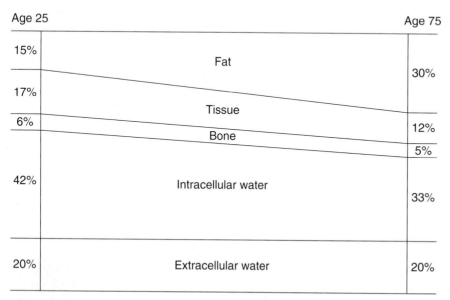

FIGURE 3.1   **Distribution of Major Body Components**
SOURCE: Reprinted with permission from the American Geriatrics Society. Speculations on vascular changes with age, by R. J. Goldman (*Journal of the American Geriatrics Society,* Vol. 18, p. 766, 1970).

Because of an increase in fibrous material, muscle tissue loses its elasticity and flexibility. After age 50, the number of muscle fibers steadily decreases; muscle mass declines by 40 percent between ages 30 and 80 (Kohrt and Holloszy, 1995). However, as described in Chapter 4 and illustrated by master athletes, older people who maintain a vigorous exercise program can prevent a significant loss of muscle tone. The loss of muscle mass and water, and increase in fat tissue, all have a significant effect on older adults' ability to metabolize many medications. Some medications are processed by muscle tissue, some in fat, and some in water throughout the human body. With the changes in body composition described here, these medications may remain in fat tissue longer than needed, or may be too concentrated relative to the available water and muscle volume.

These changes also are associated with weight alterations, from increased weight for some people in the middle years, until the later years when there is a tendency toward lower weight and lower calorie intake. This is why we rarely see people in their eighties and nineties who are obese. The balance of sodium and potassium also changes, with the ratio of sodium increasing by 20 percent from age 30 to 70. Changes in body composition also have implications for the diets of older people; although older adults generally need fewer total calories per day than active younger people, they need to consume a higher proportion of protein, calcium, and vitamin D (Blumberg, 1996). However, many older individuals do not change their diet during the later years unless advised specifically by a physician. Others, especially those living alone, eat poorly balanced meals.

CHANGES IN THE SKIN   As stated at the beginning of this chapter, changes in the appearance and texture of skin and hair are often the most visible signs of aging. These also tend to have deleterious consequences on how older people view themselves and are perceived by others. The human skin is unique among that of all other mammals in that it is exposed directly to the elements, with no protective fur or feathers to shield it from the direct effects of sunlight. In fact, ultraviolet light from the sun, which damages the elastic fibers beneath the skin's surface, is probably most directly responsible for the wrinkled, dried, and tougher texture of older people's skin, known as photoaging or extrinsic aging. Indeed, UV radiation may be the main culprit in skin aging. Human skin cells collected from exposed parts of the body grow much more slowly than skin from areas protected by the sun (e.g., underarms). This is evident when one compares the appearance of the skin of two 75-year-olds: one a retired farmer who has worked under the sun most of his life, the other a retired office worker who has spent most of his years indoors. The farmer generally will have more wrinkles; darker pigmentation known as **melanin,** which has been produced by the body to protect it from ultraviolet rays; and drier skin with a leathery texture. He is also more likely to have so-called *age spots* or *liver spots*—harmless from a health standpoint but of concern sometimes for their appearance. As one might expect, people who spend most of their lives in sunny climates are more prone to these changes. Concern about the negative consequences of extensive exposure to the sun is more prevalent today.

Besides these environmental factors, the human body itself is responsible for some of the changes in the skin with age. The outermost layer of skin, the epidermis, constantly replenishes itself by shedding dead cells and replacing them with new cells. As the person gets older, the process of cell replacement is slowed, up to 50 percent between ages 30 and 70. More importantly, the connective tissue that makes up the second layer of skin, the *dermis,* thins because the number of dermal cells diminishes and makes it less elastic with age. This results in reduced elasticity and thickness of the outer skin layer, longer time required for the skin to spring back into shape, and increased sagging and wrinkling. Sometimes women in their twenties and thirties may experience these problems earlier than men. This is because women tend to have less oil in the sebaceous glands. However, the process of skin aging varies widely, depending on the relative amount of oil in the glands, exposure to the sun, and heredity. Despite its changing appearance, the skin can still perform its protective function throughout old age.

Wound healing is also slower in older persons. Thus, people over age 65 require more time than those under age 35 to form blisters as a means of closing a wound, and more time to form new epithelial tissue to replace blistered skin.

The sebaceous and sweat glands, located in the dermis, generally deteriorate with age. Changes also occur in the deepest, or *subcutaneous*, skin layers, which tend to lose fat and water. The changes in subcutaneous skin are compounded by a reduction in the skin's blood circulation, which can damage the effectiveness of the skin's temperature regulatory mechanism and make older people more sensitive to hot and cold temperatures. As a result, older persons' comfort zone for ambient temperature is generally three to five degrees warmer than that for younger persons. It also takes longer for an older person to adjust after being exposed to either hot or cold extreme temperatures. This leaves the older individual much more vulnerable to **hypothermia** (low body temperature, sometimes resulting in brain damage and death) and **hyperthermia** (heat stroke), as evidenced by reports of increased accidental deaths among older adults during periods of extremely cold winter weather and during prolonged heat spells. For example, the long heat wave in Chicago during July 1995 resulted in more than 500 deaths; most of these were older victims who lacked adequate ventilation in their homes (*Chicago Tribune*, July 31, 1995). To prevent hypothermia, it is recommended that indoor temperatures be set above 68°F during winter months in older people's homes, and that humidity be minimized. Some older people who are concerned about conserving energy and money may not maintain this temperature and may set their thermostats below 68°F, especially at night (Collins, 1986; Macey, 1989; Macey and Schneider, 1993).

CHANGES IN THE HAIR   As we age, the appearance and texture of our hair changes. Hair is thickest in early adulthood and decreases by as much as 20 percent in diameter by age 70. This is why so many older people appear to have fine, limp-looking hair. This change is compounded by the increased loss of hair with age. Although up to 60 strands of hair are lost daily during youth and early adulthood, the hair is replaced regularly through the action of estrogen and testosterone. As we age, however, more hairs are lost than replaced, especially in men. Some men experience rapid hair loss, leading to a receding hairline or even complete baldness by their mid-forties. Some older women also find their hair thins so much that they cannot hide bald spots. Reasons for the observed variation in hair loss are not clear, but genetic factors appear to play a role.

Gray hair is a result of loss of pigment in the hair follicles. As we age, less pigment is produced at the roots. Eventually all the hair becomes colorless, or white in appearance. The gray color of some people's hair is an intermediate stage of pigment loss. In fact, some people may never experience a total loss of pigment production, but will live into an advanced old age with relatively dark hair. Others may experience graying in their twenties. In our society, graying of hair tends to have more stigma associated with it for women than for men, and women are more likely to tint or color their hair.

Changes in Organ Systems

Although some change occurs with age in all organ systems, this chapter focuses on changes in the:

- musculoskeletal and kinesthetic system
- respiratory system
- cardiovascular system
- urinary system
- gastrointestinal system
- endocrine system
- nervous system

CHANGES IN THE MUSCULOSKELETAL AND KINESTHETIC SYSTEM   Stature or height declines an average of 3 inches with age, although the total loss varies across individuals and between men and women. Indeed, the Baltimore Longitudinal Studies found that a gradual reduction in height begins around age 30, about 1/16 inch per year on average. We reach our maximum size and strength at about age 25, after which our cells decrease steadily in number and size. This decline occurs in both the trunk and the extremities, and may be attributable to the loss of bone mineral. This loss of bone mineral density is, in turn, attributed to a decline in estrogen levels with menopause in women. A decline in testosterone may explain the similar but less dramatic loss of bone mineral in older men (Rudman et al., 1991). The spine becomes more curved, and discs in the vertebrae become compacted. Such loss of height is intensified for individuals with **osteoporosis,** a disease that makes the bones less dense, more porous, and hence more prone to fractures following even a minor stress. For older people who have no natural teeth remaining, it is not unusual to lose a considerable volume of bone in the jaw or alveolar bone. This results in a poor fit of dentures and a painful feeling when chewing or biting with dentures. The loss of bone mass characteristic of osteoporosis is *not* a normal process of aging, but a disease that occurs more frequently among older women, as discussed in Chapters 4 and 15.

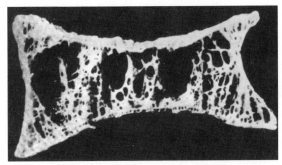

With osteoporosis, both trabecular and cortical bones become more brittle and lace-like.

Another normal change with aging is that shoulder width decreases as a result of bone loss, weakened muscles, and loss of elasticity in the ligaments. Crush fractures of the spine cause the vertebrae to collapse, such that over time, some older people (especially women) appear to be stoop-shouldered or hunched—a condition known as **kyphosis.** Stiffness in the joints is also characteristic of old age; this occurs because cartilage between the joints wears thin and fluid that lubricates them decreases. Strength and stamina also decline with aging. Maximum strength at age 70 has been found to be 65 to 85 percent of the maximum capacity of a 25-year-old. This drops to 50 percent by age 80, although older persons who maintain an active physical fitness program show much less decline in strength. Grip strength declines by 50 percent in men between age 30 and 75, and to a lesser degree in women.

The **kinesthetic system** lets an individual know his or her position in space; adjustments in body position become known through kinesthetic cues. Because of age-related changes in the central nervous system, which controls the kinesthetic mechanism, as well as in muscles, older people demonstrate a decreased ability to orient their bodies in space and to detect externally induced changes in body position. Other physiological and disease-related changes, such as damage to the inner ear, may exacerbate this problem. Comparisons of old and young subjects find that older persons need more external cues to orient themselves in space, and can be incorrect by 5 to 20 degrees in estimating their position. If both visual and surface cues of position are lost, older people experience postural sway or inability to maintain a vertical stance (Teasdale, Stelmach, and Breunig, 1991).

Not surprisingly, these changes in motor functioning and in the kinesthetic system result in greater caution among older persons, who then tend to take slower, shuffling, and more deliberate steps. Older people are more likely to seek external spatial cues and supports while walking. As a result, they are less likely to go outside in inclement

INCONGRUENCE BETWEEN THE ENVIRONMENT AND OLDER ADULTS' MOTOR FUNCTIONING AND BALANCE

Mrs. Guitierrez, age 83, lives alone and is determined to be as independent as possible. Her neighbors watch carefully, however, when she goes out to walk her small dog. She shuffles, moves very slowly, and often has to stop and grab hold of something to avoid falling. When her son and daughter-in-law visit, they shudder when she climbs on a stool to reach a can or bottle on the upper cabinet shelves. Her son has tried to make her home safer, by moving the food to lower shelves, putting grab bars in the bathroom, and removing the throw rugs. These changes are necessary to accommodate normal age-related changes in her kinesthetic and motor functioning.

weather for fear of slipping or falling. Some may complain of dizziness and vertigo. These normal, age-related changes combine with the problems of slower reaction time, muscle weakness, and reduced visual acuity to make it far more likely for older people to fall and injure themselves. However, attempts to improve balance through general and aerobic exercise, alternative approaches such as Tai Chi, and systematic programs to increase visual cues have been successful in enhancing the postural stability of healthy older persons (Hu and Woollacott, 1994). Other advantages of exercise programs for older adults are discussed in Chapter 4.

CHANGES IN THE SENSE OF TOUCH   *Somesthetic*, or touch, sensitivity also deteriorates with age. This is partially due to changes in the skin and to age-related loss in the number of nerve endings. Reduced touch sensitivity is especially prevalent in the fingertips and palms, and lower extremities. Age differences in touch sensitivity of the fingertips are much more dramatic than in the forearm. Using two-point discrimination tests (i.e., the minimum distance at which the subject detects the two points of a caliper), researchers have found that older persons need two to four times the separation of two points that younger persons do. This has significant implications for daily tasks that require sensitivity of the fingertips, such as selecting medications from a pillbox (Stevens, 1992).

Pain perception is an important aspect of touch sensitivity. Older adults are less able to discriminate among levels of painful stimuli than younger persons. One reason for this may be that nerve cells in the skin become less efficient with age. As a result, burns are often more serious in older people because they do not respond to the heated object or flame until it is too late.

The distinction between pain perception and pain behavior is a critical one. Tolerance for pain is a subjective experience, which may be related to cultural, gender, and personality factors. In older people, increased complaints of pain may be a function of depression and psychosomatic needs. On the other hand, some people may attempt to minimize their pain by not reporting above-threshold levels of unpleasant stimuli. This is consistent with a frequently observed attitude among many older adults that pain, illness, and discom-

POINTS TO PONDER

Look around your own home, or your parents' home. What physical factors can you identify that would be a problem if you were an 80-year-old woman living there? Think about lighting, stairs, floor, cabinets, and so on. What changes could make the home more congruent with an older person's needs?

fort are necessary corollaries of aging. In fact, most older adults probably underreport actual pain experienced. For example, an older person may not report symptoms of a heart attack unless or until it is severe. This has significant implications for health-seeking behaviors, as described in Chapter 4.

CHANGES IN THE RESPIRATORY SYSTEM   Almost every organ system shows some decline in **functional** (or **reserve**) **capacity** with age, as illustrated by several physiological indices in Figure 3.2. It is important to keep in mind that this graph is based on *cross-sectional* data collected from healthy men in these age groups; results from the Baltimore Longitudinal Studies of Aging show

more variability when longitudinal data for each cohort are examined. On average, many organ systems show a functional decline of about one percent per year after age 30. Complex functions that require the integration of multiple systems experience the most rapid decline. For example, maximum breathing capacity—which requires coordination of the respiratory, nervous, and muscular systems—is greatly decreased. Accordingly, normal changes in the respiratory and cardiovascular system become most evident with age. These changes are responsible for an individual's declining ability to maintain physical activity for long periods and the increasing tendency to fatigue easily. With aging, the muscles that operate the lungs lose elasticity so that respiratory efficiency is

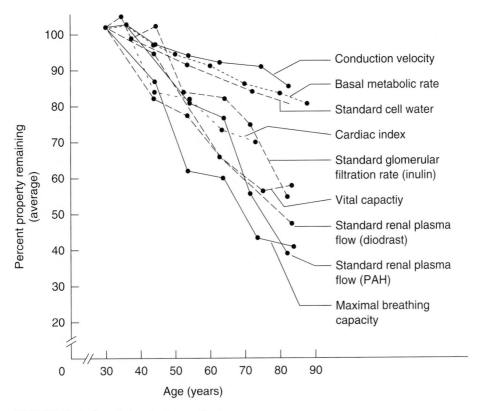

FIGURE 3.2   **Aging in Organ Systems**

SOURCE: N. W. Shock, The physiology of aging. *Scientific American, 206,* 110.

reduced. **Vital capacity,** or the maximum amount of oxygen that can be brought into the lungs with a deep breath, declines. In fact, the average decline for men is estimated to be 50 percent between ages 25 and 70, or a decline from 6 quarts of air to 3 quarts. Breathing may become more difficult after exercise, such as climbing up several flights of stairs, but it does not necessarily impair the older person's daily functions. It may simply mean that the person has to move more slowly or rest on the stairway landing. However, the rate of decline in vital capacity is slower in physically active men, such as athletes, than in sedentary healthy men. A longitudinal study that followed well-trained endurance athletes (average age 62 at baseline) and a control group of sedentary men (average age 61 at baseline) over 8 years suggests that aging per se plays only a small role in the decline of the respiratory system:

- Maximum volume of oxygen declined in master athletes by 5.5 percent.
- Maximum volume of oxygen declined in sedentary men by 12 percent (Rogers et al., 1990).

Of all the organ systems, the respiratory system suffers the most punishment from environmental pollutants and infections. This makes it difficult to distinguish normal, age-related changes from pathological or environmentally induced diseases. **Cilia,** which are hairlike structures in the airways, are reduced in number and less effective in removing foreign matter, which diminishes the amount of oxygen available. This decline, combined with reduced muscle strength in the chest that impairs cough efficiency, makes older adults more susceptible to chronic bronchitis, emphysema, and pneumonia. Older people can avoid serious loss of lung function by remaining active, pacing their tasks, taking part in activities that do not demand too much exertion, and avoiding strenuous activity on days when the air quality is poor.

CARDIOVASCULAR CHANGES AND THE EFFECTS OF EXERCISE   Structural changes in the heart and blood vessels include a reduction in bulk, a replacement of heart muscle with fat, a loss of elastic tissue, and an increase in collagen. Within the muscle fibers, an age pigment composed of fat and protein, known as *lipofuscin*, may take up 5 to 10 percent of the fiber structure (Pearson and Shaw, 1982). These changes produce a loss of elasticity in the arteries, weakened vessel walls, and **varicosities,** or an abnormal swelling in veins that are under high pressure (e.g., in the legs). In addition to loss of elasticity, the arterial and vessel walls become increasingly lined with lipids (fats), creating the condition of **atherosclerosis,** which makes it more difficult for blood to be pumped through the vessels and arteries. This buildup of fats and lipids occurs to some extent with normal aging, but it is exacerbated in some individuals whose diet includes large quantities of saturated fats. Such lifestyle risk factors for heart disease are reviewed in Chapter 4.

Walking provides many physical and emotional benefits.

HOW TO CALCULATE MAXIMUM ACHIEVABLE HEART RATE

The maximum heart rate achievable by sustained exercise is directly associated with age. An easy way to calculate this is: 220 minus age in years. For example:

- For a 25-year-old, 220–25 = 195 beats per minute
- For a 70-year-old, 220–70 = 150 beats per minute

Blood pressure is expressed as the ratio of **systolic** to **diastolic pressure.** The former refers to the level of blood pressure (in mm.) during the contraction phase (systole), whereas the latter refers to the stage when the chambers of the heart are filling with blood. For example, a blood pressure of 120/80 indicates that the pressure created by the heart to expel blood can raise a column of mercury 120 mm. During diastole, in this example, the pressure produced by blood rushing into the heart chambers can raise a column of mercury 80 mm.

In normal aging (i.e., no signs of cardiovascular disease), systolic blood pressure increases somewhat, but the diastolic blood pressure does not (see Figure 3.3). As with changes in the heart, extreme elevation of blood pressure is not normal and is associated with diet, obesity, and lifestyle, all of which have cumulative effects over the years. The harmful effects of abnormally high or low blood pressure are examined in Chapter 4.

However, heart rate varies across individuals, remaining relatively high in physically active older

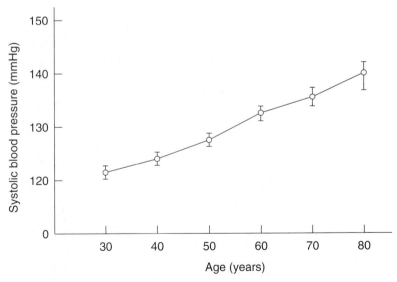

FIGURE 3.3   **Effect of Age on Systolic Blood Pressure**

SOURCE: J. D. Tobin, Physiological indices of aging. In D. Danon, N. W. Shock, and M. Marois (Eds.), *Aging: A challenge in science and society,* Vol. 1 (New York: Oxford University Press, 1981).

AN OLDER ADULT CAN IMPROVE CARDIOVASCULAR FUNCTION

Mrs. Carson had gained weight after retiring at age 66. She was never very interested in exercise. However, a medical checkup at age 68 revealed high LDL and total cholesterol, as well as marginally high blood pressure. She began an exercise program of walking 30 minutes, five times weekly, and cut down her intake of red meat. After 6 months she had lost 10 pounds, her blood lipids were in the normal range, and her blood pressure was 120/70, ideal for a woman her age.

persons. Resting heart rates also decrease with aging, although physically well-conditioned older people tend to have heart rates more similar to the average younger person.

These changes in the heart and lungs cause them to be less efficient in utilizing oxygen. This, in turn, reduces an individual's capacity to maintain physical activity for long periods. Nevertheless, physical training for older persons can significantly reduce blood pressure and increase their aerobic capacity (O'Brien and Vertinsky, 1991). Studies of master athletes have shown that physical training results in a greater volume of oxygen, more lean body weight, lower levels of low density lipoprotein (LDL) cholesterol, also known as "bad cholesterol," and higher levels of high density lipoprotein (HDL), or good cholesterol, than is found in sedentary older persons (Yataco, Busby-Whitehead, Drinkwater, and Katzel, 1997). However, these levels in master athletes are worse than in younger athletes, underscoring the reality that normal changes in the body's physiology and its operation cannot be eliminated completely. For example, world-class sprinters are generally in their late teens or early twenties, but marathon winners are normally in their late twenties or early thirties, since strength and neuromuscular coordination peak earlier than stamina. After age 30, running speed declines by a few percent each year (Hayflick, 1996).

Nevertheless, moderate exercise, such as a brisk walk three to four times per week, appears to slow down these age-related changes. Researchers have found a significant increase in aerobic capacity, as measured by maximum volume of oxygen intake, and a reduction in fat composition among sedentary older persons after 6 months of low-intensity exercise training (e.g., walking for 20 to 30 minutes), followed by 6 months of high-intensity training (e.g., jogging for 20 to 30 minutes). High-intensity exercise resulted in significant weight loss, but low-intensity exercise did not. However, high-intensity training resulted in more orthopedic injuries than did low-intensity training among older participants. For this reason, walking is often the best exercise. Both high- and low-intensity programs have been found to increase significantly the volume of oxygen consumed and to reduce blood pressure among women aged 67 to 89 (O'Brien and Vertinsky, 1991). At the same time, however, exercise may not be sufficient for reducing cholesterol and triglyceride* levels in the blood, both of which have been associated with heart disease. Instead, reduced intake of animal fats, tropical oils, and refined carbohydrates appears to be essential for lowering these elements in the blood. Although there are limitations, such findings justify optimism that physical health can be considerably improved through lifestyle changes, even after age 65. Aerobic exercise and a healthy lifestyle can significantly increase active life expectancy by postponing and shortening the period of morbidity (e.g., days of sickness) that one can expect in the later years. The significance of certain lifestyle habits for maintaining good health in old age is discussed further in Chapter 4.

Triglyceride is a molecular compound made up of three fatty acids synthesized from carbohydrates.

CHANGES IN THE URINARY SYSTEM   Both kidney and bladder functions change with age. The kidneys play an important role in regulating the body's internal chemistry by filtering blood and urine through an extraordinary system of tubes and capillaries, known as glomeruli. As blood passes through these filters, it is cleaned, and the necessary balance of ions and minerals is restored. In the process, urea (e.g., water and waste materials) is collected and passed through the ureter and the bladder, where it is excreted in the form of urine. With age, the kidneys decrease in volume and weight, and the total number of glomeruli correspondingly decreases by 30 percent from age 30 to age 65. As a result, **renal function,** defined by the rate at which blood is filtered through the kidneys, declines by up to 50 percent with age. These changes have significant implications for an older person's tolerance for certain medications such as penicillin, tetracycline, digoxin, and others that are cleared by glomerular filtration. These drugs remain active longer in an older person's system and may be more potent, indicating a need to reduce drug dosage and frequency of administration.

The kidneys also lose their capacity to absorb glucose, as well as their concentrating and diluting ability. This contributes to increased problems with dehydration and hyponatremia (i.e., a loss of salt in the blood). Of all organ systems, renal function deteriorates most dramatically with age, irrespective of disease.

Compounding this problem, bladder function also deteriorates with age. The capacity of the bladder may be reduced by as much as 50 percent in some persons older than age 65. At the same time, however, the sensation of needing to empty the bladder is delayed. The latter condition may be more a function of central nervous system dysfunction than changes in the bladder. As a result, **urinary incontinence** is common in older adults. As many as 15 to 30 percent of older people living in the community and at least 50 percent of those in nursing homes suffer from difficulties with bladder control. The problem may be made worse by a stroke, dementia, or other diseases associated with the nervous system, such as Parkinson's (Thom and Brown, 1998).

Because of these changes in the kidney and the bladder, older people may be more sensitive to the effects of alcohol and caffeine. Both of these substances inhibit the production of a hormone that regulates urine production. Ordinarily, this hormone, known as antidiuretic hormone (ADH), signals to the kidneys when to produce urine in order to keep the body's chemistry balanced. When it is temporarily inhibited by the consumption of alcohol, coffee, or tea, the kidneys no longer receive messages and, as a result, produce urine constantly. This, in turn, dehydrates the body. It appears that ADH production is slowed with aging, so substances that inhibit its production increase the load on the kidneys and the bladder. These changes can force older people to avoid social outings, even a trip to the grocery store, out of fear that they may not have access to a bathroom. Possible treatments for urinary incontinence, as well as ways that older people can alter their daily habits to accommodate bladder problems, are discussed more fully in Chapter 4.

OLDER WOMAN WITH BLADDER CONTROL PROBLEMS

Mrs. RedHorse, age 75, has experienced increasing problems with urinary incontinence, especially since she began using diuretics for her high blood pressure. This has forced her to curtail many of her favorite activities, such as her daily walks with her dog, overnight visits to her daughter's home, and her afternoon tea breaks. She feels frustrated and embarrassed to talk with her physician or daughter about this problem.

CHANGES IN THE GASTROINTESTINAL SYSTEM
The gastrointestinal system includes the esophagus, stomach, intestines, colon, liver, and biliary tract. Although the esophagus does not show age-related changes in appearance, some functions do change. These may include a decrease in contraction of the muscles and more time for the cardiac sphincter (a valvelike structure that allows food to pass into the stomach) to open, thus taking more time for food to be transmitted to the stomach. The result of these changes may be a sensation of being full before having consumed a complete meal. This in turn may reduce the pleasure a person derives from eating, and result in inadequate nutrient intake. This sensation also explains why older people may appear to eat such small quantities of food at mealtimes.

Secretion of digestive juices in the stomach apparently diminishes after age 50, especially among men. As a result, older people are more likely to experience the condition of **atrophic gastritis,** or a chronic inflammation of the stomach lining. Gastric ulcers are more likely to occur in middle age than in old age, but older people are at greater risk for colon and stomach cancer. Because of this risk, older people who complain of gastrointestinal discomfort should be urged to seek medical attention for the problem, instead of relying on home remedies or over-the-counter medications.

As with many other organs in the human body, the small and large intestines decrease in weight after age 40. There are also functional changes in the small intestine, where the number of enzymes is reduced, and simple sugars are absorbed more slowly, resulting in diminished efficiency with age. The smooth muscle content and muscle tone in the wall of the colon also decrease. Anatomical changes in the large intestine are associated with the increased incidence of chronic constipation in older persons.

Behavioral factors are probably more critical than organic causes of constipation, however, as discussed in Chapter 4. Spasms of the lower intestinal tract are an example of the interaction of physiological with behavioral factors. Although they may occur at any age, such spasms are more common among older persons. These spasms are

a form of functional disorder—that is, a condition without any organic basis, often due to psychological factors. Many gastrointestinal conditions that afflict older people are unrelated to the anatomical changes described previously. Nevertheless, they are very real problems to an older person who experiences them. For these reasons, many physicians routinely do a complete checkup of the gastrointestinal system in their patients age 50 and older, every 2 to 3 years.

The liver also grows smaller with age, by about 20 percent, although this does not appear to have much influence on its functions. However, there is a deterioration in the ability to process medications that are dependent on liver function. Jaundice occurs more frequently in older people, and may be due to changes in the liver or to the obstruction of bile in the gall bladder. In addition, high alcohol consumption may put excessive strain on the older person's liver.

CHANGES IN THE ENDOCRINE SYSTEM The endocrine system is made up of cells and tissues that produce a variety of hormones. One of the most obvious age-related changes in the endocrine system is **menopause,** resulting in a reduced production of two important hormones in women—**estrogen** and progesterone. There is strong evidence from a variety of studies that estrogen in particular protects women from heart disease, and it more recently has been shown to decrease the risk of Alzheimer's disease. Replacing it can improve cognitive performance in women with Alzheimer's (Henderson, 1997; Henderson et al., 1994; Paganini-Hill and Henderson, 1991, 1996). Estrogen replacement therapy has many important benefits, but it also can increase the risk of endometrial and breast cancer in some women. These issues are discussed further in Chapter 4 and 15.

Many other hormones besides estrogen and progesterone have been found to decline with aging. These include **testosterone,** thyroid, growth hormones, and insulin. Changes in insulin levels with aging may affect the older person's ability to metabolize **glucose** in the diet efficiently, resulting in high blood sugar levels. It is unclear if the changes in hormone production are a cause or an effect of aging. Nevertheless, much of the research aimed at reversing or delaying aging has focused on replacing other hormones whose levels decline with aging. Some support for this is found in animal studies; for example, by stimulating the hypothalamus in the brain (which produces growth hormones) of old female rats, researchers have stimulated the development of eggs and increased the synthesis of protein in these animals. Thyroid hormones administered to old rats have been found to increase the size of the thyroid and the efficiency of their immune systems (Hayflick, 1996).

CHANGES IN THE NERVOUS SYSTEM   The brain is composed of billions of neurons, or nerve cells, and billions of glial cells that support these. We lose some of both types of cells as we grow older. Neuronal loss begins at age 30, well before the period termed *old*. It is compounded by alcohol consumption, cigarette smoking, and breathing polluted air. The frontal cortex experiences a greater loss of cells than other parts of the brain. A moderate degree of neuronal loss does not create a major decline in brain function, however. In fact, contrary to popular belief, we can function with fewer neurons than we have, so their loss is not the reason for mild forgetfulness in old age. Even in the case of Alzheimer's disease and other **dementias,** severe loss of neurons may be less significant than changes in brain tissue, blood flow, and receptor organs (Thomas et al., 1996).

Other aging-related changes in the brain include a reduction in its weight by 10 percent, an accumulation of lipofuscin (i.e., an age pigment composed of fat and protein), and slower transmission of information from one neuron to another. The reduction in brain mass occurs in all species, and is probably due to loss of fluids. The gradual buildup of lipofuscin, which has a yellowish color, causes the outer cortex of the brain to take on a yellow-beige color with age. As with the moderate loss of neurons, these changes do not appear to alter brain function in old age. That is, difficulties in solving problems or remembering dates and names cannot be attributed to these slight changes in the size and appearance of the brain. Indeed, research comparing age-related changes in brain structures of healthy men and women shows that men experience greater loss of cerebrospinal fluid volume, but this does not translate to any greater or less change in memory or learning among men with normal aging (Coffey, Lucke, Saxton, Ratcliff, Unitas, Billig, & Bryan, 1998).

Age-related changes in neurotransmitters and in the structure of the synapse (the junction between any two neurons) are shown to impair cognitive and motor function. Electroencephalograms, or readings of the electrical activity of the brain, show a slower response in older brains than in the young. These changes may be at least partially responsible for the increase in reaction time with age. The Baltimore Longitudinal Studies of Aging (BLSA) found that reaction time slows by as much as 20 percent between age 20 and age 60 (Hayflick, 1996). Other hypotheses include neuronal loss and reduced blood flow; however, available data are inconclusive. Reaction time is a complex product of multiple factors, primarily the speed of conduction and motor function, both of which are slowed by the increased time needed to transmit messages at the synapses.

The reduced speed with which the nervous system can process information or send signals for action is a fairly widespread problem, even in middle age when people begin to notice lagging reflexes and reaction time. As a result, such tasks as responding to a telephone or doorbell, crossing the street, completing a paper and pencil test, or deciding among several alternatives generally take longer for older people than for the young. Most people adjust to these changes by modifying their physical environment or personal habits, such as taking more time to do a task and avoiding rush situations; for example:

- leaving the house one hour before an appointment instead of the usual 15 minutes
- shopping for groceries during times when stores are not crowded
- shopping in smaller stores
- avoiding freeway driving

Such adaptations are perhaps most pronounced in the tasks associated with driving. The older driver tends to be more cautious, to slow down well in advance of a traffic signal, to stay in the slower lane, and to avoid freeways during rush hour. Many choose to drive larger cars that can survive collisions better than compact cars. Despite this increased cautiousness, accident rates are high among older drivers, as discussed in the next chapter.

Changes in the central nervous system that accompany aging also affect the senses of hearing, taste, smell, and touch. Despite these changes, intellectual and motor function do not appear to deteriorate significantly with age. The brain has tremendous reserve capacity that takes over as losses begin. It is only when neuronal loss, inadequate function of neurotransmitters, and other structural changes are severe that the older person experiences significant loss of function. The changes in the brain that appear to be associated with Alzheimer's disease are discussed in Chapter 6.

Changes in Sleep Patterns with Aging

One of the most common complaints of older people is that they can no longer sleep well, with up to 40 percent of older persons in community surveys complaining of sleep problems. These complaints have a basis in biological changes that occur with aging. Results of laboratory studies of sleep–wake patterns of adults have consistently revealed age-related changes in electroencephalogram (EEG) patterns, sleep stages, and circadian rhythms (Vitiello, 1996). Sleep progresses over five stages:

- non-REM sleep; i.e., no rapid eye movements during sleep (stages 1–4)
- REM (rapid eye movement) sleep (stage 5)

Sleep stages occur in a linear pattern from stage 1 through stage 4, then REM sleep in stage 5. Stage 4 is when deep sleep takes place. Each cycle is repeated four or five times through the night. Brain wave activity differs in a characteristic pattern for each stage.

With normal aging, even in the absence of any predisposing diseases, many of these brain waves slow down, and the length of time in each stage changes. In particular, lab tests have shown a decline in total sleep time in stages 3, 4, and 5, and sleep is lighter. Older people have shorter cycles from stages 1 to 4 and REM sleep, with the latter stage occurring earlier in the cycle. During these stages, older people, more so than the young, are easily awakened, apparently by environmental stimuli that would not disturb a younger person (Vitiello and Prinz, 1991).

Changes in circadian rhythms, or the individual's cycle of sleeping and waking within a 24-hour period, are characterized by a movement from a two-phase pattern of sleep (awake during the day, asleep during the night) to a multiphasic rhythm that is more common in infants—daytime napping and shorter sleep cycles at night. These changes may be associated with changes in core body temperatures in older people discussed earlier in this chapter.

The older person may compensate by taking more daytime naps, which can lead to further disruptions in night sleep. More often, older people who report sleep disturbances to their primary physician are prescribed sleeping pills or sedative hypnotic medications; this age group represents the highest users of such medications, receiving almost one-half of all sedative hyponotic drugs prescribed. Yet medications do not necessarily improve their sleep patterns, especially if used long-term (Ohayon and Caulet, 1995; Vitiello, 1996). Both the incidence of sleeping difficulties and the use of sleeping pills are more common in older women than in older men. These normal, age-related changes in sleep patterns need not be disruptive to the older person's well-being. It may be disturbing for people accustomed to normal sleep in their youth to have a lighter, shorter, and more disrupted sleep pattern as they age, but individuals can adjust to these changes just as they do to other normal physiological changes without resorting to medications. Many hypnotics used to treat sleep disorders can produce a para-

---

TIPS FOR IMPROVING SLEEP

Sleep disturbances can be alleviated by improving one's **sleep hygiene.** These include:

- increasing physical exercise
- increasing exposure to natural light during the days
- reducing the intake of caffeine and other medications

- avoiding napping during the day
- improving the sleeping environment (e.g., a quieter bedroom with heavy curtains to block out the light, because exposure to light can change circadian rhythms) (Vitiello, 1996)

---

doxical effect by resulting in insomnia if used for a long time.

There are a few true *disorders of sleep* that can occur with aging; these include respiratory problems, **sleep apnea,** which is defined as a 5- to 10-second cessation of breathing, and **nocturnal myoclonus** or *restless leg syndrome (RLS),* which is a neuromuscular disturbance affecting the legs during sleep. Generally these conditions are treated with medications. More often, however, sleep disturbance is associated with poor physical health and depression (Foley et al., 1995; Livingston, Blizard, and Mann, 1993).

Sleep disorders in older persons should be treated because in some cases they can increase the risk of mortality. A large study of community-dwelling older adults found that daytime sleepiness was associated with increased death rates in men and women (1.40 times the rate for men with normal sleep, 2.12 times the rate for women with normal sleep). Frequent awakenings or early morning awakenings had no discernible effect on mortality (Newman et al., 2000).

CHANGES IN SENSORY FUNCTIONS

Our ability to see, hear, touch, taste, and smell has a profound influence on our interactions with our social and physical environments. Given the importance of our sensory functions for social interactions, and the gradual decline in our sensory

abilities with aging, it is critical that we understand these changes and how they can influence our social capabilities as we age. A popular belief is that, as we get older, we cannot see, hear, touch, taste, or smell as well as we did when we were younger. This appears to be true. The decline in all our sensory receptors with aging is normal; in fact, it begins relatively early. We reach our optimum capacities in our twenties, maintain this peak for a few years, and gradually experience a decline, with a more rapid rate of decline after the ages of 45 to 55. Having said this, we should note that there is tremendous diversity among individuals in the rate and severity of sensory decline, as illustrated earlier by Mrs. Hill and Mr. Jones. Some older persons may have better visual acuity than most 25-year-olds; many 75-year-olds can hear better than most younger persons. Although age per se does not determine deterioration in sensory functioning, it is clear that many internal changes do occur. The older person who has better visual or hearing acuity than a 25-year-old probably had even better sensory capacities in the earlier years. It is important to focus on *intraindividual* changes with age, not *interindividual* differences, when studying sensory and perceptual functions. Unfortunately, most of the research on sensory changes with age is cross-sectional—that is, based on comparing different persons who are older and younger. For this reason, the reader needs to be aware that there are tremendous individual differences in how much and how severely sensory functions deteriorate with age.

POINTS TO PONDER

Think about the wine taster who, in old age, may still be considered the master of his trade, performing a job that requires excellent taste discrimination. Perfume developers also attain their expertise over many years. What other jobs require intrinsic sensory abilities as well as skills that take years to master?

Changes in different senses also vary within the same individual. Thus, the person who experiences an early and severe decline in hearing acuity may not have any deterioration in visual functioning. Some sensory functions, such as hearing, may show an early decline, yet others, such as taste and touch, change little until well into advanced old age. Over time, however, sensory changes affect an older person's social functions.

Because these changes are usually gradual, people adapt and compensate by using other, still-intact sensory systems. For example, they may compensate by:

- standing closer to objects and persons in order to hear or see
- using nonverbal cues such as touch and different body orientations
- utilizing external devices such as bifocals or hearing aids

To the extent that people can make their environment conform to their changing needs, sensory decline need not be incapacitating. It becomes much more difficult for individuals to use compensatory mechanisms if the environment does not allow for modification to suit individual needs, if the decline in any one system is severe, or if several sensory systems deteriorate at the same time. Such problems are more likely to occur in advanced old age. There is considerable evidence that, with normal aging, a decline occurs in all sensory systems. That is, sensory and recognition thresholds increase, and discrimination between multiple stimuli demands greater distinctions between them.

Changes in Vision

Vision problems increase with age; when we compare 55- to 64-year-olds with those over age 85, the rate of visual impairments increases fourfold from 55 per 1000 people to 225 per 1000 (Bognoli and Hodos, 1991). As a result, older adults are more likely to experience problems with daily tasks that require good visual skills, such as reading small print or signs on moving vehicles, threading a needle, or adapting to sudden changes in light level. In addition, impaired vision caused by

---

DISTINCTIONS IN TERMINOLOGY RELATED TO SENSORY FUNCTIONS

- *Sensation* is the process of taking in information through the sense organs.
- *Perception* is a higher function in which the information received through the senses is processed in the brain.
- *Sensory threshold* is the minimum intensity of a stimulus that a person requires in order to detect the stimulus. This differs for each sensory system.

- *Recognition threshold* is the intensity of a stimulus needed in order for an individual to identify or recognize it. As might be expected, a greater intensity of a stimulus is necessary to recognize than to detect it.
- *Sensory discrimination* is defined as the minimum difference necessary between two or more stimuli in order for a person to distinguish between them.

untreated cataracts or glaucoma is much more likely to result in problems with activities of daily living than is hearing impairment (Rudberg et al., 1993).

EFFECTS OF STRUCTURAL CHANGES IN THE EYE
Most age-related problems in vision are attributable to changes in parts of the eye (see Figure 3.4). However, these problems are aggravated by changes in the central nervous system that block the transmission of stimuli from the sensory organs. Changes in the visual pathways of the brain and in the visual cortex may be a possible source of some of the alterations that take place in visual sensation and perception with age. The parts of the eye that show the greatest age-related changes are:

- the cornea
- the pupil
- rods and cones in the retina
- the lens

The cornea is usually the first part of the eye to be affected by age-related changes. The surface of the cornea thickens with aging, and the blood vessels become more prominent. The smooth,

rounded surface of the cornea becomes flatter and less smooth, and may take on an irregular shape. The older person's eye appears to lose its luster and is less translucent than it was in youth. In some cases, a fatty yellow ring, known as the *arcus senilis*, may form around the cornea. This is not a sign of impending vision loss; in fact, it has no impact on vision. It is sometimes associated with increased lipid deposits in the blood vessels.

At its optimal functioning, the pupil is sensitive to light levels in the environment, widening in response to low light levels and contracting when light levels are high. With aging, the pupil appears to become smaller and more fixed in size. The maximum opening of the pupil is reduced in old age, commonly to about two-thirds its original maximum. That is, the older person's pupil is less able to respond to low light levels by dilating or opening to the extent needed. The eye also responds more slowly to changes in light conditions. This problem is compounded by a slower shift from cones to rods under low-light conditions. As a result, the older person may have considerable difficulty functioning in low-light situations, or in adjusting to significant changes in ambient light. In fact, older people may need three times more light than younger persons to function effectively; for

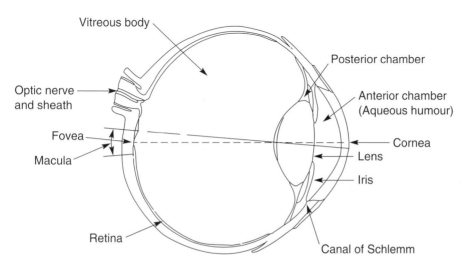

FIGURE 3.4 **The Eye**

PROBLEMS WITH RESTAURANT ENVIRONMENTS

Many older people may feel frustrated when they go to a special restaurant for an evening dinner, only to find that the tables are lit by candles. This makes it difficult to read the menu, to see the way to the table, and even to have eye contact with companions. Family and friends may be frustrated in such situations if they do not understand that the older person's complaints about the restaurant stem from these changes in vision, not from a lack of appreciation for their efforts. Some older people cope with these problems by avoiding such restaurants altogether or going there only during daylight hours.

It is important for restaurant owners to provide good lighting at each table and write their menus in large, legible print against a white background. In response to the growing number of Baby Boomers who are experiencing problems of visual accommodation, some restaurants have begun to stock reading glasses with different levels of magnification to lend to their customers!

example, highway signs must be 65 to 75 percent closer than for younger drivers to be readable at night. These changes may also reduce the older person's ability to discern images in conditions of poor light contrast (e.g., driving at twilight or under foggy or rainy conditions), and to detect details in moving objects. Even among healthy older persons who are still driving, age-related visual changes may significantly alter their abilities under marginal conditions. For example, a survey of participants aged 22 to 92 in the Baltimore Longitudinal Studies (described in Chapter 1) revealed that age was highly correlated with reports of problems with:

- sudden merging of other vehicles
- judging their own and other vehicles' speed
- driving under glare and hazy conditions
- reading street signs while driving (Kline et al., 1992)

For these reasons, older people may choose to avoid such activities, especially driving among fast-moving traffic on freeways at night when bright headlights create glare against asphalt surfaces, and in rain. Although this is a safe method of coping with age-related difficulties in low-light situations, older people must be encouraged to maintain their activity level and not become isolated because of declines in visual function. In such instances, families and professionals may have to encourage older people to use other forms of transportation, such as buses and taxis, thereby avoiding the problem of too little environmental stimulation relative to the person's competence.

PROBLEMS RELATED TO OXYGEN AND FLUID LEVELS   Problems in rod and cone function may be related to a reduced supply of oxygen to the retina. This may be due to a deficiency of vitamin A. However, there is little research evidence to suggest that increased intake of vitamin A in old age can improve visual functioning under low-light conditions.

As stated earlier, two fluid-filled chambers are in the eye: *aqueous humour* fills the anterior or front portion of the eye, and *vitreous humour* is found in the posterior chamber, behind the lens. The *aqueous humour* drains through the Canal of Schlemm. In the disease state known as **glaucoma,** drainage is less efficient, or excess production of the aqueous humour occurs. Glaucoma occurs more frequently after middle age and can be managed with regular medications. More severe cases may require surgery or, more recently, the use of laser treatment. In its later stages, glaucoma may result in tunnel vision, which is a gradual narrowing of an individual's field of vision, such that peripheral vision is lost and the individual can focus only in the center. Untreated glaucoma is the third leading cause of blindness in the United States, the United Kingdom, and Canada (Accardi,

Gombos, and Gombos, 1985), and increases in frequency with age. Among African Americans, glaucoma is the leading cause of blindness, with a prevalence rate in middle-class blacks 15 times that of whites. Even when socioeconomic differences and access to health care are controlled, glaucoma is both more prevalent and more difficult to treat in African Americans (Sommer, Tielsch, and Katz, 1991; Wilson, 1989).

EFFECTS OF AGING ON THE LENS   Perhaps the greatest age-related changes in the eye occur in the lens. In fact, the lens is a model system for studying aging because it contains some of the oldest cells in the body, formed during the earliest stages of the embryo's development. Furthermore, the lens is a relatively simple structure biochemically; all of its cells are of the same type, composed of protein.

Collagen is the primary protein in the lens, and makes up 70 to 80 percent of the total tissue composition of the entire body. As it ages, collagen thickens and hardens. This change in collagen makes the lens less elastic, thereby reducing its ability to change form (i.e., from rounded to elongated and flat) as it focuses from near to far. Muscles that help stretch the lens also deteriorate with age, thereby compounding the problem of changing the shape of the lens. This process, known as **accommodation,** begins to deteriorate in middle age and is manifested in increasing problems with close vision. By the time many people reach their forties and fifties, they need to hold their reading material at arm's length. As a result, many turn to reading glasses or bifocals.

By age 60, accommodative ability is significantly deteriorated. Decrements in accommodation may cause difficulties for the older person when shifting from near to far vision; for example, when looking across a room, walking up or down stairs, reading and glancing up, and writing notes while looking up at a blackboard or a lecturer. The hardening of the lens due to changes in collagen tissue does not occur uniformly. Rather, there is differential hardening, with some surfaces allowing more light to enter than others. This results in

uneven refraction of light through the lens and onto the retina. When combined with the poor refraction of light through the uneven, flattened surface of the cornea, extreme sensitivity to glare often results. This problem becomes particularly acute in environments with a single source of light aimed at a shiny surface, such as a large window at the end of a long, dark corridor with highly polished floors, occasional streetlights on a rain-slicked highway, or a bright, single, overhead incandescent light shining on a linoleum floor. These conditions may contribute to older people's greater caution and anxiety while driving or walking.

From childhood through early adulthood, the lens is a transparent system through which light can easily enter. With normal aging, the lens becomes more opaque, and less light passes through (especially shorter wavelengths of light); these changes compound the problems of poor vision in low light that were described earlier. Some older persons experience a more severe opacification (clouding of the lens) to the point that the lens prevents light from entering. This condition, known as **cataract,** is a leading cause of blindness in the United States and the primary cause of blindness worldwide (Sperduto, 1994). In a survey of white and black older persons in Baltimore, unoperated age-related cataracts accounted for 27 percent of all blindness among African Americans, compared with 13 percent among whites (Sommer et al., 1991). Researchers in the Framingham eye study have examined the incidence of cataracts, that is, the development of the condition in the same individual over a number of years. In a reexamination of survivors of the original Framingham eye study 13.6 years later, the incidence rate was 50 percent for people aged 55 to 59 at the beginning of the study. It jumped to 80 percent for older adults who had been age 70 to 74 at the start (Milton and Sperduto, 1991). Its prevalence increases tenfold between ages 52 and 85. There is strong evidence for a relationship between the development of cataracts with age and the lack of antioxidants such as vitamins A, C, and E (Jacques, Chylack, and Taylor, 1994; Seddon et al., 1994b).

SUGGESTIONS FOR IMPROVING PERSON–ENVIRONMENT FIT FOR PEOPLE EXPERIENCING CHANGES IN THEIR VISION

- Use widely contrasting colors on opposite ends of the color spectrum, such as red and yellow, green and orange.
- Define edges and corners such as stairs, walls, and doors clearly with color or texture.
- Avoid using blue and green together to define adjoining spaces, such as stairs and stair land-

ings, floors and ramps, and curbs and curbcuts, especially where the junction represents different levels.
- Avoid shiny floor and wall surfaces that can cause glare.
- Avoid placing a single, large window at the end of a long, dark corridor.

A cataract may occur in any part of the lens—in the center, the peripheral regions, or scattered throughout. If the lens becomes totally opaque, cataract surgery may be required to extract the lens. It carries relatively little risk, even for very old persons, and can significantly enhance quality of life. Indeed, this is the most common surgical procedure performed on people over age 65, with about 1.5 million extractions performed per year, usually as an outpatient procedure. A lens implant in place of the extracted lens capsule is the most common treatment, but a contact lens is another option. The advantage of the implant is that the older person does not need to have good finger dexterity to put the artificial lens in and out of the eye. When the older person first obtains a replacement lens, it takes some time to adjust to performing daily activities, especially if the artificial lens is not an implant, and the images form on different planes for the two eyes. Patients who receive a lens implant show improvement not just in visual function, but also in objective assessments of activities of daily living and manual function within a few months.

In addition to getting harder and more opaque, the lens becomes yellower with age, especially after age 60. The increasingly more opaque and yellowing lens acts as a filter to screen out wavelengths of light, thus reducing the individual's color sensitivity and ability to discriminate among colors that are close together in the blue-green range. Older people may have problems selecting clothing in this color range, sometimes resulting in poorly coordinated outfits. Deterioration in color discrimination may also be due to age-related changes in the visual and neural pathways.

OTHER CHANGES IN VISION   *Depth and distance perception* also deteriorate with aging, because of a loss of convergence of images formed in the two eyes. This is caused by differential rates of hardening and opacification in the two lenses, uneven refraction of light onto the retina, and reduced visual acuity in aging eyes. As a result, there is a rapid decline after age 75 in the ability to judge distances and depths, particularly in low-light situations and in the absence of orienting cues, such as stairs with no color distinctions at the edges and pedestrian ramps or curb cuts with varying slopes.

Another age-related change is narrower peripheral vision (the ability to see on either side without moving the eyes or the head). This problem becomes particularly acute when driving; for example, an older person may not see cars approaching from the left or right at an intersection.

Some older persons experiencing **age-related macular degeneration (AMD)** lose acuity in the center of their visual field. The macula is that point in the retina with the best visual acuity, especially for seeing fine detail. Macular degeneration is the fourth major cause of blindness generally, and the leading cause of blindness in Americans over age 60. It occurs if the macula receives less oxygen than it needs, resulting in destruction of the existing nerve endings. The incidence of macular degeneration increases with age, even more dramatically than cataracts. People over age 80 have 15 times the likelihood of developing AMD than people aged 60. There is evidence for both a genetic basis and environmental risk factors, such as a lack of antioxidants for age-related macular degeneration. Studies that have supplemented older people's diets with carotenoid-rich foods or used zinc supplements, have found positive effects on visual activity of AMD patients (Allikmets et al., 1997; Blumberg, 1996; Seddon et al., 1994a).

The early stages of macular degeneration may begin with a loss of detail vision; then central vision gradually becomes worse. Total blindness rarely occurs, but reading and driving may become impossible. Older persons with this condition may compensate by using their remaining peripheral vision. They may then appear to be looking at the shoulder of someone they are addressing, but actually be relying on peripheral vision to see the person's face. Laser treatment in the early stages of this disease is effective, but it carries a risk of burning away the center of the retina entirely. A new form of therapy combines a light-activated drug treatment (Visudyne) with a low-power laser light to activate the drug. This procedure is effective in destroying the abnormal blood vessels and scar tissue in the eye without damaging the retina. Although macular degeneration cannot be cured, this new treatment can slow retinal damage and improve central vision.

Some older people, most often postmenopausal women, experience reduced secretion of tears. They may complain of "dry eyes" that cause irritation and discomfort. Unfortunately, this condition has no known cure, but it does not cause blindness and can be managed with artificial tears to prevent redness and irritation. Artificial tears can be purchased at most drugstores.

The muscles that support the eyes, similar to those in other parts of the body, deteriorate with age. In particular, two key muscles atrophy. These are the elevator muscles, which move the eyeball up and down within its socket, and the ciliary muscle, which aids the lens in changing its shape. Deterioration of the elevator muscles results in a reduced range of upward gaze. This may cause problems with reading overhead signs and seeing objects that are placed above eye level, such as on high kitchen shelves.

Assisting Adaptation and Quality of Life through Environmental Modifications

As suggested above, many older adults report significant impairments in their activities of daily living, including reading small print, adjusting to dimly lit environments, tracking moving targets, and locating a sign in a cluttered background. This may mean that an older person feels compelled to give up valued social activities. To maintain person–environment congruence and psychological well-being, an aging person should be encouraged to maintain social contacts, even if new activities must be substituted for old. Family and friends also can help by improving the physical environment, such as replacing existing lightbulbs with higher wattage and three-way bulbs, moving low

---

DIAGNOSING MACULAR DEGENERATION

Mr. Lopez noticed over the past 5 years that objects appear blurry when he looks directly at them, but sharper as he glances more peripherally. He finally went for an eye exam after experiencing more problems with driving. The ophthalmologist diagnosed macular degeneration and was able to treat it with Visudyne. Mr. Lopez can now drive safely again and continue to play bridge and participate in other activities.

tables and foot stools outside the traffic flow, and putting large-print labels on prescription bottles, spices, and cooking supplies. Older people can also take advantage of:

- large-print newspapers and books
- audiotapes of books that are available in community libraries
- playing cards with large letters
- larger fonts on flat-screen computer monitors that are designed to reduce glare

Local agencies serving the visually impaired often provide low-vision aids at minimal cost. These include:

- needle threaders for sewing
- templates for rotary telephones, irons, and other appliances
- large-print phone books, clocks, and calendars
- magnifying glasses for situations where large-print substitutes are unavailable

Other environmental modifications may be more costly or require the use of a professional architect. Families and designers can help make the home and work environment safer by:

- placing contrasting color strips on stairs, especially on carpeted or slippery linoleum stairs, to aid the older person's depth perception
- color and light coding of ramps and other changes in elevation
- clearly marking changes in floor surfaces such as door sills
- increasing the number of light sources

- installing nonslip and nonglossy floor coverings
- using a flat paint instead of glossy finishes to reduce the problem of glare on walls
- installing venetian and vertical blinds to control glare throughout the day
- using indirect or task lighting (e.g., reading lamps, countertop lamps) rather than ceiling fixtures
- adding dimmer switches

Age-related vision changes need not disadvantage people if they can be encouraged to adapt their activities and environment to fit their level of visual functioning and their needs. An older adult who is having difficulty adjusting to vision-related losses may initially resist such modifications. One way to address this resistance is to involve the older person in decisions about such changes.

Changes in Hearing

In terms of survival, vision and hearing are perhaps our most critical links to the world. Although vision is important for negotiating the physical environment, hearing is vital for communication. Because hearing is closely associated with speech, its loss disrupts a person's understanding of others and even the recognition of one's own speech. An older person who is experiencing hearing loss learns to make changes in behavior and social interactions, so as to reduce the detrimental social impact of hearing loss. Many younger hearing-impaired persons learn sign language or lip reading. But these are complex skills requiring extensive training and practice, and are less likely to be learned by older adults.

POINTS TO PONDER

Consider some ways in which we rely on our hearing ability in everyday life: in conversations with family, friends, and coworkers; in localizing the sound of approaching vehicles as we cross the street or drive; and in interpreting other people's emotions through their tone of voice and use of language. How does a person function if these abilities gradually deteriorate?

THE ANATOMY AND PHYSIOLOGY OF THE EAR

It is useful to review the anatomy of the ear in order to understand where and how auditory function deteriorates with age. The auditory system has three components, as illustrated in Figure 3.5. The outer ear begins at the pinna, the visible portion that is identified as the ear. The auditory canal is also part of the outer ear. Note the shape of the pinna and auditory canal; it is a most efficient design for localizing sounds.

The eardrum, or tympanic membrane, is a thin membrane that separates the outer ear from the middle ear. This membrane is sensitive to air pressure of varying degrees and vibrates in response to a range of loud and soft sounds. Three bones, or *ossicles*, that transfer sound waves to the inner ear are located in the middle ear (the *malleus, incus,* and *stapes*).

These very finely positioned and interrelated bones carry sound vibrations from the middle ear to the **inner ear**—that snail-shaped circular structure called the cochlea. Amplified sounds are converted in the cochlea to nerve impulses. These are then sent through the internal auditory canal and the cochlear nerve to the brain, where they are translated into meaningful sounds. The cochlea is a fluid-filled chamber with thousands of hair cells that vibrate two parallel membranes to move sound waves. The vibration of these hair cells is one of several factors involved in perceiving the pitch (or frequency) and loudness (intensity) of a sound.

AGE-RELATED CHANGES   The pinna appears somewhat elongated and rigid in some older adults. These changes in the outer ear, however, have no impact on hearing acuity. The supporting walls of the external auditory canals also deteriorate with age, as is true for many muscular structures. Arthritic conditions may affect the joints between the malleus and stapes, making it more difficult for these bones to perform their vibratory function. **Otosclerosis** is a condition in which the stapes becomes fixed and cannot vibrate. It is most likely to affect older persons.

The greatest decline with age occurs in the cochlea, where structural changes result in **presbycusis,** or age-related hearing loss. Changes in auditory thresholds can be detected by age 30 or even younger, but the degeneration of hair cells and membranes in the cochlea is not observed until much later. Age-related declines in the middle ear include:

- atrophy of hair cells
- vascular changes
- changes in the cochlear duct
- loss of auditory neurons
- deterioration of neural pathways between the ear and brain (Rees, 2000)

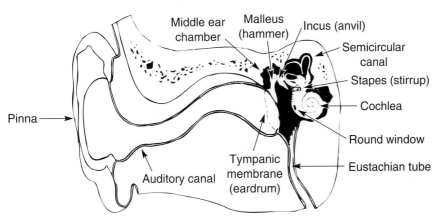

FIGURE 3.5   **The Ear**

Tests of pure-tone thresholds (i.e., the level at which a tone of a single frequency can be detected) have revealed a steady decline over 15 years. Changes in the high-frequency range are about 1 dB per year. In the range of speech, changes are slow until age 60, then accelerate to a rate of 1.3 dB per year after age 80 (Brant and Fozard, 1990). About 39 percent of the population age 65 and older in the United States is estimated to have some loss of hearing, and 13 percent suffer from advanced presbycusis (Gordon-Salant, 1996; National Academy 1999).

As with studies regarding visual changes, researchers suggest that age-related changes in the brain are primarily responsible for the deterioration in auditory functioning. These may include cellular deterioration and vascular changes in the major auditory pathways to the brain. However, aging and disease-related pathological changes can damage the auditory system itself. Together with exposure to environmental noise over a lifetime, these factors can cause presbycusis (Gordon-Salant, 1996).

Tinnitus, a high-pitched "ringing," is another problem that affects hearing in old age. It may occur bilaterally or in one ear only. The incidence increases threefold between youth and middle age, and fourfold between youth and old age, and may be aggravated by other types of hearing loss (Rosenhale and Karlsson, 1991). Tinnitus may be related to occupational noise exposure; for example, men with tinnitus have been found to have 20 to 30 years of exposure to noisy work environments. It cannot be cured, but people suffering from tinnitus can generally learn to manage it or try alternative approaches such as acupuncture (Micozzi, 1997).

In contrast to visual changes, hearing loss appears to be significantly affected by environmental causes. People who have been exposed to high-volume and high-frequency noise throughout their lives (e.g., urban dwellers and factory workers) experience more hearing decrements in old age than do those from rural, low-noise environments. Over the last three decades, hearing loss among

people age 18 to 44 has increased significantly. This means that future cohorts will include more elders with hearing loss that was environmentally induced during their youth (Wallhagen, Strawbridge, Cohen and Kaplan, 1997). As shown in Figure 3.6, women generally show less decline than men; about 61 percent of people with hearing loss are men. Gender differences are found across the lifespan:

- 3 percent of men vs. 2 percent of women at ages 18–44
- 8 percent vs. 3 percent at ages 45–64
- 19 percent vs. 10 percent among those 65 and older (National Academy on Aging, 1999)

It is interesting to speculate why these sex differences appear. Are they due to variations in noise exposure or to hormonal differences? The fact that severe hearing loss is found only in some women suggests that the former hypothesis may be more likely.

COMPENSATION AND ADAPTATION   Hearing loss can be of several types, involving limited volume and range or distortion of sounds perceived. Regardless of type, however, hearing loss results in some incongruence between the person and his or her enviornment. Older persons who have lost hearing acuity in the range of speech (250–3000 Hz) have particular difficulties distinguishing the sibilants or high-frequency consonants such as *z, s, sh, f, p, k, t,* and *g.* Their speech comprehension deteriorates as a result, which may be the first sign of hearing loss. In contrast, low-frequency hearing loss has minimal impact on speech comprehension. As Figure 3.6 illustrates, higher-frequency sounds can be heard better by raising the intensity. The recognition of consonants (*p, t, k, b, d, g*) can be increased by 50 to 90 percent among older persons simply by raising their intensity.

Thus, an individual may compensate by raising the volume of the TV and radio, moving closer to the TV, or listening to other types of music made by lower-pitched instruments such as an or-

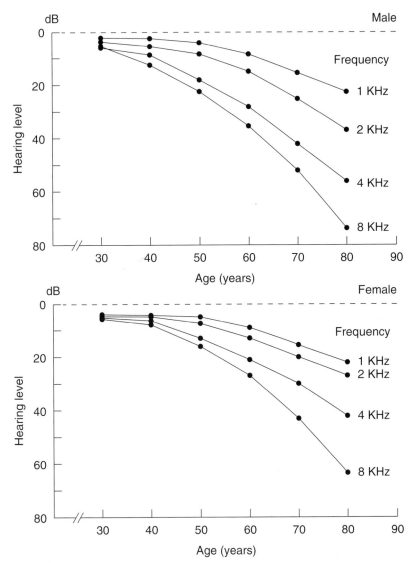

FIGURE 3.6   **Gender Differences in Hearing Thresholds**

SOURCE: J. M. Ordy, K. R. Brizzee, T. Beavers, and P. Medart. Age differences in the functional and structural organization of the auditory system in man. In J. M. Ordy and K. R. Brizzee (Eds.), *Sensory systems and communication in the elderly* (New York: Raven Press, 1979), p. 156. Reprinted with permission of the author and publisher.

gan. When this occurs, it is imperative to determine whether a hearing loss exists, to identify the cause, and to fit the individual with an appropriate hearing aid, if possible. The older design of hearing aids, using analog technology, merely in-

creases the volume of sound. A major difficulty with some hearing aids is that the volume of background noise is raised, in addition to the sound that the user of the device is trying to hear. This may compensate for loss of higher-frequency

---

RELUCTANCE TO USE HEARING AIDS

The social stigma associated with wearing a hearing aid is greater than with wearing glasses. These are undoubtedly some of the reasons why only about one-third of older people with hearing loss use them. Nevertheless, after President Clinton was fitted with a new digital hearing aid in 1997, there was a dramatic increase in the number of hearing aids sold. Sales jumped by 25 percent between 1996 and 1997; many of these were Baby Boomers like President Clinton who purchased a hearing aid for the first time (Liston, Solomon, and Banerjee, 1995; National Academy on Aging, 1999).

---

sounds, but cannot completely obliterate the problem of presbycusis. In fact, hearing aids often result in such major adaptation problems that older persons stop wearing them after several months.

Fortunately, developments in hearing aid technology are resulting in digital hearing aids with tiny computer chips that filter sounds to match each user's hearing loss profile, without amplifying background noises. These newer designs also are less obtrusive and fit well inside the ear. However, they can cost about twice as much as conventional hearing aids and are not covered by Medicare or by most private health insurance plans.

Other means of compensating for hearing loss are to design environments that dampen background noises or to select such settings for communicating with older persons. Sound levels should not exceed 80 decibels. Soundproof rooms, while costly, are beneficial, particularly if housing for older people is built on busy streets or near freeways. Offices of health professionals should have at least one quiet area without the distraction of background noises. Older people can also benefit from new designs in telephones with volume adjusters and lights that blink when the phone rings.

When conversing with people who are experiencing age-related hearing loss, the following hints can help both younger and older persons enjoy their communication:

- Face an older person directly and maintain eye contact.
- Sit somewhat close and at eye level with the older person.

- Do not cover the face with hands or objects when speaking.
- Speak slowly and clearly, but without exaggerating speech.
- Do not shout.
- Avoid distracting background noises by selecting a quiet, relaxing place away from other people, machines, and traffic sounds.
- Speak in a lower, but not monotonic, tone of voice.
- Repeat key points in different ways.
- If specific information is to be transmitted (e.g., how to take medications), structure the message in a clear, systematic manner (Kiyak, 1996).

Helping older people with hearing impairment compensate for this loss is essential to avoid harmful effects on interpersonal relationships and self-esteem. For some older adults, increasing levels of hearing impairment can disrupt functional abilities, resulting in social withdrawal and even clinical depression (Strawbridge, Wallhagen, Shema, and Kaplan, 2000; Wallhagen, Strawbridge, and Kaplan, 1996). One of the most frustrating experiences is the simultaneous deterioration of both hearing and vision. Although it is relatively rare for both functions to decline significantly with age, family, friends, and professionals must be especially sensitive to the communication techniques suggested earlier. For example, when talking with an older person who is impaired in both hearing and vision, touching a hand, arm, or shoulder may aid communication.

Changes in Taste and Smell

Although older people may complain that food does not taste as good as it once did, these complaints are probably not due to an age-associated generalized loss of taste sensitivity. It was once thought that age brought dramatic decreases in the number of taste buds on the tongue, that this loss of receptor elements led to functional loss that was experienced as a dulling of taste sensation, and that these changes accounted for older people's reduced enjoyment of food (Mistretta, 1984). Recent studies, however, have challenged each link in this chain of reasoning.

Early research on taste anatomy reported taste-bud loss (Arey, Tremaine, and Monzingo, 1935), but subsequent studies have shown that the number of taste buds does not decline with age (Miller, 1988). Early studies of taste function found large age-related changes in taste thresholds (Murphy, 1979). However, later studies found much smaller declines and concluded that threshold loss almost never involves more than one of the four basic taste qualities (Cowart, 1989).

The notion that various functions decline differentially has replaced the belief that older people experience a generalized taste loss. The research task now is to specify *which* aspects of taste function remain intact and which decline with normal aging or disease. Although the taste function of older people does not undergo a general decline in strength, it demonstrates specific changes (Weiffenbach, 1990). For example, although the relationship between taste intensity and stimulus strength is age-stable, judgments of taste intensity become less reliable with age. Even this change in reliability is specific. It affects salt but not sugar judgments. It is also important to note that in studies where the average taste performance of the older individuals is poorer, some perform as well as, or better than, many younger persons.

Appreciation of food does not depend on taste alone. The sense of smell clearly is involved. We have all experienced changes in the way food "tastes" while ill with a head cold and a stuffy nose. These changes suggest that sensitivity to airborne stimuli plays a key role in the perception of foods. Older people perceive airborne stimuli as less intense than younger persons, and do less well on odor identification. External factors such as smoking and medications contribute to these differences, but even after accounting for these factors, age differences are dominant (Ship and Weiffenbach, 1993; Weiffenbach and Bartoshuk, 1992). When parallel assessments are made in the same subject, age-related declines for smell are greater than for taste. This suggests that one way to increase older people's enjoyment of eating is to provide them with enhanced food odors. Classes in cooking with herbs and spices can be valuable for older people who are experiencing changes in their taste and olfactory abilities. These activities can also help older people in sharpening their sensitivity to tastes and odors, and enhancing their quality of life.

Cooking with spices can enhance olfactory and taste sensitivity.

SUMMARY AND IMPLICATIONS

As shown by this review of physiological systems, the aging process is gradual, beginning in some organ systems as early as the twenties and thirties, and progressing more rapidly after age 70, or even 80, in others. Even with 50 percent deterioration in many organ systems, an individual can still function adequately. The ability of human beings to compensate for age-related changes attests to their significant amount of excess reserve capacity. In most instances, the normal physical changes of aging need not diminish a person's quality of life if person–environment congruence can be maintained. Since many of the decrements are gradual and slight, older people can learn to modify their activities to adapt to their environments—for example, by pacing the amount of physical exertion throughout the day. Family members and professionals can be supportive by encouraging modifications in the home, such as minimizing the use of stairs, moving the focus of the older person's daily activities to the main floor of the home, and reinforcing the older person's efforts to cope creatively with common physical changes.

The rate and severity of decline in various organ systems vary substantially, with the greatest deterioration in functions that require coordination among multiple systems, muscles, and nerves. Similarly, wide variations across individuals in the aging process spring from differences in heredity, diet, exercise, and living conditions. Many of the physiological functions that were once assumed to deteriorate and to be irreversible with normal aging are being reevaluated by researchers in basic and clinical physiology, as well as by health educators. Examples of master athletes who continue their swimming, running, and other competitive physical activities throughout life show that age-related declines are not always dramatic. Even people who begin a regular exercise program late in life have experienced significant improvements in their heart and lung capacity. The role of preventive maintenance and health promotion in the aging process is discussed in Chapter 4.

Sleep patterns do, however, change with normal aging. Lab studies reveal changes in EEG patterns, sleep stages, and circadian rhythms with advancing years, even in the absence of disease. Sedative hypnotic drugs are widely used by older people who complain of sleep disturbance. However, improving sleep hygiene by increasing phys-

ical exercise, reducing the intake of alcohol, caffeine, and some medications, and improving the sleep environment are generally more effective methods than sleeping pills for long-term use. Medications are useful only in the case of true sleep disorders, such as sleep apnea and twitching legs during sleep.

Changes in sensory function with age do not occur at a consistent rate in all senses and for all people. Some people show rapid declines in vision while maintaining their hearing and other sensory abilities. Others experience an early deterioration in olfactory sensation, but not in other areas. All of us experience some loss in these functions with age, but interindividual differences are quite pronounced. Normal age-related declines in vision reduce the ability to respond to differing light levels; to function in low-light situations; to see in places with high levels of glare; to discern color tones, especially in the green-blue-violet range; and to judge distances and depth. Peripheral vision becomes somewhat narrowed with age, as does upward and downward gaze. Older people have more diseases of the eye, including glaucoma, cataracts, and macular degeneration; if these diseases are not treated, blindness can result. Visual impairments generally result in more problems with activities of daily living than do hearing impairments. Therefore, older persons who experience significant declines in visual function with age should be encouraged to maintain former levels of activity, either by adapting the environment to fit changing needs or by substituting new activities for those that have become more difficult. Unfortunately, some older people prefer to withdraw from previous activities, thereby becoming more isolated and at risk of depression and declining quality of life.

Decline in auditory function generally starts earlier than visual problems, and affects more people. Significant impairments in speech comprehension often result. Although hearing aids can frequently improve hearing in the speech range by raising the intensity of speech that is in the high-frequency range, many older people feel uncomfortable and even stigmatized when using them. Hence, the solutions to communicating with hearing-impaired older people may lie mostly within the environment, not within older persons themselves. These include changes in communication styles, such as speaking directly at an older person in a clear voice, but not shouting; speaking in a lower tone; repeating key points; and sitting closer to a hearing-impaired person. Environmental aids such as soundproof or quiet rooms and modified telephones can also be invaluable for older people who are experiencing significant hearing declines.

Although many older people complain that food does not taste as good as it once did, changes with age in taste acuity are minimal. The decline in olfactory receptors with age is more significant than in taste receptors, and may be responsible for the perception of reduced taste acuity. These changes are more pronounced in people who smoke or drink heavily, but the use of medications has only modest effects. There is less change in people who have sharpened their taste and olfactory sensitivity, such as professional winemakers and perfumers. This pattern suggests that older people should be encouraged to participate in activities that enhance their taste and olfactory functions.

As we learn more from studies of normal physiological changes with aging, reports that once appeared definitive are found to be less so, and a complete understanding of some areas is shown to be lacking. This is particularly true in the areas of taste, smell, and pain perception. Research is needed to distinguish normal changes in these areas from those that are related to disease, and those that can be prevented. Longitudinal research would help to answer many of these questions. Finally, research that examines the impact of sensory deterioration on the older person's interactions with the environment is also needed.

GLOSSARY

accommodation   ability of the lens of the eye to change shape from rounded to flat, in order to see objects that are closer or farther from the lens

age-related macular degeneration (AMD)   loss of vision in the center of the visual field caused by insufficient oxygen reaching the macula

atherosclerosis   accumulation of fats in the arteries and veins, blocking circulation of the blood

atrophic gastritis   chronic inflammation of the stomach lining

autoimmune theory of aging   the hypothesis that aging is a function of the body's immune system becoming defective, producing antibodies against itself

cataract   clouding of the lens of the eye, reducing sight and sometimes leading to blindness; requires surgical extraction of the lens

cellular aging theory   the hypothesis that aging occurs as cells slow their number of replications, based on the observation that cells grown in controlled laboratory environments are able to replicate only a finite number of times

cross-linkage theory   the hypothesis that aging is a function of the reduction of collagen with age, causing loss of elasticity in most organ systems

dementia   diminished ability to remember, make accurate judgments, etc.

diastolic blood pressure   the level of blood pressure during the time that chambers of the heart are filling with blood

estrogen   a female sex hormone that declines significantly with aging; can be replaced alone (ERT) or in combination with progesterone, another female sex hormone (HRT)

free radical theory   a special case of the cross-linkage theory of aging that posits that free radicals, highly reactive molecules, may produce DNA mutations

functional (or reserve) capacity   the ability of a given organ to perform its normal function, compared with its function under conditions of illness, disability, and aging

glaucoma   a disease in which there is insufficient drainage or excessive production of aqueous humor, the fluid in the front portion of the eye

hyperthermia   body temperatures several degrees above normal for prolonged periods

hypothermia   body temperatures several degrees below normal for prolonged periods

kinesthetic system the body system that signals one's position in space

kyphosis stoop-shouldered or hunched condition caused by collapsed vertebrae as bone mass is lost

master athletes individuals who have continued to participate in competitive, aerobic exercise into the later years

melanin skin pigmentation

menopause one event during the climacteric in a woman's life when there is a gradual cessation of the menstrual cycle, which is related to the loss of ovarian function; considered to have occurred after 12 consecutive months without a menstrual period

neurons nerve cells in the brain

nocturnal myoclonus a neuromuscular disturbance affecting the legs during sleep

orthopedic injuries injuries to the bones, muscles, and joints

osteoporosis a dramatic loss in calcium and bone mass resulting in increased brittleness of the bones and increased risk of fracture, more frequently found in white, small-stature women

presbycusis age-related hearing loss

renal function kidney function, defined by the rate at which blood is filtered through the kidneys

senescence biological aging, i.e., the gradual accumulation of irreversible functional losses to which the average person tries to accommodate in some socially acceptable way

sleep apnea Five- to 10-second cessation of breathing, which disturbs sleep in some older persons

sleep hygiene behaviors associated with sleep, e.g., location, lighting, regular vs. irregular bedtime, use of drugs that promote or hinder sleep

systolic blood pressure the level of blood pressure during the contraction phase of the heart

telomerase the enzyme responsible for rebuilding telomeres

telomerase inhibitors chemicals produced by the organism that block the production of telomerase

telomeres excess DNA at ends of each chromosome, lost as cells replicate

testosterone a male sex hormone

tinnitus high-pitched ringing in the ear

urinary incontinence diminished ability to retain urine; loss of bladder control

varicosities abnormal swelling in the veins, especially the legs

vital capacity the maximum volume of oxygen intake through the lungs with a single breath

wear and tear theory one of the biological theories of aging; states that aging occurs because of the system simply wearing out over time

RESOURCES

See the companion Website for this text at <www.ablongman.com/hooyman> for information about the following:

- American Foundation for the Blind, Unit on Aging
- American Printing House for the Blind
- American Speech-Language Hearing Association
- Better Hearing Institute
- International Hearing Aid Helpline of the International Hearing Society
- International Longevity Center
- Library of Congress, Blind and Physically Handicapped Division
- National Association for Continence
- Self-Help for Hard of Hearing People (SHHH)

REFERENCES

Accardi, F. E., Gombos, M. M., and Gombos, G. M. Common causes of blindness: A pilot survey in Brooklyn, New York. *Annals of Ophthalmology,* 1985, *17,* 289–294.

Allikmets, R., Shroyer, N. F., Singh, N., Seddon, J. M., and Lewis, R. A. Mutation of the Stargardt disease gene (ABCR) in age-related macular degeneration. *Science,* 1997, *277,* 1805–1807.

Arey, L., Tremaine, M., and Monzingo, F. The numerical and topographical relations of taste buds to human circumvallate papillae throughout the life span. *Anatomical Record,* 1935, *64,* 9–25.

Ausman, L. M., and Russell, R. M. Nutrition and aging. In E. L. Schneider and J. W. Rowe (Eds.), *Handbook of the biology of aging* (3rd ed.). San Diego: Academic Press, 1990.

Avery, W. M. Hypothermia and heat illness. *Aging*, 1984, *344*, 43–47.

Bjorksten, J. Crosslinkage and the aging process. In M. Rockstein, M. L. Sussman, and J. Chesky (Eds.), *Theoretical aspects of aging*. New York: Academic Press, 1974.

Blumberg, J. B. Status and functional impact of nutrition in older adults. In E. L. Schneider and J. W. Rowe (Eds.), *Handbook of the biology of aging* (4th ed.). New York: Van Nostrand, 1996.

Bodner, A. G., Ouelette, M., Frolkis, M., Holt, S. E., Chiu, C. P., Morin, G. B., Harley, C. B., Shay, J. W., Lichtsteiner, S., and Wright, W. E. Extension of life-span by introduction of telomerase into normal human cells. *Science*, 1998, *279*, 349–352.

Bognoli, P., and Hodos, W. *The changing visual system: Maturation and aging in the central nervous system.* New York: Plenum Press, 1991.

Brant, L. J., and Fozard, J. Age changes in pure-tone hearing thresholds in a longitudinal study of normal human aging. *Journal of the Acoustical Society of America*, 1990, *88*, 813–820.

Chicago Tribune: Alone in life, unclaimed in death. July 31, 1995, p. 1, 6.

Coffey, C. E., Lucke, J. F., Saxton, J. A., Ratcliff, G., Unitas, L. J., Billig, B., and Bryan, R. N. Sex differences in brain aging. *Archives of Neurology*, 1998, *55*, 169–179.

Collins, K. J. Low indoor temperatures and morbidity in the elderly. *Age and Ageing*, 1986, *15*, 212–220.

Cowart, B. J. Relationships between taste and smell across the life span. In C. Murphy, W. S. Cain, and D. M. Hegsted (Eds.), Nutrition and the chemical senses in aging: Recent advances and current research needs. *Annals of the New York Academy of Sciences*. New York: New York Academy of Sciences, 1989.

Cutler, E. D., and Cutler, R. G. Tissue auto-oxidation, antioxidants, and life span potential. *The Gerontologist*, 1983, *23* (Special Issue), 194.

Finch, C. E. *Longevity, senescence and the genome.* Chicago: University of Chicago Press, 1990.

Foley, D. J., Monjan, A. A., Brown, S. L., Simonsick, E. M., Wallace, R. B., and Blager, D. G. Sleep complaints among elderly persons: An epidemiological study of three communities. *Sleep*, 1995, *18*, 425–432.

Foster, V. L., Hume, G. J. E., Byrnes, W. C., Dickinson, A. L., and Chatfield, S. J. Endurance training for elderly women: Moderate vs. low intensity. *Journals of Gerontology*, 1989, *44*, M184–M188.

Goldstein, S., and Reis, R. J. S. Genetic modifications during cellular aging. *Molecular and Cellular Biochemical*, 1984, *64*, 15–30.

Gordon-Salant, S. Hearing. In J. E. Birren (Ed.), *Encyclopedia of gerontology*, Vol. 1. San Diego: Academic Press, 1996.

Harman, D. The aging process. *Proceedings of the National Academy of Science*, 1981, *78*, 7124–7128.

Hayflick, L. *How and why we age.* New York: Ballantine Books, 1996.

Hayflick, L., and Moorehead, P. S. The serial cultivation of human diploid cell strains. *Experimental Cell Research*, 1961, *25*, 285–621.

Henderson, V. W. The epidemiology of estrogen replacement therapy and Alzheimer's disease. *Neurology*, 1997, *48*, S27-S35.

Henderson, V. W., Paganini-Hill, A., Emanuel, C. K., Dunn M. E., and Buckwalter, J. G. Estrogen replacement therapy in older women. *Archives of Neurology*, 1994, *51*, 896–900.

Hu, M. H., and Woollacott, M. H. Multisensory training of standing balance in older adults. *Journals of Gerontology*, 1994, *49*, M52–M71.

Jacques, P. F., Chylack, L. T., and Taylor, A. Relationships between natural antioxidents and cataract formation. In B. Frei (Ed.), *Natural antioxidants in human health and disease*. San Diego: Academic Press, 1994.

Kiyak, H. A. Communication in the practitioner-aged patient relationship. In P. Holm-Pedersen and H. Loe (Eds.), *Textbook of geriatric dentistry* (2nd ed.). Copenhagen: Munksgaard, 1996.

Kline, D. W., Kline, T. J. B., Fozard, J. L., Kosnik, W., Schieber, F., and Sekuler, R. Vision, aging, and driving: The problems of older drivers. *Journals of Gerontology*, 1992, *47*, M27–34.

Kohrt, W. M., and Holloszy, J. O. Loss of skeletal mass with aging: Effect on glucose tolerance. *Journals of Gerontology: Biological and Medical Sciences*, 1995, *50*, 68–72.

Lane, M. A., Baer, D. J., Rumpler, W. V., Weindruch, R., Ingram, D. K., Tilmont, E. M., Cutler, R. G., and Roth, G. S. Calorie restriction lowers body temperature in rhesus monkeys. *Proceedings of the National Academy of Sciences*, 1996, *93*, 4159–4164.

Lane, M. A., Ball, S. S., Ingram, D. K., Cutler, R. G., Engel, J., Read, V., and Roth, G. S. Diet restriction in Rhesus monkeys lowers fasting and glucose-stimulated glucoregulatory end points. *American Journal of Physiology*, 1995, *268*, 941–948.

Lane, M. A., Ingram, D. K., Ball, S. S., and Roth, G. S. Dehydroepiandrosterone sulfate: A biomarker of primate aging slowed by calorie restriction. *Journal of Clinical Endocrinology and Metabolism*, 1997, *82*, 2093–2096.

Li, Y., and Wolf, N. S. Effects of age and long-term caloric restriction on the aqueous collecting channel in the mouse eye. *Journal of Glaucoma*, 1997, *6*, 18–22.

Liston, R., Solomon, S., and Banerjee, A. K. Prevalence of hearing problems, and use of hearing aids among a sample of elderly patients. *British Journal of General Practice*, 1995, *45*, 369–370.

Livingston, G., Blizard, B., and Mann, A. Does sleep disturbance predict depression in elderly people? *British Journal of General Practice*, 1993, *43*, 445–448.

Macey, S. M. Hypothermia and energy conservation: A tradeoff for elderly persons? *International Journal of Aging and Human Development*, 1989, *29*, 151–161.

Macey, S. M., and Schneider, D. Deaths from excessive heat and excessive cold among the elderly. *The Gerontologist*, 1993, *33*, 497–500.

McShane, T. M., Wilson, M. E., and Wise, P. M. Effects of lifelong moderate caloric restriction. *Journals of Gerontology: Biological Sciences*, 1999, *54A*, B14–B21.

Melov, S., Ravenscroft, J., Malik, S., Gill, M. S., Walker, D. W., Clayton, P. E., Wallace, D.C., et al. Extension of life-span with superoxide dismutase/catalase mimetics. *Science*, 2000, *287*, 1567–1569.

Micozzi, M. Exploring alternative health approaches for elders. *Aging Today*, 1997, *18*, 9–12.

Miller, I. J. Human taste bud density across adult age groups. *Journals of Gerontology*, 1988, *43*, B26–30.

Milton, R. C., and Sperduto, R. D. Incidence of age-related cataract: 13.6 year follow-up in the Framingham eye study. *Investigations in Ophthalmic Vision Science*, 1991, *32*, 1243–1250.

Mistretta, C. M. Aging effects on anatomy and neurophysiology of taste and smell. *Gerodontology*, 1984, *3*, 131–136.

Morales, A. J., Nolan, J. J., Nelson, J. C., and Yen, S. S. Effects of replacement dose of dehydroepiandrosterone in men and women of advancing age. *Journal of Clinical Endocrinology and Metabolism*, 1995, *80*, 2799.

Murphy, C. The effect of age on taste sensitivity. In S. Han and D. Coons (Eds.), *Special senses in aging*. Ann Arbor: Institute of Gerontology, University of Michigan, 1979.

National Academy on an Aging Society. *Hearing loss*, 1999, 2.

Newman, A. B., Spiekerman, C. F., Enright, P., Lefkowitz, D., Manolio, T., Reynolds, C. F., and Robbins, J. Daytime sleepiness predicts mortality and CVD in older adults. *Journal of the American Geriatrics Society*, 2000, *48*, 115–123.

O'Brien, S., and Vertinsky, P. Unfit survivors: Exercise as a resource for aging women. *The Gerontologist*, 1991, *31*, 347–357.

Ohayan, M. M., and Caulet, M. Insomnia and psychotropic drug consumption. *Progess in Neuro-psychopharmacology, Biology and Psychiatry*, 1995, *19*, 421–431.

Paganini-Hill, A., and Henderson, V. W. Estrogen deficiency and risk of Alzheimer's disease in women. *American Journal of Epidemiology*, 1991, 256–261.

Paganini-Hill, A., and Henderson, V. W. Estrogen replacement therapy and risk of Alzheimer's disease. *Archives of Internal Medicine*, 1996, *156*, 2213–2217.

Palmore, E. (Ed.). *Normal aging II: Reports from the Duke Longitudinal Study*, 1970–1973. Durham, NC: Duke University Press, 1974.

Palmore, E. (Ed.). *Normal aging III: Reports from the Duke Longitudinal Study*. Durham, NC: Duke University Press, 1985.

Pearson, D., and Shaw, S. *Life extension*. New York: Warner Books, 1982.

Rees, T. Health promotion for older adults: Age-related hearing loss. *Northwest Geriatric Education Center Curriculum Modules*, Seattle: University of Washington NWGEC, 2000.

Rogers, M. A., Hagberg, J. M., Martin, W. H., Ehsani, A. A., and Holloszy, J. O. Decline in VO2 max with aging in master athletes and sedentary men. *Journal of Applied Physiology*, 1990, *68*, 2195–2199.

Rosenhall, U., and Karlsson, A. K. Tinnitus in old age. *Scandinavian Audiology*, 1991, *20*, 165–171.

Rudberg, M. A., Furner, S. E., Dunn, J. E., and Cassel, C. K. The relationship of visual and hearing impairments to disability. *Journals of Gerontology*, 1993, *48*, M261–M265.

Rudman, D., Drinka, P. J., Wilson, C. R., Mattson, D. E., Scherman, F., Cuisinier, M. C., and Schultz, S. Relations of endogenous anabolic hormones and physical activity to bone mineral density in elderly men. *Clinical Endocrinology*, 1991, *40*, 653–661.

Seddon, J. M., Ajani, U. A., Sperduto, R. D., Hiller, R., Blair, H. N., and Burton, T. C. Dietary carotenoids, vitamins A, C, and E, and advanced age-related macular degeneration. *Journal of the American Medical Association*, 1994a, *272*, 1413–1420.

Seddon, J. M., Christen, W. G., Manson, J. E., Lamotte, F. S., Glynn, R. J., Buring, J. E., and Hennekens, C. H. The use of vitamin supplements and the risk of cataract among U.S. male physicians. *American Journal of Public Health*, 1994b, *84*, 788–792.

Ship, J. A., and Weiffenbach, J. M. Age, gender, medical treatment, and medication effects on smell identification. *Journals of Gerontology*, 1993, *48*, M26–M32.

Shock, N. W. The physiology of aging. *Scientific American*, 1962, *206*, 100–110.

Sommer, A., Tielsch, J. M., and Katz, J. Racial difference in the cause-specific prevalence of blindness in East Baltimore. *New England Journal of Medicine*, 1991, *325*, 1412–1417.

Sperduto, R. D. Age-related cataracts: Scope of problem and prospects for prevention. *Preventive Medicine*, 1994, *23*, 735–739.

Stevens, J. C. Aging and spatial acuity of touch. *Journals of Gerontology*, 1992, *47*, B35–40.

Strawbridge, W. J., Wallhagen, M. I., Shema, S. J., and Kaplan, G. A. Negative consequences of hearing impairment in old age: A longitudinal analysis. *The Gerontologist*, 2000, *40*, 320–326.

Strehler, B. L. Genetic instability as the primary cause of human aging. *Experimental Gerontology*, 1986, *21*, 283.

Teasdale, N., Stelmach, G. E., and Breunig, A. Postural sway characteristics of the elderly under normal and altered visual and support surface conditions. *Journals of Gerontology*, 1991, *46*, B238–B244.

Thom, D. H., and Brown, J. S. Reproductive and hormonal risk factors for urinary incontinence in later life: A review of the clinical and epidemiological literature. *Journal of the American Geriatrics Society*, 1998, *46*, 1411–1417.

Thomas, T., Thomas, G., McLendon, C., Sutton, T., and Mullan, M. Beta-amyloid-mediated vasoactivity and vascular endothelial damage. *Nature*, 1996, *380*, 168–171.

Vitiello, M. V. Sleep disorders and aging. *Current Opinions in Psychiatry*, 1996, *9*, 284–289.

Vitiello, M. V., and Prinz, P. N. Sleep and sleep disorders in normal aging. In M. J. Thorpy (Ed.), *Handbook of sleep disorders*. New York: Marcell Decker, 1991.

Wallhagen, M. I., Strawbridge, W. J., Cohen, R. D., and Kaplan, G. A. An increasing prevalence of hearing impairment and associated risk factors over three decades of the Alameda County Study. *American Journal of Public Health*, 1997, *87*, 440–442.

Wallhagen, M. I., Strawbridge, W. J., and Kaplan, G. A. Six year impact of hearing impairment on psychosocial and physiologic functioning. *Nurse Practitioner*, 1996, *21*, 11–14.

Weale, R. A. Senescence and color vision. *Journal of Gerontology*, 1988, *41*, 635–640.

Weed, J. L., Lane, M. A., Roth, G. S., Speer, D. L., and Ingram, D. K. Activity measures in rhesus monkeys on long-term calorie restriction. *Physiology and Behavior*, 1997, *62*, 97–103.

Weiffenbach, J. M. Assessment of chemosensory functioning in aging: Subjective and objective procedures. In E. L. Schneider and J. W. Rowe (Eds.), *Handbook of the biology of aging*. San Diego: Academic Press, 1990.

Weiffenbach, J. M., and Bartoshuk, L. M. Taste and smell. *Clinics in Geriatric Medicine*, 1992, *8*, 543–555.

Weiffenbach, J. M., Cowart, B. J., and Baum, B. J. Taste intensity perception in aging. *Journal of Gerontology*, 1986, *41*, 460–468.

Weindruch, R. Caloric restriction and aging. *Scientific American*, 1996, *274*, 46–52.

Wilson, D. L. The programmed theory of aging. In M. Rockstein, M. L. Sussman, and J. Chesky (Eds.), *Theoretical aspects of aging.* New York: Academic Press, 1974, 11–21.

Wilson, M. R. Glaucoma in blacks: Where do we go from here? *Journal of the American Medical Association,* 1989, *261,* 281–282.

Yataco, A. R., Busby-Whitehead, J., Drinkwater, D. T., and Katzel, L. I. Relationship of body composition and cardiovascular fitness to lipoprotein lipid profiles in master athletes and sedentary men. *Aging,* 1997, *9,* 88–94.

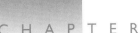

4 MANAGING CHRONIC DISEASES AND PROMOTING WELL-BEING IN OLD AGE

This chapter discusses

- Definitions of health, quality of life, ADLs and IADLs
- Social and psychological factors that affect perceptions of health and use of health services
- Distinctions among chronic diseases that occur most frequently in older adults
- Use of health services and health behaviors of older people
- Health promotion and its benefits in old age

No aspect of old age is more alarming to many of us than the thought of losing our health. Our fears center not only on the pain and inconvenience of illness, but also on its social-psychological consequences, such as loss of personal autonomy and economic security. Poor health, more than other changes commonly associated with aging, can reduce a person's competence in dealing with his or her environment.

DEFINING HEALTH

Most people would agree that good health is something more than merely the absence of disease or infirmity. As defined by the World Health Organization, health is a state of complete physical, mental, and social well-being. Thus, health implies an interaction and integration of body, mind, and spirit, a perspective that is reflected in the growth of health promotion programs.

As used by health care workers and researchers, the term **health status** refers to: (1) the presence or absence of disease, and (2) the degree of disability in an individual's level of functioning. Thus, activities that older people can do, or think they can do, are useful indicators of both how healthy they are and the services and environmental changes needed in order to cope with their impairments. Older people's ability to function independently at home is of primary concern.

The World Health Organization defines **disability** as impairments in the ability to complete multiple daily tasks. Slightly more than 20 percent of older people are estimated to have a mild degree of disability in their ADL, but only about 4 percent are severely disabled. The more disabled older population is limited in their amounts and types of major activities and mobility, such as eating, dressing, bathing, or toiletry, and requires the assistance of family or paid caregivers. The extent of disabilities and need for help in personal care activities increase with age and differ by gender, as shown in Figure 4.1.

Women aged 90 and older are twice as likely to be disabled and to require assistance than those aged 70 to 74. Men are less likely to have ADL limitations in both age groups and show a smaller increase in disability with age. For example, 24 percent of noninstitutionalized men over age 70 report ADL, compared with 32 percent of women (NCHS, 2000a). This may be because men who survive to 70, and especially to age 90, have a genetic advantage and are hardier than men who die of similar conditions earlier in life.

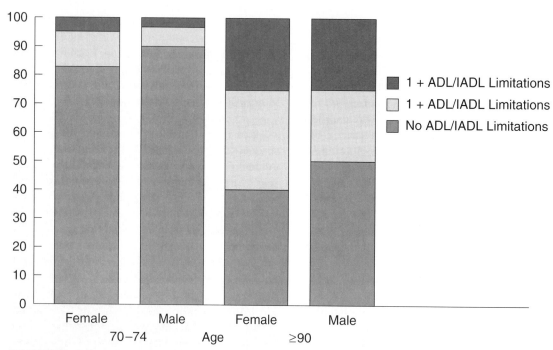

FIGURE 4.1 Comparing ADL and IADL Limitations among Men and Women, Young-Old and Oldest-Old

SOURCE: National Center for Health Statistics, 1997.

ASSESSING FUNCTIONAL HEALTH

The most commonly used measure of *functional health,* termed the **activities of daily living (ADL),** summarizes an individual's performance in personal care tasks such as:

- bathing
- dressing
- using the toilet, eating
- getting in or out of a bed or chair
- caring for a bowel-control device
- walking (the most common ADL limitation for older adults)

Instrumental activities of daily living (IADL) summarize an individual's performance vis-à-vis the environment:

- home management
- managing money
- light housework
- meal preparation
- making a phone call
- grocery shopping (the most common IADL problem)

In 2000, approximately 10 million persons 65 years or older needed some assistance to remain in the community (including 10.5 percent of those aged 65–79 and 51 percent of those over age 85). This figure is expected to reach 15 million by the year 2020 and 21 million by 2030. Another way to describe these projections is to state that 30 percent of persons over age 65 will have activity limitations that require some assistance by 2030. About 20 percent of this group will have severe limitations in ADLs (National Academy, 2000a; U.S. Administration on Aging, 2000). The implications of this growth for long-term care are described in Chapter 11.

QUALITY OF LIFE IN HEALTH AND ILLNESS

Societal values affect our attitudes toward loss of health. The importance placed by our culture on being independent and highly active may underlie our relative inability to accept illness graciously. Such values may also partially explain why healthy older people often do not want to share housing or recreational activities with those who have mental or physical disabilities.

Yet the fear of declining health may trouble us more than the actual experience of it. Although younger people assume that health issues are older adults' greatest preoccupation, most elders appear to be fairly positive about their health. The 1994–1996 National Health Interview Survey (NHIS) found that almost 72 percent of respondents aged 65–74 in the community described their health as excellent, very good, or good compared to their age peers, while only 9 percent reported their health as poor (NCHS, 1999). Even institutionalized older persons tend to rate their health positively.

A reliable evaluation of health takes into account not only a physician's assessment of a patient's physical condition, but also the older person's self-perceptions, observable behavior, and life circumstances. **Quality of life** may be defined as this combination of an individual's functional health, feelings of competence, independence in ADLs, and satisfaction with one's social circumstances. Most older people appear to adjust their perceptions of their health in response to the aging process. In the 1994–1996 NHIS, respondents aged 85 and older were twice as likely as those aged 65–74 to report fair or poor health (NCHS, 1999). Older people who must take multiple medications, who are experiencing chronic pain, or

---

WHY OLDER ADULTS RATE THEIR HEALTH POSITIVELY

- perceived comparison with peers
- sense of accomplishment from having survived to old age

- perception of competence to meet environmental demands
- a broad definition of quality of life to include social and economic factors

---

have limitations in their ADLs and their interpersonal relations are more likely to report lower quality of life. This is especially true for older women (Johnson and Wolinsky, 1994).

On the other hand, those who have recently had a successful medical or surgical intervention to *alleviate* the symptoms of their chronic conditions are more likely to report improved quality of life. It is noteworthy that physicians rate the quality of life of older persons with diabetes, arthritis, or even ischemic heart disease lower than do these elders themselves. This may indicate greater adaptation to disabling conditions among patients than physicians expect, or may suggest that medical professionals' definitions of quality of life are more constrained by health factors than are patients' own perceptions. However, a national survey of 9,000 adults with chronic diseases revealed that people with arthritis, heart disease, and chronic lung disease reported the greatest impairments in quality of life; those with hypertension reported the least (Stewart et al., 1989).

Social and psychological factors also influence people's assessments of their physical well-being. An older person's position in the social structure, for example—whether one is male or female, black or white, high or low income—affects perceptions of health. Health self-ratings as good or excellent have been found among:

- more than 72 percent of white persons age 65
- only 52 percent of older African Americans
- less than 50 percent of elderly Hispanics

Self-ratings of health as poor are found in:

- only about 5.4 percent of persons aged 65 and older with incomes over $35,000
- 14 percent of their peers who have incomes less than $10,000

In general, older women do not rate their health more poorly than men, even though they have more chronic diseases and are more likely to be institutionalized (NCHS, 1999).

Perceptions of good health tend to be associated with other measures of well-being, particularly life satisfaction. Older persons who view themselves as reasonably healthy tend to be happier, more satisfied, more involved in social activities, and less tense and lonely. In turn, lower life satisfaction is associated with lower levels of self-perceived health. It has also been found that self-ratings of health are correlated with mortality. That is, older people who report poorer health, especially poorer functional abilities, are more likely to die in the next three years than those who perceive their functional health to be good (Bernard et al., 1997).

POINTS TO PONDER

Think about your own health perceptions. To what extent do you compare your health to others of your age or gender? How does your ability to perform various ADLs affect your health perceptions? How does your day-to-day health affect your overall quality of life?

CHRONIC AND ACUTE DISEASES

As noted in Chapter 3, the risk of disease and impairment increases with age; however, the extreme variability in older people's health status, as illustrated by Mrs. Hill and Mr. Jones in the vignettes in the introduction to Part Two, shows that poor health is not necessarily a concomitant of aging. The incidence of acute or temporary conditions, such as infections or the common cold, decreases with age. Those **acute conditions** that occur, however, are more debilitating and require more care, especially for older women:

- The average number of days of restricted activity due to acute conditions is nearly three times greater for people age 65 and over than it is for those 17 to 44 years old.
- Older people report, on average, 33 days per year of restricted activity days, of which 14 are spent in bed (NCHS, 1995).

An older person who gets a cold, for example, faces a greater risk of pneumonia or bronchitis because of changes in organ systems (described in Chapter 3) that reduce his or her resistance and recuperative capacities. Thus, older people are more likely to suffer restrictions on their social activities as a result of temporary health problems.

In some cases, an acute condition that merely inconveniences a younger person may result in death for an older person. For example, respiratory infection rates are similar in young and old people, but people aged 65 and older account for 89 percent of all deaths due to pneumonia and influenza (CDC, 1995). This is why it is important for older people to be vaccinated against pneumonia and influenza. These vaccines can reduce the risk of pneumonia by 67 percent and of flu by 50 percent among older people, can save medical costs and increase days of healthy living. Yet recent surveys reveal that less than 33 percent obtain a pneumococcal vaccination and only 50 percent receive annual vaccines against influenza (CDC, 1996; Govaert, Thijs, and Masurel, 1994; Sisk et al., 1997). Recent changes in Medicare to cover the full cost of vaccinations may increase these rates.

Older people are much more likely than the young to suffer from **chronic conditions.** Chronic health conditions are:

- long-term (more than three months)
- often permanent, leaving a residual disability that may require long-term management or care rather than a cure

More than 80 percent of persons age 70 and over have at least one chronic condition, with multiple health problems being common in older adults (NCHS, 1999). Chronic problems are often accompanied by continuous pain and/or distress. At the very least, the individual is inconvenienced by the need to monitor health and daily activities, although ADLs may not always be limited. National

---

ETHNIC AND RACIAL DIFFERENCES IN CHRONIC DISEASES

Among those 70 and older:

- African American and Hispanic elders are more likely to suffer from diabetes than non-Hispanic whites.
- Diabetes is twice as common among women of color as in white women.
- Hypertension is 1.5 times more likely in African Americans than in whites.

- Rates of stroke are also higher among the former groups, but only when comparing black vs. white women.
- In contrast, white men age 70 and older are more likely to report heart disease than their Hispanic or African American counterparts (NCHS, 1999).

surveys have found that almost 40 percent of older persons with chronic diseases report limitations in their ability to perform basic ADLs (NCHS, 1999).

Although one can live a satisfying life with multiple chronic conditions, these diseases may influence the decision to continue working or to retire. An analysis of recent retirees' responses in the 1994–1996 NHIS revealed that the majority of people age 51–61 who had retired cited chronic health problems as the reason. This varied by type of disease:

- 76 percent of those with heart disease
- 62 percent with orthopedic impairments
- 61 percent with arthritis

Many of these mature but not older adults have converted to part-time work; as a result, their median income is lower on retirement, as discussed more fully in Chapter 12, than for their healthier peers (National Academy, 2000a).

Although the nature and the severity of any chronic condition vary with the individual, most older persons are capable of carrying out their normal daily routines. Only about 2 percent of those age 65 and over are confined to bed by their chronic conditions, and most older people with chronic conditions are not dependent on others for managing their daily routines. On the other hand, the small percentage who do need assistance with care have placed enormous pressures on formal health and long-term care services as well as on informal caregivers, as discussed in Chapters 10 and 17.

The most frequently reported chronic conditions causing limitation of activity in persons age 65 and over are shown in Figure 4.2. Arthritis, hypertension, and heart disease are the leading chronic conditions, but older women are less likely to suffer from heart disease and more likely to report arthritis and diabetes than older men. The most common heart condition for both men and women is ischemic heart disease.

Not surprisingly, most chronic conditions increase in prevalence with age (NCHS, 1999). For example, people age 65 and over are twice as likely

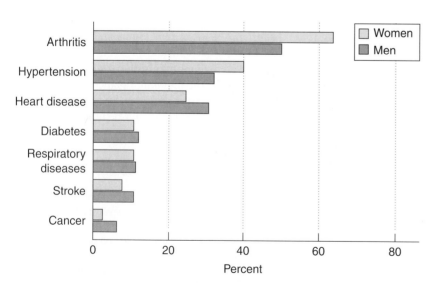

FIGURE 4.2   **Percent of Persons 70 Years and Older Who Reported Selected Chronic Conditions by Gender: United States, 1995**
SOURCE: Centers for Disease Control and Prevention, NCHS, 1999.

to suffer from arthritis as those age 45 to 64. Other conditions, such as heart disease and diabetes, show lower rates in the oldest-old, probably because of the higher mortality associated with these diseases.

Disabling chronic illnesses tend to occur earlier among African Americans, Mexican Americans, and American Indians than among whites. These conditions result in higher rates of hospitalization, longer hospital stays, and a shorter life expectancy. Therefore, it is not surprising that older persons of color with chronic conditions are more likely to describe their health as fair or poor than whites with the same conditions, as shown in Figure 4.3 (National Academy, 1999a; NCHS, 2000). Poorer self-assessments of health and lower life expectancies are explained as products of discriminatory policies, whereby nonwhites have lower incomes and inadequate nutrition throughout

their lifetimes. An additional factor is that elders of color, because of their cultural values and negative experiences with formal services, may be less likely to utilize the health care system. The effects of ethnic minority status on the incidence and treatment of chronic conditions are further discussed in Chapter 14.

Co-morbidity, or the problem of coping with two or more chronic conditions, is more common in older women than in men. Researchers have found that, among older women aged 65 and older, 50 percent have at least two chronic diseases. One-fourth of older women report three or more such conditions. (Clancey and Bierman, 2000; NCHS, 1995). Older women of color, especially in the lower socioeconomic range, have a higher prevalence of chronic illness, functional limits on their ADLs, and disability (Smith and Kingston, 1997).

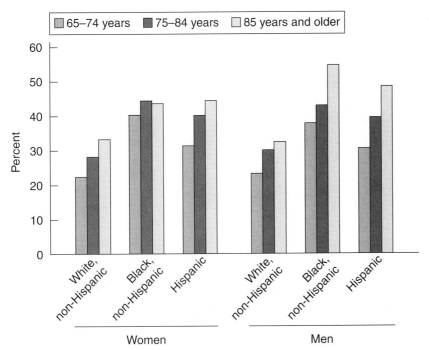

FIGURE 4.3   **Fair or Poor Health among Noninstitutionalized Persons 65 and Older, by Age, Gender, Race, and Hispanic Origin: United States, 1994–1996**
SOURCE: Centers for Disease Control and Prevention, NCHS, 1999.

Interactive Effects

Even though the majority of chronic conditions are not severely limiting, they can nevertheless make life difficult and lower older people's resistance to other illnesses. As noted earlier, the functional limits imposed by a chronic illness interact with the social limits set by others' perceptions of the illness to influence an older person's daily functioning. Therefore, it is important to look beyond the statistics on the frequency of chronic conditions to the nature of chronic illnesses, the interaction of physical changes with emotional and sociocultural factors, and the physiological differences between younger and older people.

Certain types of chronic diseases (e.g., cancer, anemia, and toxic conditions) may be related to older people's declining **immunity,** that is, reduced resistance to environmental carcinogens, viruses, and bacteria. The accumulation of long-term, degenerative diseases may mean that a chronic condition, such as bronchitis, can have different and more negative complications than the same disease would have in a younger person. With reduced resistance to physical stress, an older individual may be less able to respond to treatment for any acute disease, such as a cold or flu, than a younger person would. The cumulative effect of chronic illness and an acute condition may become the crisis point at which the older person becomes dependent on others for care. The impact of any chronic condition appears to be mediated by the physiological changes that occur with age, the sociocultural context, and the person's mental and emotional outlook.

Unfortunately, well-intentioned family members and health care professionals may assume that all chronic conditions are disabling or that a certain degree of disability is inevitable with aging. As a result, they may prematurely restrict an elder's independence or not use the same treatments that they might administer to younger adults.

In sum, disabling health changes occur at different rates in different individuals and are not inevitable with age. We turn now to an examination of the chronic conditions that are the most common causes of death in older people.

Causes of Death in Later Years

Heart disease, cancer, and strokes account for over 75 percent of all deaths among people over age 65, as shown in Table 4.1 (NCHS, 2000b). Even though there have been rapid declines over the past 30 years, heart disease remains the major cause of death. It is the number-one risk factor among adults age 65 and over, killing twice as many people as do all forms of cancer combined, and accounting for 20 percent of adult disabilities. Heart disease accounts for 18 percent of hospital admissions, and over 45 percent of deaths that occur among older people, with the highest rates among the oldest-old. Although death rates from cancer, especially lung cancer, continue to rise, it is estimated that eliminating cancer as a cause of death would extend the average life span by less than two years at age 65. Eliminating deaths due to major cardiovascular diseases, however, would add an average of 14 years to life expectancy at

---

HOW PSYCHOLOGICAL FACTORS CAN INFLUENCE REACTIONS TO DISEASE

Researchers have found that people with a pessimistic outlook toward their health and aging tend to have less physiological reserve capacity, as illustrated by comments such as, "She lost her will to live," or "He stopped fighting and gave up." There are numerous examples of the impact of an optimistic attitude on the outcome of disease, perhaps best exemplified by Norman Cousins' (1979) accounts of the positive effects of humor on treating his potentially fatal disease. Although he eventually died from this disease, medical experts generally agree that he lived far longer than predicted because of his optimistic attitude.

TABLE 4.1 **Mortality Rates for Older Women and Older Men, from the Four Leading Causes: 1998**

	DEATHS PER 100,000 POPULATION PER YEAR, 1998		
	65–74	75–84	85+*
Diseases of heart	735.5	1897	6010
Malignant neoplasms (cancer)	841	1326	1749
Cerebrovascular diseases (strokes)	130	455	1500
Chronic obstructive pulmonary disease (COPD)	169	366	569

*For the population aged 85+ pneumonia and influenza are the third leading cause of death at 1064 per 100,000.

SOURCE: National Center for Health Statistics, 2000b.

age 65. The benefits of eliminating cardiovascular diseases would be especially significant for older white women (17.4 years) and nonwhite women (22 years). This would also lead to a sharp increase in the proportion of older persons in the total population (Hayflick, 1996). Meanwhile, stroke has been decreasing as a leading cause of death among the oldest-old; it is the third leading cause for women over age 65 but fourth for men, slightly less than chronic obstructive pulmonary diseases (COPD) such as asthma and emphysema. For older African American women, diabetes is the fourth major cause of death. It accounts for more than twice the rate of deaths as COPD, which is sixth in this population group (NCHS, 2000b).

Men have higher rates of heart disease and cancer than women. In fact, gender differences in mortality are due mainly to the greater incidence of the principal fatal chronic diseases among men. However, women experience more nonfatal chronic conditions, including arthritis, incontinence, osteoarthritis, osteoporosis, and cataracts, than do men. These diseases are less likely to result in death than cancer and heart disease, but they may lead to nearly as many days spent in bed. In other words, older women are more likely to be bothered by chronic conditions, many of which can cause functional disability and impair their quality of life. However, they are less likely to face life-threatening diseases than are older men.

COMMON CHRONIC CONDITIONS

Heart Disease and the Cardiovascular System

Heart disease is a condition in which blood to the heart is deficient because of a narrowing or constricting of the cardiac vessels that supply it. This narrowing may be due to **atherosclerosis,** * in which fatty deposits (plaque formation) begin early in life and accumulate to reduce the size of the passageway of the large arteries. People in industrialized nations have higher levels of atherosclerosis, but the extent to which this is due to lifestyle factors is unknown.

*The terms *atherosclerosis* and **arteriosclerosis** are often used interchangeably, causing confusion regarding their distinction. Arteriosclerosis, a generic term, sometimes called hardening of the arteries, refers to the loss of elasticity of the arterial walls. This condition occurs in all populations, and can contribute to reduced blood flow to an area. In atherosclerosis, the passageway of the large arteries narrows as a result of the development of plaques on their interior walls; atherosclerosis has been found to be age-related and of higher incidence in industrialized populations. Arteriosclerosis and atherosclerosis can be superimposed, but there is not a causative relationship between the degree of atherosclerosis and the loss of elasticity (arteriosclerosis).

HEALTH AND BEHAVIORAL FACTORS THAT INCREASE THE RISK OF ATHEROSCLEROSIS

- hypertension or high blood pressure
- elevated blood lipids (resulting from a dietary intake of animal products high in cholesterol)
- cigarette smoking
- diabetes mellitus

- obesity
- inactivity
- stress
- family history of heart attack

As the reduced blood flow caused by atherosclerosis becomes significant, angina pectoris may result. The symptoms of angina are shortness of breath and pain from beneath the breastbone, in the neck, and down the left arm. For older individuals, these symptoms may be absent or may be confused with signs of other disorders, such as indigestion or gallbladder diseases. Treatment includes rest and nitroglycerine, which serves to dilate the blood vessels.

If deficient blood supply to the heart persists, heart tissue will die, producing a dead area known as an *infarct*. In other words, coronary artery disease can lead to a myocardial infarction, or heart attack. **Acute myocardial infarction** results from blockage of an artery supplying blood to a portion of the heart muscle. The extent of heart tissue involved determines the severity of the episode. Heart attacks may be more difficult to diagnose in older people, since their symptoms are often different from those in younger victims. These include:

- a generalized state of weakness
- dizziness
- confusion
- shortness of breath

These are different from the chest and back pain or numbness in the arms that characterizes heart attacks in younger people. Symptoms in older people may also merge with other problems, so that a heart attack may not be reported or treated until it is too late for effective help. Although women are far less likely to have heart attacks than men

prior to menopause, their rates are similar after age 65. As noted in Chapter 3, hormone replacement therapy (HRT) after menopause has been found to reduce the incidence of heart disease. This may be due to improved ratios of "good" cholesterol (HDL) to "bad" cholesterol (LDL) and increased pliability of blood vessels following regular use of HRT.

The term *congestive heart failure*, or heart failure, indicates a set of symptoms related to the impaired pumping performance of the heart, so that one or more chambers of the heart do not empty adequately during the heart's contractions. Heart failure does not mean that the heart has stopped beating. But decreased pumping efficiency results in shortness of breath, reduced blood flow to vital body parts (including the kidneys), and a greater volume of blood accumulating in the body tissues, causing edema (swelling). Treatment involves drugs, dietary modifications (e.g., salt reduction), and rest.

Most cardiovascular problems can be treated with diet, exercise, and medications. They should not prevent older people from carrying out most ADLs. Nevertheless, about 50 percent of older adults with heart diseases report limitations in their ADLs, compared with 26 percent of their aged peers who do not have this condition (National Academy, 2000a). Preventive steps are most important. For example, *hypertension*, or high blood pressure, has been found to be the major risk factor in the development of cardiovascular complications and can be affected by preventive actions. As shown in Figure 4.2, the risk of hy-

---

PREVENTIVE MEASURES TO REDUCE CARDIOVASCULAR RISK

- weight control
- daily physical activity
- treatment of diabetes
- reduced intake of salt and saturated fats
- increased intake of fruits and vegetables (rich in magnesium)

- fruits rich in potassium (e.g., bananas, oranges)
- foods high in calcium
- avoidance of cigarette smoking
- avoidance of excessive alcohol intake

---

pertension is greater for women than men after age 65 (NCHS, 1999). This may partially explain why the incidence of coronary heart disease and strokes increases with age among women, although women with these conditions, on average, live longer than men. Since 1980 the rate of coronary heart disease in women has declined by 31 percent, due mostly to better dietary habits such as eating less red meat and more fiber, as well as reducing smoking (Hu et al., 2000).

The rates of *hypertension* are higher among African Americans than whites, but whether this difference is due to lifestyle or genetic factors is unclear. Significant increases in blood pressure should never be considered normal. In some isolated primitive populations, a rise in pressure with age does not occur. Although genetic factors may come into play, this difference suggests that individuals can make lifestyle changes that may reduce their vulnerability to high blood pressure.

Most people can control their hypertension by improving these health habits, although some must also use antihypertensive medications (National Heart, Lung, and Blood Institute, 1997). Older adults who have been prescribed an antihypertensive must continue using it consistently and correctly. Because hypertension is not easily recognized by laypersons, they may stop taking their medications if symptoms such as dizziness and headaches disappear. This can lead to significant elevations in blood pressure, as well as a stroke or aneurysms.

Another cardiovascular problem, which is less frequently addressed than hypertension, is *hypotension*, or low blood pressure. Yet hypotension, characterized by dizziness and faintness from exertion after a period of inactivity and frequently related to anemia, is actually very common among older adults. Problems with hypotension may be more pronounced after sitting or lying down for a long time (postural hypotension) or suddenly standing, after which a person may appear to lose balance and sway. Hypotension is not in itself dangerous, but can increase the risk of falls. Older people who have a history of low blood pressure or who are taking some types of antihypertensive medications need to move more carefully.

COMMONLY PRESCRIBED CLASSES OF MEDICATIONS TO CONTROL HYPERTENSION

- *diuretics* (also known as "water pills"), which reduce excess water
- *beta blockers*, which reduce heart rate
- *ACE inhibitors*, which block an enzyme that constricts blood vessels

- *calcium channel blockers*, which work by preventing calcium from causing muscle contractions in the heart and inside blood vessels

Strokes and Other Cerebrovascular Problems

We have seen how heart tissue can be denied adequate nourishment because of changes in the blood vessels that supply it. Similarly, arteriosclerotic and atherosclerotic changes in blood vessels that serve the brain can reduce its nourishment and result in the disruption of blood flow to brain tissue and malfunction or death of brain cells. This impaired brain tissue circulation is called *cerebrovascular disease*. When a portion of the brain is completely denied blood, a cerebrovascular accident (CVA), or stroke, occurs. The severity of the stroke depends on the particular areas as well as the total amount of brain tissue involved. Many older adults who have heart problems also are at risk for cerebrovascular disease.

CVAs represent the fourth leading cause of death following accidents. Of the 200,000 deaths from strokes each year, 80 percent occur among persons aged 65 and over (NCHS, 1999). African American elders are at greater risk of dying from strokes than whites or other minority groups.

Atherosclerotic changes, in which fatty deposits gradually obstruct an artery in the brain or neck, are a common underlying condition. The most frequent cause of strokes in older persons is a *cerebral thrombosis*, a blood clot that either diminishes or closes off the blood flow in an artery of the brain or neck. Another cause of stroke is cerebral hemorrhage, in which a weak spot in a blood vessel of the brain bursts. This is less common in older adults, although more likely to cause death when it does occur. The risks of stroke appear to be related to social and personal factors, most prominently hypertension, but also:

- age
- previous lifestyle
- diet
- activity patterns

Regular, sustained exercise and low-fat diets are associated with the reduction of fatty particles that clog the bloodstream. The use of such over-the-counter drugs as aspirin and warfarin in preventing blood clots also reduces the risk of strokes. Indeed, the death rate from strokes has dropped by 40 percent in the last 20 years, especially among the older population, because of these preventive measures and improved and immediate treatment (Gorelick, Shanmugam, and Pajeau, 1996). The area of the brain that is damaged by a stroke dictates which body functions may be affected. These include:

- *aphasia,* or inability of the stroke victim to speak or understand speech if the speech center of the brain dies
- *hemiplegia,* or paralysis of one side of the body
- *heminanopsia,* or blindness in half of the victim's visual field

The treatment for strokes is similar to that for heart attacks and hypertension: modulated activity and supervised schedules of exercise and drugs. The FDA has approved new drugs to dissolve blood clots within three hours of the stroke. However, many victims do not receive this treatment because it generally takes longer than three hours to reach a diagnosis of the stroke and the location of the clot. An alternative method is to deliver the clot-dissolving drug directly with a long, fine tube through the artery; this can be effective within six hours after symptoms begin. These new techniques offer great hope for patients and their families, but do not entirely prevent the neurological losses caused by a stroke.

Stroke victims often require physical, occupational, and speech therapy, and their recovery process can be slow, frustrating, and emotionally draining for the victim and family. It is important to assess carefully the effects of a stroke and determine what functions can be retrained (Gresham, Duncan, and Stason, 1995). Newer, more aggressive and immediate rehabilitation methods are effective in reducing the rates of residual impairments following a stroke. Within a year, about half have regained most of their motor function, but more people report residual nonmotor impairments such as problems with vision, speech, and loss of balance (Ferrucci, Kittner, Corti, and Guralnik, 1995).

Rehabilitation must address not only physical conditions, but also the psychosocial needs for support and respite of stroke patients and their families. The recognition of this wider range of rehabilitation has led to the creation of stroke support groups in many communities.

Cancer

Among those 65 years old and over, 21 percent of deaths are due to cancer, especially cancers of the stomach, lungs, intestines, and pancreas. In fact, these malignancies in old age are the leading cause of death among women 65–74, and roughly equal to heart disease among men. Fifty percent of all cancer occurs and is diagnosed after age 65. Cancer of the bowel is the most common malignancy in those age 70 and over, and is second to lung cancer in cancer-related deaths. Lung cancer has its highest incidence in men age 65 and over, but appears to be associated more with smoking than with age. Cancer of the colon is more common in women, whereas rectal cancer is more frequent in men. Women also face increasing risks of breast and cervical cancers with age (NCHS, 1999). Both the incidence and mortality rates due to cervical and breast cancer are greater in older African American women than in older white women, primarily because of lower use of cancer screening services (Caplan, Wells, and Haynes, 1992). The greater risk of cancer with age may be due to a number of factors:

- the effects of a slow-acting carcinogen
- prolonged development time necessary for growth to be observable
- extended preexposure time
- failing immune capacity that is characteristic of increased age

Some cancers that have a high prevalence in the middle years and again in old age may have a different etiology. For example, breast cancer in pre-

menopausal women appears to have a genetic basis and is related to family history, while that in postmenopausal women may have external or environmental causes. Certain dietary and lifestyle factors may also be related to cancer in older people. Diagnosing cancer in old age is often more difficult than at earlier life stages, because of the existence of other chronic diseases and because symptoms of cancer, such as weight loss, weakness, or fatigue, may be inaccurately attributed to aging, depression, or dementia. In addition, the current older generation's fear of cancer may be so great that they do not seek medical help to address their suspicions and fears.

Arthritis

Although not a leading cause of death, arthritis is the most common chronic condition affecting older people and is a major cause of limited activity. In fact, the great majority of persons over age 70 are estimated to have some physical evidence of arthritis:

- 63 percent of women
- 50 percent of men (NCHS, 1999)

Because arthritis is so common and the symptoms are so closely identified with the normal

Gentle massage can relieve the pain of arthritis.

aging process, older people may accept arthritis as inevitable. If so, they may fail to seek treatment or to learn strategies to reduce pain and support their independent functioning. Although many treatments are used to control arthritic symptoms, little is known about ways to postpone or eliminate these disorders.

Arthritis is not a single entity, but includes over 100 different conditions of inflammations and degenerative changes of bones and joints. **Rheumatoid arthritis,** a chronic inflammation of the membranes lining joints and tendons, is characterized by pain, swelling, bone dislocation, and limited range of motion. It afflicts two to three times more women than men and can cause severe crippling. Rheumatoid arthritis is not associated with aging per se; many young people also have this condition, with initial symptoms most commonly appearing between 20 and 50 years of age.

Rheumatoid arthritis is characterized by acute episodes followed by periods of relative inactivity. Its cause is unknown; treatment includes a balance of rest, exercise, and use of aspirin, which provides relief from pain, fever, and inflammation. Use of other antiinflammatory agents, antimalarials, and corticosteroids, as well as surgical procedures to repair joints and correct various deformities, are effective for some people. There are extensive new developments in drug therapy for rheumatoid arthritis.

Osteoarthritis, which is presumed to be a universal corollary of aging, is a gradual degeneration of the joints that are most subject to stress—those of the hands, knees, hips, and shoulders. Pain and disfigurement in the fingers are manifestations of osteoarthritis, but are generally not disabling. Osteoarthritis of the lower limbs, however, can limit mobility. Heredity as well as environmental or lifestyle factors are identified as causes of osteoarthritis, particularly:

- obesity
- occupational stresses
- wear and tear on the joints

Some progress has been made in minimizing inflammation and pain through the use of several types of therapy. A natural supplement (chondroitin sulfate, or CS) has recently been shown to be effective in managing the pain associated with osteoarthritis without significant side effects (Leeb, Schweitzer, Montag, and Smolen, 2000). Unfortunately, however, none of these techniques can reverse or cure the disease.

Even on "good days" when pain subsides, an older arthritic may live with the fear of the inevitable "bad day" and may structure daily activities to avoid pain. Each day may seem to consist of a succession of obstacles, from getting out of bed and fastening clothing to opening packages, dialing the phone, and handling dishes for meals. Concentrating on coping with one obstacle after another in the completion of tasks can be exhausting, even when minimal physical exertion is involved in each task.

As a result, it is estimated that 50 percent of adults aged 70 and older who have arthritis need help with ADLs, compared with 23 percent of their peers without arthritis. Not surprisingly, the former group uses health services (physicians, hospitals, medications, nursing homes) and social services at a higher rate than the latter. Because of the

---

SYMPTOMS OF RHEUMATOID ARTHRITIS

• malaise	• joint pain
• fatigue	• redness
• loss of weight	• swelling
• fever	• stiffness affecting many joints

THERAPIES FOR OSTEOARTHRITIS

- anti-inflammatory drugs
- steroids
- mild exercise
- heat and cold

- reduction of strain on weight-bearing joints through weight loss and the use of weight-bearing appliances
- surgical procedures that restore function to the hips and knees

---

constant pain and discomfort experienced by elders with arthritis, it is highly correlated with self-reports of health. Among people in their sixties, correlates of poor subjective health include:

- arthritis
- poor vision
- few social resources

Among people in their eighties, subjective reports of poor health are correlated with:

- arthritis
- heart disease
- low education
- poor mental health (Quinn, Johnson, Poon, and Martin, 1999)

It is important to note that arthritis is the only variable that appears as an important component of subjective health for both age groups.

The prime danger for people with arthritis is reducing their physical activity in response to pain. Movement stimulates the secretion of synovial fluid, the substance that lubricates the surfaces between joints and increases blood flow to joint areas. Movement also tones the muscles that hold joints in place and that shield joints from excessive stress. When someone tries to avoid pain by sitting still as much as possible, the losses in lubricating fluid and muscular protection make movement still more painful. Eventually, the muscles surrounding immobilized areas lose their flexibility, and affected joints freeze into rigid positions called **contractures.** For these reasons, older people need

to be encouraged to maintain physical activity in spite of pain. The adage "use it or lose it" has special meaning to an arthritis victim!

The pervasive and unpredictable nature of the pain of arthritis can also result in frustration and depression. A program to teach African American elders about managing their arthritis pain resulted in fewer symptoms of depression up to two years later than in elders who received no training (Phillips, 2000). The environment may need to be restructured in these cases, so that a person with arthritis is able to walk around and keep up with daily activities, but is not burdened by extreme press or demands. For example, a smaller home on one level can reduce the environmental press. Despite the relatively low cost of physically modifying private homes, this is not widely done. A national survey revealed that only 17 percent of women and 12 percent of men aged 70 and older have installed railings; 13 percent and 11 percent respectively have installed ramps in their homes. Even the most frequently reported home modification—bathroom bars and shower seats—were not that widespread: 43 percent of women and 36 percent of older men (National Academy, 2000a).

Osteoporosis

The human body is constantly forming and losing bone through the metabolism of calcium. As noted in Chapter 3, osteoporosis involves a more dramatic loss in bone mass. The increased brittleness of the bones associated with this condition can result in diminished height, slumped posture, backache, and

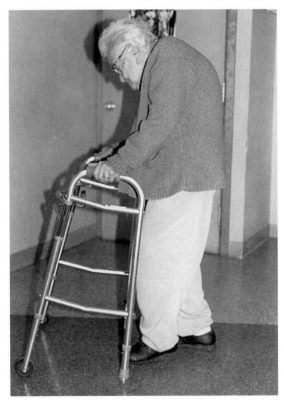

Osteoporosis can make movement difficult and painful.

many without a clinical diagnosis. Caucasian women are more likely to develop it than African American women (Looker, Johnston, Wahner, et al., 1995). The causes of osteoporosis are unclear, although several risk factors have been suggested:

- loss of calcium and estrogen in menopausal women
- a sedentary lifestyle
- cigarette smoking
- excessive alcohol and caffeine consumption
- long-term dieting or fasting
- inadequate fluoride intake
- genetic factors that determine bone density

The primary risk posed by osteoporosis is a fracture of the neck of the femur, or thigh. Many of the falls and associated hip fractures of old age actually represent an osteoporotic femoral neck that broke from bearing weight, causing the individual to fall. Osteoporosis and its less serious counterpart, **osteopenia** (a significant loss of calcium and reduced bone density but without the risk of fractures), together affect about 25 million Americans, 80 percent of whom are women. Osteoporosis results in 1.5 million fractures per year:

- 40 percent spinal
- 25 percent hip
- 15 percent wrist fractures (Looker et al., 1995; OWL, 1994)

Many older people have undiagnosed osteoporosis, often showing no symptoms until a fall or fracture occurs. Typically, no immediate precipitating event can be identified as the cause of the

a reduction in the structural strength of bones, making them susceptible to fracture. Compressed or collapsed vertebrae are the major cause of kyphosis, or "dowager's hump," the stooped look that many of us associate with aging.

Osteoporosis apparently starts well before old age (perhaps as young as age 35) and is more than four times more common in women than in men. About ten million Americans have this condition,

---

RISK FACTORS FOR HIP FRACTURES AMONG WHITE WOMEN WITH OSTEOPOROSIS

- age (especially over 70)
- family history of hip fractures
- low body weight
- use of medications that affect balance

- not using estrogen
- disabilities or weakness of the lower extremities
- stiffness affecting many joints (LaCroix, 1997)

fracture. Some 20 percent of white women experience fractures by age 65, increasing to more than 30 percent by age 90. Although both men and women lose bone mass with aging, men rarely develop symptomatic osteoporosis before age 70. White men are far less likely than white women to experience hip fractures; African American men and women have even lower rates of fractures than white men.

Hip fractures are of concern because of their impact on morbidity and mortality; it is estimated that 15 to 20 percent of people with a hip fracture die from it or from surgical complications (Josephson et al., 1991). Even when the older person does not die from a hip fracture, falls that result in hip fractures can cause long-term disability and are responsible for more days of restricted activity than any other health problem. The costs to society are also high because of necessary hospitalization and long-term care. With the growth of the older population, it is predicted that more than $45 billion will be spent over the next ten years to care for white women in the United States who sustain a fracture (Chrischilles et al., 1994).

Not all falls and fractures among older people result from osteoporosis, however. Cardiovascular disease underlies approximately 50 percent of them. Others are due to a decline in postural control, produced by impairments of the senses and the central nervous system, changes previously discussed in Chapter 3.

PREVENTING OSTEOPOROSIS: THE CASE FOR AND AGAINST ESTROGEN   In the years immediately following menopause, the rate of bone loss can be as high as 5 percent, compared to a normal rate of 1 or 2 percent. For women entering menopause, reduced estrogen—not calcium—is the primary cause of bone loss in the first 5 years after menopause. The goal in treating osteoporosis is to prevent further bone loss. Hormone replacement therapy (HRT) is the best medical means of preventing osteoporosis and bone fractures for many women, especially when started soon after menopause and continued for several years. HRT can decrease the risk of hip fractures

by 25 to 50 percent, and of spinal crush fractures by 50 to 75 percent. Since estrogen blocks the process of bone reabsorption, it can help the bones absorb dietary calcium and thereby increase bone mineral density (BMD) 3 to 5 percent in the first year. However, the effects may not be permanent, and benefits may be lost after discontinuing HRT (OWL, 1994). Of greater concern are increased risks of breast and endometrial cancer. The combination of synthetic progesterone (progestin) with estrogen can reduce the chances of endometrial cancer. For some women, however, progestin has unpleasant side effects such as a recurrence of monthly periods or breakthrough bleeding, breast tenderness, bloating, cramps, and mood swings.

HRT is far less effective if begun long after the menopause rather than immediately after it. Small, short-stature women who are postmenopausal, have high caffeine intake, smoke cigarettes, and have a family history of osteoporosis appear to be most at risk of cancer associated with hormone treatments. An additional problem is that when hormone replacement therapy is discontinued, bone loss is more rapid than prior to treatment. HRT may reduce the incidence of coronary heart disease and has no effect, positive or negative, on the risk of strokes. These conclusions are based on a large-scale, 16-year study of postmenopausal women and on several studies of women over age 70 (Henderson et al., 1991; Stampfer et al., 1991; Stampfer and Colditz, 1991). Cardiovascular disease is a greater risk for women after age 50 than is breast cancer; it accounts for 52 percent of all deaths of women over age 50 in 1990, compared with 5 percent for breast cancer.

Despite evidence of its benefits in reducing first-time heart attacks, a recent study of 309 women with a *history of heart disease* concluded that taking estrogen continuously for three years has no beneficial effect in preventing the narrowing of arteries. It is important to note that HRT *did not increase* the chances of a repeat heart attack, the average age of these women was 65, and no attempt was made to select women who had taken estrogen continuously since menopause (Herrington et al., 2000).

Women without a family history of breast cancer and other risk factors for cancer would appear to benefit from estrogen replacement. Evidence from the Framingham study suggests that HRT must take place at least 7 years continuously to demonstrate these benefits. Other studies suggest that use of estrogen supplements should be limited to 10 years or less to reduce the risk of breast cancer (Steinberg et al., 1992). Despite its proved benefits, only about 15 percent of postmenopausal women are currently undergoing HRT, and women of color are far less likely to use estrogen than are white women (Bush, 1990). This low utilization rate may be due in part to misinformation or lack of information available to women who are deciding whether to use HRT. It may also indicate greater caution because of mixed findings from longitudinal studies of women using HRT. Table 4.2 illustrates the potential benefits and risks of HRT.

For women who cannot or choose not to undergo HRT, new drugs have been approved by the Food and Drug Administration (FDA). Some of these have been found to slow the rate of bone loss and prevent vertebral fractures. However, none of these medications eliminates the need for increased intake of calcium and Vitamin D among older women. Combinations of fluoride and calcium treatments are also given, but may have negative side effects of gastrointestinal and rheumatic complaints. There is currently little research evidence that so-called "natural" estrogens are effective against osteoporosis and heart disease.

Scientists are working on new forms of estrogen that will have the benefits of current forms without the risks. These "designer estrogens," or selective estrogen receptor modulators, appear to improve bone density and reduce levels of LDL (bad) cholesterol while increasing the levels of HDL (good) cholesterol, but do not have harmful effects on breast tissue. Other researchers are exploring the effects of parathyroid hormone on advanced osteoporosis.

CALCIUM AND EXERCISE TO PREVENT OSTEOPOROSIS Certain dietary and exercise habits may help prevent osteoporosis, especially increasing the amount of calcium after age 40. A 1994 consensus conference at the National Institutes of Health concluded that women should consume:

- 1500 mg of calcium daily, if they are not on HRT
- 1000 mg per day, if they are on HRT

This is higher than previously recommended; 1500 mg of calcium is equivalent to five 8-ounce glasses of milk daily, far more than most women are ac-

TABLE 4.2 **Advantages and Disadvantages of Estrogen Replacement Therapy**

PROVED BENEFITS	LIKELY BENEFITS	PROVED RISKS	LIKELY RISKS
Relieves menopausal symptoms (e.g. hot flashes, night sweats)	Reduces risk of heart disease in women with no history of heart attacks*	Increases risk of endometrial cancer	Increases risk of breast cancer (especially if family history)
Relieves vaginal dryness	Reduces risk of colon cancer	Increases risk of benign fibroid tumors in uterus	Weight gain
Slows rate of bone loss	Reduces sudden shifts in mood	Premenstrual symptoms reappear (fluid retention, tender breasts)	Blood clots
	Improves cognitive abilities		Increases risk of gallstones
	Slows cognitive decline in Alzheimer's disease	May cause menstrual bleeding if combined with progesterone	Headaches may increase

*No apparent benefit for women with preexisting heart disease. (Herrington et al., 2000).

customed to consuming. In fact, more recent studies have recommended doses as high as 2000 mg/day in older postmenopausal women. Given the difficulty of obtaining this much calcium from dietary sources, calcium supplements may be the most effective way to get high levels. Despite concerns about side effects, such as kidney stones, related to high calcium intake, there is little evidence that such supplementation can harm older women (Chiu, 1999).

Calcium is absorbed better when combined with Vitamin D. For this reason, milk in the United States is fortified with Vitamin D. Unfortunately, many older women do not consume enough milk or milk products to obtain Vitamin D in that manner. It is also produced by the human body after 15 to 20 minutes of exposure to sunlight each day, but many older women avoid the sun or are unable to get outside every day. There is strong evidence from a large study of 3,000 older women in France that daily supplementation with Vitamin D (800 international units) and calcium (1200 mg) can reduce hip fractures by 43 percent and spinal fractures by 32 percent (Chapuy et al., 1992). For this reason, older women who do not obtain an adequate intake of fortified milk or exposure to sunshine should take daily multivitamins with at least 400 IUs of Vitamin D (600 IUs for those over age 70).

Although increased calcium appears to be an important preventive measure, low dietary calcium may be only partly responsible for osteoporosis. Therefore, increasing calcium intake may not prevent fracturing after bone loss has occurred. One reason is that an estimated 40 percent of osteoporotic women have a deficiency of the enzyme that is needed to metabolize calcium (lactose), thus making it difficult for them to absorb calcium. An additional problem is that once one fracture is present, the individual has a 70 to 80 percent chance of developing another.

A combination of calcium and exercise (twice-weekly brisk walks and once-weekly aerobics) appears to reduce bone loss over a 2-year period more than exercise alone. This combined regimen is not as effective as moderate exercise combined with hormone replacement therapy, which actually *increases* bone density almost 3 percent per year (Prince et al., 1991). Two longitudinal studies have shown that high-intensity strength training using exercise machines for one year can significantly *increase* BMD in postmenopausal women (Nelson et al., 1994; Notelovitz, Martin, and Tesar, 1991). The strength-training program was combined with estrogen therapy in the former study, but not in the latter. Another study documented that simple, vigorous walking on a daily basis reduced hip fractures by 30 percent in older women (Cummings et al., 1995). These clinical experiments demonstrate that high-intensity (i.e., twice weekly) strenuous exercise not only maintains, but also *increases,* BMD in older women (up to age 70 in both studies). The strength-training program implemented by Nelson and colleagues also resulted in increased muscle mass, muscle strength, balance, and spontaneous physical activity. Other researchers have compared the BMD of postmenopausal women who have been running regularly (at least 5 years, more than 10 miles per week) in conjunction with hormone replacement therapy or without. Bone mass does not seem to be protected with exercise alone, but the *combination of HRT and running* increased total

---

A SUMMARY OF PREVENTIVE STRATEGIES AGAINST OSTEOPOROSIS

- estrogen replacement therapy (if no risk factors for cancer)
- increased intake of calcium daily
- (1500 mg/day if not using HRT, 1000 mg/day if using HRT)
- increased intake of vitamin D
- moderate weight-bearing exercise such as vigorous walking and strength training
- fluoride

BMD and BMD in the spine. However, this combination did not significantly improve hip BMD, which is the critical issue for preventing hip fractures (Hawkins et al, 1999).

Because of the increased attention to osteoporosis today, many entrepreneurial clinics are offering bone density testing to postmenopausal women. These tests show the obvious results; that most women over 50 have less bone mass than younger women. However, they do not provide a comparison with any baseline data for a specific individual. These tests might be helpful if obtained before menopause in women at risk for osteoporosis, then redone when these women are in their sixties, seventies and eighties.

Chronic Obstructive Pulmonary Disease or Respiratory Problems

Chronic *bronchitis*, *fibrosis*, *asthma*, and *emphysema* are manifestations of chronic obstructive pulmonary diseases (COPD) that damage lung tissue. They increase with age, develop slowly and insidiously, and are progressive and debilitating, often resulting in frequent hospitalizations, major lifestyle changes, and death. In fact, by age 90, most people are likely to have some signs of emphysema, with shortness of breath and prolonged and difficult exhalation. Getting through daily activities can be extremely exhausting under such conditions. Causes of COPD are both genetic and environmental, especially prolonged exposure to various dusts, fumes, or cigarette smoke. Three to four times as many men as women have these diseases, probably due to a combination of normal age changes in the lung and a greater likelihood of smoking and exposure to airborne pollutants. This is especially true in older cohorts; men in the oldest-old group are three times more likely to die of COPD than their female counterparts. Treatment is usually continuous, and includes:

- drugs
- respiratory therapy
- breathing exercises to compensate for damage
- avoidance of respiratory infections, smoking, pollution, and other irritants

Allergic reactions to bacterial products, drugs, and pollutants also increase with age. The greater incidence of drug allergies may be a function of both decreases in physiological capacities and the increased use of many drugs, such as sedatives, tranquilizers, antidepressants, and antibiotics.

Diabetes

Compared with other systems of the body, the endocrine glands do not show consistent and predictable age-related changes, other than the gradual slowing of functioning. However, insufficient insulin, produced and secreted by the pancreas, can lead to *diabetes mellitus*. Diabetes mellitus is characterized by above-normal amounts of sugar (glucose) in the blood and urine, resulting from an inability to use carbohydrates. Diabetics may go into a coma when their blood sugar levels get very high. Low blood sugar (hypoglycemia) can also lead to unconsciousness.

Older diabetics include people who:

- have had the disease since youth (Type I);
- develop it in middle age, most often between 40 and 50, and incur related cardiovascular problems (Type II)
- develop it late in life and generally show mild pathologic conditions (Type II)

Type II diabetes is most common in older persons, and can often be managed without medication. The incidence of newly diagnosed adult-onset diabetes is highest in the 60- to 80-year-old category (NCHS, 1995). Although diabetes can occur at any age, diabetic problems related to the body's lessened capability to metabolize carbohydrates can be particularly severe in older adults. Many cases are associated with being overweight, especially due to changes in fat/muscle ratio and slower metabolism with aging. This is particularly true

---

SYMPTOMS OF DIABETES

- excessive thirst
- increased appetite
- increased urination
- fatigue

- weakness
- loss of weight
- slower wound healing

---

among older African American women, who have a higher rate of obesity and diabetes than do older white women. It is also true for Hispanics, who are 3.5 times more likely than other adults to develop Type II diabetes (NCHS, 1995). Glucose tolerance and the action of insulin are often compromised by poor diet, physical inactivity, and co-existent diseases.

A recent survey of 150,000 American households found that the rate of Type II diabetes increased between 1990 and 1998 from 4.9 percent to 6.5 percent (a change of 33 percent) of the adult population (Mokdad, et al., 2000). It is particularly disturbing that the increase is greatest among 30–39-year-olds. When rates were compared across ethnic minority groups, Hispanics showed the greatest increase (38 percent), followed by whites (29 percent) and African Americans (26 percent). The researchers attributed these increased rates of diabetes to a rise in obesity during this same interval, from 12 percent to 20 percent. These changes raise concerns about health risks for future cohorts of elders.

These symptoms may not be present in older people, however. Instead, diabetes among the older population is generally detected incidentally through eye examinations, hospitalization, and testing for other disorders. Since blood glucose may be temporarily elevated under the stress of illnesses such as stroke, myocardial infarction, or infection, people should not be labeled as diabetic unless the high glucose level persists under conditions of reduced stress.

The cumulative effect of high blood glucose levels can lead to complications in advanced stages of diabetes. These include:

- infections
- nerve damage
- blindness
- renal disorders
- stroke
- cognitive dysfunction
- harm to the coronary arteries
- skin problems
- poor circulation in the extremities, leading to gangrene

The interaction of diabetes with ordinary age-related physical problems such as hypertension can result in serious health difficulties and consequent limitations on daily activities. Atherosclerosis and coronary heart disease, for example, are more common in diabetics than in nondiabetics. The 1994-96 National Health Interview Survey revealed that 44 percent of adults aged 70 and older who had diabetes reported limitations in their ADLs, compared with 28 percent of their peers without diabetes (NCHS, 1995). On average, life expectancy among diabetics is 15 years less than in the population without diabetes (Juvenile Diabetes Foundation, 1998). Diabetes cannot be cured, but it can generally be managed at home in many ways. These include:

- a diet of reduced carbohydrates and calories
- regular exercise
- proper care of feet, skin, teeth, and gums
- monitored insulin intake for those who require it

To minimize forgetfulness and treatment errors, older people, especially those who acquire diabetes late in life, may need reminders from health care providers and family members regarding:

- the importance of diet
- daily examination of their skin
- urine testing
- the correct dosage of insulin or other drugs

Problems with the Kidneys and Urinary Tract

The various diseases and disorders of the urinary system characteristic of old age tend to be either acute infections or chronic problems resulting from the gradual deterioration of the structure and function of the excretory system with age. As seen in Chapter 3, the kidneys shrink in size, and their capacity to perform basic filtration tasks declines, leading to a higher probability of disease or infection. One of the most common age-related problems for women is the inability of the bladder to empty completely. This often results in cystitis, an acute inflammatory state accompanied by pain and irritation that can generally be treated with antibiotics.

Older men face an increased risk of diseases of the prostate gland, with cancer of the prostate being the most frequent malignancy. For this reason, the American Cancer Society and the American Urological Association recommend annual prostatic evaluations for men aged 50 and older by both a digital rectal exam and a new test to determine levels of prostate-specific antigen (PSA) in the blood. Cancer of the prostate frequently spreads to the bones, but surgery is rarely recommended for men over age 70 because the disease usually progresses slowly in this age group. Instead, more conservative treatment and more frequent monitoring are usually the treatment of choice (Albertsen, Fryback, and Storer, 1995). Treatment of prostate cancer and its effects on men's sexual functioning are described more fully in Chapter 7.

INCONTINENCE   A more difficult, noninfectious, and chronic urinary problem is **incontinence** (i.e., inability to control urine and feces). It has been estimated to occur in 5 to 19 percent of men and 7 to 38 percent of women over age 65 and living in the community (Cramer, 1993; Thom and Brown, 1998). Since older people and their families often consider incontinence a taboo topic, they tend to be unaware of methods to treat it. Most older adults do not discuss the problem with their doctors, and only a small percentage use any protective devices. Many health care providers, in turn, do not ask their older patients about incontinence. This widespread reluctance to acknowledge incontinence as a problem can have serious psychological and social implications, particularly on the decision to institutionalize an older person. Accordingly, about half of the older population living in nursing homes experience at least one episode of incontinence daily.

There are two primary types of incontinence:

- *urge incontinence,* where the person has a strong urge to urinate and is unable to hold urine long enough to reach a toilet
- *stress incontinence,* where leakage occurs during physical exertion or when sneezing or coughing, a phenomenon that can also occur among younger women

Many cases of incontinence represent a combination of these two types, referred to as *mixed incontinence.* Incontinence sometimes results from a specific precipitating factor, such as acute illness, infection, or even a change in residence. It can be treated if the cause is known. For example, temporary incontinence can be caused by bladder or urinary tract infections, which may be treated with antibiotics. Prescribed medications can also cause urgent and frequent urination. If informed of the detrimental effects of medication, a physician may reduce the drug dosage. With age, the bladder and urethra in women commonly descend, resulting in stress incontinence; leaking then occurs with the increased abdominal pressure brought on by coughing, sneezing, laughing, lifting, or physical exercise. Another type of incontinence, known as *functional incontinence,* often results from neurological changes and accompanies other problems,

---

MANAGEMENT OF INCONTINENCE

- medications to increase bladder capacity
- surgery
- dietary changes
- exercises
- behavioral management techniques, such as reducing fluid intake when bathroom access is limited

- reduction in the intake of caffeine (e.g., coffee, tea, cola, even chocolate) can prevent the stimulation of the kidneys to excrete fluids
- weight loss can also help, as obesity has been found to cause urine leakage

---

such as Parkinson's disease and organic brain syndrome. Other physical causes that should be investigated medically are prostate problems, pernicious anemia, diabetic neuropathy, and various cancers.

Since the types and causes of incontinence vary widely, thorough diagnosis and individualized treatment programs are critical. Even habitual incontinence should not be assumed to be irreversible.

Although some physicians prescribe medications to increase bladder capacity or reduce urine production, these often have unpleasant side effects such as blurred vision and dry mouth. Non-invasive behavioral management techniques, such as frequent access to toilet facilities, restriction of fluid intake before bedtime, and systematic exercise of the pelvic muscle, are often just as effective. Even incurable problems can be managed through protective products (e.g., absorbent pads) and catheters (tubes draining the bladder) to reduce complications, anxiety, and embarrassment. In fact, only about 25 percent of older persons with incontinence are so severely disabled that they are unlikely to regain continence and require a catheter or other external appliances to cope with the conditions (Cramer, 1993). Physical exercise designed to promote and maintain sphincter muscle tone can also prevent or reduce age-related incontinence, particularly among older women. All possible treatments, especially behavioral techniques, exercise, and biofeedback, should be explored, since older people's embarrassment and humiliation may result in their avoiding social

gatherings out of fear of having their incontinence detected. Support groups, such as *Help for Incontinent People (HIP)*, have chapters nationwide.

Problems with the Intestinal System

Many older people experience problems in digestion and continuing gastrointestinal distress, due particularly to age-related slowing down of the digestive process. Most intestinal problems are, in fact, related to unbalanced diets or diets with limited fiber content. **Diverticulitis** is one of the most common difficulties, affecting up to 50 percent of persons aged 80 and over, especially women (Greenwald and Brandt, 1996). It is a condition in which pouches or sacs (diverticula) in the intestines (especially in the colon) result from weakness of the intestinal wall; these sacs become inflamed and infected, leading to symptoms of nausea, abdominal discomfort, bleeding, and changes in bowel function. Management includes a high-fiber diet and antibiotic therapy. Diverticulitis, which is increasing in industrialized nations, may be associated with a highly refined diet lacking in fiber.

Many older people worry about constipation, but this is not an inevitable outcome of aging, as noted in Chapter 3. Constipation may be a symptom of an underlying disease or obstruction. If this is not the case, treatment commonly includes:

- physical activity
- dietary modification
- increased fluid intake

CAUSES OF CONSTIPATION

- overuse of cathartics
- lack of exercise
- psychological stress

- gastrointestinal disease
- an unbalanced diet with respect to bulk

Because many older people are overly concerned about having regular bowel movements, they may become dependent on laxatives. Over time, laxatives can cause problems, such as irritating the colon and decreasing the absorption of certain vitamins.

Hiatus hernia appears to be increasing in incidence, especially among obese women; this occurs when a small portion of the stomach slides up through the diaphragm. Symptoms include indigestion, difficulty in swallowing, and chest pain that may be confused with a heart attack. Medical management includes weight reduction, elevation of the upper body when sleeping, changes in the size and frequency of meals, and medication. Although hiatus hernia in itself is not especially severe, it may mask the symptoms of more serious intestinal disorders, such as cancer of the stomach.

The incidence of gallbladder disease, especially gallstones, also increases with age and is indicated by pain, nausea, and vomiting, with attacks increasing in number and severity. Most cases in older adults are asymptomatic, and physicians debate whether to perform surgery or follow a more conservative course of medical management. Medical treatment usually involves:

- weight reduction
- avoidance of fatty foods
- use of antacids

Oral Diseases

Because of developments in preventive dentistry, newer cohorts of older people have better oral health than any preceding cohort. According to the most recent National Health and Nutrition Exam Survey (NHANES III), only 30 percent over age 65 today are completely **edentulous** (i.e., no natural teeth remaining). As one might expect, edentulism increases with age:

- 25 percent of the young-old are edentulous
- 42 percent of the old-old are edentulous

This change is due entirely to historical differences in dental care delivery, not because of the aging process. Ethnic and racial differences in tooth loss are minimal in the young-old, but increase in the oldest-old, such that by age 75 the NHANES III survey (U.S. Dept. of Health and Human Services, 2000) found that all natural teeth were missing in:

- 43 percent of whites
- 44 percent of Mexican Americans
- 53 percent of African Americans

The common problems of tooth decay and periodontal diseases also appear to increase with age, although the evidence is limited and less clear. In NHANES III, the rate of root caries (cavities that develop on exposed root surfaces) was found to be more than three times greater among people over age 65 than in those under age 45. Rates of decay on the enamel surfaces of teeth, however, are not much higher among 65- to 74-year-olds compared with 35- to 44-year-olds. Differences are much greater when the older group is compared with people aged 18 to 24, who have only about 10 percent of their tooth surfaces decayed or filled, compared with 31 percent of people aged 65–74

(NCHS, 1999). These differences reflect changes over time in preventive dental care, such as the widespread use of water fluoridation. NHANES III also found an age-related increase in the incidence of periodontitis or gum disease, especially after age 45 (U.S. Dept. of Health and Human Services, 2000).

In contrast, cancers of the lip, tongue, mouth, gum, pharynx, and salivary glands increase with advanced age, regardless of ethnic minority status or sex. In North America and Western Europe, cancer of the lip is the most frequent and has the highest survival rates among those listed previously (between 65 and 90 percent over a five-year period) (U.S. Dept. of Health and Human Services, 2000). Smoking and heavy alcohol use are strongly linked to oral cancer.

AIDS in the Older Population

While it cannot be classified as a chronic disease in the same way as diabetes or chronic obstructive pulmonary disease, the growing number of older adults with AIDS (Acquired Immune Deficiency Syndrome) and the increasing time between infection, diagnosis, and death make this an important public health issue in gerontology. Over the next few years, AIDS will place greater demands on long-term care, especially home-based services. Since it is mandatory to report AIDS cases, the Centers for Disease Control and Prevention (CDC) receive reports from all state and territorial health departments on all diagnosed cases of AIDS. Because of stereotypes that older people are not sexually active, many physicians and HIV-testing programs do not routinely test older adults for AIDS. Often, cases go undiagnosed because older people do not report symptoms. Instead, they assume these are normal signs of aging.

In addition, older people are generally less knowledgeable about the transmission routes and course of HIV/AIDS (Ory and Mack, 1998). Older adults are more vulnerable to infection with the AIDS virus because their immune system deteriorates with aging. Furthermore, the progression from HIV to AIDS is more rapid among older people (62 percent compared with 21 percent of younger people). Their remaining lifespan after the diagnosis is also less (6.3 months versus 16.5 months for younger AIDS victims) (Ferro and Salit, 1992).

In 1998, of the more than one-half million diagnosed cases of AIDS, 10 percent were age 50 or older. There was an increase in diagnosed cases of 17 percent between 1990 and 1995 in this age group, compared to less than 10 percent for people under age 40. Almost one-third (29 percent) of this older group was over age 60 (Ory and Mack, 1998; Wooten-Bielski, 1999).

The most common risk factor for men at every age is homosexual or bisexual behavior. After age 65, blood transfusions are the secondary risk factor (representing 22.2 percent of cases), followed by heterosexual contact (Ory and Mack, 1998). Although widespread testing of blood products began in 1988, this has not totally eliminated the infection rate for older adults (Gaeta, Lapolla, and Melendez, 1996). Intravenous drug use is much less common in the population aged 60 and older compared with younger groups; therefore their risk of contracting AIDS in this manner is much lower.

For all the reasons described above, it is important to educate older adults about *their* risk

---

SYMPTOMS OF AIDS

- fevers
- night sweats
- skin rashes

- swollen lymph nodes
- chronic cough
- weight loss

OLDER WOMEN AND HIV/AIDS:

Although men are at greater risk today in all age groups, older women are also at increased risk. For example, among all persons over age 50 who were diagnosed with AIDS in 1995, 12 percent were women; but among those aged 65 and older, 21 percent were women (CDC, 1995). In a study of families of transfusion-infected AIDS patients, slightly more wives (18 percent) than husbands (8 percent) of AIDS patients were seropositive (i.e., the HIV antibody was detected in their blood). In addition, seropositive wives were older than seronegative wives (median age 62 versus 54, respectively) (Peterman et al., 1988). Older women are also becoming infected through hetero-

sexual transmission by their male partners who were infected in other ways. Another reason why older women may be more likely to become infected are the vaginal changes after the menopause. In particular, there is a thinning of the vaginal walls due to loss of estrogen, as described in Chapter 7. This leads to mucosal disruption and tearing of the vaginal wall, and thus makes it more susceptible for the HIV to enter the bloodstream. Older couples are far less likely to use condoms during intercourse than are younger persons, in part because they assume they are protected from AIDS (Gaeta et al., 1996).

for AIDS. Even those who know something about this disease may feel that it cannot affect them if they are not engaging in homosexual activity or intravenous drug use. Many older people have relied on the media for their knowledge in this area. Unfortunately, the media rarely reports on *older* adults contracting AIDS through heterosexual intercourse or through blood transfusions. It is therefore not surprising that many older people are unaware that they may be infected. They are also less willing to be tested for the virus, and once diagnosed, are less likely to seek out AIDS support groups or other forms of emotional support. At the same time, ageist attitudes may prevent health

providers from encouraging sexually active elders to be tested for this virus or even asking questions about their sexual history as part of a routine health screening (Emlet, 1997; Gueldner, 1995).

Accidents among Older People

Although mortality statistics suggest that older people are less likely than the young to die of accidents (only 7 per 10,000 deaths compared with 10 per 10,000 among people 21 and younger), these numbers mask the true incidence of deaths due to accident-related injuries. For example, if an older person breaks a hip after falling down a

RETRAINING OLDER DRIVERS

It may be useful for state licensing departments to test all adults annually on some of the relevant physiological and cognitive abilities, and to retrain older drivers who are experiencing significant declines in these areas. The AARP, National Safety Council, and the Automobile Association of America (AAA) have developed such courses. For example, AARP estimates that some 500,000 older drivers enroll in their

"Mature Driver Safety" program each year. This 8-hour course is offered through retirement homes, senior centers, shopping malls, libraries, and churches throughout the United States. Older persons can obtain discounts of 5 to 10 percent on their auto insurance in many states after completing such courses.

> ## DESIGN CHANGES THAT COULD HELP OLDER DRIVERS
>
> - right sideview mirrors
> - enlarged rearview mirrors
> - less complicated and legible instrument panels
> - better protection on doors

flight of stairs or breaks a leg in an auto accident, she enters a hospital, often is discharged to a nursing home, and soon after may die from pneumonia. Pneumonia is then listed as the cause of death, when in fact this acute condition was brought on by the patient's problems in recovering from the accident.

Despite this underestimate, the risk of death from physical injuries is about four times greater for 80-year-olds than for 20-year-olds. Those aged 60 and older are twice as likely as younger adults to be killed in a car crash. This is most likely due to their greater physical vulnerability (Evans, 1991). In addition, people over age 65 have the highest rates of auto injury–related hospitalization and death of any age group except teenagers. Although driving fatalities for all age groups have declined in the past decade, fatalities among drivers 65 and older have increased (Waller, 1991). This may be due to the increase in absolute numbers of older drivers as well as their greater vulnerability.

Older drivers are less likely to drive in bad weather, at night, in freeway traffic, or in rush hour. In fact, they drive fewer miles per year than younger drivers. Nevertheless, they have more accidents per mile driven. This higher rate of accidents may be attributed to:

- changes in eye-hand coordination
- slower reaction time
- impaired vision (especially diminished night vision and sensitivity to glare)
- hearing impairments
- changes in cognitive function that may impair driving abilities

Even though most accidents by older drivers occur at low speeds, age-related declines in organ systems and brittle bones make the older person more vulnerable to injuries and even death as a result of accidents. Older drivers are more likely to sustain rib and pelvic fractures, thoracic injuries, but fewer head and brain injuries in an auto accident. Regardless of their injuries, older adults have longer hospital stays and greater need for rehabilitation services following trauma (Wang et al., 1999). Some medications, especially those given for insomnia or anxiety, that have a long half-life in the bloodstream, are found to increase the risk of motor vehicle crashes in older adults by as much as 45 percent. This is a major risk, since many older people are prescribed these medications (Hemmelgarn et al., 1997).

Better environmental design can help older drivers. For example, older people have more accidents while making left turns; these could be avoided by designing better left-turn intersections with special lanes and left arrow lights. Road signs that are clearer and well lighted could reduce the high number of violations received by older drivers for improperly changing lanes or entering and exiting highways. Accident rates among older individuals could also be reduced through better auto design.

Another approach to reducing person–environment discrepancies for older drivers is to install air bags that have lower power in cars; of 68 adults killed by air bags between 1991 and 2000, 26 (40 percent) were age 70 or older. Already, the Ford Motor Company has installed "force limiters" in some models. These are part of a personal safety system to use sensors to adjust air bags and

---

RISK FACTORS FOR FALLS

- inactivity that weakens muscles
- visual impairment
- multiple diseases
- medications (e.g., cardiac conditions and medications that cause postural hypotension)
- gait disorders that are common among older persons

- low lighting levels
- hazards in the environment such as slippery floors, loose area rugs, poorly demarcated stairs, and slippery surfaces in showers and tubs

---

seatbelts according to the weight of the driver and passenger, and how close the driver is to the steering wheel.

FALLS AND THEIR PREVENTION

As noted earlier, older people are at a greater risk of falls than the young. Falls are the leading cause of injuries for people over age 65 in United States, and account for 90 percent of all hip fractures. Up to 30 percent of older adults in the community, and even more in long-term care settings, experience a fall in a given year. Many older people who fall become more fearful of falling and therefore restrict their activity levels. They may also become more rigid or overly cautious in walking. This may, in turn, increase the likelihood of subsequent falls. Therefore it is important to identify risk factors for falls and try to prevent them.

Among nursing home residents, risk factors for recurrent falls (i.e., a second or third fall several months after the first one) appear to be:

- older age (≥ 75)
- required assistance with several activities of daily living
- balance and behavioral problems (Thapa, Gideon, Fought, and Ray, 1995)

INTERVENTIONS TO PREVENT FALLS

- Environmental modifications of the homes of older people who had experienced multiple falls in the past resulted in a 72 percent decrease in falls (Tideiksaar, 1990).
- An investment of $2000 in home modifications and assistive devices saved $17,000 in health care costs for an older person over 18 months (Mann, et al., 1999).
- In a large study of 14 nursing homes, 50 percent of the homes (the experimental group) made major modifications to their physical environment, in wheelchair safety, and in the use

of psychotropic medications. No changes were made in the other seven homes (control group). A significant decline in recurrent falls occurred among older residents of the experimental homes compared with the control group. Rates of falls dropped to 19 percent among those with environmental modifications versus 54 percent in the control group in the following 2 years (Ray et al., 1997).
- Training older women how to control their balance can prevent falls (Ray et al., 1997; Tinetti et al., 1994).

USE OF PHYSICIAN SERVICES BY OLDER PEOPLE

The increased incidence of many chronic and acute diseases among the older population would seem to predict a striking growth with age in the use of health care services. As shown in Table 4.3, there is some support for a differential pattern of utilization. The probability of seeing a doctor at least once in the previous year increases slightly with age:

- 73 percent of people aged 25 to 44
- 78 percent of those aged 65 to 74
- 90 percent of those persons 75 years or older

However, the major difference across age groups is in frequency of use:

- 1.3 physician visits per person among those 65 and older
- 5.5 visits for those aged 25 to 44
- 7.3 visits for people aged 45 to 64 (NCHS, 1999)

When they visit physicians, both younger and older people do so primarily for acute symptoms and to receive similar diagnostic and therapeutic services. However, the larger number of yearly visits by older persons may indicate that they are seeking care for chronic conditions as well. It is noteworthy that only a small proportion of older adults are high users of all health services. In a longitudinal study of over 2000 older adults, only 3 percent were consistently high users of physician services over a 6-year period, while 40.5 percent were consistently low to medium users, that is, six or fewer annual physician visits (Stump, Johnson, and Wolinsky, 1995). Nevertheless, low-income older adults, regardless of ethnic minority status, report more unmet health needs than middle- or high-income elders (NCHS, 2000a). Among all races:

- Twenty-two percent of low-income elders report unmet health needs.
- Two and a half percent of middle- and upper-income elders have unmet health needs.

There is less difference between socioeconomic groups within the Hispanic population:

- Eighteen percent of low-income Hispanic elders have unmet health needs.
- Eight percent of middle- and upper-income Hispanic elders have such needs.

Use of Other Health Services

HOSPITALS   Hospital utilization apparently reflects older people's need for health care more ac-

TABLE 4.3   **Physician Utilization Rates by Age: 1994–1996**

AGE	VISITS PER YEAR*	INTERVAL SINCE LAST VISIT	
		<1 year	5+ years
25–44	5.5	73.4%	4.6%
45–64	7.3	76.8%	4.7%
65–74	10.3	78.0%	4.7%
75+	13.5	89.8%	2.5%

*Includes office and emergency room physician contacts.

SOURCE: National Center for Health Statistics, 1999.

curately than do elective visits to physicians' offices. Older people are more frequently hospitalized and for longer periods of time than younger populations, accounting for about 30 percent of all short-stay hospital days of care (NCHS, 1995). However, the average length of stay has been reduced since the introduction of **diagnosis related groupings (DRGs)** for Medicare patients in 1983 (see Chapter 17). While DRGs prompted a transfer of care from inpatient hospital settings to outpatient settings, home-based care after a hospitalization by older people has decreased overall. This reflects more stringent eligibility and reimbursement criteria rather than a diminishing need for care. Hospital emergency rooms (ER) are used for medical care more often among low-income populations. Research with low-income African Americans shows that ER users are mostly people without a regular physician, and who have an external locus of control regarding their health (i.e., the belief that others have more control than they do over their well-being) (Bazargan, Bazargan, and Baker, 1998).

PRESCRIPTION MEDICATIONS   The use of prescription medications may also be an indication of the older person's need for health care. Although

representing only 12.8 percent of the population in 1994, older people purchased approximately:

- 30 percent of all prescription drugs
- 40 percent of all over-the-counter drugs

About 25 percent of older people take three or more prescription drugs a day, compared to nine percent of younger people (Piraino, 1995). Some older people take as many as 12 to 15 different medications simultaneously, at an average cost of $450 (Noonan, 2000). Not surprisingly, because of the higher likelihood of their having many chronic conditions, nursing home residents take more prescription drugs than do community-dwelling elders.

Many older people may be taking either too many medications or inappropriate drugs, making overmedication a concern. This is because the less efficient excretion of drugs by the kidney and liver, and the changing proportions of fat and muscle tissue, as discussed in Chapter 3, may prolong the effects of some drugs. Furthermore, combinations of medications can cause adverse drug reactions. Many hospital admissions of older people result from such adverse reactions, and many falls and sudden impairments in cognitive function may be due to inappropriate medication or overmed-

---

CONCERNS ABOUT COSTS OF PRESCRIPTION DRUGS

Older people with chronic diseases spend more of their health care dollar on prescriptions. For example, those who have hypertension use 39 cents of every health care dollar for prescription drugs, compared to 20 percent without hypertension (National Academy, 2000d). Medicare, the federal government's health insurance plan for all Americans age 65 and older (described in more detail in Chapter 17), has no prescription drug benefit. However, the growing number of people who are managing chronic conditions with medications, combined with the increasing costs of prescription drugs in the United States, have made

this a volatile health care issue for many Americans. It is especially difficult for older people whose primary source of income is Social Security—who spend as much as one-third of their annual income on medications. The improvements in drug therapies for many conditions affecting older people come at a cost. The research, development, and FDA approval costs incurred by pharmaceutical companies for a single drug can exceed millions of dollars. This results in increasingly high costs to the consumer: $37.38 for an average prescription in 1998 compared with $23.68 in 1991 (Noonan, 2000).

ication. Older people who are discharged from hospitals with a large number of medications are more likely to be rehospitalized because of complications from these drugs. This is especially true if they are using seven or more medications, both prescription and nonprescription. This pattern occurs independent of the elder's diagnosis and type of medication (Flaherty, Perry, Lynchard, and Morley, 2000).

The higher rate of medication among older persons also may result in reporting errors and incorrect use. Older people admitted to a hospital often give inconsistent medication reports. For example, medication histories provided by older patients at admission differed from their reports to a research assistant within two days in 83 percent of the cases; 46 percent had three or more inconsistencies. Fully 22 percent of the drugs included in the medication history were denied by older patients in the subsequent interviews. This suggests that health and social service providers must exercise caution in obtaining self-reports of medication use from older adults (Beers, Munekata, and Storrie, 1990).

DENTAL SERVICES   An area of elective health care, ignored even more than routine medical care,

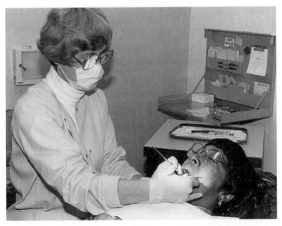

Health professionals need to be sensitive to cultural differences when caring for older patients.

is the use of professional dental services. Although the rate of preventive dental service utilization has risen significantly over the past 20 years among younger cohorts, the use of dental services by older adults has increased only slightly. In the latest national survey, older persons continued to be the lowest utilizers of professional dental care; 57 percent had not seen a dentist in the past year, and 33 percent had not obtained care in the past five years (U.S. Dept. of Health and Human Services, 2000). This rate is incongruent with the level of oral diseases that require professional attention in older persons. Yet, once older adults enter the dental care system, their average number of visits is similar to that of younger people. The current state of Medicare reimbursement, whereby physician visits are covered but dental care is not, plays an important role in this differential pattern of utilization.

HEALTH PROMOTION WITH OLDER PEOPLE

Health promotion is defined as a combination of health education and related organizational, political, and economic changes aimed at enhancing an individual's capacities for living, including moving toward greater health, not just less disease. It contrasts with disease prevention, which is focused on avoiding specific diseases that can result in impairment and disability. Health promotion emphasizes a variety of interventions in recognition of the complex social, biological, cultural, and economic factors that influence health and health behavior. Accordingly, this definition includes altering individual health practices, such as diet and exercise, as well as creating healthier environments and changing cultural attitudes and expectations toward health. Health promotion represents a shift from a biomedical model that emphasizes the physician's responsibility to treat disease, to a model in which individuals are responsible for and feel more in control of their own health and can

HEALTHY PEOPLE 2010

In September 2000, Health and Human Services Secretary Donna Shalala released a draft of *Healthy People 2010,* proposing 500 health objectives for Americans to achieve by 2010. This was a follow-up to a document released in 1990, entitled *Healthy People 2000,* which contained 319 health objectives. Two major goals of the recent publication are:

- to increase quality and years of healthy life for all Americans
- to eliminate health disparities among segments of the U.S. population

Although the 26 focus areas of *Healthy People 2010* do not specifically address elders or any particular age group, the health topics are relevant for current cohorts of older adults, as well as younger and middle-aged people today, who could improve their quality of life as they reach age 65 and beyond. For example, by promoting healthy behaviors such as increasing levels of physical activity and fitness, improving nutrition and reducing tobacco use (focus areas #1–3), future cohorts will not only increase their life expectancy, but will improve the quality of those years (www.health.gov, 2000).

optimize their quality of life. Health promotion thus makes explicit the importance of people's *environments* and *lifestyles* as determinants of good health (Breslow, 1999).

Longitudinal studies have found several unhealthy behaviors that increase chances of dying at a younger age than statistically expected. The Alameda County Study (Breslow and Breslow, 1993) which has followed community-dwelling adults for 35 years, found that mortality rates were higher among people who did not participate in regular physical activity, were obese, smoked, had high alcohol intake, did not eat breakfast, or slept less than or more than 7–8 hours per night. Similar results have been reported in another longitudinal study (Scott, Macera, Cornman and Shaupe, 1997) although it emphasized that functional abilities as reflected by independence in IADL and PADL (physical activities of daily living) are the best predictors of survival into advanced old age.

The primary rationale for health promotion programs for older adults is to reduce the incidence of *disabling chronic diseases.* This can enhance the older person's functional independence and overall quality of life, not merely prolong life. Health promotion is also a recognition that chronic conditions cannot be cured but can be pre-

vented from causing disability. As suggested in our earlier discussion of disease, as many as 80 percent of the chronic illnesses that afflict older individuals may be related to social, environmental, and behavioral factors, particularly poor health habits. In addition, 90 percent of fatal and near-fatal episodes of strokes and heart attacks are believed to be preventable.

A viable health care goal, as noted in Chapter 1, is compression of morbidity—delaying the age at which chronic illness and the infirm period of life begin (Berg and Cassells, 1992; Fries, 1980, 1984). This goal of improvement in chronic disease rates seems feasible. For example, individuals over age 75 who followed seven health-enhancing behaviors have achieved the same health index ratings as those 30 years younger who followed few or none of these behaviors (Paffenberger et al., 1986). Other evidence is shown by studies of male master athletes in their sixties. These athletes experience very little decline in their cardiovascular functions, including maximum heart rate and maximum volume of oxygen used during exercise, especially when compared with age-matched sedentary men. Furthermore, HDL cholesterol levels are higher and their triglycerides are lower than in age-matched sedentary men, and are comparable to those of healthy young men (Rogers et al.,

---

CHANGES IN HEALTH HABITS TO REDUCE RISKS

- controlling blood pressure and weight
- stopping cigarette smoking
- reducing cholesterol levels

- engaging in regular, moderate exercise
- practicing stress-management techniques such as meditation

1990; Yataco, Busby-Whitehead, Drinkwater, and Katzel, 1997).

Only about 6 percent of the national health care dollar is spent on prevention and early detection services. Medicare and most private health insurance plans do not typically pay for prevention services, although the 1997 changes in Medicare have resulted in more coverage of preventive services than in the past. An encouraging sign is the growing number of health maintenance organizations, health care clinics, universities, and work sites that are offering health promotion programs. Some of these programs have been carried into senior centers and assisted living, retirement, and nursing homes.

The Relationship of Health Practices to Health Outcomes

Considerable research demonstrates the relationship of personal health habits to health status and life satisfaction. Factors that are related to good health status include:

- not smoking
- limiting alcohol consumption
- maintaining one's weight in the ideal range
- sleeping seven to eight hours per night
- maintaining moderate levels of aerobic exercise

These relationships appear to be cumulative and independent of age, sex, and economic status (Rakowski, 1994). Additional epidemiological evidence demonstrates links between specific health habits and decreased longevity and/or increased health risks. These specific lifestyle factors, discussed briefly below, include alcohol consumption, cigarette smoking, diet, and exercise.

The relationship between drinking alcohol and physical health in old age is U-shaped, with the least healthy tending to be those who drink heavily and those who abstain, although abstainers may include former heavy drinkers who have damaged their systems. Light drinking may have some benefits to the heart. Excessive drinking (five or more drinks at a single sitting) has been found to contribute to poorer than average physical health, more frequent hospitalizations, decreased cognitive function, poorer metabolism of prescription medications, and premature death (Cummings, 1993; Wattis and Seymour, 1994).

The effects of cigarette smoking, especially in interaction with other risk factors, on heart disease, emphysema, and lung cancer have been extensively documented (Harris, 1994). Smokers who use oral contraceptives, are exposed to asbestos, have excessive alcohol consumption, or are at risk for hypertension have a greater chance of experiencing nonfatal myocardial infarction and

---

POINTS TO PONDER

Identify healthy and unhealthy behaviors in your lifestyle. Have you ever tried to modify these behaviors? If so, what techniques worked for you?

are at significant risk for cancers of the oral cavity and lung, as well as for osteoporosis. Even those who have smoked for years can benefit from smoking cessation.

Poor diet has been determined to be related to obesity, cancer, and heart disease. Obesity carries an increased risk of cardiovascular and pulmonary difficulties, aggravates other conditions such as hypertension, arthritis, and diabetes, and adds risk to surgery. Interpretation of the relationship between obesity and morbidity and mortality is difficult, however. This is because obesity is correlated with other risk factors, such as high blood pressure.

Recent clinical studies have identified the effects of specific dietary behaviors on health outcomes. A moderate reduction in dietary fat consumption, to 26 percent of total calories, may be more beneficial than a severe reduction (18 percent fat) in reducing cholesterol levels. Indeed, among men with high levels of LDL (bad cholesterol) and triglycerides (a type of fat found in blood), those who reduced their fat intake to 26 percent showed the greatest reduction in LDL and triglycerides, while maintaining their HDL (good cholesterol) levels. When fat intake decreased to 18 percent, HDL levels also declined (Knopp et al., 1997).

Another nutritional problem of older adults is insufficient intake of certain nutrients. As many as 40 percent of older people may have diets that are deficient in three or more nutrients. Up to 15 percent may have vitamin B_{12} deficiency, which is necessary for the production of blood cells and healthy functioning of the nervous system. These deficiencies are in part due to inadequate intake of

milk, eggs, vegetables, fruit, and other sources of these nutrients. They may also result from poorer absorption of nutrients by the gastrointestinal (GI) system in older adults, especially those on multiple medications that affect GI absorption (Wallace, 1997).

There is considerable evidence of the relationship between regular, moderate exercise and reduction in a person's chances of dying from heart disease and cancer, as well as hospital admissions for serious illness (LaCroix et al., 1996; Sherman, D'Agostino, Cobb, and Kannel, 1994.) Up to 50 percent of physical changes in older people that are mistakenly attributed to aging may be due to being physically unfit. Physically inactive people age faster and look older than physically fit persons of the same age, in part because of what has been termed **hypokinesia,** a disease of "disuse," or the degeneration and functional loss of muscle and bone tissue (O'Brien and Vertinsky, 1991).

Despite the known benefits of exercise, less than 30 percent of older Americans participate in *regular* physical activity. In the 1994–1996 National Health Interview Survey, 70 percent of people aged 65 and older who had no disabilities reported doing some form of exercise at least once in the past week. However, only about 33 percent of these respondents achieved recommended levels of activity and intensity in their exercise (NCHS, 2000a). Exercise needs to occur regularly, not just once a week or less. For example, in the Physicians' Health Study with 21,481 men, those who exercised less than once a week were 74 times more likely to die during exertion than men who exercised five or more times per week. This study concluded that exercise should be vigorous and last at

---

POINTS TO PONDER

Think about people you know who are between ages 75–85. What makes some of them look older, while others look younger than their chronological age? Compare their diets, smoking history, and exercise habits. Are there differences in their diets? Are any of them currently smokers or have they smoked in the past? What physical activities are they participating in, and what did they do in the past?

Older people with all levels of ability can benefit from exercise.

least 30–60 minutes each time (Albert et al., 2000). New national objectives have been established for regular exercise, stating that all adults and children over age 6 should exercise regularly (Healthy People 2010). But current activity levels among most older adults are so low that meeting objectives for *Healthy People 2010* will require significant behavioral changes among the general public.

Nevertheless, there are indications of improvements in Americans' health behaviors. For example, the National Survey of Self-Care and Aging, conducted in the early 1990s, asked older adults to describe the type and frequency of their personal health care behaviors. Researchers then examined the association between these behaviors and subsequent hospitalization rates and Medicare reimbursements. They found lower likelihood of hospitalization and lower Medicare expenses among older adults who:

- maintained a healthy weight
- never smoked
- participated in regular physical exercise
- worked in their garden
- regularly checked their pulse and blood pressure
- modified their homes to prevent falls (e.g., removing throw rugs, installing extra lighting on stairs) (Stearns et al., 1997)

The dramatic impact of self-care behaviors on hospital and physician use is an important indicator of the benefits for both individuals and society of a healthy lifestyle in the later years. Psychosocial conditions, particularly a loss of control, excessive stress, and the absence of social supports, are also linked to decreased longevity and/or poor health. As discussed in Chapter 9, epidemiologic studies also indicate that lower morbidity and greater longevity are found among people who:

- are married
- have close contacts with friends and relatives
- share common religious, ethnic, or cultural interests with others

Social networks apparently act to buffer the negative effects of stress. Translating the results of research on social supports into health services has been slow, partly because they do not fit the traditional biomedical model of disease and treatment.

Health Promotion Guidelines

Given the growing evidence about the relation of health practices to health status, most health promotion programs include components on injury prevention, nutrition, exercise, and stress management. Oral health promotion has also been implemented in geriatric dentistry. An underlying theme is taking greater responsibility for one's own health, rather than relying on medical professionals. Health contracts, some as simple as making a calendar with health promotion goals achieved each day, can help older adults maintain healthy habits. Elders who record specific behaviors (e.g., brisk walking for 30 minutes, eating five servings of vegetables) on a daily basis can increase their perceived competence and self-efficacy regarding their own health (Haber and Looney, 2000). Some health promotion programs for older adults focus on this type of individual action. Others educate participants to change the larger social environment through collective action. Several components of health promotion programs are briefly summarized.

1. NUTRITION   Although information on older people's dietary needs is incomplete and often contradictory, the basic principles are:

- Consume a wide variety of foods, especially fruits and vegetables.
- Increase consumption of unprocessed foods containing complex carbohydrates (starch and fiber), such as whole grains and legumes.
- Restrict intake of sugar, fat, and cholesterol-containing foods.
- Increase consumption of calcium, especially for postmenopausal women.

Unfortunately, there are a number of physiological, social, and emotional barriers to adequate nutrition. Any nutritional assessment of an older person must take account of such factors that can affect the amount and type of food consumed:

- inability to chew and swallow due to no teeth, missing teeth, or loose-fitting dentures
- problems with taste or smell
- poor digestion of certain foods
- social isolation that deprives the older person from mealtime socialization
- the cost of some healthy foods
- difficulty obtaining healthy foods

2. EXERCISE   Exercise programs need to be tailored to take account of variability in physical function and fitness levels. Past exercise programs for older people often have been overly cautious.

Instead, older adults need to be challenged to obtain the full benefits of an appropriately designed exercise program (National Institute on Aging, 1999). Beyond the benefits of aerobic fitness, a variety of physical activities are important for:

- maintaining overall muscle strength and endurance
- joint mobility, balance
- upright posture
- managing specific chronic diseases (Cress and Green, 1996)
- improving immune function (Shephard, 2000)

Prior to beginning a regular exercise program, older people should have a thorough medical examination, including a treadmill or other exercise tolerance test, to determine their baselines for physical fitness. Brisk walking is one of the safest and best exercises. Most ambulatory older persons, even those at a lower level of fitness, can build up their walking to one or more miles daily, and at a speed of three or four miles per hour. Indeed, even older adults with multiple chronic conditions have shown significant improvements in their speed of walking, gait, balance, and grip strength following a year of low-intensity exercise and weight training (Sharpe et al., 1997). There is evidence that greater physiological benefits, such as fat loss and cardiovascular change, require more intense and vigorous exercise, such as jogging or bicycling, which can be safely undertaken by healthy older people.

AN IDEAL EXERCISE PROGRAM

- Begins with a low level of activity.
- Includes an initial warm-up, with stretching, light calisthenics.
- Proceeds to leisurely walking.
- Consists of more strenuous exercise for 20 minutes or more.

- Ends with a relaxing cool-down period of 5 to 10 minutes of light exercise.
- This pattern should be repeated at least three times each week.

A SUCCESSFUL GROUP EXERCISE PROGRAM

Senior centers may be ideal settings for health promotion programs that emphasize exercise. At the Northshore Senior Center in Bothell, Washington, a unique program was established between the center and researchers at the University of Washington. A six-month exercise intervention was completed by 85 percent of participants, with at least 90 percent attending any one session. These rates are much higher than individually focused interventions, perhaps because of group support for continuing with the activity program. Not only did functional health improve, but participants showed fewer symptoms of depression after the intervention than a matched sample in the same center that did not participate in the exercise program (Wallace et al., 1998).

Oral Health Promotion

Preventive dentistry is included in only a few health promotion programs. One reason for this is that dental disease and tooth loss are frequently assumed to be natural concomitants of aging.

With increased preventive dentistry earlier in life, more people are retaining their natural teeth into old age, (U.S. Dept. of Health and Human Services, 2000). Those with teeth remaining should perform regular oral health care, including brushing, flossing, and appropriate visits to a dentist or hygienist. Older people, however, are not only less inclined to use professional dental services, but also to know and value preventive dentistry techniques. Therefore, prevention must be defined differently by age. In younger persons, the initiation of dental disease and tooth loss can be prevented; in older adults, the goals are to prevent *further* tooth loss and diseases that are secondary to other medical conditions and/or medications (e.g., dry mouth caused by some medications that are used to treat hypertension and depression).

Limitations of Health Promotion

Health promotion programs are sometimes criticized for their emphasis on individual responsibility for change, which minimizes the societal health disparities that underlie individual health practices such as poverty (Walker, 1994). Likewise, some educational efforts ignore the roles of policy makers, health care providers, food manufacturers, and the mass media in creating social and economic environments that may counter health promotion interventions. In addition to educating individuals to adopt healthy habits, the broader social environment must be changed.

In general, organized health promotion programs have difficulty recruiting more than 50 percent of the target population. This is true even for programs focused on people diagnosed with a potentially deadly condition such as post–myocardial infarct patients and those with high blood pressure. Attrition is also high, with rates of 30 to 60 percent. Older people most likely to participate in organized health promotion are those with a preventive attitude (e.g., regular users of physicians and dentists for checkups, nonsmokers, exercisers, and users of seat belts and smoke alarms) and those with higher participation rates in community services generally (Carter et al., 1991; Wagner et al., 1991).

Another limitation is that, although the value of health promotion is widely publicized, individuals often do not act on this information. Think about the number of people who continue to smoke despite the empirical evidence linking smoking to lung cancer, or the small proportion of women over age 45 who have a Pap smear and

---

HEALTH PROMOTION ON A LARGER SCALE

Health promotion efforts at a community and even a national level have demonstrated dramatic effects. In the early 1970s, the government of Finland responded to high rates of cardiovascular disease in its southeastern region with the North Karelia Project. Local communities passed bans on smoking in public zones. Dairy farms were converted to growing berries that reduced residents' intake of fatty milk while simultaneously increasing their intake of berries high in vita-

min C. By 1997, death rates from both lung cancer and heart disease had declined by 70 percent. On the other hand, just a few miles away, in northwestern Russia, the health of the local population has declined; death rates from heart disease, cancer, and emphysema have increased because of worsening environmental and economic conditions with the collapse of the Soviet Union (New York Times, 2000).

---

breast exam on a regular basis even though such tests are important in detecting cancer. The gap between health knowledge and health practices can be large. On the other hand, older people are more likely to change their health behaviors after learning new self-care topics than are younger people (Yusuf et al., 1996).

Even when individual behavioral change is a legitimate goal, sustaining health practices over time is difficult in the face of years of habit. In fact, little is known about the long-term benefits of health promotion, and interventions have not been long-lasting nor widely replicated. Longitudinal research is needed to assess the long-range (ten years or more) consequences of health promotion interventions for individuals and for health care costs, especially since programs may initially be very costly before they achieve long-run savings.

Nevertheless, it is encouraging that short-term educational programs that improve older participants' knowledge and preventive health behaviors

in the areas of cancer, heart disease, and oral diseases have shown continued benefits at their termination (Kiyak, 1996). The most effective prevention appears to come from two approaches: eliminating iatrogenic disease that is induced in the patient by medical care, especially with regard to the side effects of medications, and preventing the transformation from disease to disability. Health promotion is clearly a growing area, especially in light of pressure from Medicare, health maintenance organizations (HMOs), and private insurers to reduce rising health care costs for older adults.

SUMMARY AND IMPLICATIONS

Although older adults are at risk of more diseases than younger people, most older people rate their own health as satisfactory. Health status refers not only to an individual's physical condition, but also to her or his functional level in various social and psychological domains. It is affected by a person's

---

POINTS TO PONDER

Think about a health habit that you have tried to change, such as increasing your daily exercise and intake of fruits and vegetables. What difficulties did you face in making the desired changes? What are some strategies that worked for you? Could these same methods be used to help older adults change lifelong habits?

social surroundings, especially the degree of environmental stress and social support available. Although stress has been found to increase the risk of certain illnesses, such as cardiovascular disease, older people are generally less negatively affected by it; this may reflect maturity, self-control, or a lifetime of developing coping skills.

Older people are more likely to suffer from chronic or long-term diseases than from temporary or acute illnesses. The majority of older persons, however, are not limited in their daily activities by chronic conditions. The impact of such conditions apparently varies with the physiological changes that occur with age, the individual's adaptive resources, and his or her mental and emotional perspective. The type and incidence of chronic conditions also vary by gender.

The leading causes of death among persons over age 65 are heart disease, cancer, accidents, and stroke. Diseases of the heart and blood vessels are the most prevalent. Since hypertension or high blood pressure is a major risk in the development of cardiovascular problems, preventive actions are critical, especially weight control, dietary changes, appropriate exercise, and avoidance of cigarette smoking. Cancers, especially lung, bowel, and colon cancers, are the second most frequent cause of death among older persons; the risk of cancer increases with age. Cerebrovascular disease, or stroke, is the third leading cause of death among older persons. It may be caused by cerebral thrombosis, or blood clots, and by cerebral hemorrhage. Healthy lifestyle practices are important in stroke prevention.

Arthritis, although not fatal, is a major cause of limited daily activity and is extremely common among older persons. Osteoporosis, or loss of bone mass and the resultant increased brittleness of the bones, is most common among older women, and may result in fractures of the hip, spine, and wrist. Chronic respiratory problems, particularly emphysema, increase with age, especially among men. Diabetes mellitus is a frequent problem in old age, and is particularly troubling because of the many related illnesses that may result. Problems with the intestinal tract include diverticulitis, constipation, and hiatus hernia. Cystitis and incontinence are frequently occurring problems of the kidneys and urinary system. Although the majority of older persons have some type of incontinence, many kinds can be treated and controlled.

The growth of the older population, combined with the increase in major chronic illnesses, has placed greater demands on the health care system. Nevertheless, older people seek outpatient medical, dental, and mental health services at a slightly lower rate than their incidence of chronic illnesses would predict. Like younger people, the older population is most likely to seek health services for acute problems, not for checkups on chronic conditions or for preventive care. Beliefs that physicians, dentists, and mental health professionals cannot cure their chronic problems may deter many older people from seeking needed care. The problem may be compounded by the belief of some health care providers who have not been trained in geriatrics that older people are poor candidates for health services. More university and continuing education classes are needed to provide training in geriatrics and gerontology for staff in health care settings and to address their attitudes toward older people.

Health promotion has proved to be effective in improving the well-being and enhancing the quality of life of older people. The elimination or postponement of the chronic diseases that are associated with old age is a major goal for health promotion specialists and biomedical researchers. Treatment methods for all these diseases are changing rapidly with the growth in medical technology and the increasing recognition given to such environmental factors as stress, nutrition, and exercise in disease prevention. If health promotion efforts to modify lifestyles are successful, and if aging research progresses substantially, the chronic illnesses that we have discussed will undoubtedly be postponed, and disability or loss of functional status will be delayed until advanced old age.

GLOSSARY

acute condition   short-term disease or infection, often debilitating to older persons

acute myocardial infarction   loss of blood flow to a specific region of the heart, resulting in damage of the myocardium

ADL   activities of daily living summarizes an individual's performance in personal care tasks such as bathing or dressing, as well as such home-management activities as shopping, meal preparation, and taking medications

arteriosclerosis   loss of elasticity of the arterial walls

benign hypertrophy of the prostate   enlargement of the prostate gland in older men, without signs of cancer or other serious disease; may cause discomfort

chronic condition   long-term (more than three months), often permanent, and leaving a residual disability that may require long-term management or care rather than cure

comorbidity   simultaneously experiencing multiple health problems, both acute and chronic

contracture   the loss of flexibility or freezing of a joint due to lack of use

diagnosis related groups (DRGs)   a system of classifying medical cases for payment on the basis of diagnoses; used under Medicare's prospective payment system (PPS) for inpatient hospital services

disability   an impairment in the ability to complete multiple daily tasks

diverticulitis   a condition in which pouches or sacs (diverticula) in the intestinal wall become inflamed and infected

edentulous   the absence of natural teeth

good health   more than the mere absence of infirmity, a state of complete physical, mental, and social well-being

health promotion   a model in which individuals are responsible for and in control of their own health, including a combination of health education and related organizational, political, and economic changes conducive to health

health status   the presence or absence of disease as well as the degree of disability in an individual's level of functioning

hiatus hernia   a condition in which a small portion of the stomach slides up through the diaphragm

hypokinesia   the degeneration and functional loss of muscle and bone due to physical inactivity

IADL (Instrumental Activities of Daily Living)   Daily activities involving use of the environment.

immunity   resistance to environmental carcinogens, viruses, and bacteria

incontinence   the inability to control urine and feces—of two types: urge incontinence, where a person is not able to hold urine long enough to reach a toilet, and stress incontinence, where leakage occurs during physical exertion, laughing, sneezing, or coughing

osteopenia   a significant loss of calcium and reduced bone density not associated with increased risk of fractures

quality of life   going beyond health status alone, this concept considers the individual's sense of competence, ability to perform activities of daily living, and satisfaction with social interactions, in addition to functional health

rheumatoid arthritis   a chronic inflammation of the membranes lining joints and tendons, characterized by pain, swelling, bone dislocation, and limited range of motion; can occur at any age

stress   the gamut of social-psychological stimuli that produce physiological responses of shallow, rapid breathing, muscle tension, increased blood pressure, and accelerated heart rate

REFERENCES

Albert, C. M., Mittleman, M. A., Chae, C. U., Lee, I. M., Hennekens, C. H., and Manson, J. E. Triggering of sudden death from cardiac causes by vigorous exertion. *New England Journal of Medicine,* 2000, *343,* 1355–1361.

Albertsen, P. C., Fryback, D. G., and Storer, B. E. Long-term survival among men with conservatively treated localized prostate cancer. *Journal of the American Medical Association,* 1995, *274,* 626–631.

Bazargan, M., Bazargan, S., and Baker, R. S. Emergency department utilization, hospital admissions, and physician visits among elderly African American persons. *The Gerontologist,* 1998, *38,* 25–36.

Beers, M. H., Munekata, M., and Storrie, M. The accuracy of medication histories in the hospital medical records of elderly persons. *Journal of the American Geriatrics Society,* 1990, *38,* 1183–1187.

Berg, R. L., and Cassells, J. S. (Eds.). *The second fifty years: Promoting health and preventing disability.* Washington, DC: Institute of Medicine, National Academy Press, 1992.

Bernard, S. L., Kincade, J. E., Konrad, T. R., Arcury, T. A., and Rabiner, D. Predicting mortality from community surveys of older adults: The importance of self-rated functional ability. *Journals of Gerontology: Social Sciences,* 1997, *52,* S155-S163.

Breslow, L. From disease prevention to health promotion. *JAMA,* 1999, *281,* 1030–1033.

Breslow, L., and Breslow, N. Health practices and disability: Some evidence from Alameda County. *Preventive Medicine,* 1993, *22,* 86–95.

Brown, L. J., Brunelle, J. A., and Kingman, A. Periodontal status in the United States: Prevalence, extent, and demographic variation. *Journal of Dental Research,* 1996, *75,* 672–683.

Bush, T. L. The epidemiology of cardiovascular disease in postmenopausal women. *Annals of the New York Academy of Sciences,* 1990, *592,* 264–230.

Cantor, M. Family and community: Changing roles in an aging society. *The Gerontologist,* 1991, *31,* 337–346.

Caplan, L. S., Wells, B. L., and Haynes, S. Breast cancer screening among older racial/ethnic minorities and whites. *Journals of Gerontology,* 1992, *47* (Special Issue), 101–110.

Carter, W. B., Elward, K., Malmgren, J., Martin, M. L., and Larson, E. Participation of older adults in health programs and research: A critical review of the literature. *The Gerontologist,* 1991, *31,* 584–592.

Centers for Disease Control and Prevention (CDC). National Center for Chronic Disease Prevention and Health Promotion. *Physical activity and health: A report of the Surgeon General.* Atlanta: CDC Publications, 1996.

Centers for Disease Control and Prevention (CDC). Pneumonia and influenza death rates: United States 1979–1994. *Morbidity and Mortality Weekly Reports,* 1995, *44,* 535–537.

Centers for Disease Control and Prevention (CDC). Pneumonia and influenza vaccination levels among adults aged greater than or equal to 65 years: United States 1993. *Morbidity and Mortality Weekly Reports,* 1996, *45,* 859.

Chapuy, M. C., Arlot, M. E., Duboeuf, F., Brun, J., and Crouzet, B. Vitamin D3 and calcium to prevent hip fractures in elderly women. *New England Journal of Medicine,* 1992, *327,* 1637–1642.

Chiu, K. M. Efficacy of calcium supplements on bone mass in postmenopausal women. *Journals of Gerontology: Medical Sciences,* 1999, *54A,* M275–M280.

Chrischilles, E., Shireman, T., and Wallace, R. Costs and health effects of osteoporotic fractures. *Bone,* 1994, *15,* 377–386.

Clancey, C. M., and Bierman, A. S. Quality and outcomes of care for older women with chronic disease. *Women's Health Issues,* 2000, *10,* 178–192.

Cousins, N. *Anatomy of an illness.* New York: Bantam Books, 1979.

Cramer, D. Promoting continence: Strategies for success. *Perspectives in Health Promotion and Aging,* 1993, *1,* 1–3.

Cress, M. E., and Green, F. A. Exercise and aging: Physical fitness. In M. A. Stenchever (Ed.), *Health care for the older woman.* New York: Chapman and Hall, 1996.

Cummings, N. A., Chemical dependency among older adults. In F. Lieberman and M. F. Collen (Eds.), *Aging in good health: A quality lifestyle for the later years.* New York: Plenum Books, 1993.

Cummings, S. R., Nevitt, M. C., Browner, W. S., Stone, K., Fox, K. M., and Ensrud, K. E. Risk factors for hip fractures in white women. *New England Journal of Medicine,* 1995, *332,* 767–773.

Emlet, C. A., HIV/AIDS in the elderly: A hidden population. *Home Care Provider,* 1997, *2,* 22–28.

Evans, L. *Traffic safety and the driver.* New York: Van Nostrand Reinhold, 1991.

Ferro, S., and Salit, I. E. HIV infection in patients over 55 years of age. *Journal of Acquired Immune Deficiency Syndromes,* 1992, *5,* 348–355.

Ferrucci, L., Kittner, S. J., Corti, M. C., and Guralnik, J. M. Neurological conditions. In J. M. Guralnick, L. P. Fried, E. M. Simonsick, J. D., Kaspar, and M. E. Lafferty (Eds.), *The women's health and aging study.* Bethesda, MD: NIH/NIA, 1995.

Flaherty, J. H., Perry, H. M., Lynchard, G. S., and Morley, J. E. Polypharmacy and hospitalization among older home care patients. *Journals of Gerontology: Medical Sciences,* 2000, *55A,* M554–M559.

Fries, J. F. Aging, natural death, and the compression of morbidity. *New England Journal of Medicine,* 1980, *303,* 130–135.

Fries, J. F. The compression of morbidity: Miscellaneous comments about a theme. *The Gerontologist,* 1984, *24,* 354–359.

Gaeta, T. J., Lapolla, C., and Melendez, E. AIDS in the elderly. *Journal of Emergency Medicine*, 1996, *14*, 19–23.

Goldberg, A. Health promotion and aging: Physical exercise. Surgeon General's Workshop, *Health Promotion and Aging*, March 1988.

Gorelick, P. B., Shanmugam, V., and Pajeau, A. K. Stroke. In J. E. Birren (Ed.), *Encyclopedia of gerontology*, Vol. 2. San Diego: Academy Press, 1996.

Govaert, T. M., Thijs, C. T., and Masurel, N. The efficacy of influenza vaccination in elderly individuals. A randomized double-blind placebo-controlled trial. *Journal of the American Medical Association*, 1994, *272*, 1661–1665.

Greenwald, D. A., and Brandt, L. J. Gastrointestinal system: Function and dysfunction. In J. E. Birren (Ed.), *Encyclopedia of gerontology*, Vol. 1. San Diego: Academy Press, 1996.

Gresham, G. E., Duncan, P. W., and Stason, W. B. *Poststroke rehabilitation: Assessment, referral, and patient management.* Rockville, MD: USDHHS, Agency for Health Care Policy and Research, 1995.

Gueldner, S. H. The elderly: The silent population. *Journal of the Association of Nurses in AIDS Care*, 1995, *6*, 9–10.

Haber, D., and Looney, C. Health contract calendars: A tool for health professionals with older adults. *The Gerontologist*, 2000, *40*, 235–239.

Harris, J. The health benefits of health promotion. In M. P. O'Donnell, and J. Harris (Eds.), *Health promotion in the workplace*. Albany, NY: Delmar, 1994.

Hawkins, S. A., Wiswell, R. A., Jaque, S. V., Constantino, N., Marcell, T. J., Tarpenning, K. M., Schroeder, E. T., and Hyslop, D. M. The inability of hormone replacement therapy or chronic running to maintain bone mass in master athletes. *Journals of Gerontology: Medical Sciences*, 1999, *54A*, M451–M455.

Hayflick, L. *How and why we age*. New York: Ballantine Books, 1996.

Healthy People 2010. *Understanding and Improving Health*. U.S. Government Printing Office. No. 017-001-00547-9, 2000.

Hemmelgarn, B., Suissa, S., Huang, A., Boirin, J. F., and Pinard, G. Benzodiazepine use and the risk of motor vehicle crash in the elderly. *Journal of the American Medical Association*, 1997, *278*, 27–31.

Henderson, B. E., Paganini-Hill, A., and Ross, R. K. Decreased mortality in users of estrogen replacement therapy. *Archives of Internal Medicine*, 1991, *151*, 75–78.

Herrington, D. M., Reboussin, D. M., Brosnihan, B., Sharp, P. C., Shumaker, S. A., Snyder, T. E., Furberg, C. D., et al. Effects of estrogen replacement on the progression of coronary artery atherosclerosis. *New England Journal of Medicine*, 2000, *343*, 522–529.

Hu, F. B., Stampfer, M. J., Manson, J. E., Grodstein, F., Colditz, G. A., Speizer, F. E., and Willett, W. C. Trends in the incidence of coronary heart disease and changes in diet and lifestyle in women. *New England Journal of Medicine*, 2000, *343*, 530–537.

Johnson, R. J., and Wolinsky, F. D. Gender, race, and health: The structure of health status among older adults. *The Gerontologist*, 1994, *34*, 24–35.

Josephson, K. R., Fabacher, D. A., and Rubenstein, L. Z. Home safety and fall prevention. *Clinics in Geriatric Medicine*, 1991, *7*, 707–731.

Juvenile Diabetes Foundation. *Diabetes Facts*. http://www.jdfcure.org, 1998.

Kemnitz, J. W., Roccer, E. B., and Weindruch, R. Dietary restriction increases insulin sensitivity and lowers blood glucose in Rhesus monkeys. *American Journal of Physiology*, 1994, *266*, E540–E547.

Kiyak, H. A. Measuring psychosocial variables that predict older persons' oral health behavior. *Gerodontology*, 1996, *13*, 69–75.

Knopp, R. H., Walden, C. E., Retzlaff, B. M., McCann, B. S., Dowdy, A. A., Albers, J. J., Gey, G. O., and Cooper, M. N. Long-term cholesterol-lowering effects of 4 fat-restricted diets in hypercholesterolemic and combined hyperlipidemic men. The dietary alternatives study. *Journal of the American Medical Association*, 1997, *278*, 1509–1515.

LaCroix, A. Z. *Health promotion for older adults: Osteoporosis*. NWGEC Curriculum Modules, University of Washington, 1997.

LaCroix, A. Z., Leveille, S., Hecht, J., Grothaus, L., and Wagner, E. Does walking reduce the risk of cardiovascular disease and death in older adults? *Journal of the American Geriatrics Society*, 1996, *44*, 113–120.

Leeb, B. F., Schweitzer, H., Montag, K., and Smolen, J. S. A metaanalysis of chondroitin sulfate in the treatment of osteoarthritis. *Journal of Rheumatology*, 2000, *27*, 205–211.

Looker, A. C., Johnston, C. C., Wahner, H. W., Dunn, W. L., and Calvo, M. S. Prevalence of low femoral bone density in older U.S. women from NHANES

III. *Journal of Bone Mineral Research,* 1995, *10,* 796–802.

Mann, W. C., Ottenbacher, K. J., Fraas, L., Tomita, M. and Granger, C. V. Effectiveness of assistive technology and environmental interventions in maintaining independence and reducing home care costs for the frail elderly. *Archives of Family Medicine,* 1999, *8,* 210–217.

Mokdad, A. H., Ford, E. S., Bowman, B. A., Nelson, D. E., Engelgau, M. M., Vinicor, F., and marks, J. S. Diabetes trends in the U.S.: 1990–1998. *Diabetes Care,* 2000, *23,* 1278–1283.

National Academy on an Aging Society. Arthritis: A leading cause of disability. *Chronic and Disabling Conditions,* No. 5, 2000a.

National Academy on an Aging Society. Caregiving: Helping the elderly with activity limitations. *Chronic and Disabling Conditions,* No. 7, 2000b.

National Academy on an Aging Society. Chronic conditions: A challenge for the 21st century. *Chronic and Disabling Conditions,* No. 1, 1999a.

National Academy on an Aging Society. Hearing loss. *Chronic and Disabling Conditions,* No. 2, 1999b.

National Academy on an Aging Society. Heart disease. *Chronic and Disabling Conditions,* No. 3, 2000c.

National Academy on an Aging Society. Hypertension: A common condition for older Americans. *Chronic and Disabling Conditions,* No. 12, 2000d.

National Academy on an Aging Society. Workers and chronic conditions. *Chronic and Disabling Conditions,* No. 3, 2000e.

National Center for Health Statistics. *Adults' health status and health care.* NCHS website: http://www.cdc.gov/nchs, 2000a.

National Center for Health Statistics. Current estimates from the National Health Interview Survey: U.S. 1994. *Vital and Health Statistics,* Series 10, #193, 1995.

National Center for Health Statistics. Death rates and age-adjusted death rates: United States 1979, 1997 and 1998. *Vital and Health Statistics,* #48, 2000b.

National Center for Health Statistics. *Health, United States.* Hyattsville, MD: NCHS, 1999.

National Heart, Lung, and Blood Institute. *Sixth report of the Joint National Committee on Prevention, Detection, Evaluation and Treatment of High Blood Pressure.* NIH/NHLBI Publications, Nov. 1997.

National Institute on Aging. *Exercise: A guide from the National Institute on Aging.* NIH/NIA Publication No. 99-4258, 1999.

Nelson, M. E., Fiatarone, M. A., Morganti, C. M., Trice, I., Greenberg, R. A., and Evans, W. J. Effects of high intensity strength training on multiple risk factors for osteoporotic fractures. *Journal of the American Medical Association,* 1994, *272,* 1909–1914.

Noonan, D. Prescription drugs: Why they cost so much. *Newsweek,* Sept. 25, 2000, pp. 53–57.

New York Times. An ailing Russia lives a tough life that's getting shorter. Dec. 3, 2000, pp. 1–19.

Notelovitz, M., Martin, D., and Tesar, R. Estrogen therapy and variable resistance weight training increase bone mineral in surgically menopausal women. *Journal of Bone Mineral Research,* 1991, *6,* 583–590.

O'Brien, S. J., and Vertinsky, P. A. Unfit survivors: Exercise as a recourse for aging women. *The Gerontologist,* 1991, *31,* 347–357.

Ory, M. G., and Mack, K. A. Middle-aged and older people with AIDS. *Research on Aging,* 1998, *20,* 653–664.

OWL (Older Women's League). *A status report on osteoporosis: The challenge to midlife and older women.* Washington, DC: 1994.

Paffenberger, R., Hyde, R., Wing, A., and Hsied, C. Physical activity, all-cause mortality and longevity of college alumni. *The New England Journal of Medicine,* 1986, *314,* 605–613.

Pate, R. R., Pratt, M., and Blair, S. N. Physical activity and public health. *Journal of the American Medical Association,* 1996, *273,* 402–407.

Peterman, T. A., Stoneburner, R. L., Allen, J. R., Jaffe, H. W., and Curran, J. W. Risk of human immunodeficiency virus transmission from heterosexual adults with transfusion-associated infections. *Journal of the American Medical Association,* 1988, *259,* 55–58.

Phillips, R. S. Preventing depression: A program for African American elders with chronic pain. *Family and Community Health,* 2000, *22,* 57–65.

Piraino, A. J. Managing medication in the elderly. *Hospital Practice,* 1995, *30,* 59–64.

Prince, R. L., Smith, M., Dick, I. M., Price, R. I., Webb, P. G., Henderson, K., and Harris, M. P. Prevention of postmenopausal osteoporosis. *New England Journal of Medicine,* 1991, *325,* 1189–1195.

Quinn, M. E., Johnson, M. A., Poon, L. W., and Martin, P. Psychosocial correlates of subjective mental health in sexagenarians, octogenarians, and centenarians. *Issues in Mental Health Nursing,* 1999, *20,* 151–171.

Rakowski, W. The definition and measurement of prevention, preventative health care, and health promotion. *Generations*, 1994, *18*, 18–23.

Ray, W. A., Taylor, J. A., Meador, K. G., Thapa, P. B., and Brown, A. K. A randomized trial of a consultation service to reduce falls in nursing homes. *Journal of the American Medical Association*, 1997, *278*, 595–596.

Riggs, B. L., Hodgson, S. F., O'Fallon, W. M., Chao, E. Y., Wahner, H., et al. Effects of fluoride treatment on the fracture rate in postmenopausal women with osteoporosis. *New England Journal of Medicine*, 1990, *322*, 802–809.

Rogers, M. A., Hagberg, J. M., Martin, W. H., Ehsani, A. A., and Holloszy, J. O. Decline in vo_2 max with aging in master athletes and sedentary men. *Journal of Applied Physiology*, 1990, *68*, 2195–2199.

Scott, W. K., Macera, C. A., Cornman, C. B. and Sharpe, P. A. Functional health status as a predictor of mortality in men and women over 65. *Journal of Clinical Epidemiology*, 1997, *50*, 291–296.

Sharpe, P. A., Jackson, K. L., White, C., Vaca, V. L., Hickey, T., Gu, J., and Otterness, C. Effects of a one year physical activity intervention for older adults at congregate nutrition sites. *The Gerontologist*, 1997, *37*, 208–215.

Shephard, R. J. Worksite health promotion and the older worker. *International Journal of Industrial Ergonomics*, 2000, *25*, 465–475.

Sherman, S. E., D'Agostino, R. B., Cobb, J. L., and Kannel, W. B. Physical activity and mortality in women in the Framingham heart study. *American Heart Journal*, 1994, *128*, 879–884.

Sisk, J. E., Moskowitz, A. J., Whang, W., Lin, J. D., Fedson, D. S., and McBean, A. M. Cost-effectiveness of vaccination against pneumococcal bacteremia among elderly people. *Journal of the American Medical Association*, 1997, *278*, 1333–1339.

Smith, J. P., and Kingston, R. S. Race, socioeconomic status, and health in late life. In L. G. Martin and B. J. Soldo (Eds.), *Racial and Ethnic Differences in the Health of Older Americans*. Washington, DC: National Academy Press, 1997.

Speroff, L. The Heart and Estrogen/progestin Replacement Study (HERS). *Maturitas*, 1998, *31*, 9–14.

Stampfer, M. J., and Colditz, G. A. Estrogen replacement therapy and coronary heart disease: A quantitative assessment of the epidemiologic evidence. *Preventive Medicine*, 1991, *20*, 47–63.

Stampfer, M. J., Colditz, G. A., Willett, W. C., Manson, J. E., Rosner, B., Speizer, F. E., and Heinnekens, C. H. Postmenopausal estrogen therapy and cardiovascular disease: Ten-year follow-up from the Nurses' Health Study. *New England Journal of Medicine*, 1991, *325*, 756–762.

Stearns, S. C., Bernard, S. L., Konrad, T. R., Schwartz, R. J., and Defriese, G. H. *Medicare use and costs in relation to self-care practices.* Poster presented at annual meetings of the Association for Health Services Research, 1997.

Steinberg, K. K., Thacker, S. B., Stroup, D. F., Zack, M. M., Flanders, W. D., and Berkelman, R. L. A meta-analysis of the effect of estrogen replacement therapy on the risk of breast cancer. *Journal of the American Medical Association*, 1992, *265*, 185–199.

Stewart, A. L., Greenfield, S., Hays, R. D., Wells, K., Rogers, W. H., Berry, S. D., McGlynn, E. A., and Ware, J. E. Functional status and well-being of patients with chronic conditions. *Journal of the American Medical Association*, 1989, *262*, 907–913.

Stump, T. E., Johnson, R. J., and Wolinsky, F. D. Changes in physician utilization over time among older adults. *Journals of Gerontology*, 1995, *50B*, S45–S58.

Thapa, P. B., Gideon, P., Fought, R. L., and Ray, W. A., Psychotropic drugs and risk of recurrent falls in ambulatory nursing home residents. *American Journal of Epidemiology*, 1995, *142*, 202–211.

Thom, D. H., and Brown, J. S. Reproductive and hormonal risk factors for urinary incontinence in later life: A review of the clinical and epidemiological literature. *Journal of the American Geriatrics Society*, 1998, *46*. 1411–1417.

Tideiksaar, R. Environmental adaptations to preserve balance and prevent falls. *Topics in Geriatric Rehabilitation*, 1990, *5*, 78–84.

Tinetti, M. E., Baker, D. I., McAvay, C., Claus, E. B., Garret, P., and Gottschalk, M. A multifactorial intervention to reduce the risk of falling among elderly people living in the community. *New England Journal of Medicine*, 1994, *331*, 821–827.

U.S. Administration on Aging Webpage. http://www.aoa.dhhs.gov//aoa/stats, 1997.

U.S. Administration on Aging Webpage. http://www.aoa.dhhs.gov//aoa/stats, 2000.

U.S. Department of Health and Human Services, *Oral Health in America: A Report of the Surgeon General*. Bethesda, MD: NIDCR/NIH, 2000.

U.S. Public Health Service. *Promoting health/preventing disease: Year 2000 objectives for the nation.* Washington, DC: U.S. Department of Health and Human Services, 1989.

Van Nostrand, J. F., Furner, S. E., and Suzman, R. (Eds.), Health data on older Americans: United States, 1992. *Vital and Health Statistics*, Series 3: Analytic and Epidemiological Studies, No. 27, DHHS Publication 93–1411. Hyattsville, MD: NCHS, 1993.

Vogt, T. Cost-effectiveness of prevention programs for older people. *Generations*, 1994, *18*, 63–68.

Wagner, E. H., Grothaus, L. C., Hecht, J. A., and LaCroix, A. Z. Factors associated with participation in a senior health promotion program. *The Gerontologist*, 1991, *31*, 598–602.

Walker, S. Health promotion and prevention of disease and disability. *Generations*, 1994, *18*, 45–49.

Wallace, J. I. *Health promotion for older adults: Nutrition.* NWGEC Curriculum Modules, University of Washington, 1997.

Wallace, J. I., Buchner, D. M., Grothaus, L., Leveille, S., Tyll, L., LaCroix, A. Z., and Wagner, E. H. Implementation and effectiveness of a community-based health promotion program for older adults. *Journals of Gerontology: Medical Sciences*, 1998, *53A*, M301–M306.

Waller, P. F. The older driver. *Human Factors*, 1991, *33*, 499–505.

Wang, S. C., Siegel, J. H., Dischinger, P. C., Loo, G. T., Tenenbaum, N., Burgess, A. R., Schneider, L. W., and Bents, F. D. Interactive effects of age and sex on injury patterns and outcomes in elderly motor vehicle crash occupants. Paper presented at third annual CIREN (Crash Injury Research and Engineering Network) Conference, October 1999.

Wattis, J. P., and Seymour, J. Alcohol abuse in elderly people: Medical and psychiatric consequences. In R. R. Watson (Ed.), *Handbook of nutrition in the aged* (2nd ed.) Boca Raton, FL: CRC Press, 1994.

Wooten-Bielski, K. HIV and AIDS in older adults. *Geriatric Nursing*, 1999, *20*, 268–272.

Yataco, A. R., Busby-Whitehead, J., Drinkwater, D. T., and Katzel, L. I. Relationship of body composition and cardiovascular fitness to lipoprotein lipid profiles in master athletes and sedentary men. *Aging*, 1997, *9*, 88–94.

Yusuf, H. R., Croft, J. B., Giles, W. H., Anda, R. F., Casper, M. L., and Casperson, C. J. Leisure-time physical activity among older adults. *Archives of Internal Medicine*, 1996, *156*, 1321–1326.

three

THE PSYCHOLOGICAL CONTEXT OF SOCIAL AGING

The dynamic interactions between people and their environments as they age, the population trends that made gerontology such an important concern in the late twentieth century, and the historical background of social gerontology were discussed in Part One. Part Two focused on the normal biological and physiological changes that take place with aging. The types of chronic and acute health problems that afflict older people and influence their social functioning were presented. The older population's use of the health care system was reviewed. Part Two concluded with a discussion of the growing field of health promotion, and how improved health behaviors can help people achieve successful aging.

In this section, the focus is on psychological changes with aging—both normal and abnormal—that influence older people's social behavior and dynamic relationships with their physical and social environments. As we have already seen, many changes take place in the aging organism that make it more difficult to perform activities of daily living and to respond as quickly and easily to external demands as in youth. Many older people

have chronic health problems, such as arthritis, diabetes, or heart disease, that compound the normal changes that cause people to slow down. In a similar manner, some changes in cognitive functioning, personality, and sexuality are a function of normal aging. Other psychological changes may be due to the secondary effects of diseases.

Many researchers have examined changes in intelligence, learning, and memory with aging. The literature in this area, reviewed in Chapter 5, suggests that normal aging does not result in significant declines. Although older subjects in the studies described do not perform as well as younger subjects, their scores are not so poor as to indicate significant impairments in social functioning. Laboratory tests also may be less than ideal as indicators of cognitive function in older people. Suggestions for improving memory in the later years are discussed, including the use of herbal and alternative medicine, as well as vitamins that have been used with minimal systematic research as to their benefits. The chapter concludes with a review of wisdom and creativity in old age.

Chapter 6 describes personality development in the later years, the importance of maintaining self-esteem, and threats to self-esteem that result from changes in social roles. This chapter also focuses on coping and successful adaptation to the changes associated with aging. Given the normal age-related changes in physiological, sensory, and cognitive functions, in personality styles, and in older individuals' social networks, some gerontologists argue that older people experience more stress in a given time period than young adults. Furthermore, there has been considerable debate about whether aging results in the use of different types of coping strategies. However, longitudinal research in this area is insufficient to conclude with any certainty that aging is associated with more stressful life events than young adulthood. The concept of successful aging is introduced in this chapter. It is a concept that has drawn considerable research attention; it requires high levels of physical and functional health, and remaining active in cognitive and social functions. It will attract more interest as Baby Boomers age.

Some forms of psychopathology, such as schizophrenia, are more common in young adults than in old age. However, as described in Chapter 6, some older people are at high risk for major depression, paranoia, and some forms of dementia. In the case of dementia, such as Alzheimer's disease, memory and problem-solving abilities decline quite dramatically, sometimes within a few years, other times over many years. Older individuals with a diagnosis of dementia experience significant impairments in their ability to interact with other people and to control their physical and social environments. To the extent that older people do not seek mental health services for treatable disorders such as depression or paranoia, their social interactions will deteriorate. Some may become reclusive and, in the case of severely depressed older persons, at greater risk of suicide. Despite the growing number of studies that document the benefits of therapeutic interventions for older adults, the older population, especially elders of color, underutilizes mental health services. Most of the mental health care provided to older adults takes place in hospitals, not in community mental health centers or in private practice. Furthermore, most therapy is provided by family doctors who generally do not have special expertise in geriatric medicine or psychiatry.

An important aspect of personality is sexuality, the individual's ability to express intimate feelings through a wide range of loving and pleasurable experiences. Chapter 7 addresses the influence of social attitudes and beliefs, normal physiological changes, and diseases on older adults' sexuality. Contrary to popular belief, aging need not reduce sexual pleasure and capacity. More often, older people withdraw from sexual activity because of societal expectations and stereotypes. As people become better informed about aging and sexuality, and as sexual taboos are reduced, older people will express their sexuality more easily.

As with physical aging, the material in Part Three suggests that aging does not affect all people's psychological functions in the same way. Normal cognitive changes generally are not so dramatic as to impair older people's social functions. However, some people report mild forgetfulness, a condition known as "benign senescent forgetfulness." A relatively small segment of the older population experiences Alzheimer's disease or other types of dementia. Personality and patterns of coping also do not change so dramatically as to impair social functioning, although some sex-typed behaviors become less pronounced with age. Coping and adaptation skills do not become impaired with normal aging; styles of coping vary widely among older people. Indeed, aging results in increasing differences in psychological functioning among people, not greater similarity. Some older people age successfully despite chronic diseases and deterioration in cognitive function, while others experience poor adaptation to these normal and secondary changes of aging. The following vignettes illustrate the contrasts in psychological aging.

AN OLDER PERSON WITH INTACT COGNITIVE ABILITIES

Mr. Wallace, age 85, is a retired professor in a midwestern community. He retired 20 years ago, after teaching history in a large state university for 40 years. He remains active by doing volunteer work in the local historical society, teaching part-time at the university, and traveling to Europe with his wife for three months every summer, occasionally leading groups of other retirees in tours of medieval European towns. Mr. Wallace's major project that he wishes to complete before he dies is an historical novel about Charlemagne. This is a topic about which he has lectured and read extensively, and one he enjoys investigating in detail during his trips to Europe. Mrs. Wallace often remarks that he is busier these days than he was before his retirement. During the first few months after retirement, Professor Wallace experienced a mild bout of depression, but he found some relief through group therapy with other retirees. Mr. Wallace enjoys intellectual challenges today as much as he did when he was employed, in fact, more so, because he is pursuing these activities without the pressures of a day-to-day job. He vows to keep up his level of activity until he "runs out of energy." Mr. Wallace is an excellent model of successful aging.

AN OLDER PERSON WITH GOOD COPING SKILLS

Mrs. Johnson, age 83, has suffered numerous tragedies throughout her life. Born to a poor farming family in Mississippi, she moved north with her mother and eight older sisters and brothers as a child, after her father died and the family farm was lost. The family supported itself through hard work in the factories. Mrs. Johnson married young; she and her husband struggled through the years to own their home and raise their three children. Her husband died 20 years ago, leaving her with a small pension. She worked at a manual labor job until she was 70 years old, when her arthritis made it painful for her to do the heavy work needed on the job. During the past three years, Mrs. Johnson has experienced a series of losses: her son and daughter-in-law died in an auto accident; her last surviving sister died; and her oldest granddaughter, the one on whom she could most depend, moved west to attend medical school. Mrs. Johnson admits these losses are painful, but that it is "God's will" that she experience them. Her strong faith in God helps her accept these changes in her life and her deteriorating health as part

of a "master plan." When she becomes too distraught, she turns to the Bible, and looks forward to visits from her grandchildren and great-grandchildren to keep her busy.

AN OLDER PERSON WITH DEMENTIA

Mr. Adams is age 64. Several years ago he started showing signs of confusion and disorientation. He was diagnosed as having Alzheimer's disease at age 60, five years before his planned retirement. He and his wife had made plans to travel around the world during retirement; now all their plans have completely changed. While there have been some brief periods during the past four years where he has seemed to be better, Mr. Adams now is extremely agitated and disoriented, wanders during the night, and is occasionally abusive to people near him. He often does not know who his wife and children are. The slightest change in routine will upset him. In his lucid moments, Mr. Adams cries and wonders what has happened to his life; at some points, he can also carry on short conversations. His wife is determined to keep him at home, even though he often verbally abuses her and does not recognize or appreciate all that she does for him. She is able to take him to an adult day-care center during the day, where the staff try to keep him active and stimulated. Mrs. Adams also attends meetings of a support group for family caregivers of Alzheimer's disease patients. She enjoys these meetings because she can express her feelings about how hard things are and then be supported for her efforts by other caregivers. Mr. Adams expresses great fear at the thought of a nursing home, but his wife worries about how long she can manage him at home.

The next three chapters describe how the aging process influences cognitive abilities, personality styles, mental health, and intimacy and sexuality, as well as responses to major life events. They emphasize the wide variations in these processes with aging. The vastly different psychological states of Mr. Wallace, Mrs. Johnson, and Mr. Adams result in significant variations in the social aspects of their lives.

5 COGNITITVE CHANGES WITH AGING

This chapter discusses

- Research on cognitive functions with normal aging
- Measuring components of intelligence in older adults
- Individual and environmental factors that influence intelligence
- How we learn, and how aging affects the learning process
- Individual and environmental factors that affect how older people learn
- How aging affects the ability to retrieve information from secondary memory
- Cognitive retraining and other ways to help older adults improve their learning and memory skills

One of the most important and most studied aspects of aging is cognitive functioning; that is, intelligence, learning, and memory. These are critical to an individual's performance in every aspect of life, including work and leisure activities, social relationships, and productive roles. Older people who have problems in cognitive functioning will eventually experience stress in these other areas as well, along with an increasing incongruence between their competence levels and the demands of their environments. Researchers have attempted to determine whether normal aging is associated with a decline in the three areas of cognitive functioning and, if so, to what extent such a decline is due to age-related physiological changes. Much of the research on these issues has evolved from studies of cognitive development across the life span. Other studies have been undertaken in response to concerns expressed by older persons or their families that they cannot learn as easily as they used to, or that they have more trouble remembering names, dates, and places than previously.

INTELLIGENCE AND AGING

Intelligence is difficult both to define and to measure. Of all the elements of cognition, it is the least verifiable. We can only infer its existence and can only indirectly measure individual levels. **Intelligence** is generally defined as the "theoretical limit of an individual's performance" (Jones, 1959, p. 700). The limit is determined by biological and genetic factors; however, the ability to achieve the limit is influenced by environmental opportunities, such as challenging educational experiences, as well as by environmental constraints, such as the absence of books or other intellectual stimulation. Intelligence encompasses a range of abilities, including the ability to deal with symbols and abstractions, to acquire and comprehend new information, to adapt to new situations, and to understand and create new ideas. Alfred Binet, who developed the first test of intelligence, emphasized the operational aspects of intelligence: "to judge well, to comprehend well, to reason well, these are the essentials of intelligence" (Binet and Simon, 1905, p. 106). **Intelligence quotient** (or IQ) refers to an individual's relative abilities in some of these areas compared to others of the same chronological age.

Most theorists agree that intelligence is composed of many different components. Guilford's (1967, 1966) three-dimensional structure of intellect is perhaps the most complete model (see Figure 5.1). The three dimensions represent:

- the content of knowledge (e.g., figures, symbols, and words)
- the operations that an individual must perform with this knowledge (e.g., memorize, evaluate, and come up with single or multiple solutions)
- the products that are derived from these operations (e.g., relations, systems, and implications)

This model yields 120 separate components, but it is difficult to test. Nevertheless, a multidimensional structure of intelligence, although not identical to Guilford's, is assumed by most contemporary tests of intelligence. Most tests of intelligence today measure a subset of intellectual abilities known as **primary mental abilities,** which generally include:

- number or mathematical reasoning
- word fluency or the ability to use appropriate words to describe the world
- verbal meaning or vocabulary level
- inductive reasoning or the ability to generalize from specific facts to concepts
- spatial orientation or the ability to orient oneself in a three-dimensional space

A useful distinction is made between **fluid intelligence** and **crystallized intelligence** (Cattell,

---

MEASURES OF FLUID INTELLIGENCE

- spatial orientation
- abstract reasoning
- perceptual speed

MEASURES OF CRYSTALLIZED INTELLIGENCE

- verbal comprehension
- word association
- social judgment

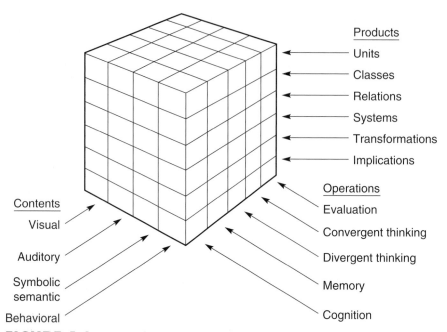

FIGURE 5.1   **A Three-Dimensional Model of Intellect**

SOURCE: J. P. Guilford, *The nature of human intelligence* (New York: McGraw-Hill, 1967) and J. P. Guilford, *Way beyond the IQ* (Buffalo, NY: Creative Education Foundation, 1977). Reprinted by permission of the author, McGraw-Hill, and the Creative Education Foundation.

1963; Horn, 1970, 1982; Horn and Donaldson, 1980). These two types of intelligence include some of the primary mental abilities described above. Fluid intelligence consists of skills that are biologically determined, independent of experience or learning, and may be similar to what is popularly called "native intelligence." It involves processing information that is not embedded in a context of existing information for the individual. It requires flexibility in thinking. Crystallized intelligence refers to the knowledge and abilities that the individual acquires through education and lifelong experiences. These two types of intelligence show different patterns with aging, as discussed in the next section.

There has been considerable controversy regarding intelligence in the later years (Schaie, 1996a). Many researchers have found significant differences between young and old persons on intelligence tests in cross-sectional studies, with older persons performing at a much lower level. Even when the same cohort is followed longitudinally, there is a decline in some intelligence tests that is independent of generational differences (Schaie and Hertzog, 1986). Others have concluded that aging is not really associated with a decline in intelligence. However, standardized IQ tests and the time pressures on test-takers may be more detrimental to older persons than to the young. Still others have pointed to methodological problems in conducting research in this area. Unfortunately, these mixed research findings have served to perpetuate the stereotype that older people are less intelligent than the young.

Many older persons are concerned that their intelligence has declined. This concern may loom so large for them that merely taking part in a study intended to "test their intelligence" may provoke sufficient anxiety to affect their test performance. Such anxieties may also influence the older person's daily functioning. Older people who are told by friends, family, test-givers or society in general that they should not expect to perform as well on intellectual tasks because aging causes a decline in intelligence may, in fact, come to perform more poorly.

The most widely used measure of adult intelligence is the Wechsler Adult Intelligence Scale (WAIS). It consists of 11 subtests, 6 of which are described as Verbal Scales (which measure, to some extent, crystallized intelligence), and 5 as Performance Scales (providing some measure of fluid intelligence). The performance tests on the WAIS are generally timed; the verbal tests are not.

Verbal scores are obtained by measuring an individual's ability to:

- define the meaning of words
- interpret proverbs
- explain similarities between words and concepts

In this way, accumulated knowledge and abstract reasoning can be tested.

Performance tests focus on an individual's ability to manipulate unfamiliar objects and words, often in unusual ways:

- tests of spatial relations
- abstract reasoning
- putting puzzles together to match a picture
- matching pictures with symbols or numbers
- arranging pictures in a particular pattern

Both psychomotor and perceptual skills are needed in performing these tasks.

A consistent pattern of scores on these two components of the WAIS has emerged in numerous studies; it has been labeled the **Classic Aging Pattern.** People beyond the age of 65 in some studies, and even earlier in others, perform significantly worse on Performance Scales (i.e., fluid intelligence), but their scores on Verbal Scales (i.e., crystallized intelligence) remain stable. This tendency to do worse on the performance tasks may reflect age-related changes in noncognitive functions, such

as sensory and perceptual abilities, and in psychomotor skills. As we have seen in Chapters 3 and 4, aging results in a slowing down of the neural pathways and of the visual and auditory functions. This slower reaction time, and the delay in receiving and transmitting messages through the sense organs, explains poorer performance on subtests requiring such capabilities. Some researchers therefore argue for the elimination of time constraints in performance tasks. Studies that have not measured speed of performance have still found significant age differences in these subtests (Salthouse, 1996). There appears to be a decline in performance-related aspects of intellectual function, independent of psychomotor or sensory factors. Speed of cognitive processing, such as the time to perform simple math problems, also declines with age and, in turn, slows an individual's responses on tests of performance.

Turning to verbal skills, the Classic Aging Pattern suggests that the ability to recall stored verbal information and to use abstract reasoning tends to remain constant throughout life. Declines, where they exist, typically do not to show up until advanced old age, or, in the case of cognitive impairment such as the dementias, they tend to begin early in the course of the disease.

When given logically inconsistent statements in cognitive studies, older subjects analyze these inconsistencies on the basis of their own knowledge, whereas younger adults tend to ignore the logic and attempt to reach conclusions quickly. Older subjects have also been found to reject simplified solutions and to prefer a complex analysis of the problem. This finding from laboratory-based research is supported by surveys of attitudes and beliefs among respondents of varying ages. Younger respondents are more willing to provide a direct response, whereas many older persons attempt to analyze the questions and give more contingency responses; that is, analyzing the question and stating that the answer could be x in one situation and y in another, rather than an all-encompassing response. For example, on a measure of environmental preference, the respondent may be asked, "How much privacy do you generally prefer?" A younger respondent is more likely to focus on the "general" situation, whereas the older respondent is more likely to consider situations both in which privacy is preferred and where it is not. It thus appears important to review older persons' responses to tests of problem solving and abstract reasoning from other perspectives beyond the traditional approaches that are grounded in cognitive theories developed with younger populations. Most tests of intelligence do not reward test-takers who provide the more analytic or complex responses typical of some older adults.

Problems in the Measurement of Cognitive Function

A major shortcoming of many studies of intelligence in aging is their use of cross-sectional research designs rather than longitudinal **approaches.** Age differences that are obtained in cross-sectional studies may be a reflection of cohort or generational differences rather than actual age changes. In particular, changes in educational systems and the development of television, computers, and high-speed travel have profoundly influenced the experiences of today's youth when compared with those of people who grew up in the early twentieth century. These historical factors may then have a greater effect on intelligence scores than age per se.

Subject attrition, or dropout from longitudinal studies of intelligence, is another problem. There is a pattern of *selective attrition,* whereby the people who drop out tend to be those who have performed less well, who perceive their performance to be poor, or whose health status and ambulatory abilities are worse than average. The people who remain in the study (i.e., "the survivors") performed better in the initial tests than did dropouts. This is consistent with our earlier observation that older persons often become unduly anxious about poor performance on tests of intellectual function. Hence, the results become biased in favor of the superior performers, indicating stability or improvement over time. They do not represent the wider population of older adults, whose performance might have shown a decline in intelligence (Schaie, 1996b).

Longitudinal Studies of Intelligence

Several major classic longitudinal studies have examined changes in intellectual function from youth to old age (Schaie, 1996a, 1983). The Iowa State Study tested a sample of college freshmen in 1919 and retested them in 1950 and 1961 (Cunningham and Owens, 1983; Owens, 1953, 1966). The researchers found general stability in intellectual functioning through middle age, with a peak in their late forties and fifties. Declines were observed after age 60 in many men, but the degree of change varied widely among the men and across variables. The New York State Study of Aging Twins began in 1946 and followed this group through 1973 (Kallmann and Sander, 1949). Average performance declined significantly on timed tests, but, as with the Iowa State Study, individual differences were pronounced. Among the individuals who were healthy enough to complete the final follow-up, performance on nonspeed intelligence tests remained stable until they reached their ninth decade. The greatest declines were observed in the test of hand-eye coordination and in fluid intelligence. Both studies had less than 25 percent of the original sample available at the final follow-up, which raises questions whether survivors are representative of their cohort in cognitive functioning.

Intellectual stimulation can help sustain higher level cognitive skills.

The Seattle Longitudinal Study began in 1956 and collected data on Thurstone's primary mental abilities every 7 years over 28 years (Schaie, 1996a). At each follow-up assessment, individuals who were still available from the original sample were retested, along with a new, randomly selected sample from the same population. The 1984 cycle included a test of some older people who had previously participated in a cognitive retraining program (Willis and Schaie, 1986). This study has provided the basis for the development of sequential research models, described in Chapter 1. Peak performance varied across tests and between men and women, ranging from age 32 on the test of Numbers for men and age 39 on the test of Reasoning for women, to age 53 for Educational Aptitude. A review of age changes for the 128 people who were observed over the entire course of this study reveals age decrements after age 60 on tests of word-fluency, space, and numbers that became progressively worse in later years. Tests of spatial abilities and inductive reasoning, both indicators of fluid intelligence, showed greater decline with age. However, other primary mental abilities, such as verbal meaning and reasoning, showed no declines until the mid-seventies. These results are consistent with cross-sectional results using the WAIS, as we have seen earlier. They are supported by other, shorter longitudinal studies that have found little change over three years (Zelinski, Gilewski, and Schaie, 1993). The findings suggest that the Classic Aging Pattern holds up in both cross-sectional and longitudinal studies, and that some performance aspects of intelligence may begin to deteriorate after age 60, although major changes are generally rare until the mid-seventies.

In all these studies, most of the significant declines occur in intellectual abilities that are less practiced. Schaie (1996b) concludes that the changes observed in the Seattle Longitudinal Study indicate a normative developmental transition from stability in general intelligence in the middle years, to a gradual decline that begins around age 60. Most people maintained their abilities in one or more areas well into their advanced years, as shown in Figure 5.2. However, Schaie found no

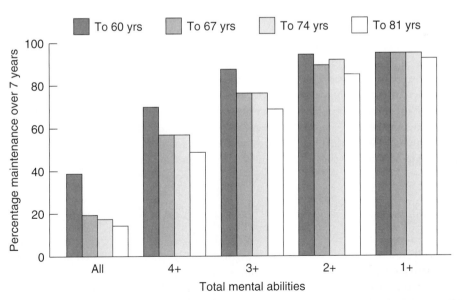

FIGURE 5.2 **Proportion of Individuals Who Maintain Scores on Multiple Abilities**
SOURCE: Schaie, K. W. The hazards of cognitive aging. *The Gerontologist,* 1989, 29, 484–493. Reprinted with permission.

SUMMARY OF AGE-RELATED CHANGES IN INTELLIGENCE

- Peak performance varies by test, usually between ages 30–55.
- Performance on timed tests declines.
- Performance on nontimed tests remains stable until the eighties.
- Rarely do people decline in all five PMATs.

- High scorers continue to do well even among oldest-old.
- Declines in tests of fluid intelligence begin earlier than in crystallized intelligence ("Classic Aging Pattern").

---

linear decline in all five primary mental abilities for any participants as old as age 88 (Schaie, 1989, 1996a, 1996b).

The Duke Longitudinal Studies, described in Chapter 1, assessed intelligence and memory, in addition to many health variables. This series of three longitudinal samples, each measured several times, provides useful information about the relationship between intellectual function and health status, especially cardiovascular disease (Palmore, 1974, 1985; Siegler, 1983). The findings regarding age changes generally are consistent with the other longitudinal studies described in this section. That is, declines in cognitive function were not observed until individuals reached their seventies. Scores on performance tests were found to decline earlier than scores on verbal measures. Another longitudinal study in Sweden examined cognitive functioning among the oldest-old (ages 84 to 90 in this study). A two-year follow-up revealed that participants who had scored high on tests of memory, attention, orientation, and ability to follow instructions continued to perform well at follow-up. However, average performance declined slightly on all these tests (Johansson, Zarit, and Berg, 1992).

FACTORS THAT MAY INFLUENCE INTELLIGENCE IN ADULTHOOD

Researchers who have compared intelligence test scores of older and younger persons found wide variations in scores of both groups. Older test-takers generally have obtained poorer scores, but age

per se is only one factor in explaining intellectual functioning.

As mentioned earlier, there is also a biological factor in intelligence, such that some people are innately more intelligent than others. However, it is difficult to determine the relative influence of biological factors, because it is impossible to measure the specific mechanisms of the brain that account for intelligence. Structural changes in the brain and in neural pathways occur with aging, as seen in Chapter 3. These changes, however, are generally diffuse and not focused in a particular region of the brain. It is therefore impossible to determine what specific changes in the brain and its pathways may account for the age-related deterioration that is observed.

Other variables that have been examined are educational attainment, involvement in complex versus mechanistic work, cardiovascular disease, hypertension, and sensory deficits. Some studies have found cohort differences on tests of intelligence, with newer cohorts of older people performing better than previous cohorts who took the same test at about the same age. These differences emerge on tests of crystallized *and* fluid intelligence (represented by verbal meaning and inductive reasoning tests), even when comparing adult children and their parents (Schaie et al., 1992; Schaie and Willis, 1995). The advantage of newer cohorts has been attributed to higher educational attainment. Therefore, it is important to control statistically for educational differences when analyzing the relationship between age and intelligence. Significant positive effects of education have been found on

INTELLECTUALLY ACTIVE ELDERS

Increasingly, more older adults continue to participate in intellectually challenging jobs well beyond their sixties and seventies. For example, college campuses are full of retired faculty who retain emeritus status and who continue to teach or conduct research well into their eighties. The recently appointed Poet Laureate of the United States is Stanley Kunitz, age 95. Another active octogenarian is Dr. Hilary Koprowski, whose research in 1948 led to the widespread adoption of a live vaccine to immunize children against polio. Koprowski, now aged 83, continues to conduct medical research at Thomas Jefferson University in Philadelphia. Meanwhile, James Wiggins, age 95, has been editor of a weekly newspaper in Ellsworth, Maine, since 1922, and comes to work every day.

all tests of cognitive function when comparing healthy independent adults aged 70 to 79 with different educational levels. In particular, participants with the highest level of education (12+ years) did three times better on a test of abstract thinking than did people with seven or fewer years of education (Inouye et al., 1993).

Occupational level, which is generally correlated with educational level, also influences intelligence test scores. Older people who still use their cognitive abilities in jobs or activities that require thinking and problem-solving (such as Mr. Wallace in the introductory vignette) show less decline on cognitive tests than those who do not use these skills. This is because most of the observed declines in intellectual abilities occur in highly challenging, complex tasks. In addition, people whose occupations demand more verbal skills (e.g., lawyers and teachers) may continue to perform very well on these apects of intelligence tests. Those who use more abstract and fluid skills in their occupations (e.g., architects and engineers) are more likely to do well on the performance tests of the WAIS, even into their seventies and eighties. In general, older people who do not participate in any intellectual pursuits perform worse on intelligence tests than do their peers who are "cognitively engaged" (Dutta, 1992; Baltes, 1993; Gold et al., 1995; Inouye et al., 1993).

The effects of declining physical health and sensory losses on intelligence become more severe in the later years, and these factors may displace any positive influence due to education and occupation for people who are 75 years and older. Several studies have identified poorer performance on intelligence tests by older people in poor health.

Older adults with cardiovascular problems tend to do worse on intelligence tests than those without such disorders, particularly in tests that demand psychomotor speed (Hultsch, Hammer, and Small, 1993). In the Seattle Longitudinal Study, participants with cardiovascular disease declined at younger ages on all tests of mental abilities than did people with no disease (Gruber-Baldini, 1991). Older people with severe or uncontrolled hypertension performed worse on these tests than did those with no hypertension. Interestingly, however, older adults with borderline hypertension showed the least decline. Mild elevations of blood pressure

HEALTH IMPAIRMENTS THAT AFFECT PERFORMANCE

- cardiovascular disease
- hypertension
- nutritional deficits
- depression
- hearing loss
- terminal drop

in older persons may be useful for maintaining sufficient blood circulation to the brain (Sands and Meredith, 1992).

Nutritional deficits may also impair an older person's cognitive functioning. One study of community dwelling, healthy older persons (ages 66 to 90) examined their performance on multiple tests of cognitive functioning and nutritional status longitudinally. Older people with low intake of vitamins E, A, B_6, and B_{12} at baseline performed worse on visuospatial and abstraction tasks 6 years later; those who used vitamin supplements did better (Larue et al., 1997). These findings reinforce the results of research on the impact of nutritional deficiencies on performance, described in Chapter 4.

Depression, or even mild dysphoria (i.e., feeling "blue" or "down in the dumps," but not clinically depressed), is a psychological variable that can influence cognitive function. Indeed, in a large study of people aged 50 to 93 that controlled for the effects of age, education, and occupation, older people with worse scores on a measure of depression had significantly lower scores on tests of both crystallized and fluid intelligence (Rabbitt et al., 1995). Given the prevalence of depression in the older population, it is important to consider this as a cause of poorer cognitive performance rather than aging per se.

As noted in Chapter 3, hearing loss is common in older persons, especially moderate levels of loss that affect their ability to comprehend speech. Visual deficits become more severe in advanced old age. Poorer performance by some test-takers who are very old may be due primarily to these sensory losses, not to a central cognitive decline. Older persons with hearing or vision loss do especially poorly on tests of verbal meaning and spatial relations (Lindenberger and Baltes, 1994).

An apparent and rapid decline in cognitive function within five years of death is another physical health factor that appears to be related to intelligence test scores. This phenomenon is known as the *terminal drop* or **terminal decline hypothesis,** first tested by Kleemeier (1962). In longitudinal studies of intelligence, older subjects whose test scores are in the lower range to start with, and who

decline more sharply, have been found to die sooner than good performers. This has been observed on many different tests, especially in vocabulary and word fluency (Berg, 1996; Cooney, Schaie, and Willis, 1988). This suggests that time since birth (i.e., age) is not as significant in intellectual decline as is proximity to death.

Finally, anxiety may negatively affect older people's intelligence test scores. As shown in the following section, older people in laboratory tests of learning and memory are more likely than the young to express high test anxiety and cautiousness in responding. These same reactions may occur in older people taking intelligence tests, especially if they think that the test really measures how "intelligent" they are. Anxieties about cognitive decline and concerns about becoming cognitively impaired may make older people even more cautious, and hence result in poorer performance on intelligence tests.

The Process of Learning and Memory

Learning and *memory* are two cognitive processes that must be considered together. That is, learning is assumed to occurr when an individual is able to retrieve information accurately from his or her memory store. Conversely, if an individual cannot retrieve information from memory, it is presumed that learning has not adequately taken place. Thus, *learning* is the process by which new information (verbal or nonverbal) or skills are encoded, or put into one's memory. The specific parts of the brain involved in this process are the hippocampus, which first receives and processess new stimuli, and the cerebral cortex, where memories are stored. Some of the most exciting research in this field is focused on the process of neuronal development as learning occurs. *Memory* is the process of retrieving or recalling the information stored in the brain when needed. Memory also refers to a part of the brain that retains what has been learned throughout a person's lifetime. Researchers have attempted to distinguish three separate types of

---

RETRIEVING OLD MEMORIES

A person may have learned many years ago how to ride a bicycle. If this skill has been encoded well through practice, the person can retrieve it many years later from his or her memory store, even in he or she has not ridden a bicycle in years.

---

memory: sensory, primary or short-term, and secondary or long-term.

Sensory memory, as its name implies, is the first step in receiving information through the sense organs and passing it on to primary or secondary memory. It is stored for only a few tenths of a second, although there is some evidence that it lasts longer in older persons because of slower reaction times of the senses. Sensory memory has been further subdivided into **iconic** (or visual) and **echoic** (or auditory) **memory.** Examples of iconic memory are:

- words or letters that we see
- faces of people with whom we have contact
- landscapes that we experience through our eyes

Of course, words can be received through echoic memory as well, such as when we hear others say a specific word, or when we repeat words aloud to ourselves. A landscape can also enter our sensory memory through our ears (e.g., the sound of the ocean), our skin (e.g., the feel of a cold spray from the ocean), and our nose (e.g., the smell of salt water). To the extent that we focus on or rehearse information that we receive from our sense organs, it is more likely to be passed into our primary and secondary memories.

Despite significant changes in the visual system with aging (as described in Chapter 3), early studies of iconic memory have found only small age differences in the ability to identify stimuli presented briefly. When old and young individuals were tested with seven-letter strings, the former were slower by a factor of 1.3, a rate similar to that found with single letters (Cerella, Poon, and Fozard, 1982). Such modest declines in iconic memory would not be ex-

pected to influence observed decrements in secondary or long-term memory. However, some researchers have suggested that even small declines in sensory memory may result in a large decline in long-term memory (Craik and Jennings, 1994). Although research on iconic memory is limited, there has been even less with echoic memory and less still that has compared older persons with younger. We have all experienced the long-term storage of memories gained through touch, taste, or smell. For example, the odor of freshly baked bread evokes memories of early childhood in many older people. However, these sensory memories are more difficult to test. As a result, very little is known about any changes experienced with these other modes of sensory memory.

Primary memory is a temporary stage of holding and organizing information, and does not necessarily refer to a storage area in the brain. Despite its temporary nature, primary memory is critical for our ability to process new information. We all experience situations where we hear or read a bit of information such as a phone number or someone's name, use that name or number immediately, then forget it. In fact, most adults can recall seven, plus or minus two, pieces of information (e.g., digits, letters, or words) for 60 seconds or less. It is not surprising, therefore, that local phone numbers in most countries are seven digits or less! In order to retain this information in our permanent memory store (**secondary memory**), it must be rehearsed or "processed" actively. This is why primary memory has been described as a form of "working memory" that decides what information should be attended to or ignored, which is most important, and how best to store it. If we are distracted while trying to retain the information for the 60 seconds that it can last in short-term memory, we immediately

AIDS TO PRIMARY MEMORY

The popularity of phones with digital memory for storing multiple phone numbers attests to the problem that people of all ages have with primary memory. Rather than looking up important phone numbers or attempting to memorize them, we can store these in the phone and retrieve them with the push of one or two buttons. Another technological development that can help reduce the information we must store in our minds is the Palm Pilot or other handheld computers. These are useful for storing phone numbers, addresses, memos and even reminders to oneself. As older adults become more comfortable with these new technologies, they will experience less stress about retaining newly acquired information.

forget it, even if it consists of only two or three bits of information. This happens because the rehearsal of such material is interrupted by the reception of newer information in our sensory memory. Most studies of primary memory have found minimal age differences in its storage capacity, which may be due to slower reaction time in older persons. It may also be that the encoding process which takes place in primary memory requires some organization or elaboration of the information received. Older persons are less likely than young people to process new information in this manner. Indeed, some argue that aging leads to a decline in "attentional resources," or mental energy, to organize and elaborate newly acquired information in order to retain it in secondary memory (Craik, 1994; Craik and Jennings, 1994; Salthouse and Babcock, 1991; Smith, 1996).

True learning implies that the material we acquire through our sensory and primary memories has been stored in "secondary memory." Thus, for example, looking up a telephone number and immediately dialing it does not guarantee that the number will be learned. In fact, only with considerable rehearsal can information from primary memory be passed into secondary memory. This is the part of the memory store in which everything we have learned throughout our lives is kept; unlike primary memory, it has an unlimited capacity.

Older people consistently recall less information than younger people in paired associate tests with retention intervals as brief as one hour or as long as eight months. Age differences in secondary memory appear to be more pronounced than in sensory or primary memory and are often frustrating to older people and their families. Indeed, middle-aged and older people are often concerned that they cannot remember and retrieve information from secondary memory (Verhaeghen, Geraerts, and Marcoen, 2000). This perception that one has poor memory can seriously harm older people's self-concept, as well as their performance on many tasks, and may even result in depression. Such concern, growing out of a fear of dementia, is generally out of proportion to the actual level of decline. Older individuals can benefit significantly from methods to help organize their learning, such as imagery and the use of mnemonics. Examples of such techniques to improve learning and memory are discussed later in this chapter.

THE INFORMATION PROCESSING MODEL

The **information processing model** of memory is presented in Fig. 5.3. This is a conceptual model; that is, it provides a framework for understanding how the processes of learning and memory take place. It is not necessarily what goes on in the neural pathways between the sense organs and the secondary memory store. Having described each of the components in this model, let us review the steps involved in processing some information that we want to retain. One example is the experience of learning new names at a social gathering. Sensory memory aids in hearing the name spoken, preferably several times by other people, and seeing the face that is associated with that name. Pri-

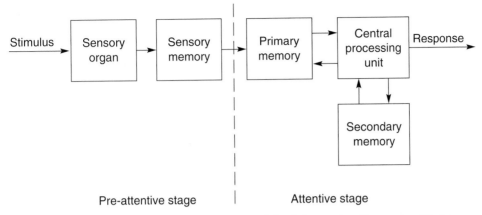

FIGURE 5.3   Schematic Representation of the Information Processing Model

mary memory is used to store that information temporarily, so that a person can speak to others and address them by name (an excellent method of rehearsing this information), or manipulate the information in order to pass it on to secondary memory. This may include repeating the name several times to oneself, trying to isolate some aspect of the person's physical features and relating it to the name, and associating the name with other people one has known in the past who have similar names. In the last type of mental manipulation, information from secondary memory (i.e., names of other people) is linked with the new information. This is a useful method because the material in secondary memory is permanent, and associating the new information with well-learned information aids in its storage and subsequent recall.

During any stage of this cognitive processing, the newly obtained information can be lost. This may occur if the sensory memory is flooded with similar information; in this case, if a person is being introduced to multiple new names and faces at a party, it is almost impossible to distinguish the names or to associate each name with a face. Information may also be lost during the primary memory stage. In our example, if a person is trying to use the newly heard name and is distracted by other names and faces, or receives unrelated but relevant information (e.g., a telephone call) while rehearsing

the new name, the name has not been sufficiently processed to pass into secondary memory.

The learning process may also be disrupted because of inability to retrieve information efficiently from secondary memory. For example, a person may associate the newly heard name with someone known in the past; if he or she has difficulty retrieving the stored name from secondary memory, however, this may be so frustrating as to redirect the individual's attention from the new name to the old name. How often have you ignored everything around you to concentrate on remembering a name that is "on the tip of the tongue" (i.e., in secondary memory) but not easily retrievable? As noted above, aging appears to reduce the efficiency of *processing* information in sensory and primary memory, as well as retrieval from secondary memory (i.e., working memory). It does *not* influence the storage capacity of primary or secondary memories. That is, contrary to popular opinion, these memory stores are not physical spaces that become overloaded with information as we age.

FACTORS THAT AFFECT LEARNING IN OLD AGE

One problem with assessing learning ability is that it is not possible to measure the process that occurs in the brain while an individual is acquiring new information. Instead, we must rely on an individual's performance on tests that presumably measure what was learned. This may be particularly disadvantageous to older persons, whose performance on a test of learning may be poor because of inadequate or inappropriate conditions for expressing what was learned (Botwinick, 1984). For example, an older person may in fact have learned many new concepts in reading a passage from a novel, but not necessarily the specific concepts that are called for on a test of learning. Certain physical conditions may affect performance and thus lead to underestimates of what the older person has actually learned. These include:

- lighting levels
- size of font
- tone and loudness of the test-giver's voice in an oral exam
- time constraints placed on the test-taker

The learning environment can be improved, however. Some ways to do this include:

- glare-free and direct lighting
- lettering of good quality
- larger fonts
- color contrast
- a comfortable test-taking situation with minimal background noise
- a relaxed and articulate test-giver

Time constraints are particularly detrimental to older people. Although the ability to encode new information quickly is a sign of learning ability, it is difficult to measure. Instead, response time is generally measured. As we have already seen, psychomotor and sensory slowing with age has a significant impact on the older person's response speed. One of the first researchers to test the effect of these conditions on learning was Canestrari (1963), who used a common test of learning, the paired associates task (i.e., linking two unrelated words, letters, digits, or symbols, such as *cat* and *82*, and asking subjects to respond with the sec-

Computers provide opportunities for active learning.

ond when the first is mentioned). He presented the paired associates at varying rates, or allowed individuals to pace the task by controlling the visual apparatus themselves. In comparing people aged 60 to 69 with those aged 17 to 35, he found striking differences between old and young individuals' performance when the task was paced fast, fewer differences in moderate pacing, and the fewest differences in self-paced conditions. Young persons did well in all conditions, but older persons in this study benefited the most from self-pacing. Decline in perceptual speed, which can be measured separately from memory skills per se, may be a major reason why older people do worse on memory tests. Research by Salthouse (1993, 1994a, 1996) has shown that perceptual speed accounts for a significant part of the observed age-related variance in memory performance. Even when older research subjects are given more time to complete tests of memory, their perceptual speed still plays a significant role in their performance.

Research on paired associates tasks has demonstrated that older persons make more *errors of omission* than *errors of commission*. That is, older persons are more likely not to give an answer than to guess and risk being wrong. This phenomenon was first recognized in middle-aged and older adults in tests of psychomotor functioning. The older the respondent, the more likely he or she was to work for accuracy at the expense of speed. This occurs even when the older learner is encouraged to guess and is told that it is acceptable to give wrong answers (i.e., commission errors). Conditions of uncertainty and high risk are particularly difficult for older persons; here they are far more cautious than the young. Low-risk situations elicit less caution from older adults and greater willingness to give responses in a learning task. The aging process may create an increased need to review multiple aspects of a problem, probably because of past experiences with similar dilemmas. Errors of omission may be reduced somewhat by giving rewards for both right and wrong answers.

Verbal ability and educational level are important factors in learning verbal information. Studies that entail learning prose passages show age deficits among those with average vocabulary abilities and minimal or no college education. In contrast, older persons with high verbal ability and a college education perform as well as younger subjects in such experiments. This may be due to greater practice and facility with such tasks on the part of more educated persons and those with good vocabulary skills. It may also reflect differences in the ability to organize new information, a skill that is honed through years of education and one that assists in the learning of large quantities of new material (Ratner et al., 1987).

Similarly, older people who have developed manual skills in a particular area have been found to perform just as well on perceptual-motor tests as do younger persons with skills. Two classic studies examined choice reaction time, tapping rate,

and accuracy by testing people aged 19 to 72 who varied in typing speed (Salthouse, 1984). These well-designed experiments measured age differences in real-life studies where professional typists were asked to type prose passages as well as random letter series. While the older typists had more years of relevant employment, there were no differences between old and young in the *recency* of this experience (i.e., older typists were just as likely to be using their skills currently). This research demonstrated that typing time remains stable with increasing age, even though choice reaction time increases and tapping rate declines. These findings are consistent with other studies of the basic components of perceptual-motor abilities (McDowd and Craik, 1988).

Such stability in performing familiar perceptual-motor tasks may also occur because the accomplished performer of a specific task makes more efficient moves in completing a task than does a less skilled person. Such differences are evident in many areas demanding skill, from typing and driving to playing a musical instrument or operating a lathe. Therefore, aging workers can overcome the effects of slower psychomotor speed and declines in learning skills by their greater experience in most occupations (Salthouse, 1993, 1994a).

The conditions under which learning takes place affect older persons more than the young, just as test conditions are more critical. Older persons respond differently to varied testing situations; people tested under challenging conditions ("this is a test of your intelligence") are likely to do worse than those in supportive conditions ("the researcher needs your help"). Positive feedback appears to be a valuable tool for eliciting responses from older adults in both learning and test situations.

Pacing information presents it at a rate suitable to the older learner and gives him or her opportunities to practice the new information (e.g., writing down or spelling aloud newly learned words). Another condition that supports learning is the presentation of familiar and relevant material compared to material perceived by the older learner to be unimportant. Older people do worse in recalling recently acquired information than do younger people when the new information is unfamiliar or confusing. Age differences also emerge when the material to be learned is low in meaning and personal significance to the learner. Laboratory studies of cognitive functioning often seem artificial and meaningless to older people who are unaccustomed to such research methods, and even more so to those with little academic experience. Many people will complain that such tests are trivial, nonsense, or that these tasks have no connection to the "real world." Indeed, it may appear odd to anyone to be learning meaningless words and symbols in a lab study. But for those older people who are unfamiliar with test-taking situations, it may appear particularly foolish and not worth the effort required. This may also serve a useful ego-defensive function for people who feel uncomfortable or threatened by a test-taking situation. It is generally easier for people to blame the environment or the test situation for their poor performance than to accept it as a sign of a decline in their intelligence or their ability to learn.

Spatial memory, that is, the ability to recall where objects are in relationship to each other in space (e.g., when finding one's way around a community or using a map), also appears to decline with aging. It is unclear, however, if older people do worse than the young because they have difficulty encoding and processing the information, or if the problem is in retrieval. It appears that there is an age-related decline in encoding ability for spatial information. Spatial recall was tested in one study following the presentation of a two-dimensional black-and-white map versus a colored map or a three-dimensional model. Older subjects in this study recalled fewer items than the young did under the condition of no visual cues, but no age differences were found when color or 3-D representations were used (Sharps and Gollin, 1988). Similarly, older people have more difficulty than younger persons in reading maps that are misaligned relative to the user. For example, when older people stand in front of a "You are here" map that is aligned 180° away from themselves,

they take up to 50 percent more time and make 30 percent more errors than younger persons in the same condition. However, when the map is aligned directly with the user, no age differences are observed. This may be attributable to increased problems with mental rotation of external images and with perspective-taking as we age (Aubrey and Dobbs, 1990; Aubrey, Li, and Dobbs, 1994).

AGE-RELATED CHANGES IN MEMORY

As we have seen, learning involves encoding information and storing it into secondary or long-term memory, so that it can be retrieved and used later. Studies of this process have focused on two types of retrieval: recall and recognition. **Recall** is the process of searching through the vast store of information in secondary memory, perhaps with a cue or a specific, orienting question. **Recognition** requires less search. The information in secondary memory must be matched with the stimulus information in the environment. Recall is demanded in essay exams, recognition in multiple-choice tests.

Not surprisingly, most researchers have found age-related deficiencies in recall, but few differences in recognition (Smith, 1996). Recall tasks have been further divided into **free recall** and **cued recall** situations. In the former, no aids or hints are provided for retrieving information from secondary memory. In the latter case, the individual is given some information to aid in the search (e.g., category labels and first letter of a word). Older people tend to do much worse than the young in tests of free recall, but are aided significantly by cueing. In particular, use of category labels (semantic cues) at the learning stage has been found to be more helpful to older persons than the use of structural cues—for example, giving the respondent the first letter of a word to be recalled (Smith, 1996). However, cued recall tests are not as helpful as recognition tests for older learners.

Of considerable controversy in aging and memory function is the question of whether older people have better recall of events that occurred in

---

EXAMPLES OF RETRIEVAL

Recall

    Free recall "List the capitals of each state." "Describe how to repair a bicycle tire."

    Cued recall "The capital of New York begins with the letter 'A'; what is it?"

Recognition "Which of these three cities is the capital of New York?"

---

the distant past than recent situations. Many events are firmly embedded in secondary memory because they are unique or so important that subsequent experiences do not interfere with the ability to recall them. The birth of a child, one's wedding ceremony, or the death of a parent, spouse, or sibling are events that most people can recall in detail 40 to 50 years later. This may be because the situation had great private significance or—in the case of world events, such as the bombing of Hiroshima or President Kennedy's assassination—had a profound impact on world history. Some distant events may be better recalled because they have greater personal relevance for the individual's social development than recent experiences, or because they have been rehearsed or thought about more. Another possibility is that cues that helped the older person recall events in the past are less effective with recalling recent occasions because of "cue-overload." That is, the same cues that were once helpful in remembering certain information are also used to recall many recent events. But the cues are so strongly associated with one's earlier life experiences that the newer information becomes more difficult to retrieve. For example, older people may have difficulty memorizing new phone numbers because the cues that helped them recall phone numbers in the past may be so closely associated with previous ones that they confuse recent phone numbers with old ones.

One problem in determining whether recall of distant situations is really better than recall of recent events is the difficulty in validating an older person's memories. In many cases, there are no sources that can be checked to determine the ac-

curacy of such recollections. We can all identify with this process of asking an old friend or family member, "Do you remember the time when . . . ?" If others have no recollection of the event, it may make us wonder if the situation really took place, or it may mean that the event was so obscure that it made no impact on other people. Hence, such memories are difficult to measure accurately.

Several theories have been offered to explain *why* older people may have problems with retrieving information from secondary memory. One explanation is that not using the information results in its loss (the **disuse theory**). This theory suggests that information can fade away or decay unless it is exercised, as in the adage, "Use it or lose it." However, this explanation fails to account for the many facts that are deeply embedded in a person's memory store and that can be retrieved even after years of disuse.

A more widely accepted explanation is that new information interferes with the material that has been stored over a period of many years. As we have noted earlier, interference is a problem in the learning or encoding stage. When the older person is distracted while trying to learn new information, this information does not become stored in memory. Poor retrieval may be due to a combination of such distraction during the learning stage and interference by similar or new information with the material being searched in the retrieval stage. Although researchers in this area have not conclusively agreed on any of these explanations, the **interference theory** appears to hold more promise than others for explaining observed problems with retrieval.

CONTINUING EDUCATION

Continuing education is an excellent way to maintain intellectual skills in old age. Elderhostel is a popular international program that offers older adults learning options based on college campuses and through tours to educational and historic sites. "Summer College for Seniors" is a program offered by Shoreline Community College in Seattle. Each summer, more than 100 elders participate in week-long college classes on topics as wide-ranging as constitutional law and classical music.

College faculty who teach these older students enjoy the perspectives they bring, and praise their maturity both intellectually and emotionally. As one 65-year-old Summer College student noted, "The people here may be gray on top but they're not dull between the ears." Another participant, age 75, added, "I think, as a senior, mental stimulation is as important as physical exercise."

Seattle Times, July 25, 2000, p. B1. (F. Vinluan, staff reporter).

IMPROVING COGNITIVE ABILITIES IN OLD AGE

Cognitive Retraining

In the Seattle Longitudinal Study described earlier in this chapter, the researchers tested the effects of **cognitive retraining**—teaching research participants how to use various techniques to keep their minds active and maintain good memory skills. This cognitive retraining was based on the premise of maximizing one's remaining potential, a widely accepted concept in physical aging but only recently applied to cognitive aging. Intellectual activities that involve problem-solving and creativity, such as Scrabble and crossword puzzles, are described by Schaie and colleagues (Schaie and Hertzog, 1986; Willis and Nesselroade, 1990; Willis and Schaie, 1988, 1986) as effective ways for older people to maximize their intellectual abilities. Cognitive performance improved in about 65 percent of participants, and 40 percent who had declined in the preceding 14 years showed a return to their predecline levels. Cognitive retraining was most effective when it focused on the specific primary mental abilities that each elder had lost. However, the oldest participants benefited least from training, even with booster sessions to assist in the retraining.

There has been considerable experimentation with techniques for improving memory. Some of the most exciting research focuses on developing drugs that enhance the chemical messengers in neu-

rons or improve the function of neural receptors. Within the next few years there may be some approved memory-enhancing drugs for older adults. **Ginkgo biloba,** a natural extract derived from leaves of the maidenhair tree, has received attention because it seems to improve memory by improving circulation in the brain. Systematic research on the effects of ginkgo biloba for mild memory loss, as well as for people with Alzheimer's disease, has recently begun (Van Dongen et al., 2000). Vitamin E is an antioxidant (described in Chapter 3) that may help enhance memory by reducing oxidative damage resulting from normal aging. No long-term human studies are yet available to support these claims for the benefits of vitamin E or other possible supplements such as lecithin, vitamin B_{12}, and folic acid.

It is also important to recognize that therapeutic doses of these and other supplements (i.e., levels that are high enough to show improved memory function) may be high enough to cause harmful side effects such as internal bleeding. Other researchers have examined practical methods such as cognitive aids. Although useful at any age, cognitive aids may be particularly helpful for an older person who is experiencing increased problems with real-world cognitive abilities, such as recalling names, words, phone numbers, and daily chores. Older persons are more likely to use external aids such as notes and lists than they are to use cognitive aids. That is, they are more likely to reduce environmental press than to enhance their competence in learning as a means of improving P–E congruence. Older adults who are most concerned about declining memory are more likely to use external and cognitive aids as a way of coping with the problem. This is particularly true for elders with a strong internal locus of control—that is, a belief that they have control over their well-being rather than attributing their problems to external forces (Verhaeghen et al., 2000).

Memory Mediators

Most memory improvement techniques are based on the concept of mediators, that is, the use of visual and verbal links between information to be encoded and information that is already in secondary memory. Mediators may be visual (e.g., the method of locations) or verbal (i.e., the use of mnemonics). **Visual mediators**—the method of locations (or loci)—are useful for learning a list of new words, names, or concepts. Each word is associated with a specific location in a familiar environment. For example, the individual is instructed to "walk through" his or her own home mentally. As the person walks through the rooms in succession, each item on the list is associated with a particular space along the way. Older persons using this technique have been found to recall more words on a list than when they use no mediators. One advantage of the method of loci is that learners can visualize the new information within a familiar setting, and can decide for themselves what new concept should be linked with what specific part of the environment. Imaging is a useful technique in everyday recall situations as well. For example, an older person can remember what he or she needs to buy at the grocery story by visualizing using these items while preparing dinner (Camp, 1988).

Another way of organizing material to be learned and to ensure its storage in secondary memory is to use **mnemonics,** or verbal riddles, rhymes, and codes associated with the new information. Many teachers use such rhymes to teach their students multiplication, spelling (e.g., "*i* before *e* except after *c*"), and the calendar ("30 days

hath September, April, June, and November/all the rest have 31, except February alone, and that has 28 days clear/except every leap year"). Many other mnemonics are acquired through experience as well as our own efforts to devise ways to learn a new concept (e.g., making up a word to remember the three components of cognition: intelligence, learning, memory might become "IntLeMe"). These can assist older people, particularly the young-old, to learn more efficiently, especially if the mnemonics are specific to the memory task at hand (Verhaeghen, Marcoen, and Goossens, 1992). Older people with mild or moderate dementia can also benefit from visual methods of recall (e.g., method of loci), but less from list-making (Yesavage, Sheikh, Friedman, and Tanke, 1990). Whatever method is used, however, it is important to train the older person in the use of a specific mnemonic and to provide easy strategies to help the person apply these techniques to everyday learning events. In one study, researchers provided half the sample with a "memory handbook" and 30 minutes of practical instruction; the other half were given just a pamphlet that gave examples of useful mnemonics (but no face-to-face instruction in their use). The former group demonstrated significant improvements in two subsequent memory tests; the pamphlet group did not (Andrewes, Kinsella, and Murphy, 1996).

Other mediators to aid memory include using the new word or concept in a sentence, associating the digits in a phone number with symbols or putting them into a mathematical formula (e.g., "the first digit is 4, the second and third are multiplied to produce the first"), placing the information into categories, using multiple sensory memories, and even combining sensory with motor function. In this last technique, one may write the word (iconic memory), repeat it aloud to oneself (echoic memory), or "feel" the letters or digits by outlining them with one's hand. Unfortunately, many older persons do not practice the use of newly learned memory techniques. They may not be motivated to use the techniques, which often seem awkward, or they may forget and need to be reminded. Perhaps the major problem is that these are unfamiliar

---

A MEMORY EXERCISE

Use the method of loci to help you remember *seven* items that you need to buy at the grocery store. Go to the store without a list, but imagine yourself walking through the kitchen at home after your trip to the grocery store, placing each of the seven items in a specific location.

---

approaches to the current generation of older people. As future cohorts become more practiced in these memory techniques through their educational experiences, the use of such strategies in old age should increase.

The most important aspect of memory enhancement may be the ability to relax and to avoid feeling anxious or stressed during the learning stage. As noted earlier, many older people become overly concerned about occasional memory lapses, viewing them as a sign of deterioration and possible onset of senile dementia. Thus, a young person may be annoyed when a familiar name is forgotten, but will probably not interpret the memory lapse as loss of cognitive function, as an older person is likely to do. Unfortunately, society reinforces this belief. How often are we told that we are "getting old" when we forget a trivial matter? How often do adult children become concerned that their parent sometimes forgets to turn off the stove, when in fact they may frequently do this themselves?

In addition to mediators, simple devices or **external aids** are often used by older people to keep track of the time or dates, or to remember to turn the stove on or off. Simple methods such as list-making can significantly improve an older person's recall and recognition memory, even if the list is not used subsequently. A list that is organized by topic or type of item (e.g., a chronological "to-do" list or a grocery list that groups produce, meats, dry-goods together) also has been found to aid older people's memory significantly. However, older adults with higher educational attainment and better vocabulary skills benefit even more from list-making methods (Burack and Lackman, 1996). Older people can develop the habit of associating medication regimens with specific activities of daily living, such as using marked pill boxes and taking the first pill in the morning before their daily shower, or just before or after breakfast, taking the second pill with lunch or before their noon-time walk, and so on. These behaviors need to be associated with activities that occur every day at a particular time, in order that the pill-taking becomes linked with that routine. Charts listing an individual's daily or weekly routine can be posted throughout the house. Alarm clocks and kitchen timers also can be placed near an older person while the oven or stove is in operation. This will help in remembering that the appliance is on without the person's needing to stay in the kitchen. With the increased availability of home computers, daily activities and prescription reminders could be programmed into an older person's computer. A fire alarm or smoke detector is essential for every older person's home, preferably one for every floor or wing of the house. Finally, for older people who have serious memory problems and a tendency to get lost while walking outdoors, a bracelet or necklace imprinted with the person's name, address, phone number, and relevant medical information can be a lifesaver.

WISDOM AND CREATIVITY

Wisdom and creativity are more difficult to define and measure. Most people have an image of what it means to be wise or creative, but it is impossible to quantify an individual's level of wisdom or creativity. It has been suggested that *wisdom* requires the cognitive development and mastery over a person's emotions that come with age (Butler and Gleason, 1985). Wisdom is a combination of experience, introspection, reflection, intuition, and

In many cultures, old age is viewed as a time of wisdom.

empathy; these are qualities that are honed over many years and that can be integrated in people's interactions with their environments. Thus, younger people may have any one of these skills individually, but their integration requires more maturity. Wisdom is achieved by transcending the limitations of basic needs such as health, income, and housing. The individual must have continued opportunities for growth and creativity in order to develop wisdom (Ardelt, 1997; Orwoll and Achenbaum, 1993). Wisdom implies that the individual does not act on impulse and can reflect on all aspects of a given situation objectively. In many cultures, older persons are respected for their years of experience, and the role of "wise elder" is a desired status. But not all older people have achieved wisdom. Wisdom suggests the ability to interpret knowledge, or to understand the world in a deeper and more profound manner. Such reflectiveness and the reduced self-centeredness that this requires allow older people to take charge of their lives and become more accepting of their own and others' weaknesses. Indeed, among older men and women in the Berkeley Guidance Study, those who scored high on the three components of wisdom (cognitive, reflective, affective thinking) also scored high

on a measure of life satisfaction. This suggests that "successful aging" (described in Chapter 6) is enhanced when wisdom has been attained (Ardelt, 1997). Older people who have achieved this level of wisdom could play a useful role in many businesses and government agencies, where their years of experience and ability to move beyond the constraints presumed by others could help such organizations succeed.

Creativity refers to the ability to apply unique and feasible solutions to new situations, to come up with original ideas or material products. A person may be creative in science, the arts, or technology. Although we can point to creative people in each of these areas (e.g., Albert Einstein in science, Wolfgang Amadeus Mozart and Georgia O'Keeffe in the arts, and Thomas Edison in technology), it is difficult to determine the specific characteristics that make such persons creative. As with intelligence in general, creativity is inferred from the individual's output, but cannot really be quantified or predicted. One measure of creativity is a test of *divergent thinking,* which is part of Guilford's (1967) structural model of intelligence. This is measured by asking a person to devise multiple solutions to an unfamiliar mental task (e.g., name some different uses for a flower). Later still, Torrance (1988) developed a test of creativity that also measures divergent thinking. Children who scored high on this test were found to be creative achievers as young adults (i.e., the test has good predictive and construct validity), but the test has not been used to predict changes in creativity across the lifespan.

Divergent thinking may be only one component of creativity, however. A creative person must also know much about a particular body of knowledge such as music or art before he or she can make creative contributions to it. However, this neglects the contributions to scientific problem-solving or the arts by people who may have expertise in one area and bring a fresh perspective to a different field. To date, there have been no systematic studies of divergent thinking among people who are generally considered to be creative. Much of the research on creativity has been performed as analyses of the *products* of artists and writers, not on their creative *process* directly. Indeed, no studies have been conducted to compare the cognitive functioning of artists, scientists, technologists, and others who are widely regarded as creative with that of persons not similarly endowed. Researchers who have examined the *quantity* of creative output by artists, poets, and scientists have found that the average rate of output at age 70–80 drops to approximately half that of age 30–40. However, a secondary peak of productivity often occurs in the sixties, although not as high as the first peak (Simonton, 1989, 1991). Indeed, Simonton's analysis of the last works of 172 classical composers in their final years revealed compositions that were judged highly by musicologists in terms of aesthetics, melody, and comprehensibility (Simonton, 1989). Mathematicians and theoretical physicists produce their major works in their late twenties and early thirties, whereas novelists, historians, and philosophers reach their peak in their late forties and fifties.

Summary and Implications

This chapter presented an overview of the major studies on cognitive functioning in the later years. Researchers have examined age-related changes in intelligence, learning, and memory, and what factors in the individual and the environment affect the degree of change in these three areas of cognitive functioning.

Of all the cognitive functions in aging, intelligence has received the greatest attention and controversy. It is also the area of most concern for many older persons. One problem with this area of research is the difficulty of defining and measuring what is generally agreed to be intelligence. In examining the components of intelligence measured by the Wechsler Adult Intelligence Scale (WAIS), fluid intelligence (as measured by performance scales) has been shown to decline more with aging than verbal, or crystallized, intelligence. This may be due partly to the fact that the former tests are generally timed, while the latter are not. However, age differences emerge even when tests are

not timed, and when variations in motor and sensory function are taken into account. This decline in fluid intelligence and maintenance of verbal intelligence is known as the Classic Aging Pattern. To the extent that older persons practice their fluid intelligence by using their problem-solving skills, they will experience less decline in this area. In contrast, aging does not appear to impair the ability for remembering word and symbol meanings. This does not imply that the ability to recall words is unimpaired, but when asked for definitions of words, older people can remember their meanings quite readily.

One problem with studying intelligence in aging is that of distinguishing age *changes* from age *differences*. To determine changes with age, people must be examined longitudinally. The problems of selective attrition and terminal drop make it difficult to interpret the findings of longitudinal studies of intelligence. These factors may result in an underestimate of the decline in intelligence with aging. The problem of cross-sectional studies of intelligence is primarily that of cohort differences. Even if subjects are matched on educational level, older persons have not had the exposure to computers and early childhood learning opportunities that have become available to recent cohorts. Other factors, such as occupation, sensory decline, poor physical health, and severe hypertension, have been found to have a significant impact on intelligence test scores.

Learning and memory are cognitive functions that are usually examined because tests of memory are actually tests of what a person has learned. According to the information processing model, learning begins when information reaches sensory memory, and then is directed via one or more sensory stores to primary memory. It is in primary memory that information must be organized and processed if it is to be retained and passed into secondary memory. Information is permanently stored in this latter region. Studies of recall and recognition provide evidence that aging does not affect the capacity of either primary or secondary memory. Instead, it appears that the aging process makes us less efficient in "reaching into" our secondary memory and retrieving material that was stored years ago. Recognition tasks, in which a person is provided with a cue to associate with an item in secondary memory, are easier than pure recall for most people, but especially for older individuals.

The learning process can be enhanced for older people by reducing time constraints, making the learning task more relevant for them, improving the physical conditions by using bright but glare-free lights and large letters, and providing visual and verbal mediators for learning new information. Helping the older learner to relax and not feel threatened by the learning task also ensures better learning. Such modifications are consistent with the goal of achieving greater congruence between older people and their environment.

Significant age-related declines in intelligence, learning, and memory appear not to be inevitable. Older people who continue to perform well on tests of intelligence, learning, and memory are characterized by: higher levels of education, good sensory functioning, good nutrition, employment that required complex problem-solving skills, and continued use of such skills in their later years. People who do not have serious cardiovascular disease or severe hypertension also perform well, although there is some slowing of cognitive processing and response speed. Even such slowing is not a problem for older people whose crystallized knowledge in the targeted area is high. Natural products and vitamins that may improve memory in older people are just now receiving research attention.

Although there is some agreement that wisdom is enhanced by age and that creativity reaches a second peak for some people in old age, there has been less research emphasis in these areas. Indeed, these concepts are more difficult to measure in young and old persons. These and other issues in cognition must be studied more fully with measures that have good construct validity before gerontologists can describe with certainty cognitive changes that are attributable to normal aging.

GLOSSARY

Classic Aging Pattern   the decline observed with aging on some performance scales of intelligence tests vs. consistency on verbal scales of the same tests

cognitive retraining   teaching research participants how to use various techniques to keep their minds active and maintain good memory skills

crystallized intelligence   knowledge and abilities one gains through education and experience

disuse theory   the view that memory fades or is lost because one fails to use the information

echoic memory   auditory memory, a brief period when new information received through the ears is stored

external aids   simple devices used by older people to keep track of the time or dates, etc., such as list-making

fluid intelligence   skills that are biologically determined, independent of experience or learning, similar to "native intelligence," requiring flexibility in thinking

ginkgo biloba   an herbal product shown to have benefits for memory

iconic memory   visual memory, a brief period when new information received through the eyes is stored

information processing model   a conceptual model of how learning and memory take place

intelligence   the theoretical limit of an individual's performance

intelligence quotient (IQ)   an individual's relative abilities in making judgments, in comprehension, and in reasoning

interference theory   the view that memory fades or is lost because of distractions experienced during learning or interference from similar or new information to the memory sought

mediators   visual and verbal links between information to be memorized and information that is already in secondary memory

mnemonics   the method of using verbal cues such as riddles or rhymes as aids to memory

primary mental abilities   the basic set of intellectual skills, including mathematical reasoning, word fluency, verbal meaning, inductive reasoning, and spatial orientation

primary (short-term) memory   a brief storage of newly acquired information; can hold 7±2 stimuli before they are processed into secondary memory or discarded

recall   the process of searching through secondary memory in response to a specific external cue

recognition   matching information in secondary memory with the stimulus information

secondary (long-term) memory permanent memory store; requires processing of new information to be stored and cues to retrieve stored information

spatial memory the ability to recall where objects are in relationship to each other in space

terminal decline hypothesis the hypothesis that persons who are close to death decline in their cognitive abilities

visual mediators the method of locations; memorizing by linking each item with a specific location in space

REFERENCES

Andrewes, D. G., Kinsella, G., and Murphy, M. Using a memory handbook to improve everyday memory in community-dwelling older adults with memory complaints. *Experimental Aging Research*, 1996, 22, 305–322.

Ardelt, M. Wisdom and life satisfaction in old age. *Journals of Gerontology*, 1997, 52B, P15–P27.

Aubrey, J. B., and Dobbs, A. R. Age and sex differences in the mental realignment of maps. *Experimental Aging Research*, 1990, 16, 133–139.

Aubrey, J. B., Li, K. Z. H., and Dobbs, A. R. Age and sex differences in the interpretation of misaligned "You-are-Here" maps. *Journals of Gerontology*, 1994, 49, P29–P31.

Baltes, P. B. The aging mind: Potential and limits. *The Gerontologist*, 1993, 33, 580–594.

Berg, S. Aging, behavior, and terminal decline. In J. E. Birren and K. W. Schaie (Eds.), *Handbook of the psychology of aging* (4th ed.). San Diego: Academic Press, 1996.

Binet, A., and Simon, T. Méthodes nouvelles pour le diagnostique du niveau intellectuel des anormaux. *Année Psychologique*, 1905, 11, 102–191.

Botwinick, J. *Aging and behavior: A comprehensive integration of research findings* (3rd ed.). New York: Springer, 1984.

Bruce, P. R., and Herman, J. F. Adult age differences in spatial memory. *Journal of Gerontology*, 1986, 41, 774–777.

Burack, O. R., and Lackman, M. E. The effects of list-making on recall in young and elderly adults. *Journals of Gerontology*, 1996, 51B, P226–P233.

Butler, R. N., and Gleason, H. *Productive aging: Enhancing vitality in later life*. New York: Springer, 1985.

Camp, C. J. In pursuit of trivia: Remembering, forgetting, and aging. *Gerontological Review*, 1988, 1, 37–42.

Canestrari, R. E. Paced and self-paced learning in young and elderly adults. *Journal of Gerontology*, 1963, 18, 165–168.

Cattell, R. B. Theory of fluid and crystallized intelligence: A critical experiment. *Journal of Educational Psychology*, 1963, 54, 1–22.

Cerella, J., Poon, L. W., and Fozard, J. L. Age and iconic read-out. *Journal of Gerontology*, 1982, 37, 197–202.

Cooney, T. M., Schaie, K. W., and Willis, S. L. The relationship between prior functioning on cognitive and personality dimensions and subject attrition in longitudinal research. *Journals of Gerontology*, 1988, 43, P12–P17.

Craik, F. I. M. Memory changes in normal aging. *Current directions in psychological science*, 1994, 5, 155–158.

Craik, F. I. M., and Jennings, J. M. Human memory. In F. I. M. Craik and T. A. Salthouse (Eds.), *The handbook of aging and cognition*. Hillsdale, NJ: Erlbaum, 1994.

Cunningham, W. R., and Owens, W. A. The Iowa State study of the adult development of intellectual abilities. In K. W. Schaie (Ed.), *Longitudinal studies of adult psychological development*. New York: Guilford Press, 1983.

Dutta, R. *The relationship between flexibility–rigidity and the primary mental abilities*. Unpublished doctoral dissertation. Pennsylvania State University, 1992.

Gold, D. P., Andres, D., Etezadi, J., Arbuckle, T., Schwartzman, A., and Chaikelson, J. Structural equation model of intellectual change and continuity and predictors of intelligence in older men. *Psychology and Aging*, 1995, 10, 294–303.

Green, R. F. Age–intelligence relationship between ages sixteen and sixty-four. *Developmental Psychology*, 1969, 1, 618–627.

Gruber-Baldini, A. L. *The impact of health and disease on cognitive ability in adulthood and old age in the Seattle Longitudinal Study*. Unpublished doctoral dissertation. Pennsylvania State University, 1991.

Guilford, J. P. Intelligence: 1965 model. *American Psychologist*, 1966, 21, 20–26.

Guilford, J. P. *The nature of human intelligence*. New York: McGraw-Hill, 1967.

Horn, J. L. The aging of human abilities. In B. B. Wolman (Ed.), *Handbook of developmental psychology*. Englewood Cliffs, NJ: Prentice-Hall, 1982.

Horn, J. L. Organization of data on life-span development of human abilities. In L. R. Goulet and P. B. Baltes (Eds.), *Life-span developmental psychology: Research and theory*. New York: Academic Press, 1970.

Horn, J. L., and Donaldson, G. Cognitive development in adulthood. In O. G. Brim and J. Kagan (Eds.), *Constancy and change in human development*. Cambridge, MA: Harvard University Press, 1980.

Hultsch, D. F., Hammer, M., and Small, B. J. Age differences in cognitive performance in later life: Relationships to self-reported health and activity lifestyle. *Journals of Gerontology*, 1993, *48*, P1–P11.

Huyck, M. H., and Hoyer, W. J. *Adult development and aging*. Belmont, CA: Wadsworth, 1982.

Inouye, S. K., Albert, M. S., Mohs, R., and Sun-Kolie, R. Cognitive performance in a high-functioning, community-dwelling elderly population. *Journals of Gerontology*, 1993, *48*, M146–M151.

Jarvik, L. F., and Falek, A. Intellectual stability and survival in the aged. *Journal of Gerontology*, 1963, *18*, 173–176.

Johansson, B., Zarit, S. H., and Berg, S. Changes in cognitive functioning of the oldest old. *Journals of Gerontology*, 1992, *47*, P75–P80.

Jones, H. E. Intelligence and problem-solving. In J. E. Birren (Ed.), *Handbook of aging and the individual: Psychological and biological aspects*. Chicago: University of Chicago Press, 1959.

Kallmann, F. J., and Sander, G. Twin studies on senescence. *American Journal of Psychiatry*, 1949, *106*, 29–36.

Kleemeier, R. W. Intellectual change in the senium. *Proceedings of the Social Statistics Section of the American Statistical Association*, 1962, *1*, 290–295.

Labouvie-Vief, G., and Blanchard-Fields, F. Cognitive aging and psychological growth. *Aging and Society*, 1982, *2*, 183–209.

Larue, A., Koehler, K. M., Wayne, S. J., Chiulli, S. J., Haaland, K. Y., and Garry, P. J. Nutritional status and cognitive functioning in a normally aging sample: A 6-year reassessment. *American Journal of Clinical Nutrition*, 1997, *65*, 20–29.

Lindenberger, U., and Baltes, P. B. Sensory functioning and intelligence in old age. *Psychology and Aging*. 1994, *9*, 339–355.

McDowd, J. M., and Craik, F. I. M. Effects of aging and task difficulty on divided attention performance.

Journal of Experimental Psychology: Human Perception and Performance, 1988, *14*, 267–280.

Orwoll, L., and Achenbaum, W. A. Gender and the development of wisdom. *Human Development*, 1993, *36*, 274–296.

Owens, W. A. Age and mental abilities: A longitudinal study. *Genetic Psychology Monographs*, 1953, *48*, 3–54.

Owens, W. A. Age and mental ability: A second adult follow-up. *Journal of Educational Psychology*, 1966, *57*, 311–325.

Palmore, E. (Ed.). *Normal aging II: Reports from the Duke Longitudinal Study*. Durham, NC: Duke University Press, 1974.

Palmore, E. (Ed.). *Normal aging III: Reports from the Duke Longitudinal Study*. Durham, NC: Duke University Press, 1985.

Poon, L. W. Differences in human memory with aging: Nature, causes, and clinical implications. In J. E. Birren and K. W. Schaie (Eds.), *Handbook of the psychology of aging* (2nd ed.). New York: Van Nostrand Reinhold, 1985.

Rabbitt, P., Donlan, C., Watson, P., McInnes, L., and Bent, N. Unique and interactive effects of depression, age, socioeconomic advantage, and gender on cognitive performance of normal healthy older people. *Psychology and Aging*, 1995, *10*, 307–313.

Ratner, H. H., Schell, D. A., Crimmins, A., Mittleman, D., and Baldinelli, L. Changes in adults' prose recall: Aging or cognitive demands. *Developmental Psychology*, 1987, *23*, 521–525.

Rebok, G. W. *Life-span cognitive development*. New York: Holt, Rinehart and Winston, 1987.

Reese, H. W. Models of memory development. *Human Development*, 1976, *19*, 291–303.

Ross, E. Effects of challenging and supportive instructions on verbal learning in older persons. *Journal of Educational Psychology*, 1968, *59*, 261–266.

Salthouse, T. A. Age-related differences in basic cognitive processes: Implications for work. *Experimental Aging Research*, 1994a, *20*, 249–255.

Salthouse, T. A. Aging of working memory. *Neuropsychology*, 1994b, *8*, 535–543.

Salthouse, T. A. Effects of age and skill in typing. *Journal of Experimental Psychology: General*, 1984, *113*, 345–371.

Salthouse, T. A. General and specific speed mediation of adult age differences in memory. *Journals of Gerontology*, 1996, *51B*, P30–P42.

Salthouse, T. A. Speed and knowledge as determinants of adult age differences in verbal tasks. *Journals of Gerontology*, 1993, 48, P29–P36.

Salthouse, T. A., and Babcock, R. L. Decomposing adult age differences in working memory. *Developmental Psychology*, 1991, 27, 763–776.

Sands, L. P., and Meredith, W. Blood pressure and intellectual functioning in late midlife. *Journals of Gerontology*, 1992, 47, P81–P84.

Schaie, K. W. Age changes and age differences. *The Gerontologist*, 1967, 7, 128–132.

Schaie, K. W. The hazards of cognitive aging. *The Gerontologist*, 1989, 29, 484–493.

Schaie, K. W. Intellectual development in adulthood. In J. E. Birren and K. W. Schaie (Eds.), *Handbook of the psychology of aging* (4th ed.). San Diego: Academic Press, 1996b.

Schaie, K. W. *Intellectual development in adulthood: The Seattle Longitudinal Study.* Cambridge: Cambridge University Press, 1996a.

Schaie, K. W. The primary mental abilities in adulthood: An exploration in the development of psychometric intelligence. In P. B. Baltes and O. G. Brim, Jr. (Eds.), *Life-span development and behavior* (Vol. 2). New York: Academic Press, 1979.

Schaie, K. W. The Seattle Longitudinal Study: A 21-year exploration of psychometric intelligence in adulthood. In K. W. Schaie (Ed.), *Longitudinal studies of adult psychological development*. New York: Guilford Press, 1983.

Schaie, K. W., and Hertzog, C. Toward a comprehensive model of adult intellectual development: Contributions of the Seattle Longitudinal Study. In R. J. Sternberg (Ed.), *Advances in human intelligence* (Vol. 3). Hillsdale, NJ: Erlbaum, 1986.

Schaie, K. W., and Labouvie-Vief, G. V. Generational versus ontogenetic components of change in adult cognitive behavior: A fourteen-year cross-sequential study. *Developmental Psychology*, 1974, 10, 305–320.

Schaie, K. W., Plomin, R., Willis, S. L., Gruber-Baldini, A., and Dutta, R. Natural cohorts: Family similarity in adult cognition. In T. Sonderegger (Ed.), *Psychology and aging: Nebraska symposium on motivation*. Lincoln: University of Nebraska Press, 1992.

Schaie, K. W., and Willis, S. L. Perceived family environments across generations. In V. L. Bengston,

K. W. Schaie, and L. Burton (Eds.), *Societal impact on aging: Intergenerational perspectives*. New York: Springer, 1995.

Sharps, M. J., and Gollin, E. S. Aging and free recall for objects located in space. *Journals of Gerontology*, 1988, 43, P8–P11.

Siegler, I. C. Psychological aspects of the Duke Longitudinal Studies. In K. W. Schaie (Ed.), *Longitudinal studies of adult psychological development*. New York: Guilford Press, 1983.

Simonton, D. K. Career landmarks in science: Individual differences and interdisciplinary contrasts. *Developmental Psychology*, 1991, 27, 119–127.

Simonton, D. K. The swan-song phenomenon: Last works effects for 172 classical composers. *Psychology and Aging*, 1989, 4, 42–47.

Smith, A. D. Memory. In J. E. Birren and K. W. Schaie (Eds.), *Handbook of the psychology of aging* (4th ed.). San Diego: Academic Press, 1996.

Spearman, C. *The abilities of man: Their nature and measurement.* New York: Macmillan, 1927.

Torrance, E. P. The nature of creativity as manifest in its testing. In R. J. Sternberg (Ed.), *The nature of creativity: Contemporary psychological perspectives*. Cambridge: Cambridge University Press, 1988.

Van Dongen, M. C. J. M., van Rossum, E., Kessels, A. G. H., Sielhorst, H. J. G., and Knipscheld, P. G. The efficacy of ginkgo for elderly people with dementia and age-associated memory impairments. *Journal of the American Geriatrics Society*, 2000, 1183–1194.

Verhaeghen, P., Geraerts, N., and Marcoen, A. Memory complaints, coping and well-being in old age: A systematic approach. *The Gerontologist*, 2000, 40, 540–548.

Verhaeghen, P., Marcoen, A., and Goossens, L. Improving memory performance in the aged through mnemonic training: A meta-analytic study. *Psychology and Aging*, 1992, 7, 242–251.

White, N., and Cunningham, W. R. Is terminal drop pervasive or specific? *Journals of Gerontology*, 1988, 43, P141–P144.

Willis, S. L., and Nesselroade, C. S. Long-term effects of fluid ability training in old-old age. *Developmental Psychology*, 1990, 26, 905–910.

Willis, S. L., and Schaie, K. W. Gender differences in spatial ability in old age: Longitudinal and intervention findings. *Sex Roles*, 1988, 18, 189–203.

Willis, S. L., and Schaie, K. W. Training the elderly on the ability factors of spatial orientation and inductive reasoning. *Psychology and Aging*, 1986, 2, 239–247.

Yesavage, J. A., Sheikh, J. I., Friedman, L., and Tanke, E. Learning mnemonics: Roles of aging and subtle cognitive impairment. *Psychology and Aging*, 1990, 5, 133–137.

Zelinski, E. M., Gilewski, J. J., and Schaie, K. W. Individual differences in cross-sectional and 3-year longitudinal memory performance across the adult life span. *Psychology and Aging*, 1993, 8, 176–186.

PERSONALITY AND MENTAL HEALTH IN OLD AGE

This chapter examines

- Normal developmental changes and stability in personality across the life span
- Theories of personality that support change or stability
- Person-environment interactions that affect personality development
- Stability versus change in self-concept and self-esteem with aging
- Older people's responses to life events and stressors
- Predictors of successful aging
- Major psychiatric disorders and dementias in old age
- The extent to which older people use mental health services

We have all had the experience of watching different people respond to the same event in different ways. For example, you probably know some students who are extremely anxious about test-taking while others are calm, and some students who express their opinions strongly and confidently while others rarely speak in class at all. All these characteristics are part of an individual's personality.

DEFINING PERSONALITY

Personality may be defined as a unique pattern of innate and learned behaviors, thoughts and emotions that influence how each person responds and interacts with the environment. An individual may be described in terms of several personality traits, such as passive or aggressive, introverted or extroverted, independent or dependent. Personality may be evaluated with regard to particular standards of behavior; for example, an adapted or maladapted, adjusted or maladjusted. Personality styles influence how we cope with and adapt to the changes when we age. The process of aging involves numerous stressful life experiences. How an older person attempts to alleviate such stress has an influence on that individual's long-term well-being. The person–environment congruence model presented in Chapter 1 suggests that our behavior is influenced and modified by the environment, and that we shape the environment around us. An individual's behavior is often quite different from one situation to another, and depends both on each situation's social norms and expectations and on that person's needs and motives.

Although personality remains relatively stable with normal aging, some older people who showed no signs of psychopathology earlier in their lives may experience some types of mental disorders in late life. For other older people, psychiatric disorders experienced in their younger years may continue or may reemerge. In some individuals the stresses of old age may compound any existing predisposition to psychopathology. These stresses may be internal, resulting from the physiological and cognitive changes, or external, that is, a function of role losses and the deaths of partners, friends, and especially one's children. These conditions significantly impact older people's competence, so that they become more vulnerable to environmental press and less able to function at an optimal level.

STAGE THEORIES OF PERSONALITY

Erikson's Psychosocial Model

Most theories of personality emphasize the developmental **stages** of personality and imply that the social environment influences development. As we focus on stages of adult development, however, it is important to avoid the image of rigid, immutable stages and transitions that are inevitable, with no room for individual differences. In fact, people *do*

make choices regarding their specific responses to common life changes. This results in numerous expressions of behavior under similar life experiences such as adolescence, parenting, retirement, and even the management of chronic diseases. There has been disagreement about whether this pattern of development continues through adulthood. Sigmund Freud's focus on psychosexual stages of development through adolescence has had a major influence on developmental psychology. In most of his writings, Freud suggests that personality achieves stability by adolescence. Accordingly, adult behavior is a reflection of unconscious motives and unsuccessful resolution of early childhood stages.

In contrast, Erik Erikson, who was trained in psychoanalytic theory, moved away from this approach and focused on psychosocial development throughout the life cycle. According to his model (Erikson, 1963, 1968, 1982; Erikson et al., 1986), the individual undergoes eight stages of development of the ego. One's unconscious goal is to achieve *ego identity*. Three of these stages are beyond adolescence, with the final one occurring in mature adulthood. At each stage the individual experiences a major task to be accomplished and a conflict; the conflicts of each stage of development are the foundations of successive stages. Depending on the outcome of the crisis associated with a particular stage, the individual proceeds to the next stage of development in alternative ways. Erikson also emphasized the interactions between genetics and the environment in determining personality development. His concept of the *epigenetic principle* assumed an innate plan of development in which people proceed through stages as they become cognitively and emotionally more capable of interacting within a wider social radius. Hence, each subsequent stage requires additional cognitive and emotional development before it can be experienced.

As shown in Table 6.1, the individual in the last stage of life is confronted with the task of **ego integrity versus despair.** According to Erikson, the individual at this stage accepts the inevitability of mortality, achieves wisdom and perspective,

TABLE 6.1   Erikson's Psychosocial Stages

	STAGE	GOAL
I	Basic trust vs. mistrust	To establish basic trust in the world through trust in the parent.
II	Autonomy vs. shame and doubt	To establish a sense of autonomy and self as distinct from the parent; to establish self-control vs. doubt in one's abilities.
III	Initiative vs. guilt	To establish a sense of initiative within parental limits without feeling guilty about emotional needs.
IV	Industry vs. inferiority	To establish a sense of industry within the school setting; to learn necessary skills without feelings of inferiority or fear of failure.
V	Ego identity vs. role diffusion	To establish identity, self-concept, and role within the larger community, without confusion about the self and about social roles.
VI	Intimacy vs. isolation	To establish intimacy and affiliation with one or more others, without fearing loss of identity in the process that may result in isolation.
VII	Generativity vs. stagnation	To establish a sense of care and concern for the well-being of future generations; to look toward the future and not stagnate in the past.
VIII	Ego integrity vs. despair	To establish a sense of meaning in one's life, rather than feeling despair or bitterness that life was wasted; to accept oneself and one's life without despair.

or despairs because he or she has not come to grips with death and lacks ego integrity. A major task associated with this last stage is to integrate the experiences of earlier stages and to realize that one's life has had meaning, whether or not it was "successful" in a socially defined sense. Older people who achieve ego integrity feel a sense of connectedness with younger generations, and share their experiences and wisdom with them. This may take the form of:

- informal visiting
- counseling
- mentoring

- sponsoring an individual or group of younger people
- writing memoirs or letters

The process of shaping one's memories and experiences with others (orally or written) has been described as **life review,** and has been found to be a useful mode of therapy with older adults, as described later in this chapter. Life satisfaction, or the feeling that life is worth living, may be achieved through these tasks of adopting a wider historical perspective upon one's life, accepting one's mortality, sharing experiences with the young, and leaving a legacy to future generations.

POINTS TO PONDER

Think about an older person you know who appears to have achieved the stage of ego integrity. What adjectives would you use to describe this individual?

Erikson's theory provides a framework for studying personality in late life because it suggests that personality is dynamic throughout the life cycle. Indeed, this theory fits the person–environment model; we interact with a variety of other people in different settings, and our personality is affected accordingly.

Jung's Psychoanalytic Perspective

Carl Jung's model of personality also assumes changes throughout life, as expressed in the following statement from one of his early writings:

> We cannot live the afternoon of life according to the program of life's morning, for what was great in the morning will be little at evening, and what in the morning was true will at evening have become a lie. (1933, p. 108).

Jung's model emphasizes stages in the development of consciousness and the ego, from the narrow focus of the child to the otherworldliness of the older person. Jung suggests that the ego moves from *extraversion,* or a focus on the external world in youth and middle age when the individual progresses through school, work, and marriage, to *introversion,* or to a focus on one's inner world in old age. Like Erikson, Jung examined the individual's confrontation with death in the last stage of life. He suggested that life for the aging person must naturally contract, that the individual in this stage must find meaning in inner exploration and in an afterlife.

Jung (1959) also focused on changes in **archetypes** with age. That is, according to Jung, all humans have both a feminine and a masculine side. An archetype is the feminine side of a man's personality (the anima) and the masculine side of a woman's personality (the animus). As they age, people begin to adopt psychological traits more commonly associated with the opposite sex. For example, older men may show more signs of passivity while women may become more assertive as they age.

Empirical Testing of These Perspectives

In testing the validity of these theories, subsequent research has contributed to our understanding of personality development in late adulthood. Many of these studies are cross-sectional; that is, they derive information on age *differences,* not age changes. There are notable exceptions to this approach, including the Baltimore Longitudinal Studies (described in Chapter 1) and the Kansas City Studies, which have examined changes in physiological, cognitive, and personality functions in the same individuals over a period of several years. Research by Costa and McCrae (1986, 1994) in the Baltimore Longitudinal Studies is related to Erikson's work, since it identifies changes in *adjustment,* with age, but stability in specific *traits* (described later in this chapter). Cross-sectional studies by De St. Aubin and McAdams (1995), and by Peterson and Klohnen (1995) examined age differences in **generativity,** Erikson's seventh stage. These researchers consistently found that middle-aged and older adults express more generative concerns (i.e., attributing more importance to the care of younger generations than self-development) than young adults. "Generative adults" exhibit concerns not just toward their own children, but toward the young in society.

Other researchers have found empirical support for Jung's observations regarding decreased sex-typed behavior in old age. David Gutmann (1977, 1980, 1992), who studies personality across the life span in diverse cultures from a psychoanalytic perspective, identified a shift from **active mastery** to **passive mastery** as men age. In contrast,

---

In contrast to the young, older persons have

"a duty and a necessity to devote serious attention to (themselves). After having lavished its light upon the world, the sun withdraws its rays in order to illuminate itself" (Jung, 1933, p. 109).

AGE CHANGES IN MASTERY

Young men tend to:

- be more achievement-oriented
- take more risks
- be more competitive
- be more concerned with controlling their environments

Compared to young men, older men:

- are more expressive
- are more nurturant
- have greater need for affiliation and accommodation

Young women tend to:

- be more affiliative
- be more expressive

Compared to young women, older women:

- are more instrumental
- express more achievement-oriented responses

(Gutmann, 1992)

---

women appear to move from passive to active mastery.

The increased passivity of older men may allow them to explore their inner worlds and move beyond the external orientation of their younger years.

The Grant Study of Harvard University Graduates longitudinal study, has identified support for stage theories of personality (Vaillant, 1977, 1994; Vaillant and Vaillant, 1990). This study followed 268 men, beginning in 1938 when they were students, through age 65 when 173 of the men were still available to take part in these life reviews and qualitative interviews. These men were observed to follow a common pattern of stages:

- establishment of a professional identity in their twenties and thirties
- career consolidation in their forties
- exploration of their inner worlds in midlife (a major transition similar to the stage of ego integrity versus despair that Erikson described as occurring in late life)

Men who were most emotionally stable and well adjusted in their fifties and sixties had experienced

- had experienced greater generativity (i.e., responsibility for and care of coworkers, children, charity)
- were less sex-stereotyped in their social interactions
- were more nurturant and expressive

These changes observed in men as they moved from youth to middle to old age have implications for contemporary family roles and responsibilities, as discussed in Chapters 9 and 10.

The Kansas City Studies

Bernice Neugarten and her associates conducted one of the first longitudinal studies of personality in middle and old age in the 1950s and 1960s. The "Kansas City Studies of Aging" have contributed to our understanding of many age-related changes in personality and coping. These researchers found that older men became more accepting of their affiliative, nurturant, and sensual side, while women learned to display the egocentric and aggressive impulses that they had always possessed but had not displayed earlier. Neugarten, similar to Jung and Gutmann, suggests that these characteristics always exist in both sexes, but social pressure and societal values encourage the expression of more sex-typed traits in youth.

The Kansas City Studies also provided the empirical basis for activity and disengagement theories described in Chapter 8. Changes in such personality characteristics as nurturance, introversion, and aggressiveness were identified in older adults. Contrary to popular stereotypes, aging was also associated with greater differences (individuation) among individuals; as people aged, they developed more unique styles of interaction. Neugarten and colleagues (1968, 1973) suggested that people do not resemble each other more in old age, but in fact become more differentiated because they grow less concerned about societal expectations. Other age-related changes observed in the Kansas City Studies included shifts toward greater cautiousness and interiority; that is, a preoccupation with one's inner life and less extroversion, as suggested by Jung. This may represent a growing concern with the meaning of life and death as one ages, to expand one's scope beyond the day-to-day details of living.

The Kansas City researchers also observed decreased impulsiveness and a movement toward using more sophisticated ego defense mechanisms with age. For example, older persons tended to use less denial and more sublimation. Attitudes toward the world were also likely to change, but these were found to relate closely to personal experiences. For instance, people do not necessarily become more conservative as they age. Based on generational (cohort) differences and personal experiences, some persons become more liberal while others adopt a more conservative social perspective during the later years. These age-related changes in impulsiveness, types of defense mechanisms used, and attitudes have been supported in studies of personality by later researchers examining a range of cultural and ethnic minority groups. Many of the changes attributed to personality in old age, such as preference for solitude or slower paced activities, are not personality traits per se, but lifestyle preferences that are influenced by life experiences, social opportunities or discrimination, and functional health status.

Dialectical Models of Adult Personality

Another model of adult personality development has been proposed by Levinson (1977, 1986) and his colleagues (Levinson et al., 1978). This model is based on secondary analyses of American men described in published biographies and in interviews with working-class men. It has also been found to apply to women (Roberts and Newton, 1987). In contrast to Erikson, who focused on stages of ego development, Levinson and colleagues have examined developmental stages in terms of **life structures,** or the underlying characteristics of a person's life at a particular period of time. Of all stage theories of adult development, this model is the most explicit in linking each stage with a specific range of chronological age. Each period in the life structure (defined as "eras" by Levinson) represents developmental stages. Levinson defines four eras, each one lasting about 20 years. These are separated by *transitions* of about 5 years, each of which generally occurs as the individual perceives changes in the self, or as external events such as childbirth and retirement create new demands on one's relationships with others (see Table 6.2.)

Levinson's model represents an example of a *dialectical approach* to personality development; it proposes that change occurs because of interactions between a dynamic person (one who is biologically *and* psychologically changing) and a dynamic environment. To the extent that an individual is sensitive to the changing self, he or she can respond to changing environmental or societal conditions by altering something within the self or by modifying environmental expectations. This process thereby reestablishes equilibrium with the environment. For example, older people who deny the normal biological and physiological changes they are experiencing may have difficulty in modifying their lifestyles and moving into a different developmental phase.

SUMMARY OF KANSAS CITY STUDIES

- Older men become more affiliative, nurturant and sensual.
- Older women accept their egocentric and assertive side.
- There is greater individuation with aging.
- There is increased preoccupation with one's inner life.
- Increased cautiousness is normal with aging.
- People become less impulsive with age.

TABLE 6.2   Levinson's "Seasons" of Life

Era I	Preadulthood (Age 0–22)
	(An era when the family provides protection, socialization, and support of personal growth)
	Early Adult Transition (Age 17–22)*
Era II	Early Adulthood (Age 17–45)
	(An era of peak biological functioning, development of adult identity)
	Entering the adult world, entry life structure for early adulthood
	Age 30 transition*
	Settling down, culminating life structure for early adulthood
	Mid-Life Transition (Age 40–45)*
Era III	Middle Adulthood (Age 40–65)
	(Goals become more other-oriented, compassionate roles, mentor roles assumed; peak effectiveness as a leader)
	Entering life structure for middle adulthood
	Age 50 transition*
	Culmination of middle adulthood
	Late Adulthood Transition (Age 60–65)*
Era IV	Late Adulthood (Age 60+)
	(An era when declining capacities are recognized, anxieties about aging, loss of power and status begin)
	Acceptance of death's inevitability

*Indicates major transitions to a new developmental era.

SOURCE: D. Levinson, C. M. Darrow, E. B. Klein, M. H. Levinson, and B. McKee, *The seasons of a man's life* (New York: Alfred A. Knopf, 1978). Reprinted with permission of the author and publisher.

TRAIT THEORIES OF PERSONALITY

Another perspective on personality is to examine characteristic behaviors specific within individuals that reflect **trait theories.** Traits are relatively stable characteristics of personality; together they make up a constellation that distinguishes each individual. For example, we can describe people along a continuum of personality attributes such as extroverted to introverted, passive to aggressive, and optimistic to pessimistic, as well as high or low on need for achievement and affiliation. Most personality theorists agree that traits do not change unless the individual makes a conscious effort to do so—for example, undergoing psychological counseling to become more nurturant.

This assumption of stability has led trait researchers to examine personality traits longitudinally in the middle and later years. Proponents of this approach are McCrae and Costa (1990), who have measured specific traits of participants in

---

AN OLDER PERSON IN DYNAMIC INTERACTION WITH THE ENVIRONMENT

Mrs. Garcia has lived in the same house for 40 years, having raised three children there and remodeling it as her family's needs changed over the years. Now that her husband has died and her children have their own homes, the four-bedroom house on two floors is too big for her. Her severe arthritis and heart problems make it difficult to go up and down stairs, and to maintain her house. However, Mrs. Garcia refuses to sell it, assuring everyone that she has always been able to take care of the house herself.

the Baltimore Longitudinal Studies (described in Chapter 1). They propose a *five-factor model of personality traits,* consisting of five primary, independent components:

- neuroticism
- extraversion
- openness to experience
- agreeableness
- conscientiousness

Within each component are six facets or subcategories of traits. For example, neuroticism consists of anxiety, impulsiveness, self-consciousness, hostility, depression, and vulnerability. People with high neurotic tendencies would also score high on these components.

Standardized tests such as the Guilford-Zimmerman Temperament Survey (GZTS) are used to compare individuals with population norms on these traits. By administering the GZTS to subjects in the Baltimore Longitudinal Studies, researchers found great stability in the five traits described above. Using a cross-sectional approach, they also identified consistency in these traits in middle-aged and older adults. Both groups differed from young adults on some personality factors (Costa and McCrae, 1994, 1995). Other studies support the lifelong stability, and even the possible heritability of some personality traits. For example, a study of middle-aged identical and fraternal twins in Sweden found similarities in their personality characteristics, whether they were reared together or apart. In particular, traits of emotionality, activity, sociability, extroversion, and neuroticism varied in the same manner within each pair of twins (Pederson et al., 1988; Plomin et al., 1988).

Cohort and cultural influences on personality traits have also been identified. Using a cross-sequential research design (described in Chapter 1), Schaie and Willis (1991) found few changes in specific traits of the same individuals over 7 years, but they did find cohort differences. That is, the oldest participants in the first wave were less flexible and adaptable than were the same older persons in the second wave of testing 7 years later. Cultural factors

Maintaining an active lifestyle can enhance an older person's self-confidence.

may also play a role in the development of certain traits. For example, traditional societies, including the United States before the women's liberation movement of the 1960s, reinforced "agreeableness" as a trait in women; the associated cluster of personality factors such as altruism, compliance, modesty, and tender-mindedness are viewed in traditional societies as important "feminine" traits. However, as women move into more diverse roles and enter occupations that were once considered "masculine," there is less gender stereotyping of traits.

SELF-CONCEPT AND SELF-ESTEEM

A major adjustment required in old age is the ability to redefine one's **self-concept** or one's cognitive image of the self as social roles shift and as new roles are assumed. Our self-concept emerges from our interactions with the social environment, our social roles, and accomplishments. Through continuous interactions with the environment, people can confirm or revise these self-images. They do so either by:

- *assimilating* new experiences into their self-concept, or
- *accommodating* or adjusting their self-concept to fit the new reality.

Accommodation is more difficult and requires greater adaptive skills (Whitbourne and Primus, 1996). For example, how does a retired teacher identify himself or herself upon giving up the work that has been that individual's central focus for the past 40 or 50 years? How does a woman whose self-concept is closely associated with her role as a wife express her identity after her husband dies?

Many older persons continue to identify with the role that they have lost (think of those who continue to introduce themselves as a "teacher" or "doctor" long after retiring from those careers). This would represent a type of *identity assimilation*. Others experience *role confusion*, particularly in the early stages of retirement, when cues from other people are inconsistent with an individual's self-concept. This may require *identity accommodation*. Still others may undergo a period of depression and major readjustment to the changes associated with role loss. To the extent that a person's self-concept is defined independently of particular social roles, one adapts more readily to the role losses that may accompany old age. Both assimilation of new social roles to a stable self-concept, and some accommodation to changing realities, are indicators of successful adaptation of one's self-concept. Indeed, research with the oldest-old demonstrates that self-concept remains essentially unchanged. Even with declining health and loss of significant others, those who survive to advanced old age maintain their identity (Troll and Skaff, 1997).

For an older person whose self-concept is based on social roles and others' expectations, role losses have a particularly significant impact on that individual's **self-esteem**—defined as an evaluation or feeling about his or her identity relative to some ideal or standard.

- *Self-esteem* is based on an emotional assessment of the self.
- *Self-concept* is the cognitive definition of one's identity.

The affective quality of self-esteem makes it more dynamic and more easily influenced by such external forces as retirement, widowhood, health status, and reinforcements (both positive and negative) from others (e.g., respect, deference, or ostracism). Social roles integrate the individual to society and add meaning to one's life. As a result, alterations in social roles and the loss of status that accompanies some of these changes often have a negative impact on an older person's self-esteem. Think, for example, of an older woman whose social roles have emphasized that of caregiver to her family. If she herself becomes dependent on others for care because of a major debilitating illness such as a stroke or dementia, she is unwittingly robbed of this "ideal self," and her self-esteem may suffer.

An individual who experiences multiple role losses must not only adapt to the lifestyle changes associated with aging (e.g., financial insecurity or shrinking social networks), but must also integrate the new roles with his or her "ideal self" or learn to modify this definition of "ideal." Older persons who are experiencing major physical and cognitive disabilities simultaneously with role losses, or worse yet, whose role losses are precipitated by an illness (e.g., early retirement due to stroke or institutionalization because of Alzheimer's disease), must cope with multiple problems at a time in their lives when they have the fewest resources to resolve them successfully. Depression is not an uncommon reaction in these cases.

Some studies have shown a generalized decrease in self-esteem from age 50 to 80, although many others have found improvement from adolescence through the young-old period. These varied findings may be attributed to the cross-sectional nature of research on self-esteem and age (Giarrusso and Bengtson, 1996). Stressful life events and disabilities such as severe hearing loss can impair self-esteem among older people (Chen, 1994; Tran, Wright, and Chatters, 1991). For example, older

PERSONALITY FACTORS IMPORTANT FOR MAINTAINING SELF-ESTEEM

• Reinterpretation of the meaning of self, such that an individual's self-concept and self-worth are independent of any roles he or she has played ("I am a unique individual" rather than "I am a doctor/teacher/wife").

• Acceptance of the aging process, its limitations, and possibilities. That is, individuals who realize that they have less energy and respond more slowly than in the past, but that they can still participate in life, will adapt more readily to the social and health losses of old age.

• Reevaluation of one's goals and expectations throughout life. Too often people establish life goals at an early age and are constantly disappointed as circumstances change. The ability to respond to internal and external pressures by modifying life goals appropriately reflects flexibility and harmony with one's environment.

• The ability to look back objectively on one's past and to review one's failures and successes. *Life review* entails an objective review and evaluation of one's life. An older person who has this ability to reminisce about past experiences and how these have influenced subsequent personality development, behavior, and interpersonal relationships can call upon coping strategies that have been most effective in the past and adapt them to changed circumstances. Life review can also help the older person come to terms with unresolved conflicts from one's past, resulting in greater ego integrity.

people who are socially isolated and have significant physical disabilities have been found to have the poorest self-esteem (Pinquart, 1991).

STRESS, COPING, AND ADAPTATION

The process of aging entails numerous life changes, as noted in this and previous chapters. These changes, both positive and negative, place demands on the aging person's abilities to cope with new life situations. Together with health and cognitive functioning, personality characteristics influence coping responses. Self-concept and self-esteem are two important elements that play a role in coping styles, and may help explain why some older people adjust readily to major life changes, while others have difficulty. Indeed, self-esteem, health, and cognitive skills all contribute to an individual's sense of competence. Major life events and situations represent environmental stressors that place demands on an individual's competence.

Some Useful Definitions

The concept of **life events** (or *life experiences*) forms the basis for this section. These terms refer to *internal or external stimuli* that cause some change in our daily lives. They may be positive or negative, gains or losses, discrete or continuous.

Improvement in one's own health or in a family member's health are examples of *positive life events*, whereas deteriorating health and death are *negative events*. Some life experiences may have

EXAMPLES OF INTERNALLY AND EXTERNALLY CREATED EVENTS

Internal
• changes in eating or sleeping habits
• effects of a chronic disease such as arthritis or diabetes

External
• starting a new job
• losing one's job
• retirement

both positive *and* negative aspects. For example, older workers may view their pending retirement with great joy and make numerous plans for the post-retirement years. However, they may also experience some negative consequences as well, such as reduced income, unstructured time, and loss of the worker role.

Another distinction is made between *on-time* and *off-time* events. This concept distinguishes life experiences that a person can anticipate because of one's stage in the life cycle (on-time) from those that are unexpected at a given stage (off-time). Other researchers have used the terms *normative* and *non-normative* events, suggesting that an individual anticipates some life experiences because they are the norm for most people of a given age. For example, a man married to a 75-year-old woman is more likely to expect the death of his wife than is the husband of a 35-year-old woman. As shown later in this chapter, researchers have found differences in how people respond to on-time and off-time events.

The concept of *stress,* as defined in Chapter 4, is also important for this chapter. Since Selye's (1946) introduction of this term, many researchers have explored the antecedents, components, and consequences of stress. In fact, Selye (1970) defined aging as the sum of stresses experienced across one's lifetime. Not everyone perceives the same events to be stressful, however. Lazarus and DeLongis (1983) have introduced the concept of *cognitive appraisal*—the way in which a person perceives the significance of an encounter for his or her well-being. Cognitive appraisal serves to minimize or magnify the importance or stressfulness of an event by attaching some meaning to it. If a situation is construed as benign or irrelevant by an individual, it does not elicit coping responses. On the other hand, if a person appraises a situation as challenging, harmful, or threatening, it becomes a stressor, and calls upon the individual's adaptation responses.

Aging and Life Events

Life events are identifiable, discrete life changes or transitions that demand adaptation by the individual, because they disrupt one's person–environment balance or homeostasis. Some researchers distinguish between life events and chronic stressors, such as poor health and financial difficulties: Both types of stressors require adaptive or coping skills (McLeod, 1996). There has been considerable discussion among researchers about the nature of life events in the later years, the older person's ability to cope with them, and whether old age is associated with more or fewer life events than youth. Significant life events that are more likely to occur in old age include widowhood, retirement, and relocation to a nursing home. The nature of such roles and the novelty associated with assuming a social role for the first time result in major changes in an individual's daily functioning and demand adaptation to the new situation.

THE IMPORTANCE OF COGNITIVE APPRAISAL

Life events can represent a positive or negative stressor for the individual. Cognitive appraisal means that different people can view the same situation differently. One may see it as a challenge (i.e., a positive stressor), while another views it as a threat (i.e., a negative stressor). This evokes different coping responses in the two people. For example, an older woman who moves voluntarily to a retirement apartment may view it as an exciting and desirable change in her lifestyle, or she may resent the change as too demanding and disruptive. In the former case, she will adapt more readily and will experience less negative stress than in the latter. On the other hand, if this person views the move as totally benign and does not expect it to place any demands on her, she will probably be unpleasantly surprised by the level of stress that she eventually encounters, no matter how minimal.

POINTS TO PONDER

Think about some life experiences that you personally have undergone. These should include both positive and negative life events. What made each event stressful to you? Did your cognitive appraisal of the situations make them easier or more difficult for you to cope with them? What specific coping techniques did you use with each event?

Few studies have compared the relative stressfulness of role losses, role gains or replacements, and role extensions in old age, although research on life stress among younger populations is extensive. Chapter 12 examines both paid and nonpaid productive roles in the later years in greater detail.

The first systematic studies of the physiological and psychological impact of increased sources and amounts of stress on humans were undertaken by Holmes and colleagues (Holmes and Masuda, 1974; Holmes and Rahe, 1967; Rahe, 1972). They introduced the concept of *life change units*, a numerical score indicating the typical level of change or stress that a particular event produces in an individual's day-to-day life. Their research with young and middle-aged adults revealed that people who experienced multiple events with life change units totaling more than 200 points within a 2-year period were more susceptible to physical illness. Whether these same life events produce the same level of stress in older persons as they do in younger people is unclear. Events such as a jail term, assuming a new mortgage, and starting school are less likely to be experienced in old age. Furthermore, the life change units assigned to some events by the young respondents may not reflect the degree of stress actually produced by events that they have not yet experienced (e.g., death of a partner). Research comparing older and younger people's ratings of life events reveals:

- Some items such as "death of spouse" are perceived to be equally stressful by all ages.
- Younger people view "death of a close friend" and "marital reconciliation" as more stressful than do older people.

- Older people who have experienced a life event such as "retirement" and "death of spouse" assign lower readjustment scores than people who have not experienced them.

These findings suggest that the anticipation of an event is more stressful than the actual experience, and that previous experience with a life event can help the person cope better when a similar event occurs. In addition, older people have developed greater resilience and maturity through their previous coping experiences; they may be the most adaptive members of their cohort if they have survived beyond the life expectancy predicted for them (McLeod, 1996).

What Determines Stress Responses in Old Age?

Both social and personal factors affect the process of coping with stressful events. The former encompasses friendships and family support, while the latter includes the individual's functional health, cognitive status, and self-esteem, as well as aspirations, values, vulnerabilities, and needs that mediate between a particular stressful situation and its outcomes. The individual's cognitive appraisal of a situation as being stressful or not is important. The relative desirability or undesirability of an event, whether or not it is anticipated, and previous experiences with similar events also determine how an individual responds to the situation. The availability of social supports is significant too (Coyne and Downey, 1991). A person who must face a crisis alone may use different coping strategies than one who has family and friends.

Personality styles also may affect responses to stress. For example, person with a passive style may not feel powerful enough to directly influence his or her fate, whereas one with an active style may rely more on personal abilities and less on others. Differences in responses to stress by older people with these different styles would be expected; however, research has not provided sufficient evidence for such hypothesized variations.

Locus of control is another personality characteristic that may influence responses to stress. This is the belief by an individual that events in his or her life result from personal actions (internal locus), or are determined by fate or powerful others (external locus). Internal locus of control and a sense of mastery appear to be related to successful coping in both young and old. It can help the individual maintain functional ability in old age and improve adjustment to widowhood (Kemper, van Sonderen, and Ormel, 1999; Thomae, 1992).

Adaptation in the Later Years

As noted earlier in this chapter, a critical personality feature in the later years is an individual's ability to adapt to major changes in life circumstances, health and social status, and social and physical environments. **Adaptation** includes a range of behaviors such as coping, goal-setting, problem-solving, and other attempts to maintain psychological homeostasis (Ruth and Coleman, 1996). Given older people's numerous experiences with life events, role loss, and environmental changes, it would appear that adaptation in old age should occur with relative ease. Indeed, in one sense, an individual who has reached age 75 or 80 has proved to be the most adaptable of his or her generation, since the ultimate proof of adaptation is survival. As we have seen thus far, older people continue to face challenges to their well-being in the form of personal and family illness, age-related declines in sensory and physiological functions, and changes in their social and physical environments. To the extent that older people are capable of using coping skills that were effective in youth and middle age, they will continue to adapt to change successfully.

Does coping change with age? Before answering, we must first define and consider the functions of **coping.** Coping is the manner in which a person responds to stress. It includes cognitive, emotional, and behavioral responses made in the face of internally and externally created events. It differs from defense mechanisms in that people are

TABLE 6.3   Major Ego Defense Mechanisms

DEFENSE MECHANISM	EXAMPLE
1. Denial (a premature defense mechanism)	Denying what one really feels to avoid punishment by the super-ego and rejection by others.
2. Projection	Feeling that others are untrustworthy when one feels unsure about one's own trustworthiness.
3. Repression	Forgetting an event that could disturb the feeling of well-being if brought into consciousness.
4. Reaction formation	Extreme display of love and affection toward someone who is actually hated.
5. Regression and fixation	Returning to a comfortable stage of life and/or way of behaving under conditions of anxiety and stress.
6. Displacement	Taking out one's anger and hostility on family because one is afraid of expressing anger toward one's supervisor at work who has humiliated the individual.

generally conscious of how they have coped in a particular situation and, if asked, can describe specific coping responses to a given stressor. Coping strategies may be described as "planful behavior" in response to a stressful situation.

These contrast with **defense mechanisms,** unconscious reactions that an individual adopts to defend or protect the self from impulses and memories that threaten one's identity. Defense mechanisms also have an underlying evaluative quality; some defenses are more primitive or less mature than others (see Table 6.3). As people mature, so do the defense mechanisms that they use. The Grant Study of Harvard Graduates found that the men in this sample used fewer primitive mechanisms (e.g., distortion and projection) as they reached middle-age, and more mature mecha-

nisms, such as sublimation, suppression, and humor (Vaillant, 1994).

Unlike defense mechanisms, coping styles cannot easily be categorized as primitive or mature. Some forms of coping, however, are aimed not at resolving the problem, but at providing psychological escape, as illustrated by the categories of coping defined by some researchers (see Table 6.4). For example, an older woman who learns that her closest friend has a terminal illness may cry and sympathize with her friend. This can alleviate the stress that both are feeling, but unless she takes some action such as searching the Internet for some newer therapies for the disease, she has not coped with the problem itself.

This example and our earlier discussion of coping responses to life events and chronic stressors

TABLE 6.4   Classification of Coping Responses

GENERAL STRATEGIES OF COPING
(Lazarus, 1975a, 1975b; Lazarus and Launier, 1978; Lazarus and Folkman, 1984)

1. Information search in an attempt to understand the situation
2. Direct action to change the situation
3. Inhibition of action
4. Psychological responses to the emotional arousal created by the situation

COPING RESPONSES TO TERMINAL ILLNESS
(Moos, 1977)

1. Searching for information
2. Setting goals
3. Denying or minimizing the problem
4. Seeking emotional support
5. Rehearsing alternative outcomes

DIMENSIONS OF COPING
(Kahana and Kahana, 1982)

1. Instrumental (taking action, alone or with the assistance of others)
2. Intrapsychic (cognitive approaches, acceptance of the situation)
3. Affective (releasing tensions, expressing emotions)
4. Escape (avoiding or denying the problem, displacement activities such as increased exercise, eating, and smoking)
5. Resigned helplessness (feeling impotent, unable to cope)

suggest that coping reactions generally serve two functions:

- *problem-focused* coping to solve a problem that has produced stress for the individual
- *emotion-focused* coping to reduce the emotional and physiological discomfort that accompanies the stressful situation (Lazarus and Folkman, 1984)

In some cases, an individual may focus only on solving the problem *or* on dealing with the emotional distress that it creates. Such reactions tend to be incomplete and do not resolve both the emotional and functional impact of the situation. Coping must fulfill both emotion-regulating and problem-solving functions in order to alleviate stress.

The question of whether coping styles change with age has not been extensively researched. Some early studies of coping among young and middle-aged persons reported few significant differences, although these groups have generally not been compared with older persons (Folkman et al., 1987). Older (ages 65 to 91) and middle-aged (ages 50 to 64) respondents in McCrae's (1989) study used more mature coping styles (e.g., problem-solving, and seeking the advice of family, friends, and professionals) and fewer escapist strategies than did younger (ages 24 to 49) respondents. Other cross-sectional studies also found age differences. For example, older adults are less likely than the young to use confrontation as a coping response, especially when the stressor could be defined as a threat. They are more likely to use distancing techniques and to reappraise the situation in a positive light. In the Baltimore and the Bonn Longitudinal Studies, cross-sectional differences were greater than intraindividual change. In both studies—the former, examining adults over a 7-year period, the latter over 10 years—coping responses remained quite stable (Thomae, 1992; McCrae, 1989). In particular, coping styles related to the personality characteristic of neuroticism were stable over 7 years, even though cross-sectional comparisons revealed that older respondents in general used *less* neurotic coping (Costa and McCrae, 1993).

Religious activity can serve a useful coping function.

Religious coping is found to be an important coping strategy in several studies of older persons, especially among African Americans (McCrae, 1989; McFadden, 1996). Indeed, in the Duke Longitudinal Study, 45 percent of the respondents aged 55 to 80 mentioned trust and faith in God, prayer, and seeking help from God as a coping strategy for at least one of three major life events. Over 70 percent of adults have been found to use religion in coping with major life events. Religious coping among church-going adults has been identified to significantly predict their recent mental health and perceived general health (Pargament et al., 1990, 1995).

Studies of coping among the old-old indicate that acceptance of change in one's life (e.g., institutionalization, divorce of children or grandchildren) may be the most adaptive coping response. Control over external events may become less important than the need to make uncontrollable events more acceptable to one's values and beliefs (Ryff, 1991). In most cases, the coping styles chosen by an older person are appropriate for the problem at hand and result in successful adaptation. When cognitive deterioration is significant, however, there is a restriction in the range of an individual's coping responses and a tendency to resort to more primitive reactions, such as denying or ignoring the problem. The majority of older people appear capable of using a wide repertoire of coping responses and can call upon the most effective ones for a given situation. In sum, most people maintain their coping styles into old age, and use appropriate responses.

SUCCESSFUL AGING

Researchers and clinicians are increasingly interested in the concept of **successful aging** (Rowe and Kahn, 1987, 1997, 1998; Seeman et al., 1994). This interest has been sparked by the growing number of older people who have avoided the chronic health problems and declining cognitive skills that afflict other older adults and have managed to cope effectively in their daily lives. What are the characteristics of such elders who age successfully that distinguish them from their less hardy peers? Successful aging is defined as a combination of:

- physical and functional health
- high cognitive functioning
- active involvement with society

This definition implies that the successful older person has low risk of disease and disability (i.e., healthy lifestyle factors such as diet, not smoking, physical activity), is actively using problem-solving, conceptualization, and language skills, is maintaining social contacts, and is participating in productive activities (e.g., volunteering; paid or unpaid work). A model of successful aging proposed by Rowe and Kahn (1997), shown in Figure 6.1, integrates these components.

The MacArthur Studies of Successful Aging examined longitudinally a cohort of men and women (aged 70 to 79 at baseline) in three East Coast U.S. communities. These people were se-

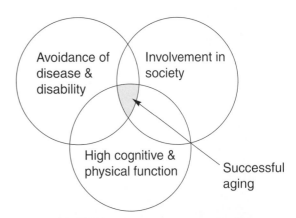

FIGURE 6.1   A model of successful aging. This model assumes that all three components must exist for successful aging to occur.
SOURCE: Reprinted with permission, Rowe & Kahn, 1997.

lected because they represented the top third of their age group in cognitive and physical function. Within this selective group of "robust" older persons, more specific tests of cognitive and physical abilities, as well as physiological parameters, were conducted in 1988 and 1991. Those with the highest performance scores in this group at follow-up and those who survived three years later had fewer chronic conditions (especially cardiovascular diseases), better self-rated health, and higher educational and income levels. The majority of these robust older adults reported no problems with daily physical activities such as walking, crouching, and stooping without help. Three-year follow-ups revealed that the majority (55 percent) maintained their baseline performance levels. Another 23 percent showed a decline on the performance tests, while 22 percent actually *improved* on these tests. Those who declined or died in the interim had greater weekly variability in their physical performance, blood pressure, balance, and gait, and had entered the study with some chronic diseases (Nesselroade, Featherman, Agen, and Rowe, 1996; Seeman et al., 1994). Participants in the MacArthur Studies were also assessed on their physical functioning over seven years. Those with more social ties and a strong support system showed less

Gerontologists have recently focused on identifying the characteristics of people who age successfully.

of maintaining cognitive abilities were *involvement in strenuous physical activity.* A higher level of **self-efficacy,** that is, a feeling of competence in one's ability to deal with new situations, was also a significant predictor of high physical and cognitive function at follow-up (Seeman et al, 1999).

The Oregon Brain Aging Study, a longitudinal assessment of a smaller number of optimally healthy persons aged 65 to 74 and 84 to 100, measured multiple physical, cognitive, neurologic, and sensory functions as indicators of healthy aging (Howieson et al., 1993). This group of older adults was selected because they had no history of diseases affecting brain function, no psychiatric disorders, or medications that could impair cognition. Very few areas of decline were found; the oldest-old differed from the youngest-old only on tests requiring visual perception and constructional skills, *not* on tests of memory or reasoning.

The concept of "robust aging" represents a broader perspective on successful aging, one that considers exceptional functioning on measures of physical health, cognitive abilities, and emotional well-being (Garfein and Herzog, 1995; Suzman et al., 1992; Vaillant and Vaillant, 1990). Others have labeled this "optimal aging," an ideal state that is theoretically but not practically possible for most people (Schulz and Heckhasen, 1996). Four important characteristics appear to distinguish robust older adults from their less robust peers:

- productive involvement (defined as 1500 hours or more of paid or unpaid work, home maintenance, or volunteer activity in the past year)
- absence of depressive symptoms (i.e., high affective well-being)
- high physical functioning
- no cognitive impairment (Garfein and Herzog, 1995)

In the survey by Garfein and Herzog, the robust group included many in the oldest-old age range. Robust elders reported more social contacts, better physical health and vision, and fewer significant life events (e.g., death of partner, child, close friend)

decline in their functional health than elders without strong ties. Such social supports were particularly valuable for men and those who had poorer physical health at baseline (Unger, McAvay, Bruce, Berkman and Seeman, 1999).

As noted above, successful aging also implies maintenance of cognitive functioning. In the MacArthur Studies, *educational level* was the best predictor of continued high levels of cognitive ability (Albert et al., 1995). Rather than innate intelligence, higher educational achievement in those who aged successfully was most likely due to lifelong interest in intellectual activities such as reading and solving crossword puzzles, as well as a beneficial effect of education on the development of complex networks in the brain. Other predictors

in the past 3 years than did poorly functioning elders. For the oldest-old, successful aging also implies the ability to independently perform both basic activities of daily living and higher-level work, as well as leisure and social activities (Horgas, Wilms and Bates, 1998)

Other researchers emphasize that a *sense of purpose or contribution to society* is a critical element of successful aging. This sense of purpose requires more than reflection, acceptance, and ego integrity as Erikson describes in the eighth stage of adult development. It requires that older persons continue their active involvement with society that is the hallmark of the seventh stage—generativity. For example, research with participants in the Foster Grandparents Program reveals that those who have aged successfully believe they have achieved higher-order needs, such as helping children, making a difference in others' lives, and feeling that one's life has purpose (Fisher, 1995). These are elements of both generativity and ego integrity, and support the importance of both types of developmental tasks for successful aging. As noted in Chapter 12, older adults who volunteer generally experience greater life satisfaction than their peers who do no volunteer work. Even those who do not volunteer but maintain social ties with family and friends can increase their chances of successful aging. A 12-year follow-up of almost 3000 community-dwelling elders showed that people who were socially disengaged (i.e., no social contacts with friends or family) were 2.4 times more likely to experience cognitive impairment over that time period than their elders of the same age, gender, ethnicity and health status who had five or six close social ties (Bassuk, Glass, and Berkman, 1999).

Mental Disorders among Older Persons

Depression is the primary affective or emotional disorder of old age, and accounts for a significant number of suicides, especially among older men. Alzheimer's disease and other dementias are cognitive disorders that are more likely to affect the old than the young. Alcoholism and drug abuse are less common in older individuals, although their effect on the physical health and cognitive functioning of older people is more detrimental than on younger persons. Paranoid disorders and schizophrenia are conditions that are first diagnosed in youth or middle age. Each of these conditions is reviewed in the following sections.

The prevalence of psychiatric disorders among older persons who are living in the community ranges from 15 to 25 percent, depending on the population studied and the categories of disorders examined. Even higher rates can occur in the institutionalized older population, with estimates of 10 to 40 percent of older patients with mild to moderate impairments, and another 5 to 10 percent with significant impairments. Twenty percent of all first admissions to psychiatric hospitals are persons over age 65. Older psychiatric patients are more likely to have chronic conditions and to require longer periods of inpatient treatment than are younger patients, as evidenced by the fact that 25 percent of all beds in these hospitals are occupied by older persons. Note the discrepancy between this proportion and the proportion over age 65 in the U.S. population—just under 13 percent in 2000. Approximately 100,000 older chronic psychiatric patients live in state mental hospitals, 500,000 in nursing homes, and the remainder (over 1 million) in the community, where they often receive inadequate treatment for their psychiatric conditions. At the same time, however, older persons are less likely than the young to use community mental health services. Older patients comprise only 4 percent of the load of psychiatric outpatient clinics and less than 2 percent of those served by private practitioners (Butler, Lewis, and Sunderland, 1991).

One problem with describing the prevalence of mental disorders of older people is the lack of criteria distinguishing conditions that emerge in old age from those that continue throughout adulthood. In fact, the major classification system for psychiatric disorders, the *Diagnostic and Statistical Manual of Mental Disorders*, fourth edition (DSM-IV), of the American Psychiatric Association (1994), makes such a distinction only for dementias that begin in late life. No other mental disorders are differentiated for old age, although other diagnostic categories are described specifically for adulthood as separate from childhood or adolescence. The problem of inadequate criteria for late-life **psychopathology** (or psychiatric disorders) is compounded by the lack of age-appropriate psychological tests for diagnosing these conditions. An increasing number of tests are being developed, especially for diagnosing depression and dementia in older people.

Depression

Depression, dementia, and paranoia are the three most prevalent forms of late-life psychopathology. Of these, depression is the most common. It is important to distinguish *unipolar* depression from *bipolar* disorders (that is, ranging from a depressed to a manic state), as well as severe conditions such as sadness, grief reactions, and other affective disorders. Most of the depressions of old age are unipolar; manic-depressive disorders are rare. Still other cases in late life are *secondary* or *reactive* depressions, which arise in response to a significant life event with which the individual cannot cope. For example, physical illness and the loss of loved ones through death and relocation may trigger depressive reactions in older people. The vegetative signs, suicidal thoughts, weight loss, and mood variations from morning to night that are observed in major depression are not found in reactive depression. Studies of older individuals in community settings and in nursing homes suggest that the prevalence of major depression is generally lower than the rates of minor or reactive depression. Estimates of depression for community-dwelling elders are:

- 20 percent for minor depression
- 1 percent for major depression
- 0.1 percent for bipolar disorder

In contrast, rates as high as 10 to 15 percent have been found among institutionalized older adults (Jefferson and Greist, 1993; Koenig and Blazer, 1996; Parmelee, Katz, and Lawton, 1992).

As noted earlier in this chapter, most role *gains* (e.g., worker, driver, voter, partner, or parent) occur in the earlier years, whereas many role *losses* may multiply in the later years. As we have seen, loss of roles may be compounded by decrements in sensory abilities, physical strength, and health. Although depression usually does not result from any one of these alone, the combination of several losses in close sequence may trigger a reactive depressive episode. This may be due to changes in the brain caused by multiple stressors that affect the production of mood-regulating chemicals in the brain. It appears that acute life events can lead to a recurrence of major depression, but do not necessarily trigger its first onset (Kessler, 1997). Older people with major physical conditions such as stroke, cancer, or chronic pain and those who do not have a supportive social network are at greatest risk. Among elders who are hospitalized for physical health problems, 10 percent have been found to have major depression, and 30 percent minor depression (Koenig and Blazer, 1996; NIH, 1994). In addition, older people who have experienced depression in the past are at risk for a recurrence, especially if it is triggered by a major life event (Gurland, 1992).

Psychiatric symptoms that persist beyond six months in these patients may indicate the development of a major depressive episode (Nacoste and Wise, 1991). Consistent with the approach of a better fit between the older person and the environment, environmental and social interventions as well as psychotherapy are more effective than antidepressant medications for minor depression. However, medications and sometimes electroconvulsive therapy are necessary to treat major depression and prevent suicide, as described later in this chapter.

Death rates appear to be greater among older persons with a diagnosis of depression, almost twice that for nondepressed people over 20 years. Even after one year, depressed older adults, especially if they have cognitive impairment, have a higher mortality risk. The more severe a patient's depressive symptoms, the more likely he or she is to die sooner (Schulz et al., 2000; Tilvis, Pitkaelae and Nevantaus, 1998). Medical hospital stays are often twice as long for those with depression. In addition, depressed older adults take longer to recover from a hip fracture or stroke (Koenig and Blazer, 1996). This may be because older persons with depression are more apathetic, less motivated to improve their health, and more likely to entertain thoughts of suicide than younger depressives. Table 6.5 lists the criteria used by the American Psychiatric Association for major depression. Below are some symptoms of depression that may be confused with normal aging:

- reports or evidence of sadness
- feelings of emptiness or detachment with no precipitating major life event such as bereavement
- expressions of anxiety or panic for no apparent cause
- loss of interest in the environment
- neglect of self-care
- changes in eating and sleeping patterns

The depressed person may complain of vague aches and pains, either generally or in a specific part of the body. Occasional symptoms or symptoms associated with a specific medication, physical illness, or alcoholism need to be distinguished from the somatic complaints associated with depression. Only when multiple symptoms appear together and persist *for at least 2 weeks* should an individual and his or her family suspect major depression, especially if an older person speaks frequently of death or suicide.

One problem with detecting depression in older people is that they may be more successful than their younger counterparts at masking or hiding symptoms. In fact, many cases of depression in older persons are not diagnosed because the individual either does not express changes in mood or denies them in the clinical interview. A *masked depression* is one in which few mood changes are reported. Instead, the patient complains of a vague pain, bodily discomfort, and sleep disturbance; reports problems with memory; is apathetic; and withdraws from others (Gallo, Anthony, and

TABLE 6.5   Summary of DSM-IV Criteria for Major Depressive Episode

At least five of the following symptoms are present during the same 2-week period and represent a change from previous function:

1. Depressed mood most of day, nearly every day[*]
2. Markedly diminished interest or pleasure in activities, apathy[*]
3. Significant weight loss or weight gain, or appetite change
4. Sleep disturbance (insomnia or hypersomnia) nearly every day
5. Agitation or retardation of activity nearly every day
6. Low energy level or fatigue nearly every day
7. Self-blame, guilt, worthlessness
8. Poor concentration, indecisiveness
9. Recurrent thoughts of death, suicide

[*]At least one of the symptoms should be these.

SOURCE: Adapted with permission from the *Diagnostic and statistical manual of mental disorders,* 4th ed. Copyright 1994 American Psychiatric Association, 327.

Muthen, 1994; Lichtenberg, Ross, Millis, and Manning, 1995). This is a common condition in older generations because many of these people were raised in environments that discouraged open expression of feelings.

Health care professionals and family members need to distinguish depression from medical conditions and changes due to normal aging. For example, an older woman with arthritis who complains of increasing pain may actually be seeking a reason for vague physical discomfort that is related to a depressive episode. People with masked depression are more likely to complain of problems with memory or problem-solving. Their denial or masking of symptoms may lead the physician to assume that the individual is experiencing **dementia,** a condition that is generally irreversible. It is for this reason that depression in older persons is often labeled *pseudodementia.*

Because of such likelihood of denial, a physician's first goal with an older patient who has vague somatic and memory complaints should be to conduct a thorough physical exam and lab tests. This is important in order to determine if an individual is depressed or has a physical disorder or symptoms of dementia. If the cognitive dysfunction is due to depression, it will improve when the depression is treated. On the other hand, some medical conditions may produce depressive symptoms. These include:

- Parkinson's disease
- rheumatoid arthritis
- thyroid dysfunction
- diseases of the adrenal glands

In some cases, depression can coexist with medical conditions such as heart disease and stroke, compounding the dysfunction associated with these medical problems and delaying the recovery process. Certain medications may also produce feelings of depression. In fact, any medication that has a depressant effect on the central nervous system can produce depressive symptoms, specifically lethargy and loss of interest in the environment. For these reasons, older adults with depressive symptoms should be examined thoroughly for underlying physical illness, hypothyroidism, vitamin deficiencies, chronic infections, and reactions to medications. Physicians must frequently conduct medication reviews to determine if their older patients begin to show side effects to a drug, even after using it for several months or years.

THERAPEUTIC INTERVENTIONS   It is important to treat both major and secondary depressions upon diagnosis, because the older depressed patient is at higher risk of self-destructive behavior and suicide. The first task of physicians or mental health professionals who diagnose depression in an older person is to provide psychological support for acute symptoms, including empathy, attentive listening, and encouragement of active coping skills. For patients with minor depression, this may be all they need to show a decrease in symptoms. For more severely depressed elders, alternative therapies may be required. There is some disagreement, however, about the efficacy of such therapies. Although short-term improvements may be achieved through treatment, the long-range prognosis is not always successful, and some older people will experience a relapse. If the onset of depression occurs before age 70, psychotherapy is generally more successful.

The most common therapeutic intervention with depressed older individuals is pharmacological, which is particularly useful for those experiencing a major depression or bipolar depression (NIH, 1994). Therapy with antidepressants is generally long-term. Although antidepressants work well for some older persons, many others cannot use these drugs because of other medications they are taking, such as antihypertensives, or because the side effects are more detrimental than the depression itself. These effects include postural hypotension (i.e., a sudden drop in blood pressure when rising from a prone position), increased vulnerability to falls and fractures, cardiac arrhythmias, urinary retention, constipation, disorientation, skin rash, and dry mouth. Because of these potentially dangerous reactions, it is important to start antidepressant therapy at a much lower dose (perhaps 50 percent lower) in older than in younger patients. Many older persons who turn to a general practitioner for treatment of depression often receive antidepressants as a first line of attack

---

MEDICATIONS THAT MAY PRODUCE SYMPTOMS OF DEPRESSION

- antihypertensives
- digoxin
- corticosteroids

- estrogen
- some antipsychotic drugs
- antiparkinsonism drugs such as L-dopa

rather than psychotherapy, which may be more appropriate. There is increased evidence that a combination of well-monitored pharmacotherapy and psychotherapy can produce a decrease in symptoms in up to 80 percent of older adults (Koenig and Blazer, 1996). This combination was found to reduce symptoms of bereavement-related depression in 69 percent of elders in a 16-week treatment program, compared with 45 percent for drugs alone, and 29 percent for psychotherapy alone (Reynolds et al., 1999). Psychotherapy lasting at least one year has also been shown to stabilize bouts of mania and depression in adults with bipolar disorder. This suggests that patients with this type of depression need consistency in their therapeutic interventions (Frank, Swartz, Mallinger, Thase, Weaver, and Kupfer, 1999).

Older people are just as likely as younger persons to benefit from the insight and empathy provided by a therapist trained in geriatric psychotherapy (Scogin and McElreath, 1994). In particular, secondary depression responds well to supportive psychotherapy that allows the patient to review and come to terms with the stresses of late life. Supportive psychotherapy is useful because it allows older patients to reestablish control and emotional stability. Older depressed persons appear to benefit from short-term, client-centered, directive therapy more than from therapy that is nondirective or uses free association to uncover long-standing personality conflicts. Cognitive-behavioral interventions, such as self-monitoring of negative thoughts about oneself, daily monitoring of moods, and increased participation in pleasant events may be especially effective (De-Vries, 1996; Teri et al., 1997).

As noted above, psychotherapy must be accompanied by **pharmacotherapy** or electroconvulsive therapy in severely depressed elders. Despite past controversy about its use, **electroconvulsive or electroshock therapy (ECT)** is sometimes used in cases of severe depression. ECT is a quick and effective method for treating major depression in patients who:

- have not responded to medications
- have a higher risk of suicide
- refuse to eat
- are severely agitated
- show vegetative symptoms
- express feelings of hopelessness, helplessness, or worthlessness
- have experienced delusions

Unilateral nondominant hemisphere ECT is often preferred because it is capable of alleviating depression without impairing cognitive functioning (Koenig and Blazer, 1996). Maintenance treatment with ECT may be necessary for older depressed persons (as often as once a month). In some cases, antidepressants are used after a course of ECT to prevent relapse.

COMBINED THERAPIES MAY BE MOST EFFECTIVE WITH OLDER ADULTS

In the six months since the death of his wife of 52 years, Mr. Simon has lost interest in all the activities that he and his wife enjoyed together. He has lost weight and sleeps irregularly. His complaints of poor memory and loss of energy have alarmed his adult children, who insisted he see his family physician. The doctor prescribed an antidepressant upon recognizing the symptoms of depression. However, Mr. Simon stopped taking these medications after two weeks because they made him feel dizzy and caused dry mouth. The physician spent time discussing the immediate benefits from medications, but also arranged for Mr. Simon to participate in one-on-one psychotherapy sessions with an expert in geriatric psychotherapy. After 2 months, Mr. Simon has already seen the benefits of combining these two therapies for his condition. He now attends a local senior center daily, and has begun a regular exercise program of walking for one hour every day.

SUMMARY OF THERAPEUTIC INTERVENTIONS FOR DEPRESSED OLDER ADULTS

Pharmacotherapy (antidepressants)

Electroconvulsive therapy

Psychotherapy
  • supportive

  • directive
  • cognitive-behavioral

Combination of therapies

Suicide among Older People

Older people are at greater risk of suicide than any other age group. It has been estimated that 17 to 25 percent of all *completed* suicides occur in persons aged 65 and older. In 1997, the national rate was 11.4 suicides per 100,000 population. The rate for persons over age 65 was over 18 per 100,000, ranging from 13.2 for those aged 65 to 70, to 21 per 100,000 among those over age 85 (McIntosh, 1997). The highest suicide rates in the United States are found among older white males. The prevalence of suicide in this group, 43.3 per 100,000, is more than:

  • twice the rate for nonwhite males (17.5 per 100,000)
  • seven times the rate for older white women (5.8)
  • 15 times the rate for older nonwhite women (2.8)

White men aged 85 and older are at greatest risk, almost double the rate for the second highest group, white men aged 15–24 (24.1 per 100,000) (NCHS, 2000). Both white and nonwhite older men account for 83 percent of all suicides among the population aged 65 and older. Note that these statistics reflect direct or clearly identifiable suicides. There are probably a significant number of indirect suicides that appear to be accidents or natural deaths (e.g., starvation or gas poisoning), and cases where family members and physicians do not list suicide as the cause of death; therefore these rates may underrepresent the actual incidence of the problem.

One explanation for the higher rates of suicide among older white males is that they gener-

ally experience the greatest incongruence between their ideal self-image (that of worker, decision maker, or holder of relatively high status in society) and the realities of advancing age. With age, the role of worker is generally lost, chronic illness may diminish one's sense of control, and an individual may feel a loss of status. Social isolation also appears to be important; suicide rates among older widowed men have been found to be more than five times greater than for married men, but no differences have been found between married and widowed women (Li, 1995). This is because older widowed men are most likely to lack strong social support networks. Older men in many populations of color such as African American and Chinese are less likely to commit suicide because of more extensive family support systems. Suicide risk is greatest among white males who are widowed, aged 85 and older, with recurrent major depression, and with chronic pain, cardiopulmonary diseases, or cancer (Blazer and Koenig, 1996; Zweig and Hinrichsen, 1993). However, contrary to popular belief, older suicide victims are no more likely than other older people to have been diagnosed with a terminal illness prior to the suicide.

Suicide rates declined among the older population from 1940 to 1980, but rose from 1980 to 1990, especially among men over age 80. They have declined slightly since the early 1990s (Surgeon General, 2000). There are fewer nonfatal suicide attempts in older men compared to their younger counterparts. That is, the rate of completed suicides is far greater among older men—one for every eight attempts, compared with one completed suicide for every 100 to 200 attempts by the young. This difference may be due to the use

---

RISK FACTORS FOR SUICIDE IN OLDER ADULTS

- a serious physical illness with severe pain
- the sudden death of a loved one
- a major loss of independence or financial inadequacy
- statements that indicate frustration with life and a desire to end it

- a sudden decision to give away one's most important possessions
- a general loss of interest in one's social and physical environment

---

of more lethal methods of suicide such as shotguns. In 1996 firearms were involved in:

- 78 percent of suicides among older men
- 36 percent among older women (McIntosh, 1997; Surgeon General, 2000)

Because attempts at suicide are more likely to end in death for older men, family members and health care providers need to be sensitive to clues of an impending suicide. The NIMH estimates that 70 percent of older persons who commit suicide had seen a primary care physician in the preceding month, but their psychiatric disturbances had not been detected or were inadequately treated. In most cases, these older persons had not sought psychiatric care. For this reason, the Surgeon General in 1999 issued a "Call to Action to Prevent Suicide." This effort, aimed at mental health providers and the older population directly, focused on increasing awareness of depression, its symptoms, and potential outcomes (Surgeon General, 2000).

Since older people are less likely to make threats or to announce their intentions to commit suicide than are young people, watching for subtle cues is even more important. Clearly, not all older people displaying such symptoms will attempt suicide, but the recognition of changes in an older family member's or client's behavior and moods can alleviate a potential disaster.

Dementia

Normal aging does not result in significant declines in intelligence, memory, and learning ability, as described in Chapter 5. Mild impairments do not necessarily signal a major loss but often represent a mild form of memory dysfunction known as **benign senescent forgetfulness.** Only in the case of the diseases known collectively as the dementias does cognitive function show marked deterioration. Dementia includes a variety of conditions that are caused by or associated with damage of brain tissue, resulting in impaired cognitive function and, in more advanced stages, impaired behavior and personality. Such changes in the brain result in progressive deterioration of an individual's ability to learn and recall items from the past. Previously, it was assumed that all these syndromes were associated with cerebral arteriosclerosis ("hardening of the arteries"). In fact, we now know that a number of these conditions occur independently of arteriosclerosis. Some features are unique to each type of dementia, but all dementias have the following characteristics:

- a change in an individual's ability to recall events in recent memory
- problems with comprehension, attention span, judgment
- disorientation to time, place, and person

The individual with dementia may have problems in understanding abstract thought or symbolic language (for example, be unable to interpret a proverb), particularly in the later stages of the disease. Although not part of normal aging, the likelihood of experiencing dementia does increase with advancing age. Depending on the criteria used, estimates range from two to three million people over age 65 having some type of dementia; almost 2 million have severe dementia, and up to 5 million are

---

CARE FOR DEMENTIA PATIENTS WITH ACUTE ILLNESS

In the late stages of many irreversible dementias such as Alzheimer's disease, the patient is often physically frail and unable to survive an acute condition such as pneumonia or a hip fracture. A recent study followed people aged 70 or older who were hospitalized for one of these conditions, and *also* had a late-stage dementing illness. Six months later, mortality rates were much higher for elders with pneumonia and dementia than for those with no dementia (53 percent vs. 13 percent). Those with hip fractures and dementia also had higher rates than elders without dementia (55 percent vs. 12 percent). Both patients with and without dementia received as many life-saving procedures. Only 7 percent of the former had written documents to forgo such treatment and only 24 percent had requested analgesics. These findings point to the need to establish guidelines for palliative treatment for an older person with dementia who is dying of an acute illness (Morrison and Siu, 2000).

---

mildly to moderately impaired (Hendrie, 1997; Teri, McCurry, and Logsdon, 1997). Because of problems in differentially diagnosing dementia, and variations in the criteria used by available tests and classification systems, prevalence rates range from 3 to 29 percent of the older population (Erkinjuntti, Ostbye, Steenhuis, and Hachinski, 1997). Nevertheless, there is general agreement among epidemiological studies that the incidence of dementias increases with age, especially between ages 75 and 90. For example, it is estimated that:

- 2 percent of the 75 to 79 age group has moderate to severe dementia
- 8.5 percent of 85- to 89-year-olds have this condition (Paykel et al., 1994)

However, as noted in Chapter 1, rates of dementia among "hardy" centenarians may actually be lower than among 85- to 90-year-olds because of genetic advantages experienced by those who live to age 100 and beyond.

The major types of dementias are shown in Table 6.6. Note the distinction between *reversible* and *irreversible* dementias. The first refers to cognitive decline that may be caused by drug toxicity, hormonal or nutritional disorders, and other diseases that may be reversible. Sources of potentially reversible dementias include tumors in and trauma to the brain, toxins, metabolic disorders such as hypo- or hyperthyroidism, diabetes, hypo- or hy-

percalcemia, infections, vascular lesions, and hydrocephalus. Severe depression may produce confusion and memory problems in some older people. Some medications may also cause dementia-like symptoms. This problem is aggravated if the individual is taking multiple medications or is on a dosage that is higher than can be metabolized by the older kidney or liver. An individual who appears to be suffering from such reactions should be referred promptly for medical screening.

Irreversible dementias are those that have no discernible environmental cause and cannot yet be cured. Although there is considerable research on the causes and treatments for these conditions, they must be labeled irreversible at the present time. Some of these are more common than others;

TABLE 6.6 **Major Dementias of Late Life**

REVERSIBLE	IRREVERSIBLE
Drugs	Alzheimer's
Alcohol	Vascular
Nutritional deficiencies	Huntington's
Normal pressure hydrocephalus	Pick's disease
Brain tumors	Creutzfeldt-Jacob
Hypothyroidism/Hyperthyroidism	Kuru
Neurosyphilis	Korsakoff
Depression (pseudodementia)	

some have identifiable causes while others do not. Pick's disease is one of the rarest; in this type, the frontal lobes of the brain atrophy. Of all the dementias, it is most likely to occur in younger persons and to result in significant personality changes. Creutzfeldt-Jacob and Kuru diseases have been traced to a slow-acting virus that can strike at any age. In the former type of dementia, decline in cognitive abilities occurs quite rapidly, as seen in the recent epidemics of "mad cow disease" that have been attributed to consuming tainted beef in Great Britain and Europe. Kuru disease is quite rare. Huntington's disease is a genetically transmitted condition that usually appears in people in their thirties and forties. It results in more neuromuscular changes than do the other dementias.

Vascular dementia is estimated to represent 15 to 20 percent of all nonreversible dementias. This form of dementia was labeled "senility" in the past. In this type, blood vessels leading to the brain become occluded, with the result that several areas of the brain show infarcts or small strokes. The primary risk factor for vascular dementia is the same as for strokes, that is, hypertension. Because of this, vascular dementia may be prevented by controlling hypertension. Nevertheless, once it occurs, this type of dementia is irreversible (Lis and Gaviria, 1997).

Delirium

Delirium is a reversible dementia experienced by some older adults. This condition has a more rapid onset than other types of dementia. Signs of delirium are:

- abrupt changes in behavior
- fluctuations in behavior throughout the day
- inability to focus attention on a task
- hallucinations
- speech that makes no sense or is irrational

Delirium is usually caused by some external variables such as a reaction to an injury (especially head injury) or infection, malnutrition, reaction to alcohol, or even a fecal impaction or urinary prob-

lems. A thorough medical assessment can help diagnose and reverse delirium and its symptoms (Logsdon and Teri, 2000).

Alzheimer's Disease

Senile dementia of the Alzheimer's type (Alzheimer's disease or AD) is the most common irreversible dementia in late life, accounting for 50 to 70 percent of all dementias. Prevalence rates are difficult to obtain, but it is estimated that about four million Americans—between 5 and 15 percent of all persons over age 65 and over, and 25 percent in nursing homes—have symptoms of AD. The prevalence of Alzheimer's disease appears to increase with age; less than 2 percent of the general population under age 60 is affected, whereas rates of 20 to 50 percent are estimated for the population over age 80 (Carr, Goate, Phil, and Morris, 1997; Hendrie, 1997). However, because of selective survival, it appears that men who survive

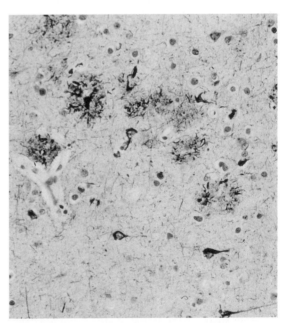

The dark patches in this brain section are neuritic plaques with a core of amyloid protein, characteristic of Alzheimer's disease.

ALZHEIMER'S DISEASE VERSUS NORMAL CHANGES IN MEMORY

Many people in middle and old age become alarmed that they may have Alzheimer's disease at the first signs of forgetting. Here are some distinctions between *normal,* age-related changes in memory (as described in Chapter 5) and AD:

Normal Aging
- Forgetting to set the alarm clock
- Forgetting someone's name and remembering it later
- Forgetting where you left your keys and finding them after searching
- Having to retrace steps to remember a task
- Forgetting where you parked your car

Possible AD
- Forgetting *how* to set the alarm clock
- Forgetting a name and never remembering it, even when told
- Forgetting places where you might find your keys
- Forgetting how you came to be at a particular location

into their nineties become less likely to develop AD after this age (Perls, 1995).

Although a distinction was made in the past between pre-senile (i.e., before age 65) and senile dementia, there is now agreement that these are the same disease. Researchers do, however, make a distinction between the more common, late-onset form of AD and a rarer form that appears in multiple generations of the same family, usually when the individual is in middle age (forties, even thirties). This is known as "familial AD."

POTENTIAL CAUSES AND RISK FACTORS FOR ALZHEIMER'S DISEASE   Several hypotheses have been proposed to explain the causes of Alzheimer's disease. Case control studies that have focused on the incidence or development of AD have not found support for environmental hypotheses, such as a previous head injury, thyroid disease, exposure to therapeutic radiation, anesthesia, or the accumulation of heavy metals (e.g., aluminum) in the brain (Kokmen, Beard, O'Brien, and Kurland, 1996). Even though the abnormal tangles (a web of dead brain cells) found in the neurons of the brains of Alzheimer's victims contain more aluminum than is found in brains of normal controls, whether such accumulation of aluminum is a cause or outcome of the disease is not easily determined.

Although it is difficult to assess with great accuracy an older person's childhood development,

two verifiable early-life characteristics may increase one's risk of AD. In a community-based case-control study comparing 393 people diagnosed with AD and 377 controls, researchers examined the effects of mother's age at patient's birth, birth order, number of siblings, and area of residence before age 18. They found only the last two variables associated with AD risk. The more children in one's family, the greater one's AD risk. Similarly, patients were half as likely as nondemented controls to have grown up in the suburbs (Moceri, Kukull, Emanuel, Van Belle, and Larson, 2000). These results suggest that receiving more attention as a child and living in a more secluded environment may serve as a protective factor against AD in old age.

In another case-control study, information was obtained about activity patterns during ages 20–60 among 193 older persons with AD and 358 healthy controls who were currently in their sixties and seventies. These activities included nonoccupational pastimes that could be classified as intellectual, physical or passive. Elders with no signs of dementia had participated in more intellectual and physical nonoccupational activities during their middle years than did those in the control group. The greatest effect was for intellectual pastimes; the more such activities an individual participated in, the lower the probability of AD. This was true regardless of educational level, gender, and current age. Although the findings must be interpreted with some caution, the dramatic differences observed suggest that participation in intellectual activities may have a protective effect against AD (Friedland et al., 2000). Recent findings from the Nun Study support the importance of intellectual activity. Among 74 men who died 50–65 years after writing their autobiographies, the linguistic complexity of their writing predicted the likelihood of AD in old age. More plaques and tangles were found in the brains of women who had less complex writing (Snowdon, Greiner, and Markesbery, 2000).

Lack of estrogen is another potential risk factor that has drawn more research interest recently. As estrogen secretion declines with aging, proteins associated with neuronal growth decrease, resulting in the synaptic impairments typical of AD. Just as estrogen replacement therapy (ERT) may prevent bone loss and cardiovascular disease in postmenopausal women, animal studies suggest that it can restore the brain proteins necessary for neuronal growth, and increase neuronal activity in the hippocampus (Brinton, Chen, Montoya, Hsieh, and Minaya, 2000; Singer, 1996a, 1996b). In one of the few large-scale longitudinal studies of the impact of estrogen replacement therapy, 248 women with a diagnosis of Alzheimer's or probable Alzheimer's disease were compared with age-matched controls in the same community (Leisure World, in southern California). Both groups had first completed a health questionnaire in 1981, so estrogen use over the subsequent 14 years could be determined. ERT significantly reduced the risk of AD and related dementias; in fact, both higher dosages and longer duration of use were associated with a much lower rate of AD among surviving women (Paganini-Hill and Henderson, 1996). Nevertheless, lifestyle differences between users and nonusers of ERT may also explain the beneficial effects of ERT. (Henderson, 1997).

The brains of AD patients experience a reduction in the number of cholinergic nerve cells (up to 80 percent loss in some key areas). These brain cells are important for learning and memory because they release an important chemical "messenger," *acetylcholine*, that transfers information from one cell to another (i.e., neurotransmitters). Their loss reduces the acetylcholine available for this important function. The noradrenergic system is another chemical messenger system that becomes impaired with Alzheimer's disease, further complicating our understanding of why and how these neurochemical systems appear to break down in this disease.

Still another neurochemical change observed in Alzheimer brains is the accumulation of *amyloid*, a protein. It appears that there may be a genetic defect in one of the normal proteins located in brain regions responsible for memory, emotions, and thinking. Amyloid is actually a group of proteins found in the neurofibrillary tangles that characterize an Alzheimer brain. The precursor protein to amyloid, *Beta-amyloid*, is coded by a gene located in chromosome 21, which is also the chromosome responsible for Down syndrome. This may explain why AD appears with greater frequency in families with a member who has Down syndrome. Deposits of amyloid or its precursor Beta-amyloid have been found in the brains of Down patients as young as age 8, and in those who die later with Alzheimer's disease. Beta-amyloid may be responsible for the death of brain cells in these patients. As with other changes observed in the brains of AD patients, it is not yet clear whether these Beta-amyloid deposits are the *cause* of AD or secondary to other structural or biochemical changes (Carr et al., 1997).

Genes on at least four different chromosomes may be involved in the development of AD. In addition to mutations of the gene encoding amyloid precursor protein on chromosome 21, presenilin 1 on chromosome 14, presenilin 2 on chromosome 1, and the apo-lipoprotein E gene on chromosome 19 have been implicated in this disease. While the mutations on chromosomes 1, 14, and 21 are associated with familial or early-onset AD, the more common late-onset form of AD appears to be linked to a genetic mutation on chromosome 19. Researchers have focused on a protein called *apo-lipoprotein* or *Apo-E* on this chromosome. Apo-E is responsible for transporting cholesterol in the blood, and Beta-amyloid in the brain. An individual with this mutation on chromosome 19 is more *susceptible* to AD, but may never develop the disease.

Of the three common allelic variations of Apo-E proteins, *E2, E3, E4,* those who inherit an E4 gene from *each* parent have eight times the risk of developing AD than the general population, and deteriorate more rapidly than AD patients who have lower levels of Apo-E4. In addition, AD patients with one or more Apo-E4 alleles have an increased risk of death due to ischemic heart disease (Carr et al., 1997; Olichney et al., 1997). Those who acquire an E3 gene from each parent also have a greater risk of developing AD, but at a later age than those with two E4 genes (at an average age of 75 versus 68).

Characteristics of Alzheimer's Disease

As illustrated by Mr. Adams in the introductory vignette, Alzheimer's disease is characterized by deficits in attention, learning, memory, and language skills and, in some instances, problems in judgment, abstraction, and orientation. These changes in cognitive function appear to be related to structural changes in the brain. They include:

- a premature loss of nerve cells in some areas of the brain
- a loss of synapses
- deterioration of the free radical metabolism process described in Chapter 3
- impaired neurotransmitter function such as the cholinergic system resulting in plaques and tangles throughout these areas

The *hippocampus* is a region in the limbic system deep inside the brain that is involved in learning new information and retrieving old information (see Chapter 5). It is one of the first regions where plaques and tangles occur, so it is not surprising that patients in the earlier stages of the disease often have difficulties with verbal memory, attention span, and orientation to the environment, as well as increased anxiety, restlessness, and unpredictable changes in mood. Family members may complain that the older person has become more aggressive or, in some cases, more passive than in the past. Depression may set in as the individual realizes that he or she is experiencing these problems. In the more advanced stages of the disease, as it spreads to the *cerebral cortex,* that controls language and movement, there may be marked aphasia (i.e., problems recalling appropriate words and labels), perseveration (i.e., continual repeating of the same phrase and thoughts), apathy, and problems with comprehension. Alzheimer's victims at this stage may not recognize their partners, children, and long-time friends. However, some patients in the moderate stages of AD may describe quite articulately and vividly events that took place many years ago. In the advanced phases, as the neurons in the motor cortex die, the patient may need assistance with bodily functions such as eating and toileting. At autopsy, there is a generalized deterioration of cortical tissue, which appears to be tangled and covered with plaque.

ARE THERE STAGES OF ALZHEIMER'S DISEASE? There have been some attempts to determine if AD proceeds through a series of stages, such that symptoms become more prevalent and severe over time. This is a difficult task because the course of AD varies so widely. Some patients may experience a rapid decline in memory, while their orientation to time, place, and people may remain relatively intact. Other patients may experience mood and personality changes early, whereas still others maintain their pre-morbid personality for many years after the symptoms first appear.

A broad distinction is often made among early, middle, and advanced stages of AD. These categories are based on the patient's levels of decline in memory, orientation, and activities of daily living. Some psychologists have provided guidelines with the use of assessment tools such as the Mini-Mental Status Exam and the Dementia Rating Scale (Folstein, Folstein, and McHugh, 1975; Mattis, 1976). These give clues to the patients' levels of deterioration on the basis of their test scores. Perhaps the most extensive research to determine the stages of AD has been conducted by Reisberg et al. (1982), who developed a Global Deterioration Scale that delineates seven stages of the disease, as shown in Table 6.7.

TABLE 6.7 **Global Deterioration Scale**

Stage 1:   No cognitive or functional decrements

Stage 2:   Complaints of very mild forgetfulness and some work difficulties

Stage 3:   Mild cognitive impairment on cognitive battery; concentration problems; some difficulty at work and in traveling alone

Stage 4:   Late confusional stage; increased problems in planning, handling finances; increased denial of symptoms; withdrawal

Stage 5:   Poor recall of recent events; may need to be reminded about proper clothing and bathing

Stage 6:   More advanced memory orientation problems; needs assistance with activities of daily living; more personality changes

Stage 7:   Late dementia with loss of verbal abilities; incontinent; loss of ability to walk; may become comatose

SOURCE: B. Reisberg, S. H. Ferris, M. J. De Leon, and T. Crook, The Global Deterioration Scale for assessment of primary degenerative dementia. *American Journal of Psychiatry, 139,* pp. 1136–1139, 1982. Copyright 1982, the American Psychiatric Association. Reprinted by permission.

Because of recent attention by the media and by researchers on Alzheimer's disease, there is some tendency to overestimate its occurrence and to assume that it is the cause of all dementias. It has even created what one neurologist has called "Alzheimer's phobia" (Fox, 1991). In many ways, it has replaced vascular dementia as a label given without a thorough diagnosis. The most confirmatory diagnosis of Alzheimer's disease today can still be made only at autopsy, when the areas and nature of damaged brain tissue can be identified. However, several psychological measures of cognitive functioning and a thorough physical exam can provide clues to its existence in the earlier stages. Or they may indicate that the observed changes in behavior and/or personality are due to a reversible condition. Early diagnosis can be made with some certainty with an extensive patient workup. In fact, it is primarily through a process of elimination of other conditions that some dementias such as AD may be diagnosed. In such diagnoses, it is particularly important to detect depression, drug toxicity, and nutritional deficiencies because, as stated earlier, these conditions may be reversed.

THERAPY FOR PATIENTS WITH ALZHEIMER'S DISEASE   Unfortunately, no completely successful treatment for AD is yet available. If the evidence for high levels of certain abnormal proteins in Alzheimer brains proves correct, future treatment might involve the use of drugs that interrupt the production of those proteins and their precursors so they cannot accumulate in brain tissue. Some researchers have focused on nerve growth factor, a naturally occurring protein that replenishes and maintains the health of nerve cells. Animal studies have shown remarkable success in repairing damaged brain cells.

Currently, many medications are being tested that may improve the cognitive functioning of victims of dementia. These medications include some drugs that restore the activity of neurotransmitters in the brain and some that even replace lost

---

DIAGNOSING ALZHEIMER'S DISEASE

- a medical and nutritional history
- laboratory tests of blood, urine, and stool
- tests for thyroid function
- a thorough physical and psychological examination

- in some cases, a CT (computerized tomography) scan, a PET (positron emission tomography) scan, or MRI (magnetic resonance imaging), in order to detect any tumors, strokes, blood clots, or hydrocephalus, and to test the response of specific areas of the brain

neurochemicals. In the last few years, one drug has been found to slow the decline of memory loss by about 5 percent, but only for a few months. This medication, donepezil (marketed as Aricept[R]), appears to slow the loss of acetylcholine in the brains of AD patients.

Some researchers have begun to explore the possibility that AD may be related to inflammation of brain tissue. This has led to the hypothesis that nonsteroidal anti-inflammatory drugs (NSAIDs), such as ibuprofen, can prevent or delay the onset of AD. Although many older people currently use low doses of NSAIDs to prevent heart attacks, few controlled clinical trials have tested whether NSAIDs have similar benefits for AD. There is, however, some correlational evidence from the Baltimore Longitudinal Studies of Aging. Older people in this study who reported that they used NSAIDs regularly for 2 or more years had less than half the risk of AD as nonusers (Stewart et al., 1997). Recent animal studies demonstrate that a daily dose of ibuprofen reduced inflammation in the brain, and resulted in about half the number of plaques and half the amyloid deposits as in the mice that were not given NSAIDs (Lim et al., 2000). The drug may act as a preventive by improving the production of chemicals that control amyloid build-up or by clearing amyloid more efficiently. Until clinical trials with humans are conducted, it will be impossible to determine if ibuprofen and other NSAIDs can really prevent AD.

Another promising pharmacotherapy for AD may be a combination of vitamin E (described in Chapter 3 as an antioxidant that appears to prevent or reduce the symptoms of other chronic diseases) and selegiline hydrochloride (marketed as Eldepryl[R] and generally prescribed for Parkinson's disease). In one clinical trial, patients in the moderate stage of AD who were given this combination did not decline as rapidly as those given a placebo (Sano et al., 1997). Ginkgo biloba is an extract from the dried leaves of the maidenhair tree. Some families have reported that regular use of this product improves the memory of an AD patient in the early to intermediate stages. However, a recent study in the Netherlands casts some doubt on the benefits of this treatment. Researchers studied 214 residents with mild to moderate AD or vascular dementia, who lived in nursing homes. Each person was given a usual dose of ginkgo biloba (84 elders) or an elevated dose (82 elders), and compared with a group (48 elders) that used a placebo over 24 weeks. No effects were observed on tests of memory or depression, but those using

---

CARING FOR AD PATIENTS AT EACH STAGE OF THE DISEASE

Depending on the stage of the disease, caregivers of elders with AD can help them in different ways. Using the GDS stages described in Table 6.7, families can try the following ways of helping the patient:

Stages 1–3 (Mild dementia)	Stages 4–5 (Moderate dementia)	Stages 6–7 (Advanced dementia)
• Set up an orientation area in the home where the patient's critical items (e.g., wallet, keys, glasses) can always be found. • Watch for signs of driving problems. • Encourage physical and social activities.	• Make changes in home environment to assure safety and independence, but maintain familiarity (e.g., improved, constant light levels). • Put labels on important doors (e.g., patient's bedroom, bathroom) and drawers. • Keep in visible areas photos of family and close friends taken with patient, names clearly written on photos.	• Visit alternative long-term care facilities that fit P–E needs of the particular patient. • Simplify daily routines but still encourage some physical activity (e.g., walks in fenced-in yard). • Try alternative means of communication (e.g., touch, sharing old family photos).

ginkgo performed slightly better on self-reported ADLs (van Dongen, van Rossum, Kessels, Siel-horst, and Knipschild, 2000).

As yet, no medication effectively restores cognitive function in the severely impaired older person for any significant period of time. Nevertheless, researchers have made dramatic strides toward understanding the neurochemical basis of this disease and are rapidly moving toward its treatment. There is even some promise of a vaccine that can help the immune system produce antibodies against amyloid proteins and clear amyloid deposits from the brain. Successful research with mice gives scientists hope that such a vaccine may be effective with humans (Schenk et al., 1999)

Medications are often prescribed to manage behavioral problems in some AD patients, including agitation, hallucinations, physical aggressiveness, and wandering. In particular, risperidone, a drug used to treat psychotic symptoms in schizophrenic patients, appears to calm aggressive, delusional behaviors in a significant segment of this population (Goldberg and Goldberg, 1997). Because of their potential side effects, however, it is important to weigh the harm caused by these patient behaviors against the possible side effects of medications. Furthermore, the prescribing physician must regularly reevaluate the need to continue or reduce the dosage of any drugs used for behavior management, perhaps as frequently as every 3 to 4 months.

Behavioral Therapies and Environmental Interventions

As noted earlier, new medications that are being approved by the FDA show some promise of slowing down the rate of decline with AD. To date, however, neither these medications nor psychotherapy can restore the cognitive functions lost with most irreversible forms of dementia. Nevertheless, many older persons can benefit from behavioral therapies such as memory retraining and from some environmental modifications.

Individual competence can be enhanced somewhat and the social and home environments sim-plified considerably in an effort to maintain P–E congruence and maintain some independent functioning. Simple changes such as removing sources of glare and making lighting levels consistent throughout the house, can prevent confusion and "sundowning," a condition that affects some AD patients as natural light levels change and they become more fatigued later in the day. It is important to maintain a regular schedule, to keep the patient active, and to prevent withdrawal from daily interactions. Written schedules of activities, simplified routes from room to room, and written directions for cooking, bathing, and taking medications can aid a person in finding his or her way around and prevent the frustration of getting lost or not recognizing once-familiar people and places. AD patients can be encouraged to perform more ADLs if their grooming supplies (e.g., toothbrush, toothpaste, comb) are kept visible and in a familiar sequence of use. These items can also help AD patients recognize their own bathroom or bedroom as the disease progresses. A useful device for patients in the intermediate stages of Alzheimer's is a "memory box" that contains photos from the individual's past on the outside and mementoes on the inside, placed on his or her door to identify the bedroom. Physical activity during the day can also help the patient sleep better through the night. Productive activities such as setting the table, folding laundry, and raking leaves in a secure backyard can also help patients maintain a sense of continuity with their past lives and use their excess energy. However, the frequency and intensity of such activities should not overwhelm or confuse the patient.

Wandering is another problem that can be prevented with some environmental changes. These can be as punitive as locking all exterior doors, or more protective, such as providing a safe backyard or garden area for the AD patient to explore, within easy sight of the home's windows and doors to orient the patient. ID bracelets with silent or audible beepers that can help locate the AD patient are becoming more common for use in the home, given their demonstrated benefits in nursing homes. One company has even developed a model where family or close friends can record a message on a tape attached to the bracelet to guide the wandering person back home. Some local chapters of the Alzheimer's Association offer the "safe return" program, which provides ID bracelets for AD patients, maintains records, and assists emergency teams in locating, identifying, and returning home the AD patient who becomes lost in the community (Alzheimer's Association, 1997).

Ultimately, the goal of managing these dementias is to slow the rate of deterioration and to prevent institutionalization for as long as possible. For the AD patient who does enter a nursing home, it is important to find a facility that can maximize the individual's remaining abilities as the disease progresses (i.e., environments that can maintain the patient's P–E congruence). In recent years, the number of special care units (SCUs) in nursing homes has grown. These units are generally designed for residents with advanced dementia, especially AD, and staffed by nurses and therapists with special training in this field. Many provide a higher staff-to-resident ratio, a safe environment where patients can wander without getting lost, and special services aimed at maintaining the patients' remaining cognitive capacities. They are less likely to use chemical and physical restraints with disruptive residents. However, because there are no national licensing regulations for SCUs, the nature of services and quality of care provided vary widely. That is, the designation of a nursing home unit as a SCU does not necessarily imply richer or more tailored services than non-SCU units that also house AD and other dementia patients (Day, Carreon, and Stump, 2000; Sloane et al., 1995). Newer options include assisted living facilities, adult family homes,

and adult day care (described in Chapter 11). However, like SCUs, families must determine if these alternative housing options can manage AD patients, especially as the disease progresses.

CAREGIVER NEEDS   One of the most important considerations with Alzheimer's disease and other dementias is to provide social and emotional support to the family as well as the patient. It is estimated that 50–70 percent of all people with Alzheimer's disease remain in the community, cared for by family. In fact, about 19 million family caregivers provide $196 billion in home care for their relatives with AD. Yet most of these costs are not reimbursed through Medicare or private health insurance, Medicaid, or through tax breaks. The typical caregiver of an AD patient is a 46-year-old woman, working full-time, caring for a 77-year-old mother with AD. On average they provide 18 hours of caregiving per week for 4.5 years. As described more fully in Chapter 10, these caregivers must balance the challenges of providing daily care to their loved ones with the need to maintain their jobs and income (Riggs, 2000).

The stress of caring for this population often results in deterioration of family members' physical and psychological health. Many caregivers feel they must shoulder this responsibility alone, resulting in increasing levels of depression, burden, and declining physical health (Pearson et al., 1993; Reese et al., 1994; Russo et al., 1995; Vitaliano et al., 1996). As family caregivers assume more responsibility for an AD patient whose functional abilities decline, perceived burden increases. This condition is aggravated and depression becomes

---

NEW WAYS OF HELPING AD PATIENTS

Until a few years ago, reality orientation was a popular therapeutic method that was used in nursing homes and by many families caring for AD patients. The emphasis was on reorienting confused older adults to the present and correcting them when they referred to a dead spouse as being alive now, or talking about getting to work despite being retired for 20+ years. However, these techniques can frustrate and agitate the patient. Most experts today agree that it is better to acknowledge the patient's memories of the past and not argue with them.

more likely if the AD patient also displays more disruptive behaviors such as aggressiveness, frequent wakings during the night, and wandering. Caregivers who experience the most depressive symptoms also report being most disturbed by such behaviors (Pearson et al., 1993). Depression and physiological and physical health outcomes of stress are most severe among spousal caregivers. Problems include higher insulin and glucose levels than age-matched controls, higher levels of lipids in blood, and cardiovascular disease (King, Oka, and Young, 1994; Vitaliano, Russo, and Niaura, 1995; Vitaliano et al., 1996).

Support groups aid their members in coping with the inevitable losses faced by the victims of AD. These groups, typically coordinated by local chapters of the national Alzheimer's Association, also provide caregivers with emotional support and respite. Depression, chronic fatigue, and anger are all common reactions among caregivers. Support groups can alleviate these stress responses for caregivers who begin participating early in the course of the disease so they are able to anticipate problems. Not surprisingly, those who attend sessions regularly benefit the most. A longitudinal study that tested the effects of a year-long weekly support-group program on depression also included individual and family counseling sessions during the first 4 months of the program. Combined individual, family, and support-group intervention was the key to significant declines in depression scores among this experimental group. Spouse caregivers in the control group, who received counseling or referrals only if they requested them (which occurred infrequently), became more depressed during this same period. The multipronged intervention was also effective in reducing the number of AD patients who were placed in nursing homes and delaying institutionalization by almost one year (Mittelman et al., 1996).

The Internet has emerged in the last few years as a way for caregivers to share their experiences with others facing similar burdens and frustrations. Some of these Websites include advice and updated information from experts, such as the Alzheimer's Association, while others encourage caregivers to offer support and suggestions to their peers who have recently become caregivers. The opportunity to log on to a chat room on the Internet also avoids the need to find alternative care for the AD patient at home while attending live support groups. The growth of adult day centers is another response to the need to keep persons with dementia in the community, to help them remain active and retain learned skills, and to provide respite for caregivers. Caregivers who regularly take their AD patients to such centers have shown lower levels of anger, depression, and stress than those who do not (Zarit, Stephens, Townsend, and Greene, 1998). The need for publicly funded daycare, respite, and support groups, however, is greater than the availability of services.

Parkinson's Disease

Parkinson's is a neurodegenerative disorder that begins as a loss of muscle control, with tremors in the feet and hands, gradually progressing to slow and limited movements. In its later stages, Parkinson's can manifest dementia-like symptoms. Today about one million Americans have this condition. It usually strikes people over age 60, although some people—such as the actor Michael J. Fox—are first diagnosed in their thirties.

Parkinson's differs from AD in many ways. First, the degeneration and loss of cells in the brain occurs mostly in the *substantia nigra*, located in the center of the brain. This is the region where dopamine is produced, the brain chemical responsible for initiating voluntary movement. This is why Levodopa (L-dopa) is the drug of choice for most people with Parkinson's, as a way of replacing dopamine. However, in some people L-dopa can cause such side effects as hallucinations, agitation, and uncontrollable movement. Newer drugs known as dopamine agonists have been developed as an alternative for such patients. One of the most exciting research developments in this area is the possibility of implanting stem cells (described in Chapter 3) into the brain of Parkinson's patients. These cells appear to revitalize damaged regions and resume production of dopamine in the substantia nigra. Another promising development is new surgical methods in the brain to stop tremors and involuntary movement. Behavioral techniques such as meditation, biofeedback, and dietary modification are also recommended.

Alcoholism

For most older people, alcohol use is associated with socializing and occurs in moderation (i.e., less than once a week, and no more than two drinks each time). However, those who consume four or more drinks per occasion and do so frequently (defined as alcoholism) are more likely to use alcohol as a way to cope with some life events and to help them relax (Krause, 1995; Mockenhaupt and Beck, 1997). Obtaining accurate statistics on the prevalence of alcoholism in older adults is difficult, because of the stigma associated with this condition among older cohorts. Estimates vary from 2 to 10 percent of all older people living in the community. A national survey in 1998 revealed that 80 percent of people over age 65 reported at least one alcoholic drink once a month or more frequently. Of this group, 10 percent reported consuming five drinks in one sitting, at least once a month. Another 5 percent have that many every time they drink (Reid, Concato, Towle, Williams, and Tennetti, 1999). Alcoholism in older adults is accompanied by depression in 30 percent of cases, and by dementia in 20 percent, although the direction of causality is not always clear (Koenig and Blazer, 1996; Osgood, Wood, and Parham, 1995). Those at greatest risk are widowers and well-educated white men who have never married. Older men are four times more likely to have alcohol problems than are older women. Women at greatest risk of alcohol abuse are those who are smokers, not married, not religious, and with little social support (Graham, Carver, and Brett, 1995; Holroyd et al., 1997).

It is important to distinguish lifelong abusers of alcohol from those who began drinking later in life. Alcoholics are less likely to be found among the ranks of persons over age 60 because of higher death rates at a young age among alcoholics. Those who continue to drink in old age tend to decrease their consumption. Surveys of alcoholism rates among older persons have revealed approximately equal proportions of those who began to drink heavily before age 40 and those who began in old age (Miller et al., 1991).

Some older persons who are diagnosed as alcoholics have had this problem since middle age, but increasing age may exacerbate the condition for two reasons:

• The central nervous system (CNS), liver, and kidneys become less tolerant of alcohol with age because of the physiological changes described in Chapter 3 (e.g., loss of muscle tissue, reduction in body mass, and reduced efficiency of liver and kidney functions). For this reason, a smaller dose of alcohol can be more deleterious in the later years.
• An individual who has been drinking heavily for many years has already produced irreversible damage to the CNS, liver, and kidneys, creating more problems than those due to normal aging alone.

Perhaps because of the damage to their CNSs, men who began drinking heavily before the age of 35 are more likely to experience depression, restlessness, sleeplessness, and tension than those who started later (Gurnack and Hoffman, 1992). It is difficult to determine the incidence of alcoholism among older persons who have no previous history of this disease. Physiological evidence is lacking, and drinking is often hidden from friends, relatives, and physicians. The older person may justify overconsumption of alcohol on the grounds that it relieves sadness and isolation. Even when family members are aware of the situation, they may rationalize that alcohol is one of the older person's few remaining pleasures. Denial is a common problem among older alcoholics who are influenced by beliefs of the prohibition era that alcoholism is a moral weakness and not a disease. In addition, many older people may feel that they should be able to cope with their alcoholism on their own and not have to rely on health professionals or even on support groups such as Alcoholics Anonymous.

Physicians may overlook the possibility that alcohol is creating a health problem because the adverse effects of alcohol resemble some physical diseases or psychiatric and cognitive disorders that are associated with old age. For example, older alcoholics may complain of confusion, disorientation, irritability, insomnia or restless sleep patterns, heart palpitations, weight loss, depression, or a dry cough. Beliefs held by health care providers that alcoholism does not occur in older people may also prevent its detection. Because of the problems caused by heavy alcohol use in old age, primary-care physicians must screen their older patients by asking questions about the quantity, frequency, and context of drinking. This can help in the diagnosis and referral of older alcoholics to treatment programs, which currently are underutilized by older adults. This can also reduce the emotional, physical, and cognitive deterioration caused by alcoholism in older people and the subsequent hospitalizations and use of emergency medical services for conditions that are secondary to heavy alcohol consumption (Adams, Barry, and Fleming, 1996; Holroyd et al., 1997).

Therapy for older alcoholics has not been differentiated from that for younger alcoholics. However, it is probably more important to focus on older alcoholics' medical conditions because of physical declines that make them more vulnerable to the secondary effects of alcohol. As with younger alcoholics, psychotherapy and occupational and recreational therapy are important for treating older people experiencing alcoholism. Recovery rates for older alcoholics are as high as for younger alcoholics.

Drug Abuse

As noted in Chapter 4, older persons use a disproportionately large number of prescription and over-the-counter (OTC) drugs, representing approximately 30 percent of prescription expenditures (Piraino, 1995). In particular, older people are more likely than the young to use tranquilizers, sedatives, and hypnotics, all of which have potentially dangerous side effects. They also are more likely to abuse aspirin compounds, laxatives, and sleeping pills, often because of misinformation about the adverse effects of too high a dosage or too many pills. It is not unusual to hear older patients state that they took twice or three times as much aspirin as they were prescribed because they did not feel that their pain was being alleviated with the lower dose. Yet, changes in body composition and renal and liver functions that occur with age, combined with the use of multiple medications, make older persons more likely to experience adverse drug reactions. Noncompliance with therapeutic drug regimens is often unintentional; older patients may take too much or too little of a drug because of nonspecific or complicated instructions by the physician, and they may use OTC drugs without reading warning labels about their side effects and interactions with other drugs they

---

MEDICATION MANAGEMENT CAN THREATEN ELDERS' INDEPENDENCE

Their inability to manage their medications can be a threat to older people's independence. Families often cannot be present at every medication administration, and neighbors may help only intermittently. Even assisted living facilities cannot provide the daily help with medications that is needed, unless the older adult pays an additional fee. Some elders use plastic pillboxes with the days of the week printed on each section, or egg cartons or other small cups that the family has labeled with instructions. However, these devices cannot help an older person remember the time of day he or she must take the medication, and are not effective at all for someone with dementia.

are using. Intentional noncompliance generally takes the form of older patients' deciding that they no longer need the medication or that it is not working for them. Such noncompliance has been found to be responsible for approximately 10 percent of all hospital admissions among the older population (Col, Fanale, and Kronholm, 1990).

Both health care providers and older people themselves are more aware of the effects of "polypharmacy" today. Older persons do not abuse drugs to the extent that younger populations do, nor use illicit drugs such as heroin, cocaine, and marijuana. Nor do they use hallucinogens, amphetamines, or mood-enhancing inhalants in noticeable numbers.

Paranoid Disorders and Schizophrenia

Paranoia, defined as an irrational suspiciousness of other people, takes several forms. It may result from:

- social isolation
- a sense of powerlessness
- progressive sensory decline
- problems with the normal "checks and balances" of daily life

Still other changes in the aging individual, such as memory loss, may result in paranoid reactions. It should also be noted that some suspicious attitudes of older persons represent accurate readings of their experiences. For example, an older person's children may in fact be trying to institutionalize him or her in order to take over an estate; a nurse's aide may really be stealing from an older patient; and neighborhood children may be making fun of the older adult. It is therefore important to distinguish actual threats to the individual from unfounded suspicions. To the extent that the individual has some control over his or her environment, the older person's perception of a threatening situation is reduced. This is consistent with the P–E competence model. The diagnosis of paranoid disorders in older people is similar to that in younger patients; the symptoms should have a duration of at least one

week, with no signs of schizophrenia, no prominent hallucinations, and no association to an organic mental disorder (APA, 1994).

Schizophrenia is considerably less prevalent than depression or dementia in old age. Most older persons with this condition were first diagnosed in adolescence or in middle age and continue to display behavior symptomatic of schizophrenia. However, the severity of symptoms appears to decrease and to change with age; older schizophrenics are less likely to manifest thought disorders and loss of emotional expression (Rabins, 1992). Late-onset schizophrenia with paranoid features has been labeled *paraphrenia* by some psychiatrists, especially in Europe and Great Britain.

Schizophrenics of any age, but especially older patients, need monitoring of their medication regimes and structured living arrangements. However, many of the current cohort of older chronic schizophrenics residing in the community were deinstitutionalized in the 1960s as part of the national Community Mental Health Services Act of 1963. After spending much of their youth and middle age in state hospitals, these patients were released with the anticipation that they could function independently in the community, with medications to control their hallucinations and psychotic behavior. Although this approach has proved effective for many former schizophrenic inpatients, some have not adjusted well to deinstitutionalization, as witnessed by the number of homeless older schizophrenics on the streets in most major cities.

As with depression, counseling can be useful for paranoid older persons. In particular, cognitive behavioral approaches, in which an individual focuses on changing negative, self-defeating beliefs or misconceptions, may be useful in treating paranoid older persons who often attribute causality to external factors (e.g., the belief that someone took their pocketbook, that they themselves did not misplace it). Therapy with paranoid older individuals may be effective in redirecting beliefs about causality to the individuals themselves. On the other hand, pharmacotherapy with antipsychotic medications is generally most effective for older schizophrenic patients.

Anxiety

Anxiety disorders are another type of functional disorder or emotional problem with no obvious organic cause. The most common forms of anxiety disorders in the older population are:

- generalized anxiety
- phobias
- panic disorders

Although more common than schizophrenia and paranoid disorders, anxiety disorders are not as frequent in older populations as they are in the young. This may be because the older person develops more tolerance and better ability to manage stressful events. More likely, however, those who have anxiety disorders in middle age may be less likely to survive to old age. Data from the Epidemiological Catchment Area study revealed a prevalence rate of 5.5 percent among those 65 and older, but late-life anxiety disorders may coexist with other medical and psychiatric disorders that can mask the underlying anxiety (Regier et al., 1988). For example, a recent study among 182 people aged 60 and older who had been diagnosed with depression found that 35 percent had also been diagnosed with an anxiety disorder at some point in their lives. A significant number (23 percent) had a current diagnosis of panic disorder or specific phobias (Lenze et al., 2000). As with other psychiatric disorders that can be masked by physical symptoms, primary-care physicians must probe further when older patients complain of diffuse pain, fast or irregular heart rate, and restlessness. Once the condition is diagnosed, older people can benefit from cognitive-behavioral therapy, psychosocial support, and in some cases, pharmacotherapy (Banazak, 1997).

OLDER ADULTS WHO ARE CHRONICALLY MENTALLY ILL

The plight of older persons who are chronically mentally ill has recently been addressed by mental health advocates. This population is defined as people who suffer mental or emotional disorders that erode or prevent the development of their functional capacities in ADL, self-direction, interpersonal relations, social transactions, learning, or recreation (Light and Lebowitz, 1991). Many chronically mentally ill older persons were institutionalized in their young adult years and released into the community after the deinstitutionalization movement began in 1963. Since then, they have been in and out of hospitals as their conditions have become exacerbated. These people have survived major upheavals in their lives under marginally functional conditions.

"It is remarkable that members of this population survive into middle age and old age" despite the social neglect they have experienced (Quam and Abramson, 1991). Of course, the social disruption and years of treatment with psychotropic drugs take their toll on many of these people, who are physiologically old in their fifties and sixties. Obtaining medical care for purely physical symptoms may be difficult because health care providers may dismiss a complaint as hypochondriasis and/or attribute it to the patient's psychiatric disorder. Health professionals in this situation need to perform a thorough exam to exclude conditions caused by the mental disorder or by aging per se, and to treat any systemic diseases that are diagnosed.

Psychotherapy with Older Persons

Despite early doubts by Freud (1924) and others about the value of psychotherapy for older patients, many researchers and therapists have developed and tested psychotherapeutic interventions specifically for this population, or have modified existing approaches. One challenge in working with older individuals is to overcome some older persons' misconceptions about psychotherapy. For this reason, short-term, goal-oriented therapies may be more effective with older patients because they can begin to experience benefits immediately. On the other hand, older patients who are reluctant and unwilling to open up to a therapist may benefit more from long-term treatment in which rapport and trust between the therapist and the client can be established gradually. Several different types of therapy have been explored with this population.

Life review is one therapeutic approach that has been successfully used with older adults. Such therapy encourages introspection through active reminiscence of past achievements and failures, and may reestablish ego integrity in depressed older persons. This method may also be used effectively by social service providers who are not extensively trained in psychotherapy. It has been found to reduce symptoms of depression, and to increase life satisfaction and self-esteem in nursing home residents up to 3 years after completion of life review therapy (Haight, Michel and Hendrix, 2000). An alternative form of life review, known as **reminiscence therapy,** has been compared with a more focused, problem-solving therapy. Although it has short-term benefits for depressed older people, it is less effective in long-term (i.e., greater than 3 months) reduction of depressive symptoms (Arean et al., 1993).

Group therapy is often advocated for older patients experiencing mental disorders, especially depression. Groups offer the opportunity for peer support, social interaction, and role modeling. Life review may be used effectively as part of group therapy. The opportunity to share life experiences and to learn that others have had similar stresses in their lives seems to enhance insight, self-esteem, and a feeling of catharsis. Group reminiscence therapy appears to reduce symptoms of depression immediately after the sessions have been completed, but its long-term benefits are unclear (McMurdo and Rennie, 1993). Groups are also established for improving memory and enhancing cognitive skills. They are an ideal setting for teaching memory skills with the use of games and puzzles as well as reminiscence exercises.

Empirical studies have been conducted to compare the efficacy of alternative therapeutic interventions. For example, *cognitive-behavioral* (i.e., active, structured, and time-limited therapy) and *brief psychodynamic therapy* (i.e., helping the patient to develop ego strength and feelings of control) both appear to be equally effective in alleviating minor depression, even up to 12 months following treatment (Gallagher-Thompson and Steffan, 1994). Psychodynamic therapy uses psychoanalytic concepts such as insight, transference, and the unconscious to relieve symptoms of depression and to prevent its recurrence by attempting to understand why the individual behaves in self-defeating ways. Each type of therapy may be appropriate for different types of older patients. For example, cognitive–behavioral therapy has been compared with brief psychodynamic therapy among depressed caregivers of Alzheimer's disease patients. Longer-term caregivers improved more with cognitive–behavioral methods, while shorter-term caregivers benefited more from psychodynamic therapy (Gallagher-Thompson and Steffan, 1994).

The therapeutic interventions just described are more frequently used in community settings than in nursing homes. The latter setting lends itself to more intense, long-term therapies: behavior-change programs, milieu therapy, and *remotivation therapy*. Behavior-change techniques using operant reinforcement and token economies have been successfully used in long-term care settings with psychiatrically impaired young and old patients. These methods have been found to increase self-feeding and self-care, and have been effective in reducing dependency. *Milieu therapy* is consistent with Lawton and Nahemow's competence model described earlier. This approach focuses on improving the therapeutic environment of the nursing home or enhancing an individual's sense of control over some important aspects of life.

Remotivation therapy has been used successfully with less confused elders. Groups of older persons with some cognitive impairment and who are withdrawn from social activities meet together under the guidance of a trained group leader. The purpose is to discuss events and experiences by bringing all group members into the discussion, emphasizing the event's relevance for each member, and encouraging them to share what they have gained from the session. This approach has been found to be effective in psychiatric hospitals and nursing homes, as well as in adult day centers.

Use of Mental Health Services

As noted in Chapter 4, older persons use physician services somewhat more than the young do, and are hospitalized at a much higher rate. In contrast, mental health services are significantly underutilized by older people, especially ethnic minorities. Community-based care is used by older people at a far lower rate than inpatient hospital treatment, far below their representation in the U.S. population and less than the estimated prevalence of mental disorders in this group. An even smaller percentage of users are elders of color.

Older persons may be more likely to seek help from their primary physicians and to be hospitalized for mental disorders than to seek community mental health services. This may be because medical care does not carry the stigma of mental health services, especially for older ethnic minorities. A disproportionate number of older persons represent the population of patients in state mental hospitals that house the chronically mentally ill. Despite the deinstitutionalization movement of the 1960s, the great majority of all psychiatric services to older people are in hospital settings.

BARRIERS TO OLDER PERSONS' USE OF MENTAL HEALTH SERVICES Older adults are generally unwilling to interpret their problems as psychological, preferring instead to attribute them to physical or social conditions or to normal aging. In addition, the current cohort of older persons may be less oriented to the use of mental health services because of societal stigmas, limited knowledge about mental disorders, and a lack of confidence in mental health workers. This requires a good "psychological ear" on the part of the older person's primary-care physician. As noted earlier, older patients may complain of physical symptoms rather than focus on psychological concerns. Therefore the physician must be attuned to the underlying emotional distress presented by the older patient.

Accessibility is perhaps the greatest barrier to older individuals' obtaining mental health services. In addition to the physical access issues of transportation and architectural barriers, there are significant problems of fragmented services and older people's lack of knowledge about seeking mental health services on their own or obtaining appropriate referrals from physicians and social service providers. Fortunately, many new and innovative programs have arisen to overcome these barriers and respond to the mental health needs of older adults. Many senior centers employ social workers trained in geriatrics to conduct support groups, education programs, and individualized sessions on coping with grief, loss, and loneliness, and on methods to improve memory. Such programs reduce the

---

OVERCOMING BARRIERS TO USING MENTAL HEALTH SERVICES

• Home visits by a psychiatrist, social worker, and a nurse are made to low-income, isolated older people in Baltimore through the "Psychogeriatric Assessment and Treatment in City Housing" (or PATCH) program.
• Rural elders in Iowa are served by mental health professionals through the Elderly Outreach Program (or EOP) of the community mental health system.
• The Family Services Program of greater Boston offers a community mental health program aimed especially at ethnic minority elders, entitled Services for Older People (or SOP).

• In Seattle, a mental health team from the community mental health network provides on-site evaluation and therapy to area nursing homes on a regular basis.
• In many communities, "gatekeepers" (nontraditional referral sources such as meter readers, postal carriers, and apartment and mobile home managers who have contact with isolated older people in the community) are trained to identify older persons who may require psychiatric care. These isolated older adults are typically chronically mentally ill.

stigma of psychotherapy by their informal structure in a familiar environment.

Reimbursement for psychological services is also a problem. For example, Medicare Part A pays for no outpatient mental health expenditures, but pays for a limited number of days for inpatient treatment. Furthermore, copayment by the subscriber for mental health services is greater than for physical health services. It should be noted that this discrepancy occurs in many health insurance programs used by younger persons as well. Because of attitudes held by older patients toward mental disorders and by therapists toward older clients, however, these reimbursement issues are greater barriers to older persons' use of mental health services than they are for the young. Future cohorts of older people may be more likely to seek such services in community mental health centers, because of increased awareness of mental disorders and treatment modalities.

SUMMARY AND IMPLICATIONS

Personality development in adulthood and old age has received increasing attention over the past 30 years. Earlier theories of personality suggested that development takes place only during childhood and adolescence, and stabilizes by early adulthood. Beginning with Erik Erikson, however, several theorists have suggested that personality continues to change and evolve into old age. According to Erikson's theory of psychosocial development, the individual experiences stages of development, with crises or conflicts at each stage, and the outcome of each has an impact on ego development in the next stage. The seventh stage, generativity versus stagnation, takes place mostly during the middle years, but increasingly researchers find that continued generativity in old age is important for successful aging. Programs such as foster grandparents encourage older people to experience ongoing generativity by working with young children. The eighth and last stage of personality development occurs in old age and poses the conflict of ego integrity versus despair in dealing with one's impending death. Both cross-

sectional and longitudinal studies have found evidence for these last two stages of development.

The work of Carl Jung also emphasizes the growth of personality across the life span, but does not specify stages of development. Jung's model, like Erikson's, focuses on the individual's confrontation with death in this last stage. In addition, Jung described a decrease in sex-typed behavior with aging. This has been supported in cross-cultural studies by Gutmann (1977, 1980, 1992) and in the longitudinal Kansas City Studies. These investigators found that men become more accepting of their nurturant and affiliative characteristics as they age, whereas women learn to accept their egocentric and aggressive impulses. Levinson's life structures model also examines personality from a developmental stage perspective. This model is consistent with the person–environment approach in emphasizing the interaction between the individual and his or her environment as the impetus for change.

Trait theories of personality have been tested systematically in the Baltimore Longitudinal Studies of Aging (Costa and McCrae, 1986, 1994, 1995; McCrae and Costa, 1990). These researchers have tested a five-factor model of personality consisting of five primary traits (neuroticism, extraversion, openness to experience, agreeableness, and conscientiousness), and several subcategories of traits. They have found considerable stability in these traits from middle age to old age when tested longitudinally, and age differences between young and old when tested cross-sectionally. The development of self-concept and self-esteem in old age has been researched even less. It is recognized that older persons' self-concepts must be redefined as they move from traditional roles of worker, partner, and parent to less well-differentiated roles such as retiree or widow. But the process by which such changes take place and, more important, how they influence life satisfaction and self-esteem in old age is unclear.

Somewhat more research has been devoted to age-related changes in the nature of life events and the stress associated with them. Cognitive appraisal is an important consideration in understanding people's reactions to life events. To the extent that people perceive a situation as a threat, or as a negative stressor, the response may be avoidance or ineffective coping. If a particular life event is viewed as benign or unimportant, coping responses will not be activated. If an event proves to be more stressful than anticipated, an older person will be unprepared to cope with these demands.

Adaptation is influenced by an individual's access to a support network, cognitive skills, and personality traits such as active versus passive "mastery style" and "locus of control." Although ego defense mechanisms have been observed to become more mature in middle and old age, it is difficult to describe coping styles in a similar manner. Age differences in the use of coping styles have been observed in cross-sectional studies, but longitudinal comparisons reveal considerable stability in coping.

Successful aging may be defined as the ability to avoid disease and disability, to function at a high level cognitively, to remain involved in society, and to cope effectively with life events and chronic hassles. An individual who has survived to the age of 75 or older has proved to be adaptable to new situations. Hence, older people who remain physically, cognitively, and socially active can achieve successful aging.

The prevalence of mental disorders in old age is difficult to determine, although estimates range from 5 to 45 percent of the older population. Research in acute and long-term care institutional settings provides higher estimates than epidemiological studies conducted in the community. This is because many older persons with mental disorders are treated in institutional settings rather than through community mental health services.

Depression is the most common mental disorder in late life, although estimates of its prevalence also vary widely, depending on the criteria used to diagnose it. Bipolar disorders are rare in old age; major depression is more common. Reactive or minor depression that is secondary to major life changes is found frequently in older persons. This condition responds well to environmental and social interventions, whereas antidepressant medications combined with psychotherapy are more effective for major depression. It is important that older adults continue treatment for several months in order to improve their condition. Electroconvulsive therapy works well for severe depression in older people who do not respond to other forms of therapy. Diagnosing depression in older people is often difficult. Many deny it, while others attribute it to medical conditions. On the other hand, it is important to screen for medical conditions and medications that may produce depressive symptoms as a side effect.

Depression is a risk factor for suicide in older people, particularly for white men over age 85. Life changes that result in a loss of social status and increased isolation may explain why this group is more likely to commit suicide than other segments of the population. The increased risk of suicide in older adults highlights the need for family members and service providers to be sensitized to clues of an impending suicide.

Dementia includes numerous reversible and irreversible conditions that result in impaired cognitive function, especially recall of recent events, comprehension, learning, attention, and orientation to time, place, and person. It is essential to perform a complete diagnostic workup of older people who have symptoms of dementia. A medical history, physical examination, assessment of medications, lab tests, psychological and cognitive testing, as well as neurological testing will aid in distinguishing "reversible" dementias that can be treated from the "irreversible" dementias such as Alzheimer's disease that currently can be managed but not cured. The biological basis of Alzheimer's disease is receiving much more research attention today. Future treatments may involve medications that replace or prevent the loss of brain chemicals, as well as vaccines and even gene therapy. Family members and service providers should be aware of changes in the older person's cognitive functioning and behavior that may signal dementia, and must avoid labeling such changes as normal aging or as—the catchall phrase—"senility."

Although cognitive functioning cannot be restored in irreversible dementias, older persons in the early stages of these conditions often benefit from some medications, memory retraining, and psychotherapy to cope with the changes they are experiencing. Environmental modifications that simplify tasks and aid in orienting the patient may slow the rate of deterioration and postpone institutionalization. It is also important to provide emotional and social support to family caregivers of elders with Alzheimer's disease and other dementias. Support groups, adult day care, and other such respite programs are valuable for spouses and other caregivers who assume full-time care for these patients at home, although they are limited by funding constraints.

Alcoholism and drug abuse are less common in older persons than in the young, although accurate estimates of prevalence are difficult to obtain. Physical health and cognitive function are significantly impaired in older alcoholics. Older men with a history of alcohol abuse also have a greater risk of suicide than do younger men or young and old women who are alcoholics. Drug abuse in older persons is rarely associated with illicit drugs, but often takes the form of inappropriate use or overuse of some prescription and over-the-counter drugs. Adverse reactions are more likely to occur in older persons because of age-related physiological changes that impair the ability to metabolize many medications and because of the greater likelihood of polypharmacy.

Paranoia and schizophrenia are far less common than depression and dementia in older persons. Most people with these conditions first developed them in middle age; life changes such as relocation and confusion that result from dementia may trigger paranoid reactions in old age, and may aggravate preexisting schizophrenic symptoms. Psychotherapy, especially using cognitive behavior strategies, may be effective in treating paranoia, although it is important first to determine and to verify the underlying causes of the condition.

Many researchers have explored the feasibility of psychotherapy with older patients. Both short-term, goal-oriented therapy and long-term approaches have been advocated. Specific modes of therapy with older patients include reminiscence, brief psychodynamic, and cognitive-behavioral techniques. These interventions have been particularly effective with depressed older people in community settings. Nursing homes are ideal settings for long-term, intense therapies using groups, but staff may not have the time or training to implement them. Behavior change and milieu therapy have resulted in significant improvements in short-term experimental interventions.

Despite the demonstrated efficacy of many forms of psychotherapy with older persons, they significantly underutilize mental health services. Most treatments for mental disorders in this population take place in hospitals. Many older people prefer to seek treatment for depression and other mental disorders from a general physician. This may result in an overuse of pharmacological treatment and an underutilization of psychotherapy in cases where the latter may be more effective. Such behavior may be attributed to reluctance among the current cohort of elders to admit they have a psychiatric problem, a lack of knowledge about such conditions and their treatment, as well as problems with accessibility. Attitudes of mental health providers and social service providers about the value of psychotherapy for older persons and, perhaps most important, the lack of effective links between mental health and social services to the older population, have been barriers in the past. As more programs evolve that integrate services, and as future cohorts become aware of mental disorders and their treatment, there will be greater acceptance and use of mental health services by older people.

GLOSSARY

active and passive mastery   interactions with one's social environment that are more controlling and competitive, versus more affiliative and docile

adaptation   ability to change personal needs, motivations, behaviors, and expectations to fit changing environmental demands or conditions

anxiety disorder   functional psychological disorder often triggered by external stress; accompanied by physiological reactivity such as increased heart rate and sleep disorders

archetypes   masculine and feminine aspects of personality, present in both men and women

benign senescent forgetfulness   mild age-related decline in memory and learning ability; not progressive as in dementia

cognitive appraisal   the individual's interpretation of an event as stressful, benign, or pleasant; determines individual's response to situation

coping (problem-focused versus emotion-focused)   conscious responses to stress, determined by nature of stressor, personality, social support, and health

defense mechanisms   unconscious responses to stress, in order to defend the ego from impulses, memories, and external threats

delirium   a reversible dementia characterized by sudden outset, generally caused by environmental factors.

dementia   progressive, marked decline in cognitive functions associated with damage to brain tissue; may affect personality and behavior; may be reversible or irreversible type

depression (major versus minor or reactive)   the most common psychiatric disorder in old age, diagnosed if several behavioral and affective symptoms (e.g., sleep and disturbances) are present for at least two weeks; bipolar disorders are less common in older people than reactive (or minor) and major depression

ego integrity versus despair   the eighth and last stage of psychosocial development in Erikson's model; aging individual achieves wisdom and perspective, or despairs because he or she views one's life as lacking meaning

electroconvulsive or electroshock therapy (ECT)   a form of therapy for severely depressed patients in which a mild electrical current is applied to one or both sides of brain

generativity   the seventh stage of psychosocial development in Erikson's model; goal of middle-aged and older persons is to care for and mentor younger generations, look toward future, and not stagnate in past

life events   identifiable, discrete life changes or transitions that require some adaptation to reestablish homeostasis

life review   a form of psychotherapy that encourages discussion of past successes and failures

life structures   in Levinson's model, specific developmental stages consisting of eras and transitions

paranoia   a psychiatric disorder characterized by irrational suspiciousness of other people

pharmacotherapy   use of medications to treat symptoms of physical or psychiatric disorders

psychopathology   abnormal changes in personality and behavior that may be caused or triggered by a genetic predisposition, environmental stress, and/or systemic diseases

reminiscence therapy   a type of psychotherapy used with depressed, anxious, sometimes confused older adults, stimulating the older person's memory of successful coping experiences and positive events in the past

schizophrenia   a psychiatric disorder characterized by thought disorders and hallucinations, psychotic behavior, loss of emotional expression.

self-concept   cognitive representation of the self; emerges from interactions with social environment, social roles, accomplishments

self-efficacy perceived confidence in one's own ability to know how to cope with a stressor and to resolve it

self-esteem   evaluation or feeling about one's identity relative to an "ideal self"; differs from self-concept in being more of an emotional, not cognitive, assessment of self

stage theories of personality   development of individual through various levels, each one necessary for adaptation and for psychological adjustment

successful aging   achievement of good physical and functional health, cognitive and emotional well-being in old age, often accompanied by strong social support and productive activity

trait theories   personality theories that describe individuals in terms of characteristic or "typical" attributes that remain relatively stable with age

RESOURCES

See the companion Website for this text at <www.ablongman.com/hooyman> for information about the following:

- **Alzheimer's Disease Education and Referral Center (ADEAR)**
- **Alzheimer's Disease and Related Disorders Association Inc. (ADRDA)**
- **Alzheimer's Research Forum**
- **American Association for Geriatric Psychiatry**
- **Eldercare Web**
- **Elder Care Locator**

- National Family Caregivers Association
- National Institute of Neurological Disorders and Stroke

REFERENCES

Adamek, M. E., and Kaplan, M. S. Firearm suicide among older men. *Psychiatric Services*, 1996, *47*, 304–306.

Adams, W. L., Barry, K. K., and Fleming, M. F. Screening for problem drinking in older primary care patients. *Journal of the American Medical Association*, 1996, *276*, 1964–1967.

Albert, M. S., Savage, C. R., Jones, K., Berkman, L., Seeman, T., Blazer, D., and Rowe, J. W. Predictors of cognitive change in older persons: MacArthur studies of successful aging. *Psychology and Aging*, 1995, *10*, 578–589.

Alzheimer's Association. *Action series: Modifying the environment*. Chicago: Alzheimer's Association, 1997.

American Psychiatric Association (APA). *Diagnostic and statistical manual of mental disorders* (4th ed.). Washington, DC: APA, 1994.

Amster, L. E., and Krauss, H. The relationship between life crises and mental deterioration in old age. *International Journal of Aging and Human Development*, 1974, *5*, 51–55.

Arean, P. A., Perri, M. G., Nezu, A. M., Schein, R. L., Christopher, F., and Joseph, T. X. Comparative effectiveness of social problem-solving therapy and reminiscence therapy as treatments for depression in older adults. *Journal of Consulting and Clinical Psychology*, 1993, *61*, 1003–1010.

Banazak, D. A. Anxiety disorders in elderly patients. *Journal of the American Board of Family Practice*, 1997, *10*, 280–289.

Bassuk, S. S., Glass, T. A., and Berkman, L. F. Social disengagement and incident cognitive decline in community-dwelling elderly persons. *Annals of Internal Medicine*, 1999, *131*, 165–173.

Blazer, D. G., and Koenig, H. G. Suicide. In J. E. Birren (Ed.), *Encyclopedia of gerontology*. San Diego: Academic Press, 1996.

Brinton, R. D., Chen, S., Montoya, M., Hsieh, D. and Minaya, J. Estrogen replacement therapy of the Women's Health Initiative promotes the cellular mechanisms of memory and neuronal survival in neurons vulnerable to Alzheimer's disease. *Maturitas*, 2000, *34*, S35–S52.

Butler, R. N., Lewis, M., and Sunderland, T. *Aging and mental health* (4th ed.). New York: Macmillan, 1991.

Carr, D. B., Goate, A., Phil, D., and Morris, J. C. Current concepts in the pathogenesis of Alzheimer's disease. *American Journal of Medicine*, 1997, *103*, 3S–10S.

Chen, H. L. Hearing loss in the elderly: Relation to loneliness and self-esteem. *Journal of Gerontological Nursing*, 1994, *20*, 22–28.

Coblentz, J. M., Mattis, S., Zingesser, L. H., Kasoff, S. S., Wisniewski, H. M., and Katzman, R. Presenile dementia: Clinical evaluation of cerebrospinal fluid dynamics. *Archives of Neurology*, 1973, *29*, 299–308.

Col, N., Fanale, J. E., and Kronholm, P. The role of medication noncompliance and adverse drug reactions in hospitalizations of the elderly. *Archives of Internal Medicine*, 1990, *150*, 841–845.

Conwell, Y., and Caine, E. D. Suicide in the elderly chronic patient population. In E. Light and B. D. Lebowitz (Eds.), *The elderly with chronic mental illness*. New York: Springer, 1991.

Costa, P. T., and McCrae, R. R. Cross-sectional studies of personality in a national sample. Development and validation of survey measures. *Psychology and Aging*, 1986, *1*, 140–143.

Costa, P. T., and McCrae, R. R. Psychological stress and coping in old age. In L. Goldberger and S. Breznitz (Eds.), *Handbook of stress: Theoretical and clinical aspects* (2nd ed.). New York: Free Press, 1993.

Costa, P. T., and McCrae, R. R. Solid ground in the wetlands of personality: A reply to Block. *Psychological Bulletin*, 1995, *117*, 216–220.

Costa, P. T., and McCrae, R. R. Stability and change in personality from adolescence through adulthood. In C. F. Halverson, G. A. Kohnstamm, and R. P. Martin (Eds.), *The developing structure of temperament and personality from infancy to adulthood*. Hillsdale, NJ: Erlbaum, 1994.

Coyne, J. C., and Downey, G. Social factors and psychopathology: Stress, social support and coping processes. *Annual Review of Psychology*, 1991, *42*, 401–425.

Day, K., Carreon, D. and Stump, C. The therapeutic design of environments for people with dementia: A review of the empirical research. *The Gerontologist*. 2000, *40*, 397–406.

De St. Aubin, E., and McAdams, D. P. The relations of generative concern and generative action to personality traits, satisfaction/happiness with life, and ego development. *Journal of Adult Development.* 1995, *2,* 99–112.

DeVries, H. M. Cognitive-behavioral interventions. In J. E. Birren (Ed.), *Encyclopedia of gerontology,* San Diego: Academic Press, 1996.

Erikson, E. H. *Childhood and society* (2nd ed.). New York: Norton, 1963.

Erikson, E. H. *Identity, youth and crisis.* New York: Norton, 1968.

Erikson, E. H. *The life cycle completed: A review.* New York: Norton, 1982.

Erikson, E. H., Erikson, J. M., and Kivnick, H. Q. *Vital involvement in old age.* New York: Norton, 1986.

Erkinjuntti, T., Ostbye, T., Steenhuis, R., and Hachinski, V. The effect of different diagnostic criteria on the prevalence of dementia. *New England Journal of Medicine,* 1997, *337,* 1667–1674.

Fisher, B. J. Successful aging, life satisfaction, and generativity in later life. *International Journal of Aging and Human Development,* 1995, *41,* 239–250.

Folkman, S., Lazarus, R. S., Pimley, S., and Novacek, J. Age differences in stress and coping processes. *Psychology and Aging,* 1987, *2,* 171–184.

Folstein, M., Folstein, S., and McHugh, P. R. Mini-mental state: A practical method for grading the cognitive state of patients for the clinician. *Journal of Psychiatric Research,* 1975, *12,* 189–198.

Fox, J. Broken connections, missing memories. Interviewed in *Time,* April 15, 1991, 10–12.

Frank, E., Swartz, H. A., Mallinger, A. G., Thase, M. E., Weaver, E. V., and Kupfer, D. J. Adjunctive psychotherapy for bipolar disorder: Effects of changing treatment modality. *Journal of Abnormal Psychology,* 1999, *108,* 579–587.

Freud, S. *Collected papers, Volume I.* London: Hogarth Press, 1924.

Friedland, R. P., Fritsch, T., Smyth, K., Koss, E., Lerner, A. J., Chen, C. H., Petot, G., and Debanne, S. M. Participation in nonocupational activities in midlife is protective against the development of Alzheimer's disease: Results from a case-control study. *Neurology,* 2000, *54,* Abstract #P05.076.

Gallagher-Thompson, D., and Steffan, A. Comparative effectiveness of cognitive-behavioral and brief psychodynamic psychotherapy for treatment of depression in family caregivers. *Journal of Consulting and Clinical Psychology,* 1994, *62,* 543–549.

Gallo, J. J., Anthony, J. C., and Muthen, B. O. Age differences in the symptoms of depression: A latent trait analysis. *Journals of Gerontology,* 1994, *49B,* P251–264.

Garfein, A. J., and Herzog, A. R. Robust aging among the young-old, old-old, and oldest-old. *Journals of Gerontology,* 1995, *50B,* S77–S87.

Giarrusso, R., and Bengtson, V. L. Self-esteem. In J. E. Birren (Ed.), *Encyclopedia of gerontology,* Vol. 2. San Diego: Academic Press, 1996.

Goldberg, R. J., and Goldberg, J. Risperidone for dementia-related disturbed behavior in nursing home residents. *International Psychogeriatrics,* 1997, *9,* 65–68.

Graham, K., Carver, V., and Brett, P. J. Alcohol and drug use by older women: Results of a national survey. *Canadian Journal on Aging,* 1995, *14,* 769–791.

Grant, L. A., Kane, R. A., and Stark, A. J. Beyond labels: Nursing home care for Alzheimer's disease in and out of special care units. *Journal of the American Geriatrics Society,* 1995, *43,* 589–576.

Gunland, B. The impact of depression on quality of life of the elderly. *Clinics in Geriatric Medicine,* 1992, *8,* 377–385.

Gurnack, A. M., and Hoffman, N. G. Elderly alcohol misuse. *International Journal of the Addictions,* 1992, *27,* 867–878.

Gutmann, D. L. The cross-cultural perspective: Notes toward a comparative psychology of aging. In J. E. Birren and K. W. Schaie (Eds.), *Handbook of the psychology of aging.* New York: Van Nostrand Reinhold, 1977.

Gutmann, D. L. Culture and mental health in later life. In J. E. Birren, R. B. Sloane, and G. D. Cohen (Eds.), *Handbook of mental health and aging* (2nd ed.). New York: Academic Press, 1992.

Gutmann, D. L. Psychoanalysis and aging: A developmental view. In S. I. Greenspan and G. H. Pollock (Eds.), *The course of life: Psychoanalytic contributions toward understanding personality development. Vol. 3: Adulthood and the aging process.* Washington, DC: U.S. Government Printing Office, 1980.

Haight, B. K., Michel, Y., and Hendrix, S. The extended effects of the life review in nursing home residents. *International Journal of Aging and Human Development,* 2000, *50,* 151–168.

Henderson, V. W. The epidemiology of estrogen replacement therapy and Alzheimer's disease. *Neurology,* 1997, *48,* S27–S35.

Hendrie, H. C. Epidemiology of Alzheimer's disease. *Geriatrics,* 1997, *52,* S4–S8.

Holmes, T. H., and Masuda, M. Life change and illness susceptibility. In B. S. Dohrenwend and B. P. Dohrenwend (Eds.), *Stressful life events: Their nature and effects*. New York: Wiley, 1974.

Holmes, T. H., and Rahe, R. The social readjustment rating scale. *Journal of Psychosomatic Research*, 1967, *11*, 213–218.

Holroyd, S., Currie, L., Thompson-Heisterman, A., and Abraham, I. A descriptive study of elderly community-dwelling alcoholic patients in the rural south. *American Journal of Geriatric Psychiatry*, 1997, *5*, 221–228.

Horgas, A. L., Wilms, H. U. and Baltes, M. M. Daily life in very old age: Everyday activities as an expression of successful living. *The Gerontologist*, 1998, *38*, 556–568.

Howieson, D. B., Holm, L. A., Kaye, J. A., Oken, B. S., and Howieson, J. Neurological function in the optimally healthy oldest old. *Neurology*, 1993, *43*, 1882–1886.

Irion, J. C., and Blanchard-Fields, F. A cross-sectional comparison of adaptive coping in adulthood. *Journal of Gerontology*, 1987, *42*, 502–504.

Jefferson, J. W., and Greist, J. H. *Depression and older people: Recognizing hidden signs and taking steps toward recovery*. Madison, WI: Pratt Pharmaceuticals, 1993.

Jung, C. G. Concerning the archetypes, with special reference to the anima concept. In *C. G. Jung, Collected works*, Vol. 9, Part I. Princeton, NJ: Princeton University Press, 1959.

Jung, C. G. *Modern man in search of a soul*. San Diego: Harcourt Brace and World, 1933.

Kemper, G. I., van Souderen, E., and Ormel, J. The impact of psychological attributes on changes in disability among low-functioning older persons. *Journals of Gerontology: Psychological Sciences*, 1999, *54B*, 23–29.

Kessler, R. C. The effects of stressful life events on depression. *Annual Review of Psychology*, 1997, *48*, 191–214.

King, A. C., Oka, R. K., and Young, D. R. Ambulatory blood pressure and heart rate responses to the stress of work and caregiving in older women. *Journals of Gerontology*, 1994, *49*, M239–245.

Koenig, H. G., and Blazer, D. G. Depression. In J. E. Birren (Ed.), *Encyclopedia of gerontology*, San Diego: Academic Press, 1996.

Kokmen, E., Beard, C. M., O'Brien, P. C., and Kurland, L. T. Epidemiology of dementia in Rochester,

Minnesota. *Mayo Clinic Proceedings*, 1996, *71*, 275–282.

Krause, N. Stress, alcohol use, and depressive symptoms in later life. *The Gerontologist*, 1995, *35*, 296–307.

Lazarus, R. S., and DeLongis, A. Psychological stress and coping in aging. *American Psychologist*, 1983, *38*, 245–254.

Lazarus, R. S., and Folkman, S. *Stress, appraisal and coping*. New York: Springer, 1984.

Lenze, E. J., Mulsant, B. H., Shear, M. K., Schulberg, H. C., Dew, M. A., Begley, A. E., Pollock, B. G. and Reynolds, C. F. Comormid anxiety disorders in depressed elderly patients. *American Journal of Psychiatry*, 2000, *157*, 722–728.

Levinson, D. J. A conception of adult development. *American Psychologist*, 1986, *41*, 3–13.

Levinson, D. J. Middle adulthood in modern society: A sociopsychological view. In G. DiRenzo (Ed.). *We the people: Social change and social character*. Westport, CT: Greenwood Press, 1977.

Levinson, D. J., Darrow, C. M., Klein, E. B., Levinson, M. H., and McKee, B. *The seasons of a man's life*. New York: Knopf, 1978.

Li, G. The interaction effect of bereavement and sex on the risk of suicide in the elderly. *Social Science and Medicine*, 1995, *40*, 825–828.

Lichtenberg, P. A., Ross, T., Millis, S. R., and Manning, C. A. The relationship between depression and cognition in older adults: A cross-validation study. *Journals of Gerontology*, 1995, *50B*, P25–P32.

Light, E., and Lebowitz, B. D. (Eds.) *The elderly with chronic mental illness*. New York: Springer, 1991.

Lim, G. P., Yang, F., Chu, T., Chen, P., Beech, W., et al. Ibuprofen suppresses plaque pathology and inflammation in a mouse model for Alzheimer's disease. *Journal of Neuroscience*, 2000, *20*, 5709–5714.

Lis, C. G., and Gaviria, M. Vascular dementia, hypertension, and the brain. *Neurological Research*, 1997, *19*, 471–480.

Logsdon, R. G. and Teri, L. *Evaluating and treating behavioral disturbances in dementia*. University of Washington: NW Geriatric Education Center Curriculum Modules, 2000.

Mattis, S. Mental status examination for organic mental syndrome in the elderly patient. In R. Bellack and B. Karasu (Eds.), *Geriatric psychiatry*. New York: Grune and Stratton, 1976.

McAdams, D. P., and De St. Aubin, E. A theory of generativity and its assessment through self-report, behavioral acts, and narrative themes in autobiography. *Journal of Personality and Social Psychology,* 1992, *62,* 1003–1015.

McCrae, R. R. Age differences and changes in the use of coping mechanisms. *Journals of Gerontology,* 1989, *44,* P161–Pl64.

McCrae, R. R., and Costa, P. T. *Personality in adulthood.* New York: Guilford, 1990.

McFadden, S. H. Religion, spirituality, and aging. In J. E. Birren and K. W. Schaie (Eds.), *Handbook of the psychology of aging* (4th ed.). San Diego: Academic Press, 1996.

McIntosh, J. L. *U.S.A. suicide: 1994 official final statistics.* 1997. http://oit.iusb.edu/~jmcintos/suicidestats.html.

McLeod, J. D. Life events. In J. E. Birren (Ed.), *Encyclopedia of gerontology,* San Diego: Academic Press, 1996.

McMurdo, M. E., and Rennie, L. A controlled trial of exercise by residents of old people's homes. *Age and Ageing,* 1993, *22,* 11–15.

Miller, N. S., Belkin, B. M., and Gold, M. S. Alcohol and drug dependence among the elderly. *Comprehensive Psychiatry,* 1991, *32,* 153–165.

Mittelman, M. S., Ferris, S. H., Shulman, E., Steinberg, G., and Levin, B. A family intervention to delay nursing home placement of patients with Alzheimer's disease. *JAMA,* 1996, *276,* 1725–1731.

Moceri, V. M., Kukull, W. A., Emanuel, I., van Belle, G., and Larson, E. B. Early-life risk factors and the development of Alzheimer's disease. *Neurology,* 2000, *54,* 415–420.

Mockenhaupt, R. E., and Beck, K. H. The social context of drinking in mid-life and older persons. Paper presented at annual meeting of the Gerontological Society of America, 1997.

Morrison, R. S., and Siu A. L. Survival in end-stage dementia following acute illness. *JAMA,* 2000, *284,* 47–52.

Muhlenkamp, A., Gress, L. D., and Flood, M. A. Perception of life change events by the elderly. *Nursing Research,* 1975, *24,* 109–113.

Nacoste, D., and Wise, W. The relationship among negative life events, cognitions and depression within three generations. *The Gerontologist,* 1991, *31,* 397–403.

National Center for Health Statistics. "Death rates and age-adjusted death rates: United States, 1998." *National Vital Statistics Report,* 2000, *486,* 68–73. 2000

Nesselroade, J. R., Featherman, D. L., Agen, S. H., and Rowe, J. W. *Short-term variability in physical performance and physiological attributes in older adults: MacArthur successful aging studies.* Unpublished manuscript, University of Virginia, 1996.

Neugarten, B. L., Personality change in late life: A developmental perspective. In C. Eisdorfer and M. P. Lawton (eds.) *The psychology of adult developmental aging,* 1973, Washington DC: American Psychiatric Association.

Neugarten, B. L., Havighurst, R. J., and Tobin, S. S. Personality and patterns of aging. In B. L. Neugarten (Ed.), *Middle age and aging.* Chicago: University of Chicago Press, 1968.

NIH (National Institutes of Health) Consensus Development Conference. *Diagnosis and treatment of depression.* Washington, DC: 1994.

Olichney, J. M., Sabbagh, M. N., Hofstetter, C. R., Galasko, D., Grundman, M., Katzman, R., and Thal, L. J. The impact of apolipoprotein E4 on cause of death in Alzheimer's disease. *Neurology,* 1997, *49,* 76–81.

Osgood, N. J., Wood, H. E., and Parham, I. A. *Alcoholism and aging: An annotated bibliography and review.* Westport, CT: Greenwood Press, 1995.

Paganini-Hill, A., and Henderson, V. W. Estrogen replacement therapy and risk of Alzheimer's disease. *Archives of Internal Medicine,* 1996, *156,* 2213–2217.

Pargament, K. I., Ensing, D. S., Falgout, K., Olsen, H., Reilly, B., Van Haitsma, K., and Warren, R. Religious coping efforts as predictors of outcomes to significant negative life events. *American Journal of Community Psychology,* 1990, *18,* 793–824.

Pargament, K. I., Van Haitsma, K., and Ensig, D. S. When age meets adversity: Religion and coping in the later years. In M. A. Kimble, S. H. McFadden, J. W. Ellor, and J. J. Seaber (Eds.), *Aging, spirituality and religion: A handbook.* Minneapolis: Fortress Press, 1995.

Parmelee, P. A., Katz, I. R., and Lawton, M. P. Incidence of depression in long-term care settings. *Journals of Gerontology,* 1992, *47,* M189–M196.

Paykel, E. S., Brayne, C., Huppert, F. A., Gill, C., Barkley, C., Gehlhaar, E., and Beardsold, L. Incidence of dementia in a population older than 75 years in the United Kingdom. *Archives of General Psychiatry,* 1994, *51,* 325–332.

Pearson, J. L., Teri, L., Wagner, A., Truax, P., and Logsdon, R. G. The relationship of problem behaviors in dementia patients to the depression and burden of caregiving spouses. *American Journal of Alzheimer's Disease and Related Disorders and Research,* 1993, *7,* 15–22.

Pederson, N. L., Plomin, R., McClearn, G. E., and Friberg, L. Neuroticism, extroversion, and related traits in adult twins reared apart and reared together. *Journal of Personality and Social Psychology,* 1988, *55,* 950–957.

Perls, T. T. The oldest-old. *Scientific American,* 1995, *272,* 70–75.

Peterson, B. E., and Klohnen E. C. Realization of generativity in two samples of women at midlife. *Psychology and Aging,* 1995, *10,* 20–29.

Pinquart, M. Analysis of the self-concept of independently living senior citizens. *Zeitschrift für Gerontologie,* 1991, *24,* 98–104.

Plomin, R., Pederson, N. L., McClearn, G. E., Nesselroade, J. R., and Bergeman, C. S. EAS temperaments during the last half of the lifespan: Twins reared apart and twins reared together. *Psychology and Aging,* 1988, *3,* 43–50.

Quam, J. K., and Abramson, N. S. The use of time lines and life lines in work with chronically mentally ill people. *Health and Social Work,* 1991, *16,* 27–33.

Rabins, P. V. Establishing Alzheimer's disease units in nursing homes: Pros and cons. *Hospital and Community Psychiatry,* 1986, *37,* 120–121.

Rabins, P. V. Schizophrenia and psychotic states. In J. E. Birren, R. B. Sloane, and G. D. Cohen (Eds.), *Handbook of mental health and aging* (2nd ed.). New York: Academic Press, 1992.

Rahe, R. H. Subjects' recent life changes and their near future illness reports: A review. *Annals of Clinical Research,* 1972, *4,* 393.

Reese, D. R., Gross, A. M., Smalley, D. L., and Messer, S. C. Caregivers of Alzheimer's disease and stroke patients: Immunological and psychological considerations. *The Gerontologist,* 1994, *34,* 534–540.

Regier, D. A., Boyd, J. H., Burke, J. S., Rae, D. S., Myers, J. K., Kramer, M., Robins, L. N., George, L. K., Karno, M., and Locke, B. Z. One month prevalence of mental disorders in the United States: Based on five epidemiologic catchment area sites. *Archives of General Psychiatry,* 1988, *45,* 977–986.

Reid, M. C., Concato, J., Towle, V. R., Williams, C. S., and Tennetti, M. E. Alcohol use and functional disability among cognitively impaired adults. *Journal of the American Geriatrics Society,* 1999, *47,* 854–859.

Reisberg, B., Ferris, S. H., De Leon, M. J., and Crook, T. The Global Deterioration Scale for assessment of primary degenerative dementia. *American Journal of Psychiatry,* 1982, *139,* 1136–1139.

Reisberg, B., Franssen, E. H., Souren, L. E., Auer, S., and Kenowsky, S. Progression of Alzheimer's disease: Variability and consistency: Ontogenic models, their applicability and relevance. *Journal of Neural Transmission Supplement,* 1998, *54,* 9–20.

Reynolds, C. F., Miller, M. D., Pasaternak, R. E., Frank, E., Perel, J. M., et al. Treatment of bereavement-related major depressive episodes in later life. *American Journal of Psychiatry,* 1999, *156,* 202–208.

Riggs, J. "Capitol Hill Forum on Family Caregivers. *Older Americans Report,* Sept. 22, 2000.

Roberts, P., and Newton, P. M. Levinsonian studies of women's adult development. *Psychology and Aging,* 1987, *2,* 154–163.

Rocca, W. A. Frequency distribution and risk factors for Alzheimer's disease. *Nursing Clinics of North America,* 1994, *29,* 101–111.

Rowe, J. W., and Kahn, R. L. Human aging: Usual and successful. *Science,* 1987, *237,* 143–149.

Rowe, J. W., and Kahn, R. L. Successful aging. *The Gerontologist,* 1997, *37,* 433–440.

Rowe, J. W., and Kahn, R. L. *Successful Aging,* New York: Pantheon Books, 1998.

Russo, J., Vitaliano, P. P., Brewer, D. D., Katon, W., and Becker, J. Psychiatric disorders in spouse caregivers of care recipients with Alzheimer's disease. *Journal of Abnormal Psychology,* 1995, *104,* 197–204.

Ruth, J. E., and Coleman, P. Personality and aging: Coping and management of the self in later life. In J. E. Birren and K. W. Schaie (Eds.), *Handbook of the psychology of aging* (4th ed.). San Diego: Academic Press, 1996.

Ryff, C. D. Possible selves in adulthood and old age: A tale of shifting horizons. *Psychology and Aging,* 1991, *6,* 286–295.

Sano, M., Ernesto, C., Thomas, R. G., Klauber, M. R., Schafer, K., and Grundman, M. A controlled clinical trial of selegiline, alpha-tocopherol or both as treatment for Alzheimer's disease. *New England Journal of Medicine,* 1997, *336,* 1216–1222.

Schaie, K. W., and Willis, S. L. Adult personality and psychomotor performance. *Journals of Gerontology,* 1991, *46,* P275–P284.

Schenk, D., Barbour, R., Dunn, W., Gordon, G., Grajeda, H., Guido, T., Hu, K., Huang, J., et al. Immunization with amyloid-B attenuates Alzheimer-disease-like pathology in the PDAPP mouse. *Nature*, 1999, *400*, 173–177.

Schulz, R., Beach, S. R., Ives, D. G., Martire, L. M., Ariyo, A. A., and Kop, W. J. Association between depression and mortality in older adults. *Archives of International Medicine*, 2000, *160*, 1761–1768.

Schulz, R., and Heckhausen, J. A life span model of successful aging. *American Psychologist*, 1996, *51*, 702–714. 1996.

Scogin, F., and McElreath, L. Efficacy of psychosocial treatments for geriatric depression: A quantitative review. *Journal of Consulting and Clinical Psychology*, 1994, *62*, 69–74.

Seeman, T. A., Charpentier, P. A., Berkman, L. F., Tinetti, M. E., Guralnick, J. M., Albert, M., Blazer, D., and Rowe, J. W. Predicting changes in physical performance in a high functioning elderly cohort: MacArthur Studies of Successful Aging. *Journals of Gerontology*, 1994, *49*, M97–M108.

Seeman, T. E., Unger, J. B., McAvay, G., and Mendes de Leon, D. Self-efficacy beliefs and perceived declines in functional ability. *Journals of Gerontology*, 1999, *54*, 214–222.

Selye, H. The general adaptation syndrome and the diseases of adaptation. *Journal of Clinical Endocrinology*, 1946, *6*, 117–230.

Selye, H. Stress and aging. *Journal of the American Geriatrics Society*, 1970, *18*, 660–681.

Singer, C. A., Pang, P. A., Dobie, D. J., and Dorsa, D. M. Estrogen increases gap-43 (neuromodulin) mRNA in the preoptic area of aged rats. *Neurobiology of Aging*, 1996a, *17*, 661–663.

Singer, C. A., Rogers, K. L., Strickland, T. M., and Dorsa, D. M. Estrogen protects primary cortical neurons from glutamate toxicity. *Neuroscience Letters*, 1996b, *212*, 13–16.

Sloane, P. D., Lindeman, D. A., Phillips, C., Moritz, D. J., and Koch, G. Evaluating Alzheimer's disease special care units: Reviewing the evidence and identifying potential sources of study bias. *The Gerontologist*, 1995, *35*, 103–111.

Small, G. W., Liston, E. H., and Jarvik, L. F. Diagnosis and treatment of dementia in the aged. *Western Journal of Medicine*, 1981, *135*, 469–481.

Snowdon, D. A., Greiner, L. H., and Markesbery, W. R. Linquistic ability in early life and the neuropathology of Alzheimer's disease: Findings from the Nun Study. In R. N. Kalaria and P. Ince (Eds.), *Annals of New York Academy of Sciences*, N.Y.: New York Academy of Sciences, 2000.

Stewart, W. F., Kawas, C., Corrada, M., Metter, E. J., Risk of Alzheimer's disease and duration of NSAID use. *Neurology*, 1997, *48*, 626–632.

Surgeon General. *The Surgeon General's Call to Action to Prevent Suicide*, 1999,. http://www.surgeon-general.gov/library/calltoaction/fact2.htm.

Suzman, R. M., Harris, T., Hadley, E. C., Kovar, M. G., and Weindruch, R. The robust oldest old: Optimistic perspectives for increasing healthy life expectancy. In R. M. Suzman, D. P. Willis, and K. G. Manton (Eds.), *The oldest old*. New York: Oxford Press, 1992.

Teri, L., Logsdon, R. G., Uomoto, J., and McCurry, S. M. Behavioral treatment of depression in dementia patients: A controlled clinical trial. *Journals of Gerontology*, 1997, *52*, P159–P166.

Teri, L., McCurry, S. M., and Logsdon, R. G. Memory, thinking, and aging: What we know about what we know. *Western Journal of Medicine*, 1997, *167*, 269–275.

Thomae, H. Emotion and personality. In J. E. Birren, R. B. Sloane, and G. D. Cohen (Eds.), *Handbook of mental health and aging* (2nd ed.). New York: Academic Press, 1992.

Tilvis, R,.S., Pitkaelae, K., and Nevantaus, H. Prognosis of depression in old age. *Archives of Gerontological and Geriatric Medicine*, 1998, *S6*, 491–498.

Tran, T. V., Wright, R., and Chatters, L. Health, stress, psychological resources, and subjective well-being among older blacks. *Psychology and Aging*, 1991, *6*, 100–108.

Troll, L. E., and Skaff, M. M. Perceived continuity of self in very old age. *Psychology and Aging*,. 1997, *12*, 162–169.

Unger, J. B., McAvay, G., Bruce, M. L., Berkman, L. and Seman, T. Variation in the impact of social network characteristics on physical functioning in elderly persons. *Journals of Gerontology*, 1999, *54*, S245–S251.

Vaillant, G. E. *Adaptation to life*. Boston: Little, Brown, 1977.

Vaillant, G. E. Ego mechanisms of defense and personality psychopathology. *Journal of Abnormal Psychology*, 1994, *103*, 44–50.

Vaillant, G. E., and Vaillant, C. O. Natural history of male psychological health: A 45-year study of predictors of successful aging. *American Journal of Psychiatry*, 1990, *147*, 31–37.

Van Dongen, M. C. J. M, van Rossum, E., Kessels, A. G. H., Sielhorst, H. J. G., and Knipschild, P. G.

The efficacy of ginkgo for elderly people with dementia and age-associated memory impairment: New results of a randomized clinical trial. *Journal of the American Geriatrics Society,* 2000, *48,* 1183–1194.

Vitaliano, P. P., Russo, J., and Niaura, R. Plasma lipids and their relationship to psychosocial factors in older adults. *Journals of Gerontology,* 1995, *50,* P18–P24.

Vitaliano, P. P., Scanlan, J. M., Krenz, C., Schwartz, R. S., and Marcovina, S. M. Psychological distress, caregiving, and metabolic variables. *Journals of Gerontology,* 1996, *51,* P290–P299.

Whitbourne, S. K., and Primus, L. A. Physical identity. In J. E. Birren (Ed.), *Encyclopedia of gerontology,* San Diego: Academic Press, 1996.

Zarit, S. H., Stephens, M. A. P., Townsend, A. and Greene, R. Stress reduction for family caregivers: Effect of adult day care use. *Journals of Gerontology,* 1998, *53,* S267–S277.

Zweig, R. A., and Hinrichsen, G. A. Factors associated with suicide attempts by depressed older adults: A prospective study. *American Journal of Psychiatry,* 1993, *150,* 1687–1693.

7

LOVE, INTIMACY, AND SEXUALITY IN OLD AGE

This chapter reviews the following

- The prevalent attitudes and beliefs about sex and love in old age that frequently affect an older person's sexuality
- Age-related physiological changes that may alter the nature of older men's and women's sexual response and performance, but do not necessarily interfere with their overall experience of sexuality
- Gay and lesbian relationships
- Importance of late-life affection, love, and intimacy
- Implications for families and professionals who work with older people

The previous chapter focused on personality: who one is and how one feels about oneself. An important aspect of one's personality is sexuality. In fact, **sexuality** encompasses many aspects of one's being as a man or a woman, including one's self-concept, identity, and relationships. **Sex** is not just a biological function involving genital intercourse or orgasm; it also includes the expression of feelings—loyalty, passion, affection, esteem, and affirmation of one's body and its functioning, which are part of one's intimate self. A person's speech and movement, vitality, and ability to enjoy life are all parts of sexuality. As with other aspects of aging discussed throughout this text, sexuality is thus comprised of biological, emotional, intellectual, spiritual, behavioral, and sociocultural components (Kingsberg, 2000).

Older people, family members, and professionals need to understand the normal physiological changes that may affect sexual functioning and intimacy across the life span. To understand and treat the effects of aging on sexuality, the three components of sexual desire need to be addressed: drive, beliefs/values, and motivation as well as the sexual equilibrium within the primary relationship (Kingsberg, 2000). Since our sexual nature goes far beyond whether we are sexually active at any particular point in life, older individuals need to be comfortable with whatever decisions they make regarding their sexuality. Accordingly, professionals need to respect older adults' choices and values regarding the expression of their sexuality. Although most older individuals can and do engage in intercourse, some genuinely have no desire to engage in the physical aspects of sexual behavior—just as varying patterns of sexual expression occur at all ages.

Nonphysiological factors affect sexual activity—self-esteem, chronic illness, psychosocial conditions, and professionals' attitudes. In many instances, these dynamic contextual factors may exert greater influence than physiological changes as such. Sexual behavior, because of the powerful role it plays in the lives of most people, is especially likely to be affected by:

- the interactions of physiological changes
- the physical and social environment
- the individual's personal sexual history, self-concept, and self-esteem
- the psychological meaning attached to one's experiences
- the degree of physical fitness (Bortz and Wallace, 1999)

ATTITUDES AND BELIEFS ABOUT SEXUALITY IN LATER LIFE

It is striking that at a time when our society is increasingly tolerant of safe sex for nearly every segment of our population, outdated ideas persist in our approach toward sex and aging (Kaye, 1993).

Widespread stereotypes, misconceptions, and jokes about old age and sexuality can powerfully and negatively affect older people's sexual experience. Jokes often center on performance "He can't get it up any more" because of our society's emphasis on productivity and physical appearance. Many of these attitudes and beliefs stem from ageism generally, such as the perceptions of older people as physically unattractive and therefore asexual. Another example of ageism is the stereotype that older people lack energy and are devoid of sexual feeling, and therefore are not interested in sex. Since sexuality in our society tends to be equated with youthful standards of attractiveness, definitions of older people as asexual are heightened for older women and for individuals with chronic illness and disability.

Other attitudes and beliefs may stem from misinformation, such as the perception that sexual activity and drive do and should decline with old age. Accordingly, older people who speak of enjoying sexuality may be viewed as sinful, exaggerating, or deviant—for example, the stereotype of the "dirty old man." Alternatively, older people who express caring and physical affection for one another may be infantilized, defined as "cute" and teased by professionals, their age peers, and family members. Such public scrutiny and ridicule frequently occur among residents and staff of long-term care facilities. The oldest-old grew up in periods of restrictive guidelines regarding appropriate sexual behavior and taboos against other forms of sexual activity, such as masturbation. Many of these attitudes and beliefs of both older people and their families may reflect a Victorian morality that views sex only as intercourse and intercourse as appropriate only for conception. Sex for communication, intimacy, or pleasure may be considered unnecessary and immoral.

Unfortunately, the widely held attitude in our society that sexual interaction between older persons is socially unacceptable and physically harmful may have negative consequences for older people. Surrounded by those with such beliefs and fearing ridicule or censure, many older people may unnecessarily withdraw from all forms of sexual

---

POINTS TO PONDER

Reflect upon jokes or stories you have heard about older adults and sexuality. What have they conveyed? How did they affect your understanding of sexuality and aging?

---

expression long before they need to, thereby depriving themselves and often their partners of the energy and vitality inherent in sexuality. For many older adults, sexual activity, in the broadest sense of encompassing both physical and emotional interaction, is necessary for them to feel alive, to reaffirm their identity, and to communicate with their partners. Yet, by accepting society's stereotypes, some older individuals may bar themselves from sexual and intimate experiences that could benefit their overall physical and mental well-being. Understanding the natural physiological alterations in sexual response associated with the aging process is an essential first step toward dispelling such myths. In future years, those myths may change, as the media, gerontologists, and other professionals convey the message that sex is permissible and desirable in old age. In fact, one sign of change is that current cohorts of older people, especially the young-old, appear more accepting of and permissive in their attitudes toward sexuality and aging than in the past (Johnson, 1997; Steinke, 1994).

MYTHS AND REALITY ABOUT PHYSIOLOGICAL CHANGES AND FREQUENCY OF SEXUAL ACTIVITY

One of the most prevalent societal myths is that age-related physiological changes detrimentally affect sexual functioning. Such misconceptions have been created by the early research on sexuality. In part because of assumptions that older people do not engage in sex or are embarrassed to talk about it, many early surveys of sexual attitudes did not even question older people about their sexuality.

Such avoidance of the topic fostered further misinformation and misperceptions.

Other early studies included questions about sexuality, but focused on changes only in the frequency of sexual intercourse. These researchers overlooked the subjective experience or more qualitative aspects of sexuality in old age. For example, from 1938 to 1948, Kinsey and his colleagues studied primarily 16- to 55-year-olds, and their discussion of respondents over age 60 focused on the frequency of sexual intercourse, not on the meaning of sexuality to older people. Using the number of **orgasms** or ejaculations as the measure of good

Sexuality and intimacy are important throughout the later years.

sex, they found that by age 70, 25 percent of men experienced sexual dysfunction. Women were portrayed as reaching the peak of their sexual activity in their late twenties or thirties, then remaining on that plateau through their sixties, after which they showed a slight decline in sexual response capability (Kinsey, Pomeroy, and Martin, 1948, 1953). Because Kinsey and colleagues overlooked the broader psychological aspects of sexuality, they failed to address the subjective experience, meaning, and importance of sex at different ages. Older individuals may have sexual intercourse less often, but it is not necessarily less meaningful than at a younger age. In fact, few age-related physiological changes prevent continued sexual enjoyment and activity in old age.

In addition to the emphasis on frequency of sexual intercourse, early research on sexuality was limited by the nonrandom and therefore nonrepresentative nature of the sample, and by comparing younger and older cohorts at one point in time. For example, the Duke Longitudinal Study, which in 1954 examined the incidence of sexual intercourse and interest in sex, found declining frequencies of sexual activity for older adults compared to their young and middle-aged counterparts, especially for women and unmarried individuals. The median age for stopping intercourse was 68 in men and 60 in women (Pfeiffer and Davis, 1972). This study had several limitations, however. The definition of sexual activity was confined to heterosexual intercourse, and the respondents constituted a cohort of individuals raised during a period of strict sexual conservatism. As discussed in Chapter 1, we now know that such cross-sectional data fail to give a lifetime picture of an individual's sexual behavior. Because the cohort effect was not identified, the low levels of sexual activity reported may not have reflected any age-related physiological changes in sexual functioning. Instead, it may have been related to the attitudes, values, and reluctance to report on their actions among a cohort of elders who grew up in the Victorian era of the late 1890s to early 1900s, rather than any age-related physiological changes in sexual functioning (Schiavi and Rehman, 1995).

A subsequent reanalysis of the 1954 Duke Longitudinal Study data to control for a possible co-

hort effect and the second Duke Longitudinal Study over a six-year period revealed stability of sexual activity patterns from mid- to late life (George and Weiler, 1981). In other words, those who were sexually conservative and inactive in young adulthood and mid-life, perhaps because of their social upbringing, carried that pattern through their later years. Similarly, those who were more sexually involved in young adulthood and middle age continued to remain active in old age. A later analysis of the Duke data also found older women to be more interested in sex than older men; however, the rate of sexual activity among older women declined, partly because of the absence of partners and because the husband tended to curtail or discontinue sexual activities. In fact, marital status and relationship issues appear to be more important in influencing women's sexual behavior than it is for men's (Matthias et al., 1997). For men, sexual dysfunction or impotence appears to be the main barrier to sexual activity (Wiley and Bortz, 1996).

One of the first large-scale studies that provided evidence for continued sexuality in old age was the work of Masters and Johnson (1981). In their classic study of sexual responsiveness across the life span, Masters and Johnson determined that, while physiological changes occur with age, the capacity for both functioning and fulfillment does not disappear. They concluded that there are no known limits to sexual behavior. Later studies have generally found that most older adults, especially men, and even among those over age 80, remain sexually active. As with most behaviors, there is a wide range; some individuals even experience an increase in sexual activity with increasing age (Matthias et al., 1997; Schiavi and Rehman, 1995; Weg, 1996). In an open-ended questionnaire completed by 800 senior center participants, Starr and Weiner (1981) found the majority of respondents to be sexually active. In fact, 99 percent desired sexual relations with varying frequencies if they could engage in sexual activity whenever they wanted. Sexual inactivity appeared to depend upon life circumstances, not lack of interest or desire. Contrary to earlier findings from the 1954 Duke study, sexual frequency did not decline sharply with age, but ranged instead from 1.5 times a week for 60- to 69-year-olds, 1.4 times a week for 70- to 79-year-olds, to 1.2 times a week for those over age 80. Some later studies have found the average frequency of sexual activity to be four times a month among those aged 65 and older (Steinke, 1994).

In sum, many of the issues that affect research designs in gerontology that were described in Chapter 1 are reflected in the area of sexuality in old age. That is, age, type of study design (longitudinal versus cross-sectional) and the possible confounding of age with cohort membership may partially account for different outcomes.

The following is a summary of general findings about older people and sexuality:

• Older people who remain sexually active do not differ significantly in the frequency of sexual relations compared with their younger selves (longitudinal data). Rather, sexual activity appears to decrease significantly when older people are compared with younger persons at the same point in time (cross-sectional data).

• When a partner is available, the rate of sexual behavior is fairly stable throughout life. And sexually active older people perceive their sex lives as remaining much the same as they grow older.

• Although good physical and mental health are predictors of sexual activity and satisfaction, even older people with chronic health problems, depression, and cognitive dysfunction can achieve sexual satisfaction (Matthias et al., 1997; Richardson and Lazur, 1995; Schiavi and Rehman, 1995).

• Regardless of the length or nature of a late-life relationship, its quality is enhanced by emotional intimacy, autonomy without too much distance, an ability to manage stress and external distrac-

tions, and achieving a satisfying sexual equilibrium (Kingsberg, 2000).

Rates of activity increase to over 80 percent for men and over 60 percent for women when sexual activity is defined more broadly than intercourse to encompass touching and caressing (Janus and Janus, 1993). Studies that include open-ended questions have identified the excitement, enjoyment, and pleasure—the passion and romance—of late-life sexuality and the value older adults place on the quality and meaning of intimate relationships. Accordingly, sexual activity and satisfaction have been found to be related to older people's sense of self-worth and competence (Weg, 1996).

To review, as our biological clocks change with age, it is not necessarily for the better or worse in terms of the frequency or the nature of the sexual experience. Individuals who have been sexually responsive all their lives will still enjoy sexual satisfaction in their later years, although their experience may differ subjectively from their earlier years (Zeiss, 1997). Yet, this difference can be positive. For example, 75 percent of the respondents in the classic Starr-Weiner study described earlier (1981) said that sex is the same or better than when they were younger. Although the majority of female respondents considered orgasm essential to a good sexual experience, they also emphasized mutuality, love, and caring as central to an enjoyable sexual relationship and willingly varied their sexual practices to achieve satisfaction. Male respondents emphasized that not only is the physical stimulation of sex important, but also that sex is necessary for them to feel alive, to reaffirm their identity, and to communicate with a person they care about. The actual level of activity may be less important than one's satisfaction

POINTS TO PONDER

When you were growing up, how did you perceive your parents'/grandparents' sexuality? What were your sources of information about older adults and sexuality? How did these affect your thinking?

with it (Matthias et al., 1997). Nevertheless, a number of physiological, age-related changes can affect the nature of the sexual response.

WOMEN AND AGE-RELATED PHYSIOLOGICAL CHANGES

With the growing numbers of women in the 45- to 54-year-old age group, increasing attention is being given to **menopause.** As noted in Chapter 4, the major changes for women as they grow older are associated with the *reduction in estrogen and progesterone*, the predominant hormones produced by the ovaries, during menopause. The **climacteric**—loss of reproductive ability—takes place in three phases: **perimenopause,** menopause, and postmenopause, and may extend over many years.

Perimenopause is marked by a decline in ovarian function in which a woman's ovaries stop producing eggs and significantly decrease their monthly production of estrogen, resulting in widely fluctuating estrogen levels and unpredictable menstrual cycles. It can occur as long as 10 years before menopause, starting as young as age 35. Only recently have researchers and health care providers recognized that perimenopause brings hot flashes around the head and upper body, concentration gaps and memory lapses, mood swings, sleep troubles, irritability, and migraines associated with menopause. Unfortunately, however, perimenopause still is not included in most medical school curricula, and some physicians still dismiss a woman's early symptoms as "all in her head" (Bagley, 1999).

Menopause, in the strictest sense as one event during the climacteric, is a period in a woman's life when there is a gradual cessation of the menstrual cycle, including irregular cycles and menses, which are related to the loss of ovarian function. Menopause is considered to have occurred when 12 consecutive months have passed without a menstrual period (**postmenopause**). The average age of menopause is 52 years, although it can begin as early as age 40 and as late as age 58. Surgical removal of the uterus—**hysterectomy**—also brings an end to menstruation.

Physiological changes related to the decrease in estrogen in menopause and postmenopause include:

- hot flashes
- urogenital atrophy
- urinary tract changes
- bone changes (osteoporosis)

Hot flashes are caused by vasomotor instability, when the nerves overrespond to decreases in hormone levels. This affects the hypothalamus (the part of the brain that regulates body temperature), causing the blood vessels to dilate or constrict. When the blood vessels dilate, blood rushes to the skin surface, causing perspiration, flushing, and increased pulse rate and temperature. Hot flashes are characterized by a sudden sensation of heat in the upper body, often accompanied by a drenching sweat and sometimes followed by chills. Gradually diminishing in frequency, hot flashes generally disappear within a year or two.

HOME REMEDIES FOR MENOPAUSAL SYMPTOMS

Sharon "Missy" Peat described herself as a 51-year-old woman on the verge of a nervous breakdown 3 years ago. After her sleep was continuously interrupted by hot flashes, one night she opened her freezer, grabbed a box of frozen peas, and applied it to the back of her neck. After a few minutes, she felt better. The sweating subsided, the panic was gone and she went back to bed in 5 minutes' time. During the night, she experienced no more perspiration or clamminess. Since then, she has manufactured a cold, flexible gel pack sold for the relief of hot flashes. The success of her cold pack suggests the growing market for menopause products (Jacobson, 2000).

Sleep disturbances can also result from hormonal changes, with sleep deprivation leading to irritability and moodiness often associated with menopause. Although 80 percent of women aged 45 through 55 experience some discomfort such as hot flashes and sweats during menopause, most find that these physiological changes do not interfere with their daily activities or sexual functioning. They also do not cause psychological difficulties, although vasomotor instability does disrupt and reduce sleep (Kaiser, 1996; Weg, 1996).

Estrogen loss combined with the normal biological changes of aging leads to **urogenital atrophy**—a reduction in the elasticity and lubricating abilities of the vagina approximately 5 years after menopause. As the vagina becomes drier and the layer of cell walls thinner, the amount of lubricants secreted during sexual arousal is reduced. Although vaginal lubrication takes longer, these changes have little impact on the quality of orgasms and do not result in an appreciable loss in sensation or feeling. Nevertheless, discomfort associated with urogenital atrophy is an important contributor to decline in sexual activity with menopause. Artificial lubricants such as KY jellies and vaginal creams can help minimize discomfort. In addition, regular and consistent sexual activity, including **masturbation,** maintains vaginal lubricating ability and muscle tone, thereby reducing discomfort during intercourse (Gelfand, 2000).

Because of thinning vaginal walls, which results from estrogen degeneration and which offers less protection to the bladder and the urethra, *lower urinary tract infections* such as cystitis and burning urination may occur more frequently. These problems can be treated and often reversed with hormone replacement therapy, most often estrogen combined with progesterone. Incontinence has been found to inhibit sexual desire and response; unfortunately, many older women are reluctant to discuss incontinence with others, which precludes their finding ways to prevent its negative impact upon sexual activity (Kaiser, 1996).

As discussed more fully in Chapters 4 and 15, **osteoporosis,** which is related to the loss of estrogen during menopause, is caused by a woman's inability to absorb sufficient calcium to strengthen her bones. The reduction in bone mass predisposes older women to fractures. Hormone replacement therapy, combined with regular exercise, has been found to prevent osteoporosis, and may actually increase bone mass by promoting new bone formation, especially in the hip and spine (PEPI Trial, 1996).

Contrary to stereotypes and taboos regarding menopause, approximately 30 to 90 percent of women have no intense symptoms such as hot flashes, while only 15 percent experience symptoms sufficiently severe to warrant treatment. The majority—65 percent—experience only mild symptoms that do not require any medical intervention. This wide variability in symptoms suggests that there is not an inevitable "menopausal syndrome" (Gonyea, 1998; Weg, 1996). Nor is there any scientific explanation for why symptoms such as hot flashes occur in some women and not in others. The primary medical response to the symptoms of hot flashes and vaginal atrophy has been **hormone replacement therapy (HRT),** which restores body hormones to levels similar to those before menopause. As noted in Chapter 4, estrogen does alleviate hot flashes and vaginal changes, including atrophy, dryness, itching, pain during intercourse, lower urinary tract problems, and frequent urination. The average amount of time spent on HRT by most women is nearly 10 years, although about 25 percent of postmenopausal women use estrogen, a rate that is far lower among women of color. There is some evidence that beneficial effects of estrogen occur even when it is started after the age of 60. These also include effects on stability of cognitive abilities and skin and hair quality, including possible reductions in the risk of Alzheimer's disease as described in Chapter 4. However, recent studies suggest that the risk of breast cancer with long-term hormonal replacement may be substantially greater and the benefits in terms of risk reduction for osteoporosis and heart disease less than previous research indicated (Colditz 1999). The benefits and risks of HRT are described in greater detail in Chapters 4 and 6, and must be carefully weighed by women as they attempt to assess their risks of bone loss, heart disease, and breast cancer. At the same time, women need to be cautious about the use of alternative therapies not yet proved to be effective. In sum, women face tough choices about what therapies to use!

Increasingly, *nutrition, exercise,* and *herbal* or *naturopathic treatments* have been found useful in moderating symptoms associated with both perimenopause and menopause. In many non-Western cultures, menopause is viewed as a time of respect and status for women. Our cultural view is that women are expected to have difficulty at this period of life. However, the incidence of insomnia, depression, and anxiety may be traced to the meaning or psychosocial significance that individuals attach to menopause, as well as the value placed on body image and on women's roles as mothers. Other symptoms reported by menopausal women, such as headaches, dizziness, palpitations, and weight increase, are not necessarily caused by menopause itself, but may be due to underlying psychosocial reasons. Most women view menopause as a potentially positive transition rather than as a loss of fertility or as a cause of depression. It can be a new and fulfilling time of opportunities, self-accomplishment and new meaning, and greater autonomy in lifestyle (Defey, Storch, Cardozo, and Diaz, 1996; Jones, 1997). Sixty percent of respondents in a recent Gallup Poll did not associate menopause with feeling less attractive, and 80 percent expressed relief with the end of their menstrual periods. The major quandary appears to be whether to use HRT (Gonyea, 1998). In sum, menopause, like other transitions experienced by women, is affected by physiological and health factors, personality, self-esteem, culture and lifestyle.

Despite some uncomfortable symptoms, menopause does not impede full sexual activity from a physiological point of view. In fact, many women, freed of worries about pregnancy and birth control, report greater sexual satisfaction postmenopause, including after a hysterectomy (Weg, 1996). Generally, an older woman's sexual response cycle has all the dimensions of her younger response, but the time it takes for her to respond to sexual stimulation gradually increases. The subjective levels of sexual tension initiated or elaborated by clitoral stimulation do not differ for older and younger women. The preorgasmic plateau phase, during which sexual tension is at its height, is extended in duration. Contrary to stereotypes, most older women enjoy orgasm; an older woman's capacity for orgasms may be slowed, but not impaired. The orgasm is experienced more rapidly, somewhat less intensely, and more spasmodically. The resolution phase, during which the body returns to its baseline prearousal state, occurs more rapidly than in younger women.

From a physiological point of view, no impediment exists to full sexual activity for postmenopausal women. Changes such as the thinning of vaginal walls and loss of vaginal elasticity may render intercourse somewhat less pleasurable, but these effects can be minimized by sexual regularity. Instead, older women's sexuality tends to be influenced more by sociocultural expectations than by physiological changes—by the limited number of available male partners, persistent stigma about lesbian relations in old age, and common cultural definitions of older women as asexual and unattractive. As another example, low self-image can

---

ALTERNATIVES TO ESTROGEN REPLACEMENT THERAPY

- herbal remedies, including soy and black cohosh, a folk medicine made from a shrub root
- drugs already proved for other conditions that may have beneficial effects on hot flashes (e.g. some antihypertensives; certain antidepressants; Neurontin, an antiseizure drug)
- combination of fluoride and calcium, but may have gastrointestinal side effects

be a barrier to intimacy (Haffner, 1994). These psychosocial barriers are discussed more fully later in this chapter.

MEN AND AGE-RELATED PHYSIOLOGICAL CHANGES

Relatively little attention has been given to men's hormonal rhythms compared to women's. One reason for less attention is that men maintain their fertility and generally do not lose their capacity to father children, making hormonal and sexual changes less abrupt and visible. There is, however, increasing evidence that **male menopause** or "viropause" occurs and can affect the psychological, interpersonal, social, and spiritual dimensions of a man's life. However, the male climacteric differs from women's in two significant ways: it comes 8 to 10 years later (typically between ages 45 and 54), and progresses at a more gradual rate. This is because the loss of testosterone (approximately 1 percent a year on average), while varying widely among men, is not as dramatic nor as abrupt as the estrogen depletion for menopausal women. Some of the effects of this loss are summarized as follows:

- reduced muscle size and strength
- increased calcium loss in the bones
- declines in response by the immune system
- lessened sexual response and interest
- fatigue, irritability, indecisiveness, depression, loss of self-confidence, listlessness, poor appetite, and problems of concentration (Diamond, 1997; Weg, 1996)
- reduced interest in sex, anxiety and fear about sexual changes
- increased relationship problems and arguments with partners over sex, love, and intimacy, and
- loss of **erection** during sexual activity.
- changes in secondary sexual characteristics such as a man's voice becoming higher pitched, his facial hair growing more slowly, and muscularity giving way to flabbiness

Combined with the loss of muscle tissue and weight in the later years discussed in Chapter 3, it is not unusual for men to become thinner and less muscular by their seventies. The changes that men experience, which occur in varying degrees, require adaptation, but in themselves do not necessarily result in reduced sexual enjoyment and desire.

The normal physiological changes that characterize men's aging alter the nature of the sexual response, but do not interfere with sexual performance. The **preorgasmic plateau phase,** or excitement stage, increases in length, so that response to sexual stimulation is slower. An erection may take longer to achieve and may require more direct stimulation. For example, in 18-year-old males, full erection is achieved on stimulation for an average of 3 seconds; at age 45, the average time is 18 to 20 seconds, while a 75-year-old man requires 5 minutes or more. Erections tend to be less full with age and the erect penis may be less firm. But these erectile changes do not necessarily alter a man's sexual satisfaction. The frequency and degree of erections can be studied while a man is sleeping. The recording of nocturnal penile tumescence—(sleep-related erections)—offers an opportunity to evaluate objectively sexual functioning under relatively controlled conditions. Such studies have found that the volume and force of the ejaculation are decreased in older men as they sleep. The two-stage orgasm—the sense of ejaculation inevitably followed by actual semen expulsion that is experienced by younger males—often blurs into a one-stage ejaculation for older men (Masters and Johnson, 1981; Schiavi et al., 1990).

Accordingly, orgasm is experienced less intensely, and more spasmodically and rapidly, occurring every second or third act of intercourse rather than every time. The length of time between orgasm and subsequent erections increases (i.e., the **refractory period** after ejaculation, before a second ejaculation is possible, is longer). However, although these changes may alter the nature of the sexual experience, none of them causes sexual inactivity or impotence. As a result, the subjectively appreciated levels of sensual pleasure may not diminish (Katchadourian, 1987;

Masters and Johnson, 1981). In recent years, as noted in Chapter 1, there has been increasing attention to hormones such as DHEA, which are produced by the adrenal glands, the brain, and the skin, to revive men's sexual interest.

Although not an inevitable consequence of aging, erectile dysfunction or **impotence** (i.e., an inability to get and sustain an erection) is the chief cause of older men's withdrawing from sexual activity. The Massachusetts Male Aging Study of 1700 men found that erectile dysfunction occurred in more than 50 percent of the men age 40 and over. Older men and their partners need to be informed that sexual dysfunctions are both common and treatable. Although impotence and lowered testosterone levels are not significantly correlated, declines in DHEA levels with aging are found to be associated with impotence (Diamond, 1997). An older man may be particularly at risk when he faces the unexpected onset of involuntary alterations in his established sexual patterns combined with the negative conditioning of cultural stereotypes related to sexual function and aging.

Despite the underlying pathologies frequently associated with impotence, it tends to be underdiagnosed because of the embarrassment and reluctance of older men and their health care providers to discuss sexual matters candidly. Since medical treatments can be effective in altering erectile dysfunction, health care providers must be sure to rule out the physical basis of impotence, which tends to be more important than psychosocial factors (Kaiser, 1996; NIH Consensus Statement, 1992; Rosen, 1996). Physical risk factors include cardiovascular disease, the effects of drugs (espe-

cially antihypertensives, antidepressants, and tranquilizers), diabetes, hypertension, endocrine or metabolic disorders, neurological disorders, depression, alcohol, or prostate disorders. Most types of prostate surgery do not cause impotence, as discussed in the next section, "Chronic Diseases and Sexual Activity." In recent years, new ways to treat impotence have drawn increased attention. The marketing of a wide range of products reflects, in part, drug companies' awareness of Baby Boomers' buying power.

Clinical trials of oral medications, such as Sildenafil or Viagra, have found that 60 to 80 percent of the men who have participated and who have varying degrees of impotence have benefited (Leland, 1997). It is important, however, that continued attention be given to the psychological factors related to intimacy and sexual enjoyment in old age, not just to chemical solutions. As noted above, the concept of sexuality in old age needs to be expanded to include more than erection and ejaculation during intercourse. For example, health care providers and counselors must encourage couples to communicate their fears about impotence and suggest ways that they can openly enjoy fulfilling sexual experiences and intimacy without an erection. Medical treatments for impotence should be carefully explored, including:

- oral medications that cause erections
- pellets inserted into the urethra with an applicator that dilate the arteries and relax the erectile tissues, thereby triggering involuntary erections
- injection therapy
- vacuum pumps

VIAGRA

Viagra has been touted as a wonder drug for men, with flashy ads typically featuring a romantic man and woman. The benefits described by the ads have been empirically supported, however. For example, a 1998 study of over 500 men, reported in the *New England Journal of Medicine,* confirmed Viagra's effec-

tiveness. The most common side effects were headache, flushing, and disturbed digestion. For men and their partners who have been frustrated by impotence, the side effects are undoubtedly viewed as minor irritants (American Federation for Aging Research, 2000).

POINTS TO PONDER

Imagine the appeal of a recent Internet ad to some older men:

Internet Advertising of Herbal Viagra—No prescription, no doctor, less than $1 a pill

Welcome to the new sexual revolution. It's the all-natural male potency and pleasure pill that men everywhere are buzzing about. Herbal V is safe, natural and specifically formulated to help support male sexual function and pleasure. You just take two easy-to-swallow tablets one hour before sexual activity. . . . Herbal V—Bringing back the magic.

- penile implants
- vascular surgery

In summary, the normal physiological changes that characterize men's aging alter the nature of the sexual response, but do not interfere with men's sexual performance. These include:

- slower response to sexual stimulation, with a longer time and direct physical stimulation more often needed for an erection
- less full or firm erections

- decreased volume and force of ejaculation
- occasional lack of orgasm during intercourse
- increased length of time between orgasm and subsequent erections

Impotence, the most common sexual disorder among older men, appears to be influenced more by physiological than psychosocial factors.

Table 7.1 summarizes the physiological changes that affect sexual activities in both older men and women, but do not necessarily alter sexual satisfaction.

TABLE 7.1   Age-Related Physiological Changes in Sexual Function

Normal changes in aging women that do not interfere with full sexual activity:
- There is reduction in vaginal elasticity and lubrication.
- Thinning of vaginal walls occurs.
- There is slower response to sexual stimulation.
- Preorgasmic plateau phase is longer.
- There are fewer and less intense orgasmic contractions.
- After orgasm, there is rapid return to prearousal state.

Normal changes in aging men alter the nature of the sexual response, but do not interfere with performance:
- Erection may require more direct stimulation.
- Erection is slower, less full, and disappears quickly after orgasm.
- Orgasm is experienced more rapidly, less intensely, and more spasmodically; there is decreased volume and force of ejaculation.
- There is increased length of time between orgasm and subsequent erections (longer refractory period).
- There is occasional lack of orgasm during intercourse.
- More seepage or retrograde ejaculation is experienced.

CHRONIC DISEASES
AND SEXUAL ACTIVITY

Although normal physiological changes do not inevitably reduce sexual enjoyment, physical well-being does appear to be associated with sexual responsiveness and activity. Not surprisingly, physical health problems, of one's own and/or one's partner, are a frequently cited reason for refraining from sexual activity. Even when an illness does not directly affect the sexual organs themselves, disease can affect sexual function because of physical decline, associated pain, iatrogenic complications of medication, and the partner's fears about causing further injuries to health. Since sexual response requires the coordination of multiple systems of the body—hormonal, circulatory, and nervous systems—if any of these are disrupted, sexual functioning can be adversely affected. And because sexual response also depends upon an individual's mental well-being, the distraction of illness may be all-consuming and deplete the psychic energy needed for sexual interest and responsiveness. On the other hand, sexual activity can be an important component of treatment following a major illness or surgery and is minimally risky to a person's health (Kaiser, 1996). In this section, the chronic illnesses that commonly affect sexual functioning—diseases of the prostate, diabetes, heart disease and strokes, and degenerative and rheumatoid arthritis—are briefly discussed.

More than 50 percent of men age 65 and over have some degree of **prostate enlargement,** known as *benign prostatic hypertrophy* or BPH. One out of every three men over age 65 will experience prostate difficulties, usually inflammation or enlargement of the prostate gland, pain in the uro-genital area, and urinary flow dysfunction (Bostwick, MacLennan, and Larson, 1996; Diamond, 1997). Infections may be successfully treated with antibiotics, and new drugs are available to shrink the prostate. Some prostate problems can be reduced through simple treatments such as warm baths and gentle massage or through antibiotics. However, when urination is severely restricted or painful, surgery

is necessary. After surgery, semen is no longer ejaculated through the penis, but is pushed back into the bladder and later discharged in the urine. After healing occurs, the capacity to ejaculate and fertility may return in some men. The feeling of orgasm or climax can still be present, and sexual pleasure is not inevitably lessened.

The rate at which prostate cancer kills men is similar to that of breast cancer in women. About 80 percent of all prostate cancers are found in men age 65 and older. Men who have a family history of prostate cancer and African American men have an increased risk of developing it, and should have more frequent screening exams. A major problem in diagnosis is that prostate cancer may have no symptoms in its early and middle stages—while it is confined to the prostate gland and more likely to be amenable to treatment. After it spreads, symptoms include pain or stiffness in the lower back, hips or upper thighs. Because the early symptoms are often masked, the American Cancer Society recommends that all men 40 years of age and older have an annual rectal exam, and that men age 50 and older receive an annual prostate specific antigen (PSA) test (American Federation for Aging Research, 2000).

The most extreme treatment for prostate cancer is radical perineal prostatectomy, when nerves are cut (Kaiser, 1996; Morra and Potts, 1996). Although most forms of prostate surgery do not cause impotence, irreversible impotence and incontinence can result from radical prostatectomy. Fortunately, there is an increasing number of alternatives for early prostate cancer, such as radioactive pellet implantation, other forms of radiation therapy, or transperineal placement of microwave antennas (Trachtenberg, Chen, Kucharczyk, Toi, and Lancaster, 1999). Nerve-sparing surgery also has been developed, and may reduce the incidence of impotence among some men who undergo radical prostatectomy. Of course, the urologist's priority is to rid the patient of cancer tissue, and nerves very close to the prostate gland must often be severed. Nevertheless, even in these cases, men who have lost their normal physiologic response can achieve orgasm. Treatments or refinements of treatments, such as penile implants, vacuum pumps, new chemotherapeutic agents, vaccines, and smooth muscle relaxants that are injected into the penis have recently been developed, but research on their effectiveness and complications is incomplete (Afrin and Ergul, 2000). A promising development is the clinical testing of a variety of vaccinations (McNeel and Disis, 2000). Health care providers must be sensitive to providing older patients with as much information as possible about the implications of surgery for sexual functioning.

Although prostate surgery does not cause impotence in the majority of cases, between 5 and 40 percent of men who have undergone such surgery can no longer achieve an erection. In addition, since treatment of prostate cancer often involves methods that lower testosterone levels or block the effects of testosterone, a large percent of men undergoing such treatment feel loss of sexual desire, and up to 40 percent actually experience hot flashes (Diamond, 1997). In such instances, psychological factors need to be addressed through counseling, and couples need to be encouraged to try alternate methods of sexual satisfaction until the man can achieve an erection. In some instances, a man's postoperative "impotence" may be a convenient excuse for not engaging in sexual activity, or may represent fears of additional illness. When impotence is irreversible, partners need to be encouraged to pursue alternate means of sexual pleasure or consider a penile implant. Masturbation, more leisurely precoital stimulation, and use of artificial lubricants can all provide satisfying sexual experiences.

While most older men fear that prostate surgery will interfere with their sexual functioning and satisfaction, women may fear that a hysterectomy (surgical removal of the uterus), an ovariectomy (surgical removal of both ovaries), or a mastectomy (surgical removal of one or both breasts) will negatively affect their sexual functioning. In most instances, however, women's sexual satisfaction and long-term functioning are not affected by these surgeries, particularly if their partners are sensitive and supportive. On the other

hand, some hormonal changes associated with a complete hysterectomy may affect sex drive. When women experience menopause as a result of a hysterectomy, perhaps earlier than the average age of onset for menopause, hormone replacement therapy is advisable except when the hysterectomy was due to cancer.

More common medical causes of male impotence than prostate surgery are *arteriosclerosis*—the vascular hardening that leads to heart attacks and strokes—and *diabetes*, particularly for those who have been diabetic most of their lives. Anything that damages the circulatory system—smoking, inactivity, poor diet—can cause erectile dysfunction. Older people who have experienced a heart attack or heart surgery may assume that sexual activity will endanger their lives and give it up. Unfortunately, many health care providers are not sensitive to such fears and fail to reassure individuals that sexual activity can be resumed after they undergo a stress test without pain or arrhythmia (Kaiser, 1996). Another precaution for post–heart attack patients who have been prescribed nitroglycerin is to take their usual dose 15 to 30 minutes before engaging in sexual activity (Schiavi and Rehman, 1995). Stroke patients may also feel compelled to abstain from sexual activity because of an unfounded fear that sex could cause another occurrence. Generally, strokes do not harm the physiology of sexual functioning or the ability to experience arousal. However, some antihypertensive drugs can cause impotence or inhibit ejaculation. Fortunately, a new class of antihypertensive drugs, called ACE inhibitors, has been reported to cause fewer side effects on sexual function.

Impotence in life-long diabetics occurs because diabetes interferes with the circulatory and neurologic mechanisms responsible for the supply of blood flowing to the penis for erection. In such instances, a penile implant may be an option. With late-onset diabetes, impotence may be the first observable symptom. When the diabetes is under control, however, potency generally returns. The sexual functioning of women diabetics appears to be relatively unimpaired. When diabetes is controlled through balanced blood chemistry, sexual problems other than impotence that are attributable to the disease should disappear or become less severe. Other less common diseases that may cause impotence are illnesses that affect the vascular and endocrine systems, kidney diseases, and neurological lesions in the brain or spinal cord (Gambert, 1987).

Arthritis does not directly interfere with sexual functioning, but can make sexual activity painful. Some medications used to control arthritic pain may also affect sexual desire and performance. Yet sexual behavior can serve to maintain some range of motion of the limbs and joints and thereby help sore joints; it can also stimulate the body's production of cortisone, which is one of the substances used to treat the symptoms of rheumatoid arthritis (Cochrane, 1989). Experimenting with alternative positions can minimize pain during sexual intercourse. A warm bath, massage of painful joints, and timing the use of pain-killing medications approximately 30 minutes prior to intercourse may also help to control some of the pain associated with arthritis. As with most chronic diseases, communication with the partner about what is comfortable and pleasurable is essential.

Closely related to the effects of chronic illness upon sexuality are those of *drugs*, including alcohol. Diagnosing drug effects on sexuality may be particularly difficult, since drugs affect individuals differently, and drug interactions frequently occur. Drugs that inhibit the performance of any one of the systems of the body can alter sexual response. For men, some medications that are prescribed for chronic conditions may cause impotence, decrease sexual drive, delay ejaculation, or result in an inability to ejaculate. Psychotropic medications used to treat depression and psychosis are particularly likely to impair erectile functioning (Corbett, 1987). Of patients taking thioridazine, 49 percent will experience impaired ejaculation, and 44 percent impotence. Yet this is one of the first drugs that a physician will prescribe for an older person who is agitated, depressed, schizophrenic, or anxious. Similarly, in 40 percent of the cases involving the drug amoxapine for treatment of depression, impotence occurs. As noted above, other types of drugs likely to affect sexual functioning are antihypertensive medications used to treat high blood pressure, drugs to control diabetes, and steroids (Gelfand, 2000).

For women, drugs may be associated with decreased vaginal lubrication, reduced sexual drive, and a delay or inability to achieve orgasm. Fortunately, physicians as well as older people are becoming more aware of potential negative effects of drug regimes on sexual functioning. Likewise, more drugs are now available that do not have negative side effects on sexual desire and/or ability. These include ACE inhibitors among the antihypertensives; fluoxetine, trazodone, and maprotiline among the antidepressants; desipramine among the tricyclic antidepressants; and lorazepam, alprazolam, and buspirone among antianxiety agents (Lewis, 1989).

Alcohol, when used excessively, can act as a depressant on sexual ability and desire. Alcohol consumption affects male sexual performance by making both erection and ejaculation difficult to attain; consequently, a man's anxiety about performance may increase and result in temporary impotence. Prolonged alcoholism may lead to impotence as a result of irreversible damage to the nervous system. Although the effects of alcohol on women's sexual performance have not been well researched, some women who abuse alcohol appear to experience less sexual desire and no orgasms.

GAY AND LESBIAN PARTNERS IN OLD AGE

Although most examples of sexual activity in this chapter are presented in terms of heterosexual marital relationships, this should not be assumed to always be the case. Although there are no reliable data, gay men and lesbians are estimated to comprise between 6 and 10 percent of the total population (Wojciechowski, 1998). Older people, their family members, and health and social service professionals need to be sensitive to heterosexual relationships outside of marriage as well as to same-gender, or **homosexual** relationships. Such

Many lesbian and gay couples maintain long-term commitments to each other.

sensitivity includes the discarding of stereotypical views of the nature of *gay* and *lesbian* relationships. Contrary to commonly held images, the varieties of gay and lesbian bonding are similar to those within heterosexual communities—ranging from monogamous life partners and non-monogamous primary relationships to serial monogamy and episodic liaisons. Gay and lesbian life partners face many of the issues that confront long-term heterosexual spouses, such as fears about the loss of sexual attractiveness, the death or illness of a sexual partner, or diminished interest or capacity for sex because of chronic disease. On the other hand, after a lifetime of discrimination or ostracism from family members, coworkers, or society generally, homosexual couples face additional issues related to in-

timacy and sexuality, which are discussed in this chapter and in Chapter 9.

Although sexual activity for gay and lesbian older people differs as much as for heterosexuals, there is also a consistent pattern of relatively high life satisfaction with being gay, good adjustment to old age, and ongoing sexual interest and activity. Older gay individuals who define the meaning of homosexuality in terms of positive self-identity and acceptance have been found to have the fewest psychosomatic complaints (Adelman, 1991). Both lesbians and gays are more likely to report a high level of life satisfaction if they are happily partnered and communicating effectively with one another, and if they have a strong social support system (Wojciechowski, 1998).

Older lesbians, often closeted about their sexual orientation, have been labeled the "invisible minority". They have generally practiced serial monogamy throughout their lives. The hiding of one's sexual orientation has been a survival strategy for some lesbians because maintaining employment was paramount to being self-sufficient. Nevertheless, most usually report a positive self-image and feelings about being identified as a lesbian (Wojciechowski, 1998). Older lesbians generally do not fear changes in physical appearance, loneliness, or isolation in old age as much as some heterosexual women do. This may be because of the strong friendship networks that characterize many lesbian relationships or flexibility in gender roles that allows them to adjust more effectively to the socially constructed beliefs of aging

---

REDEFINING SEXUAL ORIENTATION IN LATER LIFE

After her husband left her for a younger woman, a bout with breast cancer, and the death of her 26-year-old daughter, Isabel found herself increasingly drawn to spending time only with women: in a mothers' support group, in a group of midlife women coping with divorce, and through her work. She started attending workshops and lectures through the local college's Women's Information Center. At one of

those courses, she met Carla, also recovering from a bitter divorce. They began to spend nearly all their free time together, enjoying the equality and closeness in their relationship. Within a year, Carla moved in with Isabel. Although their adult children were initially shocked by their mothers' behavior, they soon saw the value of the loving support and intimacy that their mothers experienced for the next 26 years.

and being older (Dorfman et al., 1995). Most lesbians remain sexually active, although sexual frequency generally declines. The extent to which sexual activity is considered to be an integral part of a lesbian relationship varies, although sexuality in a broader sense continues to play an important role in their lives. For some, lesbianism is a wider female interdependence and sense of positive self-identity rather than a sexual relationship as such.

The number of gay men with partners increases with age and peaks among those 46 to 55 years old. After age 60, the percent of gay couples decreases because of death, illness, cautiousness, or rejection of the notion of having a single, lifelong partner (Pope and Schulz, 1991). Older gay men are more likely to be in long-term relationships (with an average length of 10 years) or none at all rather than in short-term relationships of a year or less. Similar to their heterosexual peers, gay men are devalued in their own community for the natural features of aging: graying hair, wrinkles, added weight (Yoakam, 1999). Nevertheless, they generally maintain positive feelings about themselves and their appearance in old age (Bennet and Thompson, 1990). Compared with their younger counterparts, older gay men have been found to be just as involved in the homosexual network, satisfied with their social lives and sexual orientation, and confident in their popularity with other gays. Consistent with the continuity theory of aging, sex appears to be equally important at all phases of a gay man's life. Contrary to the myth of lonely, rejected, depressed older gay men, most report that they are generally sexually active, although frequency does decline with age. They typically are satisfied with their partners and their sex lives; they report a positive sense of self-esteem, well-being, and contentment and adapt fairly well to the aging process. Despite fears of loneliness and social isolation, most gay men have closer friendships in old age than do heterosexual men, and these friends and confidants may serve to resolve any existing fear of aging (Dorfman et al., 1995; Yoakam, 1999). For many gay men, friendships may replace family ties disrupted by declaration of their homosexuality.

On the other hand, compared with their younger counterparts, *older gay men* tend to:

- fear exposure of their homosexuality
- hide their sexual orientation
- view their relatives, friends, and employers as less accepting of their homosexuality
- see their sexual orientation as outside of their personal control

However, these differences largely reflect cohort effects, rather than the aging process per se. The social support function of gay and lesbian relationships is discussed further in Chapter 9.

As noted in Chapter 4, there is growing concern about the increase in AIDS among the older population. Despite the risks, most older gay men remain sexually active, although they engage less frequently in one-night encounters and are more knowledgeable about safe sex than comparably aged heterosexual males (Pope and Schulz, 1991). With the growing public awareness about the importance of safe sex, future cohorts of gay men may be less likely to engage in high-risk sexual behavior. Older persons with AIDS have been found to be less likely to use emotional support and mental health services than the younger population. Such services may need to be reconfigured and presented differently in order to meet the emotional needs of the older population diagnosed with AIDS (Emlet, 1996).

PSYCHOSOCIAL FACTORS AND LATE-LIFE AFFECTION, LOVE, AND INTIMACY

In addition to the effects of normal physiological changes and chronic disease upon sexual activity and enjoyment, a number of psychosocial factors affect the ways in which older people express their sexuality. These include:

- Past history of sexual activity and availability of a partner. Those who were most sexually active in middle age generally remain so in old age.
- Negative attitudes toward sexual activities and intimate behavior other than intercourse such

as kissing, petting, holding and being held, dancing, massage, and masturbation interfere with the openness to try new ways of expressing intimacy.

- Reactions to physiological changes and to illness-induced or doctor-induced changes.
- Reactions to the attitudes of others, including the societal norm that one is "too old" for sex. Societal misconceptions regarding sexuality in later life can have a powerful effect on one's self-concept and perception of oneself as still being sexually attractive and interesting.
- Living arrangements. For example, older adults in long-term care facilities face numerous barriers to sexual expression, including lack of privacy and of partners, staff and family attitudes, and chronic illness (Kuhn, 1999).

A primary psychosocial factor, especially for women, is the availability of a partner. Although the nature of sexual relationships is becoming increasingly varied, most sexual activity for the current cohort of older people occurs within the context of a marital relationship (Teitelman, 1990). For women in heterosexual relationships, a central problem is differential life expectancy and the fact that most women have married men older than themselves. Because of older women's lower marriage and remarriage rates, the opportunity for sexual activity within heterosexual relationships is dramatically reduced with age, but the capacity for sexual enjoyment is not altered.

The current cohort of older women, for whom sexual activity was generally tied to marriage, have relatively few options for sexual relationships. Unfortunately, these options are made more difficult because of the lack of socially approved models of sexuality for older women. For many women, their only models for sexuality may be the young. In addition, the pairing of older women with younger men is still rare, largely because of the double standard of aging in which older men are often viewed as distinguished while older women are perceived as unattractive and asexual. Women are also more likely than men to face socioeconomic barriers to meeting new partners, given the higher incidence of poverty among women compared to men. If a

woman is preoccupied with financial or health worries, sexual activity may be a low priority.

Gender differences in sexual interest and participation may also be a barrier to finding satisfying intimate heterosexual relationships. Women report that the relational aspects of sexual activities—sitting and talking, making oneself more attractive, and saying loving words—are more important to them than to men. Men, however, view sexual activities such as erotic readings and movies, sexual daydreams, and physically intimate activities, such as body caressing, intercourse, and masturbation, as more important than do women (Johnson, 1997).

Sexual functioning in both men and women is affected by the presence of a partner. Accordingly, a man who has not had sexual intercourse for a long time following the loss or illness of a partner, especially if a result of Alzheimer's, may experience what has been called **widower's syndrome.** He may have both the desire and new opportunities for sexual activity, but his physiological system may not respond and he may be unable to maintain an erection. If he subscribes to the myth that in sex, performance counts (how many orgasms, how long an erection), rather than focusing on pleasuring and closeness, he is likely to experience performance anxiety and fear. Since anxiety tends to block sexual interest and response, he may be caught in a bind. The more he is concerned about performing well, the harder he tries and the more difficult it becomes. In such instances, older men need to be reminded that there is no right way. Rather, sex can be whatever they and their partners find satisfying at the moment. Unhurried, nondemanding sexual interaction with an understanding partner can help resolve anxieties associated with widower's syndrome.

Similarly, women may face **widow's syndrome.** After a year or more of sexual inactivity, women are likely to experience a reduction in the elasticity of the vaginal walls. With the woman less likely to respond to sexual excitement, vaginal lubrication is slowed and reduced. Although these are all symptoms that arise from estrogen deficiency, they become more severe when there is a long period of no sexual contact. For men and women, frequent contact is important to ensure sexual responsiveness and comfort. Both men and women who are grieving the loss of a partner are unlikely to have the energy or interest in someone beyond themselves—both essential features of successful sexual activity (Masters and Johnson, 1981).

Another critical factor in the physical and social environment is whether *living arrangements* provide opportunities for privacy. Such opportunities are most likely to be limited for those in long-term care facilities. Lack of privacy, negative staff attitudes, administrative difficulties, and the unromantic atmosphere of institutional environments all reduce the incentive of residents to be sexually interested or involved. On the other hand, when conjugal rooms are set aside, residents may be too embarrassed to use them.

Staff attitudes, which tend to reflect those of the larger society, may be the greatest barrier. Staff tend to assume that frail residents no longer need sexual intimacy. If older residents express a desire for sexual activity, staff may ignore, infantilize, tease, or ridicule them, or report it to administrators, thereby adding to a sense of embarrassment. Other staff may believe that chronic illness makes sexual activities impossible or harmful. Despite such obstacles, some residents in such settings are sexually active, and others would be if the opportunity allowed. The institutionalization of older persons does not necessarily mean the end of their sexual interest. Even institutionalized older people with dementia may maintain the competency to initiate sexual relationships (Kuhn, 1999). Long-term care facilities are beginning to develop policies regarding residents' sexual rights to ensure privacy, establish conjugal rooms or home visits, evaluate patients' concerns about sexual functioning, encourage varied forms of sexual expression, and educate both staff and residents about sexuality and aging (Kuhn, 1999).

Table 7.2 summarizes the psychological and social factors that may affect sexual activity among older people.

As noted throughout this chapter, sex encompasses more than intercourse. It is also important to recognize and to convey to older individuals

TABLE 7.2   Psychosocial Factors That Influence Sexual Activity in Older Adults

- Past history of sexual activity
- Attitudes toward sexual activities other than intercourse
- Reactions to physiological changes or to illness-induced changes
- Reactions to attitudes of others
- Availability of a partner, especially for women
- Performance anxiety; widower's/widow's syndrome
- Opportunities for privacy
- Staff attitudes toward those in institutional settings

that affection may be expressed in a wide variety of ways other than through sex. In fact, older people are more experienced at loving than any other age group, but this experience is often discounted. As stated above, **intimacy**—defined as the freedom to respond to and express human closeness—love, attachment, and friendship are cherished aspects of life, vital to an older person's sense of well-being. When older persons are experiencing assaults on their self-esteem, the need for affection may become even more intense. Without such affection, older individuals may feel lonely, even though they may be surrounded by other people and not physically alone.

There are many avenues for expressing intimacy: sensory, sensual, sexual. Intimacy can involve flirting, laughing, smiling, communicating love through words, singing, touching, holding, as well as genital expression (Genevay, 1999). With age, long-term relationships frequently move toward deeper levels of intimacy expressed in terms of loyalty, commitment, sharing, and mutual emotional response. This is not the case, however, in relationships characterized by conflict, emotional distance, and emotional or physical abuse throughout the years. In addition, many older people dealing with the feelings of loss and loneliness occasioned by the divorce or death of a spouse may find it difficult to reinvest the energy needed to develop intimate relationships.

THE IMPORTANCE OF TOUCH

Val, a widow for 12 years, lives in a central Boston neighborhood; her son and daughters live on the West Coast, and rarely see her. Fortunately, her neighborhood is a close-knit one and younger neighbors keep watch for her. They are accustomed to seeing her out, walking her three small dogs, talking to the dogs and giving them lots of affection.

Last week, she was out walking her dogs for the first time in 3 weeks after a severe bout of flu. One of her 35-year-old male neighbors came up to her, said how glad he was to see her, and hugged her. She began to cry in response to the human warmth of the hug. It had been nearly 2 years since someone had hugged her like that.

An important aspect of most intimate relationships is *touch*. The need to be touched is lifelong; physical contact through touching and caressing is as powerful in the sixties, seventies, and eighties as in infancy, childhood, and early adulthood. Since the sense of touch is the most basic sense, older individuals may rely upon the sense of touch to a greater extent in their social interactions than other age groups (Weg, 1996). Just beneath an older person's expression of loneliness or of missing a former partner may lie the desire for someone to touch him or her. A handclasp or hand laid gently on the shoulder or arm, a child's hug, or a back massage can all be vital to addressing older persons' needs for affection and can increase their responsiveness. Staff in long-term care facilities especially need to be sensitive to the life-affirming role of touch for most older people, including those with dementia and those who are withdrawn or disoriented. On the other hand,

helping professionals must recognize cultural differences regarding the meaning and appropriateness of touch. They need to be aware that, in some cultures, differential social status, gender, age, and the setting may influence the older person's acceptance of a friendly touch.

Friends are often important sources of intimacy, especially after a major role transition such as death of a spouse, divorce, or retirement. For example, an intimate friendship with a confidant can help prevent the demoralization often produced by widowhood. The presence of a close confidant also appears to be related to life satisfaction and a sense of belonging, worth, and identity. In any senior center or congregate meal site, gatherings of highly valued same-sex companions are frequent. Among women especially, same-sex companions frequently greet each other warmly with a hug and kiss, may join arms while walking, and spend valued time together. These contacts are nonsexual in the narrow definitions of the term, but can be important to sexual health and to a person's psychological adaptation to aging. The importance of friendship in old age is discussed further in Chapter 9.

FACILITATING OLDER ADULTS' SEXUAL FUNCTIONING

Given the importance of sexuality and sexual satisfaction, the individual's sexuality and intimacy should be part of the clinical evaluation of older persons. Concerns about sexuality surface if health

Staff in long-term care facilities can provide emotional support through touch.

care professionals initiate discussion of multiple losses and loneliness, what older people miss most in terms of intimacy, their history of loving relationships, the extent of and their interest in repairing old relationships and establishing new ones. Treatment plans should address issues relative to past, present, and potential sources of intimacy, the meaning of past intimacies, grief work over losses of intimacy, and permission to explore and repair intimate relationships (Genevay, 1999). Unfortunately, many health care providers have been taught little or nothing about sexuality and intimacy in late adulthood. Professionals may be uncomfortable or intimidated when asked to respond to the lifelong intimacy needs of people as old as their own parents or grandparents. Physicians are often in a central position to respond to concerns about sexuality and intimacy, yet they may be more likely to prescribe treatment for physical symptoms, such as vaginal dryness, than to respond to the older person's emotional concerns or need for information. It is important for physicians to recognize that the loss of intimacy may underlie other disorders that are being treated, such as depression (Genevay, 1999). This can help the physician provide treatment of the underlying cause of the problem, not just its symptoms.

When an older person raises concerns about sexual functioning, such as impotence, it is important that the physician first differentiate potential physical causes, including medications, from psychological ones. This can be done through a careful medical and social history, a thorough physical assessment, and basic hormone tests (Haffner, 1994; Kingsberg, 1998). Such an approach can help to distinguish short-term problems that many individuals experience at various times, such as transitory impotence, from problems that persist under all circumstances with different sexual partners over a prolonged time period.

Health care providers also can encourage and assure continuity of sexual expression for those for whom this has been an important part of their lives. One of the first health professionals to address this issue, Comfort (1980) noted that sexual responsiveness should be fostered but not preached.

In an AARP survey of older adults and sexual functioning, older respondents suggested guidelines for health care providers (Johnson, 1997). These included using clear and easy-to-understand terms; being open-minded, respectful, and nonjudgmental; and encouraging discussion. What an older person may want most when he or she raises sexual concerns is support, acceptance, and listening. Older people who are concerned about their sexual functioning should be encouraged to focus on giving and receiving pleasure rather than on genital sex. As noted earlier, professionals should convey that intercourse is only one way of relating sexually and that there is no prescribed way for sex to proceed. Rather, many choices can be made regarding sexuality. When a partner is not available, masturbation can be viewed as an acceptable release of sexual tension. Explicit discussion of masturbation with older people may relieve anxiety caused by earlier prohibitions during adolescence and young adulthood. Alternatively, professionals need to be sensitive to the fact that some older people do not want to engage in any sexual activity and must not put undue pressure upon them to be sexually active. It is important for practitioners to take account of an older person's values, life experiences, and right to autonomy, and support them in making their own choices about sexual behavior and sexuality.

Many older people need to be encouraged to develop alternative definitions of sexual activity that are not performance-oriented (i.e., broader than genital intercourse) in order to gain intimacy, joy, and fulfillment through a broad spectrum of sensual interactions. Sex education and opportunities for group discussion and support can increase their sexual awareness, knowledge, interest, enjoyment, and range of activities. As noted above, sex education is also important for staff who work with older people. They need to be careful not to impose their values on older people. For example, nursing home employees need to recognize that the desire for intimacy and closeness continues throughout life. With older people who are experiencing memory loss or disorientation, staff need to evaluate the competencies of the older

---

SEX THERAPY WITH OLDER PERSONS

- First, eliminate or control medical problems, including drug interference, that may directly impair genital functions or indirectly affect sexual functioning.
- Psychotherapy and sexual therapy with older adults should include practical behavioral techniques in the form of specifically structured sexual interactions that the couple can conduct in the privacy of their home (Kingsberg, 1998).

- Emphasize activities that encompass intimacy, giving pleasure, communicating with the partner, and letting the partner know when pleasure is experienced.
- Provide opportunities to discuss problems encountered as well as concerns about performance.
- Employ a holistic approach that includes exercise, nutrition, and interventions to build self-esteem.

---

person to engage in intimate relationships. These include assessing the older person's awareness of the relationship, ability to avoid exploitation, and awareness of potential risks as well as family members' attitudes (Kuhn, 1999).

In the past, sex therapists have focused on working with younger people. Fortunately, this bias is changing, and various therapies for older people who report sexual difficulties have been found to be effective.

SUMMARY AND IMPLICATIONS

As discussed throughout this chapter, sexuality is affected by physical, psychological, and disease-related changes. The normal physiological changes that men and women experience in their sexual organs as they age do not necessarily affect their sexual pleasure or lead to sexual incapacity. Even chronic disease does not necessarily eliminate sexual capacity. For example, many older persons, after adequate medical consultation, can resume sexual activity following a heart attack or stroke. Contrary to the myths about sexuality in old age, many people in their seventies and eighties participate in and enjoy sexual activities.

Older couples can adapt to age-related changes in sexual functioning in a variety of ways. Simply knowing that such changes are normal may help older people maintain their sexual self-esteem. For both older men and women, long leisurely foreplay

can enhance sexual response. Avoiding alcohol use prior to sexual activity can be helpful, since alcohol increases desire, but decreases sexual ability. Health professionals need to be alert to medications that adversely affect sexual functioning, such as antihypertensives, tranquilizers, and antidepressants.

This chapter emphasizes how psychosocial factors also can influence an older person's sexual behavior. Myths, stereotypes, and jokes pervade the area of sexuality in old age. Unfortunately, societal expectations about reduced sexual interest may mean that older people stop sexual activity long before they need to. In future years, these myths may change as the media, gerontologists, and other professionals convey the message that sex is not only permissible but desirable in old age.

In professional work with older partners, definitions of sexuality need to be broadened beyond sexual intercourse. A variety of behaviors, such as touching, kissing, hugging, massage, and lying side by side, can contribute to sexual intimacy and satisfaction, even for institutionalized older persons. Touching older people—a handclasp or back rub, for example—is especially important in home-bound and institutional settings.

Practitioners need to be sensitive to their clients' values and life experiences and to support them in making their own choices about sexual behavior and sexuality. Many of the current cohort of older persons grew up with taboos relating not only to intercourse but also to other forms of sexual activity, such as masturbation. Hence, older individuals may need encouragement from professional counselors or others if they are to be free to affirm their sexuality and to experience intimacy with others.

GLOSSARY

climacteric   in women, the decline in estrogen production and the loss of reproductive ability; in men, the decline in testosterone

erection   the swelling of the penis or clitoris in sexual excitement

heterosexuality   sexual orientation toward the opposite gender

homosexuality   sexual orientation toward the same gender

hot flashes   a sudden sensation of heat in the upper body caused by vasomotor instability as nerves over-respond to decreases in hormone level during menopause

impotence   the inability to have or maintain an erection

intimacy   feelings of deep mutual regard, affection, and trust, usually developed through long association

male menopause   a term that suggests a significant change experienced by men as their production of testosterone decreases in later life; although male fertility is maintained, some men experience both psychological and physiological changes

masturbation   erotic stimulation of the genital organs achieved by manual contact exclusive of sexual intercourse

menopause   cessation of the menstrual cycle

orgasm   climax of sexual excitement

penile implant   a device surgically implanted in the penis to reverse impotence and allow an erection

perimenopause   unpredictable menstrual cycles—up to 10 years before menopause

postmenopause   when 12 months have passed without a menstrual cycle

preorgasmic plateau phase   in men and women, the phase of lovemaking prior to orgasm and in which sexual tension is at its height

prostate enlargement   growth of the prostate, due to changes in prostatic cells with age, which can result in pain and difficult urination

refractory period   in men, the time between ejaculation and another erection

sex   in the most narrow sense, a biological function involving genital intercourse or orgasm; in a broader sense, expressing oneself in an intimate way through a wide-ranging language of love and pleasure in relationships

sexuality   feelings of sexual desire, sexual expression, sexual activity

urogenital atrophy   reductions in the elasticity and lubricating abilities of the vagina approximately 5 years after menopause

widow(er)'s syndrome   a term coined by Masters and Johnson describing sexual dysfunction following a long period of abstinence due to a spouse's illness and/or death

REFERENCES

Adelman, M. Stigma, gay lifestyles, and adjustment to aging: A study of later-life gay men and lesbians. In *Gay midlife and maturity* (Special Issue). New York: Haworth Press, 1991, 7–32.

Afrin, L. B., and Ergul, S. M. Medical therapy of prostrate cancer. *Journal of South Carolina Medical Association*, 2000, 26, 77–84.

American Federation for Aging Research, Research news on older men's health. *Lifelong Briefs*, 2000.

Bagley, S. Understanding perimenopause. *Newsweek*. Special edition on women's health. Spring/Summer, 1999, 30–34.

Bennet, K. C., and Thompson, N. C. Accelerated aging and male homosexuality. *Journal of Homosexuality*, 1990, 20, 65–75.

Bortz, W. M. 2nd, and Wallace, D. H. Physical fitness, aging and sexuality. *Western Journal of Medicine*, 1999, 170, 167–169.

Bostwick, D. G., MacLennan, G. T., and Larson, T. *Prostate cancer: What every man—and his family—needs to know.* New York: Villard, 1996.

Cochrane, M. Immaculate infection. *Nursing Times*, 1989, 26, 31–32.

Colditz, G. A. Hormones and breast cancer: Evidence and implications for consideration of risks and benefits of hormone replacement therapy. *Journal of Women's Health*, 1999, 8, 347–357.

Comfort, A. Sexuality in later life. In J. E. Birren and R. B. Sloane (Eds.), *Handbook of mental health and aging.* New York: Van Nostrand Reinhold, 1980.

Corbett, L. The last sexual taboo: Sex in old age. *Medical Aspects of Human Sexuality,* 1987, *15,* 117–131.

Defey, D., Storch, E., Cardozo, S., and Diaz, O. The menopause: Women's psychology and health care. *Social Science and Medicine,* 1996, *42,* 1447–1456.

Diamond, J. *Male menopause.* Naperville, IL: Sourcebooks, 1997.

Dorfman, R., Walters, K., Burke, P., Hardin, L., Karanik, T., Raphael, J., and Silverstein, E. Old, sad and alone: The myth of the aging homosexual. *Journal of Gerontological Social Work,* 1995, *24,* 29–44.

Emlet, C. A. Case managing older people with AIDS: Bridging systems—recognizing diversity. *Journal of Gerontological Social Work,* 1996, 27, 55–71.

Gambert, S. R. (Ed.). *Handbook of geriatrics.* New York: Plenum Medical Books, 1987.

Gelfand, M. M. Sexuality among older women. *Journal of Women's Health and Gender-based Medicine,* 2000, *9,* S15–20.

Genevay, B. Intimacy and older people: Much more than sex. *Dimensions.* San Francisco: ASA: Mental Health and Aging Network, 1999, pp. 1, 7.

George, L. K., and Weiler, S. J. Sexuality in middle and late life: The effects of age, cohort and gender. *Archives of General Psychiatry,* 1981, *38, 919–923.*

Gonyea, J. Midlife and menopause: Uncharted territories for baby boomer women. *Generations* Spring 1998, 87–89.

Haffner, D. Love and sex after 60: How physical changes affect intimate expression. *Geriatrics,* 1994, *49,* 20.

Jacobson, S., Menopause, *The Seattle Times,* November 2000.

Janus, S. S., and Janus, C. L. *The Janus Report on sexual behavior.* New York: John Wiley and Sons, 1993.

Johnson, B. Older adults' suggestions for health care providers regarding discussions of sex. *Geriatric Nursing,* 1997, *18,* 65–66.

Jones, J. B. Representations of menopause and their health care implications: A qualitative study. *American Journal of Preventive Medicine,* 1997, *13,* 58–65.

Kaiser, F. E. Sexuality in the elderly. *Urologic Clinics of North America,* 1996, *23,* 99.

Katchadourian, H. *Fundamentals of human sexuality* (4th ed.). New York: Holt, Rinehart, and Winston, 1987.

Kaye, R. A. Sexuality in the later years. *Ageing and Society,* 1993, *13,* 415.

Kingsberg, S. A. Postmenopausal sexual functioning: A case study. *International Journal of Fertility and Women's Medicine,* 1998, *43,* 122–128.

Kingsberg, S. A. The psychological impact of aging on sexuality and relationships. *Journal of Women's Health and Gender-based Medicine,* 2000, *9,* S33–38.

Kinsey, A., Pomeroy, B., and Martin E. *Sexual behavior in the human female.* Philadelphia: W. B. Saunders, 1953.

Kinsey, A. C., Pomeroy, B., and Martin, E. *Sexual behavior in the human male.* Philadelphia: W. B. Saunders, 1948.

Kuhn, D. Nursing home residents with Alzheimers: Addressing the need for intimacy. *Dimensions,* San Francisco: ASA: Mental Health and Aging Network, 1999, pp. 4–5.

Leland, J. A pill for impotence. *Newsweek,* November 17, 1997, 62–68.

Lewis, M. Sexual problems in the elderly: Men's vs. women's: A geriatric panel discussion. *Geriatrics,* 1989, 44. 75–86.

Masters, W. H., and Johnson, V. E. Sex and the aging process. *Journal of the American Geriatrics Society,* 1981, *29,* 385–390.

Matthias, R. E., Lubben, J. E., Atcheson, K. B., and Schweitzer, S. O. Sexual activity and satisfaction among very old adults: Results from a community-dwelling Medicare population survey. *The Gerontologist,* 1997, *37,* 6–14.

McNeel, D. G., and Disis, M. L. Tumor vaccines for the management of prostate cancer. *Archives,* 2000, *48,* 85–93.

Morra, M., and Potts, E. *The prostate cancer answer book.* New York: Avon Books, 1996. *NIH Consensus Statement.* National Institutes of Health Consensus Development Conference, 1992, *10,* 1–33.

PEPI Trial Writing Group. Effects of hormone therapy on bone mineral density. *Journal of the American Medical Association,* 1996, *276,* 1389–1396.

Pfeiffer, E., and Davis, G. C. Determinants of sexual behavior in middle and old age. *Journal of the American Geriatrics Society,* 1972, *20,* 151–158.

Pope, M., and Schulz, R. Sexual attitudes and behavior in midlife and aging homosexual roles. *Journal of Homosexuality,* 1991, 20, 169–177.

Richardson, J. P., and Lazur, A. Sexuality in the nursing home patient. *American Family Physician,* 1995, *51,* 121–124.

Rosen, R. C. Erectile dysfunction: The medicalization of male sexuality. *Clinical Psychology Review,* 1996, *16,* 497–519.

Schiavi, R. C., and Rehman, J. Sexuality and aging. *Urologic Clinics of North America,* 1995, *22,* 711–726.

Schiavi, R., Schreiner-Engal, P., Mandati, J., Schanzen, H., and Cohen, E. Healthy aging and male sexual function. *American Journal of Psychiatry,* 1990, *147,* 766–771.

Starr, B. D., and Weiner, M. B. *The Star-Weiner report on sex and sexuality in the mature years.* New York: Stein and Day, 1981.

Steinke, E. E. Knowledge and attitudes of older adults about sexuality in ageing: A comparison of two studies. *Journal of Advanced Nursing,* 1994, *19,* 477–485.

Teitelman, J. Sexuality and aging. In I. Parham, L. Poon, and I. Siegler (Eds.), *Aging curriculum content for education in the social-behavioral sciences.* New York: Springer, 1990.

Trachtenberg, J., Chen, J., Kucharczyk, W., Toi, A., and Lancaster, C. Microwave thermoablation for localized prostate cancer after failed radiation therapy: Role of Neoadjuvant hormonal therapy. *Molecular Urology,* 1999, *3,* 247–250.

Weg, R. B. Sexuality, sensuality, and intimacy. *Encyclopedia of gerontology: Age, aging, and the aged,* 1996, 2(L–Z Index), 479–488.

Wiley, D., and Bortz, W. M. Sexuality and aging—Usual and successful. *Journals of Gerontology,* 1996, *51,* M142–M146.

Wojciechowski, C. Issues in caring for older lesbians. *Journal of Gerontological Nursing,* July 1998, *24,* 28–33.

Yoakam, J. R. Beyond the wrinkle room: Challenging ageism in gay male culture. *Dimensions,* San Francisco: ASA, Mental health & Aging Network, 1999, pp. 3, 7.

Zeiss, A. M. Sexuality and aging: Normal changes and clinical problems. *Topics in Geriatric Rehabilitation,* 1997, *12,* 11–27.

four

THE SOCIAL CONTEXT OF AGING

Throughout the previous three sections, we have identified how changes in the physical and psychological aspects of aging have diverse consequences for older people's cognitive and personality functioning, sexuality, and mental health. We have also seen how social factors (e.g., the presence of strong family and friendship ties) can affect physical changes (e.g., being at risk for certain chronic illnesses) as well as psychological experiences (e.g., the likelihood of suicide). Within this framework of the dynamic interactions among physical, psychological, and social factors, we turn now to a more detailed discussion of the social environment of aging and its congruence with older people's level of functioning.

We begin with a review in Chapter 8 of the major social theories of aging—explanations of changes in social relationships that occur in late adulthood. Congruent with the person–environment perspective throughout the text, these theories address the optimal way for people to relate to their changing social and physical environments as they age. The early social gerontological theories, such as role, activity, and disengagement, were con-

cerned with adaptation to age-related changes. These differ substantially from later theories, including continuity, age stratification, and exchange theory, which recognized the diverse and dynamic nature of the aging experience. The most recent theories are described as taking a "qualitative leap" over prior theories; these include social phenomenology, social constructionism, and critical and feminist theory, all of which raise fundamental questions about positivist or empirical approaches to studying aging and emphasize the highly subjective nature of the aging experience. These social gerontological theories, then, provide the basis for examining the primary dimensions of older people's social environments: family, friends, and other social supports; housing and community; paid and nonpaid productive roles and activities; and changes in one's social network through death and loss. These later theoretical approaches, in particular, recognize how older people's experiences with their social environments can vary by ethnic minority status and gender.

Chapter 9 begins by examining the importance of informal social supports, particularly family, neighbors, and friends, to quality of life. Chapter 1 identified how longer life expectancies, combined with earlier marriages and childbearing, have reduced the average span in years between generations. This has also increased the number of three- and four- and sometimes five-generation families. The growth of the multigenerational family has numerous ramifications for relationships between spouses, between grandparents and grandchildren, between adult children and older relatives, and among siblings and other extended family members. Generally, these relationships are characterized by reciprocity, with older family members providing resources to younger generations and trying to remain as independent as possible. The normal physical and psychological changes of aging usually are not detrimental to family relationships, although caring for an older relative with a long-term illness can burden family members. Compared to the earlier years, late-life family relationships are more often characterized by losses that demand role shifts and adjustments. A widower may cope with the loss of his wife by remarrying, whereas a widow tends to turn to adult children and friends.

Although some older people live alone—including a growing number who are homeless—friends, neighbors, and even acquaintances often perform family-like functions for them. More conducive to reciprocal exchanges, friends and neighbors may be an even more important source of support for an older person than one's family. As gerontologists have recognized the importance of informal social networks for older people's well-being, programmatic interventions have been developed specifically to strengthen these ties, which are described in Chapter 9.

An important function of families and friends is social support. In the case of frail older adults, informal caregiving is provided by spouses, children, and sometimes by more distant relatives and friends. The impact of caregiving on both the care receiver and the caregiver is examined in detail in Chapter 10. Both the benefits and stresses of caregiving are explored. Elder abuse, although rare, can result in some cases when caregivers feel extremely stressed and lacking in social supports.

Where people live—the type of housing, urban–suburban location, and safety of the community—affects their social interactions. Chapter 11 illustrates the importance of achieving congruence between older people's social, psychological, and physical needs and their physical environment. Relocation is an example of a disruption of this congruence or fit between the environment and the older person. Another illustration of a physical environment that no longer fits a person's social needs occurs when older residents become so fearful of victimization that they dare not leave their homes. Characteristics of the neighborhood can enhance older persons' social interactions and, in some instances, their feelings of safety. Planned housing, home-sharing, congregate housing, assisted living facilities with multiple levels of care, adult family homes, home health care, and nursing homes are ways to modify the physical environment to support older people's changing and diverse needs. Chapter 11 also includes a discussion of housing policies and social and health services that affect older people, as well as an analysis of the problem of homelessness among older adults.

Throughout our discussion of the social context for aging, the effects of socioeconomic status on types of interactions and activities are readily apparent. Economic status is largely determined by past and current employment patterns and by the resulting retirement benefits. Chapter 12 shows declining rates of labor-force participation among both men and women age 65 and over, due largely to the trend toward early retirement. Most people choose to retire early, provided their public or private pensions will enable them to enjoy economic security. Although most older adults apparently do not want to work full-time, many would like the option of flexible part-time jobs, increasingly for economic reasons. For most people, retirement is not a crisis, although for those without good health, adequate finances, or prior planning, retirement can be a difficult transition. Accordingly, women, ethnic minorities, and low-status workers are most vulnerable to experiencing poverty or near-poverty in old age.

Chapter 12 also examines how people's interactions change with age in terms of their nonpaid productive roles, including involvement in community, organizational, religious, and political activities. The extent and type of participation are influenced not only by age, but also by gender, ethnic minority status, health, socioeconomic class, and educational level. Therefore, declines in participation may not necessarily be caused by age-related changes but instead represent the influence of other variables. Generally, involvement tends to be fairly stable across the life course; leisure, volunteer and community activities, and roles formed in early and middle adulthood are maintained into later life. This does not mean, however, that older people do not develop new interests and skills. Many people initiate new forms of productivity through senior centers, volunteering, civic organizations, political activism, and education programs. Or think about the reports of older athletes who complete their first marathon or mountain ascent in their sixties.

Chapter 13 examines attitudes toward death and dying, the process of dying, and the importance of palliative or end-of-life care. The impacts of social and cultural values, as well as individual factors such as the relationship between the dying person and caregivers, are discussed in reviewing grief and mourning. Recent trends in an individual's right to die, the legal and ethical debates about active and passive euthanasia and the role of advance directives also are reviewed in this chapter. It concludes by examining the process of widowhood and how adults cope with this major life event.

Because of the predominance of social problems faced by older women and ethnic minorities, their special needs and relevant practice and policy interventions are discussed in Chapters 14 and 15. Economic difficulties experienced in young and middle adulthood by these groups tend to be perpetuated in old age. These are not isolated problems, but rather of increasing concern to gerontologists and policy makers, since women over age 65 form the majority of older people, and the number of older persons of color, although a small percentage of the total older population today, is growing rapidly. These populations nevertheless display considerable strength and resiliency in the face of social problems.

The following vignettes illustrate the diversity of social interactions experienced by older people and set the stage for our discussion of the social context of aging.

AN OLDER PERSON WITH LIMITED SOCIAL RESOURCES

Mr. Valdres, age 73, has been separated from his wife for 20 years. He lives in a small room in an inner-city hotel. Since he worked odd jobs all his life, often performing migrant farm labor, he collects only the minimum amount of Social Security. Some months he finds it very hard to get by and has only one meal a day. Although he is not in contact with his former wife or his six children, he does have a group of buddies in the area who watch out for one another and who get together at night to have a beer and watch TV in the hotel lobby. Although he has smoked all his life and suffers from emphysema, he refuses to see a doctor or any other staff at the downtown medical clinic. He also will not apply for any public assistance, such as SSI or food stamps, in part because he does not understand what these programs are, but also because he does not want government "handouts." The hotel manager keeps track of his activities and will occasionally slip him some extra money or food.

AN OLDER PERSON WITH EXTENSIVE SOCIAL RESOURCES

Mrs. Howard, age 78, lives with her husband in a small town. Most of her relatives, including three of her children and eight grandchildren, live in the area, and there are large family gatherings on Sundays and holidays. She is a retired teacher; her husband was a successful local realtor until he retired. Both retired in their early seventies. They have considerable savings; in addition, they always lived simply and frugally, saving for their retirement. They have lived in the same house for the past 42 years, and their home is well maintained and recently modernized. Mrs. Howard enjoys gardening, doing housework, reading, and visiting. In addition, she is very active in her church, serves on the Advisory Board to the Area Agency on Aging, and is involved in the town's politics. She also tutors children with learning disabilities. Her days are filled with housework, talking to friends, neighbors, or relatives, or helping someone out, whether a grandchild or neighbor. Despite all her activity, she occasionally complains of being lonely and useless.

AN OLDER PERSON COPING WITH MULTIPLE LOSSES

Mr. Mansfield is 87 years old. He and his wife had six children. After having been a successful businessman in the Chicago area, he retired to the South when he turned 66. Mr. Mansfield and his wife were active in their church, and enjoyed going to plays and keeping up with their children, who had interesting careers all over the United States. He enjoyed his retirement until his wife of 50 years died when he was 80. Mr. Mansfield was heartbroken and thought that his life had ended. He then became involved in a support group offered through his church and started teaching adult education classes. Through that experience, he became involved in the ecumenical life of the small southern town and was very active in putting on an annual conference. Although he still speaks with tears when talking about his relationship

with his deceased wife, it has become clear that his life has found new meaning and purpose in his church work, and in becoming a volunteer for the Area Agency on Aging. However, Mr. Mansfield recently faced a new challenge. His youngest and his oldest children have both died. The oldest died in her early fifties of a drug overdose of pills she was taking for chronic pain. The youngest, a son, died 6 months later after a long battle with AIDS. Although these were wrenching experiences for him, he is now facing these bereavements with a supportive network. The pain is still there, but he is able to share it with others. And he continues to be an active volunteer. His own health is beginning to deteriorate, however, and he has started to talk about his own death. He is concerned about his ability to drive, as his eyesight is diminished. His faith and belief system are integral to his dealing with these concerns about death and dying.

These vignettes show the importance of informal social support networks, whether for an apparently isolated person in a low-income hotel such as Mr. Valdres, or for an older person, such as Mr. Mansfield, coping with multiple social losses. We turn now to a review of some of the social theories that address successful and satisfying aging.

8 SOCIAL THEORIES OF AGING

This chapter discusses

- The theoretical question of what is the optimal way for older people to relate to their environments
- The major social theories of aging
- Some important factors related to aging or age-related issues that serve as a guide for further inquiry and possible intervention in the aging process
- Different lenses through which to view and explain the phenomenon of aging
- A groundwork for discussions of the social aspects of aging in later chapters: social supports, caregiving, living arrangements, socioeconomic status, and changing employment and retirement roles

THE IMPORTANCE OF SOCIAL THEORIES OF AGING

All of us develop interpretive frameworks or lenses, based on our experiences, by which we attempt to explain the aging process and answer questions we all wonder about:

What makes for successful aging?

What should our society be doing with regard to older people?

What enhances older people's life satisfaction and well-being?

We observe older people in our families and communities and make generalizations about them. For example, some of our stereotypes of older people may be the result of unconscious theorizing about the meaning of growing old. Or we may devise our own recommendations for policies or programs based on our informal and implicit theories. In effect, we are developing theories based on our own experiences.

In contrast to our personal observations about age changes, the scientific approach to theory development is a systematic attempt to explain *why* an age change or event occurs. Theory-building—the cumulative development of explanation and understanding about observations and findings—represents the core of the foundation of scientific inquiry and knowledge (Bengtson, Burgess, and Parrott, 1997). By using scientific methods, researchers seek to understand phenomena in a manner that is reliable and valid across observations, and then to account for what they have observed in the context of previous knowledge in the field. Scientists never entirely prove or disprove a theory. Instead, through empirical research, they gather evidence that may strengthen their confidence in it or move them closer to rejecting the theory by demonstrating that parts of it are untrue. Scientific theories not only lead to the accumulation of knowledge, but point to unanswered questions for further research and suggest directions for practical interventions. In fact, a good theory is practical! For example, some of the biological theories of aging discussed in Chapter 3 are useful in guiding people's health behaviors. If the theory is inadequate, the research, intervention, or public policy may fail by not achieving its intended goals (Bengtson et al., 1997).

This chapter focuses on social theories of aging—explanations of changes in social relationships that occur in late adulthood. No one grand, all-encompassing social gerontological theory has emerged. Most of these theories have been developed only since the 1950s and 1960s, and some have not been adequately tested. This is because early research in the field of gerontology tended to be applied rather than theoretical, attempting to solve problems facing older people. Researchers were concerned with individual life satisfaction and older people's adjustment to the presumably "natural" conditions of old age—retirement, ill health,

or poverty. Despite their relative recency, theories of aging can be classified into first, second, and third generations (Bengtson et al., 1997; Hendricks, 1992), or first and second transformations of theoretical development or evolution of new modes of consciousness (Lynott and Lynott, 1996). The order in which they are presented in this chapter basically reflects the temporal dimensions of this intellectual history. Although there is some overlap of the central theoretical concepts across time, these theories are distinguished by a shift from:

- a focus on the individual to structural factors to interactive processes, and
- largely quantitative methods in the positivist scientific tradition to a range of more qualitative methodologies that seek to understand the meaning of age-related changes among those experiencing them.

SOCIAL GERONTOLOGICAL THEORY BEFORE 1961: ROLE AND ACTIVITY

Much of the early social gerontological research was organized around the concept of adjustment, with the term "theory" largely absent from the literature (Lynott and Lynott, 1996). The perspectives on roles and activities, however, later came to be called *theories*. Some theories of adjustment have focused on the individual and his or her personal characteristics (health, personality, needs), while others have emphasized society's demands on and expectations of the individual as he or she ages. Growing old was conceptualized as the individual encountering problems of adjustment due to role changes in later life.

Role Theory

One of the earliest attempts to explain how individuals adjust to aging involved an application of **role theory** (Cottrell, 1942). In fact, this theory has endured, partially because of its applicable and self-evident nature. Individuals play a variety of social roles in their lifetimes, such as student, mother, wife, daughter, businesswoman, grandmother, and so on. Such roles identify and describe a person as a social being and are the basis of self-concept. They are typically organized sequentially, so that each role is associated with a certain age or stage of life. In most societies, especially Western ones, chronological age is used to determine eligibility for various positions, to evaluate the suitability of different roles, and to shape expectations of people in social situations. Some roles have a reasonable biological basis related to age (e.g., the role of mother), but many can be filled by individuals of a wider age range (e.g., the role of volunteer). Age alters not only the roles expected of people, but also the manner in which they are expected to play them. For example, a family's expectations of a 32-year-old mother are quite different from their expectations of her at age 72. How well individuals adjust to aging is assumed to depend on how well they accept the role changes typical of the later years.

Age norms serve to open up or close off the roles that people of a given chronological age can play. Age norms are assumptions of age-related capacities and limitations—beliefs that a person of a given age can and ought to do certain things. As an illustration, a 76-year-old widow who starts dating a younger man may be told by family members that she should "act her age." Her behavior is viewed as not *age appropriate*. Norms may be formally expressed through social policies and laws (e.g., mandatory retirement policies that existed prior to 1987). Typically, however, they operate informally. For example, even though employers cannot legally refuse to hire an older woman because of her age, they can assume that she is too old to train for a new position. Individuals also hold norms about the appropriateness of their own behavior at any particular age, so that social clocks become internalized and age norms operate to keep people on the time track (Hagestad and Neugarten, 1985). Most people in our society, for example, have *age-normative expectations* about the appropriate age at which to graduate from school, start working, marry, have a family, reach the peak of their career, and retire. These expectations have been shifting among younger cohorts, however, with more persons marrying later, and in middle age entering second or third careers.

Every society conveys age norms through *socialization*, a lifelong process by which individuals learn to perform new roles, adjust to changing roles, relinquish old ones, learn a "social clock" of what is age appropriate, and thereby become integrated into society. Older adults become socialized to new roles that accompany old age. In addition, they must learn to deal with *role losses*,

---

AGE-NORMATIVE EXPECTATIONS

Within a five-year age range, how would you respond to the following questions *for most people, for your parents, and for yourself?* If your responses differ across these three groups, reflect upon why there are disparities:

	For Most People	For Your Parents	For Yourself
Best age for a man to marry	_____	_____	_____
Best age for a woman to marry	_____	_____	_____
When most people should become grandparents	_____	_____	_____
When most men should be settled on a career	_____	_____	_____
When most women should be settled on a career	_____	_____	_____
When most people should be ready to retire	_____	_____	_____
When a man accomplishes the most	_____	_____	_____
When a woman accomplishes the most	_____	_____	_____

such as the loss of the spouse role with widowhood or the worker role with retirement. These losses can lead to an erosion of social identity and self-esteem (Rosow, 1985). Older people may also experience *role discontinuity*, whereby what is learned at one age may be useless or conflicting with a subsequent period in one's life. For example, learning to be highly productive in the workplace may be antithetical to adjusting to leisure time in retirement. Although institutions or social situations that help older people prepare for such role changes are limited, older adults often display a considerable degree of flexibility in creating or substituting roles in the face of major changes in life circumstances. In fact, more recent research has identified a process of *role exit*, whereby individuals disengage from roles to which they have been committed and which have been central to their identity, such as the employee role. Interventions such as retirement planning can encourage a process of gradually ceasing to identify with the worker role and its demands, slowly adapting to leisure roles (Ekerdt and DeViney, 1993).

With age, roles also tend to become more ambiguous. Guidelines or expectations about the requirements of roles, such as that of nurturing parent, become less clear (Rosow, 1985). Older people have often lacked desirable role options. Until recently, few role models existed; those in the media and the public realm have tended to be youthful in appearance and behavior, maintaining middle-age standards that can hinder socialization to old age. In addition, some groups, such as women and ethnic minorities, may lack the resources to move into new roles or to emulate younger, physically attractive models. Fortunately, with the growth and visibility of the older population, there are more models of role gains and successful aging as well as alternative roles for older people to play than in the past. There is also increasing recognition that the role of "dependent person" is not inevitable with age. Rather, the life course is characterized by varying periods of greater or lesser dependency in social relationships, with most people being emotionally dependent on others regardless of age. Even a physically impaired older person may still continue to support others and may be able to devise creative adaptations to ensure competence at home. For example, older people who volunteer as "phone pals" in a telephone reassurance program for latchkey children provide valuable emotional support.

Activity Theory

Activity theory was also an attempt to answer how individuals adjust to age-related changes, such as retirement, poor health, and role loss. It views aging to a large degree as an extension of middle age in which older people seek to maintain their status in later life. Based upon Robert Havighurst's analyses of the Kansas City Studies of Adult Life

---

GIVING UP THE CAR KEYS

A major role loss for many older people, especially older men, is that of driver. Families often worry about an older relative's driving, especially if he or she has had a minor accident or some near-collisions. Or families fear that their older relative will cause an accident as a result of slow driving or abrupt shifting of lanes without first checking and signaling. Yet the older driver refuses to stop driving, blaming close calls on other drivers, poor brakes, or road conditions. The driver may deny the problem and resist giving up the keys, because the loss of role of driver carries many consequences: loss of independence, identity, personal satisfaction, the ability to carry out daily tasks, and the sense of personal power and control. For most older people, losing one's ability to drive is a major role transition, symbolizing moving from independence to dependence. Any efforts to convince an older driver to give up the car keys must take account of what this role loss means to the older person.

ROLE MODELS FOR OLDER PEOPLE

Flip through a popular magazine, noting how older people are portrayed in both the ads and in the news articles. What roles are older people playing in the national media? Are the roles largely positive ones, or negative/stereotypical images? Strive to become more sensitive in your own analysis of older adults in the media.

In the future, roles appropriate to old age may become clearer, more continuous with past roles,

and more satisfying. Cohorts of older people may also be better prepared for the role changes that often accompany the aging process. A growing number of interventions, such as preretirement counseling and peer support groups, can help to smooth role transitions. This is especially useful if the older person has the freedom and autonomy to choose particular roles after retirement, including the role to "unretire" and return to employment (Herzog and House, 1991).

(1963, 1968), it was believed that the well-adjusted older person takes on a larger number and variety of **productive roles** and age-appropriate replacements through activities in voluntary associations, churches, and leisure organizations. The more active the older person, the greater his or her life satisfaction, positive self-concept, and adjustment (Bengtson, 1969). Accordingly, age-based policies and programs were conceptualized as ways to develop new roles and activities, often consistent with middle-age behavior, and to encourage social integration. To a large extent, activity theory is consistent with our society's value system, which emphasizes work, wealth, and productivity. Losing any of these is viewed as evidence of decline. Many older people themselves have

adopted this perspective and believe it helps them to maintain life satisfaction, as illustrated by the following vignettes.

Activity theory, however, fails to take account of how personality, socioeconomic status, and lifestyle variables may be more important than maturational ones in the associations found between activity and life satisfaction, health, and well-being (Covey, 1981). The value placed by older people on being active probably varies with their life experiences, personality, and economic and social resources. Activity theory defined aging as an individual social problem that can be addressed by trying to retain status, roles and activities similar to those of earlier life stages. A challenge to this perspective was formulated in 1961 as **disengagement**

OLDER PERSONS PURSUING LEISURE ACTIVITIES

Bob lives in the Northwest region of the United States. He retired at age 62 after 30 years of work in a management position for an aerospace company. He and his wife of 40 years carefully saved money so that they could be very active in their retirement. They now spend their winters as "snowbirds," traveling in their mobile home to the "sun belt." Now at age 69, they have spent 7 years in the same community in Arizona where they are well-known and have made many friends. In the summer, they usually take one extended trip to the mountains. They enjoy good health and believe that keeping active is the key to their zest for life.

Rose was a nurse for 30 years. In her career in direct patient care and teaching, she has held positions of authority. She has always liked learning new things. Now 74 and retired, she is very active in her church and directs the adult education program. She has participated in Elderhostel four times, and has had the opportunity to visit several foreign countries. She has taken two trips with her teenage grandchildren as well. Staying active means learning to her, and she has shared slide shows of her journeys with her retired friends and the women's group at her church.

theory, which shifted attention away from the individual to the social system as an explanation for successful adjustment to aging.

THE FIRST TRANSFORMATION OF THEORY

Disengagement Theory

The development of disengagement theory represents a critical juncture—as the first public statement wherein social aging theory is treated as a form of scientific activity in its own right, separate from policy and practice applications and information-gathering (Lynott and Lynott, 1996). In fact, disengagement theory was the first comprehensive, explicit, and multidisciplinary theory advanced in social gerontology (Achenbaum and Bengtson, 1994). Cumming and Henry, in their book *Growing Old* (1961), argue that aging cannot be understood separate from the characteristics of the social system in which it is experienced. All societies need orderly ways to transfer power from older to younger generations. Therefore, the social system deals with the problem of aging or "slowing down" by institutionalizing mechanisms of disengagement or separation from society. Accordingly, older people decrease their activity levels,

seek more passive roles, interact less frequently with others, and become preoccupied with their inner lives. *Disengagement* is thus viewed as adaptive behavior, allowing older people to maintain a sense of self-worth while adjusting through withdrawal to the loss of prior roles, such as occupational or parenting roles. Since disengagement is presumed to have positive consequences for both society and the individual, this theory challenges the assumption of activity theory that older people have to be "busy" and engaged in order to be well-adjusted. In contrast to activity theory, it views old age as a separate period of life, not as an extension of middle age.

Disengagement theory has been widely discounted by most gerontologists. While attempting to explain both system- and individual-level change with one grand theory, it has generally not been supported by empirical research (Achenbaum and Bengtson, 1994). Older people, especially in other cultures, may move into new roles of prestige and power. Likewise, not everyone in our culture disengages, as evidenced by the growing numbers of older people who remain employed, healthy, and politically and socially active. As demonstrated by the MacArthur Studies, described in Chapter 6, successful aging is more likely to be achieved by people who remain involved in society. Disengagement theory also fails

---

DISENGAGEMENT AND ADAPTATION

Inga was an administrative assistant to a highly successful businessman. She has never married. When she retired at age 62, she took a creative writing class, something she had dreamed of all her life but had not had the time to pursue. At 75 she is very content to sit in her rent-controlled apartment, which overlooks a park. She has lived there for 15 years. She finds much inspiration in watching life pass before her in the park. Writing poetry and short stories gives her an outlet for her thoughts. She feels that her writing has developed greater depth as she has achieved wisdom and contemplated the meaning of her life.

John worked for 40 years on the assembly line at a factory, making cars. He believed that it was a good job that supported his family well, but he had worked many overtime hours and had had little time for leisure. Now 70, he sits in the chair in his living room and watches TV and reads the paper. This has been his pattern since his retirement 5 years ago. Occasionally, he and his wife of 45 years will go out to dinner. John is glad not to have to go to the "rat race" of work every day.

Religious leadership can be continued across the life span.

to account for variability in individual preferences, personality, and differences in the sociocultural setting and environmental opportunities within the aging population (Achenbaum and Bengtson, 1994; Estes and Associates, 2000; Marshall, 1994). Likewise, it cannot be assumed that older people's withdrawal from useful roles is necessarily good for society. Forexample, policies to encourage retirement have resulted in the loss of older workers' skills and knowledge in the workplace, especially during employee shortages. Although disengagement theory has largely disappeared from the empirical literature, as the first attempt to define an explicit multidisciplinary theory of aging, it had a profound impact on the field.

Continuity Theory

While challenging both activity and disengagement theory, **continuity theory** maintained the focus on social-psychological theories of adaptation that were developed from the Kansas City Studies. According to continuity theory, individuals tend to maintain a *consistent* pattern of behavior as they age, substituting similar types of roles for lost ones and maintaining typical ways of adapting to the environment. In other words, individuals do not change dramatically as they age, and their personalities remain similar throughout their adult lives. Life satisfaction is determined by how consistent current activities or lifestyles are with one's lifetime experiences (Atchley, 1972; Neugarten, Havighurst, and Tobin, 1968). Basically, this perspective states that, with age, we become more of what we already were when younger. Central personality characteristics become even more pronounced, and core values even more salient with age. For example, people who have always been passive or withdrawn are unlikely to become active upon retirement. In contrast, people who were involved in many organizations, sports, or religious groups are likely to continue these

---

CONTINUITY AND ADAPTATION

At age 80, Rabbi Green, who has taught rabbinical students for 40 years, still makes the trip from his suburban home into the city to work with students one day per week. He speaks with considerable excitement about the reciprocal relationship between him and his students. When students talk about their relationship with him, it becomes clear how much they value him as a mentor. Being a "teacher" is who he is now and who he has always been.

Mary, 90, has always been the "cookie jar" mother to her children and their friends. She was there to offer goodies and a listening ear. Now her children and the generation of young persons who were their friends live far away. But a new generation of younger persons has moved into the neighborhood in the small town where she lives. She has become acquainted with many of them and their parents as they stop to talk with her as she works in her beloved yard. Now many will stop by for a cookie and a glass of milk after school. She is fondly called the "cookie jar grandma." The children say that, along with giving them cookies, she always listens to them.

activities or to substitute new ones for those that are lost with retirement or relocation. An individual ages successfully and "normally" if she or he maintains a mature, integrated personality while growing old.

Continuity theory has some face validity because it seems reasonable. However, it is difficult to test empirically, since an individual's reaction to aging is explained through the interrelationships among biological and psychological changes and the continuation of lifelong patterns. Another limitation is that, by focusing on the individual as a unit of analysis, it overlooks the role of external social factors in modifying the aging process. It thus could rationalize a laissez-faire or "live and let live" approach to solving the problems facing older people.

ALTERNATIVE THEORETICAL PERSPECTIVES

Activity, disengagement, and continuity theories have often been framed as directly challenging one another (Hochschild, 1975, 1976; Lynott and Lynott, 1996), even though they differ in the extent to which they focus on individual behavior or social systems/social structure (Marshall, 1996). None fully explains successful aging nor adequately addresses the social structure or the cultural or historical contexts in which the aging process occurs. During this early period of theory development, the factors found to be associated with optimal aging were, for the most part, individualistic—keeping active, withdrawing, "settling" into old age. When macro-level phenomena were considered, they were not conceptualized as structurally linked between the individual and society. Nor were race, ethnicity, and class explicitly identified as social structural variables. A number of alternative theoretical viewpoints have emerged since the 1960s, each attempting to explain "the facts" of aging better than another (Estes and Associates, 2000; Lynott and Lynott, 1996). Many of these viewpoints place greater emphasis on a macro-level of struc-

tural analysis and include symbolic interactionism or subcultures of aging, age stratification, social exchange, and political economy.

Symbolic Interactionism and Subculture of Aging

Consistent with the person–environment perspective outlined in Chapter 1, these **interactionist theories** focus on the person–environment transaction process, emphasizing the dynamic interaction between older individuals and their social world. It is assumed that older people must adjust to ongoing societal requirements. When confronted with change, whether relocation to a nursing home or learning to use a computer, older individuals are expected to try to master the changing situation while extracting from the larger environment what they need to retain a positive self-concept.

Attempting to bridge the gap between the activity and disengagement points of view, the **symbolic interactionist** perspective of aging argues that the interactions of such factors as the environment, individuals, and their encounters in it can significantly affect the kind of aging process people experience (Gubrium, 1973). This perspective emphasizes the importance of considering the meaning of the activity, such as disengagement, for the individuals concerned. Gubrium argued that activity may be valued in some environments, while in others it is devalued. Depending upon a person's resources (health, socioeconomic status, social support) along with the environmental norms for interpreting them, there are either positive or negative consequences for life satisfaction (Lynott and Lynott, 1996). Symbolic interactionists view both the self and society as able to create new alternatives. Therefore, low morale and withdrawal from social involvement are not inevitable with aging, but are one possible outcome of an individual's interactions that can be altered. Policies and programs based on the symbolic interactionist framework optimistically assume that both environmental constraints and individual needs can be changed.

Labeling theory, derived from symbolic interaction theory, states that people derive their self-

SUBCULTURE OF AGING

Roy, 63, has resided in a downtown SRO hotel in the Pacific Northwest for the past 4 years. A logger for many years, he never married, living alone in the woods for most of his work life and coming into town only when he needed supplies. When logging was curtailed, he "retired" early. Now he lives with many other older men downtown, having only a nodding acquaintance with them. He is able to make use of a low-income clinic for health care, and goes once a week to a downtown church where they serve lunch to older adults in the area.

concepts from interacting with others in their social milieu. In other words, we all tend to think of ourselves in terms of how others define us and react to others. Once others have defined us into distinct categories, they react to us on the basis of these categorizations. As a result, our self-concept and behavior change. For example, an older person who forgets where she or he parked the car is likely to be defined by relatives as showing signs of dementia, while younger people who do so are viewed as busy and distracted.

Proponents of a **subculture of aging theory** believe that older people maintain their self-concepts and social identities through their membership in a subculture (Rose, 1965). Behavior, whether of older persons or others, cannot be evaluated in terms of some overall social standard or norm. Rather, it is appreciated or devalued against the background of its members' expectations. Older people are presumed to interact with each other more than they do with others, because they have developed an affinity for each other through shared backgrounds, problems, and interests. At the same time, they may be excluded from fully interacting with other segments of the population, either because of self-segregation in retirement communities or "involuntary" segregation, such as younger people leaving inner city or rural areas and thereby isolating older residents. The formation of an aging subculture is viewed as having two significant consequences for older people:

- an identification of themselves as old, and thus socially and culturally distant from the rest of our youth-oriented society

- a growing group consciousness that may create the possibility of political influence and social action

Although the interactionist and subculture perspectives have implications for how to restructure environments, the focus is primarily on how individuals react to aging rather than on the broader sociostructural factors that shape the experience and meaning of aging in our society. The subculture theory of aging, however, fails to recognize

Age stratification theory and the subculture of aging suggest that older people prefer socializing within their own cohorts.

that most older people have important intergenerational roles and relationships, as grandparent, parent, friend, mentor, or employer. Instead, most people move into and out of a succession of different roles and statuses as they age, which is congruent with age stratification theory.

Age Stratification Theory

Just as societies are stratified in terms of socioeconomic class, gender, and race, every society divides people into categories or strata according to age—"young," "middle-aged," and "old." Age stratification is defined in terms of differential age cohorts. This means that individuals' experiences of aging, and therefore of roles, vary with their age strata. An older person's evaluation of life cannot be understood simply as a matter of being active or disengaged. Instead, changes in the system of age stratification influence how a person's experiences affect life satisfaction (Lynott and Lynott, 1996).

The **age stratification** approach challenges activity and disengagement theories, directing attention away from individual adjustment to that of the age structure of society (Marshall, 1996). It adds a structured time component in which cohorts pass through an age structure viewed as an age-graded system of expectations and rewards (Riley, Johnson, and Foner, 1972). This recognizes that the members of one strata differ from each other in both their stage of life (young, middle-aged, or old) and in the historical periods they have experienced. Both the life course and the historical dimensions explain differences in how people behave, think, and, in turn, contribute to society. Differences due to the historical dimension are referred to as **cohort flow.** As we saw in our discussion of research designs (Chapter 1), people born at the same time period (**cohort**) share a common historical and environmental past, present, and future. They have been exposed to similar events, conditions, and changes, and therefore come to see the world in a like fashion (Riley, 1971). For example, older people who were at the early stage of their occupational and childrearing careers during the Depression tend to value economic self-

sufficiency and "saving for a rainy day," compared to younger cohorts who have experienced periods of economic prosperity during early adulthood. This may create difficulties across generations in understanding each other's behavior with regard to finances or lifestyle.

Because of their particular relationship to historical events, people in the old-age stratum today are very different from older persons in the past or in the future, and they experience the aging process differently. This also means that cohorts as they age collectively influence age stratification. When there is a lack of fit in terms of available roles, cohort members may challenge the existing patterns of age stratification. For example, as successive cohorts in this century have experienced increased longevity and formal educational levels, this has changed the nature of how they age, how they view aging, and the age stratification system itself.

Consider how the cohort retiring in the first decade of the twenty-first century may differ from the cohort that retired in the 1950s: Although heterogeneous, this later cohort will tend to:

- view retirement and leisure more positively
- be physically active and healthier
- more likely challenge restrictions on their roles as workers and community participants through age discrimination lawsuits, legislative action, and political organization than previous cohorts
- expect to be grandparents and great-grandparents
- be more planful and proactive about the aging and dying processes

These variations, in turn, will affect the experiences and expectations of future cohorts as they age. In other words, as successive cohorts move through the age strata, they alter conditions to such a degree that later groups never encounter the world in exactly the same way, and therefore age in different ways.

Age stratification theory, with its focus on structural, demographic, and historical characteristics, can help us understand the ways in which

---

FOSTER GRANDPARENT PROGRAMS

Ten-year-old Ann lives with her mother and older brother in a public housing high-rise apartment. Her mother has to work two jobs in order to make ends meet. This means that Ann is often left at home alone after school. Through the Foster Grandparent Program administered by the local senior services and available in Ann's school, Ann has someone to call after school if she is lonely or needs help with homework. And twice a week, her foster grandmother comes to visit her, taking her on neighborhood outings, making clothes for her favorite doll, buying a special treat, or tutoring her. Ann benefits from her foster grandmother's presence and love. And her foster grandmother, a widow in her mid-seventies, feels a sense of satisfaction, accomplishment, and responsibility in her relationship with Ann. She looks forward to her time with Ann and speaks with pride to her friends about Ann's accomplishments. Most of all, the young girl and the older woman love each other—an emotional component of exchange relationships that makes analysis of relationships in strictly economic terms less appropriate.

---

society uses age to fit people into structural niches in the social world, and how this age structure changes with the passage of time. By viewing aging groups as members of status groups within a social system, as well as active participants in a changing society, stratification theory can provide useful sociological explanations of age differences related to time, period, and cohort.

More recently, the concept of **structural lag** has emerged from the age and society perspective (Riley, Kahn, and Foner, 1994; Riley and Riley, 1994). Structural lag occurs when social structures cannot keep pace with the changes in population and individual lives (Riley and Loscocco, 1994). For example, with the increases in life expectancy, societal structures are inadequate to accommodate and utilize postretirement elders. In some cases, the workplace, religious institutions, and voluntary associations may fail to recognize the resources that older people could contribute. Proponents argue that an age-integrated society would compensate for structural lag by developing policies, such as extended time off for education or family across the life span, to bring social structures into balance with individuals' lives (Estes and Associates, 2000).

Social Exchange Theory

Social exchange theory also challenged activity and disengagement theory. Drawing upon economic cost-benefit models of social participation,

Dowd (1980) attempts to answer why social interaction and activity often decrease with age. He maintains that withdrawal and social isolation are not the result of system needs or individual choice, but rather of an unequal exchange process of "investments and returns" between older persons and other members of society. The balance of interactions existing between older people and others determines personal satisfaction. Accordingly, individual adjustment depends on the immediate costs and benefits/rewards between persons, although exchange may also be driven by emotional needs and resources, such as social support (Bengtson et al., 1997). Because of the shift in **opportunity structures,** roles, and skills that accompanies advancing aging, older people typically have fewer resources with which to exert power in their social relationships, and their status declines accordingly (Hendricks, 1995). Society is at an advantage in such power relationships, reflected in the economic and social dependency of older people who have outmoded skills. With fewer opportunity structures and little to exchange in value, some older people are forced to accept the retirement role and to turn to deference and withdrawal in order to balance the exchange equation (Lynott and Lynott, 1996).

Despite their limited resources, most older adults seek to maintain some degree of reciprocity, and to be active, independent agents in the management of their lives. In this model, adaptability

Both young and old can benefit from the Foster Grandparents program.

is a dual process of influencing one's environment as well as adjusting to it. Although older individuals may have fewer economic and material resources to bring to the interaction or exchange, they often have nonmaterial resources such as respect, approval, love, wisdom, and time for voluntary activities. Similarly, policies and services that are developed for older people might aim to maximize their nonmaterial resources that are valued by our society as well as to increase opportunity structures for older people. For example, the growing number of intergenerational programs recognizes the volume of social exchange between generations. Exchange theory is relevant to contemporary debates about intergenerational social support and transfer across generations through public policies such as Social Security and within families through caregiving relationships.

Political Economy of Aging

The focus of exchange theory on power and opportunity structures is related to the **political economy of aging,** a relatively recent macro-analysis of structural characteristics that determine how people adapt in old age and how social resources are allocated. According to the political economy perspective, social class is a structural barrier to older people's access to valued social resources, with dominant groups within society trying to sustain their own interests by perpetuating class in-

equities (Minkler and Estes, 1984; Olson, 1982; Overbo and Minkler, 1993). Socioeconomic and political constraints, not individual factors, thereby shape the experience of aging, and are patterned not only by age but also by class, gender, race, and ethnicity. These structural factors, often institutionalized and reinforced by economic and public policy, limit opportunities, choices, and experiences of later life (Bengtson et al., 1997). This means that the process of aging and how individuals adapt are not the problem. Rather, the major problems faced by older people are socially constructed in a capitalist society as a result of societal conceptions of aging. In fact, policy solutions, such as Social Security, Medicare, and Medicaid, are viewed as a means of social control that perpetuates the "private" troubles of older people while meeting the dominant needs of the economy (Estes and Associates, 2000; Estes, Linkins, and Binney, 1996; Olson, 1982). Estes et al. (1996) argue that the marginalization of the older population is furthered by the development of the "Aging Enterprise," a service industry of agencies, providers, and planners that reaffirms the out-group status of older adults in order to maintain their own jobs. Policy solutions have tended to focus on integrating and socializing older people to adapt to their status, rather than efforts to fundamentally alter social and economic conditions that underlie the problems facing older people.

Life Course Perspective

The **life course perspective** is not necessarily a theory, but a framework pointing to a set of problems requiring explanation (George, 1996). It attempts to bridge sociological and psychological thinking about processes at both the macro (population) and micro (individual) levels of analysis by incorporating the effects of history, social structure, and individual meaning into theoretical models (Bengtson et al., 1997; Marshall, 1996). This approach takes account of the diversity of roles and role changes across the life span, since it suggests that development is not restricted to any one part of the life span, but rather, is a lifelong and highly dynamic process. Human development cannot be solely equated with steady incremental growth or change but instead is an interactive, nonlinear process characterized by the simultaneous appearance of role gains and losses, continuity, and discontinuity. Accordingly, development is multidirectional, with stability in some functions, decline in others, and improvement in others. For example, an older person may experience some decrement in memory but still be very creative. In addition, these patterns of development are not the same in all individuals, as reflected by the considerable heterogeneity of life trajectories and transitions among older individuals. The life course perspective can provide a critical analysis of how caregiving is now a standardized part of the life course, "on-time" for increasing numbers of middle-aged adult children, because more older people are living longer and requiring care by family members (Elder, George, and Shanahan, 1996). As another example, the life course perspective has been used to examine the concept of cumulative disadvantage for women across life, because of their limited opportunities to aggregate savings and private pensions as compared to men (O'Rand, 1996).

In contrast with the more individualistic approach of role theory, the life course perspective attempts to explain:

- how aging is related to and shaped by social contexts, history, cultural meanings, and location in the social structure
- how time, period, and cohort shape the aging process for individuals and social groups (Bengtson and Allen, 1993; Elder, 1992; George, 1993)

This approach is also multidisciplinary in content and methods, bringing together seemingly disparate approaches to the life course (Bengtson et al., 1997). Although the life course perspective is not explicitly articulated throughout this text, our multidisciplinary person-in-environment approach, which encompasses biological, psychological, physiological, and social changes, draws upon many of the concepts of intra-individual change,

inter-individual variability, and historical, social, and cultural contexts or environments.

RECENT DEVELOPMENTS IN SOCIAL GERONTOLOGICAL THEORY: THE SECOND TRANSFORMATION

Social Phenomenologists and Social Constructionists

The "second transformation" in theoretical development, occurring since the early 1980s, is described as a qualitative leap in gerontological thought (Lynott and Lynott, 1996). Phenomenological theorists have taken issue with the presumed "facts of aging," questioning the nature of age and how it is described and whose interests are served by thinking of aging in particular ways. **Social phenomenologists** and **social constructionists** claim that the approach, orientation, and other subjective features of researchers and their world are significantly connected to the nature of the data as such. Therefore, the data or facts of aging cannot be separated from the researcher's perceptions about time, space, and self—or those of the individuals being studied. People actively participate in their everyday lives, creating and maintaining social meanings for themselves and those around them. No one, including researchers, directly or objectively sees a fixed reality. Rather, each of us actively constructs meanings that influence what we each call reality (Ray, 1996). For phenomenologists and social constructionists, it is not the objects or facts but rather the assumptions and interpretations of them that are critical (Lynott and Lynott, 1996). For example, this theoretical perspective would attempt to understand how legislators and other policy makers assume features about the older population in deciding whether to increase or decrease Medicare or Social Security benefits (Estes and Associates, 2000).

The emphasis of phenomenologists is on understanding, not explaining, individual processes of aging as influenced by social definitions and social structures (Bengtson et al., 1997). Instead of

---

POINTS TO PONDER

What assumptions and interpretations about middle and old age are made by politicians who argue for privatizing Social Security and allowing individuals to invest in Individual Retirement Accounts instead of paying into Social Security?

---

asking how factors such as age cohorts, life stages, or system needs organize and determine one's experience, they reverse the question and ask how individuals, whether professionals or laypersons, draw upon age-related explanations and justifications in how they relate to and interact with one another. Individual behavior produces a "reality," which in turn structures individual lives. This means that social reality shifts over time, reflecting the differing life situations and social roles that occur with maturation (Dannefer and Perlmutter, 1990). Not only do theories construct versions of reality, but people do so in their everyday lives; and in the everyday world, people often use or critique the constructions of theorists (Marshall, 1996). Gubrium (1993a) used life narratives to discern the subjective meanings of quality of care and quality of life for nursing home residents—meanings that cannot be measured by predefined measurement scales such as those used by most survey researchers. Similarly, Diamond (1992) utilized participant observation techniques as a nursing assistant to learn about the social world of nursing homes. He described the social construction of his job, how the meanings of care are constantly negotiated as the invisible work of caring for older residents' emotional needs clashes with the daily tasks of a nursing assistant. The realities of age and age-related concepts are thus socially constructed. For example, labeling older people as dependent, asexual, frail or marginal is defined socially. However, the focus is on how these definitions emerge through social interactions rather than taking account of social structure and power (Kaufman, 1994).

Social constructionists and phenomenologists, such as Gubrium and Diamond, because of their focus on individual interactions, tend to use ethno-

graphic or more qualitative methods to obtain multifaceted views of the aging experience. For example, Diamond (1992), as a participant observer as a nursing assistant, described both the social construction of the job and the negotiation of the position of patient in a nursing home. This contrasts with the **positivist** *(or quantitative) approach* of many of the earlier theories. In order to gather extensive verbal or observational data, their samples of informants are relatively small compared to the more traditional quantitative methods typically used. To positivists, however, social constructionist theories may seem impossible to test, and closer to assumptions about meaning than propositions that can be proved or disproved (Bengtson et al., 1997).

Critical Theory and Feminist Perspectives

Social constructionist theories have influenced other contemporary social gerontology theories, especially critical and feminist theories. **Critical theorists** critique the transformation of the relationships between subjects and objects from being genuine to being alienated, not the research procedures or the objective state of objects per se. With respect to age conceptualizations and theories of aging, critical theorists are concerned with how they represent a language serving to reify experiences as something separate from those doing the experiencing (Lynott and Lynott, 1996). For example, Tornstam (1996, 1992) argues that conventional gerontology draws on a limited positivist notion of knowledge and science that produces a model of aging based only on social problems. By contrast, a more critical and humane approach would allow older people themselves to define the research questions. Arguing for humanistic discourse in gerontology, Moody (1988) identifies four goals of a critical gerontology approach:

1. to theorize subjective and interpretive dimensions of aging
2. to focus not on technical advancement but on "praxis," defined as active involvement in practical change, such as public policy
3. to link academics and practitioners through praxis
4. to produce "emancipatory knowledge," which is a positive vision of how things might be different or what a rationally defensible vision of a "good old age" might be (p. xvii)

To achieve this knowledge requires moving beyond the conventional confines of gerontology to explore contributions toward theory development from more reflective modes of thought derived from the humanities (Cole, Achenbaum, Jakobi, and Kastenbaum, 1993). Dannefer (1994) suggests that critical gerontology should not merely critique existing theory but create positive models of aging that emphasize strengths and diversity. For example, Atchley (1993) maintains that critical gerontology must question traditional positivistic assumptions and measures to try to understand the multiple dimensions of retirement, including retirement as a freeing stage in the life course. What is yet unknown is what "a good old age" means, as well as how it will be attained and what type of "emancipatory knowledge" is possible. Nevertheless, critical thinking has the potential to expand the field of social gerontology. It can do so by providing insight into, and critical self-reflection on, the continuing effort to understand the aging experience (Lynott and Lynott, 1996).

Because most gerontologists have been trained in the positivist tradition, critical theory, with its abstraction, is often not cited nor yet well understood. Nevertheless, it is becoming a topic of considerable theoretical discourse in contemporary social gerontology (Cole et al., 1993; Minkler, 1996; Phillipson, 1996). By questioning traditions in mainstream social gerontology, critical theory calls attention to other perspectives relevant to

understanding aging, especially the humanistic dimension (Gubrium, 1993b), and has influenced feminist theories of aging. In addition, the self-reflexive nature of critical theory constantly challenges gerontologists to understand the impact of social research and policy on older individuals (Tornstam, 1992). With growing attention to ethnographic and other qualitative methodologies, the interpretive approach of critical theory will increasingly be brought to bear on empirical observations of aging, with researchers attempting to integrate critical theory with the strengths of positivist approaches.

From a critical theory perspective, current theories and models of aging are viewed as insufficient because they fail to include gender relations and the experiences of women in the context of aging (Bleiszner, 1993; Marshall, 1996). For example, women have traditionally been ignored in retirement research, often because paid employment is assumed to be unimportant to them (Calasanti, 1993). Or women were not included in health studies because males were defined as the norm. **Feminist theories** draw upon a number of other theories discussed thus far:

- political economy by focusing on the economic and power relations between older men and women
- symbolic interactionism, phenomenology, and social constructionism in the belief that gender must be examined in the context of social structural arrangements

Feminist theories attempt to integrate micro and macro approaches to aging through the links between individuals and social structures. In particular, they focus on power relations and the utilization of both quantitative and qualitative methodologies (Bury, 1995; Estes and Associates, 2000; Lynott and Lynott, 1996; Ray, 1996).

From a feminist perspective, gender should be a primary consideration in attempts to understand aging and older people, especially since women form the majority of the older population. Because gender is an organizing principle

A FEMINIST PERSPECTIVE ON CAREGIVING

Mrs. Reid grew up with the expectation that she would marry, have children, and take care of her family. She fulfilled this expectation, raising four children, caring for her husband when he suffered a heart attack in his early sixties, and then later caring for both her mother and her mother-in-law. She never held a full-time job, instead working occasionally and part-time in order to supplement her husband's income. When he died at age 65, she was left with only his Social Security. All her years of caregiving work, that had contributed to her family's well-being and to the economy, were not compensated in any way. If her caregiving work were valued by our society, Social Security would be altered to view such in-home care as legitimate work that contributes to society. Accordingly, caregivers such as Mrs. Reid would receive Social Security benefits in their own right in old age.

for social interactions across the life span, men and women experience the aging process differently (Bengtson et al., 1997; Ginn and Arber, 1995; Marshall, 1996). Although feminism encompasses a wide range of intellectual paradigms and political/ideological positions, most feminist theories in aging have drawn on "socialist feminism." This model argues that women occupy an inferior status in old age as a result of living in a capitalist and patriarchal society (Arber and Ginn, 1995, 1991).

Socialist feminists point to inequities in the gender-based division of labor and argue for major changes in how society defines, distributes, and rewards "work." They attempt to understand women's aging experiences in light of macro-level social, economic, and political forces rather than as isolated results of individual choices. Caregiving, women's retirement, health, and poverty across the life course are examined by feminist theorists in light of women's differential access to power in the paid labor force, childrearing, and unpaid housework throughout their lives. Such unequal access leaves women without economic resources and necessary social support for managing problems in later life (Arber and Ginn, 1995; Browne, 1998; Calasanti and Hendricks, 1999; Garner, 1999; Hooyman and Gonyea, 1995; Stoller, 1993). Social policy is criticized for defining the problems facing women as private responsibilities, rather than taking account of how existing structural arrangements create women's dependency and limited choices in old age. For example, the lack of public and private pensions for a lifelong career as homemaker and caregiver leaves older women vulnerable to society's whims in identifying social benefits to older adults. The need for feminist theory is also visible when considering the failure to take domestic labor seriously in life-course analyses of work (Marshall, 1996). From a feminist view, work in the home is integral to economic productivity, but is undervalued or devalued. As another example of a feminist approach, the consequences of caregiving should not be evaluated on the basis of individual characteristics such as caregiver burden. Instead, the underlying problem for women of all ages is inadequate and gender-based policies, not their own individual stress level; the long-range solution is reorganizing work as a societal rather than an individual responsibility. Feminists argue that caring work must be reorganized to be more equitable and humane both for the givers and the receivers (Hooyman and Gonyea, 1995; Meyer, 1997).

More recently, there are efforts to integrate **postmodern theory** into gerontology and feminism, although postmodernism is itself antitheoretical. Postmodernism theory views knowledge as socially constructed and social life as highly improvisational. Theoretically, modernism challenges positivistic science (Marshall, 1996; Ray,

1996). Postmodernists view the primary task to be the critique of language, discourse, and research practices that constrict knowledge about older women. For example, they approach caregiving not as the result of "natural" tendencies in women toward nurturing, but as the outcome of socialization processes and polices that reify gendered patterns of caring by depending on the unpaid labor of women as efficient and cost-effective (Browne, 1998; Hooyman, 1992; Hooyman and Gonyea, 1995; Stoller, 1993). A postmodern feminist approach in gerontology draws upon a variety of methodologies to understand women's experiences. Researchers acknowledge how their assumptions, values, and beliefs influence the research process. Accordingly, postmodernist research, oriented to changing conditions that face women, is conducted to benefit women, and includes women as active participants.

New to the field, broad, and often ideologically based, feminist theories are less frequently cited than established models of explanation, such as social constructionism, life course, and exchange theories. Nevertheless, they can make significant contributions to gerontology and to the development of feminist theory generally. Not only are they focusing on the needs of the majority of older adults, but they also take account of diversity by race, ethnicity, social class, education, and mental/physical status. Addressing issues that are relevant to women's lives, they draw explicit linkages to practice. In addition, they provide models for integrating micro and macro levels of analysis. They thus encompass both structural and individual levels of theory and change in order to improve the social and economic positions of women as they age. Lastly, they challenge "mainstream" feminist theories, which typically have focused on issues pertaining to younger women, to take account of age, since gender shapes everyday experiences throughout the life course (Bengtson et al., 1997; Meyer, 1997). The merger of feminist and aging scholarship has the potential for formulating politically sustainable solutions that permit women and men, young and old, to balance the burdens and satisfactions of caregiving work and paid work (Meyer, 1997).

SUMMARY AND IMPLICATIONS

This review of theoretical perspectives has highlighted the multiplicity of lenses through which to view and explain the aging process. Although we have emphasized the importance of utilizing explicit theoretical perspectives to build, revise, and interpret how and why phenomena occur, it is apparent that no single theory can explain all aging phenomena (Marshall, 1994). Instead, these theories or conceptual frameworks vary widely in their emphasis on individual adjustment to age-related changes, their attention to social structure, power, and economic conditions, the methodologies utilized, and their reflective nature on the meaning of the aging experience. As noted early in the chapter, they represent different times or historical periods in the development of social theories. Some, such as disengagement theory, have been largely rejected by empirical data, while others, such as critical theory and feminist theory, are only now evolving and capturing the attention of a new generation of gerontological researchers. Other earlier perspectives, such as social exchange and symbolic interactionism, still influence research questions and social policy. As a whole, these theoretical perspectives point to new ways of seeing aging phenomena and new modes of analysis, laying the framework for future research directions (Hendricks, 1992). As the social, economic, and political conditions affecting older people change, new theoretical perspectives must develop or former ones must be revised through the gathering of information from diverse cultures, contexts, and circumstances. Given the growing heterogeneity of the aging process, interdisciplinary research is essential. Such research must take account of both individual and macro-level changes. It must encompass the role of gender, race, and class, and allow for the dynamic nature and meaning of the aging experience. We turn now to the social context and relationships addressed by many of the social theories of aging: the vital role of social supports in old age; how physical living arrangements can affect social interactions; the concept of productive aging, which encompasses both paid and nonpaid roles and activities; and coping with loss in dying, bereavement, and widowhood.

GLOSSARY

activity theory a theory of aging based on the hypothesis that (1) active older people are more satisfied and better adjusted than those who are not active, and (2) an older person's self-concept is validated through participation in roles characteristic of middle age, and older people should therefore replace lost roles with new ones to maintain their place in society

age stratification theory a theoretical perspective based on the belief that the societal age structure affects roles, self-concept, and life satisfaction

continuity theory a theory based on the hypothesis that central personality characteristics become more pronounced with age or are retained through life with little change; people age successfully if they maintain their preferred roles and adaptation techniques throughout life

critical theory the perspective that genuine knowledge is based on the involvement of the "objects" of study in its definition and results in a positive vision of how things might be better rather than an understanding of how things are

disengagement theory a theory of aging based on the hypothesis that older people, because of inevitable decline with age, become decreasingly active with the outer world and increasingly preoccupied with their inner lives; disengagement is useful for society because it fosters an orderly transfer of power from older to younger people

feminist theory the view that the experiences of women are often ignored in understanding the human condition together with efforts to attend critically to those experiences

interactionist theory a perspective that emphasizes the reciprocal actions of persons and their social world in shaping perceptions, attitudes, behavior, etc., including person–environment, symbolic interaction, labeling, and social breakdown perspectives

labeling theory a theoretical perspective derived from symbolic interactionism, premised on the belief that people derive their self-concepts from interacting with others in their social milieu, in how others define us and react to us

life course perspective the multidisciplinary view of human development that focuses on changes with age and life experiences

opportunity structures social arrangements, formal and informal, that limit or advance options available to people based on such features as social class, age, ethnicity, and sex

political economy of aging a theory based on the hypothesis that social class determines a person's access to resources and that dominant groups within society try to sustain their own interests by perpetuating class inequities

positivism the perspective that knowledge is based solely upon observable facts and their relation to one another (cause and effect or correlation); the search for ultimate origins is rejected

postmodern theory the critique of language, discourse, and research practices that constrict knowledge

productive roles a concept central to activity theory; activities in volunteer associations, churches, employment, and politics

role theory a theory based on the belief that roles define us and our self-concept, and shape our behavior

social exchange theory a theory based on the hypothesis that personal status is defined by the balance between people's contributions to society and the costs of supporting them

social phenomenology and constructionism a point of view in studying social life that places an emphasis on the assumptions and meanings of experience rather than the "objective" facts, with a focus on understanding rather than explaining

structural lag the inability of social structures (patterns of behavior, attitude, ideas, policies, etc.) to adapt to changes in population and individual lives

subculture of aging theory a theoretical perspective based on the belief that people maintain their self-concepts and social identities through their membership in a defined group (subculture)

symbolic interactionism   a theoretical perspective based on the belief that the interactions of such factors as the environment, individuals, and their encounters in it can significantly affect one's behavior and thoughts, including the aging process

REFERENCES

Achenbaum, W. A., and Bengtson, V. C. Re-engaging the disengagement theory of aging: Or the history and assessment of theory development in gerontology. *The Gerontologist*, 1994, *34*, 756–763.

Arber, S., and Ginn, J. (Ed.). *Connecting gender and aging: A sociological approach*. Philadelphia: Open University Press, 1995.

Arber, S., and Ginn, J. *Gender and later life: A sociological analysis of constraints*. Newbury Park, CA: Sage, 1991.

Atchley, R. C. Critical perspectives on retirement. In T. R. Cole, W. A. Achenbaum, P. L. Jakobi, and R. Kastenbaum (Eds.), *Voices and visions: Toward a critical gerontology*. New York: Springer, 1993.

Atchley, R. C. *The social forces in later life*. Belmont, CA: Wadsworth, 1972.

Baltes, P. B. Theoretical propositions of life-span developmental psychology: On the dynamics between growth and decline. Baltes, P. B. (Ed.). *Developmental Psychology*, 1987.

Bengtson, V. L. Cultural and occupational differences in level of present role activity in retirement. In R. J. Havighurst, J. M. A. Munnicks, B. C. Neugarten, and H. Thomas (Eds.), *Adjustments to retirement: A cross-national study*. Assen, The Netherlands: Van Gorkum, 1969.

Bengtson, V. L., and Allen, K. R. The life course perspective applied to families over time. In P. G. Boss, W. J. Doherty, R. LaRossa, W. R. Schumm, and S. K. Steinmetz (Eds.), *Sourcebook of family theories and methods: A conceptual approach*. New York: Plenum Press, 1993.

Bengtson, V. L., Burgess, E. O., and Parrott, T. M. Theory, explanation and a third generation of theoretical development in social gerontology. *Journals of Gerontology*, 1997, *52B*, S72–S88.

Bleiszner, R. A socialist-feminist perspective on widowhood. *Journal of Aging Studies*, 1993, *7*, 171–182.

Browne, C. *Women, feminism, and aging*. New York, NY: Springer Publishing, 1998.

Bury, M. Aging, gender and sociological theory. In S. Arber and J. Ginn (Eds.), *Connecting gender and aging: A sociological approach*. Philadelphia: Open University Press, 1995.

Calasanti, T. M. Bringing in diversity: Toward an inclusive theory of retirement. *Journal of Aging Studies*, 1993, *7*, 133–150.

Calasanti, T. M. Incorporating diversity: Meaning, levels of research, and implications for theory. *The Gerontologist*, 1996, *36*, 147–156.

Calasanti, T. M. Feminism and gerontology: Not just for women. *Hallym International Journal of Aging* 1999, 44–55.

Calasanti, T. M., and Zaijicek, J. M. A socialist-feminist approach to aging. *Journal of Aging Studies*, 1993, *7*, 117–131.

Cole, T. R., Achenbaum, W. A., Jacobi, P. L., and Kastenbaum, R. *Voices and visions of aging: Toward a critical gerontology*. New York: Springer, 1993.

Cottrell, L. The adjustment of the individual to his age and sex roles. *American Sociological Review*, 1942, *7*, 617–620.

Covey, H. A reconceptualization of continuity theory: Some preliminary thoughts. *The Gerontologist*, 1981, *21*, 628–633.

Cumming, E., and Henry, W. E. *Growing old*. New York: Basic Books, 1961.

Dannefer, W. D. *Reciprocal co-optation: Some reflections on the relationship of critical theory and social gerontology*. Revised version of paper presented at the International Sociological Association, Bieleveld, Germany, July 1994.

Dannefer, W. D., and Perlmutter, M. Development as a multidimensional process: Individual and social constituents. *Human Development*, 1990, *33*, 108–137.

Diamond, T. *Making grey gold: Narratives of nursing home care*. Chicago: University of Chicago Press, 1992.

Dowd, J. J. *Stratification among the aged*. Monterey, CA: Brooks Cole, 1980.

Ekerdt, D. J., and DeViney, S. Evidence for a preretirement process among older male workers. *Journals of Gerontology*, 1993, *48*, S35–S43.

Elder, G. H., Jr. Models of the life course. *Contemporary Sociology: A Journal of Reviews*, 1992, *21*, 632–635.

Elder, G. H., Jr., George, L. K., and Shanahan, M. J. Psychosocial stress over the life course. In H. Kaplan, (Ed.), *Psychosocial stress: Perspectives on structure, theory, life-course, and methods.* San Diego: Academic Press, 1996.

Estes, C. L. *The aging enterprise.* San Francisco: Jossey-Bass, 1979.

Estes, C. L., and Associates. *Social policy and aging: A critical perspective.* Thousand Oaks: Sage, 2000.

Estes, C. L., Gerard, L. E., Zones, J. S., and Swan, J. H. *Political economy, health, and aging.* Boston: Little Brown, 1984.

Estes, C. L., Linkins, K. W., and Binney, E. A. The political economy of aging. In R. H. Binstock and L. K. George (Eds.), *Handbook of aging and the social sciences* (4th ed.). San Diego: Academic Press, 1996.

Garfinkle, H. *Studies in ethno-methodology.* Englewood Cliffs, NJ: Prentice-Hall, 1967.

Garner, J. D. "Feminism and feminist gerontology." *Fundamentals of feminist gerontology* (1999): 3–13.

George, L. K. Missing links: The case for a social psychology of the life course. *The Gerontologist,* 1996, *36,* 248–255.

George, L. K. Sociological perspectives on life transitions. *Annual Review of Sociology,* 1993, *19,* 353–373.

Gilleard, C., and Higgs, P. Ageing and the limiting conditions of the body. *Sociological Research Online,* 1998.

Ginn, J., and Arber, S. Only connect: Gender relations and aging. In S. Arber and J. Ginn (Eds.), *Connecting gender and aging: A sociological approach.* Philadelphia: Open University Press, 1995.

Gubrium, J. F. *The myth of the golden years.* Springfield, IL: Charles C. Thomas, 1973.

Gubrium, J. F. *Speaking of life: Horizons of meaning for nursing home residents.* New York: Aldine de Gruyter, 1993a.

Gubrium, J. F. Voice and context in a new gerontology. In T. R. Cole, W. A. Achenbaum, P. C. Jakobi, and R. Kastenbaum (Eds.), *Voices and visions of aging: Toward a critical gerontology.* New York: Springer, 1993b.

Gubrium, J. F., and Lynott, R. J. Rethinking life satisfaction. *Human Organization,* 1983, *42,* 30–38.

Hagestad, G., and Neugarten, B. Age and the life course. In R. H. Binstock and E. Shanas (Eds.), *Handbook of aging and the social sciences* (2nd ed.). New York: Van Nostrand, 1985.

Havighurst, R. J. Personality and patterns of aging. *The Gerontologist,* 1968, *38,* 20–23.

Havighurst, R. J. Successful aging. In R. Williams, C. Tibbits, and W. Donahue (Eds.), *Processes of aging,* Vol. 1. New York: Atherton Press, 1963.

Hendricks, J. Exchange theory in aging. In G. Maddox (Ed.), *The encyclopedia of aging* (2nd ed.). New York: Springer, 1995.

Hendricks, J. Generations and the generation of theory in social gerontology. *International Journal of Aging and Human Development,* 1992, *38,* 31–47.

Herzog, A. R., Holden, K. C., and Seltzer, M. M. *Health and economic status of older women.* Amityville, NY: Baywood, 1989.

Herzog, A. R., and House, J. S. Productive activities and aging well. *Generations,* 1991, *15,* 49–54.

Herzog, A. R., Kahn, R., Morgan, J., Jackson, J., and Antonucci, T. Age differences in productive activities. *Journals of Gerontology,* 1989, *44,* S129–S138.

Hochschild, A. R. Disengagement theory: A critique and proposal. *American Sociological Review,* 1975, *40,* 553–569.

Hochschild, A. R. Disengagement theory: A logical, empirical, and phenomenological critique. In J. F. Gubrium (Ed.), *Time, roles and self in old age.* New York: Human Services Press, 1976.

Hooyman, N. R. Social policy and gender inequities in caregiving. In J. W. Dwyer and R. T. Coward (Eds.), *Gender, families, and eldercare.* Newbury Park, CA: Sage, 1992.

Hooyman, N. R., and Gonyea, J. G. A feminist model of family care: Practice and policy directions. In J. D. Garner (Ed.), *Fundamentals of Feminist Gerontology,* New York: The Haworth Press, Inc., 1999.

Hooyman, N. R., and Gonyea, J. *Feminist perspectives on family care: Policies for gender justice.* Thousand Oaks, CA: Sage, 1995.

Kaufman, S. R. The social construction of frailty: An anthropological perspective. *Journal of Aging Studies,* 1994, *8,* 45–58.

Lynott, R. J., and Lynott, P. P. Tracing the course of theoretical development in the sociology of aging. *The Gerontologist,* 1996, *36,* 749–760.

Marshall, V. W. Sociology and psychology in the theoretical legacy of the Kansas City Studies. *The Gerontologist,* 1994, *34,* 768–774.

Marshall, V. W. The state of theory in aging and the social sciences. In R. H. Binstock and L. K. George, (Eds.), *Handbook of aging and the social sciences,* (4th ed.). San Diego: Academic Press, 1996.

Meyer, M. H. Toward a structural, life course agenda for reducing insecurity among women as they age. Book review. *The Gerontologist,* 1997, *37,* 833–834.

Minkler, M. Critical perspectives on aging: New challenges for gerontology. *Aging and Society,* 1996, *16,* 467–487.

Minkler, M., and Estes, C. *Readings in the political economy of aging.* Farmingdale, NY: Baywood, 1984.

Moody, H. R. Toward a critical gerontology: The contribution of the humanities to theories of aging. In J. E. Birren and V. L. Bengtson (Eds.), *Emergent theories of aging.* New York: Springer, 1988.

Neugarten, B., Havighurst, R. J., and Tobin, S. S. Personality and patterns of aging. In B. L. Neugarten (Ed.), *Middle age and aging.* Chicago: University of Chicago Press, 1968.

Olson, L. K. *The political economy of aging.* New York: Columbia University Press, 1982.

O'Rand, A. M. The precious and the precocious: Understanding cumulative disadvantage and cumulative advantage over the life course. *The Gerontologist,* 1996, *36,* 230–238.

Overbo, B., and Minkler, M. The lives of older women: Perspectives from political economy and the humanities. In T. R. Cole, W. A. Achenbaum, P. L. Jakobi, and R. Kastenbaum (Eds.), *Voices and visions of aging: Toward a critical gerontology.* New York: Springer, 1993.

Phillipson, C. Interpretations of aging: Perspectives from humanistic gerontology. *Aging and Society,* 1996, *16,* 359–369.

Polivka, L. Review Essay, *Journal of Aging and Identity,* 1998, *3(2),* 99–113.

Ray, R. E. A post modern perspective on feminist gerontology. *The Gerontologist,* 1996, *36,* 674–680.

Riley, M. W. Social gerontology and the age stratification of society. *The Gerontologist,* 1971, *11,* 79–87.

Riley, M. W., Johnson, J., and Foner, A. *Aging and society: A sociology of age stratification,* vol. 3. New York: Russell Sage Foundation, 1972.

Riley, M. W., Kahn, R. L., and Foner, A. (Eds.). *Age and structural lag: Society's failure to provide meaningful opportunities in work, family and leisure.* New York: John Wiley, 1994.

Riley, M. W., and Loscocco, K. A. The changing structure of work opportunities: Toward an age-integrated society. In R. P. Abeles, H. C. Gift, and M. G. Ory (Eds.), *Aging and quality of life.* New York: Springer, 1994.

Riley, M. W., and Riley, J. W. Age integration and the lives of older people. *The Gerontologist,* 1994, *34,* 110–115.

Riley, M. W., and Riley, J. W., Jr. Age integration: Update and critique. Presented at the International Sociological Association, 1998.

Roberto, K. A., Allen, K. R., and Blieszner, R. Older women, their children, and grandchildren: A feminist perspective on family relationships. In J. D. Garner (Ed.) *Fundamentals of Feminist Gerontology.* New York: The Haworth Press, Inc., 1999.

Rose, A. M. A current theoretical issue in social gerontology. In A. M. Rose and W. A. Peterson (Eds.), *Older people and their social worlds.* Philadelphia: F. A. Davis, 1965.

Rosow, J. Status and role change through the life cycle. In R. H. Binstock and E. Shanas (Eds.), *Handbook of aging and the social sciences* (2nd ed.). New York: Van Nostrand, 1985.

Stoller, E. P. Gender and the organization of lay health care: A socialist-feminist perspective. *Journal of Aging Studies,* 1993, *7,* 151–170.

Tornstam, L. Gerotranscendence: A theory about maturing in old age. *Journal of aging and identity,* 1996, *1,* 37–50.

Tornstam, L. The Quo Vadis of gerontology: On the scientific paradigm of gerontology. *The Gerontologist,* 1992, *32,* 318–326.

9

THE IMPORTANCE OF SOCIAL SUPPORTS: FAMILY, FRIENDS, AND NEIGHBORS

Consistent with the life course perspective and the person–environment model, this chapter focuses on informal social support systems:

- Family
- Different types of family relationships
  Gay and lesbian families
  The multigenerational family
  Grandparents and grandchildren
- Friends
- Neighbors and acquaintances, often in service roles
- How informal supports influence an older person's well-being
- Policy and practice issues, including the use of informal social networks to deliver services

As people age, their social roles and relationships change. Earlier chapters have noted and the introductory vignettes have illustrated that the way older people interact with others is affected by physiological, social, and psychological changes. For example, with children gone from the home and without daily contacts with coworkers, older people may lose a critical context for social involvement. At the same time, their need for social support may increase because of changes in health, cognitive, and emotional status. Such incongruence between needs and environmental opportunities can result in stress for some older people. Previous chapters have referred to formal support systems characteristic of the larger environment, such as the health care system.

THE NATURE AND FUNCTION OF INFORMAL SUPPORTS

The importance of informal social supports in older people's lives is extensively documented. The concept of social support includes the specific types of assistance exchanged (emotional or tangible support); frequency of contact with others; and how a person assesses the adequacy of the supportive exchange. Informal reciprocal relationships are, in fact, a crucial concomitant of an older person's physical and mental well-being, feelings of personal control, morale, and autonomy (Hansson and Carpenter, 1994; Hobfoll and Vaux, 1993; Krause and Borawski-Clark, 1995). As noted in Chapter 6, there is also research evidence that strong social networks contribute to successful aging. Alternatively, extreme social isolation can contribute to a higher mortality rate (LaVeist, Sellers, Brown, Elliott, and Nickerson, 1997). A common myth is that older people are lonely and alienated from family and friends. Yet, even the most apparently isolated and vulnerable older person may be able to turn to an informal network for information, financial advice, emotional reassurance, or concrete services. And aging does not necessarily result in losses in social networks, but rather affects network composition (i.e., less contact with couples) or functioning (i.e., increased need for instrumental support) (Cantor, 1994; Van Tilburg, 1998). Consistent with social exchange theory discussed in Chapter 8, most older adults try to maintain reciprocity—being able to help others—in their interactions with others. For example, even frail elders who require personal assistance from their families may still contribute to the family through financial assistance and coresidence (Boaz, Hu, and Ye, 1999). Older individuals first use informal social supports to meet their emotional needs, and move to more formal relationships only when necessary, typically when they live alone (Krause and Borawski-Clark, 1995). As suggested by the person–environment model, they draw upon these informal supports as a way to enhance their competence. In fact, too much support from others, creating inequality of exchange, can erode older adults' sense of competence. In addition, some interactions with informal networks can be negative if they are not consistent with the older person's needs and competence level (Silverstein, Chen, and Heller, 1996)—for example, disappointment that one's children are not doing enough to help their older parent following a hospitalization.

With cutbacks in formal services in the past two decades, gerontologists are more aware of the critical roles played by informal relationships. Families, friends, neighbors, and even acquaintances, such as grocery clerks and postal carriers, can be powerful antidotes to some of the negative consequences of the aging process, as in the description of Mr. Mansfield on p. 254. For example, informal networks have been found to reduce the adverse effects of stressful life events, such as bereavement and widowhood, although it is unclear whether social networks act as buffers against the negative impact of life events on health, or whether they have a more direct effect, independent of the presence or absence of major life events (Mor-Barak, Miller, and Syme, 1991).

Alternatively, loss of social support through divorce or death of a spouse can contribute to health problems. For example, older people who live alone and are not tied into informal networks are more likely to use formal services and to become institutionalized. Their self-reported well-being tends to be lower; and their burdens of adjusting to widowhood are greater than for those with strong social ties. In fact, several longitudinal studies have found an association between social support structures and reduced mortality risk (Bowling and Grundy, 1998; LaVeist et al., 1997).

Potential Outcomes of Social Supports

- Physical and mental well-being (morale, self-confidence)
- Feelings of personal control, autonomy, and competence
- Successful aging
- Reduced negative effects of stressful life events (bereavement, widowhood)
- Reduced mortality risk

The family—the basic unit of social relationships—is the first topic considered here. We examine the rapid growth of the multigenerational family and how relationships with spouses, adult children, parents, grandparents, siblings, and gay and lesbian partners change with age.

THE CHANGING CONCEPT OF THE AGING FAMILY

There has been a "structural lag" in our tendency to think of families primarily in terms of young children and to overlook the important functions and roles played by older people in contemporary **extended families** (Riley and Riley, 1994). Contrary to the myth of alienation, the family is the primary source of social support for older people. In fact, persons in all stages of life are more likely to have kin relationships involving older people and thus more likely to be part of an extended family than in the past (Uhlenberg, 1996). Nearly 94 percent of adults over age 65, similar to Mrs. Howard in the introductory vignette, have living family members—adult children, grandchildren, partners, and siblings, although this proportion

decreases with age. Although 67 percent live in a family setting (i.e., spouse, children, siblings), older men (80 percent) are more likely to do so than are older women (58 percent) (Administration on Aging, 1999b). However, the proportion living in a family setting decreases with age, with only 45 percent of those over age 85 doing so. As noted in Figure 9.1, about 13 percent (7% of men, 17% of women) are not living with a spouse, but with children, siblings, or other relations (Administration on Aging, 1999b). Older African American women, especially widows, are more likely to live in extended family households than are older white women.

Older people are not only likely to live in a family setting but also to receive assistance from them. Families provide 70 to 80 percent of the in-home care to older people with chronic illness, even when formal services are used selectively (National Alliance for Caregiving and AARP, 1997). The family not only helps directly, but also provides information and advocates for services. As an illustration of the importance of family support, it is estimated that an additional 10 percent of older people would require nursing home placement if families were not providing care in home settings

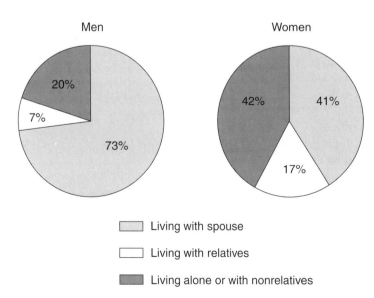

Living with spouse

Living with relatives

Living alone or with nonrelatives

FIGURE 9.1 Living Arrangements of Persons 65+, 1995
SOURCE: U.S. Bureau of the Census, March 1998.

(Hobbs and Damon, 1996). Currently, approximately 25 percent are in a nursing home at some point in time. The assistance of family members is thus often a major determinant of whether an older person lives in a nursing home or in the community. Persons without family ties, primarily widowed women and the oldest-old who have outlived other family members, are most likely to be institutionalized and to need financial assistance from their adult children (Boaz, Hu, and Ye, 1999).

The Multigenerational Family

As noted in Chapter 1, declining mortality has altered the structure of kinship relationships involving older adults. Along with the increase in life expectancy, patterns of earlier remarriage and childbearing in some generations have resulted in the growth of **multigenerational families,** spanning four, and sometimes five, generations. Among adult children, over 70 percent of married couples are part of a three-generation family with at least one living parent and one living child (Boaz et al., 1999; Juster, Soldo, Kington, and Mitchell, 1996). Accordingly, the "young-old," who may be facing their own declines in finances, energy, and health, increasingly have parents and grandparents who require some assistance. In 1900, 50-year-olds had only a 4 percent chance of having two parents still alive; this probability has increased to over 25 percent today. The changing multigenerational dynamics are reflected in the fact that a growing number of people over age 65 have a child who is also over 65, who may then be both a child and a

Family gatherings help maintain intergenerational ties.

grandparent at the same time. Given continuing technological and medical advances, these trends will undoubtedly continue.

The multigenerational family is, in turn, influenced by a number of social trends that affect interactions of family members across generations. Women's labor force participation has increased. Rates of divorce and remarriage and the consequent number of blended families have escalated, with more grandparents responsible for raising grandchildren. New and diverse family structures, such as communal living, cohabitation by unmarried couples, and gay and lesbian partnerships, affect the frequency of interactions and the potential for conflicting relationships. How these various family structures affect obligation, commitment, or resources to meet the needs of older dependents is still largely unknown. It is clear that family relationships inevitably involve both solidarity and

THE STRENGTH OF MULTIGENERATIONAL TIES

During the Summer of 2000, the governments of North and South Korea agreed to an unprecedented reunion of families that had been torn apart during the Korean War. Siblings who had not seen each other since their teens, parents now in their eighties and nineties were reunited with their children who were themselves in their sixties. The fortunate 100 families were selected by lottery from the citizens of North Korea and flown to South Korea for a brief visit. This bittersweet reunion lasted only one week, when those from North Korea were required to return home. Nevertheless, the stories shared by these families provided a dramatic illustration of the endurance of family bonds.

conflict. Cohesion or consensus appears to be based on sharing across generations along a variety of dimensions, including the extent to which they share activities, the degree of positive sentiment, and the exchange of assistance. Less is known about tensions, disagreements, or conflicts across generations over the life course (Bengtson, Rosenthal, and Burton, 1996).

The Role of Culture

Norms of intergenerational contact and **filial responsibility** affect the meaning that a culture attaches to family and care responsibilities (Choi, 1995). American culture places a high value on the family's privacy and independence. What occurs within it is generally viewed as its private affair, not to be interfered with by government or other outside sources. Similarly, family members' independence from each other is emphasized. As a result, family members' emotional interdependence tends to be overlooked. These values affect not only commonly held views of adult child–parent relationships, but also the right of the state to intervene in high-risk family situations, for example, cases of suspected elder abuse and/or neglect. They also partially underlie the relative infrequency of **intergenerational living** in our society. This contrasts with other countries, such as Japan and Mexico, where three- and four-generation families, although a small percentage of the total population, are more likely to live together under one roof. Generally, the extended family is stronger within ethnic minority groups (Markides and Black, 1996). Rapid growth of the multigenerational family, Western societies' emphasis on family privacy, and the increasing demographic, cultural, and economic diversity within our society have all created a wider range of family relationships in old age.

OLDER COUPLES

The marital relationship plays a crucial support function in most older people's lives, especially men's. Of all family members, spouses are most likely to serve as confidants, provide support, fa-

cilitate social interaction, foster emotional well-being, and guard against loneliness (Dykstra, 1995). Nearly 60 percent of the population aged 65 to 74 is married and lives with a spouse in an independent household. Significant differences exist, however, in living arrangements by gender and age. Because of women's longer life expectancy and fewer options for remarriage, 43 percent aged 65 and older are married and living with a spouse, as compared to 75 percent of men (Cohen, 1999) (see Figure 9.2). Accordingly, women represent 80 percent of the older individuals who live alone. Among noninstitutionalized older men, only about 17 percent are living without a partner, compared to 41 percent of their female counterparts. The percentages living with a spouse decline with age and among African Americans and Hispanics, as illustrated in Figure 9.2 (AOA, 1999b). Those living alone typically have higher levels of depression, loneliness, and social isolation, and are more likely to use formal social services (Mui and Burnette, 1994). Accordingly, married people typically benefit from three major health promoters: social support, health monitoring, and stress reduction (Goldscheider, 1994; Miller, Hemesath, and Nelson, 1997). On the other hand, because they often rely on each other, they tend to have smaller and less diverse networks than their unmarried counterparts (Barrett and Lynch, 1999).

Couples are faced with learning to adapt to changing roles and expectations throughout marriage. Family life is characterized by a continual tension between maintaining individual autonomy and negotiating issues of equitable exchange, dependence, and safety. Such tensions are heightened in old age. As partners change roles through retirement, postparenthood, or illness, they face the strain of relinquishing previous roles, adapting to new ones, and experiencing accumulating losses. Failure to negotiate role expectations, such as the division of household tasks after retirement, can result in disagreements and divergent paths. Other challenges that aging couples face are connecting the past with the present, anticipatory mourning, coping with acute illness, and involving adult children in their lives (Mohr, 2000). Retirement can be an especially difficult transition, especially when partners

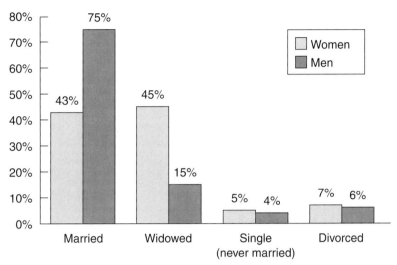

FIGURE 9.2   **Marital Status of Persons 65+, 1998**
SOURCE: AoA 1999.

do not retire at the same time, or where marital satisfaction was already low pre-retirement. Couples typically experience changes in the emotional quality of their relationship, along with conflict over too much time together and the loss of personal space (Hilbourne, 1999). On the other hand, increased time together in shared activities and with friends during retirement can have favorable effects on marital satisfaction (Mohr, 2000).

Strains may be heightened by the fact that long-lived relationships are a contemporary phenomenon. At the end of the nineteenth century, the average length of marriage at the time one's spouse died was about 28 years; now it is over 45 years. Never before in history have the lives of so many couples remained interwoven long enough to encounter the variety of life-changing events that later stages of marriage now bring. Yet most older couples are more likely than younger cohorts to view marriage as a lifetime commitment governed by obligation.

Marital Satisfaction

Despite the challenges inherent in long-lived relationships, most older partners appear satisfied, with men tending to be more pleased with mar-

riage and the degree to which their emotional needs are fulfilled than are women (Bogard and Spilka, 1996). Marital satisfaction has been found to be high among those recently married, lower among those in the childrearing period—especially in middle age—and higher in the later stages. In fact, the strongest predictor of marital satisfaction in later life tends to be the couple's level of satisfaction in the early stages of marriage. Older spouses, especially men, are more likely to report improvement in their marriages over time than younger couples. Although emotional intensity declines, positive interactions with less conflict and less negative sentiment such as sarcasm, disagreement, and criticism tend to increase (Goodman, 1999; Levenson, Cartensen, and Gottman, 1993; Miller et al., 1997).

Increases in marital satisfaction among the young-old may be partially due to children leaving home. Contrary to stereotypes, most women are not depressed when their children leave home, but rather view the **empty nest** as an opportunity for new activities, although both fathers and mothers may initially be unhappy with the change. As noted in Chapter 6, sex-role expectations and behaviors are often relaxed in old age. Men tend to become more affectionate and less career-oriented, and women more achievement-oriented. Successful negotiation of such role changes appears to be related to marital satisfaction. Happy marriages are characterized by more equality and joint decision making through a gradual relaxation of boundaries between sex roles and a decreasing division of household labor based on traditional male/female sex roles (Bogard and Spilka, 1996). Nevertheless, some areas (e.g., dependent care and family finances) typically remain gender-differentiated (Miller and Cafasso, 1992). Freed from the demands of work and parental responsibilities and with more opportunities for companionship, partners may discover or develop common interests and interdependence. As a consequence, expressive aspects of the marriage—affection and companionship—may emerge more fully (House, Mero, and Webster, 1996).

Older partners' ability to negotiate these role transitions depends, in large part, on their prior adaptability and satisfaction in their marital relationship. Studies of marital longevity have found that couples celebrating golden anniversaries (approximately 3 percent of all marriages) are characterized by intimacy, avoidance of hostile control, commitment, congruence of values, religious faith, communication, and an ability to accommodate one another (Goodman, 1999; Robinson and Blanton, 1993). Overall, the perceived rewards from being married appear to strongly influence marital satisfaction (Reynolds, 1995). For happily married older couples, their relationship is central to a "good life." Married persons appear to be happier and healthier, experience higher levels of self-esteem, make fewer demands on the health care system, and live longer than widowed or divorced persons of the same age (Goldman, Korenman, and Weinstein, 1995). In fact, marital satisfaction may be more important than age, health, life expectancy, education, or retirement in predicting life satisfaction and quality of life. These positive effects appear to emanate from three major functions that marriage performs for older couples: intimacy, interdependence, and a sense of belonging. Not surprisingly, unhappy

marriages tend to affect health negatively, especially for women (Levenson et al., 1993).

Although most older couples have been together since young adulthood, a small proportion remarry after widowhood or divorce later in life. Women have fewer options to remarry, since they generally outlive their male peers, and men tend to marry women younger than themselves. The likelihood that widowed men will remarry is seven times greater than for widowed women (Hobbs and Damon, 1996). Moreover, divorced people are more likely to remarry than are the widowed. Desire for companionship and having sufficient economic resources are central considerations in remarriage. A relationship with a partner appears to be of greater importance to men's well-being than to women's (Wright, 1994). Most older people who remarry choose someone they have previously known, with similar backgrounds and interests. Factors that appear to be related to successful late-life remarriages are long prior friendship, family and friends' approval, adequate pooled financial resources, and personal adaptability to life changes. Some older couples choose to live together but not to marry, generally for economic and inheritance reasons.

Spouses as Caregivers

With the increase in life expectancy, more older partners may end up caring for each other, frequently for long periods of time. In fact, over 12 percent of the people who care for older adults are themselves age 65 or older (National Alliance for Caregiving and AARP, 1997). Spouses account for 28 percent of the helpers of Caucasian elders, 20 percent of caregivers of Hispanics, and only 15 percent of carers of African American elders (National Academy on an Aging Society, 2000).

Gender differences exist in spousal caregiving patterns. Reflecting the fact that women outlive men by an average of 7 years, more wives than husbands over age 65 provide care for disabled, often older spouses. While men receive more care on average, they are likely to get that help from only one person, usually a wife. In contrast,

FOR BETTER OR FOR WORSE/ *Lynn Johnston*

SOURCE: © 1991 Lynn Johnston Prod. Reprinted by permission of United Press Syndicate.

women are more likely than men to be assisted by a larger number of caregivers, such as children and grandchildren. Nevertheless, husbands of wives with disabilities are more likely to provide care for their wives than are other family members. In fact, husbands comprise nearly 40 percent of spousal caregivers and are predicted to increase in the future because of declines in male mortality (Kramer and Lambert, 1999; Tennstedt, 1999; Velkoff and Lawson, 1998). Husbands tend to be the first persons called upon to care for their wives, to be the oldest subgroup of caregivers, and to spend the greatest number of hours caregiving. Caregiving husbands are found to experience more strain in the marital relationship, higher rates of depression and unhappiness, and greater declines in their emotional support than caregiving wives do (Harris, 1998; Kramer and Lambert, 1999). Recent research, however, suggests that emotional intimacy

may be more important than gender in the selection of a spouse as caregiver since the marital tie is not always a supportive one (Allen, Goldscheider, and Ciambrone, 1999).

Older caregivers not only face the 24-hour responsibilities of care, but also may be coping with their own aging, physical illnesses, or financial and legal burdens. Stresses of isolation, loneliness, and role overload may be even greater for recently married older couples who cannot draw upon a lifetime of shared experiences. These are also high for spouses who are caring for partners with cognitive impairment and personality changes. Spousal caregiver burden has been found to be associated with depression and grief. The caregiver's health and the quality of the marital relationship (e.g., high levels of spousal interaction and commitment) affect the continuation of the caregiving relationship. Most important, perhaps, is the extent to which caring

A LOVING SPOUSAL CAREGIVER

Sarah and Jim have had a loving marriage of 42 years. Devoted to family and to each other, they enjoy their summers at their island cabin surrounded by children and grandchildren. When Sarah began showing signs of forgetfulness 5 years ago, Jim would gently remind her, excuse her mistakes, and try to structure her day and outings so that others were unaware of her forgetting

things. Over time, he could no longer hide it. Nevertheless, they remained nearly as active as they had their whole lives, going to concerts, church events, and on trips. Jim would lovingly guide Sarah through events—always upbeat, occasionally joking, and never complaining. They both seemed happy and content with their lives, despite Sarah's early Alzheimer's.

for an ill or disabled spouse may be a normative experience—part of the marital contract and necessary for sustaining the quality of the marital relationship (Kramer and Lambert, 1999).

Divorce in Old Age

Even though most older marriages are reasonably happy, a small percentage are not, and an increasing proportion of older couples are choosing to divorce rather than tolerate an unhappy marriage. Although only 5 to 6 percent of older persons are divorced, the numbers have increased four times as fast as the older population as a whole since 1990. Rates are even higher among ethnic minority older adults (AOA, 1997; Hobbs and Damon, 1996).

Although most older people who are divorced were divorced before entering later life, about 5 percent are currently divorced and have not remarried (Cohen, 1999); 10 to 13 percent of persons aged 65 and over have experienced a divorce at some time. The rates are highest among African American older women (Choi, 1995). In fact, these numbers have increased 5 times as fast as the older population as a whole since 1990: 2.8 times for men, 7.4 times for women (Administration on Aging, 1999b). It appears that the frequency of divorce has changed for all ages, with more people of every age seeing divorce as an acceptable option in an unhappy marriage.

The number of divorced older persons is predicted to increase in the future, from approximately 5 percent of older men and women currently to 9 percent and 15 percent, respectively, in the year 2030, when baby boomers are over age 65 (Hobbs and Damon, 1996). There are more older adults who are either not married or are in their second or third marriage. Across all groups, three out of four divorced persons remarry within 5 years. However, the risk of that marriage ending in divorce is ten times that of someone in his or her first marriage (Hammond and Muller, 1992). For older individuals, however, the likelihood of remarriage after widowhood or divorce is relatively small compared to other age groups (Cohen, 1999). These trends clearly affect economic and social status. Being divorced in old age often means economic hardships and a sense of loss for women, as well as diminished socioemotional support at a stage when other supports are also weakened (Miller et al., 1997; Choi, 1996). Men in particular lose the "kin-keeping" function performed by their wives and have less contact with their children (Barrett and Lynch, 1999).

Lesbian and Gay Partners

As we have seen in Chapter 7, the concept of couples in old age needs to be broadened to include gay men and lesbians. Older gay men and lesbians share concerns similar to those of most older adults—loneliness, health, income, caregiving of older relatives—but what is unique is that they have lived the majority of their lives through historical periods actively hostile and oppressive toward homosexuality (Fullmer, 1995). Many older lesbians and gays have faced discrimination from family, friends, and professionals, so their later life development is not affected by sexual orientation per se, but rather by how they cope with the social stigma and low status attached to a gay identity (Adelman, 1990; Cruikshank, 1990).

Some older gay men and lesbians are concerned with "passing" or "being invisible" in a heterosexual society and only marginally accept some aspects of their homosexuality. For many gays and lesbians, they may be the only homosexual in their families of origin, which creates par-

New family structures include gay and lesbian couples with children.

CARE NETWORKS OF OLDER LESBIANS

A group of seven lesbians with varying backgrounds took turns taking care of an 84-year-old, terminally ill, single lesbian, providing transport to medical appointments and leisure activities, coordinating the access to needed services, and talking with her about her life, politics, and dying. The primary physician, a woman with a specialty in geriatrics, became part of the network by responding to calls from the group, making home visits, and supporting their role as caregivers. As death neared, one year later than expected, the woman made arrangements to die where and how she wanted.

ticular concerns because of the biased social context and unique social position in which they live. If they reveal their sexual orientation later in life, they must integrate their past lives into the coming-out process. They may need to give up part of their previously held identity, cope with their grief and that of family members, and be ostracized from children and family of origin at the stage when they most need support (Fullmer, 1995). Not all families are hostile, however, as illustrated by groups such as Parents and Friends of Lesbians and Gays, which support families in the process of accepting a family member's sexual orientation and aim to combat discrimination.

Nevertheless, the majority of older gays and lesbians, especially the young-old, emphasize positive aspects about aging, experience self-acceptance and self-esteem, and have satisfying long-term relationships (Wojciechowski, 1998; Fullmer, 1995). Through the painful process of "coming out," they often become stronger and more competent in adjusting to age-related changes, thereby buffering losses, such as friends and family moving away or dying. Experiencing greater flexibility, freedom, and differentiation in gender-role definitions throughout their lives, gay men and lesbians tend to be more independent, nontraditional, and self-affirming, and to adapt more readily to the role changes associated with aging than their heterosexual peers. Such role flexibility may ease an individual's adjustment when a partner dies or leaves (Wojciechowski, 1998).

By having confronted real or imagined loss of family support earlier in life, gays and lesbians are less likely to assume that families will provide for them in old age and more likely to plan for their own future security. Accordingly, they tend to build a "surrogate family" through a strong network of friends and significant others, which either replaces or reinforces family of origin supports (Dorfman et al., 1995). Some older gay men and lesbians share innovative housing arrangements and are part of an empowering community that may include social support and advocacy organizations. These include Senior Action in a Gay Environment (SAGE) based in New York City, the Lavender Panthers, and the National Association of Lesbian and Gay Gerontologists organized by the American Society on Aging. SAGE, for example, has grown to 20 chapters nationwide and serves old gay men and lesbians through its intergenerational friendly visitors service, housing and legal advocacy, professional counseling, as well as SAGENet, a consortium of groups offering similar services around the nation (Yoakam, 1999). Those who have the support of other gay men and lesbians as friends and confidants, in social organizations, and in housing alternatives tend to be characterized by high self-esteem and life satisfaction, less fear of aging, and greater effectiveness in managing the societal aspects of aging, such as rejection (Slusher, Mayer, and Dunkle, 1996).

Traditional health care treatments have tended to assume that all older people are heterosexual, and to be insensitive to older homosexuals (Wojciechowski, 1998; Roberts and Sorensen, 1995). Despite the fact that most gay men and lesbians have acquired skills and attitudes that facilitate their adjustment to aging, they nevertheless face more structural and legal barriers than heterosexual couples do. The partners of those who are hospitalized or in a skilled nursing facility, retirement

---

POINTS TO PONDER

If you have a brother or sister, try to imagine what your relationship will be like in old age. If you are an only child, have you created other networks that might support you as you grow older?

---

home, or assisted living, or sharing an apartment or room, may be denied access to intensive care units and to medical records; staff may be insensitive to and ignore partners, even limiting their visits and discouraging expressions of affection. Private space for conjugal visits for gay or lesbian couples in nursing homes is limited, and some institutions may admit only one member of a homosexual couple. If a durable power of attorney for health care is not in place, blood relatives, who may be unaware of or opposed to the relationship, can control visitation, treatment options, and discharge planning, and can completely exclude partners. Families may also contest a gay or lesbian partner's right to an inheritance.

SIBLING RELATIONSHIPS

Sibling relationships represent the one family bond with the potential to last a lifetime. Under contemporary mortality conditions, most persons will not experience the death of a sibling until they are past 70 years of age (Uhlenberg, 1996). Most older people, even those over age 80, have at least one sibling, and about 33 percent see a sibling monthly, although yearly visits are most typical. As with other kin-keeping responsibilities, sisters are more likely than brothers to maintain frequent contact with same-sex siblings, generally by phone or face-to-face interaction rather than by letter writing (Cicirelli, 1995).

The sibling relationship in old age is characterized by a shared history, egalitarianism, and increasing closeness, particularly among sisters. Studies based on the criterion of feelings of closeness and affection suggest that siblings often renew past ties as they age, forgive past conflict and rivalry, and become closer, frequently through

shared reminiscence (Adams and Blieszner, 1995; Bengtson et al., 1996; Cicirelli, 1995). Siblings are particularly important sources of psychological support in the lives of never-married older persons and those without children, although their ability to provide support declines with age (Barrett and Lynch, 1999). Given these ties, it is not surprising that some studies have found that bereaved siblings were more impaired and rated their overall health as worse than bereaved spouses or friends who were similarly impaired (Hays, Gold, and Peiper, 1997). Assistance generally increases after a spouse's death; such arrangements help enhance the widowed person's psychological well-being (Cicirelli, 1995). Although siblings are less frequently caregivers to each other than are spouses and adult children (with the exception of caring for the never-married), they do supplement the efforts of others during times of crisis or special need. The very existence of siblings as a possible source of help may be important, even if such assistance is rarely used (Cicirelli, 1995).

The steadily increasing rate of divorce and remarriage will undoubtedly affect sibling relationships. With the increase in blended families through remarriage, there will be more half-siblings and step-siblings. For divorced older people who do not remarry, interactions with siblings may become more important than when they were married (Goldscheider, 1994).

NEVER-MARRIED OLDER PEOPLE

Approximately 4 percent of the older population has never married (Hobbs and Damon, 1996). Contrary to a commonly held image of lonely social isolates, the majority of never-married older persons typically develop **reciprocal support** relationships with other kin, especially siblings, and with friends and neighbors. They may be more socially active and resourceful, with more diversity in their social networks, especially with younger persons, friends and neighbors, and siblings, than their married counterparts. They are also more likely to turn to formal services than others, especially if they live alone. When they need assistance from others, they are more likely to turn to siblings, friends, neighbors and paid helpers than are their married peers (Barrett and Lynch, 1999; Tennstedt, 1999). Compared to widowed peers, they tend to be more satisfied with their lives, to be self-reliant, and to be focused on the present. Accustomed to their independence, they are not necessarily lonely (Dykstra, 1995).

Increasing numbers of organizations specifically for single people have formed, although many of these are for younger singles. Alternative living arrangements, such as multigenerational share-a-home programs, and assisted living facilities may also appeal to some single older adults who choose not to live alone. The proportion of single men and women is likely to grow with the aging of the Baby Boomers (Choi, 1996).

CHILDLESS OLDER ADULTS

Although the majority of older people have living children, approximately 20 percent are childless, and thus lack the natural support system of children and grandchildren (Hobbs and Damon, 1996). The adage that "children will take care of you in your old age" contains some degree of truth. Childless older people have been found to have fewer social contacts than their counterparts with living children, yet they are not necessarily unhappy or dissatisfied (Beckman, 1985). Other relatives are most important for performing instrumental tasks, while friends typically give emotional support. When faced with health problems, childless elders turn first to their spouses (if available) for support, then to siblings, then nieces and nephews. Childless older individuals also have a higher probability of illness, living alone, and limited emotional support. Given these factors, it is not surprising that unmarried childless elders utilize social services and nursing homes more than do married childless persons (Choi-Namkea, 1994; Wu and Pollard, 1998).

On the other hand, some childless unmarried older people, particularly women, develop kin-like or "sisterly" nonkin relations and may be quite satisfied with their lives. Yet they may not want these relationships to be a source of care, fearing the change of voluntary mutuality into dependency (Rubenstein, Alexander, Goodman, and Luborsky, 1991; Wu and Pollard, 1998). The number of childless and unmarried older individuals is likely to grow, which may affect the proportion of older people who will seek both formal and informal supports in the future.

THE REALITIES OF AGING FAMILIES

- The family is the primary source of support for older people.
- Most older people have family members.
- Most older people, especially elders of color, live in some type of family setting.
- Multigenerational (4 and 5 generations) families are growing.
- The number of blended families is increasing.
- The range of alternative family structures is expanding.

- Spouses are the most important family relationship.
- Spouses are the primary family caregivers, followed by adult children.
- Sibling relationships increase in importance with age.
- Never-married and childless older adults are not necessarily lonely.
- Intergenerational relationships tend to be reciprocal.

OTHER KIN

Interaction with secondary kin—cousins, aunts, uncles, nieces, and nephews—appears to depend on geographic proximity, availability of closer relatives, and preference. Extended kin can replace or substitute for missing or lost relatives, especially during family rituals and holidays. For example, compared to their white counterparts, African American childless elders often turn to nieces and nephews when siblings are not available. Personal or historical connections that allow for remembering pleasurable events may be more important than closeness of kinship in determining interactions.

INTERGENERATIONAL RELATIONSHIPS: ADULT CHILDREN

After spouses, adult children are the most important source of informal support and social contact in old age. Typically, the flow of support is not unidirectional from adult child to older parent, but rather exchanges are reciprocal (Velkoff and Lawson, 1998). Over 80 percent of persons age 65 and over have surviving children, although the number of children in a family has decreased—a trend expected to continue. The majority of older adults live near at least one adult child, sharing a social life but not a home (Juster et al., 1996). Most older people state that they prefer not to live with their children, generally for reasons of privacy and a sense of autonomy. Although less than 20 percent of older persons live in their children's households, this percentage increases with advancing age and extent of functional disability, and for widowed, separated, and divorced older adults. Approximately 33 percent of all men and 50 percent of all women age 65 and over who are widowed, separated, or divorced share a home with their children or other family members. Some research identifies that most older adults prefer to live with their children to avoid a nursing home, although children are less willing than their par-

ents to share a residence. When older parents do live with their children, they usually live with a daughter (Boaz et al., 1999; National Alliance for Caregiving and AARP, 1997). However, less than 14 percent of those aged 65 to 75 and 4 percent of those aged 85 and older live in multigenerational households composed of parents, children, and grandchildren (Hobbs and Damon, 1996). These percentages are higher, however, among some families of color, especially African Americans (Taylor and Chatters, 1991).

Although most older parents and adult children do not live together, they nevertheless see each other frequently. Studies over the past two decades indicate the following:

- Approximately 50 percent of older people have daily contact with children.
- Nearly 80 percent see an adult child at least once a week.
- More than 75 percent talk on the phone at least weekly (AOA, 1997; Bengtson et al., 1996; Hansson and Carpenter, 1994; Hobbs and Damon, 1996).

Older children, especially daughters, are more likely to maintain contact with their parents. However, these factors are less important than proximity and socioeconomic status, with more frequent contact among higher-income families (Greenwald and Bengtson, 1995). Less is known about the quality than about the frequency of interactions between older parents and their adult children. Nevertheless, most intergenerational relationships involve some types of conflict, with parents concerned about their children's habits and lifestyle choices, and children noting differences in communication and interaction styles. Despite such widely occurring conflicts, most intergenerational families report affection and mutual support and a desire for more satisfying relationships with each other. This is the paradoxical nature of family relationships over the life course in which solidarity and conflict fluctuate (Clarke, Preston, Raskin, and Bengtson, 1999).

Geographic separation of family members is generally due to mobility of the adult children, not of the older relatives. Future cohorts of older persons may have an increasing proportion of distant children because of the growing trend toward greater residential separation between adult children and older parents. For many families, Christmas or Thanksgiving may be the only times adult children return home, and they may even miss these special events because of other commitments. Older parents who live closer to their children have more contact with them, greater affection for them, and are more involved with grandchildren, although geographic separation does not necessarily weaken socioemotional bonds and "intimacy at a distance" can occur (Silverstein and Angelelli, 1998). Older parents expect to move closer to an adult child out of need (poor health, living alone, adult child who is financially better-off than they are) and tend to select the child with the greatest potential to provide support (most often the oldest daughter). Mental health professionals and health care providers need to recognize how each generation faces its own developmental transitions as well as complex cross-generational issues (Hargrave and Hanna, 1997).

Patterns of Intergenerational Assistance

Generally, families establish a pattern of reciprocal support between older and younger members that continues throughout an individual's lifetime. Consistent with social exchange theory discussed in Chapter 8, those with more valued resources (e.g., money or good health) assist those with less. Not only concrete assistance is exchanged, but also emotional and **social support** (Rossi and Rossi, 1990). At various points, older parents provide substantial support, especially financial assistance, to their children and grandchildren, oftentimes at a geographic distance. Regardless of socioeconomic status, most **intergenerational transfers** of resources, especially of knowledge and financial support, go from parent to child (Juster et al., 1996). On the

other hand, adult children who are not married and generally have fewer financial resources than married peers are more likely to transfer resources to parents (Boaz et al., 1999; Juster et al., 1996) Contrary to stereotypes, however, most adult children are not motivated by the expectation of an inheritance when they assist their older parents (Sloan, Picone, and Hoerger, 1997).

In some instances, parents continue to provide care to adult children beyond normative expectations of "launching" one's adult children to be more independent. For example, parental care remains a central role late in life for parents of adult children who are developmentally disabled or chronically mentally ill. Yet many parents who are caregivers of adult children with disabilities are facing their own age-related limits in functional ability, energy, and financial resources, which can affect their ability to provide care. The history of and the cumulative nature of care demands can make their situation particularly stressful (Kelly and Kropf, 1995; Smith, Tobin, and Fullmer, 1995). A major worry is how their child will be cared for after their own deaths or if they themselves develop a debilitating illness. Despite their worry, most such caregiving parents do not make concrete long-term plans about where their children will eventually live (Freedman, Krauss, and Seltzer, 1997). Not surprisingly, when parental caregivers die, their adult children with mental disorders often experience housing disruptions and potentially traumatic transitions (Lefley and Hatfield, 1999). As the population of adults with chronic illness or developmental disabilities grows, both the aging and developmentally disabled service networks are initiating new support systems. These include respite care, more residential alternatives, and assistance with permanency planning (e.g., developing plans for permanent housing in the community) (Kelly and Kropf, 1995; Smith and Tobin, 1993). Fortunately, the Planned Lifetime Assistance Network (PLAN) is now available in some states through the National Alliance for the Mentally Ill. PLAN provides lifetime assistance to individuals with disabilities whose parents or other family members are deceased or no longer able to provide care (Lefley and Hatfield, 1999).

GRANDPARENTHOOD AND GREAT-GRANDPARENTHOOD

At the turn of the twentieth century, families with grandparents were rare. Now, with the increase in life expectancy, more older people are experiencing the role of grandparenthood and, increasingly, of great-grandparenthood, although they have proportionately fewer grandchildren. For women especially, the status of grandparenthood can engage 50 percent of their lives. Of the 80 percent of older people with children, 94 percent are grandparents and nearly 50 percent are great-grandparents. Another way of grasping the significance of this change is that, over 66 percent of adult children have begun life with all grandparents living, and more than 75 percent have at least one grandparent alive when they reach age 30 (Uhlenberg, 1996). In fact, the prevalence of grandparents who have adult grandchildren is historically unprecedented.

Approximately 75 percent of these grandparents see some of their grandchildren every week or two, and nearly 50 percent see a grandchild every day or so, although only about 5 percent of the households headed by older people include grandchildren (Giarrusso, Silverstein, and Bengtson, 1996). Geographic proximity appears to be more important than whether the grandparents get along with their own children in determining frequency of visits. On the other hand, geographic distance is not necessarily a barrier. This is especially true when a close relationship is established early in a child's life. Grandparent–grandchild relationships change over time; contact and expectation of closeness decline as grandchildren become older. However, some young adult grandchildren express more affection toward their grandparents as they get older. This is more likely to occur with grandmothers, particularly when the two generations are geographically near (Coony and Smith, 1996).

The meanings and functions of grandparenthood must be viewed within the societal context described previously. These include the effects of geographic mobility, divorce, reconstituted families, and employed middle-aged women who are also grandmothers. There is wide diversity among grandparents, who vary in age from late thirties to over 100 years, with grandchildren ranging from newborns to retirees. Accordingly, there are multiple grandparenting roles and meanings. A systems perspective, rather than a focus on grandparenthood as an individual attribute, better accounts for the complexity of the grandparent–grandchild relationship. This perspective takes account of the reciprocal and continually changing relationships that exist across generations, and recognizes that although nuclear families are becoming smaller, more members of more generations who share a greater part of each other's life spans are alive at one time. The grandparent–grandchild bond is initially mediated by parents, but this bond becomes more direct as time passes, and can be substantially altered by events such as divorce. The potential for direct voluntary interaction between young adult children and their grandparents benefits not only the individuals involved, but also the total kinship system.

Age, proximity, frequency of contact, and parental influences all affect the extent of satisfaction that grandparents derive from the role (Peterson, 1999). Early studies typically found the role to be peripheral and not a primary source of identity, interaction, or satisfaction (Wood and Robertson, 1976). A major study, reported by Neugarten and Weinstein (1964), found that older adults could be categorized by the meaning they gave to the role and by their style of grandparenting. The prime significance of grandparenthood was reported to be biological renewal and/or continuity (i.e., seeing oneself extended into the future), and emotional self-fulfillment, especially the opportunity to be a better grandparent than parent. In terms of style, older grandparents were more apt to be formal or distant, whereas younger ones emphasized mutuality, informality, and playfulness. Surprisingly, about 30 percent did not derive satisfaction from grandparenting, describing the role as difficult, disappointing, and unpleasant. Satisfaction with grandparenting did not vary by by gender.

More recent research has found that grandparents derive great emotional satisfaction from frequent interaction with their grandchildren and from the opportunity to observe their grandchildren's development and share in their activities. In the absence of a family crisis, grandparents' roles emphasize emotional gratification from watching their grandchildren's development and serving as a symbol of continuity and stability in family rituals and values. Grandparenthood thus provides opportunities for older people to experience feelings of immortality, relive their lives through grandchildren, indulge grandchildren with unconditional love, and develop an increased sense of well-being and morale (Peterson, 1999; Strom, Buki, and Strom, 1997).

Findings are mixed about whether the grandparent relationship differs by gender; typically grandfathers are most closely linked to sons of sons, and grandmothers to daughters of daughters. Grandmothers tend to be more expressive, having more influence on how their grandchildren relate to family and friends, while grandfathers are more instrumental. However, both express strong affection and feelings of closeness toward their grandchildren (Kivett, 1991). This reflects the increased acceptance of their nurturing side in men as they age, described in Chapter 6. Recent studies suggest that frequency of contact may be more important than gender in terms of grandparents' satisfaction (Peterson, 1999). It is unclear whether contemporary fathers who are more directly involved in parenting will become more invested in the roles of grandfather and great-grandfather in the future.

Even less is known about how the grandparenthood role and its meaning vary by ethnic minority status. In an analysis of intergenerational family relations in Mexican American families, strong ties were observed between grandparents and grandchildren. Despite the majority of grandparents living in poverty, the flow of financial assistance in these families was generally from the older to the younger generations (Dietz, 1995).

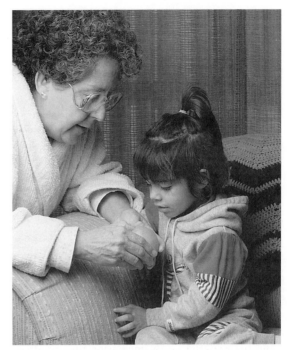

Grandparents as primary caregivers for grandchildren is a growing phenomenon.

Some studies suggest greater interactions through an extended kin network and more grandparent responsibility for childrearing among ethnic minorities. When the child's mother is a single parent, the grandmother may have responsibilities essential to the child's care (Burnette, 1997; Chalfie, 1994), especially in urban African American families. In white families and in families of color, grandparent involvement in childrearing may be a consequence of teen pregnancy, substance abuse, AIDS, incarceration, emotional problems, and parental death, combined with limited financial resources. In a growing number of instances, grandparents are the sole providers for their grandchildren.

Grandparents as Primary Caregivers of Grandchildren

Nearly 4 million children (5.5 percent of all children under age 18) now live with grandparents,

GRANDPARENTS AS CAREGIVERS

Mary long ago earned her stripes as a mom. She raised five children alone, in a tough Los Angeles neighborhood, and managed to put them through college or vocational training. She had looked forward to retirement and being a loving grandmother, to spoiling her grandchildren on visits and then sending them home. But her life has not turned out as expected. Instead, she's raising her 8-year-old grandson, James, alone, since the incarceration of her daughter and the boy's father for selling drugs.

When Mary's daughter was charged for possession of drugs, Mary could not bear the thought of her grandson being raised by strangers in the foster care system. She petitioned the courts to become his guardian. Her daughter has only contacted her son twice in the past four years. This has made the adjustment difficult for Mary and James, who often lashes out at his grandmother. Mary tries to provide as much love and stability for him as possible, helping him with his homework, assisting with his Cub Scout troop, and attending all his school events. She derives some emotional rewards from these activities with James, but misses activities with her peers. Many of her friends have dropped away, as they have more freedom to "take off and do things." She also struggles with guilt about her daughter and her situation. She has turned her anger and grief into organizing local support groups for others like herself and pressuring legislators to recognize caregiving grandparents' needs.

most often a grandmother, and in a third of these cases, neither parent is present. Many of these children have special needs, increasing the grandparents' responsibilities (Burnette, 1999). In fact, the incidence of grandparents as the custodial caregivers of grandchildren has doubled in the last decade. Ten percent of grandparents assume grandchild care for at least 6 months and often longer, typically before the child turns 5. For most custodial grandmothers, the duration of caregiving ranges from 3 to 10 years (Burnette, 1999; Fuller-Thomson, Minkler, and Driver, 1997; Pruchno, 1999; Velkoff and Lawson, 1998). The young ages of the children suggest that many grandparents may continue to be caregivers as they reach their sixties, seventies, and even eighties—and as they face increased risks of poor health (Brouard, 1995). Many older people who had looked forward to retirement and the "empty nest," and whose health and financial status may be declining, may instead be faced with the problems of sleepless nights, childhood illness, and locating child care. In addition, they may be responsible for their adult children who are coping with personal issues, such as substance abuse, incarceration, AIDS, or child abuse.

Although custodial grandparenting cuts across gender, class, and ethnic lines, there is a disproportionate representation by single women, African Americans, Hispanics, and low-income persons and those living in urban areas. For example, 29 percent of caregiving grandparents are African American, and African Americans are nearly twice as likely to assume this responsibility as their white counterparts (Burnette, 1999). This may reflect a long tradition of caring across generations that has its roots in West African culture. However, the experience of many of today's African American grandmothers may be very different from that of their foremothers, who took on caregiving under different historical circumstances. In fact, 25 percent of African American caregiving grandmothers and 81 percent of Latino custodial grandparents live below the poverty line. Caregiving grandparents are 60 percent more likely than noncustodial grandparents to report incomes below poverty and twice as likely to have major symptoms of depression as those not raising grandchildren. In addition, Latino grandparent caregivers have been found to lack reliable help with their childrearing, especially in skipped generational families (Burnette, 1999; Minkler and Fuller-Thomson, 1997; Pruchno, 1999).

Grandparents who are the sole surrogate parents may experience not only financial difficulties,

ISSUES FOR GRANDPARENTS IN RAISING THEIR GRANDCHILDREN

Legal

- Guardianship and custody, which provide parental authority, but with parental visitation rights
- Adoption, which gives grandparents all authority
- Foster parenthood

Financial

- Temporary Assistance for Needy Families (TANF)
- Food stamps
- Supplemental Security Income (SSI)
- Public housing
- Foster care payment
- Adoption assistance

Childcare (day care, preschool, babysitters)

Medical insurance
- Medicaid but not Medicare
- Private insurance

Schooling
- Public schooling
- Testing evaluation
- Remedial education

Psychological/emotional challenges for the child (loss, confusion, anger)

Psychological/emotional challenges for the grandparent
- Stress
- Parent effectiveness training
- Support groups

---

but also health problems, declines in social activities, strains in relationships with other family members, and a decrease in subjective well-being. In fact, nearly 25 percent experience depression (Burnette, 1999). Grandmothers tend to face more difficulties than grandfathers, with problems intensified for those living alone and from lower educational backgrounds (Szinovacz, DeViney, and Atkinson, 1999). The 1996 Welfare Reform Act, which limits the child welfare and Supplemental Security Income benefits that caregiving grandparents can receive, has hurt the economic health of many intergenerational households headed by grandparents. The increase in caregiving among grandparents thus often reflects differential opportunities of gender and socioeconomic class, not cultural differences. Caregiving strains are thus exacerbated by the cumulative effects of lifelong structural inequities. Even if grandparents are not the primary caregiver, more than 16 percent of preschool children with employed mothers are cared for by a grandparent, typically the grandmother (Velkoff and Lawson, 1998). Such care may be integral to family functioning, especially for Asian families, or in Afro-Caribbean countries,

where "skip" generation families are frequent, due to the migration of the middle generation to urban areas for work.

The 1995 White House Conference on Aging was the first to include resolutions related to grandparenting. Recognizing the need of grandparents for support and information, nearly 700 organizations nationally have developed newsletters, support groups, technical assistance, and seed grants to initiate services. Some of these are listed in the "Resources" at the end of this chapter.

Although these groups provide vital socioemotional support, they lack the ability to address the financial and health strain caused by such long-term responsibilities. Grandmothers have also identified the need for intergenerational senior housing, respite child care, legal counseling concerning foster care and guardianship, physical and mental health services for themselves, as well as financial assistance, and training programs for coping with drug-dependent family members (Burnette, 1999; Bengtson et al., 1996). Eighteen states now have subsidized guardianship programs, which provide financial and legal support, but these require children to become wards of the state. Fortunately, some states have enacted de facto custodian laws, giving long-term grandparent caregivers the same status as parents. And a small number of cities are developing senior housing designed exclusively for grandparent-headed households.

Despite the stress of caregiving, such intergenerational solidarity can benefit both the grandparent and the grandchild. Caregiving grandparents can ameliorate the negative impact of family disruption caused by divorce, drugs, and other social problems. Indirectly, they can influence the grandchild in symbolic ways (e.g., provide "roots") and act as "watchdogs." Children raised solely by grandparents have been found to fare well relative to children raised within other alternative family structures. They tend to be healthier and have fewer behavioral problems in school than children living with only one biological parent, although they are more likely to have difficulties in academic performance (Fuller-Thomson et al., 1997; Solomon and Marx, 1995).

Great-Grandparents

More recently, the role of great-grandparent has emerged with increasing frequency. There appear to be two predominant styles of performing this role. The most common, which tends to characterize generations separated by physical distance, is remote, involving only occasional and somewhat ritualistic contact on special occasions such as holidays and birthdays. Despite the remote nature of contacts, however, great-grandparents derive considerable emotional satisfaction and a sense of personal and familial renewal from seeing a fourth generation as representing family continuity. Living long enough to be a great-grandparent is viewed as a positive sign of successful aging or longevity. The other common great-grandparenting style occurs when great-grandparents are geographically close (within 25 miles) to the fourth generation, and thus have opportunities for emotional closeness to great-grandchildren as well. Even great-grandparents who are in their seventies and eighties may serve as babysitters, go shopping, and take trips with their great-grandchildren.

These activities provide diversions in their lives and can lead to renewed zeal. Such positive interactions will undoubtedly be more common in the future, when great-grandparenthood is the norm and the oldest-old generations are healthier than current cohorts. Consistent with the reciprocal nature of most intergenerational relationships, growing numbers of grandchildren care for great-grandparents (Roberto, 1990).

The Effects of Divorce on Grandparenthood

The growing divorce rate, discussed earlier, is a social trend that is affecting the meaning of grandparenthood. As noted above, at least 50 percent of all persons marrying today will face divorce. The consequences of this for younger generations—over 30 percent of children living in one-parent families or with neither parent—clearly influence the nature of the grandchild–grandparent relationship (U.S. Bureau of the Census, 1996). Since the tie between young grandchildren and their grandparents is mediated by the grandchildren's parents, divorce disrupts these links, changes the balance of resources within the extended family, and requires a renegotiation of existing bonds. Who is awarded custody primarily affects the frequency of interaction with grandchildren; the grandparents whose child, typically the mothers', is awarded custody have more contact (Cooney and Smith, 1996; Kruk, 1995). Controversies regarding **grandparents' rights** for visiting and proposed state legislation to ensure such rights highlight the issues faced by grandparents when the in-law is awarded custody and controls the amount of grandchild–grandparent interactions. This loss of contact often has negative consequences for the grandparents (Kruk, 1995). Groups such as Grandparents Anonymous, the Foundation for Grandparenting, and Grandparents'-Children's Rights are pressing for grandparents' visitation rights legislation in several states.

During the past two decades, most states have passed laws granting grandparents the right to petition a court to legally obtain visitation privileges

---

GRANDPARENTING AND LEGAL ISSUES

Laura and David's son was killed in an auto accident. He left behind two girls, 3 and 5 and their biological mother, who was his girlfriend. They had always been close to the grandchildren, and involved in taking care of them. After his death, his girlfriend returned to assume responsibility for the girls. In her grief and anger, the girlfriend claimed the grandparents had no legal right to visit the two girls and refused to allow contact. She later married, and her new husband felt even more strongly that Laura and David should not be allowed to visit the girls. The grandparents took their case to court, but the court ruled in favor of the biological mother.

---

with their grandchildren. In 1983, a uniform nationwide statute was passed that ensures grandparents visitation rights even if parents object. However, in June 2000, the U.S. Supreme Court ruled by a 6–3 vote that the right of responsible parents to raise their children as they see fit takes precedence over state laws that give grandparents wide visitation rights. Any state law must respect parents' wishes. These rulings raise complex issues for the involved generations and may place children in intergenerational conflicts. The long-term effects for grandchildren from visiting noncustodial grandparents over the objections of a parent are as yet unclear. What is apparent is that factors outside the family, such as the courts, are playing a larger role in how some families resolve conflicts and thus in children's development.

Conversely, complex issues have also emerged concerning the liability of grandparents and stepgrandparents for support of grandchildren in the absence of responsible parents. When divorce in the parent generation occurs, the norm of noninterference by grandparents generally disappears. Instead, grandparents, especially those on the side of the custodial parent, provide substantial assistance to their grandchildren, function as surrogate parents, and mediate tensions. Grandparents have been referred to as "the family watchdogs," who are in the background during tranquil times, but are ready to step in during an emergency (Roberto, 1990).

Despite the fact that blended families constitute about 50 percent of all households with children (National Academy on Aging, 1994), little is known about step-grandparenting relationships.

From a grandparent's perspective, the growing phenomenon of divorce-remarriage means sharing grandchildren with their newly acquired relatives under conditions in which grandchildren will be scarcer because of declining birthrates. Grandchildren, in turn, may find themselves with four or more sets of grandparents. Kinship systems are further complicated by the fact that, with the increased divorce rate after 20+ years of marriage, grandparents may no longer be married to one another. It is difficult to predict the magnitude of the effects—positive and negative—of these trends on intergenerational relations because of the relatively limited research in this area.

FRIENDS AND NEIGHBORS AS SOCIAL SUPPORTS

Although the majority of older people live with others, 30 percent of those over 65 and 46 percent of those over 85 live alone. In fact, the rate of older persons living alone increased by one-and-a-half times the growth rate for older people in general since 1970. Those living alone are most likely to be women, people of color, the oldest-old, and adults of low socioeconomic status. They tend to rely on formal services more than on support from friends and neighbors in their efforts to continue living independently in the community. They also report less satisfaction with the quality of their lives than married people (Hobbs and Damon, 1996).

As will be noted in Chapter 11, among those living alone, the most vulnerable are the homeless.

Neighbors are an important source of assistance for older adults.

While 27 percent of the homeless are estimated to be age 50 and over (including those who live in missions on skid row), their absolute numbers are increasing, especially among women. Characterized by higher rates of physical or mental disorders, economic deprivation, and alcohol misuse than the older population in general, homeless elders tend not to be tied into services and typically have fewer social supports (DeMallie et al., 1997). Coping with chronic stress, they may become further socially isolated rather than seeking social support (Hansson and Carpenter, 1994).

Men, the widowed, and the childless are the most vulnerable to being without support in times of need, often exacerbating health problems and institutionalization as a result. A small percent of older persons living alone do not even have phone conversations with friends and neighbors (Administration on Aging, 1997).

However, most older adults who live alone, and the estimated 5 percent without family ties, such as Mr. Valdres in one of the introductory vignettes to Part Four, have some friends and acquaintances to whom they can turn in emergencies. Although contact with friends tends to decline with age, the majority of older adults have at least one close friend with whom they are in frequent contact (Adams and Blieszner, 1995).

In fact, older persons who have kin may turn more to friends and neighbors for immediate assistance than to family, in part because friendship involves more voluntary and reciprocal exchanges between equals, consistent with social exchange theory described in Chapter 8 (Hatch and Bulcroft, 1992). Whether family, friends, or neighbors become involved appears to vary with the type of task to be performed, as well as the helper's characteristics, such as proximity, extent of long-term commitment, and degree of interaction. Friends and neighbors are well-suited to provide emotional support and to perform predictable tasks, such as transportation and running errands, while families are best equipped for personal care (Dykstra, 1995). Among populations of color, friends often link older persons to needed community services. In fact, African American peers have been found more likely than whites to provide and receive both instrumental and emotional support (Silverstein and Waite, 1993; Taylor and Chatters, 1991). Non-kin helpers also often link older people, particularly minority elders, to needed community services. Even friends facing chronic health problems may still be able to assist others, such as by listening and offering advice and support.

Friends are often important sources of intimacy, especially when compared to relatives other than marital partners (MacRae, 1996; Wright, 1994). This is especially true after major role transitions such as widowhood or retirement; for example, an older widow generally prefers help from confidantes because relatives may reinforce her loss of identity as "wife." To the extent that friendships can satisfy social and material needs, and allow for reciprocity in relationships, they can compensate for the absence of a partner and can help mitigate loneliness (Adams and Blieszner, 1995; Dykstra, 1995; Field, 1999). The role of friend can be maintained long after the role of worker, organization member, or spouse is lost. The extent of reciprocity and quality of interaction, not the quantity, appear to be the critical factors in the maintenance of

---

FRIENDSHIPS AMONG OLDER WOMEN

Five women had gone to high school together, married their high school sweethearts, and remained in the same Midwest town, raising their children, volunteering, and working part-time. They met occasionally to play bridge, helped watch each other's children, and shared in the joys and sadness of family life. Within an eight-year time period, all became widows. They began to meet more often than when their husbands were alive—joining each other for meals, shopping trips, and bridge. When one of the women, Marge, suffered a stroke, the other four became her primary caregivers—bringing her food, accompanying her to the doctor, visiting with her daily, and helping to clean her home. This friendship network greatly relieved the caregiving burden for Marge's daughter.

---

friendship networks. For instance, an intimate friendship with a confidant has been found to be as effective as several less intimate ones in preventing the demoralization often produced by widowhood and retirement (Lowenthal and Haven, 1968). Friendship quality, including reciprocity among friends, has been found to be strongly related to psychological well-being and happiness (Adams and Blieszner, 1995).

Older people who refuse to leave their own homes and communities in order to live with or near their adult children may recognize that friends are important sources of companionship, and that replacing lost friends can be difficult in old age. Although mortality among one's peers in the short run reduces the number of friends, most older people are steadily making new friends from acquaintances and neighbors, and close relationships generally get closer with age (Adams and Blieszner, 1995).

Gender differences in friendships are more important than life course differences. Women in general, such as Mrs. Howard in the introductory vignette to Part Four, have more intimate, diverse, and intensive friendships than men, who tend to have more acquaintances and who place a higher value on career-oriented activities (Moen, Erickson, Dempster-McClain, 2000). For many men, their wives are their only confidants, a circumstance that may make widowhood devastating for them. In contrast, women tend to satisfy their needs for intimacy throughout their lives by establishing close friendships with other women and therefore are less dependent emotionally on the marital relationship. When faced with widowhood, divorce, or separation, they can turn to these friends. Accordingly, widowed older women tend to receive more help and emotional support from friends than married older women. The resilience of some older women, in fact, may be rooted in their ability to form close reciprocal friendships (Riley and Riley, 1994). A longitudinal study of friendships found that men experienced a decline on several friendship measures as they aged: number of new friends, desire for close friendships, the intimate nature of interactions, and involvement in beyond-family activities (Field, 1999).

Both men and women tend to select friends from among people they consider their social peers—those who are similar in age, sex, marital status, sexual orientation, and socioeconomic class. Most choose age peers as their friends, even though common sense would suggest that age-integrated friendship networks can reduce their vulnerability to losses as they age. A person's adult children are not likely to be chosen as confidants, primarily because of their being from different cohorts who are at different places in the life cycle and more likely to produce an inequality of exchange. Age homogeneity plays a strong role in facilitating friendships in later life, in part because of shared life transitions, reduced cross-generational ties with children and work associates, and possible parity of exchange. Age as a basis for friendship may be most pronounced at those stages where the individual's ties to other networks are loosened. The percentage of friends providing help declines after age 85, especially for assistance with personal care (Kincade et al., 1996). For the most part, friends and neighbors play smaller roles in the long-term helping network than family. Although they are important resources when children are unavailable, their helping efforts usually do not approach those of family members in duration or intensity, and do not fully compensate for the loss of spouse or children (DeMallie, North, and Smith, 1997; Dykstra, 1995). Friendships can also be characterized by negative interactions, such as unwanted advice or assistance, and may become strained by excessive demands for assistance (Hansson and Carpenter, 1994).

INTERVENTIONS TO STRENGTHEN OR BUILD SOCIAL SUPPORTS

Because of the importance of peer-group interactions for well-being, there have been increased efforts to strengthen existing community ties or to create new ones if networks are nonexistent. Consistent with the person–environment model, such interventions are ways to alter the environment to be supportive of the older person. They can be categorized as personal network building, volunteer linking, mutual help networks, and neighborhood and community development. They aim to build upon the strengths and resources of local communities, including communities of color. Increasingly, these interventions include an intergenerational component.

Personal network building aims to strengthen existing ties, often through **natural helpers**—people turned to because of their concern, interest, and innate understanding. Such natural helpers can provide emotional support, assist with problem-solving, offer concrete services, and act as advocates. Neighbors often perform natural helping roles, and may strengthen these activities through organized block programs and block watches. Even people in service positions, often referred to as **gatekeepers,** can fulfill natural helping functions, because of the visibility of their positions and the regularity of their interactions with the older per-

son. For example, postal alert systems, whereby postal carriers observe whether an older person is taking in the mail each day, build upon routine everyday interactions. Pharmacists, ministers, bus drivers, local merchants, beauticians, and managers of housing for older people, as in the case of Mr. Valdres in the introductory vignette, are frequently in situations to provide companionship, advice, and referrals. In high-crime areas, local businesses, bars, and restaurants may have a "safehouse" decal in their windows, indicating where residents of all ages can go in times of danger or medical emergencies. These community-based supports are further described in Chapter 11.

Churches may also serve to strengthen and build personal networks, in some cases providing a surrogate family for older people. National initiatives affiliated with churches and synagogues emphasize empowering older people through caring for each other. Through intergenerational programs, church members can provide help with housework, home repair, transportation, and meal preparation, as well as psychological assurance. At the same time, older members may take on many leadership and teaching roles within the church, thereby enhancing their sense of belonging and self-worth, as in the example of Mr. Mansfield on p. 254. In many private and public programs, *volunteers* are commonly used to develop new networks or expand existing ones for older persons. For example, volunteers provide chore services in older people's homes, offer peer counseling and senior center outreach activities, and serve as Friendly Visitors. The Internet, e-mail, the Web, and interactive television also provide new opportunities for network building with peers and across generations for those with access to such information technology (Furlong, 1997).

Another approach aims to create or promote the supportive capacities of *mutual help networks,* especially through joint problem-solving and reciprocal exchange of resources. Mutual help efforts may occur spontaneously, as neighbors watch out for each other, or may be facilitated by professionals. They may also be formed on the basis of neighborhood ties or around shared prob-

---

INFORMATION TECHNOLOGY AND COMMUNITY BUILDING

When the public library in a small Massachusetts town began to offer computer training, they expected the classes to be filled with teenagers and young adults. Instead, the classes were filled with adults over age 55, eager to learn how to e-mail their friends and families spread around the country, and to use the Internet to search for information related to their town's history, medical care, and Internet classes.

---

lems, such as widow-to-widow programs, and support groups for caregivers of family members with chronic impairments. Interacting with peers who share experiences may reduce stress and expand problem-solving capacities (Pillemer and Suitor, 1996). A growing number of mutual help efforts are **intergenerational programs,** linking older people with school children, high-risk youth, and children with special needs. After-school telephone support, tutoring, and day-care programs have been initiated by Retired Senior Volunteer Programs around the country. The Foster Grandparents Program brings together low-income elders and disadvantaged youths, benefiting both young and older participants. The Internet is also providing new ways in which older adults can connect with peers and family, sharing resources, information, and peer support.

Neighborhood and community development is another approach that attempts to strengthen a community's self-help and problem-solving capabilities and may involve social action through lobbying and legislative activities. The Tenderloin Project, in a low-income area of single-room occupants in San Francisco, is an example of neighborhood development. Nearby residents acted on the immediate problem of crime and victimization of older people and then moved on to deal with issues such as nutrition and health promotion. In the process, social networks were strengthened and weekly support groups formed. Neighborhood-based intergenerational helping networks are used to connect the formal service system to provide personal care services to frail elders. More recently, Internet Websites, such as Third Age, have emerged as a means to build community connections and reduce social isolation. Chat rooms, for

example, are modeled upon community members' interests and needs; they can be altered by the changing will of the community. As noted by Hagel and Armstrong (1997), "people are drawn to virtual communities because they provide an engaging environment in which to connect with other people" (p. 18). Creating an electronic community, however, is obviously limited to those older people who have finances to access computers and the Internet (Furlong, 1997). Nevertheless, with the growing availability of networked computers at local libraries, senior centers, and community centers, many elders who cannot afford their own computer or on-line service can benefit from such services at no cost.

RELATIONSHIPS WITH PETS

Pets are another source of affection and touch, and may offer a significant relationship in some older people's lives. The mere presence of a pet appears to have little effect on psychological well-being, but emotional attachment to a pet can have benefits (Tucker, Friedman, Tsai, and Martin, 1995). Many older adults talk to their pets as if they were people, confide in them, and believe that they are sensitive to their moods and feelings. Having a pet to feed, groom, or walk can provide structure and a sense of purpose to the day, and caring for it can provide an anchor for those whose lives have undergone major change or loss. A pet may even serve as a family substitute, especially for nursing home residents. (Zasloff and Kidd, 1994). Pet owners tend to score higher on measures of happiness, self-confidence, self-care, alertness, responsiveness, and dependability than non–pet owners (Dembicki and

Anderson, 1996). These measures of well-being may be partially due to the fact that older people who care for pets, rather than being taken care of by others, can experience meaning, purpose, and a sense of control over their environment. On the other hand, the loss of a pet can result in grief as intense as that precipitated by the death of a family member or friend.

The recognition that animals fulfill many human needs has led to an increase in pet-facilitated programs for older people living in long-term care facilities, as well as in loan-a-pet programs for those individuals in their own homes. Even tropical fish and wild birds attracted to feeders have been found to evoke responses such as care and stroking from previously nonresponsive persons. Older people participating in pet therapy programs have been found to become less depressed and more communicative, and to experience higher rates of survival than do nonparticipants (Hendy, 1987; National Institutes of Health, 1988). Although a pet should never be viewed as a substitute for human relationships, pet ownership can enhance well-being and enrich older persons' quality of life, particularly in institutional environments.

SUMMARY AND IMPLICATIONS

The importance of informal social relationships for older people's physical and mental well-being has been widely documented. Contrary to stereotypes, very few older people are socially isolated. The majority have family members with whom they are in contact, although they are unlikely to live with them. Their families serve as a critical source of support, especially when older members become impaired by chronic illness. The marital relationship is most important, with more than half of all persons age 65 and over married and living with a partner in independent households. Most older couples are satisfied with their marriages, which influences their life satisfaction generally. The older couple, freed from childrearing demands, has more opportunities to pursue new roles and types of relationships.

Less is known about sibling, grandparent, and other types of family interactions in old age, although the importance of their support is likely to increase in the future. Also, comparatively little research has been conducted on lesbian and gay relationships in old age and on never-married older persons who may rely primarily on friendship networks to cope. Siblings can be crucial in providing emotional support, physical care, and a home. Interaction with secondary kin tends to depend on geographic proximity and whether more immediate family members are available.

Contrary to the myth that adult children are alienated from their parents, the majority of older persons are in frequent contact with their children, either face-to-face or by phone or letter. Filial relationships are characterized by patterns of reciprocal aid throughout the life course, until the older generation becomes physically or mentally disabled. At that point, adult children—generally women—are faced with providing financial, emotional, and physical assistance to older relatives, oftentimes with little support from others for their caregiving responsibilities. In ethnic minority and lower-income families, older relatives are most likely to receive daily care from younger relatives and to be involved themselves in caring for grandchildren.

Most families, regardless of socioeconomic class or ethnic minority status, attempt to provide care for their older members for as long as possible, and seek institutionalization only when they have exhausted other resources. Such caregiving responsibilities are affected by a number of social trends, most notable among them the increasing percentage of middle-aged women—traditionally the caregivers—who are more likely to be employed, and the number of reconstituted families resulting from divorce and remarriage. The needs of caregivers are clearly a growing concern for social and health care providers and policy makers.

With the growth of three- and four-generation families, more older persons are experiencing the status of grandparenthood and great-grandparenthood. Most grandparents are in relatively frequent contact with their grandchildren, and most derive considerable satisfaction from the grandparent role. The demands of grandparenthood are changing, however, as a result of divorce and remarriages. Perhaps the most dramatic change in the past decade has been the increase in the number of grandparents who are the primary caregivers to young grandchildren.

For many older persons, friends and neighbors can be even more critical than family members to maintaining morale and a quality of life. Generally, women interact more with friends than do men. Age-segregated settings appear to facilitate friendships rather than isolate older persons. In recognition of the importance of informal interaction to physical and mental well-being, an increasing number of neighborhood and community-based interventions have been developed to strengthen friendship and neighborhood ties. In recent years, many of these programs have attempted to foster intergenerational contacts and relationships. In sum, the majority of older persons continue to play a variety of social roles—partner, parent, grandparent, friend, and neighbor—and to derive feelings of satisfaction and self-worth from these interactions.

GLOSSARY

blended family   a family whose membership is comprised of blood and nonblood relationships through divorce or remarriage

cluttered nest   delayed departure or return of adult children to parents' home

filial responsibility   norms or expectations of what younger offspring owe older relatives

gatekeepers   people in formal (e.g., physicians, nurses) or informal (e.g., friends and neighbors) service who, because of regular interactions with older adults, can watch for signs indicating a need for assistance and mobilize help accordingly

grandparents as the custodial caregivers   grandparents who are the primary caregivers for grandchildren, when adult children are unable to provide adequate care

grandparents' rights   legal rights of grandparents to interact with grandchildren following divorce of the grandchildren's parents; liabilities of grandparent and

step-grandparents as custodians of grandchildren in the absence of responsible parents

intergenerational living   families spanning two or more generations living in the same household

intergenerational programs   services that facilitate the interaction of people across generations; for example, the Foster Grandparents Program

intergenerational transfers   exchange of knowledge, finances, and other resources among family members of different generations

intimacy at a distance   strong emotional ties among family members even though they do not live near each other

multigenerational family   a family with three or more generations alive at the same time

natural helpers   people who assist others because of their concern, interest, and innate understanding

nontraditional families   new family structures derived through gay and lesbian partnerships, communal living, cohabitation, informal adoption, etc.

reciprocal support   sharing resources and assistance among individuals

social support   interactions among family, friends, neighbors (informal), and programs (formal) that sustain and encourage individuals

women in the middle   women who have competing demands from older parents, spouses, children, and employment

RESOURCES

See the companion Website for this text at <www.ablongman.com/hooyman> for information about the following:

- AARP Grandparent Information Center
- Alzheimer's Association
- Alzheimer's Disease Education and Referral Center (ADEAR)
- Alzheimer's Disease and Related Disorders Association Inc. (ADRDA)
- Children of Aging Parents
- Foundation for Grandparenting
- Gatekeeper Program
- Generations United
- National Coalition of Grandparents, Inc. (NCOG)

REFERENCES

Adams, R., and Blieszner, R. Aging well with family and friends. *American Behavioral Scientist*, 1995, *39*, 209–224.

Adelman, M. Stigma, gay lifestyles, and adjustment to aging: A study of later-life gay men and lesbians. *Journal of Homosexuality*, 1990, *20*, 7–32.

Administration on Aging: *Aging into the 21st century*. Washington, DC: 1997.

Administration on Aging: *Family Caregiving in an Aging Society*. Washington, DC: 1999a.

Administration on Aging: *Profile of Older Americans*. Washington, DC: 1999b.

Allen, S. M., Goldscheider, F., and Ciambrone, D. A. Gender roles, marital intimacy, and nomination of spouse as primary caregiver. *Gerontologist*, 1999, *39*, 150–158.

Arno, P. S., Levine, C., and Memmot, M. M. The economic value of informal caregiving. *Health Affairs*, 1999, *18*, 182–188.

Barrett, A. E., and Lynch, S. M. Caregiving networks of elderly persons: Variation by marital status. *The Gerontologist*, 1999, 695–704.

Beckman, L. *Childlessness, Family composition and well-being of older men*. Presented at the Annual Convention of the American Psychological Association, Los Angeles, CA, August 1985.

Beery, L. C., Prigerson, H. G., Bierhals, A. J., Santucci, L. M., Newsom, J. T., Maciejewski, P. K., Rapp, S. R., Fasiczka, A., and Reynolds-Hi, C. F. Traumatic grief, depression and caregiving in elderly spouses of the terminally ill. *Journal of Death and Dying*, 1997, *35*, 261–279.

Bengtson, V. C., and Roberts, R. E. Intergenerational solidarity and aging families: An example of formal theory construction. *Journal of Marriage and the Family*, 1991, *53*, 856–870.

Bengtson, V. C., Rosenthal, C. J., and Burton, C. Families and aging: Diversity and heterogeneity. In R. H. Binstock and L. K. George (Eds.), *Handbook of aging and the social sciences* (3rd ed.). New York: Academic Press, 1990.

Benson, W. F. Administration on Aging: Public Policy on Elder Abuse. In *Silent suffering: Elder abuse in America*, 1997, Archstone Foundation, 24–26.

Boaz, R. F., Hu, J., and Ye, Y. The Transfer of Resources from Middle-Aged Children to Functionally Limited Elderly Parents: Providing Time, Giving Money, Sharing Space. *The Gerontologist*, 1999, *39*, 648–657.

Bogard, R., and Spilka, B. Self-disclosure and marital satisfaction in mid-life and late-life remarriages. *International Journal of Aging and Human Development*, 1996, *42*, 161–172.

Bouchard, G., Sabourin, S., Wright, J., Lussier, Y., and Richer, C. Predictive validity of coping strategies on marital satisfaction: Cross-sectional and longitudinal evidence. *Journal of Family Psychology*. Newbury Park, CA; March 1998.

Bowling, A., and Grundy, E. The association between social networks and mortality in later life. *Reviews in Clinical Gerontology*, November 1998, *8*, 353–361.

Brouard, Joslin D. The prevalence of grandmothers as primary caregivers in a poor pediatric population. *Journal of Community Health*, October 1995, *20*, 383–401.

Burnette, D. Grandparents raising grandchildren in the inner city. *Families in Society: The Journal of Contemporary Human Sciences*, 1997, 489–501.

Burnette, D. Physical and Emotional well-being of custodial grandparents in Latino families. *American Journal of Orthopsychiatry*, 1999, *69*, 305–318.

Burnette, D. Social relationships of Latino grandparent caregivers: A role theory perspective. *The Gerontologist*, 1999, *39*, 49–58.

Cantor, M. Family and community: Changing roles in an aging society. *The Gerontologist*, 1991, *31*, 337–340.

Chalfie, D. *Going it alone: A closer look at grandparents parenting grandchildren*. Washington, DC: American Association of Retired Persons, 1994.

Choi, N. G. Patterns and determinants of social service utilization: Comparison of the childless elderly and elderly parents living with or apart from their children. *The Gerontologist*, 1994, *34*, 353.

Choi, N. G. Long-term elderly widows and divorcees: Similarities and differences. *Journal of Women and Aging*, 1995, *7*, 69–92.

Choi, N. G. The never-married and divorced elderly: Comparison of economic and health status, social support, and living arrangement. *Journal of Gerontological Social Work*, 1996, *26*, 3–25.

Choi, N. G. Racial differences in the determinants of living arrangements of widowed and divorced elderly women. *The Gerontologist*, 1991, *31*, 496–504.

Cicirelli, V. G. Strengthening sibling relationships in the later years. In G. C. Smith, S. Tobin, E. A. Robertson-Tchabo, and P. Power (Eds.), *Strengthening aging families: Diversity in practice and policy.* Thousand Oaks, CA: Sage, 1995.

Clarke, E. J., Preston, M., Raskin, J., and Bengtson, V. L. Types of conflicts and tensions between older parents and adult children. *The Gerontologist,* 1999, *39,* 261–270.

Cohen, G. D. Marriage and Divorce in Later Life (Editorial). *American Journal of Geriatric Psychiatry,* 1999, *7,* 185–187.

Connell, B. R., and McConnell, E. S. Trating excess disability among cognitively impaired nursing home residents. *Journal of the American Geriatrics Society,* 2000, *48,* 454–455.

Cooney, T. M., and Smith, L. A. Young adults' relation with grandparents following recent parental divorce. *Journals of Gerontology,* 1996, *51B,* S91–S95.

Cruikshank, M. Lavender and gray: A brief survey of lesbian and gay aging studies. *Journal of Homosexuality,* 1990, *20,* 77–87.

DeMallie, D. A., North, C. S., and Smith, E. M. Psychiatric disorders among the homeless: A comparison of older and younger groups. *The Gerontologist,* 1997, *37,* 61–66.

Dembicki, D., and Anderson, J. Pet ownership may be a factor in improved health of the elderly. *Journal of Nutrition and the Elderly,* 1996, *15,* 15–31.

Dick-Muehlke, C., Yang, J., Yu, D. and Paul, D. Abuse of cognitively impaired elders: Recognition and intervention. In *Silent suffering: Elder abuse in America.* Long Beach, CA: Archstone Foundation, 1997.

Dietz, T. L. Patterns of intergenerational assistance within the Mexican American family. *Journal of Family Issues,* 1995, *16,* 350–355.

Dorfman, R., Walters, K., Burke, P., Hardin, L., Karanik, T., Raphael, J., and Silverstein, E. Old, sad, and alone: The myth of the aging homosexual. *Journal of Gerontological Social Work,* 1995, *24,* 29–44.

Doty, P. J., and Miller, B. Caregiving and productive aging. In S. Bass, F. Caro, and V-P Chen (Eds.), *Achieving a productive aging society.* Westport, CT: Auburn House, 1993.

Doty, P. J., Stone, R. I., Jackson, M. E., and Drabek, J. L. Informal caregiving. In C. J. Evashwick (Ed.), *The continuum of long-term care (2nd ed.)* Albany, NY: Delmar, 2001.

Dykstra, P. Loneliness among the never and formerly married: The importance of supportive friendships and a desire for independence. *Journals of Gerontology,* 1995, *50B,* S321–S329.

Ehrenberg, P. Mortality decline in the twentieth century and supply of kin over the life course. *The Gerontologist,* 1996, *36,* 681–685.

Emick, M. A., and Hayslip, B. Custodial grandparenting: New roles for middle-aged and older adults. *International Journal of Aging and Human Development,* 1996, *43,* 135–154.

Fauser, M. C. *Hospice patient perspectives regarding the implementation of advanced directives.* Dissertation Abstracts International: Section B: The Sciences and Engineering, July 1999, *60,* 0410.

Field, D. Continuity and change in friendships in advanced old age: Findings from the Berkeley older generation study. *International Journal of Aging and Human Development,* 1999, *48,* 325–346.

Finley, N., Roberts, D., and Banahan, B. Motivators and inhibitors of attitudes of filial obligation toward aging parents. *The Gerontologist,* 1988, *28,* 73–83.

Fredriksen, K. L. Family caregiving responsibilities among lesbians and gay men. *Social Work,* March 1999, *44,* 142–155.

Freedman, R. I., Krauss, M. W., and Seltzer, M. M. Aging parents' residential plans for adult children with mental retardation. *Mental Retardation,* 1997, *35,* 114–123.

Fuller-Thompson, E., Minkler, M., and Driver, D. A profile of grandparents raising grandchildren in the United States. *The Gerontologist,* 1997, *37,* 406–411.

Fullmer, E. M. Challenging biases against families of older gays and lesbians. In G. C. Smith, S. Tobin, E. A. Robertson-Tchabo, and P. Power (Eds.), *Strengthening aging families: Diversity in practice and power.* Thousand Oaks, CA: Sage, 1995.

Furlong, M. Creating online communities for older adults. *Generations,* 1997, *21,* 33–35.

Giarrusso, R., Silverstein, M., and Bengtson, V. L. Family complexity and the grandparent role. *Generations,* 1996, *20,* 17–23.

Goldman, N., Korenman, S., and Weinstein, R. Marital status and health among the elderly. *Social Science and Medicine,* 1995, *40,* 1717–1730.

Goldscheider, F. K. Divorce and remarriage: Effects on the elderly population. *Reviews in Clinical Gerontology,* 1994, *4,* 258–259.

Goodman, C. Intimacy and autonomy in long term marriage. *Journal of Gerontological Social Work,* 1999, *32,* 83–97.

Greenwald, L., and Bengston, V. L. Geographic distance and contact between middle-aged children and their parents: The effects of social class over 20 years. *Journals of Gerontology,* 1995, *52B,* S13–S26.

Hagel, J. III, and Armstrong, A. G. *Net gain: Expanding markets through virtual communities.* Boston: Harvard Business School Press, 1997.

Hammond, R. J., and Muller, G. O. The late-life divorced: Another look. *Journal of Divorce and Remarriage,* 1992, *17,* 135–150.

Hanson, E. J., Tetley, J., and Clarke, A. A multimedia intervention to support family caregivers. *The Gerontologist,* 1999, *39,* 736–741.

Hansson, R. O., and Carpenter, B. N. *Relationships in old age: Coping with the challenge of transition.* New York: The Guilford Press, 1994.

Hargrave, T. D., and Hanna, S. M. (Eds.) *The aging family: New visions in theory, practice, and reality.* New York: Brunner/Mazel, Inc. 1997.

Hatch, L., and Bulcroft, K. Contact with friends in later life: Disentangling the effects of gender and marital status. *Journal of Marriage and the Family,* 1992, *54,* 222–232.

Hays, J. C., Gold, D. T., and Peiper, C. F. Sibling bereavement in late life. *Journal of Death and Dying,* 1997, *35,* 25–42.

Hendy, H. M. Effects of pet and/or people visits on nursing home residents. *International Journal on Aging and Human Development,* 1987, *25,* 279–291.

Hilbourne, M. Living together full time? Middle class couples approaching retirement. *Aging and Society,* 1999, *19,* 161–183.

Hobbs, F. B., and Damon, B. C. *65+ in the United States.* Washington, DC: U.S. Bureau of the Census, Current Population Reports, 1996.

Hobfoll, S. E., and Vaux, A. Social support: Resources and contact. In S. Cohen and S. L. Syme (Eds.), *Social support and health.* New York: Academic Press, 1993, 685–705.

House, J., Mero, R., and Webster, P. Marital quality over the life course. *Social Psychology Quarterly,* 1996, *59,* 162–171.

Joseph, A. E., and Hallman, B. C. Over the hill and far away: Distance as a barrier to the provision of assistance to elderly relatives. *Social Science and Medicine,* 1998, *46,* 631–639.

Joslin, D., and Brouard, A. The prevalence of grandmothers as primary caregivers in a poor pediatric population. *Journal of Community Health,* 1995, *20,* 383–401.

Kelly, T., and Kropf, N. Stigmatized and perpetual parents: Older parents caring for adult children with lifelong disabilities. *Journal of Gerontological Social Work,* 1995.

Kincade, J. E., Rabiner, D. J., Bernard, S. L., Woomert, A., Konrad, T. R., DeFrisse, G. H., and Ory, M. G. Older adults as a community resource: Results from the National Survey of Self-Care and Aging. *The Gerontologist,* 1996, *36,* 474–482.

Kivett, V. R. Centrality of the grandfather role among older rural black and white men. *Journals of Gerontology,* 1991, *46,* S250–S258.

Knight, R. G., Williams, S., McGee, R., and Olaman, S. Caregiving and well-being in a sample of women in midlife. *Australia-New Zealand Journal of Public Health,* 1998, *22,* 616–620.

Krause, N., and Borawski-Clark, S. Social class differences in social support among older adults. *The Gerontologist,* 1995, *35,* 498–505.

Kruk, E. Grandparent-grandchild contact loss: Findings from a study of "Grandparent Rights" members. *Canadian Journal on Aging,* 1995, *14,* 737–754.

Kulik, L. Continuity and discontinuity in marital life after retirement: Life orientations, gender role ideology, intimacy, and satisfaction. *Families in Society,* May–June 1999, *80,* 286–294.

Langner, S. R. Finding meaning in caring for elderly relatives: Loss and personal growth. *Holistic Nurse Practitioner,* 1995, *9,* 75–84.

LaVeist, T. A., Sellers, R. M., Brown, K. A. Elliott, and Nickerson, K. J. Extreme social isolation, use of community-based senior support services, and mortality among African American elderly women. *American Journal of Community Psychology,* October 1997, *25,* 721–732.

Lefley H. P., and Hatfield, A. B. Helping parental caregivers and mental health consumers cope with parental aging and loss. *Psychiatric Services,* March 1999, *50,* 369–375.

Leutz, W. N., Capitman, J., Mac Adams, M., and Abrahams, R. *Care for frail elders: Developing community solutions.* Westport, CT: Auburn House, 1992.

Levenson, R., Cartensen, L., and Gottman, J. Long-term marriage: Age, gender and satisfaction. *Psychology and Aging,* 1993, *8,* 301–313.

Longres, J. F. *Human behavior in the social environment.* Itasca, Illinois: F. E. Peacock Publishers, 1995.

Lowenthal, M. F., and Haven, C. Interaction and adaptation. *American Sociological Review,* 1968, *33,* 20–30.

MacRae, H. Strong and enduring ties: Older women and their friends. *Canadian Journal on Aging,* 1996, *15,* 374–392.

Markides, K. S., and Black, S. A. Ethnicity and aging. In R. H. Binstock and C. K. George (Eds.), *Handbook of aging and the Social Sciences* (4th ed.). San Diego: Academic Press, 1996.

Metropolitan Life Insurance Company. *Met Life study of employer costs for working caregivers.* Westport, CT: Metropolitan Life Insurance Co., 1998.

Miller, B., Campbell, R., Farron, C., Kaufman, J., and Davis, L. Race, control, mastery, and caregiver distress. *Journals of Gerontology,* 1995, *50B,* S376–S382.

Miller, B., McFall, S., and Campbell, T. Changes in sources of community long-term care among African American and white frail older persons. *Journals of Gerontology,* 1994, *49,* S14–S24.

Miller, R. B., Hemesath, K., and Nelson, B. Marriage in Middle and Later Life. In T. D. Hargrave and S. M. Hanna (Eds.), *The aging family: New visions in theory, practice, and reality.* New York: Brunner/Mazel, 1997.

Minkler, M., and Fuller-Thomson, E. Depression in grandparents raising grandchildren. *Archives of Family Medicine,* 1997, *6,* 445–452.

Moen, P., and Forest, K. B. Family policies for an aging society: Moving to the twenty-first century. *The Gerontologist,* 1995, *35,* 825–830.

Mohr, R. Reflections on golden pond. In P. Papp et al., (Eds.), *Couples on the fault line: New directions for therapists.* New York: The Guilford Press, 2000.

Mor-Barak, M., Miller, L., and Syme, L. Social networks, life events and the health of the poor, frail elderly: A longitudinal study of the buffering versus the direct effect. *Family Community Health,* 1991, *14,* 1–13.

Mui, A. C. Caring for frail elderly parents: A comparison of adult sons and daughters. *The Gerontologist,* 1995, *35,* 86–93.

Mui, A. C., and Burnette, J. D. A comparative profile of frail elderly persons living alone and those living with others. *Journal of Gerontological Social Work,* 1994, *21,* 5–26.

National Academy on Aging. *Old age in the 21st century.* Syracuse, NY: Syracuse University, The Maxwell School, 1994.

National Alliance for Caregiving and the Alzheimer's Association. *Who cares? Families caring for persons with Alzheimer's disease,* Bethesda, MD, 1999.

National Alliance for Caregiving and MetLife Mature Market Group. *The MetLife study of employer costs for working caregivers: Findings from a national survey.* Bethesda, MD, June 1997.

National Institutes of Health. *Health benefits of pets.* Washington, DC: U.S. Department of Health and Human Services, U.S. Government Printing Office, 1988.

Neugarten, B., and Weinstein, K. The changing American grandparent. *Journal of Marriage and the Family,* 1964, *26,* 199–204.

Nokes, K. et al., (Eds.), *HIV/AIDS and the older adult.* Washington, DC: Taylor & Francis, 1996.

Peterson, Cabdida C. Grandfathers' and grandmothers' satisfaction with the grandparenting role: Seeking new answers to old questions. *International Journal of Aging and Human Development,* 1999, *49,* 61–78.

Pourat, N., Lubben, J., Wallace, S. P., and Moon, A. Predictors of use of traditional Korean healers among elderly Koreans in Los Angeles. *The Gerontologist,* 1999, *39,* 711–719.

Pruchno, R. Raising grandchildren: The experiences of black and white grandmothers. *The Gerontologist,* 1999, *39,* 209–221.

Reynolds, W. Marital satisfaction in later life: An examination of equity, equality, and reward theories. *International Journal of Aging and Human Development,* 1995, *40,* 155–173.

Riley, M. W., and Riley, J. W. Structural lag: Past and future. In M. W. Riley, R. L. Kahn, and A. Foner (Eds.), *Age and structural lag: Society's failure to provide meaningful opportunities in work, family and leisure.* New York: John Wiley & Sons, 1994.

Roberto, K. Grandparent and grandchild relationships. In T. Brubaker (Ed.), *Family relationships in later life.* Newbury Park, CA: Sage, 1990.

Roberts, S. J., and Sorensen, L. Lesbian health care: A review and recommendations for health promotion in primary care settings. *Nurse Practitioner,* 1995, *20,* 42–47.

Robinson, L., and Blanton, P. Marital strengths in enduring marriages. *Family Relations,* 1993, *42,* 38–45.

Rubinstein, R. L., Alexander, B. B., Goodman, M., and Luborsky, M. Key relationships of never married, childless older women: A cultural analysis. *The Journals of Gerontology*, 1991, 46, S270–277.

Saluter, A. *Marital status and living arrangements: March 1994*. Washington, DC: U.S. Bureau of the Census, Current Population Report. Population Characteristics, 1994.

Silverstein, M., and Angelelli, Older parents' expectations of moving closer to their children. *Journals of Gerontology: Social Sciences*, 1998, *53B*, S153–S163.

Silverstein, M., Chen, X., and Heller, K. Too much of a good thing: Intergenerational social support and the psychological well-being of older parents. *Journal of Marriage and the Family*, 1996, *58*, 970–982.

Silverstein, M., and Waite, L. Are blacks more likely than whites to receive social support in middle and old age? Yes, no and maybe so. *Journals of Gerontology*, 1993, 48, S212–S222.

Sloan, F. A., Picone, G., and Hoerger, T. J. The supply of children's time to disabled elderly parents. *Economic Inquiry*, 1997, 35, 295–308.

Slusher, M. P., Mayer, C. J., and Dunkle, R. E. Gays and lesbians older and wiser (GLOW): A support group for older gay people. *The Gerontologist*, 1996, *36*, 118–123.

Smith, G. C., and Tobin, S. S. Case managers' perceptions of practice with older parents of adults with developmental disabilities. In K. A. Roberto (Ed.), *The elderly caregiver: Caring for adults with developmental disabilities*. Newbury Park, CA: Sage, 1993.

Smith, G. C., Tobin, S. S., and Fullmer, E. M. Assisting older families with lifelong disabilities. In G. C. Smith, S. Tobin, E. A. Robertson-Tchabo, and P. Power (Eds.), *Strengthening aging families: Diversity in practice and policy*. Thousand Oaks, CA: Sage, 1995.

Solomon, J. C., and Marx, J. "To grandmother's house we go": Health and school adjustment of children raised solely by grandparents. *The Gerontologist*, 1995, *35*, 386–394.

Spillman, B. C., and Pezzin, L. E. Potential and active family caregivers: Changing networks and the "sandwich generation." *Milbank Quarterly*, 2000, *78*, 347–374.

Spitze, G., Logan, J., Joseph, G., and Lee, E. Middle generation roles and the well-being of men and women. *Journals of Gerontology*, 1994, 49, S107–S116.

Stephens, M. A., and Franks, M. Spillover between daughters' role as caregiver and wife: Interference or enhancement? *Journals of Gerontology*, 1995, *50B*, P9–P17.

Stevens, P. E. Structural and interpersonal impact of heterosexual assumptions on lesbian health care clients. *Nursing Research*, 1995, *44*, 25–30.

Stone, R., and Keigher, S. Toward equitable universal caregiver policy: The potential of financial supports for family caregivers. *Aging and Social Policy*, 1994, *6*, 57–76.

Stone, R., and Short, P. The competing demand of employment and informal caregiving to disabled elders. *Medical Care*, 1990, *28*, 513–526.

Strom, R. D., Buki, L. P., and Strom, S. K. Intergenerational perceptions of English-speaking and Spanish-speaking Mexican-American grandparents. *International Journal of Aging and Human Development*, 1997, *45*, 1–21.

Stroup, A. L., and Pollock, G. E. Economic well being among white elderly divorced. *Journal of Divorce and Remarriage*, 1999, *31*, 53–68.

Szinovacz, M. E., DeViney, S., and Atkinson, M. P. Effects of Surrogate Parenting on Grandparents' Well-Being. *Journals of Gerontology*, 1999, *54B*, S376–S388.

Taylor, R., and Chatters, L. Extended family networks of older black adults. *Journals of Gerontology*, 1991, *46*, S210–218.

Thompson, E., Futterman, A. Gallagher-Thompson, D., Rose, J., and Lovett, S. Social support and caregiving burden in family caregivers of frail elders. *Journals of Gerontology*, 1993, 48, S245–S254.

Tucker, J. S., Friedman, H. S., Tsai, C. M., and Martin, L. R. Playing with pets and longevity among older people. *Psychology and Aging*, 1995, *10*, 3–7.

Turvey, C. L., Carney, C., Arndt, S., Wallace, R. B. and Herzog, R. Conjugal loss and syndromal depression in a sample of elders aged 70 years and older. *American Journal of Psychiatry*, 1999, *156*, 1596–1601.

Uhlenberg, P. The burden of aging: A theoretical framework for understanding the shifting balance of caregiving and care receiving vs. cohort ages. *The Gerontologist*, 1996, *36*, 761–767.

U.S. Bureau of the Census. *Statistical Abstract of the United States, 116th Edition*. Washington, DC, U.S. Government Printing Office, 1996.

Van Tilburg, T. Losing and gaining in old age: Changes in personal network size and social support in a four-year longitudinal study. *Journals of Gerontology: Social Sciences*, 1998, *53B*, S313–S323.

Ward, R. Marital happiness and household equity in later life. *Sociological Abstracts*, 1992.

Whitbourne, S. K., and Cassidy, E. Achieving intimacy in late-life marriage. In G. C. Smith, S. Tobin, E. A. Robertson-Tchabo, and P. Power (Eds.), *Strengthening aging families: Diversity in practice and policy*. Thousand Oaks, CA: Sage, 1995.

Wojciechowski, W. C. Issues in caring for older lesbians. *Journal of Gerontogical Nursing*, 1998, *24*, 28–33.

Wood, V., and Robertson, J. The significance of grandparenthood. In J. Gubruim (Ed.), *Time, roles and self in old age*. New York: Human Sciences Press, 1976.

Wright, D. L., and Aquilino, W. S. Influence of emotional support exchange on caregiving wives' burden and marital satisfaction. *Family Relations*, 1998, *47*, 195–204.

Wright, L. K. Alzheimer's disease afflicted spouses who remain at home: Can human dialectics explain the findings? *Social Science and Medicare*, 1994, *38*, 1037–1046.

Wu, Z., and Pollard, M. S. Social support among unmarried childless elderly persons. *Journals of Gerontology*, 1998, *53B*, S324–S335.

Yoakam, J. R. Beyond the wrinkle room: Challenging ageism in gay male culture. *Dimensions*. San Francisco: ASA Mental Health and Aging Network, 1999, 3, 7.

Zasloff, R. C., and Kidd, A. H. Loneliness and pet ownership among single women. *Psychological Reports*, 1994, *75*, 747–752.

10

OPPORTUNITIES AND STRESSES OF INFORMAL CAREGIVING

In this chapter we address the benefits and stresses of informal caregiving—to society, to caregivers, and to care recipients themselves. The following issues are discussed:

- Economic benefits and costs of caregiving to society
- Families as caregivers
- Women as caregivers
- Families of color as caregivers
- Financial and physical demands on caregivers
- Emotional stresses associated with caregiving
- Use of formal services to supplement informal care
- Interventions to support caregivers
- Elder abuse associated with caregiving
- Institutionalization following informal caregiving
- Legal and policy issues affecting informal care

Informal caregiving, defined as unpaid assistance provided by family, friends, and neighbors in the areas of ADLs and IADLs, can help older persons remain in the community and avoid institutionalization. It is estimated that only about one-fourth of all older people with significant limitations in their activities of daily living reside in long-term care facilities. The remainder lives at home with help from informal caregivers. As many as 86 percent of older adults with three or more ADL limitations (i.e. the usual cutoff for providing long-term care services) live in the community, receiving on average 60 hours of informal care and 14 hours of paid caregiving (Doty, Stone, Jackson, and Drabek, 2001). In fact, an analysis of the 1994 National Long Term Care Survey found that two-thirds of chronically disabled older persons in the community receive *only* informal care that is not supplemented by paid caregivers (Spillman and Pezzin, 2000).

SOCIETAL BENEFITS AND COSTS

Not surprisingly, informal caregiving saves the American health care system substantial dollars. The most recent national study, conducted in 1997, estimated the cost of informal caregiving at $196 billion, or more than twice the cost of nursing home placement (Arno, Levine, and Memmot, 1999). If family and friends were not available to provide informal caregiving, long-term care costs for the older population would more than double. Given the concerns with escalating health care costs in the United States, these additional expenses could bankrupt the system and create a burden for all of society.

Yet, individual caregivers also experience tremendous costs. For example, those who are employed experience the greatest financial burdens of this situation; many modify their schedules to part-time employment, change their working hours, or take leave without pay as their older care recipient requires increasingly more assistance with ADLs. In a recent survey, more than 50 percent of caregiving employees reported making changes at work to accommodate their caregiving responsibilities (National Alliance for Caregiving and AARP, 1997). Employers must also be willing to make accommodations for these employees who are caught between conflicting roles, resulting in some loss of productivity and increased demands on the caregiver's coworkers. Indeed, a 1996 survey by the Metropolitan Life Insurance Company (1998) estimated that lost productivity associated with caregiving cost U.S. businesses nearly $11.4 billion per year. Research with caregivers of elders with dementia shows even greater

conflicts between worker and caregiver roles. These caregivers are even more likely than their counterparts who care for elders without dementia to report changing their employment patterns to part-time or to a less demanding job, or to quitting work entirely (Ory, Hoffman, Yee, Tennstedt, and Schulz, 1999).

Demographic and social changes—more older adults with chronic disabilities, more employed women, more complex family structures, and cost-cutting practices in health care—underlie many of the stresses of caregiving. Caregiving demands or stresses can be conceptualized under the domain of environmental press. Consistent with the person–environment model, these demands are likely to be stressful when there is an incongruence between the strength of the demand and the caregiver's competence (health, functional capabilities) to deal with the tasks of caregiving (Lawton and Nahemow, 1973). Unlike many transitions to new roles, caregiving is unplanned, unexpected, and not entered into by choice (Seltzer and Li, 2000).

Families as Caregivers

Families provide 70 to 80 percent of the in-home care for older relatives with chronic impairments. Likewise, nearly 75 percent of people over age 65 with a chronic disability rely exclusively on family and friends for help with everyday activities, primarily adult children (42%), followed by spouses (25%) (National Academy on an Aging Society, 2000). Adult children, especially daughters, are the primary caregivers for older widowed women and older unmarried men, and they are the secondary caregivers in situations where the spouse of an older person is still alive (Neal, Ingersoll-Dayton, and Starrels, 1997). Parent care has thus become a predictable and nearly universal experience across the life course, yet many adults are not adequately prepared for it. Approximately 51 percent of caregivers provide help every day and slightly over 20 percent assist several times a week. Women who are caregivers to older parents spend an average of 22 hours a week providing care (National Academy on an Aging

SANDWICH GENERATION

A woman in her mid-fifties with teenage children and a full-time job, Annette had cared for both her parents. Her mother, crippled with rheumatoid arthritis, lived with Annette's family for 5 years before she died. Within a year, Annette's father suffered a stroke and lived with the family for 3 years before his death. Annette's teenagers had resented the amount of time she gave to her parents, and her husband became impatient with how little time they had alone together. They had not had a vacation in 5 years. Since family and friends were not interested in helping her with the care of her parents, Annette and her husband rarely even had a night out alone together. As an employed caregiver, Annette frequently missed work and was distracted on the job whenever she had to consult doctors or take her parents for therapy during normal business hours. She felt alone, isolated, and overwhelmed by the stress. She was physically and mentally exhausted from trying to meet too many demands, unaware that some support services were available in her community, and feeling that she had to be capable of handling these responsibilities on her own. When her mother-in-law became too frail to live alone, Annette knew her family and job would suffer once again if she tried to balance household duties, a full-time job, and the care of both older and younger relatives. She began to explore assisted living options.

Society, 2000; National Alliance for Caregiving and the Equitable Foundation, 1998).

The primary forms of informal assistance are emotional support, instrumental activities inside and outside the home (e.g., transportation, meal preparation, shopping, and housework), personal care (e.g., bathing, feeding, and dressing), and mediating with agencies to obtain services. In some cases, older parents also receive financial aid from their children. The type of familial assistance is largely determined by the older member's functional level, intensity of care needed, co-residence, and the caregiver's gender, with personal care most often performed by wives, daughters, or daughters-in-law (National Alliance for Caregiving and AARP, 1997). Informal care predominates even at a level of functional disability when more formal services might be expected. Not surprisingly, the older the care recipient, the older the caregiver (Tennstedt, 1999).

Given this pattern of care, it is perplexing that the myth persists that families do not care for their older members as well as they did in the "good old days." As we saw in Chapter 2, older relatives at the turn of the 20th century were rare and valued because of their economic contributions to the family. Today, however, adult children provide more complex care to parents over much longer periods of time than they did when life expectancy was 47 years and elders comprised only 4 percent of the population. In addition, early hospital discharges, corporate fiscal constraints, managed care, and hospital downsizing contribute to the growing number of family caregivers. This is the first time in history that American couples have had more parents than children. In fact, today the average American woman can expect to spend 18 years caring for an older family member, compared to 17 years for her children. In contrast, the average woman in 1900 spent an average of 8 years on elder care (Stone, Cafferata, and Sangl, 1987). These changes are due not only to increased longevity, but also to the fact that the current cohort of frail elders who raised children during the Great Depression had a low birth rate. This resulted in fewer adult children available as potential caregivers.

The longer economic dependence of young adults combined with parents who are living longer are additional trends affecting intergenerational relationships. As a result, many contemporary middle-aged individuals, described as the **sandwich generation** (illustrated in the box above), are faced with a dilemma that is relatively new historically—the competing responsibilities of caring for parents and children, including young adult children. The "empty nest" may be filled by frail elders and by grown children who cannot afford to leave home, or who return home because of divorce, economic need, or substance-abuse problems (Cantor, 1994). This delayed departure—or return—of adult children has been referred to as the **cluttered nest** (Bengtson et al., 1996).

The growth of *blended* or *reconstituted families* as a consequence of divorce and remarriage also affects the adult child–parent relationship in later life. An increasing number of older parents are experiencing the divorce of one or more of their adult children. It is estimated that over 50 percent of all marriages that occurred during the 1970s will end in divorce, and it is this cohort of individuals who are facing caregiving responsibilities. Of the high proportion who will remarry, 44 percent are estimated to divorce again, creating the phenomenon of "serial monogamy"—persons having a series of divorces and remarriages throughout their lives (Hobbs and Damon, 1996). Adult children may thus not only be caring for their biological parents and for current parents-in-law, but, if previously divorced, may be emotionally tied to their former spouse's parents, especially through their children of the earlier marriage. Such ties may lead to caregiving responsibilities for former parents-in-law as well. Difficult definitions of family membership and loyalties may complicate the distribution of time, attention, and financial resources across generations.

Women as Caregivers

Women in the middle often face multiple cross-generational demands. Care responsibilities are usually differentiated by gender, such that women comprise over 70 percent of the family caregivers to chronically ill elders; over 50 percent of all women provide such care at some point in the life course (Pavalko and Artis, 1997). Although wives and husbands constitute the majority of the sole or primary caregivers, a hierarchy of preference exists within the female kin network, based on the centrality of the caregiver's relationship to the older person and on geographic proximity. Wives are favored over all others. If the older person who needs care is unmarried, widowed, or has an ill spouse, then an adult daughter or daughter-in-law is commonly the primary caregiver, especially for hands-on care. If a spouse or child is unavailable, then a sister is primarily responsible, and if none of these are available, a female extended family member—such as a niece or a granddaughter—or friends and neighbors assume responsibility (Matthews and Heidorn, 1998; Neal, Ingersoll-Dayton, and Starrels, 1997; Seltzer and Li, 2000; Tennstedt, 1999). Siblings, for example, tend to reduce their caregiving efforts in proportion to the number of sisters available (Wolf, Freedman, and Soldo, 1997). Even when siblings attempt to divide filial responsibilities, sisters are viewed by themselves and their brothers as being in charge. In some instances, brothers' and sons' services are seen as less important, ignored, or not acknowledged as genuine contributions (Matthews, 1995). Yet, daughters and daughters-in-law are more likely to experience caregiving costs without compensatory resources, in part because of lack of reciprocity in exchanges (Ingersoll-Dayton, Starrels, and Dowler, 1996). Even when older persons move in with the eldest son, as in East Indian, Korean, and Japanese cultures, the daughter-in-law is generally still the primary caregiver (Velkoff and Lawson, 1998). A similar pattern is found among gays and lesbians, with lesbians more likely than gay men to be caring for children and older people, and gay men more likely to assist working-age adults with an illness or disability (Fredriksen, 1999). Therefore, it is important to recognize the many ways in which families and loved ones provide care to their elders, and that the quality rather than the type of caregiving relationship is important in the caregiving experience of both biological children and children-in-law (Peters-Davis, Moss, Pruchno, 1999).

The prominence of women in the caregiving role should not obscure the 30 percent of primary caregivers who are men, or what Brody (1985) calls the "unsung heroes" committed to their caregiving roles. As noted earlier, husbands frequently provide extensive care for wives with disabilities (Bengtson et al., 1996; Kramer and Lambert, 1999).

Nevertheless, male adult children tend to be the secondary caregivers, assisting indirectly and intermittently, such as with financial management, home repair, and maintenance. Men generally become involved in personal care and instrumental tasks of cooking and cleaning only when no female relative is available.

Even when sons are involved in tasks similar to those performed by daughters, provide similar amounts of care, and use similar coping strategies, they often experience less stress from caregiving (DeVries, Hamilton, Lovett, Gallagher-Thompson, 1997; Hughes, Giobbie-Hurder, Weaver, Kubel, and Henderson, 1999; Seltzer and Li, 2000). In addition, they are less willing to travel as far or so often to assist their parents (Hallman and Joseph, 1998). This results in part because men tend to maintain more emotional distance from the care receiver, focusing primarily on instrumental assistance. In general, they are less concerned with how caregiving affects the quality of the parental relationship and wait to be asked rather than volunteer help to their parents, except during times of crisis. In such instances, they try to reestablish their parents' independence as soon as possible (Matthews and Heidorn, 1998). Men are more likely to be part of a larger network of services and to perceive more supports. In contrast, women report higher levels of burden; frequently feel responsible for an older relative's psychological well-being, and perceive greater interference between caregiving and their personal and social lives. They also are less likely to view resources as available to assist them with their care responsibilities, even though they often cope by seeking out social and recreational supports. On measures of coping, they frequently respond, "talked with a friend," "got away from things for awhile," "told myself things to feel better" (DeVries et al., 1997; Ingersoll-Dayton et al., 1996).

Women caregivers are more likely than their male counterparts to give up employment, modify their work schedules, or forgo promotions or career development to accommodate care responsibilities. More women are employed than in the past: 75 percent between the ages of 45 and 54, and 49 percent between the ages of 55 and 64. For many women, caregiving falls during the peak employment years of 35 to 64. However, being employed full-time and having a college education do not preclude women from taking on care responsibilities; they do so at rates similar to nonemployed women (Moen, Erickson, and Dempster-McClain 2000; Robison, Moen, and Dempster-McClain, 1995; Tennstedt, 1999). In fact, women employed full-time are four times more likely than working men to be the primary caregivers. Moreover, employed daughters provide nearly equal amounts and types of care as nonemployed daughters do, either directly or through purchased services (Kramer and Kipnis, 1995). Not surprisingly, work disruptions and economic strains are significant predictors of stress for female caregivers. Accordingly, caregivers who frequently adjust their work schedules to accommodate parent care demands are found to be less likely to sustain their caregiving commitment (Lechner, 1991).

In addition, 90 percent of today's middle-aged married women have children of their own to attend to—typically teenagers or young adults, compared to 66 percent of those born before the turn of the century (Cantor, 1991). These "women in the middle" may thus be juggling extensive family responsibilities along with employment and their own age-related transitions. Given the increasing mobility of our society, they also may be providing care at a geographic distance. Some researchers have countered the concept of "women in the middle": only about 33 percent of women in their early forties and 25 percent of women in their late forties were found to combine care of dependent children, elder care, and employment although, as noted above, teens or young adults may still be in the home (Bengtson et al., 1996). Findings are mixed about whether women's multiple concurrent roles enhance or reduce caregiver stress. It does appear that women's perceptions of the quality of the experience, whether the roles impose constraints or generate conflict or rewards, and whether the roles are anticipated and freely chosen are factors that affect women's experiences in multiple roles (Reid and Hardy, 1999; Penning, 1998).

CHARACTERISTICS OF WOMEN AS CAREGIVERS

- Form the majority of caregivers, even when male family members are available, except for spouses
- Feel more psychological responsibility
- Are more likely to give up or modify employment
- Face multiple demands and roles from employment and/or dependent children
- Caregiving is often a "career" over the life course

Regardless of their particular configuration of responsibilities, women try not to reduce the amount of assistance given. Instead they manage their multiple responsibilities by maintaining rigid schedules, negotiating care tasks around their employment or children, and giving up their own free time or reducing hours worked, thereby affecting current income and future retirement benefits; these consequences are discussed more fully in Chapter 15. Despite the amount of care provided, many female caregivers still feel guilty for not doing more (Pavalko and Artis, 1997).

Families of Color as Caregivers

The extent to which race and culture rather than socioeconomic status influence intergenerational relationships is unclear. In contrast to Caucasian families, multigenerational households are more prevalent among African American, Latino, and Asian American families, while spouses of color are less likely to support each other than Caucasian spouses (Tennstedt, 1999). Even when controlling for need, persons of color have been found to be more likely to live in extended families or to depend on non-kin caregivers (friends, neighbors, and paid care workers), who provide both social support and instrumental assistance with finances and activities of daily living, especially for unmarried children and unmarried parents (National Academy on an Aging Society, 2000). The greater prevalence of intergenerational co-residence in communities of color may underlie the higher levels of assistance to frail elders and the generally positive parent–adult child relationships reported by

Hispanic American, African American, and Asian American families compared to Caucasian families. In addition, even when controlling for level of disability, ethnic minority caregivers provide more assistance than Caucasian caregivers and use fewer formal resources (Dilworth-Anderson, Williams, and Cooper, 1999; Tennstedt, 1999).

Others have argued that the role of the extended family is overexaggerated or disintegrating, and that the strength of ties in families of color is more heterogeneous than has been noted in the historical literature on minority family life (Tennstedt, 1999). Some differences attributed to race may be due to socioeconomic status, education, cultural, historical, or other factors. Therefore, it is important to examine differences within and between subgroups (Connell and Gibson, 1997). For example, African American caregivers have been found to exhibit lower levels of stress, burden, and depression than other groups (Hughes et al., 1999). This may be due to:

- the cultural meanings attached to caregiving through extended family and friends
- cultural differences in support resources
- faith in religion as a way to cope with the burden of their care responsibilities
- a reluctance to ask for formal assistance (Calderon and Tennstedt, 1998; Tennstedt, 1999)

As described in Chapter 2, urbanization and modernization have weakened intergenerational ties among many families of color. In traditional Asian American families, for example, the value system emphasizes the importance of the family unit rather than individual gain and independence. However, such values of family obligation are increasingly difficult to implement in a competitive, mobile society, particularly when adult children move into a higher socioeconomic class than their parents. Many Hispanics, for example, have developed strong intergenerational cohesion and support mandated by both their cultural heritage and economic realities—patterns that have been weakened by urbanization and modernization. As the fastest-growing minority group and the most disabled in later years, Hispanic elders rely heavily on adult children. But their caregiving resources are diminished by smaller family size, increased employment of women, and the economic necessity of living at a distance from adult children. Therefore, it is important not to assume that all caregivers of color are more capable of resiliency in providing care. Researchers for example, must evaluate the sensitivity and cultural appropriateness of measures of caregiver stress to ensure that they are not underestimating the burden experienced by caregivers of color. In addition, the existence of extended family living arrangements and fictive kin may carry financial and emotional costs and divert policy makers' attention away from the need for **formal support** services. The effects of changing societal conditions and of socioeconomic class on families of color—and the wide variability within as well as among them—are explored further in Chapter 14.

Demands on Caregivers

Despite physical, financial, and emotional demands, most family members are willing to assume caregiving responsibility, and considerable variability exists in the dynamic effects on the caregiver, depending upon the timing and type of transition in a caregiving career (Seltzer and Li, 2000). For some, caregiving can be a rich and rewarding experience, characterized by greater closeness with family members. In fact, the spillover effects of caregiving on other roles vary widely. Some care-

givers express greater marital satisfaction than noncaregivers, as well as more feelings of efficacy and self-worth, increased participation in voluntary activities, greater sense of the meaning of life, pride in their ability to meet challenges, and closeness in relationships (Farkas and Himes, 1997). Multiple roles do not necessarily lead to overload and stress, because they may be associated with more extensive social support, greater access to resources (e.g., finances), and a heightened sense of personal competence (Bengtson et al., 1996; Kramer, 1997a; Seltzer and Li, 2000). Caregivers tend to experience more gains than costs of care when they define this role as enriching, possess effective problem-solving coping strategies, have social support and assistance, and are in better physical health (Almberg, Grafstroem, and Winblad, 2000; Kramer, 1997a). Not surprisingly, satisfaction in the caregiving role is greater when there is some degree of reciprocity, often when the older person lives with the caregiver and is still able to provide some assistance with household tasks (Pruchno, Burant, and Peters, 1997). However, even when caring for relatives with dementia, where reciprocity is limited, caregivers may experience satisfaction based on norms of solidarity, deeply established attachments, and rich memories (Pearlin, Anashensel, Mullon, and Whitlatch, 1996). These psychological benefits vary over time with caregiving, especially at the critical transition points of entry and exit from the caregiving role (Seltzer and Li, 2000).

Although caregiving is not universally distressing, the health, employment, personal freedom, privacy, and social relationships of many caregivers are negatively affected. The literature on caregiving differentiates between *caring for* and *caring about:* the tangible tasks associated with personal assistance versus feelings of love, worry, and concern (Bengtson et al., 1996). *Objective* and *subjective* **caregiver burdens** are also differentiated. **Objective burden** refers to the reality demands that confront the caregiver, such as symptomatic behaviors of the illness, disruptions in family relationships, income, and social life, and problems accessing services. **Subjective burden** refers to caregivers' feelings as they fulfill their functions, such as worry, sadness, resentment, anger, or guilt. This distinction recognizes that burden is qualitative; what is difficult for one caregiver may not be so for another. Although it has often been assumed that caregiving stress is related to tasks (e.g., the more care provided, the more burden for the caregiver), neither disability status nor the amount and type of care provided are related to burden. Instead, the carer's perception or appraisal of the care demands (e.g., feeling overwhelmed, perceptions of exhaustion, perceived progress) appears to be more salient than are objective burdens (Tennstedt, 1999; Yates, Tennstedt, and Chang, 1999). As another illustration of how caregiving is differentially evaluated, some caregivers of color have been found to endorse more strongly beliefs about filial support; turn to prayer, faith, and religion more readily; and consequently experience less stress, burden, and depression than Caucasian caregivers. It appears that caregiving is more stressful for wives than daughters. This is because wives are more likely to experience losses in marital and family relationships and in social involvement, although their sense of well-being tends to increase when their husband dies and they move into the bereavement phase (Seltzer and Li, 2000). The extent to which caregiving is experienced as burdensome and therefore negative is thus mediated by the following factors:

- the extent of socioemotional support
- possible co-residence
- the saliency of the role
- the timing in one's life course
- coping mechanisms used
- sense of mastery
- cultural values and beliefs (Aranda and Knight, 1997; Connell and Gibson, 1997)

Families are more likely to provide services directly than to purchase them (Tennstedt, 1999). Nevertheless, financial burdens include not only the direct costs of medical care, adaptive equipment, or hired help, but, as noted earlier, indirect opportunity costs include lost income or missed promotions. Potentially competing employment roles do not seem to decrease and actually are positively related to the likelihood of women's caregiving (Moen and Dempster-McClain, 1995). One reason for this association may be that not working—or quitting work—may be a precursor to social isolation that increases caregivers' vulnerability and their negative reaction to care (Pohl, Given, Collins, Given, 1994). Despite the advantages of employment, with 64 percent of caregivers either full- or part-time workers, it is not surprising that caregiving employees report greater job–family conflicts than non-caregiving employees.

The physical demands of providing daily personal assistance, such as frequently changing the bedding of an incontinent elder or dealing with sleep disruption, are experienced most often by caregivers who live with the care recipient and by those of older relatives with dementia (Hughes et al., 1999; Tennstedt, 1999). The physical health effects of caregiving are less clear than the mental health consequences. Physical stress and exhaustion can manifest in health problems, including headaches, depression, anxiety, stomach disturbances, and weight changes (Tennstedt, 1999; Vitaliano, Schulz, Kiecolt-Glaser, and Grant, 1997). Accordingly, they tend to use prescription drugs and medical services more than noncaregivers (Hughes et al., 1999). Not surprisingly, the physical and mental health consequences of caregiving tend to increase with the intensity of the level of care provided (National Academy on an Aging Society, 2000; National Alliance for Caregiving and AARP, 1997).

Emotional Stresses of Caregiving

The *emotional burdens* of worrying about the care recipient, feeling alone and isolated, and giving up time for oneself (e.g., vacation, leisure, hobbies) appear to be the greatest costs of caregiving, and are experienced more by women than men (National Academy on an Aging Society, 2000). Relationships with other family members and with friends

---

SUMMARY OF SOURCES OF CAREGIVER STRESS

Financial
- Direct costs of care
- Missed opportunities in career
- Reduced hours (and income) at work
- Work absenteeism
- Job–family conflicts and disruptions
- Accommodations necessary at the workplace

Physical
- Health problems (headaches, stomach disturbances, and weight changes)
- Use of prescription drugs and health services
- Sleep disorders and exhaustion
- Neglect of self and others

Emotional
- Depression
- Guilt, anger, resentment, and denial
- Anxiety
- Social isolation
- Worry
- Feelings of being alone and isolated
- Giving up of time for oneself (and family)
- Strained social and family relationships
- Negative attitude toward care recipient

---

are frequently disrupted. Rates of depression may increase, especially among long-term caregivers and those assisting relatives with dementia who evidence disruptive behaviors such as wandering and verbal outbursts (Prescop, Dodge, Morycz, Schulz, and Ganguli, 1999; Tennstedt, 1999; Vitaliano et al., 1997). Not only do dementia caregivers spend more hours providing care, but they also report more negative effects in terms of employment, caregiver strain, mental and physical health problems, reduced leisure, and family conflict (Ory et al., 1999). The psychological effects of the older dementia patient's cognitive decline and associated anticipatory bereavement of a situation that can only get worse are often as stressful or more so than the tasks of providing care. Such psychological stress can itself result in health problems and may not necessarily be alleviated by services such as respite care (Almberg et al., 2000; Pillemer and Suitor, 1996; Mittelman et al., 1995). Although wide variability exists among caregivers, it appears that it is not necessarily the duration of caregiving, but rather the increasing amounts of difficult care and lack of control that wear down and isolate the caregiver and decrease caregiving satisfaction (Ory et al., 1999; Walker, Aacock, Bowman, and Li, 1996). Caregivers use a variety of private, personal,

or informal methods to cope with stress; these include prayer, talking with friends or relatives, exercise, hobbies, and professional counseling.

FORMAL AND INFORMAL SERVICE UTILIZATION

Although men are more likely than women to utilize formal caregiving services, most families do not use them, or do so selectively to supplement informal care for limited time periods (National Alliance for Caregiving and AARP, 1997; Tennstedt, 1999). In fact, only about 5 to 10 percent of older adults depend solely on paid helpers, and those with only paid assistance tend to be institutionalized earlier (Juster et al., 1996). Eligibility for services is typically based on functional disability in the performance of specified ADLs. However, it appears important that cognitive ability also be considered. Home care is the most frequently used service, especially by caregivers who are providing higher levels of care, as for example for a relative with dementia or when there is change in the primary caregiver (Miller et al, 1996; Tennstedt, 1999; Short and Leon, 1995). In some instances, caregivers are unaware of services, do not think

---

SELF-CARE NEEDS OF THE CAREGIVER

- Learn to accept help.
- Take time for relaxing and pleasurable activities by asking others for help or utilizing respite/adult day care.
- Find ways to incorporate exercise into your daily routine.

- Take time to eat healthy food.
- Set limits on your older relative's demands.
- Attend to your spiritual needs.
- Participate in caregiver support groups.

---

they need them, or are "too proud" to use them. In others, they may find that services, such as respite care, may actually deplete their energy through the processes required to access them, or they may feel they are imposing on paid helpers. In fact, service use has been found to have minimal effects on caregiver well-being (National Alliance for Caregiving and AARP, 1997; Tennstedt, 1999; Worcester and Hedrick, 1997). Cultural differences in service utilization exist. African Americans, for example, are more likely than whites to turn to informal supports and prayer, and to use cognitive strategies to reframe the situation in positive terms. Caucasians are more likely to seek help from professionals and use problem-solving methods (Dilworth-Anderson, et al., 1999). Despite these differences, only about 4 percent of African Americans and whites use only formal services for assistance (Miller et al., 1996). In fact, the most common mechanisms used by caregivers to cope with strains are prayer and talking with relatives and friends (National Academy on an Aging Society, 2000). In some instances, caregivers may participate in support and educational groups focused on caregiving or their relative's disease as a way to relieve stress (Farkas and Himes, 1997; Tennstedt, 1999).

Although service utilization is low, most caregivers seek out information, largely from health professionals, and report that health-related information and materials on how to provide basic care are most useful. They also want more information about how to balance caregiving with work and family and ways to reduce stress. This suggests the importance of providing readily ac-

cessible information in a variety of formats (literature, video and audio tapes, phone counseling) that focus on self-care and facilitating helpful caregiving (National Alliance for Caregiving and the Equitable Foundation, 1998).

Generally, caregiving is not a shared activity, with the primary caregiver providing most of the care (Tennstedt, 1999). Most informal care networks include secondary helpers, but they are more likely to assist with intermittent and predictable tasks than with the day-to-day personal care. In fact, over 30 percent of primary caregivers have been found to report that no one is available to replace them if they become unable to continue this role (Penrod, Kane, Kane, and Finch, 1995). Lack of support resources can heighten caregivers' feelings of isolation, and, in turn, of stress. In fact, feelings of burden have been found to be strongly related to the availability of external helping resources and social support, not to the severity of the illness. Accordingly, positive and diverse informal networks and help, such as assistance with personal care and household tasks, can enhance the caregiver's well-being (Bass, Noelker, and Rechlin, 1996). Alternatively, caregivers with kin-dominated networks report less satisfaction with the support received and a high degree of conflict compared to those with more diverse networks (both kin and nonkin) (Fudge, Neufeld, and Harrison, 1997). Most caregivers report that no one in their network of family or friends regularly assists them with hands-on care. Even when family and friends help, the timing and frequency of their well-intended actions may fail to be supportive (Pearlin et al., 1996).

INTERVENTIONS TO SUPPORT CAREGIVERS

Any patient assessment should also include an assessment of the caregiver's status, especially his or her subjective appraisal of the situation rather than only availability and physical ability to provide care. In addition to the provision of services such as adult day, respite, or home health care, a wide range of psychosocial and educational interventions have been developed by both nonprofit agencies and private geriatricians to ensure the well-being of the caregiver as well as the care recipient. These include counseling in person or by phone, training programs to teach caregiving skills, self-care techniques, and support groups focused on caregiving for specific diseases such as Alzheimer's, Parkinson's or cancer. Findings regarding the efficacy of these interventions are mixed. In some cases, they appear to prolong the duration of caregiving, but not necessarily reduce the caregivers' subjective burden, in part because some problems have become too difficult to solve through short-term interventions (Given, Given, Stommel, and Azzouz, 1999; Tennstedt, 1999; Zarit, Todd, and Zarit, 1986). This is because most caregivers do not plan for changes in the situation, but rather "take it one day at a time." Interventions that develop coping skills and mobilize informal supports are likely to show more benefit than ones focused on relieving burden per se. Whether the care recipient has dementia affects the intervention, since caring for dementia patients with behavioral problems appears to be most stressful.

Increasingly, providers recognize the need for a preventive approach in training caregivers in technical skills, obtaining emotional support, and developing a sense of mastery before they actually need it. A challenge then is to identify caregivers and intervene before they define themselves as caregivers or perceive the need for outside assistance. Programs through churches, hospitals, and primary-care clinics, senior and community centers, and the workplace could be targeted to help potential caregivers plan and problem-solve before they may be abruptly thrust into a burdensome role (McKinlay, 1996; Tennstedt, 1999). Unfortunately, it is human nature that most people will not seek out information and help until they need it—and sometimes the need is critical. General information sessions about community services are frequently not well attended. An effective strategy might be to engage a caregiver in planning shortly after experiencing the first acute event or receiving the diagnosis of dementia or a fatal disease. This approach may increase caregivers receptivity to new information that could be aimed specifically at that condition.

ELDER ABUSE

In some cases, caregiving stress may become severe enough to lead to family conflict, breakdown, neglect, abuse or financial exploitation of the older person. Four to five percent of old people are abused by someone with whom they share housing, often remaining invisible within the home (Carluccio, 1997; Wold, 2000). **Elder abuse** is an all-inclusive term, representing all types of mistreatment or abusive behavior toward older adults. This mistreatment can be an act of commission (abuse) or omission (neglect), intentional

---

FORMAL SUPPORTS FOR CAREGIVERS

- Adult day care
- Respite care
- Home health care
- Counseling in person or by phone

- Training programs/skill development
- Self-care techniques
- Support groups
- Internet resources, chat rooms

WHAT IS ELDER ABUSE?

- Physical or sexual abuse: malnutrition or injuries such as bruises, welts, sprains, dislocations, abrasions, lacerations, forced sexual contact
- Psychological abuse: verbal assault, threat, fear, or isolation
- Material or financial exploitation: theft or misuse of the person or the person's money or property for another person's profit or advantage

- Medical abuse: withholding or improper administration of needed medications, or withholding of aids such as dentures, glasses, or hearing aids
- Passive or active neglect: conduct by the abuser resulting in the deprivation of care necessary to maintain physical and mental health
- Violation of rights: forcing an older person from home or into an institutional setting without his or her consent

or unintentional, and of one or more types: *physical, emotional (e.g., verbal aggression), or financial.* Neglect and physical abuse (slapping, hitting, bruising) are most common (National Center on Elder Abuse, 1998). Whether behavior is labeled as abusive may depend on its frequency, duration, intensity, severity, consequences and the cultural context. Regardless of how various state statutes define abuse and neglect, the older person's perception of the action and the cultural context in which the action occurs are primary factors in its identification and interpretation (Wold, 2000; Hudson and Carlson, 1999).

Although caregiver stress and the elder's impairment level or health status are part of the context in which the abuse often occurs, they do not in themselves lead to abusive situations. Stress is often a contributing factor, but in itself it does not explain the occurrence of abuse. Consistent with the person–environment model underlying this book, the cause lies instead in the context for interaction: in the interplay of characteristics of the abuser and the victim and thus the interplay of individual, interpersonal and societal factors. Characteristics of the abuser associated with high-risk situations include life stresses, financial or housing dependency, mental illness, substance abuse, and lack of empathy for those with disabilities (Anetzberger, et al., 2000; Brandl, 2000; Hwalek, Neale, Goodrich, and Quinn, 1996; Kosberg and Hamiash, 1996; Quinn and Tomita, 1997). Accordingly, certain characteristics of the care recipient have been found to be associated with

greater probability of abuse: behavior perceived by the caregiver as aggressive, critical, complaining, combative, excessively dependent or unrealistic in expectations (Anetzberger et al, 2000; Buckwalter, Campbell, Gardner, and Garand, 1996). Given these factors, it is not surprising that older adults with Alzheimer's or other dementias, who may display aggressive, unpredictable behavior and who are typically less able to report abuse or to access services, are the most vulnerable (McConnell, 2000).

From a feminist theoretical perspective on domestic violence, elder abuse typically involves unequal power relationships, with the abuser exerting power and control over the older dependent person. Alternatively, some abusers are dependent on the victim for financial or other types of assistance (e.g., having dinner cooked and clothes washed) (Brandl, 2000). Such power dynamics are often present in adult child–parent and spousal relationships. In almost 90 percent of the incidents with a known perpetrator, he or she is a family member, and 60 percent are adult children or spouses. Not surprisingly, female elders are abused at a higher rate than males, comprising approximately 70 percent of those abused. The oldest-old are abused at two to three times their proportion of the older population (National Center on Elder Abuse, 1998). Spousal abuse may reflect lifelong patterns with older women who are isolated and "falling between the cracks"—too old to go to shelters designed for younger women and invisible to providers of services to older people (Bengtson

---

POINTS TO PONDER

Does the state have a responsibility to monitor the lives of older people who are at risk of self-neglect? Do people have a right to live in a mess? What would you do if you knew of an older person living alone in a filthy, unhealthy house?

---

et al., 1996). An explanation that abuse reflects the marginalization of elders, especially women and the oldest-old, within society is consistent with the political economy theory described in Chapter 8.

Legally competent but mentally or physically impaired elders may fall into the category of **elder neglect or self-neglect.** In some instances, failure to care for oneself and resisting services may be a lifestyle choice, often begun when younger (Simon, Milligan, Guider, Puzan, Ellano, and Atkin, 1997). Self-neglect is often associated with dementia or other type of mental impairment, isolation, depression, and alcohol abuse (Anetzberger et al., 2000). Instances of elder abuse illustrate that it is unrealistic to expect all families to assume care functions, especially when the caregivers themselves are vulnerable—over age 75, in fair or poor health, with substance abuse problems, and low income.

Warning signs of abuse include:

- depression
- fear
- anxiety in the older patient
- illness that does not appear to be responding to treatment
- frequent trips to the emergency room

In all states but eight, physicians, other health care professionals, and service providers are required by law to report familial abuse of older relatives, although only about 16 percent of elder abuse cases are reported (Wold, 2000). The fact that abuse is not readily discernible and typically concealed by either the caregiver or the care recipient underlies the low rate of reported incidents. As an illustration, it can be especially difficult to determine if an older person is being deprived of needed medications (Reis, 2000). Another factor is that most of the validated screening measures need to be completed by the possible abused care recipient, who typically is fearful of reporting or may be too cognitively impaired to respond to such questions. A number of factors may explain this low rate, including the societal value placed on family privacy and health care providers' reluctance to suspect abuse by family members. In particular, professional codes of ethics that emphasize client confidentiality often inhibit even legally mandated individuals from contacting authorities about elder abuse reported by their clients (Anetzberger et al., 2000). When incidents are reported, over 60 percent of these are substantiated after investigation, but relatively few are prosecuted, often because of witnesses or victims who are unable or unwilling to testify (Carluccio, 1997; National Center on Elder Abuse, 1998).

Adult Protective Services (APS) is the state or county service system that becomes involved in instances of abuse or neglect, including self-neglect. Most APS agencies covered by state statutes receive reports, conduct investigations, evaluate client risk, assess clients' capacity to agree to services, develop and implement case plans, and monitor ongoing service delivery (Otto, 2000). Since mandatory reporting laws require that APS workers must accept all reports of abuse or neglect, their caseloads are often filled with the most complex and difficult cases with whom other agencies are unwilling or unable to work. An additional barrier faced by APS workers is that few community-based alternatives exist for older people who are removed from abusive situations. Another challenge is that clients' needs for medical and in-home support services may be increasingly unavailable because of managed health care. At the same time,

---

PRINCIPLES THAT SHAPE ADULT PROTECTIVE SERVICES PRACTICE

- The client's right to self-determination
- The use of the least restrictive alternative
- The maintenance of the family unit whenever possible
- The use of community-based services rather than institutions

- The avoidance of ascription of blame
- The presumption that inadequate or inappropriate services are worse than none (Otto, 2000)

---

many professionals have a bias toward home care and resist turning to institutionalization even when appropriate.

Although APS workers frequently deal with older people who are no longer competent to make decisions, they need to assess the older person's right to refuse professional assistance. This is especially critical in instances where families too readily seek guardianship or full decision-making authority over personal, financial, and estate affairs. Guardianships are often routinely approved by the courts, even though incompetence may not be demonstrated. Such family actions may be motivated by interest in preserving the estate, and role conflict in guardians often occurs (Hansson and Carpenter, 1994). Professionals and prosecutors are typically faced with how to distinguish elder abuse from competent consent. Despite fears that services may be provided against the client's will, a national survey showed that less than 10 percent of adult protection clients received services without their consent and that all states made vigorous efforts to protect clients' rights (Otto, 2000). Since mandatory reporting is seen by some as threaten-

ing client autonomy, it is a highly charged issue and does not necessarily prevent abuse (Otto, 2000).

Older people are also exploited by strangers who take advantage of their loneliness, confusion, and sense of vulnerability. **Fiduciary abuse** is especially common; this happens when a person who has care or custody, or who stands in a position of trust to a dependent adult, takes or appropriates his or her money or property to any use not in the lawful execution of the older adult's trust (Wisbaum, 1997). The abuser can be a family member or a stranger. Older people are especially prone to scams, typically of home repairs and construction, mail order, insurance, and motor vehicle complaints. Such victimization is discussed more fully in Chapter 11.

Central to an elder abuse prevention system are the elder's rights to self-determination and autonomy, but these are difficult to determine in most high-risk situations. Those working in the field of elder abuse and neglect struggle with determining *undue influence:* the substitution of a person's will for the true desires of another. It occurs when one person uses his or her role and power to

---

FIDUCIARY ABUSE

An 83-year-old woman thought she was signing loan documents to get her house out of foreclosure, but instead signed a grant deed presented to her by a mortgage loan broker, who had had his license revoked. With only an eighth-grade education, she was unaware of the licensing situation, and did not know what the words "grant deed" meant. As a result, she signed the papers but had not intended to give away the title to her house of 25 years. After her daughter discovered what had happened to her mother, she was distraught. Her mother died before the situation could go to trial.

COMPONENTS OF A MODEL INTERVENTION FOR ELDER ABUSE AND DEMENTIA

- Educational curriculum for cross-training for APS, Alzheimer's Association, and other staff
- A screening tool for use by Alzheimer's Association staff and volunteers
- Protocols for referral and intervention among these services—providing partners

- A handbook for caregivers to self-assess risk of elder abuse and to identify community resources
- Education, identification, assessment, advocacy, and collaboration among professionals are integrated in most elder abuse investigations (Anetzberger et al., 2000)

---

exploit the trust, dependency, and fear of another to gain control over the decision making of the weaker person. Undue influence can happen to older adults who would otherwise be considered capable and competent, often because they are lonely and eager for companionship (Quinn, 2000). Alternatively, professionals in this field must deal with the question: Does the family have a right to interfere if an older person who is mentally competent engages in risky behavior or makes risky investments because of what the family perceives to be others' undue influence? The ethical complexity of addressing these issues increases when cultural differences in perceptions and definitions of abuse are involved.

In some cities, multiservice centers have joined with Adult Protective Services to provide education, advocacy, and coping skills training to older adults to reduce their vulnerability. Through the Older Americans Act, long-term care ombudsmen at the city or state level have statutory authority to investigate complaints from concerned citizens, especially pertaining to nursing homes as well as board and care facilities.

INSTITUTIONALIZATION: A PAINFUL DECISION FOR FAMILY MEMBERS

The strain on caregivers, especially high levels of subjective burden, may cause them to seek relief through institutionalization of their older relatives. As noted above, most families first attempt to provide care on their own without utilizing alternative community-based services, even though use of

such services could perhaps prevent caregiver burnout and avoid nursing home admission. Although expensive, alternatives such as respite and adult day care have been found to delay or decrease the likelihood of nursing home placement and in some instances to enhance caregivers' well-being (Collins, King, and Kokinakis, 1994; Kammer, 1994; Kosloski and Montgomery, 1995; Zarit, Stephens, Townsend, and Greene, 1998).

Although living alone is a major predictor of institutionalization, some 50 percent of those in institutions have children (Tennstedt, 1999). In most cases, children and spouses resort to institutionalization only after exhausting their own resources, but adult daughters and caregiving husbands tend to turn to nursing home placement earlier than do wives (Seltzer and Li, 2000). The decision to seek institutionalization is often precipitated by the family caregiver's illness or death, or by severe family strain (Seltzer and Li, 2000). For example, the characteristics of the caregiving context—especially perceived burden, negative family feelings and relationships, and low family efficiency and confidence in care—are better predictors of whether an Alzheimer's patient will be institutionalized than are the illness characteristics or symptoms of the care receiver (Fisher and Lieberman, 1999; Tennstedt, 1999).

Most older people and their caregivers hold negative attitudes toward nursing homes and first try to bring services into the home, even though the quality of care in many nursing homes is good. Placing an older relative in a nursing home is typically a stressful life event for the family, especially for wives (Seltzer and Li, 2000). Characterized by moral dilemmas, the placement decision may arouse feelings of grief, guilt, and fear, and renew past family conflicts. As a result of reduced burden, however, some families experience improvements in their relationships with institutionalized members; they continue to visit their older relatives and assist with their hands-on care, even though the level of their activities might decline (Pearlin et al., 1996). Type of kinship care relationship appears to affect the transition to nursing home placement. For example, wives have been found to experience more benefits from exiting the primary caregiving role than daughters have (Seltzer and Li, 2000). On the other hand, "the careers of caregivers do not stop at the institution's door," largely because new stresses substitute for prior ones (Zarit and Whitlatch, 1992, p. 672). In addition, families must relinquish control over daily care decisions to staff and learn how to be an effective "visitor." These role changes for families can create dissatisfaction with their elders' institutional care.

With the growth of the oldest-old, placement in a nursing home or other long-term care setting such as assisted living or an adult family home (as discussed in Chapter 11) may come to be viewed as a natural transition in the life cycle. Professional assistance with the appropriate timing of transition to a special care environment and with negotiating a role for the caregiver's continued involvement could facilitate what might otherwise be interpreted primarily as a tremendous loss. To ease the transition to the postplacement phase, many nursing homes have developed support and educational groups for families and special training for staff. When staff–family partnerships develop, families typically experience less stress and are more satisfied with the care (Maas, 2000).

LEGAL AND POLICY QUESTIONS REGARDING CAREGIVING

The role of adult children in caring for older relatives is an increasingly important policy and practice issue. From a policy perspective, the issue of family responsibility has long been a topic of debate. Most states have had filial responsibility laws (rarely enforced) that require financially able children to contribute to their aging parents' support. Policies have been organized on the premise that the family has first responsibility for dependent older persons, and that the state should intervene only after the family's resources are exhausted. For example, ours is the only Western industrialized society without a caregiver allowance as part of the Social Security system. This is partially because policy makers fear that formal services would be overutilized and would substitute for families. Yet, as noted above, most families provide care without formal assistance, especially families of color. When families do use services, it is in addition to their own care—not to replace it (Hendricks and Rosenthal, 1993; Noelker and Bass, 1994; Tennstedt, Crawford, and McKinley, 1993).

For nearly 30 years, Congress has introduced, and in some instances passed, legislation that either requires adult children to financially support their older parents or, alternatively, supports family care through tax credits and limited cash benefits. Often this is presented as a cost-effective way to reduce institutionalization (Stone and Keigher, 1994). There is growing recognition that the costs of caregiving are too great for either the family or the state to bear alone, and more policies and programs are being developed to complement the family's efforts. More social and health care providers now assess the caregiver's status along with that of the older patient and consider caregivers' needs in the overall treatment plan. Programs have been structured to improve caregivers' abilities to manage the care situation, such as counseling, education, skills training, multimedia resources, and support groups. These programs also aim to relieve the caregiver's burden, such as through respite and adult day care (Kosloski and Montgomery, 1995; Ostwald, Hepburn, Caron, Burns, and Mantell, 1999). Broader policy changes to support caregivers, however, have been relatively limited in their impact. For example, after a lengthy political battle and compromise, the **Family and Medical Leave Act** was signed into law by President Clinton in 1993. This act offers job protection to workers requiring short-term unpaid leaves from their jobs for the care of a dependent parent or seriously ill newborn or adopted child. However, this legislation does not cover temporary or part-time workers or those in small firms, even though 50 percent of all employees in the private sector work for small businesses. In effect, it benefits only those who can afford to forgo income while on leave. In contrast, many Western European countries, particularly in Scandinavia, provide services to older people and even pay relatives to stay home to provide care. Some also offer special pensions for those who have spent many years in a caregiving role.

In the United States, some corporations have developed family leave policies, and the majority of states provide economic supports through tax credits or direct payments, although these tax supports are underutilized by caregivers of older adults. A growing number of localities have initiated services to support families:

- by decreasing the older person's needs for care (e.g., adult day care programs and in-home chore services), or
- by increasing the family's resources (e.g., educational programs, support groups, respite care, and clinical or direct service interventions).

Local area agencies on aging and information and referral services are often the best place for families to access such services. Corporations are also beginning to provide elder care information, referral, education, and adult day care, often through employee-assistance programs. Such services are often "good business," since caregiving carries costs in terms of absenteeism, shortened or interrupted workdays, and replacement of employees. Computer access to the Internet and Websites can also provide caregivers with information on community resources, including living facilities, and an opportunity to connect with other caregivers through 24-hour support. More services, however, are needed for those with the greatest subjective needs.

SUMMARY AND IMPLICATIONS

Most families, regardless of socioeconomic class or ethnic minority status, attempt to provide care for their older members for as long as possible, and seek institutionalization only when they have exhausted other resources. Without informal caregiving, the costs of long-term care to society would be staggering. Adult children—generally women—are faced with providing financial, emotional, and physical assistance to older relatives, oftentimes with little support from others for their caregiving responsibilities. In ethnic minority and lower-income families, older relatives are most likely to receive daily care from younger relatives and to be involved themselves in caring for grandchildren. But there are numerous personal costs to caregiving, including financial, physical, and emotional. Elder abuse is one tragic outcome of a stressful caregiving situation. Responsibilities for caregiving are affected by a number of social trends, most notable among them the increasing percentage of middle-aged women—traditionally the caregivers—who are more likely to be employed, and the number of reconstituted families resulting from divorce and remarriage. The needs of caregivers are clearly a growing concern for social and health care providers and policy makers.

GLOSSARY

caregiving   the act of assisting people with personal care, household chores, transportation, and other tasks associated with daily living; provided either by family members without compensation or by professionals

caregiver burden   the personal energy, time restrictions, financial strains, and/or psychological frustrations associated with assisting persons with long-term care needs

elder abuse   maltreatment of older adults, including physical, sexual, psychological, and financial exploitation

elder neglect   deprivation of care necessary to maintain elders' health by those trusted to provide the care (e.g., neglect by others) or by older persons themselves (self-neglect)

empty nest a family whose adult children have left home for a job or college or marriage

Family and Medical Leave Act federal legislation passed in 1993 that provides job protection to workers requiring short-term leaves from their jobs for the care of a dependent parent or seriously ill newborn or adopted child

informal caregiving Unpaid assistance provided by family, friends, and neighbors for persons requiring help with ADLs and IADLs

objective burden reality demands that caregivers face (income loss, job disruption, etc.).

subjective burden the caregiver's experience of caregiver burden; different caregivers appraise caregiver stress differently

women in the middle women who have competing demands from older parents, spouses, children, or employment

RESOURCES

See the companion Website for this text at <www.ablongman.com/hooyman> for information about the following:

- Caregiver Zone
- Caregiving
- Caring Concepts
- Children of Aging Parents
- Eldercare Locator
- Eldercare Web
- Family Caregiver Alliance
- The Home Care Page
- National Alliance for Caregiving
- National Center on Elder Abuse, NCEA
- National Family Caregivers Association
- National Institute on Adult Day Care

REFERENCES

Almberg, B., Grafstroem, M., and Winblad, B. Caregivers of relatives with dementia: Experiences encompassing social support and bereavement. *Aging and Mental Health*, 2000, *4*, 82–89.

Anetzberger, G. Caregiving: Primary cause of elder abuse? *Generations*, Summer 2000, *24*, 46–51.

Anetzberger, G. J., Palmisano, B. R., Sanders, M., Bass, D., Dayton, C., Eckert, S., and Schimer, M. R. A Model intervention for elder abuse and dementia. In E. S. McConnell (Ed.), Practice Concepts. *The Gerontologist*, 2000, *40*, 492–497.

Aranda, M., and Knight, B. G. The influence of ethnicity and culture on the caregiver stress and coping process: A sociocultural review and analysis. *The Gerontologist*, 1997, *37*, 342–354.

Arno, P. S., Levine, C., and Memmot, M. M. The economic value of informal caregiving. *Health Affairs*, 1999, *18*, 182–188.

Bass, D., Noelker, L. S., and Rechlin, L. The moderating influence of service use on negative caregiving consequences. *Journals of Gerontology*, 1996, *51B*, S121–S131.

Bengtson, V. C., Rosenthal, C. J., and Burton, C. Paradoxes of families and aging. In R. H. Binstock and C. K. George (Eds.), *Handbook of aging and the social sciences* (4th ed.). San Diego: Academic Press, 1996.

Brandl, B. Power and control: Understanding domestic abuse in later life. *Generations*, 2000, *24*, 39–45.

Brody, E. Parent care as a normative family stress. *The Gerontologist*, 1985, *25*, 19–30.

Buckwalter, K. C., Campbell, J., Gardner, L. A., and Garand, L. Elder mistreatment among rural family caregivers of persons with Alzheimer's disease and related disorders. *Journal of Family Nursing*, 1996, *2*, 249–265.

Calderon, V., and Tennstedt, S. L. Ethnic differences in the expression of caregiver burden: Results of a qualitative study. *Journal of Gerontological Social Work*, 1998, *30*, 159–178.

Cantor, M. Family caregiving: Social care. In M. Cantor (Ed.), *Family caregiving: Agenda for the future*. San Francisco: American Society on Aging, 1994.

Cantor, M. Family and community: Changing roles in an aging society. *The Gerontologist*, 1991, 31, 337–340.

Carluccio, T. E. Emotional Abuse: Is it a crime, civil matter or freedom of speech? A criminal and civil perspective. In *Silent suffering: Elder abuse in America*. Archstone Foundation, 1997, 8–14.

Collins, C., King, S., and Kokinakis, C. Community service issues before nursing home placement of persons with dementia. *Western Journal of Nursing Research*, 1994, *16*, 40–52.

Connell, C. M., and Gibson, G. D. Racial, ethnic and cultural differences in dementia caregiving: Review and analysis. *The Gerontologist*, 1997, *37*, 355–364.

DeVries, H. M., Hamilton, D. W., Lovett, S., and Gallagher-Thompson, D. Patterns of coping preferences for male and female caregivers of frail older adults. *Psychology and Aging,* 1997, *12,* 263–267.

Dilworth-Anderson, P., Williams, S. W., and Cooper, T. Family caregiving to elderly African Americans: Caregiver types and structures. *Journals of Gerontology: Social Sciences,* 1999, *54B,* S237–S241.

Doty, P. J., Stone, R. I., Jackson, M. E., and Drabek, J. L. Informal caregiving. In C. J. Evashivick (Ed.), *The continuum of long-term care* (2nd ed.) Albany, NY: Delmar, 2001.

Farkas, J. I., and Hines, C. L. The influence of caregiving and employment on the voluntary activities of midlife and older women. *Journals of Gerontology,* 1997, *52,* S180–S189.

Fisher, L., and Lieberman, M. A. A longitudinal study of predictors of nursing home placement for patients with dementia: The contribution of family characteristics. *The Gerontologist,* 1999, *39,* 677–686.

Fredriksen, K. L. Family caregiving responsibilities among lesbians and gay men. *Social Work,* March 1999, *44,* 142–155.

Fudge, H., Neufeld, A., and Harrison, M. J. Social networks of women caregivers. *Public Health Nursing,* 1997, *14,* 20–27.

Given, C. W., Given, B. A., Stommel, M., and Azzouz, F. The impact of new demands for assistance on caregiver depression: tests using an inception cohort. *The Gerontologist,* 1999, *39,* 76–85.

Hallman, B. C., and Joseph, A. E. Over the hill and far away: Distance as a barrier to the provision of assistance to elderly relatives. *Social Science and Medicine,* March 1998, *46,* 631–639.

Hansson, R. O., and Carpenter, B. N. *Relationships in old age: coping with the challenge of transition.* New York: The Guilford Press, 1994.

Hendricks, J., and Rosenthal, C. *The remainder of their days: Domestic policy for older families in the United States and Canada.* New York: Garland Publishing, 1993.

Hobbs, F. B., and Damon, B. C. *65+ in the United States.* Washington, DC: U.S. Bureau of the Census, Current Population Reports, 1996.

Hudson, M. F., and Carlson, J. R. Elder abuse: Its meaning to Caucasians, African Americans, and Native Americans. In T. Tattara, (Ed.), *Understanding elder abuse in minority populations.* Philadelphia: Taylor and Francis, 1999.

Hughes, S. L., Gobbie-Hurder, A., Weaver, F. M., Kubal, J. D., and Henderson, W. Relationship between caregiver burden and health-related quality of life. *The Gerontologist,* October 1999, *39,* 534–545.

Hwalek, M. A., Neale, A. V., Goodrich, C. S., and Quinn, K. The association of elder abuse and substance abuse in the Illinois elder abuse system. *The Gerontologist,* 1996, *36,* 694–700.

Ingersoll-Dayton, B., Starrels, M., and Dowler, D. Caregiving for parents and parents-in-law: Is gender important? *The Gerontologist,* 1996, *36,* 483–491.

Juster, F. T., Soldo, B., Kington, R. S., and Mitchell, O. *Aging well: Health, wealth, and retirement.* Washington, DC: Consortium of Social Science Association, 1996.

Kammer, C. Stress and coping of family members responsible for nursing home placement. *Research in Nursing and Health,* 1994, *17,* 89–98.

Kosberg, J. I., and Garcia, J. L. Confronting maltreatment of elders by their family. In G. C. Smith, S. Tobin, E. A. Robertson-Tchabo, and P. Power (Eds.), *Strengthening aging families: Diversity in practice and policy.* Thousand Oaks, CA: Sage, 1995.

Kosberg, J. I., and Hanmiash, D. Characteristics of victims and perpetrators and milieus of abuse and neglect. In L. A. Baumhover and S. C. Beall (Eds.), *Abuse, neglect, and exploitation of older persons: Strategies for assessment and intervention.* Baltimore, MD: Health Professions Press, 1996.

Kosloski, K., and Montgomery, R. The impact of respite use on nursing home placement. *The Gerontologist,* 1995, *35,* 67–74.

Kramer, B. J. Differential prediction of strain and gain among husbands caring for wives with dementia. *The Gerontologist,* 1997b, *37,* 239–249.

Kramer, B. J. Gain in the caregiving experience: Where are we? What next? *The Gerontologist,* 1997a, *37,* 218–232.

Kramer, B. J., and Kipnis, S. Eldercare and work-role conflict: Toward an understanding of gender differences in caregiver burden. *The Gerontologist,* 1995, *35,* 340–347.

Kramer, B. J., and Lambert, H. J. D. Caregiving as a life course transition among older husbands: A prospective study. *The Gerontologist,* 1999, *39,* 658–667.

Lawton, M. P., and Nahemow, L. Ecology and the aging process. In C. Eisdorfer and M. P. Lawton

(Eds.), *Psychology of adult development and aging*. Washington, DC: American Psychological Association, 1973.

Lechner, J. Predicting future commitment and care for frail parents among employed caregivers. *Journal of Gerontological Social Work*, 1991, *18*, 69–84.

Maas, M. When elders transition, so do their caregivers: Invited Commentary. *Transitions*, Wayne State University Institute of Gerontology, 2000, *7*, 2, 8.

Matthews, S. H. Gender and the division of filial responsibility between lone sisters and their brothers. *Journals of Gerontology*, 1995, *50B*, S312–S320.

Matthews, S. H., and Heidorn, J. Meeting filial responsibilities in brothers-only sibling groups. *Journals of Gerontology*, 1998, *53B*, S278–S286.

McConnell, B. R., and McConnell, E. S. Treating excess disability among cognitively impaired nursing home residents. *Journal of the American Geriatrics Society*, 2000, *48*, 454–455.

McKinlay, J. Some contributions from the social system to gender inequalities in heart disease. *Journal of Health and Social Behavior*, 1996, *37*, 1–26.

Metropolitan Life Insurance Company. *Met Life study of employer costs for working caregivers*. Westport, CT: Metropolitan Life Insurance Co., 1998.

Miller, B., and Cafasso, L. Gender differences in caregiving: Fact or artifact? *The Gerontologist*, 1992, *32*, 498–507.

Miller, B., Campbell, R. T., Davis, L., Turner, S., Giachello, A., Prohaska, T., Kaufman, J. E., Li, M., and Perez, C. Minority use of community long-term care services: A comparative analysis. *Journals of Gerontology*, 1996, *51B*, S70–S81.

Mittelman, M. S., Ferris, S. H., Shalman, E., Steinberg, G., and Levin. B. A family intervention to delay nursing home placement of patients with Alzheimer disease: A randomized controlled trial, *Journal of the American Medical Association*, 1996, *276*, 1725–1731.

Mittelman, M., Ferris, S., Shalmon, E., Steinberg, G., Ambinder, A., Mackell, J., and Cohen, J. A comprehensive support program: Effect on depression in spouse caregiving of dementia patients. *The Gerontologist*, 1995, *35*, 792–802.

Moen, P., and Dempster-McClain, D. Women's caregiving: changing profiles and pathways. *Journals of Gerontology B*, 1995, *50*, S362–73.

Moen, P., Erickson, M. A., and Dempster-McClain, D. Social role identities among older adults in a continuing care retirement community. *Research on Aging*, 2000 *22*, 559–579.

National Academy on an Aging Society. *Helping the elderly with activity limitations: Caregiving, #7:* Washington, DC: May 2000.

National Alliance for Caregiving and AARP. *Family caregiving in the U.S.: Findings from a national survey.* Washington, DC: June 1997.

National Alliance for Caregiving and the Equitable Foundation. *The caregiving boom: Baby boomer women giving care.* Bethesda, MD: September 1998.

National Center on Elder Abuse, *National Elder Abuse Incidence Study: Final report,* 1998. Washington, DC: American Public Health Services Association.

Neal, M. B., Ingersoll-Dayton, B., and Starrels, M. E. Gender and relationship differences in caregiving patterns and consequences among employed caregivers. *Gerontologist*, 1997, *37*, 804–816.

Noelker, L., and Bass, D. Relationships between the frail elderly and informal and formal helpers. In E. Kahana, D. Biegel, and M. Wykle (Eds.), *Family caregiving across the lifespan*. Thousand Oaks, CA: Sage, 1994.

Ory, M. G., Hoffman, R. R. III, Yee, J. L., Tennstedt, S., and Schulz, R. Prevalence and impact of caregiving: A detailed comparison between dementia and non-dementia caregivers. *The Gerontologist*, 1999, *39*, 177–185.

Ostwald, S. K., Hepburn, K. W., Caron, W., Burns, T., and Mantell, R. Reducing caregiver burden: A randomized psychoeducational intervention for caregivers of persons with dementia. *The Gerontologist*, 1999, *39*, 299–309.

Otto, J. The role of adult protective services in addressing abuse. *Generations*, 2000, *24*, 33–38.

Pavalko, E. K., and Artis, J. E. Women's caregiving and paid work: Causal relationships in late midlife. *Journals of Gerontology*, 1997, *52B*, S170–S179.

Pearlin, L. I., Aneshensel, C. S., Mullon, J. T., and Whitlatch, C. J. Caregiving and its social support. In R. H. Binstock and L. K. George (Eds.), *Handbook of aging and the social sciences* (4th ed.). San Diego: Academic Press, 1996.

Penning, M. J. In the Middle: Parental caregiving in the context of other roles. *Journals of Gerontology*, 1998, *53B*, S188–S197.

Penrod, J. D., Kane, R. A., Kane, R. C., and Finch, M. D. Who cares? The size, scope, and composition of the caregiver support system. *The Gerontologist*, 1995, *35*, 489–499.

Peters-Davis, N. D., Moss, M. S., and Pruchno, R. A. Children-in-law in caregiving families. *The Gerontologist*, 1999, *39*, 66–75.

Pillemer, K., and Suitor, J. J. It takes one to help one: Effects of similar others on the well-being of caregivers. *Journals of Gerontology*, 1996, *51B*, S250–S257.

Pohl, J. M., Given, C. W., Collins, C. E., and Given, B. A. Social vulnerability and reactions to caregiving in daughters and daughters-in-law caring for disabled aging parents. *Health Care Women International*, 1994, *15*, 385–395.

Prescop, K. L., Dodge, H. H., Morycz, R. K., Schulz, R. M., and Ganguli, M. Elders with dementia living in the community with and without caregivers: An epidemiological study. *International Psychogeriatrics*, 1999, *11*, 235–250.

Pruchno, R. A., Burant, C. J., and Peters, N. Understanding the well-being of care receivers. *The Gerontologist*, 1997, *37*, 102–109.

Quinn, M. J. Undoing undue influence. *Generations*, 2000, *24*, 65–69.

Quinn, M. J., and Tomita, S. K. *Elder abuse and neglect: Causes, diagnosis, and intervention strategies* (2nd ed.). New York: Springer, 1997.

Reid, J., and Hardy, M. Multiple roles and well-being among midlife women: Testing role strain and role enhancement theories. *Journal of Gerontology*, 1999, *54B*, S329–S338.

Reis, M. The IOA screen: An abuse-alert measure that dispels myths. *Generations*, 2000, *24*, 13–16.

Robison, J., Moen P., and Dempster-McClain, D. Women's caregiving: Changing profiles and pathways. *Journals of Gerontology*, 1995, *50B*, S362–S373.

Seltzer, M. and Li, L. W. The dynamics of caregiving: Transitions during a three-year prospective study. *The Gerontologist*, 2000, *40*, 165–1778.

Short, P., and Leon, J. *Use of home and community services by persons age 65 and older with functional difficulties. National Medical Expenditure Survey Research Findings 5*. Rockville, MD: Agency for Health Care Policy and Research, 1995.

Simon, M. L., Milligan, M., Guider, R., Puzan, L., Ellano, C., and Atkin, P. Self neglect: The revolving door. *Silent suffering: Elder abuse in America*. Long Beach, CA: Archstone Foundation, 1997.

Spillman, B. C., and Pezzin, L. E. Potential and active family caregivers: Changing networks and the "sandwich generation." *Millbank Quarterly*, 2000, *78*, 347–374.

Stone, R., Cafferata, G., and Sangl, J. *Caregivers of the frail elderly: A national profile*. Washington, DC: U.S. Department of Health and Human Services, 1987.

Tennstedt, S. *Family caregiving in an aging society*. Administration on Aging, 1999, Symposium.

Tennstedt, S. L., Crawford, S., and McKinley, J. Determining the pattern of community care: Is coresidence more important than caregiver relationship? *Journals of Gerontology*, 1993, 48, S74–S83.

Velkoff, V. A., and Lawson, V. A. *Caregiving: International brief on gender and aging*. Bureau of the Census, 1998, *IB/98-3*, 2–7.

Vitaliano, P. P., Schulz, R., Kiecolt-Glaser, J., and Grant, I. Research on physiological and physical concomitants of caregiving: Where do we go from here? *Annals of Behavioral Medicine*, 1997, *19*, 117–123.

Walker, A., Aacock, A., Bowman, S., and Li, F. Amount of care given and caregiving satisfaction: A latent growth curve analysis. *Journals of Gerontology*, 1996, *51B*, P130–P142.

Wisbaum, K. Financial Abuse: A trial attorney's perspective. In *Silent suffering: Elder abuse in America*, 1997, Archstone Foundation, 27–34.

Wold, R. Introduction: The nature and scope of elder abuse. *Generations*, 2000, *24*, 6–12.

Wolf, D. A., Freedman, V., and Soldo, B. The division of family labor: Care for elderly parents. *The Journals of Gerontology*, 1997, *52B (Special Issue)*, 102–109.

Worcester, M., and Hedrick, S. Dilemmas in using respite for family caregivers of frail elders. *Family and Community Health*, 1997, *19*, 31–48.

Yates, M. E., Tennstedt, S., and Chang, B. H. Contributors to and mediators of psychological well-being for informal caregivers. *Journals of Gerontology*, 1999, *54B*, P12–22.

Zarit, S. H., Stephens, M. P., Townsend, A., and Greene, R. Stress reduction for family caregivers: Effects of adult day care use. *Journals of Gerontology*, 1998, *53B*, S267–S277.

Zarit, S. H., and Whitlatch, C. J. Institutional placement: Phases of the transition. *Gerontologist*, October 1992, *32*, 665–672.

Zarit, S., Todd, P., and Zarit, J. Subjective burden of husbands and wives as caregivers: A longitudinal study. *The Gerontologist*, 1986, *26*, 260–266.

11 LIVING ARRANGEMENTS AND SOCIAL INTERACTIONS

Previous chapters have examined the relationships between older persons and their social environment. In this chapter, we focus on:

- P–E theories that describe adaptation to aging
- The impact of the natural and built environment on older persons' social functioning
- The influence of a population that is growing older on community planning and housing
- New options in long-term care for frail elders
- Services to help elders remain independent in the community
- New technology for community-dwelling elders
- Housing policy affecting older adults
- SRO housing and homelessness

As we have seen in previous chapters, successful aging depends on physical and functional health, cognitive and emotional well-being, and a level of activity that is congruent with an individual's abilities and needs. Another important element in the aging process is the environment, both social and physical, that serves as the context for activities as well as the stimulus that places demands on the individual. According to person–environment theories of aging, an individual is more likely to experience life satisfaction in an environment that is congruent with his or her physical, cognitive, and emotional needs and abilities.

AN EXAMPLE OF P–E INCONGRUENCE HARMING AN OLDER PERSON

An older man who lives with his daughter and teenage grandchildren in a small home may feel overwhelmed and unable to control the high level of activity (and choice of music!) by the younger family and their friends. In contrast, an older man who lives alone in a quiet neighborhood has greater control over the level of activity in his home, even though the house may seem too quiet and unstimulating to his grandchildren when they visit.

Age-related changes and disease conditions make the average older person more sensitive to characteristics of the setting that may have little effect on the typical younger person. They may impair the older person's ability to adapt to and interact with complex and novel environments. On the other hand, many older people function as well as younger persons do in a wide range of physical surroundings. Observation of these differences in individual responses has led to the concept of *congruence* or *fit* between the environment and the individual. This concept is explored in other person–environment theories below.

PERSON-ENVIRONMENT
THEORIES OF AGING

The impact of the environment on human behavior and well-being is widely recognized in diverse disciplines. It was in the early work of psychologist Kurt Lewin and his associates (Lewin, 1935; Lewin, Lippitt, and White, 1939) that the environment as a complex variable entered the realm of psychology. Lewin's field theory (1935, 1951) emphasizes that any event is the result of multiple factors, individual and environmental; or more simply stated, B = f(P,E) (i.e., behavior is a function of personal and environmental characteristics). Accordingly, any change in characteristics of either the person or the environment is likely to produce a change in that person's behavior.

Murray's theory of personality (1938), known as *personology*, provides the earliest framework for a person–environment congruence model. This theory depicts the individual in dynamic interaction with his or her setting, the type of interaction portrayed throughout this book. The individual attempts to maintain equilibrium as the environment changes. Murray's concepts of *need* and *press* are relevant for theories of person–environment congruence. Need is viewed as a force in the individual that works to maintain equilibrium by attending and responding to, or avoiding, certain environmental demands (i.e., the concept of press in the P–E model).

According to Murray's and other theories of person–environment congruence, the individual experiences optimal well-being when his or her needs are in equilibrium with characteristics of the environment. For example, an older woman who has lived on a farm will adjust more readily to a small nursing home in a rural area than to a large urban facility. In contrast, an older couple who are city-dwellers may be dissatisfied if they decide to retire to a small home on a lake far from town; adaptation may be more difficult and perhaps never fully achieved. To the extent that individual needs are not satisfied because of existing environmental characteristics and level of "press," it is hypothesized that the individual will experience frustration and strain.

P–E Congruence Models in Gerontology

The environment plays a more dominant role for older than for younger people, because the older person's ability to control his or her surroundings (e.g., to leave an undesirable setting) is considerably reduced. The individual's range of adaptive behaviors to a stressful environment becomes constrained because of changes in physical, social, and

COPING WITH DECLINING COMPETENCE

As competence in cognition, physical strength and stamina, health, and sensory functioning decline with advanced age, the individual would be expected to experience increased problems with high environmental press. Thus, for example, grocery shopping in a large supermarket on a busy Saturday morning may become an overwhelming task for an older person who is having increasing difficulty with hearing and walking. The older person might decide to shop in a smaller supermarket at nonpeak hours, or to avoid supermarkets altogether and use a neighborhood grocery store or order groceries by phone or on the Internet.

psychological functioning. Therefore, this perspective may be even more useful for understanding older people's behavior than for understanding the behavior of other populations.

The *competence model*, described in Chapter 1, provides an important perspective on person–environment transactions in old age. This model assumes that the impact of the environment is mediated by the individual's level of abilities and needs. Competence is defined as "the theoretical upper limit of the individual to function in areas of biological health, sensation-perception, motives, behavior, and cognition" (Lawton, 1975, p. 7). *Environmental press* refers to the potential of a given environmental feature to influence behavior (for example, the level of stimulation, physical barriers, and lack of privacy).

For the older person with Alzheimer's disease or other forms of dementia, it can be difficult to reestablish P–E congruence or to adapt to incongruence. Severe cognitive deterioration may result in an inability to recognize the incongruence experienced between one's needs and the external world. The dementia patient may become behaviorally disturbed unless others intervene to reestablish congruence. This may be accomplished by simplifying the environment to make it fit the individual's cognitive competence; for example, by providing cues and orienting devices in the home to help the person find his or her way without becoming lost or disoriented. The ultimate goal of any modification should be to maximize the older person's ability to negotiate and control the situation, and to minimize the likelihood that the environment will overwhelm the person's competence.

GEOGRAPHIC DISTRIBUTION OF THE OLDER POPULATION

As the United States and other industrialized countries have become more urbanized, a smaller proportion of all population subgroups, including those aged 65 and over, currently reside in rural communities. The great majority of older persons (77 percent) lived in metropolitan areas (i.e., urban and suburban communities) in 1995, compared with only 5 percent in communities with fewer than 2500 residents. Ethnic minority differences are particularly pronounced in the proportion of older persons who live in urban centers:

- 29 percent of non-Hispanic whites
- 55 percent of older African Americans
- 53 percent of Hispanic elders

This distribution of older minorities in central cities places them at greater risk for victimization and poor-quality housing.

There is also a "graying of the suburbs"; that is, a greater proportion of people who moved into suburban developments in the 1950s have now raised their children and have remained in these communities after retirement. Since 1977, increasing numbers of older people are living in the suburbs rather than in central cities (see Figure 11.1). Compared to their urban counterparts, elders in suburban communities tend to have higher incomes, are less likely to live alone, and report themselves to be in better functional health. However, the lower density of housing, greater distance to

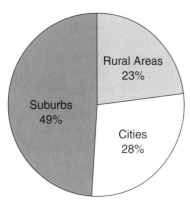

FIGURE 11.1 **Population of Older Americans Living in Urban, Suburban, and Rural Areas**
SOURCE: AARP, 2000.

social and health services, and lack of mass transit make it difficult for older suburban dwellers to continue living independently in these suburbs if they become frail or unable to drive. Many suburban communities are responding to their changing resident needs by developing community transit (e.g., vans or special buses) programs to take older adults and persons with disabilities to social and health services, senior centers, shopping, and restaurants.

Older persons who live in nonmetropolitan areas have lower incomes (near the poverty level) and poorer health than those in urban areas. A greater proportion rely on Social Security benefits for their primary source of income. This is particularly true for African Americans who reside in small towns and rural areas:

- 41.5 percent have incomes near the poverty level
- 28 percent in metropolitan areas live at or below poverty (McLaughlin and Jensen, 1993)

Consistent with these findings, limitations in mobility and activity are greater among older people in rural communities and least among elders in suburbs. This may be a function of income and cohort differences. The greater availability of medical and social services (e.g., hospitals, clinics, se-

nior centers, private physicians, transportation) in urban and suburban communities compared to rural settings may also explain these differences. Despite attempts to offset urban–rural differences in health and social services, significant gaps remain in terms of access and availability. Transportation remains a critical problem for older rural residents, both to transport them to medical and social services and to bring service providers to their homes.

Despite their lower income and poorer health, older persons in small communities have been found to interact more with neighbors and friends of the same and younger ages than do those in urban settings. Mr. and Mrs. Howard in the introductory vignette to Part Five illustrate the positive aspects of smaller communities for older people. These include the greater proximity of neighbors, stability of residents, and shared values and lifestyles. Proportionately few rural elders live near their children and most do not receive financial and social support from them. However, friendship ties appear to be stronger and more numerous among rural older people than among those in urban settings. In sum, older persons who remain in rural areas and small towns are more disadvantaged in terms of income, health, and service availability than are those in metropolitan areas. On the other hand, P–E fit suggests that those who have a high need for social interaction and have lived most of their lives in rural settings would be most satisfied in such settings, and would experience severe adaptation problems in more anonymous urban environments.

RELOCATION

Relocation, or moving from one setting to another, represents a special case of P–E incongruence or discontinuity between the individual's competence and the environment's demands. Anyone who has moved from one city or one house to another has experienced the problems of adjusting to new surroundings and to different orientations, floor plans, and design features in the home. A healthy person can usually adjust quite easily. An older

---

ADAPTING TO P–E INCONGRUENCE IN ONE'S HOME

It may seem odd to family, friends, and service providers that an older person does not wish to leave a home that is too large and too difficult to negotiate physically, especially if he or she is frail and mobility-impaired. The problem is compounded if the home needs extensive repairs that an older person cannot afford. Despite such seemingly obvious needs for relocating, it is essential to consider older people's preferences before encouraging them to sell a home that appears to be incongruent with their needs. Families should not ignore the emotional meaning of home to the older person in terms of personal identity and a treasure trove of family memories (e.g., marriage, childrearing, and grandparenting).

---

person who has lived in the same home for many years will require more time to adapt, even if the move is perceived as an improvement to a better, safer, more comfortable home. This is because the individual has adjusted to a particular configuration of P–E fit over a long period of time. The greater the change (e.g., moving from a private house in the suburbs to an assisted living facility in the city), the longer it will take to adapt. A relocation that entails extensive changes in lifestyle, such as a move to a retirement community or to a nursing home with its rules and policies governing the residents, requires even greater adjustments.

Older homeowners are far more likely than younger families to have lived in their current homes for at least 30 years (50 percent versus 4 percent). This difference also occurs among renters (16 percent versus one percent, respectively), and may explain why older people are less likely to relocate. Indeed, only 5 percent of people aged 65–85 are likely to move in a given year, compared with 32 percent of adults aged 20–29 (Administration on Aging, 1997; HUD, 1999). A national survey by AARP revealed an overwhelming desire by people aged 55 and older to remain in their own homes and community:

- 69 percent were very satisfied with their residence
- 73 percent preferred to remain in the same community

Among those who had moved in the past year, 78 percent had done so within the same state (AOA,

2000). In general, older people are less likely to move to a different community than are younger families, but are more likely to move to a different type of housing within the same community. Litwak and Longino (1994) suggest that older people generally relocate in response to changes in life conditions, such as retirement, or disabilities that make their existing home environments incongruent with their needs. As a result, the type of housing chosen varies according to the reasons for the move. They propose a three-stage model of migration:

- Stage 1 occurs most often among the young-old and recent retirees, generally to retirement communities in the sunbelt including Florida, California, Arizona or Texas. This may include "snowbirds" who spend their winters in the warmer climate and the remaining months in their home states. Both patterns have resulted in a significant increase in the over age 65 population in sunbelt states in the past 30 years.
- Stage 2 is often precipitated by chronic illness that limits the older person's abilities to perform ADLs. They may move to retirement communities or assisted living facilities nearby that offer some amenities (e.g., meals, housekeeping), but the older person remains relatively independent.
- Stage 3 is not experienced by most older adults, but occurs when severe or sudden disability (e.g., stroke) makes it impossible for the individual to live even semi-independently. In some cases the older person relocates from a sunbelt community to a nursing home near family members. One result of this shift is that Florida has the

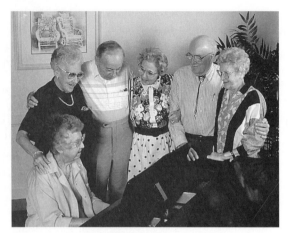

Retirement communities offer opportunities for social interaction and support.

highest population of people aged 65 and older but ranks twenty-fourth in its proportion of oldest old.

For many other elders, however, an intermediate stop may be the home of an adult child before relocating to a long-term care facility. In some cases, the older person remains in his or her own home, but receives some home care and other services (Silverstein and Zablotsky, 1996).

The problem of relocation is compounded for a person who is experiencing multiple or severe physical disabilities and dementia. As we have seen in Chapter 6, these individuals have more difficulty coping with stressful life events than healthy older people. Unfortunately, they are often the very people who must relocate to hospitals and skilled nursing facilities, environments that are most incongruent with their needs. Indeed, as suggested by the Florida data above, the oldest-old are most likely to relocate, often to their children's homes or near their children. Such moves are precipitated by widowhood, significant deterioration in health, or disability.

Concern about adapting to a new setting is one reason why many frail older people who can no longer maintain their own homes are reluctant to move, even though they may recognize that they "should" be in a safer environment. Indeed, the 1996 housing survey by AARP found greater support for the statement, "I'd like to stay in my home and never move," as age increased:

- 77 percent of respondents aged 50–64
- 89 percent of those 65–74
- 96 percent of people aged 85+ (AARP, 1996)

As anyone who has searched for a new home can attest, considerable stamina and determination are required to find housing and a neighborhood that best fits one's needs and preferences. To the extent that one is frail and unable to muster the energy to search for such housing, it becomes even more difficult to make the transition.

Some older people may choose to move to communities that were not planned for this popu-

---

NEW OPTIONS FOR RETIREMENT LIVING

Increasing numbers of new retirees in their sixties are considering options to the traditional sunbelt retirement communities. For example, Sequim is a small town with 4,400 residents on the Olympic Peninsula of Washington, backed by majestic mountains and facing Vancouver Island across the Strait of Juan de Fuca. A huge influx of retirees in the past 20 years has resulted in a population in which 40 percent are age 60 and older. Most live in single-family homes, enjoy sailing, hiking, and attending continuing education classes.

Perhaps most important, retirees in Sequim are actively engaged in intergenerational programs. The local Rotary (made up mostly of retirees) built a new facility for Sequim's Boys and Girls Club. They worked with youth and parents to build a skateboard park. They also built a new wildlife interpretive center, where retired biologists teach classes to visitors of all ages. These efforts in one community illustrate the benefits of age-heterogeneous housing not just for elders but for their younger neighbors as well (*Seattle Times*, 2000).

lation (unlike a Sun City or Leisure World, for example), but have become **naturally occurring retirement communities (NORCs).** Such places have, over the years, attracted large numbers of older people who have "aged in place" there.

THE IMPACT OF THE NEIGHBORHOOD

All of us live in a neighborhood, whether a college campus, a nursing home, a retirement park, an apartment complex, or the several blocks surrounding our homes. Because of its smaller scale, the neighborhood represents a closer level of interaction and identification than does the community. Results of the American Housing Survey by the U.S. Bureau of the Census reveal:

- Seventy-six percent of older people in general are satisfied with their neighborhoods.
- Seventy-one percent in poorer neighborhoods are satisfied (HUD, 1999).

Among those who reported problems, noise and traffic concerns topped the list, followed by complaints about people and crime in the neighborhood.

Satisfaction with one's neighborhood increases if amenities such as a grocery store, laundromat, or senior center are located nearby. These services also can provide a social network. For many older people, however, special vans or other types of transportation are necessary to access such services. Older people are willing to travel farther for physician services, entertainment, family visits (although friends need to be nearby for

regular visiting to occur), and club meetings, probably because these activities occur less frequently than grocery shopping and laundry. Because of the importance placed on family ties, visits to family members may occur more often, regardless of proximity. Distance is less important if family members drive older relatives to various places, including their homes.

Proximity and frequent contact with families may not be as critical if neighbors and nearby friends can provide the necessary social support. Indeed, the great majority of community-dwelling elders prefer mixed-age neighborhoods (AARP, 1996). As discussed in Chapter 9, neighbors play an important role in older people's social networks. When adult children are at a geographic distance, neighbors are more readily available to help in emergencies and on a short-term basis, such as minor home repairs or yard maintenance. It is often more convenient for neighbors than family to drive an older individual to stores and doctors' offices. This does not mean that neighbors can or should replace family support systems because of the family's central caregiving role. Nevertheless, neighbors are an important additional resource.

VICTIMIZATION AND FEAR OF CRIME

A common stereotype is that crime affects the older population more than other age groups. However, national surveys by the U.S. Department of Justice's Bureau of Justice Statistics consistently show that people over age 65 have the lowest rates of all types of victimization than any

---

PRACTICAL HELP FROM NEIGHBORS

Neighbors can provide a "security net," as partners in a "Neighborhood Watch" crime-prevention program, or in informally arranged systems of signaling to each other (e.g., the older neighbor who lives alone might open her living room drapes every day by 9:00 A.M.

to signal to her younger neighbors that all is well). Other neighbors might check in on the older person on a daily or weekly basis to make sure that home-delivered meals are being eaten regularly.

age group over 12. As Table 11.1 illustrates, when compared to people aged 16–19, those aged 65 and older are:

- 30 times less likely to be victims of an assault
- 23 times less likely to experience a robbery
- 3 times less likely to be attacked by a purse snatcher or pickpocket

In fact, these rates have steadily declined since 1974 for older people. Nevertheless, some segments of the older population are at greater risk for victimization:

- The young-old are more likely than those aged 75 and older to face all types of crime.
- African American elders are twice as likely as whites to experience violent and household crime.
- Older Americans with incomes less than $7500 are most likely to become victims of violent crime (twice the rate for those with incomes over $25,000).
- Not surprisingly, older people living in urban centers are 2.5 times more likely than suburban or rural elders to experience violent crime and theft.
- Urban-dwelling elders are almost twice as likely to become victims of household crime.

Contrary to common beliefs, white women aged 65 and older are at lowest risk for violent crimes:

- For aggravated assault, 0.1 per 1000 vs. 2.5 for older black women.

- For all crimes of violence, 1.7 per 1000 compared to 3.9 for their age counterparts who are white men, 4.8 for black men, and 6.2 for black women. This compares with the highest-risk group, white males age 16–19, who experience 115 violent crimes per 1000 population (Bureau of Justice Statistics, 2000).

The conditions under which crimes are committed against older people differ from those of other age groups. For example, they tend to be victimized during the day, by strangers who more often attack alone, in or near their homes, and with less use of weapons. This suggests that perpetrators of crimes feel they can easily overtake the older victim without a struggle. The sense of helplessness against an attacker may make older persons more conscious of their need to protect themselves, and produce levels of fear that are incongruent with the statistics about their relative vulnerability to violent crimes. Such fear of crime causes many elders to take protective steps. In 1996, they reported:

- Ninety percent keep their doors locked.
- Sixty-five percent avoid opening doors for strangers.
- Thirty-two percent avoid going out at night.
- Twenty percent avoid using public transportation (AARP, 1996).

Such precautions are not unrealistic, given the potential negative consequences of a physical attack or theft for an older person. Even a purse snatching can be traumatic for older women, because of the

TABLE 11.1 Victimization Rates per 100 Persons or Households, 1999

AGE	VIOLENT CRIME	ROBBERY	ASSAULT	PURSE SNATCHING/ PICKPOCKETING
16–19	77.6	11.4	91.1	2.3
25–34	36.4	4.2	43.1	1.0
50–64	14.4	1.7	16.0	1.6
65+	3.9	0.5	3.0	0.8

SOURCE: Bureau of Justice Statistics, 2000.

NEIGHBORHOOD CRIME PREVENTION PROGRAMS

In response to the problems of crime, "Neighborhood Watch" and other programs encourage neighbors to become acquainted and to look out for signs of crimes against neighbors and their homes. Such neighborhood crime prevention programs allow older people to have access to their neighbors. They break down the perception of neighbors as strangers and the fear of being isolated in a community, both of which foster fear of crime. Some large communities have established special police units to investigate and prevent crimes against older people. These units often train police to understand processes of aging, and to communicate better with older people and help them overcome the trauma of a theft or physical assault. Improvements in community design can also create a sense of security. For example, brighter and more uniform street lighting, especially above sidewalks and in alleys, can deter many would-be criminals.

---

possibility of an injury or hip fracture during a struggle with the thief and the resulting economic loss. It can also disrupt the victim's sense of competence and subjective well-being. Older women are particularly fearful of crime, even though they are least likely to be victims as described above. Although seemingly irrational, such fear of crime is an important determinant of older women's behavior that requires more societal efforts to empower and strengthen their environmental competence. For example, older women can benefit from education in self-defense and from neighborhood support networks. In sum, the significance of the fear of crime is not whether it is warranted, but the effect it has on older people's psychological well-being (Bazargan, 1994; Hollway and Jefferson, 1997).

Older people also are more susceptible to economically devastating crimes such as fraud and confidence games. Police departments in major cities report higher rates of victimization against older people by con artists and high-pressure salesmen. Medical quackery and insurance fraud are also more common, perhaps because many older people feel desperate for quick cures or overwhelmed by medical care costs. They therefore become easy prey for unscrupulous people who exploit them by offering the "ultimate medical cure" or "comprehensive long-term care insurance" coverage at cheap rates. Older adults are also more vulnerable to commercial fraud by funeral homes, real estate brokers, and investment salespeople. Perhaps more devastating than the financial consequences of fraud, such salespeople prevent the older person from seeking appropriate professional services for medical conditions, insurance, and other transactions.

HOUSING PATTERNS OF OLDER PEOPLE

In this section, we review the residential arrangements of older persons, including independent housing, planned housing, retirement communities, community residential care, and nursing homes. We also discuss newer models of long-term care. Policies that govern long-term care options are reviewed in Chapter 17.

Independent Housing

Older people are more likely than any other age group to occupy housing that they own free and clear of a mortgage. In 1997, 79 percent of all dwelling units in which older persons reside were owned by them; 77 percent were owned free and clear of any mortgage (Administration on Aging, 2000). These include condominiums, mobile homes, and even congregate facilities that offer "life care" for retired persons; but by far the greatest proportion of owned units are single-family homes. As shown in Figure 11.2, home ownership varies considerably among the older population. Married couples, non-Hispanic whites, especially those with an annual income of $25,000 or more, and those residing in rural communities are most likely to own their homes. However, the cost of utilities, taxes,

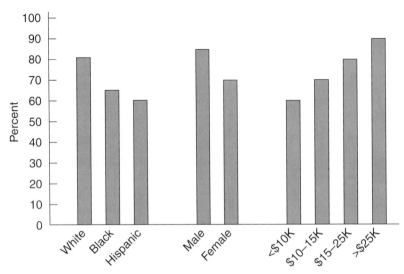

FIGURE 11.2   **Characteristics of Older Homeowners**
SOURCE: HUD, 1999.

insurance, and repair and maintenance can be prohibitive because their homes tend to be older and poorly constructed. In addition, the older person's current level of competence may be incongruent with their physical environment, so that they require a more appropriate housing situation.

One solution is the growing number of homesharing programs around the country. These are community-based programs that are operated out of the Area Agency on Aging or other governmental or voluntary service agencies. Their goal is to assist older persons who own their own homes and wish to rent rooms to others in exchange for rental income or services, such as housekeeping and assistance with other chores. The role of a homesharing agency is to serve as a "matchmaker," selecting appropriate homesharers for each older person with a home. These services are especially popular near universities and colleges, where students find low-cost or free living arrangements and benefit from intergenerational contacts. The disadvantage is that, like any other living situation where unrelated persons share housing, differences in values and lifestyles may be too great to bridge. This is particularly true when a younger person moves into an older person's home. As a result,

most intergenerational homesharing arrangements are short-lived. The success of such programs depends on appropriate matches between potential homesharers. Generally, there are more older people with homes to share than younger people wanting rooms. In some cases, a group of older people may choose to share a home.

Another implication of prolonged home ownership is that many of these houses are old, with inadequate weatherproofing and other energy-saving features, and with large indoor and outdoor spaces that are difficult to maintain. Exposed wiring, lack of sufficient outlets, and worn-out oil furnaces can be hazards. Differences exist among various subgroups of the older population, as illustrated in Figure 11.3. Elders whose homes are in the worst physical condition include:

- 8.7 percent of the oldest old vs. 5.5 percent of the young-old
- 16.7 percent of African American elders vs. 11 percent of Hispanics and 4.3 percent of white elders
- 7.5 percent of women vs. 5 percent of men (Gaberlavage and Citro, 1997; Golant and La Greca, 1995; HUD, 1999)

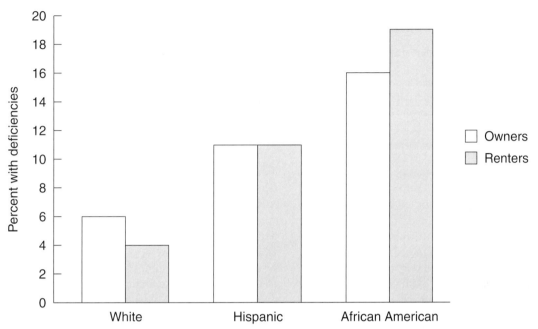

FIGURE 11.3   Housing That Is Moderately and Severely Inadequate* by Owner and Ethnic/Racial Group (1993)

*"Inadequate" is defined as regular problems with plumbing, heating, leaks, signs of rodents, and nonfunctioning kitchen sink, refrigeration, or burners inside the structure for exclusive use of unit.

SOURCE: Gaberlavage and Citro, 1997.

It is not unusual to hear news stories during winter months of fires in older homes that result from faulty wiring, overloaded circuits, and the use of space heaters because of an inadequate furnace. The latter situation is particularly troublesome for older persons who have difficulties in maintaining body heat and prefer warmer ambient temperatures (see Chapter 3). Many communities attempt to prevent these problems by providing free or low-cost home repairs for low-income elders and special assistance to all older clients to make their homes more energy efficient (e.g., no-interest loans for weatherproofing and installing storm windows). Some cities that have experienced sudden increases in their electricity and natural gas rates have also developed programs to aid low-income people of all ages, but this may become more difficult with current high energy costs.

Since 1989, HUD has had the authority to offer insurance for home equity conversion mortgages or "reverse mortgages." They are available to homeowners age 62 and older with little or no mortgage debt remaining. With insurance from the FHA, numerous lenders across the country provide reverse mortgages for older persons. In addition, it is a useful option for people aged 62 and older who are "house-rich but cash-poor." It can help older people remain in their own homes and pay for needed repairs and maintenance. Lenders estimate that 83 percent of older adults have paid off their mortgages, and the average amount of equity exceeds $55,000 for these homes. This tends to be true for older individuals of all income levels (Hobbs and Damon, 1996). In effect, reverse mortgages lend the older person money via a credit line on his or her mortgage. The title is retained by

---

REVERSE MORTGAGES ARE NOT COMMON

In its 1996 survey, AARP found that 35 percent of older homeowners had never heard of reverse mortgages. Among those who knew about this program, only 3 percent reported that they had one. Among the respondents who currently do not have one, only 27 percent would consider getting one in the future. This may change as future cohorts of elders recognize reverse mortgages as a way to retain their homes as housing prices and property taxes increase.

---

the lender, or the lender puts a lien on the home. The older person receives a lump sum or monthly payment (or annuity) from the lender and still lives in the house. This can mean an additional $1000 or more each month for many older homeowners. When the older person dies or sells the house, the lender generally deducts the portion of the mortgage that has been paid, including interest, as well as a portion (usually about 10 percent) of the home's appreciated value or equity since the date of the reverse mortgage.

Reverse mortgages for the lender may carry long-term risks; currently, there are no guidelines for the duration of such mortgage plans. For example, what if the older homeowner outlives the home's equity? Lenders do not want to evict such a person, but at the same time they do not want to lose their investment. In addition, homeowners must consider the initial costs of such a mortgage. These include a 2 percent mandatory mortgage insurance fee, a loan origination fee, and standard closing costs. Together with interest, a borrower could pay an annualized credit-line rate of 13 to 17 percent for this loan. For older people with other assets to use as collateral, other types of loans may be more cost-effective than a reverse mortgage. HUD offers information about reverse mortgages on its Website and its toll-free phone number.

On the other hand, many people in their fifties and sixties have considerable equity in their homes because of housing prices rising so steeply in the 1990s. As their children leave, some prefer to sell these homes and move to smaller dwellings. A growing trend, however, is represented by aging baby boomers, who prefer a large home but with many amenities that will help them remain independent and age in place. These include features such as master bedrooms and full bathrooms on the main floor, universal design in the kitchen and bathroom that allows independence for people in wheelchairs and walkers, and wiring for computer systems and "smart homes" (discussed later in this chapter). Builders and architects need to recognize that future cohorts of older adults will expect more options in the size and amenities of homes than any previous generation.

Planned Housing

During the past 40 years, federal and local government agencies and some private organizations, such as religious groups, have developed planned housing projects specifically for older persons. These have included subsidized housing for low-income elders and age-segregated housing for middle- and upper-income older persons. Gerontologists have attempted to understand the effects of the quality and type of housing on older persons' satisfaction level and behavior following relocation to such housing environments. It appears that planned housing can indeed improve the quality of life for low-income elders, but it is difficult to generalize to other older populations, particularly those of higher income status. Where to locate planned housing projects has no simple solution. As stated earlier in the discussion of neighborhood characteristics, older people are most likely to use services such as a senior center or laundromat if they are on site and if public transportation is easily accessible. If a particular site is not already near a bus stop, this convenience can be arranged with the local public transportation authority. Alternatively, larger developments provide van services for their older residents to obtain medical and social services, as well as planned excursions to theaters, museums, parks, and shopping centers.

Developers of planned housing for older people must also take into account such factors as whether the area is zoned for residential, commercial, or industrial use. The topography of this site, crime rates, and security of the community are important considerations, as is the need to integrate the housing project into the neighborhood. The last item is especially crucial. In a housing project that is architecturally distinct from the rest of the neighborhood, residents are likely to experience a lack of fit with their environment and to feel isolated from the larger neighborhood. Examples of this are a tall, multilevel structure in the midst of single-family homes, or a sprawling "retirement community" on the edge of an industrial area. The lack of fit may also be felt by the residents of the larger neighborhood, who often reject the presence of an entire community of older people in their midst, even if the project is architecturally consistent with other neighborhood buildings. Both physical and psychological barriers are created by walls, vegetation, and architectural features that distinguish a housing project from its surroundings, adding to the older residents' sense of separation from the neighborhood. On the other hand, the increased number of elders with higher incomes has led to the growth of retirement communities with units costing $250,000 and more, offering computer access, marinas, restaurants, golf courses, hiking trails, and some communal services. These are known as "active adult communities."

Congregate Housing

Congregate housing differs from planned housing and single-family residences in its provision of some communal services, a central kitchen, and a dining room for all residents. Some congregate facilities also provide housekeeping, social, and health services. Others may have space to establish services on site, but have not done so. In 1970, when the first federally supported congregate housing act was passed, HUD programs that financed the construction could not pay for such services but could provide the space required. Developers and planners assumed that tenants would be charged for these additional services, or that the services would be subsidized by local agencies. Recent evidence suggests that such services have indeed become necessary, as the residents of congregate housing have experienced **"aging in place,"** that is, they have stayed in the same living situation for many years as their personal competence has declined. Figure 11.4 illustrates some resources needed to reduce environmental press and permit aging in place, thereby reestablishing person–environment congruence. To the extent that a housing site has the space and resources by which to plan for such needs in the future, people are more likely to remain in such settings and to avoid or delay relocation to a long-term care facility. Congregate housing is a desirable option for many older persons who do not need regular help with medications or ADLs, but prefer having some

---

SUMMER CAMP FOR ADULTS

Many housing developers are expanding their markets by building active retirement communities for newer cohorts of older adults. Unlike the huge developments of the past, such as Sun Cities in California and Arizona with over 9,000 homes, recent projects have less than 1,000 units. They offer golf courses, tennis courts, and swimming pools for active adults aged 60 and older. Indeed, these developments have so many recreational amenities that they are marketed as "full-time summer camps for adults."

personal-care services available. Probably the most important feature of congregate housing is the availability of prepared meals. These not only provide a balanced and nutritional diet but also offer regular opportunities for socializing. Residents may also eat some meals in their own units, if they have units with a small kitchen (often a refrigerator, a range, and a few kitchen cabinets). The opportunity to eat in a congregate dining facility *or* to cook in their own kitchen is an important choice for many older persons. However, congregate housing differs from **assisted living**—described later in this chapter.

The growth of congregate housing is due in large part to the interest of private nonprofit and profit-making corporations. However, despite their increased numbers, congregate sites are inadequate in many regions of the country and for specific segments of the aging population. Federal subsidies for constructing new congregate facilities are not as readily available today. As a result, the number of congregate housing units for middle- and upper-income older persons has increased, but low-income elders who need such housing have not benefited from this growth.

Continuous Care Retirement Communities

The number of *multilevel facilities* or **continuous care retirement communities (CCRCs)** for older persons is growing. These housing projects offer a range from independent to congregate living arrangements and intermediate to skilled care facilities; with housing for 400–600 elders. Such options are more widely available in housing that is pur-

chased, less so for rental housing. As the number of oldest-old persons has increased, owners and administrators of facilities that do not provide extensive nursing services are increasingly concerned. They realize that some of their residents will eventually need to move to other facilities; they are also more aware that potential buyers of units in these facilities would prefer to have a range of services and housing options on site. Such alternatives are often of particular concern for couples, who face the likelihood that one partner will require skilled nursing care eventually. When several levels of care are available at one site, older couples can feel assured that they will be able to remain near each other, even if one becomes institutionalized.

Many housing plans for older people that offer options in living arrangements have either *lifecare contracts* or *life lease contracts*. Under these plans, the older person must pay an initial entry fee, often quite substantial, based on projections of life expectancy and on the size of the living quarters. In the case of a *lifecare contract*, the individual who eventually needs increased care is provided nursing home care without paying more for these services. This is a form of self-insurance for small groups of older adults that provides them with institutional and home-based care as needed. With a *life lease contract*, the individual is guaranteed lifetime occupancy in the apartment. However, in the latter case, if more expensive care is required, such services are generally not provided by the facility, and the older person must give up the apartment and find a nursing home. These contracts also charge monthly fees, but the monthly costs are generally not as high as those in facilities that rely only on month-to-month

Older Adult at Home

FIGURE 11.4 **Services Needed by Elders at Home with Long-Term Care Needs**

ADVANTAGES AND DISADVANTAGES OF CCRCS

Considering the high cost of CCRCs with lifecare contracts or founders' fees, it is important for potential buyers to consider the pros and cons of these commitments. Their greatest advantages are access to services that permit independent living and, for married respondents, the opportunity to continue to live together if one spouse needs institutionalization. A potential risk for older people who enter into a lifecare contract is that the facility will declare bankruptcy. In an attempt to avoid this, many states that license lifecare housing projects require providers to establish a trust fund for long-term care expenses.

---

payments. The advantage of lifecare contracts is that the individual is guaranteed lifetime care; this is important, given the actuarial tables of life expectancy for those who reach age 65 (another 17 years) and those who reach 70 (another 13 years). The older person who pays month-to-month may use up all of his or her life savings long before dying, if skilled care is needed. In contrast, the option of a lifecare contract may provide a sense of security for the older person who can pay a large lump sum. The individual is taking the chance that he or she will eventually need higher levels of care, so the costs are averaged out over a long period. For those who die soon after moving in, some facilities refund part of the entry fee to the family; in many cases, however, there is a policy of not refunding any portion of this fee. Obviously, the ability to purchase these contracts is limited to the small percentage of older people who have considerable cash assets. Indeed, older persons in these facilities are better educated and have greater financial resources than the general population of elders.

LONG-TERM CARE

Nursing Homes

Many people who are unfamiliar with the residential patterns of older people mistakenly assume that the majority live in **nursing homes;** however, the actual proportion is far smaller. According to the U.S. Bureau of the Census (1998), 4.3 percent of the 65+ population occupied nursing homes, congregate care, assisted living, and board-and-care

homes in 1998. Estimates of an older person's risk of admission to a nursing home differ by gender:

- 30 percent for men
- 50 percent for women

As shown in Figure 11.5, the rate of nursing home use increases with age:

- 1.1 percent of the young-old
- 19.8 percent of the oldest-old

Almost 50 percent of those who are 95 and older live in nursing homes (U.S. Bureau of the Census, 1998). Each year more than 1 million older persons leave long-term care institutions, almost evenly divided among discharges to the community, transfers to other health facilities, and death. Therefore, the statistic of 4.2 percent is a cross-sectional snapshot of the population in long-term care facilities that does not take account of movement into and out of such settings (Wiener, Illston, and Hanley, 1994).

With the increase in alternative long-term care options, such as assisted living and adult family homes, rates of nursing home admissions are changing substantially. More older people, even those with multiple physical and cognitive impairments, are selecting or are placed in long-term care facilities other than nursing homes, while many others receive health care in their own homes. This has resulted in a decline in the number of nursing homes in the United States from 19,100 in 1985 to 17,000 in 1997. The total number of beds and average number of beds per home

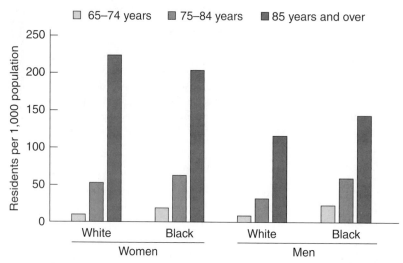

FIGURE 11.5   **Nursing Home Residents among Persons 65 Years of Age and Over, by Age, Gender, and Race: United States, 1997**
SOURCE: National Center for Health Statistics, National Nursing Home Survey, 1999.

have both increased, however. This reflects a decline in the number of smaller nursing homes (NCHS, 2000).

The lower rates of nursing home admissions in the United States will probably continue in this century, despite the significant growth in the oldest-old population. Nevertheless, nursing homes are often the best choice for the oldest, most frail, and most dependent segment of the population. As a result of more options prior to choosing a nursing home, typical nursing home residents today are much sicker and require more intensive services than their counterparts 20 to 30 years ago (Vladeck and Feuerberg, 1995–1996). The average age of nursing home residents is 81, and women are dis-

proportionately represented. The typical nursing home includes:

- 72 percent women
- 66 percent widowed or divorced elders
- 40 percent with a diagnosis of dementia
- 82 percent requiring assistance with two or more ADLs (NCHS, 2000)

The gender differential in nursing homes is due to women's longer life expectancy, their greater risk of multiple chronic illnesses, and their greater likelihood of being unmarried. The last factor is a critical one, since the absence of a spouse or other caregiver is a major predictor of institutionaliza-

---

LONG-TERM CARE IN OTHER COUNTRIES

In some countries, such as Japan and Germany, hospitals provide both long-term and acute care, so the total number of institutionalized older persons is much higher. Because hospital care is much more costly, Japanese government leaders and builders have begun to construct other types of long-term care facilities, some based on models in the United States.

BREAKING DOWN STEREOTYPES ABOUT NURSING HOMES

There is a small but growing trend to humanize or make nursing homes more homelike. This is a major paradigm shift from the medical or institutional model used in designing and operating these facilities. One such nursing home that underwent a dramatic physical and philosophical redesign is Mt. St. Vincent's in Seattle, Washington. Some of the changes in this facility include:

- Each floor is divided into "neighborhoods" of 20 residents per group.
- Each neighborhood has its own dining room, small enough for quiet meals.
- Residents with dementia are not housed separately but are usually mixed with healthier resi-

dents on each floor; ankle bracelets allow staff to monitor wanderers.
- Residents are not tied down in bed at night to keep them from falling out (a safety feature that some see as robbing elders of their dignity).
- Resident-directed care is practiced, with groups of elders deciding on meals and activities.
- Aides are assigned to a group of residents and are encouraged to become familiar with each resident's past and current life.
- Pets, plants, a day care center for young children, and an espresso stand for residents create a more homelike environment.

SOURCE: *New York Times,* 1998.

tion. This is discussed further in Chapter 15 (Freedman, 1996; Jette, Tennstedt, and Crawford, 1995).

In a 6-year follow-up of 634 community-dwelling persons aged 70 and over who had some disabilities at baseline, 41 percent had died and 23 percent had entered a nursing home for some time in those 6 years. Those whose primary caregiver was a male were more than twice as likely to enter a nursing home as elders with a female caregiver. Living with the primary caregiver reduced the risk of institutionalization by one-half. The use of formal services such as adult day care reduced the risk for cognitively impaired older persons, but increased the risk for physically frail persons by a factor of 2.5 when both formal and informal care were required. This apparent dichotomy may mean that formal services can relieve the burden of caregiving in cases of dementia (thereby postponing or preventing nursing home placement). In contrast, physically disabled older people who need both formal and informal care may have too many impairments to live in the community, even when multiple services are brought into their homes. These elders represent the segment of the population that will continue to require nursing homes in the future, even with the growth of other

less restrictive and less costly long-term care alternatives (Jette, Tennstedt, and Crawford, 1995). As noted in Chapter 10, the crucial role played by a live-in caregiver (most often a partner or adult child) in preventing or delaying institutionalization is supported by other studies where up to 25 percent of nursing home placements were precipitated by the death or serious illness of the primary caregiver (Tennstedt, Crawford, and McKinley, 1993). Unbalanced social exchange by the elder's child who is doing caregiving can also result in placement. That is, if the elder's child must help an increasingly frail parent with more ADLs, and the older adult cannot reciprocate, there is greater likelihood of moving to a nursing home (Wilmoth, 2000). Nursing home placement can be a traumatic event for some frail elders. In an analysis of 934 people aged 70 and older who moved into a nursing home, functional status declined and death rates were higher than expected within the first year (Wolinsky, Stump, and Callahan, 1997).

About 87 percent of nursing home residents are white, compared to 10.4 percent who are African American, and 3 percent who are Hispanic, American Indian, or Asian American (NCHS, 2000; Strahan, 1997). Even at age 85 and older, when the likelihood of nursing home placement is higher, proportionately fewer African American women live in nursing homes. However, African American men are slightly more likely than their white counterparts to live in such facilities, according to the following:

- 23 percent of white women
- 20 percent of black women
- 12 percent of white men
- 14 percent of black men (NCHS, 2000)

The underrepresentation of ethnic minority groups in nursing homes appears to reflect cultural differences in the willingness to institutionalize older persons, greater availability of family supports, or discrimination in admission policies (generally unofficial) against elders of color. It may also reflect the dearth of facilities that address the distinctive needs of these ethnic minorities, thereby forcing them to enter nursing homes that are incongruent with their cultural needs. In some communities with large ethnic minority populations, nursing homes have been built under the auspices of nonprofit organizations or religious groups. For example, in San Francisco and Seattle, Japanese and Chinese American elders can enter nursing homes operated and staffed by people who speak their same language and serve culturally specific foods. In most of the Chinese facilities for example, employees can communicate with residents in many dialects of Chinese.

Most nursing homes (about 67 percent) are *proprietary* or *for-profit,* and thus operate as a business that aims to make a profit for the owners or investors. The number of nursing homes owned by large multifacility chains is increasing dramatically. Another 7 percent are owned by federal, state, or local governments. *Nonprofit* homes (26 percent of the total) are generally sponsored by religious or fraternal groups (NCHS, 2000). Although making a profit is not their goal, they must be self-supporting. These are governed by a board or advisory group, rather than owners or investors, as in the case of proprietary homes. Although instances of reimbursement fraud by proprietary homes are highly publicized, the terms *proprietary* and *nonprofit* do not designate type or quality of care, but rather how the home is governed and how its earnings are distributed.

Nursing homes must follow federal guidelines to become certified by Medicare and to meet regulations that are imposed by each state. Such federal regulations have improved the quality of care in nursing homes and reduced costs (Hawes et al., 1997). Most nursing homes are not certified for Medicare, however. This is because Medicare does not reimburse for long-term care or maintenance, but only for short-term care (i.e., up to 100 days of rehabilitation following hospitalization). As a result, Medicaid is the primary payer of nursing-home care. Among those who enter a nursing home after age 65:

- Twenty-seven percent start and end their time in the facility as Medicaid recipients.
- Fourteen percent who begin as private pay residents spend down their assets and become Medicaid users (Spillman and Kemper, 1995).

Many older people with incomes below a specified level (varying across states) would not be able to afford nursing home care without Medicaid assistance. Under this program, nursing homes are reimbursed according to the level of care required by each resident. For example, residents who need more hands-on care by diverse staff are billed at a higher rate. Nursing personnel within the facility determine the level of care required on the basis of the older person's abilities to perform various ADLs and his or her mental status. Not all nursing homes accept clients who are Medicaid recipients, although many will allow elders who later become Medicaid eligible to remain in the home. In order to guard against large numbers of residents depending on Medicaid to pay for their long-term care needs and having to accept a lower reimbursement than private-pay residents are charged, some facilities have a policy that residents must demonstrate they have resources to pay for at least 2–3 years of care before they will require assistance from Medicaid.

THE EDEN ALTERNATIVE

A new approach to nursing home management focuses on enhancing residents' quality of life by encouraging them to care for plants and pets in the home; to volunteer in an attached child care center if available; and generally to have more control over the home's activities. Labeled "the Eden Alternative" by its founder, Dr. William Thomas, this philosophy posits nursing homes as habitats for elders who can continue to grow, rather than institutions where frail people come to die. According to this paradigm, residents who are surrounded by and encouraged to care for pets, plants, and children in the nursing home, and facilities that deemphasize scheduled activities, avoid the use of restraints, and practice decentralized management can improve the quality of both residents' and staff's lives (Bayne, 1998; Thomas and Stermer, 1999).

Because of stereotypes and media stories about poor-quality facilities, few older people willingly choose to live in a nursing home. Most enter after receiving informal care from family members, formal home care services, and, in some cases, following a stay in facilities such as assisted living or adult family homes. Nevertheless, their nursing home life offers some advantages over other types of long-term care. These include:

- increased social contact
- accessible social activities
- intensive rehabilitation services not provided by other long-term care alternatives
- relief from the stress of caregiving on family

Although the media reports instances of abuse and violation of regulations, there are many excellent nursing homes. Increased efforts to improve nursing homes and the development of innovative options signal an important change in skilled nursing facilities. Such options include subacute care for post-hospital discharge residents, hospice care for terminally ill persons, and special care units (SCUs) for residents with cognitive or severe physical impairments (Teresi, Holmes, and Ory, 2000). Increasingly, residents of nursing homes and their families are having more influence over their lives, through resident councils, patients' bills of rights, nursing home ombudsmen, and the advocacy of groups such as the National Citizens Coalition for Nursing Home Reform (NCCNHR). In its resident surveys, this organization has found that a major concern of cognitively intact older people is to be involved in decisions about their daily lives in the facility. Through such efforts, along with increased gerontological training, nursing home staff are also becoming more sensitive about ways to involve family, friends, and members from the larger community in their policies, procedures, and activities. New paradigms of nursing home design, as reflected in the Eden Alternative and Mt. St. Vincent's Home, described on page 345, help to humanize this type of long-term care. By adopting such a philosophy in the physical design and in staff caregiving practices, nursing homes can improve the quality of care provided for frail elders (Day, Carreon, and Stump, 2000).

Newer Options for Long-Term Care

Since the late 1980s, in response to perceived needs for more cost-effective long-term care options, there has been a dramatic growth in **community residential care options (CRCs).** This new model is defined as group housing with additional services such as meals, basic health care, and some personal assistance. Examples include **assisted living** and **adult family homes (or adult foster care).** This type of housing has increased in the past ten years as state and local builders have sought ways to provide long-term care in a cost-effective manner for elders with some limitations in their ADLs. They now number up to 28,000 facilities nationwide, with more than 600,000 beds. At a minimum, they provide room and board, at least one meal per day, and 24-hour

Chore workers and other home and community-based services can help older people remain in their homes.

security, although not as extensively as a medical model such as nursing homes (Hawes, Rose, and Phillips, 1999; Joel, 1998; Quinn, Johnson, Andress, McGinnis, and Ramesh, 1999). Community residential care can help older people maintain their independence, even if they have multiple ADL limitations. They cost less to operate and have therefore attracted more individuals and organizations to invest in this type of housing. Large health care systems, insurance companies, and nonprofit and for-profit corporations have built new CRCs or added to their existing nursing home campuses new apartment or cottage units (Meyer, 1998). The great majority of residents are age 65 and older. Indeed, a national study found that:

- Fifty-six percent are age 80 and older.
- Forty percent have dementia.
- Most need help with two or more ADLs (GAO, 1999).

As a result, more older people who, in the past, would have been placed in nursing homes are now entering CRCs. This is especially true for elders whose long-term care expenses are paid by Medicaid. The lower cost of CRCs has made them a more desirable option for states with growing numbers of frail elders who need public assistance. One reason for this is the trend toward state licensure and Medicaid reimbursement, albeit at lower levels, for these alternatives.

Assisted living is seen by its advocates as a new, more humane model of housing that is aimed at elders who need assistance with personal care (e.g., bathing and taking medications) and with some ADLs, but who are not so severely impaired physically or cognitively that they need 24-hour skilled medical care (Kane and Wilson, 1993). It is based on a social model of long-term care, rather than a medical model such as nursing homes. Residents usually live in private apartment units, generally smaller than the average nursing home, which typically include:

- a kitchen
- a full bathroom
- in some, a bedroom, sitting room, and partial bath

Some assisted living facilities offer shared units as a lower-cost alternative. Most provide congregate meals in a common dining room, as well as housekeeping, laundry, and help with some activities of daily living. Staff often include at least one nurse, a social worker, and one or more people to provide case management services. Access to health care is provided for specific tenants as needed (often contracting the services of physicians, physical therapists, mental health specialists). As a result, staffing costs are lower than in nursing homes, thereby keeping the average cost of assisted living lower by one-half to one-third.

Assisted living facilities often develop individual service plans, based on each resident's physical health and functional abilities. Families considering these options need to ask what the facility will provide as their older family members decline in their physical, cognitive, or mental functions. Like nursing homes, assisted living providers that offer a variety of services generally charge "tiered" rates,

THE DOWNSIDE OF CRCS

Despite its many advantages, housing for older adults that is based on a social model of long-term care can have its downside. These problems are aggravated in states that have few or no licensure requirements for assisted living or other CRCs. For example, state officials and industry representatives in Alabama recently agreed to enforcing stricter rules after reviewing complaints against 200 unlicensed facilities. Two particularly egregious examples are a 92-year-old man who climbed out of a window in the assisted living facility where he lived, walked away, and died of exposure; and another frail resident, in another facility, who became bedridden, lost 40 pounds and died when no medical attention was provided.

that is, increasingly costly fees for elders who need more services. As a result, some facilities can cost as much as a nursing home if they provide more amenities and health services.

Assisted living generally offers the resident more autonomy, privacy, and participation in care decisions than do nursing homes. The trade-off, of course, is that the individual may decide to participate in activities that are risky or that do not comply with health care regimens recommended by a professional. These may include choices such as refusing to use a walker or not following a rigid diet. As a result of this conflict between assuring resident autonomy versus safety, many facilities have moved toward a policy of managed or **negotiated risk.** Under such policies, residents (and often their family or guardian) must sign a written agreement that allows the resident to accept greater risk of personal injury in exchange for autonomy in decisions about his or her own lifestyle in the facility.

It is important not to place assisted living in a "continuum of care," since this type of facility can generally serve older people with a wide range of disabilities, many of whom traditionally would be placed in nursing homes. Many states are exploring the option of **Medicaid waivers** for assisted living. Some, such as Oregon and Washington, have implemented programs that encourage the use of assisted living and other community-based long-term care options. Most people in assisted living facilities today are private-pay residents, however. Many who move out do so because they have run out of funds and must turn to nursing homes that are covered by Medicaid, even though they might benefit from the greater autonomy and self-care at assisted living facilities (Kane and Wilson, 1993). As more states provide Medicaid waivers, it is anticipated that greater congruence can be achieved between needs of specific elders and available housing options. As a result of their lower costs and greater autonomy for residents, assisted living has become the fastest growing type of housing for older adults (Pynoos and Matsuoka, 2001).

Adult foster care (AFC) or **adult family homes (AFH)** are another alternative to nursing homes for older persons who do not need the 24-hour medical care of skilled care facilities. Like assisted living residents, older clients in AFCs can generally decide for themselves whether to take their medications and to exercise as much or as little as they want, unlike the more structured nursing home schedule. AFC is generally provided in a private home by the owners who may have some health care training but are not required to be professionals in the field. These homes are licensed to house up to 5 or 6 clients. Some specialize in caring for younger or older adults with physical disabilities or psychiatric disorders; others refuse to care for people with advanced dementia; while still others offer services to a small number of dementia patients only. More and more individuals are converting their homes to adult foster care. The owner and, in some cases, auxiliary staff provide housekeeping, help with some ADLs, personal care, and some delegated nursing functions, such as giving injections, distributing medications, and changing dressings on wounds if they have been trained and certified by a registered nurse. Medicaid reimbursement rates for AFC are one-third to one-half the rates paid to nursing homes. This works well for residents who do not require heavy care (e.g., those who are bedridden or with severe behavioral problems due to dementia). However, for more frail older clients, or for those who have "aged in place" (i.e., have become more impaired while living in that AFC), the reimbursement rates do not reflect the time and effort required of the facilities' caregivers. For this reason, a recent survey of 290 AFH providers in the state of Washington revealed high levels of dissatisfaction with reimbursement rates and complaints that case managers were not disclosing the severity of clients' needs when referring them to AFH (Curtis, Kiyak, and Hedrick, 2000).

This trend toward placing more impaired older persons in AFCs or AFHs is driven by states' efforts to control long-term care costs, as well as societal pressures toward a social rather than medical model of care. Evidence of the problems inherent in such motivations, however, is provided by an analysis of 1032 nursing home residents and 279 AFC residents in Oregon. After one year, 79 percent of the former and 88 percent of the latter group were still alive. However:

- Eighty-three percent of the survivors in nursing homes still lived there at follow-up.
- Fifty-three percent of those in AFC were still there.
- Twenty-nine percent of surviving AFC residents had moved to nursing homes or to other living situations.

By analyzing the 12-month change in ADL scores, the researchers concluded that almost all nursing home residents had been appropriately placed, compared with only 64 percent of AFC residents. That is, residents of AFCs who were frail at baseline generally declined more in their ADLs than did comparable residents of nursing homes. These individuals would have been more appropriately placed in nursing homes. Such differences may reflect the paucity of rehabilitation services and a greater emphasis on resident autonomy in AFC. In sum, AFC works well for the less-severely impaired older person, but not for those with multiple ADL limitations (Stark, Kane, Kane, and Finch, 1995).

SERVICES TO AID OLDER PEOPLE IN THE COMMUNITY

In recent years, the term **long-term care** has evolved from an emphasis on purely institutional care to a broad range of services to help older adults in their own homes, other community settings, and nursing homes. Under this broader definition, homemaker services, nutrition programs, adult day care, and home health care are all part of long-term care.

Home Care

Despite the increasing array of residential options for older people who need assistance with multiple ADLs, many prefer to "age in place" (i.e., remain in their own homes even though declines in physical and/or cognitive functioning reduce their P–E congruence with the home). This trend will increase dramatically as baby boomers age, with their strong values of independence and self-sufficiency.

Over the last decades, more federal, state, and local services have become available to help older people maintain their independence in the least restrictive environment feasible. This can assist the older person to maintain P–E congruence. As shown in Figure 11.4, some of these services (e.g., home care) are brought to the older person, whereas others (e.g., adult day health) require the individual to leave home to receive the service. As the older population has increased, newer cohorts of older adults have adopted the values of aging in place, and third-party payers (e.g., Medicare) have searched for alternatives to the escalating hospital and nursing home costs, home care services have grown dramatically. Medicare reimburses **home health care** services, defined as skilled nursing or rehabilitation benefits that are provided in the patient's own home and prescribed by a physician.

The three most widely used services, comprising 97 percent of Medicare reimbursements for home health care, are:

- skilled nursing (41 percent)
- home health aide (49 percent)
- physical therapy (7 percent) (U.S. DHHS, 1998).

Since 1989, when a class-action lawsuit resulted in a more flexible interpretation of Medicare home care regulations, agencies that provide home care expanded their visits and services to beneficiaries. Home care became the fastest-growing component of personal health care expenditures, increasing by 20 percent per year from 1991 until 1998. Starting in 1998, however, the Balanced Budget Act of 1997 limited home health coverage to 100 days maximum, thereby reducing the number of clients (Hughes and Pittard, 2001). Not surprisingly, the average home health client is a woman aged 70 and has 1.7 ADL impairments. The oldest-old generally receive more visits on average than any other age group, about four times as many as for those aged 65–66 (Hughes, 1996; Hughes et al., 1997).

Home health care is far less expensive than acute (hospital) care, about 40 percent less than nursing homes, and comparable to adult foster care or adult family homes. However, costs become more comparable if 24-hour care is needed. Researchers have examined the costs and impact of home care on hospitalization rates among users. In one study, home health agencies that were Medicare-certified recorded the actual costs of providing an array of services (e.g., skilled nursing care, physical therapy, home dialysis, hospice). A U-shaped curve was found to be the best model of cost-efficiency; that is, a scope of 8 to 10 different services appears to be ideal for reducing the average cost of services provided by a home health agency. Those that provide either fewer or more services do so at a higher cost per visit; this suggests that these agencies can function most economically if they provide an array of services, ideally between 8 and 10 (Gonzales, 1997). Another study examined hospital-use data among home health clients in a meta-analysis of 20 earlier studies. These studies provided a large number of home health programs and clients on which to test outcomes. When home health was defined strictly as the delivery of nursing, medical, and support services in the home of a terminally or chronically ill older person, home health users had 2.5 to 6 fewer days of hospital use, compared to similar patient populations that did not use home health care. These results support the cost-effectiveness of home health care in curtailing the use of far more expensive acute care (Hughes, 1997). As demand has increased, home care agencies have expanded their services beyond health care to include a broad array of "home- and community-based services" (HCBS):

- assistance such as chore services to maintain the home
- personal care to help the person perform ADLs
- home-delivered meals
- automatic safety response systems

PLANNING FOR AGING IN PLACE

When Mr. and Mrs. Pond bought their last home, they were in their late sixties. They chose a house on one level, installed grab bars in the bathroom, nonslip surfaces, and other safety features. When Mr. Pond was 78, he had a stroke that restricted his mobility. Mrs. Pond's vision became more impaired. However, with help from a weekly chore worker, daily meals delivered to their home, and twice-weekly visits to an adult day care facility, they were able to remain in their home until they died, he at age 82, she at 85.

Such assistance can help older people "age in place" in their own homes. Other HCBS options, such as adult day care and case management, are offered in community settings. These services provide respite to family caregivers and opportunities for social interaction for isolated elders. These additional HCBS are not covered by Medicare, but by Title XX and Title III of the Older Americans Act. These funds make each state's unit on aging (SUA) responsible for their delivery. SUAs, in turn, designate Area Agencies on Aging (AAAs) to develop and administer these services at the local level, sometimes in the form of contracts to local providers.

Adult Day Care

Adult day care (ADC) is another long-term care option that allows the older person to remain at home and receive some health and social services. In this case, users attend a local ADC center one or more times per week, for several hours each day. ADC goes beyond senior centers in providing structured health and social services for older people with cognitive impairments such as dementia and those with functional impairments due to stroke and multiple chronic illnesses. Some ADCs are based on a health rehabilitative model of long-term care with individualized care ("Adult Day Health Care" or ADHC), while others fit into a social psychological model ("social day care"). Although both may provide recreation, meals, transportation to and from the facility, and memory-retraining programs, ADHCs are more likely to offer nursing care, physical and speech therapy, and scheduled medication distribution (Tedesco, 1996). The greatest advantage of ADHCs over home health care is to bring together older people for social interaction. Equally important, they provide respite for family caregivers. Clearly, such services are not suitable for the most impaired or bedbound older person; but they are an invaluable resource for elders with moderate levels of dementia or with serious physical impairments and chronic illnesses who still benefit from living in the community.

TECHNOLOGY TO HELP OLDER PERSONS REMAIN INDEPENDENT

Adaptive technology is growing significantly, stimulated not so much by large numbers of older people, but by the increased numbers of younger people living with disabilities. The expansion and diversification of computer technology is the greatest source of **assistive technology.** Older people and those with disabilities now have greater access to resources such as libraries, service providers, support groups, health care information, and even distant family members through e-mail and the Web. For people with sensory impairments, the com-

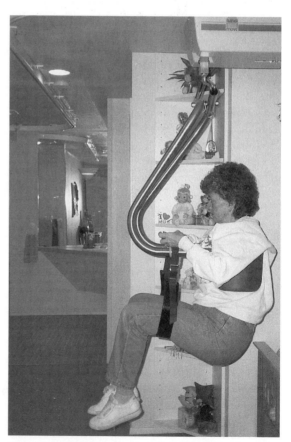

Technology can help older people with disabilities live more independently in their homes.

LESSONS FROM OTHER COUNTRIES

The United States can learn from developments in other countries with larger proportions of older adults in their population. For example, new homes in Sweden are required by housing codes to include a full bathroom on the main floor. Such foresight is important when one considers the high likelihood that a very old homeowner may no longer be able to go up and down stairs to use a bathroom in the traditional upstairs sleeping quarters (Riley, 1999).

puter itself can be adapted; for example, software is available to enlarge text or read aloud text on the screen. Telephone equipment is more user-friendly, with larger buttons, larger text, and automatic dialing capability. This growth in assistive technologies in telecommunications was stimulated by the Telecommunications Act of 1996, which requires manufacturers to make telephone equipment accessible to people with diverse disabilities. Voice-activated phones that can be dialed by voice commands and answered from across the room can help older people who have problems pressing buttons or rushing to answer the phone. Speaker- and cellular phones can make it easier for older people to place calls from any part of the house, indoors and out, as well as from their car if an emergency arises. Caller ID features can also help the older person determine if a particular call is important enough to answer (Lubinski and Higginbotham, 1997; Kaplan, 1997).

Computers can also serve a useful function for older adults who take multiple medications throughout the day. They can be programmed to remind the person when to take what specific drug and provide individualized information about drug interactions. Eventually these systems will allow the older person to report symptoms and reactions to current medications to his or her doctor, who can then review the patient's medical history, symptoms, and drug reactions in order to change or discontinue prescriptions. This innovative technology could significantly reduce the number of visits made by older people to hospital emergency rooms due to adverse drug reactions (Deatrick, 1997). Another technological innovation that can help older persons who use multiple medications

is the "smart cap," a tiny computer chip embodied in a prescription bottle cap. The cap beeps to remind the older person to take the drug; it also counts how many pills are removed each day and when. The system is connected via modem to the company that manufactures the drug so that a phone reminder can be made if the user forgets a medication. Although the cost of such a system is currently prohibitive for most older people, it offers great promise for improving medication adherence by future cohorts.

Some new trends in computer technology, developed for industry, will soon find their way into private homes. For example, computers that can detect and signal sudden changes in ambient temperature, noise, lighting levels, and air quality already exist for large workplaces. They are a valuable resource in the homes of frail and cognitively impaired older people. Robotics is another field significantly altering work environments. Robots are not yet cost-effective and practical for home use, but could play a major role in improving the quality of life for older adults with sensory and physical disabilities. If these new technologies are adapted for home use, they can help reduce the concerns of many elders and their families about leaving the older person alone.

Newer cohorts of elders are also benefiting from recent developments in **"Universal Design"** (Mace, 1998). This concept of designing the environment to allow the widest range of users possible attracts the attention of architects, landscape architects, and interior and furniture designers. What began as an attempt to make curb cuts in streets, as well as hallways and bathrooms in homes, more accessible to people in wheelchairs, has grown to a movement that makes all environments—parks, wilderness areas, automobiles, and computer workstations—accommodate people who are young and old, who are able-bodied, as well as those who are limited in their mobility, vision, and hearing.

Some architects are working on cost-effective means of applying new technology to home design, known as **smart homes.** For example, systems that make a room light up through sensors in the floor can help prevent accidents when an older person gets up in the middle of the night to use the bathroom. Remote controls for operating thermostats, windows, and their coverings can help an older person change the room temperature as needed, as well as open and close windows and shades to control the ambient temperature and to prevent glare. New systems can be installed for as little as $5000 but can cost much more as their components increase. Other design features that can be built into new homes to help future elders include:

- bathrooms with roll-in showers
- hands-free sensors on faucets
- nonskid flooring
- low-pile carpeting
- uniform lighting throughout the house
- elevator shafts that are built into the home and used as closets until they are needed as elevators

Among today's older population, however, only a small proportion have made home modifications to improve safety. The most popular effort to reduce P–E incongruence has been to install grab bars in bathrooms (in about 30 percent of homes owned by older adults). Other changes are far less frequent:

- Twenty-three percent added brighter lighting in their homes.
- Sixteen percent added more handrails.
- Four percent replaced doorknobs and water faucets with lever handles.
- Four percent installed ramps in place of steps or stairs (AARP, 1996, 2000).

In recent years, several products and services that do not depend on "high tech" have come into the marketplace to assist older people in emergency situations, especially those who are living alone. Some of these are simply pullcords in the bathroom or bedroom that are connected to a hospital or to the local emergency medical service. Others, such as the Life Safety System and Lifeline Service, are more sophisticated communication systems that use a portable medical alert device or an alarm unit to transmit specific signals for a fire, a medical emergency, or "no activity" through telephone lines or computers. These systems have been found to be cost-effective in enhancing the older person's sense of security about living alone. Other "low-tech" but helpful aids for independent living include the "Aladdin Personal Reader," which is a large electronic magnifying glass that looks like an overhead projector. It magnifies printed materials such as books, newspapers, and bottle labels up to 25 times their original size. Another simple device controls window shades and blinds without much physical force or manipulation by arthritic hands. This continuous-loop mechanism, marketed as a "Rollease," holds the window shade in position while the user pulls on one side of the loop to raise the shade or the other side to lower it. Unfortunately, while it is an option for many new shade and blind designs, currently it cannot be adapted to existing window covers (Harper, 1995).

Other products are being developed for home use that can significantly reduce the burden on family caregivers. For example, a battery-operated bathtub lift (marketed as "Libra" by Arjo, Inc.) can help people get in and out of a bathtub without human assistance. It literally lifts the user from the floor, sets him or her into the tub, and removes him or her with the press of a button (Weiner, 1995). Another device assists bedbound people out of bed and carries them to the bathroom or other parts of the house, using a harness attached to a track in the ceiling. Unfortunately, these products are not covered by Medicare, and therefore must be paid out of pocket. This makes them accessible only to a small segment of the population with disabilities and functional impairments.

HOUSING POLICY AND GOVERNMENT PROGRAMS

Housing policy for older people has received less attention than has income security and health care. This is due, in part, to the influence of well-organized interest groups, such as builders and real estate developers.

The major housing programs that benefit older people involve subsidies to suppliers of housing to enable them to sell or rent housing for less than the prevailing market price. Since 1959, a special housing program for older people and those with disabilities has given loans for the construction of housing for these groups. Known as the *Section 202* program and administered by the U.S. Department of Housing and Urban Development (HUD), it provides housing for moderate-income older persons whose incomes are just above the eligibility requirements of public housing but too low to obtain housing in the private market. Rents are set by HUD, at about 30 percent of the individual's monthly income. Under Section 202, low-interest loans are made to private nonprofit organizations or to nonprofit consumer cooperatives for the financing, construction, or rehabilitation of housing for older people. In general, these buildings include:

- safety features such as grab bars and emergency systems in each unit
- no communal services such as meals and housekeeping

An emerging concern in these housing units is their lack of P–E fit with the needs of frail older adults, many of whom have "aged in place," rather than moving to a facility that meets their increasing needs for supportive services. The average age of residents in Section 202 housing has increased to 80, and continues to rise; 90 percent are women living alone (HUD, 1999). Currently 67 percent of nonprofit groups that provide supportive housing for this population utilize Section 202 funding. However, this program has slowed as the federal government has withdrawn from supporting housing production (American Association of Homes and Services for the Aging, 1997; Pynoos and Golant, 1996).

Section 236 and *Section 8* housing programs provide private enterprise with additional means of developing quality rental and cooperative housing for low- and moderate-income persons, regardless of age, by lowering their housing costs through interest-reduction payments (*Section 236*) and rent vouchers for qualifying older adults (*Section 8*). In the latter case, landlords receive from federal and state governments the difference between the rental cost of a housing unit and 30 percent of the tenants' income available for rent. Older people form an important segment of users of this rent supplement program. However, many of these 20-year contracts with owners of low-income housing began in the 1970s and have now expired.

Federal funds have been reduced to renew the contracts, and many owners have lost interest in the low-income housing market, especially in urban centers undergoing renewal or "gentrification." Some landlords have converted their buildings into higher-rent apartments, hotels, or office spaces, or have sold the property outright to local developers. These changes in federal funding and local priorities have reduced the supply of Section 8 housing, which will continue to decline in this century. Other policies that indirectly affect older homeowners are:

- Property tax relief
- Energy assistance
- Home equity conversion or reverse mortgages described earlier in this chapter. These provide long-term homeowners with some additional income that converts their homes into more liquid assets.
- Energy assistance for low-income homeowners to offset air conditioning and heating costs is provided under the federal government's allocation of block grant money to cities and states.

As a result, less than 5 percent, or 1.5 million older people have benefited from federally funded housing assistance programs. The numbers are declining as HUD (Housing and Urban Development), the federal agency responsible for these

---

CHANGES IN SECTION 202 OBJECTIVES

During the 2000 congressional session, the Senate Appropriations Committee approved an increase of $73 million for Section 202 housing for older adults. The total allocation of $783 million for fiscal year 2002 includes $50 million for converting Section 202 housing to assisted living (AL) facilities and another $50 million for hiring service coordinators to manage them.

---

programs, reduces its subsidies directly to older adults in the form of rent vouchers (Section 8) or indirectly through low-cost loans to builders of housing for older people (Section 202). A major reason for the decline in housing subsidies is the growing public perception that older people have the financial adequacy to pay for their housing costs directly. Yet, older residents of public housing have a median income that is 35 percent of the median for all older households in the United States (HUD, 1999).

Most recent federal activity in the housing arena has maintained the programs and housing stock that currently exist, modifying programs only incrementally to serve larger numbers of older adults. The goal has been to make better use of existing housing resources through homesharing, accessory apartments, and home equity conversions, rather than to increase the overall housing supply for older adults. Another major need is for more congregate housing services. As described earlier, congregate housing is an important link in the long-term care continuum enabling frail and low-income older people to remain in the community and thereby maintain P–E congruence. The best way to achieve this may be innovations that modify existing communities and neighborhoods to meet elders' changing housing needs. This may include creating "granny flats" or accessory housing as part of existing homes to accommodate older people in smaller units near family or close friends.

SRO HOUSING

Single-room-occupancy (SRO) hotels in urban centers have traditionally served as minimal housing for the urban poor, particularly single older men, who make up the largest group of SRO res-

idents. Indeed, the typical SRO resident is a white older man with 8.7 years of education and an income level 20 percent lower than that of his non-SRO peers, who reports multiple chronic conditions, and who has lived in his room (often with incomplete kitchens and shared bathrooms) for at least 5 years. Increasing numbers of deinstitutionalized mental hospital patients have become SRO tenants as well (Rollinson, 1991). A survey in New York City found that, because of their longer tenancy, older SRO residents paid less for their SRO units than did younger tenants. Because of lower income levels, however, older residents paid a higher *proportion* of their income (44 percent) than did younger tenants (25 percent) in the same buildings (Crystal and Beck, 1992). Although overall satisfaction with SRO housing was not high, older residents liked the opportunity to have their own rooms and the physical safety afforded by such a building in an otherwise hostile city core. The lack of services such as congregate meals and counseling was not considered a disadvantage.

Yet, SRO housing is rapidly disappearing. As the process of "gentrification" of urban cores becomes more popular, and as more upper-income people discover the advantages of living downtown, the trend of demolishing SRO hotels and using this valuable land for upscale condominiums and office and retail space will continue. Over the past decade, a result of this has been a dramatic increase in the number of homeless older people in urban centers.

THE PROBLEMS OF HOMELESSNESS

Although this chapter focuses on housing and community service options for elders, a growing segment of the older population is homeless, often

Many older homeless men have no social support systems.

unable to afford basic housing and unaware of services to which they are entitled. **Homeless people** generally include those who, "for whatever reason, do not have a fixed, regular, and adequate night-time residence" (Stewart B. McKinney Homeless Assistance Act, 1987). In the mid 1960s, many homeless elders had recently been released from long-term psychiatric facilities as a result of the 1963 Community Mental Health Act. Today's homeless elders (defined as age 50 and older because physiologically they are generally 10–20 years older than their chronological age) are largely the chronic homeless who have lived on the streets for many years and have lost contact with their families. People over age 50 comprise between 10 and 20 percent of the homeless population. This includes an increasing number of women, although there are approximately four times more men in this population. Homeless men are more likely to have lived this way longer than their female counterparts. Many suffer from psychiatric disorders, alcoholism, or dementia, and lack strong social support. Those who become redomiciled (i.e., find

permanent housing) tend to be mostly older homeless women with some social support, who attend community facilities (presumably becoming more familiar to service providers), and who do not display psychotic symptoms (Cohen et al., 1997; Crane, 1996; Sokolovsky, 1997). One epidemiological study interviewed 900 homeless persons using standard diagnostic criteria for psychiatric disorders. Although the rates for other psychiatric diagnoses did not differ by age or gender, alcohol abuse was significantly more prevalent among men aged 50 and older than among younger men (81 percent versus 60 percent); the reverse was true for drug abuse (16 percent versus 43.5 percent). No differences emerged in rates of substance abuse or other psychiatric diagnoses between younger and older homelesss women (DeMallie, North, and Smith, 1997).

Not only do homeless people have no place to live, but they also lack food, clothing, medical care, and social supports. Such a disorganized lifestyle can magnify the usual age-related declines in biological and psychological processes described in earlier chapters. A life at the edge, in which the individual is constantly trying to fulfill basic human needs (food, shelter, safety from predators), does not leave much energy for these elders to maintain even a modicum of health and well-being; their problems are compounded by chronic psychiatric disorders, alcoholism, drug abuse, and cognitive impairment (often a result of long-term alcohol abuse). Homeless older persons with chronic health problems often do not have the physical, social, or psychological resources to seek regular medical care for these conditions, or even to follow the necessary medication schedules and dietary restrictions. The prevalence of chronic diseases in this group is higher than for other segments of the older population, yet their access to health services is inadequate and sporadic at best. Their ability to maintain their health and medication regimens is limited by the unstable nature of their lifestyles and frequent disruptions in psychological well-being. Their health care is typically obtained through public hospital emergency rooms, and necessary clinical appointments and follow-up visits are rarely kept. Thus, they often die because of diseases that are neglected, accidents and victimization on the streets. The number of homeless elders is estimated to double in the next 30 years, with an increase in the number of younger persons with risk factors of lifelong poverty, substance abuse, incarceration, marital disruption, and lack of family contacts (Cohen, 1999).

SUMMARY AND IMPLICATIONS

This chapter presented ways in which environmental factors affect the physical and psychological well-being of older people. Perhaps the most important lesson to be gained from this discussion is that a given environment is not inherently good or bad. Some environments are more conducive to the optimal functioning of *some* older people, while other older adults need an entirely different set of features. For example, an older person who has a high need for activity and stimulation and has always lived in an urban setting will be more satisfied with a large nursing home in a metropolitan center than will the individual who has always lived in a single-family dwelling in a rural community. Most person–environment models point to the necessity of examining each older person's specific needs, preferences, and abilities, and designing environments that can both meet the needs of this broad cross-section and, more importantly, flexibly respond to individual differences. To the degree that environmental press can be reduced to accommodate personal abilities and needs, the aging person can function more effectively and maintain his or her level of well-being. Relocation represents a special case of P–E incongruence that can disturb the well-being of an impaired older person by raising the level of environmental press.

Differences in housing quality and services for rural older residents are of concern. Current cohorts are much less likely than previous ones to live in farm and nonfarm rural communities. However, those who do, particularly African Americans, tend to have lower incomes and poorer health, with more limitations in activities of daily living. The recognition of these disparities has led to the growth of state and federally funded services for rural elders, but more are needed. Older persons in rural communities appear to have more frequent social interactions with neighbors and friends than do urban elders, but they need more formal health and social services.

The neighborhood and neighbors play a significant role in the well-being of older adults. With retirement and declining health, the older person's physical lifespace becomes more constricted. The neighborhood takes on greater significance as a source of social interactions, health and social services, grocery shopping, banking, and postal services. Neighbors represent an important component of older people's social and emotional network, especially when family is unavailable.

Fear of crime among older persons is widespread but is incongruent with actual victimization rates. Older people experience far lower rates than younger people for violent crimes, and somewhat lower for other types of crime. African American women, however, are at greater risk for crimes than any other group of elders. The potential danger of injury and long-term disability, as well as the fear of economic loss, may contribute to this incongruence between actual victimization rates and fear of crime.

The high rate of home ownership and long-term residence in their homes make it difficult for older people to relocate to new housing, even when the new situation represents a significant improvement over the old. The poor condition of many older people's homes and the high costs of renovating and maintaining them sometimes make relocation necessary, even when an older homeowner is reluctant. Better living conditions and a safer neighborhood in which several other elders reside have been found to improve older people's morale and sense of well-being, especially following a move to a planned housing project from substandard housing. The growth of planned and congregate housing for older adults has raised the issue of site selection for such housing. It is especially important when designing housing that public transportation be located nearby and that facilities such as medical and social services, banks, and groceries be within easy access of the housing facility. Services need to be integrated from the beginning, as many residents who move in as young-old persons continue to live there for many years and age in place.

As people live longer and healthier lives beyond retirement, the need for housing that provides a range of care options will continue to grow. Several alternative methods of purchasing such housing are available—some guarantee lifetime care, others do not provide personal and health services. Considering the high likelihood of using a nursing home facility at some time in old age, many retirees prefer to select the more comprehensive options.

The proportion of older people in a nursing home at any one time is very low, but up to 50 percent will need some type of long-term care before they die. Because of the greater likelihood of physical and cognitive impairments among nursing home residents, it is critical to enhance the environmental quality of these facilities at the design stage. If the facility has already been built, features can be added that increase privacy and control and allow for the expression of territoriality and other personal needs. Aging and institutionalization do not reduce the individual's needs for identity and self-expression.

Assisted living and adult foster care or adult family homes are rapidly becoming a cost-effective option for many older people who need help with ADLs but do not necessarily need 24-hour care. Many of these community residential care facilities provide greater autonomy, more options for privacy, and less direct supervision for their older tenants. Funding for assisted living is not covered by Medicaid in the majority of states, making it a viable option only for those elders with adequate personal financial resources. However, more states are offering Medicaid waivers for AFCs and, to some extent, for assisted living. Home care is now the fastest-growing component of personal health care expenditures. It is reimbursed by Medicare and Medicaid to offer more services than other long-term care options. It allows older people to "age in place" while bringing services such as skilled nursing care, rehabilitation, and personal and house-hold care to the person's home. Adult day care, both as a rehabilitative and social model, provides opportunities for social integration of frail older people who are living at home alone or with a family caregiver. The older person can attend adult day care for several hours each day and receive some nursing and rehabilitation services, while the caregiver obtains respite from caregiving tasks. Many adult day care programs also offer counseling and support groups for caregivers.

Single-room-occupancy hotels have traditionally been a low-cost housing option for older people, especially for older men living alone. However, as these buildings have been demolished or remodeled in many cities, SRO residents have become displaced; some have become homeless. Many older homeless people have chronic medical, psychiatric, and cognitive disorders that often go unattended because of lack of access to health services. As a result, these homeless elders grow physiologically older more rapidly than do their more stable peers.

GLOSSARY

adult day care (ADC)   a community facility that frail older people living at home can attend several hours each day; when based on a health rehabilitation model, it provides individualized therapy plans; those based on a social model focus on structured social and psychotherapeutic activities

adult foster care (AFC)/adult family home (AFH)   a private home facility, licensed by the state, in which the owner of the home provides housekeeping, personal care, and some delegated nursing functions for the residents

aging in place   continuing to live in a private home or apartment, even when declining competence reduces P–E congruence and more assistance with ADLs is needed

assisted living   a housing model aimed at elders who need assistance with personal care, e.g., bathing and taking medication, but who are not so physically or cognitively impaired as to need 24-hour attention

assistive technology   a range of electronic and computer technologies whose goal is to assist people with disabilities to remain independent and perform as many ADLs as possible without assistance from others

community residential care (CRC)   a general label for residential long-term care options other than nursing homes; includes adult foster care, adult family homes, and assisted living

congregate housing   a form of group housing that provides communal services, the minimum of which is a central kitchen and dining room for residents; some facilities also provide housekeeping, social, and health services

continuous care retirement community (CCRC)   a multilevel facility offering a range from independent to congregate living arrangements, including nursing home units; generally requires an initial entry fee to assure a place if long-term care is needed in the future

Eden Alternative   a new paradigm for nursing home care that encourages active participation by residents in caring for plants and animals

home health care   a variety of nursing, rehabilitation, and other therapy services, as well as assistance with personal care and household maintenance, that are provided to people who are homebound and have difficulty performing multiple ADLs

long-term care   a broad range of services geared to helping frail older adults in their own home and community settings; can include nursing homes, nutritional programs, adult day care, and visiting nurse services

Medicaid waivers   exceptions to state Medicaid rules that allow use of Medicaid funds for services that are traditionally not covered by Medicaid, such as chore services and adult family homes

naturally occurring retirement community (NORC)   a neighborhood or larger area occupied mostly by older people, but without having been planned specifically for this population

negotiated risk   agreement between a resident, family or guardian, and facility administration that the resident in a CRC setting will maintain autonomy but will assume risks if problems such as falls and accidents result from such independence

nursing homes   facilities with three or more beds staffed 24 hours per day by health professionals who provide nursing and personal-care services to residents who cannot remain in their own homes due to physical health problems, functional disabilities, and/or significant cognitive impairments

single-room-occupancy (SRO) hotels   older buildings in urban centers that have been converted to low-cost apartments; often these are single rooms with no kitchen, minimal cooking and refrigeration facilities, and bathrooms shared with other units

smart homes   technology built into a home that relies on computerized systems to monitor and maintain preferred lighting and heat levels, security, communication

universal design   designing a product or building or landscape to make it accessible to and usable by the broadest range of users

RESOURCES

See the companion Website for this text at <www.ablongman.com/hooyman> for information about the following:

- AgeNet, LLC
- American Association of Homes and Services for the Aging
- American Association of Retired Persons (AARP)
- American College of Health Care Administrators (ACHCA)
- American Seniors Housing Association
- Assisted Living Federation of America (ALFA) [formerly Assisted Living Facilities Association of America]
- Caring Concepts
- Citizens for the Improvement of Nursing Homes (CINH)
- Gatekeeper Program
- Department of Housing and Urban Development (HUD)
- National Adult Day Services Association, NCOA
- National Association for Home Care (NAHC)
- National Association of Directors of Nursing in Long Term Care (NADONAILTC)
- National Citizens Coalition for Nursing Home Reform (NCCNHR)
- National Institute on Adult Day Care
- National Shared Housing Resource Center

REFERENCES

AARP, *Fixing to stay: A national survey on housing and home modification issues*. Washington, DC: 2000.

AARP, *Understanding senior housing into the next century*. Washington DC, 1996.

Administration on Aging. *A profile of older Americans: 2000*, Web page: http://www.aoa.gov/stats/profile.

American Association of Homes and Services for the Aging (AAHSA), 1997. *Senior housing*, Web page: http://www.aahsa.org/members/backgrd2/htm

Ashley, M. J., Olin, J. S., Le Riche, W. H., Kornaczewski, A., and Rankin, J. G. Skid row alcoholism: A distinct sociomedical entity. *Archives of Internal Medicine*, 1976, *136*, 272–278.

Atchley, R. C. *Social forces and aging: An introduction to social gerontology*. (9th ed.). Belmont, CA: Wadsworth, 2000.

Auerbach, A. J. The elderly in rural areas. In L. H. Ginsberg (Ed.), *Social work in rural communities*. New York: Council on Social Work Education, 1976.

Barker, R. G., Dembo, T., and Lewin, K. Frustration and regression: An experiment with young children. *University of Iowa Studies in Child Welfare*, 1941, *18*.

Bayne, M. K. The Eden Alternative. *Contemporary Long Term Care*, 1998, *21*, 92.

Bazargan, M. The effects of health, environmental, and socio-psychological variables on fear of crime and its consequences among urban black elderly individuals. *International Journal of Aging and Human Development*, 1994, *38*, 99–115.

Bureau of Justice Statistics. *Criminal Victimization in the United States 1999: The National Crime Victimization Survey*, NCJ-174446, Sept. 2000.

Cohen, C. I. Aging and homelessness. *The Gerontologist*, 1999, *39*, 5–14.

Cohen, C. I., Ramirez, M., Teresi, J., Gallagher, M., and Sokolovsky, J. Predictors of becoming redomiciled among older homeless women. *The Gerontologist*, 1997, *37*, 67–74.

Crane, M. The situation of older homeless people. *Reviews in Clinical Gerontology*, 1996, *6*, 389–398.

Crystal, S., and Beck, P. A room of one's own: The SRO and the single elderly. *The Gerontologist*, 1992, *32*, 684–692.

Curtis, M. P., Kiyak, H.A., Hedrick, S. Resident and facility characteristics of adult-family home, adult residential care, and assisted living facilities in Washington state. *Journal of Gerontological Social Work*, 2000, *34*, 25–41.

Day, K., Carreon, D., and Stump, C. The therapeutic design of environments for people with dementia:

A review of the empirical research. *The Gerontologist*, 2000, *40*, 397–406.

Deatrick, D. Senior-Med: Creating a network to help manage medications. *Generations*, 1997, *21*, 59–60.

Demallie, D. A., North, C. S., and Smith, E. M. Psychiatric disorders among the homeless: A comparison of older and younger groups. *The Gerontologist*, 1997, *37*, 61–66.

Dibner, A. S., Lowry, L., and Morris, J. N. Usage and acceptance of an emergency alarm system by the frail elderly. *The Gerontologist*, 1982, *22*, 538–539.

Freedman, V. A. Family structure and the risk of nursing home admission. *Journals of Gerontology*, 1996, *51B*, S61–S69.

Gaberlavage, G., and Citro, J. *Progress in the housing of older persons*. Public Policy Institute, American Association of Retired Persons, Washington, DC: 1997.

GAO (General Accounting Office). *Assisted living: Quality of care and consumer protection issues*. Final Report #GAO/T-HEHS-99-111), April 1999.

Golant, S. M., and La Greca, A. J. City-suburban, metro-nonmetro, and regional differences in the housing quality of U.S. elderly households. *Research on Aging*, 1994, *16*, 322–346.

Golant, S. M., and La Greca, A. J. The relative deprivation of U.S. elderly households as judged by their housing problems. *Journals of Gerontology*, 1995, *50B*, S13–S23.

Gonzales, T. I. An empirical study of economies of scope in home healthcare. *Health Services Research*, 1997, *32*, 313–324.

Greene, V. L., and Ondrich, J. I. Risk factors for nursing home admissions and exits. *Journals of Gerontology*, 1990, *45*, S250–S258.

Harper, D. Ease and independence without stigma: Three products that work. *Generations*, 1995, *19*, 58–60.

Hawes, C., Mor, V., Phillips, C. D., Fries, B. E., Morris, J. N., Steele-Friedlob, E., Greene, A. M., and Nennstiel, M. The OBRA-87 nursing home regulations and implementation of the Resident Assessment Instrument: Effects on process quality. *Journal of the American Geriatrics Society*, 1997, *45*, 977–985.

Hawes, C., Rose, M., and Phillips, C. D. *A National Study of Assisted Living for the Frail Elderly Executive Summary: Results of a National Survey of Facilities*. Washington, DC: Public Policy Institute, AARP, 1999.

Hawes, C., Wildfire, J. B., and Lux, L. J. *The regulations of board and care homes: Results of a survey in the 50 states and the District of Columbia*. Washington, DC: Public Policy Institute, AARP, 1993.

Henretta, J. C. Retirement and residential moves by elderly households. *Research on Aging*, 1986, *8*, 23–37.

Hobbs, F., and Damon, B. L. *65+ in the United States*. Washington, DC: U.S. Department of Commerce, Bureau of the Census, Current Population Reports, 1996.

Hollway, W., and Jefferson, T. The risk society in an age of anxiety: Situating fear of crime. *British Journal of Sociology*, 1997, *48*, 255–266.

HUD (U.S. Dept. of Housing and Urban Development), Office of Policy Development and Research. *Housing our elders*. Washington, DC: 1999.

Hughes, S. L. Home health. In C. J. Evashwick (Ed.), *The continuum of long-term care*. Albany, NY: Delmar, 1996.

Hughes, S. L., and Pittard, M. A. Home health. In C. J. Evashwick (Ed.). *The continuum of long-term care* (2nd ed.). Albany, NY: Delmar, 2001.

Hughes, S. L., Ulasevich, A., Weaver, F. M., Henderson, W., Manheim, L., Kubal, J. D., and Bonarigo, F. Impact of home care of hospital days: A meta-analysis. *Health Services Research*, 1997, *32*, 415–432.

Jette, A. M., Tennstedt, S., and Crawford, S. How does formal and informal community care affect nursing home use? *Journals of Gerontology*, 1995, *50B*, S4–S12.

Joel, L. S., Assisted living: another frontier (editorial). *American Journal of Nursing*, 1998. *98:7*.

Kane, R. A., and Wilson, K. B. *Assisted living in the United States: A new paradigm for residential care for frail older persons?* Washington, DC: AARP, 1993.

Kaplan, D. Access to technology: Unique challenges for people with disabilities. *Generations*, 1997, *21*, 24–27.

Lawton, M. P. Competence, environmental press, and the adaptation of older people. In P. G. Windley and G. Ernst (Eds.), *Theory development in environment and aging*. Washington, DC: Gerontological Society, 1975.

Lewin, K. *Dynamic theory of personality*. New York: McGraw-Hill, 1935.

Lewin, K. *Field theory in social science*. New York: Harper and Row, 1951.

Lewin, K., Lippitt, R., and White, R. Patterns of aggressive behavior in experimentally created social climates. *Journal of Social Psychology*, 1939, *10*, 271–299.

Litwak, E., and Longino, C. F. Migration patterns among the elderly: A developmental perspective. In R. B. Enright (Ed.), *Perspectives in social gerontology*. Boston: Allyn and Bacon, 1994.

Lubinski, E., and Higginbotham, D. J. *Communication technologies for the elderly: Vision, hearing and speech*. San Diego: Singular Publishing Group, 1997.

Mace, R. L. Universal Design in housing. *Assistive Technology*, 1998, *10*, 21–28.

Manton, K. G., Corder, L. S., and Stallard, E. Estimates of change in chronic disability and institutional incidence and prevalence rates in the U.S. elderly population from the 1982, 1984, and 1989 National Long-Term Care Survey. *Journals of Gerontology*, 1993, *48*, S153–S166.

McLaughlin, D. K., and Jensen, L. Poverty among older Americans: The plight of nonmetropolitan elders. *Journals of Gerontology*, 1993, *48*, S44–S54.

Meyer, H. The bottom line on assisted living. *Hospitals and Health Networks*, 1998. *72*, 22–26.

Murray, H. A. *Explorations in personality*. New York: Oxford University Press, 1938.

National Center for Health Statistics (NCHS). *Advance Data*, No. 28, Jan. 23, 1997.

National Center for Health Statistics (NCHS). Data from the 1997 National Nursing Home Survey. *Vital and Health Statistics*, No. 311, 2000.

National Low Income Housing Information Service. *The fiscal year 1991 budget and low income housing* (SM-290). Washington, DC: National Low-Income Housing Information Service, 1990.

New York Times. Seattle's elderly find a home for living, not dying. Nov. 22, 1998, pp. 1, 26–27.

Pynoos, J., and Golant, S. M. Housing and living arrangements for the elderly. In R. H. Binstock and L. K. George (Eds.), *Handbook of aging and the social sciences* (4th ed.). San Diego: Academic Press, 1996.

Pynoos, J., and Matsuoka, C. A. E. Housing. In C. J. Evashwick (Ed.), *The Continuum of Long-Term Care* (2nd ed.). Albany, NY: Delmar, 2001.

Quinn, M. E., Johnson, M. A., Andress, E. L., McGinnis, P., and Ramesh, M. Health characteristics of elderly personal care home residents. *Journal of Advance Nursing*, 1999, *30*, 410–417.

Redfoot, D., and Gaberlavage, G. Housing for older Americans: Sustaining the dream. *Generations,* 1991, *15,* 35–38.

Riley, C. A. *High access home.* New York: Rizzoli International Publications, 1999.

Rollinson, P. A. Elderly single room occupancy (SRO) hotel tenants: Still alone. *Social Work,* 1991, *36,* 303–308.

Seattle Times. Growing town is bustling with high-powered seniors. July 18, 2000, pp. 1A, 8A.

Silverstein, M., and Zablotsky, D. L. Health and social precursors of later life retirement-community migration. *Journals of Gerontology,* 1996, *51B,* S150–S156.

Sokolovsky, J. One thousand points of blight: Old, female and homeless in New York City. In J. Sokolovsky (Ed.), *The cultural context of aging.* Westport, CT: Bergin and Garvey, 1997.

Spillman, B. C., and Kemper, P. Lifetime patterns of payment for nursing home care. *Medical Care,* 1995, *33,* 280–296.

Stark, A. J., Kane, R. L., Kane, R. A., and Finch, M. Effect on physical functioning of care in adult foster homes and nursing homes. *The Gerontologist,* 1995, *35,* 648–655.

Stewart B. McKinney *Homeless Assistance Act,* P.L. 100-77 (1987).

Strahan, G. An overview of nursing homes and their current residents: Data from the 1995 National Nursing Home Survey. *Vital and Health Statistics.* No. 280. Hyattsville, MD: National Center for Health Statistics, 1997.

Tedesco, J. Adult day care. In C. J. Evashwick (Ed.), *The continuum of long-term care.* Albany, NY: Delmar, 1996.

Tennstedt, S. L., Crawford, S., and McKinley, J. Determining the pattern of community care: Is coresidence more important than caregiver relationship? *Journals of Gerontology,* 1993, *48,* S74–S83.

Teresi, J. A., Holmes, D., and Ory, M. G. The therapeutic design of environments for people with dementia. *The Gerontologist,* 2000, *40,* 64–74.

Thomas, W. H., and Stermer, M. Eden Alternative principles hold promise for the future of long-term care. *Balance,* 1999, *3,* 14–17.

U.S. Bureau of the Census. *65 and older in the U.S.* Current Population Reports, Series P25-1095. Washington DC: U.S. Government Printing Office, 1996.

U.S. Bureau of the Census. *Household and family characteristics.* Current Population Reports. Series P20-515. Washington, DC: U.S. Government Printing Office, 1998.

U.S. Dept. of Health and Human Services, Health Care Financing Adm. *Health Care Financing Review* (Medicare and Medicaid Statistical Supplement), 1998.

Vladeck, B. C., and Feuerberg, M. Unloving care revisited. *Generations,* 1995–1996, *19,* 9–13.

Weiner, M. D. Bringing an award-winning product to the marketplace. *Generations,* 1995, *19,* 56–57.

Wiener, J. M., Illston, L. H., and Hanley, R. J. *Sharing the burden: Strategies for public and private long-term care insurance.* Washington, DC: Brookings Institute, 1994.

Wilmoth, J. M. Unbalanced social exchanges and living arrangement transitions among older adults. *The Gerontologist,* 2000, *40,* 64–74.

Wolinsky, F. D., Stump, T. E., and Callahan, C. M. Does being placed in a nursing home make you sicker and more likely to die? In S. L. Willis and K. W. Schaie (Eds.), *Societal Mechanics for Maintaining Competence in Old Age.* New York: Springer Publishing, 1997.

12

PRODUCTIVE AGING: PAID AND NONPAID ROLES AND ACTIVITIES

This chapter encompasses the following:

- Retirement as a status and a social process that affects economic stature, roles and activities in old age
- The employment status of older adults
- The socioeconomic status of older people, including their income and extent of poverty and near-poverty
- Activity patterns common among older adults:
    leisure pursuits
    membership in community and voluntary associations
    education
    volunteering
    religious participation and spirituality
    political involvement

Typically, we think of productivity in terms of paid work. In fact, disengagement and role theory focused on the losses associated with withdrawal from the work role. Contrary to common images, old age is not necessarily characterized by idleness or nonproductivity. Instead, many older adults are active and productive without being employed or engaged in obligatory activities. *Productivity* is broader than paid work; it includes any activity that produces goods and services such as housework, child care, volunteer work, and help to family and friends, along with training and skills to

---

POINTS TO PONDER

You may have some questions about retirement, such as what do retired adults do all day? How can one be sure to have enough money to retire, especially if a person lives a long time? How can I ensure a successful retirement for myself? Will Social Security still be around when I want to retire? Will I even want to retire?

---

enhance the capacity to perform such tasks. If there is a good fit between societal and individual expectations about roles in old age, then the activity—formal or informal, paid or nonpaid—can have a positive influence on the older person's mental and physical well-being (McIntosh and Danigelis, 1995). Consistent with the person–environment framework that undergirds this book, productive older adults appear to choose and adjust their behavior and aspirations to maintain a sense of competence in a changing environment. Many older adults are engaged in a wide range of nonpaid roles that contribute to their families, their communities, and the larger society.

As described in Chapter 8, there are many different theoretical perspectives on participation in old age—from activity theory, which stresses the beneficial effects of continued involvement, to disengagement theory, which argues the appropriateness of withdrawal. These and other theories address questions such as: Is daily activity essential

Some older people work part-time for social and financial reasons.

to successful adjustment to aging? How is use of time related to life satisfaction and to feelings of competence toward the larger environment?

Adults' living arrangements, neighborhoods, and socioeconomic status, as well as their physical capacities, attitudes, skills, and values, all influence their activity patterns. People's use of time and arenas of involvement vary with the opportunities provided by the environment and with each developmental phase in the life cycle. Young and middle-aged adults may feel that there is not enough time for all they want to do. Their days are crowded with task-oriented activities—employment, child and increasingly elder care, and household maintenance. Middle-aged adults may idealize the free time of retirement, postponing travel or classes until they have "time for things like that." With retirement, and the departure of children, most older adults experience increased discretion over their use of time. The reality of nonwork time for retirees, however, may be quite different from their middle-aged fantasies of "if only we had the time." Many retirees overestimate the extent and variety of activities they will pursue upon retirement. Poor health, reduced income, transportation difficulties, or anticipated isolated living arrangements, all may disrupt and reduce activities in old age.

Although time is less fragmented upon retirement than at earlier life stages, there still are *constraints* on how people choose to become involved in different social arenas:

• As identified in earlier chapters, normal physical and psychological changes of aging and chronic diseases may limit older adults' capacities to engage in certain activities and to maintain competence in relation to environmental demands.

• Cohort experiences and socialization, gender and race, and type of living arrangements may result in certain activities being stratified by age.

• Some older adults may believe they are "too old" and lack the skills, physical strength, or knowledge to do particular activities.

• Past activity patterns and personality dynamics shape the use of time.

• As people's interests crystallize over the life span, they generally become more selective about how they invest their time and energy in activities.

On the other hand, many individuals successfully *pursue new activities,* such as art, music, running, hiking, or skiing, for the first time in old age.

Even with decreased competence in health and physiological functioning, older people can actively maintain optimal quality of life by modifying their community and organizational activities. Consistent with the person–environment model, they re-establish congruence between their needs and abilities and environmental demands.

RETIREMENT

With increased longevity and changing work patterns, retirement is as much an expected part of the life course as having a family, completing school, or working. Men in particular, but increasingly women among younger cohorts, develop age-related expectations about the rhythm of their careers—when to start working, when to be at the peak of their careers, and when to retire; and they assess whether they are "on time" according to these socially defined schedules.

In U.S. society, the value placed on work and productivity shapes how individuals approach employment and retirement. Those over age 65 were socialized to a traditional view of hard work, job loyalty, and occupational stability. Current demographic trends and social policies mean that values and expectations about work and retirement are changing, as many of the young-old exit and re-enter the workforce through partial employment or new careers. Since more years are now spent in retirement, nearly all adults are aware that they will need to make retirement decisions, with most people in their fifties actively anticipating it (Ekerdt, DeViney, and Kosloski, 1996). As individuals live longer, a smaller proportion of their lifetime is devoted to paid employment, even though the number of years worked is longer. For example, a man born in 1900 could expect to live about 47 years. He would work for 32 years (70 percent of his lifetime) and be retired for about one year (2 percent of his lifetime). In contrast, a man born today can anticipate living about 75 years, working for about 55 percent of his life, and being retired for over 26 percent. Women, too, are living longer past the age of retirement and are devoting a smaller portion of their lives to childbearing and childrearing. A woman born in 1900 could expect that 6 years of her 48-year life span (or 12 percent) would be spent in the labor force. The comparable figure for a woman born in 1987 is nearly 40 percent of her 78-year life span (National Academy on an Aging Society, 2000).

The institutionalization of retirement is a relatively recent phenomenon in Western society. Retirement developed as a twentieth-century social institution, along with industrialization, surplus labor, and a rising standard of living. Social Security legislation, passed in 1935, established the right to financial protection in old age and thus served to institutionalize retirement. Based on income deferred during years of employment, Social Security was viewed as a reward for past economic

---

POINTS TO PONDER

How does your view of work and retirement differ from that of your parents and/or grandparents? What does retirement mean to you?

contributions to society and a way to support people physically unable to work. At the same time, Social Security served to create jobs by removing adults 65 and over from the labor market. From the perspective of critical gerontology, discussed in Chapter 8, retirement serves a variety of institutional functions in our society. It can stimulate and reward worker loyalty. In addition, it is a way to remove older, presumably more expensive, workers and replace them with younger employees, assumed to be more productive.

Some societal and individual consequences are negative, however. Earlier retirement, combined with longer life expectancies, has created prolonged dependency on Social Security and other retirement benefits as well as a loss of older workers' skills. This shift from "near-universal" work to near-universal retirement has raised concerns about Social Security's viability for future generations. Since retirement is associated in the public mind with the chronological age of 65 (the age of eligibility for full Social Security benefits), it also carries the connotation of being old, and no longer physically or mentally capable of full-time employment (Atchley, 1993). In fact, society has come to associate aging with decreased employment capacity, with little regard for the older population's heterogeneity and limited knowledge of new work arrangements and retraining opportunities (Mor-Barak and Tynan, 1993).

The Timing of Retirement

Retirement involves more than a decision to stop working full-time. The arbitrary nature of any particular age for retirement is shown by the fact that most people retire between the ages of 60 and 64, and very few continue to work past age 70. In fact, it can hardly be said that age 65 is the "normal" retirement age. Instead, 61.5 years is the average age for retirement compared to 74 years in 1910 (National Academy on an Aging Society, 2000). Almost 25 percent of those 51 to 59 years of age do not work. Seventy-five percent of all new Social Security beneficiaries each year retire before their sixty-fifth birthday, and most begin collecting reduced benefits at age 62.5. The average retirement age in heavy industries, such as steel and auto manufacturing, is even lower because of private pension inducements. Those who retire from the military in their early forties after the minimum required 20 years often move on to other careers that enable them to draw two pensions after age 65. Even though the 1983 amendments to the Social Security Act delayed the age of eligibility for full benefits and increased the financial penalty for retiring at age 62, this has not altered the overall trend toward early retirement. It is not yet clear whether the scheduled increase in the age for receipt of full Social Security benefits (age 67 by 2022), reductions in early retirement benefits of private pensions, and the partial elimination of the Social Security earnings test will result in more older adults working longer (Reitzes, Mutran, and Fernandez, 1998).

Retirement policies, labor market conditions, and individual characteristics all converge on the decision to retire and affect the timing of retirement. Prior to 1986, mandatory retirement may have influenced the retirement age. Even so, this factor was not as salient as financial incentives, since less than 10 percent of employees were forced to retire because of legal requirements (Quinn and Burkhauser, 1993). The limited effect of mandatory retirement is also shown by the fact that federal workers retire at the average age of 62, even though they have never had a mandatory retirement age.

FACTORS THAT AFFECT THE TIMING OF RETIREMENT This section discusses five person–environment characteristics that affect retirement decisions: 1) An adequate retirement income and/or economic incentives to retire; 2) health status, functional limitations, and access to health insurance; 3) the nature of the job, employee morale, and organizational commitment; 4) gender and race; 5) family and gender roles (whether a spouse is working, degree of marital satisfaction).

An *adequate income*, through Social Security, a private pension, or interest income, is a major factor affecting retirement timing. Despite our society's work-oriented values and the importance of incomes, employment and retirement/pension policies since the 1900s have encouraged early retirement. Nine out of ten U.S. pension plans, particularly for white-collar workers, provide financial incentives for early retirement. Even employees who are not planning on retirement may be offered benefits too attractive to turn down. Economic factors thus directly affect decisions about the feasibility of retirement and indirectly contribute to worker health and job satisfaction. Workers accumulate a significant proportion of the wealth that will finance their retirement in the decade preceding retirement (Mitchell and Moore, 1998). When given a choice and assuming financial security and adequate health insurance, most people elect to retire as soon as they can (Taylor and Shore, 1995). Employment experiences in the years immediately prior to retirement may be indicative of well-being throughout old age (Flippen and Tienda, 2000).

Functional limitations, health impairments, and access to health insurance are also important factors in the retirement decision, especially among those for whom retirement is least attractive (Mutchler, Burr, Massagli, and Pienta, 1999). Two categories of people who retire early have been identified: (1) those with good health and adequate financial resources who desire additional leisure time and (2) those with health problems that make their work burdensome. Poor health, when combined with an adequate retirement income, usually results in early retirement. In contrast, poor health and an inadequate income generally delay retirement by reason of necessity, as is often the case with low-income workers. Health problems are a greater motivation for retirement from physically demanding and stressful jobs for workers of color, for men with employed wives, and for men with limited, nonwork financial resources (Mutchler et al., 1999; Richardson, 1999). In fact, 55 percent of retirees age 51 to 59 say that a health condition or impairment limits the amount or type of paid work they can do. And retirees are three times more likely to be in fair to poor health than their employed counterparts (National Academy on an Aging Society, 2000). What remains unclear, however,

is whether those in poorer health are more likely to lose their jobs, or conversely, whether job loss itself leads to poorer health, or both (Kasl and Jones, 2000). Once a person is in nonworking status, poor health acts as a barrier to labor force reentry (Mutchler et al., 1999).

A third factor affecting timing is the *nature of one's job*, including job satisfaction, employee morale, and organizational commitment. Some workers retire to escape boring, repetitive jobs such as assembly line and office work. Workers who have a positive attitude toward retirement and leisure but a negative view of their jobs, often because of undesirable and stressful working conditions, are likely to retire early. Employees with a high school education or less tend to retire earlier than well-educated employees, as illustrated by Mr. and Mrs. Howard in the Part Four introductory vignette (Quinn and Burkhauser, 1993; Taylor and Shore, 1995).

While the effects of *gender and race* on the timing of retirement are not clear-cut, they do affect economic inequities in old age (Flippen and Tienda, 2000). Although both men and women overall choose early retirement, women of retirement age are less likely to be fully retired than their male counterparts. Their retirement decisions may also be determined by different variables, such as marital status and years devoted to childrearing (Szinovacz and DeViney, 1999). Nevertheless, current income and receipt of a pension other than Social Security are primary factors in women's retirement decisions (McLaughlin and Jensen, 2000). In addition, women at any age are more likely to exit the labor market to assume family care obligations (Reitzes, Mutran, and Fernandez, 1998). Women who entered the labor force in middle age or later, after performing family caregiving roles, may need to work for economic reasons. In contrast, lifelong career women, particularly the never-married, are more likely to retire early than reentry women (Flippen and Tienda, 2000; Moen, 1996). On the other hand, African American women are more likely to have worked steadily most of their adult lives, but to retire later than their white counterparts, largely for economic reasons.

Work histories that fit the expectation of life-long work with few disruptions tend to be associated with a smoother transition to retirement (Szinovacz and DeViney, 1999). In contrast, the timing of retirement for persons of color, particularly African Americans and Hispanics, differs from the traditional pattern for white males. Minorities' lifetime work patterns often yield an unclear line between work and nonwork; they tend to have lengthy periods of nonwork at an early age and lack access to pensions, in part because of diminished opportunities that "pushed" them into retirement (Flippen and Tienda, 2000). Black men up to age 61 have higher rates of retirement than Caucasian men, after which African American males have lower rates. One factor may be that moderately disabled African Americans are more likely to identify themselves as partly or fully retired. Self-identification with the retiree role has more psychological benefits and social legitimacy than identfying with a sick role (Szinovacz and DeViney, 1999). White males with a desire for leisure, low-income African Americans, and Hispanics experiencing involuntary market exits are most likely to retire (Flippen and Tienda, 2000).

Satisfaction with Retirement

For most U.S. workers, retirement is desired, and their decision is not whether to retire but when. Not surprisingly, similar factors (e.g., financial security and health status) influence the degree of satisfaction with retirement. It is useful to examine retirement as a *process* or *transition* that affects people's life satisfaction and self-identity in multiple ways. This concept encompasses not only the timing and type of retirement situation as a life stage, but also the phases and the development of a retiree identity after the event of retirement. Similarly, an individual's degree of satisfaction with the outcome depends to some extent on how the retirement process is experienced, especially the degree of choice or autonomy, the amount of preparation and planning, and the degree of congruence with prior employment roles (Szinovacz and DeViney, 1999). In his classic description of a

"typical progression of processes" in the retirement transition, Atchley (1983) suggested that an initial euphoric, busy honeymoon phase is followed by a letdown or disenchantment phase due to loss of status, income, or purpose. This, in turn, is followed by a reorientation to the realities of retired life. This sequence leads to a subsequent stable phase, when the retiree has settled into a predictable routine. Whether individuals adopt a retiree identity (e.g., what they make of the retiree role) depends upon their prior employment status, amount of retirement income, and extent of disability (Szinovacz and DeViney, 1999). Of course, not every individual will experience all the phases or in the order described. Another conceptualization of retirement as a *process of role-exit* found that as individuals approach retirement, they express increasing feelings of burden, discontent, and fatigue with the job as a way of withdrawing from their current role commitments (Ekerdt and DeViney, 1993).

Early gerontological studies emphasized the negative impacts of retirement as a life crisis due to loss (Atchley, 1976; Streib and Schneider, 1971). Later research has identified the positive effects of retirement on life satisfaction and health, especially during the first year postretirement. Although measures of physical and psychological health may decline slightly after 6 to 7 years of retirement, most retirees still report good health and overall life satisfaction (Gall, Evans, and Howard, 1995). Although retirement is a major transition, it is often blurred, with the majority of retirees experiencing minimal stress and being relatively satisfied with their life circumstances (Witt, 1998). Activities other than work that provide autonomy, some sense of control, and the chance to learn new things are all related to retirement satisfaction (Moen, 1999; Ross and Drentea, 1998). On the other hand, activities that involve less problem-solving, that are less complex and less fulfilling, have been associated with distress and depression in retirement (Drentea, 1999).

In general, financial security and health appear to be the major determinants of retirees' satisfaction with life, rather than retirement status per se.

Not surprisingly, retirees with higher incomes or at least adequate finances report being more satisfied and having a more positive retirement identity than those with lower incomes (Reitzes, Mutran, and Fernandez, 1996; Szinovacz and DeViney, 1999). Higher economic status is also associated with more positive health status in old age (Juster et al., 1996). In fact, there appears to be a dual relationship between positive health status and earned income. This suggests that programs that improve health status during the working years can, in turn, increase earned income in retirement (Okada, 1997).

Retirement does not *cause* poor health, as is commonly assumed. Although some people's functional health does deteriorate after retirement, other people's functional health improves because they are no longer subject to stressful, unhealthy, or dangerous work conditions. Contrary to stereotypes about the negative health effects of retirement, people who die shortly after retiring were probably in poor health before they retired. In fact, deterioration in health is more likely to cause retirement than vice versa. Accordingly, retirement has not been found to increase the incidence of mental health problems, and, in some instances, has improved mental health (Ross and Drentea, 1998). The misconception that people become ill and die as a consequence of retirement undoubtedly persists on the basis of findings from cross-sectional data, as well as reports of isolated instances of such deaths. In addition, the traditional American ideology that life's meaning is derived from paid work may reinforce the stereotype that retirement has negative consequences. Retirees may also be motivated to exaggerate their health limitations to justify their retirement. In fact, health status is interconnected with other factors, such as the normative acceptability of not working and the desire for a retirement lifestyle (Mutchler et al., 1999).

Personal and social characteristics that contribute to satisfaction in retirement include:

- perceptions of daily activities as useful
- internal locus of control

- a sense of having chosen the timing of retirement
- living in a suitable environment
- access to an adequate social support system of friends and neighbors (Drentea, 1999; National Academy on an Aging Society, 2000)

Consistent with continuity theory, *preretirement self-esteem and identity* influence postretirement self-esteem (Reitzes, Mutran, and Fernandez, 1996). Individuals whose primary source of meaning was not employment and who have weaker work values adjust to a satisfying routine more readily than do those with strong work ethics who did not develop leisure activities when employed. Conversely, retirees who do not adjust well have been found to have poor health, inadequate family finances, marital problems, and difficulties making transitions throughout the life span. Those who retire early because of poor health or lack of job opportunities or who are experiencing other stressful events in their life are less satisfied with being retired. But, they are also dissatisfied with other aspects of their lives, such as their housing, standard of living, and leisure (Bossé et al., 1991).

Occupational status, which is frequently associated with educational level, is also an important predictor of retirement satisfaction; lower-status workers have more health and financial problems and therefore less satisfaction than higher-level white-collar workers. The more meaningful work characteristics of higher-status occupations may "spill over" to a greater variety of satisfying nonwork pursuits throughout life. These are conducive to more social contacts and more structured opportunities during retirement. For example, a college professor may have a work and social routine that is more readily transferable to retirement than that of a construction worker. Differences between retirees in upper- and lower-status occupations do not develop with retirement, but rather reflect variations in social and personal resources throughout the life course. This view of retirement as a long-term process that presents continual challenges as retirees adapt is consistent with continuity theory.

SUMMARY OF FACTORS AFFECTING RETIREMENT SATISFACTION

- Retirement process that involves choice, autonomy, adequate preparation and planning, and congruence with prior job roles
- Retirement activities that provide autonomy, sense of control, chance to learn and to feel useful
- Financial security

- Good health
- A suitable living environment
- Strong social support system of reciprocal relationships
- Higher-status occupation prior to retirement
- Gender and race
- Individual personality traits (e.g., personal resources, positive outlook)

Less is known about how gender or race influences retirement satisfaction. Women's retirement plans and well-being, like men's, are influenced by their health and their own pension and Social Security eligibility, not by their husbands'. The slightly lower levels of retirement satisfaction among women seem to be due to their lower retirement incomes, typically because of the lack of a private pension. In addition, adjusting to a full-time stay-at-home role during retirement can be difficult for women accustomed to the routine, rewards, and sociability of paid employment. In such instances, women's role transition may not be in synchrony with their husband's (Johnson, Sambamoorthi, and Crystal, 1999).

African Americans and Hispanics with a lifetime of discontinuous work patterns and ongoing need are unlikely to define themselves as retired. As "unretired-retired," they spend a greater percentage of their lives both working and disabled, employed intermittently beyond retirement because of their low wage base. Older nonwhites are both more vulnerable to job displacement and more adversely affected by it; they experience lower reemployment rates, lower personal and household income, and lower rates of health insurance coverage following displacement than white workers (Reitzes et al., 1998). For these workers retirement is not a single, irreversible event that represents the culmination of career employment. Instead, it is a blurred transition from employment to unemployment, partial retirement, or partial employment

that may be temporary. In addition, African American males tend to have higher rates of disability and mortality across the life span and especially in the years preceding retirement, which result in retirement inequities (Flippen and Tienda, 2000; Hayward, Friedman, and Chen, 1996).

More recent literature portrays retirement not as a single transition in a person's life course but as a dynamic process with several stages where the retired/nonretired roles may overlap, and individuals move in and out of the workforce through **serial retirement.** Instead of a "crisp" or unidirectional one-step movement from work to retirement, transitions are "blurred," involving complex patterns such as returning to employment, "unretirements," and later, second or third partial or full retirements. The exit and then reentry into the workforce reflect the increasing numbers of older people who want to return to employment, typically on a part-time or part-year basis, because they lack pensions and other types of nonwage resources. The propensity to work part-time for economic reasons appears to be generalized, not specific to a particular job. Those who change jobs shortly before retirement are the most likely to work afterward, suggesting that "unretirement" is part of a repertoire of adaptive behavior in the later years. In sum, consistent with the life-course perspective discussed in Chapter 8, there is growing diversity regarding the timing and flexibility of retirement, with changing norms about the timing and sequencing of paid and nonpaid roles or repeated work exits and reentry (Henretta, 1997; Mutchler et al., 1997; Settersten, 1998).

The Importance of Planning

Since retirement is a process, preparation and planning for productive roles in old age are important for transitioning to retirement. In fact, preparation, an orientation toward the future, and a belief in one's ability to adapt to change are associated with a more positive retirement experience (Ekerdt, Kosloski, and DeViney, 2000; Taylor and Shore, 1995). Retirement affects identity, self-esteem, and feelings of competence to the extent that it influences opportunities for new nonpaid roles and activities. In addition, occupations that demand more complex thinking, decision making, and intellectual challenge (e.g., professional and highly paid positions) may better prepare people for retirement decision-making and planning (McLaughlin and Jensen, 2000). If nonwork interests and skills are not developed prior to retirement, cultivating them afterward is difficult (Drentea, 1999).

Comprehensive *retirement planning programs* that address social activities, financial well-being, health promotion, and family relationships are one way of encouraging a positive transition. Unfortunately, such programs are not widespread. Government employees and older men with more years of education, higher occupational status, and private pensions have greater access to these programs. Accordingly, older workers who especially need retirement preparation—single people, women, and those facing the probability of lower retirement incomes—are the least likely to have access to or utilize such services (Walker, 1998).

Another approach to retirement preparation is for employers to *restructure work patterns* during the preretirement years, gradually allowing longer vacations, shorter work days, job-sharing, and more opportunities for community involvement, thereby easing the transition to more leisure time. Most retirees seem not to want the constraints inherent in full-time employment. Instead, 75 percent of workers prefer to retire gradually, phasing

down from full-time to part-time work. This preference is contingent upon whether their employers will retrain them for a new job, make pension contributions after age 65, or transfer them to jobs with less responsibility, fewer hours, and less pay as a transition to full retirement (Juster et al., 1996). Until recently, relatively few firms offered opportunities to transfer to jobs with reduced pay and responsibility, or for phased retirement through a gradual decrease in hours worked. Fortunately, more companies are now recognizing that older workers are eager for new career directions or for part-time and other flexible work.

In fact, options for increasing flexibility in work schedules are offered by about 33 percent of companies, as illustrated in Figure 12.1. These include part-time work, job sharing, flextime, and incremental retirement through reduced work weeks or "gliding out" plans of staged retirement that permit a gradual shift to a part-time schedule.

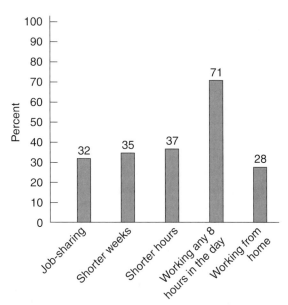

FIGURE 12.1 **Proportions of Companies Offering Flexible Work Schedules**
SOURCE: McKonnell, K., P. Fronstein, K. Olsen, P. Ostrow, J. VanDerhei, and P. Yakoboski (1997). *EBRI Databook on Employee Benefits* (4th ed.). Washington, DC: Employee Benefit Research Institute.

PHASED RETIREMENT PROGRAMS GROW

A recent issue of the *New York Times* featured the growth of phased retirement programs. Early retirement packages have been offered for many years to university professors. However, many large companies such as Lockheed Martin and PepsiCo have begun phased retirement packages that offer workers in their fifties a chance to work shorter hours and

receive some pension income. This approach allows employers to retain skilled employees at a lower cost than full-time work, while older workers benefit from the flexibility of part-time employment with an adequate income.

SOURCE: *New York Times*, April 15, 2001, p. 1, 17.

EMPLOYMENT STATUS

As noted above, some older adults never fully retire, and employment remains the primary means by which they are productive. Among those over age 65, approximately 16 percent of men and 8 percent of women are in the labor force (Administration on Aging, 1999). As illustrated in Figure 12.2, these percentages represent a decline from 1950, when nearly 46 percent of older men and 10 percent of older women were employed. In fact, the pattern of more men retiring early and more middle-aged and young-old women entering the labor force means that older Americans' labor force experiences are becoming similar for men and women. This pattern of declining labor-force participation, especially among men, is expected to continue. Composing less than 3 percent of the total labor force, older workers are concentrated in service-oriented jobs and in positions that initially require considerable education and a long training process (e.g., managerial and professional positions or self-employment), or those with flexible retirement policies (Administration on Aging, 1999). Compared with their younger counterparts, older workers are less likely to be in physically demanding or high-tech jobs (National Academy on an Aging Society, 2000).

While full-time employment has declined, part-time work among older women has expanded to 62 percent of those age 65 and over, but declined among their male counterparts, as illustrated in Figure 12.3. As noted above, part-time work that

allows gradual retirement is perceived by the working public of all ages as a desirable alternative, especially when a flexible work schedule is combined with the ability to draw partial pensions (Simon-Riesinowitz, Wilson, Marks, Krach, and

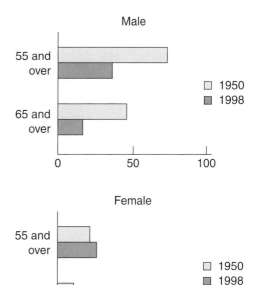

FIGURE 12.2 **Percentage of Civilian Noninstitutional Population in the Labor Force, by Age and Sex: 1950–1998**
SOURCE: AoA, 1999.

Welch, 1998). Although the number of older people working part-time is smaller than the number who report they would like to do so, the proportion of part-time workers increases with age. Similarly, more older workers (23 percent) are self-employed compared to younger workers (7 percent) (National Academy on an Aging Society, 2000). The availability of part-time jobs, created in part by a healthy economy, more flexible work schedules, and the recent elimination of the Social Security earnings test, also make employment more attractive to older workers (National Academy on an Aging Society, 2000). Depending upon one's definition of career, 25 to 50 percent of all Americans, especially those who are self-employed, remain in the labor force in some capacity after they leave their primary career jobs. It is unclear whether part-time work represents underemployment of adults whose hours of work have been reduced because of slack work or feeling pressured to leave full time work, or who cannot find full-time employment (Quadagno and Hardy, 1996).

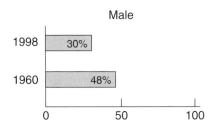

Male

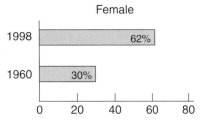

Female

FIGURE 12.3 **Persons 65 Years and Over Who Work Part-Time**
Source: AoA, 1999.

Unemployment among Older People

Unfortunately, approximately 3 percent of older adults who seek employment are unable to find a job; this rate increases for older persons of color. Several factors partially explain why more older people, especially among the young-old, seek employment, despite the trend toward early retirement, as follows:

Financial Need: A primary factor is that many people choose to retire and then find it harder to live on their retirement income than they had anticipated. In fact, some studies found that over 52 percent of retired workers return to work within 4 years, largely for economic reasons. They move back and forth from full or partial retirement into nonretirement, or accept jobs in the service sector and in smaller firms at substantially lower pay in order to get by financially (Quadagno and Hardy, 1996). This movement in and out of the labor force is a common pattern with negative economic and health consequences in old age for African Americans and Hispanics.

Desire to Feel Productive: Others work after retirement in order to feel productive, share expertise, and reduce boredom. In such instances, retirees are often more willing to work in lower-status positions (Quadagno and Hardy, 1996). Continued employment into old age has been found to be associated with higher morale, happiness, adjustment, and longevity, in part because of the friendship networks with coworkers (Mor-Barak and Tynan, 1993). For some older people, a job can be a new career, a continuation of earlier work, or a way to learn new skills and form friendships.

Job Restructuring and Contingent, Temporary Service Jobs: Older workers seeking to reenter the workforce are more likely than younger workers to be forced out of work because of company closures, technological change, downsizing, mergers, or reorganization. When older workers feel pushed out of their jobs by workplace changes, retirement is not "voluntary," may border on age discrimination, and can be associated with poorer physical and mental health (Cascio, 1998; Gallo, Bradley,

Siegel, and Kasl, 2000). In the past decade, more employers have tried to reduce costs and increase productivity by creating labor-force structures that can be readily altered at management discretion. This has resulted in the growth of a contingent or temporary workforce, even for highly skilled professional positions, that does not provide security and benefits based on workers' seniority or skills. Contingent employees work less than 34 hours a week and may be on-call workers or independent contractors. Workers displaced by these market changes may be too old to have good job prospects, but may nevertheless need to work and accept temporary work just to make ends meet. Those who do find jobs, often in the service industry, typically experience downward mobility to low wages and to temporary or part-time work in smaller firms with fewer benefits (Cascio, 1998; Quadagno and Hardy, 1996). This trend disproportionately affects women and older adults of color (Dodson, 1996).

Even though the unemployment rate is lower among older workers than younger, they stay out of work longer, suffer a greater loss of earnings in subsequent jobs, experience longer periods of unemployment, and are more likely to become discouraged and stop looking for work. For older adults needing to work for economic reasons or wanting to stay active, unemployment is associated with life dissatisfaction and higher rates of morbidity (Gallo et al., 2000).

Barriers to Employment

Why do unemployed older workers have a difficult time with their job search?

- They may have been in one occupation for many years and therefore lack experience in job-hunting techniques.
- They are more vulnerable to skill obsolescence with changes in the economy, including the shift away from product manufacturing and medium-wage jobs in manufacturing toward low-wage positions in the service industries and high-wage positions in high-tech fields (National Academy on an Aging Society, 2000).
- Until recently, many businesses did not alter the work environment to prepare older workers for rapid changes. This is shifting, however, with the current shortage of qualified workers and the state of the economy.
- Only a few programs, such as the federal Senior Community Service Employment Program, specifically target low-income older adults through retraining and subsidized employment.
- Age-based employment discrimination persists, even though mandatory retirement policies are illegal. Despite federal legislation, age discrimination alleged as the basis for loss of employment is the fastest-growing form of unfair dismissal litigation. The Age Discrimination in Employment Act has been somewhat ineffective in promoting

---

IS THIS AGE DISCRIMINATION?

A bank announces that it is opening a new branch and advertises for tellers. Jane Feld, age 53 with 22 years of banking experience, applies. The employment application includes an optional category for age. Rather than pausing to think about whether to indicate her age, she answers the question voluntarily and truthfully. The next week, Ms. Feld receives a polite letter from the bank, complimenting her on her qualities, but turning her down because she is overqualified. She later finds out that a 32-year-old woman with only 4 years' experience is hired.

Sarah Nelson, age 55, is a manager with a large advertising company. For the past 5 years, she has received outstanding performance reviews. Two months after a strong review and pay increase, she was abruptly fired for "poor performance." Her replacement, age 35, started a week after she was fired.

LAWS TO PREVENT OR ADDRESS DISCRIMINATION BASED ON AGE

- The Age Discrimination in Employment Act (ADEA), passed in 1967, is to protect workers age 45 and over from denial of employment strictly because of age.
- This act was amended in 1978 to prohibit the use of pension plans as justification for not hiring older workers and to raise the mandatory retirement age to 70. In 1986, mandatory retirement was eliminated.

- In 1990, the Older Workers Benefit Protection Act prohibited employers from treating older workers differently from younger workers during a reduction in workforce.
- The Americans with Disabilities Act of 1990 also offers protection to older adults. Employers are expected to make work-related adjustments and redesign jobs for workers with disabilities, including impairments in sensory, manual, or speaking skills.

---

the hiring of older workers, although it has reduced blatant forms of age discrimination (e.g., advertisements that restrict jobs to younger people) (Quadagno and Hardy, 1996).

- More subtle forms of discrimination endure, such as expectations of attractiveness in dress, makeup, and hairstyle or making a job undesirable to older workers by downgrading it.
- Negative stereotypes about aging and productivity persist. Some employers assume that older workers will not perform as well as younger ones because of poor health, declining energy, diminished intellectual ability, or different work styles.
- Others perceive older workers as less cost-effective, given their proximity to retirement; less flexible in a changing workplace; uncomfortable

with new technology; and expensive to train. Despite such concerns, however, most employers rate older workers highly on loyalty, dependability, emotional stability, and ability to get along with coworkers (Quadagno and Hardy, 1996).

In addition to these general barriers to employment, *obstacles exist to part-time work:*

- Older persons may not be able to find part-time work at a wage level similar to full-time work.
- Employer policies against part-time workers drawing partial pensions (e.g., defined-benefit pension plans do not permit a worker to stay on the job and collect a pension).
- Employer resistance about the additional administrative work and higher health insurance

---

WHAT IS UNLAWFUL UNDER THE AGE DISCRIMINATION IN EMPLOYMENT ACT (1967)?

Employers with 20 or more employees, including state and local governments, may not:

- Discriminate against workers age 40 and older in hiring, firing, compensation, benefits, terms, conditions, or any other aspect of employment because of age.

- Indicate age preferences in notices or advertisements for employment.
- Retaliate against any individual for complaining about age discrimination or for helping the government investigate an age discrimination charge.

costs entailed in hiring part-time or temporary older workers, (e.g., it is more costly to insure older than younger workers). Those costs, however, may be tempered by the advantage of fewer employer-paid benefits for dependents among older workers (Quadagno and Hardy, 1996).

Creating New Opportunities for Work

Advocacy organizations for older people maintain that judging a person's job qualifications solely on the basis of age, without regard to job suitability, is inequitable, and that chronological age alone is a poor predictor of job performance. Not hiring older workers deprives society of their skills and capacities. To address future labor shortages changes in government and corporate policies and pensions are needed to extend employment opportunities for older workers and modify the financial incentives for work. For example, tax incentives could be given to employers who hire older workers. With willing supportive employers, work environments can be modified and job-referral, training, and counseling programs provided to link older adults and potential employers.

A primary reason for increased hiring of older workers is that the strong economy of the late 1990s created labor market shortages, especially in service and temporary jobs. Other reasons include a decreasing pool of younger workers, a healthier and better educated cohort of older persons who are oriented toward lifelong careers, economic expectations to continue a similar lifestyle, and increasing health and long-term care expenses. Already, older people are moving into jobs traditionally filled by youth (e.g., providing service at fast-food restaurants), in part because

of the decline among young people available to work in such positions.

ECONOMIC STATUS: SOURCES OF INCOME IN RETIREMENT

Economic status in old age is largely influenced by environmental conditions in the larger society, especially past and current employment patterns and resultant retirement income and benefits. Although economic resources in themselves do not guarantee satisfaction, they do affect older people's daily opportunities and competence that can enable them to lead satisfying lives—their health, social relationships, living arrangements, community activities, and political participation. For most people, economic status is consistent across the life course. For example, workers of color in low-paying jobs in young and middle adulthood generally face a continuation of poverty in old age. Other older people, including widowed or divorced women who depended on their husbands' income, or retirees with only Social Security as income, may face poverty or near-poverty for the first time in their lives. Alternatively, those in higher-paying careers with private pensions and assets continue to enjoy economic advantages in old age, reflecting a pattern of cumulative advantage across the life course (Crystal, 1996; Park and Gilbert, 1999).

The median household income of people age 65 and over in 1998 was $17,777, compared to a median figure of approximately $35,000 for all households. Over 20 percent had incomes below $10,000, and 13 percent above $50,000 (Social Security Administration, 1998). Older adults are estimated to need 65 to 80 percent of their preretirement income to maintain their living standard in retirement. Since retirement can reduce individual incomes by one-third to one-half, most retirees must adjust their standard of living downward—while their out-of-pocket spending for items such as health care typically increases.

Sources of income for the older population include Social Security earnings, savings, assets, investments, and private pensions. The percent of aggregate income for persons over age 65 from these sources is illustrated in Figure 12.4.

The distribution of income sources varies widely, however, with women, elders of color, and the oldest-old most likely to rely on Social Security. The incremental privatization of retirement income (i.e., a slow decline in the proportion of retirement income from Social Security relative to that derived from employer-provided pensions and Individual Retirement Accounts) has affected income distribution. For example, older people in the bottom 40 percent of the income distribution have experi-

enced a minimal increase in private sources of pension, while the upper ranges have shown steady gains in private benefits (Park and Gilbert, 1999). Those at the bottom of the income range rely largely on Social Security and/or Supplemental Security Income (SSI), as described below.

Social Security

Older people depend most on **Social Security** for their retirement income.

- In 1998, nearly 40 percent of all income received by older units (i.e., a married couple with one or both members aged 65 or older and living together, or a person aged 65 or older not living with a spouse) was from Social Security.
- Approximately 90 percent of all older people receive Social Security (Administration on Aging, 1999).
- Of those age 65 and over, 66 percent received at least 50 percent of their income and 18 percent all their income from Social Security (Social Security Administration, 1998). (See Figure 12.5.)
- Among low-income households and the oldest-old, 85 percent of their income is from Social Security.
- In contrast, only 18 percent of those in the highest income categories receive Social Security (Binstock, 2000; Gramlich, 2000).

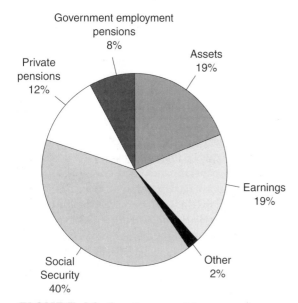

FIGURE 12.4 **Percent of Aggregate Income of the Population 65+ from Various Sources, 1998**
SOURCE: AoA, 1999.

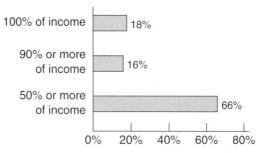

FIGURE 12.5 **Percent of Beneficiary Units with Social Security Benefits as a Major Source of Income, 1998**
SOURCE: AoA, 1999.

Social Security was never intended to provide an adequate retirement income, but only a floor of protection or the first tier of support. It was assumed that additional pensions and individual savings would help support people in their later years. This assumption has not been borne out, as reflected in the proportionately lower income received by retirees from savings and private pensions. Without Social Security, poverty rates among the older population would increase from 11 percent to nearly 50 percent (Social Security Administration, 1998). Not surprisingly, older individuals with the lowest total income have Social Security as their *sole* income source.

The Social Security system is a public trust into which all pay and from which all are guaranteed an income floor in old age or disability. In order to be insured, a worker retiring now must be age 62.5 or older and must have been employed at least 10 years in covered employment. The level of benefits received is based on a percentage of the retired worker's average monthly earnings that were subject to Social Security tax. Insured persons are eligible for full benefits at age 65 (note that the age is rising from 65 to 67 at a rate of two months each year, beginning with workers and spouses born in 1938—who must be 65 years and two months for a full benefit). If workers choose to retire at age 62.5, their monthly benefits are permanently reduced and are not increased when they reach age 65. Most recipients currently receive reduced benefits because they retired before the age of 62. Since 1975, Social Security benefits are automatically increased annually whenever the Consumer Price Index increases by 3 percent or more. This is known as the cost-of-living adjustment, or COLA, which protects benefits from inflation. Since benefits are related to a worker's wage and employment history, women and people of color, with patterns of intermittent or part-time work, tend to receive less than the average monthly benefit. Some of the oldest-old persons never qualify for Social Security, because they were employed in occupations such as domestic work not covered by the system.

The Social Security payroll tax is regressive (i.e., requiring the same rate for both the rich and the poor). This means that low-income workers, often women and people of color, pay a larger proportion of their monthly salary for the Social Security tax compared to higher-income workers. On the other hand, proportionately, lower-income workers benefit more from Social Security when they retire, receiving benefits equal to 90 percent of their working wages, while high-income workers' benefits on average are only 19 percent of their prior salary. In addition, they must now pay

---

GENDER INEQUITIES AND SOCIAL SECURITY

• A widow may start to collect surviving dependents' benefits when she reaches age 60; however, she will lose about 28 percent of what she would have received if she had waited until age 65. But for each additional year after age 60, a widow receives a larger percentage of Social Security benefits. And after age 65, she receives full benefits even if she has been getting only 72 percent for the past 4 years.

• Widows and divorcees under age 60 who are not disabled and who do not have children under age 18 entitled to Social Security, or who are not responsible for disabled persons, cannot receive Social Security benefits. This group of women, who generally do not

have a paid work history and do not qualify for any public benefits, are often referred to as **displaced homemakers.** Since the average age at widowhood is 66 years, many women face this "widow's gap" (Martin-Matthews, 1996).

• A woman who is divorced after at least 10 years of marriage and who reaches retirement age may collect up to 50 percent of her ex-husband's retirement benefits, but only when he turns 62 and if she remains single. Because many widows or divorced women do not meet these criteria, a large percentage of single older women live in poverty or near-poverty conditions.

income tax on 50 percent of their Social Security benefits. Unfortunately, most people do not plan sufficiently for their retirement income, because they presume that Social Security will be adequate and fail to assess the impact of inflation and reduced income levels. Some are able to supplement their Social Security income with assets, pensions, or job earnings.

Asset Income

Income from assets (e.g., savings, home equity, and personal property), the next most important source of income, is received by about 66 percent of older adults. Assets compose about 20 percent of the total income of older people (Social Security Administration, 1998). Not surprisingly, the median income of those with asset income is more than twice the median income of those without it (Social Security Administration, 1998). Asset income is unevenly distributed, with larger income disparities intensified by race and gender. Nearly 37 percent of the older households—typically the oldest-old, women, and persons of color—report no asset income (Administration on Aging, 1999).

Older people's assets consist primarily of home equity, representing 40 to 50 percent of their net worth. Currently 76 percent of older people own their homes, although this percentage declines among elders of color. Yet 50 percent of older homeowners spend at least 45 percent of their incomes on property taxes, utilities, and maintenance (Smith 1997a). Home equity therefore does not represent liquid wealth or cash and cannot be relied on to cover daily expenses.

Even though most older people with fixed incomes cannot depend on assets to meet current expenses, their net worth tends to be greater than for those under age 35. In fact, the median net worth (assets minus liabilities) of older households is $86,300, well above the U.S. average. As an indicator of vast income differences among older people, net worth is below $10,000 for nearly 20 percent of older households (largely households of color), but above $250,000 for 17

percent (largely white households) (Administration on Aging, 1999).

Pensions

Although most jobholders are covered by Social Security as a general public pension, some also have *job-specific pensions*. Most such pensions are intended to supplement Social Security, not to be the sole source of income. They are available only through a specific employment position and are administered by a work organization, union, or private insurance company. Job-specific pensions include public employee pensions (for those who work for federal, state, or local governments) and private pensions. Since 1950, pension plans have increased from 25 to 50 percent among private sector workers and from 60 to 90 percent among civilian government workers. Overall, 43 percent of older units receive some income from public and/or private pension benefits, other than Social Security. However, only 50 percent of those eligible for benefits have had enough years of service to be fully vested in a plan and thus entitled to future benefits. Relatively few workers are enrolled in private pension programs that provide the replacement rate of income necessary for retirement. Instead, job-specific pensions compose approximately 20 percent of the older population's aggregate income, with the average annual private pension income less than $5,000. Only about 3 percent of pension plans provide for cost-of-living increases, with most such plans adversely affected by inflation (Gramlish, 2000). Economic recessions, escalating health care costs, and inflation in the past two decades have reduced pension assets. In recent years, employee pension coverage, especially among persons of color, has declined, although this may have shifted with the economic boom of the late 1990s and early twenty-first century (Gramlish, 2000; Johnson, Sambamoorthi, and Crystal, 1999; Hardy and Kruse, 1998).

Pension benefits are generally based on earnings or a combination of earnings and years of ser-

PENSIONS AND GENDER INEQUITIES

- The mean pension benefit for men is 76 percent greater than for women (Johnson et al., 1999).
- Women are more likely than men to be "in and out" of the labor force and therefore less likely to achieve the required length of service and level of seniority for vesting.
- Women's earnings in their longest career job, used as the base for calculating a pension, tend to be relatively low.

- Nonemployed women face an additional problem: Most pension plans reduce benefits for those who elect to protect their spouses through survivors' benefits. In the past, many men chose higher monthly benefits rather than survivors' benefits; when they died, their wives were left without adequate financial protection. As married women's employment experiences increasingly resemble those of men, the gender gap in pensions is expected to narrow.

vice. Eligibility is usually between ages 60 and 65, with a range from ages 50 to 70. Federal policies support private pension programs by postponing taxation of pension benefits, as well as allowing benefits to be invested to generate earnings that are not taxed. Tax is paid only when the pension is drawn, after the money has produced many years of earnings.

Private pensions go to workers with long, continuous service in jobs that have such coverage. In general, these are higher-income, relatively skilled positions of 30 or more years concentrated among large, unionized firms or service and financial sectors. As a result, retirees who benefit from private pensions tend to be white, well-educated males in the middle- and upper-income brackets, with the lowest-income older persons receiving, on average, only 3 percent of their income from pensions (Johnson et al., 1999). Pension coverage varies dramatically by class, race, gender, and age. It is relatively low for women, workers of color, and lower-income workers in small nonunion plants and low-wage industries such as retail sales and services, and for retirees currently over age 65. In particular, African Americans and whites with the lowest wages are ten times less likely to have a pension compared to those with the highest wages (Juster et al., 1996).

The **Employment Retirement Income Security Act (ERISA)**, enacted in 1974 to strengthen private pension systems, was the first comprehensive effort to regulate them. As a result, private pension plans must vest benefits (*vesting* refers to the amount of time a person must work on a job in order to acquire rights to the pension). When vested, all covered workers are guaranteed a full pension upon retirement after 10 or 15 years with the company, regardless of whether they remain with that organization until retirement. This means that a person could work for one firm for 12 years, move to a second company until retirement at age 65, and then receive pensions from both based on years of service. Although vesting options increased under ERISA, *portability* (whereby pension contributions and rights with one organization can be transferred to another) remains low. This policy has been criticized for penalizing worker mobility and career changes. For example, an individual who serves 40 years with one company will receive a higher pension than one who spent 20 years with one firm and 20 with another.

ERISA also strengthened standards for financing, administering, and protecting pension plans. Tax-exempt individual retirement accounts (IRAs) were made available to all workers in 1981, in an effort to increase personal savings for retirement. Under the 1986 tax reform plan, employees with other private pensions are no longer able to use an IRA as a tax deduction. Yet IRAs are not an option for most workers; instead, they are used primarily by those earning $50,000 or more who have disposable income. Lower-income workers generally cannot spare the money, and the tax benefit is considerably less for them. Ironically, then, the people who need retirement income the most generally cannot take advantage of IRAs. As with employer pension plans, the tax deferral of IRAs provides the equivalent of a long-term interest-free loan (e.g., tax shelter) to the predominantly high-income taxpayers who use IRAs.

Earnings

Overall, current job *earnings* form approximately 20 percent of the income of older units, and earnings are reported by about 20 percent of older adults (Administration on Aging, 1999). This low percentage is consistent with the declining labor-force participation generally among people age 65 and over. Although earnings are an important income source to the young-old and to those with the highest income from assets and pensions, they decline in importance with age. For example, over 40 percent of young-old individuals receive income from earnings, compared with only 3 percent for those 80 years and older (Social Security Administration, 1998).

In sum, the equity goals of Social Security are outweighed by private pensions, asset income, IRAs, and other preferential tax treatment for a small percentage of wealthy older adults. This creates greater economic inequality among the older population over time. The basic facts about older American household wealth are: modest wealth holdings by the typical older household, large inequities in wealth, and little evidence of prior savings by poor and even middle-class households (Smith, 1997b).

POVERTY AMONG OLD AND YOUNG

The economic status of older people has improved since the 1960s. In 1959, 35.2 percent of those age 65 and over fell below the official poverty line. Today, 11 percent of older people are poor, compared to 13.3 percent for all those under age 65, and 19.9 percent of children under age 18.

At the same time, wealth has accumulated among a small percent of older adults, with the older population increasingly dichotomized into rich and poor. Between 1979 and the present, approximately 20 percent of older families with lowest incomes experienced a decline in real income, while older families in the top 20 percent enjoyed increases in real income. As a result, the top 5 percent of older people with financial means possess 27 percent of all the wealth among Americans over age 70 (Smith, 1997a; Villa et al., 1997). As noted above, these high-income elders depend primarily upon assets, earnings, private pensions, and savings, not on Social Security.

Nevertheless, the overall economic status of older adults is improved today. This is due to the following factors:

- the strong performance of the economy in the 1950s and 1960s
- accumulation of home equity
- existence of Medicare
- expansion of Social Security and other pension protection
- improved and longer coverage by pensions
- the 1972 increases in Social Security benefits

WHO ARE THE OLDER POOR?

- Nearly 9 percent of older whites
- 14 percent of older Asian Americans/Pacific Islanders
- 26 percent of older African Americans
- 21 percent of older Hispanics

- 35 percent of older American Indians
- 14 percent of those who live in central cities
- 12.5 percent of those in rural areas
- 12 percent of those living in the south (Administration on Aging, 1999)

- the 1975 automatic annual cost of living adjustments (COLAs) in Social Security
- implementation of the Supplemental Security Income program

When all sources of income are considered (including tax and in-kind benefits), fewer older families have subpoverty resources than younger families. In addition, the majority of poverty "spells" among older adults are 3 years or less (Rank and Hirschl, 1999). As a result of such gains, a widely held public perception is that *all* older persons are financially better off than other age groups. This perception is also fueled by the increase of poverty among children under age 18, who are the poorest age group. However, this decline in the income status of children is largely structural, caused by economic and demographic forces, not by the older population itself (Ozawa, 1996).

Poverty Differentials over Time

When looked at over time, many older people are not financially comfortable, despite the overall improved income status. Forty percent of Americans between the ages of 60 and 90, experience at least one year below the poverty line, and 48 percent at least a year in which their income falls below 125 percent of the poverty line (Rank and Hirschl, 1999). A larger proportion (6.3 percent) of older people than younger (4.5 percent) fall just above the poverty line and thus are "near poor" and at risk for poverty; approximately 17 percent are poor or near poor (Administration on Aging, 1999). These "tweeners" are caught between upper-income and poor older people—not well enough off to be financially secure but not poor enough to qualify for the means-tested safety net of Medicaid and Supplemental Security Income. Paradoxically, the only way that they can improve their economic well-being is to qualify for Medicaid and Supplemental Security Income by spending down (using up their assets). As noted earlier, the poverty rate for older adults would be about 50 percent without Social Security (Abramoritz, Grossinger, and Sachs, 2000). The percentage of subgroups

who are poor, even with Social Security, and the percentage kept out of poverty by Social Security are illustrated in Figure 12.6.

These figures also do not reflect that the federal poverty standard for a single adult younger than age 65 is higher than for an older individual. The U.S. Bureau of the Census assumes that the costs of food and other necessities are lower for older people, even though they spend proportionately more on housing, transportation, and health care than do younger groups. If the same standard were applied to the older population as to the other age groups, the poverty rate for older people would increase to over 15 percent (Administration on Aging, 1999). In addition, older people spend a greater share of their income than younger adults do on the basic necessities of food, utilities, and health care—areas particularly hard hit by inflation. Older adults are also less likely to have reserve funds to cover emergencies such as catastrophic medical expenses. As a result, low-income elders are at risk of malnutrition, poorly heated and inadequate housing, homelessness, and neglect of medical needs.

Contrary to the static nature of poverty that is suggested by cross-sectional data, many older people move in and out of poverty over time. When such individual movements are identified, the risk of falling below the poverty line at some time during a specified period is more than double the highest average risk for older couples, and is raised by almost 30 percent for widows. For example, many women become poor for the first time in their lives after depleting their assets while caring for a dying partner. Once an older person moves into poverty, she or he is less likely to exit than are younger age groups. Many "hidden poor" among the older population are either institutionalized or living with relatives and thus not counted in official census statistics. In sum, more older people are at marginal levels of income and at greater risk of poverty than the population 18–64 years; they are also more likely to be trapped in long-term poverty (Administration on Aging, 1999). In addition, wide socioeconomic diversity exists within the older population, with economic marginality most pronounced among older women, those who live

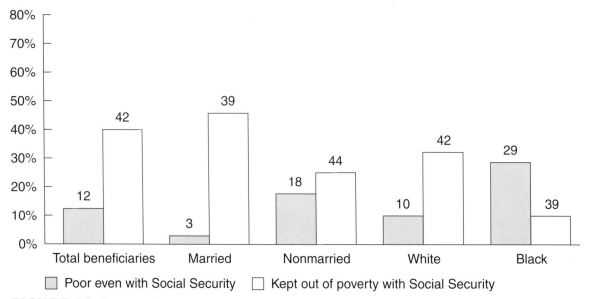

FIGURE 12.6 Aged Units and Poverty Status

SOURCE: Social Security Administration. *Income of the Aged. Chartbook, 1994.* Washington, DC: U.S. Government Printing Office, 1996.

alone, those outside metropolitan areas, ethnic minorities, and the oldest-old.

Poverty Differentials by Gender

Older women comprise one of the poorest groups in our society. In fact, the risk of poverty among couples and single men has sharply fallen, leaving poverty in old age a characteristic primarily of single frail women over age 85, especially women of color, in nonmetropolitan areas, who have outlived their husbands (McLaughlin and Jensen, 2000). Although women account for approximately 50 percent of the older population, they compose nearly 75 percent of the older poor. Nearly 13 percent of older women are poor, compared to approximately 7 percent of older men.

Widows account for over 50 percent of all older poor, reflecting the loss of pension income and earned income often associated with the death of a wage-earner spouse (Administration on Aging, 1999; Simon-Rusinowitz, Wilson, Marks, Krach, and Welch, 1998). In contrast, the wife's

death reduces the risk of poverty for widowers (McLaughlin and Jensen, 2000). As implied above, the *primary reasons for women's lower retirement income are:*

- their interrupted work histories related to family responsibilities
- the greater likelihood of being divorced, widowed, and unmarried
- lower wages and their resultant lower Social Security benefits
- less likelihood of their having private pensions to supplement Social Security
- the gradual erosion of assets and interest income
- their lower likelihood of having worked in higher-level or professional occupations that demand complex decision making and therefore better prepare them to plan for retirement (McLaughlin and Jensen, 2000)

These factors that lead to higher proportions of poor older women are referred to as the **feminization of poverty.**

POVERTY DIFFERENTIALS AMONG OLDER WOMEN

- Of women age 85 and over living in metropolitan areas, 19.7 percent are poor.
- Of widowed women, 21 percent are poor.
- Of women living alone, 23 percent are poor.
- Of those divorced or separated, 26 percent are poor.

- Fifty percent of older African American women not living with family have incomes below the poverty line.
- Almost 70 percent of rural African American women live in poverty, making them the most economically deprived group in our society.

Poverty Differentials by Race

African American and Hispanic elders of both sexes have substantially lower incomes than their white counterparts, as shown in Figure 12.7. Over 26 percent of older African Americans and over 21 percent of older Hispanics are poor compared to 8.2 percent of older whites (National Institutes of Health, 2000). The median income of older African American and Hispanic men living alone is about 33 percent lower than older white men living alone. Although the differences are less pronounced among women, the median incomes of older African American and Hispanic women are generally 25 to 33 percent lower than those of white women. Minority women's slight economic advantage compared to white women and relative to that of their male peers stems from the higher rates of unemployment and unsteady work histories among their male peers. Not only are median incomes lower, but the average black or Hispanic households have no financial or liquid assets (Smith, 1997b). Within each population of color, poverty is more common for women, especially unmarried women, than for men (Administration on Aging, 1999).

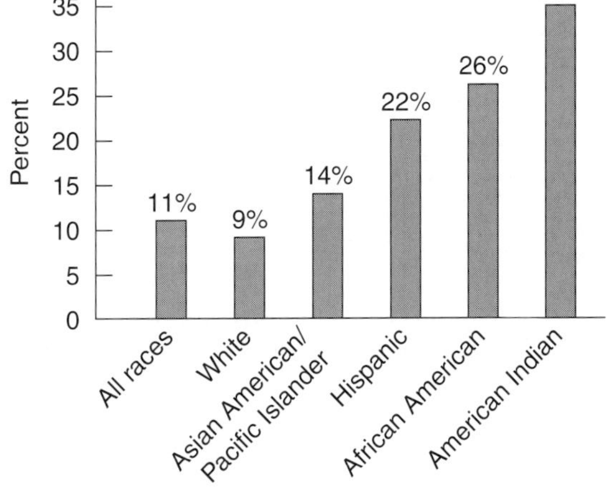

Poverty Differentials by Age and Living Status

The poverty rates among the young-old are lower, in part due to continued employment or the greater likelihood of retirement with good pension plans. In contrast, older cohorts continue to experience income loss as they age, and therefore economic deprivation relative to younger cohorts. The poverty rate for those 65 to 74 years is over 10 percent; for those over age 85, nearly 20 percent. The fact that median income declines with age is due in part to the disproportionate number of nonmarried women among the oldest-old. The economic hardships of older cohorts are often compounded by a lifetime of discrimination, by historical factors such as working at jobs with no pension or inadequate health insurance, and by recent stressful events such as loss of spouse or declining health. Accordingly, older cohorts are more likely to live alone, which is associated with poverty. Of all older people living alone, 20 percent are poor, compared

FIGURE 12.7 **Percent of Population below Poverty by Race, 1998**
SOURCE: AoA, 1999.

to 6 percent of those living with others. When the poor and the near-poor are grouped together, 45 percent of older people living alone fall into this category. In every successively older age group, nonmarried women have a lower median income than nonmarried men or married couples. Since the poverty rate increases with age, nearly 50 percent of those age 85 and over are either poor or near-poor (Administration on Aging, 1999; Social Security Administration, 1998). To illustrate from the introductory vignettes, Mr. Valdres worked as a migrant farm laborer and therefore relies on the minimum Social Security level for his income.

In sum, despite the overall improved financial situation of the older population, large pockets of poverty and near-poverty exist, particularly among women, groups of color, those over age 75, those who live alone, and those who live in rural areas. As a result, economic inequities are actually greater among older people than among other age groups. Aging advocates maintain that strategies to alleviate poverty among today's older Americans cannot rely on an improving labor market. Instead, they must be immediate, such as increasing levels of Social Security for those with low lifetime earnings and ensuring that women and men have full access to benefits accrued by their spouses (Smith, 1997b).

Public Assistance

Only about 5 percent of the older population receives some type of public assistance, primarily in the form of *Supplemental Security Income* (**SSI**) (Social Security Administration, 1998). This percentage increases among persons of color and women. SSI was established in 1974 to provide a minimum income for elders living on the margin of poverty. The basic federal payment in 1999 was $500 a month for a single person and $751 for a couple. These payments change each year to reflect cost-of-living increases (National Committee to Preserve Social Security and Medicare, 2000).

In contrast to Social Security, SSI does not require a history of covered employment contributions. Instead, eligibility is determined by a cat-

egorical requirement that the recipient be 65 years of age, blind, or disabled, with limits on amount of monthly income and assets determining eligibility. Nevertheless, many eligible older poor do not participate in SSI. For those who do so, the federal SSI benefits fall substantially below the poverty line. Even when states supplement federal benefits, levels remain low, so that SSI supplies only 14 percent of the income of poor older people (Social Security Administration, 1996). Those who receive SSI may also qualify for Medicaid and food stamps. The amount of SSI benefits depends upon income, assets, and gifts or contributions from family members for food, clothing, or housing. These gifts may be counted as income and may result in a reduction in benefits. Becoming eligible for SSI is a time-consuming and often demeaning process, requiring extensive documentation and the ability to deal with conflicting criteria for benefits from SSI, Medicaid, and food stamps. Despite these barriers, increasing numbers of "poor" or "near-poor" older adults rely on public assistance, through either SSI, Medicaid, or food stamps.

As noted earlier, economic status, along with health, living arrangements, and marital status, influences the nonpaid roles and activities in old age—particularly voluntary association membership, voluntarism, religious participation and spirituality, and political involvement. We turn now to discuss these other forms of productive aging.

PATTERNS AND FUNCTIONS OF NONPAID ROLES AND ACTIVITIES

Leisure

The term **leisure** evokes different reactions in people. For some, it signifies wasting time. For others, it is only the frenzied pursuit of "leisure activities" on the weekends that sustains them through the work week. Leisure can be defined as any activity characterized by the absence of obligation that is inherently satisfying. Free time alone is not necessarily leisure. Instead, the critical variable is how a person defines tasks and situations

Leisure activities for many older people include maintaining their gardens.

to bring intrinsic meaning. Accordingly, leisure implies feeling free and satisfied. Individuals who do not experience such feelings may still be at "work" rather than at "leisure." People's reactions to the concept of leisure are clearly influenced by cultural values attached to work and a mistrust of non-work time. Because of American values of productivity and hard work—especially among the current generation of older persons—many older adults have not experienced satisfying nonwork

activities at earlier phases in their lives. Societal values are changing, however, with more legitimacy given to nonwork activities throughout the life cycle, as evidenced by the growing number of classes and businesses that specialize in leisure. For low-income or ethnic minority elders or for older people in developing countries, however, leisure may be a meaningless concept if they have to continue working to survive or lack resources for satisfying recreational time.

Disagreement regarding the value of leisure pursuits for older people is reflected in the gerontological literature. Most definitions of productive aging do not include activities of a personal enrichment nature, thereby excluding leisure activities such as watching television, attending a concert, and travel (Caro, Bass, and Chen, 1993; Danigelis and McIntosh, 1993; Herzog and Morgan, 1993). An early perspective was that leisure roles cannot substitute for work roles because they are not legitimated by societal norms. Since work is a dominant value in U.S. society, it was argued that individuals cannot derive self-respect from leisure. It was also observed that older individuals, fearing the embarrassment of failing in a leisure activity, avoid pursuits that are common to younger people—such as biking or dancing (Miller, 1965).

A closely related perspective is that retirement is legitimated in our society by an ethic that esteems leisure that is earnest, occupied, and filled with activity—a "busy" ethic, which is consistent with the activity theory of aging (Ekerdt, 1986). For those with strong work values, worklike activities are probably important for achieving satisfaction in retirement. The prevalence of the "busy" ethic is reflected in a question commonly asked of retirees: What do you do to keep busy? "Keeping busy" and engaging in productive activities analogous to work are presumed to ease the

---

POINTS TO PONDER

What does leisure mean to you? How have values and culture influenced your definition of leisure? How is this different from your parents' or grandparents' definition?

adjustment to retirement by adapting retired life to prevailing societal norms, although the "busy" ethic is contrary to the definition of leisure as intrinsically satisfying. A counterargument is that leisure can replace the work role and provide personal satisfaction in later life, especially when the retired person has good health and an adequate income, and their activities build upon preretirement skills and interests.

Although wide variations exist, *patterns of meaningful nonpaid activity* among older individuals are identified.

- Most activity changes are gradual, reflecting a consistency and a narrowing of the repertoire of activities as individuals age.
- Compared to younger people, older adults are more likely to engage in solitary and sedentary pursuits, such as watching television, visiting with family and friends, and reading.
- The time spent on personal care, sleep and rest, hobbies, and shopping composes a larger fraction of older adults' days than among younger and middle-aged individuals (Verbrugge, Gruber-Baldini, and Fozard, 1996).

When judged by younger persons or by middle-class standards, these essential and universal activities may be viewed as "boring and nonproductive." Yet, the ability to perform these more mundane activities—personal care, cooking, doing errands, puttering around the house or garden, or sitting in quiet reflection—can be critical to maintaining older people's competence, self-esteem, and life satisfaction. Furthermore, these routines may represent realistic adjustments to declining energy levels and incomes. Such routine leisure pursuits, consistent with the broader concept of productive aging, may thus reflect rational choices about ways to cope congruent with environmental changes and may also enhance quality of life.

Leisure activities also vary by gender and socioeconomic status. Older men tend to do more household and yard maintenance and paid work outside the home, while older women perform more housework, child care, and volunteer work, and participate in more voluntary associations. Not surprisingly, higher-income older people, especially those living in planned retirement communities, tend to be more active in leisure pursuits than low-income elders (Riddick and Stewart, 1994; Verbrugge et al., 1996). Such differences in activities are attributable primarily to the costs of pursuing them, not necessarily to inherent differences by socioeconomic status. Several benefit programs are designed to reduce financial barriers to leisure. For instance, Golden Passports give older people reduced admission fees to national parks. Similar programs at the local or state level provide free admission to parks, museums, and cultural activities, and reduced prices from businesses and transportation. Not surprisingly, a wide range of leisure-oriented businesses, including group travel programs, are marketing services to higher-income older adults.

The *psychological benefits of leisure* perceived by older participants include:

- companionship (e.g., playing cards or going dancing)
- compensation for past activities (e.g., picnicking instead of hiking)
- temporary disengagement (e.g., watching TV)
- comfortable solitude (e.g., reading)
- expressive solitude (e.g., knitting and crocheting)
- expressive service (e.g., volunteer service, attending meetings of social groups) (Tinsley, Teaff, Colbs, and Kaufman, 1985)

The major benefit of nonpaid activities may be maintaining ties with others and providing new sources of personal meaning and competence. Not surprisingly, leisure activities are associated with a positive identity and self-concept among older people. Accordingly, activities that result in a sense of being valued and contributing to society are found to be positively related to life satisfaction and mental well-being in retirement (Riddick and Stewart, 1994). This relationship does not mean, however, that leisure activity itself creates well-being, since older people who are active also tend to be healthier and of higher socioeconomic status. The quality of interactions with others in nonwork may be more salient roles than the number or frequency of interactions (Cutler and Hendricks, 1990).

Membership in Voluntary Associations

Given our societal emphasis on being an active and productive participant, voluntary association membership is often presumed to be a "good" leisure activity. Based on such assumptions, association members often go to considerable lengths to recruit older people. Overall, older people may be more involved in voluntary organizations than are younger people. Membership is most closely tied to social class and varies among cultures. When socioeconomic status is taken into account, older people show considerable stability in their general level of voluntary association participation from middle age until their sixties (Cutler and Hendricks, 2000).

Characteristics that appear to influence voluntary association membership include age, gender, race, prior activities and memberships, health, and socioeconomic status.

The kinds of organizations in which older people participate vary by gender and race. Older women are more active in voluntary associations than older men. Women's multiple roles at earlier phases of the life span, such as volunteer work, have been found to be positively related to health and occupying multiple roles in old age (Caro and Bass, 1997). Older African Americans have higher rates of organizational membership than do older whites or members of other groups of color; although for both blacks and whites, membership is most frequent among those with better health and higher income and education levels. Some racial differences exist in the types of associations joined. Older African Americans are especially likely to belong to church-related groups and social and recreational clubs; older whites frequently are members of nationality organizations and senior citizen groups. Hispanics participate in fraternal and service-oriented organizations, mutual aid societies, and "hometown" clubs.

Senior centers encourage voluntary association activities. These vary greatly in the type of services offered, ranging from purely recreational events to social action, or the delivery of social and health services, including health screening and health promotion. In fact, the Older Americans Act identifies senior centers as preferred focal points for comprehensive, coordinated service delivery. Despite the range of activities, only about 15 percent of older persons participate in senior centers.

Furthermore, centers typically draw from a relatively narrow population, reaching primarily healthy, lower- to middle-class individuals under age 85 with a "lifetime of joining clubs." Nationwide, individuals who are generally less advantaged, but not the least advantaged, are most likely to participate in senior center activities. Those who participate tend to do so out of a desire for social interaction and to have been invited by friends (Wagner, 1995; Bazargan, Barbre, and Torres-Gil, 1992).

Senior centers face programmatic challenges. Their membership has become "older" as their users have "aged in place," and the young-old are less inclined to attend at the same time that the oldest-old are too frail to participate. Centers are criticized for not doing more to reach elders of color and older people who are frail, low-income,

Older adults often tutor children in the classroom.

**REASONS FOR LOW LEVELS OF PARTICIPATION
IN SENIOR CENTERS BY OLDER ADULTS**

- Lack of interest in the center's activities
- Poor health
- Inadequate transportation

- Desire not to be with only old people
- The low proportion of men in many centers

---

or disabled. Although African American elders are slightly more likely than whites to attend centers, most programs need to become multicultural. Some senior centers, established in neighborhoods of color, have successfully attracted diverse elders who would not otherwise participate. In contrast, some observers contend that such targeting of services runs counter to the universal nature of the Older Americans Act and may reduce the participation of those relatively more-advantaged older people who currently attend centers.

Older persons who are active in community organizations such as senior centers derive a variety of benefits. Socializing appears to be the primary reward, and aids in achieving successful aging, as described in Chapter 6. Because these organizations are typically age-graded, people interact with others who are similar in age and interests. These interactions often result in friendships, support, a sense of belonging, mutual exchanges of resources, and collective activity. Consistent with the broader concept of productivity, voluntary associations can also serve to maintain the social integration of older people, countering losses in roles and in interactions with others. Older people in voluntary organizations are found to have a sense of well-being and higher morale, although this may be attributed to their higher levels of health, income, and education. When these other characteristics are taken into account, organizational membership is apparently unrelated to overall life satisfaction (Cutler and Hendricks, 2000). The most satisfied members of organizations are those who become involved in order to have new experiences, achieve something, be creative, and help others. Such members, in turn, participate actively through planning and leadership. Opportunities for more active partici-

pation are found in senior advocacy groups such as the Older Women's League or in organizations such as advisory boards to Area Agencies on Aging where older people must, by charter, be in leadership roles. Overall, voluntary association membership appears to be more satisfying when it provides opportunities for active, intense involvement and significant leadership roles.

Volunteer Work

With cutbacks in public funding, nonprofit, service, educational, and religious organizations increasingly rely upon volunteers to accomplish their missions and provide services. Because current retirees are younger, in better health, and better educated than earlier cohorts, they tend to have the time, energy, and skills to contribute to society through volunteer work. Such activity is consistent with the concept of productive aging, whereby older people, even though unpaid, produce valued goods and services (Hendricks, Hatch, and Cutler, 1999). Similar to participation in voluntary associations, volunteering is more characteristic of U.S. society than others.

About 40 percent of older people volunteer, a rate that is fairly stable but lower than adults as a whole (70 percent). Those who do volunteer invest more hours into their volunteer work than do younger volunteers, in part because of having more uncommitted time (Van Willigen, 2000). Among the older population, *rates of community involvement and of volunteerism* are highest among adults with the following characteristics:

- higher income and education
- more leisure time

AN ACTIVE VOLUNTEER AT AGE 80

Edna was an elementary school librarian, forced to retire in 1986, when mandatory retirement still existed. After a few months at home, she was back in the local school, working four or five days a week as a substitute librarian. She is widely loved by the kids, and the parents and teachers respect her ability to relate to a wide range of children, managing to hook them into "listening to reading."

- better health
- a history of volunteering throughout their lives (e.g., activists of the 1960s)
- a broad range of interests
- a belief that they can make valuable contributions

The primary type of volunteer work is through religious organizations, followed by direct service such as tutoring, handiwork, raising money, serving on a board or committee, or assisting in an office; most volunteers serve in only one organization. The majority volunteer only a few hours a week, but for some, volunteer work is equivalent to a full-time job (Chatfield, 1999; Cutler and Hendricks, 2000; Warburton, LeBrocque, and Rosenman, 1998).

GENDER DIFFERENCES IN VOLUNTARISM   As is the case generally in voluntary activities, women (especially widows) are more likely to volunteer than men. This may shift, however, as more women enter the paid workforce. Although women generally view volunteering as a way to help others, men more frequently define it as a substitute for the worker role.

RACIAL DIFFERENCES IN VOLUNTARISM   Volunteering as a way to help others through informal networks is frequent in communities of color, such as through African American churches. It may represent a history of self-reliance and incorporation of a lifetime of hard work into leisure experiences and services to others (Allen and Chin-Sang, 1990). Mutual aid (e.g., providing food and lodging to older persons) is common in American Indian communities. Volunteer activities among Pacific Asian elders reinforce the continuation of their value systems. Older Chinese, for example, often work through family associations or benevolent societies. Some Japanese elders participate in clubs that are an extension of the "family helping itself" concept rooted in traditional Japanese culture. The Hispanic community emphasizes self-help, mutual aid, and neighborhood assistance for their older members.

Within the past 30 years, a number of public and private initiatives have been designed to expand community service by older persons. One of the best-known of the government-sponsored initiatives is the Foster Grandparents Program, which pairs seniors with children with disabilities; it is found to be beneficial to both. This mutual aid concept was extended to the Senior Companion Program, in which able-bodied seniors serve older adults with disabilities. The participation of people over 40 in the Peace Corps has increased from 2 percent in 1960 to 13 percent today (King, 2000). The Older American Volunteer Program of ACTION recruits older people to work with disadvantaged groups within the United States. One of the largest of the volunteer networks is the Retired Senior Volunteer Program (RSVP), which has projects in schools, hospitals, adult and child daycare centers, and nursing homes.

Within the private sector, programs sponsored by the American Association of Retired Persons (AARP) volunteers are matched with jobs through a nationwide Volunteer Talent Bank (Chambré, 1993). Other private sector programs are the National and International Executive Services Corps of Retired Executives (SCORE), where retired executives use their technical and financial expertise to consult with small businesses in the United States

VOLUNTEERING AS A SUBSTITUTE FOR PAST ROLES

Ted was a teacher of sixth-grade science in an inner-city public school for 35 years. When he retired at age 57, he began a successful second career selling real estate. Now at age 72, he continues to work on average 2 days per week. He enjoys the contact with people and finds his work very different from teaching. Because he believes it is important to give back to his community, he also volunteers as a tutor in an after-school program run by his church for neighborhood "latchkey" children.

and abroad, and Civic Ventures, a nationwide organization dedicated to mobilizing older adults to work in inner-city schools.

Volunteer programs serve *two major social benefits:* 1) provide individuals with meaningful social roles; and 2) furnish organizations with experienced, reliable workers at minimal cost (Hendricks et al., 1999).

Older volunteers appear to experience greater psychological benefits than do younger volunteers. These benefits include greater life satisfaction, physical and mental well-being, and sense of accomplishment and feelings of usefulness. The difference may be due in part to the greater meaning that older volunteers attach to this role (Willigen, 2000). In fact, a recent study determined that volunteering has a protective effect on mortality among those who volunteered for one organization or for 40 hours or less over the past year. These protective effects appear to be strongest for those who report low levels of informal social interaction and who do not live alone (Musick, Herzog, and House, 1999). This curvilinear relationship between volunteering and mortality is undoubtedly due to other factors, such as self-identity, role strain and meaningfulness.

Contrary to the assumptions of activity theory, the desire to replace lost roles (e.g., employee or spouse) is not a primary motivator. Instead, older people are more likely to volunteer if they are married, involved in other organizations, and employed part-time, while nonemployed older people tend to volunteer less. For most retirees, volunteering is apparently not a work substitute, although it may protect them from any negative effects of retirement, physical decline, and inactivity

(Fischer and Schaffer, 1993). Consistent with the continuity theory of aging, most older volunteers have volunteered earlier in their lives and have a sense of responsibility. Volunteerism is part of an overall productive lifestyle that unfolds in the formal arenas of work and organized activities, with volunteers' long-standing involvement either remaining constant or expanding as they age. Nevertheless, it is still possible to recruit new volunteers in old age, especially if those who are about to leave or have recently left their jobs are targeted (Caro and Bass, 1997). From the perspective of social exchange theory, volunteering may ensure valued social resources as a basis of exchange, primarily by assisting others rather than being perceived as dependent.

The experience of Ted and Edna illustrate how some older adults achieve life satisfaction by substituting volunteering for previous professions as teachers and mentors. Mary's activities, described in the following box, illustrate how volunteering can support older adults in helping roles. A number of trends will influence the meaning and functions of volunteerism for older persons. If government service cutbacks continue, volunteers are essential to meeting the service needs of a wide range of disadvantaged groups (Musick et al., 1999; Wheeler, Gorey, and Greenblatt, 1998). Simultaneously, with the growing emphasis nationally on self-help and mutual aid, some people may choose to become more active in neighborhood and community advocacy groups. The young-old are likely to be more involved in advisory councils and commissions, lobbying efforts, and national senior organizations such as those described later in this chapter. These volun-

---

VOLUNTEERING AS A SOURCE OF SUPPORT

Mary, a homemaker and mother of four children, spent her early years being involved with Scouts and PTA and teaching Sunday school. Her last child left home when Mary was 52, and she felt "lost" because there was no one to "need" her in the same ways the children had. At 53, she began volunteering, answering the phone for a community center that served children and elders, and found a new role. When she was widowed at age 70, she increased the hours of volunteering to fill the lonely hours when she especially missed her husband. Since she has never driven, she takes the bus one day a week to the community center. Now at age 80, she was recently honored by the city at a special reception for her 8,000 hours of volunteer service.

---

teer and advocacy efforts will continue to face the challenge of how to involve older people who are low-income, persons of color, living alone, frail and disabled, or from areas with inadequate public transportation. Regardless of the type of voluntarism, the documented benefits suggest that efforts to encourage volunteering among older persons should continue (Van Willigen, 2000).

Educational Programs

Many educational programs have been oriented toward enrichment or practical personal assistance in such areas as health and finances, and therefore have not necessarily supported the movement of older people into new productive roles (Caro et al., 1993). A primary reason for the limited role of education in productive aging is that most higher education institutions have not viewed older learners as a priority, nor have they fully recognized the market potential for education among senior boomers. Even though 80 percent of state universities offer tuition-free, space-available enrollment in college classes for older people, state legislatures typically have provided little funding for older adult programs, or such programs have been cut.

Fortunately, some creative late-life learning initiatives have developed in higher education that are constructed around images of productive aging, not of decline or need. One of the best known is **Elderhostel,** where older learners attend special seminars or institutes on campuses and affiliated locations throughout the country and the world. Each one of these has an educational component and is associated with a college or university, whether the group is studying architecture in London, seals in Antarctica, monkeys in Belize, antiquities in Rome, or art in the Southwest. Elderhostel involves over 250,000 participants a year at over 1500 different academic institutions. To cater to the young-old and boomers, Elderhostel now offers private rooms and baths rather than dormitory accommodations.

Some gerontology certificate programs are committed to preparing significant numbers of older people for roles as advocates and service

---

INTERGENERATIONAL SERVICE LEARNING IN GERONTOLOGY

The Association for Gerontology in Higher Education sponsored service-learning courses at ten universities. Coursework affiliated with over 100 community agencies attracted students ranging in age from 18 to the mid-seventies. The students, in turn, had a significant impact on local communities and agencies serving older adults. Learners of all ages, within the classroom and in community settings, benefited (McCrea, Nichols, and Newman, 1998).

POINTS TO PONDER

Think about the kinds of educational or learning experiences that you would like to pursue when you are retired. What qualities characterize them?

---

providers. Community colleges, because of their accessibility, are ideal settings in which to develop educational programs that offer older adults ways to be productive. A few states recognize the market for lifelong learning and are funding a range of programs, including liberal arts education, peer learning groups, health promotion, training of older volunteers, intergenerational programming, and seniors' mentoring of younger undergraduates for career guidance. With the growth of distance learning and Web-based instruction, the Baby Boomers will be a growing market for educational programs. Even for the current cohort, programs such as Senior Net teach computer skills and how to communicate on-line.

As suggested in Chapter 5, educational programs need to take account of older learners' particular needs, such as flexibility, avoidance of time pressures, self-paced learning, and sensitivity to hearing and vision problems. Senior learning programs represent an area in need of further development and funding, especially with the increase in healthy, active older people who seek new opportunities to contribute to society after retirement.

Religious Participation, Religiosity, and Spirituality

Of the various options for organizational participation, the most common choice for older persons is through their *religious affiliation*. After family and government, religious groups are an important source of instrumental and emotional support for older people (Cutler and Hendricks, 2000). Across the life span, church and synagogue attendance is lowest among those in their thirties, peaks in the late fifties to early sixties (with approximately 60 percent of this age group attending), and begins to decline in the late sixties or early seventies. Despite

this slight decline, the level of organizational religious involvement for older adults exceeds that of other age groups, with 50 percent of persons over age 65 attending church or synagogue in an average week, and many more attending less frequently. Furthermore, people age 65 and over are the most likely of any age group to belong to church-affiliated groups that can provide a loving, supportive community and a way to contribute. In contrast to other types of voluntary organizations, leadership positions in churches and synagogues tend to be concentrated among older people.

Such formalized religious involvement is found to be related to general measures of personal adjustment, mental well-being, better physical functioning, and subjective health and life satisfaction, (Neill and Kahn, 1999). As an illustration of this, a study of older women with breast cancer found that religious faith provided them with emotional support and a way to cope with the illness (Feher and Maly, 1999). Similarly, studies of low-income older women show that religious beliefs help them cope with hardships (Barusch, 1999). Rates of church attendance in themselves do not indicate the extent of religiosity among older persons, however (Levin, Chatters, and Taylor, 1995; Kaye and Robinson, 1994).

Religiosity can be examined in terms of three factors:

1. Participation in religious organizations
2. The personal meaning of religion and private devotional activities within the home
3. The contribution of religion to individuals' adjustment to the aging process and their confrontation with death and dying

Slight declines in rates of religious participation after age 70 may reflect health and transportation difficulties and functional limitations more than lack of religiousness and spirituality per se (Barusch, 1999). In fact, while attendance at formal services declines slightly with age, older individuals apparently compensate by an increase in internal religious practices—reading the Bible or other religious books, listening to religious broadcasts, praying, or studying religion. Older adults pray, asking help from God, more often than other age groups. The emotions of hope, gratitude, and forgiveness may represent significant components by which prayer exerts a salutary influence on mental health. For many elders, **spirituality**—defined broadly as encompassing trust and faith in a power greater than oneself, prayer, and strength from a greater being—is an effective way to cope (Barusch, 1999; Koenig et al., 1998; Levin and Taylor, 1997). Religious beliefs, as contrasted with church attendance, appear to be relatively stable from the late teens until age 60 and to increase thereafter. Thus, some older people who appear to be disengaged from religious organizations may be fully engaged nonorganizationally, experiencing a sense of spirituality and strong and meaningful subjective ties to religion (Barusch, 1999). Although religion appears to be important to older people, many also valued it when they were young. That is, contrary to popular stereotypes and consistent with continuity theory, we do not necessarily become more religious as we age.

Most surveys on religiousness are limited by cross-sectional research, as discussed in Chapter 1. That is, they do not attempt to measure adults' past religious values and behaviors. The few available longitudinal studies suggest that cohort differences may be more important than the effects of age, although one 16-year study found increased participation in religious services as people entered

their sixties and early seventies, then declined by age 75 (Atchley, 1995). Thus, although religious convictions appear to become more salient over the years, this may be a generational phenomenon captured by the cross-sectional nature of most of the research. The current cohort of older persons, raised during a time of more widespread religious involvement, had their peak rates of attendance in the 1950s, when this country experienced a church revival. All cohorts, not only older people, have shown a decline in church or synagogue attendance since 1965, although this is now changing.

Studies of religious activity identify both gender and racial differences. Consistent with patterns of involvement in other organizations, women, particularly African American women, have higher rates of religious involvement than men (Levin, Taylor, and Chatters, 1994). Religion appears to be central to the lives of most older African Americans of both sexes and to be related to their life satisfaction, feelings of self-worth, personal well-being, and sense of integration in the larger community. The high esteem afforded African American elders in the church may partially underlie these positive associations. Historically, African Americans have had more autonomy in their religious lives than in their economic and political lives. The negative effects of life stress for older African Americans are found to be offset by increased religious involvement through prayer, other private religious activities, and a cognitive reframing of the situation in positive terms (e.g., "I have been through a lot before and I'll get through this too") (Black, 1999; Chatters and Taylor, 1994; Levin and Taylor, 1997).

For some African American caregivers, the church and God are considered part of their informal system of support and respite (Dilworth-Andersen, Williams, and Cooper, 1999; Wood and

FUNCTIONS SERVED BY RELIGION IN AFRICAN AMERICAN COMMUNITIES

- Identity, self-esteem, and meaning
- Social services
- Political participation
- Social support
- Sense of community and belonging

Wan, 1993). The church also provides social services such as in-home visitation, counseling, meals, household help, and transportation for African American elders, and links them with formal agencies (Porter, Garong, and Armey, 2000). Such instrumental support reflects the African American church's historical responsibility for improving its parishioners' socioeconomic and political conditions.

Although the relationship between religious involvement and life satisfaction is not clear-cut, religious attitudes, beliefs, and participation generally are positively associated with well-being, happiness, a sense of usefulness, and morale. The strength of these relationships increases over time. In fact, for some individuals age 75 and over, religion is second to health in its relationship to morale, especially for women (Mickley, Carson, and Soeken, 1995). Across all religions, the more religiously devout are usually less afraid of death, more effective at coping with chronic illness, and less prone to depression and loneliness than the less devout (Leifer, 1996). Accordingly, individuals for whom faith provides meaning experience greater feelings of internal control and a more positive self-concept (Mickley et al., 1995). Findings regarding the relationships between religiosity and self-esteem are mixed, however. Among African American women, for example, spirituality is found to engender self-esteem and positive interpretations of life circumstances (Black, 1999). Self-esteem is identified to be highest among older persons with the greatest and the least religious commitment, and lowest among older adults with only modest levels of religiosity. Therefore, it is unclear if the changes in religiosity precede changes in self-worth, or whether those with initially positive self-evaluations are more capable of mustering the effort needed for mature faith (Krause, 1995).

It is also not clear whether religiousness itself is beneficial, or if the organizational aspects of the sense of belonging and social support are the determinants, since religious participation is associated with other types of group involvement (Idler and Kasl, 1997). Satisfaction, serenity, or acceptance of death may result not from faith or spirituality per se, but rather from participation in social networks and reference groups that offer support and security. Older people themselves list among its benefits both the meaning religion gives to life and the social interaction it affords. Therefore, it is important to consider how social support through churches and synagogues complements and interacts with religious beliefs and activities. In addition, as public social services continue to be cut, religious institutions can play a vital role in providing counseling, referral to services, and prevention/health promotion. Unfortunately, these institutions may be asked to play this role without adequate resources.

The Value of Spiritual Well-Being

Spirituality or *spiritual well-being* can be differentiated from organized religion and defined in a wide variety of ways:

- self-determined wisdom in which the individual tries to achieve balance in life
- self-transcendence or crossing a boundary beyond the self, being supported by some power greater than oneself
- achievement of meaning and purpose for one's continued existence
- sense of the wholeness of life and connectedness to the universe
- awe or unconditional joy
- intuitive nonverbal understanding of how to cope with life's circumstances

People can be spiritual, believing in a relationship with a higher power, without being religious in the sense of organized religion. In fact, the dimensions of spirituality are applicable to older adults who are nonreligious or even antireligious. Listening to music, rituals, viewing a sunset or a painting, and loving and being loved can all be profound spiritual experiences. Accordingly, spirituality can be expressed in trying to find the meaning and purpose of life, looking at the significance of past events, and wondering what will happen after death. High levels of spirituality (e.g., closeness to

---

SPIRITUALITY AND QUALITY OF LIFE

A key theme in narratives from a small sample of African American women is that their relationship with God, perceived as personal, reciprocal, and empowering, allows them to take an active and positive stance in viewing and interpreting the circumstances of their lives. Their spirituality imbues their hardship with meaning, engenders self-esteem, and gives hope for rewards in both this life and the next (Black, 1999).

God) are found to be associated with mental health indicators such as purpose in life, self-esteem, and social skills (Burke, 1999; Kavanaugh, 1997). Spirituality is also identified as an important factor in an individual's perception of quality of life (irrespective of age or socioeconomic status) and in maintaining a healthy lifestyle.

Spiritual well-being is related not only to the quality of life but also to the will to live. Some gerontologists and theologians maintain that the person who aims to enhance spiritual well-being and to find meaning in life will have a reason to live despite losses and challenges associated with aging (Fallon, 1998). When death is near, spirituality is important for coping with disease, disability, and pain (Burke, 1999). Mr. Mansfield, in the introduction to Part Four, illustrates the role of spirituality in helping older persons cope with tragic losses in their lives.

Aging can be characterized as a spiritual journey in which the person aims to achieve integration across a number of areas of life—biological, psychological, social, and spiritual. An ageless self, that is, a person who is not preoccupied or discouraged by his or her aging, has an identity that maintains continuity and is on a spiritual journey in time, despite age-related physical and social changes. For such an individual, being old per se is neither a central feature of the self nor the source

of its meaning. Confronting negative images of aging, loss, and death is believed to be essential for psychological-spiritual growth and successful aging. In fact, dealing with loss can be one of aging's greatest spiritual challenges. Autobiographical storytelling, journal keeping, and empathic interactions with others are useful in supporting older persons' spiritual integration.

The central role of spirituality in many older adults' lives has numerous implications for professionals working with them. Spirituality is a quality that can be acknowledged in any situation, including professional practice with older adults. Many faith traditions emphasize the importance of silence in creating space to experience spirituality, with the silence of meditation or prayer as a way to nourish our spirituality. In hospice programs, for instance, patients, workers, and families can experience profound togetherness out of shared silence. In nursing homes, staff and families may find that silence when they are together has value. Spiritual deepening can also come from confronting and working through doubt and uncertainty. For others, spirituality is a state of being rather than of doing, of approaching each other with kindness and openness to their unique way of manifesting their spirituality. It is a way to experience others authentically with little tendency to judge or evaluate them. Spiritual reflections and

---

Carl, age 68, is an active volunteer and employed part-time. No matter how busy he is, however, he always manages to set aside a half hour in the morning to meditate. Since he started meditating at age 62, his blood pressure has decreased; he has fewer health problems, and he has a calm, positive outlook on life. He describes his meditation to his friends as the center of his spiritual journey.

experiences can also be a source of insight for both practitioners and older clients. Contemplative understanding includes feelings and thoughts, and can counterbalance overly rational decision-making processes. In some instances, spirituality can provide a more balanced understanding of what is compared to what is needed. When practitioners learn to focus on experiences of spirituality with older adults, they can create common experiential ground that can transcend the confines of specific faith traditions and open opportunities for incorporating spirituality into all aspects of everyday life (Atchley, 1999).

Historically, the medical profession has taken a predominantly biological perspective toward aging, overlooking psychological, emotional, and spiritual factors. Fortunately, more health care providers are attending to the spiritual dimensions of health care and dying (Nordquist, 1999). Health care practitioners who view spiritual well-being as important to older people's physical and mental health have developed instruments to measure an individual's spiritual interests and resources, such as personal values, philosophy, and sense of purpose. Some health-promotion screening tools include questions on the individual's spiritual or philosophic values, life goal-setting, and approach to answering questions, such as: What is the meaning of my life? How can I increase the quality of my life? Similarly, spiritual beliefs influence definitions of health, the prevention of illness, and health promotion and coping with illness, and give meaning in life (Koenig, 1995). For example, a study of older women diagnosed with breast cancer found that spirituality was an effective coping strategy. It provided emotional and social support, and the ability to make meaning in their everyday lives, especially during their cancer experience (Feher and Maly, 1999). Increasingly, health care providers are

encouraged to be sensitive to, and to ask questions about, spiritual well-being that may guide health care choices. Similarly, they often encourage patients to seek religious support or to reconnect with a spiritual community (Feher and Maly, 1999).

Political Participation

Another major arena of participation is political life. Political acts range from voting, to participation in a political party or a political action group, to running for or holding elective office. In an examination of older people's political behavior, three factors make any interpretation of the relationship between age and political behavior complex:

1. stages in the life cycle,
2. cohort effects, and
3. historical or period effects, as discussed in Chapter 1.

Historical effects influence interpretations of older people's political behavior, particularly analyses of the extent of conservatism. Some early studies found older people to be more conservative than younger people, as measured by preference for the Republican party and voting behavior (Campbell, 1962; Dobson, 1983). Older people's apparent conservatism partially reflects the fact that people born and raised in different historical periods tend to have perspectives reflecting those times—in this instance, the historical effect of party realignments in the late 1920s and 1930s. Before the New Deal of the 1930s and 1940s, people entering the electorate identified with the Republican party to a disproportionate extent; they have voted Republican ever since, and form the majority of the oldest-old population. This apparent association of Republicanism with age thus

---

POINTS TO PONDER

Ask an older person—a relative, neighbor, close friend—whether he or she perceives himself or herself as spiritual. What does spirituality mean to the individual? How has that meaning developed over time?

reflects cohort differences, not the effects of aging per se. Conclusions about older people's political behavior and attitudes are thus limited by the cross-sectional nature of most research, which has not taken account of historical and cohort effects. In short, how a person thinks and acts politically can be traced largely to environmental and historical factors, not to that person's age.

Age differences in conservatism/liberalism are less a matter of people becoming more conservative than of their maintaining these values throughout life (Binstock and Day, 1996). Successive generations entering the electorate since World War II have become comparatively more liberal, with more older people identifying with the Democratic party since the mid-1980s. This shift may be due in part to increases in low-income and retired blue-collar people who are opposed to the fiscal conservatism of the Republican party, especially on issues such as Social Security and health care. In fact, older adults are more likely to favor major health care reforms than are younger people, in part because of escalating costs. At the same time, increasing numbers of young people, including many among the Baby Boom generation, have identified with the conservative Republicans and with independent candidates since the 1980s (Binstock, 2000; Alwin, 1998).

Overall, individuals of all ages are not ideologically consistent in their issue-specific preferences, such as Medicare, Social Security, or taxes. Furthermore, both older and younger people may hold beliefs on specific issues that contradict their views on more general principles. Given the older population's heterogeneity, differences of opinion on any political issue are likely to equal or exceed variations among age groups and are more likely to be due to economic status and partisanship than age (Binstock, 2000; Binstock and Day, 1996).

Voting Behavior

Older Americans are more likely than younger adults to vote in national elections, although rates of electoral participation are low for all age groups in our society. They currently compose 20 percent

of all votes, though only 17 percent of the general electorate. The participation rate of older people in the last three presidential elections has averaged 68.6 percent, almost three times the rate of 18- to 20-year-olds. Although voting participation declines for those age 75 and older, the 75-plus group was still more likely to vote in the last six presidential elections than people younger than age 35 (Alwin, 1998; Binstock, 2000). The most important factor for the increase in the portion of votes cast by older people is that turnout rates of younger age groups have declined. Several reasons underlie the older population's higher rate of registration and voting:

- Older people are more likely to pay attention to the news and to be more knowledgeable about politics and public affairs generally, demonstrating higher levels of "civic competence" (Binstock, 2000; Strate, Parrish, Elder, and Ford, 1989).
- Strong partisans are more likely to vote, and older people identify with the major political parties more strongly than younger persons, who are more likely to identify with independent parties (Binstock, 2000; McManus and Tenpas, 1998).

In instances where voter turnout is declining among older adults, factors other than aging are probably the cause, including gender, race, education, and generational variables. For example, the voter turnout of populations of color is lower than that of whites, with Hispanics the least likely to vote (Hobbs and Damon, 1996). Their political acculturation appears to influence their participation; for example, Mexican American elders, historically fearful of deportation, have a more cautious, conservative approach to political involvement. On the other hand, older African Americans who are active in their communities, with a strong sense of citizen duty, an identity as Democrats, and higher levels of education, are more likely to vote (Bazargan et al., 1992). These and earlier findings suggest that differences in the rates of political participation among older people of color do not reflect age

Many older people advocate for their rights.

or ethnic minority identity per se, but rather lower educational levels, feelings of powerlessness, cohort experiences, and real or perceived barriers to voting and other political activities. To public officials and the media, the older electorate is viewed as exerting substantial political influence beyond what their numbers might suggest.

Senior Power

Research on "senior power" reflects an ongoing debate about whether age serves as a catalyst for a viable political movement.

PROPONENTS OF THE "SENIOR POWER" MODEL OF POLITICS   Older people can be a powerful political constituency in the policy-making process because legislators and appointed officials are influenced by public opinion—especially by those who vote and are political party leaders, as is the case with older people (Torres-Gil, 1993). As perceived by a Democratic pollster, "It's virtually impossible to take back the House or win the Presidency without taking back seniors. . . . That makes them the key battleground, and both parties know it" (Toner, 1999). Since the 1980s, older Americans have been portrayed by the media and by some

policy makers as an organized group of "greedy geezers," acting as a monolithic bloc to achieve their interests (Binstock, 1993). Those who believe that older adults have benefited economically at the expense of younger age groups perceive the "tyranny of America's old," united to maintain old-age benefits at the expense of the young, as "one of the most crucial issues facing U.S. society" (Preston, 1984; Smith, 1992).

This perspective of senior power is consistent with the subculture theory of aging, discussed in Chapter 8. This theory suggests that older people, because of common values and experiences, develop a shared political consciousness that is translated into collective action on old-age-related issues (Rix, 1999; Street, 1999). Since future cohorts of older adults will be better educated and healthier and may retire earlier with higher incomes, it is argued that they will have more resources essential to political power. It also assumes that older people in the future will experience increasing pride, dignity, and shared consciousness about old age and thus define problems collectively. From this perspective, age is viewed as becoming a more salient aspect of politics, even if all older persons and their organizations do not speak (or vote) with a unified political voice. Heterogeneity among the older population does not preclude age—as with gender and race—from exerting political influence (Binstock and Day, 1996).

Admittedly, old-age advocacy groups enjoy a number of advantages in the political arena, including (1) large active memberships that can be mobilized to contact policy makers, (2) policy information and expertise, (3) ready informal access to public officials, and (4) widespread public support and legitimacy as public benefit recipients (Day, 1993a). "Senior citizens" have traditionally been one of the prime targets of campaign efforts focused on critical states with large blocs of electoral votes, as vividly illustrated in the 2000 presidential election in Florida. This is because of their aggregate numerical importance and the relative ease with which they can be accessed through age-segregated housing and existing programs such as senior centers, AARP chapters, and congregate meal sites. In fact, an important form of power available to old-age interest groups is "the electoral bluff": the perception of being powerful is, in itself, a source of political influence, even though old-age organizations have been unable to swing a decisive bloc of older voters (Binstock, 2000).

COUNTERARGUMENT: OLDER PEOPLE DO NOT CONSTITUTE A SIGNIFICANT AGE-BASED POLITICAL FORCE

Early critics of the subculture theory argue that the diversity of the older population precludes their having shared interests around which to coalesce. Most older people, especially the young-old, do not identify themselves as "aged," nor do they perceive their problems as stemming from their age. In addition, they are not captives of any single political philosophy, party, or mass organization. In fact, some argue that "The Elderly" is really a category created by policy analysts, pension officials, and outdated models of interest group politics (Heclo, 1988). Since age is only one of many personal characteristics, age alone cannot predict political behavior or age-group consciousness based on differential access to resources. Nor are these self-interests or old-age policy issues the most important factors in their electoral decisions (Binstock, 2000; Torres-Gil, 1992, 1993).

Instead, differences by socioeconomic class, race, gender, and religion increasingly influence older people's political interests. For example, contrary to widely held perceptions, older people are rarely unified about issues affecting the young, such as school levies, and do not vote as a bloc against increasing property taxes to support public schools (Binstock and Day, 1996). Instead, they generally recognize the importance of education for economic productivity. This example suggests that old-age–related issues are not necessarily more important to them than other issues, partisan attachments, or the characteristics of specific candidates. In fact, it appears that older and younger people are more likely to form alliances along economic, racial, ethnic, and ideological lines than to unite horizontally on the basis of age (Binstock and Day, 1996). The national organization Generations United, composed of over 120 organizations of different age groups, represents one such vertical across-age coalition.

As an example of a cross-age, cross-class alliance, poor older people may work with younger welfare beneficiaries for better health insurance for all ages, while upper-income older adults may be more interested in long-term care (Achenbaum, 1993). In the face of federal cuts, future subgroups of older people may become more politically organized, with political agendas different from most of today's senior organizations, especially around issues of means-testing and higher eligibility ages for benefits such as Social Security. For example, lower-income older people have a greater stake in the maintenance and enhancement of Social Security, since it accounts for a larger proportion of their income (Binstock, 1993; Torres-Gil, 1993). Accordingly, the failure of the 1988 Medicare Catastrophic Coverage Act illustrates the fragility of interest-group politics when upper-middle-class older adults were asked to sustain a program that benefited primarily low-income older people.

HISTORICAL DEVELOPMENT OF AGE-BASED GROUPS

At first glance, the number, variety, and strength of age-based national organizations appear to support the perspective that older people are a powerful political force. Age-based organizations are able to build memberships, conduct policy analyses, marshal grassroots support, and utilize direct mail and political action. Conscious organizing of older individuals is not without historical precedent. The first age-based politically oriented interest group grew out of the social and economic dislocations of the Depression. The Townsend Movement proposed a tax on all business transactions to finance a $200/month pension for every pensioner over age 60. However, passage of the Social Security Act in 1935, in which groups of older people played a supporting but not a leading role, took away the Townsend Movement's momentum, and the organization died out in the 1940s. Most political divisions during the turbulent period of the Depression were class- and labor-based rather than age-based. The Townsend

Movement did demonstrate, however, that old age could be a short-term basis for organizing (Binstock and Day, 1996). The McClain Movement, another early age-based organization, aimed to establish financial benefits for older persons through a referendum in the 1938 California elections, but lost followers after economic conditions improved in the 1940s. These early groups did furnish older people with a collective voice and identity, however (Torres-Gil, 1993).

Organized interest groups representing older people did not reemerge until the 1950s and 1960s. Currently, over 1000 separately organized groups for older adults exist at the local, state, and national levels, with at least 100 major national organizations involved in political action on behalf of older persons. In many ways, the diversity of the older population is reflected in the variety of organizations themselves, ranging from mass membership groups to nonmembership staff organizations and associations of professionals or service providers. Yet, the very diversity of these groups reduces their potential to act together as a unified bloc. For example, the National Caucus for the Black Aged, the National Hispanic Council on Aging, and the National Indian Council on Aging were created to address political inequities facing elders of color. They may not act in concert with organizations such as the American Association of Retired Persons (AARP) that represent primarily a white, middle-class constituency.

Three of the largest *mass-membership organizations* are the **National Council of Senior Citizens (NCSC), the National Association of Retired Federal Employees (NARFE),** and the **American Association of Retired Persons (AARP),** together with the National Retired Teachers' Association (NRTA). The National Council of Senior Citizens

(NCSC) was developed by organized labor in the early 1960s with the objective of passing Medicare. Although anyone may join, most members of NCSC are former blue-collar workers who receive insurance and other tangible membership benefits. The National Association of Retired Federal Employees (NARFE) was also formed for a specific political purpose—the passage of the Federal Employees Pension Act in the 1920s. It has since concentrated on bread-and-butter issues for federal employees, such as labor/management relations, rather than broader political issues affecting older persons generally.

The best known and largest of these organizations is the **American Association of Retired Persons (AARP),** with a membership of approximately 33 million—which encompasses 47 percent of the nation's population over age 50, and 13 percent of the population generally. With a modest annual fee, members are attracted by the benefits of lower-cost health insurance, credit cards, travel discounts, and mail-order drugs, and by a myriad of programs related to retirement planning, crime prevention, housing, and widowhood. AARP's magazine, *Modern Maturity,* is the most widely circulated membership periodical in the world. AARP was instrumental in helping to end mandatory retirement based on age and in the initial passage of catastrophic health care legislation, though both pieces of legislation are largely attributable to the initiatives of federal public officials (Binstock, 2000; Binstock and Day, 1996). Others have criticized AARP for moving away from advocacy on behalf of diverse older populations and becoming big business, with questionable organizational practices, despite its tax-exempt status (Binstock, 2000). In the past few years, AARP has lowered the age for membership eligibility to 50, spending

AARP ads feature themes such as "Age is just a number, and life is what you make it" or "You're ready to make this the time of your life. We help make it happen." A recent cover of AARP's magazine, *Modern Maturity,* promised "Great Sex," and carried a picture of actress Susan Sarandon wearing a deep V-necked sweater.

millions of dollars to advertise in popular magazines such as *Time* and *Newsweek* to inform readers and attract new members. AARP no longer uses its full name (American Association of Retired Persons) but only its acronym. These ads attempt to counter the image of AARP as an organization of "old" and "retired" persons. AARP members who appear to be healthy, robust, and successful in their aging, and who resemble only the "young-old," are portrayed in these ads. In this spirit, AARP now sponsors 10K runs and marathons. Such ads and programs reflect AARP's recognition of the huge market for their products with the Baby Boomers.

A wide range of trade associations, professional societies, and coalitions concerned with aging issues also exists. *Trade associations* include:

- the American Association of Homes and Services for the Aged
- the American Nursing Home Association
- the National Council of Health Care Services (consisting of commercial enterprises in the long-term care business, such as the nursing home subsidiary of Holiday Inns)
- the National Association of State Units in Aging (NASUA), which is composed of administrators of state area agencies on aging

The emphasis of trade associations is to obtain federal funds and influence the development of regulations for long-term care facilities and the delivery of public services. Two *professional associations* active in aging policy issues, the Gerontological Society of America (GSA) (which now also includes the Association for Gerontology in Higher Education) and the American Society on Aging (ASA), are composed primarily of gerontological researchers, educators, and practitioners from many disciplines. The major confederation of social welfare agencies concerned with aging is the National Council on the Aging (NCOA), which encompasses over 2000 organized affiliates, including public and private health, social work, and community action agencies.

Several organizations that began at the grassroots level now have nationwide membership and recognition. The Older Women's League (OWL), founded in 1981, brings together people concerned about issues affecting older women, especially health care and insurance, Social Security, pensions, and caregiving. It advocates for older women both in the federal policy-making process and within the programs of national associations such as the Gerontological Society of America. Women activists within OWL represent a trend away from the comparatively lower rates of past political participation among older women. The Gray Panthers, founded by the late Maggie Kuhn, aimed to form grassroots intergenerational alliances around issues affecting all ages. Since Maggie Kuhn's death, the Gray Panthers' social change efforts have declined.

POLITICAL ACTIVISM AND OLDER WOMEN

Tish Sommers is an example of the increasing political activism of older women. Sommers, a long-time homemaker, learned about the vulnerability of older women when she was divorced at age 57. She found that newly single homemakers her age had a hard time getting benefits that people who have been employed take for granted. She coined the term *displaced homemaker* and built a force of women. They successfully lobbied for centers where displaced homemakers had job training during the late 1970s.

In 1980, she and Laurie Shields founded the Older Women's League, a national organization that has grown to over 14,000 members and over 100 chapters. Her maxim always was "Don't agonize, organize." During the 6 years of organizing OWL, Sommers also fought a battle with cancer. Even at her death in 1986, she was still fighting, organizing groups nationally around the right to maintain control over the conditions of one's death.

On certain issues such as health care reform, the influence of organizations of older people has been limited relative to powerful interest groups such as the insurance, medical, and pharmaceutical industries. For example, none of President Clinton's 1997 appointments to the National Bipartisan Commission on the Future of Medicare was representative of organized old-age interests (Binstock, 2000; Day, 1993a). Nevertheless, until recently, most politicians did not want to offend age-based organizations and constituencies. After higher-income older people organized to influence Congress to repeal the 1988 Medicare Catastrophic Coverage Act, no proposals concerning seniors got out of committees in the next Congressional election year.

Whether older people act as a unified bloc, many policy makers act as if there were a "politics of age" founded on cohort-based interest groups, and politicians continue to count the votes of older persons. Presidential candidates in the 2000 election actively courted the senior vote, advocating widely different proposals for Social Security and prescription drug coverage. Even if older people cannot effect the passage of legislation, they can at least block changes in existing policies, especially when programs such as Social Security and Medicare are threatened. Perceptions of such influence then affect whether major changes in policies on aging are viewed as feasible, even though the political legitimacy of old-age interest groups has eroded over the past decade (Binstock, 2000; Binstock and Day, 1996).

Some national age-based organizations are criticized for being biased toward the interests of middle- and upper-working-class older people. AARP, for example, is criticized for advancing only the interests of its primarily middle-class membership, for recruiting members largely on the basis of selective incentives and direct member services (e.g., insurance, drug discounts, and travel), and for imposing its policy agenda on its members (Pear, 1995). In recent years, however, age-based organizations have not only reached out to lower-income older persons, but also collaborated with other groups; this is reflected by the cross-age coalitions that have formed around health and long-term care. In addition to national associations, a wide range of organizations at the local and state levels have mobilized around intergenerational and cross-class issues such as affordable public transportation, safe streets, and low-cost health care (Binstock and Day, 1996).

In sum, despite the growth of age-based organizations, the senior power model appears to have little validity with respect to older adults' voting behavior and political attitudes. Old age per se is currently not a primary basis for political mobilization, despite images of homogenous senior groups put forth by politicians, the media, and age-based organizations. With regard to the future, it can be predicted that the senior boomers will cast a higher total vote in national elections than occurs today; on the other hand, the heterogeneity of the Baby Boom cohort suggests that age will not form the primary basis for political behavior (Binstock, 2000). Intergenerational alliances and policies are likely to be most important in influencing policies, as further discussed in Chapter 16.

SUMMARY AND IMPLICATIONS

Paid employment is typically associated with productivity in our society. Increasingly, however, Americans are retiring in their early sixties and looking forward to two to three decades of leisure time in relatively good health. Health status, income, and attitudes toward the job influence the decision about when to retire. Most retirees adjust well to this important transition and are satisfied with the quality of their lives. Those with good health, higher-status jobs, adequate income, and existing social networks and leisure interests are most likely to be satisfied. Not all retirement is desired, however; many older people would prefer the opportunity for part-time work, but are unable to find suitable and flexible options. Preparation for the retirement transition is beneficial, but planning assistance is generally not available to those who need it most—workers who have less education, lower job status, and lower retirement incomes. Retirement by itself does not cause poor health or loss of identity and self-esteem. Dissatisfaction in this stage of life is more often due to poor health and low income.

Although a smaller percentage of older people have incomes below the poverty line than was true in the past, more older than younger people live at marginal economic levels. Social Security is the major source of retirement income for a large proportion of the older population; those who depend on Social Security alone are the poorest older group. Private pensions tend to be small in relation to previous earnings, be subject to attrition through inflation, and go primarily to workers in large, unionized, or industrialized settings. Income from assets is distributed unequally among the older population, with a small number of older persons receiving sizable amounts from savings and investments, whereas the most common asset of older people is their home, which provides no immediate income. In addition to those older adults who are officially counted as living below the poverty line, many others live near this level, and many are "hidden" poor who live in nursing homes or with their families. Frail, unmarried women—ethnic minority women, especially—are the most likely to live in or near poverty. Public assistance programs such as SSI have not removed the very serious financial problems of the older poor.

The trends toward greater longevity, early retirement, low rates of labor-force participation, and pockets of poverty among older women, ethnic minorities, and the oldest-old suggest that a growing problem for the United States is the increase in the relative size of an older population encouraged not to work. The increased segmentation of life into a period of full-time work and one of total or partial retirement is, to a great extent, a product of our present pension systems. Changes that are needed include greater flexibility in the workplace, part-time work options, and a gradual transition from full-time productive work to leisure activities and retirement.

As earlier chapters have documented, changes in employment and parenting roles, income, and

physical and sensory capacities often have detrimental social consequences for older adults. Nevertheless, there are arenas in which older people may still experience meaningful involvement and develop new opportunities and skills, consistent with the broader definition of productive aging that includes nonpaid contributions to society. This chapter has considered six of these arenas: leisure pursuits, voluntary association membership, volunteering, education, religious involvement, and political activity. The meaning and functions of participation in these arenas are obviously highly individualized. Participation may be a means to strengthen and build informal social networks, influence wider social policies, serve other persons, and substitute for role changes. The extent of involvement is influenced not by age alone, but also by a variety of other salient factors including gender, ethnic minority status, health, socioeconomic status, and educational level.

Because of the number of interacting variables, age-related patterns in participation are not clearly defined. There are some general age-related differences in types of leisure pursuits; with increasing age, people tend to engage in more sedentary, inner-directed, and routine pursuits in their homes than social activities or obligations outside the home. Changes in organizational participation and volunteering are less clearly age-related. Participation in voluntary associations stabilizes or declines only slightly with old age; declines that do occur are likely to be associated with poor health, inadequate income, and transportation problems. Volunteering, which is higher among the older population than other age groups, tends to represent a lifelong pattern of community service.

Past research on religious and political participation has pointed inaccurately to declines in old age. Although formal religious participation such as church or synagogue attendance appears to diminish slightly, other activities such as reading religious texts or listening to religious broadcasts increase. Religiosity appears to be an effective way of coping, particularly among ethnic minority elders. Spirituality is differentiated from religion as a positive factor in older people's physical and mental well-being and their quality of life.

Voting by older people has increased since the 1980s. Declines in voting and political participation in the past may have been a function of low educational status or physical limitations, not of age per se. In fact, older persons' skills and experiences may be more valued in the political arena than in other spheres. The extent to which older people form a unified political bloc that can influence politicians and public policy is debatable. Some argue that older adults form a subculture with a strong collective consciousness; others point to their increasing diversity and political inequity, as apparent with the Medicare Catastrophic Health Care legislation.

Most forms of organizational involvement appear to represent stability across the life course; the knowledge and skills necessary for a varied set of activities in old age are generally developed in early or middle adulthood and maintained into later life. On the other hand, preretirement patterns of productivity are not fixed; individuals can develop new interests and activities in later life, often with the assistance of senior centers, continuing education programs, or community or special interest organizations.

GLOSSARY

Age Discrimination in Employment Act (ADEA) federal law that protects workers age 45 and over from denial of employment strictly because of age

American Association of Retired Persons (AARP) national organization open to all adults age 50 and over, offering a wide range of informational materials, discounted services and products, and a powerful lobby

American Society on Aging (ASA) association of practitioners and researchers interested in gerontology

assets an individual's savings, home equity, and personal property

displaced homemakers widowed or divorced women under age 60 who do not yet qualify for Social Security benefits but may lack the skills for employment

Elderhostel program in which older adults can take inexpensive, short-term academic programs associated with colleges and universities around the world

Employment Retirement Income Security Act (ERISA) 1974 legislation to regulate pensions

feminization of poverty variety of factors that lead to higher proportions of poverty among women than men

Foster Grandparents Program volunteer program pairing seniors with children with special needs

Generations United a national intergenerational coalition

Gerontological Society of America (GSA) an association of researchers, educators, and practitioners interested in gerontology and geriatrics

Gray Panthers a national organization, founded by Maggie Kuhn, that encourages intergenerational alliances around social issues

leisure time (not devoted to "work") when one has options in selecting activities

National Association of Retired Federal Employees (NARFE) national organization of adults retired from the federal government, primarily involved in political and social issues

National Council of Senior Citizens (NCSC) mass-membership organization involved in political action for older adults

National Council on the Aging (NCOA) national organization of over 2000 social welfare agencies concerned with aging that provides technical consultation and is involved in federal legislative activities

Older American Volunteer Program federally sponsored volunteer program that recruits older people to work with disadvantaged groups

Older Women's League (OWL) a national organization, formed by Tish Sommers and Laurie Shields, concerned about issues affecting older women

Retired Senior Volunteer Program (RSVP) federally sponsored program in which older adults volunteer in schools, hospitals, and other social agencies

retirement the period of life, usually starting between age 60 and 65, during which an individual stops working in the paid labor force

Senior Community Services Employment Program (SCSEP) programs sponsored by government or business that encourage the employment of older workers

Senior Companion Program   a volunteer program in which seniors assist other seniors

senior learning programs   academic programs specially designed for older adults, or programs of tuition waivers that allow older adults to take college courses at no cost

Senior Net   national educational program that teaches computer skills and provides opportunities for on-line communication

serial retirement   term to describe individuals who move in and out of the workforce

Service Corps of Retired Executives (SCORE)   a program that links executives as technical and financial consultants with companies in the United States and abroad asking for assistance

Social Security   federal program into which workers contribute a portion of their income during adulthood and then, beginning sometime between age 62 and 65, receive a monthly check based on the amount they have earned/contributed

spirituality   believing in one's relationship with a higher power without being religious in the sense of organized religion

Supplemental Security Income (SSI)   federal program to provide a minimal income for low-income older people (and other age groups with disabilities)

vesting of pension benefits   amount of time a person must work on a job in order to acquire rights to a pension

RESOURCES

See the companion Website for this text at <www.ablongman.com/hooyman> for information about the following:

- ACTION
- American Association of Retired Persons (AARP)
- Elderhostel
- Federal Council on Aging
- Generations United
- Grey Panthers
- National Association of Retired Federal Employees
- National Council on the Aging Inc. (NCOA)
- National Council of Senior Citizens (NCSC)

REFERENCES

Abramoritz, M., Grossinger, K., and Sachs, J. S. *The Social Security primer: An advocacy tool.* For the Social Welfare Action Alliance, 2000.

Achenbaum, W. A. Generational relations in historical context. In V. L. Bengtson and W. A. Achenbaum (Eds.), *The changing contract across generations.* New York: Aldine de Gruyter, 1993.

Achenbaum, W. A., and Morrison, M. H. Is unretirement unprecedented? In S. A. Bass, F. G. Caro, and Y-P Chen (Eds.), *Achieving a productive aging society.* Westport, CT: Auburn House, 1993.

Administration on Aging. *Profile of Older Americans: 1999.* Washington, DC: 1999.

Administration on Aging. *Aging into the 21st century.* Washington, DC: 1997.

Allen, K., and Chin-Sang, V. A lifetime of work: The context and meaning of leisure for aging black women. *The Gerontologist,* 1990, *30,* 734–740.

Alwin, D. The political impact on the baby boom: Are there persistent generational differences in political beliefs and behaviors? *Generations,* Spring 1998, *22,* 46–54.

American Association of Retired Persons (AARP). *A profile of older Americans, 1990.* Washington, DC: AARP, 1991.

Atchley, R. C. *Aging: Continuity or change.* Belmont, CA: Wadsworth, 1983.

Atchley, R. C. Continuity of the spiritual self. In M. A. Kimble (Ed.), *Aging, spirituality, and religion: A handbook.* Minneapolis, MN: Fortress Press, 1995.

Atchley, R. C. Critical perspective on retirement. In T. Cole, W. A. Achenbaum, P. L. Jakobi, and R. Kastenbaum (Eds.), *Voices and visions of aging: Toward a critical gerontology.* New York: Springer Publishing, 1993.

Atchley, R. C. Retirement and leisure participation: Continuity or crisis? *The Gerontologist,* 1971, *11,* 13–17.

Atchley, R. C. Incorporating spirituality into professional work in aging. *Aging Today,* July/August 1999, 17.

Atchley, R. C. *The sociology of retirement.* New York: Wiley/Schenkman, 1976.

Bammel, L. L. B., and Bammel, G. Leisure and recreation. In J. E. Birren and K. W. Schaie (Eds.), *Handbook of the psychology of aging* (2nd ed.). New York: Van Nostrand Reinhold, 1985.

Barusch, A. S. Religion, adversity and age: Religious experiences of low income elderly women. *Journal of Sociology and Social Welfare*, March 1999, *26*, 125–142.

Bazargan, M., Barbre, A., and Torres-Gil, F. Voting behavior among low-income black elderly: A multi-election perspective. *The Gerontologist*, 1992, *32*, 584–591.

Binstock, R. H. The 1996 election: Older voters and implications for policies on aging. *The Gerontologist*, 1997, *37*, 15–19.

Binstock, R. H. The aged as scapegoat. *The Gerontologist*, 1983, *23*, 136–143.

Binstock, R. H. The implications of population aging for American politics. Paper delivered at the annual meeting of the American Political Science Association, Chicago, September 1987.

Binstock, R. H. Older people and voting participation: past and future. *The Gerontologist*, 2000, *40*, 18–31.

Binstock, R. H. Older voters and the 1992 Presidential election. *The Gerontologist*, 1993, *32*, 601–606.

Binstock, R. H. Reframing the agenda of policies on aging. In M. Minkler and C. Estes (Eds.), *Readings in the political economy of aging*. Farmingdale, NY: Baywood, 1984.

Binstock, R. H., and Day, C. L. Aging and politics. In R. H. Binstock and L. K. George (Eds.), *Handbook of aging and the social sciences*. San Diego, CA: Academic Press, 1996.

Binstock, R. H., Levin, M. A., and Weatherley, R. The political dilemmas of social intervention. In R. H. Binstock and E. Shanas (Eds.), *Handbook of aging and the social sciences* (2nd ed.). New York: Van Nostrand Reinhold, 1985.

Binstock, R. H., and Murray, T. The politics of developing appropriate care for dementia. In R. H. Binstock, S. G. Post, and P. Whitehouse (Eds.), *Dementia and aging: Ethics, values and policy choices*. Baltimore, MD: Johns Hopkins University Press, 1991.

Black, H. K. Life as gift: Spiritual narratives of elderly African-American women living in poverty. *Journal of Aging Studies*, Winter 1999, *13*, 441–455.

Blazer, D. Spirituality and aging well. *Generations*, Winter 1991, *15*, 61–65.

Burke, K. J. *Health, mental health, and spirituality in chronically ill elders*. Dissertation Abstract, University of Chicago, 1999.

Button, J. W., and Rosenbaum, W. A. Seeing gray: School bond issues and the aging in Florida. *Research on Aging*, 1989, *11*, 158–173.

Campbell, A. Social and psychological determinants of voting behavior. In W. Donohue and C. Tibbits (Eds.), *Politics of age*. Ann Arbor: University of Michigan, 1962.

Caro, F. G., and Bass, S. A. Receptivity to volunteering in the immediate postretirement period. *Journal of Applied Gerontology*, 1997 Dec., *16*, 427–441.

Caro, F. G., Bass, S. A., and Chen, Y-P. Introduction: Achieving a productive aging society. In S. A. Bass, F. G. Caro, and Y-P Chen (Eds.), *Achieving a productive aging society*. Westport, CT: Auburn House, 1993.

Cascio, W. F. Learning from outcomes: Financial experiences of 300 firms that have downsized. In M. Growling, J. Kraft, and J. C. Quick (Eds.), *The new organizational reality: Downsizing, restructuring and revitalization*. Washington, DC: American Psychological Association, 1998.

Chambré, S. M. Is volunteering a substitute for role loss in old age? An empirical test of activity theory. *The Gerontologist*, 1984, *23*, 292–299.

Chambré, S. M. Volunteerism by elders: Past trends and future prospects. *The Gerontologist*, 1993, *33*, 221–228.

Chatfield, D. L. Expectations of civic intrastructure in an age-restricted retirement community: Implications for community development. *Dissertation Abstracts International, A: The Humanities and Social Sciences*, 1999, *60*, 2250A–2251A.

Chatters, L. M., and Taylor, L. J. Religious involvement among older African-Americans. In J. S. Levin (Ed.), *Religion in aging and health: Theoretical foundations and methodological frontiers*. Thousand Oaks, CA: Sage, 1994.

Choi, N. G. Racial differences in timing and factors associated with retirement. *Journal of Sociology and Social Welfare*, Sept. 1994, *21*, 31–52.

Choi, N. Long-term elderly widows and divorcees: Similarities and differences. *Journal of Women and Aging*, 1995, *7*, 69–72.

Clark, R. L., Ghent, L., and Heeden, A. Retiree health insurance and pension coverage: Variations by firm characteristics. *Journals of Gerontology*, 1994, *49*, S553–561.

Couch, K. A. Late life job displacement. *The Gerontologist*, 1998, *38*, 7–17.

Crystal, S. Economic status of the elderly. In R. H. Binstock and L. K. George (Eds.), *Handbook of aging and the social sciences*. San Diego, CA: Academic Press, 1996.

Cutler, N. E. Introduction: Financial dimensions of aging—and middle age. *Generations*, 1997, *21*, 5–8.

Cutler, S. J., and Hendricks, J. Age differences in voluntary association memberships: Fact or artifact. *Journals of Gerontology*, 2000, *55B*, S98–S107.

Cutler, S. J., and Hendricks, J. Leisure and time use across the lifecourse. In R. Binstock and L. K. George (Eds.), *Aging and the social sciences* (3rd ed.). New York: Academic Press, 1990.

Danigelis, N. C., and McIntosh, B. R. Resources and the productive activity of elders: Race and gender as contexts. *Journals of Gerontology*, 1993, *48B*, S192–S203.

Day, C. L. Older Americans' attitudes toward the Medicare Catastrophic Coverage Act of 1988. *Journal of Politics*, 1993b, *55*, 167–177.

Day, C. L. The organized elderly: Perilous, powerless, or progressive. *The Gerontologist*, 1993a, *33*, 426–427.

Day, C. L. *What older Americans think: Interest groups and aging policy*. Princeton, NJ: Princeton University Press, 1990.

Devlin, S., and Arye, L. The Social Security debate: A financial crisis or a new retirement paradigm. *Generations*, Summer 1997, *21*, 27–34.

Dietz, B. E., and Carrozza, M. *Gender differences in retirement planning: The influence of status, human capital, and occupational structure*. American Sociological Association, 1999.

Dilworth-Anderson, P., Williams, S. W. and Cooper, T. Family Caregiving to Elderly African Americans: Caregiver Types and Structures. *Journals of Gerontology*, 1999, *54B*, S237–S241.

Dobson, D. The elderly as a political force. In W. Browne and L. K. Olson (Eds.), *Aging and public policy*. Westport, CT: Greenwood Press, 1983.

Dodson, D. The Contingent workforce: Implications for today's and tomorrow's midlife and older women. *AARP Women's Initiative Fact Sheet*, 1996, D14561.

Drentea, P. The best or worst years of our lives? The effects of retirement and activity characteristics on well-being. *Dissertation Abstracts International, A: The Humanities and Social Sciences*, 1999, *60*, 1771A.

Ekerdt, D. J. The busy ethic: Moral continuity between work and retirement. *The Gerontologist*, 1986, *26*, 239–244.

Ekerdt, D. J., and DeViney, S. Evidence for a pre-retirement process among older male workers. *Journals of Gerontology*, 1993, *48B*, S35–S43.

Ekerdt, D. J., DeViney, S. S., and Kosloski, K. Profiling plans for retirement. *Journals of Gerontology*, 1996, *51B*, S140–S149.

Ekerdt, D. J., Kosloski, L., and DeViney, S. The normative anticipation of retirement by older workers. *Research on Aging*, Jan. 2000, *22*, 3–22.

Erickson, M. A., and Dempster-McClain, D. The aging self: Role identities following the transition to a continuing care retirement community. American Sociological Association, 1998.

Fallon, P. E. An ethnographic study: Personal meaning and successful aging of individuals 85 years and older. *Dissertation Abstracts International: Section B: The Sciences and Engineering*, Feb. 1998, *58*.

Feher, S., and Maly, R. C. Coping with breast cancer in later life: The role of religious faith. *Psycho-Oncology*, Sept.-Oct. 1999, *8*, 408–416.

Feuerbach, E., and Erdwins, C. Women's retirement: The influence of work history. *Journal of Women and Aging*, 1994, *6*, 69.

Fischer, K. *Winter grace. Spirituality for the later years*. New York: Paulist Press, 1985.

Fischer, L. R., and Schaffer, K. B. *Older Volunteers: A guide to research and practice*. Newbury Park, CA: Sage Publications, 1993.

Flippen, C., and Tienda, M. Pathways to Retirement: Patterns of Labor Force Participation and Labor Market Exit Among the Pre-Retirement Population by Race, Hispanic Origin, and Sex. *Journal of Gerontology*, 2000, *55B*, S14–S27.

Floyd, F. J., Haynes, S. N., Doll, E. R., and Winemiller, D., et al. Assessing retirement satisfaction and perceptions of retirement experiences. *Psychology and Aging*, Dec. 1992, *7*, 609–621.

Forbes, L. Spirituality, aging and the community-dwelling caregivers and care recipients. *Geriatric Nursing*, 1994, *15*, 297–302.

Fudge, E. Recently retired non-professional men and their perceptions of retirement. *Australasian Journal on Aging*, 1998, *17*, 90–94.

Gall, T. L., Evans, D. R., and Howard, J. The retirement adjustment process: Changes in the well-being of male retirees across time. *Journals of Gerontology*, 1995, *52B*, P110–P117.

Gallo, W. T., Bradley, E. H., Siegel, M., and Kasl, S. V. Health effects of involuntary job loss among older workers: Findings from the health and retirement survey. *Journals of Gerontology*, 2000, *55B*, S131–S140.

Gallup, G. J., and Jones, J. *One hundred questions and answers: Religion in America.* Princeton, NJ: Princeton Research Center, 1989.

Glass, J. C., Jr., and Kilpatrick, B. B. Financial planning for retirement: An imperative for baby boomer women. *Educational Gerontology,* Sept. 1998, *24,* 595–617.

Goyer, A. Intergenerational Shared-Site Programs. *Generations,* Winter 1998–99, 79–80.

Gramlish, E. M. *Social Security in the 21st Century.* The Nineteenth Leon and Josephine Winkelman Lecture Presentation, University of Michigan, 2000.

Gurin, P., Hatchett, S., and Jackson, J. S. *Hope and independence: Blacks' response to electoral and party politics.* New York: Russell Sage Foundation, 1989.

Hardy, M., and Kruse, K. Realigning retirement income: The politics of growth. *Generations,* Spring 1998, *22,* 22–28.

Hardy, M., and Quadagno, J. Satisfaction with early retirement: Making choices in the auto industry. *Journals of Gerontology,* 1995, *50B,* S217–S228.

Hayward, M. D., Friedman, S., and Chen, H. Race inequities in men's retirement. *Journals of Gerontology,* 1996, *51B,* S1–S10.

Hendricks, J., Hatch, L. R., and Cutler, S. J. Entitlements, social compacts, and the trend toward retrenchment in U.S. old-age programs. *Hallym International Journal of Aging,* 1999, *1,* 14–32.

Henretta, J. C. Changing perspectives on retirement. *Journals of Gerontology,* 1997, *52B,* S1–S3.

Herzog, A. R., and Morgan, J. N. Formal volunteer work among older Americans. In S. A. Bass, F. G. Caro, and Y-P. Chen (Eds.), *Achieving a productive aging society.* Westport, CT: Auburn House, 1993, 119–142.

Hobbs, F., and Damon, B. L. *65+ in the United States.* Washington, DC: U.S. Department of Commerce, Bureau of the Census, Current Population Reports, 1996.

Hogan, R., and Perrucci, C. C. Producing and reproducing class and status differences: Racial and gender gaps in U.S. employment and retirement income. *Social Problems,* 1998, *45,* 528–549.

Hudson, R. B., and Binstock, R. Political systems and aging. In R. Binstock and E. Shanas (Eds.), *Handbook of aging and the social sciences.* New York: Van Nostrand Reinhold, 1976.

Hudson, R. B., and Strate, J. Aging and political systems. In R. Binstock and E. Shanas (Eds.), *Hand-*book of aging and the social sciences (2nd ed.). New York: Van Nostrand Reinhold, 1985.

Hyer, L., Jacob, M. R., and Pattison, E. M. Later life struggles: Psychological/spiritual convergence. *Journal of Pastoral Care,* 1987, *41,* 141–149.

Idler, E. L., and Kasl, S. V. Religion among disabled and nondisabled persons II: Attendance at religious services as a predictor of the course of disability. *Journals of Gerontology,* 1997, *52B,* S306–S316.

Johnson, R. W., Sambamoorthi, U., and Crystal, S. Gender Differences in Pension Wealth: Estimates Using Provider Data. *The Gerontologist,* 1999, *39,* 320–333.

Juster, F. T., Saldo, B., Kington, R. S., and Mitchell, O. *Aging well: Health, wealth, and retirement.* Washington, DC: Consertium of Social Science Associations, 1996.

Kasl, S. V., & Jones, B. A. The impact of job loss and retirement on health. In L. F. Berkman and I. Kawachi (Eds.), *Social epidemiology.* New York: Oxford University Press, 2000.

Kasper, J. *Aging alone: Profiles and projections.* Baltimore, MD: Commonwealth Fund, 1988.

Kaufman, S. R. *The ageless self.* New York: New American Library, 1986.

Kavanaugh, K. M. The importance of spirituality. *Journal of Long-Term Care Administration,* 1997, *24,* 29–31.

Kaye, J., and Robinson, K. M. Spirituality among caregivers. *Image Journal Nursing Scholarship,* 1994, *26,* 218–221.

Kaye, L. W., and Alexander, L. B. Perceptions of job discrimination among lower-income, elderly part-timers. *Journal of Gerontological Social Work,* 1995, *23,* 99–120.

Koenig, H. G. *Aging and God: Spiritual pathways to mental health in midlife and later years.* New York: Haworth Pastoral Press, 1995.

Koenig, H. G., Cohen, H. J., Blazer, D. G., Pieper, D., Meador, K. G., Shelp, F., Goli, V., Veeraindor, G., and DiPasquale, B. Religious coping and depression among elderly, hospitalized medically ill men. *American Journal of Psychiatry,* 1992, *149,* 1693–1700.

Koenig, H. G., Kvale, H., and Ferrel, C. Religion and well-being in later life. *The Gerontologist,* 1988, *28,* 18–28.

Koenig, H. G., Pargament, K. I., and Nielsen, J. Religious coping and health status in medically ill hospitalized older adults. *Journal of Nervous and Mental Disease,* Sept. 1998, *186,* 513–521.

Krain, M. A. Policy implications for a society aging well: Employment, retirement, education, and leisure policies for the 21st century. *American Behavioral Scientist,* Nov.-Dec. 1995, *39,* 131–151.

Krause, N. Religiosity and self-esteem among older adults. *Journals of Gerontology,* 1995, *50B,* P236–P246.

Krout, J. *Senior centers in America.* Westport, CT: Greenwood, 1989.

Krout, J., Cutler, S. J., and Coward, R. T. Correlates of senior center participation: A national analysis. *The Gerontologist,* 1990, *30,* 72–79.

Lawton, M. P., Moss, M., and Fulcomer, M. Objective and subjective uses of time by older people. *International Journal of Aging and Human Development,* 1986–87, *24,* 171–188.

Leifer, R. Psychological and spiritual factors in chronic illness. *American Behavioral Scientist,* 1996, *39,* 752–66.

Levin, J. S. *Religion in aging and health: Theoretical foundations and methodological frontiers.* Thousand Oaks, CA: Sage Publications, 1994.

Levin, J. S., Chatters, L. M., and Taylor, R. J. Religious effects on health status and life satisfaction among Black Americans. *Journals of Gerontology,* 1995, *50B,* S154–S169

Levin, J. S., and Taylor, R. J. Age differences in patterns and correlates of the frequency of prayer. *The Gerontologist,* 1997, *37,* 75–88.

Levin, J. S., Taylor, R. J., and Chatters, L. M. Race and gender differences in religiosity among older adults: Findings from four national surveys. *Journals of Gerontology,* 1994, *49,* S137–S145.

Levine, S. The hidden health care system. *Medical Care,* 1983, *21,* 378.

Martin-Matthews, A. Widowhood and widerhood. *Encyclopedia of Gerontology,* 1996, *2,* 621–625.

McCrea, J. M., Nichols, A., and Newman, S. (Eds.). *Intergenerational Service-Learning in Gerontology: A Compendium.* The Corporation for National Service, Generations Together, University Center for Social and Urban Research, University of Pittsburgh, 1998.

McFadden, S., and Gerl, R. Approaches to understanding spirituality in the second half of life. *Generations,* Fall 1990, *14,* 35–38.

McKenzie, R. The retreat of the elderly welfare state. *Wall Street Journal,* March 12, 1991, 29.

McIntosh, B. R., and Danigelis, N. C. Race, gender and the relevance of productive activity for elders' affect. *Journals of Gerontology,* 1995, *50B,* S229–S239.

McLaughlin, D., and Jensen, C. Poverty among older Americans: The plight of non-metropolitan elders. *Journals of Gerontology,* 1993, *48,* S44–S54.

McManus, S. A., and Tenpas, K. D. The changing political activism patterns of older Americans: "Don't throw dirt over us yet." In J. S. Steckenrider and T. M. Parrott (Eds.), *New directions in old-age policies* (pp. 111–130). Albany: State University of New York Press, 1998.

Mickley, J. R., Carson, V., and Soeken, K. Religion and adult mental health. *Issues in Mental Health and Nursing,* 1995, *16,* 345–360.

Middleton, F. Computers for seniors. In R. Harootyan (Ed.), *Resourceful aging: Today and tomorrow, Vol. V* (pp. 75–78). Washington, DC: American Association of Retired Persons, 1991.

Miller, S. The social dilemmas of the aging leisure participant. In A. Rose and W. Peterson (Eds.), *Older people and their social world.* Philadelphia: F. A. Davis, 1965.

Mitchell, O. S., and Moore, J. F. Can Americans afford to retire? New evidence on retirement saving adequacy. *The Journal of Risk and Insurance,* 1998, *65,* 371–400.

Moen, P. Gender, age and the life course. In R. H. Binstock and L. K. George (Eds.), *Handbook of aging and the social sciences.* San Diego, CA: Academic Press, 1996.

Moen, P. *Retirement and well-being: Does community participation replace paid work?* American Sociological Association, 1999.

Moen, P., Erickson, M. A., and Dempster-McClain, D. *Role occupancy, role identity, and role satisfaction in a continuing care retirement community.* International Sociological Association, 1998.

Moody, H. R. A strategy for productive aging: Education in later life. In S. A. Bass, F. G. Caro, and Y-P Chen (Eds.), *Achieving a productive aging society.* Westport, CT: Auburn House, 1993.

Mon-Barak, M., and Tynson, M. Older workers and the workplace: A new challenge of occupational social work. *Social Work,* 1993, *38,* 45–55.

Muffels, R. J. A. Aging and flexibilization. Caveats or Challenges for the welfare state? *Sociologicky-Casopis,* 1998, *34(3),* 285–302.

Musick, M. A., Herzog, A. R., and House, J. S. Volunteering and mortality among older adults: Findings from a national sample. *Journals of Gerontology,* 1999, *54B(3),* S173–S180.

Mutchler, J. E., Burr, J. A., Massagli, M. P., and Pienta, A. Work Transitions and Health in Later Life. *Journals of Gerontology,* 1999, *54B(5),* S252–S261.

Mutchler, J. E., Burr, J. A., Pienta, A. M., and Massagli, M. P. Pathways to labor force exit: Work transitions and work instability. *Journals of Gerontology,* 1997, *52B,* S4–S12.

National Academy on Aging. *Facts on Social Security: The old age and survivors trust fund.* Washington, DC, July 1996.

National Academy on an Aging Society. *Who are young retirees and older workers?* Data Profile. Washington, DC, June 2000.

National Committee to Preserve Social Security and Medicare. *Facts on SSI.* Washington, D.C. 2000.

National Economic Council, Interagency Working Group on Social Security. *Women and Retirement Security,* 1998.

Neill, C. M., and Kahn, A. S. The role of personal spirituality and religious social activity on the life satisfaction of older widowed women. *Sex Roles,* 1999, *40(3–4),* 319–329.

Nordquist, G. 1999. American health care and the medicalization of dying. *Journal of Applied Social Sciences,* 1999, *23(2),* 31–42.

Okada, S. Health and earned income: Recursive and non-recursive models. *Dissertation Abstracts International, Section A: Humanities and Social Sciences,* Sept. 1997, *58(3-A),* 1095.

Ozawa, M. N. *The economic well-being of the elderly in a changing society.* The Seventeenth Annual Leon and Josephine Winkelman Lecture, Ann Arbor: University of Michigan, School of Social Work, December 2, 1996.

Ozawa, M. N., and Lum, Y. S. Marital status and change in income status 10 years after retirement. *Social Work Research,* June 1998, *22(2),* 116–128.

Paloutzian, R. F., and Ellison, C. W. Loneliness and quality of life measures: Measuring loneliness, spiritual well-being and their social and emotional correlates. In L. A. Peplau and D. Perlman (Eds.), *Loneliness: A sourcebook of current theory, research and therapy.* New York: Wiley Inter-Science, 1982.

Park, N. H., and Gilbert, N. Social Security and the incremental privatization of retirement income. *Journal of Sociology and Social Welfare,* 1999, *26(2),* 187–202.

Pear, R. Senator challenges the practices of a retirees association. *New York Times,* p. A14, June 14, 1995.

Pratt, H. J. *Gray agendas: Interest groups and public pensions in Canada, Britain and the United States.* Ann Arbor: University of Michigan Press, 1993.

Preston, S. H. Children and the elderly in the United States. *Scientific American,* 1984, *251,* 44–49.

Quadagno, J., and Hardy, M. Work and retirement. In R. H. Brinstock and L. K. George (Eds.), *Handbook of aging and the social sciences.* San Diego, CA: Academic Press, 1996.

Quinn, J. F., and Burkhauser, R. V. Labor market obstacles to aging productively. In S. A. Bass, F. G. Caro, and Y-P Chen (Eds.), *Achieving a productive aging society.* Westport, CT: Auburn House, 1993.

Ralston, P. Senior centers and minority elders: A critical review. *The Gerontologist,* 1991, *31,* 325–331.

Ramirez, A. Making better use of older workers. *Fortune,* January 1989, 179–182.

Rank, M. R., and Hirschl, T. A. Estimating the proportion of Americans ever experiencing poverty during their elderly years. *Journals of Gerontology,* 1999, *54B(4),* S184–S193.

Reitzes, D. C., Mutran, E. J., and Fernandez, M. E. The decision to retire: A career perspective. *Social Science Quarterly,* 1998, *79(3),* 607–619.

Reitzes, D.C., Mutran, E., and Fernandez, E. Preretirement influences on post-retirement self-esteem. *Journals of Gerontology,* 1996, *51B,* S242–S249.

Reitzes, D. C., and Reitzes, D. C. Metro services in action: A case study of a citywide senior organization. *The Gerontologist,* 1991, *31,* 256–266.

Richardson, V. E. How circumstances of widowhood and retirement affect adjustment among older men. *Journal of Mental Health and Aging,* Summer 1999, *5(2),* 165–174.

Riddick, C., and Stewart, D. An examination of the life satisfaction and importance of leisure in the lives of older female retirees: A comparison of blacks to whites. *Journal of Leisure Research,* 1994, *26,* 75–87.

Rix, S. E. The politics of old age in the United States. In A. Walker and G. Naegele (Eds.), *The politics of old age in Europe* (pp. 178–196). Buckingham, PA: Open University Press, 1999.

Ross, C. E., and Drentea, P. Consequences of retirement activities for distress and the sense of personal control. *Journal of Health and Social Behavior,* Dec. 1998, *39(4),* 317–334.

Ruhm, C. J. Gender differences in employment behavior during late middle life. *Journals of Gerontology,* 1996, *51B,* S11–S17.

Settersten, R. A., Jr. Time, age, and the transition to retirement: New evidence on life course flexibility? *International Journal of Aging and Human Development,* 1998, *47(3),* 177–203.

Simon-Riesinowitz, L., Wilson, L., Marks, L., Kroch, C., and Welch, C. Future work and retirement needs: Policy experts and baby boomers express their views. *Generations,* Spring 1998, *22,* 34–40.

Smith, J. *The changing economic circumstances of the elderly: Income wealth and Social Security.* Syracuse, NY: Maxwell School Center for Policy Research, 1997b.

Smith, J. P. Wealth inequality among older Americans. *Journals of Gerontology,* Special Issue, 1997a, *52B,* S74–81.

Smith, L. The tyranny of America's old. *Fortune,* 1992, *125,* 68–72.

Social Security Administration. *Fast facts and figures about Social Security.* Washington, DC: U.S. Government Printing Office, 1996.

Social Security Administration. *Income of the Aged, Chartbook, 1994.* Washington, DC: U.S. Government Printing Office, 1996.

Social Security Administration. *Income of the population 55 or older.* Washington, DC: Social Security Administration Office of Research and Statistics, 1998.

Social Security Administration. *Social Security: Understanding the benefits.* Washington, DC: U.S. Government Printing Office, 1996.

Statistical Abstract of the United States, 114th Edition. Washington, DC: U.S. Department of Commerce, Bureau of the Census, 1994.

Sterns, H., and McDaniel, M. Job performance and the older worker. In S. Rix (Ed.), *Older workers: How do they measure up?* Washington, DC: AARP, 1994.

Strate, J. M., Parrish, C. J., Elder, C. D., and Ford, C. Life span civic development and voting participation. *American Political Science Review,* 1989, *83,* 443–464.

Street, D. Special interests or citizens' rights? Senior power, Social Security, and Medicare. In M. Minkler and C. L. Estes (Eds.), *Critical gerontology: Perspectives from political and moral economy* (pp. 109–130). Amityville, NY: Baywood Publishing Company, 1999.

Streib, G., and Schneider, C. J. *Retirement in American society. Impact and process.* Ithaca, NY: Cornell University Press, 1971.

Stuckey, J. D. *The Sunday school class: The meaning of older women's participation in church.* Presented at the Annual Scientific Meeting of the Gerontological Society, Boston, MA, November 1990.

Szinovacz, M. E., and DeViney, S. The retiree identity: Gender and race differences. *Journals of Gerontology,* July 1999, *54B(4),* S207–S218.

Taylor, H., and Bass, R. *Productive aging: A survey of Americans age 55 and over.* New York: Louis Harris and Associates, 1992.

Taylor, M., and Shore, L. M. Predictors of planned retirement age: An application of Baehr's model. *Psychology and Aging,* 1995, *10,* 76–83.

Taylor, R. J., and Chatters, L. M. Nonorganizational religious participation among elderly black adults. *Journals of Gerontology,* 1991, 46, S103–110.

Thomson, D. Generations, justice and the future of collective action. In P. Laslett and J. Fishkin (Eds.), *Philosophy, politics and society, Relations between age groups and generations.* New Haven, CT: Yale University Press, *Vol. VI:* 1993.

Thorson, J. Spiritual well-being in the secular society. *Generations,* 1983, *8,* 10–11.

Tinsley, H., Teaff, J., Colbs, S., and Kaufman, N. A system of classifying leisure activities in terms of the psychological benefits of participation reported by older persons. *Journal of Gerontology,* 1985, *40,* 172–178.

Torres-Gil, F. M. Interest group politics: Generational changes in the politics of aging. In V. L. Bengtson and W. A. Achenbaum (Eds.), *The changing contract across generations.* New York: Aldine de Gruyter, 1993.

Torres-Gil, F. M. *The new aging: Politics and change in America.* Westport, CT: Auburn House, 1992.

Torres-Gil, F. M. *Political behavior: A study of political attitudes and political participation among older Mexican Americans.* Unpublished dissertation, Heller School, Brandeis University, 1976.

U.S. Senate Special Committee on Aging. *Aging America: Trends and projections.* Washington, DC: U.S. Department of Health and Human Services, 1992.

Van Willigen, M. Differential trends among elderly persons and implications for the future. *The Journals of Gerontology,* *55B,* No. 5 (2000). p. S308.

Verbrugge, L., Gruber-Baldini, A. C., and Fozard, J. L. Age differences and age changes in activities: Baltimore Longitudinal Study of Aging. *Journals of Gerontology*, 1996, *51B*, S30–S41.

Villa, V. M., Wallace, S. P., and Markides, K. Economic diversity and an aging population: The impact of public policy and economic trends. *Generations*, 1997, *21*, 13–18.

Wagner, D. L. Senior center research in America: An overview of what we know. In D. Shollenberger, *Senior centers in America*. Washington, DC: The National Council on the Aging, 1995.

Walker, A. Age and employment. *Australasian Journal on Ageing*, 1998, *17(1)*, 99–103.

Warburton, J., Le-Brocque, R., and Rosenman, L. Older people—The reserve army of volunteers?: An analysis of volunteerism among older Australians. *International Journal of Aging and Human Development*, 1998, *46(3)*, 229–245.

Wheeler, J. A., Gorey, K. M., and Greenblatt, B. The beneficial effects of volunteering for older volunteers and the people they serve: A metaanalysis. *International Journal of Aging and Human Development*, 1998, *47(1)*, 69–79.

Witt, V. G. *Life satisfaction in late adulthood: Role transitions and social integration.* American Sociological Association, 1998

Wood, J. B., and Wan, T. Ethnicity and minority issues in family caregiving to rural black elders. In C. Barresi and D. Stull (Eds.), *Ethnic elderly and long-term care*. New York: Springer, 1993.

Worthington, E. L. Religious faith across the life span: Implications for counseling and research. *Counseling Psychology*, 1989, *17*, 555–612.

Zsembik, B., and Singer, A. The problem of defining retirement among minorities: The Mexican Americans. *The Gerontologist*, 1990, *30*, 749–757.

13

Death, Dying, Bereavement, and Widowhood

This chapter examines

- Age-related attitudes toward death in our culture
- The dying process and its meaning to the dying person
- The conditions for care of the dying (palliative or end-of-life care)
- The concept of the right to die (active and passive euthanasia)
- The increasing ethical, medical, and legal issues raised by whether to continue life-sustaining technologies
- The legal options of advance directives available to individuals
- The rituals of bereavement, grief, and mourning
- The experience of widowhood

Y ou have probably heard of people who "lost their will to live" or "died when they were ready." Such ideas are not simply superstitions. Similar to other topics addressed throughout this book, death involves an interaction of physiological, social, and psychological factors. The social context is illustrated by the fact that all cultures develop beliefs and practices regarding death in order to minimize its disruptive effects on the social structure. These cultural practices influence how members of a particular society react to their own death and that of others. Although measures of death are physical, such as the absence of heartbeat or brain waves, psychosocial factors, such as the will to live, can influence the biological event. For instance, terminally ill people have been found to die shortly after an important engagement, such as a child's wedding, a family reunion, or a holiday, suggesting that their social support systems, enthusiasm for life, and "will to live" prolonged life to that point (McCue, 1995). How people approach their own death and that of others is closely related to personality styles, sense of competence, coping skills, and social supports, as discussed in Chapter 6.

THE CHANGING CONTEXT OF DYING

In our culture, dying is associated primarily with old age. Although we all know that aging does not cause death, and younger people also die, there are a number of reasons for this association. The major factors are medical advances and increased life expectancy. In pre-industrial societies, death rates were high in childhood and youth, and parents could expect that one-third to one-half of their children would die before the age of ten. Now it is increasingly the old who die, making death predictable as a function of age. Death has thus come to be viewed as a timely event, the completion of the life cycle in old age.

Others view death not only as the province of the old, but also as an unnatural event that is to be fought off as long as medically possible. In this sense, death has become medicalized, distorted from a natural event into the end point of untreatable or inadequately treated disease or injury. Prior to the 1900s, the period of time spent dying was relatively short, due to infectious diseases and catastrophic events. With improved diagnostic techniques and early detection, individuals are living for longer periods of time with terminal illnesses. At the end of a prolonged illness, when medicine may care for but not cure the patient, dying may seem more unnatural than if the person had been allowed to die earlier in the progression of the disease. With expanded technological mastery over the conditions of dying, chronically ill people have often been kept alive long beyond the point at which they might have died naturally in the past. As noted by Callahan (1993), achieving a peaceful death is difficult because of the complexity in drawing a clear line between living and dying—which is partially a result of technology

and of societal and professional ambivalence about whether to fight or accept death.

The surroundings in which death occurs have also changed with increased medical interventions. In pre-industrial society, most people died at home, with the entire community often involved in rituals surrounding the death. Now approximately 75 percent of all deaths occur in institutions where aggressive treatment is common, generally in hospitals and nursing homes, and with only a few relatives and friends present. The majority of dying patients, regardless of age, experience severe, undertreated pain, and nearly 40 percent spend at least 10 days in an intensive care unit. This is the case even though most people express a preference to die at home, without pain, surrounded by friends and family (Preston, 2000).

Attitudes toward Death

More insulated from death than in the past, most people are uncomfortable with talking about it, especially the prospect of their own death. This discomfort is shown even in the euphemisms people use—"sleep, pass away, rest"—instead of the word "death" itself. Freud, in fact, recognized that although death was natural, undeniable, and unavoidable, people behaved as though it would occur only to others; that is, "they" will die, but not "me." Fear of death has been defined as the anxiety experienced in daily life caused by the anticipation of the state in which one is dead (Tomer, 1994). As such, it is ongoing in everyday life, in contrast to a more acute fear stimulated by an immediate threat to one's life (Cicirelli, 1999). Fear and denial are natural and comforting responses to our inability to comprehend our own death and lack of physical existence. Such fear tends to make death a taboo topic in our society. Although in recent years death has become a more legitimate topic for scientific and social discussion, most people talk about it on a rational, intellectual level rather than discuss and prepare for their own deaths or those of loved ones. When diagnosed with a terminal illness, nearly 30 percent of patients remain in denial, and 15 percent in fear (Butler, 2000).

POINTS TO PONDER

Do you talk about death, your own or others, with someone else? If so, whom do you talk with? What kinds of concerns, fears, hopes, or questions do you express? How comfortable are you in talking about death? What might increase your feelings of comfort?

Whether people's fear of death is natural or learned is unclear. When asked what they fear most about death, respondents mention suffering and pain, loss of their body and personality, loss of self-control, concern over an afterlife and the unknown, loneliness, and the effect on survivors. In general, people fear the inability to predict what the future might bring (e.g., fear of the unknown afterlife, of nonexistence) and the process of dying, particularly of a painful death, more than death itself (Cicirelli, 1999; Maro, 1996). Generally, older patients tend to choose *quality* of life in their end-of-life decision making, while younger patients tend to select *quantity* of life. Older African Americans, however, are the least likely to employ advanced directives and more likely to want lifesaving technology (Fauser, 1999). When questioned directly, people typically are more concerned with the death of close friends and family than with their own, and generally express an acceptance of their own death. Although the validity of responses to questions about one's own death is difficult to ascertain, it appears that most people both deny and accept the reality of dying. These ambivalent views reflect the basic paradox surrounding death, in which we recognize its universality, but cannot comprehend or imagine our own dying. Dying is one of the few events in life certain to occur, but not one for which we plan.

Variation by Age and Gender

Multiple factors, particularly age and gender, influence socioemotional responses to death and dying. Younger women tend to express significantly greater fear than older women regarding both their own death and the death of others. Older women more often report anxiety and fear of dying, but less fear of the unknown than their male counterparts, although this may reflect gender differences in religiosity and socialization, and greater ability to express emotions such as fear (Cicirelli, 1999; Straub, 1997). In research utilizing metaphors for death, women fear pain and bodily decomposition, but may view death as peaceful, like a "compassionate mother" or an "understanding doctor." Men tend to perceive death as antagonistic, a "grinning butcher" or a "hangman with bloody hands." Findings are mixed regarding fear of death among older adults compared to younger persons (Cicirelli, 1999). In general, older people think and talk more about death and appear to be less afraid of their own death than are younger people; they are concerned about a painful death, loss of control, and the uncertainty of an afterlife. When they face "unfinished business," however, they tend to be more likely to fear death (Rasmussen and Brems, 1996; Thorson, Powell, and Samuel, 1998a, 1998b). Regardless of age, the most universal fear

---

POINTS TO PONDER

We spend more time planning for a two-week vacation than we will for our last two weeks of life. What factors might explain this?

Spirituality can assist older people in facing their own mortality.

is concern over an afterlife—the possibility of either no afterlife or a threatening one (Cicirelli, 1999).

A number of factors may explain this apparent paradox of a lessened fear of death in the face of its proximity. Having internalized society's views, older people may see their lives as having ever-decreasing social value, thereby lowering their own positive expectation of the future. Those who are unmarried and depressed tend to worry about the circumstances of dying more than other old people (Rao, Dening, Brayne, and Huppert, 1997). If they have lived past the age they expected to, they may view themselves as living on "borrowed time." A painless death tends to be viewed as preferable to deteriorating physically and mentally and being socially useless or a burden on family. In addition, dealing with their friends' deaths, especially in age-segregated retirement communities or nursing homes, can help socialize older people toward an acceptance of their own. Experiencing death and other losses more frequently, they are more likely to think and talk in a matter-of-fact way about death on a regular basis and to develop effective means of coping, including humor, than are younger people (Ingebretsen and Solem, 1998). Many older people are already experiencing "bereavement overload" through the increased frequency of family and friends' deaths, and thus worry less about the impact of their death on others (Thorson, Powell, and Samuel, 1998a, 1998b). On the other hand, sustained family contacts tend to create a greater desire to prolong life (Mutran, Danis, Bratton, Sudha, and Hanson, 1997). If they achieve the developmental stage of ego integrity, as described in our discussion of Erikson in Chapter 6, and engage in life review, they are able to resolve conflicts and relieve anxiety, becoming more accepting of death as fair and a release.

Older adults also have been found to react differently to perceptions of limited remaining time, and thus to death as an "organizer of time." Compared to youth, older people confronting death may conclude that little of meaning can be accomplished, because all activities will be short-lived and unfinished. Accordingly, many older people whose death is imminent make less effort than younger people to alter their way of life or to attempt to complete projects. Instead, they are more likely to turn inward to contemplation, reminiscence, reading, or spiritual activities. The awareness of one's mortality can stimulate a need for the "legitimization of biography," to find meaning in one's life and death. People who successfully achieve such legitimization experience a new freedom and relaxation about the future and tend to hold favorable attitudes toward death. Many older people consider a sudden death to be more tragic

---

POINTS TO PONDER

What thoughts, feelings, or images do you experience when you hear that a baby has died? What about the death of a young adult just graduating from college? A 50-year-old mother just starting her new career? An 80-year-old who has advanced dementia? A 79-year-old who is hit by a car while crossing the street? What variables or factors might explain differences in your reactions?

than a slow one, desiring time to see loved ones, say good-bye, settle their affairs, and reminisce. Older people generally can accept the inevitability of their own death, even though they tend to be concerned about the death of relatives.

It is unclear whether variability in the acceptance of death is due to age or to cohort differences. For example, the current cohort of older people has fewer years of formal schooling than younger generations, a factor that affects attitudes toward death. The interactive effects of other variables with age need to be further probed. For instance, in all age groups the most religious persons who hold the greatest belief in an afterlife have less anxiety about dying (Sullivan, Ormel, Kemper, and Tymstra, 1998). For the religious, they have less fear of the unknown and view death as the doorway to a better state of being. Those most fearful about death are irregular participants in formal religious activities, or those intermediate in their religiosity whose belief systems may be confused and uncertain or those whose religious motivation is extrinsically rather than intrinsically motivated (Cicirelli, 1999; Clements, 1998). Religion apparently can either comfort or create anxiety about an afterlife, but it provides some individuals with one way to try to make sense of death. The age of the person who died is also a factor in how survivors react to death. Because the death of older people is often anticipated, it may be viewed as a "blessing" for someone whose "time has come" rather than as a tragic experience.

THE DYING PROCESS

As noted earlier, most older people do not fear being dead as much as the painful process of dying. The stages of death, one of the most widely known

and classic frameworks for understanding the **dying process,** was advanced by Kübler-Ross (1969, 1981). Each stage represents a form of coping with the process of death.

Denial is initially a healthy buffer, but it can prevent dying persons from moving to subsequent stages if others are unwilling to talk with them about their concerns. In the second stage, anger ("Why me?") may be displaced on family or medical staff and can lead to withdrawal and avoidance. This stage may be the most difficult for caregivers to tolerate. In the bargaining stage, the dying person may try to make a deal with God to live long enough to attain some goal or to postpone death as a reward for good behavior. The fourth stage is depression, which represents a natural grieving process over the final separation of death. The dying person may withdraw from loved ones as a way to prepare for this separation. The final stage, acceptance, is achieved only if the dying person is able—and allowed—to express and deal with earlier feelings, such as anger and depression. The dying person thereby achieves a sense that personal tasks have been accomplished and the struggle is over. Rather than a happy stage, the acceptance phase is almost devoid of feelings, and should not be confused with wishing to die. Although Kübler-Ross cautioned that these stages were not invariant, immutable, or universal, she nevertheless implied that progression from one to the other is normal and adaptive. She encouraged health care providers to help their patients to advance through them; and she depicted the final stage as consummate. Kübler-Ross (1975) also emphasized that dying can be a time of growth and profound spirituality. By accepting death's inevitability, dying persons can use life meaningfully and productively and come to terms with who they really are. Values change and things once ignored

---

FIVE STAGES EXPERIENCED BY A DYING PERSON

1. Denial and isolation
2. Anger and resentment
3. Bargaining and an attempt to postpone

4. Depression and sense of loss
5. Acceptance

"Once you learn how to die, you learn how to live." Moyers, 2000.

become more important (Teno, 1999). Since the dying are "our best teachers," those who work with them can learn from them and emerge from such experiences with fewer anxieties about their own death (Kübler-Ross, 1969).

The religious assumptions and allegations about life after death that are embedded in Kübler-Ross's writings have evoked scientific and theological criticism, and often detracted from the importance of her work with dying patients. The empirical usefulness and generalizability of these stages continue to be debated and it is now recognized that there is no "typical," unidirectional way to die through progressive stages. Instead, alternates may occur between acceptance and denial, between understanding what is happening and magically disbelieving its reality (Kastenbaum, 1985, 1991).

Although her work is controversial, Kübler-Ross has been a pioneering catalyst, increasing public awareness of death and the needs of the dying and their caregivers. Her framework can be a helpful cognitive grid or guideline of possible modes and ways of coping with death and loss, not a fixed sequence that determines a "good death." Apathy, apprehension, and anticipation have been found as well as acceptance of death. Moreover, any of these feelings and behaviors may occur at any time during the dying process, and the person may move back and forth between them, displaying several of the feelings simultaneously up until the point of death. In fact, many patients remain at one of the first stages (denial or anger)

and never pass through all five stages. Family members and health care providers must be cautious about implying that the dying person must follow Kübler-Ross's stages, and thus creating an illusion of control by naming phases. Instead, they should be open to the dying person's choice of whether and how to move through these stages.

Consistent with the framework of dynamic interactions discussed throughout this book, the dying process is shaped by:

- an individual's own personality and philosophy of life
- the specific illness
- the social context (e.g., whether at home surrounded by family who encourage the expression of feelings, or isolated in a hospital)

CARE OF THE DYING

The concept of the dying process highlights the importance of the ways in which end-of-life care is provided. As noted earlier, although most dying people prefer to be at home, the common practice has been to hospitalize them, with most deaths occurring in hospital intensive care units or, in the case of older people, nursing homes (Butler, 2000). Rather than death as sudden from accident or infection, it is now the culmination of years with chronic illness, such as dementia, congestive heart failure, or cancer. The majority of older people die of chronic disease, with the focus of medicine on

---

POINTS TO PONDER

If you have experienced the dying process of someone close to you or for whom you provided care, what phases did you observe? Did you observe the dying process as flowing, alternating between different stages, or rather unidirectional? Did the person ever reach the stage of acceptance? How did you know?

A "GOOD" DEATH

The Institute of Medicine Committee on Care at End of Life defined a "good death" as one that is

- free from avoidable distress and suffering for patients, families, and caregivers

- in general accord with patients' and families' wishes
- reasonably consistent with clinical, cultural, and ethical standards (Field and Cassel, 1997)

---

the treatment of the underlying disease, while older patients often suffer debilitating symptoms such as nausea, delirium, or severe pain. Physicians and families may see death as a defeat, not an inevitable culmination. The traditional problem-oriented model of health care that emphasizes life-enhancing therapies falls short in guiding end-of-life care. What is necessary is for more people to give up rescue medicine, when the hope of a cure is miniscule, and to seek comfort care.

The **Dying Person's Bill of Rights,** developed over 20 years ago, states that individuals have the right to personal dignity and privacy; informed participation, including to have their end-of-life choices respected by health care professionals; and considerate, respectful service and competent care. As highlighted below, the **right to die** with dignity and without pain, rather than to endure prolonged suffering through life extension, is currently emphasized more than it was at the time the Dying Person's Bill of Rights was first introduced. Although controversy surrounds the use of life-sustaining technology, both sides agree that the dying person's self-determination and right to be free from physical pain are essential to humane care. As articulated by the Ethics Committee of

the American Geriatrics Society (1997), dying persons should be provided with opportunities to make the circumstances of their dying consistent with their preferences and lifestyles.

The U.S. Supreme Court ruled in 1997 that Americans have a constitutional right to palliative care. **Palliative care** focuses not on lifesaving measures, but on relief of pain and other physical symptoms by addressing the patient's emotional, social, and spiritual needs. Physicians, nurses, and social workers use both pharmacological and psychosocial approaches to cope with symptoms. Pain management is a major component of such care.

With palliative care, both the patient and health care providers recognize that, although the disease cannot be cured, quality of life can be enhanced. It does not treat the terminally ill patient as on the brink of death. And it neither hastens nor postpones death. Instead, it simply recognizes that life can be meaningful and rewarding even with a diagnosis of a terminal illness (Payne, 2000). Listening to music, art therapy, and reminiscences through photos and mementos may all be encouraged as a way to add enjoyment and meaning at the end-of-life. Such care is characterized

---

FACING DEATH ON YOUR OWN TERMS

Ruth, age 85, was diagnosed with incurable cancer. She told her family and doctor that she wanted to live long enough (five months) to see her first granddaughter married. Her doctor arranged for low-dose chemotherapy that did not cause much discomfort, and she experienced a remission. After her grand-

daughter's wedding, the doctors found that the cancer had returned and spread. Her response was that she was now ready to die. She received excellent palliative care, lived three months without pain through morphine, and was alert almost to the end, sharing memories and saying good-bye to her family.

by respect for the patient's own values and choices about privacy and end-of-life care, candid and sensitive communication, encouragement to express feelings, and a multidisciplinary team approach (Cicirelli, 1997a; Zuckerman, 1997). The social support of friends and family can be a major source of strength and enhance the quality of the dying process (Kavanaugh, 1996–97). Improved tools for prognosis and to measure quality of life at its last stages are needed to document the effectiveness of palliative care and to enhance such care (Teno, 1999).

In recent years, more training has been provided to health care providers who work with the dying. For example, the American Medical Association launched a nationwide continuing education effort regarding end-of-life care, which contrasts with an emphasis on technological interventions to prolong life. Similarly, the American Geriatrics Society calls for the development and study of instruments that measure quality of care at end of life and suggest domains for measurement and study, such as patient and family satisfaction and bereavement. The Soros Foundation in New York City, through its Death in America project, provides national fellowships in end-of-life care to physicians and social workers. And the accrediting body for hospitals now requires them to implement pain management plans for terminally ill patients.

Medical professionals are more open in talking about death with their patients as well as among themselves than in the past. Most now believe that dying persons have the right to know their condition and prognosis and to have some control over their death, although they also state

they are not adequately prepared to work with the dying (Abrams, 1998; American Medical Association, 1996; Christ and Sormanti, 1999). Increasingly, the pursuit of a peaceful death is viewed as the proper end of medicine, even though less agreement exists on how this is to be achieved. This breaking of "professional silence" is in part a reaction to external pressures, including patients who insist on being informed about their illnesses, and current public affirmations about the "right to know" and the "right to die."

Hospice Care

Another trend toward being more responsive to dying patients and their families is the expansion of the **hospice** model of caring for the terminally ill. Hospice is not a "place" but a philosophy of, and approach to, care that is offered through a range of organizational settings, primarily in the home. It provides physical, medical, emotional, and spiritual care not only to the patient but also to his or her support system. As such, it is a central component of palliative care services through the home, although its principles can also be enacted as inpatient services (e.g., hospital, nursing home). As one type of end-of-life care, hospice is dedicated to helping individuals who are beyond medicines curative power to remain in familiar surroundings where pain is reduced and personal dignity and control over the dying process maintained. Ensuring the patient's quality of life, and assessment and coordination of the physical, psychosocial, and spiritual needs of patient and family, are fundamental to the hospice approach. In

---

How can cities create a context for better end-of-life care? Missoula Montana's Quality of Life's End project is one such model.

- Physicians, lawyers, clergy, and students are educated about what it means to die well.
- Hospitals treat pain as a fifth vital sign, ensuring that medical staff will take it seriously.

- Lawyers receive instruction on writing advance directives.
- End-of-life issues are incorporated into high school classes.
- Educational programs for the public are implemented in churches, synagogues, physicians offices or health care clinics, and community centers or educational settings.

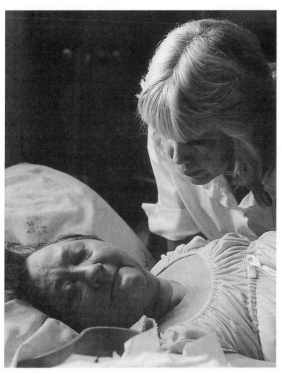

Hospice care can enhance quality of life for the dying person.

- use of volunteers as central to the team
- inpatient care when needed
- bereavement counseling for family and friends

St. Christopher's Hospice, started in Great Britain in 1967, was the first formal hospice in the world, although TB asylums for younger people had informally performed similar functions. The first hospice in the United States was developed in 1974 in New Haven, Connecticut, and now nearly 3,200 hospices exist nationwide (Johnson and Slaninka, 1999). The majority of these provide in-home services for cancer and HIV/AIDS patients with a prognosis of 6 months or less. Most hospices, however, are small, not-for-profit community-based organizations, often depending upon volunteers and contributions. In 1986, Congress passed legislation making hospice a permanent Medicare benefit, including reimbursement for prescriptions, and granting a modest increase in reimbursement rates. Medicare's guidelines are strict. However, some private insurance plans cover hospice, and some states provide hospice benefits under Medicaid. Nevertheless, coverage is limited, even though hospice is considerably less expensive than other forms of care. Ironically, insurance companies are more likely to reimburse costly chemotherapy than prescriptions for pain relief. An end-of-life health insurance plan has been discussed in Congress, but is unlikely to be approved in the near future.

Even though hospice patients tend to receive at least 3 hours a day more attention than nursing home residents, only 17 percent of dying Americans of all ages participate in hospice (Cloud, 2000). Although older people are both providers and recipients of hospice care, the population over 75 years of age is generally underserved by hospice compared to other age groups with terminal illnesses. For example, patients with dementia are unlikely to receive hospice care, even when they are hospitalized for hip fracture or pneumonia, which significantly increase mortality. Others resist hospice because it requires that people abandon hope of full recovery and acknowledge that they are dying. As a result, the average length of stay in a

recent years, more nursing homes, responsive to a changing market, are providing hospice care and pain management programs (Castle, 1998).

Most hospice programs share the following characteristics:

- focus on quality of life
- service availability on a 24-hour per day, 7-day per week, on-call basis
- respite care for the family
- management of physical symptoms, including pain management through medications
- psychological, social, and spiritual counseling for the patient and the family
- coordination of skilled and homemaker home care services and collaboration among providers (home health care, hospitals, nursing homes)
- physician direction of services by a multidisciplinary team

hospice for Medicare patients tends to be less than 60 days. This suggests that most patients are not utilizing the services as early or fully in the dying process as they might (Morrison and Siu, 2000).

Low-income individuals and persons of color also appear to be underserved, even though groups such as African Americans have a higher overall incidence of death from cancer, and presumably a greater likelihood of inadequate treatment of pain from cancer (Freeman and Payne, 2000). Culturally specific end-of-life care programs are needed. African Americans are less likely than other groups to prepare a living will, to talk to their doctors about end-of-life care, or to participate in a hospice program. When death is inevitable and imminent, blacks are twice as likely as whites to request life-sustaining treatments—which can make dying a miserable experience for both them and their families. In some cases, this may occur because African Americans perceive palliative care as "giving up

hope," or not respecting their cultural and personal values. Some may fear that hospice or palliative care is a code word for "no care" or "less care," or "trying to get rid of them" (Payne, 2000). Aggressive medical treatment is viewed as a sign of respect, even if it means food tubes, pain, and losing life savings. Providers need to be sensitive to cultural differences in the ways the patient chooses to die and be able to discuss alternatives to life-sustaining treatments in order to give African Americans the gift of a "good death." Despite the different definitions of "death with dignity" among culturally diverse groups, underutilization of hospice may also be due to inadequate knowledge of this service and the lack of providers who are trained to discuss end-of-life care with persons of color. Working through African American ministers and community centers may be a way to provide hospice information to African American communities (Kurent, 2000). In addition, medica-

A GOOD DEATH

Anne was a 68-year-old retiree who had battled breast cancer for over 4 years. She had received radiation and chemotherapy, but the cancer had metastasized and spread to other organs in her body. She had lost more than 40 pounds, had no appetite, and had difficulty breathing, even with the aid of an oxygen tank. She had decided to end her suffering and wanted to die.

Her husband contacted the local office of Compassion in Dying. The case management staff arranged for a visit and included medical staff to verify the primary physician's diagnosis. Mentally alert, Anne assured the staff that she understood and met the requirements outlined in Compassion's Guidelines and Safeguards. She indicated that her physician had already prescribed half the necessary medications needed to hasten her death; the rest would be obtained within 2 weeks. The physician carefully reviewed with Anne the procedures to follow to self-administer the required medications. She hoped for a hastened death within the next 6 weeks. Her husband, Ed, confirmed that he

supported Anne's decision to choose when the end would come rather than watch her continue to suffer.

A month later, Ed phoned the Compassion staff and indicated that Anne was ready. Upon their arrival, the staff reminded Anne that she need only tell them if she had changed her mind. She was clear and adamant in her decision to proceed: "Today is the day." According to Compassion's protocol, she ate some food to be certain she had something in her stomach before taking the first dose of medications. Anne began to take the pills with a glass of orange juice, according to Compassion's guidelines that patients must be able to ingest all of the medications by themselves. As suggested in the protocol, Anne asked for some vodka to speed the effect of the drugs. She expressed her appreciation to the Compassion staff for their assistance, kissed her husband and two sons, laid her head back on the pillow, and looked as if she were going into a peaceful sleep. In about 15 minutes, she stopped breathing. She had died what Compassion calls a good death.

"The good death: We only get one time to get it right."

tions for managing pain must be affordable and accessible in pharmacies in minority neighborhoods. Religious organizations in a range of culturally diverse communities may be the locus for discussion about death, dying, and end-of-life care, even though religious leaders are not necessarily comfortable with initiating such topics (Braun, Pietsch, and Blanchette, 2000).

Hospice professionals and volunteers, working as an interdisciplinary team, advocate for giving dying persons full and accurate information about their condition. They also try to develop supportive environments in which people can tell their life stories (e.g., life review), attain resolution and reconciliation in relationships, and find meaning in their deaths. Listening, touching the dying person, music and art, family involvement, and ritual celebration of special events such as birthdays and weddings are all emphasized by the staff. For those who value spirituality, staff support them in their quest for meaning and the intrinsic quality of dignity in the last stage of life (Simmons, 1998). In addition, hospice staff work directly with family and friends to help them resolve their feelings, clarify expectations, relate effectively to the dying patient, and provide bereavement counseling after the death. Hospice programs also offer counseling and support to staff members to help prevent "burnout." There is increasing evidence that hospice provides better quality of life for both end-of-life patients and their caregivers than hospitals (Bretscher, et al., 1999). Savings to Medicare is also associated with hospice care relative to conventional care (Miller, 1996). With the growing proponents of right to die, hospice must now address not only concerns about pain, but also fears of suffering and of loss of dignity and physical and cognitive capacities through a slower dying process (Caplan, 1997).

One of the barriers to a "good death," however, is that doctors often refer patients to hospice too late. A primary reason for this is that doctors are no better at predicting length of survival of terminally ill patients than they were 30 years ago. In addition, some physicians remain uncomfortable with telling a person that he or she is dying. In fact, physicians tend to convey an optimistic bias when discussing prognoses with each other and sharing them with patients and families. They are likely to overestimate survival and future quality of life, in part because they may fear that a short prognosis will be self-fulfilling. Partially because of this bias, the actual length of stay for most hospice patients is usually two to three weeks, despite eligibility for hospice care when estimated life expectancy is six months or less (Christakis and Lamont, 2000). Most patients come to hospice during a period of rapid physical change and often in crisis. At such times, the immediate management of symptoms and relieving the family overshadows the need to address the emotional and spiritual issues of remembering, forgiving, and bringing closure to a person's life. When more time is available, the dying person can participate in the process of validating the past and planning for the future, and this gives the family the chance to enjoy or repair family relationships. The National Hospice Organization tries to educate physicians on how to predict appropriate entry points to hospice for various conditions.

THE RIGHT TO DIE OR HASTENED DEATH

Along with increased attention to the ways in which people choose to die and the meanings they assign to their deaths, the right-to-die movement is growing; this has given rise to new ethical and legal debates regarding the right to a "good death." Advocates of the right to die increasingly use the term *hastened death* rather than

euthanasia, because it hastens the inevitable (Compassion in Dying, 2000). Whether others have a right to help people die, and under what conditions, has been discussed throughout history, but recent debates about the complex ethical, social, and legal issues raised by euthanasia or hastened death have intensified with increased medical advances used to prolong life. These issues revolve around three different types of patients:

1. the terminally ill who are conscious
2. the irreversibly comatose
3. the brain-damaged or severely debilitated who have good chances for survival but have limited quality of life (e.g., Alzheimer's patients, patients with Lou Gehrig's disease)

Central to these debates is the doctrine of **informed consent,** which establishes a competent patient's right to accept or refuse medical treatment based on his or her understanding of the benefits and harms of that treatment. Standard informed-consent procedures work best in the acute-care setting, where they involve treatment choices that lead to cure, significant improvement, or death. Decision making for older people with chronic illness, often in long-term care settings, is much more ambiguous than in acute-care environments, and long-term care providers tend to disagree about patients' rights to end their lives (McClain, Tindell, and Hall, 1999; Walker, 1997). Findings are mixed regarding the acceptability of a range of end-of-life decision options among older people. Some research has found that the majority of elders want to live for as long as possible, undergoing whatever treatments might extend their lives (Cicirelli, 1997b; Walker, 1997). Other studies have reported that increased age is associated with preferring quality over quantity of life (Fausar, 1999).

The value of autonomy, articulated in informed consent and advance directives, may conflict with cultures that are more collectivist than individualist in nature. For example, decisions about end-of-life care in Asian and Pacific Islander cultures are influenced by the value placed on shared or deferred decision making within families; filial piety; silent communication, whereby it is improper to discuss

issues of death and dying with parents; and preservation of harmony, whereby families may be unwilling to share bad news if it disrupts the group's harmony. When patients have difficulty making independent health care decisions and defer to the family or doctor, they may unfortunately be labeled noncompliant by traditional Western medicine. To take account of such cultural variations, family-centered, shared, or negotiated models of medical decision making recognize the legitimacy of multiple points of view (McLaughlin and Braun, 1998).

Passive Euthanasia (Voluntary Elective Death)

Euthanasia can be passive (allowing death) or active (causing death). In **passive euthanasia,** treatment is withdrawn, and nothing is done to prolong the patient's life artificially, such as use of a feeding tube or ventilator. Suspension of medical interventions or physician aid in dying allows the natural dying process to occur, but no active steps are taken to bring about death. In order to relieve pain, medications are sometimes given that may hasten death, but the object is to relieve suffering, not to bring about death. Withholding or withdrawing useless or unwanted medical treatments, or providing adequate pain relief, even if it hastens death, has been determined to be neither illegal nor unethical. The legal context for this is the 1990 U.S. Supreme Court case of *Cruzan v. Director, Missouri Department of Health*, which recognized the right of a competent patient to refuse unwanted medical care, including artificial nutrition and hydration, as a "liberty" interest, and therefore as constitutionally protected. The Supreme Court later delegated regulation of this constitutional right to the states.

Another indicator of changing legal interpretations is the position of the American Medical Association (AMA). Their 1984 statement on euthanasia presented two fundamental guidelines:

- The patient's role in decision making is paramount.
- A decrease in aggressive treatment of the hopelessly ill patient is advisable when treat-

---

COMPASSION IN DYING

Compassion in Dying is a nonprofit national organization with local chapters created to support the right of terminally ill patients to choose to die without pain, without suffering, and with personal assistance, if necessary, to intentionally hasten death. Its mission is to provide counseling and support about end-of-life choices to individuals who have been diagnosed by their physicians with either a terminal illness or an incurable illness that will lead to a terminal diagnosis. Through education and advocacy, Compassion will uphold the individual's right to aid in dying.

---

ment would only prolong a difficult and uncomfortable process of dying.

In 1989, the American Medical Association adopted the position that, with informed consent, physicians could withhold or withdraw treatment from patients who are close to death. Most physicians agree that withholding and withdrawing nutrition and hydration are permissible in certain circumstances and that it is the physician's duty to initiate discussion of these issues with patients and their families. Consistent with this changing medical position, almost 60 percent of the American public support the option of physician-assisted suicide for patients with incurable diseases (*Seattle Times*, 1997).

In contrast to passive euthanasia, where deliberate decisions are made about withholding or withdrawing treatment, there is also a form of hastened death whereby older people may voluntarily make decisions that are equivalent to choosing to die. For example, an older person may refuse extra help at home or insist on hospital discharge directly to the home, in spite of the need for skilled nursing care. When an older person commits suicide through the process of **self-neglect,** the effects of his or her decisions are subtle and gradual. If older people neglect their care needs or choose an inappropriate living situation because of impaired judgment, involuntary treatment laws can sometimes be used to move them to protected settings. If their "failure to care," however, is not immediately life-threatening, they usually have to be allowed to deteriorate to that point before being legally compelled to comply with treatment.

Active Euthanasia

Active euthanasia refers to positive steps taken to bring about someone else's death, by administering a lethal injection or by some other means. Sometimes called *mercy killing*, the legality of active euthanasia has been tested by several highly controversial court cases, voter initiatives, and state legislation. As noted above, a subject of intense controversy is *physician-assisted suicide* or *assisted suicide;* this occurs when someone else provides the means by which an individual ends

---

THE CONTROVERSIAL DR. KEVORKIAN

One of the states in which the legality of assisted suicide has been the focus of public attention is Michigan, where Dr. Jack Kevorkian has assisted over 100 people to commit suicide. In the first case, involving a woman with Alzheimer's disease, the court dismissed the murder charges on the grounds that no law in Michigan prohibited assisting in a suicide. Subsequently, the legislature passed a bill to stop Dr. Kevorkian's activities. Some cases have been dismissed on the grounds that the law is unconstitutional; others are pending. Although controversial, Kevorkian's crusade to legalize active euthanasia has served to push the debate on physician-assisted suicide to the forefront of the American political scene.

his or her life. For example, a physician may prescribe medication, typically barbiturates, knowing that the individual intends to use it to commit suicide, but it is the individual who decides when and whether to take it.

Those who argue against the legalization of assisted suicide fear a "slippery slope," that a "right to die" could become a "duty to die" and be inappropriately applied to older adults and other dependent members of society. They fear that a law made to convey permission could come to be seen as prescriptive, with assisted suicide viewed as a solution to solve societal problems faced by the poor, persons of color, or individuals with disabilities. The American Medical Association, based on the historical role of physicians as advocates for healing, officially oppose physicians' directly assisting their patients in committing suicide (AMA, 1996).

Citizen initiatives and recent legislation in several states reflect increasing public support for physician-assisted suicide. In fact, 60 percent of adults in national polls believe that doctors should be allowed to help terminally ill patients in severe pain take their own lives. The degree of support, however, varies by religious affiliation and ethnic minority status (Braun et al., 1996; McMahon and Koch, 1999; *Seattle Times*, 1997). Most believe that forcing people to endure prolonged suffering is inhumane and cruel. *Compassion et al. v. Wash-*

ington State was the first case to challenge in a federal court the constitutionality of a state law on assisted suicide insofar as it applies to mentally competent, terminally ill patients seeking prescribed medications with which to hasten death. An initiative in Washington State to permit physician aid in dying was only narrowly defeated in 1992. Patients could request such assistance in writing at the time they wanted to die, as long as two witnesses would certify that the request is voluntary and two doctors would state that the patient would die within 6 months. However, 4 months after the initiative was defeated at the polls, the legislature passed a bill giving comatose and dying people the right to have food and water withdrawn (*Seattle Times*, 1992). In 1994, the federal district court ruled that the Washington State ban on physician-assisted suicide violates the patient's constitutional right to liberty, but this ruling did not protect physicians from prosecution if they assisted in a terminally ill patient's suicide (Hudson, 1994). In 1996, a federal appeals court struck down both Washington and New York statutes banning physician-assisted suicide. The plaintiffs (near-death patients and physicians) argued that no public interest is served by prolonging pain in truly hopeless situations and that to do so is to subject patients to potential abuse. The courts linked the right to facilitate death with the right to refuse medical treatment. They argued that the Four-

---

OREGON: THE ONLY STATE TO LEGALIZE PHYSICIAN-ASSISTED SUICIDE

The Death with Dignity Act, passed by Oregon voters in 1994 and again in 1997, allows doctors to write a prescription of lethal drug doses for an aware, terminally ill adult who asks for it, orally and in writing. Nevertheless, doctors are not compelled to comply with this request, and there are numerous safeguards. A 15-day waiting period is required for the first oral request, and two witnesses are necessary for the written request, along with agreement of a second doctor. The doctor must inform the patient about options, including pain control, and make sure

that the request really is voluntary. At the end of this elaborate process, only the patient can decide whether and when to take fatal drugs and must do so him- or herself. This citizen initiative made Oregon the second entity (after the Netherlands) to legalize physician-assisted suicide. Since the second passage of the law in 1997, about 30 patients, most of whom were suffering from cancer, have taken their lives with barbiturates; their average age was 69. At the same time, there are ongoing threats to overturn the Oregon Death with Dignity Act.

teenth Amendment protects the individual's decision to hasten death with physician-prescribed medication and that statutes prohibiting physician-assisted suicide deny equal protection guaranteed by the Fourteenth Amendment to competent terminally ill adults who are not on life supports (Tucker, 1999).

These conflicting state rulings and pressure from advocacy organizations such as Compassion in Dying brought the issue of assisted suicide to the U.S. Supreme Court. In June 1997, the Court ruled that there is no constitutional or fundamental "right to die." They thus upheld the Washington and New York laws that make it a crime for doctors to help patients kill themselves, although several justices indicated that they are willing to revisit the issue in specific cases. This ruling by the Supreme Court, however, does not preclude states from deciding on their own to pass laws allowing doctor-assisted suicide. By returning the debate to the states, the justices apparently opened the way for other jurisdictions to follow Oregon, the only state to legalize the physician-assisted suicide choice for patients who are diagnosed by two doctors as having less than 6 months to live. Several states—Maine, California, and Alaska—are considering legalization of physician-assisted suicide. The Supreme Court ruling also left open the possibility that the court might extend federal constitutional protection in the future (Tucker, 1999).

Nor will the Supreme Court ruling stop patients from seeking physicians to prescribe lethal medications or stop doctors from providing them illegally. The court ruled that prescribing medication with the intent to relieve suffering is legal and acceptable, but presenting drugs with the intent to cause death is not. Since "intent" is difficult to determine, the Court does give significant discretion and latitude to physicians to use adequate pain medication and explicitly endorses "terminal sedation." Nevertheless, many physicians incorrectly assume that they can be censured or prosecuted for giving patients controlled substances. A dying patient who is suffering and is in pain, wrote Justice Sandra Day O'Connor, "has no legal barriers to obtaining medication from qualified physicians

to alleviate that suffering, even to the point of causing unconsciousness and hastening death" (Ostrom, 1998). In many ways, this solution, known as the "double effect," is an old one. In the Supreme Court's definition, this occurs when a physician, intending to relieve pain or suffering, gives a terminally ill patient medication that has the unintended—but foreseeable—side effect of hastening death. Often, this medication is morphine. It is estimated that about 25 percent of doctors have had patients ask for assistance with suicide, and of these, about 25 percent actually did so by prescribing pain medication, despite the possibility of legal penalties (Ostrom and Westnext, 1997).

In spite of individual physicians' assistance with suicide, the American Medical Association continues to oppose such actions. Instead, the AMA advocates compassionate, high-quality palliative care and assistance in addressing fears as a way to reduce the expressed need for physician-assisted suicide (Compassion in Dying, 2000). Some critics of physician-assisted suicide fear that it will be used to the detriment of the oldest-old and persons with disabilities, some of whom could be pressured to feel that it's "their duty to die" (Callahan, 1996). Some health care providers believe that if patients are afforded compassionate care and assistance in addressing fears, the need for assisted suicide would diminish (Hornik, 1998). Others argue that a health care system driven by both profits and cost containment poses a greater risk to frail elders than does physician-assisted suicide (Olson, 1998).

Oregon voters' support of a law allowing doctors to prescribe lethal medications to terminally ill patients also conveyed the public's lack of confidence in physicians' pain management. As a result, Oregon leads the nation in aggressive pain management through a 1995 Intractable Pain Act, which set new rules to ease doctors' fears about prescribing controlled substances for pain control. In fact, the state's medical board shocked professionals around the country by disciplining a doctor for not prescribing enough pain medication! Not surprisingly, Oregon leads the country in lowest in-hospital death rates, better attention to advance planning, more referrals to hospice, fewer barriers to prescribing narcotics, and a smaller percentage of dying patients in pain (34% compared to 50% nationally) (Ostrom, 2000). Nationwide accreditation standards for hospitals and institutions are also changing to require medical staff to assess pain in all patients and make sure it is treated.

Although there is growing public support for physicians to provide aggressive pain control and palliative care, most health care providers are not well informed about how to minimize suffering. Some physicians view the use of aggressive pain relief as an admission of failure in an effort to cure. Patients and families are often unaware that pain-killing narcotics are legally available, (even though Websites now exist for "pain control" or "death and dying.") Many physicians assume wrongly that they will be censured or prosecuted for giving controlled substances to the terminally ill even when the controlled drug is the approved treatment. In fact, the Supreme Court has cited two legal methods for more aggressive pain management:

1. the "morphine drip," a continuous administration of morphine at a dose that will abolish pain, and, if that is not effective,
2. physician-prescribed "terminal sedation" with barbiturates or other drugs providing continuous anesthesia.

Increasing numbers of medical organizations, such as the American Medical Association and the American College of Physicians, have released recommendations on standards for palliative or end-of-life care, formulated guidelines for quality pain-management technologies, or created expert panels to make recommendations. A 1997 report by the Institute of Medicine criticizes physicians and other providers for failing to provide competent palliative and supportive care (Institute of Medicine, 1997). The American Geriatrics Society has issued a statement of principles to measure quality of life at the end of life, including physical and emotional symptoms, advance care planning, aggressive care near death, and global quality of life. Last Acts, a coalition of 72 organizations, seeks reforms to improve communication and decision making among physicians and other health care providers, payers, hospitals, nursing homes, and consumers regarding end-of-life issues. Many of these initiatives assume that if individuals can be assured that pain is not inevitable in the dying process, they are less likely to request physician-assisted suicide.

Another sign of the ongoing debate about the links between assisted suicide and pain management is *The Pain Relief Promotion Act* proposed by Congress in Spring 2000. Prohibiting physician-assisted suicide with federally controlled drugs (barbiturates), the bill would have overruled Oregon's law. The bill, which allows controlled drugs to be prescribed only to control pain, not to hasten death,

---

IS THIS PHYSICIAN-ASSISTED SUICIDE?

An 89-year-old man was in tremendous pain from the end stages of pancreatic cancer. He had been diagnosed only 6 weeks earlier, and nothing could be done to halt the spread of this deadly cancer. His daughter flew him cross country to her house in order to provide daily care and to have her beloved grandsons nearby. The day before his 90th birthday, he cried out for better relief from the pain. His daughter called the hospice doctor, who delivered a bottle of morphine to her home, because he wanted to check in on the patient. He advised the daughter to start a heavy dosage right after dinner. In leaving, he gently said to her, "and if he does not wake up, that may be a blessing." The next morning, her father did awaken, but he was very disoriented, appeared to have suffered a mild stroke during the night, and was crying from the pain. Anxious to relieve the pain, his loving daughter gave him another dose of morphine. Within a few hours, he was dead. Did the morphine hasten his death? What was the doctor's role? The daughter's?

was supported by the American Medical Association, although opposed by about 12 state chapters. Others have opposed the bill as an unwarranted expansion of federal authority over states' rights to self-determination. This legislation is likely to be reintroduced into Congress (Compassion in Dying, 2000). The American Civil Liberties Union has put forth the "End of Life Care Act of 1998"; this would remove legal liability from physicians who offer patients a full range of end-of-life care choices, including palliative sedation. The ACLU argues that if a patient is uncomfortable, then it is appropriate to offer stronger pain medication. Overall, recognition is growing of the need for more training and research related to aggressive end-of-life care to ensure the patient's comfort.

LEGAL OPTIONS REGARDING END-OF-LIFE CARE

While active euthanasia continues to be debated in courtrooms and the ballot box, all 50 states have laws authorizing the use of some type of **advance directive** to avoid artificially prolonged death. This refers to patients' oral and written instructions about end-of-life care and someone to speak on their behalf if they become incompetent; it may include proxy directives (see medical power of attorney, below). Both federal and state laws govern the use of advance directives. The federal law, the **Patient Self-Determination Act,** requires health care facilities (hospitals, skilled nursing facilities, hospice, home health care agencies, and health maintenance organizations) that receive Medicaid and Medicare funds to inform patients in writing of their rights to execute advance directives regarding how they want to live or die; state regulations vary widely. State-specific advance directives can be ordered from the national organization, Choices in Dying, or downloaded from their Website. However, these facilities do not require that the patient make an advanced directive; the law specifies only that people must be informed of their right to do so.

This act assumes that increased awareness of advance directives will generate discussion between patients and their health care providers and result in more completed advance directives (Galambos, 1998). Despite this act, few patients issue advance directives, and those who do tend to be white, female and middle to upper socioeconomic class. Only 9 percent of patients under age 30 and 35 percent of those over age 75 have an advance directive (Butler, 2000; Compassion in Dying, 2000). In fact, most individuals, regardless of age, do not have wills or engage in estate planning. As noted earlier, racial differences still exist at the end of life.

Nor has increased education about advance directives expanded the completion rate beyond 15 percent (Weinberg and Brod, 1995). Although older people are presumed to want advance directives, some studies indicate that they prefer informal discussion with family. In fact, they tend to delay the completion of a finalized advance directives process and defer to others to make health care decisions (Galambos, 1998). Many assume their "family will know what to do." Unfortunately, it is human nature to delay such discussions until "later," even though it is preferable that they occur when individuals are still healthy (Johnston, Pfeifer, and McNutt, 1995). Even when patients complete advance directives, noncompliance by health care providers often occurs. This may be because of lack of awareness of the directive's existence (e.g., patients kept the only copy in a safe deposit box and not available in their medical records), complying with the family's preference rather than the written directive, or the physician's decision overriding both patient and family preferences (Galambos, 1998; Asch, Hansen-Flaschen, and Lanken, 1995). Another problem is when individuals who designate a health care agent as surrogate decision-maker fail to make their preferences known to this proxy (Weinberg and Brod, 1995).

In an attempt to resolve some of the problems with the Patient Self-Determination Act, the **Uniform Health Care Decision Act** was passed in 1993 to provide uniformity and a minimum level of standards in statutes across state lines. This act promotes autonomous decision making by acknowledging individuals' rights to make health care decisions in all circumstances, including the right to decline or discontinue health care. Given people's preference for informal methods, oral directives as well as written are honored. To safeguard the patient's end-of-life autonomy, providers, agents, surrogates, and guardians are mandated to comply with an individual's instructions. Even with such safeguards, compliance is not guaranteed. A health care provider may decline to honor an advance directive (1) for reasons of conscience if a directive conflicts with institution policy or values, and (2) if the instruction is contrary to accepted health care standards. However, according to the act, reasonable efforts must be made to transfer the patient to a facility that can honor the directive. In such situations, the act provides for court mechanisms for dispute resolution. A major limitation of this act is that each state may choose whether to replace its own advance directive mandates with the Uniform Health Care Decisions Act. Without federal mandates, the number of states that have done so is limited.

The most frequently used type of advance directive is a **living will.** An individual's wishes about medical treatment are put in writing in the case of terminal illness or the prognosis of a permanent vegetative (unconscious) state. Living wills can direct physicians at hospitals to withhold life-sustaining procedures in the event of an irreversible terminal condition and can assist family members in making decisions when they are unable to consult a comatose or mentally incompetent relative. Such stipulations apply only to care in hospitals, although some states have drafted laws that would exempt emergency medical technicians from liability for not resuscitating patients who have legal do-not-resuscitate (DNR) medical directives (Gianelli, 1994). In many states, the person can specify particular treatments or details of care not included in a standard living will form, or can write additional comments on the document.

The majority of Americans appear to approve of living wills; yet only about 50 percent of older people have them on file. Of those who do, very few even tell their doctors about the directive. As previously stated, many older people trust their families to know what to do. Of those who designate someone to make medical decisions if they are unable, 30 percent of those designees do not know they have been selected (Cloud, 2000; Cole and Holstein, 1996). Given this gap between intent and action, the impact of advance directives such as living wills on end-of-life decision making is limited (Butler, 2000). Health care providers, oftentimes with conflicting beliefs, do not always follow a living will but instead implement their own values, especially if no one advocates for the dying individual. Or family members may later change their minds about adhering to a living will. If so, physicians are more likely to comply with the family's preference than the written directive (Galambos, 1998). It is important to note that federal law does not require that the provider follow such directives, only that the provider follow state laws or court decisions that deal with advanced directives. Patients and their families can access their state's particular law and forms through national organizations, such as **Choice in Dying** and **Compassion in Dying,** local hospitals,

---

STEPS TO TAKE TO AVOID AN ARTIFICIALLY PROLONGED DEATH

- Order state-specific, advance-directive documents from Choice in Dying or download them free at choices.org.
- Issue an advance directive, witnessed or notarized according to state laws.
- Give copies to your personal physician and family members.

- While healthy, make sure that your family understands your wishes.
- Be sure that your desires are also noted in your medical record.
- Begin this process while you are still healthy, your thought processes are clear, you are not in crisis, and time is available.

state attorney generals' offices, or the Internet through Websites (choices.org). (See the example of Florida State Health Care Directive or Living Will on pages 435 and 436.)

In situations where there is no living will, the family of an incompetent patient must go to court to obtain legal authority if they wish to refuse life support on the patient's behalf. This expensive and time-consuming process is viewed as necessary where doctors and health care facilities are unwilling to make decisions to remove life-sustaining treatment because of the perceived risk of liability. To obviate this court process, 24 states and the District of Columbia have passed statutes governing a **surrogate decision maker.** The surrogate has a duty to act according to the known wishes of the patient; if those wishes are not known, the surrogate must act according to the patient's "best interest." Such laws support the concept that the people closest to the patient are in the best position to know his or her wishes or to act in the patient's best interest. Each state's law includes a prioritized list of people connected to the patient who are potential surrogates. The doctor must approach these individuals, in order of priority, to find someone who is willing to make decisions about life support (Choice in Dying, 1994).

Durable power of attorney is another type of written advance directive, usually in addition to a living will. This authorizes someone to act on an individual's behalf with regard to property and financial matters. The individual does not relinquish control with a power of attorney since it is granted only for the financial matters specifically set forth in the relevant document. An advantage of durable power of attorney is that a living will cannot anticipate what might be wanted in all possible circumstances.

A **medical power of attorney** (or durable power of attorney for health care) specifically allows for a health care surrogate to make decisions about medical care if the patient is unable to make them for him- or herself. A durable power of attorney for healthcare may be used instead of, or in addition to, a living will because it is more broadly applicable to nearly any type of health care during

periods of incapacitation. *Durable* means that the arrangement continues even when the person is incapacitated and unable to make his or her own medical decisions. A durable power of attorney agreement may be written either to go into effect upon its signing or only when the disability occurs. At that point, bills can continue to be paid and revenues be collected while other more permanent arrangements are being made, such as the appointment of a conservator or guardian.

Conservatorship generally relates to control of financial matters. In this instance, probate court appoints a person as a **conservator** to care for an individual's property and finances because that person is unable to do so due to advanced age, mental weakness, or physical incapacity. Such a condition must be attested to by a physician. Once appointed, the conservator will be required to file an inventory of all the assets and to report annually all income and expenses. The individual, however, loses control over his or her property and finances.

Guardianship is a legal tool that establishes control over a person's body as well as financial affairs. In a guardianship, a probate court appoints someone to care for the individual's person, property, and finances because of the individual's mental inability to care for him- or herself. The **guardian** has a responsibility for directing the individual's medical treatment, housing, personal needs, finances, and property. To establish guardianship, a medical certificate from a physician must state that the individual is mentally incapable of caring for him- or herself. As with conservatorships, the medical certificate by the physician must be made not more than 10 days before the probate court hearing, so in this sense, guardianship cannot be arranged in advance of need. However, through a medical power of attorney, an individual may nominate someone he or she would like to act as guardian if such a need develops. Since the guardian manages all the individual's affairs, guardianship is generally considered a last resort. This is because the process essentially eliminates an individual's legal rights, since consent is not required, and it is costly and rarely reversible.

FLORIDA DESIGNATION OF HEALTH CARE SURROGATE

Name: _____
      (Last)   *(First)*   *(Middle Initial)*

In the event that I have been determined to be incapacitated to provide informed consent for medical treatment and surgical and diagnostic procedures, I wish to designate as my surrogate for health care decisions:

Name: _____

Address: _____

_____ Zip Code: _____

Phone: _____

If my surrogate is unwilling or unable to perform his duties, I wish to designate as my alternate surrogate:

Name: _____

Address: _____

_____ Zip Code: _____

Phone: _____

I fully understand that this designation will permit my designee to make health care decisions and to provide, withhold, or withdraw consent on my behalf; to apply for public benefits to defray the cost of health care; and to authorize my admission to or transfer from a health care facility.

Additional instructions (optional):

FLORIDA DESIGNATION OF HEALTH CARE SURROGATE—PAGE 2 OF 2

I further affirm that this designation is not being made as a condition of treatment or admission to a health care facility. I will notify and send a copy of this document to the following persons other than my surrogate, so they may know who my surrogate is:

PRINT THE NAMES AND ADDRESSES OF THOSE WHO YOU WANT TO KEEP COPIES OF THIS DOCUMENT

Name: _____

Address: _____

Name: _____

Address: _____

SIGN AND DATE THE DOCUMENT

Signed: _____

Date: _____

WITNESSING

Signed: _____

Address: _____

TWO WITNESSES MUST SIGN AND PRINT THEIR ADDRESSES

Witness 2:

Signed: _____

Address: _____

Courtesy of **Choice In Dying, Inc.** 6/96
1035 30th Street, NW Washington, DC 10007 800-989-9455

Family members who are concerned about finances may move too quickly through these options. However, families and service providers should try, as long as possible, to respect the older person's wishes with regard to living arrangements, legal will, and other financial decisions. In other words, the older person should be encouraged to exercise as much control as possible, to the extent that his or her cognitive status allows. In general, less restrictive approaches than guardianship, which balance the need for protection with self-determination, are needed (Wilber and Reynolds, 1995).

Some nursing homes include a statement with their admissions packet that, unless otherwise noted in writing, there will be "no code" for the patient. This type of advance directive means that if the patient quits breathing or his or her heart stops, the staff will not "call a code" to initiate cardiopulmonary resuscitation (CPR). In other nursing homes or hospitals, this type of statement must be written in the patient's chart and signed by the patient and witnesses.

A wide range of organizations exist to educate the public, health care providers, and lawmakers regarding right-to-die issues and advance directive options. The largest of these is **Choice in Dying, Inc.,** a national not-for-profit organization that was created in 1991 by a merger of the nation's two oldest organizations advocating the rights of dying patients, Concern for Dying and Society for the Right to Die. These two organizations pioneered patients' rights to refuse unwanted life support and developed the first living will document in 1967. Choice in Dying has provided national leadership on living wills, guided the enactment of advance directives in all states, and lobbied for the passage of the Patient Self-Determination Act. Its goal is to achieve full societal and legal support for the right of all individuals to make decisions regarding the nature and extent of life-sustaining measures as well as the conditions under which dying occurs, and to have those decisions recognized and honored. Another national patient advocacy group that promotes legal strategies for death with dignity is the **Compassion in Dying Federation.** It also established a Center for End-of-Life Law and Policy that assists in the development of challenges to state laws that bar patients from requesting aid in dying from their physicians. Compassion in Dying aims to provide a safe, respectful environment for the consideration of end-of-life choices, as well as the personal presence of case management volunteers who form relationships with terminally ill individuals as they explore end-of-life possibilities.

An organization that has actively attempted to change the law in order to legalize assisted suicide for the terminally ill is the **Hemlock Society.** The society's popular publication, *Final Exit*, by its founder, Derek Humphry, is a manual on nonviolent methods to commit suicide with prescription barbiturates to assure a gentle, peaceful death. The Hemlock Society distinguishes between "rational or responsible suicide" (i.e., the option of ending one's life for good and valid reasons) and suicide that is caused by a rejection of life because of emotional disturbance. In response to prohibitions against physician-assisted suicide, the society also advocates nonfelonious methods, such as gas masks and paper bags. It views the right to request assistance in dying as merely an extension of the individual's right to control the kind of treatment he or she receives when dying. Rejecting remote chances of recovery as a basis to justify prolonging life, the society also discards the notion of any

---

POINTS TO PONDER

Have you and your family members ever discussed how to die, your preferences and fears? If not, how could you initiate such a discussion, either with your parents, your partner, or your adult children?

ETHICAL DILEMMAS

"With the use of our moral imagination, we can reshape the way we behave toward people with any kind of disability. It goes back to Aristotle's question, How does one live a good life? How does ethical thinking help older people live a good life? Ethics is part of what we do every day. It's so much more than making a decision about putting in a feeding tube...." (Holstein, 1998, p. 4). On a personal and practical level, many dying people find that the medical technol-ogy that prolongs their lives may financially ruin their families. It is important that families discuss in advance such issues as who should assume medical care deci-sion making on the patient's behalf, if necessary, or under what circumstances one would prefer or not prefer life support. However, most families find it emotionally difficult to do such planning, especially if the older adult refuses to do so or cannot make a rational decision because of dementia.

ethical distinction between stopping treatment and assisting someone to die.

Societal cost-benefit criteria inevitably come into play in discussions of active and passive euthanasia. As society seeks to contain rising health and long-term care costs, physicians are subject to demands for financial restraint. Admittedly, a significant proportion of the money spent on medical care in a person's lifetime goes to services received during the last years and months of life. In spite of that, even if such end-of-life care were eliminated, the nation's health care expenditures would be reduced by only one-half of one percent—or even less (Alliance for Aging Research, 1997; Butler 2000). Nevertheless, the public often perceives that the costs to keep alive a comparatively small number of people are prohibitively high (Cole and Holstein, 1996).

Rapid improvements in medical technology are not matched by refinements in the law and the ethics of using those therapies. This is the case even though the field of **bioethics** or medical ethics, which focuses on procedural approaches to questions about death, dying, and medical decision making, has grown in the past 20 years. Hastened death raises not only complex ethical and legal dilemmas, but also resource-allocation issues. Both policy makers and service providers face the issue of how to balance an individual client's needs for personal autonomy with the community's demand to conserve resources. A fundamental question is whether the doctrine of personal privacy under the

U.S. Constitution and related state laws extends to individuals' decisions about their physical care, even when those decisions involve life or death choices for themselves or others. Alternatively, as older people seek to remain at home to die, what are equitable ways to allocate community services such as home care in the face of a growing public distrust of broad-based "entitlements" and perceptions of shrinking resources (Weinberg, 1998)? From another perspective, is home care always the best care, especially in instances of highly impaired elders and burdened caregivers?

As noted by Holstein (1998), providers, policy makers and families are taking ethics beyond autonomy and decision making into the broader realm of how we treat the terminally ill—how we look at them, what we expect of them, and how we talk to them.

BEREAVEMENT, GRIEF, AND MOURNING RITUALS

Death affects the social structure through the dying person's survivors, especially spouses and partners, who have social and emotional needs resulting from that death. Some early studies found that the intensity of these needs is reflected in the higher rates of suicide, hospitalization for psychiatric disorders, visits to physicians, and somatic complaints among survivors (Kalish, 1982; Marshall, 1986). As a whole, however, the research on the relationship between widowhood (for both men and women) and morbidity and mortality is fraught with contradictory findings. Despite early research findings of high mortality, suicide, and morbidity rates among widowers, more current epidemiological studies have found few significant relationships between bereavement and mortality. Following loss of a spouse, health status and perceived health are found to decrease, while mortality and suicide rates increase, but only in the short term. Long-term (e.g., after two years) physical and mental health appears largely unaffected (Martin-Matthews, 1996; Raveis, 1999; Rosenzweig, Prigerson, Miller, and Reynolds, 1997). In fact, some studies suggest that the resiliency and ability of the grieving spouse to cope effectively are often underestimated (Caserta and Lund, 1992; Lund, 1993).

The long-term impacts of widowhood on mental health are also unclear, although the early bereavement period is generally associated with depression, anxiety, appetite loss, mood alterations, disruptive sleep patterns, obsessive thoughts of the deceased, and disorientation (Martin-Matthews, 1996). Accordingly, findings are equivocal about the relationship between bereavement and suicide; the first 6 months of widowhood appear to be the most stressful, especially when spouses face multiple losses and are at risk of poor health, psychiatric disorders, death, and suicide (Bennett, 1997; Raveis, 1999). To minimize these disruptive effects, older survivors need help from both formal (e.g. professional counseling and education) and informal networks in dealing with their grief. Such supportive efforts must take account of cultural values and belief.

Bereavement refers to both the situation and the long-term process of adjusting to the death of someone with whom the person felt close (Lund, 1993). The **grief process** is the complex emotional response to bereavement and can include shock and disbelief, guilt, psychological numbness, depression, loneliness, fatigue, loss of appetite, sleeplessness, and anxiety about one's ability to reorganize and carry on with life. **Mourning** signifies culturally patterned expectations about the expression of grief. What is believed about the meaning of death, how it should be faced, and what happens after physical death vary widely by culture and its associated religion (Braun, Pietsch, and Blanchett, 2000). With the increasing diversity of American society and worldwide globalization, professionals working with older people and their families need to be sensitive to the influences of multiple cultures and to the patient's generation and acculturation level. For example, among Asian Americans, there tends to be reluctance to talk about death; grief is kept within the family, and the body is not to be moved nor organs removed for donation until the soul has had time to travel from it (Braun and Nichols, 1997).

Although there are clusters or phases of grief reactions, the progression is more like a roller coaster—with overlapping responses and wide individual variability—rather than orderly stages or a fixed or universal sequence. To expect grieving individuals to progress in some specified fashion is inappropriate, and can be harmful to them. The highs and lows within broad phases can occur within minutes, days, months, or years, with grieving individuals moving back and forth among them. Even within the individual, there can be mixed reactions, with a person simultaneously experiencing anger, guilt, helplessness, loneliness, and uncontrolled crying—along with personal strength and pride in their coping—all within a matter of hours. Emotions change rapidly, begin-

---

Bereaved persons are like ducks: Above the surface . . . looking composed and unruffled. Below the surface, paddling like crazy!

Northwest Geriatric Center Newsletter, 2000.

ning with shock, numbness, and disbelief, followed by an all-encompassing sorrow. Early months following the loss are the most difficult, with early indicators often serving as predictors of longer-term adjustment (Lund, 1993; Lund, Caserta, and Dimond, 1993). However, even when a grieving person has tried to work through early phases and move toward integrating the loss into his or her life, a picture, a favorite song of the deceased, or a personal object may evoke more intense grief.

An intermediate phase of grief often involves an idealization and searching for the presence of the deceased person, as well as an obsessive review to find meaning for the death and to answer the inexplicable "why"? Anger toward the deceased, God, and caregivers may also be experienced, as well as guilt and regrets for what survivors did not do or say. When the permanence of the loss is acknowledged and yearning ceases, anguish, disorganization, and despair often result. The grieving person tends to experience a sense of confusion; a feeling of aimlessness; a loss of motivation, confidence, and interest; and an inability to make decisions. Simply getting out of bed in the morning can require intense effort. These feelings may be exacerbated if the grieving person tries to live according to others' expectations, including those of the deceased. Instead, successful adjustments require active coping strategies in which the be-

reaved individual finds his or her own best way to live with grief (Lund, 1993).

The final phase—reorganization—is marked by a resumption of routine activities and social relationships, while still remembering and identifying with the deceased, and recognition by the bereaved individual that life will never be the same. The ability to communicate effectively one's thoughts and feelings to others, form new relationships, and learn new skills and competencies enhances the adjustment process (Lund, 1993). *Integration of the loss into one's life* might be a more appropriate description than the term *recovery* to describe changes in the person's identity and emotional reorganization to ordinary levels of functioning (Weiss, 1993).

Estimates of the duration of time for the completion of grief among the bereaved range from 2 to 4 years, depending upon the nature of the relationship and the circumstances surrounding the death. On the other hand, some people never fully resolve their loss or cease grieving, but learn to live with the pain (Martin-Matthews, 1996; Thompson, Gallagher-Thompson, Futterman, Gilewski, and Peterson, 1998). Unresolved grief may be misdiagnosed as illness and lead to depression, as described in Chapter 6. For most people, some of the pain of loss remains for a lifetime. Older adults' experiences with grief may be even more complex than other age groups' for several reasons. As

---

STRATEGIES FOR GRIEVING

- Remember that grief is an emotion and needs to be felt; it cannot be worked out in the head.
- Tears are not a sign of weakness; they are an emotional first aid.
- Only the individual can decide what's right for him or her during this time.
- Grief is a life-changing experience; it takes time and patience to adjust.
- Be kind to oneself and lower expectations of what one can do. Grief

takes up a lot of emotional and physical energy.
- Lack of concentration, difficulty sleeping, forgetfulness, confusion, and anger toward others and the deceased are normal.
- It can be comforting to carry or wear something that belonged to the person who has died.

SOURCE: Northwest Geriatric Education Center, 2000.

noted in Chapter 6, they are more likely to experience unrelated, multiple losses over relatively brief periods, at a time when their coping capacities and environmental resources are often diminished. The cumulative effects of losses may be greater, especially if the older person has not resolved earlier losses, such as a child's death, or interprets current losses as evidence of an inevitable continuing decline. Health care providers must be careful not to misdiagnose grief symptoms as physical illness, dementia, or hypochondria. Not surprisingly, loneliness has been found to be the greatest difficulty for older bereaved spouses and cannot be managed simply by surrounding oneself with others (Lund et al., 1993).

Whether adjustment to bereavement is more difficult when death is sudden or unexpected is unclear. In comparison to the young, older people may be less affected by a sudden death because they have rehearsed and planned for widowhood as a life-stage task. They have also experienced it vicariously through the deaths of their friends or spouses of friends. An expected death can allow survivors to prepare for the changes through **anticipatory grief,**

but it does not necessarily minimize the grief and emotional strain following the death. In fact, some studies indicate that a longer period of anticipatory grief, through caring for an individual with chronic illness, can actually create barriers to successful adaptation and increase the risk of depression and other psychiatric disorders (Raveis, 1999). Family members who experience the death as a relief from long-term demands of care may feel premature detachment, ambivalent and hostile feelings, guilt, depression, and a reduced ability to mourn publicly. Other researchers have concluded that the overall adjustment process is similar whether the loss is expected or unexpected, although suddenness may make a difference early in the process of bereavement (Randolph, 1997; Lund et al., 1993). Some preventive predeath psychosocial interventions have been developed to minimize postdeath complications. These include facilitating communication with the ill partner, preparing the survivor for the practical aspects of life without one's spouse, and enabling the surviving spouse to deal with his or her own illness-related demands and losses.

HOW PROFESSIONALS AND FAMILIES CAN SUPPORT THE GRIEVING PROCESS

- Listen without judgment or giving advice to the bereaved individual's expression of feelings including guilt, anger, and anxiety, rather than suggesting what he or she *should* feel.
- Realize that the grieving process can be a lengthy and emotional roller-coaster, not a fixed progression in which one learns to live with grief.
- Be careful to avoid endless chatter or simplistic statements ("I know just how you feel." "She is happier now." "God loved him more than you did." "You should feel better in six months." "You can marry again/you'll meet someone else").
- Resist telling your own stories.
- Listen carefully to the silences, to what is not said as well as said.

- Encourage sharing of memories.
- Sometimes the most helpful response is simply "to be there" for the bereaved.
- Time itself does not heal. Healing takes place only through grief work, which can be painful and exhausting.
- Recognize that one never completely gets over a loss but one can learn to live with grief.
- Don't tell the bereaved to stop crying or not be sad; provide time and space to cry; sometimes hugging or patting the crying person's hand actually shuts down the crying.
- Identify concrete tasks by which to help, such as organizing meals, child care, and house cleaning, so the bereaved has time and space to grieve.
- Recognize gender differences in grieving.

Factors that are found to help manage grief and minimize negative effects are whether the death is viewed as natural, the degree to which relationships seem complete, and the presence of surviving confidants to provide emotional support. A central dynamic in caregiver bereavement is the support experienced while providing care, as well as the possibility of continued support (Almberg, Grafstroem, and Winblad, 2000). To work through grief successfully requires facing the pain and fully expressing the related feelings. Fortunately, understanding is growing about how grief and loss affect the bereaved individual's life and how to respond appropriately. Health care providers now recognize the importance of grief work and counseling, and view grieving as a natural healing process. Assistance in grief resolution, perhaps through life review and encouragement of new risk-taking, is especially important for older adults.

Unfortunately, most research of bereavement is case studies or retrospective studies during the early phase of grief. There are few well-controlled longitudinal studies of the bereavement process. An additional limitation is that few researchers have controlled for the effects of variables such as gender, race, age, social class, and education. Our understanding of the emotional components of bereavement is based largely on middle-aged, middle-class Caucasians, thereby limiting the cultural relevance of interventions to address the emotional aspects of grieving.

Mourning involves cultural assumptions about appropriate behavior during bereavement. Mourning rituals develop in every culture as a way to channel the normal expression of grief, define the appropriate timing of bereavement, and encourage support for the bereaved among family and friends. Professionals need to be sensitive to cultural and ethnic differences regarding the form and meaning of death and the burial or cremation of the dead. Grief rituals, such as sorting and disposing of personal effects and visiting the grave site, are important in working through the grief process.

The funeral, for example, serves as a rite of passage for the deceased and a focal point for the expression of the survivors' grief. Funerals also allow the family to demonstrate cohesion through sharing rituals, food, and drink, and thus to minimize the disruptive effects of the death. Funerals and associated customs are more important in societies with a high mortality throughout the life cycle than in societies where death is predominantly confined to the old. Money donations instead of flowers, memorial services and celebrations of the deceased person's life instead of funerals, and cremations instead of land burial signal the development of new kinds of death rituals. Traditional funeral ceremonies are criticized for being costly, for exploiting people at a time when they are vulnerable, and for elaborate cosmetic restorations of the body. Legislation has been enacted to control some of the excesses of the funeral industry; organizations such as the People Memorial Association ensure lower funeral costs to its members. Despite criticisms of the funeral industry, however, most people approve of some type of ceremony to make the death more real to the survivors and to offer a meaningful way to cope with the initial grief.

WIDOWHOOD

A spouse's death (or that of a partner, in the case of gay and lesbian couples or unmarried heterosexual couples) may be the most catastrophic and stressful event experienced by older adults, altering one's self-concept to an "uncoupled identity" (Raveis, 1999). Widowhood for both men and women not only represents the obvious loss, but numerous other dramatic changes in the survivor's life: loss of the role or status of married; lack of a sexual partner; loss of companionship, social networks, and a confidant; and especially for women, loss of economic security.

Among women age 65 and over, 50 to 70 percent are widowed, more than three times the rate among their male peers (Cohen, 1999). The average age of widowhood is 66 years for women and 69 years for men; when combined with women's greater life expectancy, this means that the average duration of widowhood for women is 15 years compared with 6 years for men. Widows

Older widows generally have more extensive peer support than widowers.

outnumber widowers 5 to 1; among people of color, the proportion of widows is twice that among whites; nonwhite women are also widowed earlier (Martin-Matthews, 1996). This is a reflection of the shorter life expectancy of nonwhite men in our society. Generally, bereaved individuals (especially men), are observed to manifest higher levels of psychiatric distress, anxiety, substance abuse, physical illness and utilization of health services, and lower well-being and morale, especially for the first 2 years after a partner's death (Nieboer, Lindenberg, Siegwart, and Ormel, 1999; Raveis, 1999). Rates of depression and somatic complaints (e.g., headaches, dizziness, muscular aches, weight changes, sleep disturbances, memory problems, and difficulty concentrating) are found to be nearly nine times as high among the newly bereaved, especially among men, as among married individuals (Raveis, 1999; Turvey, Carney, Arndt, Wallace, and Herzog, 1999). Quality of the prior relationship appears to affect how partners experience loss of a spouse. Psychological adjustment is also more difficult for those whose marriage was characterized by warmth and emotional dependence. Accordingly, grief appears to be less for those whose spousal relationship was conflictual (Carr, House,

Kessler, Nesse, Sonnega, and Wortman, 2000). In addition, harmonious marriages appear to have a protective benefit in terms of health service use and health care costs, until after widowhood, when health costs are higher than for survivors of discordant marriages (Prigerson, Maciejewski, and Rosenheck, 2000).

Despite the stress, the course of spousal bereavement is often characterized by resiliency and effective coping, which allows feelings of self-confidence, self-efficacy, and personal growth to follow short-term depression, loneliness, and sadness. In fact, only 15 to 25 percent of bereaved spouses have long-term (e.g., more than two years) difficulties in coping, or experience long-term negative impacts on physical and mental health (Lund, 1993). One exception is that the bereaved tend to experience loneliness more than the nonbereaved (Arbuckle and deVries, 1995).

The negative impact of widowhood can be attenuated through a number of complex social-psychological variables. These include the adequacy of the social support network, including professional support and closeness to children and intimate friends; the individual's characteristic ways of coping with stress; and religious commitment (Barrett and Lynch, 1999). Although family plays an important role following widowhood, 20 percent of widowed persons report not having a single living relative to whom they feel particularly close. Older widows are more likely to use social supports as a coping strategy when their social networks are characterized by reciprocity and reliability, but men generally do not. At the same time, friendships developed on the basis of marital relationships may not survive widowhood. In fact, the ability to make new friends may be an important indicator of how an individual is coping with the loss of a spouse (Ducharme and Corin, 1997; Martin-Matthews, 1996). Other variables that appear to affect the degree of stress of widowhood are age, gender, and health status of the widowed person. Age by itself, however, is found to have little effect on bereavement outcomes. Differences between younger and older widows can be explained by the relationship of age to employment status

Darlene became a widow at age 56. Although she was too young to qualify for her husband's Social Security, her dependent children at home received a monthly benefit of approximately $1,000 per child. A successful career woman, Darlene sought refuge in her work, her friends, and her children. She learned skills that she had not mastered during her marriage, such as home and car repairs, and appeared to be self-sufficient and "moving on" to her friends and children. During the day, she did function well. It was only at the end of the day, when other family members were asleep and she was climbing into the bed she had shared with her husband for many years, that she would be overcome by feelings of intense loneliness, hopelessness, and regret. At times, she felt overwhelmed by all the years ahead where she would bear both responsibilities and pleasure alone, without an intimate with whom to share. For more than two years, she cried every night before she fell asleep.

and income. Age is associated, however, with a greater need to learn new life skills, such as an older woman's mastering of financial-management tasks after the death of her husband. Gender has fairly consistent effects on personal functioning; women tend to exhibit lower levels of completing plans, lower self-efficacy, and higher levels of depression, and to express greater fatalism and more vulnerability than their male counterparts (Arbuckle and deVries, 1995).

Whether the stress of bereavement is greater for the young than for the old is unclear. Psychological distress tends to be greater for younger widows than older ones, since the death of one's spouse is more likely to be unanticipated and few of their peers are experiencing similar loss. Although younger spouses are found initially to manifest more intense grief, a reverse trend is noted after 18 months, with older spouses showing exacerbated grief reactions. A lifelong relationship has been lost, and the basic loss with bereavement continues to exist like a "phantom limb after an amputation" (Horacek, 1995). As noted earlier, older people are more likely to experience other losses simultaneously, or "bereavement overload" (Kastenbaum, 1991), which may intensify and prolong their grief. On the other hand, spousal bereavement in later life is an "on-time" or normative event, especially for older women, who typically have had other opportunities to develop appropriate coping strategies for a variety of losses. In such instances, widowhood may be less stressful, even among the oldest-old, and different death circumstances do not appear to have a significant impact on long-term adjustment (Lund, 1993).

Preventive psychoeducational interventions initiated predeath, such as through hospice, have been found to prevent or minimize problems in mourning as opposed to interventions postdeath, after problems have surfaced. Interventions postdeath focus on helping the surviving spouse review and reflect on the loss, providing support for grieving, and helping the surviving spouse to withdraw emotionally from his or her dead partner (Raveis, 1999). Since bereaved partners who have extensive contacts with friends and family and belong to church groups and other voluntary associations are less likely to die soon after the death of a spouse, interventions need to encourage network building and affiliations. Community mental health centers, primary care clinics, and senior centers are suitable venues for such cost-effective interventions.

Gender Differences in Widowhood

Whether widowhood is more difficult for women or men is unclear. Certainly, coping or adaptation to widowhood is related to income for both men and women. Adequate financial resources are necessary to maintain a sense of self-sufficiency and to continue participation in meaningful activities. Older widows are generally worse off than widowers in terms of finances, years of education, legal problems, and prospects for remarriage. Women who have been economically dependent on their husbands often find their incomes drastically

---

DEVELOPING NEW ROLES IN WIDOWHOOD

Martha had always seen her role as wife and mother and left the paying of the bills and "business" aspects of family life to her husband. Her "job" was to keep the home a comfortable place for him and their daughter. When he died 5 years ago, she was 63. She felt ill-prepared to take on paying the bills and managing other financial matters. She sought the advice of her banker on the best way to set up a bookkeeping system. After paying the bills, ordering some appliances for the house, and taking care of the Medicare paperwork for the past few years, she now sees herself as being in the role of "manager" for herself, and is pleased with what she has learned.

---

reduced, especially if they do not yet qualify for Social Security or if their husbands had not chosen survivors' pension benefits. Financial hardships may be especially great for women who have been caring for a spouse during a long chronic illness or who have depleted their joint resources during the spouse's institutionalization. Furthermore, older widows generally have few opportunities to augment their income through paid employment. Insurance benefits, when they exist, tend to be exhausted within 2 years of the husband's death. Not surprisingly, higher income has been found to be associated with better bereavement outcomes (Sanders, 1993). Accordingly, more years of schooling are related to higher levels of personal functioning, since education tends to provide the ability to clarify problems, identify resources, and take action toward solutions (Lopata, 1993). For both men and women, social support is positively associated with successful grief resolution (Thornton, 1997).

Some women, however, do not depend on a man for economic or social support. Because women generally have more diverse, extensive friendship networks than men do, and because widowhood is a more typical component of the life cycle for women, older women form strong support networks with other widows. These friendship groups can compensate for the loss of a husband's companionship and ease the adjustment to living alone. Friends are of greatest support, in some instances more so than children. This is especially true when friends accept the widow's emotional ambivalence, do not offer advice, and respond to what she defines as her needs. Adjust-

ing to the loss of a spouse is likely to be most difficult for women who are in poor health, have had few economic and social resources throughout their lives, and perceive themselves as dependent (Raveis, 1999). It is also problematic for women whose identity as a wife is lost without the substitution of other viable roles and lifestyles. A closely related factor appears to be whether a gap exists between how a woman was socialized to be dependent upon a man and how she must now live more independently as a widow (Lopata, 1987). For example, in a classic study, Lopata (1973) found that widows who did not have their own friends or who had only couple-based friendships before the husband's death generally had difficulty forming new friendships and developing satisfying roles. They also tended not to access social services. In our couples-oriented society, such women were lonely and isolated, and turned primarily to their children for emotional support. Friendships were thus the least frequent and the least deeply involving among the most disadvantaged and uneducated of the urban widows studied by Lopata. However, because more women have entered the workforce in the past 30 years, future cohorts of older women may be better prepared to live independently than the women in Lopata's early studies.

Among women over age 70, two-thirds of whom are widowed, the married person is the unusual case, but she may still have an extensive helping network (Barrett and Lynch, 1999). Whether widows have strong friendship networks appears to vary with socioeconomic class and race, whether they had a social network and satisfying roles before their husbands' deaths, and the prevalence of widowhood among a person's own age, sex, and class peers. Hispanic and Asian American widows are more likely to live with others and thus to have more active support systems than do Caucasian widows or those from other ethnic minority groups (Moen, 1996).

While older widowed men are seven times more likely than older widows to remarry (Cohen, 1999), many widows have no interest in remarriage. Even among Lopata's (1973) study of widows described above, 36 percent said they would not marry again. Although many persons feel great loss following a spouse's death, for some who have been restricted in their marriage or who faced long-term caregiving responsibilities, widowhood can bring relief and opportunities to develop new interests. Although a husband's death is devastating, personal growth can be a positive result of the loss (Salahie and Sakinah, 1996).

A woman's change in status inevitably affects her relationship with her children and other relatives. Most widows move in with their children only as a "last resort," although their children may view them as "helpless" and urge them to make the move. Older widows tend to grow closer to their daughters through patterns of mutual assistance, but sons may provide instrumental support (home repairs, yard work) for mothers in their own homes. Nevertheless, although children provide both socioeconomic support and assistance with tasks, this may not necessarily reduce their widowed parent's loneliness. For example, interactions with an adult child are less reciprocal, while friends and neighbors are better suited for sharing leisure activities and providing compan-

ionship. Such reciprocity tends to be associated with higher morale. What is clear is the importance of diverse social networks that include age-generational peers, whether family or nonfamily (McCandless and Conner, 1997).

Research on widowhood has focused on women, since there are five widows to every widower in our society. Less is known about the effects of widowhood on older men, for whom their wife's death tends to be unexpected (think about how many widowers will say "I always thought I was the one who would go first"). Men more often complain of loneliness and appear to make slower emotional recoveries than do women. Accordingly, they are more likely to experience declines in mental health, morale, and social functioning (Bennett, 1998). They may have more difficulty expressing their grief and adjusting to the loss than women do. This is because of their lower degree of involvement in family and friendship roles throughout life, their lifelong patterns of restraining emotions, their limited prior housekeeping and cooking, and the greater likelihood of a double role loss of worker and spouse (Patterson, 1996). On the other hand, some men experience pride and enhanced self-esteem from mastering new housekeeping skills (Lund et al., 1993). Many older men depended on their wives for emotional support, household maintenance, and social planning. Given these factors, men appear to "need" remarriage more than women do, and perhaps have been socialized to move more quickly into restructuring their lives through remarriage. Men, however, experience more medical problems (as measured by increased physicians'

MEN AND WIDOWHOOD

George's first wife died in childbirth; his second wife; who suffered a long bout of cancer, when he was 79, and his third wife, when he was 85. After the deaths of his first two wives, he quickly sought out someone else who could help fill the void left by their deaths. Each time, he looked for someone who would attend to his needs, listen to his stories, and join him on short outings and trips. He was seeking a companion, not a lover. After the death of his third wife, he became socially isolated and depressed. She had been the one who kept their social life going. Without her, friends seemed to drop away.

visits and use of medications, and higher rates of depression) and are at greater risk of dying during the 6 months following their wife's death (Lee, Willetts, Seccombe, 1998). Higher rates of illness may result from hormonal responses to the stress of loss, which can lead to depression of the body's immune system. Although the death of their wives may significantly impair older men's emotional and medical well-being, it is less likely to place men at an economic disadvantage. More research is needed on how men cope with the loss of their wives. Even less is known about how older men's experience of widowhood varies by social class or ethnic minority status.

Generally, widowhood increases social isolation for both men and women, with loneliness perceived as a major problem. In order to provide such support for persons coping with loneliness and isolation, mutual help groups and bereavement centers are developed by both mental health professionals and lay organizations. Women are the most frequent participants. These widow-to-widow groups are based on the principle of bringing together people who have the common experience of widowhood and who can help each other identify solutions to shared concerns. They recognize that a widowed person generally accepts help from other widowed people more readily than from professionals or family members. Support groups thus can provide widows with effective role models and can help integrate them into a social network and enhance their sense of competence toward their environment. Similar groups also need to be developed for gay men and lesbian women who are coping with the loss of a partner. Some studies, however, have suggested that a widowed person's sense of self-esteem, competence, and life satisfaction may be as important resources as the self-help intervention—or more so. One implication is that group interventions should focus upon ways for the bereaved to draw upon and enhance their internal resources, to experience increased confidence, and to learn new skills, not just serve as a forum to address the disruptive effects of the loss (Caserta, Lund, and Rice, 1999). Clearly, more research is needed on how support-

group dynamics and structure relate to specific adjustment outcomes.

SUMMARY AND IMPLICATIONS

Although death and dying have been taboo topics for many people in our society, they have become more legitimate issues for scientific and social discussion in recent years. At the same time, there is a growing emphasis on how professionals should work with the dying and their families, as well as a movement to permit death with dignity. A major framework advanced for understanding the dying process is the concept of stages of dying. However, the stage model is only an inventory of possible sequences, not fixed steps.

Most people appear both to deny and to accept death, being better able to discuss others' deaths than their own, and fearing a painful dying process more than the event of death itself. Different attitudes toward dying exist among the old and the young. Older people are less fearful and anxious about their death than younger people and would prefer a slow death that allows them time to prepare. Likewise, survivors tend to view an older person's death as less tragic than a younger individual's.

Professionals and family members can address the dying person's fears, minimize the pain of the dying process, and help the individual to attain a "good death." One of the major developments in this regard is hospice, a philosophy of caring that can be implemented in both home and institutional settings, and which provides people with more control over how they die and the quality of their remaining days.

The movement for a right to a dignified death has prompted new debates about euthanasia. Both passive and active euthanasia raise complex moral and legal questions that have been only partially addressed by the passage of living will legislation and a growing number of judicial decisions, including the June 1997 Supreme Court decision that ruled that there is no constitutional "right to die." Economic issues are also at stake; as costs for health care escalate, questions about how much public money should be spent on maintaining chronically ill people are likely to intensify. Bioethics, with its emphasis on informed consent, patient rights, and autonomy, addresses the moral issues raised by the health care of older people.

Regardless of how individuals die, their survivors experience grief and mourning. The intensity and duration of grief appear to vary by age and sex, although more research is needed regarding gender differences in reaction to loss of spouse and adjustment to widowhood.

By age 70, the majority of older women are widows. A much smaller number of older men become widowers, generally not until after age 85. The status of widowhood has negative consequences for many women in terms of increased legal difficulties, reduced finances, and few remarriage prospects. Although men are less economically disadvantaged by widowhood, they may be lonelier and have more difficulty adjusting than women do. For both men and women, social supports, particularly close friends or confidants, are important to physical and mental well-being during widowhood. In addition to mourning rituals to help widows and widowers cope with their grief, services such as widows' support groups are also needed. Comprehensive and diverse service formats are essential, given the variety of grief responses, and interventions should be available early in the bereavement process and continue over relatively long periods of time to ensure maximum effectiveness. Health and social service professionals can play a crucial role in developing services for the dying and their survivors that are sensitive to cultural, ethnic minority, sexual orientation, and gender differences.

GLOSSARY

active euthanasia   positive steps to hasten someone else's death, such as administering a lethal injection; assisted suicide, perhaps by a physician

advance directive   documents such as living wills, wills, and durable power of attorney for health care decisions that outline actions to be taken when an individual is no longer able to do so, often because of irreversible terminal illness

anticipatory grief   grief for a loved one prior to his or her death, usually occurring during the time that the loved one has a terminal illness that may allow survivors to prepare; may be a barrier to adaptation

bereavement   state of being deprived of a loved one by death

bereavement overload   an experience of older adults who are exposed to the increased frequency of family and friends' deaths and become desensitized to the impact of death

bioethics   discipline dealing with procedural approaches to questions about death, dying, and medical decision making

Choice in Dying, Inc.   national organization supporting passive euthanasia and providing information on advance directives

Compassion in Dying Federation   national organization supporting the right to die and working to educate health care providers about aggressive pain management

conservator   person designated by a court to manage the affairs, either personal or fiscal or both, of persons unable to do so for themselves

death crisis   an unanticipated change in the amount of time remaining to live

death with dignity   dying when one still has some independence and control over decisions about life

durable power of attorney   legal document that conveys to another person designated by the person signing the document the right to make decisions regarding either health and personal care or assets and income, or both, of the person giving the power; it is a durable power that does not expire, as a power of attorney normally does, when a person becomes incompetent

Dying Person's Bill of Rights   affirms dying person's right to dignity, privacy, informed participation, and competent care

dying process   as advanced by Kübler-Ross, five stages experienced by the dying person: (1) denial and isolation, (2) anger and resentment, (3) bargaining and an attempt to postpone, (4) depression and sense of loss, and (5) acceptance

dying trajectory   the pace of dying, sudden or slow, regular or erratic, usually shaped by the cause of death and by how much information is disclosed to the dying person

euthanasia   the act or practice of killing (active euthanasia) or permitting the death of (passive euthanasia) hopelessly sick or injured individuals in a relatively painless way; mercy killing

grief process   intense emotional suffering caused by loss, disaster, misfortune, etc.; acute sorrow; deep sadness

grief reaction   a state of shock, disbelief, and depression experienced following the death of a loved one

guardian   person who establishes legal control over another person's body as well as finances

Hemlock Society   national organization that promotes the right to die for terminally ill persons, calls for legalizing assistance for those who decide to take their own lives, and publishes information on nonviolent painless methods to commit suicide

hospice   a place or a program of care for dying persons that gives emphasis to personal dignity of the dying person, reducing pain, sources of anxiety, and family reconciliation when indicated

informed consent   written or oral document that states indications/reasons for treatment, its benefits, risks, and alternatives

living-dying interval   the time that occurs between the death crisis and the actual time of death, characterized by three phases: acute, provoking anxiety; chronic, characterized by decline of anxiety and facing death's reality; and terminal, eliciting withdrawal

living will   legal document in which an individual's wishes about medical treatment are put in writing should he or she be unable to communicate at the end of life, directing physicians and hospitals to withhold life-sustaining procedures, take all measures to sustain life, or whatever seems appropriate to the person executing the document

medical power of attorney   similar to "durable power of attorney," but focuses on a health care surrogate to make decisions about *medical* care

mourning   culturally patterned expressions of grief at someone's death

palliative care   treatment designed to relieve pain provided to a person with a terminal illness for whom death is imminent

passive euthanasia   voluntary elective death through the withdrawal of life-sustaining treatments or failure to treat life-threatening conditions

Patient Self-Determination Act   federal law requiring that health care facilities inform their patients about their rights to decide how they want to live or die; for example, by providing them information on refusing treatment and on filing advance directives

right to die   the belief that persons have a right to take their own lives, especially if they experience untreatable pain, often accompanied by the belief that persons have a right to physician assistance in the dying process

self-neglect   a process by which a person voluntarily makes decisions that are equivalent to choosing to die (e.g., refusing help, not eating)

surrogate decision maker   person legally designated to act according to patient's known wishes or "best interest"

RESOURCES

Web Resources on Grief and Loss   Web pages dedicated to grief and loss are increasing in both quantity and quality. Sites offer information on the grief process and provide opportunities to share feelings, questions, and concerns with others. Below is a small sampling of some of these sites. See the companion Website for this text at <www.ablongman.com/hooyman> for information about the following:

- Choice in Dying
- Griefnet
- Griefshare Grief Recovery Support Groups
- Hemlock Society
- Hospice Association of America
- Mr. Long Term Care
- National Alliance for Caregiving
- National Hospice Organization (NHO)
- AARP Grief and Loss Programs
- National Hospice and Palliative Care Organization
- Willowgreen
- www.caregivertips.com
- www.griefworks.com
- www.petloss.com

REFERENCES

Abrams, R. C. Physician-assisted suicide and euthanasia's impact on the frail elderly: Something to think about. *Journal of Long Term Home Health Care:*

The Pride Institute Journal, Summer 1998, *17*, 19–27.

Alliance for Aging Research. *Seven deadly myths: Uncovering the facts about the high costs of the last year of life*. Washington, DC: 1997.

Almberg, B. E., Grafstroem, M., and Winblad, B. Caregivers of relatives with dementia: Experiences encompassing social support and bereavement. *Aging and Mental Health*, 2000 4, 82–89.

American Geriatrics Society. The care of dying patients: A position paper from the American Geriatrics Society. *Journal of the American Geriatrics Society*, 1994.

American Medical Association, Report 59(A-96). Physician-assisted suicide. Reference Committee on Amendments to Constitution and Bylaws. *Journal of the Oklahoma State Medical Association*, 1996, *89*, 281–293.

Arbuckle, N. W., and deVries, B. The long-term effects of later life spousal and parental bereavement on personal functioning. *The Gerontologist*, 1995, *35*, 637–645.

Asch, D. A., Hansen-Flaschen, J., and Lanken, P. N. Decisions to limit or continue life sustaining treatment by critical care physicians in the United States: Conflicts between physician's practices and patient's wishes. *American Journal of Respiratory and Critical Care Medicine*, 1995, *151*, 288–292.

Barrett, A. E., and Lynch, S. M. Caregiving networks of elderly persons: Variation by marital status. *The Gerontologist*, 1999, *39*, 695–700.

Benedict, A., and Zhang, X. Reactions to loss among aged men and women: A comparison. *Activities, Adaptation and Aging*, 1999, *24*, 29–39.

Bennett, K. M. A longitudinal study of well-being in widowed women. *International Journal of Psychiatry*, 1997, *12*, 61–66.

Braun, K., Look, M., Yang, H., Onaka, A., and Horiuchi, B. Native Hawaiian mortality in 1980 and 1990 in the State of Hawaii. *American Journal of Public Health*, 1996, *86*, 888–889.

Braun, K. L., and Nichols, R. Death and dying in four Asian American cultures: A descriptive study. *Death Studies*, 1997, *21*, 327–359.

Braun, K. L., Pietsch, J. H., and Blanchette, P. L. (Eds.). An introduction to culture and its influence on end-of-life decision making. In *Cultural Issues in end-of-life decision making*, Thousand Oaks, CA: Sage, 2000.

Bretscher, M., Rummans, T., Sloan, J., Kaur, J., Bartlett, A., Borkenhagen, L., and Loprinzi, C. Quality of life in hospice patients: A pilot study. *Psychosomatics*, July-August 1999, *40*, 309–313.

Butler, R. Keynote Address, Presented at the Open Society Institute. *Project on Death in America*, Lake Tahoe, CA: July 17–22, 2000.

Callahan, D. *The troubled dream of life: Living with mortality*. New York: Simon and Schuster, 1993.

Callahan, S. A feminist case against euthanasia: Women should be especially wary of arguments for "the freedom to die." *Health Progress*, 1996, 21–29.

Caplan, A. L. Will assisted suicide kill hospice? *Hospice Journal*, 1997, *12*, 17–24.

Carr, D., House, J. S., Kessler, R. C., Nesse, R. M., Sonnega, J., and Wortman. C. Marital quality and psychological adjustment to widowhood among older adults: A longitudinal analysis. *Journals of Gerontology*. 2000, *55B*, S197–S205.

Caserta, M. S., and Lund, D. A. Bereavement, stress and coping among older adults: Expectations versus the actual experience. *Omega*, 1992, *25*, 33–45.

Caserta, M. S., and Lund, D. A. Intrapersonal resources and the effectiveness of self-help groups to bereaved older adults. *The Gerontologist*, 1993, *33*, 619–629.

Caserta, M. S., Lund, D. A., and Rice, S. J. Pathfinders: A self-care and health education program for older widows and widowers. *The Gerontologist*, 1999, *39*, 615–620.

Castle, N. G. Innovations in dying in the nursing home: The impact of market characteristics. *Journal of Death and Dying*, 1998, *36*, 227–240.

Choice in Dying, *Fact Sheets: National Advance Directive Campaign*. New York: Choice in Dying, 1994.

Christ, G. H., and Sormanti, M. Advancing social work practice in end-of-life care. *Social Work in Health Care*, 1999, *30*, 81–98.

Christakis, N. A., and Lamont, E. B. Extent and determinants of error in doctors' prognoses in terminally ill patients: Prospective cohort study. *Journal of Behavioral Medicine*, 2000, *320*, 469–473.

Cicirelli, V. G. Elders' end-of-life decisions: Implications for hospice care. *Hospice Journal*, 1997a, *12*, 57–72.

Cicirelli, V. G. Personality and demographic factors in older adults' fear of death. *The Gerontologist*, 1999, *39*, 569–579.

Cicirelli, V. G. Relationship of psychosocial and background variables to older adults' end-of-life decisions. *Psychology and Aging*, March 1997b, *12*, 72–83.

Clements, R. Intrinsic religious motivation and attitudes toward death among the elderly. *Current*

Psychology: Developmental, Learning, Personality, Social, 1998, *17,* 237–248.

Cohen, G. D. Marriage and divorce in later life (Editorial). *American Journal of Geriatric Psychiatry,* Summer 1999, *7,* 185–187.

Cole, T. R., and Holstein, M. Ethics and aging. In R. H. Binstock and L. K. George (Eds.), *Handbook of aging and the social sciences* (4th ed.). San Diego, CA: Academic Press, 1996.

Compassion in Dying. Senate bill threatens Oregon's death with dignity act & pain care nationwide. *Compassion in Dying,* Summer/Fall 2000, Issue 13.

Ducharme, F., and Corin, E. Widowed men and women—An exploratory study of the significance of widowhood and coping strategies. *Canadian Journal on Aging,* 1997, *16,* 112–141.

Fauser, M. C. Hospice patient perspectives regarding the implementation of advanced directives. *Dissertation Abstracts International: Section B: The Sciences and Engineering,* 1999, *60,* 0410.

Feher, A. Wills and estate planning. *Access. A Guide to Resources,* 2000, Senior Services Newsletter.

Freeman, H., and Payne, R. Racial injustice in health care: An editorial. *The Washington Post,* March 2000, 1–2.

Galambos, C. M. Preserving end-of-life autonomy: The patient self-determination act and the uniform health care decisions act. *Health & Social Work,* 1998, *23,* 275–281.

Gianelli, D. Right-to-die debate turns to out-of-hospital DNR order. *American Medical News,* November 7, 1994, *37,* 3.

Gordon, A. K. Hospice and minorities: A national study of organizational access and practice. *Hospice Journal,* 1996, *11,* 49–70.

Holstein, M. Ethics and aging: Bringing the issues home. *Generations,* Fall 1998, *22,* 4.

Hornik, M. Physician-assisted suicide and euthanasia's impact on the frail elderly: A social worker's response. *Journal of Long Term Home Health Care: The Pride Institute Journal,* Summer 1998, *17,* 34–41.

Hudson, T. Court strikes down assisted suicide ban in Washington State. *Hospitals and Health Networks,* August 5, 1994, *68,* 180.

Ingebretsen, R., and Solem, P. E. Death, dying, and bereavement. In I. H. Nordhus and G. R. VandenBos et al., *Clinical geropsychology.* Washington, DC: American Psychological Association, 1998.

Institute of Medicine. *Approaching death: Improving care at the end of life.* Washington, DC: National Academy Press, June 1997.

Johnston, S. C., Pfeifer, M. P., and McNutt, R. The discussion about advance directives: Patient and physician opinions regarding when and how it should be conducted. *Archives of Internal Medicine,* 1995, *155,* 1025–1030.

Kalish, R. Death and survivorship: The final transition. *Annals of the American Academy of Political and Social Sciences,* 1982, *464,* 163–173.

Kastenbaum, R. *Death, society and human experience* (4th ed.). New York: Macmillan/Merrill, 1991.

Kastenbaum, R. Dying and death: A life-span approach. In J. Birren and K. W. Schaie (Eds.), *Handbook of the psychology of aging.* New York: Van Nostrand Reinhold, 1985.

Kavanaugh, K. I. M. The importance of spirituality. *Journal of Long-Term Care Administration,* 1996–97, *24,* 29–31.

Kübler-Ross, E. *On death and dying.* New York: Macmillan, 1969.

Kübler-Ross, E. (Ed.). *Death: The final stage of growth.* Englewood Cliffs, NJ: Prentice-Hall, 1975.

Kübler-Ross, E. *Living with dying.* New York: Macmillan, 1981.

Kurent, J. E. The Institute for Community and Professional Education in End-of-Life Care. Presented at the Open Society Institute, *Project on Death in America,* Lake Tahoe, CA: July 17–22, 2000.

Lee, G. R., Willetts, M. C., and Seccombe, K. Widowhood and depression: Gender differences. *Research on Aging,* September 1998, *20,* 611–630.

Lloyd, M. Dying and bereavement, spirituality and social work in a market economy of welfare. *British Journal of Social Work,* 1997 April, *27,* 175–190.

Lopata, H. Z. The support systems of American urban widows. In M. Stroebe, W. Stroebe, and R. Hanson (Eds.), *Handbook of bereavement: Theory, research and intervention.* New York: Cambridge University Press, 1993.

Lopata, H. Z. *Widowhood in an American city.* Cambridge, MA: Schenkman, 1973.

Lopata, H. Z. *Widows.* Durham, NC: Duke University Press, 1987.

Lund, D. A. Widowhood: The coping response. In R. Kastenbaum (Ed.), *Encyclopedia of adult development.* Phoenix, AZ: Onyx Press, 1993.

Lund, D. A., Caserta, M., and Dimond, M. The course of spousal bereavement in later life. In M. Stroebe,

W. Stroebe, and R. Hanson (Eds.), *Handbook of bereavement: Theory, research and intervention.* New York: Cambridge University Press, 1993.

Maro, R. Victory through the courts. *Compassion in Dying,* Spring 1996, 1.

Marshall, V. A sociological perspective on aging and dying. In V. Marshall (Ed.), *Later life: The social psychology of aging.* Beverly Hills, CA: Sage, 1986.

Martin-Matthews, A. Widowhood and widowerhood. *Encyclopedia of Gerontology,* 1996, 2, 621–625.

McCandless, N. J., and Conner, F. P. Older women and grief: A new direction for research. *Journal of Women and Aging,* 1997, 9, 85–91.

McClain, V. R., Tindell, S., and Hall, S. H. Ethical dilemmas in right to die issues. *American Journal of Forensic Psychology,* 1999, 17, 77–88.

McCue, J. D. The naturalness of dying. *Journal of the American Medical Association,* 1995, 273, 1039–43.

McLaughlin, L. A., and Braun, K. L. Asian and Pacific Islander Cultural Values: Considerations for Health Care Decision Making. *Health and Social Work,* 1998, 23, 116–126.

McMahon, P., and Koch, W. Assisted suicide: A right or a surrender. *USA Today,* November 29, 1999, 1, 21A.

Miller, G. Hospice. In C. Evashwick (Ed.), *The continuum of long-term care: An integrated systems approach.* Albany, NY: Delmar Publishers, 1996.

Moen, P. Gender, age and the life course. In R. H. Binstock and L. K. George, *Handbook of aging and the social sciences* (4th ed.). San Diego, CA: Academic Press, 1996.

Morrison, R. S., and Siu, A. L. Survival in end-stage dementia following acute illness. *Journal of the American Medical Association,* 2000, 284, 47–52.

Moyers, B., and Moyers, J. *On our own terms: Moyers on dying.* Public Affairs Television, September 2000.

Muir, J. C. No title. Presented at the Open Society Institute, *Project on Death in America,* Lake Tahoe, CA: July 17–22, 2000.

Mutran, E. J., Danis, M., Bratton, K., Sudha, S., and Hanson, L. Attitudes of the critically ill toward prolonging life: The role of social support. *The Gerontologist,* 1997, 37, 192–199.

Nieboer, A. P., Lindenberg, S. M., and Siegwart Ormel, J. Conjugal bereavement and well-being of elderly men and women: A preliminary study. *Journal of Death and Dying,* 1999, 38, 113–141.

Nordquist, G. American health care and the medicalization of dying. *Journal of Applied Social Sciences,* Spring-Summer 1999, 23, 31–42.

Northwest Geriatric Education Center, Dealing with grief and loss, *NWGEC Viewpoint,* Winter 2000, 9, 1–3.

Olson, E. Physician-assisted suicide and euthanasia's impact on the frail elderly: A physician's reply. *Journal of Long Term Home Health Care: The Pride Institute Journal,* Summer 1998, 17, 28–33.

Ostrom, C. New focus on debate on assisted suicide. *The Seattle Times,* January 1998, 1, A18.

Ostrom, C. The war on pain. *The Seattle Times,* May 14, 2000, pp. 1, A15, A17.

Ostrom, C., and Westnext, D. Next target of assisted suicide efforts: State laws. *The Seattle Times,* June 27, 1997, A2.

Patterson, J. Participation in leisure activities by older adults after a stressful life event: The loss of a spouse. *International Journal of Aging and Human Development,* 1996, 42, 123–142.

Payne, R. At the end of life: Color still divides. *The Washington Post,* February 15, 2000.

Preston, T. A. Facing death on your own terms. *Newsweek,* May 22, 2000, 82.

Prigerson, H. G., Maciejewski, P. K., and Rosenheck, R. A. Preliminary explorations of the harmful interactive effects of widowhood and marital harmony on health, health service use, and health care costs. *The Gerontologist,* 2000, 40, 349–357.

Randolph, J. D. Timing of conjugal loss in late life and successful outcome: A life-span perspective. *Dissertation Abstracts International: Section B: The Sciences and Engineering,* February 1997, 57, 5366.

Rao, R., Dening, T., Brayne, C., and Huppert, F. A. Attitudes toward death: A community study of octogenarians and nonagenarians. *International Psychogeriatrics,* June 1997, 9, 213–221.

Rasmussen, C. A., and Brems, C. The relationship of death anxiety with age and psychosocial maturity. *The Journal of Psychology,* 1996, 130, 141–144.

Raveis, V. H. Facilitating older spouses' adjustment to widowhood: A preventive intervention program. *Social Work in Health Care,* 1999, 29, 13–32.

Reibstein, L. Matters of life and death. *Newsweek,* July 7, 1997, 18, 30.

Rosenfeld, K. Los Angeles Healthcare System, Presented at the Open Society Institute, *Project on Death in America,* Lake Tahoe, CA: July 17–22, 2000.

Rozenzweig, A., Prigerson, H., Miller, M. D., and Reynolds, C. F., 3rd. Bereavement and late-life depression: Grief and its complications in the elderly. *Annual Review of Medicine*, 1997, *48*, 421–428.

Salahu-Din, S. N. A comparison of coping strategies of African American and Caucasian widows. *Journal of Death and Dying*, 1996, *33*, 103–120.

Sanders, C. M. Risk factors in bereavement outcome. In M. Stroebe, W. Stroebe, and R. O. Hanson (Eds.), *Handbook of bereavement: Theory, research and intervention*. New York: Cambridge University Press, 1993.

Seattle Times, "Death with dignity" bill approved by Senate, March 6, 1992, 1-B2.

Seattle Times. "No right to die, say justices." June 26, 1997, 1, 23A.

Silverman, H. J., Tuma, P., Schaeffer, M. H., and Singh, B. Implementation of the Patient Self-Determination Act in a hospital setting. *Archives of Internal Medicine*, 1995, *155*, 502–510.

Simmons, H. C. Spirituality and community in the last stage of life. *Journal of Gerontological Social Work*, 1998, *29*, 73–91.

Straub, S. H. Fear of death after the loss of a spouse: A study of the effects of age and mode of death. *Dissertation Abstracts International: Section B: The Sciences and Engineering*, October 1997, *58*, 1794.

Sullivan, M., Ormel, J., Kemper, G. I. J. M., and Tymstra, T. Beliefs concerning death, dying, and hastening death among older, functionally impaired Dutch adults: A one-year longitudinal study. *Journal of the American Geriatrics Society*, 1998, *46*, 1251–1257.

Teno, J. M. Putting patient and family voice back into measuring quality of care for the dying. *Hospice Journal*, 1999, *14*, 167–176.

Thompson, L. W., Gallagher-Thompson, D., Futterman, A., Gilewski, M. J., and Peterson, J. The effects of late-life spousal bereavement over a thirty-month interval. In M. P. Lawton and T. A. Salthouse et al. (Eds.), *Essential papers on the psychology of ag-*

ing. Essential papers in psychoanalysis. New York: New York University Press, 1998.

Thornton, J. C. B. *The hospice widow and grief resolution: Perceived marital satisfaction and social support as factors influencing bereavement*. Barry University Ph.D. dissertation, May 1997.

Thorson, J. A., and Powell, F. C. Elements of death anxiety and meanings of death. *Journal of Clinical Psychology*, 1988, *44*, 691–701.

Tucker, K. L. Physician-assisted dying: A constitutionally protected form of "rational suicide." In J. L. Werth et al. (Eds.), *Contemporary perspectives on rational suicide. Series in death, dying, and bereavement*. Philadelphia: Brunner/Mazel, Inc., 1999.

Walker, G. C. The right to die: Healthcare workers' attitudes compared with a national public poll. *Journal of Death and Dying*, 1997, *35*, 339–345.

Weinberg, J. Balancing autonomy and resources in healthcare for elders. *Generations*, Fall 1998, *22*, 92–96.

Weinberg, J. K., and Brod, M. Advance medical directives: Policy perspectives and practical experiences. *Journal of Ethics, Law, and Aging*, 1995, *1*, 15–35.

Weiss, R. S. Loss and recovery. In M. Stroebe, W. Stroebe, and R. O. Hanson (Eds.), *Handbook of bereavement: Theory, research and intervention*. New York: Cambridge University Press, 1993.

Weitzner, M. A., and McMillan, S. C. The caregiver quality of life index—cancer (CQOLC) Scale: Revalidation in a home hospice setting. *Journal of Palliative Care*, Summer 1999, *15*, 13–20.

Wilber, K. H., and Reynolds, S. C. Rethinking alternatives to guardianship. *The Gerontologist*, 1995, *35*, 248–256.

Wojciechowski, C. Issues in caring for older lesbians. *Journal of Gerontological Nursing*, 1998, *24*, 28–31.

Zuckerman, C. Issues concerning end-of-life care. *Journal of Long Term Home Health Care: The Pride Institute Journal*, Spring 1997, *16*, 26–34.

14

THE RESILIENCY OF ELDERS OF COLOR

This chapter covers the following:

- Definition of ethnicity, minority status, and people of color
- Research history on ethnic minorities
- Challenges faced by older African Americans, Hispanic Americans, American Indians, Asian Americans, and Pacific Islanders
- Barriers to service delivery
- Implications for culturally sensitive services

When discussing the physiological, psychological, and social changes experienced by older adults, there is a tendency to speak about them as if they were a homogeneous group. Yet, as illustrated throughout this book, the older population is more heterogeneous than any other. Two primary variables in this heterogeneity are gender and ethnic minority status; both influence an individual's position in the social structure and typical lifetime experiences (Angel and Hogan, 1994). To be an older person of color, or an older woman, is to experience environments substantially different from those of a white male across the life span. For example, both older women and African American elders are more likely to live alone, which places them at greater risk of economic insecurity, poorer health status, and social isolation.

The interaction of gender, ethnicity/race, living arrangements, and social class is illustrated by the following facts:

- The poverty rate for women who live alone is five times greater than that for their peers who live with a spouse.
- The mean income of older African American households is about half that of older white households.
- Older women of color are more likely to obtain health care from hospital outpatient units, emergency rooms, and neighborhood centers than from private physicians.
- Older women of color who live alone form the poorest group in our society (Administration on Aging, 1999).

Consistent with the *life course perspective* outlined in Chapter 8, such economic and health disparities in old age are typically related not only to current living arrangements, but also to early experiences in education, labor-force participation, health status and access to health care, and cultural beliefs and practices. Elders of color bring to old age the cumulative effects on their health of being ethnic minorities in a society where they face disadvantages because of their race. Inequities from earlier in life are usually intensified in old age.

Relevant differences among older people arising from their gender and their ethnic minority status are noted throughout this text. Chapters 14 and 15, however, focus specifically on these factors because of their interactive effects with age and the resulting higher incidence of poverty, poor health, and inadequate living arrangements. In this sense, both older women in general and persons of color of both genders are affected by environmental changes that are not always congruent with their needs as they age. Socioeconomic status, along with race and gender, creates inequities across the life course. Socioeconomic status also influences variation within groups, not only between groups. Despite the greater problems facing both women and people of color, both groups display strengths and resiliency in old age.

Defining ethnicity*

Ethnicity involves three components:

1. culture, values, and beliefs, as well as an internalized common heritage, which are not fully understood or shared by outsiders
2. social status
3. support systems (Barresi and Stull, 1993)

These components influence the way people feel about themselves and how they interact with their environments, resulting in particular patterns of adjustment to aging. Ethnicity serves the following functions:

- an integrating force in passing through significant life changes
- a buffer to stresses of old age, especially when the environment supports the expression of ethnicity
- a filter to the aging process, influencing beliefs, behaviors, and interactions with professionals

Given these various functions, social and health-care providers need to understand ethnicity and how it influences values and behaviors such as help-seeking.

By identifying culturally conditioned values in an older person's heritage, we can gain a better understanding of that person's attitudes and behaviors in the face of aging. For example, many Japanese American elders emigrated from small farming villages where ancestor worship was practiced, reflecting the respect traditionally accorded elders. They have grown old in a country where youth is more highly valued than age, and thus may experience conflicts between their views and those of their

---

*Throughout the book, we refer interchangeably to ethnic minorities and people of color.

children and grandchildren. Based on its unique history, each ethnic minority population has developed its own methods of coping with the inevitable conflicts between traditional and adopted ways of life, leading to both vulnerabilities and strengths.

Defining Minority and People of Color

For purposes of this chapter, *ethnic minority elders* include older people of color belonging to groups whose language and/or physical and cultural characteristics make them visible and identifiable, who have experienced differential and unequal treatment, who share a distinctive history and bonds of attachment among group members, and who regard themselves as objects of collective discrimination and oppression *by reason of their race*. Specifically, this chapter examines the life conditions and adaptation to aging among people of color who are defined by the federal government as protected groups—African Americans, Hispanic Americans (including Mexican Americans/Chicanos, Puerto Ricans, Cubans, and Latin Americans), American Indians, and Asian Americans and Pacific Islanders. Although we consider how ethnicity or cultural homogeneity in general influences the aging process, our focus is on people of color who have experienced economic and racial discrimination, and thus often face greater problems.

Two distinct issues should be kept in mind in this discussion of ethnic minority elders:

1. the unique historical calendar of life events and culture and their impact on lifestyles, many of which are positive
2. the consequences of racism, ageism, discrimination, and prolonged poverty, most of which are negative

For people of color, race is a social status that shapes an individual's values, behaviors, and distribution of resources. In fact, race may interact with individual conditions (e.g., functional impairment) and social structural factors (e.g., socioeconomic status) to influence the receipt of help, including the use of informal and formal care (Nor-

gard and Rodgers, 1997). It is not only their ethnic and cultural traditions that influence their socialization process, but also their experience of being a racial minority within a white majority culture (Wykle and Kaskel, 1994). Accordingly, the aging process and quality of life of elders of color are inevitably affected by the experiences of a lifetime of racial discrimination.

The use of the term "people of color" recognizes, however, that in most instances, by the middle of the twenty-first century, groups that are currently numerical minorities will become the numerical majority in many areas. They may, however, continue to face oppression and discrimination. For example, Hispanics are already the numerical majority in Los Angeles and in some Texas cities, but continue to be poorer and less healthy than their Caucasian counterparts. And the 2000 Census captured the dramatic growth of populations of color nationwide.

There are recurring themes in analyses of ethnic minority status and older people, such as family structure, coping behavior, and values. Nevertheless, variations *within* as well as *among* these groups must be understood. Differences in immigration patterns, birthrates, region, social class, rural or urban location, gender, and acculturation level add to the intragroup variations. Hispanics, for example, who are defined by the U.S. Bureau of the Census as Spanish-speaking persons, include people from many different cultures and a high percentage of recent immigrants. Accordingly, no one term for persons of Spanish heritage is accepted by all. Persons of Hispanic descent can be from any of the following racial groups: Caucasians, Native American, Indian/African. Mexican Americans are generally of Spanish Caucasian/Indian descent, while Cubans/Puerto Ricans are of Spanish Caucasian/African descent. American Indian refers to the indigenous peoples of North America, including Indians, Eskimos, and Aleuts and over 500 recognized tribes, bands, or Alaskan Native villages. African Americans differ from one another in terms of cultural background, socioeconomic status, and geographic location—especially recent immigrants from Africa, Haiti, or the Caribbean Islands. Recent immigrants from Laos, Cambodia, and Vietnam have a higher proportion of elders than do other Asian American/Pacific Islander groups.

Today, ethnic minorities comprise 15.7 percent of the population over age 65, as shown in Table 14.1 (AoA, 1999). They include a smaller proportion of older adults and a larger proportion of younger adults than the white population. This differential results primarily from higher rates of fertility and higher mortality rates, as well as patterns of immigration, among the nonwhite population under age 65 than among the white older population. Although relatively small in size, populations of color are of increasing concern to gerontologists because of the disproportionately greater number of social problems that they face relative to whites. In addition, the proportion of elders of color is expected to increase at a higher rate than for the white population, forming more than 33 percent of the total older population by 2050 (NIH, 2000). As noted in Chapter 1, this is occurring partially because of the large proportion of children in these groups, who, unlike their parents and especially their grandparents, are expected to reach old age. The greatest growth will occur in those 85 and over. Currently, less than one in ten ethnic minority elders are among the oldest-old; this percentage will increase to one in five by the year 2050, with the greatest increase among Hispanic oldest-old, to triple to nearly 15 percent of ethnic minority older adults. Although immigrants are generally younger persons, many have brought or sent for their older parents and relatives, especially from countries experiencing political oppression. Accordingly, it is predicted that the immigrant groups of the twentieth century—Hispanics, Asian Americans, and Pacific Islanders—will redefine American culture in the twenty-first century (Angel and Hogan, 1994).

RESEARCH HISTORY

Ethnogerontology, a growing field of social gerontology, is the study of the causes, processes, and consequences of race, national origin, and culture on individual and population aging. From 1940 to 1970, when both scholarly and political concern with older adults grew, little was written about the special circumstances of ethnic minority elders; this was, in part, because of their relatively small size compared to Caucasian older adults (Markides and Black, 1996). In 1956, Tally and

TABLE 14.1 **Ethnic Minority Distribution of the Older Population**

	% OF TOTAL POPULATION, 65+	% OF THE ETHNIC MINORITY POPULATION, 65+	PROJECTED PERCENTS IN 2050
Whites	84.3	—	
African Americans	8.0	8.4	10.0
Asian Americans/Pacific Islanders	2.1	7.5	7.0
American Indians	0.4	7.2	0.6
Hispanic Americans	5.1*	5.8	16.0

*The sum of the specific percentages reported here will never round off to approximately 100 percent if a Hispanic percentage is included. The reason for this anomaly is that the U.S. Bureau of the Census does not treat the Hispanic category (which includes Mexicans, Venezuelans, and Latinos who self-designate themselves as being white) as one that is mutually exclusive from the racial categories. Thus, the Hispanic data are also included within each of the racial categories. Persons of Hispanic origins may be of any race, and represent 3 percent of the older population.

SOURCE: AoA, 1999.

Kaplan first raised the **double jeopardy hypothesis:** Are African American elders doubly jeopardized relative to their white counterparts? That is, do lifetime factors of economic and racial discrimination make adjusting to old age more difficult for African Americans (and other minorities) than for whites? As a result of such double jeopardy, do minorities experience lower life satisfaction (Cuellar and Weeks, 1980)? Debates about double jeopardy—whether it exists and is related to socioeconomic status or to race per se—have been central in research and policy discussions in ethnogerontology.

A second but related position asserts that patterns of racial inequality are changing, and that minorities' opportunities throughout their lives are related more to their economic class position than to their race. Social class, not minority status, jeopardizes them. The **multiple hierarchy stratification** perspective encompasses both views, defining race as one source of inequality along with class, gender, and age itself (Bengtson, 1979). Ethnogerontologists argue that double jeopardy should not be a central concept because cross-sectional studies have rarely produced useful information about age changes as opposed to age differences (Markides et al., 1990). They suggest that double jeopardy may be time-bound, resulting largely from major social and political changes in the status of minorities, not from racial differences. They also point to the lack of empirical support for widening differentials in health and socioeconomic status with age (Markides and Black, 1996). Since cross-sectional studies have rarely produced useful information about age changes as opposed to age differences, more longitudinal studies are required to determine the effects of ethnic minority group status on age changes.

A counterargument to the double jeopardy hypothesis is that age is a leveler of differences in life expectancy. This mortality **crossover effect** refers to the fact that people of color experience poorer health and higher death rates than whites at all ages until very old age. After age 75, the death rates for African Americans, Asian Americans, and American Indians are actually lower than for

whites. Accordingly, life expectancy for these survivors is greater, due to a combination of biological vigor, psychological strength, and resources for coping with stress, such as religious practices that link individuals to the community. Thus, the oldest-old segment of the ethnic minority population may represent successful or robust aging, as described in Chapter 6. In fact, although people of color may experience increasing income and health disparities with age, they nevertheless display considerable strengths and may experience higher levels of psychological well-being and emotional support than do Caucasian elders. This may result from selective survival and adaptation factors that cause those who survive to be more hardy (Wykle and Kaskel, 1994). It is unclear, however, if the apparent racial crossover and selective survival are due to enumerative errors and reliance on cross-sectional data to compare advantaged and disadvantaged populations, rather than to health differences per se. The apparent racial crossover effect also raises questions about the usefulness of chronological age as a measure of aging. Given these issues, the relative status and mortality risks of whites and nonwhites are still debated. What is clear is that tremendous variation occurs both across and within ethnic minority categories (Markides and Black, 1996).

The year 1971 marked a turning point in the recognition of ethnic minority elders as a special area of gerontological study. In that year, the National Caucus on the Black Aged was formed (later becoming the National Center and Caucus on the Black Aged), and a session on "Aging and the Aged Black" was held at the White House Conference on Aging. This conference, especially important from a policy perspective, highlighted the need for income and health care supports. Since 1971, the National Association for Spanish-Speaking Elderly, the National Indian Council on Aging, and the National Asian Pacific Center on Aging have been established. These associations function as advocacy groups for elders of color and as research and academic centers.

The census is the primary source of information for organizations planning services for ethnic

---

THE CHARACTERISTICS OR PATTERNS SHARED ACROSS POPULATIONS OF COLOR

Cumulative disadvantages of being people of color:

- limited resources throughout their lives to meet health care needs
- influence of socioeconomic status on health differences between people/populations of color and whites
- women outnumbering men, and more likely to be widowed than their male peers

Centrality of family/kin values:

- preference for in-home services
- reluctance to use out-of-home services, especially nursing homes
- more likely to turn to informal supports than formal services

Lower rates of insurance coverage and health care utilization, especially preventive services:

- lower rates of Medicare coverage, especially among immigrant populations
- sociocultural and political barriers to health care (different communication styles, history of racism and discrimination, language barriers)
- preference for non-Western methods of healing (especially among Asian Americans, American Indian elders)

Chronic illness:

- major causes of death: diabetes and hypertension
- greater number of functional disabilities (e.g., restricted activity and bed-disability days)
- may be recognized as old prior to chronological age
- more likely to experience psychosocial distress and erroneous diagnoses of mental health problems

---

minority elders. Census data, however, are criticized for undercounting minority subgroups, misclassifying individuals, or merging data about various nonwhite groups. For example, the Census Bureau has often grouped people by race as "white," "black," or "other." However, how mixed race or multiracial individuals should be classified in the census is changing, with the 2000 census the first to include multiracial categories. In addition, research on ethnic minorities generally does not break down data by gender, and studies on older women do not cross-classify data by minority status. From the feminist perspective discussed in Chapter 8, it is difficult to determine how racism and sexism interact to produce "gender-specific race effects and race-specific gender effects" (Gould, 1989). Another limitation is that studies in the 1970s and 1980s were based on small, nonrepresentative samples. Fortunately, research methodology in recent years has improved, especially in the areas of cross-cultural measurement and sampling (Markides and Black, 1996).

Because of census data limitations and the wide diversity of cultural patterns, few other generalizations are valid for ethnic minority older populations as a whole. Using race per se as a variable may not lead to straightforward interpretations, because cultural values (e.g., the meaning attached to caregiving or to spirituality) and socioeconomic status are interdependent and difficult to separate. Within the overall context of these limitations, we next briefly review the life conditions of each of the four major ethnic minority groups in the United States.

OLDER AFRICAN AMERICANS

Although African Americans are the largest population of color in the United States, only about 8 percent of them are over 65 years of age, compared to 14 percent of the white population. The young outnumber the old, due primarily to the higher fertility of African American women and blacks' higher mortality, including homicide, in their younger years. The median age of African Americans (29.5 years) is 5 years younger than the median age for whites (34.6). The life expectancy

Oldest-old African American men are remarkable survivors.

for African American men and women is 65 and 74.5 years, respectively, compared with the life expectancy of 73.5 years for white men and 80 years for white women (Administration on Aging, 1997). Although these disparities in life expectancy reflect differences in childhood and youth mortality rates, differences in life expectancy after age 75 are less dramatic. African American men who live to age 65 can expect to live another 14 years; African American women, 18 years. This is only slightly less than for their white counterparts (15.5 and 19 years, respectively). This narrowing of difference in life expectancy after age 75 (the crossover effect discussed earlier) may be explained by the fact that African Americans who survive to this age tend to be the most robust of their cohort.

Although they are a relatively small percentage of the total African American population, adults over age 65 form the fastest-growing segment of that group. While the overall African American population is expected to grow by 45.6 percent by 2020, the proportion of older people generally will likely increase by 90 percent, from 8 percent to 15.3 percent in the year 2020, and to 21.3 percent by 2050. The greatest proportion (nearly 60 percent) are young-old, although as with other groups, the oldest-old is the fastest-growing segment of African American elders. The ratio of

men to women is slightly lower than among whites, 62 males for every 100 females, compared to 67 per 100 among the Caucasian population. Oldest-old women are the most rapidly growing group of African American elders, and they have the longest average remaining life span (NIH, 2000).

Economic Status

Nearly three times the proportion of older African Americans live below the poverty line compared to older whites: 26 percent vs. 9 percent respectively (AoA, 1999). The poverty rate across groups is shown in Figure 14.1. The incidence of poverty increases dramatically among households composed of unrelated black individuals, especially females age 65 and over. The median income of African American males over 65 is approximately 60 percent of white men; that of black women about 66 percent that of white women, with the proportion of older African American female-headed families in poverty increasing in the past 20 years (Miller et al., 1996). Differences in education do not explain the gaps in income, which have persisted since 1985. In fact, these inequities are increasing, due to general economic conditions from the 1970s to the mid-1990s, such as the lack of growth in real wages, decline in pension coverage, and reductions in public supports such as Supplemental Security Income (SSI).

As noted in Chapter 12, the primary reasons for the lower socioeconomic status of older African Americans are:

- pattern of limited employment opportunities and periods of unemployment throughout their lives
- concentration in low-paying, sporadic service jobs, especially in nursing homes and hospitals
- greater likelihood of leaving the workforce earlier, frequently because of health problems
- decreased likelihood of receiving pension income
- likelihood of receiving only minimum Social Security benefits compared to whites

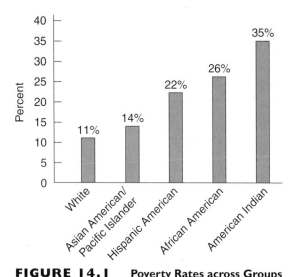

FIGURE 14.1 **Poverty Rates across Groups**
SOURCE: AoA, 1999.

As noted in Chapter 12, African Americans often return to work after retirement out of economic necessity, creating the phenomenon of the "unretired/retired." In effect, they spend a greater proportion of their lives both working and disabled, with fewer years in retirement (Hayward, Friedman, and Chen, 1996). This pattern reduces not only their lifetime earnings, but also their Social Security and pension benefits. Accordingly, more older African Americans than white persons rely on SSI.

Health

By most measures, the health of African American adults is worse than that of their white counterparts, which is oftentimes a continuation from middle age and an outcome from cumulative effects of poverty, racism, and genetics. Being either black or poor is a powerful predictor of mortality. The socioeconomic disadvantages experienced by African Americans explain much of the variance in their lower utilization of health services, reduced access to health care, poorer health status, and higher rates of mortality. Gaps in mortality are re-

duced when social class is controlled for. In fact, marginal increases in socioeconomic status and education generally have larger positive effects on the health of blacks than on whites (Schoenbaum and Waidman, 1997).

The prevalence of chronic diseases is estimated to be twice as high among African Americans as among whites, and the former more often perceive themselves as being in poor health than do their white counterparts. Older African Americans experience hypertension, cancer, heart disease, stroke, and diabetes more frequently than do their white peers, although these differences are greatest at age 45 and decline with age, especially after age 85 (Freeman and Payne, 2000; National Institutes of Health, 2000). In addition, they have more undetected diseases such as depression. The stresses of constantly struggling to make ends meet may translate into higher rates of depression, especially among women For example, obesity is a frequent health problem among African American women, which can lead to complications of hypertension and diabetes. The rate of diabetes mellitus among black women is twice that among white women, and has been described as an epidemic (NIH, 2000). Kidney failure, which may result from hypertension and diabetes, is more common in older African Americans. They also experience more rapid declines in functional ability, more days of functional disability (i.e., substantially reduced ability to complete daily activities) and bed disability (i.e., being confined to bed for at least half of the day), and at earlier ages than whites. Proportionately more African American older people are completely incapacitated and unable to carry on any major activity (e.g., paid employment, keeping house), although still residing in community-based households (Belgrave, Wykle, and Choi, 1993).

African American elders also appear to have less access to health care than their white counterparts, although they are more likely to use hospital emergency rooms as a way to enter the health care system. An important predictor of health service utilization is the availability of health insurance. Older blacks are more often dependent on Medicaid, less likely to have private supplemental health insurance than their white counterparts, and therefore less likely to receive adequate care at hospitals (Kahn, Pearson, and Harrison, 1994). Alternatively, they are more likely to turn to kin and friends for information and use self-care health practices, such as home remedies, lay consultations, and folk medicines (Davis and Mc-Gadney, 1993; Hopper, 1993).

There is a wide range of social and political barriers to health care for African American elders:

- With the legacy of history of discrimination within health care systems, especially in the South, health care providers are perceived as unwelcoming.
- Individuals are reluctant to report poor care for fear of being ignored or retaliation.
- They turn to friends and kin, rather than health care, for support and information.
- Indirect communication styles used to function in a racist society may interfere with the open of information-sharing needed for diagnosis, and make it difficult for health providers to understand health concerns in misdiagnosis of conditions.
- Providers may be unaware of how skin color can affect the presentation or manifestation of a disease.
- Potentially significant conditions may not be detected until advanced stages, or benign conditions may be misdiagnosed as more serious than they are.

Black–white differences in mortality rates are notable for the three leading causes of death. Thus, while heart disease, stroke, and cancer are the leading causes of death for both races at age 65 and older, rates for African Americans are 5, 17, and 24 percent higher, respectively, for each of these conditions (NCHS, 1992). African Americans have higher death rates for cancers of the lungs, prostate, and cervix than do other groups of color. Similarly, their 5-year survival rate for cancer of the cervix,

uterus, and esophagus is lower than for any other population segment. They have many of the risk factors for cancer: higher occupational and residential exposure to cancer-causing substances, higher rates of obesity (e.g., 60 percent of black women over age 45 are obese), higher prevalence of smoking, and less knowledge about cancer and its prevention (NIH, 2000). This greater vulnerability is compounded by their lower access to health care and higher rate of undetected diseases, so that many cancers are not detected early enough to prevent metastasis. Blacks are less likely than whites to receive curative surgery for early-stage lung, colon, and breast cancer, and are inadequately treated for pain from cancer (Freeman and Payne, 2000). Once diseases are detected, however, due to the crossover phenomenon, the higher likelihood of death for blacks from these conditions occurs only until about age 75, when both men and women begin to have a lower incidence of death than their white counterparts (Gibson, 1994). Deaths in late life due to lifestyle and environmental hazards, including accidents and homicides among men, are also much higher in blacks than in whites, except for those who survive into their eighties. In addition, they face a number of sociocultural and political barriers to health care.

Social Supports and Living Situations

Living arrangements affect blacks' health and socioeconomic status. The proportion of married African Americans is lower than that of any other population. This is because of lower life expectancy for black men in particular and high rates of widowhood among black women; (48% are widowed compared to 19% among their male peers) (NIH, 2000). Among African Americans over age 65, 54 percent of men and 25 percent of women are married. This compares with 80 percent and 41 percent, respectively, among whites (Rawlings, 1993). Almost 50 percent of African American women live alone, a higher proportion than that of their white counterparts or older black males. Those who live alone are more likely to be impoverished, marginally housed, and even homeless (Killon, 2000). In addition, rates of remarriage are lower than in other groups. One reason for these differences is that widowhood, separation, and divorce are more prevalent among older African Americans and more likely to have occurred at an earlier age compared to other groups (NIH, 2000).

Even though most older African Americans do not live in extended families, approximately 20 percent, compared to 12 percent of their white counterparts, live with a family member other than their spouse. Comparative studies have found that older African Americans have larger, more extended families than do whites, a higher frequency of family-based households, and higher levels of social support from their extended families, including friends, neighbors, and coworkers. Accordingly, older African American women are more likely than white women to have family living with them in their homes. Most often, these are three-generation households, with older women at the top of the family's power hierarchy, playing an active role in the management of the family (Smith, 1997). As noted in Chapter 9, older women often provide financial assistance and care for grandchildren, as well as children of other family members and friends.

Similar to whites, adult children remain a primary source of assistance and support for older African Americans. For childless older adults, siblings are the most important kin tie (Johnson, 1999). The family has flexible definitions of membership and more elastic boundaries that can potentially expand the numbers to include **fictive kin.** Creation of fictive kin is another source of loving support. This includes foster parents or children who function in the absence of blood relatives or when family relationships are unsatisfactory. As an illustration, African American women active in church are more likely to turn to nonrelatives in times of need than to their children, but these nonkin may be considered part of an extended family network. Similarly, they are more likely than whites to have larger, looser social networks that include nonimmediate family members among

their pool of unpaid caregivers (Johnson, 1999). By redefining distant kin and friends as primary kin, they increase the number of close relationships. The process of enlarging their extended family beyond lineal ties thus expands their pool of supportive resources.

Although many African American elders live alone, they generally tend to draw from a more varied pool of friends, fellow church members, and other associated contacts, and are more likely to use them interchangeably than are whites (Johnson, 1999). Although blacks are more likely to receive help from children and grandchildren, and to take children into their homes, intergenerational assistance is a function not just of race, but of age, marital and socioeconomic status, and level of functional disability. In some instances, such multigenerational households may be an adaptation to poverty or other problems rather than an indicator of a supportive extended family. Indeed, an increasing number of older blacks are affected by stressors influencing members of their social networks, such as crime and substance abuse by children and grandchildren, and face caregiving responsibilities as a result. On the other hand, intergenerational households that develop out of financial necessity illustrate the resourcefulness of black families whose domestic networks expand and contract according to economic resources. Even though socioeconomic factors partially explain race differences in intergenerational exchanges, there is strong adherence to norms of filial support and attitudes of respect toward elders among African Americans across social classes (Smith, 1997).

In sum, African American elders appear to have a broader range—not just a larger number—of informal instrumental and emotional supports than is characteristic of Caucasian older people. Norms of reciprocity are strong and have evolved from a cooperative lifestyle that served as a survival mechanism in earlier times and which continues to be a source of support.

Studies of psychological and general well-being among African American elders illustrate the benefits of social support. Despite significant economic hardships, the majority of older blacks, especially those age 75 and older, report high life satisfaction and happiness compared to their white counterparts, regardless of living conditions. This may reflect the decreasing demands of family and employment responsibilities in this oldest group, and the associated perception of few significant stressors affecting them. At the same time, however, older African Americans are more likely to report high levels of life satisfaction and happiness if they perceive their physical health to be good; this is consistent with other evidence of the link between physical and psychological health generally among the older population. Black elders who survive to age 75, are in good health, and are relieved of the burdens of family caregiving are most likely to experience life satisfaction.

Older African Americans' life satisfaction is also explained in terms of their spiritual orientation and their religious participation. As noted in Chapter 12, spirituality and religion, which are important in the lives of many black elders for adaptation and support, are related to feelings of well-being, self-esteem, and personal control. The church also provides a support network of spiritual help, companionship, advice, encouragement, and financial aid. Faith in God is one way that older African American women living in poverty cope with hardship and enhance self-esteem. For example, qualitative interviews with 50 women identified their belief that they enjoy a partnership with God in which God responds to their faith with reciprocal blessings, both in this life and the next. They believe that their hardship is part of a divine plan that will eventuate in rewards both in this life and the next; the women are thereby released from despair. God is regarded as a personal friend who knows each woman intimately and cares for her (Black, 1999).

Accordingly, African Americans prefer formal services in the home rather than institutional care, which is considered a last resort, and are less likely to enter a nursing home than whites. Only 3 percent of all African Americans age 65 and older and only 12 percent of those over age 85 are institutionalized, compared to 5 and 23 percent of their white counterparts, respectively (NIH, 2000). African American nursing home residents are found to be more limited in their ability to carry out activities of daily living and less often receiving the appropriate level of care than are whites. Once admitted to a nursing home, older blacks are less likely to be discharged, largely because informal resources have been exhausted.

Low rates of nursing home placement may reflect the following factors:

- lack of nursing homes in African American communities
- inadequate income to pay for private nursing home care
- perceptions that nursing home services are not culturally compatible
- greater probability that an African American elder, dependent upon Medicaid, has fewer institutional options
- current or historical racist practices among medical providers and nursing home staff
- preference for traditional folk medicine and/or informal supports (NIH, 2000)

OLDER HISPANIC AMERICANS

Hispanic Americans are the largest ethnic minority population following African Americans. They are also the fastest-growing group in the United States. They are highly diverse and include many groups, each with its own distinct national/cultural heritage: Mexicans, Puerto Ricans, Cubans, Central or South Americans, and the native Mexican American or Chicano population, whose history in the United States predates settlement by English-speaking groups. They thus encompass native-born, legal, and undocumented immigrants with varying lengths of residence in the United States. The recency of immigration affects the needs of these groupings for various supports and services. For example, the Dominican population is growing rapidly. Their elders' pressing needs are for housing, assistance with the naturalization process, and obtaining basic medical and social services. Any

Grandparents in the Hispanic community often play vital intergenerational roles.

such services will need to take account of the Dominican population's strong sense of spirituality as a way to cope with stressful events (Paulino, 1998). The greatest proportion of Hispanics (64 percent)—and also the poorest—are Mexican Americans, or Chicanos, who are concentrated in five, primarily rural, southwestern states. Central and South Americans form 14 percent, Puerto Ricans 10 percent, and Cubans 14 percent of the Hispanic population. A sizable proportion of Cubans have immigrated at age 55 or older and represent the wealthiest and most educated; they also have the largest proportion of foreign-born older adults among Hispanics (NIH, 2000). The remaining 8 percent are "other Hispanics," descendents of the early Spanish colonists. Although bonded by a common language, each Hispanic grouping differs substantially by geographic concentration, income, education, length of residence in the United States, cultural heritage, history, and dialect.

Hispanic elders' needs may be underestimated, since many studies include Hispanics in either black or white categories. Those that have an Hispanic classification often fail to differentiate among the diverse subgroups. The Hispanic older population is projected to grow much faster than their white or black counterparts. In fact, the percentage of oldest-old among the Hispanic population will triple by 2050. Compared to other ethnic groups, the Spanish-speaking population is youthful, with a median age of 26 years, 8 years younger than the norm in the United States (NIH, 2000). A number of factors underlie their relative youthfulness. One variable is lower average life expectancy, which may be partially explained by poor economic and health status among Mexican Americans and Puerto Ricans. The most important contributing factor, however, is their generally high fertility rate. The number of children born and the average family size among Hispanics exceed the national average. High levels of net immigration and repatriation patterns are secondary factors, with the youngest (and often poorest) people most likely to move to a new country, and some middle-aged and older Mexican Americans moving back to Mexico. Despite its current relative youthfulness, the Hispanic population experienced the greatest increase in median age of all ethnic groups from 1960 to the late 1990s. As noted above, this suggests that the percentage of older Hispanic Americans will rise steeply in the future, as younger cohorts reach old age. Accordingly, the parent support rate is expected to triple by 2030, with more middle-aged and young-old adults faced with family care responsibilities (NIH, 2000).

Within the overall Hispanic population, the sex ratio varies because of the gender imbalance in previous immigration streams and women's survival rates. As a whole, there are proportionately more Hispanic men to women over age 65 than among the white older population, but this is due to the higher mortality rate of Hispanic women than white women at earlier ages, not to increases in longevity among Hispanic men. Nevertheless, the overall gender patterns of this population are similar to those of other older people. Women live longer and outnumber men, comprising over 60 percent of the population age 65 and over, and 62 percent of the oldest-old (NIH, 2000). They more often remain widowed and live alone than men do. Older Hispanic men marry or remarry more often than men in other groups: over 80 percent of older Hispanic males are married, compared with 33 percent of older Hispanic women (Angel and Hogan, 1994). Those female-headed households are most likely to be poor.

Economic Status

Sociocultural conditions underlie Hispanics' poor economic and health status. More than any other group, they have retained their native language, partially because of geographic proximity to their home countries, combined with the availability of mass communication. In fact, approximately 40 percent of older Hispanics speak only Spanish (NIH, 2000). Although serving to preserve their cultural identity, their inability to speak English is a major barrier to their education, employment, and utilization of health services. Mexican Americans and Puerto Ricans are also the most educationally deprived group, with approximately 30 percent having less than a fourth-grade education. Another barrier encountered by those who entered the country illegally is the inability to apply for Social Security, Medicare, or Medicaid. All these factors partly explain why such large numbers of Mexican American and Puerto Rican elders have minimal education and have worked in unskilled, low-paying jobs with few benefits. Nearly 20 percent receive neither Social Security nor pension income, and nearly 10 percent have no public or private medical insurance, although Social Security and SSI are the primary sources of retirement income for other Hispanics. Such patterns have been intensified by the 1996 Welfare Reform Act, which restricts benefits for immigrants.

These employment and educational conditions contribute to the high rate of poverty among older Hispanics. In 1990, approximately 22 percent lived below the poverty level, compared to approximately 9 percent of older whites. Another 33 percent, compared to 18 percent of older whites, hover just above the "near poverty" threshold at incomes below 125 percent of the poverty line. The median personal income of Hispanic men age 65 and over

is about 65 percent of white males; for Hispanic older women the median income is 68 percent of white females (AoA, 1999).

Health

The poverty of Hispanic Americans undoubtedly contributes to their generally poor health across the life span, which reduces their opportunities for employment and education and lowers their chances of a lifetime accumulation of income. Given the high proportion who have been migrant farm workers, exposure to potentially harmful pesticides may put them at further risk of health problems. Eighty-five percent of older Hispanics report at least one chronic condition; 45 percent indicate some limitation in their activities of daily living. Physiological aging tends to precede chronological aging, with those in their early fifties experiencing health disabilities typical of 65-year-old whites. Because they age "faster" than whites, 66 percent of a sample of older Mexican Americans viewed themselves as old beginning at or below 60 years of age (Espino, 1993). Such earlier functional aging can be attributed to harder working conditions, poor nutrition, and inadequate health care. Diabetes, kidney disease, circulatory disorders, heart disease, chronic liver disorders, and motor vehicle accidents are the main causes of higher death rates than for their white counterparts (NIH, 2000). Women are more likely than men to suffer multiple illnesses. Higher rates of depression are identified among Puerto Rican and Dominican elders, especially among those who are female, live alone, and have a higher number of health problems (Falcon and Rucker, 2000). Hispanic women have higher mortality rates from cervical cancer and cancer of the uterus than do white women (NIH, 2000). As with African Americans, this may be due to lower access to health care and preventive services, resulting in cancer detection occurring too late for successful treatment. Some studies, however, suggest that immigrants among the Hispanic population, regardless of age, are healthier than their peers who remain in their home countries. This may be due to protective cultural factors and selective immigration (e.g., those who immigrate tend to be healthier than those who remain at home) (Stephen, Foote, Hendershot, and Schoenbaum, 1994).

Early studies suggested that Hispanic elders are least likely among all groups of older adults to utilize formal health services (Miranda, 1990). However, recent research on health service utilization found that Hispanic elders made more physician visits than whites. The authors caution against assuming homogeneity among Hispanics, however (Lum, Chang, and Ozawa, 1999). For example, Cuban Americans and Puerto Ricans are more likely to see a physician than are Mexican Americans, in part because of a higher probability of insurance coverage (Burnette and Mui, 1999). Barriers to health service utilization exist, such as mistrust of mainstream medical providers, reliance on folk medicine and religious healing, and language difficulties among some Hispanic subpopulations. Nevertheless, wide heterogeneity in immigration experiences and socioeconomic status affect both how Hispanics perceive their health and what services they utilize.

Only about 3 percent are in nursing homes, with 10 percent of those over age 85 institutionalized, compared to 23 percent of oldest-old whites. Since families attempt to provide support as long as possible, when older Hispanics do enter nursing homes, they tend to be more physically and functionally impaired than their Caucasian counterparts (NIH, 2000).

Social Supports and Living Situations

Historically, the extended family has been a major source of emotional support to older Hispanics, especially in rural areas. Older Hispanics are more likely than whites to believe that elders should be cared for in the community. They are more than four times as likely as Anglos between the ages of 65 and 74, and more than two times as likely as those 74 years of age and older, to live with their adult children. Widowed women over 75 are the most likely to live in extended family households. Hispanic older couples are more likely to head

households containing relatives, and Hispanic older singles more likely to live as dependents in someone else's household than are other ethnic minority groups (Choi, 1999).

Family caregiving is influenced by the cultural values and beliefs of:

- *familism* (family as central to the life of the individual)
- *marianismo* (female superiority and the expectation that women are capable of enduring all suffering)
- *machismo* (socially learned and reinforced set of behaviors that guides male behavior)
- *respect* (expectations of how others should treat us and vice versa)

Family caregiving behaviors are affected by perceptions of gender inequities and self-identification as a member of a minority group (Cuervo, 1999; Vasquez and Rosa, 1999). As a whole, Hispanics highly value family relations, believing that the needs of the family or its individual members should take precedence over one's own. Although patterns of intergenerational assistance are strong compared to Caucasian populations, the percentage of Hispanics living in multigenerational households has declined recently. With their urbanization and greater acculturation, younger Hispanics are increasingly unable to meet their older parents' expectations to support an extended family in one location. Those who live alone are often inadequately housed, with substandard housing rates substantially greater among Hispanics than among whites (NIH, 2000).

When families are living apart, elders often still perform parental roles; assist with child care, advising, and decision making; and serve as role models (Johnson, 1995). Socioemotional help and advice are typically sought across generations. Although families remain the most important support for their older members, a division of labor is emerging. This takes place between the family, which provides emotional support and personal care, and public agencies, which give financial assistance and medical care, along with churches and mutual-aid, fraternal, and self-help groups. These community-based groups provide outreach, advocacy, and information about resources, socialization opportunities, financial credit for services, and folk medicine. The supportive social and cultural context of neighborhood and community is congruent with Hispanics' strong sense of cultural identity. Being part of "La Raza" encompasses a shared experience, history, and sense of one's place in the world that can be a powerful base for community and political mobilization (Torres-Gil and Kuo, 1998).

Older American Indians

American Indian refers to indigenous people of the United States, including Eskimos and Aleuts (i.e., Alaskan Natives). Their median age is 27 years (approximately half of all Indians are under the age of 27.6 years), compared to 34 years for the general population. Only 6 percent of this population is 65 years of age and older. Their current life expectancy at birth is 65 years, approximately 8 years less than for the white population, although women tend to live longer than men. Life expectancy tends to be even lower in nonreservation areas. Not surprisingly, with a gender ratio of approximately 64.5 men to every 100 women age 65 and over, women comprise almost 60 percent of American Indian elders (NIH, 2000). More than 75 percent of American Indian men, but less than 50 percent of their female counterparts, are married. Although only 13 percent of the American Indian population will enter the 65-plus age category, compared to 19.5 percent of the U.S. population, by the end of this century the number of American Indians who are in the oldest-old category will at least double. In fact, between 1940 and 1980, life expectancy for American Indians at birth increased by 20 years, from 50 to 71.1 years, compared to a 10-year increase for whites to 74.4 years (Administration on Aging, 1997; NIH, 2000). This increase is due, in large part, to efforts of the **Indian Health Service** (IHS) to eliminate infectious diseases and meet acute-care needs earlier in life. The greatest reduc-

Congregate meal sites offer an important source of social support and cultural continuity.

tions have occurred in death rates due to tuberculosis, gastrointestinal disease, and maternal and infant mortality. Nevertheless, mortality rates for the major killers of older people—heart disease, cancer, and stroke—have not been reduced in the American Indian population.

Less systematic data are available for American Indians than for other populations. The two federal agencies responsible for collecting data, the Bureau of Indian Affairs (BIA) and the Census Bureau, frequently have different estimates, making it difficult to generalize about American Indian older people. An additional complication in generalizing findings is that there are nearly 535 federally recognized tribes, an estimated 100 nonrecognized tribes, and approximately 300 federally recognized reservations (NIH, 2000). Also, many urban Indians do not live on reservations, and therefore their conditions and needs are less visible. A further complication is that approximately 20 percent of American Indian elders who live in federally recognized areas are not enrolled in a tribe, and thus would not be seen by providers within the Bureau of Indian Affairs (BIA) or the Indian Health Service (IHS) (John, 1994). Among this highly diverse population, nearly 300 native languages are spoken, and cultural traditions vary widely. More American

Indian elders live in rural areas than do other older populations of color, with nearly 25 percent on reservations or in Alaskan Native villages. On the other hand, most do not return to their reservations as they age, instead preferring to age in place, similar to many elders. Relatively high levels of residential stability characterize the older American Indian population. Over 50 percent are concentrated in southwestern states, with the remainder mostly in states along the Canadian border.

Economic Status

Over 35 percent of older American Indians are estimated to be poor, with per capita incomes that are 40 to 59 percent less than those of whites. The median income is barely above the poverty threshold. Although about 50 percent of older urban American Indians live with family members, their families are also more likely to be poor than their white counterparts (Manson, 1993). Similar to other ethnic minority populations, the poverty of older American Indians tends to reflect lifelong patterns of unemployment, employment in jobs not covered by Social Security, especially on reservations, and poor working conditions. Of all populations, American Indian elders are the most likely to have never been employed. By age 45, incomes have usually peaked among men in this group, and decline thereafter. In addition, historical circumstances and federal policies toward tribes have intensified the pattern of economic underdevelopment and impoverishment in "Indian country," which has led to a steady net migration to urban areas (John, 1994).

American Indian women are generally less educated than their male counterparts, and seldom earn even half the income of the men, putting them in a severely disadvantaged position. Another factor that negatively affects their socioeconomic and living conditions is that more than 50 percent of women age 60 and over are widowed. High unemployment and low income levels tend to necessitate intergenerational living arrangements, with the elders often the sole provider of the family through their Social Security or Supplemental Security Income. Yet only about 50 percent of American Indian elders receive Social Security and Medicare benefits, and less than 40 percent receive Medicaid, even though such public supports appear to be essential to their survival (John, 1994).

Health

American Indians may have the poorest health of all Americans, due in part to inadequate housing conditions and the isolation of many of their communities. Their elders have a higher incidence than their white counterparts of diabetes, hypertension, accidents, tuberculosis, heart disease, liver and kidney disease, strokes, pneumonia, influenza, hearing and visual impairments, and problems stemming from obesity, gall bladder, or arthritis. In fact, nearly 75 percent suffer limitations in their ability to perform activities of daily living. Cancer survival rates are the lowest among all U.S. populations (NIH, 2000). The primary risk factors for disease are smoking and diet, especially consumption of alcohol. The death rate from alcoholism is seven times higher than that of the United States generally. Alcoholism, however, usually takes its toll before old age. Alcohol-related deaths drop sharply among American Indians who have reached age 55. Automobile accidents also take a disproportionately heavy toll on American Indian men (Barresi and Stull, 1993; John, 1994). In addition, poverty has combined with the historical suppression of indigenous religions and medical practices to place American Indians/Alaska Natives at higher health risks due to environmental degradation. These risks result from living in poor-quality housing, being exposed to local toxins, and lacking safe water supplies and sewage disposal systems.

For traditional American Indians, medicine is holistic and wellness-oriented. It focuses on behaviors and lifestyles through which harmony can be achieved in the physical, mental, spiritual, and personal aspects of one's role in the family, community, and environment (Kramer, 1992; Manson, 1993). The loss of access to traditional environments and the suppression of religious and medical practices also threaten traditional knowledge de-

Characteristics of American Indians/Alaska Natives that influence their use of health services:

- Strong values favoring tribal autonomy
- Nonlinear thinking, especially about time

- Use of indirect communication and styles
- Historical suspicion of authority

rived from the use of plants and herbs. Fortunately, the IHS is allowing medicine men and other traditional healers to treat patients in some of their clinics. This may help foster and preserve their heritage and enhance IHS professionals' learning of non-Western healing practices. Unfortunately, most procedures that focus on treating specific diseases rather than the whole person have typically not incorporated healing elements, such as the medicine wheel. This then reduces the effectiveness of such programs with American Indian elders.

Given these health problems, it is not surprising that people on reservations appear to be physiologically old by 45 years of age, and in urban areas, by age 55. In fact, three times as many American Indian persons die before reaching the age of 45 than non-Indians (NIH, 2000). American Indians are less likely than non-Indians to define aging chronologically. Social functioning and decline in physical activities are generally used to identify an elder. As a result, a significant barrier to using publicly funded health services is that eligibility is typically based on chronological, not functional, age.

Because of the importance of tribal sovereignty, many American Indians believe that health and social services are owed to them as a result of the transfer of land and that these services derive from solemn agreements between sovereign nations. Despite this attitude, the majority of elders rarely see a physician, often because of living in isolated areas, lacking transportation, and mistrusting non-Indian health professionals. Accordingly, the prevailing life circumstances for many elders—of poverty, low self-esteem, alcoholism, and substance abuse—may interfere with their ability to seek preventive health care. In addition, language remains a barrier. For example, some of the languages of indigenous people contain no words for

cancer. Many feel that talking about the disease will bring it on, hold fatalistic views of it, or believe that their culture may stigmatize cancer survivors. In addition, many prefer traditional health care from their tribal medicine people and resist using non-Indian medical resources.

To understand their health care patterns, a life-course perspective is necessary that considers their experiences with racism and discrimination. The urbanization of the American Indian population during and after World War II created two worlds of aging. For American Indian elders who are dispersed among the general urban population, there is no tribal community or government concerned with their welfare. Nor do they have special government institutions, such as the Indian Health Service or the Bureau of Indian Affairs, responsible for the well-being of American Indians on reservations.

In contrast, those on reservations have access to the *Indian Health Service* for health care. As noted earlier, the IHS is effective in controlling infectious diseases and providing acute care earlier in life, thereby extending life expectancy. The IHS, however, tends to emphasize services to youth and families and acute care, rather than addressing elders' needs or providing long-term care (skilled- and intermediate-care facilities) (NIH, 2000). As a result, the majority of American Indian elders receive social and medical services from the BIA and IHS only periodically. For example, the IHS operates only 10 nursing-homes on reservations, as compared to 49 hospitals. This means that older American Indians who need nursing home care may find themselves in long-term care facilities that are at a geographic distance and not oriented to Indian peoples. Such cultural and geographic barriers have resulted in a pattern of repeated short-term stays or revolving-door admissions for chronic conditions. Accordingly, among those over 85 years of age, only 13 percent of American Indians are in nursing homes, compared to 24.5 percent of whites (Manson, 1993).

The sociocultural and political barriers to health care among American Indians encompass the following:

- They ascribe ill health and debility to the normal aging process and are therefore less likely to seek care for conditions that are treatable and curable.
- There is a distrust of medical care that is not native.
- They encounter professionals' lack of sensitivity to ritual folk healing and cultural definitions of disease.
- There have been past experiences with racism, discrimination, and stereotyping and with being turned away from public clinics where staff insist that IHS is the sole agency responsible for them.
- They anticipate adverse contacts and being treated unfairly by non-Indian health professionals.
- They are unwilling to sit through long waits at non-native clinics.
- They perceive health care providers as rude because of such behaviors as getting right down to business, addressing strangers in a loud voice, confident tones, and frequent interruptions of the patient.

American Indian elders perceive their physical and mental health to be poorer than do white older adults. Some studies document a higher incidence of suicide, but findings are mixed. Depression appears to be a major mental health problem but is difficult to diagnose because of cultural factors. American Indians' low utilization of mental health services is not necessarily a reflection of fewer emotional problems, but may represent barriers to treatment and lack of information about available psychological services from their health care providers (Markides and Black, 1996). On the other hand, maintaining a tribal identity may serve to buffer various stresses. With age, American In-

dians appear to shift to a more passive relationship with their world, accepting age-related changes as a natural part of life and utilizing passive forbearance to cope. This movement from active mastery to passive accommodative styles is consistent with Gutmann's findings for diverse cultures, described in Chapter 6. It is also an adaptation to the decreasing P–E congruence experienced by many minority elders as they age.

Emotional problems may be intensified by the degree to which older American Indians' lives are dictated by government bureaucratic policies. Unlike any other group, various tribes are sovereign nations that have a distinct and special relationship with the U.S. government, based largely, but not exclusively, on treaties agreed to by the two parties. Congress and the Bureau of Indian Affairs, not the individual states, largely determine daily practices on the reservations. Although the Bureau's regulations are intended to ensure basic support, it is criticized for expending the majority of its budget on maintaining the bureaucracy, with only a small percentage actually going to services. It is also criticized for denying traditional cultural values. As an example, land-grazing privileges were historically extended to all tribal members for as long as they desired. Today, older American Indians must transfer their grazing rights to their heirs before they qualify for supplemental financial assistance. Although extra income may be welcome, the program serves to deprive the old of their traditional position within the tribal structure. In 2000, the head of the BIA apologized to tribal leaders for the agency's "legacy of racism and inhumanity," including attempts to eliminate Indian languages and cultures, but this apology was not made on behalf of the federal government as a whole (Kelly, 2000). The history of American Indian elders and their relationship with the federal bureaucracy must be considered in developing culturally appropriate social and health services.

Social Supports and Living Situations

Historical and cultural factors also strongly influence family and community relationships. Family is the central institution; "honoring" and giving re-

---

SHARED EXPERIENCES AMONG THE HIGHLY DIVERSE
AMERICAN INDIAN/ALASKA NATIVE ELDERS

- The rapid and forced change from a cooperative, clan-based society to a capitalistic and nuclear family–based system
- The outlawing of language and spiritual practices

- The death of generations of elders to infectious disease or war
- The loss of the ability to use the land walked by their ancestors for thousands of years

---

spect to elders and sharing family resources are an integral part of their ethos. American Indians' deep reverence for nature and belief in a supreme force, the importance of the clan, and a sense of individual autonomy as a key to noncompetitive group cohesion all underlie their practices toward their elders. Historically, as described in Chapter 2, the old were accorded respect and fulfilled specified useful tribal roles, including that of the "wise elder" who instructs the young and assists with child care, especially for foster children and grandchildren. They also maintained responsibility for remembering and relating tribal philosophies, myths, and traditions, and served as religious and political advisors to tribal leaders. These relationships have changed, however, with the restructuring of American Indian life by the BIA and by the increasing urbanization of native populations.

Despite these changes, many American Indian older people, particularly in rural settings, continue to live with an extended family, often as its head. Approximately 66 percent of all American Indian elders live with family members (e.g., spouse, children, grandchildren, and foster children), and over 40 percent of these households are headed by an older woman. Some 25 percent of Indian elders, typically the grandmother, care for at least one grandchild, and 67 percent live within 5 miles of relatives. Given cultural values and norms of intergenerational assistance, family caregivers may feel less anger and guilt toward relatives for whom they provide care, accepting such care as reciprocity for the help they and their children have received from now-aging relatives. As noted above, this pattern of helping family members, combined with mistrust of government programs, probably underlies American Indians' comparatively low utilization of ser-

vices. In turn, these factors put undue pressure on families to keep their elders at home, even when they lack sufficient resources to do so (John, 1994).

OLDER ASIAN AMERICANS AND PACIFIC ISLANDERS

Asian American and Pacific Islander elders encompass at least 30 distinct cultural groups who speak more than 100 different languages:

1. Asian Americans include Burmese, Cambodian, Chinese, East Indian, Filipino, Indonesian, Japanese, Korean, Laotian, Malaysian, Thai, and Vietnamese.
2. Pacific Islanders encompass Fijian, Guamanian, Hawaiian, Micronesian, Samoan, and Tongan populations.

Some classifications include Native Hawaiians and other Pacific Islanders under Native Americans. Each group represents a culture with its own history, religion, language, values, socioeconomic status, lifestyle, and patterns of immigration and adaptation. Adding to this diversity is the timing of immigration. Some Asian American and Pacific Islanders first settled in the United States in the 1850s; others have immigrated here in the past 20 years. Asian American elders who were born in this country around the turn of the twentieth century or who came to the United States during the early 1900s share the experience of discrimination and isolation. Laws discriminating against Asians are numerous:

- the Chinese Exclusion Act of 1882
- the Japanese Alien Land Law of 1913

- denial of citizenship to first-generation Asians in 1922
- the antimiscegenation statute of 1935
- the Executive Order of 1942 for the internment of 110,000 persons of Japanese ancestry during World War II
- more recently, Public Law 95-507 excluding Asians as a protected minority under the definition of "socially and economically disadvantaged"

Such legislation, combined with a history of racism, contributes to feelings of mistrust, injustice, powerlessness, and fear of government—and thus to a reluctance to utilize services among many Asian American/Pacific Islander elders.

In 1965, immigration quotas based on race and nationality were repealed. These changes resulted in a rapid growth of Southeast Asian immigrants, primarily after 1975, as the conflicts in Cambodia, Laos, and Vietnam were winding down. The majority of refugees were Vietnamese, (60 percent), followed by Cambodians and Laotians (20 percent each). The earlier waves during the post-1975 period were better educated and wealthier than later arrivals; Hmong and Laotians, especially, were poor, illiterate, and unaccustomed to Western culture at the time of their settlement. In addition, the trauma of dislocation and resettlement may contribute to the health problems of these groups (NIH, 2000). In addition, the direct immigration of older Asian Americans has increased, often as parents or grandparents of younger immigrants from the Philippines, China, Korea, and Vietnam. These four countries are the source of 30 percent of all older immigrants to the United States (Tanjasiri, Wallace, and Shibata, 1995). The 1996 welfare legislation poses new barriers, however, because legal alien and immigrant older persons are restricted from receiving government assistance for 5 years.

Approximately 6 percent of the Asian American/Pacific Islander population is 65 years of age and over. They are the fastest-growing ethnic minority group over age 65, due mostly to immigration rates. As with other groups, the oldest-old are the most rapidly growing segment (NIH, 1999). As the largely young immigrant population of Asian Americans ages over the next 50 years, the number who are old is expected to increase by 1,000 percent (Tanjasiri et al., 1995). Within the Asian American/Pacific Islander population, the percentage of foreign-born varies widely.

Economic Status

A widely held perception is that Asian Americans and Pacific Islanders are a "successful" minority because, as a whole, they are better educated and better off financially than other ethnic minority groups (Braun and Browne, 1998). The model minority epithet tends to trivialize the health problems of Asians, suggesting that they can take care of these on their own. It overlooks the socioeconomic and educational diversity among Asians and the problems faced by the newest refugees. In other words, the success of some mask the severe problems of

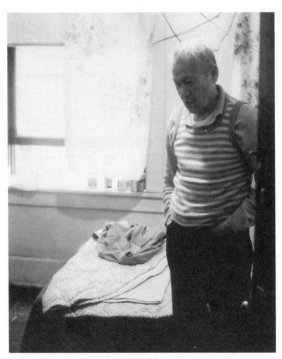

Many older Asian men have never married and lack family ties.

others. Asians who immigrated prior to 1924, especially Japanese and Chinese, generally differ substantially in their occupational and educational backgrounds from those who came later. As a result of denial of property rights and discrimination against them for public jobs, most older Asians who immigrated earlier are less educated and more economically deprived than their white counterparts. In addition, subgroups of poverty exist among recent immigrants; for example, the Vietnamese tend to have incomes below the poverty level and high rates of no education. Older Asian Americans/Pacific Islanders have, on average, 6 years of school, with the exception of the Japanese, who average 8.5 years. Many still speak only their native language. In fact, 30 percent of all Asian Americans and Pacific Islanders who are age 65 and over live in households where no adults speak English. This reduces their ability to interact with most public services (Tanjasiri et al., 1995). Their social worlds may be limited to ethnic enclaves, such as Chinatown and Korea-town where they have developed small retail and service businesses, mutual-aid or benevolent societies, and recreational clubs, and have access to traditional health care. Although segregated from the general society, these ethnic enclaves are a center for social interaction and the delivery of services to elders. These functions, however, may not exist for future generations of Asian Americans/Pacific Islanders, who will be more geographically and socially mobile and more socioeconomically diverse (NIH, 2000).

Another factor that will work against such cohesive enclaves in the future is that Chinese Americans are increasingly diverse in terms of social class, occupation, and linguistic and regional background. Differences between foreign born and American born, urban residents and suburbanites, old timers and newcomers, northerners and southerners, Christians and Buddhists, professionals and laborers, and rich and poor frequently override a common ethnic identity, making unity at times an elusive goal.

Although U.S.-born Chinese American and Japanese American older people tend to be economically better off than other groups, approximately 14 percent of Asian American and Pacific Islander elders live below the poverty level (Dhooper, 1997; Nishi, 1995; Young and Gu, 1995). The poverty rate may be even higher than that reflected in official statistics, since the number of employed adults, often self-employed as farmers or in small businesses, is greater than in other groups, thereby inflating "family" income. Noted above, the poverty figures are highest among recent immigrants, particularly among the Chinese and Vietnamese (Rumbaut, 1995). Many older Chinese and Filipinos have experienced a lifetime of low-paying jobs, often in self-employment, garment factories, and service or farming work not covered by Social Security or other pensions. Filipino males, in particular, were concentrated in live-in domestic, migrant agricultural, or other unsettled work, often living in homogeneous male camps. This prevented them from gaining an insured work history and developing close ties with family and neighbors.

As is the case with older Hispanics, many older Asian Americans/Pacific Islanders qualify for public financial supports, such as Supplemental Security Income, but do not apply. After years of living under discrimination and fear of deportation, they resist seeking help from a government bureaucracy that they distrust. Their reluctance to seek nonfamilial assistance is also influenced by cultural and linguistic traditions emphasizing hierarchical relationships, personal social status, and self-restraint. When unsure of others' social status, some older Asian Americans and Pacific Islanders avoid interacting with them. In the past, they turned to their families and the benevolent societies and clubs in their tightly knit communities. Now many are caught between their cultural traditions of group and familial honor and the values of their adopted culture that stress independence and self-sufficiency, making them loath to seek support from others (Braun and Browne, 1998).

The cultural values of Asian Americans/Pacific Islanders also underlie reluctance to utilize services. Filipino Americans, for example, are guided by values of both respect and shame. Respect includes listening to others, self-imposed restraints, loyalty to family, and unquestioning obedience to authority; shame involves fear of being left exposed, unprotected, and unaccepted. Filipino Americans are also very concerned with good relations or the avoidance of disagreement or conflict. The high value they place on personal relationships may impede their accepting formal assistance, including institutional care. For first-generation Japanese, or Issei, a value that transcends that of family is group conscience, characterized by cohesiveness, strong pride, and identity through a devotion to and sense of mutuality among peer-group members. This value has been preserved through the residential and occupational isolation of older Japanese American cohorts from mainstream American culture. Even among the second generation (Nissei), the Japanese vision of Buddhism endures in the cherishing of filial devotion and the loving indulgence of the old toward young children. Such interdependence with and respect for elders who have greater life experience, knowledge, and wisdom are widely accepted values. Accordingly, Japanese American older people tend to value social interaction, hierarchical relationships, interdependency, and empathy—all values that may not characterize formal services. These situations illustrate a lack of person–environment fit between a group's cultural values and the service system's insensitivity to cultural differences (Browne, Fong, and Mokuau, 1994).

Health

Information on the health of Asian Americans/ Pacific Islanders is limited. Less comparative research has been conducted on their health status and behaviors because of difficulties in collecting epidemiological data on the relatively small Asian groups. Given the wide variability within population groupings, their overall health status compared to the general population is unclear. Nevertheless, immigrants appear to be healthier than native-born Americans, and some studies have defined the Asian American/Pacific Islander population as a whole as healthier than the general

U.S. population (Braun, Yang, Onaka, and Horiuchi, 2000; Markides and Black, 1996). As noted earlier, in terms of socioeconomic and health status, there appears to be a bimodal distribution. Some Asian American/Pacific Islanders (e.g., Japanese and Chinese Americans) fare quite well, while others have very low income and poor health status (e.g., Vietnamese and Hawaiians) (Braun et al., 2000; Chen and Hawks, 1995; Min, 1995; Tanjasiri et al., 1995). When health data are disaggregated, Native Hawaiian mortality rates are generally higher than other groups for heart disease and all causes of death (Braun et al., 2000). Asian Americans/Pacific Islanders tend to face higher rates of hypertension, cholesterol, osteoporosis, and cancer, especially among low-income subgroupings. A higher incidence of osteoporosis among Asian American women may be due to inadequate exercise (NIH, 2000). The incidence of strokes in Chinese and Japanese living in the United States is lower than in China and Japan. The relatively better health status of these two Pacific Asian groups may be due to their diet, with lower fat and higher carbohydrate intakes compared with whites, and lower obesity rates compared with other groups. On the other hand, the rates of digestive system cancers, diabetes, and suicide are higher in Japanese Americans than among their white counterparts (Wright and Mindel, 1993). Asian Americans/Pacific Islanders report greater emergency room use and longer hospitalizations than other groups, suggesting that they are less likely to have a regular source of care or that they wait too long to use it (Braun and Browne, 1998). With respect to health status for this highly diverse group especially, the relative impact of socioeconomic status and other variables that confound race and ethnicity needs to be tested.

There is even less research on the mental health of Asian Americans/Pacific Islanders. The average level of depression is slightly higher than that for whites, with the highest rate among Koreans. This is attributed to their recent immigration status and difficulties in adjusting to American society (Markides and Black, 1996). The suicide rate among

Korean American women is higher than for whites. Suicides are often explained by perceived incongruities between the elders' values and the reality of their relatively isolated lives in an alien culture (NIH, 2000). Older Japanese males in California have been hospitalized for schizophrenia more frequently than their white counterparts. However, since cultural factors influence the diagnosis of mental health problems, these findings may not necessarily reflect the true mental health status of this highly diverse population. For example, some groups somaticize mental distress, in part because of the shame and stigma attached to mental illness (Braun and Browne, 1998).

Asian American/Pacific Islanders tend to underutilize Medicare and Medicaid, relying on non-Western medicine or family and friends. It is estimated that 33 percent of Asian American/Pacific Islander elders have never seen a Western doctor or a dentist, and only about 2 percent are in nursing homes (Braun and Browne, 1998). This low utilization of Western health services is probably due to:

- a combination of their having fewer chronic diseases than do their majority group peers
- sociocultural and structural barriers to health care
- traditional values such as endurance and looking the other way
- elders' reluctance to use formal Western health services
- greater likelihood of turning to traditional healers (Pourat, Lubben, Wallace, and Moon, 1999)

The health problems of Asian Americans/Pacific Islanders are worsened by a complex and wide set of cultural, linguistic, structural, and financial barriers to care, as illustrated below:

Health-Seeking Behaviors
- They lack knowledge of risk factors or preventive behaviors.
- They are less likely than whites or African Americans to get checkups or have blood pressure measured.

- They lack knowledge of what blood pressure is, and what can be done to prevent heart disease.
- There are low rates of breast self-exams or screening for breast or cervical cancer.
- They are unfamiliar with cancer risk factors.
- They perceive illness as focusing on symptoms of pain, weakness, dizziness, or nausea and therefore do not seek treatment for diseases that cannot be seen: cancer, hypertension, diabetes mellitus.
- They experience increased difficulty in accepting their diagnoses as real or accepting Western treatment regimens for them.
- They hold themselves and their families (especially Korean Americans) responsible for their health status rather than turning to providers.

Belief Systems
- They believe in the supernatural powers of ancestral and natural spirits.
- Hospitals are seen as places to die, not get well, among Chinese Americans.
- The use of public services is seen as shameful and an indicator of dependency and inability to care for oneself.
- There is a belief that cancer is inevitably fatal.
- There is stigma associated with cancer and with mental illness, especially among Japanese Americans.
- There is a reluctance to visit medical professionals for a checkup without getting prescriptions for medications, since this is contrary to Chinese expectations of medical providers.
- They use over-the-counter or traditional home remedies rather than go to physicians.
- There is discomfort with male physicians among women, since 90 percent of obstetricians and gynecologists in China are female.
- Reverence for authority may result in not questioning a physician's diagnosis and treatment and indicating agreement when there is none.
- The desire to "keep up appearances" results in low utilization of mental health and addiction treatment services.

- Culturally accepted medical models (e.g., acupuncture and herbal medicines) are not covered by insurance.
- There is high noncompliance with Western prescription medications.
- There is a fear of communication problems.
- There are difficulties in translating English medical/health terminology into Southeast Asian languages and translating Asian health concerns to English (e.g., cancer is not mentioned as a disease in texts on Chinese medicine).
- Health care providers are viewed as "impatient, disrespectful" of their ethnicity.
- If residing illegally, they fear that seeking medical care will expose their illegal status and result in deportation.

On the other hand, cultural values can provide a source of mutual support and pride. For example, *Bayanihan* is the Filipino concept of a community working together, doing heroic deeds and lending helping hands for community betterment. As Filipino immigrants encountered the individualistic spirit of the United States, the *Bayanihan* spirit faded. The economic value placed on time hampered volunteerism and devalued unpaid community work. However, in some communities, advocates are seeking to resurrect the spirit of *Bayanihan* to promote the health and well-being of Filipino elders. The concept of this spirit is also promoted as a culturally significant health advocacy tool (Bagtas, 2000). Similarly, traditional healers provide broader social benefits for Korean elders compared to Western medicine. For example, healers typically spend a longer time with older patients, discuss personal situations thoroughly, are more accessible after hours and on weekends, and have personal contact with family members and friends (Pourat, Lubben, Wallace, and Moon, 1999).

Social Supports and Living Situations

Compared to the national average, Asian American/Pacific Islander groups show higher proportions of extended family arrangements, although the majority of elders live by themselves or with a spouse, not with children. In contrast to other ethnic minorities and to white older persons, men living alone constitute a larger percent of the older Asian American/Pacific Islander population. This reflects the continuing influence of disproportionate male immigration in the early part of the century and past restrictions on female immigration, rather than a higher life expectancy for men. In contrast to other subgroups of older adults, the ratio of men to women among Asian Americans/Pacific Islanders increases with age, controlling for gender, social class, and levels of functional ability. On the other hand, women in this group are much more likely to be married than their white counterparts, with a smaller proportion remaining single in their later years (Angel and Hogan, 1994).

Advancing age increases the probability of living alone, although the rate of institutionalization among older Asian Americans is significantly lower than for their white counterparts (Manson, 1993). Some 2 percent over age 65, and 10 percent over age 85, are in nursing homes, compared to 23 percent of whites. Intergenerational living arrangements have declined as younger generations of Asians are acculturated into the larger society. For example, many Chinese older people prefer to remain in their ethnic communities rather than live with children who have moved to the suburbs or across the country. Despite their strong commitment to family and filial responsibility, Chinese American elders can no longer offer financial support, land, or other material goods as they would have in their homeland. They generally live with their children only in cases of extreme poverty or poor health. Living with adult children may also be a function of their dependency on them for translation. In contrast, Korean American elders often accept separation from their children as a way to promote the children's happiness and success.

Although Asian Americans/Pacific Islanders represent tremendous diversity in terms of country of origin, degree of acculturation, and transcending values and religion, they all share the erosion of the **law of primogeniture.** This refers to the relationship between aged parents and the oldest son, who provides care for them and, in turn, inherits their wealth. This is a value that is still prevalent in most Asian countries today, as discussed in Chapter 2, although it is diminishing there as well. Today, all children, not just the eldest son, are expected to display filial piety and to repay their parents for sacrifices made for them (Braun and Browne, 1998). A strain faced by many families is the duality of cultures and the inevitable clashes when generations have different languages, values, and ethos. As a result, traditional cultural values regarding care of elders by adult children are weakening (Antonucci and Cantor, 1994). Nevertheless, compared with the majority culture, Asian Americans/Pacific Islanders place a higher value on reciprocal exchanges between young and old and the prestige of being old, and seek outside assistance only in desperate circumstances (Braun and Browne, 1998). Any discussion of family caregiving should also take account of differences in culture, economic circumstances, and generations among Asian Americans/Pacific Islanders.

This chapter highlights only a few characteristics of Asian American/Pacific Islander elders, because of the large inter- and intra-group differences that exist. Because of population and political pressures in Asia, the high rate of immigration is likely to continue, and the diversity under the label of Asian American/Pacific Islander to increase. A major challenge for researchers and service providers is to recognize this diversity of history and cultural values when developing culturally sensitive research and practice models (Braun and Browne, 1998).

IMPLICATIONS FOR SERVICES

Because it is important that services are responsive to ethnic minority elders, we consider further the implications of sociocultural factors for service delivery. As noted above, findings are mixed regarding whether elders of color underutilize social and health care services (Markides and Black, 1996; Miller et al., 1996). On the one hand, Medicaid is not fully used by potentially eligible

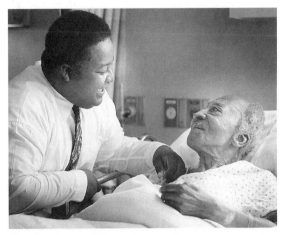

Shared cultural backgrounds can enhance communication between health care providers and older patients.

minority elders. Such underutilization is attributed to lack of knowledge about the program, difficulties in applying, and an aversion to accepting publicly funded benefits (Wykle and Kaskel, 1994). Nevertheless, an analysis of three national data sets found that living arrangements, health status, number of functional limitations, region, and insurance/income status affect use of services more than race or ethnicity (Markides and Black, 1996). On the other hand, service use by minority elders may vary more in the cultural contexts of local and regional levels than at the national level.

Although some service providers rationalize that elders of color do not utilize formal services because of their families' assistance, patterns of underutilization cannot fully be explained in this way. Underutilization of in-home services, for example, may result more from perceptions of culturally inappropriate alternatives within long-term care than to the existence of family supports. In fact, when medical and psychosocial interventions are culturally sensitive, ethnic minority service utilization is increased (Miller et al., 1996). Barriers to service utilization can be conceptualized at the level of service recipients and the delivery system, as illustrated in the box on the next page.

BARRIERS TO UTILIZATION

I. Cultural and Economic Barriers

• Cultural isolation, including language differences.

• Perceived stigma of utilizing services, especially mental health, and embarrassment and fear in attempting to describe symptoms.

• Confusion, anger at, and fear of health care providers and hospitals, which may be related to present or historical acts of racism by medical providers.

• Lack of trust and faith in the efficacy of service professionals within a Western biomedical health care system, which may be intensified by cohorts' experiences. For example, segregated health care and explicit policies, such as the Tuskegee experiment with African Americans and the internment of Japanese Americans on the West Coast, underlie a distrust of the health care system.

• Lack of knowledge of services, including how to make appointments, how to negotiate a clinic visit, and how to describe symptoms.

II. Structural Barriers within the Service System

• The 1996 Welfare Reform Bill that eliminated some public benefits to legal immigrants.

• Lack of services that are specifically oriented toward and operated by members of respective ethnic minority groups.

• Real or perceived discrimination by service providers.

• Assessment instruments whose meaning is altered in translation.

• Geographic distance of services from ethnic minority neighborhoods.

• Lack of transportation to services.

• Nonminority staff who are not bilingual, are insensitive to ethnic and cultural differences, and serve meals that conflict with customary dietary preferences.

Gerontologists generally agree that services need to be designed to take account of inter- and intra-cultural and geographic differences within and across groups. From this perspective, preferential consideration is needed to reduce social inequities between the elders of dominant and minority groups, to respond to the diversity of needs, and to increase the participation of various groups. Accordingly, service providers need to be trained to be culturally competent, and the importance of cross-cultural care or **ethnogeriatrics** is increasingly being recognized (Yeo, 1996–97).

Fortunately, many health providers recognize and respect older ethnic minorities' adherence to traditional paradigms of health and illness, as well as to associated folk beliefs and behaviors that diverge from mainstream Western scientific medical concepts. Some elders combine these with orthodox or scientific treatments. As noted earlier, such folk treatments can enhance psychological well-being (Braun and Nichols, 1997; Cheng, 1997). Accordingly, current health promotion efforts aimed at older whites may not be appropriate for populations of color. For example, social entities that play a key role in older African Americans' lives, such as the church and religious leaders, are more likely to influence health beliefs and behaviors than are traditional approaches to health promotion. The involvement of health-promotion experts from the same culture may also help bridge the gap between cultural values and scientific knowledge about the causes and treatment of disease. This is particularly true for American Indian and Asian American/Pacific Islander cultures, where traditional ways of treating disease are still widely practiced among older cohorts. Health-promotion efforts that ignore traditional beliefs about harmony between the individual, nature, and the universe are unlikely to be effective in these cultures. For example, the Chinese believe that health represents a balance between Yin and Yang energy forces; certain foods are assumed to bring about this balance. Believing that the aging process predisposes people to Yin (or cold forces), Chinese elders avoid eating many cold foods such as leafy green vegetables (Yee and Weaver, 1994). Health-

---

GUIDELINES FOR CULTURALLY APPROPRIATE ASSESSMENT

• With the growth of immigrant populations, it is very important to be sensitive to issues of acculturation and language when administering assessment measures and interpreting test results.

• Both the content of the test as well as the language in which it is administered affects a test's multicultural applicability.

• To enable accurate translations, test instructions should be written in simple, concise terminology.

• Use "back translation" to obtain an equivalent fair battery for any language: Material produced in one language is translated into another language by a bilingual translator, then translated back into English by a second individual, and then the original and back-translated English versions are compared.

• Bilingual staff should be required to administer the measures in the client's native language.

• All staff assessing the cognitive and functional status of the older adult must be trained to deal appropriately with the client's cultural background and be closely monitored for any class, race, and other biases, of which they may be unaware, that could imperil the assessment.

(Adapted from Arguelles and Lowenstein, 1999)

---

promotion facilitators must recognize the basis for such avoidance if they are to encourage healthier diets among older Asians. Accordingly, Western assessment measures may not be appropriate for elders of color. For example, most research on caregiving among populations of color has described lower levels of burden. However, caregivers of color may express their burden in different ways than Caucasian caregivers, and available measures of caregiver burden may not adequately measure the impact of caregiving on them. In fact, some qualitative studies have found that African American and Puerto Rican caregivers express anger, frustration, loneliness, and resignation similar to their white counterparts, despite their appearance of coping effectively through religion (Calderon and Tennstedt, 1998).

Service use by elders of color is increased by the following conditions:

• Services should be located in ethnic minority communities, easily accessible, and near complementary supports; transportation should be easily available.

• Services should adhere to the cultural integrity of the elders' lifestyles; for example, nutrition programs should include appropriate ethnic foods, and nursing homes should offer culturally sensitive recreation.

• The organizational climate should be informal and personalized.

• Staff should include bilingual, bicultural, and/or indigenous workers, or translators who are culturally sensitive, who convey respect and who use personalized outreach methods to establish trust and rapport. Medical and insurance forms, newsletters, and descriptions of services should be bilingual.

• Ethnic minorities should be involved in both the planning and the delivery of services to be accountable to the community served.

• Services should be advertised in ways to reach ethnic minorities, such as through minority-oriented television, radio programs and newspapers, and announcements made through churches, neighborhood organizations, civic and social clubs, natural support systems, and advocates. For example, black churches, linked with other agencies, can recruit more African American elders to use social and health care services.

• Given major differences in the epidemiology and risk factors of certain diseases (such as diabetes), screening, prevention, and education are essential.

In sum, rather than a deficits model, in which interventions are developed to ameliorate personal or social problems, service providers should identify community strengths to supplement and augment existing services. This also suggests the value of utilizing existing organizational structures, such as churches, to provide services and to link informal and formal sources of help.

Underlying such strategies are assumptions that the needs of elders of color are best understood by members of their own groups, that these elders should be treated as distinct populations, and that research and training programs should give special attention to them. It is also important to employ ethnic minority practitioners as service providers, and to state explicitly minority-specific statutes in federal regulations for aging programs.

Due to increasing longevity and recent waves of immigration, growth rates of minority elders are expected to far exceed those of same-aged whites in the twenty-first century. To advance research on populations of color and thus provide an empirical basis for service interventions, clear and consistent terminology is needed to define and target populations. Issues related to design, data collection, and measurement for and across different groups must be resolved (Burnette and Mui, 1999). The National Institute on Aging's strategic plan for fiscal years 2001–2005 proposes ways to eliminate health disparities among populations of color over time (NIH, 2000). Such a focus will provide a better basis for review and evaluation of proposed future directions in minority aging research and practice.

SUMMARY AND IMPLICATIONS

Although age is sometimes called the great equalizer, today's elders are highly diverse. As we have seen throughout this book, differences in income, health, and social supports significantly affect older adults' quality of life. An important source of this diversity is ethnic minority status. Ethnogerontology is the study of the causes, processes, and consequences of race, national origin, and culture on individual and population aging. One of the earliest debates in that field continues: whether ethnic minorities experience double jeopardy because of

their race or whether age is a leveler of differences in income and life expectancy. Recent studies indicate a narrowing of differences in health status and life expectancy after age 75, or a crossover effect.

This chapter reviewed the social, demographic, economic, and health status of African Americans, Hispanic Americans, American Indians, and Asian American/Pacific Islander elders. Although there are variations among these groups, several common themes also emerge. For most ethnic minority older adults, their resources and status reflect social, economic, and educational discrimination experienced earlier in life. Those who immigrated to the United States, especially, experience cultural and language differences. As a whole, they face shorter life expectancy and increased risks of poverty, malnutrition, substandard housing, and poor health, although within-group variations exist. Nevertheless, many ethnic minority elders, especially among the oldest-old, display considerable strengths and resiliency. Social and health care assistance is of particular concern. Cultural and language difficulties, physical isolation, and lower income, along with structural barriers to service accessibility, contribute to their underutilization of health and social services. Efforts must continue to modify services to be more responsive to the particular needs of ethnic minority older adults.

In recent years, the older population has been growing faster among ethnic minorities than among whites—a trend that is expected to continue. Still, white elders outnumber their ethnic minority peers. The status of ethnic minority elders is not likely to improve greatly in the immediate future. The factors that largely determine the older population's quality of life—education, employment, income, and health—will not vary considerably among the ethnic minority cohort now approaching retirement age. This trend suggests the importance of targeting services to meet the needs of ethnic minority elders. On the other hand, some advocates maintain that policies and programs should increase for education and employment opportunities among younger minorities to ensure that the next generation will enjoy a higher quality of life than that of their predecessors.

GLOSSARY

crossover effect the lower death rates among African Americans, Asian Americans, and American Indians after age 75

double jeopardy hypothesis the hypothesis that aging persons of color are in jeopardy in our society due to both growing old and being part of an ethnic minority

ethnogeriatrics cross-cultural geriatric care that recognizes cultural differences in response to health and disease

ethnogerontology study of causes, processes, and consequences of race, national origin, and culture on individual and population aging

fictive kin foster parents of children, close friends, or neighbors who function in the absence of blood relatives or when family relationships are unsatisfactory

Indian Health Service federal program that provides health care for Native Americans and Alaskans of all ages through hospitals and community clinics

multiple hierarchy stratification the theory that social class, in addition to ethnic minority status, can jeopardize older minorities

primogeniture, law of the exclusive right of the eldest son to inherit his father's estate

RESOURCES

See the companion Website for the text at <www.ablongman.com/hooyman> for information about the following:

- National Asian Pacific Center on Aging
- National Association for Hispanic Elderly
- National Caucus and Center on Black Aged
- National Indian Council on Aging
- U.S. Public Health Service
- www.healthywomen.org

REFERENCES

Administration on Aging. *Aging into the 21st century.* Washington, DC: Administration on Aging, 1997.

Administration on Aging. *Profile of older Americans.* Washington, DC: Administration on Aging, 1999.

Angel, J. L., and Hogan, D. P. The demography of minority aging populations. In *Minority elders: Five goals toward building a public policy base* (2nd ed.). Washington, DC: The Gerontological Society of America, 1994.

Antonucci, T. C., and Cantor, M. H. Strengthening the family support system for older minority persons. In *Minority elders: Five goals toward building a public policy base* (2nd ed.). Washington, DC: The Gerontological Society of America, 1994.

Arguelles, T., and Lowenstein, D. Making assessment culturally appropriate. *Diversity Curren,* San Francisco: American Society on Aging, Multicultural Aging Network, Fall 1999, *2,* 6.

Bagtas, A. P. Filipino elders community promotes health with dose of bayanihan. *Asian Pacific Affairs,* 2000, *8(3),* 1.

Baker, F. M. Ethnic minority issues: Differential diagnosis, medication, treatment and outcomes. In M. S. Harper (Ed.), *Minority aging.* DHHS Publication #HRS (P-DV-90–4). Washington, DC: U.S. Government Printing Office, 1990.

Baquet, C. R. Cancer prevention and control in the black population. In J. S. Jackson (Ed.), *The black American elderly.* New York: Springer, 1988.

Barresi, C., and Stull, D. Ethnicity and long-term care: An overview. In C. Barresi and D. Stull (Eds.), *Ethnic elderly and long-term care.* New York: Springer, 1993.

Belgrave, L. L., Wykle, M. L., and Choi, J. M. Health, double jeopardy, and culture: The use of institutionalization by African-Americans. *The Gerontologist,* 1993, *33,* 379–385.

Bengtson, V. L. Ethnicity and aging: Problems and issues in current social science inquiry. In D. E. Gelfand and A. J. Kutzik (Eds.), *Ethnicity and aging: Theory, research and policy.* New York: Springer, 1979.

Black, H. K. Poverty and prayer: Spiritual narratives of elderly African-American women. *Review of Religious Research,* 1999, *40,* 359–374.

Braun, K. L., and Browne, C. Cultural values and caregiving patterns among Asian and Pacific Islander Americans. In D. E. Redburn and L. P. McNamara (Eds.), *Social gerontology.* Westport, CT: Greenwood Press, 1998.

Braun, K. L., and Nichols, R. Death and dying in four Asian American cultures: A descriptive study. *Death Studies,* July-August 1997, *21,* 327–359.

Braun, K. L., Yang, H., Onaka, A. T., and Horiuchi, B. Y. Asian and Pacific Islander mortality difference in Hawaii. In K. Braun, J. Pietsch, and

P. Blanchette (Eds.), *Cultural issues in end-of-life decision making.* Thousand Oaks, CA: Sage Publications, 2000.

Browne, C., Fong, R., and Mokuau, N. The mental health of Asian and Pacific Island elders: Implications for research and mental health administration. *Journal of Mental Health Administration,* 1994, *21,* 52–59.

Burnette, D. Physical and emotional well-being of custodial grandparents in Latino families. *American Journal of Orthopsychiatry,* 1999a, *69,* 305–318.

Burnette, D. Social relationships of Latino grandparent caregivers: A role theory perspective. *The Gerontologist,* 1999b, *39,* 49–58.

Burton, L., Kasper, J., Shore, A., Cagney, K., LeVeist, T., Cubbins, C., and German, P. The structure of informal care: Are there differences by race? *The Gerontologist,* 1995, *35,* 744–752.

Chen, M. S., and Hawks, B. L. A debunking of the myth of healthy Asian Americans and Pacific Islanders. *American Journal of Health Promotion,* 1995, *9,* 261–268.

Chen, Y. P. Improving the economic security of minority persons as they enter old age. In *Minority elders: Five goals toward building a public policy base* (2nd ed.). Washington, DC: The Gerontological Society of America, 1994.

Cheng, B. K. Cultural clash between providers of majority culture and patients of Chinese culture. *Journal of Long Term Home Health Care: The Pride Institute Journal,* Spring 1997, *16,* 39–43.

Choi, N. G. Living arrangements and household compositions of elderly couples and singles: A comparison of Hispanics and Blacks. *Journal of Gerontological Social Work,* 1999, *31,* 41–61.

Cochran, D. L., Brown, D. R., and McGregor, K. C. Racial differences in the multiple social roles of older women: Implications for depressive symptoms. *The Gerontologist,* 1999, *39,* 465–472.

Cook, C. D. American Indian elderly and public policy issues. In M. S. Harper (Ed.), *Minority aging.* DHHS Publication #HRS (P-DV-90-4). Washington, DC: U.S. Government Printing Office, 1990.

Cuellar, J. Hispanic American aging: Geriatric educational curriculum development for selected health professions. In M. S. Harper (Ed.), *Minority aging.* DHHS Publication #HRS (P-DV-90-4). Washington, DC: U.S. Government Printing Office, 1990.

Cuellar, J., and Weeks, J. Minority elderly Americans: The assessment of needs and equitable receipt of public benefits as a prototype in area agencies on aging. Final report. San Diego, CA: Allied Home Health Association, Grant AOA/DHHS 90-A-1667(01), 1980.

Davis, L., and McGadney, B. Self-care practices of black elders. In C. Barresi and D. Stull (Eds.), *Ethnic elderly and long-term care.* New York: Springer, 1993.

Dhooper, S. S. Poverty among Asian Americans: Theories and approaches. *Journal of Sociology and Social Welfare,* March 1997, *24,* 25–40.

Espino, D. Hispanic elderly and long-term care: Implications for ethnically sensitive services. In C. Barresi and D. Stull (Eds.), *Ethnic elderly and long-term care.* New York: Springer, 1993.

Ferraro, K. F., and Farmer, M. M. Double jeopardy, aging as leveler or persistent health inequality? A longitudinal analysis of white and Black Americans. *Journals of Gerontology,* 1996, *51B,* S319–S328.

Freeman, H. T., and Payne, R. Racial injustice in health care. *New England Journal of Medicine,* March 2000, *11,* 17–20.

Gallagher-Thompson, D. Service delivery and recommendations for working with Mexican American family caregivers. In G. Yeo and D. Gallagher-Thompson (Eds.), *Ethnicity and the dementias.* Washington, DC: Taylor Frances, 1996.

Garcia, J. L., Kosberg, J. I., Mangum, W. P., Henderson, J. N., and Henderson, C. C. Caregiving for and by Hispanic elders: Perceptions of four generations of women. *Journal of Sociology and Social Welfare,* 1999, *26,* 169–187.

Gibson, R. Minority aging research: Opportunity and challenge. *Journals of Gerontology,* 1989, *44,* S52–53.

Gibson, R. C. The age-by-race gap in health and mortality in the older population: A social science research agenda. *The Gerontologist,* 1994, *34,* 454–462.

Gould, K. H. A minority-feminist perspective on women and aging. *Journal of Women and Aging,* 1989, *1,* 195–216.

Greene, V. L., and Ondrich, J. I. Risk factors for nursing home admissions and exits: A discrete-time hazard function approach. *Journals of Gerontology,* 1990, *45,* S250–S258.

Guralnik, J. M., Land, K. C., Blazer, D. G., Fillerbaum, G. G., and Branch, L. G. Educational status and active life expectancy among older blacks and whites.

New England Journal of Medicine, 1993, *329,* 110–116.

Gutmann, D. Use of informal and formal supports by white ethnic aged. In D. E. Gelfand and A. J. Kutzik (Eds.), *Ethnicity and aging: Theory, research and policy.* New York: Springer, 1979.

Harper, M., and Alexander, C. Profile of the black elderly. In M. S. Harper (Ed.), *Minority aging.* DHHS Publication #HRS (P-DV-90–4). Washington, DC: U.S. Government Printing Office, 1990.

Hayward, M. D., Friedman, S., and Chen, H. Race inequities in men's retirement. *Journals of Gerontology,* 1996, *51B,* S1–S10.

Hobbs, F., and Damon, B. L. *65+ in the United States.* Washington, DC: U.S. Department of Commerce, Bureau of the Census, 1996.

Hopper, S. V. The influence of ethnicity on the health of older women. *Clinics in Geriatric Medicine,* 1993, *9,* 231–259.

John, R. The state of research on American Indian elders' health, income security, and social support networks. In *Minority elders: Five goals toward building a public policy base* (2nd ed.). Washington, DC: The Gerontological Society of America, 1994.

Johnson, C. L. Fictive kin among oldest old African Americans in the San Francisco Bay area. *Journals of Gerontology,* 1999, *54B,* S368–S375.

Johnson, R. W., Sambamoorthi, U., and Crystal, S. Gender differences in pension wealth: Estimates using provider data. *The Gerontologist,* 1999, *39,* 320–333.

Johnson, T. Utilizing culture in work with aging families. In G. Smith, S. Tobin, E. A. Robertson-Tchabo, and P. Power (Eds.), *Strengthening aging families: Diversity in practice and policy.* Thousand Oaks, CA: Sage, 1995.

Kahn, K., Pearson, M. L., and Harrison, E. R. Health care for black and poor hospitalized Medicare patients. *Journal of the American Medical Association,* 1994, *271,* 1169–1174.

Kelly, M. BIA head issues apology to Indians. *The Seattle Times,* September 9, 2000, p. 3A.

Killon, C. M. *A broken or crystal stair? Life histories of marginally housed elderly African American women.* University of Michigan, Ann Arbor: Program for Research on Black Americans, 2000.

Kim, P. Asian-American families and the elderly. In M. S. Harper (Ed.), *Minority aging.* DHHS Publication #HRS (P-DV-90–4). Washington, DC: U.S. Government Printing Office, 1990.

Kramer, B. J. Cross-cultural medicine a decade later: Health and aging of urban American Indians. *Western Journal of Medicine,* 1992, *157,* 281–285.

Lacayo, C. G. Hispanic elderly: Policy issues in long-term care. In C. Barresi and D. Stull (Eds.), *Ethnic elderly and long-term care.* New York: Springer, 1993.

Lum, Y. S., Chang, H. J., and Ozawa, M. N. The effects of race and ethnicity on use of health services by older Americans. *Journal of Social Service Research,* 1999, *25,* 15–42.

Manson, J. Long-term care of older American Indians: Challenges in the development of institutional services. In C. Barresi and D. Stull (Eds.), *Ethnic elderly and long-term care.* New York: Springer, 1993.

Manson, S. M., and Callaway, D. G. Health and aging among American Indians. In M. S. Harper (Ed.), *Minority aging.* DHHS Publication #HRS (P-DV-90–4). Washington, DC: U.S. Government Printing Office, 1990.

Markides, K. S., and Black, S. A. Race, ethnicity and aging. In R. H. Binstock and L. K. George (Eds.), *Handbook of aging and the social sciences* (4th ed.). San Diego, CA: Academic Press, 1996.

Markides, K., Liang, J., and Jackson, J. Race, ethnicity and aging: Conceptual and methodological issues. In R. Binstock and L. K. George (Eds.), *Handbook of aging and the social sciences* (3rd ed.). New York: Academic Press, 1990.

Mayers, R. S., and Souflee, L. Utilizing social support systems in the delivery of social services to the Mexican-American elderly. *Journal of Applied Social Sciences,* Fall/Winter 1990–91, *15,* 31–50.

Miller, B., Campbell, R. T., Davis, L., Turner, S., Giachello, A., Prohaska, T., Kaufman, J. E., Li, M., and Perez, C. Minority use of community long-term care: A comparative analysis. *Journals of Gerontology,* 1996, *51B,* S70–S81.

Miller, B., McFall, S., and Campbell, R. T. Changes in sources of community long-term care among African American and white frail older persons. *Journals of Gerontology,* 1994, *49B,* S14–S24.

Min, P. G. *Asian Americans: Contemporary trends and issues.* Thousand Oaks, CA: Sage Publications, 1995.

Minkler, M., and Roe, K. *Grandmothers as caregivers.* Newbury Park, CA: Sage, 1993.

Miranda, M. Hispanic aging: An overview of issues and policy implications. In M. S. Harper (Ed.), *Minority aging.* DHHS Publication #HRS (P-DV-90–4). Washington, DC: U.S. Government Printing Office, 1990.

Mui, A. C., and Burnette, D. Long-term care service use by frail elders: Is ethnicity a factor? *The Gerontologist*, 1994, *34*, 190–198.

National Academy on an Aging Society. Helping the elderly with activity limitations. Washington, DC: *Caregiving #7*, May 2000.

National Center for Health Statistics. *Health: United States, 1990*. Hyattsville, MD: NCHS, 1992.

National Institutes of Health. *Women of color health data book*. Washington, DC: Office of Research on Women's Health, 2000.

Nishi, S. M. Japanese Americans. In P. G. Min (Ed.), *Asian Americans: Contemporary issues and trends*. Newbury Park, CA: Sage Publications, 1995.

Norgard, T. M., and Rodgers, W. C. Patterns of in-home care among elderly black and white Americans. *Journals of Gerontology*, 1997, *52B*, S93–S101.

Pourat, N, Lubben, J., Wallace, S., and Moon, A. Predictors of use of traditional Korean healers among elderly Koreans in Los Angeles. *The Gerontologist*, 1999, *39*, 711–719.

Quinn, J. F., and Smeeding, T. M. Defying the averages: Poverty and well-being among older Americans. *Aging Today*, September/October 1994, *XV*, 9.

Rawlings, S. Household and family characteristics: March 1992. *Current Population Reports*, Series P-20, No. 463. Washington, DC: U.S. Bureau of the Census, 1993.

Rhoades, E. Profile of American Indians and Alaska natives. In M. S. Harper (Ed.), *Minority aging*. DHHS Publication #HRS (P-DV-90–4). Washington, DC: U.S. Government Printing Office, 1990.

Rumbaut, R. G. Vietnamese, Laotian, and Cambodian Americans. In P. G. Min (Ed.), *Asian Americans: Contemporary issues and trends*. Newbury Park, CA: Sage Publications, 1995.

Schoenbaum, M., and Waidman, T. Race, socioeconomic states and health: Accounting for race differences in health. *Journals of Gerontology*, 1997, *52B*, 61–73.

Silverstein, M., and Waite, C. J. Are blacks more likely than whites to receive and provide social support in middle and old age? Yes, no and maybe so. *Journals of Gerontology*, 1993, *48*, S212–S222.

Smith, S. H. Now that mom's gone: African-American middle-aged daughters' experiences of bereavement. *Dissertation Abstracts International: Section A: Humanities and Social Sciences*, May 1997, *57(11-A)*: 4933.

Stephen, E. H., Foote, K., Hendershot, G. E., and Schoenbaum, C. A. Health of the foreign born population: United States 1989–90. *Advance data from vital and health statistics*; No. 241. Hyattsville, MD: National Center for Health Statistics, 1994.

Tanjasiri, S. P., Wallace, S. P., and Shibata, K. Picture imperfect: Hidden problems among Asian Pacific Islander elderly. *The Gerontologist*, 1995, *35*, 753–760.

Torres-Gil, F. M., and Kuo, T. Social policy and the politics of Hispanic aging. *Journal of Gerontological Social Work*, 1998, *30*, 143–158.

U.S. Bureau of the Census. *Statistical Abstract of the United States*, 116th edition. Washington, DC: Current Population Reports, 1996.

U.S. Senate Special Committee on Aging. *Aging America: Trends and projections. 1990–91*. Washington, DC: U.S. Department of Health and Human Services, 1992.

Walls, C., and Zarit, S. Informal support from black churches and the well-being of elderly blacks. *The Gerontologist*, 1991, *31*, 490–495.

Wood, J. B., and Wan, T. Ethnicity and minority issues in family caregiving to rural black elders. In C. Barresi and D. Stull (Eds.), *Ethnic elderly and long-term care*. New York: Springer, 1993.

Wright, R., and Mindel, C. Economics, health and service use policies: Implications for long-term care of ethnic elderly. In C. Barresi and D. Stull (Eds.), *Ethnic elderly and long-term care*. New York: Springer, 1993.

Wykle, M., and Kaskel, B. Increasing the longevity of minority older adults through improved health status. In *Minority elders: Five goals toward building a public policy base* (2nd ed.). The Gerontological Society of America, 1994.

Yee, B. W. K., and Weaver, G. D. Ethnic minorities and health promotion. *Generations*, 1994, *18*, 39–44.

Yee, E., Kim, K., Liu, W., and Wong, S-C. Functional abilities of Chinese and Korean elders in congregate housing. In C. Barresi and D. Stull (Eds.), *Ethnic elderly and long-term care*. New York: Springer, 1993.

Yeo, G. Ethnogenetics: Cross-cultural care of older adults. *Generations*, Winter 1996–97, *20*, 72–77.

Young, J. J., and Gu, N. *Demographic and socio-economic characteristics of elderly Asian and Pacific Island Americans*. Seattle: National Asian Pacific Center on Aging, 1995.

15

THE RESILIENCY
OF OLDER WOMEN

This chapter covers

- The economic conditions faced by older women
- Their health and social status
- How these factors interact
- The strengths and resiliency of older women
- Program and policy options to reduce older women's vulnerability to poverty, poor health, and social isolation

Previous chapters illustrate how women's experiences with aging differ from men's: in patterns of health and life expectancy, marital opportunities, social supports, employment, and retirement. This chapter elaborates on these gender differences, with attention to how personal and environmental factors interact vis-à-vis the particular problems facing women in old age. The impact of social factors, particularly economic ones, on physiological and psychological variables is vividly illustrated in terms of women's daily lives.

RATIONALE FOR A FOCUS ON OLDER WOMEN'S NEEDS

A major reason for gerontological research and practice to take account of older women's needs is

Many older women have overcome a wide range of obstacles and are remarkable survivors.

that they form the fastest-growing segment of our population, especially among the oldest-old (Diczfalusy and Bengiano, 1997; Velkoff and Lawson, 1998). As noted in Chapter 1, the aging society is primarily a female one. Women represent 56 percent of the population aged 65 to 74 and 72 percent of those over age 85. They outnumber men age 65 and over by three to two, men age 85 and over by five to two; and centenarians by three to one. These ratios differ among ethnic minorities, as described in Chapter 14. Chapter 1 noted that these disproportionate ratios result from a nearly 7-year difference in life expectancy between women and men; this is due to a combination of biological factors, such as the genetic theory that the female's two X chromosomes make her physiologically more robust, and to lifestyle factors, such as women's greater likelihood of consulting doctors

and their lower rates of smoking, problem drinking, and other high-risk behaviors across the life span. At age 65, women can expect to live about 19 more years compared to 15.5 more years for male counterparts. At age 75, the comparable figures are 12 more years for women and 9 for men. Even at age 85, female life expectancy is 1.5 years more than that for males (U.S. Bureau of the Census, 1996). However, men who survive beyond age 85 are likely to be in better health and to have a similar life expectancy—or even more remaining years than women (Moen, 1996).

Another reason to focus on the status of older women is that gender structures opportunities across the life course, making the processes of aging and the quality of life in old age markedly different for men and women. Consistent with the feminist perspective described in Chapter 8, research on women and aging recognizes that gender and age interact to affect the distribution of power, privilege, and social well-being, and resulting in distinctive patterns for men and women throughout the life course. Feminists note that, as more women reach old age in our culture, age compounds a woman's already devalued status and increases her powerlessness (Browne, 1998; Garner, 1999; Holstein, 1993; Moen, 1996; Pohl and Boyd, 1993). Since gender and age are powerful systems for patterning inequities, neither can be understood fully without reference to the other (Hess, 1994). Given this interaction, it is not surprising that the problems of aging are increasingly women's problems. Older women are more likely than older men to be poor; to have inadequate retirement income; to be widowed, divorced, and alone; to live in assisted living or a nursing home; and to be caregivers to other relatives. Women are viewed as experiencing double jeopardy—they are discriminated against both for being old and for being female. In addition, the emphasis on youth and beauty in our society, which traditionally values women for their sex appeal and ability to bear children, is particularly difficult for older women. In fact, it is this cultural emphasis that underlies the growing popularity of expensive chemical skin peels, laser treatments, and antiwrinkle creams, available only to upper-middle-class women. In recent years, older women's vulnerability to social, economic, and health problems has been made visible, primarily as the result of the educational and advocacy efforts of such groups as the Older Women's League (OWL).

Despite the underlying interconnections among gender, age, and socioeconomic class, a number of strategies could be taken to reduce the poverty rate among older women:

- Increasing survivor's benefits would improve the status of widowed women.
- Improving benefits for low earners would help many divorced and never-married women.
- Improving the Supplemental Security Income Program would assist the poorest older women. (e.g., increase asset limits)
- Targeted benefits could be established within Social Security, such as an income-tested minimum benefit guarantee of $600 per month for beneficiaries taking home less than $400 a month.
- Regarding divorce benefit eligibility, the number of years of marriage required for qualification for spousal benefit under Social Security could be lowered.
- Earnings sharing could be instituted by combining a couple's earnings and dividing the credits.
- There could be Social Security plans that would provide a better return on earnings and better survivor's benefits.

Women are also less likely to have private pensions than men, because of their concentration in low-paying positions and shorter employment careers. In addition, mandatory pension laws were not in effect when women of the oldest-old cohort were employed (i.e., in the 1920s and 1930s). As discussed in Chapter 12, pension plans reward the long-term steady worker with high earnings and job stability, a pattern more characteristic of men than of women who are more likely to interrupt their careers to marry, rear children, and perhaps care for older relatives. This continues to be the

trend even among the current cohort of women. Over 40 percent of men are covered by private pensions, compared with fewer than 20 percent of women who have been employed. Women with pensions receive approximately half the benefit income of men because of salary differentials during their working years (AARP, 1999). A woman whose family role resulted in economic dependence on her husband can benefit from his private pension only if the following conditions exist:

- He does not die before retirement age.
- He stays married to her.
- He is willing to reduce his monthly benefits in order to provide her with a survivor's monthly annuity.

Given the economic vicissitudes of aging, some older men choose higher monthly benefits rather than survivor's benefits. Such a choice can be detrimental to older women, since, as noted earlier, most wives outlive their husbands by an average of 8 years. Fortunately, pension provisions enacted by Congress in 1984 (Retirement Equity Act) benefit older women by shortening the time it takes to earn a pension and improving coverage for lower-income workers, for those who begin work after age 60, and for those who continue to work after age 65. Most of these provisions, however, are not effective for years worked before 1988, and thus do not affect the current cohort of older women. In addition, federal laws designed to provide protection to spouses of private pension recipients do not apply to state government plans. As a result, 26 states do not have a **spousal consent requirement** before a plan participant can waive survivor benefits. Thus, a wife may discover only after her husband's death that she will no longer be entitled to pension benefits that were paid prior to that point (AARP, 1999). Another limitation is that policies to address women's vulnerability as nonemployed or late-entry workers focus on benefiting women at risk of impoverishment as they age, not those who have been poor throughout life.

Not surprisingly, older women who have never married and who have been employed tend to have a higher average annual income than their divorced or widowed counterparts. They are also far more likely to derive their income from pensions, annuities, interest, and dividends. In addition, never-married employed women spend less on housing and health care than do their widowed women peers (Schwenk, 1992). These figures do not hold true, however, for never-married mothers.

Older women without private pensions and whose Social Security income falls below the poverty line may turn to Supplemental Security Income (SSI). In fact, women comprise nearly 75 percent of older SSI recipients (Older Women's League, 1995). For women who value economic self-sufficiency, dependency on government support can be stigmatizing. On the other hand, some older low-income women cope by reducing the stigma associated with poverty. They "count their blessings," redefine poverty to exclude oneself, compare themselves to others less fortunate, and describe poverty as temporary (Older Women's League, 1998).

The economic outlook for women in the future remains bleak: Poverty and insecurity will be as much a problem of older women in the middle of the twenty-first century as for women retiring today (Smeeding et al., 2000). The Social Security system was designed nearly 70 years ago at a time when women had limited employment prospects (and therefore depended upon the marriage benefit); They were widowed young, and divorce was unusual. These conditions are dramatically different today. Even though more middle-aged and older women are employed, they are more likely to hold part-time and poorly paid jobs in the service sector. In fact, more than 66 percent of working women age 55 and over are employed in three traditionally female job categories: sales; administrative support, including clerical; and services (Quadagno and Hardy, 1996). These rates are much higher among older women of color. It is predicted that by the year 2020, poverty will remain widespread among older women living alone—those who are divorced, widowed, or never married—while Social Security and pension systems will have practically eliminated poverty among older men and couples (Smeeding

et al., 2000). Accordingly, fewer women will receive either spousal or survivor benefits due to their increased earnings, declines in marriage rates, and better health of older men. Poverty rates will increase among divorced women and never-married mothers.

In summary, women's traditional family roles and limited job options in the past tend to result in discontinuous employment histories. This pattern, combined with fewer pension opportunities and lower Social Security benefits, produces a double jeopardy for older women's economic status. These structural barriers and the interaction of gender and age (and race/ethnicity) mean that government policies (e.g., Social Security, SSI, and public pensions) are differentially effective in raising men and women and persons of color out of poverty. Accordingly, women of color remain at the lowest income levels across decades (Gonyea, 1996). Since most changes in Social Security and pension laws have improved the benefits of women as dependents rather than as employees, they do not address structural inequities across the life span. A feminist perspective on retirement would (1) examine the interconnections between family (private) and work (public) roles, (2) investigate the personal and political spheres in order to free women from a substantial investment in unpaid work (caregiving, home labor), and (3) promote parity among men and women during retirement (Richardson, 1999).

Older Women's Health Status

Women's disadvantaged economic status increases their health risks. They may live longer than men, but they have higher rates of illness, physician visits, and prescription drug use as a result of more acute illnesses and nonfatal chronic conditions (Moen, 1996). As described in Chapter 4, older people who are poor, represented primarily by women and ethnic minorities, tend to be less healthy than higher-income older adults. Their living conditions are not conducive to good health. Compared to their wealthier peers, low-income elders are more likely to be living alone, have inadequate diets, have less access to information about how to maintain their health, and have fewer dental visits and physician contacts per year. In fact, older women of color are more likely to obtain health care from hospital outpatient units, emergency rooms, and neighborhood clinics than from private physicians. Since women, especially the divorced and widowed, predominate among the older poor, women's health status is more frequently harmed by the adverse conditions associated with poverty than is men's. In turn, poor health combined with inadequate insurance can deplete the limited resources of the low-income poor.

Less Access to Health Insurance

Previous family and employment patterns affect older women's access to adequate health care and health maintenance information. Specifically, the workplace determines such access through opportunities to enroll in group insurance plans. Most insurance systems exclude the occupation of homemaker, except as a dependent. Accordingly, more women than men lack health insurance. This is often because women have never been, or have sporadically been, employed or in part-time positions that do not provide health benefits. Low-income divorced and/or widowed women, unable to rely on their husbands' insurance, are especially disadvantaged. Divorced women are about twice as likely to lack health insurance as married women, and are more likely than widows to be uninsured (Costello and Krimgold, 1996). Women of color, especially Hispanics, also have lower rates of insurance coverage, including Medicare, than their white counterparts (NIH, 2000).

Some uninsured women gamble on staying healthy until qualifying for Medicare coverage at age 65. Since the incidence of chronic disease is higher among older women than among men, many women do not win this gamble. They may not qualify for Medicaid at an earlier age nor for Medicare at age 65. For example, if a divorced woman is diagnosed with cancer in her late fifties, she is too young to qualify for Medicare and too sick to ob-

tain private insurance; yet she may fall just above the income limits for Medicaid; and, as a divorcee, unable to turn to her former husband's insurance. Fortunately, groups such as Older Women's League have succeeded in advocating for **conversion laws** that require insurance companies to allow women to remain in their spouse's group insurance for up to 3 years after divorce, separation, or widowhood (Consolidated Omnibus Budget Reconciliation Act or COBRA). Even with adequate health insurance, older women spend more of their annual income for out-of-pocket health care costs compared to their male peers.

Because of their lower socioeconomic status, older women are more likely than men to depend on Medicaid (Costello and Krimgold, 1996). An insidious negative effect of this dependency is that health care providers, concerned about low reimbursement rates and extensive paperwork, may be unwilling to accept Medicaid patients. This makes it difficult for older women to obtain adequate health care. Male–female differences in longevity, marital status, and income are central in assessing the impact of recent increases in Medicaid copayments and deductibles. Women outnumber men two to one among frail elders, for whom health and long-term care use and costs are greatest. For example, white women living alone have the highest utilization of nursing homes and home health services and for longer periods of time than white males. As more Medicaid costs are shifted to the patient, more low-income frail women will be unable to afford health care, especially for prescription drugs.

Higher Incidence of Chronic Health Problems

Limited insurance options and greater dependence on Medicaid are especially problematic since 85 percent of older women have a chronic disease or disability. Although men tend to experience fewer daily aches and pains than do women, when they do become ill, men are more likely to face life-threatening acute conditions and to require hospitalization. In contrast, women are more likely to experience the disabling effects of multiple chronic conditions. These differences in types of health problems may be one reason why women live longer than men, even though they are less healthy (National Center on Women and Aging, 1999). Since many chronic conditions can be prevented through early detection and treatment or through changes in health behavior, older women may be healthier in the future (Falik and Collins, 1996).

Contrary to common perceptions that men are at higher risk of heart attacks and strokes than are women, cardiovascular disease is the number-one killer for both men and women, although men experience the symptoms of coronary heart disease at younger ages. In fact, cardiovascular disease kills more women than the next 16 causes of death combined. The primary causes are unhealthy diets and sedentary lifestyles. The rate of heart disease triples for women age 65 and over, while remaining nearly equal for men and women between the ages of 45 and 64. In fact, five times as many women die from heart disease than from breast cancer. This is because, as noted in Chapter 4, women lose the advantage of estrogen's protection against heart disease after menopause and have a longer life expectancy than do men after ages 45 to 55.

Women also increasingly face health problems specifically associated with their reproductive functions, such as breast, cervical, and uterine cancers—as well as high-risk complications from hysterectomies. Of women with breast cancer, 75 percent are over age 50 (National Policy and Resource Center on Women and Aging, 1997). In the past 25 years, the chances of a woman developing breast cancer have grown from 1 in 16 to 1 in 8, while prevention, diagnosis, and treatment have lagged. One improvement in Medicare made by Congress in 1990 was to include **mammography** screening as a biennial Medicare benefit. In addition, the 1997 changes in Medicare provided for fuller reimbursement for mammograms. Yet, physicians frequently do not refer older women for mammography, even though yearly mammograms generally are recommended after age 40 (physicians vary in whether it is recommended at age 40 or 50). In fact, in 1995, only 50 percent of women

obtained regular mammography checkups in accordance with established medical guidelines. One reason for this low rate is that many older women believe that they will not get breast cancer because of their age. In reality, the longer a woman lives, the more likely she is to develop breast cancer, although it may be slow-growing. A similar pattern can be seen where women over age 60, who are most at risk of cancers of the reproductive system, are least likely to have annual pap smears (National Policy and Resource Center on Women and Aging, 1997).

As noted above, although women suffer from more chronic health conditions, most of these are not life-threatening; they do, however, interfere with daily functioning and require frequent physician contacts. For example, over 50 percent of women age 70 to 74 find it difficult or impossible to lift or carry 25 pounds, and 60 percent of women over age 65 have been screened out of random public physical fitness testing for reasons of health risk. This lack of basic strength increases the likelihood of falls that may increase their probable need for nursing home care (O'Brien and Vertinsky, 1991). On the other hand, the National Institutes of Health Women's Health and Aging Study found that the majority of women respondents, despite high levels of disability, engage in some form of physical activity, typically related to household chores (Simonsick, Phillip, Skinner, Davis, and Kasper, 1995). Furthermore, women who begin an exercise program even in their seventies and eighties can improve their fitness and strength.

Some studies find that older women also experience more injuries and more days of restricted activity and bed disability compared to their male counterparts. These measures are generally indicators of chronic disorders, such as high blood pressure and arthritis, although they may reflect women's greater readiness to take curative action and spend more time in bed recuperating when they are ill. Among people aged 85 and over, gender differences in patterns of illness become even more striking, with 65 percent of women age 85 and over likely to enter a nursing home compared to 50 percent of men (National Policy and Resource Center on Women and Aging, 1997). Women comprise about 75 percent of nursing home residents, and 66 percent of home care consumers (Adams et al., 1999). Several factors besides health status that may account for such differences, however. As discussed in Chapter 9, old men are more likely to be married, with wives to care for them at home instead of being placed in a nursing home. Women over age 75, on the other hand, have few available resources for home-based care, and are often unable to afford private home health services. In addition, as noted earlier, men who survive to age 75 and older are the healthiest and hardiest of their cohort.

More recent analyses of gender and health suggest that the pattern of women outliving men and experiencing more chronic health problems may not be immutable. Scholars on gender and health are urging a shift away from equating "gender" solely with "women" toward a "relatively undifferentiated model of consistent sex differences" in morbidity (Hunt, and Annandale, 1999; MacIntyre, Hunt, and Sweeting, 1996). For example, a strong association has been found between indicators of gender inequality (e.g., women's position in relation to men for employment and earnings, indicators of women's economic status) and mortality for both women *and* men. Some of these socioeconomic gradients of macroindicators show a stronger association with male rather than female mortality (Hunt and Annandale, 1999; MacIntyre and Hunt, 1997). A growing body of research seeks to question empirically whether important influences on health (e.g., working conditions, social and material circumstances) show similar associations in men and women, rather than simply assuming a difference. Some studies have discovered a "new paradox." Men are more likely than women to assess their health as being poor, despite women's higher level of functional impairment (Arber and Cooper, 1999; Hunt and Annandale, 1999; National Center on Women and Aging, 1999). In sum, the relations between gender and health are not necessarily clear-cut, and may not be in the direction commonly assumed: that women experience more health and mental health difficulties in their longer lives. This also suggests the limitations of trying to make "all things

equal" in a social order where gender remains such a powerful influence on life chances. Proponents of this gender-based approach also recognize the importance of considering race, ethnicity and social class along with gender in terms of health status (Hunt and Annandale, 1999).

Osteoporosis

As noted in Chapter 4, the majority of older people with osteoporosis are women. In fact, 25 percent of women over age 65 have osteoporosis in their hips or spine (Williams, 1999). Osteoporosis has been called the silent disease because a woman feels no pain as her bones gradually thin to the point where even a slight bump or fit of coughing can cause a fracture. The higher incidence of wrist, spinal, and hip fractures related to postmenopausal osteoporosis is one reason for the greater number of injuries and days of restricted activity among older women. Spinal fractures frequent and severe enough to cause dowager's hump (loss of up to 8 inches in height) occur in 5 to 7 percent of women. Over 50 percent of postmenopausal women are estimated to fracture a hip and 25 to 40 percent will suffer spine shortening and often painful vertebral fractures (Speroff, Rowan, Symons, Genant, and Wilborn, 1996). The incidence of hip fractures in older women doubles every 5 years after the age of 60 (National Policy and Resource Center on Women and Aging, 1996). The threat of hip fractures can create numerous fears and losses among older women—and circumscribe their social world.

The case for and against hormone replacement therapy discussed in Chapter 4 is not clear-cut. Women who do not replace their estrogen can lose 3 to 4 percent of their bone mass every year; for the first 5 years after menopause. HRT has been found to increase bone mass in the spine and hip by 3 to 5 percent in the first year; this increase is maintained as long as the individual takes hormones. It can reduce the risk of both hip and forearm fractures by 50 percent, and the risk of spinal fractures up to 75 percent. These benefits decline somewhat after age 75, the period when women are most at risk. This pattern holds even among women who start using HRT in their sixties (Williams, 1999).

WAYS TO PREVENT OSTEOPOROSIS AND RELATED INJURIES

- Be physically active through weight-bearing and strength-training exercises (brisk walking, running, hiking, dancing, climbing stairs, lifting weights, and jumping rope).
- Don't smoke, since smoking weakens bones.
- Get enough calcium (1200–1500 mg) and vitamin D (400–800 mg) through supplements, but do not exceed recommended daily allowances for women.
- Eat yogurt, milk, cheese, sardines, dry roasted soybeans, or collard greens, which are high in calcium and vitamin D.

- Prevent falls:
  - Avoid high-heeled or loose-fitting shoes, loose throw rugs, slippery bathtubs, and wet steps.
  - Turn on lights when the room is dark; move things that one could trip on; use nonslip bathmats and bathroom grab rails.
- Talk to your health care provider about cutting down on drugs that make you more likely to fall and those that lead to bone loss (pain and sleep medications, steroids, epilepsy medicines, and thyroid hormones).

However, women with the greatest bone density in their hips, spines, and wrists also have been found to have the highest incidence of breast cancer, illustrating the ongoing controversy about the risks of estrogen replacement therapy (Speroff et al., 1996). Because of growing concern about estrogen replacement therapy on risk of breast cancer, diet (increased calcium and vitamin D) and exercise are increasingly emphasized as a way to reduce bone loss. Low-impact aerobics and weight-bearing upper body strength training can boost bone density 3 to 5 percent a year in those who previously did not exercise (Williams, 1999). Accordingly, women with calcium supplementation have higher bone mineral densities than those without, and fewer fractures if residing in nursing homes (Meunier, 1999). In addition, several drugs can halt bone loss and may result in a 2 or 3 percent yearly increase in bone mass (Williams, 1999). Fortunately, increasing attention is directed toward both the prevention and treatment of osteoporosis, including bone-mineral-density tests, which are covered by Medicare and use sophisticated X-rays or sonograms.

Menopause

The physiological changes associated with menopause were discussed in Chapters 3 and 7. Social and cultural attitudes can also make menopause troublesome, since many of its associated discomforts result from our society's tendency to view menopause as a disease rather than a normal biological process. Hence, many women anticipate that depression, loss of sexual desire and sexual attractiveness, and such signs of aging as wrinkled skin and weight gain are inevitable. Contrary to such expectations, menopause is not an illness or a deficiency, and 30 to 50 percent of women have no symptoms as they pass into menopause. In fact, for most women, it can be a positive transition (Gonyea, 1998). Increasingly, women find that menopause can bring a renewed sense of living and time for oneself, or what the anthropologist Margaret Mead termed **postmenopausal zest.** Menopausal symptoms thus provide another example of the interaction of normal physiological changes with psychological conditions and societal expectations.

The culturally prevalent model of menopause as a disease attributes changes to loss of estrogen. When it is thus defined as a "deficiency disease," the treatment implication is that estrogen must be replaced. Accordingly, the primary medical response to treating symptoms such as hot flashes has been hormone replacement therapy. When menopause is viewed as a normal life transition, however, lower estrogen levels among postmenopausal women can

---

NONMEDICAL APPROACHES TO MENOPAUSE

- Hypnosis, meditation, biofeedback, acupuncture, paced respiration, and muscle relaxation techniques
- Exercise
- Support groups, and use of humor
- Herbal remedies, such as black cohosh roots to reduce hot flashes; kava to reduce mood swings, irritability, and stress; St. John's wort for depression and anxiety. Despite the growing popularity of herbal approaches, most herbs sold in health food stores

(as capsules, teas, tinctures, extracts, or infusions) are not regulated by the Food and Drug Administration. Caution also needs to be exercised in terms of possible interactions with prescription drugs
- Vitamin E to alleviate hot flashes
- Dietary changes to reduce fats and preservatives and increase fiber, calcium, soy (through tofu, soymilk, tempeh, miso), or wheat flour (Murkies, 1998)

---

be considered normal. Recently, many women have been using nonmedical approaches to minimize uncomfortable symptoms.

Although the disease model of menopause links depression with the endocrine changes, depression among postmenopausal women appears to be more closely associated with psychosocial variables, particularly changes in women's roles and relationships, than with physiological factors. Women who have had prior episodes of depression, especially during other periods of hormonal fluctuation (e.g. postpartum depression), those with poor social supports, and those who experience menopause at a younger age are at higher risk, but menopause alone is *not* a risk factor for depression. Health care providers have often treated the symptoms of depression with drugs, or have assumed that women were "too old" to benefit from therapeutic interventions. More recently, efforts have been made to provide women with

ways of exerting control over their lives, and to develop counseling and social support interventions as a means of combating depression. Social support groups are found to reduce women's feelings of isolation and to enhance their self-esteem and self-efficacy.

Unfortunately, a recent national survey shows that many women are not getting useful information for coping with menopause. Doctors are unlikely to talk about the long-term health effects of decreased estrogen unless women are experiencing unpleasant menopausal reactions, such as hot flashes or mood swings. This then puts women at a disadvantage in making careful decisions about ways to reduce risks. In addition, nonmenopausal health conditions may be ignored because they are attributed to the "change of life" (National Center on Women and Aging, 1999). Not surprisingly, the National Women's Information Center, a resource center that can be accessed by phone or Internet,

---

PLANNING PROACTIVELY FOR A POSITIVE OLD AGE

- Protect your health (diet, exercise, screening tests).
- Improve your skills (e.g., computer literacy).
- Maximize your workplace benefits (e.g., Simplified Employee Pension plan).
- Learn as much as you can about your retirement income.

- Take charge of your finances.
- Determine if you are eligible for public benefits.
- Research your housing options and alternatives.
- Learn about resources to assist with caregiving.
- Be prepared for changes in your marital status.
- Protect yourself through safety strategies.

reports that the topic on which they receive the highest number of inquiries is menopause. Increasingly, newer cohorts of middle-aged women are proactive in seeking accurate information about what to expect, what therapies work, and what the risks and benefits are (Clinton, 1999).

Regardless of age and marital or socioeconomic status, if you are a woman, steps can be taken to ensure a positive old age.

Older Women's Social Status

Older women's problems are frequently intensified by the greater likelihood of their living alone. For example, those who live alone are more likely to be diagnosed as malnourished. This is not surprising when the social functions of eating are considered. The older person living alone may derive no pleasure from eating and may skip meals, subsisting instead on unhealthy snacks. The high poverty rates among older women who live alone may also account for their poor diet. Even mild nutritional deficiencies may produce disorientation, confusion, depression, and reduced ability to respond to stress. In addition, a person with few immediate social supports may be less likely to resist infections and viral diseases. Her ability to live in the community may thus be sharply curtailed. In fact, socially isolated African American women are found to have higher rates of mortality than their peers with strong social networks (LaVeist, Sellers, Brown, Elliott, and Nickerson, 1997).

Approximately 41 percent of older women (compared to 17 percent of older men) live alone for nearly one-third of their adult lives, primarily because of widowhood or divorce. When never-married older women are included, the percentage living alone increases to over 70 percent. At the turn of the century, widows lived alone for 5 to 10 years; now the average is 24 years, yet fewer adult children are available to provide care (Velkoff and Lawson, 1998). In fact, only 40 percent of all women aged 65 and over live with their spouses, compared to 72 percent of men, and only 16 percent live with other family members, generally a

daughter. Among women aged 75 and over, the percentage living with their spouses drops to less than 25 percent compared to 70 percent of men; and the proportion living alone increases to over 54 percent, a rate at least twice that of their male counterparts. Only about 2 percent live with non-relatives, although a growing number say they would consider asking a friend if they needed help around the house or with personal care (Chalfie, 1998). In contrast, older women of color who are divorced and widowed are more likely to live in extended family households, with children and/or grandchildren living in their home. For example, African American (36%) and Hispanic (34%) women live with relatives compared to only 14 percent of older white women. Women of color often extend their households to include children and grandchildren, assuming child care and housekeeping responsibilities into old age (Cochran, Brown, and McGregor, 1999). This may help them meet housing and food costs.

Divorce

Divorced women are even more vulnerable. Compared to both their married and widowed peers, divorced women aged 65 and over are found to have poorer health, lower income and rates of home ownership, lower levels of life satisfaction, and higher mortality rates. Many of the assets that middle-aged and older women have accumulated over the years of marriage are lost in late-life divorce. If women were divorced earlier in life, the disadvantages of having no financial support and often being employed in low-paying positions may result in a lifetime of marginal economic security.

Widowhood

As discussed in Chapter 13, the average age of widowhood for women is 66 years. Because women generally marry men older than themselves, live longer than men, and, in their later years, seldom remarry after the death of their husbands, 85 percent of all wives outlive their husbands. Some 52 percent of women aged 65 and over are widowed, in contrast to 14 percent of men in this age group; this gap increases dramatically with age. The expected years of widowhood are far more than the 8-year difference in life expectancy between women and men at these ages. At age 65 a widow can anticipate living another 18 years; at age 70, 11 years; and at age 85, another 9 years. Not surprisingly, after age 85, 66 percent of women live alone (National Policy and Resource Center, 1996). Moreover, this increased time living alone is accompanied by shrinking family size, with fewer children available as potential caregivers (Moen, 1996). The probability of widowhood increases among older women of color.

As noted previously, the primary negative consequence of widowhood is low socioeconomic status (Smith, 1997). These economic conditions have social implications: Low-income women have fewer options for social interactions, fewer affordable and safe accommodations, and fewer resources to purchase in-home support services. The most negative consequence may be that older women's economic situation precludes continued independent living when health problems arise. In fact, widowhood has been found to result in increased health service use and costs (Prigerson, Maciejewski, and Rosenbeck, 2000). Despite these objective disadvantages of widowhood, the "lonely widow" may be a stereotype to some extent, and widowhood may not necessarily produce the major, enduring negative emotional effects typically reported (Moen, 1996).

Limited Opportunities to Remarry

Although remarriage may be viewed as a way to ensure economic security, older widowed and divorced women have fewer remarriage options than do their male peers. The primary obstacles to remarriage are the disproportionate number of women age 65 and over to men and the cultural stigma against women marrying younger men. With the ratio of 80-year-old women to men being three to one, the chances for remarriage decline drastically with age. These gender differences lead to differential needs for support in the face of fail-

Group exercise offers physical and social benefits.

ing health; most older men are cared for by their wives, whereas most older women rely on their children, usually daughters, for help and may turn later to paid assistance. Increasingly, adult daughters who assist their widowed mothers are themselves in their sixties and seventies, and are faced with their own physical limitations. One consequence of this pattern is that older women may have to depend more on public support services, even though these are not well funded. As invisible laborers, women's work is essential to the health care system and to their relatives' long-term care, but it is not adequately supported by public policies.

In addition to high rates of widowhood and increasing rates of divorce, the current cohort of older women has relatively high proportions of unmarried women throughout their lives (approximately 5 percent for those now in their seventies and eighties). Therefore, a cohort effect also may explain the large numbers of older women living without spouses. Another factor that increases the probability of being alone among this current cohort is that approximately one in five has either been childless throughout her life or has survived her offspring (Saluter, 1994). In the future, the proportion of old women living alone, including those unmarried throughout their adult lives, will increase.

The absence of children and a spouse also increases the chance of being placed in a nursing home. This suggests that women may be institutionalized for social rather than medical reasons,

FORMATION OF COMMUNITY AMONG OLD WOMEN IN A BEAUTY SHOP

An unintentional community of older women is formed at an old-fashioned beauty shop, based on a shared universe of meaning as Jewish mothers, housewives, and caregivers in a society that expects women to be attractive, despite the realities of aging and physical decline. Women in a beauty shop are brought together around a common concern with appearance as a source of self-worth. The face and the body are used to maintain self-respect and community status. Taking care of oneself is a moral imperative for these old women. Friendships formed in the beauty shop illustrate the diversity of women's connectedness and their varied expression of mutual supportiveness and caring. They talk about illness, aches, and pains, expe-

riencing an outlet for subjects that they feel they cannot discuss with family. Discursive personal stories permit exchange of lived experiences and strengthen social bonds. Shows of physical and verbal affection, humor about the inevitability of wrinkles, sags and bags, and food shared further strengthen social ties. The beauty shop is a search for a good old age among women disadvantaged by age and gender. In the process of seeking beauty, the women gain a sense of belonging, affirmation, and being cared for. The beauty shop thus also acts as a community of resistance against being old and female in a gendered society.

Adapted from Markson, B. 1999.

and may be inappropriately placed in a nursing home when alternative community supports might have permitted more independent lifestyles. As noted in Chapter 11, women in nursing homes are typically widowed or single, often dependent on Medicaid, and lacking family members to assist them either socially or financially. After age 85, 25 percent of women, especially never-married and widowed women, are in nursing homes (NIH, 2000).

Sources of Support

In general, older women have fewer economic but more social resources and richer, more intimate relationships than do older men. Men tend to have larger nonkin networks, perhaps as a result of employment, but are less resourceful in planning social get-togethers and building networks that substitute for the sociability in marriage (Moen, 1996). Widowed women, in particular, and women in retirement communities generally have frequent and intimate contacts with friends and social activities. One reason for this is that retirement communities provide women with peers at the same stage of life and shared similar experiences (Perkinson and Rockemann, 1996). Even when their

friends die, women generally establish new relationships, exchanging affection and material support outside their families, although they may not be able to call upon such relationships to care for them. Instead, they value the mutuality of their friendships and do not want to become dependent for personal care upon friends (Roberto, 1996). Support groups for widows and family caregivers build on such reciprocal exchange relations among peers. In addition, with age, some women first become comfortable with being open about their lesbianism and their strong emotional bonds with other women. One function of the affirmation of women's competencies by the women's movement has been to encourage them to support each other rather than depend on men. This is evidenced by the growth of shared households, older women's support and advocacy groups, support groups for caregiving grandmothers, and intergenerational alliances (Fullmer, 1995).

Consistent with feminist theory discussed in Chapter 8, a feminist analysis of older women's social status would articulate their strengths and resilience, as well as their vulnerabilities. Feminist research seeks to "rediscover, revalue, and bring to public view women's experiences that have been obscured, occluded or devalued because they have been seen as socially insignificant or morally irrelevant" (Furman, 1997, p. 6). Although cohort, period, historical, and gender-based life circumstances mold older women, they are not passive. By studying gender and age power differentials, feminists seek to deepen our understanding of both women and men, their uniqueness, and their similarities in active meeting life's challenges (Markson, 1999).

FUTURE DIRECTIONS

Since women's socioeconomic status compounds problems they face in old age, fundamental changes are needed to remove inequities in the workplace, Social Security, and pension systems. Most such changes, however, will benefit future generations of older women, rather than the current cohort, which was socialized for work and family roles that no longer prevail. For example, recent efforts in some states to assure that women and men earn equal pay for jobs of comparable economic worth and to remove other salary inequities may mean that future generations of older women will have retirement benefits based on a lifetime of more adequate earnings, and will have more experience in handling finances. Some businesses and government agencies have initiated more flexible work arrangements with full benefits, which will allow men and women to share employment and family responsibilities more equitably. When such options exist, women may have fewer years of zero earnings to be calculated into their Social Security benefits, and will be more likely to hold jobs covered by private pensions. Even so, it is predicted that 60 percent of women in the year 2030 will still have 5 or more years of zero earnings averaged into the calculation of their Social Security benefits. This will widen the current gap between older women living alone and all other groups (Crystal, 1996). This is in large part due to the fact that despite three decades of legislation, women have not achieved equality in the workforce. Women remain disproportionately in the secondary labor market, marked by low

wages, few benefits, part-time employment, and little job security (Holstein, 1993). Even the entrance of more women into previously male-dominated positions has not resulted in a significant restructuring of the distribution of roles within families, with women still responsible for the majority of child care and housework (Moen, 1996).

Changes in Social Security to benefit women workers have been proposed by federal studies and commissions. The current Social Security system is based on an outmoded model of lifelong marriage, in which one spouse is the paid worker and the other is the homemaker. As the prior discussion of divorce and changing work patterns suggests, this model no longer accommodates the emerging diversity of employment and family roles. Nor, for that matter, has this model ever represented the diversity of American families. The most commonly discussed remedy is **earnings sharing,** whereby each partner in marriage is entitled to a separate Social Security account, regardless of which spouse is employed in the paid labor force. Covered earnings would be divided between the two spouses, with one-half credited to each spouse's account. Credits for homemaking, partial benefits for widows under age 62, full benefits for widows after age 65, and the option of collecting benefits as both worker and wife have also been discussed by senior-citizen advocacy groups and by some legislators. The likelihood of any such changes being instituted in the future is small. Instead, the greater risk is that efforts to privatize Social Security will disproportionately hurt older women.

Pension reforms have also been passed on the federal level that would increase by more than 20 percent the number of women covered by private pensions, through a reduction of the amount of time required for vesting. In the long run, more fundamental changes are needed in society's view of work throughout the life cycle, so that men and women may share more equitably in caregiving and employment responsibilities. At the same time, employers must value skills gained through homemaking and voluntary activity as transferable to the marketplace. As discussed in Chapters 9 and 12, the ways in which women contribute to society through their volunteerism, caregiving, housekeeping responsibilities, and informal helping of others need to be recognized under a broad concept of productivity, rather than equating productivity with only paid work (Holstein, 1993).

An important development in the quality of older women's lives is that more women of all ages are increasingly supporting one another, as illustrated by the intergenerational advocacy efforts of the Older Women's League. Another promising change is the growth of social support groups among older women. Groups of older widows and women caregivers are found to be effective in reducing isolation. They encourage group members to meet their own needs and expand women's awareness of public services to which they are entitled. This function of educating and politicizing older women also helps many to see the societal causes of the difficulties that they have experienced as individuals. Awareness of external causes of their problems may serve to bring together for common action women of diverse ages, ethnicity, race, socioeconomic classes, and sexual orientation. Cross-cultural evidence shows that age permits women in a wide range of cultures to become more dominant and powerful, with fewer restrictions on their behavior and mobility and increased opportunities to engage in roles outside the home. Rather than passivity, growing numbers of older women are aiming to resist denigration and invisibility (Markson, 1999). As women unite to work for change, they can make further progress in reducing the disadvantages of their economic and social position.

SUMMARY AND IMPLICATIONS

Older women are the fastest growing segment of our population, making the aging society primarily female. In addition, the problems of aging are increasingly the problems of women. Threats to Social Security, inadequate health and long-term care, and insufficient pensions are issues for women of all ages. Increasingly, older women are not only the recipients of social and health services, but also are cared for by other women, who are unpaid daughters and daughters-in-law, or staff within public social services, nursing homes, and hospitals.

Women's family caregiving roles are interconnected with their economic, social, and health status. Women who devoted their lives to attending to the needs of children, spouses, or older relatives often face years of living alone on low or poverty-level incomes, with inadequate health care, in substandard housing, and with little chance for employment to supplement their limited resources. Women face more problems in old age, not only because they live longer than their male peers, but also because, as unpaid or underpaid caregivers with discontinuous employment histories, they have not accrued adequate retirement or health care benefits. If they have depended on their husbands for economic security, divorce or widowhood increases their risks of poverty. As one of the poorest groups in our society, women account for nearly three-fourths of the older poor. The incidence of problems associated with poverty increases dramatically for older women living alone, for ethnic minority women, and for those age 75 and over. Frequently outliving their children and husbands, they have no one to care for them and are more likely than their male counterparts to be in nursing homes.

On the other hand, many women show remarkable resilience in the face of adversity. Fortunately, the number of exceptions to patterns of economic deprivation and social isolation is growing. With their lifelong experiences of caring for others, for example, women tend to be skilled at forming and sustaining friendships, which provide them with social support and intimacy. Recently, increasing attention has been paid to older women's capacity for change and to their strengths, largely because of efforts of national advocacy groups such as the Older Women's League. Current efforts to expand the employment and educational opportunities available to younger women will undoubtedly mean improved economic, social, and health status for future generations of women.

GLOSSARY

conversion laws   legal requirement for insurance companies to allow widowed, divorced, and separated women to remain on their spouses' group insurance for up to 3 years

earnings sharing   proposed change in Social Security whereby each partner in a marriage is entitled to a separate Social Security account, regardless of employment status

mammography   an X-ray technique for the detection of breast tumors before they can be seen or felt

postmenopausal zest   renewed sense of life and time for oneself that many women experience at menopause

postmenopause   in women, referring to the period of life after menopause

spousal consent requirement   federal law requiring that a spouse must consent to or agree to waiving survivor's benefits; not true of state government pension plans

RESOURCES

See the companion Website for this text at <www.ablongman.com/hooyman> for information about the following:

* AARP Women's Initiative
* National Black Women's Health Project
* National Center on Women & Aging
* National Women's Health Network
* Pension Rights Center
* Older Women's League

REFERENCES

AARP. *A Woman's Guide to Pension Rights.* American Association of Retired Persons, 1999.

Abel, S. L. Social Security retirement benefits: The last insult of a sexist society. *Family and Conciliation Courts Review,* 1998, *36,* 54–64.

Adams, S., Nawrocki, H., and Coleman, B. Women and long-term care. AARP Public Policy/Institute, 1999.

Aging Research and Training Newsletter, 1999, 22.

Arber, S., and Cooper, H. Gender differences in health in later life: The new paradox? *Social Science and Medicine,* January 1999, *48,* 61–76.

Barer, B. M. Men and women aging differently. *International Journal in Aging and Human Development,* 1994, *38,* 29–40.

Barusch-Smith, A., Self-concepts of low-income older women. *International-Journal of Aging and Human Development,* 1997, *44,* 269–282.

Bound, J., Duncan, G., Laren, D. S., and Oleinick, L. Poverty dynamics in widowhood. *Journals of Gerontology,* 1991, *46B,* S115–S124.

Bush, T. L., Wells, H. B., James, M. K., Barrett-Connor, E., Marcus, R., Greendale, G., Hunsberger, S., and McGowan, J. Effects of hormone replacement therapy on endometrial histology in postmenopausal women: The postmenopausal estrogen/progestin interventions (PEPI) trial. *Journal of the American Medical Association,* 1996, *275,* 370–375.

Chalfie, D. Facts about Older Women: Housing and Living Arrangements. *AARP Fact Sheet* D12880, 1998.

Choi, N. Racial differences in the determinants of living arrangements of widowed and divorced elderly women. *The Gerontologist,* 1991, *31,* 496–504.

Clinton, H. Essay: The next frontier. *Newsweek,* Special Edition on Women's Health, Spring/Summer 1999, 94–95.

Cochran, D. L., Brown, D. R., and McGregor, K. C. Racial differences in the multiple social roles of older women: implications for depressive symptoms. *The Gerontologist,* 1999, *39,* 465–472.

Costello, C., and Krimgold, B. K. (Eds.). *The American woman 1996–97: Women and work.* New York: W. W. Norton and Company, 1996.

Crystal, S. Economic status of the elderly. In R. H. Binstock and L. K. George (Eds.), *Handbook of aging and the social sciences* (4th ed.). San Diego, CA: Academic Press, 1996.

DeViney, S., and Solomon, J. C. Gender differences in retirement income: A comparison of theoretical explanations. *Journal of Women and Aging,* 1995, *7,* 83–100.

Diczfalusy, E., and Bengiano, G. Women and the third and fourth age. *International Journal of Gynecology and Obstetrics,* 1997, *56,* 177–188.

Dietz, B. E., and Carrozza, M. *Gender differences in retirement planning: The influence of status, human capital, and occupational structure.* Paper presented at meeting of the American Sociological Association, Chicago, IL, 1999.

Falik, M., and Collins, K. *Women's health: The Commonwealth Fund survey*. Baltimore, MD: John Hopkins University Press, 1996.

Fullmer, E. M. Challenging biases against families of older gays and lesbians. In G. C. Smith, S. Tobin, E. A. Robertson-Tchabo, and P. Power (Eds.), *Strengthening aging families: Diversity in practice and policy*. Thousand Oaks, CA: Sage, 1995.

Furman, F. K. *Facing the mirror: Older women and beauty shop culture*. New York: Rutledge Press, 1997.

Gonyea, J. G. Making gender visible in public policy. In E. H. Thompson, Jr., et al. (Ed.), *Older men's lives. Research on men and masculinities series*. Thousand Oaks, CA: Sage, 1996.

Gonyea, J. G. Midlife and menopause: Uncharted territories for baby boomer women. *Generations*, Spring 1998, 87–89.

Gordon, M. H. *The aging of an immigrant generation: A preliminary exploration into the experiences of post-1965 immigrant women in the United States*. International Sociological Association, 1998.

Guralnik, J. M., Fried, L. P., Simonsick, E. M., Kasper, J. D., and Lafferty, M. E. (Eds.). *The women's health and aging study: Health and social characteristics of older women with disabilities*. Bethesda, MD: National Institute on Aging, 1995.

Hatch, L., and Bulcroft, K. Contact with friends in later life: Disentangling the effects of gender and mental status. *Journal of Marriage and the Family*, 1992, *54*, 222–232.

Healy, B. Essay: A medical revolution. *Newsweek*, Special Edition on Women's health, Spring/Summer 1999, 64–67.

Hess, B. Gender and aging: The demographic parameters. In Robert Enright (Ed.), *Perspectives in social gerontology*. Boston: Allyn and Bacon, 1994.

Hobbs, F., and Damon, B. L. *65+ in the United States*, Washington, DC: U.S. Department of Commerce, Bureau of the Census, Current Population Reports, 1996.

Holstein, M. Women's lives, women's work: Productivity, gender, and aging. In S. A. Bass, F. G. Caro, and Y-P Chen (Eds.), *Achieving a productive aging society*. Westport, CT: Auburn House, 1993.

Hooyman, N., and Gonyea, J. A feminist model of family care: Practice and policy directions. In J. D. Garner, *Fundamentals of feminist gerontology. Journal of Women and Aging*, 1999, *11*, 149–170.

Hooyman, N., and Gonyea, J. *Feminist perspectives on family care: Policies for gender justice*. Thousand Oaks, CA: Sage, 1995.

Huckle, P. *Tish Sommers, activist and the founder of the Older Women's League*. Knoxville: The University of Tennessee Press, 1991.

Hunt, K., and Annandale, E. Relocating gender and morbidity: Examining men's and women's health in contemporary Western societies. Introduction to Special Issue on Gender and Health. *Social Science and Medicine*, 1999, *48*, 1–5.

Kingson, E. R., and O'Grady-LeShane, R. The effects of caregiving on women's Social Security benefits. *The Gerontologist*, 1993, *33*, 230–239.

LaVeist, T. A., Sellers, R. M., Brown, K. A., Elliott, and Nickerson, K. J. Extreme social isolation, use of community-based senior support services, and mortality among African American elderly women. *American Journal of Community Psychology*, 1997 October, *25*, 721–732.

Leonard, F. The course. *The Owl Observer*, September/October 1991, 7.

Macintyre, S., and Hunt, K. Socioeconomic position, gender and health: How do they interact? *Journal of Health Psychology*, 1997, *2*, 315–334.

Macintyre, S., Hunt, K., and Sweeting, H. Gender differences in health: Are things really as simple as they seem? *Social Science and Medicine*, 1996, *42*, 617–624.

Markson, B. Communities of resistance: Older women in a gendered world. Review of Frida Furman, Facing the Mirror. *The Gerontologist*, 1999, *39*, 496–497.

Meunier, P. J. Calcium, vitamin D and vitamin K in the prevention of fractures due to osteoporosis. *Clinical Pearls News*, 1999, 223.

Moen, P. Gender, age and the life course. In R. H. Binstock and L. K. George (Eds.), *Handbook of aging and the social sciences* (4th ed.). San Diego, CA: Academic Press, 1996.

Moen, P., Dempster-McClain, D., and Williams, Jr. R. M. *Pathways to women's well-being in later adulthood: A life course perspective*. Unpublished manuscript, 1995.

Moody, H. Aging: *Concepts and controversies* (3rd ed.). Thousand Oaks, CA: Pine Forge Press, 2000.

Murkies, A. L. Postmenopausal hot flashes decreased by dietary flour supplementation: Effects of soy and wheat. *American Journal of Clinical Nutrition*, 1998, *68*, 1533S.

National Center on Women and Aging, *Women are Aging Better*, Waltham, MA: Brandeis University, 1999.

National Institutes of Health. *Women of Color: Health Data Book*, Washington, DC: U.S. Department of Health and Human Services, 2000.

National Policy and Resource Center on Women and Aging. Half of America's women are not getting the mammograms they should. *The Women and Aging Letter*, Waltham, MA: Brandeis University, May 1997, 2, 8.

National Policy and Resource Center on Women and Aging. Osteoporosis. *The Women and Aging Letter*, Waltham, MA: Brandeis University, March 1996, 1, 8.

National Policy and Resource Center on Women and Aging. *Planning for retirement security.* Waltham, MA: Brandeis University, May 1996, *1*, 1–6.

Neill, C. M., and Kahn, A. S. The role of personal spirituality and religious social activity on the life satisfaction of older widowed women. *Sex Roles*, 1999, *40*, 319–329.

O'Brien, S., and Vertinsky, P. Unfit survivors: Exercise as a resource for aging women. *The Gerontologist*, 1991, *31*, 347–348.

Older Women's League. *The path to poverty: An analysis of women's retirement income.* Washington, DC: Older Women's League, 1995.

Older Women's League. Path of poverty: An analysis of women's retirement income. In C. L. Estes and M. Minkler (Eds.), *Critical gerontology: Perspectives from political and moral economy.* Amityville, NY: Baywood, 1998.

Ovrebo, B., and Minkler, M. The lives of older women: Perspectives for political economy and the humanities. In T. R. Cole, W. A. Achenbaum, P. L. Jakobi, and R. Kastenbaum (Eds.), *Voices and visions of aging: Toward a critical gerontology.* New York: Springer, 1993.

Perkinson, M. A., and Rockemann, D. D. Older women living in a continuing care retirement community: Marital status and friendship formation. In K. A. Roberto (Ed.), *Relationships between women in later life.* Binghamton, NY: The Haworth Press, 1996.

Pohl, J. M., and Boyd, C. J. Ageism within feminism. *IMAGE: Journal of Nursing Scholarship*, 1993, *25*, 199–203.

Prigerson, H. G., Maciejewski, P. K., and Rosenheck, R. A. Preliminary explorations of the harmful interactive effects of widowhood and marital harmony on health, health service use, and health care costs. *The Gerontologist*, 2000, *40*, 349–357.

Quadagno, J., and Hardy, M. Work and retirement. In R. H. Binstock and L. K. George (Eds.), *Handbook of aging and the social sciences* (4th ed.). San Diego, CA: Academic Press, 1996.

Richardson, V. E. Women and retirement. *Journal of Women and Aging*, 1999, *11*, 49–66.

Roberto, K. A. Friendships between older women: Interactions and reactions. In K. A. Roberto (Ed.), *Relationships between women in later life.* Binghamton, NY: The Haworth Press, 1996.

Roberto, K. A., Allen, K. R., and Blieszner, R. Older women, their children, and grandchildren: A feminist perspective. In J. D. Garner (Ed.), *Fundamentals of feminist gerontology.* Binghamton, NY: The Haworth Press, Inc., 1999.

Rubenstein, R., Alexander, B., Goodman, M., and Lubovsky, M. Key relationships of never-married, childless older women: A cultural analysis. *Journals of Gerontology*, 1991, 46, S270–277.

Rushing, B., Ritter, C. and Burton, R. Race differences in the effects of multiple roles on health: Longitudinal evidence from a national sample of older men. *Journal of Health and Social Behavior*, 1990, 33, 126–139.

Saluter, A. *Marital status and living arrangements: March 1994.* Washington, DC: U.S. Bureau of the Census, Current Population Reports, Population Characteristics, 1994.

Schwenk, F. N. Income and expenditures of older, widowed, divorced, and never-married women who live alone. *Family Economics Review*, 1992, *5*, 2–8.

Simonsick, E. M., Phillip, C. L., Skinner, E. A., Davis, D., and Kasper, J. D. The daily lives of disabled older women. In J. Guralnik, L. P. Fried, and E. M. Simonsick (Eds.), *The women's health and aging study: Characteristics of older women with disability.* Bethesda, MD: National Institute on Aging, NIH Publication No. 95—4009, 1995.

Smeeding, T., Estes, C., and Glasse, L. *Social Security in the 21st century: More than deficits: Strengthening security for women.* Washington, DC: The Gerontological Society of America, 2000.

Smith, J. *The changing economic circumstances of the elderly: Income, wealth and Social Security.* Syracuse, NY: Maxwell Center for Policy Research, 1997.

Speroff, L., Rowan, J., Symons, J., Genant, H., and Wilborn, W. The comparative effect on bone density, endometrium, and lipids of continuous hormones as replacement therapy (CHART Study): A randomized controlled trial. *Journal of the American Medical Association,* 1996, 276, 1397–1403.

Thorson, J. *Aging in a changing society.* Omaha: University of Nebraska Press, 2000.

U.S. Bureau of the Census *Statistical abstract of the United States, 116th edition.* Washington, DC: U.S. Government Printing Office, 1996.

U.S. Bureau of the Census *Statistical abstract of the United States,* (118th ed.). Washington, DC: U.S. Government Printing Office, 1998.

Velkoff, V. A., and Lawson, V. A. *Caregiving: International brief, gender and aging.* U.S. Bureau of the Census, 1998, IB/98–3, 2–7.

Weber, P. The role of vitamins in the prevention of osteoporosis—A brief status report. *Clinical Pearls News,* 1999, 222

Whittaker, R. Re-framing the representation of women in advertisements for hormone replacement therapy. *Nursing Inquiry,* 1998, 5, 77–86.

Wiener, J. M., and Illston, L. H. Financing and organization of health care. In R. H. Binstock and L. K. George (Eds.), *Handbook of aging and the social sciences* (4th ed.). San Diego, CA: Academic Press, 1996.

Williams, S. Preventing osteoporosis. *Newsweek,* Special Edition on Women's Health, Spring/Summer 1999, 60–63.

THE SOCIETAL CONTEXT OF AGING

The final section of this book examines aging and older people from a broader context. The values and beliefs that policy makers and voters hold toward a particular group or issue are often the basis for developing policies and programs. To the extent that these policies also are grounded in empirically based knowledge, they can enhance the status and resources of that group. On the other hand, policies that are based on stereotypes or generalizations may be inadequate and even harmful.

Throughout this book, the current state of knowledge about the physiological, psychological, and social aspects of aging has been reviewed. We have examined variations among older ethnic minority groups, between older men and women, and among other segments of older adults. The diversity in the aging process has been emphasized. Differences in lifestyle, work patterns, and family interactions in earlier periods of life can significantly impact health and social functioning in old age. As a result, variations among the older population are greater than among any other population group. As Chapter 16 points out, increasingly this diversity affects the development, implementation and effectiveness of social policies and programs.

Some age-based programs such as Medicare are directed toward all people who meet age criteria, whereas others such as Supplemental Security Income (SSI) and food stamps are based on financial need. Eligibility criteria and services are often determined by the prevailing social values and by those of the political party and presidential administration in power. These values, in turn, reflect society's attitudes toward older people, their contributions, and their responsibilities to society. For example, attitudes and values regarding older people's rights and needs, whether chronological age is an appropriate basis for services, and whether care of the aging population is a societal or individual responsibility all influence the development of social, health, and long-term care policies. The historical development of aging policy and alterations in existing programs are also reviewed within the context of larger societal changes that influence such values. One societal change examined in this section is the growing economic security

503

of a proportion of older adults. This change, in turn, has fueled an attitude that they are financially better off than other age groups. As noted in Chapter 12, such an attitude also stereotypes older adults as being "all alike"; it overlooks both the economic and racial/ethnic diversity among older people and the fact that younger and older generations engage in reciprocal exchanges and share interests throughout life.

Health and long-term care policies toward older people also have evolved incrementally in response to society's values and expectations of responsibility and need. Chapter 17 describes these policies; their rising costs; the growing need for long-term care; obstacles to their public funding; and current cost-containment initiatives in Medicare and Medicaid, especially managed care and health maintenance organizations.

Finally, the Epilogue discusses the implications of a changing older population for future social, health, and long-term care policy and programming. As noted throughout this book, society is undergoing major transitions regarding the roles and contributions of older people. Changes such as the termination of mandatory retirement, the growing numbers of older adults desiring part-time work, often in low paying, temporary positions, and the increased proportions of workers covered by employer pension plans suggest that the cohort entering old age in the mid-twenty-first century will be far different from previous ones. These changes will dramatically impact society as a whole. Conversely, the tremendous technological advances in medicine raise hopes of a longer life but also profound questions about the quality of such extended years. Moreover, computers will play an increasing role in older people's social and physical well-being. The following vignettes illustrate the impact of changing societal attitudes and policies regarding the older population on individuals who have been raised in different eras.

AN OLDER PERSON BORN EARLY IN THE TWENTIETH CENTURY

Mr. O'Brien was born in 1920 in New York City. His parents had migrated to the United States from Ireland

ten years earlier, in search of better employment opportunities for themselves and a better life for their children. One of Mr. O'Brien's brothers died during a flu epidemic while still in Ireland; a sister and brother who were born in New York died of measles. Mr. O'Brien and his three surviving siblings worked from the age of 12 in their parents' small grocery store. He could not continue his education beyond high school because his father's death of tuberculosis at age 45 left him in charge of the family store. Mr. O'Brien thought of signing up for the newly created Social Security program in 1945, but he was confident that he would not need any help from the government in his old age. The family grocery was supporting him and his wife quite well; he planned to work until the day he died. And besides, his family had all died in their forties and fifties anyway. He has been a heavy smoker all his life, just as his father had been. As he approaches his eighty-second birthday, however, Mr. O'Brien has been having second thoughts about old age. His emphysema and arthritis make it difficult for him to manage the store. He has had two heart attacks in the past ten years, both of which could have been fatal if it had not been for the skills of the emergency medical team and their sophisticated equipment in his local hospital. Mr. O'Brien's savings, which had seemed substantial a few years ago, now are dwindling as he pays for his wife's care in a nursing home and for his medications and doctor's care for his heart condition, emphysema, and arthritis. Despite these struggles, Mr. O'Brien is reluctant to seek assistance from the government or from his children and grandchildren. They, in turn, assume that Mr. O'Brien is financially independent because he still works part-time, and never seems to require help from anybody.

AN INDIVIDUAL BORN IN THE POSTWAR BABY BOOM

Ms. Smith was born in 1949, soon after WWII ended and her father returned from his military duty. Her father took advantage of the GI bill to complete his college education and purchase a home in one of the newly emerging suburbs around Chicago. As Ms. Smith grew up, her parents gave her all the advantages they had missed as children of the Depression: regular medical and dental check-ups, education in a private school, a weekly allowance, and a college trust fund. She completed college, obtained a master's degree in business, and now holds a middle-level management position in a bank. She has already begun planning a "second career" by starting work on a master's degree in systems analysis. Recognizing the value of health promotion at all ages, she has been a member of a health club for several years, participating in aerobic exercise classes and jogging every day. She has also encouraged her parents, now in their mid-seventies, to participate in health promotion activities in their local senior center. Her parents both receive pensions, are enrolled in Medicare Parts A and B, and have planned for the possibility of catastrophic illness by enrolling in a supplemental health insurance program. Ms. Smith has encouraged her parents to get on the waiting list of an excellent retirement community nearby, which includes a life contract for residential and nursing home care, should they ever need it. She is also examining her investments and pension plan while she is in her prime earning years. She realizes that Social Security cannot be her primary source of income after retirement. She recently purchased private long-term care insurance for herself. In this way, both Ms. Smith and her parents are planning for an independent and, to the extent they can control it through prevention, a healthy old age.

These vignettes illustrate the changing social and economic status of older people today and in the future. The implications of these changes for the development of policies and programs, as well as on individuals' planning for their own aging, are discussed in the remainder of this book. We conclude with a brief discussion of career opportunities in gerontology.

16

SOCIAL POLICIES TO ADDRESS SOCIAL PROBLEMS

Chapter 16 focuses on the following topics:

- Definitions of policy
- Differentiation of types of policies
- Factors that affect policy development
- The relatively slow development of aging policies prior to the 1960s, with the rapid expansion of programs in the 1960s and 1970s and the federal budget cuts of the 1980s, 1990s and early in this century
- Policy impact of the White House Conferences on Aging and of public perceptions about the "deservingness" of older persons
- Social Security benefits, the fiscal challenges, and proposed reforms, including privatization
- Direct social services funded through the Administration on Aging and Title XX
- Major policy dilemmas and implications for future directions

A wide range of policies, established within the past 70 years, aim to improve the social, physical, and economic environments of older people. Approximately 50 major public programs are directed specifically toward older persons, with an-

other 200 affecting them indirectly. Prior to the 1960s, however, the United States lagged behind most European countries in its development of public policy for its older citizens. For example, Social Security benefits were not awarded to retirees in the United States until 1935, whereas alternative Social Security systems were instituted in the nineteenth century in most Western European countries. The United States has slowly and cautiously accepted the concept of public responsibility, albeit only partial, for its older citizens.

Since the 1960s, however, federal spending for programs for older adults rapidly expanded, resulting in the "graying of the federal budget" and a dramatic change in the composition of expenditures. For example, some defense expenditures have been reallocated to health and retirement benefits, although this may shift under the current Republican administration. The growth in federal support for these services is vividly illustrated through budgetary figures (see Figure 16.1). In 1960, only 13 percent of federal expenditures went to general health, retirement, and disability programs, compared to approximately 50 percent in 2000 (Samuelson, 2000).

Raising public concern is that approximately 66 percent of federal spending goes toward **entitlement programs**—those for which spending is determined by ongoing eligibility requirements and benefit levels rather than by annual Congressional appropriations. These programs—Social Security, Medicare, Medicaid, and civil service and military pensions—are growing so fast that they are predicted to consume nearly all the federal tax revenues by 2012 (see Figure 16.2). Already, Social Security represents 22 percent of the federal budget, and Medicare 12 percent (Bryce and Friedland, 1997). By 2030, Social Security, Medicare, and Medicaid are expected to compose up to 70 percent of total federal outlays (Smeeding, Estes, and Glasse, 2000). The long-term increase in the share of the budget spent on older adults occurred primarily because of legislative improvements in income protection, health insurance, and services enacted in the late 1960s and early 1970s to reduce poverty among older persons. Since then, the rapid growth of the older population raises concern about the long-term financial viability of these programs and whether older adults are benefiting at the expense of younger groups. Such concern is reflected in contemporary debates in Congress about changes in Social Security and Medicare, including increased privatization, to reduce age-based public expenditures.

It is important to recognize, however, that when Social Security and Medicare are excluded from these federal allocations, only about 4 percent of the total federal budget is devoted to programs that benefit older adults. These growing expenditures also mask the fact that funded aging services are often fragmented, duplicated, and do not reach those with the greatest need, thus leaving health and income inequities. Despite growing allocations, the United States lacks an integrated, comprehensive, and effective public policy to enhance the well-being of all older adults, and faces complex policy challenges.

VARIATIONS AMONG POLICIES AND PROGRAMS

Policy refers generally to the principles that govern action directed toward specific ends. The purview of social policy is not only to identify problems, but also to take action to ameliorate them. The development of policy thus implies a change in situations, systems, practices, beliefs, or behaviors. The procedures that governments develop for making such changes encompass planned interventions, bureaucratic structures for implementation, and regulations governing the distribution of

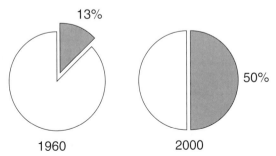

FIGURE 16.1   **Changes in Percentage of Federal Budget for Health, Retirement, and Disability Programs**

public funds. Policy for the older population thus reflects society's definition of what choices to make in meeting their needs and the division of responsibilities between the public and private sectors. Each policy development serves to determine which older persons should receive what benefits, from which sources, and on what basis.

Social programs are the visible manifestations of policies. The implementation of the 1965 Older Americans Act, for example, resulted in numerous programs—senior centers, nutrition sites, Meals-on-Wheels, homemaker and home health services, and adult day care. Some programs are designed specifically for older people, whereas others benefit them indirectly. Programs can be differentiated from each other in many ways; these dimensions are presented in Table 16.1 and described next.

1. *Eligibility Criteria for Benefits:* When **eligibility** for benefits depends on age alone (i.e., a person is entitled to Medicare benefits at age 65), **age-entitlement programs** are categorical and specifically for older adults. In contrast, in **need-based entitlement programs**, eligibility depends on financial need (i.e., a person's financial resources entitles him or her to benefits, such as Medicaid, Supplemental Security Income (SSI), food stamps, and public housing). Most programs for older adults are age entitlements, with the government automatically paying benefits to anyone who is "entitled" to the benefits on the basis of age. In contrast, programs for children and for younger persons with disabilities are typically discretionary and **means-based**, which limits participation.

2. *Form of Benefits:* Another variation is the form in which benefits are given, either as **direct benefits** or as **indirect benefits** through a cash transfer or substitute. Social Security benefits are a *direct cash transfer,* and vouchers for the purchase of goods, such as food stamps and rent supplements, are a *direct cash substitute.* Tax policies that affect selected groups (e.g., personal income tax exemptions for older persons) are *indirect cash transfers* of funds from one segment of the population to another. Medicare payments to

TABLE 16.1   Dimensions along Which Programs and Policies Vary

	EXAMPLES
Eligibility	
On basis of age	Medicare
On basis of financial need	Supplemental Security Income
	Medicaid
Form of benefits	
Cash	
Direct cash transfers	Social Security
Indirect cash transfers	Income tax exemption
Cash substitute	
Direct cash substitutes	Vouchers
Indirect cash substitutes	Medicare payments to service providers
Method of financing	
Contributory (earned rights)	Social Security
Noncontributory	Supplemental Security Income
Universal or selective benefits	
Universal—for all persons who belong to a particular category	Older Americans Act
Selective—determined on an individual basis	Food stamps

health care providers, rather than directly to beneficiaries, are *indirect cash substitutes*.

3. *Method of Financing:* Programs also vary in how they are financed. Social Security and Medicare are **contributory programs;** benefit entitlement is tied to a person's contributions to the system as a paid worker across the life span. In contrast, Supplemental Security Income (SSI) is a **noncontributory program** available to older persons and adults with disabilities who meet financial need criteria, regardless of their prior contributions through payroll taxes.

4. *Universal or Selective Benefits:* Programs differ according to whether they benefit populations on a universal or selective basis. **Universal benefits** are available as a social right to all persons belonging to a designated group. Eligibility for Medicare, the Old Age Survivors Insurance of Social Security, and the Older Americans Act is established by virtue of belonging to the older population. In contrast, **selective benefits** are determined individually. These include Supplementary Security Income, Medicaid, food stamps, and housing subsidies, which use economic need as a criterion. Whether or not aging services should be targeted to low-income elders and subsidized by higher-income older adults is debated. Public consensus on the best approach to service delivery does not exist, as reflected in the following discussion of the factors that influence social policy.

FACTORS AFFECTING THE DEVELOPMENT OF POLICIES

Despite the orderliness of these dimensions, the policy-development process is not necessarily rational nor part of an overall plan. Approaches to the financing and delivery of aging services evolved in a very different time period, when life expectancy was shorter and federal revenues were of less concern. A major characteristic of our public policy process is its shortsightedness—its general inability, because of annual budgetary cycles and the frequency of national elections, to deal with long-term economic, demographic, and social trends, or to anticipate future consequences of current policies to meet needs or political imperatives. In an aging society, shortsightedness in policy development has resulted in a fragmented array of services with separate entitlements and eligibility requirements. In fact, this diversity can be so complex and confusing to older people and their families that it has spawned the growth of private case managers to locate, access and coordinate services for them.

The complexity of the public policy formation process is also magnified by the variety of societal factors influencing it. These factors include:

- individual and societal values and beliefs
- economic, social, and governmental structures
- the configuration of domestic and international problems
- powerful interest groups and their lobbyists

Two different sets of values have been played out in American social policies:

1. Individual welfare is essentially the *person's responsibility* within a free-market economy unfettered by government control. This belief in individual freedom and autonomy, self-determination, and privacy is deeply rooted in our history and culture, is widely embraced by many segments of our society, and underlies many public policies.

2. Individual welfare is the responsibility *of both the individual and the community* at large. Government intervention is necessary to protect its citizens and to compensate for the free market's failure to distribute goods and opportunities more equitably. Given the belief in individual productivity and competitiveness, however, some degree of income disparity is accepted as inevitable.

Our society's emphasis on individual and family responsibility has resulted in a "public burden" model of welfare, whereby older persons are often viewed as a burden on the taxpayers rather than entitled to services as a matter of right. Accordingly, government performs a *residual* or "back-up" role to informal support systems. Programs are developed to respond *incrementally* to crises, not to prevent problems or to attack their underlying causes. This contrasts with the approach of many other countries, where national health and welfare polices represent a consensus that citizens are universally entitled to have certain needs met. Even when our government intervenes, it is justified because of the failure of the market economy, the family, or the individual to provide for themselves or their relatives (Gill and Ingman, 1994). Accordingly, solutions tend to be patterned after private-sector initiatives, as illustrated by many of the proposed changes in both Social Security and Medicare.

Since the New Deal of the 1930s, policy has oscillated between these two value orientations as public mood and national administrations have shifted. American cultural values of productivity, independence, and youthfulness, public attitudes toward government programs and older citizens, and public perceptions of older people as "deserving" converged to create universal categorical programs (e.g., Administration on Aging, Medicare) that are available only to older persons, regardless of income. In contrast, policies that use income (e.g., means-testing of Medicaid) to determine if a person is "deserving" of services reflect our cultural bias toward productivity and independence. Although Social Security was the first federal initiative to address older adults' income needs, it succeeded largely because it is perceived as an insurance plan for "deserving" elders who have contributed through their prior employment, not a means-tested income maintenance policy for all vulnerable citizens. In the past, the American public tended to perceive older people as more deserving of assistance than other populations. Accordingly, Social Security and Medicare have, until recent years, been viewed as inviolate and not to be cut drastically. The passage of such otherwise unpopular programs as a national health insurance for older people (i.e., Medicare) and guaranteed income (i.e., Supplemental Security Income) can be partially explained by the fact that older persons aroused public support. In addition, older adults are often viewed as a powerful, organized constituency. As a

result, they are more likely than low-income or homeless families, for example, to arouse a favorable response from politicians. As noted in Chapter 12, this also reflects a model of interest-group politics to advance one's agenda in our political system, although the increasingly diverse older population is now less likely to act as a unified block to influence legislation than in the past.

Ongoing debate about the nature and extent of public provisions versus the responsibility of individuals, families, and private philanthropy often has moral overtones. Judgments about the relative worth of vulnerable populations that compete for a share of limited resources (e.g., older persons within the prison system as undeserving) and about the proper divisions between public and private responsibilities are ultimately based on individual or group values (or preferences). A major policy issue therefore revolves around the question of whose values shape policy.

Society's technical and financial resources, and current economic conditions also significantly influence policy development. Adverse economic conditions can create a climate conducive to the passage of income-maintenance policies. For instance, Social Security was enacted in part because the Great Depression dislodged the middle class from financial security and from their belief that older adults who needed financial assistance were undeserving. A strategy to increase the number of persons retiring at age 65 was also congruent with economic pressures to reduce widespread unemployment in the 1930s. With economic constraints, program cost factors were also salient; Social Security as a public pension was assumed to cost less than reliance on local poorhouses, as had been the practice prior to the 1920s. Thus, a variety of economic and resource factors converged to create the necessary public and legislative support for a system of social insurance in the 1930s. In contrast, periods of economic growth can be conducive to new social and health care programs. Both Medicare and the Older Americans Act were passed during the 1960s and early 1970s. During economic growth and social consciousness, government resources expanded under the so-called War on Poverty on behalf of both the younger poor and older people. Funding for the National Institute on Aging increased during the economic boom of the late 1990s.

The influence of both economic resources and cultural values is also evident in the current public emphasis on smaller government, tax cuts, private responsibility, program cost-effectiveness and cost containment, and targeting services to those most in need. Under the fiscal conservatism of a Republican Congress in the 1990s (and now in the early twenty-first century), the concept of states' rights and prerogatives was emphasized. States assumed a stronger role in the development and financing of social programs. Unfortunately, this resulted in increased variability of eligibility criteria and benefits such as SSI and Medicaid among the states. Periods of scarcity tend to produce limited and often punitive legislative responses, as occurred in the 1980s and early 1990s. As illustrations of the erosion of public support for universal age-based benefits in the 1980s and 1990s, Medicare copayments, deductibles, and Part B premiums increased; Social Security benefits for higher-income older people were taxed; and many legislators proposed cutting Medicare, Medicaid, and Social Security to reduce federal expenditures. Growing preoccupation since the 1990s with ways to limit public funding has meant that priority is placed on the most efficient and least expensive solutions, rather than equity and the common good.

In sum, these values, economic conditions, and the consequent resource capacity underlie a *categorical, residual, and incremental* policy approach for older adults. One of the most vocal critics of this approach, Estes (1979, 1984, 1989; Estes, Linkins, and Binney, 1996) maintains that our conceptions of aging socially construct the major problems faced by older people, and thereby adversely influence age-based policies. These conceptions, discussed briefly as the political economy perspective in Chapter 8, are shown in the box below. According to Estes, our societal failure to develop a comprehensive, coordinated policy framework reinforces older persons' marginality and segregates them. For example, Social Security and employer-sponsored pensions have ensured that most older adults leave the labor force even though they could still be productive workers (Estes et al., 1996).

In contrast to Estes, others maintain that the older population has benefited at the expense of other age groups and is "busting the budget." Benefits for older persons are viewed as a primary reason for growing federal expenditures and for the declining economic status of some younger groups (Marmor, Cook, and Scher, 1997; Quinn, 1996). Spending for entitlement programs is perceived as "mortgaging the future" of succeeding generations. In reality, however, Social Security and Medicare's actual contribution to the federal deficit has been

---

POLITICAL ECONOMY OF AGING

1. Older individuals, not economic or social structural conditions, are defined as a "social problem."
2. Older people are seen as special and different, requiring separate programs.
3. Through categorical and age-segregated services, public policy has promoted an "aging enterprise" of bureaucracies and providers to serve older people.
4. A perception is growing that problems of older adults cannot be solved by national programs,

but rather by initiatives of state and local governments, the private sector, or the individual.
5. The problems of older people are individually generated and best treated through medical services to individuals. This has resulted in the medicalization of aging and limited public funding for home- and community-based social services as alternatives to institutional care.
6. The use of costly medical services is justified by characterizing old age as a period of inevitable physical decline and deficiency.

nearly the same since 1980 and many younger groups have thrived in the current high tech economy. Within this context of the factors affecting policy development, we turn now to the formulation of public policy for older persons.

THE DEVELOPMENT OF POLICIES FOR OLDER PEOPLE

1930 to 1950

Prior to 1930, the United States had few social programs for older adults. Family, community, charity organizations, and local government (e.g., county work farms) were expected to respond. Factors such as the lower percentage of older adults, a strong belief in individual responsibility, and the free-market economy partially explain why our government was slow to respond. Table 16.2 traces these historical policy developments. The Social Security Act of 1935, the first national public bene-

National debates on social policy draw older citizens and key political leaders.

fits program, established the federal government as a major player in the social welfare arena (Bryce and Friedland, 1997). The act is based on an implicit guarantee of social insurance—that the succeeding generation will provide for its older

TABLE 16.2   Major Historical Developments of Policies That Benefit Older People

1935	Social Security Act
1950	Amendments to assist states with health care costs
1959	Section 202 Direct Loan Program of the Housing Act
1960	Extension of Social Security benefits
1960	Advisory commissions on aging
1961	Senate Special Committee on Aging
1961	First White House Conference on Aging
1965	Medicare and Medicaid, Older Americans Act, establishment of Administration on Aging
1971	Second White House Conference on Aging
1972 & 1977	Social Security amendments
1974	Title XX
1974	House Select Committee on Aging
1974	Change in mandatory retirement age
1974	Establishment of the National Institute on Aging
1980	Federal measures to control health care expenditures
1981	Third White House Conference on Aging
1981	Social Services Block Grant Program
1986	Elimination of mandatory retirement
1987	Nursing Home Reform Act
1989–90	Medicare Catastrophic Health Care Legislation passed, then repealed
1995	Fourth White House Conference on Aging
1999	United Nations: International Year of Older Persons

members through their Social Security contributions as employees. The original provisions of the act were intended to be only the beginning of a universal program covering all "major hazards" in life. However, this broader concept of the program, including a nationwide program for preventing sickness and ensuring security for children, was never realized.

After the passage of Social Security, national interest in policies to benefit older persons subsided. One exception was President Truman's advocacy to expand Social Security benefits to include farmers, self-employed persons, and some state and local government employees. He also proposed a national health insurance plan, but was opposed by organizations such as the American Medical Association. President Truman did succeed, however, in his push for a 1950 Social Security amendment to financially assist states that choose to pay partial health care costs for needy older persons. This amendment then became the basis for the establishment of Medicare in 1965.

Program Expansion in the 1960s and 1970s

Since the 1960s, programs for older people have rapidly evolved, including Medicare, Medicaid, the Older Americans Act, Supplemental Security Income (SSI), the Social Security Amendments of 1972 and 1977, Section 202 Housing, and Title XX social services legislation. The pervasiveness of "compassionate stereotypes"—which assumed that most older adults are deserving poor, frail, ill-housed, unable to keep up with inflation, and therefore in need of government assistance—created a "permissive consensus" for government action on age-based services in the 1960s and 1970s. A negative consequence of "compassionate ageism," however, was the development of programs that obscured individual and subgroup differences among the older population. A large constituency—including older adults who are not poor, frail, or inadequately housed—has benefited from the policy consensus built upon the "compassionate stereotype" in the 1960s and 1970s (Binstock and Day, 1996). Since old-age constituencies have been viewed as relatively homogeneous (white, English-speaking, and male), many older people with the greatest needs—women, ethnic minorities, the oldest-old, and those living alone—have not always benefited from program improvements. Some of these inequities were described in Chapters 14 and 15.

The first White House Conference on Aging and the establishment of the Senate Special Committee on Aging in 1961 highlighted older people's distinctive needs. Four years later, Medicare and the Older Americans Act were passed, for which eligibility is determined by age, not by need. Although the Older Americans Act established the Administration on Aging at the federal level, as well as statewide area agencies and advisory boards on aging services, funding to implement these provisions has remained low. Therefore, one of the primary objectives of the 1971 White House Conference on Aging was to strengthen the Older Americans Act. In 1972, Social Security benefits were expanded 20 percent, and the system of *indexing* benefits to take account of inflation ("**cost of living adjustments**" or **COLA**) was established. Additional funding was provided for the Older Americans Act in 1973.

The 1970s, with its prevailing liberal ethos, propelled more developments to improve older people's economic status:

- the creation of the Supplemental Security Income (SSI) program
- protection of private pensions through the Employee Retirement Income Security Act (ERISA)
- formation of the House Select Committee on Aging; increases in Social Security benefit levels and taxes
- the change in mandatory retirement from age 65 to 70 (As noted in Chapter 12, mandatory retirement was later abolished for most jobs in 1986.)

As described by Hudson (1997), public policy on aging begat more public policy, by creating its own constituencies. During this period of federal government expansion, more than 40 national committees and subcommittees were involved in legislative efforts affecting older adults. As a result of the expansion of age-related programs, agencies, and benefits, along with more age-based interest groups, individuals grew to expect that they were entitled to receive certain benefits such as Social Security and Medicare automatically, based on age rather than on income or need. Yet, the presumed influence of many aging advocacy organizations appears to result more from their defense of existing policy rather than their affecting the development of these policies (Hudson, 1997). Paradoxically, many older adults assumed that they were entitled to continued political support and public benefits, even though their needs, along with their political efficacy, had declined.

Program Reductions in the 1980s and 1990s

Although compassionate stereotypes and a "permissive consensus" underlay the growth of age-entitlement programs in the 1960s and 1970s, fiscal pressures and increasing concern about the well-being of younger age groups in the 1980s and 1990s brought into question the size and structure of these programs. In those years, a new stereotype of older people as relatively well-off resulted in their being scapegoats and blamed as "greedy geezers." In fact, older people were seen as responsible for the increasing poverty rates among younger age groups (Bengtson, 1993; Torres-Gil, 1992).

The impact of tax cuts, reductions in federal programs, the huge federal deficit, and an overemphasis on economic growth prevented consideration of any large or bold programs for domestic spending in social and health services during the Reagan Administration (1980–1988). At the same time, public perceptions of and support for aging programs varied widely. Senior advocates urged more funding, particularly for social services, and watched closely to see that Social Security not be cut. Concern over the future of Social Security was fueled by the near-term deficit facing the Social Se-

curity trust fund in the 1980s. As a result, Social Security was amended in 1983 to address short-term financing problems. As public scrutiny of the costs of Social Security, Medicare, and Medicaid grew, *cost-efficiency* measures were implemented, such as taxation on Social Security benefits and less generous cost-of-living increases.

During the 1980s, the political reality of the economic and social diversity of the aging population—that chronological age is not an accurate marker of economic status—became more apparent. The variability in distribution of income is reflected among three different groupings of older people:

- those ineligible for Social Security, including both the lifelong underclass and the working poor who have interrupted employment histories, hourly wages without benefits, and few personal assets
- those who depend heavily on Social Security, with small or no private pensions and few assets except for their own home
- those with generous private pensions, personal savings investments, and Social Security benefits

A number of policies passed in the 1980s recognized that the older population has differential capabilities for helping to finance public programs, so that both age and economic status began to be considered as eligibility criteria for old-age benefit programs (Binstock, 1994). For example, the Social Security Reform Act of 1983 taxed Social Security benefits for higher-income recipients. The Tax Reform Act of 1986 provided tax credits on a sliding scale to low-income older adults and eliminated a second or third exemption on federal tax income previously available. Meanwhile, programs funded under the Older Americans Act have been gradually targeted toward low-income individuals. These policy changes, combined with public perceptions that older people are better off than younger ones, reflect a transition from the legacy of a modern aging period (1930–1990) to a new period in which old age alone is not sufficient grounds for public benefits (Torres-Gil and Puccinelli, 1994).

The Politics of Diversity and Deficit Spending in the 1990s and the Twenty-First Century

The growing federal deficit profoundly affected public policy development in the 1990s. To reduce the deficit, there were two major options—reductions in spending through program cutbacks, or revenue enhancement through higher taxes. National groups that cut across the political spectrum, such as the Bipartisan Commission on Entitlement and Tax Reform and the Concord Coalition, maintained that entitlement programs for older people were growing so fast that they would consume nearly all the federal tax revenues by the year 2012, leaving government with little money for anything else. Increasingly such groups argued that programs such as Social Security, Medicare, and Medicaid must be drastically curtailed to balance the federal budget early in the twenty-first century. Such a perspective, for example, is reflected in the Balanced Budget Act of 1997 where Medicare and Medicaid were cut, but not Social Security. In reality, since Social Security is financed by its own dedicated payroll tax, none of the federal deficit has ever been caused by Social Security spending. In other words, Social Security is a *creditor,* not a debtor, of the federal government—a reality that is not portrayed by the media (National Committee to Preserve Social Security, 1999).

In the 1996 Personal Responsibility Act, President Clinton signed restrictive welfare legislation, but vetoed the bill containing changes to alter the nature of entitlements to Medicare and Medicaid. Social Security remained basically untouched. Resistance against dramatically changing these entitlement programs for older people remained strong in the Clinton/Gore Administration. However, it is now being challenged by the Republicans in the White House and Congress who favor privatization of Social Security

and other programs. The fact that such entitlement programs are "under attack" (although not yet dramatically altered) reflects a societal shift toward the older population. In the early twenty-first century, they are less likely to be perceived as a "politically sympathetic" group (Binstock, 1993, 1994; Peterson, 1993). At the same time, disparities within the older population are more evident, with subgroups of poor, ethnic minorities, women, and persons living alone likely to join political alliances around class, race, or ethnity that compete with groups of more affluent elders. The "politics of diversity" may thus fragment the political influence of established aging organizations, further eroding support for universal programs. In fact, incremental changes in Social Security, the Older Americans Act, and Medicare to target benefits toward relatively poor older people reflect recognition of this diversity (Binstock, 1995).

Such diversity among the older population, combined with a focus on reducing federal expenditures, has resulted in a greater emphasis on private sector initiatives that can be supported by higher-income older adults (e.g., individual retirement accounts instead of Social Security). With more older adults able to self-finance or privately insure against the social and health costs of later life, the base of support for high-quality government programs appears to be eroding. This could result in limiting services to elders without retirement plans and health insurance and thus lead to increasing inequality among the older population. A policy challenge in the 1990s was targeting policy responses to those who risk losing a significant part of their income and who have never had economic stability, while maintaining public support for the financing of quality universal programs. These complex issues set the framework for the 1995 White House Conference on Aging. Delegates at the 1995 conference voted to maintain Social Security, the Older Americans Act, the basic features of Medicaid and Medicare, and some advocacy functions under the Older Americans Act. These directions fundamentally conflicted with the emphasis of the Republican Congress on cutting entitlement programs to reduce the federal deficit. Now that the federal deficit is relatively under control, due largely to the booming economy of the late 1990s, Republicans seek to reduce taxes and allow more individual control over Social Security investments, while Democrats want to preserve basic programs such as Social Security and Medicare.

Social Security and SSI

We next review the specific programs that account for the majority of age-based federal expenditures:

- Social Security (OASDI) and Supplemental Security Income (SSI)
- tax provisions and private pensions that provide indirect benefits
- social services through Title XX *block grants* and the **Aging Network** of the Older Americans Act

As noted earlier, Social Security (Older Age Survivors and Disability Insurance), federal employee retirement, and Medicare and Medicaid combined represent the largest and most rapidly growing federal entitlements, as was illustrated in Figure 16.2. However, many younger people also benefit from OASDI and Medicaid, as described on page 529.

INCOME SECURITY PROGRAMS: SOCIAL SECURITY AND SUPPLEMENTAL SECURITY INCOME

Social Security

As indicated earlier, the 1935 Social Security Act aimed to establish a system of income maintenance for older persons through individual insurance. A secondary purpose was to provide a basic level of protection for the most needy older adults, initially

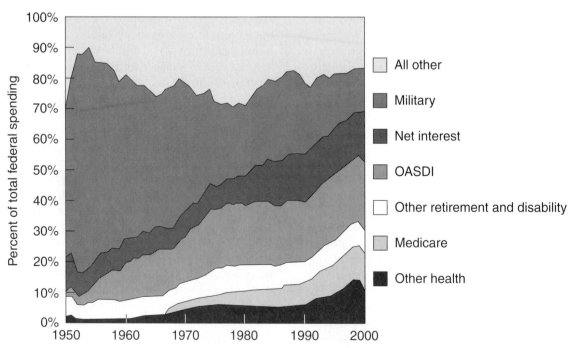

FIGURE 16.2 Change in the Composition of the Federal Budget, 1950–2000

through state plans for Old Age and Survivors Insurance (OASI) and, since 1974, through the federally funded Supplemental Security Income (SSI) program. A more recent objective is to provide compensatory income to persons, regardless of age, who experience a sudden loss of income, such as widows, surviving children, and persons with disabilities.

To meet these objectives, Social Security has four separate *trust funds:*

1. Old Age and Survivors Insurance (OASI)
2. Disability Insurance (DI)
3. Hospital Insurance (HI), which is funded through Medicare
4. revenues for the supplemental insurance portion of Medicare

Social Security is financed through separate trust funds; revenues raised equally from the taxing of employees and employers; and income based on current tax revenues. As illustrated in Figure 16.3, out of every tax dollar from *payroll taxes* that a worker pays into Social Security and Medicare:

- Sixty-nine cents goes to a trust fund that pays monthly benefits to retirees and their families and the equivalent of a $307,000 life insurance policy to surviving widows, widowers, and children of workers who have died.
- Nineteen cents goes to a trust fund that pays some of the cost of hospital and related care of Medicare beneficiaries.
- Twelve cents goes to a trust fund that pays benefits to people with disabilities and their families.

Every worker contributing to Social Security, regardless of age, has disability insurance worth about $207,000—a fact often overlooked by younger critics of Social Security (Social Security Administration, 1996a, 1996b). This discussion focuses on the combined OASDI fund, of which programs for persons with disabilities are only 7 percent of the combined obligation. Funding for Medicare is discussed in Chapter 17.

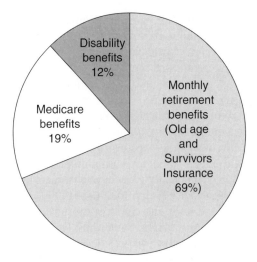

FIGURE 16.3　　**Where Our Social Security Tax Dollars Go**
SOURCE: Social Security Administration, Secondary Benefits. Washington DC: U.S. Government Printing Office, 1996.

As described in Chapter 12, the Social Security system is based first on the concept of earned rights. In fact, only 60 percent of the labor force was initially eligible to earn future benefits on the basis of the 1935 law. Coverage has since expanded to insure 90 to 95 percent of the labor force, reflecting nearly universal protection across socioeconomic classes (Bryce and Friedland, 1997). In addition, wage-price indexing protects recipients against economic changes over which they have no control. Although Social Security provides a mechanism to pool resources and share the risk, no one is excluded no matter how "bad" a risk he or she may be. This is a fundamental difference from private insurance or welfare programs (Kingson and Schulz, 1997). Social Security can be described as similar to fire or collision insurance. You might not ever need to collect on your policy, but that does not mean you do not need to pay the premiums!

Contrary to public perceptions, Social Security is not an investment program or the sole source of retirement income, but rather a minimum floor of protection. Yet, it is the major source of income (providing for at least 50 percent of total income) for 66 percent of total beneficiary units, and the only source for about 40 percent. Retirees typically need 70 percent of their preretirement income to continue living comfortably. Social Security's average older recipients are paid 42 percent of their income, a figure that is projected to remain stable through the year 2040 (Zebrowski, 2000). This average percentage varies with income, however. Social Security provides 75 percent of the aggregate income of older households with annual incomes of less than $10,000, 42 percent of the aggregate income for those earning $30,000–$40,000, and only 12 percent of income for those earning $80,000 plus (Villa, Wallace, and Markides, 1997). While higher-income workers receive higher benefits, lower-income workers are assured a greater rate of return for what they have paid into the system (e.g., the proportion of earnings that is replaced after retirement is higher for lower-paid workers). Social Security therefore is most helpful to those at the lowest end of the income scale—oldest-old, elders of color, and women (Devlin and Arye, 1997).

This distribution of benefits reflects Social Security's dual goals of social adequacy and individual equity.

- *Social adequacy* refers to a shared societal responsibility to provide a basic standard of living for all potential beneficiaries, or a "safety net," regardless of the size of their economic contributions.
- *Individual equity* refers to an individual's receiving benefits that reflect that person's actual monetary contributions proportionate to what workers have paid into the system.

Today's retirees generally recoup their Social Security contributions within seven years. Actuaries expect that today's young workers will recoup their contributions after eleven years of retirement (National Committee to Preserve Social Security, 1999).

It is a myth that Social Security is a funded pension system in which retirees are merely paid back, with interest, the "contributions" that they made during their working years. Instead, it is a system whereby current workers support retired or disabled workers. This "pay-as-you-go" system is like a pipeline; payroll taxes from today's workers flow in, are invested in special U.S. government bonds, and then flow out to current beneficiaries. In short, consistent with the conclusion of the National Commission on Social Security Reform, Social Security's nearly universal coverage and predictability of income make it the foundation of economic security for most retirees.

Payroll taxes, however, have risen enormously, from a combined 3 percent on employers and employees in 1950 to 15.3 percent with Medicare (12.4 percent without). But the average return that a worker can expect has declined dramatically. An average earner born in 1915 could expect to get back at age 65 approximately $60,000 more than he or she paid into the system (adjusted for inflation and interest), while today's retirees will just about break even and recoup their contributions (Miller, 1998). By 2030, up to 50 percent of one's payroll may be needed to support Social Security and Medicare (Sass and Triest, 1997).

This pay-as-you-go method of financing partially underlay the fiscal crisis in the early 1980s, when the Social Security reserves were inadequate for projected benefits. Primary factors behind threats of bankruptcy were:

1. The economic recession; High unemployment and low productivity resulted in fewer taxes collected, so that less money was available in the Social Security trust funds.
2. There was increased longevity and more retired workers in proportion to younger employees, with fewer workers paying into Social Security.

This changing *dependency ratio*, discussed in Chapter 1, means that the ratio of taxpayers to older retired adults is projected to drop to fewer than 4 to 1 by 2020. When Social Security was enacted, life expectancy was 61 years and the average recipient collected for 12 years, compared to 78 years and 19 years, respectively, today. Social Security was never intended to support individuals for up to a third of their lives (Devlin and Arye, 1997; Mathews, 1995).

Pessimistic interpretations of these shifts argue that "apocalyptic demography" will make it difficult for our nation to sustain all age-related benefits through the first half of this century. The "graying of the welfare state" is perceived as having catastrophic consequences for the after-tax living standards of most working-age Americans (Howe, 1995; Quinn, 1996). This view, fostered by the media, is put forth by groups such as the Third Millennium, who point to a survey in which people under age 35 stated that they believed in UFOs more than in Social Security's future viability (Conte, 1997). Data such as these, however, are misrepresented as public support for "radical reform". In fact, many polls consistently show that Americans overwhelmingly support protecting Social Security, even though they lack confidence in its future and are confused about eligibility criteria (National Committee to Preserve Social Security and Medicare, 1999; Quinn, 1996, 2000).

An alternative, more optimistic view is that projected shortfalls—25 to 30 years in the future—are a warning that can be addressed with relatively minor adjustments in the program. They are not a crisis requiring major structural changes (Conte, 1997; National Committee to Preserve Social Security and Medicare, 2000). One minor change, for example, is a 0.7 percent reduction in annual cost-of-living adjustments that will, over time, result in enormous cost savings. Accordingly, future benefits to older people will not depend solely on the proportion of workers to retirees. In addition, it will depend on whether the economy generates sufficient resources to be transferred and whether the political will to transfer them to older adults exists (Binstock, 1994).

As noted above, the short-term danger of bankruptcy was averted through remedial legislation passed in 1983, which resulted in benefit reductions and increased the age of full Social Security eligibility from 65 years to age 67 by the year 2003. These reforms allowed the system to accumulate reserves, which currently exceed the benefits paid. The latest report of the Social Security actuaries predicts that a funding shortfall will not occur until at least the year 2034. If, however, the fund continues to grow well above the actuaries'

projections, a shortfall could be smaller or even nonexistent. Despite such solvency, a long-range concern is that the federal government debt is turning the surplus into paper savings. This concern stems from the fact that the Treasury Department borrows and then spends the Social Security reserves by investing them in Treasury bonds. In effect, it gives Social Security an IOU, so that the reserves accumulated now may be consumed by deficits in later years.

When and if Social Security expenditures (or the "outgo") will exceed funds collected through current taxes is unknown. At that point, Social Security will be funded through a combination of payroll taxes and interest generated by the trust fund. If and when the benefit payouts are projected to exceed taxes and interest, the reserves in the trust fund would be drawn down. The exhaustion of the trust fund, however, would not mean that Social Security benefits would stop; this would happen only if Congress passed legislation ending Social Security payroll taxes. In fact, even by 2034, the benefits would not end, but the financial security of a trust fund would be lost and benefits would be lower. Congress would be able to pay only around 70 percent of its obligations promised to future retirees (e.g., 75 cents for every dollar of benefits). Most proposals for change suggest that the only way to repay the reserves in the future within the current system is for the federal government to raise payroll taxes, increase the age of eligibility, use means testing, increase borrowing, reduce benefits, or rely on economic growth (Wheeler and Kearney, 1996).

Points of view vary widely about the magnitude of the Social Security crisis, along with proposed solutions. Variations in Social Security reform proposals can be attributed to differing perspectives regarding program goals, whether as:

- *social insurance* (e.g., provide benefits upon disability or death), or
- *income redistribution* (transfer resources from the wealthier to those with fewer resources, both within and between generations).

In recent years, the goal of increasing national savings has grown (Sass and Triest, 1997). Those

---

POINTS TO PONDER

How much will *your* Social Security benefits be when you retire? Since 1988, the Social Security Administration has sent individual statements to every U.S. worker age 25 and older, listing their years of employment, earnings, and Social Security taxes paid each year. Best of all, it lists each person's estimated benefits if they retire at age 62, 67, or 70, based on past contributions to the system, current age, and income. Individual workers can also estimate their benefits by checking SSA's Website: www.ssa.gov/planners/calculators.htm.

---

who focus on the traditional social insurance and income-adequacy goals tend to favor addressing the fiscal imbalance within the current structure. For example, the 1997 Social Security Advisory Council suggested changes to lower Social Security benefits within the current system, such as increasing the tax rate. Currently, workers pay 6.2 percent on earnings up to $65,400 in taxes to support OASDI, with employers paying a matching 6.2 percent, for a combined tax rate of 12.4 percent. Even if taxes had to be raised to pay benefits for the next 75 years, the combined tax would only have to be raised to 14.6 percent of earnings, which is defined as a "problem" but not a "crisis" (Moon, 1997; Stern, 1997).

Others argue that an income or means test for Social Security is needed to exclude or sharply lower benefits to the well-off and target resources to those in greatest need. This approach, however, undermines Social Security's universal nature and the basic principle that workers at all income levels will receive some reasonable return in exchange for their payroll tax contributions (Kingson and Schulz, 1997).

Contemporary critics of Social Security prefer to view it as a savings program that maximizes the "rate of return" to beneficiaries and fosters economic growth by encouraging savings. Such advocates of Social Security as a savings instrument argue for the privatization of Social Security by greater reliance on individual savings. They predict, that individuals can obtain higher rates of return on individual contributions through investments in the stock market. *Privatization* would divert payroll taxes (or general revenue income tax credits) to new systems of Social Security investment accounts. One proposal is to allow workers to invest half or more of their Social Security retirement money in the stock market and set aside the remainder in individual retirement accounts. Such proposals are criticized for putting workers at risk of failing investments, especially in light of the stock market's performance in 2000-2001, and losing disability and survivor insurance, particularly since historical experience indicates that many workers are unable to deal with the complexities of retirement planning (Wheeler and Kearney, 1996). Another proposal is a "double decker" system. The lower deck would provide a flat benefit for those meeting eligibility requirements, equal to 47 percent of benefits paid to an average worker, and therefore would address the goals of social adequacy. The upper deck would require payment into a government-supervised retirement plan that would offer choices about where money was invested. This proposal does not include a redistribution component but would address individual equity concerns by providing a benefit proportionate to contributions (Devlin and Arye, 1997).

Proposals that privatize or individualize Social Security and reduce government control tend to be supported by Republican lobbyists—including insurance companies, investment companies, and big business that would profit from it—as well as the CATO Institute, a conservative Washington, D.C.–based think tank (Deets, 1997; Dentzer, 1997; Stern, 1997). It is important to recognize that privatization is counter to the basic philosophy of a social insurance plan with universal eligibility. This philosophy represents societal willingness to

AN OVERVIEW OF PROPOSALS TO REFORM SOCIAL SECURITY

Changes within the current system:

- Diversify the trust funds to invest a larger portion privately in the stock market.
- Lower benefits.
- Tax Social Security benefits as ordinary income.
- Raise the payroll tax up to 14.6 percent (split between employer and employee contributions).
- Compute benefits on a 38-year work history instead of 35 years. Thus would further reduce benefits to women who tend to have shorter work histories than men.
- Raise the age for full benefits to age 69 or 70.

- Raise the early retirement age to 65.
- Cut spousal benefits from 50 percent to 33 percent. (Atchley, 1997; Bale, 1997).
- Establish an income or means test.

Changes to the underlying principles of the system:

- Privatization of savings programs and individual investment in the stock market
- "Double-decker system": flat benefit as first tier, government-supervised retirement plan as second tier
- Numerous other privatization models

---

compensate those whose income has been destroyed or lowered by marketplace forces, regardless of the individual's actual contribution. As such, these proposed changes challenge the fundamental notion that governments subsidize programs deemed to be in the common good. (Goyin, 2000). Instead, older Americans are viewed as being able to fend for themselves until they fall to "safety net" status. Efforts to delegitimize public policies in effect attack Social Security and Medicare's roles in preventing poverty and ill health. In contrast to these challenges to public policy, more liberal policy makers view Social Security as a "sacred entitlement," not to be altered, even at the expense of other groups.

A wide range of negatives or "downsides" associated with the privatization of Social Security are identified by policy analysts and economists:

- Transition costs of moving from current system to privatized plan.
- High administrative costs of managing individual accounts.
- Funds used to pay current retirement benefits would have to be replaced (e.g., by tax increases, massive government debt, or benefit costs).

- Current workers would be double-taxed: They would have to pay for their own retirement plus benefits of today's retirees.
- Uncertainty about how well one will do on stock market; two-thirds of all mutual funds return less than market average; with the vicissitudes of the current market, investment income may not last until a person dies.
- Low-income workers have only a small amount to invest.
- Uncertainty for the young worker who is disabled early in his or her career before investments yield profit.
- The primary beneficiaries of privatization will be higher-income, unmarried men who will not be born until 2025.
- Women are biggest losers under privatization, regardless of age, race, income level, or marital status.
- Few African American households would benefit (National Committee to Preserve Social Security and Medicare, 1999).

Despite the rhetoric of some urging alteration of Social Security, the majority of the public does not perceive that older people benefit inequitably, or that benefits are too costly. In fact, over 80 percent of the U.S. population in most national polls support protection of Social Security (National Academy on Aging, 1997). This support may reflect recognition of how Social Security also benefits younger family members by reducing their financial responsibility to older relatives. Intergenerational transfer programs may actually receive more support than typically portrayed by the media and politicians, an issue discussed below vis-à-vis the intergenerational-equity framework.

Supplemental Security Income

As described in Chapter 12, about 6 percent of Social Security recipients also receive Supplemental Security Income (SSI). This program is financed fully by the federal government under the Social Security Administration, although states may supplement the federal payment; this results in benefit variability among states. SSI is intended to be a protective system or "safety net" for the least economically fortunate, but it has not eliminated poverty among older people and reaches only 50 percent of the older poor. A primary reason for this is that SSI only brings needy individuals up to 75 percent and couples up to 90 percent of the poverty level, even in states that supplement the federal payment. About 17 percent of low-income older adults receive food stamps; of these, approximately 20 percent have lost their benefits due to the Personal Responsibility and Work Opportunity Reconciliation Act, also known as the Welfare Reform Act of 1996 (Kassner, 1996).

PRIVATE PENSIONS AND INCOME TAX PROVISIONS

Private Pensions

Some older persons receive a combination of government-supported public and/or private pensions to supplement Social Security. As described in Chapter 12, about 50 percent of the current labor force, primarily middle- and high-income workers, is covered by an employer-sponsored pension plan. This translates into nearly 40 percent of

Older people who have multiple sources of income are generally financially secure.

older adults receiving some income from public or private pensions. However, only about 10 percent of these receive in private pensions an amount equivalent to that of Social Security. About 55 percent of retirees early in this century will have private pension income, only a small increase from the late-twentieth century (Bryce and Friedland, 1997). Overall, the rate of pension growth has slowed due to the changing nature of the workforce. Manufacturing jobs that historically provided pensions have declined, and service sector and part-time, temporary contingent jobs in high-tech firms have grown, but in a growing number of instances, may flourish only for a short time.

As noted in Chapter 12, the pension system tends to perpetuate systematic inequities across the life span by income, ethnic minority status, and gender. Lower-income workers, often women and persons of color, are least likely to be in jobs covered by pensions and to have attained the vesting requirements (e.g., 10 years on the same job). Another inequity is that retired military veterans, civil service workers, and railroad employees also receive cash benefits in addition to Social Security. This means that cash benefits from government-supported private savings plans and favorable tax

DEFINED BENEFIT PLAN

Social Security is a defined benefit plan. Such plans can also be employer sponsored. Benefits are paid from a common trust. Beneficiaries are guaranteed a set of benefits once they qualify. Customarily, the guarantee is based on number of years of service, contributions, or other factors. The risks for fulfilling the guarantee fall upon the sponsor of the plan.

DEFINED CONTRIBUTION PLAN

IRAs and 401(k) plans are defined contribution plans. Under these, the beneficiary bears the plan's investment risk. The amount that participants have for retirement depends on the performance of their individual investment portfolios through securities market ups and downs. More corporations are shifting to defined plans.

policies accrue to those who are already relatively well off, intensifying economic disparities over time (Wheeler and Kearney, 1996). Although private pensions help upper- or middle-income workers to replace more of their income when they retire, they do not meet the value of adequacy inherent in Social Security, since lower-income workers generally do not participate (Wheeler and Kearney, 1996).

As described in Chapter 12, the Employee Retirement Income Security Act of 1974 (ERISA) established standards for participation, vesting, and minimum funding to protect workers. Since then, corporate contributions to pension plans have declined, and many businesses have instead used pension funds to pay for employee health care expenses and to increase their own profitability. *Defined benefit plans* beneficial to employees have been terminated and replaced by **contributory plans,** such as 401(k)s, increasing uncertainty for the employee. This represents a shift in pension responsibility away from the company and toward the individual (Bryce and Friedland, 1997; Woods, 1994).

Income Tax Provisions

Pension plans are not the only "tax expenditures" related to aging. Some older individuals also enjoy extra tax deductions and pay on average a smaller percent of their income in taxes. Many older

people who file tax returns benefit from not paying a tax on railroad retirement and other government pensions, for example. Higher-income older persons enjoy property-tax reductions and preferential treatment of the sale of a home (e.g., exemption from capital gains taxation for the sale of a home after age 55). The 1997 Tax Reform Act also benefits wealthy older adults who own stocks and bonds. Capital gains realized from the sale of stocks and mutual funds now are taxed at lower rates than ever before—20 percent in 1998 for those in the highest income brackets. Tax benefits go to the majority of the older population who have an annual income of over $20,000, and only a small percentage goes to persons with incomes less than $5,000. Tax provisions are thus another way that public benefits to older people are inequitably distributed.

SOCIAL SERVICES

Social service programs for older adults have developed in response to needs unmet by income maintenance, health, and housing programs. Despite these developments, federal and state expenditures are primarily oriented toward medical care. Less than 1 percent of the older population's share of the federal budget is spent on social service programs. From a political economy perspective, as discussed in Chapter 8, social services are underfunded because they do not fit within the dominant medical model (Estes et al., 1996).

Funding for social services for older people derives from four federal sources: Medicare, Medicaid, amendments to the Social Security Act (Title XX), and the Older Americans Act of 1965. This section will focus on Title XX (or Social Services Block Grants) and the Older Americans Act as the primary basis of social service funding.

Title XX, established in 1974, provides social services to all age groups. Entitlements are means tested, with most services to older adults going to those who receive SSI. In terms of the program classification system discussed earlier, Title XX is a universal program aimed at redressing needs. Yet it is also means tested by income as an eligibility criterion. This means older people compete with a diverse group of Title XX recipients—primarily families with dependent children and persons who are blind or mentally and/or physically disabled. Title XX encompasses basic life-sustaining, self-care services to compensate for losses in health and the capacity for self-maintenance: homemaker and chore services, home-delivered meals, adult protective services, adult day care, foster care, and institutional or residential care services. These have generally ensured a minimum level of support for vulnerable older adults.

Under the federal Omnibus Budget Reconciliation Act of 1981, Title XX was converted to the Social Services Block Grant program, while federal funds allocated to the states were reduced on average by 30 percent (Estes et al., 1996). The Social Services Block Grant program was one of the initial decentralization efforts emerging from the 1980s new federalism under President Reagan. Block grant funding increased the states' discretion in determining clients' needs and allocating Title XX funds among the diverse eligible groups. For example, national income-eligibility guidelines aimed at targeting programs to needy persons were eliminated. Accordingly, the competition for funds, along with variability in services between and within states, increased. As a result, most states al-

located a greater percentage of block grant funds to children than to older adults. Limits to federal funding under decentralization decreased revenues for social services under Title XX for older people while the demand for services increased. Competition for limited funds is likely to intensify under the Bush administration, and may pit the poor and their allied service providers against the older population.

The **Older Americans Act (OAA)** seeks to alter state and local priorities to ensure that older adults receive a proportionate share of social services allocations. Title III of the Older Americans Act is the single federal social service statute designed specifically for older people. Entitlements to services are universal for all people over age 60, regardless of income or need. The OAA was intended to create a national network for the comprehensive planning, coordination, and delivery of aging services. At the federal level, the act charges the Administration on Aging (AOA), through the Assistant Secretary on Aging, to oversee the activities of the aging network (i.e., the system of social services for older people) and to advocate for them nationally.

The Older Americans Act also established State Units on Aging (SUAs), which now number over 700. Each of these has a state advisory council to engage in statewide planning and advocacy on behalf of older adults' service needs. State Units on Aging designate local **Area Agencies on Aging** (AAAs) to develop and administer service plans within regional and local areas. Their advisory boards must include older adults. In addition to federal, state, and local agencies that are responsible for planning and coordination, a fourth tier is composed of direct service providers in local communities. As described in Chapter 11, these include information and referral, case management, transportation, outreach, homemaker services, day care, nutrition education and congregate meals (both hot meals at senior centers and home-delivered meals), legal services, respite care, senior centers, and part-time community service jobs. Many of these OAA services, central to long-term care, overlap with the goals and provisions of the Social Services Block Grants. Within this wide range of programs, the relatively low level of funding requires the OAA

SERVICES PROVIDED UNDER THE OLDER AMERICANS ACT

Access Services: Information and referral; care management.

In-Home Services: Homemaker assistance, respite care, emergency response systems, home health care, friendly visiting, and telephone reassurance.

Senior Center Programs: Social, physical, educational, recreational, and cultural programs.

Nutrition Programs: Meals at senior centers or nutrition sites; in-home meals (Meals on Wheels).

Legal Assistance Advocacy: For individual seniors and on behalf of programs and legislation. The Older Americans Act is the only major federal legislation that mandates advocacy on behalf of a constituency.

Additional services provided based on local community needs and resources.

---

to target services to low-income, ethnic minority, rural elders, and frail older adults at risk of institutionalization, even though it still retains its original goal of universality.

Because participation rates in many OAA services are highest among middle-income older individuals, proposals for cost sharing of services have been introduced. This raises fears among some OAA program staff and advocates that cost sharing would introduce means testing and stigmatize OAA programs as "welfare," thereby discouraging their use. However, an implicit means test is already being employed by targeting services to low-income older people. Another goal is to increase participation by elders of color through targeted outreach and increased recruitment of ethnic minority staff and board members of local agencies receiving OAA funds. Proponents of the political economy perspective fear that the current focus on indirect services (care assessment and management) rather than direct service delivery may impede the achievement of improving quality of life among older Americans (Estes et al., 1996).

POLICY DILEMMAS

Age-Based versus Needs-Based Programs

Longtime debates about the need for age-based programs have influenced policy developments in the aging field. These debates highlight choices about whom to serve and how to restrict benefits eligibility. Advocates of age-based programs view them as an efficient way to set a minimum floor of protection, less stigmatizing than means-tested services, and supporting the values of individual dignity and interdependence. Efficiency is presumably enhanced by the fact that age-based policies exclusively or predominantly affect older people. Similarly, age-based programs are assumed to involve fewer eligibility disputes and be less administratively intrusive into applicants' lives (Holstein, 1995).

Neugarten (1982; Neugarten and Neugarten, 1986), in particular, argued strongly against age-based services. She maintained that they reinforce the perception of "the old" as a problem, thereby stigmatizing older people and adding to age segregation. The Older Americans Act, for example, implicitly views anyone over age 60 as vulnerable and therefore needing services. Yet, as we have seen, growing numbers of adults over age 60 are healthy, have adequate incomes, and do not need services. As a result, many universal age-based programs benefit the young-old who are relatively healthy and in the top third of the income distribution. In fact, Torres-Gil (1992) argues that with up to 25 percent of the population qualifying for age-related benefits, a purely age-based approach is politically and economically unfeasible. The use

Meals-on-Wheels is an age-based program that can help older people remain independent.

of age as a benefits criterion assumes that older people are homogeneous and different from other age groups; but Neugarten contends that old age in itself does not constitute a basis for differential treatment. As noted in Chapter 1, chronological age is a poor predictor of the timing of life events and of health, income, and family status—and therefore of needs. An inadequate indicator of changes within a person, age is an arbitrary criterion for service delivery.

An alternative view is that economic and health needs that increase the need for services should be the basis for selectively targeting services, rather than age. Proposals for income eligibility for Social Security and Medicare are congruent with a needs-based approach. Some advocates for targeting services to high-risk older persons favor a combination of categorical and group eligibility mechanisms. For example, a portion of OAA service funds could be restricted for allocation to SSI and older Medicaid recipients, thereby reaching individuals with the lowest incomes and presumably the most service needs. Given the increasing economic inequality within the older population, means-testing programs that comprise the "safety net" for the least well-off older adults, (e.g. SSI and Medicaid) are viewed as priorities for improvement.

The Politics of Productivity versus the Politics of Entitlement

Closely related to the ongoing debate about age-based versus needs-based programs is the politics of productivity versus entitlement (Moody, 1990). As implied throughout this chapter, the **politics of entitlement** is characterized as follows:

- In a "failure model of old age," older people, solely because of their age, are defined as needy, worthy, and deserving of public support.
- Issues are defined in terms of needs and rights.
- The emphasis is on what older people deserve to receive as their right rather than what they can give.
- Resources are transferred to the older population as a categorical group.
- Other groups must pay for the benefits due the older population.

The **politics of productivity,** as discussed in Chapters 8 and 12, is characterized this way:

- The older population is increasingly diverse.
- The implementation of new policies requires an expanding economy toward which older adults can contribute.
- Older people are defined as a resource in an interdependent society and can contribute to younger populations. Old age is a time for giving assistance and advice to the young.
- "Investing in human resources" across the life span is essential to future economic growth to benefit all ages.

As noted earlier, national groups as well as members of Congress, particularly among the "New Right," are questioning entitlement programs for all age groups. While they point to the increased socioeconomic diversity of the older population as a rationale for means testing, they do not agree on how much to target resources to benefit those most at risk, such as women and elders of color. In other words, most advocates for changing entitlement programs appear to be motivated by fiscal goals, not by a desire to reduce status inequities within the older population.

Intergenerational Inequity Framework

Closely related to the debate about both age-based entitlement programs and a politics of productivity is the argument that older persons benefit at the expense of younger age groups, who lack the political clout represented by senior organizations. The **intergenerational inequity** debate began in 1984 with Samuel Preston's analysis of poverty rates among the young and old and public expenditures on behalf of older people. The old were perceived to be thriving, at the expense of children, as a result of expanded Social Security benefits and inflationary increases in real estate and home equity (Preston, 1984). This generated a rather simplistic picture of generational conflict, expounded in a growing number of newspaper and magazine editorials. It also resulted in the formation of groups such as **Americans for Generational Equity** (AGE), which later merged with the American Association of Boomers (AAB) and the National Taxpayers Union. These organizations maintain that the Baby-Boom generation (i.e., those born between 1946 and 1964) will collectively face a disastrous retirement, and its children will, in turn, be disproportionately burdened with supporting their parents as no other generation has been historically. More recently, advocates for the Baby Boomers are joined by the Third Millennium and PAC 20/20, groups that are concerned about the future of *Generation X*, young adults in their twenties.

Underlying their arguments is the assumption that our country faces significant distribution choices, especially related to Social Security and other retirement incentives, about how to pay the costs of an aging society. Policy questions then frequently become framed in terms of competition and conflict between generations. This creates a backlash against the gains experienced by the older population and polarizes younger and older generations.

Even though the economy flourished in the late 1990s, many young adults still struggle to start jobs and families and to buy a home. Similarly, the growing divorce rate has thrown millions of children into one-parent households and poverty. At the same time, older people are perceived by some critics as benefiting from generous entitlement programs that policy makers have been loath to cut. As described in earlier chapters, the average older person today is financially better off than in the past. In many ways, the improved economic status of the older generation actually represents a success story of government interventions rather than a basis for criticism. Yet, beneath the appearance of a dramatic decline in poverty is the reality that many of those who "moved out" of poverty have shifted from a few hundred dollars below the poverty line to a few hundred above it, forming the "near poor"

THEMES OF THE BACKLASH ARGUMENT

- America's older citizens, now better off financially than is the population as a whole, are selfish and concerned only with personal pension and income benefits and their share of the federal budget.
- Programs for older people are a major cause of current budget deficits, economic problems, inadequate schools, and increases in poverty among mothers and children.

- Children are the most impoverished age group.
- Younger people will not receive fair return for their Social Security and Medicare investments.
- The future of younger generations is also threatened by declining expenditures for national defense.

and "hidden poor." In addition, the distribution of income among the older population is extremely diverse, and the level of inequality extraordinarily high.

Critique of the Intergenerational Inequity Framework

The intergenerational inequity framework that attempts to measure the relative hard times of one generation against the relative prosperity of another has been widely criticized by advocates for older adults. The major criticisms are as follows:

• Contrary to the pessimistic argument that society will not be able to provide for future generations, the economy of the future, barring unforeseen disasters, will be able to support a mix of programs for all age groups. The distribution of benefits extends far beyond the older population; 50.5 percent of all American families receive at least one benefit from entitlements or other safety-net programs, and 23 percent receive at least one need-related benefit (Wu, 1995).

• Evidence of significant intergenerational conflict is limited. Younger and older generations appear to recognize their interdependence and to support benefits for each other across the life span. For example, the Children's Defense Fund argues that funding for programs for the young should be increased at the cost of military spending, not at the expense of programs for the old. The AARP concurs, and maintains that older people's well-being contributes to the welfare of all other generations.

• The definition of fairness put forth by groups such as Americans for Generational Equity is narrow and misleading. When fairness is equated with numerical equality, this assumes that the relative needs of children and older adults for public funds are identical, and that equal expenditures are the equivalent of social justice. Even if needs and expenditures for each group were equal, this would not result in equal outcomes or social justice.

• By framing policy issues in terms of competition and conflict between generations, the intergenerational inequity perspective implies that public

benefits to older individuals are a one-way flow from young to old, and that reciprocity between generations does not exist.

• The intergenerational debate is a convenient mechanism to justify shifting responsibility for all vulnerable groups to individuals, the private sector, and local governments.

• It overlooks other ways to increase public resources through economic growth, increased tax revenues, or reduced defense spending, and that future generations' economic well-being will ultimately depend on growth rates of real wages (Kingson, 1988; Kingson et al., 1986; Kingson et al., 1987; Quinn, 1996).

Nevertheless, some advocates for older adults acknowledge that it is no longer realistic to proceed on the assumption that all benefits are sacrosanct. They now recognize that it is counterproductive to oppose all measures imposed on financially better-off older persons, such as treating part of Social Security as taxable income or subjecting Social Security and Medicare to means testing.

The Interdependence of Generations Framework

Consistent with social exchange theory described in Chapter 8, a continuing human dilemma is the "contract between generations." Typically, this is defined as parents to children and children to aging parents. What is different today is the focus on relationships between age groups in society rather than individuals within the family. This shift from generations to age groups has increased the magnitude and complexity of the issues involved, so that it is no longer youth versus elders, but rather elders versus middle-aged adults and youth. Never before have so many individuals lived so long, and never have there been so relatively few members of the younger generation to support them.

The **interdependence of generations framework** recognizes the changing societal and political context: increases in life expectancy, decreases in fertility, and growing concerns about public ex-

A major way in which older generations provide assistance is through child care.

penditures targeted by age. Within this larger context, public and private intergenerational transfers are viewed as central to social progress. A major way in which generations assist one another is through the family; for example, through care for children and dependent adults, financial support, gifts to children and grandchildren, and inheritances. Private intergenerational transfers are essential to meeting families' needs across the life course and to transmitting legacies of the past (e.g., culture, values, and knowledge). In addition, the growing number of intergenerational programs, such as Foster Grandparents, reflects how both generations benefit from these social exchanges.

Transfers based on public policy (e.g., education, Social Security, and health care programs) also serve intergenerational goals. For example, Social Security benefits are distributed widely across all generations and protect against risks to families' economic well-being across the life span, such as when a younger worker becomes disabled. Social Security is not simply a one-way flow of resources from young to old. Instead, younger generations benefit from programs that support their older relatives' autonomy and relieve them from financial responsibilities. Grandchildren cared for by grandparents also benefit from Social Security. In addition, long-term care affects all age groups—particularly younger adults with AIDS or who are developmentally disabled or chronically mentally ill—and thus benefits all generations. Likewise, it is erroneous to think of education as a one-way flow to children that is resisted by older people. Instead, older adults have contributed to public education throughout their working careers. In addition, they now enjoy access to a growing range of lifelong learning opportunities. Older adults' support for school levies reflects recognition that they benefit from education programs that increase workforce productivity.

Within the framework of interdependence, other paradigms are proposed as ways to conceptualize how burdens and opportunities within our society can be fairly shared among generations. One paradigm is the concept of **generational investment,** in which age-based services and other social programs, such as public education, play an integral part in the system of reciprocal contributions that generations make to one another. Programs such as Social Security and Medicare are mechanisms through which generations invest in one another and publicly administer returns to older cohorts for the investments

---

THE INTERGENERATIONAL COMPACT

- More than 3 million children under the age of 18 receive Social Security benefits because their parents are retired, disabled, or deceased.
- Temporary Assistance to Needy Families (TANF) assists children and their caretaker relatives (parents or grandparents).

- More than 3 million minor children live in households where an adult, often a grandparent, receives Social Security (Weill and Rother, 1998–1999).
- A growing percentage of older Americans help children by volunteering.

INTERGENERATIONAL POLICY AGENDA OF GENERATIONS UNITED

- Prevent cuts in Title XX Social Service Program.
- Stop effort to change Medicaid to a block grant program.
- Keep and expand the dependent care tax credit.

- Forbid landlords from discriminating in housing rentals against families with children while also allowing legitimate senior housing to stay exempt.

---

made in the human capital of younger groups. As such, old-age benefits represent claims based on merit and social contributions and should not be subject to means testing (National Academy on Aging, 1997).

Similarly, older people can be the vanguard of renewed efforts to ensure a decent standard of living for all Americans, perhaps through measures such as a universal family-allowance program and paid parental leaves that recognize the societal contributions of childrearing (Kingson, 1988; Kingson et al., 1987; Kingson et al., 1986). This assumes that enhancing people's opportunities earlier in their lives can reduce intergenerational competition. A broadened welfare consensus also can be fostered through an understanding of the life-course experiences that lead to problems in old age. This perspective of our common human vulnerability across the life course is not a new one. In fact, President Lyndon B. Johnson's charge to the 1968 Task Force Report on Older Americans was to determine the most important things to be done for the well-being of most older Americans. Since vulnerability in old age is the product of lifetime experiences, the task force concluded that providing social and economic opportunities for young and middle-aged persons is a priority (Binstock, 1995; Jacobs, 1991).

Similar to the "politics of productivity" and the interdependence framework, Torres-Gil (1992; Torres-Gil and Puccinelli, 1994) argues for a paradigm of "New Aging" in the post-1990s. The politics of the New Aging aims to identify how all generations can contribute to a new society. In contrast to the prior focus on the older population from 1930 through the 1990s, our society must alter both our view of older adults to acknowledge their growing diversity and the manner in which we provide for them. With such increased heterogeneity, intergenerational conflict of old versus young cannot be assumed. While some tensions between young and old will remain, the *politics of diversity* will become the norm, whereby some older adults have more in common with younger age groups than with their peers. Differences of political opinions among older people and between age cohorts will increase, with more linkages based on political priorities, not age per se (Torres-Gil, 1992).

In the politics of the New Aging, advocacy and lobbying should be rechanneled from special-interest issues toward policies to benefit all future generations. Groups of older adults should shift from the horizontal alliances that characterize interest-group politics to new vertical alliances, representing common needs between aging and nonaging groups (Binstock, 1995). Previously underrepresented groups of older persons—ethnic minorities, women, and rural residents—must establish alliances with nonaging groups (Ozawa, 1999). In fact, this is already occurring. For example, the Child Welfare League of America, the National Council on the Aging, and the Children's Defense Fund helped establish *Generations United*, a coalition of consumer, labor, children, and senior groups, to reframe policy agendas around our common stake in cross-generational approaches. AARP is also forming networks with populations of color and supports policies to benefit children cared for by grandparents. The United States Student Association and the Gray Panthers have joined together to support policies that enhance quality of life for all. Not only should older adults be viewed as a resource able to contribute to the economy and their own income security, but the young should be educated to assume full adult responsibilities and prepare for their own aging. The real potential of cross-generational advocacy depends on whether the approach pioneered by Generations United is adopted by mainstream age-based and social service organizations (Weill and Rother, 1998–99).

For the interdependence framework to address the problems of the disadvantaged, an ideological consensus is required that government should help people in need, regardless of age. Given that such consensus does not exist, some policy analysts argue that the real issue for the future is not intergenerational interdependence but rather redefining the role of the public sector in caring for its vulnerable citizens and the relationship between the public and private sectors.

WHO IS RESPONSIBLE?

As noted, many of these policy debates revolve around the division of responsibility between the public sectors of federal and state governments, and the private realms of family and business. The current public–private debate is not new, but long-standing, reflected even in the passage of Social Security. Until recently, Social Security benefits, Medicare, Medicaid, SSI, and services under the Older Americans Act settled the question of responsibility for older citizens. It was to be a collective responsibility, exercised through the national government, and a protection to which every older citizen was entitled, simply by virtue of age.

A growing view held by public officials is that the problems of older adults and other disadvantaged groups cannot be solved with federal policies and programs alone. Instead, solutions must come from state and local governments and from private-sector and individual initiatives, such as advocacy, self-help, family care, personal retirement planning and private investments, and faith-based organizations. Individuals are assumed to be responsible for

their own problems, and federal government interventions are considered too costly. An anti-tax mentality, combined with growing public concern about the use of federal reserves, has resulted in legislative changes to reduce federal funds and to rely increasingly upon the states through block grants. The assumption that states can most efficiently and creatively respond to local needs is used to justify such cuts. This decentralized approach, however, is flawed by the fact that states have the fewest resources for services. Accordingly, they are least likely to respond to the needs of the most disadvantaged. Historically, decentralization has not assured policy uniformity and equity for powerless groups across different states. We have already seen evidence for such inequality in state-funded education and nutrition programs for children and youths. National initiatives that establish stable, uniformly administered federal policies are necessary to bring the states with the lowest expenditures up to a minimum standard, but are highly unlikely in the near future.

Reductions in Government Support

What is more important than federal-state relations, however, is the level of public spending. Although public spending has increased in terms of total dollars, it has declined when measured as a percentage of the gross national product or as government expenditures per capita, corrected for inflation. Economically disadvantaged older persons have been hurt the most by the budget cuts of the past 25 years, especially under the Republican "Contract with America" and the 1996 "Personal Responsibility and Work Opportunity Legislation" (welfare reform).

Public spending levels are being reduced at the same time that private and local spheres are being expected to be more responsible for older people with chronic disabilities. Policy makers often assume that public programs reduce family involvement and that families could do more for their older relatives. However, as discussed in Chapter 10, the family has consistently played a major role in elder care. Family members provide all the support that they are able or willing to do, although such assistance is not necessarily financial. When resources become scarce, the family should not be viewed as simply a cost-effective alternative to nursing home placement and to publicly funded social services.

Not only are families unable to carry expanded responsibilities on their own, but the private nonprofit service sector, especially faith-based organizations, lack the resources to fill the gaps created by federal cuts or changed priorities. In fact, federal tax laws have reduced incentives for corporate giving. In addition, private contributions traditionally have not been concentrated on social services, so that increased private giving would not automatically flow into areas most severely cut, nor would this benefit the most disadvantaged. The challenge is that, as the older population's need for services increases, both public and private funds will be needed.

SUMMARY AND IMPLICATIONS

Rapid demographic and social changes mean that U.S. society is faced with complex, difficult policy choices. It is increasingly apparent that the older population is not one constituency but several, in which race, gender, socioeconomic class, and rural/urban residence may be greater unifiers than age. A political agenda must be drafted that can unite different older constituencies—low-income, middle-class, and wealthy—as well as different racial and ethnic groupings with common needs. Limited public resources in itself is not the primary barrier to action, however. For example, the cost of eliminating poverty among both older people and children is well within our societal resources, but our society lacks the public will to do so. The greater challenge is to frame the political consensus to ensure a minimal level of economic security and health for all Americans. Progress could be made in both areas largely by improving the basic income support of SSI and expanding Medicaid eligibility—changes that are fiscally possible. Unfortunately, such gains are unlikely to occur without major

changes in our political structures and belief systems of democratic pluralism, states' rights, and individual freedom. Until then, Americans will continue to be personally generous but reluctant to support income-maintenance programs for an entire class of needy persons or a national health care system that is perceived to threaten individual choice.

This chapter has reviewed federal programs that benefit older persons. Since 1960, age-specific spending has increased significantly, mostly through Medicare and Old Age and Survivors and Disability Insurance of Social Security. In the past, such age-entitlement programs have been based on cultural values and public beliefs that older people are deserving. However, the rapid expansion of these programs, combined with the improved economic status of the majority of older adults, has created a growing public and political sentiment that such age-based entitlement programs must be reduced, perhaps through means testing to minimize the benefits received by higher-income older adults.

The United States developed policies aimed at older populations more slowly than European countries. The Social Security Act of 1935 was the first major policy benefit for older people. Social Security was expanded slightly in 1950 to support partial health care costs through individual states. These changes led to the enactment of Medicare in 1965. Since then, the number of programs aimed at improving the welfare of older people has grown significantly: the Older Americans Act, Supplemental Security Income, the Social Security Amendments of 1972 and 1977, and Title XX social services legislation. National forums such as the 1961 and 1971 White House Conferences on Aging strengthened these programs. During the 1980s, however, social service funding declined despite recommendations from the 1981 White House Conferences on Aging to increase funds for aging services. Allocations for homemaker, nutrition, chore services, adult day care, low-income energy assistance, respite, and volunteer programs such as Retired Senior Volunteer Programs all diminished. These cost-efficiency measures were based on a national perception that the older population has greater financial security than younger age groups. The fiscal crisis faced by the Social Security system in the early 1980s fueled this stereotype through speculations that the growing number of older persons would drain the system before future generations could benefit. However, numerous structural factors are responsible for the problems. Changes that have subsequently been made in this system assure its future viability until approximately 2029.

The debate over age-based versus needs-based programs has also led to the emergence of organizations that expound arguments about older people benefiting at the expense of younger age groups. Yet, evidence for such inequities is weak; numerous other organizations such as the Children's Defense Fund and Generations United recognize generational interdependence and the importance of seeking increased public support for all ages through other sources. This framework, known as the interdependence of generations, assumes that assistance from young to old and old to young benefits all ages and supports the role of families across the life span.

The policy agenda for older Americans for the beginning of the twenty-first century is full and complex. The current federal emphasis on fiscal austerity and decentralized government underlies all policy debates about how much the federal government should be expected to provide and for whom. Increasing public perceptions of older people as well off, combined with decreased government expenditures, will undoubtedly affect the types of future programs and policies developed to meet older adults' needs. Older adults are less likely to act as a unified bloc in support of age-based programs. Instead, their increased diversity suggests that alliances will be formed between at-risk elders and other age groups. Consistent with the frameworks of interdependence and generational investment, such alliances may foster policies that benefit both older people and future generations. Threatening such cross-age efforts, however, is the anti-tax mood of the public and the fiscal conservatism of the current administration. These pressures suggest that advocates for older adults will need to find new ways to address the complex needs created by their increased life expectancy and diversity. A major challenge is the development and funding of health care, especially home- and community-based forms of long-term care, the topic addressed next in Chapter 17.

GLOSSARY

age-entitlement (age-based) programs   programs only available to people of a certain age

Aging Network   the system of social services for older adults funded by the Older Americans Act

Americans for Generational Equity   a group that questions age-entitlement programs for older people, since such programs are perceived as reducing the resources available to other age groups

Area Agencies on Aging   offices on aging at the regional and local levels that plan and administer services to meet the needs of older adults within that area; established and partially funded through the Older Americans Act

cash substitute   a benefit given in a form other than cash, such as a voucher, which may be exchanged for food, rent, medical care, etc.

cash transfer   a benefit paid by cash or its equivalent

categorical   in this context, a manner of dealing with public problems by addressing the problems of specific groups of persons rather than attempting solutions that are comprehensive or dealing with problems as they affect the entire population

contributory plans   programs providing benefits that require the beneficiary to contribute something toward the cost of the benefit

cost-of-living adjustments (COLA)   changes in benefits designed to maintain steady purchasing power of such benefits

dependency ratio   the number of people who are "dependent" compared to the number who are employed; a ratio calculated by dividing the number of people under age 18 plus people over age 65 by the number of workers (i.e., people between age 18 and 65)

direct benefit   a benefit given directly, in the form of either a cash payment or of some commodity such as food or housing

eligibility criteria   factors that determine the ability of programs to deliver benefits to people

entitlement programs   government programs organized in such a way that appropriations from a legislative body are not required; rather, eligibility on the part of applicants triggers receipt of benefits regardless of the total cost of the program

generational investment investments made by one generation for the benefit of another, such as the payment of Social Security taxes by the working population for the benefit of retirees, the services provided by older persons for the care of children, and the payment of property taxes that benefit school children

indirect benefit a benefit given through tax deductions or exemptions or other indirect means

interdependence of generations framework recognition of intergenerational transfers that occur across the life span

intergenerational inequity the view that one generation or age group receives benefits that are disproportional to those received by another

need-based (or means-based) entitlement programs social programs delivered to persons who meet defined criteria of eligibility based on need or ability to pay for the benefits

noncontributory programs programs providing benefits that do not require the beneficiary to contribute toward the cost of the benefit

Older Americans Act federal legislation for a network of social services specifically for older people

policy principles that govern action directed toward specific ends, designed to identify and ameliorate problems and implying changes in situations, systems, practices, beliefs, or behaviors

politics of entitlement political preferences, especially as applied to the aged, for the allocation of resources based on notions of older persons as needy, worthy, and deserving of public support

politics of productivity political preferences, especially as applied to the aged, for the allocation of resources based on a recognition of the diversity of the aging population (some are well-off, others are poor; some are capable of continued productive work, while others are ill or disabled)

selective benefits benefits available on an individually determined need or means basis

social programs the visible manifestations of policies (see policy)

Title XX or the Social Services Block Grant funding for social services (e.g., homemaking chores, adult day care) based on need, not age

universal benefits benefits available on the basis of social right to all persons belonging to a designated group.

RESOURCES

See the companion Website for this text at <www.ablongman.com/hooyman> for information about the following:

- AgeWork
- Administration on Aging (AOA)
- Gatekeeper Program
- International Federation on Aging
- National Academy on Aging
- National Association of Area Agencies on Aging
- National Committee to Preserve Social Security and Medicare
- National Policy and Resource Center on Women and Aging
- U.S. Senate Special Committee on Aging

REFERENCES

Atchley, R. Retirement income security: Past, present and future. *Generations*, Summer 1997, *21*, 9–12.

Ball, R. The case for maintaining benefits plan for Social Security. In D. Salisbury, *Assessing Social Security reform alternatives*. Washington, DC: Employee Benefits Research Institute, 1997.

Bengtson, V. L. Is the contract across generations changing? Effects of population aging on obligations and expectations across age groups. In V. L. Bengtson and W. A. Auchenbaum (Eds.), *The changing contract across generations*. New York: Aldine de Gruyter, 1993.

Binstock, R. H. Changing criteria in old-age programs: The introduction of economic status and need for services. *The Gerontologist*, 1994, *34*, 726–730.

Binstock, R. H. The deficit entitlements and policies on aging. *Gerontology News*, Washington, DC: Gerontological Society of America, February 1993, 2.

Binstock, R. H. A new era in the politics of aging: How will the old-age interest groups respond? *Generations*, Fall 1995, *19*, 68–74.

Binstock, R. H. The politics and economics of aging and diversity. In S. Bass, E. Kutza, and F. M. Torres-Gil (Eds.), *Diversity in aging*. Glenview, IL: Scott, Foresman and Co., 1990.

Binstock, R. H., and Day, C. L. Aging and politics. In R. H. Binstock and L. K. George (Eds.), *Handbook of aging and the social sciences* (4th ed.). San Diego, CA: Academic Press, 1996.

Bryce, D. V., and Friedland, R. B. *Economic and health security: An overview of the origins of federal legislation.* Washington, DC: The National Academy on Aging, January 16, 1997.

Clark, R. L. Retirement policy for an aging society. American Sociological Association, 1998

Conte, C. Executive Summary: Assessing Social Security reform alternatives. In D. Salisbury, *Assessing Social Security reform alternatives.* Washington, DC: Employee Benefit Research Institute, 1997.

Deets, H. B. Social Security reform? Just follow the money. *AARP Bulletin*, May 1997, 3.

Dentzer, S. Social Security reform: Gaps in perception. In D. Salisbury, *Assessing Social Security reform alternatives.* Washington, DC: Employee Benefits Research Institute, 1997.

Devlin, S., and Arye, L. The Social Security debate: A financial crisis or a new retirement paradigm. *Generations*, Summer 1997, *21*, 27–34.

Dugger, W. M. Old age is an institution. *Review of Social Economy*, 1999, *57*, 84–98.

Estes, C. L. *The aging enterprise.* San Francisco: Jossey-Bass, 1979.

Estes, C. L. Aging, health and social policy: Crisis and crossroads. *Journal of Aging and Social Policy*, 1989, *1*, 17–32.

Estes, C. L. Austerity and aging: 1980 and beyond. In M. Minkler and C. L. Estes (Eds.), *Readings in the political economy of aging.* Farmingdale, NY: Baywood, 1984.

Estes, C. L., Linkins, K. W., and Binney, E. A. The political economy of aging. In R. H. Binstock and L. K. George (Eds.), *Handbook of aging and the social sciences* (4th ed.). San Diego, CA: Academic Press, 1996.

Estes, C. L., Swan, J. H., and Associates. *The long-term care crisis.* Newbury Park, CA: Sage, 1993.

Feldstein, M. A new era of Social Security. *Public Interest*, 1998 *130*, 102–125.

Friedland, R. B. *Investing in Our Future.* Washington, DC: National Academy on an Aging Society, 2000.

Gill, D., and Ingman, S. *Eldercare, distributive justice, and the welfare state: Retrenchment or expansion.* Albany: State University of New York, 1994.

Gorin, S. A Society for all ages: Saving Social Security and Medicare. *Health and Social Work*, 25: 69–73. February 2000.

Goyer, A. Intergenerational Shared-Site Programs. *Generations*, Winter 1998–99, 79–80.

Gramlish, E. M. *Social Security in the 21st Century.* The Nineteenth Leon and Josephine Winkelman Lecture Presentation, University of Michigan, 2000.

Gran, B. Public and private pensions: Survival or retrenchment. *International Sociological Association*, 1998

Henkin, N., and Kingson, E. Advancing an intergenerational agenda for the twenty-first century. *Generations*, 1998/1999, *22*, 99–105.

Holstein, M. The normative case: Chronological age and public policy. *Generations*, Fall 1995, *19*, 11–14.

Howe, N. Why the graying of the welfare state threatens to flatten the American dream—or worse. *Generations*, Fall 1995, *19*, 15–20.

Hudson, R. B. The history and place of age-based public policy. *Generations*, Fall 1995, *19*, 5–10.

Hudson, R. B. The reconstitution of aging policy. Donald P. Kent Lecture. *Gerontological Society of America.* Cincinnati, Ohio. November 15, 1997.

Hudson, R. B. The role of government in "A Society for all Ages." *Health and Social Work*, 1999, *24*, 155–160.

Jacobs, B. Public policy and poverty among the oldest old: Looking to 2040. *Journal of Aging and Social Policy*, 1991, *2*, 85–99.

Johnson, M. L. Dignity for the oldest old: Can we afford it? *Journal of Gerontological Social Work*, 1998, *29*, 155–168.

Kassner, E. *The impact of food stamp cuts in the welfare reform bill on older persons.* Washington, DC: AARP, Public Policy Institute, 1996.

Kingson, E. R. Generational equity: An unexpected opportunity to broaden the politics of aging. *The Gerontologist.* 1988, *28*, 765–772.

Kingson, E. R. Testing the boundaries of universality: What's mean? What's not? *The Gerontologist*, 1994, *34*, 736–742.

Kingson, E. R., Hirshorn, B. A., and Cornman, J. C. *Ties that bind: the interdependence of generations.* Cabin John, MD: Seven Locks Press. 1986.

Kingson, E. R., Hirshorn, B. A., and Harootyan, L. K. The common stake: The interdependence of generations (A policy framework for an aging society). Washington, DC: *The Gerontological Society of*

America. Reprinted in H. R. Moody (1994), *Aging: concepts and controversies.* Thousand Oaks, CA: Pine Forge Press, 1987.

Kingson, E. R., and Quadagno, J. Social Security: Marketing radical reform. *Generations,* Fall 1995, *19,* 43–47.

Kingson, E. R., and Schulz, J. H. Should Social Security be means-tested? In E. R. Kingson, and J. H Schulz. (Eds.), *Social Security in the 21st century.* New York: Oxford Press, 1997.

Luna, A., and Riemer, H. The 2030 Center: An intergenerational agenda. *Generations,* Winter 1998–99, 76–78.

Marmor, T. R., Cook, F. L., and Scher, S. Social Security politics and the conflict between generations. Are we asking the right questions? In E. R. Kingson, and J. H. Schulz, *Social Security in the 21st century.* New York: Oxford University Press, 1997.

Mathews, J. The retirement crisis. *The Seattle Times,* Friday, January 6, 1995, B5 (Special to *The Washington Post*).

Miller, M. Rebuilding retirement. *US News and World Report,* April 20, 1998, 20–26.

Moncada, A. The Americanization of retirement. International Sociological Association, 1998.

Moody, H. R. The politics of entitlement and the politics of productivity. In S. Bass, E. Kutza, and F. M. Torres-Gil (Eds.), *Diversity in aging.* Glenview, IL: Scott, Foresman and Co., 1990.

Moon, M. Are Social Security benefits too high or too low? In E. R. Kingson, and J. H. Schulz (Eds.), *Social Security in the 21st century.* New York: Oxford Press, 1997.

Moon, M. Social Security: Critics get it wrong. *AARP Bulletin,* October 1997, *38,* 14.

National Academy on Aging. *Facts on the Older Americans Act.* Washington, DC: The National Academy on Aging, 1995.

National Academy on Aging. *Facts on Social Security: The Old Age and Survivors Trust Fund, 1996.* Washington, DC: The National Academy on Aging, 1997.

National Committee to Preserve Social Security and Medicare. *Update on Congress: A synopsis of legislation important to seniors.* Washington, DC. November 12, 1999.

Neugarten, B. Policy in the 1980s: Age or need entitlement. In B. Neugarten (Ed.), *Age or need: Public policies for older people.* Beverly Hills, CA: Sage, 1982.

Neugarten, B., and Neugarten, D. Changing meanings of age in the aging society. In A. Pifer and L. Bronte (Eds.), *Our aging society: Paradox and promise.* New York: W. W. Norton, 1986.

Ozawa, M. N. The economic well-being of elderly people and children in a changing society. Abstract. George Warren Brown School of Social Work, Washington University, St. Louis. *Social Work.* January 1999, *44,* 9–19.

Park, N. H., and Gilbert N. Social Security and the incremental privatization of retirement income. *Journal of Sociology and Social Welfare,* 1999, *26,* 187–202.

Peterson, P. G. *Facing up: How to rescue the economy from crushing debt and restore the American Dream.* New York: Simon and Schuster, 1993.

Preston, S. H. Children and the elderly in the United States. *Scientific American,* 1984, *251,* 44–49.

Quadagno, J. Generational equity and the politics of the welfare state. *International Journal of Health Services,* 1990, *20,* 631–649.

Quinn, J. *Entitlements and the federal budget: Securing our future.* Washington, DC: National Academy on Aging, 1996.

Rosen, E. I. American exceptionalism and the dismantling of the welfare state. *Critical Sociology,* 1998, *24,* 154–155.

Samuelson, R. J. It's more than a drug problem: *Newsweek,* September 25, 2000, 37.

Sass, Steven A., and Triest, Robert K. Social Security: How Social and Secure Should It Be? *Conference Proceedings of 1997 conference sponsored by the Federal Reserve Bank: "Social Security Reform: Links to Saving, Investment and Growth."*

Schorr, A. L. Income supports across the life course. *Generations,* 1998/1999, *22,* 64–67.

Schulz, J. H., Rosenman, L., and Rix, S. E. International developments in Social Security Privatization: What risk to women? *Journal of Cross Cultural Gerontology,* 1999, *14,* 25–42.

Smeeding, T. M., Estes, C. L., and Glasse, L. More than deficits: Strengthening security for women. Washington, DC: The Gerontological Society of America, *Social Security in the 21st Century,* 2000.

Social Security Administration. *Fast facts and figures about Social Security.* Washington, DC: U.S. Government Printing Office, 1996a.

Social Security Administration. *Social Security: Understanding the benefits.* Washington, DC: U.S. Government Printing Office, 1996b.

Spitz, G. N. Social Security doesn't need saving. *Social Policy*, 1998, *29*, 19–28.

Stern, L. Can we save Social Security? *Modern Maturity*, January–February 1997, 28–36.

Torres-Gil, F. M. *The new aging: Politics and change in America*. New York: Auburn House, 1992.

Torres-Gil, F. M., and Puccinelli, M. Mainstreaming gerontology in the policy arena. *The Gerontologist*, 1994, *34*, 749–752.

Villa, V. M., Wallace, S. P., and Markides, K. Economic diversity and an aging population: The impact of public policy and economic trends. *Generations*, Summer 1997, *21*, 13–17.

Wheeler, P. M., and Kearney, J. R. Income protection for the aged in the 21st century: A framework to help inform the debate. *Social Security Bulletin*, 1996, *59*, 3–19.

Woods, J. Pension coverage among the baby boomers: Initial findings for the 1995 Survey. *Social Security Bulletin*, Fall 1994, *57*, 12–25.

Wu, K. B. *Recipiency of Entitlement and other safety-net program benefits among families in 1993*. Washington, DC: AARP Public Policy Institute, 1995.

Zebrowski, J. Social Security: You've been warned. *Business Monday, Seattle Times*, Monday, November 20, 2000. p. C6.

17

HEALTH AND LONG-TERM CARE POLICY AND PROGRAMS

This chapter covers

- Definitions, status, and expenditures for acute and long-term care
- Medicare, its rising costs, and current efforts to reduce costs
- The growing need for long-term care, especially home care
- Improving the quality of care
- Medicaid and the growth of community-based services
- Private long-term care insurance, its costs and limitations
- New cost-attainment initiatives under Medicaid and Medicare, especially Social Health Maintenance Organizations (SHMOs) and Medicare HMOs

Throughout this book we have examined the interplay of social, physiological, and psychological factors in how older people relate to their environment, and how health status affects this interaction. Technological advances oriented toward cure have created the paradox that, while adults now live longer, they face serious, often de-

bilitating or life-threatening disabilities that create the need for ongoing care. Although Chapter 4 notes that disability per se in old age does not create dependency, growing numbers of older adults, especially among the oldest-old, are physically or mentally frail, and depend on informal supports as well as medical and nonmedical services. This dependence is often intensified by the interaction of age, race, gender, and poverty, as well as changes in family structure described in Chapter 9. And, as we have seen, the oldest-old, persons of color, women, and those who are low-income are more likely to have chronic disabilities that affect their ability to function.

As described in Chapter 11, *long-term care* (LTC) refers to a wide range of supportive services and assistance provided to persons who, as a result of chronic illness or disability, are unable to function independently on a daily basis. The need for LTC does not necessarily correspond to medical conditions, but rather to problems with performing *activities of daily living (ADLs)*—bathing, dressing, toileting, eating, and transferring—and *instrumental activities of daily living (IADLs)*—shopping, cooking, and cleaning. In addition, adults with cognitive impairments such as Alzheimer's disease may need nearly constant supervision. Long-term care is characterized by services to minimize, rehabilitate, or compensate for the loss of independent functioning and to enhance functional capabilities. Although largely "low-tech," long-term care services are increasingly complicated because those with complex medical needs are being discharged home earlier than was previously the case. In effect, long-term care aims to integrate health care treatment and assistance with daily life tasks and to address social, environmental and medical needs over a prolonged period (Kane, Kane, and Ladd, 1998).

Because nursing homes are the major institutional setting for long-term care, many older people and their families first think of them when they consider such care. However, as seen in Chapter 11, the boundaries between long-term care in institutional and noninstitutional environments are far from clear. For example, long-term care services are provided in:

- nursing homes
- home and community-based care settings
- noninstitutional settings, such as congregate care and residential care (assisted living, board and care, and adult family homes)
- adult day centers

Services provided within *home and residential care settings* include:

- personal assistance (home-delivered meals, visiting nurse or social work services, chore services, homemaker/home health aides, in-home respite, friendly visiting, and telephone reassurance)
- assistive devices (canes, walkers), home modifications
- technology (computerized medication reminders and emergency alert systems)

Services delivered in *community-based settings* encompass:

- nutrition programs
- senior centers
- adult day care
- respite
- hospice
- transportation

While the long-term care system also encompasses younger adults with AIDS, serious and chronic mental illness, and developmental disabilities, the focus of our discussion is on the structural, funding, staffing, and regulatory aspects of long-term care that affect older people. Overall, nearly 60 percent of those who report using long-term care are age 65 or older (Moon, 1996). The need for long-term care services is growing rapidly, especially among the oldest-old. While only 5 percent of those age 65 and over are in nursing homes at any one point in time, 12 percent in the community have ADL or IADL restrictions. Among those age 85 and over, the corresponding rates increase to 21 and 49 percent, respectively. When all adults age 65 and over are considered across their lifetimes, almost 65 percent of them will be in a nursing home, if only for a short time period (for over 50 percent, less than a year) before they are discharged to community settings. This translates into 75 percent of those over age 65 requiring some degree of home health care or personal assistance (Feder, Komisar, and Niefeld, 1999; Stone,

---

CHARACTERISTICS OF LONG-TERM CARE

- It is targeted at persons of all ages who have functional disabilities.
- Disabilities may be physical or mental, temporary or permanent.
- Aim is to enhance independence in functional abilities and quality of life, including the right to die with dignity for those who are terminally ill.

- It encompasses a wide range of services, professions, and settings of care.
- Care addresses physical, mental, social, and financial aspects of a person's life.
- Care is organized around the distinctive needs of each individual and family.
- Services change over time as the patient's and family's circumstances change.

1999). Although the health care system has traditionally emphasized primary and acute care, the boundaries with long-term care are blurred. In fact, our "acute" health care system is increasingly devoted to chronic care by various providers in a range of settings (Stone, 2000). Given the high incidence of chronic health needs among the growing population of older adults, it is not surprising that health and long-term care costs are one of the most critical and controversial policy issues facing our nation.

Although home-based long-term care services are available in nearly all communities, family and friends are the major providers of care. As many as 80 percent of older adults in need of long-term care live in their own homes or community settings. Of those who reside in the community, about 54 percent with severe disabilities rely exclusively on help from family and friends (Graves, 1997). The burdens faced by caregiving relatives are illustrated by the case of Kay Ruggles and her daughter in the vignette on page 547.

After informal supports, most paid providers are paraprofessionals such as certified nursing assistants in nursing homes or home care workers who deliver low-tech personal care and assistance with daily life tasks. Women predominate among both the unpaid and underpaid service providers, comprising up to 80 percent of family caregivers and 90 to 96 percent of paraprofessionals (Stone, 2000). In contrast to physicians who play a key role in acute-care hospital settings, nurses and ancillary therapists are the primary providers within

chronic-care facilities. We turn next to examining the rising health and long-term care costs and the factors underlying these.

HEALTH AND LONG-TERM CARE EXPENDITURES

Policy makers, service providers, and the general public are all concerned about the "crisis in health care." This refers mostly to the costs of care, the growing numbers of uninsured individuals, and the status and future of health care systems (Zis, Jacobs, and Shapiro, 1996). The consumer price index for health care is growing at about twice the rate of all consumer prices (Moon, 1996). People over 65 account for over 30 percent of the nation's annual federal health care expenditures (Wiener and Illston, 1996). In fact, the average expenditure for health services for adults age 65 and over is nearly four times the cost for those under age 65 and increases even more among the oldest-old. This is largely attributable to their greater chronic disease needs and use of hospital and nursing home services. Of all long-term care expenditures in the United States (e.g., nursing home, home health care), 70 percent are for people age 65 and over (Evashwick, 2001).

Although cost-containment changes in the private health care marketplace, especially through managed care, appear to have slowed the rate of medical costs, expenses are still rising faster than the national income. Medicare and Medicaid are expanding at several times the economic growth rate, adding to the pressure to change them in order to cut federal spending. Based on current trends, it is projected that spending on Medicare and Medicaid will consume 26.4 percent of the federal budget in the year 2003, up from 16.5 percent in 1994 (Driscoll, 1996). Nevertheless, most analysts do not fear a fiscal crisis in the Medicare trust fund in the near future. While public expenditures for health and long-term care rise, older individuals and their families continue to pay more out-of-pocket for their care than do younger Americans. Only 67 percent of total personal health care costs of older people are covered by government funding (Medicare, Medicaid, and other sources such as Veterans Administration), as illustrated in Figure 17.1. As mentioned in Chapter 12, older Americans now spend a higher proportion (and more in actual dollars) of their incomes on acute health care services than they did before Medicare and Medicaid were established three decades ago (23% versus

11%, respectively) (National Academy on Aging, 1997a). Over the same period that the median income of the older population rose 18 percent, real out-of-pocket spending on health care more than doubled (Moon, 1996; Wiener and Illston, 1996). In addition, long-term care costs are a growing proportion of total personal health care expenditures, increasing from less than 4 percent in 1960 to more than 11 percent in 1999 (Stone, 2000). The distribution and source of personal health care expenditures are illustrated in Figure 17.1.

Over 50 percent of out-of-pocket health care expenditures are for prescription drugs, which are not covered by Medicare. This lack is a historical accident. When Medicare was created in 1965, few private insurance policies covered prescriptions, because drugs were less numerous and important in medical treatment. Now, prescription drugs are a primary means of treatment. Adults over age 65 account for 42 percent of total drug spending (Ostrom, 2000). Because there are no restrictions on

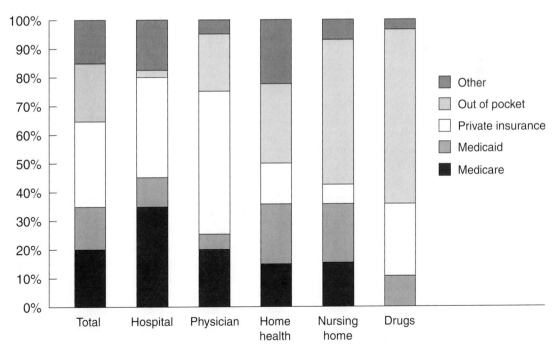

FIGURE 17.1 **Estimated Personal Health Care Expenditures, 1998**

drug prices in the United States, the profit margins for drug companies surpass those of nearly every economic sector. *Families USA,* a nonprofit health care research group, report that the average wholesale prices of 15 of the 50 drugs used most frequently by older people to treat arthritis, diabetes, and other common problems rose more than three times the rate of inflation between January 1999 and 2000. For example, Premarin, an estrogen replacement treatment that prevents osteoporosis, jumped 12.1 percent in price that year. Many Americans are shocked to learn that they can buy the same drugs in Canada for a fraction of the cost. The drug company lobbyists argue that such costs are necessary to cover research and testing of new, high-risk drugs. Admittedly, the research to produce new drugs is expensive and may yield only one or two FDA-approved drugs out of years of testing. However, critics of the drug industry argue what good is research and new drugs if no one can afford them? They maintain that too many dollars are spent on marketing and advertising drugs. Prescription drug costs and lack of coverage were among the hottest issues in the 2000 presidential campaign. If drug benefits are eventually covered under Medicare, this would nearly triple Medicare's costs by 2030. In contrast, some policy makers advocate higher eligibility ages for Medicare coverage, reduced benefits for the affluent, and targeting Medicare to the poor and near poor as a way to control costs, especially if drugs are covered (Samuelson, 2000). Regardless of specific strategies, government price controls on prescription drug costs are likely in the future.

In sum, the burdens of health care are expected to expand faster than the older population's ability to pay. At the same time, private health insurance costs are growing more rapidly than Medicare spending, and increases are greatest for home health and skilled nursing facility care (Driscoll, 1996; Moon, 1996).

Factors Underlying Growing Costs

A number of structural factors underlie escalating health care costs.

- The success of modern medical care: Costs have grown not so much in terms of the overall number of visits to health care providers, but in the type and complexity of services. Although advances in medical science produce cost-saving breakthroughs, they also make possible more sophisticated and expensive medical treatments. These tend to be in addition to prior services rather than replacements for old technologies or procedures. For example, an older patient now may receive X-rays, CAT scans, and MRIs to diagnose a problem, whereas before only X-rays would have been used.
- Related to the success of medical technology in prolonging life is the conflict between the curative goals of medicine and the chronic-care needs of older adults. As a result, there is a poor fit between the medical and related social service needs of the older population (e.g., long-term care needs) and the funding mechanisms, regulations, and fragmented services of the health care system.
- The system of public financing is biased toward acute care.
- Comprehensive, coordinated health and long-term care policy and programs that integrate acute and chronic care are lacking.

Because of the rapid growth of the older population, along with the public funding of their care through Medicare and Medicaid, older people have often been "blamed" for escalating costs. Yet, contrary to media portrayals that medical costs in the last year of life escalate for the oldest-old, hospital and physician costs actually *decline* for those age 80 and over, although "custodial" or personal-care costs are high (Blanchette, 1996–97). This is because, as noted in Chapter 1, the very old are generally survivors and the strongest of their cohort.

As seen in Chapter 16, some powerful beliefs and assumptions underlie these structural factors. These include a growing distrust of government and its ability to fund health care, and a strong belief in the private sector. These combine to produce an approach to service delivery that is determined largely by the market or who provides the best services at lowest cost (Moon, 1996). In other words, the shape of health care is largely influenced by

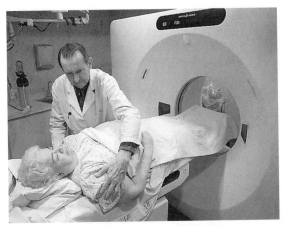

Expensive diagnostic techniques are one of the factors influencing growing health care costs.

its method of payment. The private provision of health services, without effective market control or uniform government regulation of expenditures, is emphasized. Nevertheless, most health services are financed by a mix of public programs, private insurance, and direct patient payments. Patients have been largely free to choose the health care providers they prefer. In turn, physicians have been able to charge patients whatever they choose. Only recently has Medicare, and subsequently most private health insurance companies, instituted a system of Preferred Provider Plans (PPPs) that require physicians to accept a set fee for each procedure in order to be paid by that insurer. Patterns of variable costs are even more pronounced with regard to the "non-system" of long-term care, which assumes that individuals are financially responsible for costs until their assets are exhausted. At that point, welfare in the form of Medicaid takes over. Funding mechanisms are now shifting with the growth of **managed care,** which aims to control the level of resources devoted to health care and is described more fully on page 561.

Even with managed care and attempts at cost control, acute and long-term care remain largely two separate fragmented systems, with distinct caregivers, treatment settings, financing structures, and goals. Physicians are the primary care providers in hospitals and outpatient settings, and Medicare

covers most of the costs. Nursing staff, paraprofessionals, and family members are the principal caregivers in nursing homes and private home settings. Medicaid pays for a large percentage of institutional care and, increasingly, home-based care. In the acute-care setting, intensity of services determines costs, compared to duration of treatment in long-term care. As noted by Vladeck (1994), the irony with long-term care is that the better the care, the longer the individual lives and remains in the system accruing costs. The different purposes between Medicaid and Medicare, which are the primary sources of funding and regulation for health and long-term care for older adults, are primary barriers to the integration of these two systems.

MEDICARE

As a social insurance system, **Medicare,** or Title XVIII of the Social Security Act of 1965, is intended to provide financial protection against the cost of hospital and physician care for people age 65 and over. Prior to the passage of Medicare, only about 50 percent of older adults had health insurance. Many could not afford insurance, or were denied coverage because of their age. In contrast, a value underlying Medicare is that older people are entitled to access to *acute medical care*, and society has an obligation to cover the costs associated with inpatient hospital care. Medicare's focus on the older population grew out of a compromise with the medical profession, which successfully opposed comprehensive health insurance for the general public. Yet Medicare was also viewed as the "first step" toward increasing access to health care for all age groups. Despite Medicare's goal of financial protection, it covers less than 50 percent of the total health expenditures of older adults, since it explicitly does not pay for long-term care or for prescription drugs; it also does not provide a maximum out-of-pocket cap to limit liability for medical expenses (Aaronson, 1996; Driscoll, 1996; Moon, 1996). As noted above and illustrated in Figure 17.1, the remainder is paid by older people out-of-pocket, by private supplemental insurance, by Medicaid, and by other public payers such as the Veterans Administration.

Contrary to many older adults' assumptions that their health care costs will be covered, Medicare pays only 80 percent of the allowable charges, not the actual amount charged by health providers. The patient must pay the difference between "allowable" and "actual" charges, unless the physician accepts "assignment" and agrees to charge only what Medicare pays. Beneficiaries whose doctors do not accept Medicare assignments are responsible for the amount that their doctor charges above the Medicare-approved rate, as illustrated by the vignette about Mr. Fox on p. 549.

Individuals with both Parts A and B must also pay an annual deductible and, in recent years, increasing copayments. About 90 percent of Medicare beneficiaries, such as Mr. Fox, now have supplemental insurance ("medigap") coverage to help pay for additional health care costs, especially for the catastrophic costs of extended hospitalization. However, the purchase of such private coverage is not a solution to health costs. Instead, it means that the average spending on health care is increased. Since the majority of older people pay fully for this insurance, they effectively still bear the burden of health care costs (Moon, 1996).

Medicare's major limitation is its focus on acute care (e.g., inpatient hospital and physicians), as illustrated in Figure 17.2. As noted above, it either excludes or gives little coverage to significant long-term care expenses, such as nursing homes, preventive health measures, outpatient costs of prescriptions, mental health services, and custodial or nonmedical services. Instead, the majority of Medicare dollars pay for hospital care, typically for catastrophic illness and increasingly for home care. Nursing home care is restricted to 100 days of skilled nursing care or skilled rehabilitation services, with eligibility contingent on acute illness or injury after hospitalization and requiring copayments. As a result, Medicare covers 45 percent of all health care spending for older people overall, but less for the oldest-old who require more nursing home care. In fact, less than 29 percent of the total Medicare budget covers nursing home expenditures. Accordingly, Medicare covers the long-term care expenses of only 3 to 5 percent of the

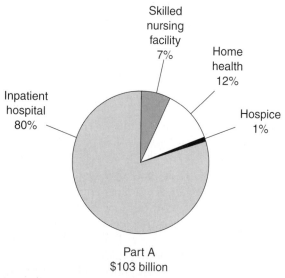

Part A
$103 billion

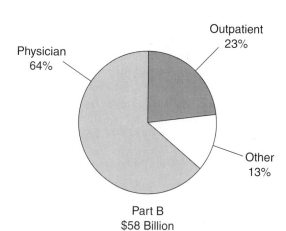

Part B
$58 Billion

FIGURE 17.2 *Medicare Benefit Payments*
SOURCE: HCFA, Office of the Actuary, 1995.

ELIGIBILITY FOR MEDICARE-REIMBURSED HOME CARE

- Older person must be homebound.
- Person must be capable of improvement.
- Person must require short-term intermittent nursing care, physical therapy, or speech therapy.

- All services, including occupational therapy, medical social work, and home health aide services, must be prescribed by a physician.

---

institutionalized older population. Believing that Medicare pays for long-term care, some older adults become aware of its lack of protection only upon their first hospitalization or admission to a nursing home.

A past gap in Medicare funding had been home- and community-based care, but now this is the most rapidly growing Medicare benefit. With over 20 percent of nursing home placements estimated to be incongruent with older persons' needs, home care is widely advocated as the lower-cost preferred alternative to inappropriate institutionalization. Even those in nursing homes or hospitals may require home care at some point, since 50 percent of those elders who stay less than 3 months are able to return to live in the community (Kane and Kane, 1990). As described in Chapter 11, home care permits earlier discharge, reduces the number of days of hospital care, and thus can cut costs. However, the costs of home care can easily exceed nursing home care if 24-hour daily care is necessary. Whether home care is cost-effective varies with the person's condition and the range and duration of services. Not only do most older people require home care, but they also prefer it and tend to recover faster at home, when there is continuity of care (Hughes, Ulasevich, Weaver, Henderson, Manheim, Kubal, and Bonango, 1997; Stone 2000).

Given the preference for home care, it is not surprising that the number of beneficiaries (almost one in ten Medicare beneficiaries have a home health visit during a year) and the average number of visits per user have grown dramatically. This translates into Medicare financing almost 60 percent of home care compared to funding by state and local sources, including Medicaid (14%) and out-of-pocket (20%). Home health care services are available for as long as beneficiaries remain eligible, without any burden of copayments or deductibles. As a result, long home health episodes are increasingly common under Medicare, with only about 60 percent of these episodes preceded by a hospital stay in the thirty days before services. From 1990 to 1996, annual expenditures grew, on average, 29 percent a year (Gage, Stevenson, Lui, and Aragon, 1998). The majority of these expenditures are for a small percent of users who have over 200 visits a year (Komisar and Feder, 1997). Home care services are delivered by over 11,000 agencies nationwide, many of which are dually certified to serve the needs of both Medicare and Medicaid. The field, however, has shifted from primarily Visiting Nurses Associations and public agencies to hospital-based and private for-profit or nonprofit agencies. The data suggest that Medicare beneficiaries are using home health for longer periods and less medically intensive services (e.g., more long-term, unskilled personal care by home health aides) for a recovery period after hospital discharge. This translates into home health aide visits that are lucrative for the agencies; this is because less skilled care is still highly compensated. Whether this shift indicates better coverage of chronic disabilities for older persons requiring unskilled care after early discharges or greater provision of more discretionary services is unclear. Nevertheless, the data appear to support the critics who contend that Medicare is beginning to approximate a system of long-term care rather than an acute care insurance program. It also appears that incentives for agencies to spend as little as possible could place at greatest risk the patients who need the most skilled care (Feder et al., 1999).

CHECKLIST FOR CHOOSING HOME HEALTH CARE SERVICES

- Is the agency licensed, accredited and certified to give home health care?
- Is the agency Medicare certified/approved?
- Does it have a written statement about its services, eligibility, costs, and payment procedures?
- Are homemakers and home health aides trained? For how long? By whom?
- How are employees supervised?
- Will the same person provide care on a regular basis?

- What are the hourly fees? Minimum hours required?
- How does the agency handle theft and other unacceptable behaviors?
- Will you be given a copy of the treatment/service plan?
- Does the agency have a Bill of Rights for patients?

The checklist above summarizes factors that families should consider in selecting home health care services.

A number of factors underlie the extraordinary growth in Medicare-funded home care services:

1. Earlier hospital discharges as a result of the 1983 Prospective Payment Systems mean that patients require more technical care at home, such as intravenous therapy and ventilation therapy. Home care serves as the "safety net" for patients being discharged from acute and rehabilitation institutional settings after shorter lengths of stay (Schlenker, 1996).

2. A 1989 class action lawsuit created a more flexible interpretation of definitions (homebound), scope of services (both management and evaluation), and regulations (part-time or intermittent care) and skilled nursing judgment, not just skilled nursing care. In addition, some home health care remains a brief recovery "subacute" service, usually after a hospital stay. Medicare-funded home health benefits thus serve a dual purpose, caring for both the short- and long-term needs of beneficiaries (Hughes, 1996; Moon, 1996).

3. The number of **proprietary** or for-profit home health agencies that are reimbursed under Medicare has grown dramatically. In the past, home care was dominated by nonprofit agencies such as the Visiting Nurses Association. For-profit chains grew in response to the 1980 and 1981

Omnibus Budget Reconciliation Acts. These eliminated the requirement for state licensing as a basis for reimbursing proprietary agencies. These regulatory changes served to stimulate competition for the provision and contracting out of services to new proprietary agencies. Such agencies, however, are less likely to concentrate on the ambulatory care of older people after hospital discharge.

4. There are isolated instances of Medicare–home health agencies not complying with federal health and safety standards, overcharging, fraud and abuse, and providing substandard care (Pear, 1997).

5. High-technology home therapy, such as intravenous antibiotics, oncology therapy, and pain management, continues to grow. Such care involves expensive pharmaceuticals and equipment that require special staff expertise to use and monitor, and is costly to the patient or insurer.

The number of private home health agencies that serve primarily private-pay and contract patients is also growing dramatically. These are not certified for payment by Medicare and, accordingly, are not bound by Medicare regulations. Instead, they often contract with managed care agencies. They fill the demand for home care by patients who do not qualify for Medicare or Medicaid, and offer more services than Medicare-certified agencies. In contrast to the intermittent skilled visits of Medicare home care agencies, noncertified private

Kay Ruggles, age 87, suffers from severe osteoporosis and arthritis. Although she worries about falling, she wants to stay in her home as long as possible. Since she is not eligible for any publicly funded home care program, she must pay out of pocket for daily assistance with bathing, walking, and cooking. Her daughter is employed and has a family to care for, but tries to stay with her mother on weekends and assist her with the household chores. Because the cost of home care is so much greater than her income, Mrs. Ruggles's savings are dwindling. She and her daughter worry that she will have to go into a nursing home as a Medicaid patient as the only way to fund her care.

agencies typically provide 24-hour daily care for an indefinite period, as well as specialty services. They also offer homemaker/home health aide care services, typically on an on-call basis. Referrals for private agencies come through social service agencies, Medicare-certified home health agencies, relatives, friends, and the Yellow Pages. As with all long-term care services, there are problems of recruiting and retaining quality part-time contractual staff. A dilemma for families, however, is that many private agencies, especially those affiliated with large nationwide chains, require a minimum number of hours of care, which can become prohibitively expensive. Another expense is durable medical equipment, ranging from walkers to electric beds. Medicare covers such equipment only if prescribed by the patient's physician.

Another Medicare growth area is for **subacute care**—intensive coordinated services to post–acute care patients to minimize or avoid expensive hospital stays. Subacute care may refer to:

- certain types of services (rehabilitation)
- patients (those who no longer require acute services)
- level of services between acute hospital care and skilled nursing care

The verdict is still out on whether subacute care is an innovative practice or a repackaging of previous services (Stone, 2000).

Along with the costs of home and subacute care, Medicare expenditures in general are spiraling. This overall growth is due primarily to significant

---

COMPONENTS OF MEDICARE

Hospital Insurance (Part A)
- Covers 99 percent of the older population.
- Financed through the Social Security payroll tax.
- Available for all older persons who are eligible for Social Security.
- Pays up to 90 days of hospital care and for a restricted amount of skilled nursing care, rehabilitation, home health services (if skilled care is needed), and hospice care.
- Recipients are responsible for their first day's hospital stay and for copayments for hospital stays exceeding 60 days.
- When the 90 days of hospital care are used up, a patient has a "lifetime reserve" of 60 days.

Supplemental Medical Insurance (Part B)
- Covers 97 percent of the older population.
- Paid voluntarily through a monthly premium.
- Annual $100 deductible.
- Generally pays 80 percent of physician and hospital outpatient services; home health care limited to certain types of health conditions and specific time periods; diagnostic laboratory and X-ray services, and a variety of miscellaneous services, including 50 percent of the approved amount for outpatient mental health care.

increases in hospital costs into the early 1990s. Medicare currently forms over 12 percent of the federal budget. Total Medicare spending is projected to grow by 8 to 10 percent per year over the next decade, just to maintain the same level of services for a growing Medicare population that is living longer (Driscoll, 1996). The Trustees of the Hospital Insurance Trust Fund continue to warn Congress of the need to restore the balance between income and spending in order to reduce insolvency. The threats to the trust fund are due, in part, to the fact that the number of workers paying taxes relative to the number of beneficiaries is decreasing as the population continues to age (e.g., the age-dependency ratio discussed in Chapters 1 and 16). As one of the fastest-growing programs in the federal budget, Medicare became a target for budget cuts in the 1997 Balanced Budget Act. Nevertheless, even greater spending reductions may be necessary, since legislative cuts of even billions of dollars have been outweighed by spending growth, albeit at a slower rate of increase. These Medicare expenditure problems are due, in part, to the much larger, more intractable problem of rising health care costs generally in the United States.

Efforts to Reduce Medicare Costs

A number of measures attempt to reduce costs under Medicare, as follows:

1. A **prospective-payment system (PPS)** was instituted in 1983 to reduce incentives for physicians to provide more hospital-bed services under fee-for-service payment plans. Instead of reimbursing providers for each service for each patient, the Health Care Financing Administration (HCFA) determines payment by the diagnostic category in which each patient is placed. These categories, which classify patients by medical condition and thus establish Medicare payments prior to admission, are called **diagnostic related groupings, or DRGs.** Under the prior cost-based reimbursement system, hospitals were paid more if they provided more and longer services, resulting in higher subsequent costs. With DRGs, a hospital is paid a fixed

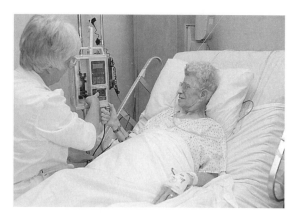

Recent legislation seeks to reduce Medicare's share of hospital costs.

amount per admission, according to the diagnostic category. The rates for DRGs are, in turn, based on an expected length of stay for each condition. A hospital that keeps patients longer than needed, orders unnecessary tests, or provides care inefficiently must absorb the differential in cost between the care provided and the amount reimbursed by Medicare. Alternatively, hospitals that provide care at a cost below the established DRG can keep the financial difference. This serves as an incentive for hospitals to release patients as soon as possible. In effect, DRGs were an early form of managed care, designed to curb skyrocketing costs (Abramson, 1998).

2. Congress passed the *Medicare Catastrophic Health Care Act* (MCHCA) in 1988 to reduce costs associated with physician services, hospitalizations, and after-care for acute illness. Expanded benefits were to be financed by a mandatory supplemental premium. This surtax, ranging from $4 to $800 a year based on income, affected approximately 40 percent of older adults, specifically those with incomes over $30,000 or couples with incomes over $50,000 a year. Although AARP supported this legislation, none of its supporters anticipated the negative grassroots reaction among older persons nationwide. Many reacted against changes in the basic premise of Medicare financing—that higher-income older adults would pay a surtax for benefits serving primarily low-income older people, and that financing was entirely through a transfer of funds within older and disabled populations, not shared across groups. In addition, the legislation failed to address what older people want—protection from the bankrupting expenses of long-term care. In 1989, Congress voted to repeal the legislation, leaving many legislators wary of making changes in Medicare.

3. In 1992, a physician payment reform was implemented to limit Medicare spending on physician care. This established a physician fee schedule and a system of limiting payment increases when the total cost of physician services billed in a year exceeds estimated levels. The physician payment reform program also limits the amount doctors can charge above the approved Medicare rate.

4. The 1997 Federal Balanced Budget Agreement included an increase in Part B premiums and cuts of $115 billion in Medicare payments to doctors, hospitals, and HMOs, the largest reduction in the program's history. Such changes are intended to postpone the financial crisis of the Medicare Trust Fund until 2007. Yet after 2010, when the baby boomers begin receiving benefits, the financial outlook is extremely unfavorable (Rosenblatt, 1997).

5. The National Bipartisan Commission on the Future of Medicare was created by Congress in 1998 to study how Medicare can accommodate Baby Boomers in this first century.

Concerns over increased home care costs resulted in a 1997 decision by the **Health Care Financing Administration** (HCFA), the federal agency that approves or denies Medicare claims, to freeze the licensing of new home health agencies. In addition, Congress passed the *Balanced Budget Act of 1997*, which substantially changed Medicare's payment system for home health care. Instead of separate payments for each visit, Medicare adopted the prospective-payment system (PPS), with fixed, limited payments in advance for a general course of treatment. Another iteration of PPS is the *interim payment system (IPS)*; this sets limits on the number of visits by home health agencies. Even though the regulations were not issued until 1998, the new IPS rates were applied retroactively to all payments after October 1, 1997. In addition, agencies have been restrained to historical cost patterns since 1994, even if their current costs are higher. Such limits may unintentionally limit access to care, especially for those who are sickest and needing the most costly care (Komisar and Feder, 1998; The Lewin Group, 1998).

The prospective payment system operates in a manner similar to the DRG system in hospitals; agencies are reimbursed at a capitated rate per patient per episode of service. Anecdotal reports suggest that many home health agencies, especially nonprofits, are closing due to low Medicare payments relative to patient costs, and that patients are being dropped from care. The greatest concern is that chronically ill older people who need ongoing home care on a regular basis are the least desirable patients for an agency because of the financial burden. Regardless of any future changes in the IPS, it is important to monitor whether beneficiaries continue to have access to services prescribed by their physicians (Gage, 1998).

Mr. Fox went to his physician for a sigmoidoscopy, a procedure to examine the large colon for polyps or cancer. His physician charges $300 for this procedure. Medicare determined that the going rate for the procedure in Mr. Fox's community is $180, which means that Medicare pays the physician 80 percent of that amount, or $144. If Mr. Fox's physician accepts the assignment, then Mr. Fox owes his doctor the difference between $180 and $144, or $36. Fortunately, Mr. Fox has private "medigap" insurance that covers this difference. If Mr. Fox's physician had not accepted assignment, then Mr. Fox would have been responsible for paying $300 less the amount paid by Medicare ($144) or a total of $156.

Despite these reforms, Medicare expenditures continue to grow, albeit at a slower rate than might have occurred otherwise (National Academy on Aging, 1997b). This growth is partially because the prospective payment system has not altered Medicare's basic approach or the structural arrangements that depend upon fee-for-service financing. Nor have DRGs reduced all the incentives for applying costly technologically oriented care. In fact, there has been an *increase* in the use of specialists and improved procedures such as hip replacement and cataract surgery that result in higher utilization rates. Costs have also grown because of increased federal oversight and regulatory control through hospital rate setting and the regulation of physician behavior. Other Medicare costs have increased, for example, by shifting medical procedures to ambulatory settings and doctors' offices, which thus far are restricted by the prospective payment system.

Although findings are mixed, both lengths of stay per admission and number of admissions appear to have fallen under PPS and DRGs. The total number of inpatient hospital days under Medicare has declined since 1991, even though hospital admissions have risen (Moon, 1996). This is partially explained by the trend toward more frequently performing simple surgical and diagnostic procedures on an outpatient basis. What is less clear is how the PPS and DRGs have affected utilization of nursing homes, home care by families, and home health care. Initially, it appeared

that these groups faced increased pressures to provide care for patients discharged from the hospital on average 2 days earlier and, therefore, sicker. Since families and home health agencies often cannot provide these more complex and intensive levels of care, some early studies found that premature discharges resulted in a "revolving door" pattern of more patients in and out of hospitals (Gaumer, Poggio, Coelen, Sennett, and Schmitz, 1989; Hing, 1989; Sager, Easterling, Kindig, and Anderson, 1989). On the other hand, findings of greater need for care and higher rates of mortality may be due, in part, to differences in risk factors (e.g., the inpatient population is now older and sicker than before the prospective payment system), not because of shorter stays or declining quality of care. Nevertheless, quality of care as a whole appears to be affected by earlier hospital discharge and restrictions on physician payment levels (Moon, 1996), as illustrated by the experience of Mr. Jones, below. This is partly because DRGs discourage the extra time required to make appropriate discharge plans and the use of ancillary personnel such as social workers, except to expedite hospital discharges.

The 2000 presidential and congressional elections set the tone, temperament, and direction of budget, tax and entitlement politics in the future, and especially in the fiscal years 2002 through 2004. Not surprisingly, Republicans and Democrats differ on the nature and size of cuts in Medicare, although both agree on the need for re-

---

Mr. Jones underwent major surgery—a radical prostatectomy for prostate cancer. Despite the pain that he was still experiencing, he was discharged after 3 days in the hospital and had to return home with a catheter in place that required careful monitoring by a physician or nurse. His wife was in her late 80s and unable to provide the skilled care that a catheter requires. He was extremely fatigued. With only his frail wife to care for him, he required the services of a visiting nurse. He continued to experience considerable pain for which his medication was inadequate; if he could have remained in the hospital, his pain could have been relieved by an anesthesiologist. Perhaps the most difficult issue was his uncertainty and anxiety about a variety of symptoms, such as loss of appetite, which could have been resolved with a somewhat longer hospital stay.

STRATEGIES TO REDUCE MEDICARE COSTS

- Limit eligibility for the next cohort of Medicare recipients by increasing the age of eligibility to 67.
- Bill enrollees $5 for home health visits.
- Ration services by age.
- Use an income test as a basis for eligibility.

- Increase coinsurance and deductibles to shift more financial risk onto the beneficiaries.
- Increase Supplemental Medical Insurance premiums (Part B) for higher-income beneficiaries.
- Reduce the coverage of services and the reimbursement given to providers.

---

forms. Republicans advocate increased application of market principles to the health care market, more HMOs, additional managed care, increased privatization, and more coverage choices. Both parties agree that managed care is a way to slow Medicare costs, and that new payment methods and improved beneficiary services are both necessary, along with measures to combat health care fraud and abuse. The fact that a substantial amount of the current budget surplus is in Social Security and Medicare trust funds means that using the trust funds to reduce the public debt would result in a corresponding increase in the debt held by the government. In other words, the publicly held debt would be replaced by government-held debt. Until the long-range implications of such a shift are more clearly identified, the public needs to be cautious about proposals to use the surplus to reduce public debt. The projected surplus in federal taxes and its implications for Medicare will undoubtedly remain controversial under the new administration and Congress.

The New Medicare

The Federal Balanced Budget Act of 1997 also established **Medicare Choice.** This allows Medicare to pay for a wider range of preventive services, including mammograms, PAP smears, cervical exams, prostate screening, bone density measurement procedures, diabetes screening and self-care, and enhancement of the vaccination program. The major change, however, is that beneficiaries have more choice in where and how they obtain health care. The choices available include:

1. Medicare **Health Maintenance Organizations/Preferred Provider Organizations (HMOs/PPOs):** Networks of independent hospitals, physicians, and other health care providers who contract with an insurance entity to provide care at discount rates. Medicare beneficiaries who join HMOs are given incentives to use the HMO/PPO physicians, but also may use providers outside the network at higher out-of-pocket costs. (See page 561 for more descriptions of Medicare HMOs.)

2. Purchase of *private insurance plans,* including long-term care insurance (see page 557 for a discussion of such insurance).

3. Establishment of **medical savings accounts,** which allow beneficiaries to put Medicare dollars into a tax-exempt account to pay for qualified medical expenses.

The medical savings account is combined with a high-deductible insurance policy to cover catastrophic injuries or illness. Advocates of these accounts believe that older adults will become more cost-conscious by their deciding, not their insurers, where to seek care. Critics fear that only the wealthier and healthier older adults can afford such a plan. With all the options under Medicare Choice, Medicare begins to look more like a private health care system than a publicly funded base of services for all older adults. What is unclear is how many adults age 65 and over will migrate to these new forms of care rather than rely upon the past Medicare model of reimbursement.

Other strategies to reduce Medicare costs continue to be debated at the national level, as illustrated in the box on page 551. Contrary to these proposed changes, 83 percent of 1,000 respondents in a 1997 national poll agreed that the federal government has a basic responsibility to guarantee adequate health care for older people. Of these respondents, 58 percent favored adding dollars to Medicare from new taxes or general government funds and opposed all the strategies for cutting costs (Bernstein, 1997). It is also noteworthy that while Medicare is the current focus of many cost-cutting debates, costs remain below those of private insurers on a per capita basis. One major reason for this is that Medicare is administratively more efficient (less than 2 percent on overhead) than most private insurers or HMOs (average of 15 percent on overhead) (Stone, 2000).

MEDICAID

In contrast to Medicare, **Medicaid** is not a health insurance program specifically for older people, but rather a federal and state means-tested welfare program of medical assistance for the poor, regardless of age (e.g., to recipients of Aid to Families with Dependent Children and Supplemental Security Income). Unlike Medicare, it covers long-term care but only for the poor or those who become poor by paying for long-term or medical care. Medicaid also differs from Medicare in that federal funds are administered by each state through local welfare offices, which can carry a stigma for some older recipients. As such, it is the major public program covering long-term care for older adults and for disabled people of all ages, as illustrated in Figure 17.3. By assisting more than 10 percent of people over age 65, Medicaid plays three essential roles:

1. Makes Medicare affordable for low-income beneficiaries by paying Medicare's premiums, deductibles, and other cost-sharing requirements ("dual eligibles").

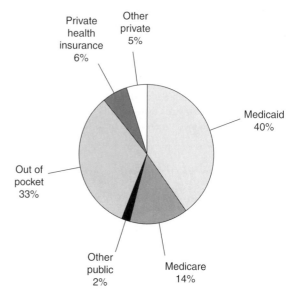

FIGURE 17.3 **Approximate Sources of Long-Term Care Expenses**
SOURCE: National Academy on Aging, 1997.

2. Provides coverage of medical benefits that Medicare does not cover, such as prescription drugs and long-term care.
3. Stands alone as the only public source of financial assistance for long-term care in both institutional and community settings (Lyons and Rowland, 1996).

Federal regulations require that all state Medicaid programs provide the following: hospital inpatient care, physician services, skilled nursing facility care, laboratory and X-ray services, home health services, hospital outpatient care, family planning, rural health clinics, and early and periodic screening. In contrast to Medicare, home health care services are a mandatory area of coverage for Medicaid, while personal-care services and home and community-based services are optional. Although Medicare covers only skilled nursing care for patients with rehabilitative potential in nursing homes, Medicaid can cover both skilled care for rehabilitation and intermediate nursing home care of a more custodial nature. However, to qualify for Medicaid-reimbursed nursing home care, the older person must first spend down his or her income to a certain level (determined by each state) and must contribute almost all personal income to the cost of nursing home care. Yet most nursing home occupants have already depleted their resources and are eligible for Medicaid at the time of admission. And for those who are not, states vary on the limit on one's income to be eligible for Medicaid nursing home coverage; homes, businesses, and cars are exempt from eligibility rules. Nevertheless, we have all heard stories of older people, oftentimes women, who first had to become impoverished to qualify for Medicaid-financed nursing home care. For some segments of the older population, those stories are true.

Moses (1998), however, presents a different view of Medicaid spend down than that of impoverished elders. He maintains that middle-class Americans fail to buy long-term care insurance because they view Medicaid as a way to save their estates and inheritances. He suggests that this group views Medicaid as a means to pay for their long-term care without selling their homes or, if they can afford a good lawyer, their assets. He contends that the almost universal availability of publicly financed nursing home benefits enables widespread public denial concerning long-term care risks and the need to plan for such care. Accordingly, he argues that the middle class and well-to-do should pay privately for long-term care to the extent that they are able, without suffering financial devastation.

Although states are the major financiers of Medicaid long-term care, they vary widely in the services included and the groups eligible to receive them. For example, states may elect to provide coverage for personal care services but are not required to do so. States differ greatly in the provision of "optional" services, such as intermediate care, prescription drugs outside the hospital, dental services, eyeglasses, and physical therapy. Similar to Medicare, coverage for mental health and social services is limited. Because of such limitations, Medicaid, like Medicare, provides only 60 to 80 percent of daily care charges, even though Medicaid public expenditures have grown more rapidly than inflation (Burwell et al., 1996). For example, in over 30 states, spending on older people accounts for 25 percent or more of the overall Medicaid budget (Lyons et al., 1996). As with Medicare, the growth in expenditures is due primarily to price increases by health providers and fragmented funding mechanisms, not population growth per se or expansion of care.

Older adults may qualify for Medicaid in the following ways:

1. Participation in Supplemental Security Income (SSI), which encompasses the provision of Medicaid. Although Medicaid is the principal health care insurance provided for the poor and is viewed as a "safety net" program, only 33 percent of poor older persons meet the stringent categorical eligibility requirements. Most of these are residents in nursing homes (Lyons et al., 1996). Those who do qualify for cash assistance are provided the broadest coverage under Medicaid, including payment of Medicare premiums, cost sharing, and payment for additional services, such as prescription drug, vision-care, and dental-care coverage under state Medicaid programs.

2. Having incomes above welfare cash assistance levels, but facing such high medical or long-term care expenditures that older adults **spend**

POINTS TO PONDER

What is your position on Medicaid spend down? Do you think that it unjustly impoverishes older people and their families needing nursing home care? Or do you think that those with assets find ways to protect them and still get Medicaid to cover the cost of nursing home care? Reflect on family members or others you know who have used the Medicaid spend down to access nursing home care. What were some of their experiences?

down to Medicaid eligibility requirements. These income levels are established by each state and therefore differ. However, before Medicaid will pay for services, an older person must deplete almost all personal assets and apply all monthly income, except for a small personal allowance, toward the cost of nursing home care.

3. Being eligible for both Medicare and Medicaid, typically those whose income falls 100 percent below the federal poverty guidelines and yet having limited financial assests. Those beneficiaries are often very ill, less likely to have a spouse or any living children, and more likely to live in a nursing home. Known as qualified medicaid beneficiaries (QMB) or specified low-income Medicaid beneficiaries (SLMB), they get help from Medicaid to cover Medicare's copayments and deductibles (e.g., out-of-pocket expenses) and their monthly premiums for physician and outpatient coverage. In other words, even though they have too many financial resources to be eligible for Medicaid full benefits, Medicaid does pay for what Medicare does not cover (National Academy on Aging, 1997).

Older persons constitute a minority (approximately 12 percent) of the total users of Medicaid, yet they account for about 30 percent of the total expenditures (Lyons et al., 1996). The predominant cause of this disproportionate rate of expenditures is that Medicaid is the primary public funding source (40 percent) of long-term care, largely institutional care, with only about 20 percent for home and community-based care (Feder, Komisar, Niefeld, 1999) (see Figure 17.3). In most states, Medicaid spending on long-term care services comprises 30 to 50 percent of total Medicaid spending. Of these total Medicaid expenditures, nursing home costs comprise approximately 80 percent, as illustrated in Figure 17.4 (National Academy on Aging, 1997b). The fastest-growing category of Medicaid costs, nursing home expenditures are increasing at an average annual rate of 10 percent (currently averaging over $127 a day or $46,000 a year). Nevertheless, about 33 percent of

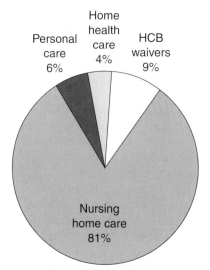

FIGURE 17.4 **Proportion of Medicaid Long-Term Care Spending by Service,*** 1995

*Personal care refers to services to assist a person with activities of daily living such as bathing and dressing; home health care generally refers to skilled nursing care and care provided by home health aides; and home and community-based (HCB) waivers refer to services that a state provides to persons at risk of needing nursing home care.

SOURCE: Brian Burwell, The MEDSTAT Group, 1996.

nursing home care is still paid by individuals out of pocket (Feder et al., 1999).

As noted above, only a small percent of Medicaid expenditures go to community-based home health services, even though the average cost of home health care is significantly less (approximately $500 a month) than nursing home care. The *financing of home care services* under Medicaid occurs under three different coverage options:

1. Home health services, which are skilled services typically provided by a Medicaid-certified home health agency
2. Personal care services, which are semiskilled or unskilled services provided to Medicaid beneficiaries who need assistance with basic activities of daily living in their own home (typ-

ically provided by nonlicensed individuals, these constitute the majority of total spending of home care services under Medicaid)
3. Home- and community-based waiver services

The home- and community-based waiver services were first authorized under the 1981 Omnibus Budget Reconciliation Act. This permits the waiver of Medicaid statutory requirements so that states can provide community-based options by targeting benefits to limited geographic areas and to specific groups and numbers of beneficiaries. The waiver program specifies seven core services that have not been traditionally considered "medical," but which allow people to remain at home—case management, homemaker, home health aide, personal care, adult day care, rehabilitation, respite care—and other services approved by the federal government as "cost-effective." The primary criterion is that states must demonstrate that the costs of such home- and community-based services are less than care in institutions, and also that they serve to divert at-risk individuals from nursing home placement. Although nearly all the states have an array of waivers, the program's cost-containment goals mean that most states restrict the scope of services and the number of recipients (Coleman, 1996; Lyons et al., 1996). Despite such limits, Medicaid spending for home care has increased, especially in states that have widely implemented waivers. For example, Washington and Oregon, which view nursing homes as the setting of last resort, have deliberately reduced the number of nursing home beds and have chosen to support more case management, assisted living, and adult family homes. Despite reductions in nursing home use, total long-term spending has continued to rise. Other states augment or create their own separate home care programs with state funds, a few through lottery revenues or county levies for long-term care. Most state policy initiatives have, however, a modest impact on the allocation of resources between nursing homes and home- and community-based care (Feder et al., 1999).

Medicaid is the primary source of public funding for nursing home care.

Medicaid is a highly visible target for federal and state cost cutting, because it forms a growing proportion of state budgets at the same time that federal funds allocated to states for Medicaid have declined (Wiener and Illston, 1996). States attempt to limit expenditures in a wide variety of ways:

- limits on the supply of nursing home beds through certificate of need requirements for nursing homes and moratoria on construction of new nursing home beds or facilities
- preadmission screening and tightening the medical and functional eligibility requirements for nursing home admission, thereby limiting the number of people entering nursing homes
- unlinking Medicaid from welfare benefits and using managed-care models with **capitated payments** to control Medicaid expenditures
- reducing benefits covered (for example, eliminating coverage of prescription drugs), restricting eligibility and utilization, and increasing copayments
- rationing or limiting services only to those proved most cost-effective

The most successful approach to monitoring quality in nursing homes is the long-term care ombudsman. An ombudsman office in each state develops nonregula- tory approaches to monitoring care in nursing homes. Their influence is constrained, however, by limited funding and reliance on volunteers.

Such benefit reductions, however, fail to address rising hospital and nursing home costs caused by providers' price increases. In addition, efforts to control Medicaid spending for nursing homes are difficult because of not only the continued increase in the oldest-old but also resistance by nursing home lobbyists. Rather, Medicaid cuts have created a growing number of older adults who lack access to care and who are at risk of declining health status and increased mortality. In fact, aging advocates contend that when nursing home care is restricted, some older consumers, with fewer choices, receive lower quality of care (Coleman, 1997). Medicaid is thus faced with how to provide coverage for acute and long-term care for low-income and vulnerable populations at a time of intense pressure to limit public spending. In sum, achieving a better balance across services appears to require a substantial investment in long-term care, which is unlikely in the near future.

SOCIAL SERVICES BLOCK GRANTS AND THE OLDER AMERICANS ACT (OAA)

In addition to the limited allocations of Medicare and Medicaid for community-based services, Title XX Amendments to the Social Security Act (Social Services Block Grants) and Title III of the Older Americans Act provide some funding for nonmedical, custodial services for older people with disabilities.

As noted in Chapter 16, most services to older persons under Title XX go to those who receive Supplemental Security Income, and are viewed as necessary to carry out basic ADLs. They include:

- homemaker and chore services
- home-delivered meals (Meals on Wheels)

- adult protective services
- adult day care
- foster care
- institutional or residential care

With federal reductions in block grant funding to the states, competition for decreasing funds at the local level has increased. Services funded under Title III of the Older Americans Act include, for example, information and referral, case management, transportation, homemaker and home-based chore services, adult day care, nutrition education and congregate meals, respite care, and senior centers. OAA services may be provided without the restrictions of Medicare and the means test of Medicaid, since the primary eligibility criterion is age 60 regardless of income. However, services must be targeted to persons with the greatest social or economic need and to frail older adults. With Medicaid cuts, some states are targeting their resources to only the most severely disabled.

Both Title XX and Title III are limited in their impact by the relatively small allocation of federal resources and constraints on nonmedical services (e.g., homemaker, chore, and personal care). Despite the demand for aging network programs, the Administration on Aging (AoA) remains a relatively small federal government unit. Federal dollars for AoA programs have been essentially "flat" for over a decade. Many Area Agencies on Aging now turn to funding through other federal, state, and local appropriations. Funding constraints through the Social Services Block Grant and the Older Americans Act, along with changes in Medicare and Medicaid, have reduced overall access to long-term care, especially for low-income women and elders of color. The general approach under both programs is to give a few services to as many people as possible, which does not necessarily reach the most vulnerable older persons nor remove inequities.

PRIVATE INSURANCE

Although the U.S. health and long-term care system is based on the assumption that individuals are first responsible for paying for their care, 44 million Americans under age 65 lack insurance for hospital and physician costs. A substantially greater number—over 200 million—have no insurance for long-term care. Therefore, as noted earlier, about 30 percent of all long-term care expenditures are paid on an out-of-pocket basis (Feder et al., 1999). Those paying out of pocket use a combination of pension income, Social Security benefits, savings, and investments, including reverse mortgages which allow them to tap the equity in their homes to pay for care.

Among the older population, wide disparities exist in terms of their ability to purchase private supplemental and **long-term care insurance.** For older adults who can afford more extensive coverage than Medicare, private "medigap" supplemental insurance is available to pay for protection that Medicare does not cover. As noted above, these basic gaps are:

1. Medicare deductible and copayments
2. Items and services not covered by Medicare (prescription drugs and hearing aids)
3. Charges exceeding the amount approved by Medicare (in excess of Medicare's "allowable" or "reasonable" charges)

Despite the 1990 passage of the Medigap Fraud and Abuse Prevention Act, older people and their families need to be careful and explore options before purchasing Medicare supplemental insurance. About 75 percent of the older population has purchased some private supplemental insurance. Of these, about 50 percent were able to obtain coverage through their former place of employment (National Academy on Aging, 1997b; National Committee to Preserve Social Security

and Medicare, 1999). This translates into unequal access to private health insurance for higher-income elders or those who have access through employment/unions. Eleven percent of Medicare's recipients have neither assistance from Medicaid nor supplemental health coverage to help pay for Medicare's coinsurance, deductibles, and uncovered services. Not surprisingly, this group is more likely to have low incomes and/or to be in poor health (Rowland, Feder, and Keenan, 1998). Of poor or near-poor older persons, who suffer from more chronic illness and disability, only 47 percent have private insurance, compared to 87 percent of their higher-income and healthier peers. Less than 18 percent of older persons of color have private coverage, compared to 48 percent of poor older whites. Furthermore, older women are less likely than men to have access to group health insurance through employment (Moon, 1996).

Even those who carry supplemental coverage can suffer burdensome medical expenses if they are seriously ill, since Medicare does not cover the full costs of care. Few "medigap" policies pick up physician charges in excess of Medicare's allowable fees, nor do they ordinarily cover prescriptions in full, dental care, or nursing home care—all services essential to the long-term maintenance of the older population. In fact, less than 6 percent of the expenditures for nursing home care and home- and community-based services are paid by private insurance. Instead, nearly 37 percent of such expenditures are out of pocket. As a result, 36 percent of all older people admitted to nursing homes in 1995 incurred catastrophic financial expenses prior to admission (National Academy on Aging, 1997b).

As older adults become more aware of the limits of public funding, an increasing number of insurance companies are selling *private long-term care insurance plans.* Most policies are written to exclude people with certain conditions or illnesses and contain benefit restrictions that limit access to covered care. The period of coverage is usually only 4 or 5 years. The majority of policies pay a fixed amount for each qualified day in a nursing home (at a range of $40 to $120 a day). Home health and adult day-care services, which are often

---

FRAGMENTED SOURCES OF FUNDING FOR LONG-TERM CARE

- Public funding from health, mental health, social services, Social Security—often involving four to five state and federal agencies—which means lack of pooled funding streams

- Individuals and families
- Private insurers and managed care companies

---

preferred by older adults and their families, are usually reimbursed at 50 to 80 percent of the selected nursing home benefit. Indeed, high-quality policies cost as much as $2,500 annually when purchased at age 67 and $7,700 for those age 79. The high premiums and copayments mean that most policies are out of the financial reach of up to 20 percent of Americans age 55 to 79. The policies are expensive for two reasons: nine out of 10 are sold individually and therefore carry high administrative costs, and most are bought by older people whose risk of needing long-term care is great. Given these costs, only 10 to 20 percent of older people can afford private long-term care insurance. Among those policies purchased, it is estimated that 50 percent lapse due to high premiums (Driscoll, 1996; Wiener and Illston, 1996). As with health insurance, women are less likely than men to be able to afford long-term care insurance, and they spend a higher proportion of their income when they do, reflecting both gaps in coverage and their lower median income (Allen, 1993). People who are most likely to purchase and benefit from long-term care insurance are those with assets and

a spouse to protect. Those who are covered by private insurance form only about 1 percent of older individuals with chronic health care needs.

Resultant Inequities

Because public funding is biased toward institutional and acute care, and private policies are beyond the financial reach of most low-income elders, a *two-tier system of health care delivery* has resulted: one level for those with private health insurance or the means to pay for expensive medical treatment, and another for those forced to rely on Medicaid or Veterans' Assistance, or to do without health care altogether.

Even with Medicare recipients, there are disparities. Older people who have Medicare only, many of whom may be near-poor, tend to have fewer doctor visits and hospital stays, and buy fewer prescription medications than those who can afford cost-sharing provisions and other private insurance. In fact, low-income Medicare beneficiaries are nearly twice as likely to delay getting care than those with private or Medicaid coverage

---

OUT-OF-POCKET HEALTH EXPENDITURES BY SOCIOECONOMIC CLASS

- Fifty-four percent of the annual income of poor older Americans pays for fee-for-service health care.
- Forty-eight percent of the annual income of poor older Americans pays for Health Maintenance (HMOs).
- Eight percent of the annual income for those with Medicaid pays for health care.

- Poor older Americans spend 35 percent of their income on acute care compared to 10 percent of income for middle- and upper-class families (above 400 percent of poverty) (Rowland et al., 1998).

EXAMPLES OF OUTREACH TO UNDERSERVED MEDICARE BENEFICIARIES

- "Medicare University," funded by the National Asian Pacific Center on Aging, offers training workshops for providers and community leaders to update their knowledge of Medicare and other health benefits.
- "Help for Health" bilingual booklets are available in Chinese, Khmer, Korean, Samoan, Tagalog, Tongan, and Vietnamese and are funded by the Health Care Financing Administration (HCFA).
- These are bilingual Websites with information on Medicare and Medicaid.

- HCFA funds pamphlets on "Dual Eligible Buy-in Programs."
- "Voices of Minority Elderly" for consumers and advocates on Medicare and managed care issues is funded by the Kellogg Foundation.
- These publications can be obtained through the National Asian Pacific Center on Aging (see resources, Chapter 16).

(Khamvongsa, 2000).

---

to supplement Medicare (Rowland et al., 1998). Not surprisingly, the proportion of income spent on health care increases as income decreases.

These inequities are intensified for elders of color who tend to underutilize services that could enhance their health and quality of life. Even in programs designed for the poor, they are represented far less than their reported objective needs indicate (Mui and Burnette, 1994).

Medicaid, in particular, has been criticized for perpetuating class inequities. In fact, less than 50 percent of all poor Medicare beneficiaries benefit from Medicaid's financial protections (Rowland et al., 1998). Low participation levels in Medicaid are attributed to lack of awareness and understanding of the assistance provided by Medicaid, complex enrollment processes, limited outreach activities by federal and state governments, and reluctance to apply for help from a welfare-linked program. About 25 percent of physicians refuse to take Medicaid patients, especially those with a high level of need. This is because the reimbursement rates are generally below prevailing cost levels. Physicians who accept Medicaid patients typically limit them to 20 percent of their patient load. Since the number of Medicaid beds in nursing homes is limited, these patients must often wait longer for placement than do private-pay patients. Further, the homes available to them are frequently of lower quality. These burdens disproportionately fall on older women and ethnic minorities. As

stated earlier, these individuals must spend down their assets to be eligible for Medicaid. Older persons who have been private-pay patients in a nursing home may find that the facility will no longer accept them after they have "spent down." Moreover, some 40 percent of the older population have incomes that are too high to be eligible for Medicaid, yet they typically lack the resources to pay out of pocket for long-term care. Those who fall in this "Medicaid gap" frequently receive inadequate care or must depend on families (Wiener, Illston, and Hanley, 1994). In fact, results from a 1995 national survey indicate that nearly 20 percent of home-dwelling older people with long-term care needs reported that they need help, or more help, with ADLs and IADLs. They found services too expensive, had difficulty locating help, or were ineligible for assistance because of income or medical eligibility criteria. Such reported unmet needs were disproportionately high among the severely impaired, those living alone, and the poor or near-poor (Feder et al., 1999). Fortunately, long-term care providers are now recognizing the need for targeted outreach to underserved populations.

HEALTH AND LONG-TERM CARE REFORMS

Given these gaps, national reform in health and long-term care is widely debated. Such debates are

HISTORY AND STATUS OF LONG-TERM CARE LEGISLATION AT THE NATIONAL

LEVEL

- **1988:** The first comprehensive long-term care legislation was introduced by the late Florida Representative Claude Pepper, who linked an initiative to fund long-term care in the home to the ill-fated catastrophic health care legislation.
- **1990:** The Pepper Commission recommended public funding of home, community, and nursing home care for seriously disabled Americans.
- **1992:** The Democratic leadership in the House and the Senate introduced bills for long-term care known as the Long Term Care Family Security Act.

- **1992:** Bill Clinton was the first presidential candidate to call for expanded public funding for home care services provided on a non–means-tested basis.
- **1990–94:** The National Committee to Preserve Social Security and Medicare and the Leadership Council of Aging Organizations proposed universal and comprehensive long-term care plans for all people with disabilities; this encompassed institutional, home- and community-based care, and personal assistance.
- **1993:** President Clinton's National Health Security Act offered new long-term care benefits and set forth the principles of universal access,

often polarized between those advocating private-sector strategies and those who look to the public sector or some combination of public and private coverage. In some respects, the debates are not new, but rather more visible. In fact, since 1912, there have been efforts to create a program of access to health care for all Americans. In 1986, Wilbur Cohen, assistant secretary of Health, Education, and Welfare, noted that major social legislation occurs in 30-year intervals, with Social Security (1935) followed by Medicare and Medicaid (1965) and national health care reform embracing universal coverage and continuity of care in 1995 (Brody, 1994). Yet the United States and South Africa remain the only industrialized nations that do not provide some form of universal health coverage, regardless of ability to pay. After the 1992 federal elections, health care reform moved from academic debates to the legislative process, but ended in gridlock, without even modest changes in insurance industry practices. In spite of escalating costs, growing numbers of uninsured citizens, and restrictive insurance policies, attempts to change the health care system clash over the goals of cost containment versus guaranteeing access to all. Although the majority of Americans support health care reform in the abstract and believe that government should guarantee adequate health care for

all, they are generally satisfied with their own care. Their ambivalence is expressed further by their unwillingness to accept government interference and any restriction of their own choice of doctors or hospitals, even if doing so would reduce health care costs or make universal coverage possible (Zis, Jacobs, and Shapiro., 1996).

What ultimately killed national health care reform was the disproportionate influence of powerful special-interest lobbies, particularly insurance companies and small businesses that sought to protect their financial interests and ways of doing business. Resistance to large-scale change in the health care system has grown since the Republican sweep in the November 1994 federal elections. Today, for all intents and purposes, fundamental health care reform at the national level is a "dead" issue. Nevertheless, the growing alliance between senior organizations, such as AARP, and groups serving other populations has been a positive development in the long-term care arena, despite the present lack of a successful outcome.

Although major changes in long-term care have been stalled at the national level, most states have moved to plan, finance, and implement their own long-term care packages. They often did so to overcome the bias in federal funding toward institutional care, to contain costs, and to address the

---

HOW SOME OTHER COUNTRIES APPROACH LONG-TERM CARE

- **Japan:** Public Long Term Care Insurance Act: universality of coverage, freedom of choice, reliance on a service market, and availability of comprehensive care
- **Germany:** Universal long-term care insurance, with focus on home care services

- **Great Britain:** Royal Commission on Long Term Care, proposed reforms of long-term care are currently debated (Cuellar and Wiener, 1999; Davey, 1999, Stone, 1999).

---

growing numbers of individuals who lack access to adequate care. In addition, states such as Washington and Oregon are dramatically restructuring their long-term care delivery system, usually through consolidation of financing and delivery systems into more streamlined, coordinated, and efficient administrative structures (Burwell et al., 1996). At the same time, the market has moved more quickly to achieve the goals of competitiveness and reduced costs, largely through managed health care (HMOs or PPOs) that provides an established package of services for enrollees for a single monthly capitated (limited) rate.

Health Maintenance Organizations (HMOs)

As noted earlier, the 1997 Balanced Budget Act created, under Medicare Choice, managed care options for older people. Medicare managed care refers to a health plan option in which Medicare beneficiaries receive care from a network of providers employed by or under contract to an HMO. Under HMOs, coverage of health care costs and delivery of health care are provided through a prepaid premium. This means that a single payment per user covers all services, rather than fee for service. Because consumers pay on a capitated basis, HMOs overcome the access barriers of fragmented funding from the consumer's perspective for packaged services. As private plans, Medicare HMOs offer services such as prevention, education, eye glasses, hearing aids, and prescription drug coverage—in addition to a traditional Medicare benefits package. Most plans offer these benefits for no additional

premiums and limit cost sharing. Financial incentives encourage providers to be efficient in getting the necessary services to patients. As a result, HMOs have typically served primarily younger, healthier populations because of the presumed higher costs associated with older patients. Less than 20 percent of Medicare recipients today are enrolled in HMOs or a similar type of managed care plan.

Many HMOs offer consumers lower costs and broader coverage (e.g., some preventive services and prescription drug coverage) than Medicare, or private medigap policies (Quinn, 2000). Not surprisingly, enrollment in HMOs is highest among those who are near-poor or have modest incomes. This pattern reflects the financial incentives and protection to join HMOs for expanded coverage and to avoid rapidly rising medigap premiums. It also reflects the lack of Medicaid coverage for many above the poverty level (Rowland et al., 1998). While they may have been able to negotiate lower prices from health providers, HMOs take on the risk of providing the full range of Medicare-covered services in return for a fixed payment that approximates 95 percent of the costs for similar enrollees in fee-for-service systems.

Because HMOs are a capitated system and thus charge a fixed payment per beneficiary, costs to Medicare are presumed to be more predictable. Findings are mixed on whether Medicare expenditures are decreased under HMOs. After controlling for factors such as health status, some studies find that the costs to Medicare associated with HMO enrollment are actually *higher* than through Medicare per se. This is because Medicare only "saves" 5 percent on each HMO participant, since the capitated rate is set at 95 percent of the expected expenditure level (Driscoll, 1996; Moon, 1996). HMO Medicare enrollment is associated with reduced health care utilization (e.g., hospital length of stay), but this may result from HMO beneficiaries being healthier than the average older adult. This means HMOs may selectively attract and contract with enrollees who are healthier than average, or have fewer propensities to use health services, and thus lower than expected costs. As a result, they may skim off enrollees who would never have cost Medicare the estimated expenditure level even if they had remained in the regular fee-for-service part of Medicare. When this occurs, Medicare is not saving dollars under the HMO program (Baker, 2000; Newhouse, Buntin, and Chapman, 1997). Thus, it is increasingly apparent that managed care does not necessarily deliver promised cost savings nor reduce the regulatory burden on government (Oberlander, 1997). Greater administrative costs (e.g., 15 percent to marketing, billing, debt collection, and close evaluation of medical treatments compared to Medicare's overhead costs of 2 percent) and federal payments to providers that do not cover the costs of care have resulted in thin profits for many Medicare HMOs. In an effort to recruit members to HMOs in the 1980s, many offered zero premiums and free pharmaceutical benefits, which they now are unable to sustain. With declining profits, most HMOs have reduced benefits, such as prescription drug coverage; increased premiums and copayments; and, in growing instances, dropped out of Medicare (Stone, 2000). They contend this is necessary because the federal government is not paying enough to reimburse the cost of care. As a result, approximately 10 percent of Medicare managed care beneficiaries have been forced to return to traditional fee-for-service Medicare, even though many cannot afford the high premiums and prescription drug costs associated with the traditional plan (National Committee to Preserve Social Security and Medicare, 1999). These closures have made many older adults wary of HMOs, especially if they do not realize that they remain covered by Medicare regardless of their use of HMOs versus fee-for-service health providers.

A greater concern is that chronically ill elders may be denied benefits and access to care (Dallek, 1998; Stone and Niefeld, 1998). Some studies identify reduced HMO use and worse outcomes for older people with chronic disabilities and for poor patients treated in HMOs (Miller and Luft, 1997; Newcomer, Manton, Harrington, Yordi and Vertees, 1995; Rowland et al., 1998; Ware, 1996). For example, those receiving managed care are less likely to receive home health care and, following a stroke, more likely to be treated in nursing homes than rehabilitation facilities (Retchin, 1997). While the effects on quality of care are unclear, critics fear that incentives are greater to reduce costs than to improve quality (Escarce, Shea, and Chen, 1997; Miller and Luft, 1997). Consumers in HMOs are also less satisfied with their care than those utilizing the fee-for-service system. But these same people are more satisfied with their out-of-pocket expenses being reduced by their HMO membership. Given mixed findings about costs and outcomes, older people may be confused by increased options (Gage, 1998; Nichols, 1998). AARP and other consumer advocacy groups are working to ensure through disclosure requirements and ratings of HMO services that older adults are accurately informed about the benefits and the quality of care through HMOs. Congressional members have pushed for better and more accessible information available through plans and access to emergency services and specialty care. Means of dispute resolution to redress grievances and quality concerns, as well as to be fair, timely, consistent, accessible, and easily understood, are also needed (Rowland et al., 1998; Karp and Wood, 1998).

If Medicare managed care continues, it will undoubtedly cost more to consumers, offer fewer benefits, and require a substantial cash infusion from the federal government. This means that older adults need to be better informed about managed care options. The ability of HMOs or other managed care systems to control health costs is limited by the development of medical technology that continues to drive cost and by consumers' expectations for immediate access to all types of care. It is becoming increasingly clear that managed care, per se, is unlikely to obviate the need for other strong policy measures to solve the long-term costs of health care.

Approximately ten states allow, through waivers, low-income Medicare beneficiaries with supplemental Medicaid coverage to be enrolled in Medicaid managed care while remaining in fee-for-service Medicare services. If low-income beneficiaries are locked into a restricted set of providers, they lose their Medicare rights to choose their providers and may receive inadequate care. Government oversight is critical to assuring both fiscal accountability and other consumer protections.

Social Health Maintenance Organizations (SHMOs) and Other Model Innovative Programs

Because of growing awareness of the inadequacies of the current system, there is increasing policy interest in bringing the acute-care and long-term care sectors together into a single integrated system. Some of the best known of these initiatives are **Social Health Maintenance Organizations (SHMOs),** On Lok, and The Program for All-inclusive Care for the Elderly (PACE). SHMOs are demonstration projects initiated in 1985 by the Health Care Financing Administration (HCFA). As prepaid health plans, they try to integrate acute and long-term care to voluntarily enrolled Medicare beneficiaries. They offer all Medicare benefits, as well as home- and community-based care, prescription drugs, and case management to prevent nursing home placement. SHMOs test whether comprehensive health services, linking acute and chronic care under an integrated financing scheme within a managed care setting, can be provided at a cost that does not exceed the public costs of Medicare and Medicaid and can reduce nursing home placement (Aaronson, 1996). In other words, they are examining the relative cost-effectiveness of a capitated payment system that includes chronic and extended benefits and medical services. Concerns are raised, however, about the quality of care of SHMOs, the lack of

real coordination between acute and long-term care providers, and whether mortality rates are higher among SHMO patients (Wiener, 1996). Some studies suggest that service integration may be more idealistic than realistic, especially if a capitated system (a single payment per user to control all services) is used to contain costs (Feder et al., 1999). SHMOs are characterized by:

- A single organizational structure provides a full range of acute and long-term care services to voluntarily enrolled Medicare beneficiaries.
- Long-term care services for members who meet disability criteria are authorized by a coordinated case management system.
- They are designed to reach a cross-section of older people, including both functionally impaired and those without impairments. They thus try to spread the risk of service use over a representative population (5,000 to 10,000 at each site).
- Financing is through prepaid capitation by pooling funds from Medicare, Medicaid, and member premiums.

The Health Care Financing Administration (HCFA) is funding a second generation of SHMOs that will set reimbursement rates based on an individual's impairment and illness profile at the time of enrollment and annually thereafter. By establishing geriatric health programs for all enrollees, HCFA aims to better coordinate acute care with a set of flexible, user-friendly and efficient long-term care services (Stone, 1999). Early findings suggest that integrated home care based on comprehensive geriatric assessment and case management can reduce the number of hospitalizations as well as hospital costs (Landi, Gambassi, Pola, Tabaccanti, Cavinato, Carbonin, and Bernabei, 1999).

Another model tested in a wide range of communities is San Francisco's On Lok model of social care. **On Lok** aims to integrate a full continuum of acute and chronic care into one agency, and thus to prevent institutionalization of frail elders who are certified as needing a nursing home level of care. As a capitated system, On Lok is paid a flat

---

CHARACTERISTICS OF INTEGRATED SERVICES

- Broad, flexible benefits (primary, acute, and long-term care)
- Far-reaching delivery systems that encompass community-based long-term care, care management, and specialty providers
- Mechanisms that coordinate various services, such as care management and care planning protocols, interdisciplinary care teams, centralized records, and integrated information systems

- Overarching quality control and management information systems with a single point of accountability
- Flexible funding that enables pooling of funds and has incentives to integrate funding streams and minimize cost shifting (Booth, Fralich, Saucie, and Mollica, 1997).

---

amount for each person served, similar to the way that HMOs are paid. A comprehensive day health program is integrated with home care, including nursing, social work, meals, transportation, personal care, homemaker, and respite care. The On Lok model is effective at serving low-income and elders of color in their communities and is widely replicated to varying degrees nationwide.

The **Program for the All-inclusive Care for the Elderly (PACE)** is funded by HCFA as a 15-site federal demonstration project that aims to replicate the On Lok model. It differs from SHMOs by its focus on only a relatively small number of frail elders (120–300 per site) who are eligible for nursing home placement. It is a publicly funded approach to long-term care for frail elders who are eligible for Medicaid and nursing home certifiable. It aims to keep individuals in community care and out of nursing homes by "one-door access" to a comprehensive care package of preventive, acute, and long-term care services. Interdisciplinary teams of physicians, nurses, social workers, aides, therapists and even van drivers coordinate their care through adult day health centers and case management at predetermined reimbursement rates. In effect, PACE is built around the day health model, which combines primary care with long-term care. The 1997 Balanced Budget Amendment made PACE a permanent Medicare provider. To date, evaluations of both On Lok and PACE reveal cost savings to Medicare and Medicaid, as well as some success in integrating the delivery of acute and long-term care

(Stone, 1999). Because these programs rely upon voluntary enrollment, reaching persons with the most limitations in ADLs is difficult (Wiener, 1996). Nevertheless, such model programs that aim to control costs and integrate services need to be expanded to a larger population.

Unfortunately, a wide range of barriers make service integration difficult to achieve:

- lack of a national policy or program on long-term care; responsibility left to individuals
- fragmentation of funding sources, especially Medicare and Medicaid
- different eligibility requirements and coverage rules that impede the development of a rational plan of care
- fear of financial risk on the part of providers involved in integrating acute and long-term care
- lack of training and knowledge among providers on how to coordinate and manage an array of services
- lack of communication between acute and long-term care providers
- no recognized authority for managing care across time, place, and profession
- absence of management information systems and patient data bases that span time and place

States are also attempting to integrate acute and long-term care, especially for the population that is "dual eligible" for both Medicare and Medi-

---

AN EXAMPLE OF PROVIDERS' INTEGRATED CARE PLANS

The National Chronic Care Consortium (NCCC) is an alliance of over 30 nonprofit health systems that share a vision of integrated care. Member organizations serve as laboratories for establishing chronic-care networks. It advocates the creation of integrated administration, information, financing, and care man-agement arrangements to help providers work to-gether to minimize costs while maximizing long-term health of the populations being served. It has developed the Self-Assessment for Systems Integration, funded by the John A. Hartford Foundation, that identifies nine key objectives for chronic care integration.

---

caid. Some are experimenting with innovative financing and service delivery of acute and long-term care for older people on Medicaid and younger people with disabilities. However, gaps in care are unlikely to be filled by the states' share of Medicaid and by programs funded entirely by states (Stone, 2000). In addition, some providers are attempting to create integrated service systems, in part for altruistic reasons and in part for market incentives. Hospitals are integrating vertically—buying nursing homes, rehabilitation centers, and home health agencies—in an effort to become an all-purpose provider in the community. Skilled nursing facilities and, to some extent, home health agencies are integrating horizontally—building alliances with hospitals, physicians groups, assisted living developers, and other community-based providers.

A promising direction is the growth of consumer-directed care, where persons with long-term care needs take an active part in choosing their care. Consumer direction emphasizes privacy, autonomy, and the right "to manage one's own risk." It is seen as a way to level the playing field between institutional- and home- and community-based care, and has been found to increase service satisfaction, feelings of empowerment, and perceived quality of life among older participants who are or have disabilities. Nevertheless, some people have raised questions about the ethics of this approach to long-term care. Examples of consumer-directed care are shown in the box below.

Agreement is emerging about the major components of an ideal long-term care system, but there is not the national political will to achieve it. These components include:

- integrated acute and long-term care
- easy access at a single point of entry
- case or care management
- uniform client needs assessment
- home- and community-based care
- nonmedical social services
- supportive housing

The rapid changes in health and long-term care make predictions about future directions difficult.

CONSUMER-DIRECTED CARE

- In-Home Supportive Services Program, funded by Medicaid, where participants hire and fire their own workers through a state registry of home care workers; can also hire their family caregivers.
- At least 35 states provide some type of financial payment to relatives and other informal caregivers: wage and allowance programs.
- State Medicaid waivers to "cash out" home- and community-based care benefits for consumers to use to purchase services directly.

ETHICAL ISSUES SURROUNDING CONSUMER DIRECTION

- The balance between autonomy and safety
- Potential exploitation of personal care workers
- The appropriateness of this option for cognitively impaired older adults

- The potential for fraud or abuse by family members (Stone, 1999)

What other ethical conflicts can you envision?

Clearly, health care has shifted from a system oriented toward acute care, independent providers, and fee-for-service insurance to one that is focused on chronic care, disability prevention, and managed care. Because of market changes and the growth of managed care, these patterns of consolidation and cost savings will continue at the local level. This will occur even without the passage of national legislation to ensure health and long-term care as a right, regardless of income or age. As noted earlier, the current dichotomy between long-term care and acute care is not functional for either older persons or care providers, since long-term care is a health crisis for which virtually every American is uninsured. From the perspective of older people, an ideal is a national health plan that integrates preventive, acute, hospital, ambulatory, community-based, and home care to ensure continuity of care across the life span. In the short run, however, legislation at the federal level will be focused on ways to reduce Medicare and Medicaid expenditures, on delegating more financing responsibility to the state level, and on funding demonstrations that attempt to integrate acute and long-term care.

Workforce Shortages

A component often overlooked in efforts to reform long-term care is the shortage of paraprofessional workers—certified nursing aides in nursing homes and home care aides. This shortage has intensified in the booming economic conditions of the late 1990s and tight job market where nursing homes and home care agencies compete with fast-food restaurants that pay higher wages and offer better benefits (Stone, 1999). Paraprofessionals are not only poorly paid, but they also face other unattractive job characteristics: heavy workloads, lack of benefits, limited career advancement, inadequate training, high potential for injury (back injuries from inappropriate lifting and transferring), and exposure to high emotional stress. Such stress includes abuse by cognitively impaired clients and racial tensions between white care recipients and aides who are people of color or foreign-born. For example, in urban areas, a growing proportion are recent immigrants whose language and customs differ from those of the frail elders for whom they provide care, a pattern that can lead to misunderstandings and conflicts. Not surprisingly, annual turnover exceeds that of other types of employees in the service industry, reaching as high as 100 percent in some nursing homes and home health agencies. In fact, Stone (2000) contends that the lack of a well-trained, well-qualified workforce for long-term care is an even greater challenge to ensuring quality care than are financing and delivery problems. The problem will be intensified by the increased educational status of women, which provides them with access to better jobs, and the tightening of federal policies to limit immigration. Incentives are needed to recruit and retain paraprofessional workers in long-term care, as well as to develop alternative labor pools, such as retired men and women, former welfare recipients and employees of temporary agencies. Some long-term care facilities have begun to advertise for employees in the Philippines and other countries where people with health care experience are available and unemployment is high. Legislation has been introduced in Congress to increase staffing and training levels in nursing homes, establish minimum staffing requirements for homes, and require facilities to post the number of health care personnel serving patients. However, such legislation fails to address the underlying problem of the declining pool of paraprofessional workers and the overall negative work environment in many homes.

SUMMARY AND IMPLICATIONS

The growing health and long-term care expenditures by both federal and state governments and by older people and their families are a source of concern for most Americans. Escalating hospital and physician costs have placed enormous pressures on Medicare—the financing mechanism through which almost half of the funds for the older population's acute care flows. The government's primary response to these Medicare costs has been cost-containment, especially through diagnostic-related groupings (DRGs), financial incentives for shortening the hospital stays of Medicare patients, greater deductibles and copayments, and cuts in Medicare funding. Efforts have also been made to provide more choices for Medicare recipients, including managed care or HMO options. For most older adults, Medicare fails to provide adequate protection against the costs of home- and community-based care. In fact, changes in Medicare funding have affected the availability of nonprofit home care agencies. They have also meant that more older persons and their families have either had to pay privately for home care or do without. As the fastest-growing portion of the federal budget, Medicare is under intense scrutiny.

Medicare is the major payment source of hospital and physician care for older adults, but it is almost absent from nursing home financing. The reverse applies to Medicaid, however. The largest portion of the Medicaid dollar goes to services needed by older persons, but not covered by Medicare—nursing home, home and personal care, and prescription drugs. However, as Medicaid has been increasingly subject to cost-cutting measures at the state level, benefits have been reduced. For example, copayments for health care services have increased as a way to reduce Medicaid spending, but this cost is borne disproportionately by low-income elders. Another disadvantage for Medicaid recipients is that most nursing homes and doctors limit the number of Medicaid recipients they will accept. Although waivers by the federal government have allowed state funding of some community-based alternatives to institutionalization, Medicaid remains biased toward nursing home care. Other federal programs that fund community-based services are relatively limited in terms of the numbers of older people reached. Given the gaps in public funding for long-term care, private insurers are offering long-term care insurance options, but these are beyond the financial reach of most older adults and fail to provide comprehensive home-care benefits.

Although concern about the costs and gaps in public funding is widespread, there is little agreement about potential solutions. The critical policy question is thus how care will be provided and funded. Since 1992, there has been increased visibility and legislative debate about health care reform, although most proposals have been oriented to acute care and not toward the greatest need of the older population for long-term care. Currently, the prospects for a comprehensive health and long-term care reform bill that guarantees universal access along with cost containment are virtually nil. Instead, many states, hospitals, and agencies have moved ahead with reforms that seek to integrate acute and chronic care and to reduce costs through managed care models. At the federal level, the emphasis in the near future will be on cutting Medicare and Medicaid deficits and on incremental insurance reforms. However, as illustrated in earlier chapters, long-term care reform in the next decade will become an issue that Congress and the president cannot ignore. This is the case because of the senior boomers and the continued growth of other vulnerable populations, such as older adults with developmental disabilities and chronic mental illness. Given the magnitude of both the need and the potential changes, it is not surprising that no other part of the health care system generates as much passionate debate as does long-term care. How to meet the needs of growing populations with chronic disabilities will require creative solutions that integrate acute and long-term care. What is less clear is the balance that will be achieved between public and private financing for future solutions and how the shortage of paraprofessional workers will be addressed.

GLOSSARY

capitated payments   payments for services based on a predetermined amount per person per day rather than fees for services

Health Care Financing Administration   the federal agency that administers the Medicare and Medicaid programs

Health Maintenance Organizations (HMOs)   health plans that combine coverage of health care costs and delivery of health care for a prepaid premium, with members typically receiving services from personnel employed by or under contract to the HMO

long-term care insurance   private insurance designed to cover the costs of institutional and sometimes home-based service for people with chronic disabilities

managed care   policies under which patients are provided health care services under the supervision of a single professional, usually a physician

Medicaid   a U.S. federal and state means-tested welfare program of medical assistance for the categorically needy, regardless of age

medical savings accounts   proposed Medicare program that will allow beneficiaries to carry private "catastrophic" insurance for serious illness and pay routine costs from a special account

Medicare   the social insurance program, part of the Social Security Act of 1965, intended to provide financial protection against the cost of hospital and physician care for people age 65 and over

Medicare Choice   starting in 2002, Medicare beneficiaries would choose between traditional Medicare and a Choice Plan that includes HMOs

On Lok   a comprehensive program of health and social services provided to very frail older adults, first started in San Francisco, with the goal of preventing or delaying institutionalization by maintaining these adults in their homes

PACE   federal demonstration program that replicated On Lok's integrated services to attempt to prevent institutionalization

Preferred Provider Organizations (PPOs)   networks of independent physicians, hospitals, and other health care providers who contract with an insurance entity to provide care at discount rates

prospective-payment system (PPS)   a system of reimbursing hospitals and physicians based on the diagnostic category of the patient rather than fees for each service provided, as applied to inpatient services

Social Health Maintenance Organizations (SHMOs)   prepaid health plans that provide both acute and long-term care to voluntarily enrolled Medicare beneficiaries

spend down   to use up assets for personal needs, especially health care, in order to become qualified for Medicaid

subacute care   intensive health services to patients after a hospital stay

RESOURCES

See the companion Website for this text at <www.ablongman.com/hooyman> for information about the following:

- American Health Care Association
- American Medical Directors Association
- American Physical and Occupational Therapy Association. (Section on Geriatrics)
- American Society for Long Term Care Nurses
- Families USA
- Medical Matrix: Geriatrics
- Medicare
- National Association for Home Care (NAHC)
- National Association of Directors of Nursing in Long Term Care (NADONAILTC)
- National Association of Professional Geriatric Care Managers
- National Association of Residential Care Facilities (NARCF)
- National Citizen's Coalition for Nursing Home Reform (NCCNHR)

REFERENCES

Aaronson, W. Financing the continuum of care: A disintegrating past and an integrating future. In C. J. Evashwick (Ed.), *The continuum of long-term care:*

An integrated systems approach. Albany, NY: Delmar Publishers, 1996.

Abramson, K. B. Understanding the world of managed care: Opportunities and obstacles for rehabilitation teams. *Topics in Stroke Rehabilitation*, 1998, *5*, 1–10.

Administration on Aging. *Profile of older Americans: 1999*. Washington, DC: Administration on Aging, 1999.

Allen, J. Caring, work and gender: Equity in an aging society. In J. Allen and A. Pifer (Eds.), *Women on the front lines: Meeting the challenge of an aging America*. Washington, DC: The Urban Institute Press, 1993.

Baker, L. C. Association of managed care market share and health expenditures for fee-for-service Medicare patients. *Journal of the American Medical Association*, 1999, *281*, 432–437.

Berenson, R., The doctor's dilemma revisited: Ethical decisions in a managed care environment. *Generations*, Summer 1998, 63–68.

Bergthold, L., Estes, C., and Villanueva, A. Public light and private dark: The privatization of home health services for the elderly in the U.S. *Home Health Care Services Quarterly*, 1990, *11*, 7–33.

Bernstein, J. *Restructuring Medicare: Values and policy options*. Washington, DC: National Academy of Social Insurance, 1997.

Blanchette, P. L. Age-based rationing of health care. *Generations*, Winter 1996–97, *20*, 60–65.

Booth, M., Fralich, J., Saucie, P., and Mollica, R. *Integration of acute and long-term care for dually eligible beneficiaries through managed care*. Robert Wood Johnson Foundation Medicare/Medicaid Integration Program, 1997.

Brody, S. A responsible geezer's analysis of the Clinton health proposal. *The Gerontologist*, 1994, *34*, 586–589.

Bryce, D. V., and Friedland, R. B. *Economic and health security: An overview of the origins of federal legislation*. Washington, DC: The National Academy on Aging, January 16, 1997.

Burwell, B., Crown, W. H., O'Shaugnessy, C., and Price, R. Financing long-term care. In C. J. Evashwick (Ed.), *The continuum of long-term care: An integrated systems approach*. Albany, NY: Delmar Publishers, 1996.

Coleman, B. *New directions for state long-term care systems. Volume I: Overview*. Washington, DC: AARP, Public Policy Institute, 1996.

Coleman, B. *New directions for state long-term care systems. Volume IV: Limiting state Medicaid spending on nursing home care*. Washington, DC: AARP, Public Policy Institute, April 1997.

Cuellar, A. E., and Wiener, J. M. Implementing universal long-term care insurance in Germany. Washington, DC: The National Academy on Aging, Gerontological Society of America, Fall 1999, *10*, 1–12.

Dallek, G. Shopping for managed care: The Medicare market, *Generations*, Summer 1998, *22*, 19–23

Davey, A. *With respect to old age—Findings of the Royal Commission on Long-term Care in the United Kingdom*, Washington, DC: National Academy on an Aging Society, Gerontological Society of America, Fall 1999, *10*, 5–7.

Driscoll, L. *The Medicare program*. Washington, DC: AARP, Public Policy Institute, 1996.

Eng, C., Pedullo, J., Eleazer, G. P., McCann, R., and Fox, N. Program of all-inclusive care for the elderly (PACE): An innovative model of integrated geriatric care and financing. *Journal of the American Geriatrics Society*, 1997, *45*, 223–232.

Escarce, J. J., Shea J. A., and Chen, W. Segmentation of hospital markets: Where do HMO enrollees get care? *Health Affairs*, 1997, *16*, 181–192.

Evashwick, C. J. (Ed.), *The continuum of long-term care: An integrated systems approach*. 2nd ed. Albany, NY: Delmar Publishers, 2001.

Feder, J., Kolmisar, H. L., and Neifeld, M. *Long-term care in the United States: An overview*. Commonwealth Fund International Symposium on Health Care Policy, October 1999, Washington, DC.

Feder, J., and Moon, M. Managed care for the elderly: A threat or a promise? *Generations*, Summer 1998, 6–10.

Gage, B. The history and growth of Medicare managed care. *Generations*, Summer 1998, 11–18.

Gage, B. Medicare home health: An update. *The Public Policy and Aging Report*, 1998, Vol. 9, 12–15.

Gage, B., Moon, M., and Nichols, L. *Medicare Savings: Options and Opportunities*. Washington, DC.: Urban Institute, 1997.

Gaumer, G. L., Poggio, E. L., Coelen, C. G., Sennett, C. S., and Schmitz, R. J. Effects of state prospective reimbursement programs on hospital mortality. *Medical Care*, 1989, *27*, 724–736.

Graves, N. R. *Long-term care*. Washington, DC: AARP, Public Policy Institute, 1997.

Hing, E. Effects of the prospective payment systems on nursing homes. *Vital health statistics*. Hyattsville, MD: National Center for Health Statistics, 1989.

Hughes, S. Home health. In C. J. Evashwick (Ed.), *The Continuum of long-term care. An integrated systems approach*. Albany, NY: Delmar Publishers, 1996.

Hughes, S. C., Ulasevich, A., Weaver, F., Henderson, W., Manheim, L., Kubal, J., and Bonango, F. Impact of home care on hospital days: A meta analysis. *Health Services Research*, 1997, *32*, 416–431.

Kane, R. A. Kane, R. L. and Ladd, R. C. *The heart of long-term care*. New York: Oxford University Press, 1998.

Kane, R. C., and Kane, R. A. Health care for older people: Organizational and policy issues. In R. Binstock and L. K. George (Eds.), *Aging and the social sciences* (3rd ed.). New York: Academic Press, 1990.

Karp, N., and Wood, E. Resolving managed care consumer disputes: Where do we stand? *Generations*, 1998, *22*, 79–81.

Khamvongsa, C. Translated Help for Health books reach thousands. *Asian Pacific Affairs Newsletter*, National Asian Pacific Center on Aging, February 2000, *1*, 10.

Komisar. H. L., and Feder, J. *The Balanced Budget Act of 1997: Effects on Medicare's home health benefit and beneficiaries who need long-term care*. New York: The Commonwealth Fund, 1998.

Komisar, H. L., and Feder, J. *Medicare Chart Book*, Washington, DC.: Institute for Health Care Research and Policy, 1997.

Landi, F., Gambassi, G., Pola, R.,, Tabaccanti, S., Cavinato, T., Carbonin, P., and Bernabei, R. Impact of integrated home care services on hospital use. *Journal of the American Geriatrics Society*, 1999, *47*, 1430–1434.

The Lewin Group. *Implications of the Medicare Home Health Interim Payment System of the 1997 Balanced Budget Act*. Washington, DC.: National Association for Home Care, 1998.

Lyons, B., and Rowland, F. Medicare, Medicaid, and the elderly poor. *Health Care Financing Review*, 1996, Vol. 18, 61–85.

Miller, R., and Luft, H. Managed Care Plan Performance Since 1980: A Literature Analysis. *Journal of the American Medical Association*, 1997, *271*, 1512–1519.

Miller, R., and Luft, H. Managed care performance: Is quality of care better or worse? *Health Affairs*, 1997, *16*, 7–25.

Moon, M. *Medicare now and in the future* (2nd ed.). Washington, DC: The Urban Institute Press, 1996.

Moses, S. A. Long-term care choice: A simple, cost-free solution to the long-term care financing puzzle. *The Public Policy and Aging Report*. Washington, DC: National Academy on an Aging Society, Gerontological Society of America, 1998.

Mui, A. D. and Burnette, D. Long-term care service use by frail elders: Is ethnicity a factor? *The Gerontologist*, 1994, Vol. 34, 190–198.

National Academy on Aging. *Facts on long-term care*. Washington, DC: The National Academy on Aging, 1997a.

National Academy on Aging. *Facts on Medicare: Hospital insurance and supplementary medical insurance*. Washington, DC: The National Academy on Aging, 1997b.

National Committee to Preserve Social Security and Medicine. *Medicare Managed Care*, Washington, DC: 1999.

National Committee to Preserve Social Security and Medicare. *Passages: Planning for long-term care*. Washington, DC, February 2000.

Newcomer, R., Manton, K., Harrington, C., Yordi, C., and Vertees, J. Case mis controlled service use and expenditures in the social/health maintenance organization demonstration. *Journals of Gerontology*, 1995, *50A*, M35–M44.

Newhouse, J. P., Buntin, M. B., and Chapman, J. D. Risk adjustment and Medicare: Taking a closer look. *Health*, 1997, *16*, 26–43.

Nichols, L. M. Building a marketplace for elderly consumers. *Generations*, Summer 1998, *22*, 31–36.

Oberlander, J. Managed care and Medicare reform, *Journal of Health Politics, Policy and Law*, 1997, *22*, 595–631.

Ostrom, C. M. Lower drug prices in Canada a prescription for outrage in U.S., *The Seattle Times*, September 5, 2000, *1*, A12.

Pear, R. Medicare-paid home health care rife with fraud, investigation finds. *The Seattle Times*, July 27, 1997, *1*, A18.

Quinn, J. B. What Medicare really needs, *Newsweek*, September 2000, 36.

Retchin, S. Outcomes of stroke patients in medicare fee for service and managed care. *Journal of the American Medical Association*, 1997, *278*, 119–124.

Riley, T., and Mollica, R. L. *The impact of health reform on vulnerable adults: Volume II. An analysis of national health reform proposals*. Waltham, MA: Brandeis University, Center for Vulnerable Populations, 1994.

Rosenblatt, R. A. Medicare: "Savings," "Choices," and worries. *Aging Today*, Sept/Oct 1997, *XVIII*, 1–2.

Rowland, D., Feder, J., and Keenan, P. S. Managed care for low-income elderly people. In managed care and older people: Issues and experience, *Generations*, Summer 1998, 43–50.

Sager, M. A., Easterling, D. U., Kindig, D. A., and Anderson, O. W. Changes in the location of death after passage of Medicare's prospective payment system. *New England Journal of Medicine*, 1989, *320*, 433–439.

Samuelson, R. J. It's more than a drug problem. *Newsweek*, September 2000, 37.

Schlenker, R. *Home health payment legislation: Review and recommendations*. Washington, DC: AARP, Public Policy Institute, 1996.

Smolka, G. *Medicare Hospital Insurance (HI) Trust Fund: The trustees' 1997 annual report*. Washington, DC: AARP, Public Policy Institute, 1997.

Stewart, S., Pearson, S., Luke, C. G., and Horowitz, J. D. Effects of home-based intervention on unplanned readmissions and out-of-hospital deaths. *Journal of the American Geriatrics Society*, 1998 February, *46*, 174–180.

Stone, R. I. *Long-term care for the elderly with disabilities: Current policy, emerging trends and implications for the twenty-first century*. New York: The Milbank Memorial Fund, 2000.

Stone, R. I. *Long-term care in Japan: A window on the future?* Washington, DC: National Academy on Aging, Gerontological Society of American, Fall 1999, *10*, 1–3.

Stone, R. L., and Niefeld, M. R. Medicare managed care: Sinking or swimming with the tide. *Journal of Long-term Home Health Care*, 1998, *17, 1*, 7–16.

Temkin-Greener, H., and Meiners, M. Transitions in long-term care. *The Gerontologist*, 1995, *35*, 196–206.

Vladeck, B. Overview: The case for integration. Conference Proceedings, *Integrating acute and long-term care: Advancing the health care reform agenda*. Washington, DC: AARP, Public Policy Institute, 1994.

Ware, J. Differences in 4-year health outcomes for elderly and poor, Chronically ill patients treated in HMO and fee-for-service systems. *Journal of the American Medical Association*, 1996, *276*, 1039–1047.

Wiener, J. M. Managed care and long-term care: The integration of financing and services *Generations*, Summer 1996, *20*, 47–51.

Wiener, J. M., and Illston, L. H. Financing and organization of health care. In R. H. Binstock and L. K. George (Eds.), *Handbook of aging and the social sciences* (4th ed.). San Diego, CA: Academic Press, 1996.

Wiener, J. M., and Illston, L. H. Health care reform in the 1990s: Where does long-term care fit in? *The Gerontologist*, 1994, *34*, 402–408.

Wiener, J. M., Illston, L. H., and Hanley, R. *Sharing the burdens: Strategies for public and private long-term care insurance*. Washington, DC: The Brookings Institute, 1994.

Wright, I. S. *The role of the older citizens in the society of 2000 A.D.* American Federation for Aging Research, 1973.

Zis, M., Jacobs, L. R., and Shapiro, R. Y. The elusive common ground: The politics of public opinion and health care reform. *Generations*, Summer 1996, 7–12.

EPILOGUE

In this final section, we turn toward this century to study how future cohorts, specifically the aging Baby Boomers, will differ from the current population. We also attempt to anticipate how societal conditions and social and health policies will influence older adults' quality of life. Central to any predictions are the concepts of successful aging, productive aging, and extending the quality of life that were presented in earlier chapters. The major changes examined are:

- Demographics, particularly the growth of the "senior boomers"
- Health status and the delivery of health care
- Alternative family relationships
- Work and productivity
- Innovative design and living arrangements
- Ethical dilemmas posed by the increased ability to extend life
- The impact of technology on the ways in which older people live and how services will be delivered
- Career opportunities in gerontology

DEMOGRAPHICS

As noted throughout, the growth of the population over age 65, and the increased numbers who will survive to age 85 and beyond, provide a major challenge to society and to individuals themselves. The greatest increase in the aging population will occur around 2010 as the "Baby Boom" generation (those individuals born between 1946 and 1964) begins to reach old age and creates the "senior boom." The oldest among this cohort will reach age 65 in 2011 and age 85 in 2031, and the younger members will reach age 65 in 2029 and 85 in 2049. Baby Boomers will represent about 60 million of the projected 69 million people age 65 and over in 2030. In that same period, the proportion of the oldest-old will increase dramatically. Currently, 4.1 million people in the United States are age 85 or older; these numbers will probably more than double by the year 2020. By 2050, when the Baby Boomers are age 85 and over, the oldest-old are expected to number 19 million. An even more dramatic increase is expected among centenarians, with 1 in 26 of the Baby Boomers living to be over 100 (U.S. Bureau of the Census, 1996).

Even without this demographic bulge due to the Baby Boomers, the number and proportion of people living longer would have continued to increase, as they have since the turn of the twentieth century. It is the unprecedented rapid jump in the number of older people through the first half of

1973 PROJECTIONS FOR THE YEAR 2000

Which of these predictions have now become true? What kinds of predictions might we make for the year 2030?

Almost 30 years ago, the Director of the American Federation for Aging Research joined President Nixon, Governor Ronald Reagan, and others in predicting how the world would change for older people in the year 2000. Among his predictions, many of which have become reality, are:

- Great advances in the scientific aspects of medical care will take place. The quality of health care ... will improve to such a degree that our infants now achieve maturity and our mature adults reach old age in numbers undreamed of.

- The numbers of individuals reaching 90 and 100 years will be multiplied many times.
- Home health care will be a burgeoning field.
- A more widespread acceptance of euthanasia will occur.
- Physicians, nurses, and allied health personnel will have special training in the care of geriatric patients.
- Medical schools will include consideration of the problems of geriatric patients in their curriculum.
- Retirement will be on the basis of biological age (degree of disability), not chronological age (Wright, 1973).

this century that has created the sense of a demographic or aging crisis. As noted in Chapter 1, these changes mean an increasing rectangularization of the age pyramid, with more older people becoming self-sufficient, and proportionately fewer young persons available to care for frail elders. However, it is the economy, not demography, that holds the key to the ability of the United States to "afford" the aging society and sets the parameters for decisions about how to prepare for the aging boomers. Demographic changes must be viewed within the context of:

- Recent budget cuts in federal and state programs, including Medicare and Medicaid, despite a booming economy in the late 1990s
- The current "slowing down" of national and global economies
- Increasing competition for limited public dollars, with more emphasis on accountability
- Growing expectations that the private sector, including nonprofits and faith-based organizations, will meet the gaps in responding to the needs of vulnerable populations
- Increasing income inequities across households, with the top 20 percent of families benefiting disproportionately from the economic growth of the late 1990s

These demographics, along with increases in longevity and the variability in the aging process, are changing the definition of "old age," with 65 no longer considered old. As noted in Chapter 1, biological age is more important than chronological age in determining an individual's health status. In turn, functional age (i.e., the ability to carry out activities of daily living) is more critical in terms of developing services than chronological age. Accordingly, some have argued that the study of aging should not be restricted to persons 65 and over but rather should cover the entire life course, since the nature of old age is substantially influenced by one's circumstances earlier in life (Cornman and Kingson, 1996). This suggests the importance of life span research and education.

A central question confronting individual citizens as well as policy makers is: What will life be like for the senior boomers? Unfortunately, we do not have a crystal ball to predict the future with certainty. Some factors are well beyond the control of social gerontologists, including economic conditions, international conflicts, globalization of markets, fatal diseases such as AIDS, and natural disasters. Nevertheless, there is adequate knowledge about the Baby-Boom generation to begin to speculate about the future (Morgan, 1998). And most researchers agree that boomers

---

RETHINKING THE WAY WE GROW OLD

Boomers have always embraced the new and unknown, especially compared to their parents. Adults 50 to 60 years old are now challenging what it means to grow old. They are reassessing, shaking life up, taking chances, and doing the things they always wanted to do, especially when they confront their own mortality through watching their parents age. In response, a new industry—*coaching* for reinventing oneself—has emerged to help older boomers (and those just a few years ahead of them) to start over as teachers, business entrepreneurs, community volunteers, students of the dot.com culture, and adventurers in foreign travel. Coaches help them plan a meaningful last half of life and pursue unfinished business. However, these services are not available to most people because coaches charge several hundred dollars an hour.

---

are likely to transform the last decades of life just as they have already dismantled other conventional milestones.

The future cohort of older people will differ from current cohorts in ways other than living longer. Already, they are a highly diverse cohort, with 50-year-olds who are parents of toddlers and 45-year-olds retiring early after cashing out "dot.com" stock. Most have had more than one career. Some Baby Boomers are likely to enter old age in a better economic position than pre-boom cohorts (e.g., their parents and grandparents) because of deferred marriage, reduced childbearing, greater pension coverage, higher education levels, profitable stocks, and increased labor-force participation of women (Cutler, 1997). They will have diverse sources of income other than Social Security

or limited pensions. Nevertheless, there will be tremendous disparity in income and education among the senior boomers, especially between "early" (e.g., those who remember John F. Kennedy's death) and "late" baby boomers (e.g., those whose youth was influenced by Watergate and the energy crisis of the early 1970s). The "older Baby Boomers" are likely to be better off economically and in terms of home ownership than younger boomers. They entered a growing economy, benefited from lower housing costs and investments, and were more likely to have private pensions and higher net earnings than the "younger" boomers who followed them (Cornman and Kingson, 1996). Those likely to have lower retirement income than their parents are boomers who are poorly educated, single parents, or unable to buy a house. Baby Boomers face

---

THE BOOMER'S ECONOMIC STATUS:
WHAT ARE THE IMPLICATIONS FOR THE FUTURE?

- In 71 percent of boomer households, both spouses worked, 1998.
- Thirty-nine percent of boomer households made $60,000 or more, 1997.
- Seventy-one percent of boomers owned their own homes, 1998.
- The net worth of householders age 45 to 54 was $90,500 in 1995.

- Sixty-nine percent of Baby Boomers were satisfied with their current standard of living, 1998.
- Sixty-nine percent have some form of health insurance for all members of their families, 1998.

(Princeton Survey Research Associates, 2000).

Senator John Glenn charted new frontiers for older people.

population that will remain predominantly white. Ethnic minorities among the Baby-Boom cohort are, on average, poorer than their Euro-American counterparts and therefore likely to bring fewer financial resources and often poorer health to old age (Cornman and Kingson, 1996).

Women will predominate among senior boomers, with more than 50 percent of them living alone. Although the status of women and ethnic minorities in the early decades of this century will represent an improvement over current cohorts, gains in education and employment have not necessarily been widely distributed. Women, for example, are still paid only about 70 cents for every dollar earned by their male counterparts, and they remain concentrated in secondary sector industries and traditionally female-oriented, lower-paying occupations. In fact, the Department of Labor projections identify five service occupations, dominated by women and characterized by low wages, as more likely to experience large-scale growth in this century than higher-paying occupations. More women will be employed out of economic necessity for longer periods, but their earnings profile will not necessarily improve. Despite the increased number of women in the paid workforce and the relatively greater affluence of some younger women, older women in the future are predicted to remain significantly poorer than older men. Seventy percent of Baby-Boom women will outlive their husbands by 15 years, but on average will earn only two-thirds of what their husbands earn. When today's 25-year-old woman retires, after having been employed for as long as 35 years, she can expect to receive, on average, the same retirement benefits—adjusted only for inflation—that her mother did, even though she will have paid more into Social Security (National Academy on an Aging Society, 2000; National Economic Council, 1998).

the possibility that they will need more retirement income for longer periods of time than their parents did (Manchester, 1997). On the other hand, they may supplement their income through freelancing, contract or part-time work, or starting their own companies. They may need to do so because of longer life expectancy, rising out-of-pocket health care costs, and the probability of high college tuition for their children at a time when they need to be preparing for retirement.

Another difference from prior generations will be the growing number—at least 18 million—of persons of color among the boomers. They are expected to comprise nearly half of the United States population by the year 2050, growth fueled in part by increased immigrant and refugee populations. The number of older Hispanics and Asians will increase by factors of more than 5 from 1990 to 2050, compared to a doubling of whites and a tripling of African Americans (Morgan, 1998). Accordingly, in all sections of the country, a "minority" population will be the majority, raising questions about the identity and meaning of "minority" and community. There will be proportionately more persons of color in the younger, employed population than today, supporting an older

HEALTH STATUS

Most older people in the future will undoubtedly be healthier than current cohorts, because of the

STEM CELL RESEARCH

Advances in stem cell research were recognized as the "scientific breakthrough of the year" in 1999 by the journal *Science*. This is because of significant advances in guiding such cells into becoming organ-specific tissues. Nevertheless, this new technology, even more than other emerging areas of genetic research, is fraught with ethical dilemmas. In order to obtain human embryonic stem cells by current methods, it is necessary to use human embryos. Such embryos are often derived from aborted fetuses, so this has stirred debate among people opposed to abortion. Indeed, in 1995, Congress banned the National Institutes of Health (NIH) from funding research using human stem cells. Researchers in private biotech firms that do not receive government funding continued their work in this area. In 2000, the NIH issued new rules that federally funded researchers could use stem cells derived from frozen embryos that are due to be discarded by fertility clinics. These rules were accompanied by strict guidelines on how embryonic cells are to be harvested. This makes them valuable for replacing cells in diseased or dead tissues as in Parkinson's disease, Alzheimer's disease, or strokes. Ethical concerns regarding the harvesting of stem cells from embryonic tissue may be alleviated in the future as research with adult stem cells finds ways of differentiating them into organ-specific tissues as successfully as embryonic cells (Bloom, 1999).

advantages of medical technology, preventive medicine, health promotion, and widely available knowledge about ways to maintain health. Older adults and their health care providers will be less concerned with surviving chronic disease than achieving successful aging and adding years to life (e.g., the quality of life)—rather than life to years. As discussed in Chapter 6, the number of people who achieve successful aging is growing. Researchers have found that successful agers remain active both physically and mentally in late life, continue their social interactions with a rich social network, and maintain a strong sense of "self-efficacy," or the feeling that they can achieve whatever they set their minds to do (Rowe and Kahn, 1998). It is noteworthy that studies of successful aging have concluded that the determining factor is not heredity, but the individual's own determination and desire to live well in old age. An underlying focus will be better understanding or differentiating the effects of disease from the declines of aging alone and developing interventions that postpone aging-related dysfunction. As we have seen in Chapter 1, identifying methods to extend the quality of life will be increasingly emphasized, including research on growth hormones, caloric restriction, gene therapy to forestall disease, and stem cell therapy to repair organs such as the pancreas or brain.

Recent developments in cell biology are heralded as "the discovery of the fountain of youth." Indeed, the discovery of a method to force cells to continue producing an enzyme called *telomerase* (described in Chapter 3 as useful for keeping a cell alive, but which normal cells can no longer produce as they age) catapulted the researchers to sudden fame. Accordingly, the biotech company producing it dramatically increased its value on the stock market (de Lange, 1998)! This is an example of how new methods in gene therapy will not necessarily add years to life, but will add life to years. By extending the life of specific cells, scientists, and eventually medical geneticists, can prevent the rapid deterioration caused by many diseases, including cancer and atherosclerosis. In fact, some researchers argue that altering telomerase can slow the process of aging at its very basic, cellular level. Combining this with dietary changes may result in extending the maximum life span, in addition to postponing or preventing many diseases and disabilities (Banks and Fossel, 1997).

These new developments in cell biology and genetic engineering will someday allow more people to achieve successful or robust aging. Even today

UNITED FLYING OCTOGENARIANS

An organization calling itself "United Flying Octogenarians" (UFOs) is made up of pilots over the age of 80 who are still flying small planes. Although airline pilots are among the few professionals today who must retire at a certain age—in this case, from flying for the airline by age 60—there is no restriction on flying small private planes. UFO boasts 1000 members over the age of 80 who have valid medical certificates to fly small planes. They are required to obtain a physical exam and perform a test ride with an instructor every 2 years. The oldest active pilot who is a member of UFOs is 94!

there are numerous examples of older people achieving milestones that were previously believed to be impossible beyond a certain age. For example, the decision by NASA to invite Senator John Glenn, a former astronaut, on a space mission in 1999 served to redefine "old." Not only did this signal the end of defining physiological capacities in terms of chronological age, but the mission provided a natural experiment in helping us understand the effects of aging on the ability to function in space. It also gave scientists an understanding of the impact of weightlessness on aging. The increase in the number of "master athletes," described in Chapter 3, including marathon runners, mountain climbers, and long-distance cyclists, is no longer a phenomenon but a reality for newer cohorts of older people. This pattern will certainly continue to grow as the baby boomers become senior boomers.

For the majority of older people, however, access to adequate health care will continue to exacerbate disparities in health status. Those with adequate health care will enjoy longer periods of functionality followed by more rapid decline. Those who do not have access to quality health care will endure years, even decades, of a long and slow decline from chronic illness. If disability rates remain relatively stable, the number of older persons needing help with basic tasks was expected to double between 1990 and 2030, and the number of older individuals requiring nursing home care more than triple (Wiener, Illston, and Hanley, 1994).

The difference in life expectancy between women and men may be narrowed by younger women's tendency to engage in riskier behaviors and lifestyles, as well as more young men pursuing healthier lifestyles by avoiding smoking, limiting alcohol and fat intake, and increasing exercise levels. This pattern has reduced death rates due to heart disease and hypertension. On the other hand, if AIDS continues to affect more younger men than women, the sex differential in life expectancy could increase. Although the interaction of these trends is unknown, it is clear that women will continue to live longer and will consequently predominate among the frailest and sickest (Cornman and Kingson, 1996).

Despite the increased knowledge about the health benefits of exercise and diet, only about 10 percent of boomers are currently following a prescription for good health in terms of diet and fitness. Although boomers may consume less fat and alcohol than people did 40 years ago, they are not health conscious by the following measures:

- Twenty-seven percent of men and 41 percent of women say they rarely or never exercise.
- Only 32 percent rate their health as excellent.
- Fifteen percent or more do not engage in more strenuous exercise such as biking, running, or swimming.
- Boomers report eating more fat and less fruit than older cohorts did.
- Fifty-four percent of boomers are overweight; 26 percent of male boomers are clinically obese (Blanchette and Valcour, 1998).

Health care researchers contend that boomers are negatively affected by environmental changes. For example, in car-based suburbs or with long commutes in jobs, more time is spent in cars than walking. Work often consists of sitting before a computer terminal. At home, labor-saving gadgets make housework less strenuous and therefore diminish any aerobic benefits. Given the fast-paced nature of many boomers' lives, they eat more meals away from home and snacks, which results in more fat, salt, and calories than if eating at home. As long as people are short on time, technology will continue to make food faster and domestic life easier. Nevertheless, even modest changes, such as taking the stairs at work, parking a distance from the office entrance, drinking water instead of reaching for a Coke, or snacking on apples instead of candy, can make a difference in slowing the aging process.

In addition to the higher rates of chronic illness and mortality among ethnic minorities and women, other populations are of concern. These include people who are affected by AIDS and those facing long-term developmental disabilities or mental illness. Although the AIDS epidemic affects only about 1 percent of the current cohort of older adults, this proportion will grow. This is because of the probability of Baby Boomers who contracted the infection earlier in their lives, largely because they defined themselves as low risk and did not use adequate protection. The onset of AIDS may occur when senior boomers are experiencing other age-related changes, since the median interval between HIV infection and full-blown AIDS is nearly 10 years. Preventive education about AIDS among the young-old population is critical.

As noted in Chapter 10, another population that will require specialized care is older persons with developmental disabilities (e.g., cerebral palsy or Down syndrome). As a result of improved health care, life expectancy for persons with Down syndrome has increased dramatically, from 9 years in 1929 to 18.3 years in 1963, to 55 years today (Adlin, 1993). The population with developmental disabilities over age 65 is projected to double by 2030. They will probably require services from agencies serving older adults and persons with developmental disabilities, as well as care by family members who may be among the oldest-old (Kelly and Kropf, 1995). What old age will be like for the growing number of adults who are chronically

mentally ill or homeless is also unknown and of concern to planners and policy makers.

Health care delivery

Baby Boomers as a group face considerable uncertainty about health care expenditures. Although tremendously concerned about costs, they are not well informed about how to pay for health and long-term care. Boomers who have been employed part-time as temporary workers or have been self-employed lack access to employer-funded health care benefits. Compared to earlier generations, boomers are more likely to view health care as a responsibility shared by government and the individual, and to place a higher value on individual responsibility for health (e.g., health promotion) (Blanchette and Valcour, 1998). The increasingly high costs of hospitalization and nursing homes have already resulted in the growth of various community-based options in health and long-term care, many of which are private pay.

As noted in Chapters 11 and 17, a major area of expansion is *home health care* provided by hospitals, private and nonprofit agencies, or local governments, or privately contracted by the older person. Home health, adult day centers, and adult day health programs provide respite to families and allow older people to remain as self-sufficient as possible—values that future generations may be more likely to hold because of their greater opportunities for choice. Despite these benefits for older adults and their families, public funding for such community-based options is relatively limited. More comprehensive, coordinated, accessible, in-home and community-based supportive services are needed, along with changes in public financing of long-term care. What is unknown is the extent to which Medicare and Medicaid will be modified to cover more such community-based programs in the future. The current partisan splits and cost-containment mood in Congress, however, suggest that this is unlikely, at least in the next decade.

The growth in the number of hospitals, along with the surplus of physicians and an excess of hospital beds in some communities, has led to greater competition for older patients. At the same time, financial limitations on the provision of care have resulted in an increase in ambulatory services. We have moved from an era of reduced hospital days following major surgery to *no* hospital stays following many surgical procedures. Many changes in hospital use are taking place within the context of managed care. In recent years, there have been greater pressures to move Medicare beneficiaries into private managed care systems and for the Health Care Financing Administration, which administers Medicare and Medicaid, to operate more like a private business "managed choice model." Although the overall percent of HMO (Health Maintenance Organization) enrollees over age 65 is currently low compared to younger populations, HMOs actively recruit older adults by offering comprehensive health care at lower average costs than private hospitals and physicians can offer. Many existing private hospitals are converting to HMOs and some provide attractive health-promotion and health-education programs. The federal demonstration projects, SHMOs, add home care to the standard managed care package and allow earlier discharge from acute-care facilities; whether these will prove to be cost-effective and therefore more widely available in the future is unknown. Pressures to discharge patients quickly have created demands for a new type of facility for the person who is too sick to go home but not sick enough for a hospital. As a result, subacute-care facilities, as described in Chapter 17, are growing, whereby nursing homes are becoming less like homes and more like hospitals, to provide stroke rehabilitation, cardiac care, and intravenous feeding. This shift, however, means that in many facilities, spaces for long-term Medicaid patients are being filled by higher-paying Medicare patients, furthering inequities in access to health care (Fritz, 1995).

Rapid innovations in computer applications will continue to change health care service dramatically. Already, consumers and professionals alike can access data bases that contain medical information about chronic conditions, care needs,

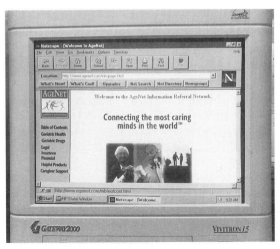

The Internet is making health care information accessible to both consumers and providers.

and products through the Internet and Websites. Health-education and health-promotion projects, decision-support programs, access to technical expertise, and mutual support from other patients and families are all available "on line." In fact, over 25,000 Websites relate to health information and mutual support, a number that will grow dramatically. In addition, a 1997 study found more than 3.5 million Web documents using health-related key words. Some health care organizations maintain the Internet exclusively for members, providing plan information and directories of plan providers (Kelly, 1997). An example of an effective stand-alone system is CHESS, the Comprehensive Health Enhancement Support System. By entering the system through a personal computer from home, users can obtain brief answers to standard health questions as well as detailed articles and descriptions of services. They can anonymously ask questions of experts and communicate and read personal stories of people with similar problems. Preliminary evaluations indicate that CHESS has been extensively used, even by underserved patients of color with low levels of education (Gustafson, Gustafson, and Wackerbarth, 1997). One advantage of such stand-alone systems is that patients do not need to learn how to navigate the Internet.

COMPUTER-BASED MONITORING OF PATIENTS WITH HEART FAILURE

Cardiologists at the University of Illinois at Chicago taught their older patients with heart failure how to use a home-based monitor of blood pressure, heart rate, and weight, and then transmit this information via a telephone modem (even if they had no home computers) to the hospital. If these vital signs exceed acceptable levels, an alarm sounds at the central monitoring station and immediate action is taken by the physician. For most patients, however, the system allows regular monitoring by their cardiologist without costly hospital and physician visits.

Most academic medical centers offer detailed information about various diseases on their Websites. The Senior-Med Project, which creates a network to help manage and monitor medications, adds accessing the Internet to a stand-alone system with basic information about medications (Deatrick, 1997). All these technology-based approaches point to a collaborative or partnership model between health care providers and older people and their families. The concepts of client empowerment and breaking down traditional boundaries between health care providers and patients are furthered when a client can readily access information from physicians or nurses via e-mail.

Indeed, new experiments in *telemedicine,* which originally was developed for health providers in remote communities to consult with medical specialists, demonstrate this to be a useful tool for homebound patients to communicate with their physicians. Computer-based systems, such as Help Innovations and Healthdesk Online, allow patients to "visit" an office nurse by sending their health report, vital signs, and any problems with medications. A major advantage is that this does not involve extra time spent by nurses for in-home visits and reduces trips by chronically ill elders to physicians' offices and clinics.

The use of technology will undoubtedly affect the training and allocation of health care providers. Even without technology, we have seen increasing use of personnel such as geriatric nurse practitioners who are less costly than traditional physician-based care. The growth of geriatric education in colleges of medicine, nursing, dentistry, social work, pharmacy, and in other areas such as nutrition and physical therapy, suggest that a well-trained cadre of health care providers will increase, although they may not meet projected needs. Most of them will be trained in the use of information technology as a way to communicate with patients and their families. Since the potential for misuse and misinformation on the Internet is high, health care providers will need to be aware of the sources and types of computer-based information accessed by their clients. Nevertheless, all of these developments offer hope for cost containment and quality of care.

More broadly, the need to expand our intellectual and conceptual approaches to health and healing is increasingly recognized. This encompasses a multidimensional approach to health care that takes account of both physical and psychosocial factors, such as self-efficacy. A striking indicator of people's desire for different health care modalities is the decline in the number of individuals who rely solely on modern Western medicine. In fact, 33 percent of people in the United States (even though they often pay out of pocket), 50 percent of those in Europe, and 80 percent worldwide use some type of alternative medicine (Micozzi, 1997). Complementary and Alternative Medicine (CAM) is generally understood as diagnostic or therapeutic techniques considered to be outside mainstream Western medicine but that may enhance conventional treatment. This represents a "reverse technology transfer," whereby useful medical systems and techniques from other countries make their way into popular usage in the United States. As a reflection of growing recognition of CAM, a Presidential Commission on Complementary and Alternative Medicine has been formed.

Alternative medicines encompass two broad types:

1. healing systems, such as homeopathy, herbal treatments, chiropractic medicine, osteopathy, and acupuncture
2. well-developed systems represented by ancient health traditions such as tai chi and massage therapy

These techniques are generally considered less invasive, lower tech, and less expensive than traditional medicine. For example, acupuncture or chiropractic techniques rather than surgery may be used to treat chronic back pain. Tai chi, the fluid meditative movement routine from China, has been found to be effective in preventing falls by keeping older people limber and improving their balance; it also has been used in nursing homes and by people in wheelchairs (Jahnke, 1997). Nontraditional approaches may be especially effective with long-term conditions for which there is no cure (e.g., Alzheimer's, arthritis, living with chronic pain). Research to assess the effectiveness of alternative medicine is growing. In fact, institutions such as the University of California at San Francisco, Stanford, and Columbia are integrating complementary and alternative medicine into their medical curricula and examining the use of alternative treatments for musculoskeletal diseases, cancer, and heart disease. An Office of Complementary and Alternative Medicine within the National Institutes of Health is funding scientific studies to understand why some alternative therapies are effective.

CHANGING FAMILY RELATIONSHIPS

The Baby-Boom generation has been characterized by a wide variety of family forms and lifestyles. Family structures have become more diverse because of:

- higher rates of divorce, remarriage, step-family relationships, and never-married adults
- more couples or single mothers delaying childbearing until their thirties or forties, or choosing to have fewer children or not to have children at all
- more households with both adults employed
- more children being raised in single-parent households
- more gay and lesbian partners raising children
- more couples cohabitating, rather than marrying

Such diversity creates more choices and options for members (Cornman and Kingson, 1996; Pillemer and Suitor, 1998). Diversity also characterizes family structure by ethnicity and class, as well as by life stage. In addition, "family" no longer simply means coresidents of the same household, particularly in the later phases of the life cycle. As these changes take place, more consideration needs to be given to life course variations in household and kinship arrangements as men and women move in and out of various communities, living and employment situations, and primary relationships (Moen, 1998; Moen and Forest, 1995). Families united by love rather than blood will become more common.

Increases in life expectancy complicate the diversity of family structures. These added years serve to prolong a person's relationships to others—spouse, parents, offspring, friends—whose lives are also extended. In the year 2000, a 50-year-old had an 80 percent chance of having at least one parent alive and a 27 percent chance of having both alive. In fact, a 60-year-old had a 44 percent chance of having a parent alive (Cutler, 1997). It will not be unusual to find retired people in their seventies and eighties caring for a centenarian parent. These dramatic changes mean that a growing proportion of parents, children and perhaps even grandchildren within multigenerational families will share such critical adulthood experiences as school, work, parenthood, and even retirement and widowhood. For example, for current generations of young women, the death of a mother and the last child leaving home for college may occur close to the daughter's retirement age. Similarly, grandparents or great-grandparents may survive to experience many years of their grandchildren's or great grandchildren's adulthood. Women will experience more years of the "empty nest," with more postparenting years than active parenting. However, the "empty nest" is likely to be filled by care responsibilities for older relatives, many of whom desire to "age in place" (Dennis and Migliaccio, 1997). With the delay in the onset of morbidity and need for care among the oldest-old, caregivers of the future are likely to be young-old themselves. They will also be more likely to remain employed, given improved health status, higher living standard expectations, a smaller pool of younger workers, and a lower likelihood of caring for young children at home.

As members of a person's social network survive longer, the vertical links that cross generational lines increase in complexity. Individuals in a multi-generational family line interact in a much more complex set of family identities than is the case in a lineage with only two generations, those of parent and child. Kinship networks will become even more attenuated and diffuse than currently. The verticalized or "beanpole family structure" will grow—that is, an increasing number of living generations in a family (though they probably will not physically live together), accompanied by a decreasing number of family members within the same generation due to declining fertility rates. Increased life expectancy combined with reduced fertility means that future cohorts of adult children will have a greater number of aging parents and grandparents to care for while having fewer siblings to call on for assistance. Kin networks, as a result, will be top-heavy. Simultaneously, intergenerational relations are to a much greater extent voluntary and individually negotiated (Pillemer and Suitor, 1998; Uhlenberg, 1996; Bengtson, Rosenthal, and Burton, 1996). Such patterns raise questions about multigenerational responsibilities. For example, who is responsible for a great-grandparent who falls and needs daily care—the grandparents who may themselves be frail, the parents who may both be employed, or grandchildren who are often still in school? These trends of declining family size, combined with increases in the number of unmarried persons and childless couples (the "truncated family"), are likely to continue, reducing the pool of potential family caregivers. Figure E.1 illustrates the expected decline in numbers of younger family members available to care for an increasingly older population.

Delayed childbearing and smaller family size have resulted in a larger-than-average age difference between each generation and a blurring of demarcations between generations, particularly among Caucasian families. For example, active involvement in the daily demands of raising children is now likely to be fully completed by the time women are grandmothers. Women who marry and give birth later in life are less likely to divorce, and more likely to have economic, educational, and emotional advantages that benefit their children. However, generational differences of 30 to 40 years may, over time, contribute to difficulties in building affective bonds across multiple generations due to different values or lifestyles. In contrast to this phenomenon of later-life marriage and childbearing is the age-condensed family, where young women are bearing children in the teenage years, which is accompanied by higher rates of divorce. This may result in a blurring of roles and relationships, particularly the growth of young grandmothers and great-grandmothers who are the primary caregivers for grandchildren. Some of these differences in family structure vary by socio-economic status.

Reduced fertility rates also mean fewer individuals within each generation in which to invest emotionally. As a result, intergenerational relationships are not only more extensive, but also more emotionally intensive. At the same time, siblings, who are closer in age and think of themselves as peers, may be more likely to share care tasks than to expect the oldest child or the unmarried daughter to be the primary caregiver—a pattern more common in large families in the past. In turn, adults may experience richer social relationships with their peers and be more likely to form nontraditional intimate relationships (Silverstone, 1996).

The increase in longevity has also significantly changed grandparent–grandchildren roles. For example, we now anticipate that our grandparents

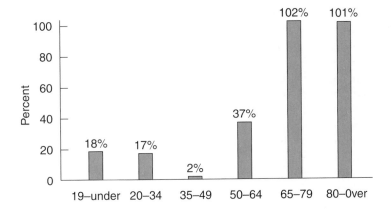

Americans 65 and older will be the fastest-growing age group ...[1]

... but they will have fewer offspring to care for them.[2]

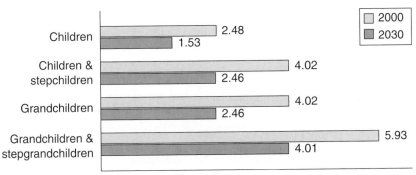

FIGURE E.I **Who Will Provide Care in the Future?** Two trends in the next 30 years—an America growing older, on average, and baby boomers having fewer children—raise questions about future caregiving trends.
[1]Projected change in population, 2000–2030.

[2]Projected average number of offspring for each white resident of the U.S.A. aged 70–85.

SOURCE: U.S. Census Bureau: Kenneth Watcher, University of California, Berkeley; USA TODAY analysis by Anthony DeBarros.

will not die until our early adulthood, but until quite recently most grandparents did not live long enough to know their grandchildren well. Now, as more women have their first children anywhere from the early teens until their mid-forties, first-time grandparenthood occurs for persons ranging in age from 35 to 75. Accordingly, grandchildren encompass both infants and retirees, and grand-

parents include active middle-aged adults as well as frail, very old persons. For the first time in history, a woman can be both a granddaughter and a grandmother simultaneously. Additional complicating factors are that grandparents and grandchildren are often separated by geographic distance, and by divorce and remarriage of the grandchildren's parents. As a result, the two generations may rarely see each other. These patterns, which are likely to increase in the future, raise questions about grandparents' rights and obligations. Without historical precedence, there are few clear culturally shared expectations about grandparent–grandchildren relationships when parents divorce.

The widened gap between the mortality rates of men and women is another demographic change that influences family relationships. Chapters 9 and 15 demonstrated that the world of the very old is a world of women, both in society and within families. Some five-generation families may include three generations of widows. Most older women are widows living alone; most older men live with their wives. Such differences in widowhood and remarriage mean that men are more likely to maintain horizontal, intragenerational ties, primarily through their wives. In contrast, women turn more to intergenerational relationships for support throughout their lives, especially in old age. Although more women are entering the marketplace traditionally dominated by men, they continue to put greater emphasis on interpersonal relationships. This, combined with the value placed by the women's movement on friendships and social support, suggests that women will continue to build diverse and extensive social networks to which they can turn in old age. For example, more older women in the future may choose to live with other women, forming intergenerational households as a way to reduce housing costs and strengthen their support networks. Another factor that may contribute to this trend is the growing number of women who choose not to marry or who are lesbians. For these women, friends often represent a stronger social bond than relatives.

The increasing divorce rate interacts with these demographic changes. This increase may be inevitable in aging societies, because modern longevity makes marriage a greater long-term commitment than in the past. The chance of couples who married in the 1930s and 1940s reaching their golden wedding anniversary has been less than 5 percent. In spite of increased life expectancy, no more couples reach this 50-year marker nowadays than did a century ago. But whereas before 1974, most marriages ended with death, now, more marriages end with divorce (Hobbs and Damon, 1996). Among the 75 percent of men and 60 percent of women who remarry, more than 40 percent are estimated to divorce yet again, creating complex step-family relationships. An increasing number of children, parents, and grandparents will thus devote substantial effort toward building reconstituted families and step-relationships, only to find them eventually dissolved.

Trends in divorce and remarriage are shaping the life course and social networks of young and old, but they differentially affect men and women. For women, divorce reduces their standard of living and creates an uncertain financial future. The more resources (e.g., education and income) that a divorced woman has available, the less likely she is to remarry, whereas this is reversed for men (Choi, 1995). Among women divorcing in the future will be growing numbers of resourceful individuals who will already have lived for many decades on their own as they face old age in a new century. Although they may experience financial

---

QUESTIONS RAISED BY TRENDS IN DIVORCE AND REMARRIAGE

How will children of divorce, remarriage, redivorce, and cohabitation approach relationships during their own adult years? What patterns of support will exist between aging parents and children in families disrupted by divorce? To what extent will younger members of "blended" families and those unrelated by blood, but joined by years of sharing familial responsibilities, assume the role of caregivers? Will the divorced and remarried receive the same support from adult children, particularly stepchildren, as those who stayed in intact families?

TRENDS THAT POSE TROUBLING QUESTIONS

What will be the nature of relationships between aging fathers and their children with whom they have had only sporadic contact for many years? What sort of responsibility will adult children feel toward an aging father who never paid child support and was largely absent from their lives? Will the mother–daughter relationship become even more important as the mainstay of family cohesion? And how will these changes affect the development of policies regarding the care of frail elders?

---

struggles as single mothers, they also may be innovative and adept at coping with the changes that aging brings.

For men, the primary consequence of divorce is disruption of intergenerational family networks. Most common is reduced contact with and financial support for children, because most mothers, whether by choice or out of necessity, assume primary childrearing responsibility. Divorced fathers, for example, are less likely to keep in touch with their children or to be named as a source of support. This reduced responsibility also translates into less involvement across generations, such as diminished interaction between paternal grandparents and grandchildren. Social values toward gender equality have increased, but demographic and social changes have created very different family worlds for men and women. An increasing proportion of men have only tenuous vertical ties along generational lines, yet women have retained strong links to both young and old generations. This suggests that divorced fathers will have fewer children or stepchildren to provide care.

FAMILY CAREGIVING RESPONSIBILITIES

As more women, both as single parents and as caregivers for older relatives, are assuming more intergenerational responsibilities, their employment demands are also expanding. The expectation and necessity for women to enter the paid workforce have grown, without any significant diminution in women's family responsibilities, as evidenced by the fact that women devote nearly as much time to household tasks as they did 50 years ago. Seventy-five percent of married mothers with children work outside the home, and women with children under age 6 are the fastest-growing component of the female labor force (Coontz, 1997). Traditional expectations about family caregiving have not changed, however, and the demands on employed women can be an unbearable burden. Although such sex-based roles are slowly changing in terms of child care, and more men are caregivers for older relatives, the fact that women still assume primary responsibility for children tempers any unrealistic expectations that men will soon become the primary care providers of frail elders.

A symmetry exists between husbands and wives in their distinctive work–family interfaces over the life course (Han and Moen, 1999). Occupational careers represent a "structural lag" (see Riley, Chapter 8) in which norms and practices have not kept pace with demographic realities. The concept of career as an orderly occupational status ladder contains hidden assumptions about jobs and social relationships that create value dilemmas between individualism and the family, women's careers and family responsibilities, and paid and productive work. Yet our understanding of these issues is no longer congruent with the changing economy, modern gender roles, and a lessened distinction between work and retirement.

Who will provide what care for older dependents is a critical policy issue currently and for the future. Federal cutbacks and the devolution of responsibility for services to the states suggest publicly funded supports for family caregivers will diminish. At the same time, the number of senior boomers who will provide long-distance care is expected to double to 14 million in the next 15 years.

WORKPLACE MODIFICATIONS TO SUPPORT CAREGIVERS

- Elder-care referral and counseling services, especially for caregivers at a geographic distance
- On-site day care programs for older parents and young children of employees

- Because of the federal Family and Medical Leave Act, flexible hours and unpaid leave options for employees with care responsibilities

Accordingly, the need for policies conducive to family well-being at all stages of the life course and to sustaining ties within and across generations is likely to grow dramatically (National Council on the Aging, 1997). Fortunately, the private sector is beginning to respond to the growth of employees who have caregiving responsibilities, and elder care will be an important employee benefit. Corporations have responded because they recognize the relationship between caregiving demands and productivity; elder care is estimated to cost businesses about $29 billion a year. These costs, which include replacing employees, absenteeism, workday interruptions, and supervisory time, will increase (De Martino, 1997).

Modifications in the workplace, however, are the exception, not the norm; the trend toward cost-cutting and reduction of employee benefits may, at least in the short run, counteract such improvements. This suggests that new, more open

Growing numbers of younger women will assume both elder-care and employment responsibilities.

and flexible institutional arrangements are required for structuring the work–family interface for both, as well as for women at all life course and career stages (Han and Moen, 1999).

Elder-care services are increasingly coordinated by for-profit geriatric care management businesses. Most often it is adult children, typically at a geographic distance, who contract for a private care manager to locate services for an aging parent, visit regularly, and handle emergencies. However, their fees range from $150 to $500, thereby limiting their service to middle- and upper-class families. These marketplace initiatives will undoubtedly expand, although adult children, typically women, will continue to be involved in assuring that appropriate services are provided as needed. Closely related will be an increase in public–private partnerships, including churches and synagogues. For example, Area Agencies on Aging, faced with reduced federal funds, are likely to reach out increasingly to for-profits to establish collaborative initiatives for older adults (Gray, 1995).

The use of information technology to forge intergenerational communities and to provide family caregivers with information and mutual support also will increase. The Internet provides ways for older adults to communicate with others who share similar concerns, purchase products, and research aging resources. Living in a networked society, senior boomers, facile with computers throughout most of their adult lives, will be comfortable accessing information and support from others through computer-based technology. In fact, older users of the Internet already do so more than younger users. Accordingly, computer-based resources for family caregivers are likely to increase and provide a means to reduce feelings of isolation. For example, the Family Caregiver Alliance for caregivers of cognitively impaired adults offers "Factsheets," a Website of resources and peer support (Kelly, 1997). Websites such as "Total Living Choices" can provide free information on long-term care resources. Alzheimer's networks provide free e-mail, question-and-answer functions, and a bulletin-board structure. In fact, users appear to benefit more from the 24-hour-a-day mutual support of other caregivers than from their access to medical information (Hunt, 1997).

The growth of assistive technology, as described in Chapter 11, will enable more frail elders to remain in their own homes. This technology includes devices such as pagers, tracking devices, and emergency call buttons in private homes and apartments. All of these technological developments will have profound implications for how family members relate to each other and to health care professionals. Indeed, as they age, Baby Boomers will have increasing electronic access to medical information and for communicating with their physicians as needed.

WORK AND PRODUCTIVITY

Baby Boomers entered the workforce during a slowing economy that could not absorb the large number of new workers, resulting in a decline in the growth of work incomes and consequent decrease in future Social Security benefits. In addition, Baby Boomers saved less and borrowed more than their parents, which could lessen their ability to maintain their standard of living in retirement (Kutza, 1998).

Despite these patterns, on average this cohort is likely to enter old age in a better economic position than did preboom cohorts. This is because of economic and demographic adjustments, such as deferred marriage, reduced childbearing, increased labor-force participation of wives, and greater pension coverage, all of which have compensated for the baby boomers' relatively lower wages and savings in a slower economy in their earlier years. They will also benefit from the lifting of the Social Security cap on outside earnings, which will allow them to keep working without penalty.

The majority of senior boomers will also be better educated. Because of the association between education, occupation, and income, those with degrees are likely to earn more during their lifetimes. More people over age 70 may choose to continue to be employed, preferably on a part-time basis, although the pattern of early retirement will probably persist. In fact, Baby Boomers indicate that their preferred retirement age is 58 (Merrill Lynch, 1995)! The Baby Boom generation is the first cohort of workers expected to assume more direct responsibility for financing their own retirement (Hardy and Kruse, 1998). Nevertheless, most Baby Boomers express little confidence about their financial futures and are concerned about outliving their retirement savings (Cutler, 1998). Paradoxically, relatively few of this cohort are actively planning financially for their retirement. In fact, many are saving only about one-third of what they will need to maintain their current standard of living (Cutler, 1997; Manchester, 1997). Whether the extent of financial planning will increase with the dramatic growth of planning resources available

---

CHANGING LIFESTYLES

Some Baby Boomers who have benefited from the strong economy have chosen a new lifestyle and developed income opportunities. After John retired from an engineering position in aerospace, he and his wife, Susan, sold their 3-acre home to a developer and relocated to a small community on the Olympic Peninsula in Washington state. There, they are growing a garden where customers can cut dahlias, have renovated a farmhouse for weddings, and are actively involved in fighting encroaching development in their small town.

on the Internet and Websites is as yet unclear (Sherman, 1997). A financial industry eager to garner pension funds into the private equity market and an anti–government-spending political environment may propel many Baby Boomers into greater financial planning (Hardy and Kruse, 1998).

These differential opportunities, however, will benefit middle- and upper-class older persons more than those with limited financial resources. The numbers of economically vulnerable elders will not diminish dramatically. Instead, a permanent underclass of boomers is projected, with disproportionate representation of African Americans, those with a sporadic work history, single women, and the poorly educated (Dennis and Migliaccio, 1997). In contrast to their better-off counterparts, they will want Social Security continued as a risk-free contributory system and will worry about Medicare's and Medicaid's copayments and deductibles. The extent to which the public sector will focus on the needs of this underclass is unclear, given the increasingly more conservative political climate and the trends toward less federal support and devolution of responsibility to the states and nonprofit organizations. And those in the middle, the "tweeners"—who have too many resources to qualify for public programs, yet are unable to pay fully for their health and long-term care—will increase. In fact, the expansion of "tweeners" is predicted to create future intergenerational competition for scarce resources.

Increasingly, questions are being raised about whether people should retire, under what conditions, and for what purposes. As people begin to comprehend how much of the adult lifetime is spent in retirement, there is growing awareness that formal retirement does not end the need for involvement in the larger society. With declines in well-paid and part-time work opportunities for older adults, pressures have mounted for socially rewarding, productive roles in the larger community.

The concept of the "Third Age" denotes the stage in life that occurs after middle age but before the final stage; it is conceptualized as a time of continued involvement and development in areas of life beyond work and family. With growing recognition of the potential of older people to contribute to society, new public values regarding their opportunities and responsibilities are needed (Fahey, 1996). Increasingly, questions will be raised about how "work" should be defined and "contributions" measured. For example, volunteer effort may be perceived as contributing more to the common good than paid work and therefore as deserving greater rewards than currently exist. The concept of productive aging, defined in Chapter 12 as paid and unpaid activities that contribute to society in diverse ways, is consistent with that of the Third Age. However, flexible options for productive activity by older persons are unevenly distributed across all sectors of society.

As members of successive cohorts retire at younger ages, are better educated, and are perhaps healthier than their predecessors, it seems predictable that pressures from age-based organizations and from the general public will modify

---

WORKPLACE CHANGES TO RECRUIT AND RETAIN OLDER WORKERS

- Incentives to maintain the older workers' productivity
- Ways to ease the transition to retirement ("gliding out" phase)
- Redesigning jobs (e.g., job sharing, flexible and part-time schedules, and conducting work at home) to accommodate older workers' abilities and needs

- Retraining in new technologies such as computers and robotics
- Counseling and other support services for new careers and for voluntarism
- Additional forms of compensation (health benefits or tax credits)
- Data banks of retiree skills for temporary employment and job sharing

existing work, retirement, and leisure roles. In fact, modifications in the workplace are underway to offset the lag between changes in social structures and the recognition of older people's skills and productivity. Many of these efforts seek to encourage people to work longer without undermining the self-esteem of those no longer able to work. A very pragmatic reason for developing incentives for older workers is the projected labor shortage among youth, particularly in the service sector. From 1993 to 2004, the population comprised of workers over age 40 will increase by over 28 million; the aging of the Baby Boomers will raise the median age of the labor force by 3 years. By 2005, 15.1 percent of workers will be over age 55, compared to 11.9 percent in 1998 (Moen, 1998).

More companies are therefore beginning to modify the workplace in order to retain older workers longer and to encourage multiple careers. To date, however, such workplace modifications do not adequately meet growing interest in part-time employment. This suggests the need for new forms of public–private collaboration in the future to create viable options for older adults.

New Paradigms of Retirement

Viewing retirement as a process involving successive decisions may be more useful than traditional conceptions of a single and irreversible event. The transition to retirement can be eased through financial planning and comprehensive retirement-preparation programs—for example, IBM has a Retirement Education Assistance plan that provides tuition to employees and their spouses 3 years prior to retirement eligibility and 2 years after retirement to enable employees to develop new interests and prepare for new careers. Another model, common in some European countries and in Japan, is a "gliding out" plan of phased retirement that permits a gradual shift to a part-time schedule. Some Scandinavian countries give workers year-long sabbaticals every 10 years as a time to reevaluate their careers or to take a break instead of working straight through to retirement.

Jobs can also be restructured, gradually allowing longer vacations, shorter work days, and more opportunities for community involvement during the preretirement working years.

Volunteer opportunities that draw upon retirees' competence as well as provide them with chances to learn new skills can also blur the line between paid employment and retirement. In recognition of these challenges, the Administration on Aging funded the "Redefining Retirement Initiative: The Baby Boomer Challenge." This initiative seeks to resocialize and inspire Baby Boomers and middle-aged individuals to prepare for their retirement and projected longer life, and to develop new ways of contributing to a better society (Dennis and Migliaccio, 1997). This emphasis on individual and community responsibility reflects the changing ethos about the role of government.

Other changes in work and retirement patterns are the increased number of people in their forties and fifties who are electing to move into second and even third careers. As noted above, more organizations are providing sabbaticals, extended vacations and leaves, retraining programs, and career-development alternatives. More of these adult education opportunities will become available through distance-learning formats that use information-based technology. Such educational options benefit employees by allowing them to explore new careers and volunteer and leisure interests; this, in turn, can serve to prevent job burnout or boredom, so that early retirement is not perceived as the only viable option. These programs also benefit employers in companies that are undergoing rapid technological changes—such as automobile manufacturing, where robotics and computerized assembly lines are already in place. By retraining their older, more experienced workers, such organizations can retain employees who have proved capable in the past.

A work–retirement continuum for a population with a longer life span will involve lifelong education and training. Changing social values about the "appropriate age" for education, employment, retirement, and leisure demand a reexamination of employment policies and norms. The

---

REDEFINING RETIREMENT

A year ago, Diane took a leave from her job with a large corporation to serve with the Peace Corps in Ghana. Although she had a good income, new condo, and lavish annual vacations, she felt that her life was lacking purpose and meaning. She hoped to get clearer about her values through contributing to those considerably less fortunate than she. The Peace Corps experience helped her to sort out her priorities. She came back to work a changed person, energized and motivated by her time in Ghana, and determined to find a way to retire at age 55. She wants to dedicate herself to helping young African Americans. Earlier in her life, she tried to prove to everybody, especially those superior to her, that she could hold down a big corporate job and be successful. Now she is clear that she wants her legacy to be about making a difference, not about money.

---

traditional linear life cycle of education for the young, employment for the middle aged, and retirement for the old is already undergoing major changes. This is occurring as more middle-aged and older persons enter college for the first time, move into new careers, or begin their studies for graduate or professional degrees. From a developmental perspective:

- temporary "retirement" may be a more viable option for the young worker just starting a family; employment may be desirable for the teenager who is bored with school; and
- education may be attractive to the older person who can integrate his or her life experiences with the knowledge gained in a formal learning situation.

Instead of the linear career trajectory traditionally followed in our society, movement in and out of the workforce, schooling, and family care may all need to be defined as legitimate options in a cyclical life plan.

Women have moved in and out of the workforce for years, largely because of family responsibilities; but they have often been penalized for their discontinuous work patterns through lower salaries and retirement benefits, (e.g., the feminization of poverty). However, movement in and out of the workforce may come to be viewed as a legitimate alternative for both men and women because of the following factors:

- increasing numbers of career-oriented women who are committed to an ideology of shared family responsibilities
- growing awareness of the possibility of two or three careers over the life course

This trend may also encourage individuals to better integrate their work and family lives.

Modifications in work patterns and organizational opportunities for career development, described above, suggest that traditional definitions of leisure will also change. Employment and leisure are becoming less compartmentalized and more evenly distributed across the life span through modified work schedules, job sharing, and phased retirement, as well as the increasing number of retirees who work part-time and also volunteer. This "blurring" of work and leisure is reinforced by increased organizational awareness of employee needs, such as on-the-job exercise and fitness programs, child care, staff training, and psychological counseling. To some extent, these factors reflect a shift from the traditional work ethic to a more balanced view of employment and leisure. Therefore, future cohorts of older adults may view leisure in retirement merely as a continuation of prior leisure activities and not regard it as a new stage in life. Such integration of leisure throughout the life span will undoubtedly mean a smoother transition to retirement.

There is disagreement, however, on the economy's ability to create such work and leisure al-

"My vision is to use the aging of this cohort as the way to educate and inspire them to think about themselves and others, plan ahead to grow old with the sense of responsibility not just to themselves but to their community and to the nation."

Torres-Gil in Dennis and Migliaccio, 1997, p. 46.

ternatives, despite declines in unemployment and a general economic boom in the late 1990s. Many new jobs are in the service sector (e.g., health and social services, food, and recreation), rather than in manufacturing. As a result, they are less likely to provide older workers with financial security. Uncertainties exist about whether technological advances will produce new jobs or result in net job losses. What is certain is greater labor-market diversity among the older population and greater variations in reasons for retirement. Definitions of the nature of work, family, careers and retirement will gradually reshape cultural and organizational expectations. Diversity will also increase among the unemployed by social class and in economic well-being before and after retirement.

Rather than focusing on altering work roles, a more humanistic approach, consistent with the politics of productivity, is to ask how to develop and use our human potential in old age as part of a productive society. The vitality of the older population must be recognized as a way to involve their skills and wisdom, through both paid and unpaid positions, for societal benefits. Arguing that national policies and attitudes must change, advocates of a productive aging society point to the need for a national consensus that encourages older people to create their own roles and use their talents more productively and in a more satisfying manner (Morris, 1993). Changes must include placing a real value on unpaid volunteer and caregiving activities, and taking practical steps such as publicly emphasizing that technology does not necessarily displace older workers. This perspective also reflects the goals of the federally funded Redefining Retirement Initiative, which emphasizes individual behavioral change and responsibility within a larger public policy framework.

Such redefinitions of old age and aging can move citizens and policy makers beyond the artificially framed policy debates about young and old competing for scarce resources. As suggested in Chapter 16, the interdependence of generations across the life span, if made more explicit, can provide a new paradigm for policy and program development. Older people are becoming more aware of the creative and central roles that they can play in leaving a legacy for future generations—for example, through their active participation in environmental and energy issues. Likewise, intergenerational programs in schools, community centers, nursing homes, retirement facilities, and adult day care centers are growing. Such programs serve to utilize older adults' skills, as well as to provide children and youth with opportunities to interact with elders. In other words, these interactions build on the inherent reciprocity that exists between generations. Such cooperative, intergenerational efforts may, in the long-term, reduce ageism and competition among age groups, so that young and old work together to benefit the most needy in our society, regardless of age. These interactions can also enhance the older person's developmental needs for generativity, as noted in Chapter 6. In the future, it may be less necessary to develop age-based social and long-term care health policies, but rather to establish programs that address special needs across the life span.

CHANGES IN LIVING ARRANGEMENTS

The movement away from farms and city centers to the suburbs has also resulted in the graying of the suburbs, with many people who had moved to these areas after World War II reaching retirement.

Shared housing between young and old can benefit both generations.

Older residents in these suburbs have lower average incomes and lower home values than those in newer communities, as seen in Chapter 11 (Longino, 1998). These trends will continue as the children of these migrants to the suburbs—who, in turn, built their homes in the suburbs and worked in nearby satellite communities—themselves age. Until now, most health and social services have been built near city centers. Future cohorts will expect these services to be located closer to their homes in the suburbs, just as shopping centers, banks, and jobs have been moved outward from urban centers to these areas. Boomers with adequate resources, however, are likely to move to retirement communities, frequently in the current retiree destination states that offer numerous amenities, leisure activities, and a moderate climate. These communities will eventually expand to include assisted living and health services. Geographic mobility will also expand in unknown ways. Trailblazers among Baby Boomers will engage in educational travel, search the Internet for new living opportunities, engage in volunteer activities that keep them "on the road" most of the year, and engage in virtual reality travel. This means the expansion of new mobility trends based on experience rather than only on location (Longino, 1998). And some will seek new types of living arrangements that they lacked in their childrearing years, such as the couple described in the box on page 593.

Regardless of geographic location, new home buyers are increasingly demanding "flexible housing." Indeed, a recent annual meeting of the National Association of Home Builders focused on designing housing that can be used throughout a lifetime. This interest on the part of home builders is clearly more than academic. It reflects the trend of first-time buyers to select neighborhoods where they will want to live for many years, and the decline in relocation rates among all ages (Longino, 1998). As a result, architects and builders are already designing homes with movable walls that can expand or shrink a room as needs change, or plumbing that can convert a small room on the main floor of the house into a bathroom. This gives families the flexibility to adapt their homes as they assume caregiving roles, or if one of the current residents needs long-term care in the future. Other options that can be built into a home are modifiability in the number and size of bedrooms, using a cluster design so that multiple generations and even unrelated renters can live under the same roof while retaining their privacy.

Knowledgeable of the requirements of the Americans with Disabilities Act (ADA), builders and architects are aware of the need to make main-floor hallways and doorways in private homes wide enough for wheelchair access. Even though the ADA does not require accessibility in private homes, these trends are occurring because builders recognize the growing market for such housing features. Computerized controls for heat, artificial

NEW OPTIONS IN HOUSING

Darien and Carey raised their four children in a large home in a neighborhood with good schools and nearby amenities. After the deaths of their own parents, they found their normal lives suspended and began talking about changes they wanted to make while they had the opportunity. They abruptly sold their large home and moved into a new public housing project that has been developed around a new concept of community; this project offers low-income housing, apartments, duplexes and single-family homes aimed at all income levels. Their new home is accessible for people with disabilities and convenient to public transportation. They like living in a racially diverse, family-oriented community. The physical closeness of the houses provides opportunities to be actively involved in civic life and engaged with new neighbors.

lighting, window coverings, and music are too costly for most of today's home buyers, but will become more prevalent in homes of the future. With portable keypads, these features can help frail older persons maintain ambient temperatures, lighting, and music at levels that are comfortable and congruent with the older person's competence level.

Although these home building patterns will help future cohorts of older adults, low-cost structural modifications, communication, and transportation systems are needed now to assist current cohorts' independence. Consistent with the person–environment model, older people's home environment can be modified to reduce the level of environmental press and enhance their level of competence and quality of life. For example, currently nearly 35 percent of individuals age 75 and older use at least one assistive device or have their home modified for accessibility, a proportion that will increase dramatically. Given trends toward computerized home-based banking and shopping services, future cohorts may not need to leave their homes to obtain many services.

The Alliance for Technology Access focuses on assistive technology for older persons with chronic illness. ThirdAge.com offers chat rooms, bulletin boards, speak-outs, a Market Square on quality products, and Invest Tools for financial planning. Unfortunately, however, many of these computer-based services will be available only to higher-income elders, since government regulations and medical reimbursement programs have not kept pace with the growth of technology and rarely reimburse for such products (Bowe, 1995).

Computer programs have also been developed to describe potential side effects of various medications and interactions among them. Currently, these software programs are aimed at physicians, pharmacists, and other health professionals. However, it will soon be possible to buy such a program written in layman's language, type in the names and doses of medications one is taking, and then obtain a printout of potential side effects and special precautions. This would be particularly useful to the many older adults who are using numerous prescriptions and over-the-counter medications. Although too costly to implement at present, it is technically possible to conduct remote monitoring between a patient's home and a local health care facility for such things as blood pressure and heart-rate measures.

Technology also can be used to enhance options for older adults' recreation and enrichment. For example, computers are commonly used for obtaining information via the Web and for leisure (e.g., games linked by telecommunication channels or books read on microchips). Interactive television, CD-ROM and DVD, closed-caption TV programming, and open university via television can greatly expand the social worlds of homebound elders and stimulate intellectual functioning through active participation in learning. For example, Senior Net is a nationwide computer network that encourages discussion on diverse topics and offers hands-on classes in computer use. For a small membership fee, users can attend local classes on computer literacy, word processing, database management, and how to access useful sites on the Internet.

OLDER ADULTS, HEALTH INFORMATION, AND THE WEB

A three-day workshop on this topic was sponsored by the National Institutes of Health, the Administration on Aging, the Health Care Financing Administration, and a range of nonprofits in February 2001. It was targeted at older adults, researchers, and Web designers interested in improving the quality of information on health, education, caregiving, and social issues relevant to aging. The human-factor issues associated with computer use, vision, and cognitive changes affecting older users were also addressed.

Technological advances will also benefit younger family caregivers. As robotics and computer systems become more cost-effective and user-friendly, they can assist frail elders and reduce reliance on family caregivers. Frail elders may also be freer to use less intensive and less costly housing options that offer such technological assistance to their residents. Through the Internet, home-bound elders can not only send verbal messages and family photos, but also create greeting cards. They can even play bridge and other games on the computer with friends in distant places! In this way, the computer can replace TV-watching with a tool that actively engages older adults' cognitive skills. These developments will be readily adopted by future generations of elders who have grown up with computers and rapid technological advances in their work and leisure. On the other hand, older people do not necessarily want technology that saves time or replaces activity, such as automatic tellers or shopping via television. This is because household tasks and shopping are not necessarily seen as onerous by many older adults, but rather as interesting time-fillers. As a result, older people may be more interested in technology that makes life easier and safer, and improves their quality of life, but does not necessarily save time (Gitlin, 1995).

Although equipment will increasingly be used to supplement or replace personal assistance, there are financial barriers to the use of these technologies. Currently, third-party sources (private insurance, Medicare, Medicaid, Veterans Administration, or other private or public sources) cover about 50 percent of the assistive devices in use, with the rest paid out of pocket. In fact, more than 75 percent of home-accessibility features are paid for entirely by the user and family. Not surprisingly, finances are the primary reason given for not utilizing needed assistive devices. Since reimbursement and regulatory issues are also a barrier to companies entering this marketplace, producers and consumers may share common goals in changing reimbursement mechanisms. Advocates for these new products and designs will also find support for their cause in federal legislation such as the Americans with Disabilities Act (ADA). The ADA emphasizes the economic and social advantages of increasing the use of assistive technologies and accessible environmental design (Emerman, 1994).

Shared housing is another means of helping older people remain in their own homes and making the cost of housing affordable to a wider cross-section of persons. These intergenerational programs also provide security for frail older people who need occasional assistance, but do not require the 24-hour nursing home care. Future cohorts of elders may also continue the trends of their younger years by sharing housing with unmarried companions. As society has become more accepting of unmarried couples and gay and lesbian partners living together, the advantages of such arrangements for older couples are more evident. Thus, for example, sharing a home without marrying can reduce an older couple's expenses while they maintain their separate incomes from pensions and Social Security benefits. Most important, shared housing provides much-needed social companionship.

This growth in the number and variety of long-term care options and ways to maintain older adults in their own homes is exciting. However, it raises major policy dilemmas for the twenty-first century. These policy issues inevitably raise ethical dilemmas about the distribution of resources among various segments of society.

ETHICAL DILEMMAS

At the forefront of ethical dilemmas in an aging society is the issue of the prolongation of life at a time of escalating medical costs, increasing use of high-technology treatments, and fears that managed care will foster rationing of services. As a society, we have valued finding cures for dreaded diseases and forestalling death as long as possible. Many older people are now saved, often at considerable cost, from diseases that previously would have killed them, only to be guaranteed death from another disease at equally high or even higher cost. Physicians have been taught to spare no effort in keeping a patient alive. Increasingly, however, health professionals and lay persons are questioning whether dying should be prolonged indefinitely when there is no possibility of recovery. Life-support systems, organ transplants, and other advances in medical technology make it possible to prolong the life of the chronically and terminally ill but blur definitions of when life ends. For example, technology now allows the transplantation of various human organs, and life can be prolonged by machines that keep the body functioning even if the conscious mind has died. In other words, as a society, we have accomplished more at adding years to life than life to years.

The timing, place, and conditions of death are increasingly under medical control. For almost any life-threatening condition, some interventions can now delay the moment of death, but not its inevitability. Doctors and nurses have always dealt with dying, but not until the present technical advances have they had so much power and responsibility to control how long life lasts and to determine when treatment is medically futile. These new medical capabilities demand a new set of ethics and practices. As noted in Chapter 13, the field of *bioethics* was born out of the dilemmas surrounding the introduction and withdrawal of invasive treatments, the patient's decision-making capacity to participate in treatment decisions, and the quality of the patient's life. Health-care facilities

ETHICAL DILEMMAS

- Who decides what for whom (which raises issues of power and authority)?
- Whether and how intervention should occur in a terminal illness
- At what point should efforts to prolong life be stopped, when the alternative is so final?
- How much suffering is "worth it" to stay alive?
- Which is more important: quality or quantity of life?
- How do we measure or determine quality of life?
- Under what conditions and for which decisions should the patient's wishes supersede those of family members?
- What institutional mechanisms should be employed to resolve ethical conflicts?

are now required to have the capacity to address such bioethical issues for patients, families, and staff, typically through ethics committees. Bioethics is a field that will grow in this century, encompassing a wider range of professionals in debates about end-of-life care.

Concerns about when and whether treatment should be withheld frame the debates regarding the right to die and to assisted suicide. Proponents of the right to die maintain that no public interests are served by prolonging excruciating pain and threatening dignity in extending hopeless situations. These decisions become even more complex when the older person is mentally incompetent—cross-cultural differences can also affect how life-sustaining treatment is interpreted and the value and respect accorded elders' lives.

The increased visibility of medicine and the media attention on bioethical issues means that more people know their legal rights as patients and have thought about the personal moral principles that govern their individual choices. In most cases, the debate centers not on *if* such activity should be condoned but *under what circumstances* and what is meant by terminal and medical finality. Public support is growing for individual determination regarding life-sustaining treatment through advanced directives such as living wills. The Supreme Court in 1997 moved the debate about a person's right to die from the national level back to the states, but left open the possibility of future appeals. In fact, five justices acknowledged that in the future the court may well find that a hastened death might be entitled to constitutional protection. The Supreme Court decision also put at the forefront of the debate the issue of aggressive pain management and how well health care professionals are trained in end-of-life care. All 50 states have laws authorizing the use of *advance directives*, supplemented by a federal law, the Patient Self-Determination Act. Nevertheless, these citizen initiatives and state laws have not necessarily been successfully implemented and are often contested, suggesting that ethical issues surrounding the dying process cannot easily be legislated.

Although less than 1 percent of total health care expenditures go to individuals in the last year of life, economic issues often are raised along with ethical considerations (Alliance for Aging Research, 1997). Many policy makers and the lay public, concerned about scarce public resources, continue to question how benefits should be distributed among various groups in society. Critics of costly lifesaving techniques for older adults, such as transplants, argue that with over 40 million people under age 65 without health care insurance and many more who cannot afford high-tech care, our health care system should first address such basic needs. This should take priority over spending disproportionate resources for expensive procedures for only a few. Yet the total savings achieved by denying high-cost acute care to older people would apparently have little impact on overall health care expenditures. Nevertheless, intense debates continue regarding who should decide, in the aggregate and in individual instances, who receives what type of health care. Some fear that in the absence of legal protection for the right to die, economic considerations will override compassionate concerns, especially under managed care, with its fixed fees and capitation as incentives to save costs.

Rationing decisions tend to be made at a societal level, while decisions about whether treatment is *medically futile* are made at the patient's bedside. In other words, rationing specifically acknowledges that a treatment offers a benefit, but the issue is how to distribute beneficial but limited resources fairly, while medical futility signifies that a treatment offers no therapeutic benefit to a patient (Schneiderman, 1994). Some argue that states already ration health care through physicians who refuse to treat Medicaid recipients. In fact, the state of Oregon implemented a federally authorized policy experiment in which it operates with a fixed Medicaid budget and classifies specific categories of health care as not reimbursable. Even if rationing is not formal policy, some evidence suggests that physicians may ration medical care to the oldest-old. As doctors attempt to provide adequate care within capitated systems of care, colleagues and administrators may pressure them not to make available the same expensive tests and medical specialties as exist for younger patients (Binstock, 1994; Kane and Kane, 1994). Debates about an equitable provision of services versus targeting lifesaving interventions for a few will undoubtedly intensify in the future.

Opponents of rationing maintain that a major cost would be the removal of moral barriers against placing any group of human beings in a separate category. If older adults can be denied access to health care categorically, then this action could happen to other groups as well. They argue that suggestions that older people are unworthy of lifesaving care start us down a "slippery slope" (Binstock, 1994, p. 40). Not only are the moral costs of rationing too great, but older people's potential contributions to society are lost.

Ultimately, these larger ethical questions translate into daily practice dilemmas for those who are faced with caring for chronically ill and dying older people, as well as for children with acute medical needs, in an era of diminishing public resources. As noted by Zuckerman (1994), much of health care is carried out in settings where the need for timely, practical solutions outweighs the need for abstract philosophical debate about patients' ethical and legal rights. The question of who should control decisions about life and death will continue to be argued among doctors, families, and often lawyers. Conflicting pressures for change may give way to the creation of new norms, whereby more people will support the removal of life supports for the terminally ill and will want to have control over their own deaths.

A reflection of the growing national debate at the grassroots level is the number of Internet resources on death and dying. The Website of Choices in Dying offers a comprehensive resource for those wanting to understand the right-to-die movement and a way to download advance-directive packages geared to the laws and regulations in a particular state. DeathNET, founded by Derek Humphry, offers the largest collection of "right to die" material and services on the Internet. A smaller number of Websites are maintained by the anti-euthanasia groups, such as LifeWEB of the International Anti-Euthanasia Task Force. Such Internet resources will undoubtedly proliferate in this decade.

As the older population increases, decisions regarding the allocation and withholding of health care will assume greater importance. These decisions must be made by an informed and humanistic society; they cannot be left only to policy makers, physicians, and attorneys. What many today consider to be only geriatric issues will increasingly influence the lives of most Americans. For these reasons and consistent with the underlying assumptions of this book, it is important to understand the processes of aging, as well as the policies and services that affect the older population. This will ensure that society as a whole can make informed choices. In the final section, we review some of the opportunities for careers in gerontology. Whether or not gerontology is chosen as a career, however, all of us need to become informed about this field so that we can be better consumers, citizens, advocates, and caregivers to frail elders within our families and communities, and can better prepare for our own aging.

CAREERS IN GERONTOLOGY

One reason for studying social gerontology is to determine the types of career opportunities in this field. It should be clear by now that gerontology holds great promise for practitioners, researchers, and teachers in diverse aspects of the field. As we have seen throughout this book, specialists in geriatric health care will assume a greater role in helping the growing population of older people to maintain their quality of life, in terms of both treating chronic diseases and preventing health problems. The increasing number of geriatric training programs in schools of medicine, nursing, dentistry, pharmacy, social work, and public health attest to the importance of this field. Geriatric medicine is now a recognized subspecialty of internal medicine. Although the number of universities offering courses in aging has grown, these are not necessarily part of the core curriculum and are rarely taught in depth to students in the health professions.

Specialists in geriatric nutrition and in physical and occupational therapy will be in greater demand in the future as options expand in housing and long-term care. Attorneys with training in medical ethics and aging will become critical members of the gerontological team. In fact, elder law has become a specialty in many law schools, focusing on trusts and estates, age discrimination, and elder abuse. The increased interest in leisure activities in old age will call for more recreation specialists. Architects and planners will be expected to design housing that is sensitive to the needs of an aging population. Social workers and psychologists will be needed to work with older people and their families as counselors, advocates, support-group facilitators, and care or case managers who coordinate services. Program planners, developers, and managers will have opportunities in a myriad of areas such as assisted living, senior centers, adult day

health programs, chore services, home health care, and respite care. And opportunities will multiply for computer programmers and Web designers to design new products to maintain older people's independence. With the growing number of older adults who have investment income, financial planners and stockbrokers will find growing business opportunities with older clients.

In addition, there will be an ongoing shortage of low-tech workers, such as nursing aides and home health workers, who provide most of the personal daily long-term care services. Better pay and benefits, training, and working conditions are needed to address this shortage. Figure E.2 illustrates the broad array of employment opportunities for gerontologists. These range from direct services to education and research (Klein, 1994).

As noted throughout this book, more research is needed on the normal aspects of aging and on how age-related changes influence older people's social functioning. Researchers trained in sociology, psychology, economics, social welfare, and politi-

---

FIGURE E.2   **What Does a Gerontologist Do?**

1. *Direct Service*
- Assesses needs of older adults
- Provides services directly to the older person and family
- Coordinates services with other agencies and institutions
- Works to assure that the older adult and family receive appropriate services that are of a high quality
- Evaluates and modifies the services needed
- Conducts outreach to expand and enhance client base
- Carries out advocacy on behalf of older persons

2. *Program Planning and Evaluation*
- Identifies the needs of the community
- Plans the programs and facilities
- Determines the level and timing of funds required
- Develops the staffing and management plans
- Determines the evaluation plan for the program
- Consults and coordinates with other agencies and programs

3. *Education and Training*
- Plans and conducts educational programs for older persons, their caregivers, and families

- Plans and conducts continuing education programs for paraprofessionals and professionals interested in serving older people
- Instructs preprofessionals
- Provides intergenerational programs

4. *Administration and Policy*
- Designs the structure, motivates and supervises the activities of staff members
- Determines, monitors, and modifies organizational expenditures
- Coordinates activities within the organization and outside organizations
- Conducts analyses of current and proposed programs
- Increases public awareness of needs and services

5. *Research*
- Designs and carries out research on basic processes of aging
- Conducts demonstration projects and clinical trials
- Evaluates effectiveness of demonstration and intervention programs

cal science must work with biologists, geneticists, nutritionists, neuroscientists, and others in the basic and clinical sciences to understand and develop models of the interactive effects of biological, psychological, and social influences on how people age successfully. In many ways, the field of gerontology is limited only by one's imagination. For those of you motivated and concerned about improving the quality of life for current and future generations of older people, we hope that the issues raised in this book encourage you to join this exciting and challenging field.

REFERENCES

Adlin, M. Health care issues. In E. Sutton, A. Factor, B. Hawkins, T. Heller, and G. Seltzer (Eds.), *Older adults with developmental disabilities*. Baltimore, MD: Paul H. Brookes Publishing, 1993.

Administration on Aging: *Family caregiving in an aging society,* Washington, DC: 1999.

Alliance for Aging Research. *Seven deadly myths: Uncovering the facts about the high cost of the last year of life*. Washington, DC: 1997.

American Geriatrics Society. The care of dying patients: A position paper from the American Geriatrics Society. *Journal of the American Geriatrics Society,* 1995, *43*, 577–578.

Banks, D. A. and Fossel, M. Telomeres, cancer and aging: Altering the human life span. *Journal of the American Medical Assocation*, 1997, *278*, 1345–1348.

Bengtson, V. C., Rosenthal, C. J., and Burton, C. Paradoxes of families in aging. In R. H. Binstock and L. K. George (Eds.), *Handbook of aging and the social sciences* (4th ed.). San Diego, CA: Academic Press, 1996.

Binstock, R. H. Old-age-based rationing: From rhetoric to risk? *Generations*, 1994, *18*, 37–41.

Blanchette, P. L., and Valcour, V. G. Health and aging among baby boomers, *Generations*, 1998, *22*, 76–80.

Bloom, F. Breakthroughs 1999. *Science*, 1999, *286*, 2267.

Bowe, F. Is it medically necessary: The political and economic issues that drive and derail assistance technology development. *Generations*, Spring 1995, *19*, 37–40.

Bulcroft, K. A., and Bulcroft, R. A. The timing of divorce: Effects on parent child relationships in later life. *Research on Aging*, 1991, *13*, 226–243.

Burnette, D. Social relationships of Latino grandparent caregivers: A role theory perspective. *The Gerontologist*, 1999, *39*, 49–58.

Callahan, D. *The troubled dream of life: Living with mortality*. New York: Simon and Schuster, 1993.

Caro, F. G., Bass, S. A., and Chen, Y. P. Introduction. In S. A. Bass, F. G. Caro, and Y. P. Chen (Eds.), *Achieving a productive society*. Westport, CT: Auburn House, 1993.

Choi, N. Long-term elderly widows and divorcees: Similarities and differences. *Journal of Women and Aging*, 1995, *7*, 69–72.

Coontz, S. *The way we really are: Coming to terms with America's changing families*. New York: Basic Books, 1997.

Cornman, J. M., and Kingson, E. R. Trends, issues, perspectives and values for the aging of the baby boom cohorts. *The Gerontologist*, 1996, *36*, 15–26.

Cutler, N. E. The false alarms and blaring sirens of financial literacy: Middle-agers' knowledge of retirement income, health finance, and long-term care. *Generations*, Summer 1997, *21*, 34–40.

Cutler, N. E. Preparing for their older years: The financial diversity of aging boomers. *Generations*, Spring 1998, *22*, 81–86.

Day, J. Population projections of the United States by age, sex, race and Hispanic origin: 1992 to 2050. *Current Population Reports*, Series P25, No. 1092, Washington, DC: U.S. Government Printing Office, 1992.

Deatrick, D. Senior-med: Creating a network to help manage medications. *Generations*, Fall 1997, *21*, 59–60.

de Lange, T. Telomeres and senescence: Ending the debate. *Science*, 1998, *279*, 334–335.

De Martino, B. *The MetLife study of employee costs for working caregivers*. Westport, CT: MetLife Mature Market Group, 1997.

Dennis, H., and Migliaccio, J. Redefining retirement: The baby boomer challenge. *Generations*, Summer 1997, *21*, 45–50.

Emerman, J. Demand grows for technology that helps. *Aging Today*. September/October 1994, *XV*, 11.

Fahey, Msgr. Charles J. Social work education and the field of aging. *The Gerontologist*, 1996, *36*, 36–41.

Friedland, R. B. *Investing in our Future*. National Academy on an Aging Society, 2000.

Fritz, M. Nursing homes chase big profits in subacute care. *The Seattle Times*, March 19, 1995, A4.

Furlong, M. Creating on-line community for older adults. *Generations*, Fall 1997, *21*, 33–35.

Gitlin, L. Why older people accept or reject assistive technology. *Generations,* Spring 1995, *19,* 41–47.

Goldscheider, F. K. Divorce and remarriage: Effects on the elderly population. *Reviews in Clinical Gerontology,* 1994, *4,* 258–259.

Gray, J. What the business community and the aging network can learn from each other. *Generations,* Spring 1995, *19,* 20–25.

Gustafson, D., Gustafson, R., and Wackerbarth, S. CHESS: Health information and decision support for patients and families. *Generations,* Fall 1997, *21,* 56–58.

Han, S. K., and Moen, P. Work and family over time: A life course approach. *Annals of the American Academy of Political and Social Science,* 1999 *(562),* 98–110.

Hardy, M. A., and Kruse, K. S. Realigning retirement income: The politics of growth. *Generations,* 1998, *22,* 22–28.

Hobbs, F., and Damon, B. C. *65+ in the United States.* Washington, DC: U.S. Bureau of the Census, Current Population Reports, 1996.

Hunt, G. C. Cleveland Free-net Alzheimers Forum. *Generations,* Fall 1997, *21,* 37–39.

Jahnke, A. Hospital offers integrated therapies. *Aging Today,* November/December 1997, *6,* 11–12.

Johnson, M. L. Dignity for the oldest old: Can we afford it? *Journal of Gerontological Social Work,* 1998, *29,* 155–168.

Kane, R. L., and Kane, R. A. Effects of the Clinton health reform on older persons and their families: A health care systems perspective. *The Gerontologist,* 1994, *34,* 598–606.

Kelly, K. Building aging programs with on-line information technology. *Generations,* Fall 1997, *21,* 15–18.

Kelly, T., and Kropf, N. Stigmatized and perpetual parents: Older parents caring for adult children with lifelong disabilities. *Journal of Gerontological Social Work,* 1995, *24,* 3–17.

Klein, M. *Where do gerontologists work and what do gerontologists do? A model illustrating alternative careers in gerontology.* Unpublished manuscript, University of Southern California, Andrus Gerontology Center, 1994.

Krain, M. A. Policy implications for a society aging well: Employment, retirement, education, and leisure policies for the 21st century. *American Behavioral Scientist,* November-December 1995, *39,* 131–151.

Kutza, E. A. A look at national policy and the baby boom generation. *Generations,* 1998, *22,* 16–21.

Longino, C. Geographic mobility and the baby boom. *Generations,* Spring 1998, *22,* 60–64.

Lubitz, J. D., and Riley, G. F. Trends in Medicare payments in the last year of life. *New England Journal of Medicine,* 1993, *328,* 1092–1096.

Manchester, J. Aging boomers and retirement: Who is at risk? *Generations,* Summer 1997, *21,* 19–22.

Matthews, J. The retirement crisis. *The Seattle Times,* January 6, 1995, B5.

Merrill Lynch. *The seventh annual Merrill Lynch retirement and financial planning survey: Confronting the savings crisis.* Princeton, NJ: 1995.

Michel, V. Factoring ethnic and racial differences into bioethics decision making. *Generations,* 1994, *18,* 23–26.

Micozzi, M. Exploring alternative health approaches for elders. *Aging Today,* November/December 1997, *18,* 9–12.

Moen, P. Recasting careers: Changing reference groups, risks, and realities. *Generations,* 1998, *22,* 40–45.

Moen, P., and Forest, K. B. Family policies for an aging society: Moving to the twenty-first century. *The Gerontologist,* 1995, *35,* 825–830.

Morgan, D. Introduction: The aging of the baby boom. *Generations,* Spring 1998, *22,* 5–10.

Morris, R. Conclusion: Defining the place of the elderly in the twenty-first century. In S. A. Bass, F. G. Caro, and Y. P. Chen (Eds.), *Achieving a productive society.* Westport, CT: Auburn House, 1993.

National Academy on Aging. *Old age in the 21st century.* Syracuse University and the Administration on Aging, 1994.

National Academy on an Aging Society. *Helping the elderly with activity limitations,* Washington, D.C.: Caregiving #7, May 2000.

National Academy on an Aging Society. *Who are young retirees and older workers?* Washington, D.C. 2000.

National Council on the Aging (NCOA). *Long Distance Caregiving.* Washington, DC: National Council on the Aging, 1997.

National Economic Council, *Women and retirement security.* Washington, D.C. Interagency Working Group on Social Security, 1998.

Ozawa, M. N. The economic well-being of elderly people and children in a changing society. *Social Work,* 1999, *44,* 9–19.

Pillemer, K., and Suitor, J. Baby boom families: Relations with aging parents. *Generations*, Spring 1998, 22, 65–69.

Rix, S. *Older workers: How do they measure up? An overview of age differences on employee costs and performances*. Washington, DC: AARP, 1994.

Rowe, J. W., and Kahn, R. L. *Successful aging*. New York: Pantheon Books, 1998.

Schneiderman, L. J. Medical futility and aging: Ethical implications. *Generations*, 1994, 18, 61–65.

Scofield, G. R. Medical futility: Can we talk? *Generations*, 1994, 18, 66–70.

Sherman, R. Sources of help in financial preparation for retirement: AAAs to Web sites. *Generations*, 1997, 21, 55–60.

Silverstone, B. Older people of tomorrow: A psychosocial profile. *The Gerontologist*, 1996, 36, 27–32.

Tennstedt, S. *Family caregiving in an aging society*. Administration on Aging, 1999, Symposium.

Twigg, J., and Atkin, K. *Carers perceived: Policy and practice in informal care*. Buckingham, UK: Open University Press, 1994.

Uhlenberg, P. I. Mortality decline over the twentieth century and supply of kin over the life course. *The Gerontologist*, 1996, 36, 681–685.

U.S. Bureau of the Census. Marital status and living arrangements: March 1992. *Current Population Reports*, Series P-20, No. 468. Washington, DC: U.S. Government Printing Office, 1992.

U.S. Bureau of the Census. Population projections of the U.S. by age, sex, race and Hispanic origin data: 1996–2050. *Current Population Reports*, P25, No. 1130. Washington, DC: U.S. Government Printing Office, 1996.

Ward, C. R., and Smith, T. Forging intergenerational communities through information technology. *Generations*, Fall 1997, 21, 38–42.

Wiener, J. M., Illston, L. H., and Hanley, R. J. *Sharing the burden: Strategies for public and private long-term care insurance*. Washington, DC: The Brookings Institute, 1994.

Wright, I. S. *The role of the older citizens in the society of 2000 A.D.* New York: American Federation for Aging Research, 1973.

Zuckerman, C. Clinical ethics in geriatric care settings. *Generations*, 1994, 18, 9–12.

INDEX